MANUAL OF ONLINE SEARCH STRATEGIES

# Manual of Online Search Strategies
# Second edition

**Edited by**
**C.J. Armstrong**
**and**
**J.A. Large**

Routledge
Taylor & Francis Group

LONDON AND NEW YORK

First published 1992 by Ashgate Publishing

Reissued 2018 by Routledge
2 Park Square, Milton Park, Abingdon, Oxon, OX14 4RN
711 Third Avenue, New York, NY I 0017, USA

*Routledge is an imprint of the Taylor & Francis Group, an informa business*

Publisher's Note
The publisher has gone to great lengths to ensure the quality of this reprint but points out that some imperfections in the original copies may be apparent.

Disclaimer
The publisher has made every effort to trace copyright holders and welcomes correspondence from those they have been unable to contact.

A Library of Congress record exists under LC control number: 92002908

ISBN 13: 978-1-138-32495-4 (hbk)
ISBN 13: 978-0-429-45061-7 (ebk)

# Contents

# Notes on authors

**Chris Armstrong** worked as a research officer at the (then) College of Librarianship Wales for about ten years before leaving and setting up his own research and consultancy company. Information Automation Limited specialises in all aspects of online and CD-ROM information provision and handling with an emphasis on training. Chris Armstrong is a frequent writer of papers in the areas of online and CD-ROM information and is also responsible for the compilation and production of *CD-ROM Information Products: an Evaluative Guide*. Chris Armstrong is a Fellow of the Institute of Analysts and Programmers (FIAP) and a Member of the Institute of Information Scientists (MIInfSc).

**Judith Barton** has worked as a local government officer for the past nine years, first at the Greater London Council Research Library and then at the London Research Centre. She has at various times held responsibility for answering queries in housing, social services, health services, arts and recreation, and is at present responsible for information on European affairs and local government policy. As well as compiling and editing current awareness bulletins on Europe and local government finance, she has wide experience of online searching on all major hosts over many years. In addition, she abstracts and indexes material for the London Research Centre's ACOMPLINE and URBALINE databases.

**David Bawden** was until recently Principal Information Scientist with the Research Information Services of Pfizer Central Research, a pharmaceutical research organisation in the United Kingdom. He was responsible for the introduction of online searching at Pfizer and for the applications of information technology within the organisation as a whole. He is now Senior Lecturer in Information Science at City University, London. He publishes widely in the online area.

**Jamshid Beheshti** is Assistant Professor at the Graduate School of Library and Information Studies, McGill University, Montreal, where he teaches in the areas of information storage and retrieval, quantitative methods and information technology. He has been a member of the Editorial Board of *Canadian Library Journal* and has served as a consultant for several national projects. He has published articles on information uses of students and interface design for CD-ROMs, and is currently on a research team investigating the impact of multimedia on information retention of children.

**Veronica Calderhead** has been Reference Librarian in the Physical Sciences and Engineering Library at McGill University, Montreal, Quebec since 1989. She provides training in online searching for the researchers in the University's Chemistry Department in addition to other reference and collection services. She has also worked as a special librarian at C.I.L. Explosives Research Laboratory, McMasterville, Quebec.

**Jacqueline Cropley** is a consultant specialising in information, technology, management and public relations. She has worked in a variety of libraries and information services, most recently for international financial institutions in the City of London. An expert in business information, she has been responsible for introducing several CD-ROM products to librarians and end users in the business community.

**Claire Drinkwater** has been Assistant Librarian at the Institute of Education, University of London since 1978, and Head of the Computer Search Service there since 1980. She is Committee member and past Chairperson of the Education Librarians Group of the Library Association, and editor of the *Education Libraries Journal*.

**Joyce Garnett** has been Director of the Library at Laurentian University, Sudbury, Ontario since 1991. She was formerly Area Librarian (Physical Sciences and Engineering) at McGill University, Montreal, Quebec and Chief Librarian at Pratt & Whitney Canada, Longueuil, Quebec. She has taught courses covering scientific and technical information sources, and online searching at Concordia University and McGill University since 1976. She is active in the Special Libraries Association and has held office at the regional and national levels.

**Gary D. Gott** is Assistant Professor of Law and Director of the Thormodsgard Law Library at the University of North Dakota School of Law. Prior to this he held positions at the University of Texas Tarlton Law Library and the Brigham Young University Law Library. In addition to his library reponsibilities, he teaches courses in Legal Research and Writing, and Introduction to Law. He is a member of the American Association of Law Libraries and the North Dakota Library Association.

**Yve Griffith** is Manager of Library and Information Services for the law firm of Winston & Strawn, Chicago, Illinois. She was formerly Information Manager for the Marketing Intensive Practice at Booz-Allen & Hamilton in Chicago. Ms. Griffith is an adjunct professor at Rosary College, where she teaches online searching, and is also President of the Alumnae Association of the Graduate School of Library and Information Science. She has a continuing interest in online searching and the marketing and financial management of information services.

**Mike Koenig** is Dean of the Graduate School of Library and Information Science at Rosary College. He has held various managerial positions in the information industry including those of Manager of Information Services for Pfizer Inc., Director of Operations for the Institute for Scientific Information, Vice President Operations (US) for Swets and Zietlinger and Vice President Data Management for Tradenet. He has many years experience in business database searching; in fact, as Pfizer was SDC's first paying customer, he can legitimately claim to be the very first commercial online database searcher. He is author of more than fifty professional publications.

**Sherry Koshman** is currently a Doctoral student at the School of Library and Information Science at the University of Pittsburg. Prior to September 1991, she was Professional Associate with responsibility for the Information Technology Laboratory at the Graduate School of Library and Information Studies, McGill University, Montreal. She has also served on the Information Technology Committee of the Special Libraries Association.

**Andy Large** is Professor and Director, Graduate School of Library and Information Studies, McGill University, Montreal. Prior to joining McGill he was Principal Lecturer at the College of Librarianship Wales. He has directed a number of research projects in the online and CD-ROM areas and is currently investigating the effectiveness of multimedia information in an educational environment. As well as publishing widely in the journal literature, he is joint author of *Online Searching: Principles and Practice* (Bowker-Saur, 1990) and joint editor of *CD-ROM Information Products,* volumes 1-2 (Gower, 1990-1991) and the quarterly journal, *Education for Information.* He has acted as consultant for a number of national and international organisations.

**John Luedtke** is Director of Computer Services at the Kurt F. Wendt Engineering Library, University of Wisconsin-Madison. As Director, he established the library's online search services, and recently, he developed a system to provide access to a variety of CD-ROM products both from a local area network within the library and via the campus ethernet network. He was Coordinator of the Water Resources Information Program at the University, and a former member of the Ad Hoc Environmental Information Systems Committee; he has published widely on environmental information matters.

**Mary Moon** is a Senior Librarian with United Technologies Library and Information Services managing the greater Hartford area libraries at Pratt & Whitney and International Fuel Cells. Prior to this she was an Information Broker in the Boston area specializing in scientific research. She has held office at the regional and national levels in the Special Libraries Association and has considerable experience with technical research, including the evaluation of online and CD-ROM databases.

**Mary Muenkel** is Vice President and Director of Information Services at BBDO in New York. Prior to her current association with the advertising industry, she has been affiliated with the consulting firms of Towers Perrin and Booz-Allen and with the investment bank, Morgan Stanley.

**John Parkinson** is presently Librarian at the Home Office, Emergency Planning College in North Yorkshire; immediately prior to this he was Librarian at the Ministry of Agriculture, Fisheries and Food, Central Science Laboratory at Slough. He has also worked as Assistant Librarian at the Royal Botanic Gardens, Kew and has considerable experience in online and CD-ROM information sources in agriculture.

**David Raitt** is in charge of library and information services for the European Space Agency in The Netherlands. He is Chairman of the International Online Information Meeting Organizing Committee, editor of *The Electronic Library* and European news editor of *Online Review*. He has published extensively in the information science and technology fields.

**Candy Schwartz** holds degrees in linguistics, library science and information science and teaches courses in online and optical information services, database management, cataloguing, indexing and records management. Dr Schwartz has served as a consultant to software publishers, and has published and spoken at national conferences on topics relating to indexing, database design and optical disc publishing. She is a member of the Board of Directors of the American Society for Information Science, and is President of the Board of Directors of Documentation Abstracts, Inc. Current research interests include the use of electronic networks for access to library resources and subject access to audio and image collections.

Correspondence should be directed to the author at GSLIS, Simmons College, 300 The Fenway, Boston MA 02115 USA; e-mail: schwartz@babson.bitnet; *or* cschwartz@lucy.wellesley,edu

**Edlyn S. Simmons** serves as Patent Information Supervisor in the Patent Law Department of Marion Merrell Dow Inc., in Cincinnati, Ohio. She is a registered patent agent and her work involves online and manual searching of the chemical, pharmaceutical and patent literature as well as the preparation and prosecution of United States and international patent applications. She serves as Chair of the Patent Information Users Group, is a member of the Pharmaceutical Manufacturers Association Patent Information Committee and the ORBIT Advisory Panel, and has served on advisory committees for Derwent Chemical Abstracts Service. She has published extensively in the field of chemical and patent information.

**Bonnie Snow** is Manager of the Mid-Atlantic Region in the United States for DIALOG Information Services, Inc., with an office based in Philadelphia, Pennsylvania. Prior to joining DIALOG in 1980, she worked at the Philadelphia College of Pharmacy and Science as Head of Reference Services and Search Analyst. She has also served as a Consulting Education Officer for Excerpta Medica (1980) and as Lecturer in Library and Information Science at the Catholic University of America (1984). Ms. Snow has been a Continuing Education Instructor for the Medical Library Association since 1979 and has taught courses on drug information worldwide. She serves on the editorial boards of *Medical Reference Services Quarterly* and *Journal of Pharmacy Teaching* and has been editor of the CADUCEUS column in *Online* and *Database* since 1985. Ms Snow has written extensively on biomedical information retrieval and online education; her latest book is entitled *Drug Information: A Guide to Current Resources*.

**Ian Snowley** is Senior Librarian: Services at the Ministry of Agriculture, Fisheries and Food in central London. He has been with the Ministry since 1986, holding posts as both Assistant Librarian and Librarian in Whitehall Place Library. He started his career with the London Borough of Redbridge, at Seven Kings Branch Library.

**John Williams** is Senior Lecturer in Law at University College of Wales Aberystwyth where he specialises in Family Law and International Law. He is author of *Social Services Law* (Fourmat, 1988) and *Law of Mental Health* (Fourmat, 1990), as well as many articles on family and international law.

**Patricia M. Young** is Law Librarian at McGill University Law Library and Past President of the Canadian Association of Law Libraries. During her twenty-year career, Ms. Young has worked in a variety of law libraries, including the Library of Parliament, the law firm of Courtois, Clarkson, Parsons & Tétrault and the Bell Canada Law Library. She has also frequently contributed to *Canadian Law Libraries/Bibliothèques de droit canadiennes*.

# Acknowledgements

We should like to acknowledge the support of the various database producers and search services who have given permission to reproduce their searches. Copyright for all figures and searches remains with the individual producers.

C.J. Armstrong
and J. A. Large

# Introduction

It is incumbent upon editors of a second edition to identify at the outset differences between the new work and its predecessor. The most dramatic change which has occurred since the first edition appeared in 1988 is the emergence of CD-ROM as a major publishing medium for databases. With more than two thousand databases now available on CD-ROM this new edition could no longer confine its scope to databases accessible from remote vendors via telecommunication networks. The importance of CD-ROM alongside online has now been acknowledged in this new edition; due attention is paid to the problems of searching databases on CD-ROM as well as online.

Partly as a consequence of CD-ROM, but also as a result of a more eclectic approach in the online field, databases now cover practically every subject area from a bibliographic, numeric and full-text perspective. They include illustrations, maps, software, sound and moving images as well as text, and cater for the specialist and the generalist, the young and the old.

The fixed costs of CD-ROM searching, in such marked contrast to variable online costs, has largely explained the growth of end-user searching. The slower but more readily grasped retrieval interfaces such as menu screens, pull-down and pop-up menus together with window and mouse environments have brought CD-ROMs within reach of the mass audience which has always eluded their online counterparts. Such searchers may no longer have to grapple with the idiosyncrasies of command languages but they still need advice on which databases to use for a particular query and how to find the relevant information contained in those databases. The need for help with search strategies, then, is heightened by the democratisation of database retrieval.

The online industry has not remained static since 1988. New databases have appeared or in some cases disappeared, retrieval software has been enhanced, hosts have acquired new owners, and so on. These changes are reflected in this new edition.

These changes have inevitably affected some chapters more than others. In a few instances, indeed, they have prompted structural changes in the new edition. Two chapters found in the first edition are no longer included in this volume. Full-text journals are now encountered in growing numbers in many subject fields and are best dealt with in subject-based chapters rather than separately as in the first edition. At the same time, interactive electronic journals such as BLEND, discussed by Harry Collier in 1988, have not yet emerged from the research environment into the commercial world. Likewise, a special chapter on office and home use now seems superfluous with growing end-user searching, especially of CD-ROMs, in many fields (although it is interesting to note that most end-user searching takes place in the library rather than home or office). An appendix of databases and the hosts on which they could be found has been scrapped for the more useful tables covering the same information but within individual chapters. Overlap between the biological sciences and health sciences prompted a merger of these two fields in the second edition under the title 'The Biosciences'.

All our authors have struggled to cover broad subject remits and in some cases such as the humanities and the social sciences the boundaries are especially far flung. Nevertheless, a desire to establish links between related fields as well as considerations of size and cost have deterred the editors from fragmenting the book into more narrowly defined subject divisions.

With the passage of time individual lives are every bit as exposed to change as are databases and online hosts. It is therefore not surprising that a number of authors from the first edition were unable on this occasion to accept the invitation to participate. It has been a pleasure to work with a number of new colleagues as well as our faithful collaborators from the first edition. The chapters written by the former are especially likely to present new perspectives when compared with the previous edition.

Like the first edition, this new one is not intended as an introductory textbook to command-driven, Boolean searching (although in fact it contains a wealth of searching advice illustrated with well-chosen examples which should prove invaluable in the classroom). It is primarily targeted at online searchers who already have some knowledge of command languages and may be proficient searchers on databases in one or two subject areas, but when required to venture into new and less familiar territory still need guidance. It is also offered to end users who possess the subject expertise but lack information retrieval know-how. The *Manual* is offered as a guide to database selection and a navigational aid through the twists and turns of the retrieval maze; at least some of the dead ends and back-tracking may thereby be avoided. This volume, written by experts in their various fields, deals with the subject coverage and record structures of specific databases, offers comparisons between databases (content, indexing procedures, updating policies, etc.), discusses the choice between online and CD-ROM sources (and between hosts if online is selected), and illustrates strategies with numerous search extracts.

Chapter 1 deals with two themes of relevance to all subsequent chapters: the evaluation of databases and the choice between online and CD-ROM versions. It would have been unduly repetitive to disperse such information throughout the book.

Chapters 2 and 3 concentrate on searching by form rather than subject. Special techniques are required when searching citation index and patent databases and it is therefore better to dedicate chapters to these topics rather than attempt to do them justice in the subject-based chapters.

Chapters 4 to 15 then deal with the retrieval of information from online and CD-ROM databases in a number of broad subject areas: chemistry, the biosciences, agriculture, energy and the environment, engineering, computer science and information technology, the social and behaviourial sciences, law, business and economics, and the humanities. Their authors inevitably cannot deal with every online database or CD-ROM product which might impinge upon such broad intellectual fields but have rather striven to identify major sources which are likely to satisfy the overwhelming majority of searches. The rule of one chapter per subject has been breached in two cases: law, and business and economics. The marked national orientations in these fields has necessitated in each case chapters dedicated to North America and to Europe.

Chapter 16 departs from the subject approach in order to deal with strategies for answering quick-reference questions which acknowledge no demarcation by discipline.

An appendix containing a bibliography of reference works relevant to online and CD-ROM database searching completes the volume.

The book, perforce, is divided principally by subject but the databases themselves often defy such neat categorisation. Many are multidisciplinary in scope and are relevant to several broad subject areas; their coverage may indeed be broader than their titles suggest. Databases of patents and citations are relevant to any subject and are therefore frequently mentioned throughout the book although two chapters are specifically dedicated to them. Many of the chapters (agriculture and the humanities are good examples) explicitly remind the reader that on occasion searchers may have to range far from the obvious databases in the field to find all that is available online or on CD-ROM. Unnecessary duplication between chapters has been eliminated but no attempt has been made to excise valuable, embedded cross references by one author to another's chapter. The indexes are intended to collocate databases and subjects which the primary chapter division has scattered.

At the same time, each chapter, whilst a part of the whole, is intended to stand by itself and a reader should be able to turn to any chapter and find a self-contained treatment of the topic.

Authors have been given discretion to select the databases - online and CD-ROM - and the online hosts which they consider are most relevant. The selection inevitably reflects the authors' national base (Canada, the United States, the Netherlands and the United Kingdom) and heaviest emphasis is given to databases and hosts from these countries. Selection has also been influenced by local availability of CD-ROMs, access to hosts on which relevant online databases are installed and, ultimately, author preferences and prejudices.

This book deals with a field which, while relatively recent, is already plagued by inconsistencies of terminology. It also unites authors who might share one language - English - but whose spelling is fractured into three (at least) variants. The editors and publisher have striven for consistency but would be rash to claim full standardisation/standardization.

Authors have represented their subjects as they found them at the time of writing. This book is primarily about search strategies; the reader in search of the latest information on CD-ROM titles and prices, database availability, etc, should always turn to sources like host newsletters and publishers' catalogues. The *Manual of Online Search Strategies* is intended to supplement, not replace, such vital sources of current information.

Many people are responsible for the appearance of a book such as this and it is one of the pleasant tasks afforded the editors to express their thanks and appreciation. The database producers and online hosts not only grant copyright permission to reproduce search extracts but also in many cases provide constructive comments to authors. The authors themselves, of course, must take most credit for this volume; their expertise, enthusiasm and diligence have made it possible. Sue McNaughton at Gower has played an active role in the planning and production at every stage and the editors are indebted to her for such constant support. Since the first edition appeared in 1988 the twelve miles then separating the two editors have been stretched to some 3,500. Editorial meetings in the local village pub have become a thing of the past (the global village is somehow not quite the same) and in this Introduction acknowledgement must be given to British Telecom and Bell Canada for making (usually) communication possible. One thing remains constant, however; our gratitude to our families - Kathy, Ben, Dan, Joel, Val, Amanda and Kirsty.

C.J. Armstrong
and J. A. Large

December 1991

# 1 Database evaluation and selection

*Chris Armstrong and Andy Large*

The individual chapters within the *Manual* discuss the retrieval of information from online and CD-ROM databases in a variety of subject fields. In so doing they consider database selection: which database, for example, offers the best coverage of Japanese patent information in English, or where should a search for bibliographic data on diabetes in Hispanic Americans be conducted? (Anyone seeking answers should turn to Chapters 3 and 5 respectively.) A different kind of decision must also be taken in a growing number of cases: when a database is available both online and on CD-ROM, which should be used? This first chapter offers some general guidance on the pros and cons of these alternative formats and some views on the evaluation of databases in general. Readers seeking more precise guidance regarding the use of individual titles on CD-ROM or online should consult the relevant chapters in the remainder of this volume.

## EVALUATION

Printed reference tools have traditionally been evaluated according to a number of criteria: for example, Katz has used purpose, authority, scope, audience, cost and format (arrangement, indexing, binding, typography, illustrations, etc.) [1]. Most of these criteria can be applied to online and CD-ROM titles, although it might prove more difficult to assess such factors as scope and audience with a medium which is less easily browsed than print. It is also necessary, however, to consider additional criteria if the evaluation is to be comprehensive, such as search software and help facilities (online and offline) [2].

Indeed portable (as opposed to online) databases extend the problem still further. Their ease of production and distribution has opened up the marketplace to a significant array of new vendors. Many, with roots firmly in the library/information industry are simply making available traditional databases in a new medium. In this case, the problem from the user's point of view is only to discern any differences which might be apparent in terms of coverage in time or in terms of access. For example, MEDLINE online is available with retrospective coverage to 1966 while one producer's CD-ROM coverage only goes back to 1984. Other publishers are responsible for a range of databases - such as Electronic Text's LIBRARY OF AMERICA COLLECTION (the works of American authors) and Columbia Granger's WORLD OF POETRY - which have not previously been available through the traditional route of online.

It might be supposed that a database on CD-ROM or online is always justified by enhancements to the print product: the electronic version would be expected to offer value-added features. The additional retrieval facilities provided by Boolean-driven engines as well as the speed at which an inverted file can be searched online or on CD-ROM normally ensure that bibliographic databases can be more easily exploited than printed indexing/abstracting journals or published bibliographies. Many databases, and especially those on CD-ROM, are not bibliographic however, but contain encyclopedias, dictionaries, monographs, newspapers, etc. It should not be assumed that these electronic versions are necessarily superior: some are and some are not. The OXFORD ENGLISH DICTIONARY on CD-ROM does provide a number of useful facilities which are absent from the multi-volume print version. The standard search on headwords, for example, has been expanded to permit searching on sub-headings and even reverse look-up: words can be found anywhere in an entry. The DICTIONARY contains numerous quotations and is indeed as rich a source of this kind of information as many a dedicated dictionary of quotations. These quotations in the print version, however, are locked away from the user except when found as a by-product of a search on headwords. As Grogan points out, these quotations on the CD-ROM can now be searched directly by author, date of source work or the text words themselves. Answers to questions like what did Dickens have to say about wine or John Stuart Mill about slavery can be answered with ease. The DICTIONARY also contains a wealth of etymological information which again has been unlocked on CD-ROM. How many words in English are related to the game of cricket or which English words are derived from the Chinese? These kinds of questions are straightforward to search (257 in the case of cricket and a surprising number from Chinese such as sampan, typhoon, and chop-stick as well as more surprisingly cash, hun and ketchup) [3].

Despite these added-value features, the OXFORD ENGLISH DICTIONARY is not free from problems. As Grogan comments, it is far easier to run your eye down the printed page to identify relevant information than to scroll through many screens. Some entries are very long; the verb 'set' has an entry of more than seventy thousand words and requires more than five hundred screens [3]! Other CD-ROMs are questionable in terms of offering any advantage over their print equivalents. The OXFORD TEXTBOOK OF MEDICINE, for example, at over twice the price of the print product provides only minimally better access to the text in its electronic format but robs users of all figures and tables.

The increasing use of multimedia facilities in CD-ROM databases offers an ideal opportunity to enhance a print product - or even an online product - with capabilities not possible in other media. Producers can add sound, video sequences, still photographs and animation to text-based products. Both the GUINNESS DISC OF RECORDS and the NEW GROLIER ELECTRONIC ENCYCLOPEDIA are instances of this trend where the added facets actually give added value. Unfortunately, for every product usefully launched, there are many which simply exploit the capabilities of optical publishing to increase the market share for their producers. Quanta Press markets a series with the title USA WARS; so far VIET-NAM, KOREA and the CIVIL WAR have appeared. Of the last, Desmarais has said that while the disc could hardly support the requirements of any detailed historical research containing as it did only brief accounts or descriptions, its value came from its collection of photographs and period music samples. However, he went on to add that 'at US$129, buyers could purchase books of Civil War photographs or recordings of Civil War songs more economically elsewhere' [4]. The CD-ROM in this case has brought together several related archives, but it remains questionable whether the resulting assemblage has any intrinsic value.

In the CD-ROM publishing arena, it has frequently been argued that for a medium which can only be updated remotely and via a postal service, static products such as encyclopedias, dictionaries, workbooks and manuals would be more appropriate and marketable than those containing frequently changing data such as business statistics or frequently updated data such as bibliographic citations. Indeed, TFPL data at the end of 1990 showed that of 1,522 CD-ROM databases, four hundred were bibliographic and 164 were in the business and financial sector [5]. But while such traditional databases have proliferated, many textual databases not available online and requiring less frequent updating have also been produced: Maxwell Electronic Publishing is producing a range of medical journals and BDC Technical Services has produced a range of aircraft maintenance manuals under their DRUID (Dynamic Retrieval Using Interactive Databases) software which allows hypertext-like links between textual material, parts lists and technical drawings.

Product development should be preceded by a substantial investment in market research: new products have to be targeted and not simply scattered in the hope that someone somewhere will buy. One is tempted to speculate on the market research that suggested users either reading on screen or printing their favourite Sherlock Holmes stories from CD-ROM; as with SHAKESPEARE ON DISC the versions used and the editorial decisions made as the texts where transplanted to their new medium mean that neither can be used for serious literary study. Titles such as PRAVDA ON DISC, TEACHINGS OF KRISHNAMURTI, TERRORIST GROUP PROFILES, THE UNABASHED HISTORY OF EROTICA or the numerous versions of *The Bible* which are available suggest that relatively few sales are necessary to justify a title, while ABOUT COWS must surely lie close to the frivolous end of the publishing spectrum.

In other cases, lack of research may be less serious reflecting only the inability of publishers to visualise their market in terms of kind of users: information specialists versus end users [6]. The search interface on which ultimately access to the data depends may be inappropriate for the real users of a database. If the producer has no clear sight of the potential user, the user interface may become a barrier to an otherwise valuable database. If end users will be the chief market - or the main users after the product has been marketed to libraries and information units - the interface should be self-explanatory and intuitive with plenty of readily-apparent help screens on call.

While lack of marketing direction may be irritating, perhaps the most serious failing in any database is poor or poorly validated data. It is also the most difficult aspect of any product to evaluate. Most problematically, such failings may not even be apparent to users. In examining a prospective product users must ask: Are the data factually accurate? Are the data textually accurate? Is the text precise rather than verbose, presented in a fashion appropriate to the content, indexed using a controlled language (and if so are the thesaurus and any indexing guidelines published)? A series of questions on which to base a purchase decision. Even when talking to the supplier (who may not be the database publisher), answers may not be clear: frequently data are input 'offshore' using cheap labour to key multiple copies which are then compared to discover anomalies; frequently, too, spelling checkers are used on textual data - but who offshore will decide which is the correct figure and what spelling check will highlight UNCLEAR rather than NUCLEAR?

While many of these evaluation problems mirror those questions traditionally asked by librarians of new print reference tools, the spurious authority frequently vested in electronic media often prevents users from positing such doubts. And yet, it is these very media (CD-ROM, diskette and online) - removed from user's eyes by a software interface which could hide a multitude of sins - that most demand such exploration.

EUSIDIC (the European Association of Information Services) has suggested a series of guidelines which, while not guaranteeing data quality, may at least enable users to see and understand exactly what is being presented in a database. One suggestion is that the initial screen visable when a CD-ROM is used will announce clearly the scope and currency of the database; statements such as 'This database has no data added after [date]' or 'The earliest data stem from [date]' should be complemented by 'The latest corrections and updates to these data were made [date]'. A clear statement of the aims, subject scope and intended uses of the database should also be included. A second guideline suggests that where amendments have been made, these should be in the form of added, dated addenda which will be located automatically at the same time as the original item. Thus an audit of changes is available to all users who may then make their own decisions as to the value to put on such data.

Some evaluations of CD-ROMs *do* bring poor data to light, and a review of the British POSTCODE ADDRESS FILE CD-ROM, for example, discovered that five variations of a Bank's name had to be used to locate all its addresses; that it would take considerable imagination to locate the hundred or so entries which began in error with an ampersand; and that some interpretation would be necessary to translate 4950 to 49-50 or 9011 to 9-11 [7]. Nor were the addresses comprehensive despite the accompanying publicity which suggested that they could be used to compile reliable area mailing lists. Most of these peculiarities came to light by viewing the indexes - at least nonce words show up this way.

The problem of quality management in databases is not new and is being tackled on both sides of the Atlantic. Reva Basch reporting on discussions which took place at the Southern California Online User Group's annual retreat in 1990 described its goal as being to develop a framework for judging quality and reliability of databases in terms of, among other things, consistency, timeliness, accuracy and error rates [8]. In the United Kingdom, the Library Association and the United Kingdom Online User Group are working towards a methodology for a database quality infrastructure in which the terms 'fitness for purpose or use' and 'reliability' can be applied meaningfully so that users can confidently rely on the databases purchased.

## SELECTION

### Coverage

One important point must be emphasised: it should not be assumed that a common title means that coverage in various formats is identical. This is most obvious in terms of retrospective coverage, where the CD-ROM, as the newest format, may not extend as far back as its online or print equivalents. Differences in retrospective coverage may also distinguish two rival CD-ROM versions of the same title. NTIS, for example, is available on CD-ROM from two companies - DIALOG and SilverPlatter - but only from 1980 and 1983 respectively; online it is available on several vendors from 1964.

Illustrative material can enhance certain kinds of CD-ROM databases whose online equivalents must rely simply on text. Encyclopedias and dictionaries make particularly good use of illustrations on CD-ROM. A relatively new development in the CD-ROM industry is the multimedia product which combines sound and/ or animation alongside pictures and text. WEBSTER'S NINTH NEW COLLEGIATE DICTIONARY, for example, includes synthesised pronunciation of words while COMPTON'S MULTIMEDIA ENCYCLO-PEDIA has both sound and animation sequences (consult, for example, the articles on earthquakes, Martin Luther King and whales).

### Cost

Like books and journals but in contrast to online databases, CD-ROMs are a publishing medium. Once acquired, there are no incremental costs related to usage. This is quite different from online databases where costs are directly related to use (by connect time, number of records retrieved and/or printed, number of commands issued, etc.). A title which is likely to get heavy use may well, therefore, be better purchased on CD-ROM; conversely, it may be more economical to access a lightly-used title online where a payment is only incurred during the online connection. A reviewer of ABI/INFORM ONDISC has calculated that the CD-ROM would be cheaper than online access if more than one online search per week was to be undertaken [9]. The decision as to whether a title currently accessed online should be purchased on CD-ROM may be complicated because usage might increase once the CD-ROM is purchased, partly because a lower (or no) searching charge is imposed upon users, and partly because users may be allowed to undertake their own searching rather than having to rely upon the intervention of an information professional.

The actual price of CD-ROM titles varies greatly; some are relatively inexpensive, costing less than one hundred pounds sterling while others may be much more expensive, exceeding ten thousand pounds.

## Currency

CD-ROMs, like books and journals, must be published and delivered to the customer. There are limits, therefore, to the currency of any title. The medium cannot compete with online services where databases can be updated in real time if necessary. One of the major differences between an online and a CD-ROM version of a database is likely to be the former's edge in currency. AGRICOLA, for example, is updated monthly online but only quarterly on disc. Nonetheless, update frequency is improving as production costs fall and user expectations rise; OG/PLUS (US patents), for example, is updated weekly. In some cases magnetic diskettes rather than CD-ROM are used to supply very current data to users, reducing costs and thereby facilitating more frequent updating. An invisible gateway to an online service may also be offered so that CD-ROM updating can be achieved online (as with Wilson products such as the MLA INTERNATIONAL BIBLIOGRAPHY or the Compact Cambridge MEDLINE).

## Storage capacity and database size

The capability to search an entire database online at one go even though it might contain more than eight million bibliographic records (as with BIOSIS PREVIEWS on DIALOG) has always been a great attraction for the online user when compared with retrospectively searching volume after printed volume. The introduction of cross-file searching dramatically increased the quantity of information which can be searched simultaneously. Although CD-ROMs have an impressive storage capacity (around 550 Mbytes or enough to hold the entire multi-volume 1933 edition of the *Oxford English Dictionary*) current data compression techniques will not permit very large databases to be held on a single disc. In cases like OG/PLUS and INSPEC multiple discs are required, each of which must be searched, a problem simplified but not totally eliminated if a CD-ROM stack or juke box rather than a one-disc player is available. Acknowledging this problem, SilverPlatter has produced a version of MEDLINE which although supplied on CD-ROMs, is designed expressly for transfer to the fixed disk of a microcomputer where the complete database since 1966 can be searched (if networked, by thirty-five users) at one go. On the other hand, the relatively large storage capability of CD-ROMs has encouraged publishers to utilise space by packaging a number of print titles on one disc. For example, HARRAP'S MULTILINGUAL DICTIONARY and the MCGRAW-HILL CD-ROM SCIENCE AND TECHNICAL REFERENCE SET each contains the equivalent of both a print encyclopedia and a dictionary. The CANADIAN PATENT INDEX from the University of British Columbia contains nine databases including: the Patent Index: the CONSUMER HEALTH BIBLIOGRAPHY, UNION LIST OF BRITISH COLUMBIA NEWSPAPERS, CANADIAN POLITICS BIBLIOGRAPHY, POISON INFORMATION REFERENCE, INDEX TO THE VANCOUVER CITY COUNCIL MEETINGS, and a VANCOUVER CENTENNIAL BIBLIOGRAPHY. The ARCTIC AND ANTARCTIC REGIONS DATABASE from the National Information Services Corporation combines material from nine source databases into a single database and also includes a separately accessed database from the United States Department of Energy on the one disc; and in a similar way TOXLINE PLUS from SilverPlatter includes material from the National Library of Medicine, BIOSIS, the American Society of Hospital Pharmacists and the Chemical Abstracts Service as well as a secondary database, RISKLINE from Sweden.

## Retrieval

CD-ROMs typically offer very similar retrieval facilities to their online counterparts: Boolean matching, field and proximity searching, truncation and so on are often available. Nevertheless, there may be differences. The command-driven mode provided by H.W. Wilson for its CD-ROM products does not offer command stacking, proximity searching or sorting, all of which are available on the online version of its retrieval software.

When retrieval from CD-ROM databases is compared with retrieval from online equivalents a major shortcoming is often revealed - response time. Response time is the number of seconds from the moment that a user initiates an activity until the computer begins to display the results. Generally speaking, the faster the response time the better. Shneiderman comments: 'It seems clear that lengthy response times (longer than fifteen seconds) are generally detrimental to productivity, increasing error rates and decreasing satisfaction' [10]. If so, users are facing problems with some CD-ROMs. It can still be relatively slow to execute complex searches on bibliographic databases stored on CD-ROM, and certainly slower than their online equivalents. The problem is more evident with CD-ROMs such as SUPERMAP (a statistical/cartographic database) which can take many minutes to execute complex instructions such as to draw a map of Arkansas and then plot crime rates by county. But, of course, this kind of facility is not usually available online. CD-ROM producers are very aware of criticisms concerning response rates and are trying, with some success, to improve retrieval speed. It should be emphasised that response times with CD-ROMs are related to the speed of the processor used in the workstation as well as, in some cases, whether some or all of the indexes have been transferred from the CD-ROM to the hard disk (which should improve retrieval times). The installation of a CD-ROM on a local area network may cause a dramatic loss of speed and some producers for this reason caution against networking their products.

## Interfaces

Although the majority of CD-ROM drives are located in libraries rather than homes or offices, in many cases it is the end user rather than the librarian or information officer who sits at the workstation and searches the database. Such users are unlikely to have either the time or the inclination to master complicated retrieval systems or to use them frequently enough to retain any acquired expertise. This is in contrast to print products, which are often searched by end users rather than librarians but which are normally fairly straightforward to use, and online databases whose pricing encourages searching by experienced information professionals rather than end users.

The user interface, which controls the interaction between the searcher and the software, is therefore a crucial feature in any CD-ROM product. Much ingenuity has been applied to the design of CD-ROM interfaces [11]. Unfortunately one consequence is that rival producers have designed different interfaces for their products. Some software such as that designed by SilverPlatter and DIALOG Ondisc is used with many different CD-ROMs but in other cases unique software has been designed for just one title. The diversity of interface design is much greater than with online databases where a relatively small number of vendors account for the majority of databases. Indeed, the interface is an area of competition between publishers, each trying to produce a simpler interface to more powerful retrieval facilities. Such competition is most evident, of course, when the same database is available with different software on rival CD-ROMs.

Traditionally online systems have opted to transact the dialogue between the searcher and the retrieval engine through a command language which has its own vocabulary and syntax. Such languages are flexible (with a small number of commands it is possible to execute a wide range of instructions) and efficient, enabling instructions to be given quickly. This latter quality is important for systems which charge by connect time. Unfortunately, command languages have to be learned, practised and regularly used if they are to be effective.

This makes them much more suitable for information professionals than end users. As a consequence, most CD-ROM producers have opted for other methods of dialogue transaction, though some such as DIALOG Ondisc provide a command language as well as an alternative (interestingly, the online vendors are now frequently offering a menu-driven alternative to command languages largely in order to attract end users).

The full-screen menu interface as used by DIALOG with databases like CANADIAN BUSINESS AND CURRENT AFFAIRS (CBCA) relies upon successive menu screens, each menu offering a number of choices one of which must be selected by the user. The menus guide the user through the search process step-by-step and are effective with users who have little or no training. Terms can be combined using Boolean operators but this is masked from the user. On CBCA, for example, the Boolean AND is activated by choosing 'Limit with additional concepts or terms' and OR by selecting 'Include alternate terms', both included in the 'Modify Existing Search' menu. The process can be long, however, involving many menus, and after a while it can become tedious. Menus also lack flexibility; it may be necessary to re-cycle several times through the same menus in order to complete a search. Finally, it is difficult to encapsulate a complex search process in a series of short menus each of which must be accommodated on one screen. Menus are therefore most suitable for CD-ROMs which can be searched using simple and short strategies.

Pull-down or pop-up menus are also widely used by CD-ROMs such as the Canadian OCCUPATIONAL HEALTH AND SAFETY INFORMATION. In such cases the user must activate each menu (normally with a mouse). This provides more flexibility but demands more knowledge of the user who has to know which menu to activate at which point in the search process.

A different approach, and one exemplified by SilverPlatter with its many CD-ROMs, is the command menu. Commands must be selected and implemented by the user but the commands are listed on the screen as an aide-memoire. The command menus may be context-sensitive so that only those commands which can be used at that point in the search are available to the user. Even so, users must learn what each command does and when to use it in the search process. This involves self-study of manuals and/or training sessions.

Window and icon environments are increasingly being implemented by CD-ROM producers to give users direct manipulation. By placing the cursor over an icon (a graphic representation of an object, concept or message) or word, usually with a mouse, it is possible to carry out a variety of tasks quickly and efficiently. COMPTON'S MULTIMEDIA ENCYCLOPEDIA displays icons on the left-hand side of the screen which can be selected to display illustrations or activate sound and animation sequences.

CD-ROM interfaces, unlike their online cousins, tend to make good use of colour; it is therefore important to have a colour monitor. Furthermore, products which make heavy use of illustrations, like National Geographic's MAMMALS require high quality VGA or Super VGA monitors. Hardware suitable for online searching, therefore, may be less satisfactory with CD-ROMs.

## CONCLUSION

Clearly, in the first instance products are measured against the information needs of an individual, department or company; but just as print-based reference works should be evaluated, so too should those available electronically. Indeed it is arguable that products which rely on the intervention of computer software to release their wealth of information need a more stringent and disciplined examination. Once they have been noted as 'of interest', a second series of decisions must be made: should they be purchased online or ondisc? If available from various hosts/publishers, which should be chosen? Does the electronic version offer anything which cannot be found in print? Or indeed, does the electronic version have any defects not apparent in the original print? At the time of writing, at least one database producer has expressed a *caveat emptor* philosophy, underlining the need for evaluation. It certainly should not be assumed that print always takes second place to its newer electronic rivals. It is not Ludite, simply prudent, to select the old fashioned when the new cannot measure up to it!

Katz suggested the following evaluation criteria for print-based sources: purpose, authority, scope, audience, cost and format. From these it would be wise to select authority and scope for particular attention and mention specifically coverage, timeliness, visible standards, accessibility, accuracy, design appropriateness, fitness of purpose and finally reliability (of both entrée and content) for electronic products. When new databases - be they online or ondisc - have to be added to the portfolio in use by a company, some if not all of these considerations should be exercised.

This *Manual* sets out to help users select databases in areas unfamiliar to them but clearly it is impossible for authors to deal with every database extant. Other reference works contain subjective information on databases and many journals contain reviews of databases - these are an excellent source of unbiased assessments [12]. While this chapter has highlighted those considerations that should be applied when looking at and evaluating databases in general, the remainder of the *Manual* sets out in the various chapters a selection of evaluated databases which can be used to advantage in various subject areas.

## REFERENCES

1.   William A Katz. *An introduction to reference work,* vol. 1, 5th ed. New York: McGraw-Hill, 1987, 23-30

2.   J A Large. Evaluating online and CD-ROM reference sources. *Journal of Librarianship* 21(2) April 1989, 87-108

3.   Denis J Grogan. Oxford English Dictionary. *In* C J Armstrong & J A Large (eds). *CD-ROM Information Products: an Evaluative Guide and Directory* vol. 1. Aldershot: Gower, 1990, 213-238

4.   Norman Desmarais. USA Wars: The Civil War (Review). *CD-ROM Librarian* 6(9) October 1991, 40-41

5.   CD-ROM Facts & Figures [Pamphlet]. London: TFPL Publishing, 1990

6.   Steven D Zink. Towards More Critical Reviewing and Analysis of CD-ROM User Software Interfaces. *CD-ROM Professional* 4(1), 1991, 16-24

7.   Chris Armstrong. Postcode Address File on Compact Disc. *In* C J Armstrong & J A Large (eds). *CD-ROM Information Products: The Evaluative Guide* vol. 2. Aldershot: Gower, 1991, 331-348

8.   Reva Basch. Measuring the quality of the data: report on the Fourth Annual SCOUG Retreat. *Database Searcher* 6(8) October 1990, 18-23

9.   Joan Day. ABI/Inform Ondisc. *In* C J Armstrong & J A Large (eds). *CD-ROM Information Products: an Evaluative Guide and Directory* vol. 1. Aldershot: Gower, 1990, 3-21

10.  Ben Shneiderman. *Designing the User Interface: Strategies for Effective Human-Computer Interaction.* Reading, Mass: Addison-Wesley, 1987, 273-274

11.  Andy Large. The user interface to CD-ROM databases. *Journal of Librarianship and Information Science* 23(4) December 1991, 203-217

12.  See for instance, the journals: *CD-ROM Librarian* or *CD-ROM Professional;* and *CD-ROM Information Products: The Evaluative Guide* series edited by C J Armstrong & J A Large as well as the *World Databases in [topic]* series currently in production by Bowker-Saur.

# 2 Citation indexing*

*David Bawden*

## INTRODUCTION

This chapter differs from others in this book as it deals with a type of index and searching technique of general applicability, rather than with searching in one subject area. Citation searching, a form of searching offering both unique capabilities in itself, and also an ideal complement to other searching techniques, well merits individual treatment. This is especially so because the advantages of citation searching are still not well-recognized, despite the fact that citation indexes have been available for many years.

Citation indexes are at present only available online in the forms of the files produced by the Institute of Scientific Information (ISI). This chapter is intended to be both an introduction to the concept of citation searching and an exposition of its advantages, as well as a primer on the use of the ISI files. It is intended to be balanced in the weight given to the three subject areas covered by the ISI files (science and technology, social sciences and arts and humanities), while emphasising the value of citation searching for multi-disciplinary and cross-disciplinary searching. The references in the bibliography therefore include both detailed treatments of the specifics of citation searching in particular situations, and also more discursive discussions of the value of citation indexes *per se*.

## NATURE AND PRINCIPLES OF CITATION SEARCHING

The basic idea of citation searching is extremely simple. Virtually all scholarly documents (journal and magazine articles, books and chapters in them, reports, etc.) include references to related work in the form of

* I am grateful to the editors of this volume and to Robert Kimberley of ISI's European branch for helpful suggestions during the preparation of this chapter.

footnotes or lists of references. These references, or citations, are usually bibliographic descriptions of other documents in which related material may be found although they may sometimes be more informal, for example, 'personal communication'. Necessarily they must be older than, or at best contemporaneous with, the citing document.

Citations are of obvious value in referring the reader to related older material; following up references is perhaps the most widely used technique of information retrieval. Citation indexing stands this process on its head by allowing a search for documents which have cited a particular reference. So, if Professor Blue refers to an article by Dr. Black in a paper, it will be easy for a reader of Blue's paper to follow up the reference to Black's previous related writings. Conversely, a reader knowing of, and interested in, Black's article could find Blue's paper from a citation index, using the bibliographical reference of Black's paper as the starting point; a kind of index term.

A citation index is therefore a list of bibliographical references, sorted initially by first author's name and then by date, volume, etc, so that a particular cited document is uniquely identified. Alongside that document's identification are listed details of those documents which have cited it, in a manner analogous to any subject index.

It is important to note that the time coverage of a citation index refers to the publication dates of the citing papers. The dates of the cited documents are unrestricted, since authors can (and do) cite work of any age. A citation index may include as entry points - index terms - documents from the most up-to-date which could be cited in a published paper to the oldest works recognized as scholarly documents. Humanities scholars, in particular, cite old material very often; ISI's ARTS AND HUMANITIES SEARCH contains hundreds of citations to authors such as Socrates, Herodotus, and Aristotle.

We should also note that operational citation indexes note merely that a document has been cited but give no indication of the reason for the citation. There must be some relation, but what it is will only become clear from an examination of the citing document. There have been proposals for citation indexes which would include such information, as discussed later in this chapter, but these have never been put into practice.

A good deal of research has been carried out on the citation practices of authors in different disciplines in an attempt to clarify types of citation. This work is summarized and discussed by Oppenheim [1], Cronin [2], Cano [3], Sen [4] and Garfield [5].

Weinstock [6] lists fifteen principal reasons for citation, and many of the other classifications are variants on these:

1.    Paying homage to pioneers.
2.    Giving credit to related work.
3.    Identifying methods, equipment, etc.
4.    Providing background reading.
5.    Correcting one's own work.
6.    Correcting the work of others.
7.    Criticising previous work.
8.    Substantiating claims.
9.    Alerting readers to forthcoming publications.
10.   Providing leads to poorly disseminated work.
11.   Authenticating data and facts.
12.   Identifying the original publications in which an idea was discussed.
13.   Identifying the original publication describing an eponymic concept or term, for example, Hodgkin's disease.
14.   Disclaiming work or ideas of others.
15.   Disputing priority claims by others.

There are therefore many valid reasons for one document to cite another. A somewhat cynical view of human nature, supported by a good deal of sociological research [2], suggests that authors often include inappropriate citations and omit appropriate ones for a variety of rather dubious reasons. These include:

- inclusion of irrelevant citations to impress readers with the author's breadth of knowledge
- citation of irrelevant work by respected authors to lend a spurious validity to an argument
- citation only of work by the author's friends, colleagues and compatriots

and • failing to cite relevant work through simple ignorance or forgetfulness.

Citation practices of authors, both individually and en masse, are clearly of importance given the increasing tendency for citation analysis to be used for sociometric and scientometric studies. The use of citation analysis for studies of the sociology of science, for the mapping of scientific disciplines and (most notoriously) for the assessment of research quality, in order to distribute funding and to develop a national research policy, is a highly controversial topic [2, 7-11].

Even from the viewpoint of simple information retrieval, the searcher should be aware of the lack of rigour and consistency in citation practices. This is hardly a fatal flaw, particularly considering the known deficiencies of other access points, for example, human intellectual indexing. As with other searching techniques, searchers need to allow for the problems and develop flexible strategies to overcome them.

The unspecified nature of the relation between citing and cited documents is a perennial problem. As Cronin [2] expresses it:

'A feature of citation-based information retrieval systems (from the user's point of view) is that a large number of unproductive or irrelevant leads are included ... because authors cite in different ways and for different reasons, not all the connections prove to be useful.'

This is not invariably so by any means. Citation searching, used in appropriate circumstances, can give admirably precise retrieval: examples are given later in the chapter. This problem must, however, always be borne in mind.

Synge [12] sums up the situation well:

'[citation indexing] depends for intellectual content on citations by authors, who are sometimes prodded by editors and referees. Its patchiness is therefore not surprising, but frequently it gives access to relevant and up-to-date documents not easily accessible by other means.'

On the other hand, there are very clear advantages in being able to carry out a search for documents related in some way to a starting document, without any need to consider indexing policies, etc. As White [13] puts it:

'In return for the inevitable false drop, one almost always finds some nice surprises - relevant papers whose existence would not be revealed by subject indexing of the usual kind.'

When used in the right way, to answer the right sort of question, citation searching can prove uniquely useful. It is, in fact, a virtually indispensable tool for effective online searching of bibliographic material, particularly if used in conjunction with other types of databases and other search techniques.

## CITATION INDEXES IN PRACTICE

The historical development of the idea of citation indexing, an interesting topic in itself, has been described in detail [6, 7, 14].

The first practical example of a citation index was *Shepard's Citations*, an American legal reference tool, in use as long ago as 1873 [15]. A legal system based on precedents set in previous cases is clearly an obvious application for citation indexing, since it will usually be important to ensure that a decision of importance has not been overturned, reversed, limited or otherwise commented upon. The document references in *Shepard's* are the case numbers quoted in legal reports. Shepard's index is available in computerized form as part of the WESTLAW® system [16].

Statistics is another field of study well suited to citation indexing and searching because of the high occurrence of method papers being referred to descriptions of their applications [17]. A number of citation indexes covering various aspects of statistics were produced from the 1950s onwards, but none proved viable in the longer term and none is publicly available in computerised form.

A few other citation indexes have been produced, some in computer form, but only on an experimental basis [6, 7, 14].

### The ISI databases

Listed below is a summary of the present (1990) state of availability of the ISI citation databases. Details are, of course, liable to change with time.

| Database | Vendor | Dates |
|---|---|---|
| Arts and Humanities Search | DIALOG | 1980-date |
| | BRS | 1980-date |
| Scisearch | DIALOG | 1974-date |
| | Data-Star | 1980-date |
| | DIMDI | 1974-date |
| | ORBIT | 1974-date |
| | CD-ROM | 1980-date |
| Social Scisearch | DIALOG | 1972-date |
| | BRS | 1972-date |
| | DIMDI | 1973-date |
| | Data-Star | 1972-date |
| | CD-ROM | 1981-date |
| Computer and Mathematics Search | BRS | 1980-date |

## TECHNIQUES OF CITATION SEARCHING

In this section, some of the main ways of accessing information from online citation databases are outlined. The techniques of searching the ISI databases are described in a number of publications [18-22]. For the most part, the techniques do not differ in principle between the online and CD-ROM implementations. Where features are significantly different, this is explicitly noted here. The CD-ROM implementations of citation databases are discussed in detail by Garfield [23] and Cawkell [24].

### Simple citation searching

The most straightforward use of a citation index is to find documents citing a known starting-point document. This, in principle, is done by searching directly for the cited reference description. In practice, this is not such a good idea. The full cited-reference description (author, year, volume, page, title) is a long string to type, and the searching languages are unforgiving of misplaced spaces, missing commas, etc. It can be difficult to know whether a null result means that there are no citations, or that a typing error has been made. Also, and perhaps more significant, variability in the description of the cited reference means that some citations will almost inevitably be missed by a precise search command. The problems of variant, and downright erroneous, citations have been discussed in detail [25, 26].

It is therefore *always* a good idea to display the section of the citation index around the required cited reference, using the appropriate system command (EXPAND on DIALOG, etc), and then select the entries required. This enables the searcher to spot variations in author's initials and bibliographic details. If comprehensive recall is important, the searcher should consider the possibility of variations of surname which could cause the record to appear in very different parts of the index. This is particularly possible with hyphenated surnames, and those beginning with VAN, DE, etc.

Truncation can, of course, be used for a fairly general search, for example (with DIALOG syntax):

BLUE A, 1984?      [citations to all   A. Blue's 1984 documents]
BLUE A, 198?       [citations to all   A. Blue's papers of the 1980s]
BLUE A,?           [citations to all   A. Blue's papers]

It is important to remember that only the first author's name is used in the cited reference record. To find citations to all of an author's works, it will be necessary first to do an author search to identify all potential cited documents, then construct a search strategy to cover all of them.

One or more key papers must be known as the starting point for a citation search, which can therefore be carried out only with some knowledge of publications in the area. If none are known, then an initial search must be carried out to identify one or more references; either on the ISI databases, using conventional access points such as title words, or on alternative subject-oriented databases.

It is always necessary to consider alternative cited references as starting points, since authors will not always choose the same paper to cite, even to make the same point. Often an original paper is no longer referenced, having been replaced for citation purposes by later publications or by review articles, or having simply passed into common knowledge and thus there being considered no need to reference; the so-called obliteration phenomenon [1]. These factors mean that older publications are less cited than more recent ones. This effect varies greatly with subject discipline, being most evident in the experimental sciences.

An example is a search for applications of a data analysis method termed non-linear mapping, first described in a paper by J.W. Sammon in 1969. This paper has one hundred and thirty citations in SCISEARCH. A slightly modified version of this algorithm was introduced by R.J. Howarth in 1973, and has been cited thirty-one times.

It is increasingly being used as a standard method reference, in place of Sammon's paper. If a complete bibliography on this topic were required, citations to either of these papers would have to be found.

Different citation databases have varying searching facilities, appropriate to their subject matter. ARTS AND HUMANITIES SEARCH, for example, has a specific citation convention for works of art without specification of date; this allows for different editions, etc. For example, to find citations to Charles Dickens' *Mystery of Edwin Drood*, the DIALOG search statement would be:

    CR=DICKENS? AND CW=DROOD

The truncation ? after Dickens' name allows for all possible edition dates, pagination, etc. The single term, DROOD, allows for variant citations of the title, even for different languages. The sixty-five references retrieved had such varying forms of citations as:

    DICKENS C, EDWIN DROOD
    DICKENS C, 1974, EDWIN DROOD
    DICKENS C, 1982, EDWIN DROOD
    DICKENS C, 1983, MISTERO EDWIN DROOD
    DICKENS C, MYSTERE DEDWIN DROOD

The ARTS AND HUMANITIES SEARCH database has special features [27, 28] giving particular treatment to certain types of cited reference, of importance in the humanities. Sacred texts, book reviews and musical scores are examples. The ISI user guide should be consulted for full details, but some examples are given here to illustrate the sort of facilities offered.

A searcher wishing to find articles discussing Botticelli's painting 'Primavera', for example, could use the direct search statement (BRS syntax):

    BOTTICELLI-S$ WITH PRIMAVERA.CR

to find twenty-five citing references, the titles of which are listed in Figure 2.1.

**Figure 2.1: Results of Botticelli search using ARTS AND HUMANITIES SEARCH.**

```
BOTTICELLI, SANDRO PRIMAVERA RESTORED
IMAGES OF SPRING IN BOTTICELLI AND HORACE
THE SOURCE OF BOTTICELLI PRIMAVERA
THE TWO MAYINGS IN CHAUCER'S KNIGHT'S TALE - CONVENTION AND INVENTION
MOVING PICTURES (MOVIES, PAINTING AND PHOTOGRAPHY) AS ART
BOTTICELLI PRIMAVERA
A WOMAN SEEING
METAPHOR IN EARLY RENAISSANCE ART
THE PRESENCE OF BOTTICELLI PRIMAVERA
IN DETAIL - BOTTICELLI PRIMAVERA
RENAISSANCE VARIANTS ON A THEME BY KEATS
BOTTICELLI PRIMAVERA AND THE TRADITION OF DANTE
THE PORTICO FRIEZE OF LORENZO IL-MAGNIFICO
BOTTICELLI PRIMAVERA - CHE VOLEA SINTENDESSE
THE CARE AND RESTORATION OF ART WORKS ON PAPER
A BRIGHT AND HAPPY 400TH BIRTHDAY YEAR FOR THE REMARKABLE UFFIZI
THE UFFIZI - FOUR CENTURIES OF A GALLERY
```

**Figure 2.1:** (cont.)

```
BOCCACCIO  EXPERIMENTATION  WITH  VERBAL  PORTRAITS  FROM  THE  FILOCOLO  TO
THE  DECAMERON
IN DETAIL - MATISSE DANCE
A MAENAD FROM PISA IN THE PRIMAVERA
THE CENTRAL FIGURES IN BOTTICELLI'S PRIMAVERA
OBSERVATIONS ON THE RECEPTION OF THE ANTIQUE IN RENAISSANCE PAINTING
BOTTICELLI PRIMAVERA AND VENERE - 18 LITERARY READINGS
CEZANNE BATHERS - FORM AND CONTENT
WHAT IS A MASTERPIECE
```

This list of titles indicates the wide range of material of relevance (particularly marked in humanities information), and the virtual impossibility of retrieving it by use of subject indexing.

A further elaboration is possible - if the searcher or enquirer has no reproduction of the painting to hand, the search statement:

BOTTICELLI-S$ WITH PRIMAVERA WITH JLLUSTRATION.CR

will restrict the output to those articles giving a reproduction (in this case fifteen out of the twenty-five).

Reviews of works of art can easily be found by citation search. The search statement:

TANNER-A$ WITH MESSIDOR.CR

retrieves fourteen documents referring to Alain Tanner's 1979 film 'Messidor'; combining this set with the publication type, film review, gives four reviews.

Of course, there is no certainty that reviews found in this way will be reviews of the particular work sought, since reviewers may well cite other works in the course of their discussion. A search:

TOLKIEN-JRR$.CR and PT=B [that is, publication type = book review]

retrieves forty-one documents, thirty-six of which are indeed reviews of Tolkien's works, while five are reviews of works by other authors in which the reviewer has, incidentally, cited works of Tolkien. Though potentially irritating, this can in fact be a valuable way of following up an author's work, given the importance of book reviews in the humanities.

**Finding related records**

This is a means of searching currently only available in CD-ROM implementations of the ISI citation databases. It offers a powerful and convenient means of browsing among sets of related documents.

Documents are related if they have one or more cited references in common. These relationships are set up by the database producer's processing as part of database creation, and are therefore immediately, and automatically, available for use. Up to twenty related references can be displayed in order of the strength of the relation; that is, the number of cited references in common. It is then possible for the user to browse through five levels of related records, returning to the starting point when desired.

To give an example, using the 1989 SCISEARCH CD-ROM, the starting point was an article by A.J. Lawson entitled 'Chemical Structure Browsing'. This was shown as having six related records. A single command in the CD-ROM search software displays these. Their titles are:

CLUSTERING A LARGE NUMBER OF COMPOUNDS. 1. ESTABLISHING THE METHOD
ON AN INITIAL SAMPLE.
CHEMICAL DATABASE PROCESSING USING PARALLEL COMPUTER HARDWARE.
CHEMICAL STRUCTURE INFORMATION SYSTEMS - INTRODUCTION.
CREATIVITY AND SCIENCE. 2. THE PROCESS OF SCIENTIFIC DISCOVERY.
CORCHOP - AN INTERACTIVE ROUTINE FOR THE DIMENSION REDUCTION OF
LARGE QSAR DATA SETS.
MULTIVARIATE QSAR METHODS WHICH MAY BE APPLIED TO PESTICIDE RE-
SEARCH.

It is clear that we have here a fairly diffuse set of records, with some relation, but no very tightly defined common subject. This is ideal for loose browsing for inspiration.

If we assume that our interests are most closely met by the first of these articles, dealing with the clustering of large sets of chemical structures, we find that this has seventeen related records which we can display. These lead to articles from the chemical, statistical and computing literature, all dealing in some way with the algorithms involved in the clustering of structures. This is a good example of the way in which this form of browsing, based on citation relationships, can lead very rapidly to interdisciplinary analogies.

## SEARCHING FOR COMBINATIONS OF CITATION - CO-CITATIONS

A search for documents citing a combination of references can be a powerful means of identifying information on very specific topics, especially in interdisciplinary areas. The strategy is simple. Citation searches are carried out for documents or authors reflecting each subject concept of interest, and the results ANDed together. It is rare, in practice, to find any answers when trying to combine three or more specific citations, unless they are unusually heavily cited or correspond to a tight subject topic.

An example shows the specificity obtained by combining just two sets of citing references. C.J. van Rijsbergen and G. Salton have both written books giving overviews of the development of research on document retrieval systems. B.S. Everitt, A.D. Gordon and P.H.A. Sneath have all written standard texts on cluster analysis algorithms and programs. Searching for documents citing either information retrieval book and any one of the clustering texts should identify work applying clustering methods to document retrieval.

On SOCIAL SCISEARCH, seven such references are found with the titles:

RECENT TRENDS IN HIERARCHIC DOCUMENT CLUSTERING - A CRITICAL REVIEW
RETRIEVAL TECHNIQUES
THE CONTRIBUTION OF EXPERIMENTAL INFORMATION RETRIEVAL TO LIBRAR-
IANSHIP AND INFORMATION STUDIES
SIMILARITY MEASURES IN SCIENTOMETRIC RESEARCH
QUERY SPECIFIC AUTOMATIC DOCUMENT CLASSIFICATION
HIERARCHICAL AGGLOMERATIVE CLUSTERING METHODS FOR AUTOMATIC
DOCUMENT CLASSIFICATION
SIMILARITY COEFFICIENTS AND WEIGHTING FUNCTIONS FOR AUTOMATIC
DOCUMENT CLASSIFICATION - AN EMPIRICAL COMPARISON

Clearly, the combination of cited references from different fields of study has led rather precisely to the literature of an interdisciplinary topic. Four of the seven papers are, in fact, reviews, and hence particularly useful as a lead-in to the literature. The full search is shown in Search 2.1.

## Search 2.1: Co-citation search

```
File 7:SOCIAL SCISEARCH _ 72-90/WK36
      (COPR. ISI INC.1990)

      Set     Items    Description
      ---     -----    -----------
?e cr=vanrijsbergen cj, 1979

Ref  Items    Index-term
E1     8      CR=VANRIJSBERGEN CJ, 1978, V14, P75, DREXEL LIBRA
E2     1      CR=VANRIJSBERGEN CJ, 1978, V34, P294, J DOCUMENTA
E3     0     *CR=VANRIJSBERGEN CJ, 1979
E4     2      CR=VANRIJSBERGEN CJ, 1979, CH6, INFORMATION RETRI
E5   131      CR=VANRIJSBERGEN CJ, 1979, INFORMATION RETRIEVA
E6     1      CR=VANRIJSBERGEN CJ, 1979, INFORMATION RETREVAL
E7     1      CR=VANRIJSBERGEN CJ, 1979, P167, INFORMATION RETR
E8     1      CR=VANRIJSBERGEN CJ, 1979, P17, INFORMATION RETRI
E9     1      CR=VANRIJSBERGEN CJ, 1979, P38, INFORMATION RETRI
E10    1      CR=VANRIJSBERGEN CJ, 1980, V1, P91, PROG COMMUN S
E11    5      CR=VANRIJSBERGEN CJ, 1980, INFORMATION RETRIEVA
E12    1      CR=VANRIJSBERGEN CJ, 1980, NEW MODELS PROBABILI

      Enter P or E for more
?s e4-e9,e11
                 2      CR=VANRIJSBERGEN CJ, 1979, CH6, INFORMATION RETRI
               131      CR=VANRIJSBERGEN CJ, 1979, INFORMATION RETRIEVA
                 1      CR=VANRIJSBERGEN CJ, 1979, INFORMATION RETREVAL
                 1      CR=VANRIJSBERGEN CJ, 1979, P167, INFORMATION RETR
                 1      CR=VANRIJSBERGEN CJ, 1979, P17, INFORMATION RETRI
                 1      CR=VANRIJSBERGEN CJ, 1979, P38, INFORMATION RETRI
                 5      CR=VANRIJSBERGEN CJ, 1980, INFORMATION RETRIEVA
      S1       142      E4-E9,E11
?e cr=salton g, 1983

Ref  Items    Index-term
E1     1      CR=SALTON G, 1982, 5TH P INT C INF RETR
E2     2      CR=SALTON G, 1982, 82511 CORN U DEP COM
E3     0     *CR=SALTON G, 1983
E4     1      CR=SALTON G, 1983, ACCESS INFORMATION H
E5     1      CR=SALTON G, 1983, CH4, INTRO MODERN INFORMA
E6     1      CR=SALTON G, 1983, CH5, INTRO MODERN INFORMA
E7     1      CR=SALTON G, 1983, COMP 2 METHODS BOOLE
E8     1      CR=SALTON G, 1983, DYNAMIC INFORMATION
E9     3      CR=SALTON G, 1983, INTRO INFORMATION RE
E10  183      CR=SALTON G, 1983, INTRO MODERN INFORMA
E11    1      CR=SALTON G, 1983, P145, INTRO MODERN INFORMA
E12    1      CR=SALTON G, 1983, P151, MAY MAY P SIGIR ACM

      Enter P or E for more
?p
Ref  Items    Index-term
E13    2      CR=SALTON G, 1983, P151, RES DEV INFORMATION
E14    1      CR=SALTON G, 1983, P252, P ACM SIGIR C
E15    1      CR=SALTON G, 1983, P257, INTRO MODERN INFORMA
E16    1      CR=SALTON G, 1983, P258, INTRO MODERN INFORMA
E17    1      CR=SALTON G, 1983, P267, INTRO MODERN INFORMA
E18    1      CR=SALTON G, 1983, P52, COMPUT SCI SERIES
E19    1      CR=SALTON G, 1983, P59, INTRO MODERN INFORMA
E20    1      CR=SALTON G, 1983, P63, INTRO MODERN INFORMA
E21    1      CR=SALTON G, 1983, P66, INTRO MODERN INFORMA
E22    1      CR=SALTON G, 1983, P75, MODERN INFORMATION R
```

**Search 2.1:** (cont.)

```
E23     1    CR=SALTON G, 1983, P755, INFORMATION PROCESSI
E24     2    CR=SALTON G, 1983, RES DEV INFORMATION

      Enter P or E for more
?s e5-e6,e9-e11,e15-e17,e19-e22
              1    CR=SALTON G, 1983, CH4, INTRO MODERN INFORMA
              1    CR=SALTON G, 1983, CH5, INTRO MODERN INFORMA
              3    CR=SALTON G, 1983, INTRO INFORMATION RE
            183    CR=SALTON G, 1983, INTRO MODERN INFORMA
              1    CR=SALTON G, 1983, P145, INTRO MODERN INFORMA
              1    CR=SALTON G, 1983, P257, INTRO MODERN INFORMA
              1    CR=SALTON G, 1983, P258, INTRO MODERN INFORMA
              1    CR=SALTON G, 1983, P267, INTRO MODERN INFORMA
              1    CR=SALTON G, 1983, P59, INTRO MODERN INFORMA
              1    CR=SALTON G, 1983, P63, INTRO MODERN INFORMA
              1    CR=SALTON G, 1983, P66, INTRO MODERN INFORMA
              1    CR=SALTON G, 1983, P75, MODERN INFORMATION R
    S2      196    E5-E6,E9-E11,E15-E17,E19-E22
? e cr=everitt bs, 1980
Ref  Items    Index-term
E1      28    CR=EVERITT BS, 1979, V9, P581, PSYCHOL MED
E2       3    CR=EVERITT BS, 1979, V9, P581, PSYCHOLOGICAL MEDI
E3       0   *CR=EVERITT BS, 1980
E4       1    CR=EVERITT BS, 1980, ADV METHODS DATA EXP
E5      28    CR=EVERITT BS, 1980, CLUSTER ANAL
E6       1    CR=EVERITT BS, 1980, FINITE MIXTURE DISTR
E7       1    CR=EVERITT BS, 1981, CLUSTER ANAL
E8      41    CR=EVERITT BS, 1981, FINITE MIXTURE DISTR
E9       1    CR=EVERITT BS, 1981, P279, INTERPRETING MULTIVA
E10     24    CR=EVERITT BS, 1981, V138, P336, BRIT J PSYCHIAT
E11     10    CR=EVERITT BS, 1981, V16, P171, MULTIVAR BEHAV RE
E12      1    CR=EVERITT BS, 1982, V120, P143, BRIT J PSYCHIAT

      Enter P or E for more
?s e5,e7
             28    CR=EVERITT BS, 1980, CLUSTER ANAL
              1    CR=EVERITT BS, 1981, CLUSTER ANAL
    S3       29    E5,E7
?e cr=gordon ad, 1981
Ref  Items    Index-term
E1       1    CR=GORDON AD, 1980, P161, ANAL DONNEES INFORMA
E2       1    CR=GORDON AD, 1980, P161, ANAL DONNES INFORMAT
E3       0   *CR=GORDON AD, 1981
E4      24    CR=GORDON AD, 1981, CLASSIFICATION
E5      16    CR=GORDON AD, 1981, CLASSIFICATION METHO
E6       1    CR=GORDON AD, 1981, OCT UPST WOM HIST C
E7       1    CR=GORDON AD, 1986, V3, J CLASSIFICATION
E8       5    CR=GORDON AD, 1987, V150, P119, J ROY STAT SOC A
E9       1    CR=GORDON AD, 1987, V150, P119, J ROYAL STATISTI
E10      1    CR=GORDON AD, 1987, V150, P119, J ROYAL STATISTIC
E11      1    CR=GORDON AD, 1987, V4, P85, J CLASSIF
E12      1    CR=GORDON ADD, 1978, BUSINESS POLITICS RI

      Enter P or E for more
?s e4,e5
             24    CR=GORDON AD, 1981, CLASSIFICATION
             16    CR=GORDON AD, 1981, CLASSIFICATION METHO
    S4       40    E4,E5
?e cr=sneath pha, 1973
```

**Search 2.1:** (cont.)

```
Ref  Items   Index-term
E1       1   CR=SNEATH PHA, 1972, V7, P29, METHODS MICROBIOLO
E2       1   CR=SNEATH PHA, 1972, V72, P377, J GEN MICROBIOL
E3       0  *CR=SNEATH PHA, 1973
E4       1   CR=SNEATH PHA, 1973, COMMUNICATION
E5       1   CR=SNEATH PHA, 1973, NUMERIAL TAXONOMY
E6       1   CR=SNEATH PHA, 1973, NUMERICAL TAXONOMY
E7     289   CR=SNEATH PHA, 1973, NUMERICAL TAXONOMY
E8     114   CR=SNEATH PHA, 1973, NUMERICAL TAXONOMY P
E9       5   CR=SNEATH PHA, 1973, PRINCIPLES NUMERICAL
E10      2   CR=SNEATH PHA, 1973, PRINCIPLES PRACTICE
E11      1   CR=SNEATH PHA, 1973, P1, NUMERICAL TAXONOMY
E12      1   CR=SNEATH PHA, 1973, P115, NUMERICAL TAXONOMY P

         Enter P or E for more
?p
Ref  Items   Index-term
E13      1   CR=SNEATH PHA, 1973, P119, NUMERICAL TAXONOMY P
E14      4   CR=SNEATH PHA, 1973, P131, NUMERICAL TAXONOMY
E15      1   CR=SNEATH PHA, 1973, P150, NUMERICAL TAXONOMY
E16      1   CR=SNEATH PHA, 1973, P178, NUMERICAL TAXONOMY
E17      1   CR=SNEATH PHA, 1973, P188, NUMERICAL TAXONOMY
E18      1   CR=SNEATH PHA, 1973, P201, NUMERICAL TAXONOMY P
E19      2   CR=SNEATH PHA, 1973, P216, NUMERICAL TAXONOMY
E20      1   CR=SNEATH PHA, 1973, P490, NUMERICAL TAXONOMY
E21      1   CR=SNEATH PHA, 1973, P573, NUMERICAL TAXONOMY
E22      1   CR=SNEATH PHA, 1974, NUMERICAL TAXONOMY
E23      1   CR=SNEATH PHA, 1974, NUMERICAL TAXONOMY P
E24      1   CR=SNEATH PHA, 1974, P354, BERGEYS MANUAL DETER

         Enter P or E for more
?s e5-e23
                   1   CR=SNEATH PHA, 1973, NUMERIAL TAXONOMY
                   1   CR=SNEATH PHA, 1973, NUMERICAL TAXONOMY
                 114   CR=SNEATH PHA, 1973, NUMERICAL TAXONOMY P
                   5   CR=SNEATH PHA, 1973, PRINCIPLES NUMERICAL
                   2   CR=SNEATH PHA, 1973, PRINCIPLES PRACTICE
                   1   CR=SNEATH PHA, 1973, P1, NUMERICAL TAXONOMY
                   1   CR=SNEATH PHA, 1973, P115, NUMERICAL TAXONOMY
                   1   CR=SNEATH PHA, 1973, P119, NUMERICAL TAXONOMY P
                   4   CR=SNEATH PHA, 1973, P131, NUMERICAL TAXONOMY
                   1   CR=SNEATH PHA, 1973, P150, NUMERICAL TAXONOMY
                   1   CR=SNEATH PHA, 1973, P178, NUMERICAL TAXONOMY
                   1   CR=SNEATH PHA, 1973, P188, NUMERICAL TAXONOMY
                   1   CR=SNEATH PHA, 1973, P201, NUMERICAL TAXONOMY P
                   2   CR=SNEATH PHA, 1973, P216, NUMERICAL TAXONOMY
                   1   CR=SNEATH PHA, 1973, P490, NUMERICAL TAXONOMY
                   1   CR=SNEATH PHA, 1973, P573, NUMERICAL TAXONOMY
                   1   CR=SNEATH PHA, 1974, NUMERICAL TAXONOMY
                   1   CR=SNEATH PHA, 1974, NUMERICAL TAXONOMY P
      S5       429   E5-E23
?c (1 or 2) and (3 or 4 or 5)
                 142   1
                 196   2
                  29   3
                  40   4
                 429   5
      S6         7   (1 OR 2) AND (3 OR 4 OR 5)
?t6/3/1-7
```

**Search 2.1:** (cont.)

```
   6/3/1
02006142     Genuine Article#: AB438     Number of References: 13
   SIMILARITY MEASURES IN SCIENTOMETRIC RESEARCH - THE JACCARD INDEX VERSUS
SALTON COSINE FORMULA
   HAMERS, L; HEMERYCK Y; HERWEYERS G; JANSSEN M; KETERS H; ROUSSEAU R;
VANHOUTTE A
      KATHOLIEKE IND HOGESCH W VLAANDEREN,ZEEDIJK 101/B-8400
      OOSTENDE//BELGIUM/
   INFORMATION PROCESSING & MANAGEMENT, 1989, V25, N3, P315-318
   Language: ENGLISH                    Document Type: ARTICLE


   6/3/2
01922513     Genuine Article#: Q4140 Number of References: 119
   RECENT TRENDS IN HIERARCHIC DOCUMENT CLUSTERING - A CRITICAL-REVIEW
   WILLETT P
      UNIV SHEFFIELD,DEPT INFORMAT STUDIES/SHEFFIELD S10 2TN/S
      YORKSHIRE/ENGLAND/
   INFORMATION PROCESSING & MANAGEMENT, 1988, V24, N5, P577-597
   Language: ENGLISH                    Document Type: REVIEW, BIBLIOGRAPHY


   6/3/3
01870400     Genuine Article#: NO501 Number of References: 174
   RETRIEVAL TECHNIQUES
   BELKIN NJ; CROFT WB
      RUTGERS STATE UNIV,SCH COMMUN INFORMAT & LIB STUDIES,4 HUNTINGDON
      ST/NEW BRUNSWICK//NJ/08903; UNIV MASSACHUSETTS,DEPT COMP & INFORMAT
      SCI/AMHERST//MA/01003
   ANNUAL REVIEW OF INFORMATION SCIENCE AND TECHNOLOGY, 1987, V22, P109-145
   Language: ENGLISH                    Document Type: REVIEW, BIBLIOGRAPHY


   6/3/4
01735860     Genuine Article#: G8040 Number of References: 49
   THE CONTRIBUTION OF EXPERIMENTAL INFORMATION-RETRIEVAL TO LIBRARIANSHIP
AND INFORMATION STUDIES
   ENSER PGB
      COLL LIBRARIANSHIP WALES,DEPT MANAGEMENT & INFORMAT SYST/ABERYSTWYTH
      SY23 3AS//WALES/
   EDUCATION FOR INFORMATION, 1987, V5, N1, P3-14
   Language: ENGLISH                    Document Type: ARTICLE


   6/3/5
01489552     Genuine Article#: AMD10 Number of References: 19
   QUERY-SPECIFIC AUTOMATIC DOCUMENT CLASSIFICATION
   WILLETT P
      UNIV SHEFFIELD,DEPT INFORMAT STUDIES/SHEFFIELD S10 2TN/S
      YORKSHIRE/ENGLAND/
   INTERNATIONAL FORUM ON INFORMATION AND DOCUMENTATION, 1985, V10, N2, P
28-32
   Language: ENGLISH    Document Type: ARTICLE


   6/3/6
01410921     Genuine Article#: TT749 Number of References: 81
   HIERARCHIC AGGLOMERATIVE CLUSTERING METHODS FOR AUTOMATIC DOCUMENT
CLASSIFICATION
   GRIFFITHS A; ROBINSON LA; WILLETT P
      UNIV SHEFFIELD,DEPT INFORMAT STUDIES/SHEFFIELD S10 2TN/S
      YORKSHIRE/ENGLAND/
   JOURNAL OF DOCUMENTATION, 1984, V40, N3, P175-205
   Language: ENGLISH    Document Type: ARTICLE
```

**Search 2.1:** (cont.)

```
 6/3/7
 01301335      Genuine Article#: RY044 Number of References: 16
   SIMILARITY COEFFICIENTS AND WEIGHTING FUNCTIONS FOR AUTOMATIC DOCUMENT
 CLASSIFICATION - AN EMPIRICAL-COMPARISON
   WILLETT P
     UNIV SHEFFIELD,DEPT INFORMAT STUDIES/SHEFFIELD S10 2TN/S
     YORKSHIRE/ENGLAND/
   INTERNATIONAL CLASSIFICATION, 1983, V10, N3, P138-142
   Language: ENGLISH    Document Type: ARTICLE
```

A more general method of co-citation searching involves searching for co-cited authors, rather than particular documents. This method has been discussed by several authors [13, 29-31], with search strategies described in detail by White [31] and by Knapp [30]. The method involves a search for documents in which any item by each of two authors is cited, rather than specific items as in the above example. It is obviously important to choose authors prominent enough to have been cited frequently, whose work is sufficiently related for them to have been cited together, and whose names together imply some topic or aspect of a topic. These aspects may not be adequately described by conventional subject indexing; White [13] gives examples from SOCIAL SCISEARCH such as critical elections and voting behaviour; curiosity and exploration in animals; and geographical diffusion of innovation.

Although citations to all of an author's work may cover a wide subject area, the ANDing of two cited reference sets usually gives good discrimination. It also removes the false matching resulting from the (not uncommon) occurrence of individuals with the same surname and initials. For very highly cited authors, Knapp [30] recommends an intermediate step between co-cited author and co-cited document retrieval: the inclusion of publication year in the cited reference search statement.

Co-cited author searching has the limitation of including only those documents for which the author specified is the first author. For complete account to be taken of all citations to any author, it is necessary to work at the level of individual cited documents.

Three strategies for co-cited author retrieval have been proposed. The first simply involves a single pair of co-cited authors. White exemplifies this by a search for papers co-citing the work of the philosopher Hannah Arendt and the historian Ernst Nolte, to find material dealing with Nazism and fascism [13]. Chapman and Subramanyan [29] compared using SCISEARCH, a subject search, a co-cited document search, and a co-cited author search, to find references to cyclic adenosine monophosphate. Both of the co-citation searches found papers which could not have been retrieved from the subject (title word) search; admittedly not a sophisticated form of subject searching. A co-cited authors strategy retrieved more relevant material than a strategy based on co-cited documents. These authors recommend that cocitation searching be used alone, if precision of searching is very important, or in addition to a conventional subject search for good recall.

A second co-citation strategy involves the systematic pairing of co-citations to a small group of related authors. This is straightforward to carry out online. To give an example, consider the case of four cited authors, retrieved as sets 1 to 4 respectively. The required combinations are then:

| | |
|---|---|
| 1 AND (2 OR 3 OR 4) | giving set 5 |
| 2 AND (3 OR 4) | giving set 6 |
| 3 OR 4 | giving set 7 |
| 5 OR 6 OR 7 | giving set 8 |

Set 8 contains the final result.

It may be more useful to search for papers citing at least three of a set of authors, in which case the strategy is a little more complicated; for example, in the case of a set of five authors, with their citing references in sets 1 to 5:

|                              |                 |
|------------------------------|-----------------|
| 1 AND 2 AND (3 OR 4 OR 5)    | giving set 6    |
| 1 AND 3 AND (4 OR 5)         | giving set 7    |
| 1 AND 4 AND 5                | giving set 8    |
| 2 AND 3 AND (4 OR 5)         | giving set 9    |
| 2 AND 4 AND 5                | giving set 10   |
| 3 AND 4 AND 5                | giving set 11   |
| 6 OR 7 OR 8 OR 9 OR 10 OR 11 | giving set 12   |

with the final result in set 12.

White [13] gives an example of the pairs strategy, using four social psychologists as co-cited authors to find papers dealing with attribute theory (a description of the processes by which people arrive at causal explanations for behaviour). This strategy, on SOCIAL SCISEARCH, found many references additional to those retrieved by a subject search on the PSYCINFO database, including a substantial proportion which the author considered could not have been found in any other way. Knapp [30] gives an example of this technique, using five co-cited authors in conjunction with title terms to find references to boundary spanning (techniques by which organizations deal with activities beyond their boundaries). Again the co-citation search found references which would be very difficult to retrieve by subject indexing, and also showed an alternative terminology, boundary roles, which could be fed back into a subject indexing search.

White [31] gives a further example, using six authors writing on social indicators. Combining all pairs gives a broad bibliography of the area, while searching on particular pairs of cited authors finds papers with a specific slant, for example mathematical modelling, an indication of the subtlety of retrieval possible with these co-citation methods.

A third co-cited author searching strategy is the free pairing of many related authors from two or more separate lists; the so-called Chinese Menu strategy. This is done by ORing together the sets of cited references for the authors in each list separately, and ANDing the results.

White [13] exemplifies this method by the construction of a bibliography of science and technology indicators, using one list of authors regarded as specialists in the field, and a second more varied list, including sociologists, historians, information scientists, etc. The resulting large set of references, citing at least one author from each list, was judged to be at least fifty per cent relevant, and encompassed a very broad subject area. Again, much of this material could not be found using titlewords or subject indexing.

Knapp [30] describes this technique being used to construct a bibliography of material dealing with the socialisation of women physicians, but points out that this is the least precise method of co-citation searching.

Examples of the use of the various methods of co-cited author searching to find review articles are given below.

## Combining citations with other access points

Although the majority of publications receive few, if any citations, a particularly significant document may be cited tens or even hundreds of times, and the searcher may want to restrict the output in some way. In general, this can be done more efficiently and conveniently online rather than in a printed index.

If particular authors or institutions are of interest, these can be searched directly online and combined with the results of the citation search. In a printed citation index, only the name of the first author is accessible without extensive cross-checking in the Source Index.

Words or phrases from the title can be searched online and combined with the citation search results. In a printed citation index, of course, the references to citing papers would have to be checked individually in the Source Index.

If citing references are required to come from particular journals, this can be done directly by scanning the citing reference list. Online, the output can be similarly scanned, or a search directly carried out on journal name. Online, the language of publication, year of publication, document type, and number of cited references can all be used directly to restrict a large set of citing references to manageable proportions.

It is therefore clear that any search involving a combination of access points is best carried out online. The one arguable exception is a search involving a browsing inspection of a set of citing references, to select those in interesting or accessible journals. Examples of this technique are given later in this chapter.

Some of the ISI databases have specific access points such as a Journal Subject Category, a broad classification of journals by subject coverage. ARTS AND HUMANITIES SEARCH, for example, has groupings for archaeology, folklore, information/library science, literature and urban studies. These categories, though necessarily imprecise and referring to a journal rather than an individual article, can be useful in focusing on a particular aspect of citations to a highly cited original document.

Janke [32] gives the example of a search to find business- or economics-related documents citing the Canadian politician Pierre Trudeau. Using SOCIAL SCISEARCH on BRS, the search took the form:

```
1_:TRUDEAU-P$.CR
    result 40
2_:1 AND (DI,GY).CC
    result 2
```

The category codes DI (business and finance) and GY (economics) very effectively increase the precision of the search. Another example of the use of category codes is given later.


## Iterative citation searching

This is a way of thoroughly examining the influence of an initial document and of producing a bibliography on a given topic.

One or more starting documents, which should be some years old at least, are identified and all the references to documents citing them are retrieved. Any which are judged to be not relevant to the topic of interest are discarded. The remainder are used as starting points for a new iteration: references to papers which cited them are retrieved. The process continues until the search has been brought up to date, and the only references left are too recent to have been cited. This does not usually take more than three or four iterations. It is advisable to be quite stringent in rejecting irrelevant papers to prevent the size of sets retrieved growing to unmanageable proportions.

Garfield [7] describes a three-iteration search resulting in a bibliography of sixteen papers dealing with the antibiotic compound trimethoprim. A starting reference is cited ten times. When each of these ten documents is used in a citation search, one gives three new relevant references, two give one relevant citation each, and the remaining seven have no relevant citations. The five newly-found documents give no new relevant citing documents. This is an unusually neat and tidy example, with the documents covering a time span of nine years.

The whole procedure can be carried out online as each cited reference search statement must be explicitly typed in, the process can soon become tedious and time-consuming if large numbers of references are involved.

**Forward and backward citation searching - cycling**

Like the previous iteration technique, with which it has a good deal in common, cycling is a method for thoroughly exploring the literature of a topic.

An older starting document, central to the topic of interest, is chosen, and citing documents found. The reference lists in these citing documents are examined to find older relevant material, and these publications are used as the starting points for further citation searches. The search can move backward in time (by following up references in relevant papers) and forward (by iterative citation searching). The process continues until no further relevant material is being found (or the searcher's stamina is exhausted).

It is not possible to carry out the cycling procedure entirely online. Although online implementations of citation databases allow the reference lists to be displayed, these do not include titles, so that relevance judgments cannot be made immediately. In any case, it is essential to remove all except the most relevant material from the cycle as soon as possible, to avoid being swamped. This requires examination of the full text of at least some documents.

This sort of search should not be undertaken lightly since it will almost always be very time-consuming. It should be reserved for the compilation of a definitive bibliography, when it will be carried out together with searches on a variety of other databases using other searching techniques. Synge [12] gives examples of this method in the area of natural product chemistry and Garfield [7] illustrates its use in the compilation of a bibliography of serum measurement of iron and ferritin.

## APPLICATIONS OF CITATION SEARCHING

Some of the more important applications of citation searching are described in this section. There is inevitably some overlap between the categories since searches do not always fit neatly into this sort of classification. The ordering of the applications does not indicate any order of importance.

**To identify subsequent developments to a publication**

New information, directly related to material already published, will almost invariably appear in print with a reference to the earlier work. A citation search on the older document will lead directly to identification of the newer work. This is, perhaps, the most straightforward use of a citation index.

New information may take several forms, among them:

- corrections, retractions and amendments
- criticism and refutation
- confirmation and support
- provision of new, relevant data
and   - inclusion in a review, setting the original work in context.

Citation searching is the only efficient means of finding this sort of updating information, and online searching on the frequently updated ISI files is the best method. A citation search should be carried out as a matter of course on any publication which is of particular significance to avoid the embarrassment of basing a research project, major report, etc. on outdated or erroneous information.

Three scientific examples show this point quite well.

A paper by R.J. Adams *et al.* (*Journal of the American Chemical Society*, 1984, 106, 6296) deals with the structures and reactivity of certain organometallic compounds. Use of the SCISEARCH database shows that this paper has been cited twenty times. One of these references is a correction by the original authors, which states, among other things: 'Table IX in the text is incorrect in its entirety. These were the fractional atomic coordinates for a very similar, but different, molecule.' It is tempting to speculate how many hours of confusion, for anyone working with the information from this paper, would have been saved by a five-minute citation search.

It is to be hoped that no student based a project on the work of M.B. Wise *et al.* (*Journal of the American Chemical Society*, 1985, 107, 1590) on metal cluster ions, without first carrying out a citation search on this paper. *Inter alia,* there is a correction by the original authors beginning: 'We wish to retract this paper. What we believed to be $Sc_4+$ has been shown subsequently to be $Ta+$.'

Eugene Garfield [7] gives an interesting example of the use of the *Science Citation Index* to check whether a published idea has been confirmed or not. A paper by P.M.M. Rae in the *Proceedings of the National Academy of Sciences* in 1970 predicted the existence of repetitive DNA sequences. Using this article as the starting point for a citation search, several papers were found with titles indicating that they describe such repetitive sequences in the DNA of various organisms - thus neatly answering the question.

## To identify the latest developments in a topic

The use of citation indexes, by their very nature, leads the searcher forward in time, from older publications to more recent. It is a particularly useful way of rapidly acquainting oneself with new developments in a subject area, providing only that the area can be associated with one or more key documents to be used as starting points in citation searching.

These key documents may be books (particularly in the humanities and the social sciences), classic journal articles (often the first substantial articles to deal with a topic) or review articles. Reviews occupy a particularly important place in the scholarly communication process, especially in the physical and biological sciences [33]. From the viewpoint of citation searching they are rather special, since they almost invariably have a large number of references (and therefore can be readily found by citation searching) and are themselves more frequently cited than other types of document, since a reference to a review article neatly captures and summarises a large amount of literature. Reviews and surveys of progress in an area are therefore excellent starting points for citation searches to find the latest developments.

An example comes from the statistics literature. In 1979, B.S. Everitt wrote a stimulating article entitled 'Unresolved problems in cluster analysis' (*Biometrics*, 1979, 35, 169) in which he discussed both theoretical methods and aspects of the practical application of this multivariate statistical technique. A citation search on this paper in SOCIAL SCISEARCH shows that it has been cited fifty-four times. Twenty titles from these references are shown in Figure 2.2, clearly covering a wide range of theoretical and practical aspects of cluster analysis, and including up-to-date reviews and literature surveys. It is not comprehensive; the inconsistencies of citation practice mean that no single search of this nature can give complete recall. However, a perusal of these papers would be an excellent way of gaining a quick overview of advances in the topic since Everitt's review was published.

## Figure 2.2: Sample set of references citing Everitt

```
A MULTIVARIATE STATISTICAL ANALYSIS OF COUNTRY CLASSIFICATION - THE
IDENTIFICATION OF SMALL DEVELOPING COUNTRIES.
STAGES OF CHANGE IN PSYCHOTHERAPY - A FOLLOW-UP REPORT.
IDENTIFYING THE COARSE AND FINE STRUCTURES OF MARKET SEGMENTS.
```

**Figure 2.2:** (cont.)

```
COMPOSITIONAL  DATA  ANALYSIS  IN  ARCHAEOLOGY.
THE EVALUATION OF VERBAL MODELS.
TRUE LOVE WAYS - THE SUBJECTIVE EXPERIENCE AND COMMUNICATION OF ROMANTIC
LOVE.
APPLYING CLUSTER ANALYSIS IN COUNSELLING PSYCHOLOGY RESEARCH.
THE CONTRIBUTION OF EXPERIMENTAL RETRIEVAL TO LIBRARIANSHIP AND INFORMATION
STUDIES.
A CRITICAL ANALYSIS OF EMPIRICAL SUBTYPING RESEARCH IN LEARNING DISABILITIES.
DESIGNING AN AUTOMOBILE INSURANCE CLASSIFICATION SYSTEM.
AN EXAMINATION OF PROCEDURES FOR DETERMINING THE NUMBER OF CLUSTERS IN
A DATA SET.
TAXONOMY OF LIFESTYLES. 2. HOMES WITH SLOW LEARNING CHILDREN.
STANDARDISATION OF MEASURES PRIOR TO CLUSTER ANALYSIS.
DOCUMENT CLUSTERING USING AN INVERTED FILE APPROACH.
CLASSIFICATION OF CLIMATE IN GREAT BRITAIN.
A SURVEY OF THE LITERATURE OF CLUSTER ANALYSIS.
PROPOSITIONS REGARDING THE USE OF CLUSTER ANALYSIS IN CLINICAL TRIALS.
NUMERICAL PHENETICS - ITS USES IN BOTANICAL SYSTEMATICS.
APPROXIMATIONS TO BAYESIAN CLUSTERING RULES.
A COMPARATIVE STUDY OF THE MULTIVARIATE STRUCTURE OF TOWNS.
```

## To find applications of techniques and methods

Finding information on applications of methods (for example, scientific laboratory procedures, statistical analysis techniques, use of computer software packages) by searching conventional indexes is notoriously difficult. Unless the technique itself is a central topic within a document, which is not usually the case, it will neither be mentioned in the title, nor indexed. However, it is usual for a reference to be given whenever a particular method or technique is mentioned; the reference will be either a research paper describing the method, or perhaps supplier's documentation, instruction manual, etc. If the usual form of citation is known, then it can be used for a citation search which stands a good chance of retrieving a reasonably complete set of documents describing applications. This is a particularly powerful and valuable way of using a citation database.

One example of this application is a search carried out on both SCISEARCH and SOCIAL SCISEARCH to find citations to a paper by D.A. Williams (*Biometrics*, 1972, 28, 519). This paper describes a statistical procedure for the analysis of the results of experiments involving administration of several dose levels of a chemical substance. Thirty-five references were found only in SCISEARCH, two only in SOCIAL SCISEARCH, and ten in both. This is a reminder of the value of searching more than one of the ISI databases for comprehensive recall when the topic is multidisciplinary. The forty-seven references could be roughly assigned to the following subject classes:

| | |
|---|---|
| Toxicology | 20 |
| Statistics | 13 |
| General Biology | 7 |
| Environmental Science | 6 |
| Horticulture | 1 |

This spread of application area reiterates the value of multidisciplinary citation indexes for this sort of search. Of the papers in the statistics category, only one, with a reference to the technique in the title, could have been found readily other than by a citation search. The full search is shown in Search 2.2.

## Search 2.2: Search for use of statistical procedure

```
System:OS - DIALOG OneSearch

        File 34:SCISEARCH _ 1990 WK 1-36
                 (COPR. ISI INC. 1990)
 * See also files 434 (1987-89), 433 (1980-86) & 432 (1974-79)
 * Use 'BEGIN SCISEARCH' to search all of SciSearch

        File 434:SCISEARCH _ 1987-1989
                 (COPR. ISI INC. 1990)
 * See also file 34 (1990-), 433 (1980-86) & 432 (1974-79)
 *** SORTS ARE NOT WORKING ***

        File 433:SCISEARCH - 1980-1986
                 (COPR. ISI INC. 1988)
 * See also file 34 (1990-), 434 (1987-89) & 432 (1974-79)

        File 432:SCISEARCH - 1974-1979
                 (COPR. ISI INC. 1988)
 * See also file 34 (1990-), 434 (1987-89) & 433 (1980-86)

        Set    Items    Description
        ---    -----    -----------
?e cr=williams da, 1972

Ref    Items    Index-term
E1        4     CR=WILLIAMS DA, 1971, V91, P225, OBSERVATORY
E2        1     CR=WILLIAMS DA, 1971, V91, P226, OBSERVATORY
E3        0    *CR=WILLIAMS DA, 1972
E4        2     CR=WILLIAMS DA, 1972, V10, P17, AP LETT
E5        4     CR=WILLIAMS DA, 1972, V10, P17, ASTROPHYS LETT
E6        2     CR=WILLIAMS DA, 1972, V10, P17, ASTROPHYSICAL LET
E7        1     CR=WILLIAMS DA, 1972, V28, P315, BIOMETRICS
E8      110     CR=WILLIAMS DA, 1972, V28, P519, BIOMETRICS
E9        1     CR=WILLIAMS DA, 1972, V92, P174, OBSERVATORY
E10       1     CR=WILLIAMS DA, 1973, CAVENDISH TEST RANGE
E11       1     CR=WILLIAMS DA, 1973, P349, STOCHASTIC ANAL TRIB
E12       1     CR=WILLIAMS DA, 1973, SPECTROSCOPIC METHOD

        Enter P or E for more
?s e8
        S1      110    CR=WILLIAMS DA, 1972, V28, P519, BIOMETRICS
?t1/6/1-20

 1/6/1        (Item 1 from file: 34)
10329555      Number of References: 51
  ALTERATIONS IN THE ENERGY-METABOLISMS OF AN ESTUARINE MYSID
(MYSIDOPSIS-BAHIA) AS INDICATORS OF STRESS FROM CHRONIC PESTICIDE EXPOSURE

 1/6/2        (Item 2 from file: 34)
10329549      Number of References: 27
  FISH EMBRYOS AS TERATOGENICITY SCREENS - A COMPARISON OF EMBRYOTOXICITY
BETWEEN FISH AND BIRDS

 1/6/3        (Item 3 from file: 34)
10236698      Number of References: 77
```

**Search 2.2:** (cont.)

```
    U-SHAPED DOSE-RESPONSE CURVES - THEIR OCCURRENCE AND IMPLICATIONS FOR
RISK ASSESSMENT

    1/6/4        (Item 4 from file: 34)
10196896        Number of References: 27
    INFLUENCE OF AN INSECT GROWTH-REGULATOR ON THE LARVAL DEVELOPMENT OF AN
ESTUARINE SHRIMP

    1/6/5        (Item 5 from file: 34)
10175921        Number of References: 30
    QUANTITATIVE STRUCTURE-ACTIVITY-RELATIONSHIPS FOR FISH EARLY LIFE STAGE
TOXICITY

    1/6/6        (Item 6 from file: 34)
10171140        Number of References: 26
    PULMONARY EFFECTS DUE TO SUBCHRONIC EXPOSURE TO OIL FOG

    1/6/7        (Item 7 from file: 34)
10133017        Number of References: 12
    TOXICITY OF 4-VINYL-1-CYCLOHEXENE DIEPOXIDE AFTER 13 WEEKS OF DERMAL OR
ORAL-EXPOSURE IN RATS AND MICE

    1/6/8        (Item 8 from file: 34)
10093568        Number of References: 15
    SUBCHRONIC STUDIES OF THENYLDIAMINE IN FISCHER 344 RATS

    1/6/9        (Item 9 from file: 34)
10091614        Number of References: 41
    DEVELOPMENTAL TOXICITY EVALUATION OF ACRYLAMIDE IN RATS AND MICE

    1/6/10       (Item 10 from file: 34)
10091530        Number of References: 13
    PHARMACOKINETIC AND PHARMACODYNAMIC STUDIES IN MAN WITH AN ANTIANGINAL
AGENT VISACOR

    1/6/11       (Item 11 from file: 34)
10041274        Number of References: 13
    EFFECTS OF ULTRASOUND ON DNA AND RNA-SYNTHESIS IN PREIMPLANTATION MOUSE
EMBRYOS

    1/6/12       (Item 12 from file: 34)
09980565        Number of References: 40
    ROBUSTNESS STUDY ON WILLIAMS-PROCEDURE AND SHIRLEY-PROCEDURE, WITH
APPLICATION IN TOXICOLOGY

1/6/13          (Item 13 from file: 34)
09980071        Number of References: 43
    ON THE BEHAVIOR OF FLIGNER-WOLFE-TREND TEST CONTROL VERSUS-K TREATMENTS
WITH APPLICATION IN TOXICOLOGY

    1/6/14       (Item 14 from file: 34)
09937530        Number of References: 32
    THE DEVELOPMENTAL TOXICITY OF ORALLY-ADMINISTERED THEOPHYLLINE IN RATS
AND MICE

    1/6/15       (Item 15 from file: 34)
09885928        Number of References: 32
    DEVELOPMENTAL TOXICITY OF 1,1,1-TRICHLOROETHANE IN CD RATS

    1/6/16       (Item 1 from file: 434)
```

**Search 2.2:** (cont.)

```
09834127        Number of References: 172
  COMPARISONS OF TREATMENTS AFTER AN ANALYSIS OF VARIANCE IN ECOLOGY

 1/6/17          (Item 2 from file: 434)
09828775        Number of References: 12
  COMPARATIVE INHALATION TOXICITY OF TECHNICAL CHLORDANE IN RATS AND
MONKEYS

 1/6/18          (Item 3 from file: 434)
09819429        Number of References: 41
  CLONIDINE-INDUCED HYPOACTIVITY AND MYDRIASIS IN MICE ARE RESPECTIVELY
MEDIATED VIA PRESYNAPTIC AND POSTSYNAPTIC ALPHA-2-ADRENOCEPTORS IN THE
BRAIN

 1/6/19          (Item 4 from file: 434)
09819428        Number of References: 40
  CLONIDINE PRODUCES MYDRIASIS IN CONSCIOUS MICE BY ACTIVATING CENTRAL
ALPHA-2-ADRENOCEPTORS

 1/6/20          (Item 5 from file: 434)
09714612        Number of References: 19
  CONTRASTS FOR IDENTIFYING THE MINIMUM EFFECTIVE DOSE
 ?b7
        25sep90 09:35:18 User200796 Session A242.3
             $3.18 0.020 Hrs File34
                $0.00 15 Type(s) in Format 6
             $0.00 15 Types
     $3.18 Estimated cost File34
             $1.59 0.010 Hrs File434
                 $0.00 5 Type(s) in Format 6
             $0.00 5 Types
     $1.59 Estimated cost File434
             $0.00 0.000 Hrs File433
     $0.00 Estimated cost File433
             $0.16 0.001 Hrs File432
     $0.16 Estimated cost File432
          OneSearch, 4 files, 0.033 Hrs FileOS
     $0.33 DialnetE
     $5.26 Estimated cost this search
     $5.93 Estimated total session cost 0.044 Hrs.

 File 7:SOCIAL SCISEARCH   72-90/WK36
        (COPR. ISI INC.1990)

     Set    Items   Description
     ---    -----   -----------
 ?e cr=willaims da, 1972

 Ref Items   Index-term
 E1     1    CR=WILLAIME JP, 1989, V1, P536, ASS INT SOCIOLOGU
 E2     1    CR=WILLAIME P, 1964, CONTRIBUTION ETUDE S
 E3     0   *CR=WILLAIMS DA, 1972
 E4     1    CR=WILLAIMS EB, 1964, V69, P47, J ABNORM PSYCHOL
 E5     1    CR=WILLAIMS EE, 1983, BUSINESS PLANNING EN
 E6     1    CR=WILLAIMS R, 1980, PROBLEMS MATERIALISM
 E7     2    CR=WILLAIMS WW, 1987, V27, P77, Q REV ECON BUS
 E8     1    CR=WILLAISMDEAN G, 1975, V41, P97, KIVA
 E9     1    CR=WILLAM FM, 1960, ARISTOTELISCHE ERKEN
 E10    1    CR=WILLAM HA, 1967, C ZEISS 1816 1888
 E11    1    CR=WILLAMAN J, 1925, P397, AM J PHYSIOLOGY
```

**Search 2.2:** (cont.)

```
    E12     1    CR=WILLAMAN JJ, V1234, TECHNICAL B

        Enter P or E for more
?e cr=williams da, 1972

Ref  Items    Index-term
E1      1    CR=WILLIAMS DA, 1971, V87, P1, CORNELL DAILY S 03
E2      0   *CR=WILLIAMS DA, 1972
E3     11    CR=WILLIAMS DA, 1972, V28, P519, BIOMETRICS
E4      1    CR=WILLIAMS DA, 1973, PSYCHOL DETERMINISM
E5      3    CR=WILLIAMS DA, 1973, V22, P407, APPL STATIST
E6      1    CR=WILLIAMS DA, 1973, V22, P407, APPLIED STATISTI
E7      1    CR=WILLIAMS DA, 1973, V29, P695, BIOMETRICS
E8      1    CR=WILLIAMS DA, 1973, V37, P273, WESTERN SPEECH
E9     13    CR=WILLIAMS DA, 1975, V31, P949, BIOMETRICS
E10     9    CR=WILLIAMS DA, 1976, V63, P33, BIOMETRIKA
E11     1    CR=WILLIAMS DA, 1977, P25, NEWSWEEK 0523
E12     1    CR=WILLIAMS DA, 1977, V64, P9, BIOMETRIKA

        Enter P or E for more
?s e3
    S1        11    CR="WILLIAMS DA, 1972, V28, P519, BIOMETRICS"
?t1/6/1-11

 1/6/1
01391853       Number of References: 3
  DEGREES OF FREEDOM IN A NONPARAMETRIC TEST

 1/6/2
01350819       Number of References: 28
  COMPUTER-BASED ONLINE INFORMATION-RETRIEVAL FOR STATISTICAL LITERATURE

 1/6/3
01277857       Number of References: 17
  RANK ANALYSIS OF COVARIANCE - ALTERNATIVE APPROACHES

 1/6/4
00776555       Number of References: 21
  CYTO-TOXICITY TO ALVEOLAR MACROPHAGES OF TRACE-METALS ADSORBED ON FLY-ASH

 1/6/5
00625155       Number of References: 18
  INFLUENCE OF CADMIUM, NICKEL, AND CHROMIUM ON PRIMARY IMMUNITY IN MICE

 1/6/6
00489796       Number of References: 14
  NONPARAMETRIC EQUIVALENT OF WILLIAMS-TEST FOR CONTRASTING INCREASING DOSE
LEVELS OF A TREATMENT

 1/6/7
00388978       Number of References: 65
  COMPARING TREATMENT MEANS - COMPENDIUM

 1/6/8
00373519       Number of References: 17
  APPROXIMATION TO MAXIMUM MODULUS OF TRIVARIATE-T WITH A COMPARISON TO
EXACT VALUES

 1/6/9
00337452       Number of References: 13
```

**Search 2.2:** (cont.)

```
    POWERS OF SOME TESTS OF EQUALITY OF NORMAL MEANS AGAINST AN ORDERED
    ALTERNATIVE

    1/6/10
    00304372      Number of References: 1
      CORRECTION

    1/6/11
    00208777      Number of References: 8
      TESTING FOR ORDERED ALTERNATIVES WITH INCREASED SAMPLE SIZE FOR A CONTROL
```

A second example involves the Kostick Perception and Performance Inventory, a psychometric test designed to assist in recruitment and career counselling. A citation search was carried out to find examples of its use in varying types of organization. There is no single key reference to this technique, and so the cited reference field was displayed around the name KOSTICK (the EXPAND command on DIALOG) to see what would turn up.

In SOCIAL SCISEARCH there was one citation to an early article by the technique's originator, N.M. Kostick, published in *Management Review* in 1977. The citing reference, a review article in the *Training and Development Journal*, entitled 'Styles of Work', includes a discussion and evaluation of Kostick's work.

In SCISEARCH there was one citation to an instruction manual for applying the technique. The citing reference, an article from *Technovation* entitled 'Managing change in pharmaceutical industry R&D', includes a description of the application of the technique in promoting career development (Search 2.3).

## Search 2.3: Search for examples of the application of psychometric test

```
    File   7:SOCIAL SCISEARCH _ 72-90/WK36
           (COPR. ISI INC.1990)

         Set     Items     Description
         ---     -----     -----------
    ?e cr=kostick nm

    Ref  Items     Index-term
    E1      1      CR=KOSTICK MM, 1968, APPLIED PSYCHOL ASS
    E2      1      CR=KOSTICK MM, 1980, KOSTICKS PERCEPTION
    E3      0     *CR=KOSTICK NM
    E4      1      CR=KOSTICK NM, 1977, V66, P48, MANAGEMENT REV
    E5      1      CR=KOSTICKDA, 1926, CASE, DEP LABOR IND
    E6      1      CR=KOSTIK MM, 1954, V45, P449, J EDUCATIONAL PSYC
    E7      1      CR=KOSTIKA, 1975, CASE, CUOMO
    E8      1      CR=KOSTIKA, 1977, CASE, CUOMO
    E9      1      CR=KOSTIKAS A, 1974, J PHYS PARIS
    E10     1      CR=KOSTIKAS A, 1974, V12, P537, J PHYSIQUE
    E11     4      CR=KOSTIKAS A, 1974, V35, P107, J PHYS
    E12     1      CR=KOSTIKAS A, 1974, V35, P107, J PHYSIQUE C

         Enter P or E for more
    ?s e2,e4
                       1     CR=KOSTICK MM, 1980, KOSTICKS PERCEPTION
                       1     CR=KOSTICK NM, 1977, V66, P48, MANAGEMENT REV
         S1            2     E2,E4
    ?t1/3/1-2
```

**Search 2.3:** (cont.)

```
    1/3/1
    01892630       Genuine Article#: P0938    Number of References: 15
      SPURIOUSER AND SPURIOUSER - THE USE OF IPSATIVE PERSONALITY TESTS
      JOHNSON CE; WOOD R; BLINKHORN SF
        PSYCHOMETR RES & DEV LTD,36-38 LONDON RD/ST ALBANS AL1 1NG//ENGLAND/;
        UNIV LONDON/LONDON//ENGLAND/; HATFIELD POLYTECH/HATFIELD AL10
        9AB/HERTS/ENGLAND/
      JOURNAL OF OCCUPATIONAL PSYCHOLOGY, 1988, V61, N2, P153-162
      Language: ENGLISH                     Document Type: ARTICLE



    1/3/2
    01099919       Genuine Article#: NR867    Number of References: 8
      STYLES OF WORK
      BIES JD; TURETZKY JA
        HUMAN RESOURCES DEV CONSULTANTS/MEMPHIS//TN/00000
      TRAINING AND DEVELOPMENT JOURNAL, 1982, V36, N6, P76&
      Language: ENGLISH                     Document Type: ARTICLE

    ?begin scisearc
            25sep90 09:37:35 User200796 Session A242.5
                    $1.92      0.016 Hrs File7
                     $1.12 2 Type(s) in Format 2
                     $1.12 2 Type(s)
          $3.04 Estimated cost File7
          $0.16 DialnetE
          $3.20 Estimated cost this search
         $13.42 Estimated total session cost      0.094 Hrs.


    System:OS - DIALOG OneSearch


        File 34:SCISEARCH _ 1990 WK 1-36
                (COPR. ISI INC. 1990)
    * See also files 434 (1987-89), 433 (1980-86) & 432 (1974-79)
    * Use 'BEGIN SCISEARC' to search all of SciSearch


        File 434:SCISEARCH _ 1987-1989
                (COPR. ISI INC. 1990)
    * See also file 34 (1990- ), 433 (1980-86) & 432 (1974-79)
    *** SORTS ARE NOT WORKING ***


        File 433:SCISEARCH - 1980-1986
                (COPR. ISI INC. 1988)
    * See also file 34 (1990- ), 434 (1987-89) & 432 (1974-79)


        File 432:SCISEARCH - 1974-1979
                (COPR. ISI INC. 1988)
    * See also file 34 (1990- ), 434 (1987-89) & 433 (1980-86)


        Set    Items    Description
        ---    -----    -----------
    ?e cr=kostick nm

    Ref Items    Index-term
    E1     1     CR=KOSTICK JA, 1978, STEADY STATE IMAGING
    E2     1     CR=KOSTICK MM, 1952, V30, P209, PEABODY J ED
    E3     0     *CR=KOSTICK NM
    E4     1     CR=KOSTICK PERCEPTION P, 1961
    E5     1     CR=KOSTICPODGORSKA V, 1955, V8, P169, ZBORN RAD G
```

**Search 2.3:** (cont.)

```
      E6      1    CR=KOSTICPODGORSKA V, 1957, V9, P49, ZBORN RAD GE
      E7      1    CR=KOSTICPODGORSKA V, 1958, V4, GEOL GLASNIK
      E8      1    CR=KOSTIE P, 1964, V15, P467, GYNECOL PRAT PARIS
      E9      1    CR=KOSTIE S, 1985, V22, P117, P EDTA
      E10     1    CR=KOSTIENKO AI, 1959, V4, P482, RADIOTEK EL
      E11     4    CR=KOSTIENKO AI, 1959, V4, P482, RADIOTEKHNIKA EL
      E12     2    CR=KOSTIENKO AI, 1967, P146, ELEKTRONNAYA TEKHN 1

          Enter P or E for more
      ?s e4
          S1          1    CR=KOSTICK PERCEPTION P, 1961
      ?t1/3

      1/3/1           (Item 1 from file: 433)
      06607120    Genuine Article#: AMY34    Number of References: 26
        MANAGING CHANGE IN PHARMACEUTICAL-INDUSTRY R-AND-D
        LOVEDAY DEE
          FISONS PLC,DIV PHARMACEUT,BAKEWELL RD/LOUGHBOROUGH LE11
          0RH/LEICS/ENGLAND/
        TECHNOVATION, 1985, V3, N2, P89-109
        Language: ENGLISH    Document Type: ARTICLE
```

### To find information on topics not well described by indexing terminology

Some kinds of search are difficult to carry out using a conventional subject indexing approach. These include:

- very new topics whose terminology is not yet clarified and generally accepted and which will not have been incorporated into thesauri and classifications, nor recognised by database producers' indexing policies.
- interdisciplinary topics, where the terminology used may depend on the background and viewpoint of the author
- searches involving general concepts, whose nature is difficult to tie down in specific terminology
- searches for material presented from a specific aspect, or with a particular slant, which may not be reflected in the terminology used.

Citation searching, because of its independence of terminology, is capable of finding related papers in these difficult areas. It is not, of course, a general panacea. If a subject area is very new there may not have been time for the publication process to generate a citation network. In interdisciplinary areas, authors may tend to cite only papers from their own discipline or school of thought.

With these provisos, citation searching should always be considered as a potentially valuable resource for difficult queries of this sort. The rapidly updated ISI files are, of course, very well suited to searching new and rapidly developing topics.

One example of this kind of search is based around a paper by M.W. Bernadt *et al.* (*Lancet*, 1982, 325-328) which describes a comparison of questionnaire and laboratory tests in the detection of alcoholism. An underlying theme is the diagnostic advantage of combining biomedical and psychosocial data in the detection of such medicosocial problems. This would be a difficult concept to search for using title words or indexing terms.

A citation search on this paper, using SCISEARCH, gives ninety-nine citing references. A sample of ten of these is shown in Figure 2.3, indicating that the search has indeed produced material relevant to the theme.

**Figure 2.3: Sample set of titles of references citing Bernadt.**

```
ALCOHOL - LOOKING FOR PROBLEMS.
LIFESTYLE ASSESSMENT - JUST ASKING MAKES A DIFFERENCE.
VALUE AND JUSTIFICATION OF ALCOHOLISM SCREENING.
COMPARISON OF CAGE QUESTIONNAIRE AND COMPUTER-ASSISTED LABORATORY PROFILES IN
SCREENING FOR COVERT ALCOHOLISM.
DERIVATION AND VALIDATION OF A PREDICTIVE RULE FOR IDENTIFYING HEAVY
CONSUMERS OF ALCOHOL.
LIFESTYLE ASSESSMENT - APPLYING MICROCOMPUTERS IN FAMILY PRACTICE.
ALCOHOL CONSUMPTION IN ARTHRITIC PATIENTS - CLINICAL AND LABORATORY  STUDIES.
THE ACCURACY AND SIGNIFICANCE OF MEDICAL TESTING.
COMPARISON OF GAMMA-GLUTYLTRANSFERASE AND QUESTIONNAIRE TESTS AS ALCOHOL
INDICATORS IN DIFFERENT RISK GROUPS.
IDENTIFICATION OF ALCOHOL ABUSE USING LABORATORY TESTS AND A HISTORY OF
TRAUMA.
```

Searching for applications of a specified chemical reaction is another example. This information can be very difficult to find in conventional indexes, as the means of describing chemical reactions are neither well developed nor standardized. Very often the names of the originators are used - for example, the Friedel-Crafts reaction or the Eschenmoser hydrolysis - a considerable barrier to searching for anyone other than an expert. Citation searching on the original publications is a very useful way of finding applications of, modification to, and analogies of specific reactions [14, 34].

Another example of this type of application is Synge's use of the *Science Citation Index* to overcome problems of nomenclature in the field of natural product chemistry [12].

Garfield [7] gives a further example: a citation search to find papers dealing with the highly specific subject of the use of Kerr4 geometry to describe black holes. This was a rapidly developing topic in astrophysics, so that indexing terminology could not be up-to-date. Title terms would not be, for the most part, specific enough. A *Science Citation Index* search, however, rapidly produced a number of relevant references.

Journal category codes can be combined with citations searching to find material of a particular kind, or with a particular bias. Michael Polanyi's well-known book, *Personal Knowledge,* has been cited many times in different contexts. To find material dealing specifically with the significance of these ideas in a religious aspect, the category code for religion can be used. On DIALOG, the statement:

CR=POLANYI M? AND CW=KNOWLEDGE AND SC=RELIGION

gives seventy-one apparently relevant references.

Co-citation searching is also a useful way of focusing on a very specific topic. An example is the use of SOCIAL SCISEARCH to find articles on education and training for online systems. Six United Kingdom authors in this area are S. Keenan, L.A. Tedd, A. Vickery, F.E. Wood, J.A. Large and C.J. Armstrong. The search was carried out to find documents citing references by any pair of these authors, using the methods described earlier in this chapter. A total of twenty-eight papers was found, the titles of a sample of ten being shown in Figure 2.4.

Despite the cited authors all being based in the United Kingdom, of these twenty-eight references, nine came from the United States and one from the Soviet Union. The subject area is defined quite tightly, since there are few papers on closely related aspects such as online training for end-users in industry, or information technology in the library/information curriculum. Several of these retrieved documents are reviews, pointing to the value of co-citation searching for this kind of material, as was mentioned above.

**Figure 2.4: Results of online training search.**

```
EDUCATION  AND  TRAINING  OF  THE  INFORMATION  PROFESSIONAL.
COMPUTER ASSISTED INSTRUCTION IN USER EDUCATION.
EDUCATION FOR LIBRARIANSHIP AND INFORMATION SCIENCE - A RETROSPECT AND A
REVALUATION.
OPTIONS AND TRENDS IN THE TRAINING OF INFORMATION PROFESSIONALS.
TEACHING ONLINE INFORMATION RETRIEVAL IN UNITED KINGDOM LIBRARY SCHOOLS.
ONLINE SEARCHING IN LIBRARY EDUCATION.
EDUCATION AND TRAINING FOR ONLINE SYSTEMS.
TEACHING AIDS DEVELOPED AND USED FOR EDUCATION AND TRAINING FOR ONLINE
SEARCHING.
THE EVALUATION OF A DRILL AND PRACTICE PROGRAM FOR ONLINE RETRIEVAL.
USE OF THE INSTRUCT TEXT RETRIEVAL PROGRAM AT THE DEPARTMENT OF INFORMATION
STUDIES, UNIVERSITY OF SHEFFIELD.
```

**To find information comprising only a small part of a publication**

Very often information which is not itself the main subject of a document can be of special interest to the searcher. Examples include:

- techniques, methods or apparatus used
- data and property values

and
- comparisons and analogies.

Because these all comprise only a minor part of a publication, they are not likely to be mentioned in the title, or included in the indexing of secondary services. Very often, however, a reference will be given to documents relating to the minor topic, making it accessible to citation searching.

One example is based on a 1979 IUPAC publication, authored by E.P. Sergeant, which lists an extensive compilation of ionization constants for organic acids in aqueous solution. A citation search (which must include citation variants such as specification of page number) on SCISEARCH shows that this work has been cited one hundred and seventeen times since 1981. The titles of a sample of ten citing papers are shown in Figure 2.5.

**Figure 2.5: Citations to IUPAC compilation.**

```
BASICITY  AND  ACIDITY  OF  AZOLES.
CARCINOGENICITY ASSESSMENT AND THE ROLE OF STRUCTURE-ACTIVITY RELATIONSHIPS.
KINETICS OF THE REACTION BETWEEN SORBIC ACID AND THIOLS.
THE DEVELOPMENT OF AN ENVIRONMENTAL FATE DATABASE.
THE SYNTHESIS AND IONISATION CONSTANTS OF SOME DERIVATIVES OF 1-BIPHENYLENOL.
ISOCRATIC  CHROMATOGRAPHIC  RETENTION  DATA  FOR  ESTIMATING  AQUEOUS
SOLUBILITIES  OF  ACIDIC,  BASIC,  AND  NEUTRAL  DRUGS.
AN INFRA-RED SPECTROSCOPIC STUDY OF AQUEOUS SOLUTIONS OF L(+)- GLUTAMIC
ACID.
QUANTUM MECHANICALLY CALCULATED PROPERTIES FOR THE DEVELOPMENT OF
QUANTITATIVE STRUCTURE-ACTIVITY RELATIONSHIPS.
DEVELOPMENT  OF  A  GENERAL  KINETIC  MODEL  FOR  BIODEGRADATION  AND  ITS
APPLICATION  TO  CHLOROPHENOLS  AND  RELATED  COMPOUNDS.
REACTIVITY  OF  HO2/0-2  RADICALS  IN  AQUEOUS  SOLUTION.
```

They include both reports of newly measured ionization constants, techniques for measuring or calculating such constants, and applications of known data; for example, in chromatography and in predicting reactivity, carcinogenicity, and environmental fate. Some documents include the concept of ionization constant in the title, but most do not. The search could, of course, include title-words or co-citations to identify the type of data or application more closely.

Citation searching is a valuable adjunct to more conventional subject indexing for this application. It may be a particularly useful way of updating from a standard data compilation to find newly reported data of the kind sought.

A further example is given by an extension to the search (described earlier) to find articles citing Botticelli's painting 'Primavera', using ARTS AND HUMANITIES SEARCH. The search can be refined to find whether any recent articles have commented on the views on this painting expressed by the art critic and historian H.P.Horne, who wrote the classic study of Botticelli at the turn of the century. By combining the set of twenty-five references citing the painting with the set citing Horne as an author (twenty in all), two potentially relevant papers are found, entitled:

> THE PRESENCE OF BOTTICELLI'S 'PRIMAVERA'

and

> A MAENAD FROM PISA IN THE 'PRIMAVERA'.

Alternatively, the same technique could be used to assess any influence this painting is thought to have had on the work of Cezanne. In this case, combination of the twenty-five 'Primavera' citations with the set of documents citing any work of Cezanne produces a single document, entitled:

> CEZANNE BATHERS - FORM AND CONTENT.

In both cases, the concept of interest (that is, the comments of Horne on the 'Primavera'and the suggested influence of that painting on Cezanne) are minor elements of the respective citing documents, but are readily retrieved by a citation search. The full search is shown in Search 2.4.

## Search 2.4: Search for references with a particular slant

```
     File 439:ARTS & HUMANITIES SEARCH_1980-1990WK36
            (COPR. ISI INC.1990)

        Set      Items    Description
        ---      -----    -----------
   ?s cr=botticelli s? and cw=primavera
                   78     CR=BOTTICELLI S?
                  193     CW=PRIMAVERA
        S1         25     CR=BOTTICELLI S? AND CW=PRIMAVERA

   ?t1/6/1-25


    1/6/1
    00925293        Number of References: 139
      UNITED ON THE THRESHOLD OF THE 20TH-CENTURY MYSTICAL IDEAL,
    LAURENCIN,MARIE  INTEGRAL  INVOLVEMENT  WITH  APOLLINAIRE,  GUILLAUME  AND
    THE
    INMATES OF THE BATEAU-LAVOIR
```

**Search 2.4:** (cont.)

```
   1/6/2
00923115        Number of References: 3
  BOTTICELLI,SANDRO 'PRIMAVERA' RESTORED

   1/6/3
00890472        Number of References: 68
  IMAGES OF SPRING IN BOTTICELLI AND HORACE

   1/6/4
00708782        Number of References: 28
  THE SOURCE OF BOTTICELLI 'PRIMAVERA'

   1/6/5
00700150        Number of References: 45
  THE 2 MAYINGS IN CHAUCER 'KNIGHTS TALE' - CONVENTION AND INVENTION

   1/6/6
00668365        Number of References: 7
  MOVING PICTURES (MOVIES, PAINTING, AND PHOTOGRAPHY AS ART)

   1/6/7
00663710        Number of References: 1
  'BOTTICELLI PRIMAVERA'

   1/6/8
00615942        Number of References: 7
  A WOMAN SEEING

   1/6/9
00587330        Number of References: 64
  OF ANTIQUE AND OTHER FIGURES - METAPHOR IN EARLY-RENAISSANCE ART

   1/6/10
00527294        Number of References: 23
  THE PRESENCE OF BOTTICELLI 'PRIMAVERA'

   1/6/11
00371269        Number of References: 2
  IN DETAIL BOTTICELLI 'PRIMAVERA'

   1/6/12
00369649        Number of References: 12
  RENAISSANCE VARIATIONS ON A THEME BY KEATS

   1/6/13
00369552        Number of References: 12
  BOTTICELLI 'PRIMAVERA' AND THE TRADITION OF DANTE

   1/6/14
00350166        Number of References: 112
  THEMES OF TIME AND RULE AT POGGIO-A-CAIANO - THE PORTICO FRIEZE OF
LORENZO-IL-MAGNIFICO

   1/6/15
00306934        Number of References: 42
  BOTTICELLI 'PRIMAVERA' - CHE-VOLEA-SINTENDESSE

   1/6/16
00292668        Number of References: 6
  THE CARE AND RESTORATION OF ART WORKS ON PAPER
```

**Search 2.4:** (cont.)

```
  1/6/17
00284865        Number of References: 12
  A BRIGHT AND HAPPY 400TH-BIRTHDAY YEAR FOR THE REMARKABLE UFFIZI
(FLORENCE GALLERY)

  1/6/18
00264496        Number of References: 1
  THE UFFIZI - 4 CENTURIES OF A GALLERY

  1/6/19
00254303        Number of References: 26
  BOCCACCIO EXPERIMENTATION WITH VERBAL PORTRAITS FROM THE 'FILOCOLO' TO
THE 'DECAMERON'

  1/6/20
00180674        Number of References: 13
  IN DETAIL - MATISSE 'DANCE'

  1/6/21
00147186        Number of References: 11
  A MAENAD FROM PISA IN THE 'PRIMAVERA'

  1/6/22
00138591        Number of References: 14
  THE CENTRAL FIGURE IN BOTTICELLI 'PRIMAVERA'

  1/6/23
00046182        Number of References: 110
  MASACCIO AND THE SPINARIO, PIERO AND THE POTHOS - OBSERVATIONS ON THE
RECEPTION OF THE ANTIQUE IN RENAISSANCE PAINTING

  1/6/24
00023834        Number of References: 118
  CEZANNE BATHERS - FORM AND CONTENT

  1/6/25
00005122        Number of References: 23
  WHAT IS A MASTERPIECE
?s cr=horne hp?
     S2        20     CR=HORNE HP?
?c1 and 2
               25     1
               20     2
     S3         2     1 AND 2
?t3/3/1-2

  3/3/1
00527294     Genuine Article#: TV172     Number of References: 23
  THE PRESENCE OF BOTTICELLI 'PRIMAVERA'
  COOK A
    BROWN UNIV/PROVIDENCE//RI/02912
    STANFORD ITALIAN REVIEW, 1984, V4, N1, P55&
  Language: ENGLISH    Document Type: ARTICLE

  3/3/2
00147186     Genuine Article#: LZ481     Number of References: 11
  A MAENAD FROM PISA IN THE 'PRIMAVERA'
    LUCHS A
      MITTEILUNGEN DES KUNSTHISTORISCHEN INSTITUTES IN FLORENZ, 1980,
V24, N3
```

**Search 2.4:** (cont.)

```
     P369-371
     Language: ENGLISH     Document Type: NOTE
?s cr=cezanne p?
     S4          264     CR=CEZANNE P?
?c 1 and 4
                 25     1
                264     4
     S5           1     1 AND 4
?t5/3

     5/3/1
     00023834      Genuine Article#: JR526     Number of References: 118
     CEZANNE BATHERS - FORM AND CONTENT
     KRUMRINE ML
       ARTS MAGAZINE, 1980, V54, N9, P115-123
     Language: ENGLISH     Document Type: REVIEW, BIBLIOGRAPHY
```

It should be noted that the techniques searches discussed earlier are also good examples of this use of citation indexes, since the techniques used are not, for the most part, central to the subject matter of the papers which cite them.

**To assess influence**

One of the most controversial aspects of the use of citation indexes is their application for the assessment of the quality and significance of published work, and by implication of its authors, as was noted earlier. This is not central to the subject matter of this chapter, and will not be discussed further.

From time to time, however, it may be necessary for the online searcher to try to gain an appreciation of the influence of particular publications, individuals, institutions and ideas. Citation searching is one way of doing this, though it is unwise to use it in isolation; it should be combined with a consideration of publication records, informed assessment of quality, etc.

In principle, the searcher need only identify a set of publications whose influence is to be investigated, carry out a citation search on it, and contemplate the results. The first stage may prove time consuming since it will be necessary to identify all papers from a given author or institution by some initial search, and then to enter these as separate citation searches. The most difficult part is the assessment of the results. It will be best to consider them qualitatively: to try, for instance, to see the degree of influence in different subject areas by looking at the range of source journals, category codes, etc. If the matter is important, it is essential that the citing documents be read to see why the citation has been made. Quantitative comparisons of citation counts are fraught with difficulty and are best avoided by those with no expertise or experience in this sort of analysis.

Used carefully and informally, citation searching can illuminate the influence and importance of ideas and authors in a uniquely valuable way. A good example is a study of citation analysis as one of a number of measures of the productivity and creativity of pharmaceutical research organizations [35].

A smaller scale example deals with chemical notation systems. Linear notations are a method of describing chemical structure in a more rigorous and systematic fashion than is possible with conventional nomenclatures. They enjoyed a wide usage in early generations of chemical information systems.

Of the many chemical notations devised, only three gained any amount of operational use: those due to W.J. Wiswesser, G.M. Dyson, and H.W. Hayward. All were originally devised in the late 1940s and 1950s. A citation search on SOCIAL SCISEARCH, which has a good coverage of the information science literature, reveals the extent of their continuing influence in the 1970s and 1980s.

The original papers, and other relevant documents, were used as the starting point. Some citations were to the notations themselves, rather than to documents: WISWESSER LINE FORMULA, for example. Many authors referring to Wiswesser's notation cite a manual of notation rules authored by E.G. Smith. There are, in fact, over twice as many citations to this book as to all of Wiswesser's publications, a striking example of the obliteration phenomenon referred to above.

The total numbers of relevant citations are:

| | | |
|---|---|---|
| Wiswesser / Smith | - | 81 |
| Dyson | - | 19 |
| Hayward | - | 5 |

The references to the notations of Dyson and Hayward turn out to be largely historical reviews. Many of the references to the Wiswesser notation, by contrast, describe the use of the notation in operational information systems, emphasizing the predominance of this notation during the time period covered by SOCIAL SCISEARCH.

This is a good illustration of how a citation search can give a quick indication of the relative influence and persistence of ideas, and an equally good illustration of the need for great care in choosing starting cited references for this purpose.

Burdrick [36] gives an example of the use of a citation index to assess the importance of individual documents. In this case they are library books being considered for disposal, which may be reprieved if citation data shows that they are still commonly referred to, and hence of arguable importance.

## To identify review articles

Reviews, surveys, overviews ... regardless of the term used, this type of publication is particularly valuable to the scholar, researcher and teacher, and is therefore often the target of an online search [33]. By their very nature, such documents cite many related publications and are therefore readily found by citation searching.

The searcher may simply carry out a citation search on one or more references on the subject of interest and scan the citing papers to identify reviews by their titles. However, the ISI databases include two searchable fields which allow more precise searching: publication type and number of cited references. The publication type distinguishes different types of document - one such type is REVIEW OR BIBLIOGRAPHY, and this can be searched directly or, on certain host systems, used to limit a large set. Of course, there will inevitably be differences of opinion as to exactly what constitutes a review, but this is a very useful way of finding precisely what is required.

The number of cited references refers to the number of references cited by each document, that is those which would be retrieved as citing references from a citation search. It is therefore possible to restrict the items which cite the starting point papers to those which have more than, say, fifty references. These will necessarily include a substantial literature survey, even if the paper is not styled a review.

A simple example is a search for reviews dealing with the anti-schistosomal drug, oxamniquine. The first major paper describing this drug is by H.C. Richards and R. Foster, published in 1969 (*Nature*, 222, 581).

In SCISEARCH, there are nineteen references to this paper. Combining this set with the term for REVIEW OR BIBLIOGRAPHY gives three papers entitled:

CHEMOTHERAPY OF SCHISTOSOMIASIS MANSONI.
THE CHEMOTHERAPY OF SCHISTOSOMIASIS.

DRUGS FOR TROPICAL DISEASES IN THE THIRD WORLD.

Examination of these papers reveals them to be useful reviews, written from different viewpoints, of the development and use of oxamniquine.

Restricting the original citing set to those having over one hundred references would also retrieve these three articles. Restricting it to those having over fifty references would add a fourth, entitled:

HISTORY OF CHEMOTHERAPY OF BILHARZIA

not encoded as a REVIEW/BIBLIOGRAPHY, but apparently from its title a relevant review, as is confirmed by examination of the actual document.

A shorter review article, by Richards himself, entitled

OXAMNIQUINE - A DRUG FOR THE THIRD WORLD

might well be of use, but is not coded as a REVIEW/BIBLIOGRAPHY. It has only twenty-six references, less than several papers in the original citing set which are reviews in the accepted sense of the word.

This example indicates that citation searching can be a good way of finding review articles, but that there may be problems with comprehensiveness, particularly in finding shorter and more specific reviews without extensive bibliographies. If the set of citing references is not too large, scanning those with more than, say, twenty references may be worthwhile.

The technique of co-cited author searching was described earlier. Knapp [30] points out that a search for documents citing three of a set of relevant authors is an effective way of finding review articles. She gives the example of a search for articles on organizational boundary spanning (that is, operating beyond the normal bounds of the organization) on SOCIAL SCISEARCH, using five cited authors. In this case, more than half of the thirty-eight papers retrieved were reviews.

A smaller-scale example of the use of co-citation searching for reviews comes from the area of physical organic chemistry. L.P. Hammett, J. Hine, and S. Winstein are all classic authors, well-known and widely-cited for their work on quantitative studies of chemical reactivity. A search was carried out on SCISEARCH from 1981 to date for articles citing all three of these authors. The resulting seven papers are entitled:

THE COLLAGE OF SN2 REACTIVITY PATTERNS.
SOLVENT EFFECTS IN ORGANIC REACTIONS.
SUBSTITUENT AND SOLVENT EFFECTS ON ORGANIC REACTIVITY.
DEPENDENCE OF EQUILIBRIUM AND RATE CONSTANTS ON TEMPERATURE AND PRESSURE.
THE MECHANISM OF ALKYLATION REACTIONS.
MECHANISM AND CATALYSIS OF NUCLEOPHILIC SUBSTITUTION IN PHOSPHATE ESTERS.
BASICITY, NUCLEOPHILICITY AND ELECTROPHILICITY IN THE PROTONATION OF AMINES.

These are all relevant review articles, though not all are categorised as REVIEW/BIBLIOGRAPHY in the database.

This cannot be regarded as a means of conducting a comprehensive search because of the first author-only problem, but it is a rapid and reliable method of identifying at least some relevant reviews. It would be a useful adjunct to a conventional subject search if completeness were required.

Another example of this application of co-cited author retrieval is a search to find articles reviewing education and research in librarianship and information studies in the United Kingdom, using SOCIAL SCISEARCH. Among the best-known educators and authors on this topic are W.L. Saunders, T.D. Wilson, R.T. Bottle, B. Cronin, and D. Davinson. A search was carried out to identify references citing at least three of these authors. Five documents were found, entitled:

EDUCATION AND TRAINING OF THE INFORMATION PROFESSIONAL.
CURRICULUM DEVELOPMENT.
THE MANAGEMENT AND DEVELOPMENT OF INFORMATION AND LIBRARY PRO-
VISION IN THE SOCIAL SCIENCES.
EDUCATION FOR LIBRARIANSHIP AND INFORMATION SCIENCE - A RETROSPECT
AND REVALUATION.
EDUCATION FOR INFORMATION SCIENCE. 1. UNITED KINGDOM.

Four of these are clearly relevant reviews. The third in the list is also a review, but reflecting another common interest of several of these authors, social sciences information.

Restricting the search to documents citing four of the authors leads to the retrieval of a single reference, the fourth in the list. This is a major review, with 183 references.

## To identify individuals and institutions working in a particular subject area

The most usual way of doing this kind of search is simply to search by subject in a conventional index. Use of a citation index offers a particular advantage, based on the ways in which authors refer to other work; so-called citation patterns.

Citations are likely to be given to material which not merely deals with a relevant topic, but which approaches it in a particular way, or from a particular viewpoint. This factor is especially pronounced in social science and humanities, with well-established schools of thought, but is not entirely absent from science and technology. Looking for authors who cite papers central to a particular topic is therefore a way of identifying, with precision, those active in a specific aspect of research or scholarship. It is a fruitful means of identifying potential colleagues, collaborators and competitors. The ISI databases are particularly useful in this respect, since they provide institutional information for all authors, not merely for the first-named, as do so many other databases.

An example of this application of citation searching is given by the field of study known as chemometrics. This is a relatively new and rapidly developing area, involving the application of appropriate statistical techniques to multivariate chemical data. The search was carried out to find details of individuals and research groups working in this subject area in the Nordic countries.

Most chemometrics researchers cite the pioneering work of B.R. Kowalski, and this offers a straightforward way into the literature of the area. The set of documents citing any of Kowalski's publications is combined with the terms: Norway, Sweden, Denmark or Finland from the organizational source field.

Using SCISEARCH from 1985 to date, sixteen references result. These indicate the existence of chemometrics research groups in Umea in Sweden, (six references), in Bergen in Norway (five references), and in Stockholm in Sweden (two references), and well as to the work of three individual authors.

**For current awareness**

Online citation indexes, because of their timeliness in processing the primary literature and their frequent updating, are particularly useful for current awareness. The most convenient means, of course, is to store a search profile with the host system, to be run each time the database is updated.

The inclusion of citation searching in current awareness profiles, as well as, or even instead of, subject descriptors and author names, can prove very effective. Many users of current awareness services find it relatively easy to give a list of documents central to their interests (not least their own publications!), so that any document citing any of them will most probably be of interest. Profiles of this sort may often be easier to construct and more successful in operation than profiles of subject terms. The vagaries of citation retrieval, owing to the inconsistencies of authors' citation practices, can be a positive advantage for current awareness, with peripheral and unexpected material sparking off ideas in the recipients. The lack of comprehensive recall to be expected from simple citation searching is not likely to be of importance here, since most people are over-loaded with material to be read.

**For verification of bibliographic references**

At first sight this seems an odd application for a citation index, since reference checking is most usually carried out in a conventional index, searching by author name, or by title or index terms if the identity of the author is one of the points in doubt.

However, one should bear in mind the point made earlier about the great breadth of material (both in terms of time period and of documents included) in a citation index, as compared with a corresponding conventional index. There is, all other things being equal, a much greater chance of finding a reference in a substantial citation index, than in other sources. This is, of course, dependent on the reference which is being checked having been cited during the time period when the citation index was compiled.

This method is particularly useful for checking older references and obscure references; those, in fact, less likely to have been included by secondary services. Note that it is not necessary for the reference being checked to appear in a source covered by the ISI databases; merely for it to have been referred to by a document in one of those sources.

An example is the use of SOCIAL SCISEARCH to find the full reference to an article written during the 1940s by Vannevar Bush, which had a considerable influence on thinking during the development of information science as a discipline. The publication date is, of course, far too early for inclusion in any online database, and would necessitate a lengthy hunt through printed sources. Because of the time-independence of citation records, a citation search rapidly solves the problem.

Scanning the cited references to Bush's work in SOCIAL SCISEARCH, two highly cited articles are seen, both dating from 1945. One of them, an article from *Atlantic Monthly* (volume 176, page 101) is cited over eighty times, and a perusal of the citing documents shows almost all of them to be articles in library/information journals, many dealing with the development of the subject. The problem is thus neatly solved. This is shown in Search 2.5.

**Search 2.5: Verification of a Vannevar Bush reference**

```
File 7:SOCIAL SCISEARCH   72-90/WK36
      (COPR. ISI INC.1990)
   Set    Items   Description
   ---    -----   -----------
```

**Search 2.5:** (cont.)

```
?e cr=bush v, 1940

Ref  Items   Index-term
E1      1    CR=BUSH V, 1935, COMMUNICATION 0620
E2      1    CR=BUSH V, 1939, MECHANIZATION RECORD
E3      0   *CR=BUSH V, 1940
E4      1    CR=BUSH V, 1940, COMMUNICATION
E5      1    CR=BUSH V, 1940, COMMUNICATION 0502
E6      1    CR=BUSH V, 1940, COMMUNICATION 0621
E7      1    CR=BUSH V, 1940, COMMUNICATION 0703
E8      1    CR=BUSH V, 1941, MECHANIZATION RECORD
E9      1    CR=BUSH V, 1942, COMMUNICATION 0202
E10     1    CR=BUSH V, 1943, COMMUNICATION 0308
E11     1    CR=BUSH V, 1943, COMMUNICATION 1117
E12     1    CR=BUSH V, 1943, V22, P83, BIOGRAPHICAL MEMOIRS

        Enter P or E for more
?p

Ref  Items   Index-term
E13     1    CR=BUSH V, 1943, V98, P571, SCIENCE
E14     1    CR=BUSH V, 1944, AEC186, DOC
E15     1    CR=BUSH V, 1944, COMMUNICATION 1113
E16     1    CR=BUSH V, 1944, COMMUNICATION 1229
E17     1    CR=BUSH V, 1944, MEMORANDUM C 1208
E18     1    CR=BUSH V, 1944, SAL POINTS FUT 0930
E19     2    CR=BUSH V, 1944, ATLANTIC MONTHLY
E20     7    CR=BUSH V, 1945, ATLANTIC MONTHLY JUL
E21     1    CR=BUSH V, 1945, COMMUNICATION 0607
E22     1    CR=BUSH V, 1945, ENDLESS FRONTIER
E23     2    CR=BUSH V, 1945, ENDLESS FRONTIER REP
E24     1    CR=BUSH V, 1945, NSF6040 NAT SCI F

        Enter P or E for more
?p

Ref  Items   Index-term
E25     1    CR=BUSH V, 1945, PERSPECTIVE COMPUTE
E26     1    CR=BUSH V, 1945, POLITICS SCIENCE
E27     1    CR=BUSH V, 1945, P1, SCI ENDLESS FRONTIER
E28     1    CR=BUSH V, 1945, P101, ATLANTIC MONTHLY
E29    21    CR=BUSH V, 1945, P101, ATLANTIC MONTHLY JUL
E30     2    CR=BUSH V, 1945, P106, ATLANTIC MONTHLY JUL
E31     1    CR=BUSH V, 1945, P12, SCI ENDLESS FRONTIER
E32     2    CR=BUSH V, 1945, P13, SCI ENDLESS FRONTIER
E33     1    CR=BUSH V, 1945, P147, SCI ENDLESS FRONTIER
E34     2    CR=BUSH V, 1945, P176, ATLANTIC MONTHLY
E35     1    CR=BUSH V, 1945, P25, SCI ENDLESS FRONTIER
E36     1    CR=BUSH V, 1945, P34, SCIENCE ENDLESS FRON

        Enter P or E for more
?p

Ref  Items   Index-term
E37     1    CR=BUSH V, 1945, P7, SCI ENDLESS FRONTIER
E38     1    CR=BUSH V, 1945, P80, SCI ENDLESS FRONTIER
E39     1    CR=BUSH V, 1945, P86, SCI ENDLESS FRONTIER
E40     1    CR=BUSH V, 1945, REPORT PRESIDENT
E41     1    CR=BUSH V, 1945, SCI ENDLESS FRON JUL
E42     1    CR=BUSH V, 1945, SCI ENDLESS FRONTIE
```

**Search 2.5:** (cont.)

```
E43     51    CR=BUSH V, 1945, SCI ENDLESS FRONTIER
E44      6    CR=BUSH V, 1945, SCIENCE ENDLESS FRONT
E45      1    CR=BUSH V, 1945, V175, P101, ATLANTIC MONTHLY
E46      1    CR=BUSH V, 1945, V176, P10, ATLANTIC MONTHLY
E47      2    CR=BUSH V, 1945, V176, P101, ATLANTIC MONTHL 0700
E48     75    CR=BUSH V, 1945, V176, P101, ATLANTIC MONTHLY

     Enter P or E for more
?s e29,e43,e48
                21    CR=BUSH V, 1945, P101, ATLANTIC MONTHLY JUL
                51    CR=BUSH V, 1945, SCI ENDLESS FRONTIER
                75    CR=BUSH V, 1945, V176, P101, ATLANTIC MONTHLY
     S1     147    E29,E43,E48
?t1/6/1-25

1/6/1
02149939      Number of References: 10
  THE KNOWLEDGE HYPERMAP - AN ALTERNATIVE TO HYPERTEXT

1/6/2
02144439      Number of References: 23
  HYPERTEXT HYPERMEDIA - JONASSEN,DH

1/6/3
02139646      Number of References: 18
  PRINCIPLES OF GEOMATIC HYPERMAPS

1/6/4
02129257      Number of References: 51
  DEMOCRATIZING SCIENCE - A HUMBLE PROPOSAL

1/6/5
02128428      Number of References: 14
  HYPERLOG - HYPERTEXT SYSTEM WITH LOGIC-SEMANTIC NAVIGATION

1/6/6
02110256      Number of References: 5
  PLANNING WITH HYPERMEDIA - COMBINING TEXT, GRAPHICS, SOUND, AND VIDEO

1/6/7
02097675      Number of References: 45
  UNITED-STATES TECHNOLOGICAL LEADERSHIP - WHERE DID IT COME FROM AND WHERE
DID IT GO

1/6/8
02092976      Number of References: 18
  COMPUTERS AND QDA - CAN THEY HELP IT - A REPORT ON A QUALITATIVE
DATA-ANALYSIS PROGRAM

1/6/9
02049453      Number of References: 29
  HYPERTEXT AND INFORMATION-RETRIEVAL - TOWARDS THE NEXT GENERATION OF
INFORMATION-SYSTEMS

1/6/10
02046757      Number of References: 18
  FROM MEMEX TO MEDIAMAKER

1/6/11
02032784      Number of References: 15
  INFORMATION-SCIENCE IN THE INFORMATION AGE
```

**Search 2.5:** (cont.)

```
  1/6/12
02026875      Number of References: 8
  EXPANDING THE SEARCHING POWER OF CD-ROM - ISIS NEW
SOCIAL-SCIENCES-CITATION-INDEX COMPACT DISK EDITION IS COMPATIBLE WITH THE
SCIENCE-CITATION-INDEX ON COMPACT DOSK - NEW SOFTWARE STREAMLINES SEARCHING

  1/6/13
02026204      Number of References: 14
  ADVANCES IN HYPERMEDIA

  1/6/14
02006945      Number of References: 32
  THE REEMERGENCE OF THE NATIONAL-SCIENCE-FOUNDATION IN AMERICAN-EDUCATION
- PERSPECTIVES AND PROBLEMS

  1/6/15
02005909      Number of References: 74
  THE CHANGING-ROLE OF DIRECTORS OF UNIVERSITY-LIBRARIES

  1/6/16
02001489      Number of References: 37
  MAKING THE TRANSITION FROM PRINT TO ELECTRONIC ENCYCLOPEDIAS - ADAPTATION
OF MENTAL MODELS

  1/6/17
01998338      Number of References: 97
  THE NATIONAL LIBRARY IN HISTORICAL-PERSPECTIVE

1/6/18
01996716      Number of References: 23
  THE ELECTRONIC BOOK EBOOK3

  1/6/19
01993974      Number of References: 3
  GOVERNING SCIENCE AND TECHNOLOGY IN A DEMOCRACY - GOGGIN,ML

  1/6/20
01989239      Number of References: 59
  INTRODUCING HYPERTEXT IN PRIMARY HEALTH-CARE - A STUDY ON THE FEASIBILITY
OF DECISION SUPPORT FOR PRACTITIONERS

1/6/21
01989181      Number of References: 23
  INNOVATION, PRAGMATICISM, AND TECHNOLOGICAL CONTINUITY - VANNEVAR BUSH
MEMEX

  1/6/22
01989179      Number of References: 16
  SUPPORTING COLLABORATION IN HYPERMEDIA - ISSUES AND EXPERIENCES

  1/6/23
01989176      Number of References: 41
  WRITING AND READING HYPERTEXT - AN OVERVIEW

  1/6/24
01989175      Number of References: 16
  PERSPECTIVES ON - HYPERTEXT - INTRODUCTION AND OVERVIEW
```

**Search 2.5:** (cont.)

```
    1/6/25
01984040       Number of References: 26
   TO LINK OR NOT TO LINK - EMPIRICAL GUIDANCE FOR THE DESIGN OF NONLINEAR
TEXT SYSTEMS

  ?t1/6/125-135

    1/6/125
00792029       Number of References: 12
   RESEARCH-LIBRARIES ENTER THE INFORMATION AGE/

    1/6/126
00708270       Number of References: 56
   REORGANIZATION OF FEDERAL-AGENCIES

    1/6/127
00699430       Number of References: 47
   ESSAY ON THE PAST AND FUTURE (QUESTIONABLE) OF INFORMATION-SCIENCE
EDUCATION .1. HISTORICAL OVERVIEW

    1/6/128
00682993       Number of References: 10
   HOW WILL NEW TECHNOLOGY CHANGE CHARACTERISTICS OF LIBRARIES AND THEIR
USERS

    1/6/129
00668748       Number of References: 37
   READING OVERLOAD AND COGENCY

    1/6/130
00662569       Number of References: 32
   COMPUTER-SYSTEMS - PROSPECTS FOR A PUBLIC INFORMATION NETWORK

    1/6/131
00646899       Number of References: 22
   RESEARCH SYSTEM - COMPARATIVE SURVEY OF ORGANIZATION AND FINANCING OF
FUNDAMENTAL RESEARCH .1. FRANCE, GERMANY, UNITED-KINGDOM .2. BELGIUM,
NETHERLANDS, SWEDEN, SWITERLAND .3. CANADA, UNITED-STATES, GENERAL
CONCLUSIONS - CATY,G, DRILHON,G, FERNE,G, WALD,S, ENOCH,R, FLORY,M,
KAPLAN,N

    1/6/132
00590570       Number of References: 18
   ENDLESS FRONTIER OR BUREAUCRATIC MORASS

    1/6/133
00581449       Number of References: 22
   RELATIONSHIPS BETWEEN HARD-SOFT, PURE-APPLIED, AND LIFE-NONLIFE
DISCIPLINES AND SUBJECT BOOK USE IN A UNIVERSITY-LIBRARY

    1/6/134
00523270       Number of References: 121
   HISTORY AND FOUNDATIONS OF INFORMATION-SCIENCE

    1/6/135
00508663       Number of References: 54
   CONTEMPORARY-ISSUES IN BIBLIOGRAPHIC-CONTROL/
```

## FUTURE PROSPECTS FOR CITATION INDEXES

A good deal of research has been done on new and improved types of citation indexes and databases, and on citation searching techniques [2]. The findings have suggested the potential value of approaches such as:

- including in a citation index the reason why the document is cited, to allow greater precision in searching; several classification schemes have been devised to allow for this
- automatically generating citations from text in computerized form, to avoid authors' idiosyncratic decision of when, and what, to cite

and
- improving citation searching by, for example, displaying the whole of a citing sentence, again with the aim of improving precision of searching.

There seems no likelihood as present that these improvements will be incorporated in operational retrieval systems in the forseeable future, despite their apparent advantages.

Nor is there any indication that any organization, apart from ISI, is considering the introduction of new citation searching capabilities into generally-available information systems. This is regrettable, in view of the unique capabilities of this sort of index, as outlined in this chapter.

## THE SIGNIFICANCE OF CITATION SEARCHING

This chapter has illustrated the range of searches for which a citation index can be a valuable searching tool. These fall into two categories. There are some searches for which a citation index is a uniquely valuable source, answering questions which cannot be effectively dealt with by any other sort of information resource; finding subsequent developments to a publication is a good example. There are others for which a citation index is a useful complement or alternative to other forms of index; identifying individuals active in a particular field of study is one particular example. Several recent studies have emphasized this complementary nature of citation searching [37-39], pointing out its value as an alternative and support to conventional subject retrieval.

Citation searching should not be regarded as a thing apart, to be utilized only for certain specific sorts of query. Rather, it should be an integral part of the resources of all online searchers, to be used in conjunction with other searching options. If more use were made of citation searching, the result would be a generally higher level of information provision.

## ADDENDUM

Abstracts have now been added in the ISI citation databases, including Current Contents, on the main online hosts. This will now enable relevance decisions to be made more easily.

## REFERENCES

1.     C. Oppenheim and S.P. Renn. Highly cited old papers and the reason why they continue to be cited. *Journal of the American Society for Information Science* 29(5) 1978 226-231
2.     B. Cronin. *The Citation Process*. London: Taylor Graham, 1984

3.     V. Cano. Citation behaviour: classification, utility and location. *Journal of the American Society for Information Science*  40(4) 1989 284-290

4.     S.K. Sen. A theoretical glance at citation process. *International Forum on Information and Documentation* 15(1) 1990 3-7

5.     E. Garfield. Citation behaviour - aid or hindrance. *Current Contents*  May 1989 (editorial)

6.     M. Weinstock. Citation indexes. *Encyclopedia of Library and Information Science*, Vol. 5. New York: Dekker, 1971, pp 16-40

7.     E. Garfield. *Citation Indexing: Its theory and application in science, technology, and humanities* (2nd ed.) Philadelphia: ISI Press, 1983

8.     L.C. Smith. Citation analysis. *Library Trends*  30 (1) 1981 83-106

9.     E. Garfield. Uses and abuses of citation frequency. *Current Contents*  28(43) 1985 3-9

10.    L. Leydesdorff. The Science Citation Index and the measurement of national performance in terms of numbers of scientific publications. *Scientometrics*  17(1-2) 1989 111-120

11.    D. Lindsey. Using citation counts as a measure of quality in science - measuring what's measurable rather than what's valid. *Scientometrics*  15(3-4) 1989 189-203

12.    R.L.M. Synge. 25 years of Science Citation Index - some experiences. *Journal of Chemical Information and Computer Sciences*  30(1) 1990 33-35

13.    H.D. White. Cocited author retrieval. *Information Technology and Libraries.* 5 1986 93-99

14.    E. Garfield. History of citation indexes for chemistry: a brief review. *Journal of Chemical Information and Computer Sciences*  25(3) 1985 170-174

15.    R.G. Logan (ed.) *Information Sources in Law*. London: Butterworth, 1986

16.    C. Franklin. Searching LEXIS and WESTLAW. *Database*  9(1) 1986 13-20

17.    D. Bawden. Computer-based online information retrieval for statistical literature. *Journal of the Royal Statistical Society*, Series A, 147 1984 78-86

18.    B. Snow. Online cited reference searching. *Online*  10(2) 1986 83-88

19.    C. Bonnelly and G. Drolet. Searching the social science literature online: Social Scisearch. *Database* 1(2) 1978 10-25

20.    J. Bradshaw. Evaluations of Biomed and ISTPB, two new literature databases from the Institute for Scientific Information. *Online Review*  7(3) 1983 221-226.

21.    G.S. Savage. Scisearch on DIALOG. *Database*  1(1) 1978 50-67

22.    E. Garfield. ABCs of cluster mapping. Parets 1 and 2. In *Essays of an information scientist*, Vol. 4. Philadelphia: ISI Press, 1981, pp 634-649

23.    E. Garfield. CD-ROM. *Current Contents*  September 1989 (editorial)

24.    A.E. Cawkell. Automatic indexing in the Science and Social Science Citation Index CD-ROM. *Electronic Library*  7(6) 1989 345-350

25.    M. Thompson. Incorrect citations: a problem and a challenge for librarians. *Australian Academic and Research Libraries*  9(1) 1978 45-57

26.    H.F. Moed and M. Vriens. Possible inaccuracies occurring in citation analysis. *Journal of Information Science* 15(2) 1989 95-107

27.    E. Garfield. How to use the Arts and Humanities Citation Index and what's in it for you and your mate. *Current Contents* 16(6) 1985 3-12

28.    E. Garfield. Is information retrieval in the arts and humanities inherently different from that in science? *Library Quarterly*  50(1) 1980 40-57

29.    J. Chapman and K. Subramanyam. Cocitation search strategy. In *Proceedings of the National Online Meeting 1981*. Medford NJ: Learned Information, 1981, pp 97-102

30.    S.D. Knapp. Cocitation searching: some useful strategies. *Online*  8(4) 1984 43-48

31.    H.D. White. Cocited author retrieval online: an experiment with the social indicators literature. *Journal of the American Society for Information Science*  32(1) 1981 16-21

32.    R.V. Janke. Searching the Social Sciences Citation Index on BRS. *Database* 3(2) 1980 19-45

33.    A.M. Woodward. The role of reviews in information transfer. *Journal of the American Society for Information Science* 28(3) 1977 175-180

34.    E. Garfield and G. Vladutz. Citation-based fact rertrieval in chemistry: retrieval of chemical reactions using citation indexes. *Abstracts of Papers of the American Chemical Society Congress,* Hawaii, 1979

35.    M.E.D. Koenig. Bibliometric indicators versus expert opinion in assessing research performance. *Journal of the American Society for Information Science* 34(2) 1983 136-145

36.    A.J. Burdrick. Science Citation Index data as a safety net for basic science books considered for weeding. *Library Resources and Technical Services* 33(4) 1989 367-373

37.    M.L. Pao and D.B. Worthen. Retrieval effectiveness by semantic and citation searching. *Journal of the American Society for Information Science* 40(4) 1989 226-235

38.    K.W. McCain. Descriptor and citation retrieval in the medical behavioural sciences literature: retrieval overlaps and novelty distribution. *Journal of the American Society for Information Science* 40(2) 110-114

39.    S.R. Venkataraman. Improving retrieval results through analysis. *Canadian Jornal of Information Science* 13(3-4) 1988 40-46

# 3 Patents

*Edlyn S. Simmons*

## AN INTRODUCTION TO PATENTS

Patents reside at the intersection of technology, law and commerce as governmental guarantees that companies and individuals who develop new products and processes may take legal action to prevent others from manufacturing, selling or using their inventions. A patent describes the invention, identifies its owner, and specifies the limits of the grant of exclusivity. Thus patents are valuable sources of information about advances in science and technology, about the research interests of businesses and individuals, and about the legal limits to one's own business activities. Patents are uniquely valuable sources of information about the ownership of inventions: inventions that are claimed in patents cannot be used without authorization from the patent owner. They are invaluable sources of information about technology, and most of the information can be used in research without infringing the patent. They are also rich stores of information about businesses, they identify the areas of research and development activity in industry, and thereby facilitate the prediction of market changes.

Patents contain vast stores of practical scientific and engineering information, much of it unique. Research is often missing from the journal literature, for many inventors refuse to teach the world about discoveries that have not been protected by a patent. It is not unusual for corporations to delay submission of manuscripts to scientific journals until after a patent application has been published, and many manuscripts submitted to journals are refused publication because they do not meet a referee's standards of scientific sophistication. Patent applications are published by many countries about eighteen months after they are filed. They are subject to screening on the basis of national security considerations in most countries, but they are normally published promptly without any other editing or restriction. As a result, a large share of research and development is described first in patents or indeed only in patents. By combining the technical information in patents with the names of inventors and corporate patent owners, it is possible to track the research and business interests of companies and other institutions. With the addition of legal status information it is also possible to determine which products and processes are being emphasized by competitors and which have been abandoned. Most important, of course, patents tell us which products and processes are the exclusive domain of others.

The word 'patent' refers to the grant of patent rights and also to the patent specification, the document that describes the invention. The first page of the specification of US patent 4 532 250 is illustrated in Figure 3.1. A patent is a form of intellectual property. The grant of a patent by a national government gives the owners of the invention the right to exclude others from making, using or selling the thing invented and the right to sell or license those rights to others. The property rights are granted for a limited time and are limited to the product or process claimed in the patent specification. Patent rights are limited by the scope of the allowed claims, by the geographical borders of the granting country, and by the obligation, in most countries, to pay maintenance fees during the life of the patent. Patent terms are not renewable; they can be extended beyond the statutory expiration date in some countries only under very special circumstances. The owner of a patent has the right to practise the invention only to the extent that he or she does not infringe other patents while doing so. When it is necessary to practise inventions claimed in earlier patents in order to practise the invention claimed in a later patent, for example, to use a patented pigment in a newly patented paint formulation, the earlier patents are said to 'dominate' the invention and the patent owner must obtain a licence from the owner of the dominating patent to avoid infringement. Patent rights are defended from infringers through civil court suits.

## Figure 3.1: Title page of US Patent 4 532 250

| **United States Patent** [19] | [11] **Patent Number:** 4,532,250 |
|---|---|
| Stout et al. | [45] **Date of Patent:** **Jul. 30, 1985** |

[54] 5-HETEROARYLIMIDAZOL-2-ONES
HAVING CARDIOTONIC ACTIVITY

[75] Inventors: **David M. Stout**, Vernon Hills; **Diane M. Yamamoto**, Gurnee, both of Ill.

[73] Assignee: **American Hospital Supply Corporation, Evanston, Ill.**

[21] Appl. No.: **554,498**

[22] Filed: **Nov. 23, 1983**

[51] Int. Cl. .....................................**A61K 31/44**
[52] U.S. Cl...........................................514/341; 544/237
544/284; 546/144; 546/167; 546/278; 548/127
548/128; 548/134; 548/137; 548/317; 548/318
548/322; 548/202; 548/206; 514/259; 514/248
514/307; 514/311; 514/392

[58] Field of Search .............................546/278; 424/263

[56] References Cited
U.S. PATENT DOCUMENTS
3,538,104 11/1970 Gossenfeld et al. ....... ...546/278
3,850,944 11/1974 Tanaka et al. ................ 546/278

FOREIGN PATENT DOCUMENTS
59948 3/1982 European Pat. Off. .
78545 11/1982 European Pat. Off. .
78546 11/1982 European Pat. Off. .

OTHER PUBLICATIONS
Burger, Medical Chemistry, 2nd edition, 1960, p. 77.
*Primary Examiner*--Jane T. Fan
*Attorney, Agent, or Firm*--Gildo E. Fato

[57] ABSTRACT
Described are compounds of the formula

wherein R is heteroaryl and R1 is hydrogen or loweralkyl, or a pharmaceutically acceptable salt thereof. The compounds exhibit cardiotonic activity.

3 Claims, No Drawings

One right that is not conferred by the grant of a patent is a copyright on the patent specification itself. It is the claimed invention that belongs to the patent owner, not the words used to describe it. Governments grant patents in order to encourage innovation and to encourage the spread of knowledge. The right to exclude others is balanced by a requirement that the invention be described fully in a published patent specification. To obtain a patent, the inventors are required to file a patent application that consists of a specification that describes the invention, an oath or declaration signed by the applicants, and an application fee. The term 'patent application' is commonly used to refer either to the act of applying for a patent or to the text of the patent specification. In most countries, no patent is granted until the application has been examined to determine whether the claimed invention is new, useful and inventive as the terms are understood in the patent laws of that country, but in many countries the patent specification is published before the examination proceedings are begun, usually eighteen months after the original filing or priority date.

Published applications are often referred to as 'patents', although many of them never mature into granted patents. Many inventions claimed in patent applications are found to be unpatentable during examination and others are abandoned because they are discovered not to be worth further development. In some countries the application may be abandoned before examination is begun by failing to submit a formal request for examination. Most patent applications that do result in granted patents are amended during examination, changing the scope of the claims and even the details of the supporting disclosure. Patent databases commonly index the published application, assuming in doing so that the application contains all of the information that will appear in the issued patent.

Patents have legal effect only within the country that grants them, and each country has its own patent laws, which are occasionally amended. There are variations from country to country in the kinds of inventions that may be patented and in the breadth of the claims that are allowed. In some countries, for example, new chemical compounds may not be claimed and must be protected by claims directed to methods of synthesis, and in many countries pharmaceutical agents and methods of treating disease may not be patented. Some countries allow patent claims to be written in broadly generic language, so as to cover embodiments of the claim language that are not exemplified in the patent specification, while other countries restrict the claims to the exemplified species. There is also great variability in the Patent Office procedures of the various countries. An inventor who files patent applications on a single invention in several countries often obtains patents over a period of several years, each protecting a different claim scope. In some cases an application will result in more than one patent from a single country, as many Patent Offices restrict each patent to what they consider to be a single invention, requiring that the original claims be separated into two or more divisional applications. Patent laws in most countries do not permit the applicant to insert new information into a pending patent application, but do allow the filing of modified applications. The resulting documents may be 'patents of addition' or, in the United States, 'continuations-in-part' of the original patent application. Some countries offer more than one kind of patent, each subject to different standards. In the United States, for example, manufactures, compositions of matter and processes that are found to be new, useful and non-obvious are covered by utility patents; new, decorative and non-obvious designs are covered by a separate series of design patents; and new asexually reproduced plants are covered by a series of plant patents. A general description of the world's patent laws may be found in the monograph on 'Patents literature' by John W. Lotz [1].

**Table 3.1: Patent databases**

| DATABASE | COVERAGE | SYSTEMS | PRODUCER |
|---|---|---|---|
| WORLD PATENTS INDEX | International | ORBIT Questel DIALOG | Derwent Publications Ltd |
| INPADOC | International | INPADOC ORBIT DIALOG STN PATOLIS | International Patent Documentation Center (INPADOC) |

**Table 3.1:** (cont.)

| DATABASE | COVERAGE | SYSTEMS | PRODUCER |
|---|---|---|---|
| EDOC | International | Questel | Institut National de Propriété Industrielle (INPI) |
| CLAIMS | US | DIALOG ORBIT STN | IFI/Plenum Data Co. |
| US PATENTS | US | ORBIT | Derwent Publications Inc. |
| PATDATA | US | BRS | BRS Information Technologies |
| LEXPAT | US | NEXIS | Mead Data Central |
| EPAT | EPO | Questel | Institut National de Propriété Industrielle (INPI) |
| FPAT | France | Questel | Institut National de Propriété Industrielle (INPI) |
| PATDPA | Germany | STN | Deutsches Patentamt |
| CHINESE PATENT ABSTRACTS | China | ORBIT DIALOG | INPADOC |
| JAPIO | Japan | ORBIT | Japan Patent Information Organization (JAPIO) |
| APIPAT | International, petroleum | STN DIALOG | American Petroleum Institute (API) |
| World Patents Index/APIPAT | International | ORBIT | Derwent Publications Ltd/ American Petroleum Institute (API) |
| CA SEARCH | International, chemistry | STN DIALOG ORBIT Questel BRS Data-Star et al. | Chemical Abstracts Service (CAS) |
| MARPAT | International, chemistry | STN | Chemical Abstracts Service (CAS) |
| PHARMSEARCH | International, pharmaceutical | Questel | Institut National de Propriété Industrielle (INPI) |
| CURRENT PATENTS | International, pharmaceutical | Data-Star ORBIT | Current Patents Ltd. |
| DRUG PATENTS INTERNATIONAL | International, pharmaceutical | ORBIT | IMSworld Publications Ltd. |

In the years since the invention of the computer it has become increasingly easy to find information about patents, as machine-readable Patent Office records and computer typeset patent documents have been converted into an ever increasing number of patent databases. In addition, most of the abstracting and indexing services that index patents have made their databases available online. The databases listed in Table 3.1 will be discussed in detail in this chapter.

Patent databases include many kinds of documents, not all of them having the legal force of granted patents. Recognizing the various types of documents was made somewhat easier by the work of an organization called ICIREPAT, which developed a series of internationally recognized codes for identification of patent data. ICIREPAT country codes (now replaced by a nearly identical list of ISO codes) use two-letter codes for country names. A list of current and discontinued country codes applied to the countries whose patents are indexed by the databases listed in Table 3.1 may be found in Table 3.2. ICIREPAT Numbers for the Identification of Data (INID) are placed on the cover page of patents so that it is possible to tell what names and numbers signify without being able to read the language of the patent. There are also 'patent kind' codes that identify the type of patent document. These codes consist of a letter, sometimes followed by a number, and the meaning of a particular code depends upon the laws of the country issuing the document. The first publication of a patent in the regular series of utility patents is usually identified by the letter A, sometimes followed by a numeral. Patents republished after examination are usually labelled B, also sometimes followed by a number.

## Table 3.2: Country coverage of patent databases

| COUNTRY | ISO CODE | WPI | INPADOC | EDOC* | APIPAT* | CA | OTHER SEARCH DATABASES |
|---|---|---|---|---|---|---|---|
| ARGENTINA | AR | 1975 | 1973- | | * | | |
| ARIPO (Africa, English) | AP | | 1984- | | | | |
| AUSTRALIA | AU | 1963-1969, 1983- | 1973- | 1973- | * | 1967- | |
| AUSTRIA | AT [OE] | 1975- | 1969- | 1971- | * | 1967- | |
| BELGIUM | BE | 1963- | 1964- | 1964- | 1964- | 1967- | CLAIMS: 1950-1979 |
| BRAZIL | BR | 1976- | 1973- | * | * | 1976- | |
| BULGARIA | BG | | 1973- | | | | |
| CANADA | CA | 1963- | 1970- | 1970- | 1964- | 1967- | |
| CHINA | CN | 1985- | 1985- | | | | CHINAPATS 1985- |
| CUBA | CU | | 1974- | | | | |
| CYPRUS | CY | | 1975- | | | | |
| CZECHOSLOVAKIA | CS | 1975- | 1973- | * | * | 1967- | |
| DENMARK | DK | 1974- | 1968- | * | * | 1967- | |
| EGYPT | EG [ET] | | 1976- | | | | |
| EUROPE | EP | 1978- | 1978- | 1978- | 1978- | 1979- | EPAT: 1978-; PHARMSEARCH: 1986-; CURRENT PAT.: 1989- |
| FINLAND | FI [SF] | 1974- | 1968- | * | * | 1967- | |
| FRANCE | FR | 1963- | 1968- | 1968- | 1964- | 1967- | FPAT: 1969-; CLAIMS: 1950-1979; PHARM-SEARCH: 1986- |
| GERMANY, EAST | DD [DL] (EG) | 1963- | 1973- | * | 1983- | 1967- | |
| GERMANY, F. R. | DE [DT] (DS,GE) | 1963- | 1967- | 1968- | 1964- | 1967- | PATDPA: 1968-; CLAIMS: 1950-1979 |
| GREECE | GR | | 1977- | | | | |

**Table 3.2:** (cont.)

| COUNTRY | ISO CODE | WPI | INPADOC | EDOC* | APIPAT* | CA | OTHER SEARCH DATABASES |
|---|---|---|---|---|---|---|---|
| HONG KONG | HK | | 1976- | | | | |
| HUNGARY | HU | 1975- | 1973- | * | * | 1967- | |
| INDIA | IN | | 1975- | | * | 1967- | |
| IRELAND | IE [EI] | 1963-1969 | 1973- | | | | |
| ISRAEL | IL | 1975- | 1968- | * | * | 1967- | |
| ITALY | IT | 1966-1969, 1977- | 1973- | * | * | 1967-74 | |
| JAPAN | JP (J#) [JA] | 1963- | 1973- | 1973- | 1968- | 1967- | JAPIO: 1976- |
| KENYA | KE | | 1975- | | | | |
| KOREA, SOUTH | KR [KS] | 1986- | 1978- | | | | |
| LUXEMBOURG | LU | 1984- | 1960- | 1961- | | | |
| MALAWI | MW | | 1973- | | | | |
| MALAYSIA | MY | | 1953- | | | | |
| MEXICO | MX | | 1981- | | | | |
| MONACO | MC | | 1975- | | | | |
| MONGOLIA | MN [MO] | 1972- | | | | | |
| NETHERLANDS | NL | 1963- | 1964- | 1965- | 1964- | 1967- | CLAIMS: 1950-1979 |
| NEW ZEALAND | NZ | | 1978- | | | | |
| NORWAY | NO | 1974- | 1968- | * | * | 1967- | |
| OAPI (Africa, French) | OA | | | 1964- | | | |
| PATENT COOPERATION TREATY | WO (WP) | 1978- | 1978- | 1978- | 1978- | 1979- | CURRENT PAT.: 1989- |
| PHILIPPINES | PH [RP] | | 1975- | | | | |
| POLAND | PL [PO] | | 1973- | | * | 1967- | |
| PORTUGAL | PT | 1974- | 1976- | * | * | | |
| ROMANIA | RO [RU] | 1975- | 1973- | * | * | 1967- | |
| SINGAPORE | SG | | 1983- | | | | |
| SOUTH AFRICA | ZA (SA) | 1963- | 1971- | * | 1964- | 1968- | |
| SPAIN | ES | 1983- | 1968- | * | * | 1967- | |
| SWEDEN | SE [SW] | 1974- | 1968- | 1973- | * | 1967- | |
| SWITZERLAND | CH (SW) | 1963- | 1969- | 1968- | * | 1967- | |
| TURKEY | TR | | 1973- | | | | |
| UNITED KINGDOM | GB (BR) | 1963- | 1969- | 1968- | 1964- | 1967- | CLAIMS: 1950-1979; CURRENT PAT.: 1989- |
| UNITED STATES | US | 1963- | 1968- | 1969- | 1964- | 1967- | CLAIMS: 1950-; USPATENTS: 1970-; LEXPAT: 1975-; PATDATA: 1975-; PHARM-SEARCH: 1986-; CURRENT PAT.: 1989- |
| USSR | SU (RU) | 1963- | 1972- | * | 1983 | 1967- | |
| VIET-NAM | VN | | 1984- | | | | |
| YUGOSLAVIA | YU | | 1973- | | | | |

**Table 3.2:** (cont.)

| COUNTRY | ISO CODE | WPI | INPADOC | EDOC* | APIPAT* | CA | OTHER SEARCH DATABASES |
|---------|----------|-----|---------|-------|---------|-----|------------------------|
| ZAMBIA | ZM [ZB] | | 1968- | | | | |
| ZIMBABWE | ZW [RH] | | 1980- | | | | |

**NOTES:**

Country Codes in brackets are obsolete ICIREPAT Codes. Country Codes in parentheses were used by Derwent Publications prior to the adoption of Standard Country Codes. For Japanese Patents, Derwent replaces the second character of the Country Code with the first digit of the publication year.

* Not covered systematically. In addition, patents from some of the systematically covered countries may have been indexed in earlier years.

The following countries are members of the European Patent Organization, the African Intellectual Property Organization (OAPI) or the Patent Cooperation Treaty whose national patents are not indexed separately, but which may be found as Designated States in the records of EP, OA and WO documents:

| | | |
|---|---|---|
| BARBADOS BB [BD] | CONGO CG [GF] | NORTH KOREA KP [KN] |
| BENIN BJ [DA] | GABON GA | SENEGAL SN |
| BURKINA FASO BF [HV, UV] | LIECHTENSTEIN LI | SRI LANKA LK [CL] |
| CAMEROON CM [KA] | MADAGASCAR MG [MD] | SUDAN SD |
| CENTRAL AFRICAN REPUBLIC CF [ZR] | MALI ML [MJ] | TOGO TG [TO] |
| CHAD TD [TS] | MAURITANIA MR [MT] | |

There are also codes for design patents and 'utility models', for patents of addition and for 'inventors' certificates', which are issued as alternatives to patents in some Communist countries. Lists of the kinds of patents issued by the various countries may be found in the manuals issued by INPADOC, in the WIPO *Patent Information and Documentation Handbook*, in the publication, *Patent Information from Chemical Abstracts Service Coverage and Content*, and in the *Manual of Patent Examining Procedures* of the United States Patent and Trademark Office.

Legally valid patents can be obtained only on inventions that have not been described in a printed publication before the effective filing date of the patent application, so it is important to file a patent application on a useful discovery before publishing a description of it anywhere else. On the other hand, if one wishes to reserve the right to practise an invention without patenting it, one has only to publish a description of it before anyone else has a chance to file a patent application on it. This can be done with a publication in a scientific journal, but there are also publications devoted specifically to 'defensive disclosures'. Two of these, *Research Disclosures* and *International Technology Disclosures*, are abstracted by Derwent Publications, Ltd. in WORLD PATENTS INDEX. Published patent applications that are abandoned before grant also serve as defensive publications. In the United States a programme for the publication of *Defensive Publications* has been superseded by a series of *Statutory Invention Registrations* which are published through the same channels as United States patents and are included in some databases that index United States patents.

Because any publication will prevent the grant of a valid patent, searches that aim to discover whether a prior publication will prevent the issuance of a patent must include not only patent databases but databases in the non-patent literature of the relevant technology. The state of technology before the filing of a patent application and the publications that describe it are referred to as the 'prior art'. In most countries an invention that has not been described in a printed publication is unpatentable if the invention was used publicly before the patent application was filed. In most cases, public use is brought to the attention of the Patent Office or the courts by persons with inside information. It is very difficult to find information about prior public use by searching online, although in cases where prior use is suspected it may be possible to document it by searching the periodical literature. More important from the point of view of a patent searcher is the statutory requirement for non-obviousness or inventiveness. This requirement prevents the grant of a patent unless the claimed invention is sufficiently different from what is already known that a person of ordinary skill would not arrive at it through a simple modification of the nearest prior art product or process. It is often unnecessary to retrieve a reference that describes an invention in every detail to determine that the invention is likely to be unpatentable. Since the legal requirement for inventiveness or unobviousness is applied differently in every country, however, an invention that is similar to one described in a published reference is likely to be patentable in some countries and not in others.

## PATENT DATA FIELDS

Patents are more complex than other publications because they function both as technical documents and as legal documents. The information in a patent divides itself into three general kinds of data: bibliographic information identifying the document itself; technical information describing the claimed invention; and information about the history of the patent application with regard to its prosecution by the applicant's representative in the national or international patent office and its legal status. In searches for technical information alone, the bibliographical and technical information found in the patent specification are sufficient to answer any possible question. If the searcher needs to know whether or not a patent is currently in force, however, legal status information is also needed. At the present time it is not possible to answer all questions about the current status of a patent by searching online, as only limited information is available in the databases about changes in patent ownership, the expiration of patent terms, or the lapse of patents prior to the end of their statutory terms. Some countries publish every change in the status of a pending patent application; some even announce the serial number, title and applicant before the specification itself is published. These announcements of filing, usually with the patent kind code A0, are not actually publications of the patent specification. Other countries, notably the United States, keep all details of pending patent applications secret until a patent is granted. In order to guess whether an American patent application on a particular invention has been filed it is necessary to search for equivalent applications published by other countries.

### Bibliographic data fields

In patent databases, as in other bibliographic databases, the bibliographic data tells the searcher who wrote the cited publication, where it can be found, and when it was published. But a patent is a legal document, and its bibliographic information also identifies the owner of the claimed invention and the extent of his or her rights.

*Country or patent convention*

Historically, patents are published by the patent granting authority of a national government and have legal effect only in that country. Each patent document bears the name of the granting country and recent patent documents also bear a two letter ISO (formerly ICIREPAT) code identifying the country. Current and obsolete ISO codes for the countries covered by the patent databases discussed in this chapter are listed in Table 3.2. Some databases use standard ISO codes to identify the patent country, but others, especially databases that are not devoted primarily to patents, identify the patent country by the full name of the country or an abbreviation that may or may not be ambiguous.

In recent years there has been a move toward international cooperation in the processing of patent applications. The Patent Cooperation Treaty (PCT), which came into force in 1977, provided for the filing of a single patent application to be processed by the Patent Offices of several countries. As of 1991, forty-five countries had signed the treaty. PCT applications are published eighteen months after filing with the ISO code WO, but the published document is not a granted patent. Using the results of a single prior art search, each of the countries designated in the PCT application examines the application separately and issues a patent if the invention meets the national standards of patentability. The European Patent Convention created a centralized European Patent Office empowered to grant patents having effect in each of the member countries and enforced by the courts of each country. European patent applications are published with the ISO code EP about eighteen months after filing and, if the claimed invention is found to be patentable, republished after allowance for any amendments made during prosecution. Negotiations toward the creation of a European Community patent, enforceable by the Community rather than the national courts, are under way, and it is expected that the Community Patent will come into being in the early 1990s. In Africa there are similar regional Patent Offices: OAPI, the African Intellectual Property Organization, which provides for patents in twelve French-speaking countries, and ARIPO, the African Regional Industrial Property Organization, which provides for patents in seven English-speaking countries.

## Designated states

Applicants for patents who file PCT or European patent applications may elect to obtain patent coverage in as few or as many of the member countries as they desire. The selections, indicated on the patent application as 'designated states', define the geographical boundaries of the area for which protection is sought. PCT applications may designate some countries through national Patent Office procedures and others through the regional European Patent Office procedures. Patent databases usually provide a field to identify the designated states for WO and EP documents.

## Document number and publication date

Patents and published patent applications are issued with a document number that is used in combination with the country name or ISO country code to identify it. This number and the date of publication are printed on the face of the document. Some countries, the United States and the United Kingdom, for example, issue patents in single continuous series. Others issue a new series of patent numbers every year, with the year as part of the document number. Japanese patents use the Japanese imperial year, representing the year of the reign of the Emperor. For patents published prior to 8 January 1989, the imperial year refers to the Showa era and is equal to the Gregorian year minus 1925, the year before Emperor Hirohito was crowned. Patents published since the accession of Emperor Akihito refer to the Heisei era, equal to the Gregorian year minus 1988. Patents published during the first few months of the Heisei era were printed with the year 64, but are indexed with the 'correct' year designation 01.

Databases vary in the way they handle patent number formats. Some databases use a fixed field length for all patent numbers. The nine-character format used by Derwent until the end of 1990 has been adapted to many of the other patent databases carried on ORBIT and Questel. For patent numbers that incorporate the publication year, Derwent's patent number format places the last two digits of the publication year at the front of the serial number. Derwent's format incorporates the Imperial year for published Japanese applications and the Western year for granted Japanese patents to differentiate between them. DIALOG has adopted a standard patent number format of its own, consisting of the ISO code followed by a space and the document number

The hosts that have adopted a standard format permit the searcher to use either the standard format or the format provided by the database producer. ORBIT and DIALOG automatically select the standardized format for crossfile searching, while Questel allows the searcher to select either format. Since DIALOG does not reverse Derwent's formatting algorithm when reformatting patent numbers, crossfile searching between WPI and other databases with the MAPPN command is relatively inefficient.

In indexing published patent applications, databases sometimes use the application serial number rather than the publication number to represent the document. This can cause serious problems in crossfile searching between databases with different input policies. No matter how carefully the vendor has standardized formats, for example, it will not be possible to cross an Austrian patent number between CA SEARCH and WPI; the 'patent number' cited by WPI is indexed by Chemical Abstracts as the application serial number if it is in the record at all. Searchers who fail to retrieve the correct patent by searching for a known number in the patent number field should try reformatting the number, searching in the application or priority number field, or, if all else fails, searching a different database or host system.

Patent publication dates are very important in some countries such as the United States and Canada (for patents applied for prior to the 1989 patent law revisions) because the patent term is measured from the issue date. In most other countries, however, the patent expiration date is calculated from the date of filing, and the publication date indicates only the date that the document became available to the public. The publication dates of patents retrieved as references in prior art searches are important in deciding the patentability of a claimed invention, as only patents published before the application was filed can be considered as references.

*Patent kind or level of publication*

A patent document number is not always sufficient to identify a particular patent. Some countries issue two or more series of documents with identical serial numbers, while others assign a unique serial number to a patent application and use the same number to identify the corresponding granted patent after it has been changed by amendment. Modern patent numbers have associated with them a one or two character ISO code that indicates the kind of patent or level of publication of the document. This code, a letter or a letter followed by a numeral, indicates whether the document is an announcement of filing, a published application, an examined patent, a patent granted after opposition, a patent of addition or a reissued granted patent and whether it is a utility patent, a utility model, a design patent or a plant patent, depending upon the choices available in the country in question. The codes are defined separately for each country: an 'A' document in the United States is a granted patent, while an 'A' document in France is a published application.

The patent kind codes are not strictly bibliographic identifiers. Their main purpose is to indicate the legal status of the document. But the code is usually printed with the document number on the face of the patent and it is often an essential bibliographic element. In countries where the same document number follows a patent application through several levels of publication, the code (or an indication of the level it represents) is necessary for unambiguous identification of the patent document. An indication of the level of publication is essential for countries like Japan that use an identical numerical sequence to identify a patent application, an unrelated published specification and an unrelated granted patent.

*Application number and date*

Patent applications are assigned a serial number when they are filed. This serial number identifies the application in the Patent Office before it is published. Both the serial number and the application date are printed on the document. The date of filing is of great legal importance, as a valid patent will be granted only if the invention has not been described elsewhere prior to the application date. In most countries the term of the patent is calculated from the application date, the most common term being twenty years from filing to expiration. Databases that treat patents only as sources of technical information frequently omit application numbers and dates from their records.

*Priority application number and date*

Only one patent can be granted in each country for any invention, and in most countries the first applicant is entitled to that patent. Applicants for patents on a single invention in several countries that are members of international patent treaties such as the Paris Convention for the Protection of Industrial Property can rely on the filing of a single application to establish the effective filing date in all of the countries. A convention priority date is established by filing an application in one country and making a formal claim for priority based on that original filing in applications filed within one year in other countries. The national application number and date of the original patent application appears on each of the resulting patents as the priority number and date. The original application and any other application that is filed on the invention without claiming priority are published without a priority number and priority date, but many patent databases treat the local application data as priority data in order to establish patent families. Most countries allow applicants to claim more than one priority. Databases generally index multiple priorities so all of them can be used to search for members of a patent family.

Application numbers are printed on patents in a format characteristic of the country of publication. The priority application number may be printed in a different format when priority is claimed in another country, and it may appear in yet another format when the priority information is put into computer-readable form by a database producer and modified still further by the host system when it is offered online. The difficulty this creates for searchers is due in large part to the practice of treating the final two digits of the year as a part of the standardized priority application number format. When the priority application is Japanese, the Imperial year designation complicates the problem still further. Each of the records in Figures 3.12 and 3.14 through 3.16 and Search 3.1 describes a patent based on Japanese patent application number 58-207128, filed on 4 November 1983. The priority application number is represented in FPAT as JP20712883, in PATDPA as JP 83-207128, in JAPIO in the Japanese Patent Office format and in the Derwent format 83JP-207128, in APIPAT as JP 207128 and in Derwent format, and in the WORLD PATENTS INDEX/APIPAT record in Derwent format alone. Searchers will sometimes notice that queries based upon patent application numbers fail to retrieve the expected patents even though the numbers are formatted correctly for the database being searched. This usually means that no patent based upon that priority has been issued in the countries covered by the database, but the possibility that the priority data have been indexed incorrectly should not be overlooked.

*Patent family members*

Patents that are filed in a number of countries on a single invention by a single applicant form families of equivalent patents. Such patents usually have the same technical information, although the claims may vary from country to country. Since each country requires that patent applications be filed in its official language, equivalent patents are useful as translations. In many countries the law permits applicants to claim more than one priority. To minimize the number of patents they index, some databases fully analyse only the first patent on an invention to reach the indexers, referred to as the 'basic patent'. Patents are treated as equivalent family members when they claim the same priority application numbers as a patent that was indexed earlier or because they seem to the indexer to cover the same invention despite the absence of a common priority.

Because patent databases differ in their treatment of multiple priorities, in their policy toward intellectually identified equivalent patents, and in the number of countries they index, the number of patents in a family may be different in the various databases that index its members. It is important to recognize the fact that 'equivalent' patent applications may differ considerably in content, either because the original specification was modified before the later applications were filed or because the various Patent Offices have required amendment of the applications after filing.

*Patentee names*

All patent documents bear the name and residence of the applicant who becomes the owner of the patent when it issues. As units of property, patents may be sold or given to another by the original patentee and they may be owned jointly by two or more companies or individuals. All inventions have inventors - individuals or teams of individuals who conceived of the invention and reduced it to practice - but most inventions are made at the behest of the inventors' employers. Patent applications may be filed by the inventors or by the contractual owner of the invention, depending upon the national laws and upon the individual circumstances. In countries like the United States, where the inventors are required to apply for the patent, many patents are assigned to the inventors' employer or financial backer prior to the publication of the patent document and the name of the assignee as well as that of the inventor appears on the patent. Some countries categorize patentees, indicating whether the patent owner is, for example, a corporation or a foreign government. The patentee field in most databases indexes the patent assignee or corporate patent applicant listed on the face of the patent specification. Almost invariably the indexed patentee is the original owner of the patent: subsequent sale or reassignment of the patent is rarely indexed by patent databases. Changes of corporate name or affiliation, on the other hand, are tracked by some database producers so that the record for a patent often will be found to identify the patent owner by a name different from the one on the face of the patent specification.

Some patent databases have established a series of patentee codes for organizations that have a substantial number of patents. These may be used to group all patents belonging to the various divisions of a corporation, as they are by Derwent, or each company name may have a unique code. The codes are usually continued when the name of the company changes. Some databases also use a list of standardized company names, applying the preferred form of the name along with, or instead of, a company code.

Inventors are not always identified on patent documents published by countries that treat the corporation as the patentee, and inventor names are not always indexed by patent databases. Therefore, a search for a patent claiming subject matter developed by a particular scientist or engineer will be incomplete if it requires that the inventor's name be present in the record of every patent it retrieves.

*Cross-reference citation*

Patent Offices publish bulletins or gazettes in which they announce the publication of patent documents. The Patent Office gazette citation is not an essential bibliographic element, but it is cited in some patent databases. Databases based on abstracting services, such as WPI, CA SEARCH and JAPIO, include the accession number or citation of the printed abstract in the online record. Cross-reference citations to these abstracting services are present in records in some of the other patent databases.

**Technical data fields**

Patents are required to describe the claimed invention in sufficient detail that it can be practised without undue experimentation by a hypothetical person of ordinary skill in the art to which the invention pertains. At the same time, patents are written with an eye toward the eventual need to defend them from infringers in the courts. In order to obtain protection for the broadest possible invention, patent agents and attorneys normally draft patent applications using generic language in place of specific language that would be easy for an infringer to design around. A patent will refer to a leg as a 'supporting means' and a spade as a 'digging implement'. That kind of language is helpful when a competitor introduces a similar product or process using a cantilevered bracket or a hoe, but it complicates free-text searching enormously. A common form of generic description is the Markush structure, named after a patent applicant whose claims were approved in a landmark decision of the United States Patent Office. Markush structures are usually employed in chemical patents; they consist of a central substructure and one or more groups of optional substructures.

*Title*

Patents are published with short titles in the language of the patent. These are often so general and so concise that they offer no clue about the details of the invention: 'Cleaning Composition' or 'Mining Apparatus', for example. Some patent databases translate the titles, augment the original titles with explanatory phrases, or replace the original title with a new one that summarizes the gist of the invention.

*Abstract*

Most countries now require that patent applications include an abstract that summarizes the invention. The abstract submitted by the applicant is of uncontrolled quality: it may be extremely vague or it may be a restatement of the broadest claim in the application as filed. It is nearly always in generic language and it seldom contains a specific example.

Some databases write their own abstracts. These may be longer than the ones supplied with the patent application and they commonly include specific language and examples taken from the body of the patent specification. Because each database indexes patents from its own point of view and in its own native language, the content of the abstracts it produces may differ markedly from the content of the author abstract and from the abstract produced for another database. In Figures 3.5, 3.7 and 3.8, the original abstract of United States patent 4 532 250 is reproduced in citations from the CLAIMS UDB, USPA, and PATDATA databases; Derwent's abstracts of this patent and the equivalent PCT application, WO 85/02402, reproduced from WPIL in Figure 3.2, are considerably more informative.

*Claims*

Patent claims define the scope of the patent grant. A patent usually contains one or more broad generic claims and a series of narrower sub-generic and specific claims that cover embodiments of the broader claims. The broadest claim must be an independent claim, one that defines the invention fully, although it may be necessary to refer to the body of the specification for the limits of some of the generic language. The narrower claims are usually written as dependent claims, where some of the features of the invention are defined by referring back to an earlier claim.

In published applications, the claims define the invention for which the applicant hopes to obtain protection. They often include unpatentable material. Granted patent claims have been examined for patentability and have often been amended after filing. Claims in a valid granted patent define a product or process that cannot be made, used or sold without the consent of the patent owner. Products and processes that are described in the patent and not claimed are not protected by the patent and can be used by the public unless they are claimed in some other patent in the same country. Within a family of patents filed by an applicant in several countries, the scope of the granted claims may vary widely. This occurs because the laws that define patentable subject matter and the standards for judging whether an invention is disclosed in sufficient detail to support a patent claim differ from one country to the next. If it is important to know whether your company is permitted to practise an invention disclosed in a patent, it is essential to obtain a copy of the granted patent document from the country in which you wish to do business.

Most sources of patent information that publish patent claims use only one or two of the claims, not all claims published in the document. The claim that is chosen is usually the first claim, which is conventionally assumed to be the broadest claim. In many cases, however, the patent contains several broad claims covering different aspects of the invention, such as a product and the process for making it or a class of compounds and method for treating a disease with the compounds. In databases where a single 'main claim' is reproduced, one should never assume that the claim summarizes the patented invention in its entirety.

*Disclosure*

The bulk of a patent specification is in the disclosure, which teaches how to make and use the claimed invention. A typical patent disclosure consists of a description of the problem the claimed invention seeks to solve, a summary of the prior art, a detailed description of the claimed invention with definitions for all new or obscure terms, a general description of the ways the invention can be made and used, and examples of the production and use of specific embodiments of the generic invention. The disclosure usually teaches how to prepare sub-assemblies and chemical intermediates as well as the final product. Although patent abstracts and claims often contain only obscure generic language, the disclosure contains clear specific language. It is not unusual for a patent disclosure to contain speculative or prophetic examples that describe embodiments of the invention that were never made. These are educated guesses and they are sometimes in error.

It is in their treatment of prophetic disclosures that national patent examining procedures and patent databases differ the most. The patent claims may be allowed to issue as filed or the applicant may be required to delete the unexemplified scope from the patent claims before grant. Likewise, the abstract or indexing prepared by the database may either include the 'paper examples' or the database's indexing policy may require that they be ignored. Thus the content of the patent claims will differ significantly from country to country and the depth of indexing will differ significantly from database to database.

*Drawings*

Electrical and mechanical patents normally contain pages of drawings for the claimed invention. The parts of the drawings are identified by reference symbols, and the disclosure explains what the drawings depict in terms of the reference symbols. Chemical structures are usually integrated into the disclosure and claims. The drawings and chemical structures are an essential part of the patent disclosure, but they are especially difficult to depict online. Patent drawings for German patents indexed in PATDPA are available in the PATGRAPH database. While the STN mounting of the CAS database contains drawings of chemical structures from some patents, these are the illustrations used in the printed *Chemical Abstracts* publication and may not correspond to structures shown in the abstracted patents. Chemical structures illustrated in MARPAT and in WPIM and MPHARM, the auxiliary chemical structure databases for WPIL and PHARMSEARCH, are notations that represent the indexing conventions and do not necessarily correspond to structures shown in the patents. Each database has its own procedures for dealing with drawings in the abstracts and claims that appear in the online record. The database may ignore the structure, translate the structure into a linearized form that can be shown in the printout, reproduce only alphanumeric substructures, or refer the reader to the printed patent specification. Differences in the way drawings are treated can make a significant difference to the amount of information available in the online record and in its cosmetic appearance, as can be seen by comparing the treatment of the chemical structure diagram shown in Figure 3.1 by WPIL, CLAIMS/U, USPA and PATDATA in the records reproduced in Figures 3.2, 3.5, 3.7 and 3.8.

*Subject indexing*

The technical content of patents is made more accessible to searchers through subject indexing applied by both the patent issuing authorities and some database producers. Patent information is found in two distinct types of databases: those that catalogue the patents of one or more countries as legal documents; and those that index patents as technical disclosures. Databases in the first group include INPADOC and the national patent databases. In such databases, the subject indexing is usually limited to patent classification codes and such words as happen to occur in the title, abstract or claims of the patent. Databases in the second group include WORLD PATENTS INDEX, the CLAIMS UNITERM and COMPREHENSIVE databases, APIPAT, PHARMSEARCH, and many databases like CA SEARCH that index both journal and patent literature in a technological field. These databases index the patent disclosure in considerable depth and some replace the original patent abstract with a comprehensive abstract based on the technical data present in the specification. The deepest indexing is applied to chemical patents; even databases that index chemical patents intensively provide relatively superficial indexing for patents without chemical aspects.

*Patent classification codes*

Patent indexing has traditionally been done in patent offices by means of hierarchically-based patent classification codes. The classification codes appear on the patent document and are used to identify the field of technology to which the patent belongs. The classification schemes were designed to subdivide the files of paper copies of patent documents used by examiners and searchers in the Patent Office search rooms. Patent classification systems are modified frequently to keep up with changes in technology.

Each national patent office has traditionally designed and used its own patent classification system. The national systems do not necessarily have similar guidelines for subdividing technologies and they do not use the same kinds of symbols to identify classifications. The most common national patent classification codes in patent databases are United States classes, which are formatted as a three-digit numerical class code followed by a slash or hyphen and a sub-class code consisting of from one to three numbers occasionally followed by a letter or by a decimal point and additional numerals. Patents are given a single 'original classification' and usually are given one or more 'cross reference classifications'. The United States patent classification system is under constant revision and as the purpose of the system is to provide a useful arrangement of the patents on the shelves of search rooms, file copies of the patents are moved to their new places and the indexes are revised when new classifications are assigned to existing patents. The printed patent specification is not changed, of course, when a patent is reclassified; some databases change the records of reclassified patents while others retain the original classification codes.

The World Industrial Property Organization, WIPO, designed an International Patent Classification (IPC) system for patents that has been adopted by most of the industrially-advanced countries of the world. Even countries that continue to use the national classification system as the basis for the organization of the patent search files print a corresponding IPC classification on the patent documents. Although the IPC is used by most countries, these countries do not all follow the same guidelines for applying the codes and they do not all use the finest divisions of the classification system. Patents with identical claims may be classified differently in each country in which the patent application was filed.

The IPC, in the format ANNA-NNN/NN, where A represents a letter and N represents a numeral, represents a hierarchical system in which each successive character narrows the definition of the invention. Some countries index patents only to the four-character sub-class level, while others use the full IPC. In searching, it is usually necessary to truncate IPC codes unless the level of specificity used by the country of interest is known. A hybrid system of classification has been introduced for more specific indexing of patents; countries that use the hybrid system append indexing codes in the format NNN:NN to IPC codes for some technologies. The IPC has been revised four times since it was introduced in 1968 and is now in its fifth edition. Some patent offices and some databases, but not all, identify the edition of the IPC used in classifying a patent. The European Patent Office has reclassified all of the patents in its search documentation files according to its own standards, using a somewhat modified version of the IPC, and has made the resulting index of reclassified patents available in the EDOC database.

*Database-supplied indexing*

Patent databases run the gamut in the depth of indexing supplied by their producers. Many patent databases have no information in their records that is not present in the patent document, and the majority contain no more than the original text of the title, the abstract and a single claim. A few patent databases, notably Derwent's WORLD PATENTS INDEX, APIPAT and the CLAIMS UDB and CDB, index the entire patent specification by means of controlled thesaurus terms and chemical compound coding. The deepest indexing is provided at great expense, so it is not surprising that access to such indexing is usually restricted to organizations that have paid a subscription fee for access and is made available to non-subscribers, if at all, at a higher cost or for limited connect time. Indexing is common in databases produced from literature abstracting services that include patents because of their technical content. Many of these databases are described in Chapters 4 to 10. Since an especially large proportion of the records in CA SEARCH, the online version of *Chemical Abstracts*, are patents, it is discussed in this chapter as a major patent database.

## Prosecution history and legal status data fields

After a patent application is filed in a national patent office its legal status changes frequently. Prosecution history information is extremely valuable to those who are interested in the commercial exploitation of the invention claimed in the patent. If a valid patent grant is in force, the use of the patented invention can lead to a lawsuit. If the patent has lapsed or if the patent application has been abandoned, the invention is freely available.

*Prior art search results*

Patent examiners search the prior art for patents or other publications that disclose or suggest the claimed invention in each patent application. The examiner records citations in the patent application file to the most pertinent references found in the search, and some patent offices print the citations on the patent document when it is published. If the document is a granted patent, the cited references describe related art; if the examiner had discovered a reference that described the claimed invention, the applicant would have been required to amend the claims before the patent was issued. If the document is a published application, some of the cited references may describe exactly the same product or process being claimed, and the application may never mature to a granted patent. Search reports made for European patent applications and PCT applications are issued as documents separate from the published application itself, and are not always available at the time the published application is indexed by a database.

Cited references are useful in searches for technical information, as they represent the most relevant prior publications on the claimed subject matter found by a skilled searcher. Even more useful are citing references, those later patents in which the patent examiner has cited a publication known to be relevant to the search in progress. Patent examiners still rely heavily on manual searches of patent documents, so they often cite valuable references that are not retrievable online in any other way, especially patents published before the online era. On the other hand, some cited references relate to aspects of the citing patent that are irrelevant to the subject of the search in progress.

The patent classifications searched by the examiner are printed on the face of United States patents to indicate the scope of the examiner's search. It is not customary to publish any information about the additional non-patent sources of information that may have been used, although the references that were found are cited on the document.

*Prosecution details*

Before a patent is granted the application passes through a number of stages in its prosecution. Monitoring the progress of a patent application can provide useful information to potential licensees or competitors. No information about the status of a United States patent application is available to the public before the patent is issued, but the title and applicant of newly filed patent applications and/or progress in the prosecution of published applications are treated as public records in some countries. Before the application is examined in many countries, the applicant must make a formal request for examination of the application. Patent examiners issue office actions in which they report the results of the prior art search, make any necessary comments on the format of the application, and either allow or reject the claims. The applicants may abandon the application or file amendments, and they may file documents containing data supporting the patentability of the claimed invention. Applications that have been finally rejected by the examiner may be appealed to the courts, which eventually issue decisions on the patentability of the invention. In many countries, the public is invited to oppose the grant of a patent on an invention during a period of time after the examined patent specification is published. The usual route of publication for patent prosecution information is the printed patent office gazette.

*Amendments and certificates of correction*

Many patent databases obtain information about the technical content of patents from published patent applications. But after a patent application has been filed and before a patent has been granted, the scope of the claims and the content of the supporting disclosure are often changed by amendment. Published applications therefore differ from the patent that eventually protects the claimed invention. In some countries the granted patent may be changed radically, either through the deletion of material found not to be pertinent to the allowed claims or through the addition of supporting data that was not in the application when it was filed. Patent databases do not usually index granted patents in sufficient depth to identify the changes wrought by amendments. If the legal scope of a patent indexed from the published application is important, it is essential to obtain a copy of the granted patent specification.

When a patent is published, errors are sometimes found in the document. In the United States, these can be corrected through the issuance of a Certificate of Correction. The existence of a Certificate of Correction is not usually noted in patent databases.

*Patent term lapse or extension*

Patents expire at the end of their statutory term. The expiration date does not appear on the face of the patent, so it does not appear in patent databases. The expiration date is generally calculated by adding the length of the statutory term to the date from which that country measures patent terms.

Most of the world's patent laws require that periodic fees be paid to maintain a patent in force throughout its entire statutory term. Failure to pay these fees causes the patent to become void. Most patent databases do not record the lapse dates of patents, although the fact that a particular patent is no longer in force is of the greatest importance.

Sometimes a patentee gives up the right to some or all of the claims in the patent, either by dedicating the patent to the public before it expires or by disclaiming the unwanted claims. In the United States, some patent applications are found to be so closely related to other commonly owned patents that they are allowed to issue only on condition that the resulting patent expire no later than the related patent. In such cases a terminal disclaimer, a statement that the patentee's rights will expire on a date earlier than the end of the statutory seventeen-year patent term, appears on the face of the patent. Although the patent becomes partly or wholly ineffective as of the disclaimer date, most patent databases do not record that information.

Patents may also be nullified as the result of a court decision. Although the decisions may be published in legal databases, the invalidation of the patent is not commonly reported in patent databases.

In some countries it is also possible to obtain an extension of a patent if it can be shown that the patentee was prevented from exercising its rights. The only patent term extensions now available in the United States cover pharmaceutical and agricultural products kept from the market place by government regulatory delays, and the extension applies only to the approved product and not to the entire scope of the patent. Patent term extensions are not usually recorded in patent databases, but information about patent term extensions may be available online in government regulations or business news databases.

*Patent examiner and applicant's representative*

Patents usually record the name of the patent attorney or agent who represented the patentee in the prosecution of the patent and sometimes record the name of the patent examiner who examined the patent application. This information may be useful to persons who are planning strategies for a patent suit or who are evaluating the persons involved for employment opportunities, but it is not important for searches into the technical content of the patent.

## PATENT DATABASES

The data fields contained in the databases listed in Table 3.1 are summarized in the following sections. Databases are illustrated by a sample citation in full format from one of the host files. The print field tags shown in the figure appear in brackets in the discussion of the corresponding data elements; the illustrated field tags may not be applicable to the database on a different host. The figures illustrate citations from only a few patent families, so that the differences in record content can be seen readily. US 4 532 250 and equivalent patents are shown in Figures 3.2, 3.5, 3.7 and 3.8; US 4 851 417 and equivalent patents are shown in Search 3.1 and Figures 3.3, 3.4 and 3.17 through 3.20; US 3 826 728 is shown in Figure 3.6 and Search 3.2; US 4 306 289 and equivalent patents are shown in Figures 3.6, 3.9 and 3.10; and JP 60-179169 and equivalent patents are shown in Figures 3.11, 3.12,, 3.14 and 3.15.

## WORLD PATENTS INDEX

The WORLD PATENTS INDEX database, (WPI), produced by Derwent Publications Ltd., covers the technological content of patents from thirty-four patent-issuing authorities and invention disclosures from two defensive publication journals. The database was designed to give access to the technical information in the patents, not to provide bibliographic documentation of every patent in the database. For that reason, each record represents a family of patents that claims a single invention. The database corresponds to a complex of subscription services: the thirteen sections of the *Chemical Patents Index (CPI*, formerly known as the *Central Patents Index), the three sections of the *Electrical Patents Index (EPI)*, and the two sections of *General & Mechanical Patents Index (GMPI)*. Subscribers may purchase print, microfilm and magnetic tape versions of abstracts, indexes and complete specifications. They are given access to special in-depth coding for online retrieval and discounted rates for online searches. The database is mounted on ORBIT, DIALOG and Questel as two files, a backlog file covering 1963-1980, and the WORLD PATENTS INDEX LATEST file (WPIL) covering 1981 to the present. The two files may be searched as one using OneSearch on DIALOG or file WPAT on ORBIT. Figure 3.2 shows the record for the patent family based on WO 85/02402 from Questel's file WPIL.

## Figure 3.2: WORLD PATENTS INDEX citation - Questel file WPIL

```
1/1  -  (C) Derwent
AN   -  85-146530 [24]
XA   -  C85-063786
TI   -  New 5-heteroaryl:imidazol-2-one(s) - having cardiotonic activity
DC   -  B05
AW   -  HETERO ARYL IMIDAZOLONE
PA   -  (AHSC ) AMER HOSPITAL SUPPL CORP
IN   -  STOUT D M; YAMAMOTO D
NP   -  4
PN   -  WO8502402 A 850606 DW8524
        AU8436783 A 850613 DW8533
        US4532250 A 850730 DW8533
        EP-162102 A 851127 DW8548
DS   -  CH DE FR GB SE CH DE FR GB LI SE
DN   -  AU JP
LA   -  E E
PR   -  83US-554498 831123
AP   -  84WO-U01854 841113; 83US-554498 831123; 84EP-900282 841113 [Based on
        WO8502402]
CT   -  US3538104 US3850944 EP-78545 EP-78546 EP-59948 US4053480
        US4405635 US3505350 US3641049 US3488423 US3303199 US2585388 US3538104
        US3850944 EP--78545 EP--78546 EP--59948 US4053480 US4405635 US3505350
        US3641049 US3488423 US3303199 US2585388
IC   -  A61K-031/41 C07D-233/54 C07D-401/04 C07D-403/04
AB   -  WO8502402 Cpds. of formula (I) and their salts are new. R =
        heteroaryl; R1 = H or 1-6C alkyl; "Heteroaryl" includes bicyclic
        heteroaryl such as phthalazine, quinazoline, quinoline or
        isoquinoline, and opt. substd. phenyl, naphthyl, thiazole,
        thiadiazole, thiophene or pyridyl.
          Specifically R = pyridyl; R1 = 1-6C alkyl.
          USE - (I) have cardiotonic activity and are useful for treating
        cardiac disorders. Dosage is 10-100 mg/kg (parenteral). The cpds. have
        minimal effects on blood pressure and heart rate.
          In an example, soln. of 4-propionylpyridine oxime tosylate (7.9 g)
        in EtOH (40 ml) was added to a soln. of KOEt (2.4 g) in EtOH (25 ml),
        stirred for 3.5 hrs. at room temp., then treated with 400 ml Et2O and
        filtered. The filtrate was exted. with several portions of 2N HCl and
        the aq. extracts conc. to give 2.64 g 4-(alpha-aminopropionyl)pyridine
        dihydrochloride (II). 6NHCl (0.84 ml) and a soln. of KOCN (0.81 g) in
        water (5 ml) were added to (II) (1.115 g) in water (5 ml) and refluxed
        for 2 hrs. The prod. was filtered and dried to give 0.47 g (40%)
        4-methyl-5-(4-pyridyl)-2 -imidazolone hydrochloride. (15pp Dwg.No.0/0)
USAB -  US4532250  5-heteroarylimidazol-2-ones of formula (I) are new. In
        (I), R is pyridyl; R1 is H or 1-6C alkyl (Me). (I) are prepd. from
        4-cyanopyridine by a multi stage reaction scheme involving treatment
        with Grignard reagent, hydroxylamine hydrochloride, potassium
        ethoxide, and potassium cyanate in turn.
          USE - (I) have good cardiotonic activity and are used to increase
        ventricular myocardial contractility without undesirable peripheral
        vascular effects. (vaso-constriction) and in this are advantageous
        over cardiac glycosides (e.g. digitalis) and over sympathomimetic
        amines (e.g. dobutamine and dopamine). Nor does (I) induce ischemia as
        does amrinone. (4pp)
MC   -  B06-H B07-D09 B12-F01
```

Derwent began the database in 1963 with patents from fifteen countries in the field of pharmaceuticals, and has gradually increased the scope of coverage over the years. Abstracts were printed on punched cards and all the indexing was represented by punch coding. Indexing has been expanded greatly, but the constraints of the punched card system are still evident in the fixed field formats. Derwent's fixed field formats have become the de facto standard for online systems as hosts have converted patent data in other databases to Derwent's formats either as the only searchable format or as an alternative to the format provided by the database producer. Derwent has recently revamped its data processing system, enlarging the data fields so that data elements that have historically been truncated can be entered in full. Although the changed formats will be apparent in Derwent's current products, it is possible that the host systems will not convert the online databases to the new formats, as much effort has been expended to standardize patent data formats for all databases on each host system. The formats described below are those in use in early 1991.

Patents from various countries are not treated equally, being divided for depth of indexing into 'major' and 'minor' countries. Indexing is based on the earliest publication of the patent specification in a covered country, the indexed patent being treated as the basic patent and later patents as equivalent. The patents indexed for the database are the first published document in each country. For some major countries (the United Kingdom, Netherlands, Germany and, for chemical patents, Japan) as well as for the European Patent Office, the examined patent is also indexed. Patent families are defined by the latest priority application cited on the patent documents. Patents that do not claim priority are sometimes made equivalent to other patents on the basis of their technical content, date of filing and ownership. Abstracts [AB] are prepared for basic patents and for equivalent granted patents from the United Kingdom, Germany, the European Patent Office and the United States [USAB].

In the WPI database, the patent country code for basic and equivalent patents is searchable both alone and in combination with the publication number in a fixed nine-character format [PN]. A status letter, the first character of the one or two character ISO code that indicates the level of publication, is appended to each patent number in the patent family. Designated states for European and PCT documents [DS, DN] are searched and printed in an additional field, and a language field that represents the language of the specification by a single letter [LA] is also present in records that include these documents. ORBIT also provides the language indicator 'E' for patent families where an English-language document is present, but the indicator is occasionally incorrect because it is applied on the basis of the country of issue, and some predominantly English-speaking countries also publish patent specifications in a second language. Document numbers and Derwent's entry week are indexed for both basic and equivalent patents. The entry week corresponds to the week the patent was processed for the database, not to the date the document or its abstract was published. The 'number of patents' field [NP] gives only the number of entries in the [PN] field, not the number of countries the patents cover. Application numbers other than priority application numbers [AP] have been indexed only since 1984, and they are now indexed only for basic patents and selected equivalent patents. The application number of the priority application, or the national application number if priority is not claimed, is indexed as a priority [PR], as are earlier and later applications relied upon to establish filing dates of continuing applications. The national application numbers of patents that have been indexed as equivalent on the basis of technical content are also searchable as priorities. Priority application numbers are searchable in a fixed eleven-character format. Publication dates of basic and equivalent patents are provided in the PN field for patents indexed since 1974.

Derwent's indexers use a thesaurus of standard company names for major patentees, and have recently begun to integrate the more complete company name thesaurus used by INPADOC into the Derwent system. In addition to company names, Derwent uses a four- or five-character company code to index patent owners [PA]. In the early punch code-based years, the company code was the only searchable patentee name, and standard codes were assigned to all patentees. Later, rules were developed for the assignment of non-standard codes to patentees without large patent portfolios, and standard codes are now used only for major patenting organizations. New standard company codes are added rather infrequently as Derwent has no regular procedure for identifying new companies with significant patent activity. Since non-standard codes are applied to more than one patentee, searches using these codes do not give precise answers. Codes are maintained when organizational name changes take place and, in most cases, recognized corporate affiliates are assigned the code belonging to the parent organization. In cases where equivalent patents name different patent assignees, all appropriate company codes and names are indexed. The patentee name field is of limited length, and names are often truncated. It is best to use the NEIGHBOR or EXPAND command to locate possible truncated forms of names and to check for the company code in the printed *Company Code Manual*. Individual inventor names [IN] appear only in the online database, not in the corresponding printed abstract. Inventor names have been indexed only since 1978 and are taken only from basic documents other than Japanese patents, so a 'NO POSTINGS' message in a search for a patent by a particular inventor should never be taken as evidence that the invention has not been patented.

Accession numbers in WPI [AN] refer to the entire patent family and take the form ##-X####X, where # is a numeral and X is either a letter or a numeral. The first two digits refer to the entry year of the basic patent and correspond to the terminal letter that designated the year of publication from 1970 to mid-1983. Before a unified chemical patents service was established in 1970, Derwent produced three separate patent services: Farmdoc, with accession numbers terminating in F; Agdoc, with accession numbers terminating in G or H; and Plasdoc, with accession numbers terminating in P or Q. Dummy year designations were assigned to records from these three services, so that the year '66' corresponds to all 'pre-CPI' pharmaceutical patents, '67' corresponds to agricultural patents, and '68' corresponds to polymer patents. Because the records were created from three independent databases, there are two or three records for some families of patents from the pre-CPI era. In the ORBIT WPI file there are accession numbers with the dummy year '65', assigned to records incorporated into the file through the merger of the APIPAT file with WPI. Related accession numbers are reported in the XR field for some patent families, but they are not provided for most of these pre-CPI records. Throughout most of its history, Derwent's system for assigning equivalent patents to families assigned them to only one of the multiple pre-CPI records; if a full patent family is needed it is necessary to search for a second record based upon the same priority or having overlapping patent families. Since 1983, Derwent has assigned two series of secondary accession numbers in addition to the primary accession numbers. These are in the format ##-C##### for chemical patents [XA] and ##-N##### for non-chemical patents.

Derwent abstractors write descriptive titles [TI] for all basic patents. The titles of all but the earliest records include an indication of the inventive concept stressed in the patent specification. Abstracts are available online for most patent families. Derwent produces two kinds of abstracts for chemical patents: short abstracts are published in *Alerting Bulletins*, and longer documentation abstracts of basic chemical patents are published a few weeks later in *Documentation Abstracts Journals*; only the alerting abstracts are online. The printed abstracts include drawings and chemical structures and describe the invention in terms of them. Drawings and chemical structures are omitted from the online record, but the verbal descriptions of the symbols in the drawings are online. Abstracts are not written for most basic patents from 'minor' countries or for non-chemical Japanese patents, although the expanded titles are often sufficient to allow retrieval. The notation 'NoAbstract' appears in the title of unabstracted patents to allow their exclusion from sets of records whose abstracts are to be printed. In addition to the title and abstract text, additional words [AW] are added to the online file if they are thought to be likely search terms. A thesaurus of heavily posted terms has been devised, and the preferred form of a significant title term is searchable in addition to the form that appears in the text. The title, abstract and index terms are written, with British spelling, as summaries of the entire patent specification. The novel features of the claims are stressed, but the claims are not reproduced verbatim except as the abstracts of some equivalent granted patents.

International Patent Classification codes [IC] are indexed from the basic patent, and additional IPC codes are added to the online record when they are found in equivalent patents. Derwent assigns IPC codes to patents published without IPC codes and to non-patent references indexed from *Research Disclosure* and *International Technology Abstracts*. Derwent also applies several of its own indexing schemes to patents. The Derwent Classification Codes [DC], used for subdividing technologies in the printed abstract books, are useful for limiting searches to a general field. Use of the more precise special coding schemes is limited to subscribers. There is a system of 'Manual Codes' [MC]: hierarchical classification codes designed to sort printed documents for manual searching. A polymer code is used for patents classified in Section A (Plasdoc) of CPI; a chemical fragmentation code is applied to patents in Sections B, C and E, known as Farmdoc, Agdoc and Chemdoc respectively. Derwent Registry Numbers have been applied to a few thousand common chemical compounds since 1981. Since 1987, most chemical structures in patents indexed in Sections B, C and E have been indexed for the WPIM structure file using Markush DARC software to provide topological storage and retrieval of both generically defined chemical structures and specific compounds. As of early 1991, WPIM was available only on Questel.

Patents cited as references in European and PCT patent applications [CT] are indexed, but journal references and patents cited in other countries are not. The grant of a patent in the United Kingdom, Germany, the European Patent Office, the Netherlands and, for chemical patents, Japan, is indicated by the additional posting of a B or C level document among the equivalent patents. United States reissue patents and re-examined patents are indexed as equivalents to the original patent.

The WPIL database is updated on a weekly basis with bibliographic information, abstracts, IPC codes and subscriber Manual Codes. The remainder of the subscriber coding is added to the records several months after the bibliographic data. Patent families are updated whenever new equivalent patents are found. Equivalent patents are added to the backfile on a monthly basis, so that the patent family data for the few pre-1981 families still being updated lags behind the information in the current file. New information is taken from the weekly CPI, EPI and GMPI publications, and update codes correspond to the volume number of the printed abstract books. The actual publication date of the patents added to the file in a particular week varies from country to country; for example, week 9001 contains United Kingdom patents published during the first week of January and patents published in other countries from one week to several months earlier.

While ORBIT and Questel have retained all of Derwent's fixed length fields, and employ them as crossfile searchable formats in other patent databases, DIALOG has modified Derwent's Japanese patent numbers by including the full country code, JP, and reformatted Derwent's patent, priority, and application numbers for crossfile searching into standard DIALOG formats by separating the country code and serial numbers. In DIALOG format, the numerical sequence can be searched separately from the bound format of the country code, number and year. If one has an application serial number without an associated year of filing, this is a welcome improvement, but because DIALOG's format does not reverse Derwent's modifications to published patent numbers, some crossfile searches do not retrieve the correct documents in other databases. To address this problem, the MAPPN command converts Japanese patents to both the Imperial year and the Gregorian year for crossfile searches, resulting in the retrieval of unrelated patents as false drop when a database coincidentally contains the same serial number for a different level of publication.

## INPADOC

INPADOC is a databank of bibliographic patent information compiled by the International Patent Documentation Center (INPADOC), an agency of the European Patent Office formerly run by the Austrian Patent Office and the World Industrial Property Organization of the United Nations (WIPO). Tapes of data on all patents published by fifty-six patent offices are forwarded to Vienna and reformatted for entry into the database and the weekly *INPADOC Patent Gazette*. The starting date for coverage varies, as each country began submitting data to INPADOC at a different time and some countries submitted retrospective data. Bibliographic data differ somewhat from country to country as well, because some countries omit certain information from the records they provide to INPADOC. Information is added to the INPADOC computer whenever it is received from the contributing patent offices, with a lag time of a few days or many months after publication of the patents, depending on the country.

INPADOC is searchable on the INPADOC PFS/PRS service in Vienna, operated by the European Patent Office, the Japanese PATOLIS system, ORBIT, DIALOG and STN but the database differs radically according to the individual host. INPADOC has a file of patent status information on British, United States, West German, European Patent Office, French, Dutch, PCT, Danish, Swiss, Belgian and Austrian patents. The history of the progress of the patent application through the patent system of each country is tracked. Status information for the patent family is searchable in the INPADOC databases on the INPADOC and PATOLIS computers as well as on DIALOG and STN. On ORBIT, legal status data are segregated into the LEGSTAT database, where they may be searched directly. Legal status information is displayable in the ORBIT INPADOC file only by using the PRINT FAMSTAT command after a family search has been done.

As mounted in Vienna, the INPADOC PFS/PRS is a patent family database, searchable only by means of patent number, application, and priority data, and yields a list of all patent documents in the file with a common priority. Titles, names, IPCs and dates are printable, but not searchable. A substantial fee is charged for each family searched. A search using the INPADOC computer is not exclusively a computer search. Online searches of the database are monitored by INPADOC staff members in Vienna, who back up each search with a manual search that sometimes identifies additional, equivalent non-priority patents. Searchers who attempt to use an unacceptable query are notified by INPADOC that they have made an error.

The INPADOC file on ORBIT is a complete bibliographic database, containing all the bibliographic and technical information in INPADOC's patent family database, but not the patent status information. The database is updated weekly. Each record in the database describes a single patent. In INPADOC all bibliographic data are printable and all data except priority application numbers and dates are searchable. As in the INPADOC PFS/PRS, a substantial surcharge is made for searches that generate patent families. In order to collect the surcharge, ORBIT permits searches for patent family information only through four special commands: FPRI, which generates the patent family through input of a priority application number; FPAT, which locates equivalents to a patent number; FSET, which locates equivalents to a patent already retrieved by some other search strategy; and FSEL, which locates equivalents to a patent number SELECTed from a record in any ORBIT patent database. A family search yields a set of records that may be manipulated further or printed in any available format. In Search 3.1 a search that retrieved United States patent 4 851 417 is followed by the FSET command, yielding all the patents with a common priority. Patents reported in the *INPADOC Patent Gazette* within the last six weeks are duplicated in the INPANEW file. The INPANEW database has no restrictions on searching with priority data.

## Search 3.1: INPADOC records - ORBIT File INPADOC

```
YOU ARE NOW CONNECTED TO INPADOC.
CURRENT THROUGH UPDATE 9035.

SS 2?
FSET SS 1/1

FAMILY SEARCH FOR PATENT NUMBER 'US 4851417-A'.  THE SURCHARGE IS
 $20.  DO YOU WISH TO CONTINUE? (Y/N)

Y

SS 2 RESULT (3)

SS 3?
PRINT FAMSTAT
```

**Search 3.1:** (cont.)

```
*** FAMILY PATENT INFORMATION ***

-1-
PN   - AU 37593/89-A1 [AU8937593] 89.12.12
TI   - SUBSTITUTED 6H-PYRIDO (4,3-B) CARBAZOLES
IN   - ARCHER SYDNEY
PA   - RENSSELAER POLYTECH INST
AP   - 89.05.25   37593/89-A  [89AU-037593]
PR   - 89.05.25   WO 8902333/89(US)-A   [89WO-U02333]
       88.05.26   US 198976/88-A    [88US-198976]
IC   - C07D-471/04; A61K-031/475
ND   - AR


-2-
PN   - US 4851417-A [US4851417] 89.07.25
TI   -  9-SUBSTITUTED 6H-PYRIDO(4,3-B)CARBAZOLES
IN   - ARCHER SYDNEY [US]
PA   - RENSSELAER POLYTECH INST [US]
AP   -  88.05.26   198976/88-A   [88US-198976]
PR   -  88.05.26   US 198976/88-A   [88US-198976]
IC   - A61K-031/475; C07D-471/04
CXR  - CA12-35839(05)
WXR  - 89-270442 (C)


-3-
PN   -  WO 8911480-A1.10000 [WO8911480] 89.11.30
TI   - SUBSTITUTED 6H-PYRIDO (4,3-B) CARBAZOLES
LA   - ENG
IN   - ARCHER SYDNEY [US]
PA   - RENSSELAER POLYTECH INST [US]
AP   - 89.05.25   8902333/89(US)-A   [89WO-U02333]
PR   - 88.05.26   US 198976/88-A   [88US-198976]
IC   - C07D-471/04;  A61K-031/475
DS   - *AT *AU *BB *BG *BR *CH *DE *DK *FI *GB *HU *JP *KP *KR *LK
        *LU *MC *MG *MW *NL *NO *RO *SD *SE *SU AT BE BF BJ CF CG CH
        CM DE FR GA GB IT LU ML MR NL SE SN TD TG

*** LEGAL STATUS INFORMATION ***

-LS 1-
PN   - US 4851417 [US4851417]
DT   - US-P
ACT  - 88.05.26 US/AE-A
        APPLICATION DATA (PATENT)
         {US 198976/88 [88US-198976] 88.05.26}
ACT  - 89.07.25 US/A
        PATENT
UP   - 8942

-LS 2-
PN   - WO 8911480 [WO8911480]
DT   - WO-P
ACT  - 89.05.25  WO/AE-A
        APPLICATION DATA
         {WO 8902333/89(US) [89WO-U02333] 89.05.25}
ACT  - 89.11.30  WO/AK-A1 [+]
        DESIGNATED STATES CITED IN A PUBLISHED APPLICATION WITH
        SEARCH REPORT
        AT AU BB BG BR CH DE DK FI GB HU JP KP KR LK LU MC MG MW NL
        NO RO SD SE SU
ACT  - 89.11.30  WO/AL-A1  [+]
```

**Search 3.1:** (cont.)

```
           DESIGNATED COUNTRIES FOR REGIONAL PATENTS CITED IN A
           PUBLISHED APPLICATION WITH SEARCH REPORT
           AT BE BF BJ CF CG CH CM DE FR GA GB IT LU ML MR NL SE SN TD
           TG
   ACT   - 89.11.30  WO/A1  [+]
           PUBLICATION OF THE INTERNATIONAL APPLICATION WITH THE
           INTERNATIONAL SEARCH REPORT
   UP    - 8950
```

The STN version of the INPADOC database permits searching for priorities, and a search automatically generates a single record for a full patent family which can be printed in a tabular format. Patents from the four latest weekly updates are also searchable in the INPAMONITOR database, which has individual records for the newly added patents rather than family records. Priority data can be searched directly; charges are determined not by the search that generates the family, but by the amount of information printed. Patents forming a 'family' from a particular country can be extracted for printing at a lower price than the entire family by designating a numerical code corresponding to the country that is used exclusively in this database. On STN, the Chemical Abstracts accession number can be searched in the INPADOC file, and patent families identified by the CA accession number are available at a lower charge than in the standard bibliographic format.

DIALOG's File 345 also permits searching for priorities without generating a search fee. An INPADOC record on DIALOG is stored as a complete family; the charge for displaying a record is determined by the format chosen for the display. DIALOG records can be printed in tabular format, as shown in Figure 3.3. Individual 'country families' can be extracted from the record for less expensive display using the standard ISO country code to designate the display format. The record for the 'patent basic' can also be displayed inexpensively, but unfortunately the earliest patent entered into a family is often the announcement of an unpublished patent application filing, and titles are often meaningless. A full citation from DIALOG File 345 of the patent family that includes United States 4 851 417, complete with the legal status of the US and WO documents, is shown in Figure 3.3. The same patent family, as retrieved on ORBIT, is shown in Search 3.1.

**Figure 3.3: INPADOC record - DIALOG File 345**

```
   1/39/1
   9268848
   Basic Patent (No,Kind,Date): US 4851417 A 890725 <No. of Patents: 003>
   Patent Family:
        Patent No    Kind  Date     Applic No    Kind Date
        AU 8937593    A1   891212   AU 8937593    A    890525
        US 4851417    A    890725   US 198976     A    880526 (BASIC)
        WO 8911480    A1   891130   WO 89US2333   A    890525
   Priority Data (No,Kind,Date):
        WO 89US2333 A 890525
        US 198976 A 880526


   PATENT FAMILY
   AUSTRALIA (AU)
       Patent (No,Kind,Date):  AU 8937593  A1  891212
           SUBSTITUTED 6H-PYRIDO (4,3-B) CARBAZOLES (English)
           Patent Assignee: RENSSELAER POLYTECH INST
           Author (Inventor): ARCHER SYDNEY
           Priority (No,Kind,Date): WO 89US2333 A 890525; US 198976 A
             880526
           Applic (No,Kind,Date): AU 8937593 A 890525
           IPC: * C07D-471/04; A61K-031/475
```

**Figure 3.3:** (cont.)

```
          CA Abstract No: * 112(05)035839P
          Derwent WPI Acc No: * C 89-270442
          Language of Document: English

    UNITED STATES OF AMERICA (US)
       Patent (No,Kind,Date):  US 4851417  A    890725
          9-SUBSTITUTED 6H-PYRIDO(4,3-B)CARBAZOLES (English)
          Patent Assignee: RENSSELAER POLYTECH INST (US)
          Author (Inventor): ARCHER SYDNEY (US)
          Priority (No,Kind,Date): US 198976 A 880526
          Applic (No,Kind,Date): US 198976 A 880526
          National Class: * 514285000; 546070000
          IPC: * A61K-031/475; C07D-471/04
          CA Abstract No: ; 112(05)035839P
          Derwent WPI Acc No: ; C 89-270442
          Language of Document: English

       Legal Status (No,Type,Date,Code,Text):
          US 4851417    P   880526 US AE        APPLICATION DATA (PATENT)
                               (APPL. DATA (PATENT))
                               US 198976  A    880526
          US 4851417    P   890725 US A         PATENT
    WORLD INTELLECTUAL PROPERTY ORGANIZATION, PCT (WO)
       Patent (No,Kind,Date):  WO 8911480  A1  891130
          SUBSTITUTED 6H-PYRIDO (4,3-B) CARBAZOLES (English)
          Patent Assignee: RENSSELAER POLYTECH INST (US)
          Author (Inventor): ARCHER SYDNEY (US)
          Priority (No,Kind,Date): US 198976 A 880526
          Applic (No,Kind,Date): WO 89US2333 A 890525
          Designated States: (National) AT; AU; BB; BG; BR; CH; DE; DK; FI; GB;
             HU; JP; KP; KR; LK; LU; MC; MG; MW; NL; NO; RO; SD; SE; SU
             (Regional) AT; BE; BF; BJ; CF; CG; CH; CM; DE; FR; GA; GB; IT; LU; ML
             ; MR; NL; SE; SN; TD; TG
          Filing Details: WO 10000 With international search report
          IPC: * C07D-471/04; A61K-031/475
          Derwent WPI Acc No: * C 89-270442
          Language of Document: English

       Legal Status (No,Type,Date,Code,Text):
          WO 8911480    P   880526 WO AA        PRIORITY (PATENT)
                               US 198976  A    880526
          WO 8911480    P   890525 WO AE        APPLICATION DATA  (APPL. DATA)

                               WO 89US2333 A 890525
          WO 8911480    P   891130 WO AK        DESIGNATED STATES CITED IN A
                               PUBLISHED APPLICATION WITH SEARCH REPORT
                               (DESIGNATED STATES CITED IN A PUBLISHED APPL.
                               WITH SEARCH REPORT)
                               AT AU BB BG BR CH DE DK FI GB HU JP KP KR LK
                               LU MC MG MW NL NO RO SD SE SU
          WO 8911480    P   891130 WO AL        DESIGNATED COUNTRIES FOR
                               REGIONAL PATENTS CITED IN A PUBLISHED
                               APPLICATION WITH SEARCH REPORT  (DESIGNATED
                               COUNTRIES FOR REGIONAL PATENTS CITED IN A
                               PUBLISHED APPL. WITH SEARCH REPORT)
                               AT BE BF BJ CF CG CH CM DE FR GA GB IT LU ML
                               MR NL SE SN TD TG
          WO 8911480    P   891130 WO A1        PUBLICATION OF THE INTERNATIONAL
                               APPLICATION WITH THE INTERNATIONAL SEARCH
                               REPORT  (PUB. OF THE INTERNATIONAL APPL. WITH
                               THE INTERNATIONAL SEARCH REPORT)
```

Although the data in INPADOC are the same on all hosts, records are quite different in their organization. Field tags indicated in the following descriptions are those shown in the ORBIT citations in Search 3.1. Patent country and number are indexed for each patent using the ISO country code and the document number in the same format that appears on the patent document as well as in Derwent format [PN], and the patent kind code and publication date are also provided. Designated states are listed in the record of European and PCT documents [DS], where ORBIT uses an asterisk to identify each country designated for a national patent and not for coverage by a European or other regional patent. A separate record is provided for each level of publication of a patent document, but not every country provides INPADOC with the details of all levels of publication. INPADOC's Manual 002 lists the types of patents documented by each country. Each record carries the full patent kind code [PN], which is necessary to identify the latest version of the document for countries in which the various levels of publication keep the same number. Later publications of the same patent in countries that assign different numbers to the various levels of publication can be correlated with the earlier publications through the application number. Each record bears the local application number and date [AP] as well as priority application numbers and dates [PR]. The national application number is duplicated in the priority field if no Convention priority is claimed. Patent applicant and assignee names [PA] are standardized for organizations with many patents. For countries that report them, inventor names are also present [IN]. The country of origin of the patentee and inventors is also present in the records of some countries' patents.

In addition to the bibliographic information relating to the patent documents themselves, INPADOC records contain cross-reference accession numbers [CXR, WXR] for patents indexed in CHEMICAL ABSTRACTS, JAPIO, or the Derwent WORLD PATENTS INDEX. Cross-reference accession numbers are not provided for all equivalent patents in the family. Derwent accession numbers are represented in the form A##-######, where A represents the letter 'C' for patents classified in one of the chemical sections of the WORLD PATENTS INDEX database and 'G' for patents that are classified only in the electrical or general and mechanical sections. The numerical part of the accession number is Derwent's primary accession number; these Derwent accession numbers should not be confused with Derwent's secondary accession numbers which begin with the letters 'C' and 'N.'

The title [TTL] is given in its original language. Titles in non-Roman alphabets are translated into English. Some records have no titles; Japanese titles are provided as updates to the records after several months' delay. The International Patent Classification codes applied to the patents by the issuing patent office [IC] are listed. INPADOC contains neither abstracts nor additional indexing. The language of the document is provided if the issuing patent office provides the information [LA]. The [ND] field indicates fields for which no data are provided.

## EDOC

The EDOC database on Questel is produced by INPI, the French Patent Office, from the European Patent Office's search documentation files. Patents from sixteen patent-issuing authorities are covered systematically and patents from many other countries are included on a non-systematic basis. Coverage of German patents begins in 1877, with other countries added over the years. Most of the patents in the European Patent Office files have been reclassified for the convenience of its patent examiners, using a refined version of the International Patent Classification code (ECLA) or, for some technologies, using the Netherlands' national patent classification code. Japanese patent records are indexed with their original IPC codes. The classification codes are applied in a consistent manner to all of the patents in the files, including those patents that were published before the IPC system was created. Figure 3.4 illustrates the EDOC records of the patents claiming priority from United States patent application 198 976 of 1988.

**Figure 3.4: EDOC citations - Questel File EDOC**

```
1/3  -  (C) INPI/OEB
PN   -  WO8911480 A 891130
AP   -  WOUS8902333 W 890525
PR   -  US19897688 A 880526
DT   -  CD
EC   -  C07D-471/04 C07D-221:00A C07D-209:00A

2/3  -  (C) INPI/OEB
PN   -  AU3759389 D 891212
AP   -  AU3759389 D 890525
PR   -  US19897688 A 880526
IC   -  A61K-031/475
        C07D-471/04

3/3  -  (C) INPI/OEB
PN   -  US4851417 A 890725
AP   -  US19897688 A 880526
PR   -  US19897688 A 880526
DT   -  BAS
EC   -  C07D-471/04 C07D-221:00A C07D-209:00A
IC   -  A61K-031/475
        C07D-471/04
```

EDOC records relate to a single patent and contain the patent document [PN], application [AP] and priority [PR] numbers and dates, one-letter patent kind codes, and patent classification codes [EC, IC]. For patents that do not claim priority, the national application number and date are repeated in the priority field. The European Patent Classification codes can be searched either with full ECLA codes or with truncated IPC codes. Patent document and priority numbers are indexed in their original format in the /PN and /PR fields and in Derwent format in the /XPN and /XPR fields, which do not print in any of the standard formats. The database has no title, patentee or inventor information and no claim or abstract text. The database is normally used only to search for patent families, to generate a list of commonly classified patents that includes patents from many countries and patents too old to have been classified with IPC codes, and to discover missing publication, application or priority data for patents cited elsewhere. EDOC is especially useful for retrieving information about the status of Japanese patents as it contains not only the numbers of patent applications published before and after examination, but also the number of the granted patent which is omitted from most other patent family databases. Bibliographic information that is absent from the EDOC database can be found for many patents by using the ..MEM and *MEM commands to search the /XPN fields in Questel's WPI/L, FPAT, EPAT and CAS databases.

EDOC records contain document type codes [DT] that indicate the status of the document in the EPO files. A basic patent [BAS] is indexed for each patent family, family members are linked by one or more common priorities, and patents that are identified as equivalent on the basis of technical content are indexed as members of an intellectual family. The records for older patents do not contain the priority links that are used to create patent families, so the dates of coverage for the various countries shown in Table 3.2 should not be considered as the earliest dates of patents retrievable by means of patent family searches. Patent family searches can be done by searching normally for patents with a common priority or, for a surcharge, by means of a special ..FAM command, which automatically searches all common priorities for equivalents to a patent designated by a priority number.

## CLAIMS

The CLAIMS family of databases, produced by IFI/Plenum Data Co., covers United States patents issued since 1950. The CLAIMS BIBLIO/ABSTRACT database, the CLAIMS UNITERM database (UDB) and the CLAIMS COMPREHENSIVE database (CDB) are three parallel databases containing records of chemical patents from 1950, electrical and general or mechanical patents from 1963, and design patents from 1980 to the present. The bibliographic and text data of the BIBLIO/ABSTRACT database are included in full in both the UNITERM and COMPREHENSIVE databases. The UDB also contains detailed indexing of chemical and chemically-related patents, including fragmentation coding of chemical compounds. The CDB, available by subscription only, indexes chemical and chemically related patents with the same thesaurus of general terms used for the UNITERM database and provides more precise coding of chemical structures and linked indexing of the roles of the indexed substances. CLAIMS subscribers are encouraged to participate in the development of the database and the indexing system; changes and improvements are made, retrospectively in most cases, with every annual database reload. The databases are mounted on DIALOG, ORBIT and STN, and the bibliographic data in CLAIMS is also available on CD-ROM. The CLAIMS family of databases also includes the CLAIMS/REASSIGNMENT AND RE-EXAMINATION and CLAIMS/CITATION databases on DIALOG and CLAIMS reference files on all three systems.

The CLAIMS databases are updated weekly with bibliographic data one or two weeks after the publication date of the patents. The original records are replaced once a month by edited records that have expanded titles and company coding. On DIALOG, the preliminary records are isolated in a separate CLAIMS PATENT ABSTRACTS WEEKLY database, and each of the BIBLIO/ABSTRACT, UNITERM, and COMPRE-HENSIVE databases is available both as a combined file lacking the unedited records and divided into three time-limited files that begin in 1950, 1971 and 1982. All of the records from 1950 to the present are consolidated in a single file on STN and ORBIT.

Until 1991, CLAIMS contained only standardized bibliographic data fields, the title, abstract, and exemplary claim, classification codes and IFI's coding. An enhanced version of CLAIMS with the non-exemplary claims as well as all bibliographic and prosecution history data on the first page of the patent was introduced. At the time this chapter was written, DIALOG was mounting the additional data for 1991 patents, with the backfile of patents from 1975 to be added gradually, and neither of the other hosts had announced plans for the enhanced database. The full unenhanced record of US 4 532 250 is shown in Figure 3.5 as it appeared in the CLAIMS/U file on ORBIT.

## Figure 3.5: CLAIMS/UNITERM citation - ORBIT File CLAIMS/U

```
    -1-
AN   -  1612192
CHAN -  8512858
PN   -  US4532250
TI   -  5-HETEROARYLIMIDAZOL-2-ONES HAVING CARDIOTONIC ACTIVITY
IN   -  STOUT DAVID M; YAMAMOTO DIANE M
PA   -  AMERICAN HOSPITAL SUPPLY CORP (03104)
PD   -  85.07.30 AP - 83.11.23 83US-554498
PCL  -  514/341.000,   CROSS REFS:  514/248.000,   514/259.000,
        514/307.000,   514/311.000,   514/392.000,   544/237.000,
        544/284.000,   546/144.000,   546/167.000,   546/278.000,
        548/127.000,   548/128.000,   548/134.000,   548/137.000,
        548/202.000,   548/206.000,   548/317.000,   548/318.000,
        548/322.000
IC   -  A61K-031/44
PT   -  C (Chemical)
DT   -  UTILITY
```

**Figure 3.5:** (cont.)

```
AB    - DESCRIBED ARE COMPOUNDS OF THE FORMULA
               2-(O=),4-R1,5-R-4-IMIDAZOLINE
        WHEREIN R IS HETEROARYL AND R1 IS HYDROGEN OR LOWERALKYL, OR
        A PHARMACEUTICALLY ACCEPTABLE SALT THEREOF. THE COMPOUNDS
        EXHIBIT CARDIOTONIC ACTIVITY.
CLM   - 1. A METHOD OF TREATING OR RELIEVING THE SYMPTOMS ASSOCIATED
        WITH CARDIAC INSUFFICIENCY IN A PATIENT BY A SELECTIVE
        INCREASE IN THE CARDIAC CONTRACTILE FORCE COMPRISING
        ADMINISTERING TO A PATIENT IN NEED OF SUCH A TREATMENT A
        THERAPEUTICALLY EFFECTIVE AMOUNT OF A COMPOUND OF THE FORMULA

               2-(O=),4-R1,5-R-4-IMIDAZOLINE
        WHEREIN R IS PYRIDYL AND R1 IS HYDROGEN OR LOWERALKYL, OR A
        PHARMACEUTICALLY ACCEPTABLE SALT THEREOF.
GN    - 00097; 00863; 01273; 01773; 02295; 05859; 06154; 06232;
        06909; 10030; 22042; 22052
FN    - 30003; 34236; 40001; 40002; 40004; 40005; 40023; 40026;
        40079; 40144; 40305; 40473; 40516; 40531; 40537; 40549
```

The CLAIMS databases index the patent number [PN] and publication date [PD] for all patents and the application [AP] and priority numbers and dates for patents published from 1971 to the present. Patent numbers of equivalent British, West German, Dutch, French and Belgian patents published up to 1979 are reported in the record of the corresponding American patent. Both inventor names [IN] and assignee names [PA] are indexed. CLAIMS applies five-digit numerical assignee codes and standardized company names to records for chemical and chemically-related patents, and these codes are generally applied to other patents belonging to the same companies. The names associated with the codes are changed when company names are found to have been changed, and the new names are posted retrospectively to the online files with subsequent reloads. When a patent is reassigned to a new owner and the reassignment is recorded at the USPTO, a flag is added to the record for that patent and a record of the reassignment is added to the CLAIMS REASSIGNMENT AND REEXAMINATION file.

In addition to the information relating to the patent documents themselves, CLAIMS records corresponding to patents that have been indexed by *Chemical Abstracts* are cross referenced to the *Chemical Abstracts'* accession number of the indexed patent, and CLAIMS records that correspond to patents indexed by *Chemical Abstracts* from mid-1979 contain CAS registry numbers. The STN version of the databases also has CAS Registry Numbers for patents indexed since 1979. This information is added to the records with other corrections and modifications in annual reloads.

The original titles [TI] are present in the database and are augmented by descriptive phrases for patents published since 1971. The author abstract [AB] and the claim or claims printed in the *Official Gazette* of the United States Patent and Trademark Office [CLM] are present in the records. Chemical structures that occur in the claim are replaced in the online record by a linearized representation of the drawn structure. This allows the reader to visualize the structure without referring to the full text of the patent specification and allows structural features of the claim to be used as search terms.

The original and cross reference United States Patent Classification codes [PCL] are present in all records. Each yearly reload includes any changes in patent classification announced by the United States Patent and Trademark Office, so that the classification codes in the database correspond to the latest revision of the classification system. Records of patents published since 1971 also contain the International Patent Classification codes assigned at the time of publication by the USPTO [IC].

The UNITERM and COMPREHENSIVE databases contain extensive indexing for patents that are chemical and chemically-related. A thesaurus of general terms [GT], extensively cross-indexed and frequently revised to accommodate new technologies, identifies general concepts, processes and substances. A fragmentation code [FT] is used to define the structure of specifically identified monomeric compounds, polymers and generic chemical structures from the examples and the claims of the patents. All general terms and fragment terms are identified by five-digit numeric codes and may be searched by the term name or code number. Common chemical substances are not indexed by fragmentation coding every time they occur, but are indexed through their own five-digit compound terms. One may discover whether a compound term exists by searching the separate CLAIMS REFERENCE or REGISTRY database with the fragmentation codes appropriate to the compound or with the name and/or molecular formula of the compound. In addition to the level of indexing supplied by the UNITERM database, the COMPREHENSIVE database provides further refinements of the chemical fragmentation coding system and a system of role identifiers that are linked to the fragment terms and to general terms that identify chemical substances. The roles indicate whether the compound is produced in the patent, used as a chemical intermediate, or present in some other role. For polymers, role identifiers link the coding for the structure of the polymer's monomeric unit with the type of polymeric structure being indexed.

Patents cited by the examiner are indexed in the separate CLAIMS Citation database, which is available only on DIALOG. Records in the BIBLIO/ABSTRACT, UNITERM and COMPREHENSIVE databases on all three hosts contain a flag 'Cited in # Later Patents' to indicate whether a citation search would yield any references to the patent, but they do not identify the citing patents. The CLAIMS Citation database is produced by Search Check Inc. and marketed by IFI/Plenum, and indexes patents cited in US patents since 1947, the year the examiners' citations were first printed in US patents. There are three CLAIMS Citation files, comprising patents issued from 1790 to 1946, from 1947 to 1970, and from 1971 to the present. A CLAIMS Citation record consists of only a patent number and a list of cited or citing patents. United States patents issued since 1947 are searchable and printable as citing and cited patents; those issued earlier can be searched only to determine whether they have been cited in patents published after 1946. Foreign patents cited in American patents are printable, but are not searchable; information about the nature of the cited patents must be obtained by searching other databases or by consulting the patent specifications.

For reissue patents and for patents that were filed as divisions, continuations or continuations-in-part of earlier patent applications, the CLAIMS record contains the application and/or patent numbers and dates of the parent applications. These related patents are retrieved automatically when the application or patent numbers are searched on DIALOG and STN; they are indexed in the priority field on ORBIT. Patents which have been republished after re-examination proceedings are flagged in the CLAIMS records and the re-examination certificate is indexed in the separate CLAIMS REASSIGNMENT AND RE-EXAMINATION database.

The CLAIMS REASSIGNMENT AND RE-EXAMINATION database includes the text of the re-examination certificate of all patents re-examined by the United States Patent and Trademark Office, the first having been issued in 1981, and the reassignment records of all patents whose change of ownership has been recorded with the USPTO since 1980. The database is updated bimonthly. The record for a reassigned patent, US 4 306 289, and for a re-examined patent, US 3 826 728, are reproduced in Figure 3.6. The reassignment record contains only the patent number and date, the reassignment record and date, and the nature of the change of assignment. The name of the original assignee prints in the ORBIT and STN records, but not in the DIALOG record. The re-examination record contains the patent number and date, the name and address of the entity that requested re-examination, the dates and numbers of the re-examination request and certificate, and the result of the re-examination of the claims. An exemplary re-examined claim, showing the amendments, is reproduced in the record. Since late 1985, United States patents have been subject to lapse for failure to pay periodic maintenance fees. The expiration dates of lapsed patents announced in the *Official Gazette* of the USPTO are reported in the CLAIMS REASSIGNMENT AND RE-EXAMINATION file. Patents whose term has been extended under the Drug Price Competition and Patent Term Restoration Act of 1984 are also indexed. Records of extensions and lapses are very brief.

**Figure 3.6: CLAIMS/REASSIGNMENT & REEXAMINATION citations - DIALOG File 123**

```
   1/5/1
   1367372
   Assignee: AT&T TECHNOLOGIES INC      REASSIGNED
   Reassignment (Seq,Date,Kind,Co):
      840319  CHANGE OF NAME  AT & T TECHNOLOGIES, INC.,
                Patent      Issue
                Number      Date
                ----------  ------
   Patent:      US 4306289  811215


   1/5/2
   0875866
   Reexamination requested by: SHATTERPROOF GLASS CORP DETROIT MI US
   Assignee: SHATTERPROOF GLASS CORP
                Patent      Issue
                Number      Date
                ----------  ------
   Patent:      US 3826728  740730
   REEXAMINED
   Reexamination Certificate (Date): 860610 (No,Seq): B13826728 (514TH)
   Reexamination Request (No,Date): 90/000529 MAR 19 1984
   Claim:
      AS  A  RESULT  OF  REEXAMINATION,  IT  HAS  BEEN  DETERMINED  THAT: THE
   PATENTABILITY OF CLAIMS 1 AND 2 IS CONFIRMED. NEW CLAIMS 3-16 ARE ADDED AND
   DETERMINED  TO BE PATENTABLE. 1. A TRANSPARENT ARTICLE HAVING REDUCED SOLAR
   RADIATION  TRANSMITTANCE  AND  REDUCED  GLARE,  WHICH  COMPRISES:  (A)  A
   TRANSPARENT  GLASS  SHEET  FOR  USE  AS A WINDOW PANE AND THE LIKE HAVING A
   SMOOTH  CONTINUOUS  SURFACE; AND (B) A CONTINOUS SPUTTER-COATED FILM ON SAID
   CONTINUOUS GLASS SHEET TO A THICKNESS OF FROM 200 TO 400 A. A A., SAID FILM
   BEING  A METAL SELECTED FROM THE GROUP CONSISTING OF NICKEL AND NICKEL-BASE
   ALLOYS;  (C)  SAID  COATED  GLASS  SHEET  HAVING  A  SUBSTANTIALLY  UNIFORM
   TRANSMITTANCE  OVER  THE RANGE OF 0.75 TO 2.0 MICRONS AT A LEVEL RELATIVELY
   LOWER  THAN  THE  LEVEL  OF  TRANSMITTANCE  IN  THE  VISIBLE  RANGE AND THE
   TRANSMITTANCE  ALSO BEING SUBSTANTIALLY UNIFORM IN THE VISIBLE RANGE OF 0.4
   TO  0.75  MICRONS  RESULTING  IN  EXCELLENT  COLOR  FIDELITY  AND  NATURAL
   VISIBILITY THERETHROUGH SUBSTANTIALLY FREE FROM DISTORTION.
```

Companion CLAIMS files contain the registry of specific common compounds indexed for the UNITERM and COMPREHENSIVE databases, the United States patent classification titles from the *Manual of Classification* and its Index, and the CLAIMS Thesaurus. All three of these are included in STN's IFIREF database; DIALOG's CLAIMS/REFERENCE file includes the *Manual of Classification* and the *CLAIMS Thesaurus,* and the CLAIMS Compound Registry is a separate file. The Compound Registry can be searched in the CREGISTRY file on ORBIT, while the CLAIMS/Class file on ORBIT contains only the US patent classification data.

## US PATENTS

The US PATENTS database is produced by Derwent Inc. and mounted on ORBIT. It includes all United States utility patents and defensive publications published since August 1970. The database is divided into a current file, USPA, and a backfile, USPB, and can also be searched in its entirety as USPM. The file is updated weekly with patents issued one or two weeks earlier. Figure 3.7 illustrates the USPA citation for US 4 532 250.

**Figure 3.7: US PATENTS citation - ORBIT File USPA**

```
-1-
PN  - US4532250
TI  - 5-Heteroarylimidazol-2-ones having cardiotonic activity
IN  - Stout, David M., Vernon Hills (IL) US; Yamamoto, Diane M.,
      Gurnee (IL) US
PA  - American Hospital Supply Corporation, Evanston, IL, US
PD  - 85.07.30
AP  - 83.11.23 83US-554498
NO  - 3 Claims, Exemplary Claim 1, 0 DRAWINGS, 0 Figures
      Examiner: Fan, Jane T.
      Atty/Agent: Fato, Gildo E.
PCL - 514/341.000, Cross Refs: 544/237.000 X, 544/284.000 X,
      546/144.000 X, 546/167.000 X, 546/278.000 X, 548/127.000 X,
      548/128.000 X, 548/134.000 X, 548/137.000 X, 548/317.000 X,
      548/318.000 X, 548/322.000 X, 548/202.000 X, 548/206.000 X,
      514/259.000 X, 514/248.000 X, 514/307.000 X, 514/311.000 X,
      514/392.000 X
IC  - A61K-031/44
FLD - 546/278.000, 424/263.000
DT  - INVENTION PATENT
FS  - To US Company or Corporation
CT  - US3538104, 11/1970, Gouenfeld et al., 546/278.
      US3850944, 11/1974, Tanaka et al., 546/278.
      EP59948, 3/1982.
      EP78545, 11/1982.
      EP78546, 11/1982.
      Burger, Medicinal Chemistry, 2nd edition, 1960, p. 77.
AB  - Described are compounds of the formula  NHR/sup 1/RNHO


          wherein R is heteroaryl and R/sub 1/is hydrogen or
      loweralkyl, or a pharmaceutically acceptable salt thereof.

          The compounds exhibit cardiotonic activity.
MCLM- What is claimed is: 1. A method of treating or relieving the
      symptoms associated with cardiac insufficiency in a patient
      by a selective increase in the cardiac contractile force
      comprising administering to a patient in need of such a
      treatment a therapeutically effective amount of a compound of
      the formula NHR/sup 1/RNHO

          wherein R is pyridyl and R/sub 1/is hydrogen or
      loweralkyl, or a pharmaceutically acceptable salt thereof.
CLM - 1. See Main Claim.
CLM - 2. The method of claim 1 where R is pyridyl and R/sup 1/is
      loweralkyl.
CLM - 3. The method of claim 2 wherein R/sup 1/is methyl.
```

US PATENTS records include the patent document [PN], application [AP] and priority numbers and dates of the indexed patents in Derwent format. Patent assignee [PA] and inventor [IN] names are indexed. Records include the address of the inventors and the assignee. Patent assignees are classified by type as United States or non-United States corporations, governments or individuals. The 'Notes' field [NO] includes the number of claims, drawings and figures in the patent.

The original title [TI] and abstract [AB] of the patent are provided in the record. All of the patent's claims [CLM] are searchable. In the current file, USPA, all claims are also printable. Only the exemplary claims

[MCLM], those reproduced in the Official Gazette, are printable in USPB. Where chemical structures occur in the claims, alphanumeric symbols are reproduced, subscripts and superscripts being indicated as 'sub' and 'sup', and the remainder of the structure is ignored. The United States Patent Classifications [PCL] and International Patent Classifications [IC] assigned at the time of publication are present.

Both patent and literature citations [CT] made by the examiner during examination of the patent application are searchable and printable. All names and numbers in the citation are searchable, but foreign patent numbers and literature citations are not in a standardized format. The examiner's field of search [FLD] is also searchable and printable.

The database includes United States reissue patents. Patent and application numbers for parent applications of United States divisional, continuation and continuation-in-part patents are indexed in the priority field.

In patents that are published with a terminal disclaimer, the date on which the shortened term of the patent will expire prints in the Notes field. The Notes field also includes the name of the examiner and attorney or agent of record.

## PATDATA

The PATDATA database, produced by BRS Information Technologies, covers United States utility patents from 1975 to the present and is updated weekly. All printable fields are directly searchable. Figure 3.8 illustrates the PATDATA citation for US 4 532 250.

### Figure 3.8: PATDATA citation - BRS File PATDATA

```
    1
 PN  US 4532250.
 PD  JUL 30, 1985
 TI  5-Heteroarylimidazol-2-ones having cardiotonic activity.
 IV  Stout-David-M. Yamamoto-Diane-M.
 IA  Vernon Hills IL.
 AS  American Hospital Supply Corporation.
 AP  554498 NOV 23, 1983.
 OR  514/341.
 XR  544/237. 544/284. 546/144. 546/167. 546/278. 548/127. 548/128.
     548/134. 548/137. 548/317. 548/318. 548/322. 548/202. 548/206.
     514/259. 514/248. 514/307. 514/311. 514/392.
 IC  A61K 31/44. EDITION 3.
 RU  3538104, NOV 1970. 3850944, NOV 1974.
 RF  59948 EUROPEAN PATENT OFFICE (EPO). 78545 EUROPEAN PATENT OFFICE
     (EPO). 78546 EUROPEAN PATENT OFFICE (EPO).
 AB  Described are compounds of the formula (*SEE PATENT FOR CHEMICAL
     STRUCTURE*) (*SEE PATENT FOR TABULAR PRESENTATION*) (*SEE PATENT FOR
     CHEMICAL STRUCTURE*) (*SEE PATENT FOR CHEMICAL STRUCTURE*) NHR(1)RNH
     (*SEE PATENT FOR CHEMICAL STRUCTURE*) O (*SEE PATENT FOR CHEMICAL
     STRUCTURE*) wherein R is heteroaryl and R(1)is hydrogen or
     loweralkyl, or a pharmaceutically acceptable salt thereof. The
     compounds exhibit cardiotonic activity.
```

PATDATA indexes all patent document [PN, PD], application [AP] and priority numbers and dates. Inventor and assignee names [IV, AS] are indexed, as is the address of the first named inventor, in the form of a city and state or country [IA].

The original title [TI] and author abstract [AB] are included in the record. Chemical structures are treated especially awkwardly. The original and cross reference United States Patent Classification codes [OR, XR] and the International Patent Classification codes, including an indication of the IPC edition [IC], are indexed.

United States and foreign patents cited by the Examiner [RU, RF] are reproduced as they appear in the patent. The publication dates of the cited American patents are included in the record.

## LEXPAT

LEXPAT is a full-text database of United States patents published from July 1975, to the present, produced by Mead Data Central as one of the libraries in its NEXIS databank. The LEXPAT library contains a file of utility patents, a file of design patents, a file of plant patents, a combined patents file, a file that indexes patents to their current United States Patent Classification codes, the text of the *Manual of Classification,* and the text of the *Index to the Manual of Classification.* The database is updated weekly with patents published the previous week. Figure 3.9 illustrates excerpts from the full citation for US 4 306 289 showing the bibliographic and examination information from the first page of the patent and a short passage from the 'Background of the Invention' section of the disclosure.

**Figure 3.9: LEXPAT citation - MEAD DATA CENTRAL LEXPAT LIBRARY**

```
                              4,306,289

                           Dec. 15, 1981

          Digital computer having code conversion apparatus for an
                           encrypted program

     INVENTOR: Lumley, Robert M., Lawrence Township, Mercer County, New Jersey

     ASSIGNEE: Western Electric Company, Inc., New York, New York (02)

          [See Patent and Trademark Office Documents for Details of Assignments]
     *** Assignments updated as of Jun. , 1984 ***

          Mar. 19, 1984, Name Change, AT & T TECHNOLOGIES, INC.,

     APPL-NO: 118,003

     FILED: Feb. 4, 1980

     INT-CL: [3] G06F 5#00

     US-CL: 364#200; 400#90

     CL: 364;400

     SEARCH-FLD: 364#200MSFile, 900MSFile; 375#2; 178#22

      REF-CITED:
                              U.S. PATENT DOCUMENTS

          3,846,763      11/1974      Riikonen          364#200
          3,889,242       6/1975      Malmer, Jr.       364#200
          4,042,972       8/1977      Gruner et al.     364#200
          4,064,554      12/1977      Tubbs             364#200
          4,120,030      10/1978      Johnstone         364#200
```

**Figure 3.9:** (cont.)

```
    4,168,396        9/1979         Best                364#200

PRIM-EXMR: Zache, Raulfe B.

LEGAL-REP: Sheffield; B. W.
                 * * * * * * *
    Of course, vendors of proprietary software attempt to protect their
interests by copyrighting the software and/or by requiring the purchaser to
execute some form of contractual agreement which limits his right to
duplicate the software or use it on some other CPU. Unfortunately, due to the
proliferation of microprocessor-based computer systems, such agreements are
difficult to police; indeed, they become impossible to police with respect to
"personal computers."

In view of the above, various attempts have been made to solve the software
piracy problem. For example, U.S. Pat. No. 4,168,396, which issued on Sept.
18, 1979 to Robert M. Best, discloses a microprocessor which deciphers and
executes an encrypted program, one instruction at a time, through a
combination of substitutions, transpositions and exclusive-or additions in
```

As a full text database, LEXPAT contains the document, application, and priority numbers and dates of all patents in the file and of all related patents and applications mentioned in the specification. The names and addresses of the inventors and assignees are included. For patents whose reassignment has been recorded, the name of the new assignee is also in the record.

The original title, abstract, disclosure and claims are searchable and printable in full. All United States Patent Classifications and International Patent Classifications are present. The number of drawings published in the patent is noted, but the drawings are not reproduced. Searchers are referred to the printed specification for chemical structure diagrams.

Because the full text of the specification is reproduced, searching for common terms inevitably retrieves an enormous volume of irrelevant material. The vocabulary is completely uncontrolled, so obscure information is as accessible in LEXPAT as prominent information. It is a particularly good place to find patents dealing with specific plants, animals or micro-organisms, as the biosystematic name can usually be used as an unambiguous search term.

LEXPAT records include all the patent and literature citations made by the examiner as well as the field of search. The names of the examiner and the applicant's legal representative are both searchable and printable. Terminal disclaimers are noted, as are disclaimers and dedications of a patent to the public that are registered after publication of the patent. When a patent has been the subject of a request for re-examination or of litigation in a federal court, the filing is noted in the record and the result of the proceeding is reported. Reissue patents and re-examination certificates are in separate records and their issuance is noted in the record of the original patent.

## EPAT

EPAT is the database of the European Patent Office, mounted on Questel by the French Patent Office, L'Institut National de Propriété Industrielle (INPI). It contains the EPO's record for all European patents and patent applications and all PCT applications designating the EPO published since the latter's establishment in 1978. The file is updated every Wednesday with the current day's patent publications and updates of the existing records. Figure 3.10 illustrates the EPAT citation for EP 44 866.

## Figure 3.10: EPAT citation - QUESTEL File EPAT

```
1/1  - (C) INPI/OEB
PN   - EP44866 A1 820203
AP   - EP81900597 810122
PPN  - WO8102351 810820
PAP  - US8100084 W
PR   - US11800380 800204
BPN  - 8205
GAZ  - 8120
ET   - DIGITAL COMPUTER
FT   - ORDINATEUR NUMERIQUE
GT   - DIGITALE RECHENANLAGE
IC1  - G06F-005/00
DS   - DE FR NL
PA   - Western Electric Company, Incorporated / 222 Broadway / New
       York, NY 10038 (US)
IN   - LUMLEY, Robert Miller / 2826 Princeton Pike / Lawrenceville,
       NJ 08648 (US)
RP   - Weitzel, David Stanley et. al / Western Electric Company
       Limited 5, Mornington Road / Woodford Green Essex IG8 0TU
       (GB)
DRR  - 820203
DRRS - 821125
RR   - EUROPEAN SEARCH REPORT
     - See also references of WO810235
BRR  - 8205
DDWD - 850430 Deemed to be Withdrawn
DREX - 820125 Request for Examination
DNEX - 841018 First Examination Report
PNL  - EN
APL  - EN
PCL  - EN
```

The document [PN], application [AP] and priority [PR] numbers and dates of the patent are recorded, as are the country codes of the designated states [DS]. Records for European patents originating from PCT applications carry the document [PPN] and application [PAP] numbers of the PCT application. Patent document and priority numbers are indexed in their original format in the /PN and /PR fields and in Derwent format in the /XPN and /XPR fields, which do not print in any of the standard formats. The patent kind code indicates the current status of the indexed patent. Inventor [IN] and patentee [PA] names and addresses are given. The issue of the *EPO Bulletin* and of the *PCT Gazette* in which the publication was announced [BPN, GAZ] is also indicated.

The original title of the patent in English [ET], French [FT], and German [GT] is given, as are the International Patent Classification codes [IC1] assigned by the EPO. Abstracts are provided for applications published since 1988, and the English and French text of the first claim of granted patents is added to the record within one month of the grant date. The language of the application, the published document and the proceedings in the EPO are indicated [APL, PNL, PCL].

The current status of the patent or application is indicated by the patent kind code and by entries in fields that give the date of publication of the search report and supplementary search reports [DRR, DRRS], the date the applicant requested examination of the application [DREX], and other events in the prosecution of the application [DNEX]. The references cited in the search report or, as here, a cross reference to the PCT search report [RR] are provided along with the corresponding Bulletin issue [BRR].The filing of an opposition to the grant of the patent is indicated by the name of the opposer and the filing date. The date of the grant of the patent or the abandonment [DDWD] of the application is provided when applicable. The name and address of the patent agent [RP], but not those of an examiner, are given. Subsequent to patent grant, information about transfer of rights or licences recorded by the EPO are added to the record. If the patent lapses for failure to pay maintenance fees, the lapse date is recorded. In addition to the status of the European patent itself, EPAT contains information about the French legal status of granted European patents.

## FPAT

FPAT is the database of the French Patent Office, L'Institut National de Propriété Industrielle (INPI), and is mounted on Questel. It contains records for all French patents and patent applications published since 1966, and is updated every Friday with the current week's patent publications and updates of the existing records. Records are additionally present for medicinal patents published from 1961 to 1965. Figure 3.11 illustrates the citation for FR 2 554 364.

## Figure 3.11: FPAT citation - QUESTEL File FPAT

```
     1/1   - (C) INPI
     PUB   - FR2554364 - 850510
     EN    - FR8416673 841031
     BPD   - 8519 NAT - Brevet
     PR    - JP20712883 831104
     DDL   - 881014 BDL - 8841
     DRR   - 870821 BRR - 8734
     RR    - RAP. RECH.
           - US3895604(A)(Cat. A); FR2381657(A)(Cat. A)
     CIB   - B05C-007/08 B05C-009/10 B08B-009/06 G05D-003/10
     TI    - APPAREIL DE REVETEMENT DE SURFACE INTERIEURE DE TUYAUX
     AB    - L'INVENTION CONCERNE UN APPAREIL DE REVETEMENT DE SURFACE
             INTERIEURE DE TUYAUX DU TYPE TELECOMMANDE.
           - L'APPAREIL COMPREND UN VEHICULE AUTOPROPULSE 1 DEPLACABLE A
             L'INTERIEUR D'UN TUYAU PAR UN MECANISME A CHENILLES SANS FIN
             24, UN DISPOSITIF DE TRAVAIL 110 MONTE SUR UNE EXTREMITE
             AVANT DU VEHICULE, UNE UNITE A SUBSTANCE RADIOACTIVE 2
             PLACEE SUR LE VEHICULE DE FACON A PERMETTRE LA DETECTION
             D'UNE POSITION DU VEHICULE DANS LE TUYAU DE L'EXTERIEUR DE
             CELUI-CI, UN DISPOSITIF DE NETTOYAGE DE L'INTERIEUR DU TUYAU
             QUI EST RELIE AU VEHICULE, UN MOTEUR ELECTRIQUE
             D'ENTRAINEMENT DU MECANISME CHENILLES ET UN DISPOSITIF DE
             TELECOMMANDE DU FONCTIONNEMENT DU DISPOSITIF DE TRAVAIL, DU
             DISPOSITIF DE NETTOYAGE ET DU MOTEUR D'ENTRAINEMENT.
     DEP   - NIPPON KOKAN KK
     ADEP  - JP
     INV   - SACHIO TABE, YOSHINOBU SATO, OSAMU KOBAYASHI, KEISUKE
             MOTOSUGI, TOSHIRO NAKAMURA, SHINTARO IKEDA, KAZUHIRO TAKASU,
             SHUJI CHIBA, RYOJI IMAI ET TOSHIKUNI FUKAMI
     MND   - REGIMBEAU CORRE MARTIN SCHRIMPF
```

The document [PUB], application [EN], and priority [PR] numbers and dates of the patent and its current status [NAT] are recorded. Patent document and priority numbers are indexed in their original format in the /PUB and /PR fields and in Derwent format in the /XPN and /XPR fields, which do not print in any of the standard formats. Inventor [INV] and patentee [DEP] names and the country of origin of the patentee [ADEP] are provided.

The original French title [TI] of the patent is given, as are the International Patent Classification codes assigned by INPI [CIB]. FPAT has French-language abstracts [AB] for patents published since 1981, but does not contain the text of the claims. English and French keywords are provided for patents published since 1987.

The current status of the patent or application is indicated as the legal nature of the document. The date of grant of the patent [DDL] and date of publication of the examination search report [DRR] are given, as are the corresponding issue numbers of the *Bulletin Officiel de Propriété Industrielle*. The patents and literature citations reported in the search report are in the online record [RR]. The name of the applicant's agent [MND] is listed. If the patent lapses for failure to pay maintenance fees, the lapse date is recorded.

## PATDPA

The PATDPA database is produced by the Deutsches Patentamt, the Patent Office of the Federal Republic of Germany, and supplied on STN by FIZ Karlsruhe. The database covers German patents and European and PCT patent documents designating Germany. The database includes full bibliographic information, abstract text and status information for all published applications, granted patents and utility models reported in the *Patentblatt* since 1968. Patent applications pending in the former East German patent office at the time of reunification are included. The drawings from the first page abstract of Offenlegungsschriften published from 1983 to the present are printable in a companion file, PATGRAPH. Figure 3.12 illustrates the PATDPA record for DE 34 40 250.

**Figure 3.12: PATDPA citation - STN INTERNATIONAL File PATDPA**

```
L1      ANSWER 1 OF 1
AN      Datenbankschluessel       DE-Patentblatt Datum und Woche
        85(21):5603 PATDPA        ED   861204  EW    8649
SN      (21) Aktenzeichen    --- Datum der letzten Veraenderung
        DE3440250.0               UP   861204
TI      (54) Bezeichnung der Erfindung/Titel (aktueller und vorheriger)
        (C2)(A1) Vorrichtung zur Beschichtung der Innenflaeche von Roehren
IN      (72) Erfinder (aktuelle Angaben und vorherige)
INC     Tabe, Sachio (*JP Musashino, Tokio/Tokyo)
        Sato, Yoshinobu (*JP Kamakura, Kanagawa)
        Kobayashi, Osamu (*JP Yokohama, Kanagawa)
        Motosugi, Keisuke (*JP Yokosuka, Kanagawa)
        Nakamura, Toshiro (*JP Yokohama, Kanagawa)
        Ikeda, Shintaro (*JP Sagamihara, Kanagawa)
        Takasu, Kazuhiro (*JP Yokohama, Kanagawa)
        Chiba, Shuji (*JP Yamato, Kanagawa)
        Imai, Ryoji (*JP Kanagawa)
        Fukami, Toshikuni (*JP Yokohama, Kanagawa)
PA      (71,73) Anmelder / Inhaber (aktuelle Angaben und vorherige)
PAC     Nippon Kokan K.K. (*JP Tokio/Tokyo)
PAN     Anmeldernummer von aktuellem(n) Anmelder(n)/Inhaber(n)
        1003941 JP
PAT     Anmelderstatus von aktuellem(n) Anmelder(n)/Inhaber(n)
        (CORP) Juristische Person
AG      (74) Anmeldervertreter
        Westphal, K. 'Dipl.Ing.' (7730 Villingen-Schwenningen)
        Mussgnug, B. 'Dipl.Phys. Dr.rer.nat.' (7730 Villingen-Schwenningen)
        Buchner, O. 'Dr.rer.nat., Pat.Anw.' (8000 Muenchen)
EXF     Patentabteilung DPA (Pruefungsgebiet)
        51 Akustik, Optik, Photographie
SO      Quellenangabe
        Patentblatt 105 (1985) Heft 21, DE A1 Offenl.-Schrift, 1. Veroeff.
        Textseiten 25; Blattzahl 18; Zeichnungsseiten 9; Filmlochkarten 5
```

**Figure 3.12:** (cont.)

```
        Patentblatt 106 (1986) Heft 49, DE C2 Patentschrift, 2. Veroeff.
DT    Dokumenttyp
        P
LA    (26) Sprache der Publikation
        German
NTE   Ausgewaehlte Rechtsstandsdaten
        831104: FPRD (32) Erstes Prioritaetsdatum
        841103: ADP  (22) Anmeldetag d. DE-Patentanm.
        850523: AO   (43) Offenlegungstag der DE-Anmeldung (OS)
        861204: PG   (45) Veroeff.-Tag der DE-Patenterteilung
        861204: SRP  (56) Veroeff. d. Entgegenhaltungen auf DE-PS
NTL   Letzte Rechtsstandsdaten
        861204: SRP  (56) Veroeff. d. Entgegenhaltungen auf DE-PS
        861204: PG   (45) Veroeff.-Tag der DE-Patenterteilung
PIT   (12) Schriftart
        PS EF DE-Patentschrift, 2. Veroeff., Einspr.-Frist 3 Mon.
PI    (10) Patentinformation (Publ.-Daten der letzten Hauptanmeldung)
        DE 3440250    C2 861204   PG OP3 (10) letzte Publ./ DE-Schrift
AI    (20) Anmeldeinformation
        DE 84-3440250 A 841103   ADP      (22) DE-Patentanmeldung
PRAI  (30) Prioritaetsinformation
        JP 83-207128 A 831104   CP       (32) Unionsprioritaet
FI    (20,35,40,86,87) Familieninformation
FIA   DE 84-3440250 A 841103   ADP      (22) DE3440250
FIP   DE 3440250    A1 850523  AO       (43) DE-Offenlegung
      DE 3440250    C2 861204  PG       (45) DE-Patenterteilung
RE    (56) Zitierte Patent- und Nichtpatentliteratur
REP   DE 2444863    A          SRP      (56) Aus nation. Pruefungsverf.
      DE 1750782    A          SRP      (56) Aus nation. Pruefungsverf.
      US 3056155    A          SRP      (56) Aus nation. Pruefungsverf.
IC    (51) internationale Patentklassifikation (aktuelle und vorherige
        Angaben)
ICM   (ID2) B05B013-06              (511) IPC-Hauptklasse
ICS   (ID2) B05D007-22              (512) IPC-Nebenklasse
AB    (57) Zusammenfassung
        (C2) Eine Vorrichtung zur Beschichtung der Innenflaeche von Roehren mit
        mit Fernsteuerung umfasst ein Fahrwerk mit Eigenantrieb, wobei eine
        Endlosraupe ueber ein Spannrad und ein Antriebsrad und ueber
        mehrere Fuehrungsrollen auf jeder Seite gespannt ist und die
        Bewegung des auf das Fahrwerk montierten Antriebsmotors auf die
        Endlosraupe uebertragen wird, wodurch das Fahrwerk innerhalb einer
        Roehre frei bewegbar ist. Die Vorrichtung enthaelt eine
        Arbeitseinheit zum automatischen Schleifen und Reinigen sowie zum
        Beschichten, die am vorderen Ende des Fahrwerks befestigt ist, eine
        auf das Fahrwerk montierte radioaktive Substanz zur Bestimmung der
        jeweiligen Lage des Fahrwerks, eine auf das Fahrwerk montierte
        Fernsehkamera zur Beobachtung des Innenzustands der Roehre sowie
        eine auf den hinteren Teil des Fahrwerks montierte
        Reinigungseinheit.
PST   Passat - Terme (Stammwortzerlegung fuer Titel und Abstact)
        ANTRIEB; ANTRIEBSMOTOR; ANTRIEBSRAD; ARBEIT; ARBEITSEINHEIT;
        AUTOMATISCH; BEFESTIGEN; BEOBACHTEN; BEOBACHTUNG; BESCHICHTEN;
        BESCHICHTUNG; BESTIMMUNG; BEWEGBAR; BEWEGUNG; EIGENANTRIEB;
        EINHEIT; ENDE; ENDEN; ENDLOSRAUPE; ENTHALTEN; FAHRWERK;
        FERNSEHKAMERA; FERNSTEUERUNG; FREI; FUEHRUNG; FUEHRUNGSROLLE;
        HINTERE; INNENFLAECHE; INNENZUSTANDS; LAGE; MONTIEREN; MOTOR;
        RADIOAKTIV; REINIGEN; REINIGUNG; REINIGUNGSEINHEIT; ROEHRE;
        ROEHREN; ROLLE; SCHLEIFE; SCHLEIFEN; SEITE; SPANNEN; SPANNRAD;
        SUBSTANZ; UEBERTRAGEN; UMFASSEN; VORDER; VORRICHTUNG
FA    Feldbesetzung von nicht obligatorisch besetzten Feldern
        INC; PAC; PAN; AG; EXF; AB; REP; ICS; PAS; PAT
```

PATDPA has a single record based on the serial number of each patent application [SN]. Stripped of the final digit and decimal point, the German serial number becomes the document number of the patent [PI, FI]. The Family Information [FI] field records the document number and a description of each level of publication of the German patent document; it does not include family members from other countries. The patent application number and date [AI] are identical to the serial number for German national applications, but differ for European and PCT applications, whose records also include a list of the ISO country codes of designated states. Priority application numbers and dates [PRAI] are reported, the German national application being used when foreign priority is not claimed. When a related German patent application exists, it is identified in the record. The patent assignee [PA] field includes the name of the assignee and its address [PAC] and an indication of the type of organization to which the patent is assigned [PAT]. All the inventors and their addresses [IN] are listed. Where a change of inventors or assignee is recorded, both old and new names are indexed. The *Patentblatt* date and week [ED] and a full citation to each edition of the *Patentblatt* reporting on the cited patent [SO] is given. The CAS accession number is given in the records of patents that appeared in *Chemical Abstracts* prior to the last update of the record.

The original title [TI] and author abstract [AB] of the patent application are given in German. Index terms consisting of the uninflected forms of the terms in the abstract [PST] are given as an aid to searching. The IPC codes [ICM, ICS] and the IPC edition from which the codes are taken are identified. Patent and literature citations made by the examiner are indexed and the examiner's field of search is identified [EXF].

All the patent status information on file with the Patent Office is reported in the database [NTE, NTL]. This includes the publication of the examined application corresponding to a published patent application, changes in ownership, licensing agreements, patent lapse dates, and each step in the prosecution of a patent application. The name and full address of the German patent agent representing the applicant [AG] is given. When a change in the status of the patent application is reported in the *Patentblatt*, the record is amended and all new data are added to the existing record.


## CHINESE PATENTS ABSTRACTS IN ENGLISH

The online version of *Patent Abstracts of China,* produced by INPADOC, is mounted as CHINAPATS on ORBIT and as File 344 on DIALOG. It covers all patent applications published by the People's Republic of China, the first of which appeared in September 1985. Figure 3.13 shows the record for CN 85101435 from DIALOG File 344.

**Figure 3.13: CHINESE PATENTS ABSTRACTS IN ENGLISH record - DIALOG File 344**

```
      1/5/1
       101435
       PREPARATION OF N,N'-METHYLENE-BIS(2-AMINO-5-MERCAPTO-1,3,4-THIODIAZOLE)
   Patent Assignee: SICHUAN INST OF CHEMICAL INDUS (CN)
   Author (Inventor): WANG LOYU (CN); TU YONGFU (CN); ZHU LIANGYAO (CN)
   Number of Patents: 004
   Patent Family:
        CC   Number   Kind    Date
        CN  85101435   A     860709 (Basic)
        GB  8607783    A0    860430
        GB  2173193    A1    861008
        JP  61229875   A2    861014
   Application Data:
        CC   Number   Kind    Date
       *CN  85101435   A     850401
```

**Figure 3.13:** (cont.)

```
Abstract:  The  present  invention  relates  to  preparation  method of a new
       compound N,N'-methylene-bis(2-amino-5-mercapto-1,3,4-thiodiazole). Vari
       ous  types  (such as wettalbe powder or suspensoid) of bactericides can
       be  composed  of  this  new  compound as effective component with other
       conventional components. The presently invented bactericide can inhibit
       effectively  leaf  spot of rice and other bactorial plant diseases, and
       is non-toxic to human-being, animal, fish and environment.
IPC: C07D-285/08; A01N-043/10
```

All patent document, application, and priority numbers and dates are indexed in the original published format. The patent kind code A0 is present in all records. All patent assignee and inventor names are indexed with their countries of residence; when no corporate or governmental assignee is present the assignee field contains the names of the inventors in uninverted form. For patent applications claiming the same priority as other patent publications indexed in the INPADOC database, the record includes the document number, patent kind code, and publication date of all equivalent patents indexed before the Chinese patent was added to the INPADOC file. A warning that the patent family data is not current is provided in the ORBIT CHINAPATS file, but not in DIALOG File 344, where the 'Number of Patents' field counts the family members provided by INPADOC at the time the Chinese patent application is indexed. For patents equivalent to those whose INPADOC record contains a cross-referenced *Chemical Abstracts* or Derwent accession number at the time the Chinese patent is indexed, the cross-reference accession numbers are provided in the CHINESE PATENTS ABSTRACTS record.

The original title is translated into English, and the International Patent Classification [IPC] codes assigned by the Chinese Patent Office are given. English language abstracts produced by the Patent Documentation Service Centre of the Chinese Patent Office are prepared for all patents issued to Chinese inventors; only the bibliographic record is available online for patents issued to non-Chinese applicants.

## JAPIO

JAPIO covers published Japanese patent applications, 'kokai', issued from October, 1976 to the present. It is produced by the Japanese Patent Information Organization (JAPIO), an agency of the Japanese Patent Office, and mounted on ORBIT. The database contains abstracts published in the printed publication *Patent Abstracts of Japan* and bibliographic citations for all kokai not selected for abstracting. It is updated monthly with data from the printed abstracts, which are published about five months after the issue date of the patents. Figure 3.14 shows the full JAPIO citation for JP 60-179169.

**Figure 3.14: JAPIO citation - ORBIT File JAPIO**

```
     -1-
AN  - 85-179169
TI  - DEVICE FOR PAINTING INNER SURFACE OF PIPE
PA  - (2000412) NIPPON KOKAN KK; (2399763) NIHON KOUKAN KOUJI KK
IN  - TANABE, YUKIO; SATOU, YOSHINOBU; KOBAYASHI, OSAMU; MOTOSUGI,
      KEISUKE; NAKAMURA, TOSHIROU; IKEDA, SHINTAROU; TAKASU,
      KAZUHIRO; CHIBA, SHIYUUJI; IMAI, TAKASHI; FUKAMIZU, TOSHIKUNI
PN  - 85.09.13    J60179169, JP 60-179169
AP  - 83.11.04    83JP-207128, 58-207128
SO  - 86.02.04    SECT. C, SECTION NO. 326; VOL. 10, NO. 28, PG. 36.
IC  - B05C-007/00; B08B-009/04
```

**Figure 3.14:** (cont.)

```
JC  - 14.7 (ORGANIC CHEMISTRY—Coating Material Adhesives); 24.1
      (CHEMICAL ENGINEERING—Fluid Transportation); 28.1
      (SANITATION—Sanitary Equipment)
AB  - PURPOSE: To paint with remote manipulation while detecting
      correctly the painting position by furnishing an automatic
      polishing machine or a painting machine to the front end of a
      self-traveling vehicle and a cleaner to the rear end, further
      providing an radioisotope and an in-pipe television camera.
      CONSTITUTION: An automatic polishing machine 110 or a
      painting machine is furnished to the front end of a
      self-traveling vehicle 1, and an radioisotope 2 for detecting
      the traveling position of the self-traveling vehicle 1 and an
      in-pipe television camera 7 for inspecting the state of the
      interior of the pipe are provided. A cleaner is also
      furnished to the rear end of the self-traveling vehicle 1.
      The coating position at the inside of the pipe can be
      correctly detected in this way, and the inside of the
      long-sized pipe can be painted. In addition, painting can be
      rapidly carried out with remote manipulation from the outside
      of the pipe.
```

JAPIO indexes all patent [PN], application [AP], and priority numbers and dates in the original published format and in Derwent format, and both formats print in the record. The document and application numbers incorporate the year as the Japanese Imperial year, the current Western year minus 1988, and for dates before 8 January 1989, the current Western year minus 1925. Derwent's format for the patent number retains the Imperial year, contracting the ISO code to 'J' in order to fit the entire patent number into the fixed nine-character format. All patent applicant [PA] and inventor [IN] names are indexed. JAPIO has standard seven-digit patentee codes for companies with many patents, and the names of the companies that have codes are printed in a standardized format. Because the names are transliterated from the Japanese alphabet, company and inventor names, especially those of non-Japanese origin, are often spelled in unfamiliar ways. Searches in JAPIO for non-Japanese names should rely on the printed company code manual, liberal use of the NEIGHBOR command, and an open, imaginative mind. The record also includes a citation [SO] to the printed version of the abstract in *Patent Abstracts of Japan*. JAPIO accession numbers [AN] consist of a six-digit serial number that corresponds to the document serial number, preceded by the last two digits of the Gregorian year. The accession number is a convenient alternative to the patent document number for searchers who are unfamiliar with Japanese imperial history.

JAPIO includes an English translation of the original title [TI] of all patents. An abstract [AB], written in English as a summary of the complete specification and claims, is provided for patents applied for by Japanese nationals in selected chemical, mechanical, electrical and physics technologies. Approximately sixty per cent of the records in the database have abstracts.

All records include the International Patent Classification codes [IC] assigned by the Japanese Patent Office. Patents published from 1976 to 1979 also have Japanese national patent classification codes. JAPIO Classification Codes [JC] are given to each record and alphanumeric Fixed Keyword Codes are applied by JAPIO to some records. Lists of JAPIO Classification Codes and Fixed Keyword Codes are provided in the ORBIT database documentation chapter.

## APIPAT

APIPAT is a database of patents relating to all aspects of petroleum technology, produced by the Central Abstracting and Indexing Service of the American Petroleum Institute (API). The database is mounted on DIALOG and STN. APIPAT was founded in 1964, and in its early years API screened patent specifications and prepared abstracts for indexing. Since 1972 most of the records have been derived from the Derwent *World Patents Index* or from *Chemical Abstracts*. APIPAT is the online version of the printed *API Technical Index*; it may be searched by non-subscribers for a maximum of three hours a year, but only subscribers are authorized to display abstracts. STN and DIALOG have separate non-subscriber files without displayable abstracts. The database is updated monthly; records are necessarily delayed several months after the publication of the patents, as the patents are indexed by API only after the original delay for processing by Derwent or CAS. Figure 3.15 illustrates the APIPAT record for DE 34 40 250.

### Figure 3.15: APIPAT citation - STN File APIPAT2

```
AN      85:7394     APIPAT;APIPAT2
DN      8541331
TI      PIPELINE  CLEANING  AND  INTERNAL  COATING APPTS.  -  ON REMOTELY  CONTROLLED
        CRAWLER  CARRIAGE  WITH  RADIOACTIVE  LOCATING  DEVICE  AND  TV  CAMERA
PA      NIPPON  KOKAN  KK
OS      DERWENT  85129357
PI      DE    3440250    850523
PRAI    JP 83-207128    831104
AB      Pipeline  cleaning  and  internal  coating  appts.  -  on  remotely  controlled
        crawler  carriage  with  radioactive  locating  device  and  TV  camera.  A
        remotely  controlled  apparatus  for  internally  cleaning  and  grinding  and
        coating  (painting)  pipes  comprises  a  crawler  with  electric  drive  motor
        mounted  thereon  and  carrying  a  radioactive  emitter  enabling  the  exact
        position  to  be  detected  by  a  receiver  positioned  outside  the  pipe.  The
        carriage  also  carries  a  television  camera  and  necessary  control
        equipment  and  is  supplied  by  electric  cables,  pneumatic  pipes,  paint
        hoses, etc.connected  to  it  with  a  guide  wire.  At  the  front  the  carriage
        carries,  alternately,  a  grinding  and  cleaning  apparatus  which  can  be
        removed  after  the  grinding  operations,  and  a  paint  spraying  or  coating
        apparatus  inserted  into  the  same  mounting  socket  at  the  front  of  the
        carriage.  The  carriage  is  mounted  on  a  starting  ramp  which  is  coupled
        to  the  front  end  of  the  pipe,  the  carriage  then  being  launched  into  the
        pipe.  Cleaning  operations  are  executed  under  careful  locating  control
        by  the  radioactive  emitter  and  receiver,  so  that  a  weld  seam  alone  can
        be  cleaned  without  the  remainder  of  the  internal  pipe  surface.  After
        cleaning  the  various  sections  or  zones  of  the  pipe  the  carriage  is  retracted
        to  the  starting  ramp  and  the  grinding  head  is  replaced  by  the  spraying  head.
        Using  the  same  controls  and  monitoring  equipment,  the  carriage  then
        advances  to  the  same  programme  and  coats  the  already  cleaned  zones.USE/
        ADVANTAGE  -  For  internally  cleaning  pipes,  esp.  those  less  than  approx.
        60  cm  diameter,  where  man  access  is  virtually  impossible.  The  apparatus
        can  be  easily  remotely  controlled  and  exactly  positioned  to  enable
        specific  local  operations  to  be  carried  out  inside  the  pipe  at  a
        considerable  distance  from  the  start.  (36pp  Dwg.No.0/19)
IC      B05B013-06;  B05D007-22
CC      CONSERV-TRANSP-STOR-ENG;  PIPELINES
CT      CABLE;  CAMERA;  *CLEANING;  COATING  MATERIAL;  *COATING  PROCESS;
        COMMUNICATION  SYSTEM;  CONTROL  EQUIPMENT;  DETECTOR;  DRIVE;  ECONOMIC
        FACTOR;  ELECTRIC  CIRCUIT;  ELECTRICAL  EQUIPMENT;  FASTENER;  HOSE;
        INSIDE;  INSTRUMENT;  MAINTENANCE;  *MECHANICAL  CLEANING;  MONITORING;
        NONE;  PAINT;  PERSONNEL;  PHOTOGRAPHIC  EQUIPMENT;  PIGGING;  PIPE;
```

**Figure 3.15:** (cont.)

```
        *PIPELINE; *PIPELINE PIG; PNEUMATIC SYSTEM; PROCESS CONTROL;
        RADIATION;  RADIOACTIVITY;  REMOTE;SIZE  REDUCTION;  SPRAYER;  SPRAYING;
        TELEVISION;  USE;  WELDING;WIRE
LT      INSIDE;  PIPELINE
LT      PROCESS  CONTROL;  REMOTE
LT      ECONOMIC  FACTOR;  NONE;  PERSONNEL
```

Patent [PN, PD, SO] and priority [PR, SO] numbers and dates are indexed in Derwent format. Priority numbers may also be searched as individually indexed country codes and serial numbers. The Source field, which is not present in the STN files, contains patent numbers in a non-standard format, sometimes with obsolete country codes. Records of patents indexed before 1978 include equivalent patent numbers. The records of European patents and PCT applications carry the ISO country codes of designated states in a separate field. Patent assignee names [OS] are provided for all records and inventor names are in the records of patents indexed before 1972.

Cross-reference accession numbers from WORLD PATENTS INDEX [XR] are present in records from 1972 to the present, and may be used for crossfile searching on ORBIT. Cross reference accession numbers for *Chemical Abstracts* and *Petroleum Abstracts* are included in the Source field.

The title [TI] is taken from the source abstract, and the abstract [AB] is reproduced for records indexed from 1980 to the present. International Patent Classification codes [IC] present in the source record are indexed. APIPAT references are intensively indexed by API, using the Derwent or CA abstract as a basis for indexing. Controlled index terms [IT,LT] from the *API Thesaurus* are searchable alone, linked in groups of related concepts, and with the role qualifiers /A for reactants, /P for products and /N for substances that are neither reactant nor product. For index terms of narrow scope, broader index terms are automatically posted to the record. Individual words from multiword index terms may be searched. The API controlled vocabulary includes terms for the advantages expected from an invention, for processes, apparatus and chemical substances taking part in the invention, and for structural features of chemical substances. Generic chemical structures are indexed by linked structural fragment codes. When appropriate, supplementary index terms that are not in the API Thesaurus are applied to the record. Category codes [BH] and headings from the *API Thesaurus* and printed abstract publications may be searched to limit searches to major fields. Specific compounds may be searched by use of CAS Registry Numbers, and role qualifiers may be applied to the registry numbers.

## WORLD PATENTS INDEX/APIPAT

ORBIT Search Service has merged the WORLD PATENTS INDEX files with APIPAT to form files, WPIA, WPILA, and the combined file WPAM, in which the indexing applied by both Derwent and API is searchable in the records of patents covered by both services. Records carry the Derwent primary [AN] and secondary [XRAM, XRPX] accession numbers and contain the API accession number in the XR field. Records are included in the database that were not indexed by Derwent and these carry a Derwent accession number beginning with '65'. Abstracts provided to API by Chemical Abstracts are omitted from these files, but all other data present in the WPI files or APIPAT are included. Figure 3.16 shows the WPAM citation for DE 3 440 250, which corresponds to the APIPAT citation in Figure 3.15.

**Figure 3.16: WORLD PATENTS INDEX/APIPAT citation - ORBIT File WPAM**

```
    -1-
AN  - 85-129357/22
XR  - API 8541331
XRAM - C85-056224
XRPX - N85-097331
TI  - Pipeline cleaning and internal coating appts. - on remotely
      controlled crawler carriage with radioactive locating device
      and TV camera
DC  - H03 J06 K08 P42 P43 R26
PA  - (NIKN ) NIPPON KOKAN KK
IN  - TABE S,SATO Y,KOBAYASHI O,MOTOSUGI K,NAKAMURA T,IKEDA
      S,TAKASU K,CHIBA S
NP  - 5
PN  - DE3440250-A     85.05.23 (8522)
      GB2149051-A     85.06.05 (8523)
      FR2554364-A     85.05.10 (8524)
      DE3440250-C     86.12.04 (8649)
      GB2149051-B     87.10.28 (8743)
LA  - E
PR  - 83.11.04 83JP-207128
AP  - 84.11.03 84DE-440250  84.11.01 84GB-027647  84.10.31
      84FR-016673 84.11.03 84DE-440250 84.11.01 84GB-027647
IC  - B05B-013/06 B05D-007/22 B08B-009/04 B05C-007/08 B05C-009/10
      G05D-003/10
AB  - (DE3440250)
      A remotely controlled apparatus for internally cleaning and
      grinding and coating (painting) pipes comprises a crawler
      *
      *
EQAB - (DE3440250)
      An arrangement for coating the inner surface of tubes,
      includes a unit for grinding and cleaning the tubes and for
      coating them, while in inserted into the pipe and controlled
      remotely. A transsporting unit is located in the pipe,
      driven by an endless caterpillar, and the workpiece is fixed
      to the front of the unit. A radioactive substance is located
      in the transport unit in order to detect its position. The
      caterpillar is driven by an electric motor, and the cleansing
      unit is also attached to the unit.
          USE/ADVANTAGE - The arrangement is efficient and
      reliable, and is easy to locate. It is used in nuclear power
      plants. (17pp)
EQAB - (GB2149051)
      Appts. for coating the inside surface of a pipe, comprising
      *
      *
MC  - H03-B J06-C02 K09-L
BH  - CONSERV-TRANSP-STOR-ENG; PIPELINES
IT  - CABLE/N; CAMERA/N; *CLEANING/N; COATING MATERIAL/N; *COATING
      PROCESS/N; COMMUNICATION SYSTEM/N; CONTROL EQUIPMENT/N;
      DETECTOR/N; DRIVE/N; ECONOMIC FACTOR/N; ELECTRIC CIRCUIT/N;
      ELECTRICAL EQUIPMENT/N; FASTENER/N; HOSE/N; INSIDE/N;
      INSTRUMENT/N; MAINTENANCE/N; MONITORING/N; NONE/N; PAINT/N; PERSONNEL/N; PHOTOGRAPHIC
      EQUIPMENT/N; PIGGING/N; PIPE/N; *PIPELINE/N; *PIPELINE PIG/N;
      PNEUMATIC SYSTEM/N; PROCESS CONTROL/N; RADIATION/N;
      RADIOACTIVITY/N; REMOTE/N; SIZE REDUCTION/N; SPRAYER/N;
      SPRAYING/N; TELEVISION/N; USE/N; WELDING/N; WIRE/N
LT  - ECONOMIC FACTOR/N; NONE/N; PERSONNEL/N
LT  - INSIDE/N; PIPELINE/N
LT  - PROCESS CONTROL/N; REMOTE/N
```

The bibliographic data in the merged file are taken from WPI/L, thus enhancing the APIPAT record with equivalent patent data [PN, NP, AP], inventor names [IN], and Derwent company codes [PA].

Because the title and abstract in most APIPAT records were provided by Derwent, it is not surprising that these are identical in the merged file. Unlike APIPAT records, WPAM records are updated with abstracts of the granted equivalent patents [EQAB]. Derwent's collected IPC codes [IC] are searchable. In addition to the controlled indexing applied by API, WPAM records contain Derwent's controlled indexing [DC, MC].

## CA SEARCH

CA SEARCH, the online version of *Chemical Abstracts,* is available on most of the major online systems, and an enhanced version is available on STN International as the CA File. Over fifteen per cent of the references included in the database since its beginning in 1967 are patents. CA SEARCH is described in detail in Chapter 4; only special features of CA SEARCH as a patent database are addressed here. Figure 3.17 illustrates the CA File citation for US 4 851 417.

**Figure 3.17: CHEMICAL ABSTRACTS citation - STN INTERNATIONAL File CA**

```
L1 ANSWER 1 OF 1
COPYRIGHT (C) 1990 AMERICAN CHEMICAL SOCIETY

AN    CA112(5):35839p
TI    9-Substituted 6H-pyrido[4,3-b]carbazoles, i.e. ellipticine
      derivatives, useful as schistosomicides and antitumor agents
AU    Archer, Sydney
CS    Rensselaer Polytechnic Institute
LO    USA
SO    U.S., 9 pp.
PI    US 4851417  A  25 Jul 1989
AI    US 88-198976  26 May 1988
IC    ICM  A61K031-475
      ICS  C07D471-04
NCL   514285000
SC    28-2 (Heterocyclic Compounds (More Than One Hetero Atom))
SX    1, 31
DT    P
CO    USXXAM
PY    1989
LA    Eng
GI    Diagram(s) available in offline prints and/or printed CA Issue.
AB    Title carbamates I (R = H, alkoxy, OH, aryloxy; R1 = H, alkyl; R2 =
      alkyl, aryl) are prepd. as antitumor agents and schistosomicides.
      Thus, condensation of Me indole-2-acetate with 3-acetylpyridine in
      H2SO4/MeOH gave [(carbomethoxymethyl)indolyl]pyridylethene II, which
      underwent quaternization, cyclization., dequaternization, and LiAlH4
      redn. of the ester group to give
      (hydroxymethyl)methylpyridocarbazole III.  Acylation of III by MeNCO
      in pyridine gave I (R = R1 = H, R2 = Me) (IV).  In tests against 4
      lung cancer cell lines, IV was superior to adriamycin, ellipticine,
      and III; it was also superior to ellipticine and III against
      Schistosoma mansoni in vitro.
KW    pyridocarbazole prepn antitumor schistosomicide; ellipticine deriv
      prepn antitumor schistosomicide
IT    Neoplasm inhibitors
          (ellipticine derivs.)
```

**Figure 3.17:** (cont.)

```
IT    Anthelmintics
          (schistosomicides, ellipticine derivs.)
IT    108320-78-1P
          (prepn. and antitumor and schistosomicidal activity of)
IT    27798-66-9P    77251-57-1P    91653-14-4P    108320-73-6P
      108320-76-9P    108320-77-0P    120106-40-3P    120106-41-4P
      124549-43-5P    124549-44-6P    124549-45-7P    124549-46-8P
      124549-47-9P    124549-48-0P    124549-49-1P    124549-50-4P
          (prepn. and reaction of, in prepn. of antineoplastic and
          schistosomicidal ellipticine derivs.)
IT    108320-79-2P    124549-40-2P    124549-41-3P    124549-42-4P
          (prepn. of, as schistosomicide and antitumor agent)
IT    519-23-3DP, Ellipticine, derivs.
          (prepn. of, as schistosomicides and antitumor agents)
IT    100-11-8, p-Nitrobenzyl bromide 350-03-8, 3-Acetylpyridine
      624-83-9, Methyl isocyanate 917-64-6, Methylmagnesium iodide
      21422-40-2, Methyl indole-2-acetate 75525-73-4
              (reaction of, in prepn. of antineoplastic and schistosomicidal
              ellipticine derivs.)
```

Chemical Abstracts Service abstracts the first member of a family of equivalent patents to become available. Members of patent families are identified by INPADOC, and patent family information is published by CAS in a printed *Patent Concordance* but is not currently online. The patent number and date [PI] are indexed, and the publication year is indicated [PY]. Patent countries are represented as both the country name [SO] and the ISO code. Designated states for European and PCT patent applications and patent kind codes have been indexed only since 1982. The application number and/or a priority number [AI] and the corresponding date are present in the record of most patents, with the priority country represented as the country name and ISO code. For patents indexed from 1967 to 1981, only the earliest priority or the national application number is indexed; multiple priorities and the national application numbers of patents that claim priority are indexed for later patents. Patent and application number formats are not standardized in the printed *Chemical Abstracts;* the numbers are printed as they appear on the patent document. As a result, some of the patent numbers have not been converted properly to the standardized formats used by online hosts.

Inventor names are recorded in the Author field [AU] and corporate patentees and assignees are recorded in the Corporate Source field [CS]. Names in non-Roman alphabets are transliterated by CAS staff using the same conventions they use to transliterate names in literature citations. These may not use the same spelling that appears in other patent databases. The residence country of the patentee is indicated in the Location field [LO]. CA SEARCH patent records also include a language indicator [LA] and a CODEN [CO] appropriate to the patent country and document type.

CA SEARCH contains the title of the patent in English [TI], the International Patent Classification codes [IC] and some United States Patent Classification codes [PCL] from the indexed patent. Titles for recent patents are enhanced by CA indexers with an indication of the claimed subject matter. The abstract of the patent is currently available only in STN's CA FILE. Chemical structures in the abstract [GI] do not represent the full scope of the patent claims or disclosure, but are a summary of the compounds discussed in the abstract. Large structures, such as the one belonging to the abstract in Figure 3.17, do not display online. Patent documents are indexed in depth by CAS in the same way as other documents [SC, SX, KW, IT]. The abstract and indexing concentrate on new chemical concepts, not on the aspects of the disclosed invention that are claimed as new. The compounds synthesized in the patent's examples are indexed in the CA Registry file, and may be retrieved by searching on their registry numbers. Although it is possible to search topologically for generic structures in the REGISTRY file on STN or in the Generic DARC EURECAS file on Questel, what is retrieved is a set of specific compounds encompassed by the generic structure. Generic structures are not indexed topologically for CA SEARCH or the CA File, and the verbal indexing of generic structures is necessarily imprecise.

## MARPAT

Chemical Abstracts Service introduced MARPAT as an enhanced patents database on STN International in 1990. Patents indexed by Chemical Abstracts from the beginning of 1988, with the exception of those from the USSR, are selected for inclusion in MARPAT. The new patent service contains a searchable and displayable representation of the generic chemical structures in the patent along with an indication of the location of the indexed structure in the patent. The full bibliographic record and abstract appear as in the CA File. Only patents that illustrate organic and organometallic Markush structures are included in MARPAT. One of the structure records corresponding to US 4 851 417 is shown in Figure 3.18.

### Figure 3.18: Structure record - STN INTERNATIONAL File MARPAT

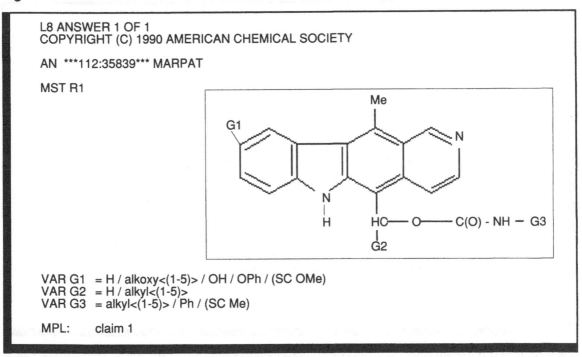

```
L8 ANSWER 1 OF 1
COPYRIGHT (C) 1990 AMERICAN CHEMICAL SOCIETY

AN  ***112:35839*** MARPAT

MST R1
```

VAR G1  = H / alkoxy<(1-5)> / OH / OPh / (SC OMe)
VAR G2  = H / alkyl<(1-5)>
VAR G3  = alkyl<(1-5)> / Ph / (SC Me)

MPL:     claim 1

MARPAT is a document-based, structure-searchable database, intended to supplement a search of the Registry file by making the entire scope of a generic chemical structure available. The only searchable data in the MARPAT file are the chemical structure, which is always a generic structure, and the associated text fields. MARPAT can be searched with the same query used in the REGISTRY file. A search in MARPAT retrieves the record of the document in which the indexed structure appears. Structure records in MARPAT closely resemble the query language used for retrieval in STN structure files. Bibliographic data in the MARPAT file is displayed in the same format as in the CA FILE, but is not currently searchable in MARPAT. Crossfile searching of the CA FILE is available if a search requires bibliographic limitations as well as structural ones. Specific compounds must be searched in the Registry file and crossed into the CA FILE to display the bibliographic record.

## PHARMSEARCH

PHARMSEARCH is a database of French, European and United States pharmaceutical patents produced by the French Patent Office , L'Institut National de Propriété Industrielle (INPI), and is mounted on Questel. A companion file of chemical structure records, MPHARM, is searchable on the Markush DARC system. When it was released in 1989 the database contained patents published since the beginning of 1987, but the coverage of the database is being extended retrospectively and will eventually cover United States and European Patent Office documents published since 1978 and all French pharmaceutical patents, including the series of French Medicinal patents that began in 1961. Patents found to be equivalent to previously indexed patents do not normally appear in the database. When a patent claiming the same priority as a previously indexed document has a different claim scope, the 'equivalent' patent is indexed without reference to the earlier record. The database is updated every two weeks. Figure 3.19 illustrates the citation for US 4 851 417.

**Figure 3.19: PHARMSEARCH citation - QUESTEL File PHARMSEARCH**

```
1/1   - (C) INPI
AN    - 89070361
CN    - 89070361-01
PN    - US4851417 - 890725
AP    - US19897688 880526
PA    - RENSSELAER POLYTECHNIC INSTITUTE
PAC   - US
IC    - A61K-031/475; C07D-471/04
EAB   - N-(alkyl or-aryl) carbamates of 9-substituted
        5-hydroxy-alkyl-11-methyl-6H-pyrido[4,3-b]carbazole. Process of
        preparation thereof. Their use as antitumoral agents
IT    - PYRIDOCARBAZOLE; METHYLPYRIDOCARBAZOLE; HYDROXYPYRIDOCARBAZOLE;
        METHOXYPYRIDOCARBAZOLE; ETHYLPYRIDOCARBAZOLE;
        CARBAMOYLOXYETHYLPYRIDOCARBAZOLE; METHYLCARBAMOYLOXYETHYLPYRIDOCAR
        BAZOLE; CARBAMOYLOXYMETHYLPYRIDOCARBAZOLE;
        METHYLCARBAMOYLOXYMETHYLPYRIDOCARBAZOLE; ETHYLCARBAMOYLOXYMETHYLPY
        RIDOCARBAZOLE; PROPYLCARBAMOYLOXYMETHYLPYRIDOCARBAZOLE;
        ISOPROPYLCARBAMOYLOXYMETHYLPYRIDOCARBAZOLE;
        BUTYLCARBAMOYLOXYMETHYLPYRIMIDOCARBAZOLE;
        TERTIOBUTYLCARBAMOYLOXYMETHYLPYRIMIDOCARBAZOLE;
        PENTYLCARBAMOYLOXYMETHYLPYRIDINOCARBAZOLE;
        PHENYLCARBAMOYLOXYMETHYLPYRIDINOCARBAZOLE
PROC  - SYNTHESIS PROCESS; SYN
EFF   - CLAIMED EFFECT; CLEF; TUMOR; CANCER
PHC   - 03
```

The document [PN], application [AP], and priority [PR] numbers and dates of the patent are recorded. Patent document and priority numbers are indexed for crossfile searching in Derwent format in the /XPN and /XPR fields, which do not print in any of the standard formats. Patentee [PA] names and the country of origin of the patentee [PAC] are provided, but the names of inventors are not.

Patent titles are not given. Each record has a short English-language abstract [AB], and patent documents in the French language also have a French-language abstract. International Patent Classification codes are searchable [IC]. INPI's indexers assign uncontrolled index terms [IT] for chemical structures, process steps and pharmaceutical components, controlled terms corresponding to three-letter codes describing therapeutic effects [EFF] and processes [PROC], and numeric Pharmsearch Classification codes [PHC]. Compound numbers [CN] correspond to structure records in the Markush DARC companion file MPHARM. Specific compounds and generic structures from the claims together with examples are indexed topologically, and the

# Figure 3.20: MARKUSH DARC structure record - File MPHARM

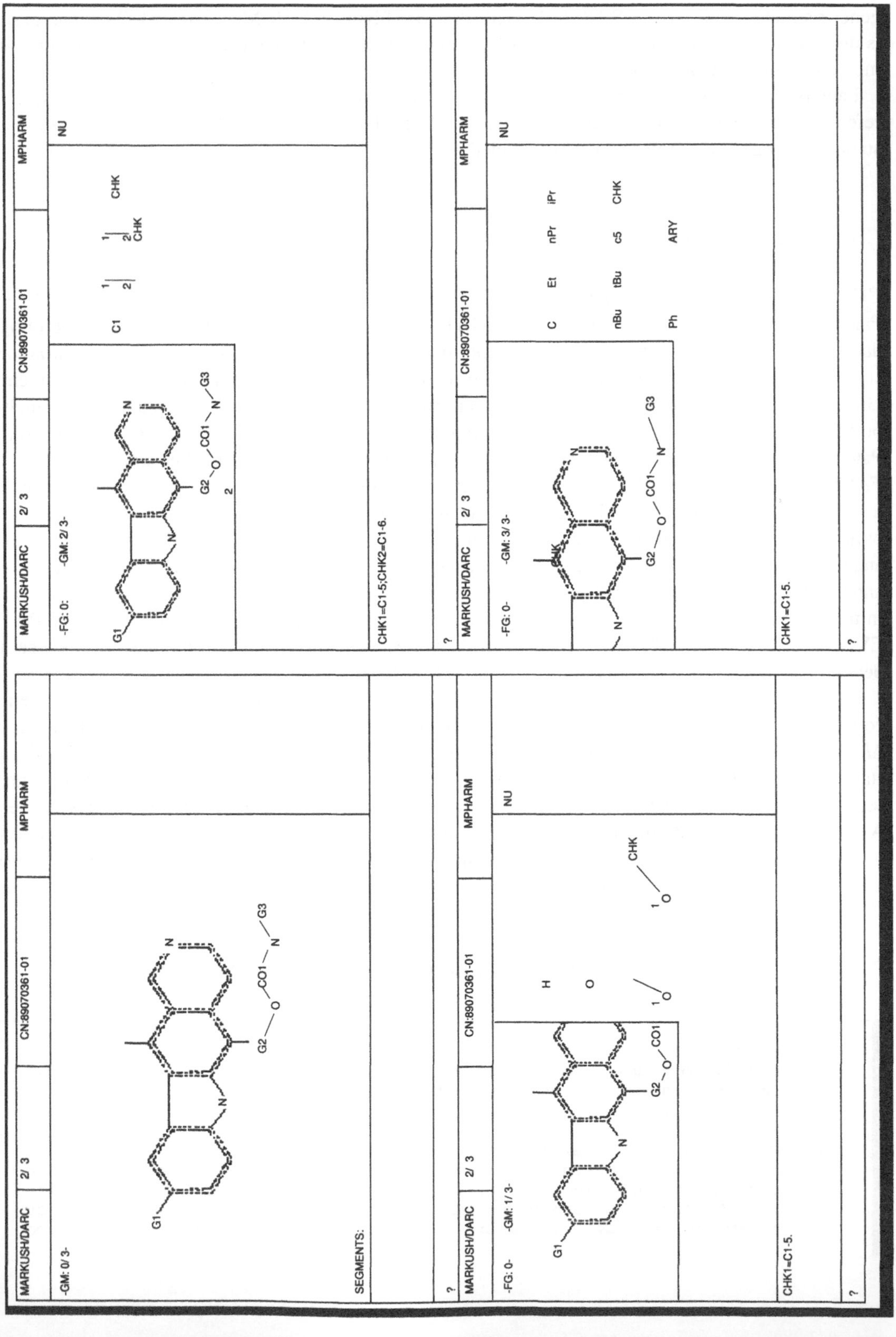

structure records are searchable and displayable in the MPHARM file. The Markush DARC record for the generic structure indexed in US 4 851 417 is illustrated in Figure 3.20. In Markush DARC, the parent structure is displayed and each variable group for a Markush structure is shown as a separate screen along with the molecular sub-structure to which it is attached.

Patents cited as prior art references in the indexed documents are listed [RF], but non-patent literature references are not searchable. The PHARMSEARCH database was designed as a tool for prior art searching, so no other legal status information is provided.

## CURRENT PATENTS

CURRENT PATENTS FAST-ALERT and CURRENT PATENTS EVALUATION, produced by Current Patents Ltd, and mounted on Data-Star and ORBIT, are databases of 'informed summaries' and bibliographic data for agrochemical and pharmaceutical patents in selected therapeutic areas. Antimicrobial, cardiovascular, central nervous system, anticancer, metabolic disease, biotechnology, immunology patent documents from Great Britain, the United States and the European Patent Office, as well as PCT applications are included in both databases, with coverage of the various therapeutic categories beginning at various times since July 1989. Patents on herbicides, plant growth regulators, insecticides and fungicides published since late 1990 are in the FAST-ALERT database only, where the latest six weeks are provided in a current file, and older patents are in a less expensive archive file. Discounts are available online to subscribers to the printed Current Patents' bulletins in two or more therapeutic areas. Summaries of patents in Current Patents' *FAST-ALERT* bulletins and the online database are provided less than ten days after the patents are available to the database producer, and the database is updated weekly. Critical evaluations of selected pharmaceutical patents are later printed in the monthly *Current Opinion in Therapeutic Patents*, which forms the basis of CURRENT PATENTS EVALUATION (CPEV). The focus of these services is to inform the scientific community of advances in drug development rather than to provide access to patents as legal documents or prior art.

Figure 3.21 illustrates the CPEV record for US 4 954 494. Fields shown in bold face are present in the corresponding FAST-ALERT record. Accession numbers are assigned for the printed Current Patents' *FAST-ALERT* bulletins and carry the database update code in the [AN] field. The patent number [PN], designated states [DS], and the priority country and number [PR] are searchable, with the number and ISO country code separately searchable. The patent assignee or, for unassigned patents, the inventor, appears in the Patent Assignee field [PA], and a maximum of three inventors [IN] are listed as the surname followed by a maximum of two initials. The priority data field [PY] includes the date, country and serial number of the first priority of the patent, with each being searchable independently. The priority date [PY], the filing date of the application [FD] and the publication date of the patent document [PD] are searchable in the YYMMDD format.

**Figure 3.21: CURRENT PATENTS EVALUATION citation - Data-Star File CPEV**

```
AN  CV2975 910121.
TI  Pyridyl-pyridazinone and pyridyl-pyrazolinone compounds and their use
    in the treatment of congestive heart failure.
AT  Pyridyl-pyrazolinones to treat congestive heart failure.
SO  Current-Cardiovascular-Patents, Vol. 2, Iss. 12.
AB  Novel pyridyl-pyrazolinone compounds, possessing positive inotropic
    activity and useful as cardiotonic agents for treating cardiac
    disorders including congestive heart failure, are disclosed. The
    effectiveness of the compounds as inotropic agents was determined by
    measuring changes in cardiac contractile force in the anaesthetised
```

**Figure 3.21:** (cont.)

       **dog procedure and in the conscious instrumented dog procedure. In vitro evaluation using guinea-pig atria is also described; no specific results are detailed. 2,4-Dihydro-4-(N-morpholinomethyl)-5-(6-(1H-imidazol-1-yl)pyrid-3-yl)-3-pyrazolinone is one of three specifically claimed compounds.**

EV   Chemical and therapeutic : Treatment of congestive heart failure (CHF) has been limited historically to use of cardiac glycosides such as digitalis. Problems of this mode of therapy lie in the fact that the therapeutic and toxic doses are very similar. In the past decade or so, alternative approaches including the use of angiotensin converting enzyme (ACE) inhibitors such as captopril (1), fast sodium channel activators such as DPI 201106 (2), vasodilator combinations of hydralazine and nitroprusside (3) and phosphodiesterase (PDE) inhibitors such as the prototype milrinone (4) have been investigated in clinical settings for improved efficacy and for both improved quality and duration of life for CHF patients. More than 15 pharmaceutical companies have studied modifications of PDE inhibitors that might improve potency, selectivity and duration of action. In addition to the bipyridine milrinone (Sterling), one class of compounds that has been well-represented in this concerted effort is a group of pyridazinones including imazodan (5; Warner-Lambert), pimobendan (6; Boehringer Ingelheim) and indolidan (7; Lilly) among many others. Rorer has been investigating PDE inhibitors for some time and several patents concerning pyridazinones have appeared in the last year (WO-A-90/03790, US 4859698 (1989)). In the current case, Rorer describes interesting pyrazolinone derivatives which are essentially ring-contracted pyridazinones. Especially interesting is that despite a Markush description that also includes pyridazinones, only pyrazolinones are claimed with the three most interesting compounds including the above-shown derivative. Unfortunately, while the structural type is a very interesting extension of the structure-activity relationship of PDE inhibitors, no biological data are provided. Thus, while their testing methods in vitro (guinea pig atria) and in vivo (anaesthetised and conscious dogs) are standards which would allow comparison with other known inotropic agents, no such comparison may be made. Consequently, potential advantages of potency, selectivity or duration of action of this new class of heterocycles are not defined. Unless there are some remarkable properties associated with this class of compound, it is unlikely that another PDE inhibitor would be developed. Besides milrinone which is approved for some therapy, there are a great number of compounds already in Phase II-III clinical trials.

KR   (1) Chatterjee K et al., Am J Heart, 1985, 110:137; (2) Schotysik G, J Cardiovasc Pharmacol, 1989, 14(Suppl 3):524; (3) Cohn et al., N Engl J Med, 1986, 314:1547; (4) Lejemtel et al., Circulation, 1986, 73.

**PA**  **Rorer Pharmaceutical Corporation.**
**IN**  **Kuhla-D-E, Campbell-H-F, et-al.**
**PN**  **US-4954494.**
**DS**  **None.**
**PD**  **900904.**
**PR**  **US-303879.**
**PY**  **890130.**
**FD**  **890130.**
**SC**  **Cardiovascular (CV).**
**DE**  **Cardiostimulant; Positive-inotrope; Pyridyl-pyrazolinone.**
**IC**  **C07D-401-14 A61K-31-44.**

The original titles [TI], with an English-language abstract [AB] for all patents except Japanese-language PCT applications, are provided in both CPEV and FAST-ALERT, with additional terms in the Annotated Title field in CPEV [AT]. The emphasis in the *Current Patents* abstracts is on the pharmaceutical utility disclosed in the patent and focuses on the specific compounds exemplified in the patent; although the abstract identifies the novel features of the claims in a general sense there is no attempt to define the generic scope of the claims. In CPEV, there is an extensive evaluation of the claimed invention [EV]. An expert in pharmaceutical research evaluates the scientific disclosure in the patent. The evaluation takes into account the pharmacological data provided in the patent specification and compares the invention with products currently available and under clinical development in the same therapeutic category. Much of the material in the evaluation is taken from sources outside the patent under discussion and is based upon the subjective opinion of the expert author. Patents judged to cover potential products of value receive a Merit Rating. Key References [KR] listed in the record relate to the Evaluation; these are not the references cited by the examiner or discussed in the patent specification. *Current Patents* section codes [SC] and descriptors [DE] are provided. The descriptor terms are not based upon a controlled thesaurus. A maximum of six IPC codes are listed, each searchable at the sub-class, group, and sub-group level.

## DRUG PATENTS INTERNATIONAL

DRUG PATENTS INTERNATIONAL, produced by IMSworld Publications Ltd., and mounted on ORBIT, is a database of patents covering marketed drugs. IMSworld provides pharmaceutical business information to subscribers, with emphasis on the marketing aspects of the industry rather than the scientific aspects addressed by *Current Patents*. This database has been designed to provide pharmaceutical executives with information about the patents that cover marketed single-entity drugs. There were only 750 drugs in the database as of early 1991, with individual records for each indexed patent. Data is derived from searches in other databases to identify patents claiming a drug, the patent specification is 'evaluated' to determine the scope of its claims, and equivalent patents are found by consulting INPADOC and/or Derwent's patent family databases. The expiration date of the patent, with information about the availability of patent term extensions, is calculated for each patent, and the data is published in the printed *Patents International*. The data from the 1987-1989 publications was made available online in early 1991, with additional information to be added through monthly updates. It should be understood that the currency of the database update has nothing to do with the currency of the patents added to the file. Newly added records will cover additional drugs, and most drugs have already been patented by the time they are eligible for coverage by this database. This database does not purport to provide the entire patent status of the drug; comments on additional patent families are provided only as Notes and Comments in the record for the original patent on the drug. Since most marketed drugs are eventually covered by numerous patents on pharmaceutical compositions and production processes, this database does not provide the entire answer for most questions, but it does have the information deemed most important by senior managers.

Figure 3.22 illustrates the record for French medicinal patent 296. Although a record in this database relates to a patent, the title of the record is the generic name of the compound the patent covers [NA], provided in several official versions. The patent [PN] number can be searched in Derwent format or as the publication number independent of the ISO country code. For countries that grant patents after unexamined publication, both numbers are provided, but dates may not be provided for unexamined publications. The patent country [PC] can be searched by name or ISO code. Application dates are searchable, but the application serial number is not provided. Priority numbers and dates [PR] are provided, with the priority number searchable in Derwent format or as the serial number recorded from the patent. The name of the assignee [PA] and its country of residence [AR] can be searched, and the corporate producer of the marketed drug [CP] is indexed. It should be noted that the database producer does not identify producers other the original marketer of the drug except when a licence agreement is noted in the Country Comments field [CM] or when patents belonging to other companies are discussed in the Notes field [NO].

## Figure 3.22: DRUG PATENTS INTERNATIONAL citation - ORBIT File DPIN

```
AN - 9001-003698
NA - KETOPROFEN; KETOPROFEN [INN]; KETOPROFEN [USAN]
PN - FR—296 [296]  70.02.23
PC - FRANCE (MEDICAL) [FR]
APD - 67.01.27
PR - 67.01.27 FR92828/67 [67FR-092828]
     67.12.15 FR132526/67 [67FR-132526]
PT - PRODUCT; PATENT OF ADDITION
CM - THE FRENCH MEDICAL PATENT QUOTED IS A PATENT OF ADDITION (CAM) TO FRENCH
     MEDICAL PATENT 6444 AND CLAIMS OPTICALLY ACTIVE DEVIVATIVES. BOTH FRENCH
     MEDICAL PATENTS EXPIRE AT THE SAME TIME.
EX - 87.01.27
PA - RHONE POULENC
AR - FRANCE
SY - PROFENID; ALRHEUMUN; FASTUM; REMAURIC; SECTOR; KNAVON; FLEXEN;
     KETARTRIUM; KETO-50; KETOFEN; PROFENIL; VELOZINA; MENAMIN; RP 19583
TN - PROFENID; BI PROFENID
DE - ANTIRHEUMATIC NON-STEROIDAL
TC - M01A; R05C; M02A
RN - 22071-15-4
NO - RHONE POULENC HAS A LATER PROCESS PATENT WHICH IS VERY WIDELY FILED
     THROUGHOUT THE WORLD. THESE PATENTS HAVE A 1971 PRIORITY AND WOULD
     THEREFORE NORMALLY EXPIRE IN APPROXIMATELY 1992 IN MOST COUNTRIES.
```

Technical information about the patent is sparse. The type of patent claim [PT], for example, product, process, or product-by-process, is reported. The CAS registry number [RN] of the compound is provided along with synonyms for its generic name [SY], trade names [TN], descriptors for the drug's activity [DE], and IMSworld's therapeutic class codes [TC]. There is no title, abstract or claim text.

The expected expiration date is given in the [EX] field. For most patents this data has been estimated, but some extended terms are noted. The availability of patent term extensions or imposition of licences of right is indicated where the patent law provides for them. IMSworld does not promise that the expiry data reflects the actual status of the patent. The expiry field is accessible online only to hardcopy subscribers, and thus others must obtain this information from other sources.

Since the fee for displaying a single record in DPIN is nearly as much as the fee for a patent family search in INPADOC, it is extremely expensive to display all of the records for a given drug, especially in light of the fact that marketed drugs have usually been patented worldwide. Unless the information in the [CM] field of each country is of special value, it would be wise to display only one patent record in DPIN and to search for equivalent patents and expiry information elsewhere. DPIN differs from other ORBIT patent databases in that the PRINT SELECT command is not effective. Thus one cannot retrieve a member of the patent family and cross into other files to search for additional family members and status information without re-keying the patent or priority number.

## OTHER DATABASES THAT INCLUDE PATENTS

The databases summarized above are not the only ones that provide patent information online. Patent office online databases exist for limited searching in many countries, some of them available to the public. Complete Japanese patent data are available in Japanese on PATOLIS. German, European and PCT patent publications are covered in databases on Bertelsmann Informations Service GmbH.

Many databases available through the major host systems treat patents as technical literature. As a rule, databases that treat patents as technical literature index them in the same way that they index journal articles, making little distinction between background disclosures and claims. Many of these databases omit most of the special bibliographic fields in patents, making it difficult to obtain a copy of the abstracted patent or to identify an equivalent patent. Some of the databases obtain patent information from the Patent Office gazette or from another abstracting service and identify the secondary source as the abstracted publication. In addition to databases that make patents or their surrogates the subject of individual records, there are many databases that index articles that discuss patents or report on patents as news.

Patent numbers are reported as references in many technical publications. Although SCISEARCH does not index patents, it is an excellent source of patents related to scientific research reported in the journal literature, as the reference citations indexed from the literature by SCISEARCH include many patents. Full-text databases include patents as cited references and sometimes discuss the content of the patents in the text.

The monographs reproduced in such databases as the MERCK INDEX, BEILSTEIN and HEILBRON, which describe the synthesis and properties of chemical compounds, refer the reader to patents as the source of much of the information in the database. The PHARMAPROJECTS database, which describes pharmaceutical products under development, includes patent numbers supplied by the developers of the new drugs in some monographs. One is often asked to find the patent that claims a particular product. Patents cited in PHARMAPROJECTS are likely to be the actual patent relied upon for protection. A patent cited in the MERCK INDEX, on the other hand, usually represents the earliest publication describing the synthesis of the compound. Citations in these databases should never be accepted without verification as an indication that the compound or its synthesis is actually claimed in that patent.

### Databases offering information about patents

In addition to the many databases that index patents as legal and technical documents, there are a number of databases that serve as sources of information about patents or as aids to the use of other patent databases. Such databases include thesauri to the patent classification systems and legal databases that document the fate of patents that have been involved in litigation.

*International Patent Classification: CIB*

The text of the fifth edition of the *International Patent Classification* definitions and a keyword index, in French, is online in the CIB database on Questel. The database may be searched to determine what class code covers a particular subject by means of text terms from the definitions and it may be searched by means of IPC codes to determine their definitions. The definitions are written in generic language. Consequently, it is not always possible to retrieve a class code by searching with the term that appears to describe the subject matter of interest.

*European Patent Classification: ECLATX*

The full text of the *European Patent Classification (ECLA) Manual* is online in the ECLATX database mounted by INPI on Questel. The classification scheme is based on the hierarchical structure of the IPC, and has additional sub-divisions for the convenience of European Patent Office search staff, with monthly updates to adapt the classification to technological evolution. The database may be searched by means of text terms to determine what class code covers a particular subject, and it may be searched by IPC codes or European Patent Classification codes to find definitions. The definitions are written in the same generic language as the IPC code definitions in CIB, but the text in this file is in English. The file may be used to find current IPC codes by determining the ECLA class and ignoring final characters designating the subdivisions. ECLATX is most useful when searched for code definitions, which may be viewed in their full context. The definitions for classification codes in EDOC records can easily be found by transferring them into ECLATX with the ..MEM command. The reverse procedure is not possible as classification codes are indexed in the basic index and every level of the code is indexed in the /TF field; the full codes do not have a unique field identifier. The definition of IPC class F02M-051/02 is illustrated in Figure 3.23.

### Figure 3.23: ECLATX citation - Questel File ECLATX

```
1/1   - (C) INPI/OEB
GR      F02M-051/00 Fuel-injection apparatus characterised by being
        operated electrically
SG      . ***F02M-051/02*** specially for low-pressure fuel-injection
        (pumps per se 51/04; injectors per se 51/08)
```

*United States Patent Classification*

The full text of the *Manual of Classification* and the *Index to the Manual of Classification* of the United States Patent Classification system are searchable in Mead Data Central's LEXPAT library. The text of the class definitions for the United States Patent Classification system and the *Index to the Manual of Classification* comprise the CLAIMS/CLASS database on ORBIT and are incorporated into the CLAIMS/REFERENCE database on DIALOG and the IFIREF database on STN, which also contain the thesaurus to the CLAIMS UNITERM and COMPREHENSIVE databases. These files can be searched by means of text terms from the definitions to determine what classification code covers a particular subject or by means of classification codes to find their definitions. Searching with free text is unrewarding, as the definitions are written in generic language and anticipating the terms associated with a concept within the hierarchy of the classification definitions is often impossible. The United States Patent Classification definition databases are reloaded with revised class definitions when these are announced by the USPTO. Obsolete class definitions are removed from the databases and their definitions cannot be retrieved online.

The USCLASS database, produced by Derwent Inc. and mounted on ORBIT, and an additional file in the LEXPAT library contain the patent numbers of all United States patents published since 1790 with their US Patent Classification codes. The codes are current with the latest reload of the database. The files may be searched by means of the classification code or the patent number, yielding either a list of all patents that have been assigned the code or of all classification codes that have been assigned to the particular patent.

**Patent litigation databases**

Patents exist in order to protect inventions from exploitation by infringers. They are enforced by filing civil suits in the national court systems. Infringers typically defend themselves by countersuing on the grounds that the patents are not valid or that the owners of the patents have lost the right to enforce them. Legal battles also occur before the grant of a patent in interferences and oppositions to patent grant. Such legal duels often involve high stakes: the life or death of a company may even depend on the outcome of a patent suit. For persons involved in the practice of patent law, the outcome of patent litigation is the most important aspect of patent information.

The most complete sources of legal information are full-text legal databases such as WESTLAW® and LEXIS® which contain statutes, court decisions, and the full text of the BNA's *Patent, Trademark & Copyright Journal*. CANADIAN PATENT REPORTER, produced by Canada Law Book Inc. and available on QL/SEARCH, contains decisions rendered in intellectual property cases litigated in the Canadian courts. JURINPI, produced by INPI and mounted on Questel, contains published and unpublished French and European Patent Office jurisprudence concerning patents and trademarks, with coverage beginning in 1952.

PATENT STATUS FILE (PAST) and LITALERT, produced by the Rapid Patent Service of Research Publications and mounted on ORBIT, contain records of post-issuance activity related to United States patents. The printed version of *Patent Status File* and the online counterpart report all post-issue status changes to United States patents reported in LITALERT or in the USPTO *Official Gazette* from 1973 to the present. Changes include dedications, disclaimers, patent term lapses and extensions, the filing of reissue applications and requests for examination, the issuance of reissue patents, re-examination certificates and certificates of correction, the filing of patent suits, and adverse decisions in patent litigation. Many of these events are not reported in INPADOC legal status records. LITALERT contains records of pending patent and trademark suits filed in United States Federal District Courts. The PATENT STATUS FILE is essentially a cumulative index to LITALERT and Research Publications' CDR microfilm file of US patent Certificates of Correction, Disclaimers, and Reissued and Reexamined patents. Backlog information from PATENT STATUS FILE and LITALERT are available on CD-ROM as PATENT HISTORY. Updates of both publications are incorporated in Research Publications' CD-ROM subscription service, OG PLUS, along with searchable bibliographic data and images of the full text of the *Official Gazette* of the USPTO.

The PATENT STATUS FILE and LITALERT records for US 3 826 728 are included in Search 3.2. There is a substantial search fee for each patent number searched in PATENT STATUS FILE, so it is wise to NEIGHBOR each patent number you wish to search to determine whether data are available. PATENT STATUS FILE records relate to a particular action and contain the patent number [PN] and document type [DT] of the patent and a code [CO], action name [AC] and subject heading [SH] for the action. In most records these three fields are redundant. Records for actions reported in the *Official Gazette* include the publication date of the notice [OG], but not the content of the notice. Reissue patent numbers are provided. Actions recorded in LITALERT are indicated in the Notes field [NO], and the searcher must refer to that database for details. Records for certificates of correction, disclaimers, reissued patents and reexamination certificates contain the number of the appropriate CDR microfilm reel in the Notes field.

LITALERT reports the details of pending cases on file with the Office of the Solicitor of the United States Patent and Trademark Office. LITALERT records include the patent numbers and other bibliographic data of the patents in suit, as well as the names of the litigants. The Solicitor's records of pending cases are not complete, so failure to retrieve a record of a pending suit from LITALERT cannot be taken as evidence that no suit has been filed.

## Search 3.2: **PATENT STATUS FILE and LITALERT citations - ORBIT Files PAST and LITALERT**

```
YOU ARE NOW CONNECTED TO PAST.
 COVERAGE FROM 1973 THRU UPDATE 9005.

PATENT NUMBER SEARCH TERMS (PN) WILL BE CHARGED
$9.50 FOR EACH TERM ENTERED.

SS 1?
NBR US3826728/PN

SELECT# RESULTS    TERM
     1        1    US3826717/PN
     2        1    US3826724/PN
     3        8    US3826728/PN
     4        1    US3826729/PN
     5        1    US3826736/PN
UP N OR DOWN N?

SELECT 3

SS 1 RESULT (8)

SS 2?
PRINT FULL 8

-1-
AN  - 8900-206516
PN  - US3826728
DT  - A (UTILITY)
OG  - 89.11.07
CO  - RXA
ACT - REQUEST FOR REEXAMINATION FILED
SH  - REQUEST FOR REEXAMINATION FILED
    .
    .
    .
-4-
AN  - 8900-145055
PN  - US3826728
DT  - A (UTILITY)
OG  - 86.06.10
CO  - RXC ACT - REEXAMINATION CERTIFICATE
SH  - REEXAMINATION CERTIFICATE NO - 055

-5-
AN  - 8900-125546
PN  - US3826728
DT  - A (UTILITY)
OG  - 84.04.24
CO  - RXA
ACT - REQUEST FOR REEXAMINATION FILED
SH  - REQUEST FOR REEXAMINATION FILED

-6-
AN  - 8900-090704
PN  - US3826728
DT  - A (UTILITY)
OG  - 80.04.01
CO  - COR
```

**Search 3.2:** (cont.)

```
ACT - CERTIFICATE OF CORRECTION
SH  - CERTIFICATE OF CORRECTION
NO  - 032

-7-
AN  - 8900-001756
PN  - US3826728
DT  - A (UTILITY)
CO  - PS
ACT - PATENT SUIT
NO  - LitAlert

-8-
AN  - 8900-001755
PN  - US3826728
DT  - A (UTILITY)
CO  - PS
ACT - PATENT SUIT
NO  - LitAlert

SS 2?
FILE LITALERT

ELAPSED TIME ON PAST: 0.04 HRS.
YOU ARE NOW CONNECTED TO LITALERT.
 CURRENT THROUGH UPDATE 9031.


SS 1?
SELECT 3

SS 1 RESULT (2)

SS 2?
PRINT FULL 2


-1-
AN  - P87-06-11
FS  - PATENT (P)
PN  - US3826728 74.07.30
TI  - Transparent Article Having Reduced Solar Radiation
      Transmittance and Method of Making the Same
PCL - 204192000R
IN  - Chambers Douglas L; Carmichael Donald C; Wan Chong T
PA  - Shatterproof Glass Corp
IT  - Chemistry, Electrical and Wave Energy
PF  - Shatterproof Glass Corp
DF  - Guardian Industries Corp
CT  - DE
DN  - C.A. 86-607
FD  - 86.12.29
ACT - A complaint was filed.
UP  - 8706

-2-
AN  - P86-29-20
FS  - PATENT (P)
PN  - US3826728 74.07.30
TI  - Transparent Article Having Reduced Solar Radiation
      Transmittance and Method of Making the Same
```

**Search 3.2:** (cont.)

```
PCL  -  204192000R
IN   -  Chambers Douglas L; Carmichael Donald C; Wan Chong T
PA   -  Shatterproof Glass Corp
PF   -  Shatterproof Glass Corp
DF   -  Ford Motor Co
CT   -  MI, Eastern Dist.
DN   -  86CV73039-DT
FD   -  86.07.16
ACT  -  On July 16, 1986, a complaint was filed.
UP   -  8608
```

## SELECTING A DATABASE

Patents cover every aspect of applied art, science and technology, so patent databases can be used to answer questions that arise in almost any field of knowledge. The best retrieval is obtained from databases that provide deep indexing and/or abstracts that summarize the factual content of the patent without the awkward generic language of the claims or the verbosity of full text. Databases that write their own patent abstracts do not cover every patent issued in the countries they index; most such databases are devoted to a restricted field of knowledge. The least selective source of comprehensive abstracts, WORLD PATENTS INDEX, has been providing abstracts in an increasing number of technologies for one member of each patent family and some equivalent granted patents since 1963. JAPIO provides descriptive English-language abstracts for Japanese patent applications published in most technologies since 1980, but only for patents belonging to Japanese nationals. Patent databases such as WPI, APIPAT and the CLAIMS UNITERM and COMPREHENSIVE databases that supply controlled indexing can be extremely powerful for searching the technologies they cover in depth.

Because patents are so complex and current information is so important, it is unlikely that online searching of patent databases will be replaced by CD-ROM patent databases. CASSIS, the US *Manual of Classification* and an index of US patents with their current classification code, is available from USPTO. Bibliographic information from current United States patents is available on CD-ROM on Research Publications' OG PLUS service, which also provides patent status and litigation data. United States patent bibliographic information without the images or status data is available from Chadwyck-Healey as MICROPATENT, APS. Other MICROPATENT databases contain the claims of United States patents, the full text of the patents without images, and images of the patent documents in full. European and PCT patent CD-ROM products are being produced by the European Patent Office. The EPO European and PCT patent specifications are available as images of the first page and of the full specification, but these products are not fully searchable. With the exception of the CLAIMS CD-ROM, which contains forty years of bibliographic data on United States patents, the CD-ROM databases available as of 1991 are valuable chiefly as current awareness tools for bibliographic searches and for high-quality document delivery. For searches in large databases or for the technological information retrievable from text terms or indexing, it is necessary to search online.

For online searches in any field, searchers may employ the free text and patent classification codes provided in the databases that document all of the patents issued in one or more countries. The main claim and/or abstract of West German patent applications is provided by PATDPA for applications published since October, 1968. LEXPAT provides the full text of United States patents issued since 1975, and several United States patent databases provide claim or abstract text. US PATENTS has the full text of the abstract and all claims of United States patents issued since August, 1970; CLAIMS has the abstract and/or main claim of American chemical patents published since 1950 and of other American patents published since 1963, is in the process of adding the full text of all claims for patents published since 1975 on at least one host, and has augmented the original title of patents published since 1971 with additional descriptive phrases; PATDATA has abstracts of United States patents published since 1975.

For free-text searching, it would seem that the more text the database provides the more likely the search will be to retrieve every relevant patent. Searching both the main claim and the abstract, however, does not always double one's chance to retrieve a particular patent. In many patents the abstract is simply a summary of the main claim, written in the same generic language, and provides little additional information. Dependent claims, on the other hand, often contain specific language that is missing from the main claim. Full-text searching, while it gives access to all the details in the patent disclosure, retrieves irrelevant details as readily as important ones. Free-text searching gives good results only when the terms in the query include all possible synonyms for the concept being searched and when all the terms are unambiguous.

INPADOC has only titles and IPC codes as guides to the subject matter disclosed in patents, while EDOC and USCLASS have only current patent classification codes, so they are of little use in searches for technical content. Most patent titles are too short to yield reliable search terms. Although patent classification codes are sufficiently precise for manual searching, they are too highly posted to use alone for online retrieval. Subject searches in these databases should be attempted only when no other database covers the appropriate country and time range. INPADOC is a valuable source of updated patent family and legal status information, however, as patents are indexed sooner in INPADOC than in databases that prepare abstracts and indexing.

If both technical and legal status information is needed, it is usually advisable to search a combination of databases, using a database with enough searchable text or indexing to retrieve patents covering a particular technical subject and a database with full bibliographic citations and/or legal status information to determine the claim scope and status of equivalent patents issued in the countries of interest. It is also advisable to search more than one database whenever comprehensive retrieval is needed. Many patents are long and complex; patents of over one hundred pages are not uncommon. It is difficult to index such long documents comprehensively, and the indexing policies of patent databases are so diverse that a search of any one database may fail to retrieve vital references that can be retrieved elsewhere. Searches for technical information, even when only patent references are desired, ought not to be restricted to patent databases. Many of the databases discussed in Chapters 4 to 10 contain patents, and normal search strategies will retrieve any pertinent patent references that are present in the database.

The number of databases to be searched and the time range to be searched for the answer to a particular question depends upon the use that is to be made of the information. In searches directed to the technical information in the patent disclosure, patent databases merely supplement databases that index the journal literature. In searches intended to discover whether an invention is patentable, both patent and literature databases should be searched exhaustively, for no published information is too old or too obscure to prevent a patent from issuing. When the objective of the search is to discover whether a product or process is covered by one or more patents, the search must focus on the patent claims. Only unexpired patents are relevant to such searches; older patents are of interest only when it is possible that an equivalent patent in another country may still be in force. When a patent that seems to cover the product or process is found, a supplementary search should be made to determine that patent's current legal status.

The most common patent question, 'What patent covers this product?', is unfortunately the most difficult to answer. Patents do not customarily name the commercial product they protect and it may be very difficult to determine whether a specific product is actually covered by the claims of a patent written in generic terms. IMSworld's DRUG PATENTS INTERNATIONAL database on ORBIT provides the results of searches in other databases for the patent claiming about 750 marketed drugs, but such databases are unavailable for other industries. The most convenient way to find the patent that claims a product is often the most obvious way - obtain a sample of the product and look for a patent number stamped on the product or printed on its packaging. It should never be forgotten that many products are marketed without patent protection and that other products are protected by more than one patent. Even when a patent covering a product in one country has been identified, it is not safe to assume that the product is covered in all countries where equivalent patents are in force.

Almost all of the subject fields discussed in Chapters 4 to 16 can be searched advantageously in patent databases of one kind or another. In addition to the databases that provide full coverage of the publications of a national or international Patent Office, there are databases that are especially suited to each field.

## Chemistry

Most new chemical compounds and chemical process technology is reported in patents, usually long before it is reported in chemical journals, but retrieving chemical information from patents presents special problems. Searching for all references to a compound by using free text is bound to fail: a single compound can be named a great many ways, Markush structures in patents include vast numbers of compounds which are never named at all, and most chemical structures are represented in patents only as diagrams. Only controlled indexing of the structural features of a compound can guarantee that all documents that describe it will be retrieved.

Because patents are so important to the chemical industry, the first patent databases were developed specifically to provide access to chemical patents. WORLD PATENTS INDEX provides English-language titles and abstracts that summarize the novel aspects of patents published in thirty-four countries. For Chemical Patents Index subscribers, WPI provides controlled indexing of products and processes, including fragmentation code indexing or topological structure indexing of the broadest generic chemical structure in the patent. The CLAIMS UNITERM and COMPREHENSIVE databases provide controlled indexing of the claims and examples of United States chemical patents. There are terms for specific chemical substances, fragmentation codes for generic chemical structures, and *Chemical Abstracts* Registry Numbers for specific compounds in some of the records. There are terms for aspects of chemical and chemical engineering processes and for all kinds of chemically related products, and there are property descriptors for chemically related products and processes. The CLAIMS COMPREHENSIVE database, accessible only to subscribers, is particularly good for identifying polymers. Chemical aspects of pharmaceutical patents can be retrieved using both topological structure indexing and keywords in PHARMSEARCH. Patents related to the petroleum industry are deeply indexed in APIPAT, using a controlled thesaurus of product, process, and compound terms tailored for petroleum patents. The WORLD PATENTS INDEX/APIPAT files on ORBIT combine the strengths of both files. Most chemical kokai belonging to Japanese persons and organizations are abstracted in JAPIO.

Chemical patents can also be retrieved from databases that are not limited to patents. Chemical Abstracts provides structural indexing of chemical compounds in its registry file, and the registry numbers retrieved there can be used to retrieve patents indexed in CA SEARCH, CAOLD, CLAIMS, APIPAT and the MERCK INDEX. *Chemical Abstracts* patent citations can be retrieved directly by searching the generic structure records in MARPAT. Derwent's CHEMICAL REACTIONS DOCUMENTATION SERVICE (CRDS) on ORBIT includes reactions reported in patents since 1975 and allows searching for products, reactants and transformations with structural fragment codes and reaction codes. Chemical information is also retrievable without special coding in many other databases that include patents. Among these, the CURRENT PATENTS files are devoted entirely to pharmaceutical patents, most of them relating to chemical substances.

## Biological and health sciences

PHARMSEARCH, DRUG PATENTS INTERNATIONAL and CURRENT PATENTS are devoted entirely to pharmaceutical patents. Biopolymers from patents in the WORLD PATENTS INDEX database are indexed structurally in the GENESEQ database, produced by Derwent Publications Ltd., and available through

IntelliGenetics. Polypeptide structures have been added to the CAS REGISTRY file on STN, and are directly searchable for transfer to the CA File. Patent references are included in many of the bioscience databases, including BIOTECHNOLOGY ABSTRACTS, CURRENT BIOTECHNOLOGY ABSTRACTS, SUPERTECH, IRL LIFE SCIENCES COLLECTION, PASCAL, TOXLINE and BIOBUSINESS. Most bioscience-related kokai belonging to Japanese persons and organizations are abstracted in JAPIO, but those relating to medical devices are represented by only titles and a few index terms. There are also references to bioscience patents in many databases that index chemical patents. The guidelines for selecting chemical patents for deep indexing in the CLAIMS UNITERM and COMPREHENSIVE databases and in the Chemical Patents Index sections of WPI include most patents in bioscience fields. Pharmaceutical patents are included in WPI's Farmdoc section, and are searchable by subscribers with a special Galenic code that was introduced in 1976 and with the other retrieval codes that have been available since 1963. Microbiology and biotechnology patents and patents relating to foods and nutrition published since 1970 are classified in WPI's section D. Patents on medical devices are included in the non-chemical sections of WPI that have been available since 1974.

## Agriculture

Agricultural patents are indexed by many of the agriculture databases, including CAB ABSTRACTS and AGRIS. Most agricultural kokai belonging to Japanese persons and organizations are abstracted in JAPIO. Patents relating to agricultural chemicals and veterinary science are included in CURRENT PATENTS FAST-ALERT and in databases that index chemical patents, including the CLAIMS UNITERM and COMPREHENSIVE databases and the Chemical Patents Index sections of WPI. Agriculture patents with chemical or veterinary medical features have been included in WPI's Agdoc section since 1965, and are searchable by subscriber coding. Other agricultural patents have been included in WPI's non-chemical sections since 1974.

## Energy and the environment

Patents relating to energy and the environment are indexed in a great many databases. DOE ENERGY, INIS, TULSA and SOVIET SCIENCE AND TECHNOLOGY feature patents on energy. Patents relating to the petroleum industry are indexed in depth in APIPAT and the combined WORLD PATENTS INDEX/APIPAT files. ENVIRONLINE, POLLUTION ABSTRACTS and WATER RESOURCES ABSTRACTS feature patents on pollution control. Patents in these areas can also be found in chemical, agricultural and engineering databases.

## Engineering

Patents relating to engineering are included in a great variety of databases that index patents, including INIS, PHYSICS BRIEFS, PASCAL, INSPEC, ISMEC, FLUIDEX, CHEMICAL ENGINEERING ABSTRACTS and CA SEARCH. Kokai in the field of physics and most engineering fields are abstracted by JAPIO. Chemical engineering patents are included in the guidelines for selecting patents for deep indexing in the CLAIMS UNITERM and COMPREHENSIVE database, and other engineering patents have been included without indexing in CLAIMS since 1963. Chemical engineering patents have been indexed in the Chemical Patents Index of WPI since 1970 and other engineering patents have been included in WPI since 1974. Electrical engineering patents have been indexed for subscribers to the Electrical Patents Index sections of WPI since 1982.

## Computer science and information technology

United States patents on electronic data processing published since 1984 are abstracted in INFORMATION SCIENCE ABSTRACTS. In addition, patents on computer science and information technology are included in other databases that index electrical patents, including the Electrical Patents Index sections of WPI.

## Social and behavioural sciences

Patents relevant to the social and behavioural sciences include those claiming psychological testing methods and devices, educational aids, behaviour modification programmes, toys and games. In addition to patents that claim inventions such as these, there are a great many patents in areas such as pharmacy and medicine that disclose the results of experiments that test the behavioural responses of animals to various stimuli.

## Humanities

Patentable subject matter includes new art forms and techniques for their application, musical instruments, games, toys, clothing and furnishings. In addition to patents that claim new apparatus or new methods for using or producing them, there are design patents that claim actual decorative designs. Design patents are indexed in CLAIMS and LEXPAT, but the claimed subject matter in the patents is defined by the drawings, which are not in the online records. Although LEXPAT and the enhanced records in CLAIMS have brief descriptions of the drawings, searching for design patents is more efficient if done manually.

## Business and economics

Methods of managing assets can be patented, as shown in Search 3.8, but the most important uses for patent information in business and economics are as guides for business development and as sources of competitive intelligence. Monitoring the expiration dates of patents that protect competitive products allows a company to enter the market as soon as the patents expire. A company can identify sources of equipment or raw materials by discovering which companies own patents on the equipment or materials, and it can identify customers for its products by discovering which companies have patented technology that uses the products. By studying the patent portfolio of a competitor or a potential acquisition, one can learn what kind of research it has been pursuing and what kind of products it can sell exclusively.

Statistical manipulation of patent assignee data and patent classification codes can be used to create summaries of industrial trends. Information can be downloaded from patent databases for manipulation with statistical software programs. Derwent Publications Ltd. offers its PATSTAT PLUS software package specifically for analysing data downloaded from WPI. Some host systems provide statistical software online. STN's SELECT command automatically ranks the terms it extracts from a set of records. ORBIT allows online manipulation of data with the GET command. Data from the databases mounted on Questel can be manipulated

## Search 3.3: Analysis with the GET command - ORBIT File INPADOC

```
SS 1?
ATLAS COPCO:/PA

SS 1 RESULT (4426)

SS 2?
1 AND 87/AY AND SE/PC/DS

        OCCURS      TERM
        876617      87/AY
        823823      SE/PC, DS
SS 2 RESULT (66)

SS 3?
GET IC(1-8) GT 2

THERE ARE 25 UNIQUE VALUES.
14 TERMS SUPPRESSED - FREQUENCY LESS THAN 3.
OCCURRENCES       TERM
          5         B25B-023
          5         F15B-013
          4         F04C-029
          3         B01D-013
          3         B05B-005
          3         B24C-001
          3         B24C-005
          3         B25H-003
          3         B62D-065
          3         E21C-005
          3         G01S-005
```

online with the ..MEMSORT command. Search 3.3 illustrates a search in ORBIT's INPADOC file to determine what kind of technology is being developed at Atlas Copco AB. After a search for all Atlas Copco patents having effect in Sweden and applied for in 1987, the GET command is used to determine what technical areas were being developed, as indicated by the International Patent Classification codes assigned to the patents. The resulting ranked listing of IPC codes can be compared with the patenting activity of competing companies or with Atlas Copco data from other years to find out how the emphasis at Atlas Copco has varied over time.

Search 3.4 illustrates an application of the ..MEMSORT command in Questel's WPIL file. After a search for patents covering the compound minoxidil, the names of the patent assignees are analysed to discover which companies are most actively developing the compound. Here the ..MEMSORT command extracts the patent assignee name, which is the second term in the /PA field, creating a list of companies ranked according to the number of patent families they own. Sorting on the basis of the first element of the patentee field, the Derwent company code, could have given a different ranking, since the same company code can be used for several operating units of a corporation.

Statistical manipulation of patent data can be misleading. Because patent publications from different countries differ in their significance, the results are meaningless if all patent documents in a multinational file are given equal weight. A granted patent is the first publication in the United States, for example, while a granted German patent is the third publication covering the invention; if each ORBIT INPADOC record is treated equally, a granted German patent will be given three times as much weight as a granted American patent. A company that begins filing European patent applications in place of national patent applications appears to be filing fewer equivalent patent applications if only the number of eventual publications is counted

**Search 3.4: Analysis with the MEMSORT command - QUESTEL File WPIL**

```
   ** SS 3: Results 101

   Search statement   4

?..MEMSORT /PA RK 2

   Total number of terms extracted: 51
   Number of terms now sorted in MEMSORT: 30

   Search statement   4

?..LI MEMS

   # FREQ  TERM

        1      9 L'OREAL SA
        2      5 UPJOHN CO
        3      3 KANEBO KK
        4      3 MERCK & CO INC
        5      3 UNILEVER PLC
        6      2 KANEKO T
        7      2 PROCTOR P H
        8      2 TAISHO PHARMACEUT KK
        9      1 CIRD CENT INT RECH
       10      1 CRINOS IND FARMACO SPA
       11      1 DI SCHIENA M G & C
       12      1 FABRE COSMETIQUE P
       13      1 FARMOS-YHTYMA OY
       14      1 GONG-HWAN L
       15      1 HATZENBUHLER D A

   Continue: Y / N

?N
```

without factoring in the number of designated states. The 'number of patents' data in patent family records is particularly misleading in such cases. Differences among the various editions of the *International Patent Classification Manual* can lead to apparent discontinuities in statistical trends when one IPC is replaced by a number of more precise codes. The set of patents analysed in Search 3.3 includes both Swedish national patent applications and European or PCT applications that designate Sweden, the underlying assumption being that Atlas Copco files all its patent applications in its home country. All publications based on 1987 applications would have been published applications rather than granted patents at the time this search was done; if the set of patents retrieved for analysis had included granted patents as well as published applications, it would have been necessary to eliminate duplicate records. Statistics derived from a database that covers only one country or that represents an entire family of equivalent patents in a single record, while they are based upon more uniform units of intellectual property, still fail to distinguish between patents that protect valuable products and those that are filed defensively.

## SELECTING A HOST

Crossfile searching is particularly useful in patent searches. Full bibliographic and legal status information is not available in the databases that provide deep indexing. Most databases index only one member of a patent family and others cover only selected patents. After a relevant patent has been found, a supplemental search is often needed in order to determine whether there is an equivalent or related patent in another country or to locate a readable copy of the patent disclosure. The ease with which one may complete a patent search online varies from host to host, depending upon the databases that are available on the system, the extent to which the databases have been harmonized for crossfile searching, and the software provided for crossfile searching. The examples of crossfile searches that follow are intended to illustrate the usefulness of crossfile searching in patent databases in a general sense as well as the capabilities of the host systems at the time they were performed. Most of the patent databases discussed in this chapter are mounted on ORBIT, Questel, STN and/ or DIALOG. The availability of patent databases on the various hosts has been changing at an enormous rate: new files are being introduced and old ones are being reloaded, existing databases have been loaded by new vendors, and search software is being modified.

## ORBIT

ORBIT has nearly all of the deeply indexed patent databases. WPI, CLAIMS, APIPAT, and JAPIO are mounted on ORBIT, as well as INPADOC, US PATENTS, USCLASS, and many chemistry, energy, and engineering databases that contain substantial numbers of patents. Files WPI and WPIL can be searched separately or together as file WPAT. ORBIT has combined the WPI/L files with the APIPAT database, merging the API records with the Derwent records so that the indexing can be used in a single search rather than a sequential crossfile search. In addition to technical databases like CA SEARCH and INSPEC that are carried by other host systems, ORBIT has several exclusive databases with substantial numbers of patents, including TULSA and CRDS. All the patent information fields in the ORBIT patent database cluster are being standardized in Derwent format. Terms in fields designated for crossfile searching in each database can be converted to search terms with the PRINT SELECT command and the resulting list of terms can be requalified or edited before being searched with the SELECT command. Sets may be manipulated statistically with the GET command, with the resulting sets placed in a SELECT list for crossfile searching. It is possible to transfer temporarily out of one file and into another with the TFILE command and to transfer searches from the CLAIMS/U file to the less expensive CLAIMS BIBLIO/ABSTRACTS file with the XCLAIM command.

Search 3.5 illustrates a crossfile search on ORBIT for patents belonging to Mitsubishi and covering electrically controlled internal combustion ignition apparatus. The search is begun in JAPIO, where all published Japanese patent applications are indexed. The IPC main group code, F02M-051, truncated to retrieve all of the subgroups below it in the IPC hierarchy, is used to define the subject of the patents. The definition of the IPC code is shown in Figure 3.22. The company codes for Mitsubishi Motors Corp. and Mitsubishi Electric Corp. are searched to avoid the translation and transliteration problems that would be encountered if the company name were searched. The resulting fifty Japanese patent applications may or may not have been filed in other countries. To find out, the patent application numbers are extracted with the PRINT SELECT command and requalified with the REQUAL command so that they can be searched in the priority field in WPAT. The search is repeated in WPAT with Derwent's company codes in place of the JAPIO codes, after which the fifty Japanese patent application numbers retrieved in JAPIO are SELECTed. The search retrieved twenty-eight patent families, only five of which claim priority from the applications retrieved in JAPIO. Most of the Japanese patents were not retrieved because WORLD PATENTS INDEX includes Japanese patents only in the chemical and electrical sections of the database. The WPAT search therefore retrieved only the inventions patented by Mitsubishi outside Japan, but it retrieved twenty-three Mitsubishi patents that were missed by the search in JAPIO. Some of these patents may have received a different JAPIO company code, some may have been based on Japanese utility model applications, and some will have been published before October, 1976, but most will have had the IPC F02M-051 code assigned to an equivalent patent in the Derwent family and not to the Japanese priority document.

## Search 3.5: Crossfile searching on ORBIT

```
YOU ARE NOW CONNECTED TO JAPIO.
COVERS PATENT APPLICATIONS FROM OCT 1976 THROUGH MARCH 1990 (9009).
COPYRIGHT JAPAN PATENT INFORMATION ORGANIZATION.

SS 1?
F02M-051:/IC AND (/CC 2351404 OR 2000601)

        OCCURS    TERM
          3646    F02M-051:/IC
          3506    2351404/CC
        110971    2000601/CC
SS 1 RESULT (50)

SS 2?
PRINT 1

-1-
AN  - 90-009946
TI  - FUEL INJECTION VALVE FOR INTERNAL COMBUSTION ENGINE
PA  - (2000601) MITSUBISHI ELECTRIC CORP
IN  - ASAYAMA, YOSHIAKI
PN  - 90.01.12 J02009946, JP 02-9946
AP  - 88.06.27 88JP-159816, 63-159816

SS 2?
PRINT SELECT 1-50 AP

TERMS 1 THRU 50 ADDED TO SEL LIST.

SS 2?
REQUAL 1-50 PR

SS 2?
FILE WPAT

YOU ARE NOW CONNECTED TO WPAT.
COVERS 1963 - DATE: UPDATED TO
9026/UP, 9026/UPEQ, 9013/UPA, 8946/UPB;
WPI 9022/UPEQ.

SS 1?
F02M-051:/IC AND (/CC MITM OR MITQ)

        OCCURS    TERM
          3213    F02M-051:/IC
           817    MITM/CC
         54427    MITQ/CC
SS 1 RESULT (26)

SS 2?
SELECT 1-50

        OCCURS    TERM
             0    88JP-159816/PR
             .
             .
             0    75JP-149914/PR
SS 2 RESULT (5)

SS 3?
1 OR 2
```

**Search 3.5:** (cont.)

```
SS 3 RESULT (28)

SS 4?
PRINT 1

-1-
AN    - 89-179408/25
XRPX  - N89-137019
TI    - Measuring equipment for air-fuel ratio for IC engine -
        includes measurement element producing electrical signal
        corresp. to concn. of component in exhaust gas
DC    - X22 Q52 Q53
PA    - (MITQ ) MITSUBISHI DENKI KK
IN    - SUZUKI H,NISHIYAMA R,NISHIDA S
NP    - 2
PN    - DE3840247-A    89.06.15 (8925)
        US4889098-A    89.12.26 (9008)
PR    - 87.12.01 87JP-304960
AP    - 88.11.29 88DE-840247    88.12.01 88US-278403
```

## Questel

Questel carries WORLD PATENTS INDEX and INPI's French, European and European Patent Office patent documentation files as well as the IPC and European patent classification definitions in CIB and ECLATX. CA SEARCH is loaded on Questel in the CAS file and may be searched with CAS Registry Numbers transferred from the Generic DARC EURECAS database, which contains the structure records for compounds registered by CAS from 1965 to the present. Questel has adopted the Derwent formats for crossfile searching of patent and priority numbers and has introduced additional fields into its CAS, EPAT, EDOC and FPAT records for the cross reference formats. Crossfile searches employ the ..MEM and *MEM commands to 'memorize' a list of search terms and search the terms. MEM lists can be created from any field in the record; the list can be edited by deleting items and terms can be truncated, limited, requalified and searched selectively. With the ..MEMSORT command, it is possible to perform statistical analyses of any data in records obtained from a search.

The full strength of the Generic DARC and Questel crossfile searching capabilities can be used to retrieve patent families from WORLD PATENTS INDEX by searching topologically in the EURECAS file for compounds indexed in CA SEARCH. Search 3.6 began by searching EURECAS for the compound minoxidil and any minoxidil salts, isomers or mixtures registered by CAS. Sixty-seven compounds and mixtures were retrieved and saved in a file named 'essminox'. After switching to the bibliographic CAS file, the saved file of registry numbers is searched with the *DARC command and limited to patent documents, retrieving 114 records. The MEM command is used to extract the patent numbers from the /XPN field of patent records, specifying the length of the patent number format as nine characters to avoid numbers that may have been formatted incorrectly. Priority numbers are also extracted in order to retrieve any patents indexed by CAS under a patent number that does not correspond to the number indexed by Derwent. 111 Unique priority numbers are extracted from the 114 patent records. The lists of patent and priority terms are searched in the WPIL file, where 109 patent families are retrieved. The search strategy is saved and re-executed in the WPI backfile to retrieve four additional patent families. This search will have missed any patents that were not indexed by Chemical Abstracts as well as any patents in which minoxidil was described generically, but the only possible false drops are patents where the role of minoxidil is irrelevant to the question being answered. If the searcher is interested in the current legal status of the French or European patents in these 109 patent families, the patent numbers can be extracted from the Derwent family records and searched in FPAT or EPAT.

## Search 3.6: Crossfile searching on Questel

```
          PRIOR TO SEARCHING THE BIBLIOGRAPHIC DATABASES ON QUESTEL, THE
          DARC EURECAS FILE WAS SEARCHED FOR THE CHEMICAL STRUCTURE OF
          MINOXIDIL. THE CAS REGISTRY NUMBERS OF THE COMPOUNDS RETRIEVED IN
          THE SEARCH WERE STORED IN A FILE NAMED ESSMINOX


   Selected file: CAS

   CA SEARCH : VOL 66/113-10 (1990-09-08)
   Copyright 1990 by the American Chemical Society

   Search statement  1

?*DARC ESSMINOX AND P/DT

   ** SS 1: Results 114

   Search statement  2

?..MEM /XPN LG 9

   Total number of terms extracted: 114
   Number of terms added to MEM: 114
   First term introduced for this extraction: 1

   Search statement  2

?..MEM /XPR

Total number of terms extracted: 114
   Number of terms added to MEM: 111
   First term introduced for this extraction: 115

   Search statement  2

?..FI WPIL

   Selected file: WPIL

   Last DERWENT week available:
   - basics: 9027; equivalents: 9027
   - plasdoc: 9014; chemical codes: 8947

   Search statement  1

?*MEM 1-114 /XPN

   ** SS 1: Results 102

   Search statement  2

?*MEM 115-226 /XPR

   ** SS 2: Results 106
```

**Search 3.6:** (cont.)

```
   Search statement   3

?1 OR 2

  ** SS 3: Results 109

?..LI 1

  1/109 - (C) Derwent
  AN  - 90-139425 [18]
  XA  - C90-061247
  TI  - Promotion or acceleration of wound heating - by treatment with
        minoxidil, effective for promoting migration of epithelial cells in
        wound
  DC  - B03 D12 E13
  PA  - (UPJO ) UPJOHN CO
        (USSH ) DEPT OF HEALTH & HUMAN S
  PN  - ***US4912111*** A 900327 DW9018
        WO9006117 A 900614 DW9027
  DS  - AT BE CH DE ES FR GB IT LU NL SE
  DN  - AU DK FI HU JP KR NO SU
  PR  - ***88US-281129*** 881207


   Search statement   4

?..FI WPI SV


  Selected file: WPI

  Last DERWENT week available:
  - basics: 8052; equivalents: 9026

  Search statement   4

?..EX


  ** SS 1: Results 4

  ** SS 2: Results 3

  1 OR  2

  ** SS 3: Results 4
```

## STN INTERNATIONAL

The STN computer in Columbus, Ohio, is the home of the CA FILE, the exclusive version the CA SEARCH database enhanced with abstracts, and of the CAOLD file with references to chemical compounds indexed in *Chemical Abstracts* prior to 1965. The MARPAT database, available only on STN, contains topological indexing for generic structures in patents in the CA File. Only STN has CAS Registry Numbers in CLAIMS records indexed since 1980. STN has mounted the CLAIMS databases with their entire time range in a single file and has combined the *CLAIMS Thesaurus and Compound Registry* with the US *Manual of Classification* in a single IFIREF file. The STN computer in Karlsruhe, Germany, has the PATDPA German patents database and PATGRAPH, the corresponding graphics file. On STN, the registry numbers of chemical substances retrieved from the Registry file through both topological and text searches are automatically placed in crossfile searchable answer sets. The Chemical Abstracts Service has provided many of the databases on STN with registry numbers that were not present in the records supplied by the database producers, so that crossfile searching with registry numbers can be done in these databases only on STN and not on other host systems. CAS has determined corresponding CAS registry numbers for most of the compounds in the CLAIMS Compound Registry and posted them in the IFICDB and IFIUDB files with the qualifier URN. These converted registry numbers are automatically retrieved when a list of registry numbers is crossed over from the Registry file. Terms can be extracted from records in STN databases with the SELECT command and the list of terms can be edited to change their qualifiers before they are searched in another database.

Search 3.7 illustrates a search of the CLAIMS UNITERM file on STN for toothpaste formulations containing sodium pyrophosphate. CAS Registry Numbers are searchable directly in the CLAIMS file; to find the registry numbers for all forms of sodium pyrophosphate, the REGISTRY file is searched using the CAS index name, 'diphosphoric acid, sodium salt', retrieving 221 registry numbers. CLAIMS compound numbers are assigned in the UNITERM and COMPREHENSIVE databases to common chemical substances; to find the registry numbers for sodium pyrophosphate salts, the IFIREF file is searched with the common name, retrieving ten UNITERM numbers, which are extracted under the numbers E1-E10 with the SELECT command. Transferring to the IFIUDB file, the ten Uniterm numbers are searched, yielding 2,851 patents in L3. The registry numbers in L1 are searched, yielding 2,728 patents, which are combined in L5 with those retrieved through the UNITERM numbers to give 2,890 patent records. Of these, ninety-eight also contain UNITERM number 01577, IFI's controlled index term for dentifrices.

## Search 3.7: Crossfile searching on STN International

```
    FILE 'REGISTRY' ENTERED AT 15:52:03 ON 12 SEP 90
    USE IS SUBJECT TO THE TERMS OF YOUR CUSTOMER AGREEMENT
    COPYRIGHT (C) 1990 AMERICAN CHEMICAL SOCIETY

    STRUCTURE FILE UPDATES: HIGHEST RN 129260-79-3
    DICTIONARY FILE UPDATES: 8 SEP 90 (900908/ED) HIGHEST RN 129238-77-3

    =>S DI(W)PHOSPHORIC(L)SODIUM
            4811084   DI
              36622   PHOSPHORIC
             157305   SODIUM
    L1          221   DI(W)PHOSPHORIC(L)SODIUM

    =>FILE IFIREF

    FILE 'IFIREF' ENTERED AT 15:54:14 ON 12 SEP 90
    COPYRIGHT (C) 1990 IFI/PLENUM DATA CORPORATION

    FILE COVERS CURRENT DATA.  LAST UPDATE: MAY, 1990.

    =>S SODIUM(W)PYROPHOSPHATE
              785   SODIUM
               79   PYROPHOSPHATE
    L2         10   SODIUM(W)PYROPHOSPHATE

    =>SELECT L2 1-10 UN
    E1 THROUGH E10 ASSIGNED

    =>FILE IFIUDB
```

**Search 3.7:** (cont.)

```
FILE 'IFIUDB' ENTERED AT 15:56:22 ON 12 SEP 90
COPYRIGHT (C) 1990 IFI/PLENUM DATA CORPORATION

FILE COVERS 1950 TO DATE.
FILE LAST UPDATED: 11 SEP 90 (900911/ED) PATENT PUBLICATION 08/28/90
HIGHEST NO.: 4953230 INDEXING CURRENT THROUGH 31 JUL 1990 (900911/UP)

=>S E1-10
            2542   51762/UN
             292   59629/UN
             138   64509/UN
              83   66603/UN
              10   67120/UN
               6   67121/UN
               1   67357/UN
               2   68005/UN
               3   70014/UN
               4   71455/UN
L3          2851   (51762/UN OR 59629/UN OR 64509/UN OR 66603/UN OR 67120/UN
                   OR 67121/UN OR 67357/UN OR 68005/UN OR 70014/UN OR 71455/UN)

=>S L1
L4          2728   L1

=>S L3 OR L4
L5          2890   L3 OR L4

=>S L5 AND 01577/UN
            1634   01577/UN
L6            98   L5 AND 01577/UN?

=>DISPLAY L6 1 BIB

L6  ANSWER 1 OF 98

AN   2013357  IFIPAT;IFIUDB;IFICDB
TI   Peroxide gel dentifrice compositions; STABILITY
IN   Drucker Jacob
PA   Carter-Wallace Inc (14520)
PI   US  4895721  900123
AI   US  88-146902  880122
FI   US  4895721  900123
DT   UTILITY
FS   CHEMICAL
```

Even though most of the UNITERM compound numbers had been converted to CAS Registry Numbers, the UNITERM numbers retrieved 162 patents that were not retrieved by registry numbers. Searching the CLAIMS database directly for CAS Registry Numbers added thirty-nine patents that had not been assigned a compound registry number by IFI's indexers.

# DIALOG

DIALOG carries the WORLD PATENTS INDEX, INPADOC, CLAIMS and CHINESE PATENTS AB-STRACTS databases along with a great many patent-containing technical databases. DIALOG'S CLAIMS databases are fragmented into several files that may be searched separately and a merged file covering all but the unedited patents from the latest month, which must always be searched in File 125. Only DIALOG has the CLAIMS CITATION databases. DIALOG's OneSearch feature allows the searcher to combine the CLAIMS bibliographic files and REEXAMINED AND REASSIGNED US Patents file in a single search, to search the split WPI/L files together, or to combine any other group of patents databases in a single search. It is possible to transfer back and forth between databases with the FILE command without erasing the previous search strategy. A search in WPI can be done using either Derwent's format (with the exception of Japanese patent numbers) or DIALOG's. Most bibliographic patent data fields can be converted to search terms using the MAP command to create saved searches to be executed in other databases. Priority, application and publication numbers MAP in DIALOG format. Since the DIALOG format in the WPI files is derived from Derwent's modified numbers, some patents cannot be transferred successfully from other files. DIALOG has modified the MAP protocol for Japanese patent numbers so that all possible versions of the number are searched, often retrieving entirely unrelated patents as a false drop. Because DIALOG's format for application and priority numbers does not integrate the year of filing as Derwent's format does, searches for patents based on United States applications (which are assigned in series of 100,000, that re-start every ten years or so) retrieve patents from every series in the database, another source of unrelated false drop.

## Search 3.8: Crossfile searching on DIALOG

```
System:OS  - DIALOG OneSearch

     File 351:World Patents Index, Latest 1981+_
             DW=9026, UA=9013, UM=8946

     File 350:WORLD PATENTS INDEX 1963-1980
             EQUIVALENTS THRU DW=9022

        Set   Items  Description
        ---   -----  -----------
?S SECURITIES OR INVEST? OR STOCK? ? OR BOND? ?
              89    SECURITIES
           14581    INVEST?
           18702    STOCK? ?
           90008    BOND? ?
        S1 122991   SECURITIES OR INVEST? OR STOCK? ? OR BOND? ?
?S S1 (S) (ACCOUNT? ? OR TRANSACTION? ?)
          122991    S1
           10989    ACCOUNT? ?
            1338    TRANSACTION? ?
        S2    112   S1 (S) (ACCOUNT? ? OR TRANSACTION? ?)
?S S2 AND DC=R27 AND PC=US
             112    S2
           78061    DC=R27
         1253177    PC=US
        S3     12   S2 AND DC=R27 AND PC=US
?MAPPN TEMP

3 select statement(s)
serial#TB002

?BEGIN CLAIMS

System:OS  - DIALOG OneSearch

     File 125:CLAIMS/US PATENT ABSTRACTS WEEKLY - Jul 03 1990 to Aug 21 1990
*** Patent Numbers: 4937879 - 4951315 ****
```

**Search 3.8:** (cont.)

```
      File 340:CLAIMS/U.S. PATENTS ABSTRACTS_
Chemical patents from 1950 - Jun/90,
Electrical and Mechanical patents 1963 - Jun/90
Patent number: 2492948-4937878

*** This file has been reloaded as of November 1989 ***

      File 123:CLAIMS/Reassignment & Reexamination
               REASSIGN 1980-06/90
REEXAM - 1981 - 04/90
EXPIRE - 09/85 - 04/90

This file has been reloaded as of August 1989.

*** AU= (Author Field) has been removed from this file ***

      Set   Items   Description
      ---   -----   -----------
?EXECUTE
Executing TB002
                      ******
             12   PN=CH 670716 + PN=DE 3072077 + PN=DE 3539545 + PN=DK
                  8004925 + PN=EP 29569 + PN=GB 2180380 + PN=US 3941985 +
                  PN=US 4316257 + PN=US 4346442 + PN=US 4376978 + PN=US
                  4597046 + PN=US 4642768 + PN=US 4674044 + PN=US 4694397 +
                  PN=US 4722055
                      ******
              4   PN=US 4742457 + PN=US 4751640 + PN=US 4774663 + PN=US
                  4910676
             15   S1:S2
      S1     15   Serial: TB002
?TYPE 1/9/1


1/9/1 (Item 1 from file: 340)
2029464 3016174
E/ Processing system for managing bi-media investments
Inventors: Alldredge Robert L (US)
Assignee: Unassigned Or Assigned To Individual Assignee Codes: 68000
Document Type: UTILITY
                    Applic    Applic    Patent     Issue
                    Number    Date      Number     Date
                    --------  ------    ----------  ------
Patent:             US 31590  870330  US 4910676   900320
Priority Applic: US 31590  870330
Claim:
        D R A W I N G
```

1.  A  system  for supervising and processing buy- and sellinvestment transactions  of bi-media investments in a plurality of investment accounts, wherein  a  bi-media  investment  comprises both a first-media-investment of revenue  generating character having a predetermined qualified value for bi-media  representation,  and  a  second-media-investment of a negotiable draft character, issued by and drawn against a financial institution or associated entity  other  than  the investor, the present and future value of which said system  creates,  manages,  and  ensures  to  be  fully supported against the qualified  value  of  the  first-media-investment, said system comprising: a first investment account file containing current information identifying bi-media  investments  of  a  first account holder; transaction entry means for requesting  buy-and  sell-investment  transactions  to  said first investment account  file;  investment-transaction-generating  means  responsive  to the transaction entry means for initiating a requested investment transaction of a  first-media-investment  in said first investment account file; qualified-

**Search 3.8:** (cont.)

```
investment-identification  means  responsive to said transaction entry means
for  characterizing  the requested firstmedia-investment as to predetermined
qualified  value;  second-media-investment-generating  means responsive to a
determination  by  the  qualified-investment-identification  means  of  said
predetermined  qualified  value  of  the requested firstmedia-investment for
initiating   an  investment  transaction  of  a  second-media-investment  of
negotiable   draft   character,   issued  by  and  drawn  against  a financial
institution  or  associated  entity other than the investor, the present and
further value of which said system creates, manages, and ensures to be fully
supported  against  the  qualified  value of the first media investment, of a
value corresponding to the predetermined qualified value; means undating the
investment   account file in response to the qualified-investment-identificat
ion means, the investmenttransaction-generating means, and the second-media-
investmentgenerating  means  to  show  the  status of the resulting bi-media
investment.
```

Search 3.8 illustrates a search for United States patents that claim computerized systems for managing securities accounts. The search was begun in the combined WPI and WPIL files, where the Derwent Classification code R27, applied to patents dealing with digital computing, is combined with free-text terms for securities accounts. Twelve patent families are retrieved. The patent numbers are mapped with the MAPPN command into a saved strategy which is executed in the combined CLAIMS BIBLIO/ABSTRACTS files, where the actual main claim can be displayed. The fifteen records retrieved in the combined CLAIMS files may include divisional patents present in the same WPI family or records of re-examination certificates or reassignments. To be complete, the search should include a strategy for searching the CLAIMS files directly to find any other patents that were missed by the WPI strategy or published before 1974.

## REFERENCES

1.    John W. Lotz. Patents literature. In *Encyclopedia of Chemical Technology*, vol. 16. 3rd. ed. New York: Wiley, 1981, pp. 889-945; reprinted in M. Grayson, ed. *Information Retrieval in Chemistry and Chemical Patent Law*. New York: Wiley, 1983, pp. 60-116.

## ACKNOWLEDGEMENTS

The author wishes to express thanks to STN International, Questel Inc., DIALOG Search Service, and Maxwell Online Inc. for providing computer access, and to the producers of the databases discussed in this chapter for permitting the publication of exemplary records.

# 4 Chemistry

*Joyce Garnett and Veronica Calderhead*

## INTRODUCTION

Chemistry is the physical science that is concerned with the composition, structure, properties and transformations of matter at the atomic and molecular levels, and with the utilization of natural substances and the creation of artificial ones. Chemistry is both a pure science and an applied science. Many of the concepts of physics and the methods of mathematics are basic to chemistry, while chemistry in turn is of fundamental importance to many other disciplines, including biology, geology, metallurgy, medicine and pharmacology. Chemistry plays a major role in the petroleum, polymer and pharmaceutical industries.

Chemistry has traditionally been divided into four broad areas of specialization, dating from early in its history: analytical chemistry, dealing with the identification of substances and the quantitative measurement of their compositions; inorganic chemistry, concerned with the compounds of elements other than carbon; organic chemistry, which deals with the compounds of carbon; and physical chemistry, which treats the physical laws and energetics governing chemical reactions. During the twentieth century new areas of specialization have emerged, including polymer, environmental and medical chemistry. Understanding the organization and language of chemistry is essential for effective retrieval. Selected guides to the literature that provide background reading on the subject and its information resources are listed at the end of this chapter as Further Reading.

In keeping with the theme of this book, the chapter is directed at the experienced searcher who is new to the field of chemistry. The organization and interdisciplinary scope of chemistry are reflected in the range and choice of databases available for searching a chemical topic. In common with the majority of subject areas, the online searcher in chemistry cannot rely solely on any one single database or vendor. This chapter focuses on the databases and strategies of particular relevance to online searching in chemistry. Databases where the primary subject is biology, engineering or medicine will have content of interest to chemists, but are not examined in depth because of the coverage in other chapters. Similarly, while both patent and citation searching are essential to chemistry, these forms are not covered because of the comprehensive treatment in separate chapters devoted to them.

Chemistry and its literature present unique challenges not found in other fields. Among these are variances in nomenclature, graphic or structural presentations, and combinations of alphanumerics and punctuation in a single term. The storage, retrieval and transmission of these special formulations require software and techniques not used in online searching outside chemistry. To balance these specialized approaches are the familiar access methods of author, title and keyword common to all subjects. Following this introduction, the chapter covers:

- systems and databases (vendor systems, types of databases, portable databases);
- pre-search preparation (selection of databases, front-end software, documentation);
- retrieval methods (nomenclature, structure, bibliographic, referral, reaction and toxicology searches);
- primary chemistry databases; and
- references and further reading.

To unify examples across databases and systems with various search strategies, the same compound was used frequently - although not exclusively. Dinitrochlorobenzene, or to give its Chemical Abstracts name, 1-chloro-2,4-dinitro-benzene, is a good choice to demonstrate nomenclature input being a compound neither overly simple nor too complex.

## SYSTEMS AND DATABASES

### Vendor systems

Chemistry databases are available from all major vendor systems, each of which has its particular emphases and strengths. A selection of host systems that offer at least CHEMICAL ABSTRACTS is given in alphabetical order:

**BRS** - BRS Information Technologies, a division of Maxwell Online Inc., has strengths in the areas of health and life sciences, including pharmacology, medicine and toxicology.

**CAN/OLE** - Canadian-based system available from the Canada Institute for Scientific and Technical Information (CISTI). Emphasis is placed on scientific databases, as well as some unique files in the environmental and resource technology areas.

**CIS** - Chemical Information Systems is an American-based system with twenty or more chemistry-related databases including a structure and nomenclature file, and an excellent chemical properties numeric file.

**Data-Star** - European-based system that excels in areas of prime concern to the European Community, with the chemical industry well covered; pharmaceutical databases are this system's strong suit.

**DIALOG** - United States-based system offering close to four hundred databases, with those covering chemistry and the chemical industry being well-represented.

**ESA-IRS** - the European Space Agency-Information Retrieval Service based in Italy offers about one hundred databases.

**NLM** - the National Library of Medicine's chemistry files have a medical orientation, including toxicology, medical research, clinical medicine and pharmacological information. Although NLM does not offer CHEMICAL ABSTRACTS, those databases available are sufficiently significant to chemistry to warrant its inclusion.

**ORBIT** - ORBIT Search Service, a division of Maxwell Online Inc., provides access to approximately one hundred databases in science and technology, including many covering chemistry and patents.

**Questel** - European-based system that developed DARC, software designed for chemical structure searching (now adopted by DIALOG); also has a strong pharmaceutical content.

**STN** - Vendor system owned by Chemical Abstracts Service which provides features for CHEMICAL ABSTRACTS not available on other systems including abstracts and locator fields, and offers numerous related scientific databases. Numeric files are well represented on STN. STN offers an after-hours discount to academic institutions.

## Types of databases

Databases fall into five broad categories: bibliographic, referral, numeric, factual and full-text. These categories are not mutually exclusive; for example, a bibliographic file can lead to factual data in a source document, and a referral database may be full-text in nature.

### Bibliographic databases

The bibliographic database is the type of file most familiar to the librarian/information scientist. It provides a surrogate record of the parent document with enough information to allow the end-user to judge the pertinency of the work to his/her own research and to locate the complete document if needed.

Chemistry is extremely well covered by bibliographic databases (a selective list can be found in Table 4.1). Indeed, one of the most heavily used databases world-wide is CHEMICAL ABSTRACTS. The vast majority of indexing/abstracting publications for chemistry are available online. Chemistry is such a large discipline that its pure and its applied areas are covered by different vendor systems. STN has the most comprehensive coverage but no one single system offers all chemistry databases. A thorough search may require knowledge of three, sometimes four different command languages.

Online bibliographic records will sometimes contain an abstract. At present STN is the only vendor providing abstracts for CHEMICAL ABSTRACTS. English currently accounts for about eighty per cent of documents abstracted by the Chemical Abstracts Service. Abstracts can overcome language barriers. The CHEMICAL ABSTRACTS abstract (when available) is always provided in English, and many other chemical literature databases also provide abstracts; for example, CHEMICAL ENGINEERING AND BIOTECHNOLOGY ABSTRACTS and ANALYTICAL ABSTRACTS. Records on some databases, such as CHEMICAL ABSTRACTS (STN) and CHEMLINE (NLM) include a field indicating other databases offered by the vendor with information relating to that compound or subject.

### Referral databases

Referral databases are the online equivalents of reference works. As seen from Table 4.2, chemistry referral databases includes directories, handbooks and dictionaries. Referral sources particular to chemistry include Questel's JANSSEN database, which is an electronic version of the *Janssen Chimica Catalog*, made more flexible by being online.

**Table 4.1:  Selected bibliographic databases**

| Database | Vendor |
|---|---|
| ANALYTICAL ABSTRACTS | Data-Star, DIALOG, ORBIT |
| BIOSIS PREVIEWS | BRS, CAN/OLE, Data-Star, DIALOG, STN |
| BIOTECHNOLOGY ABSTRACTS | DIALOG, ORBIT |
| CHEMICAL ABSTRACTS | BRS, CAN/OLE, Data-Star, DIALOG, ORBIT, Questel, STN |
| CHEMICAL BUSINESS NEWSBASE | Data-Star, DIALOG |
| CHEMICAL ENGINEERING AND BIOTECHNOLOGY ABSTRACTS | Data-Star, DIALOG, ESA-IRS, ORBIT |
| CHEMICAL EXPOSURE | DIALOG |
| CHEMICAL INDUSTRY NOTES | DIALOG, ORBIT, STN |
| CHEMICAL REGULATIONS AND GUIDELINES SYSTEM | DIALOG |
| CHEMICAL SAFETY NEWSBASE | Data-Star, DIALOG, ESA-IRS, ORBIT, STN |
| CLAIMS | DIALOG, ORBIT, STN |
| COMPENDEX | BRS, CAN/OLE, Data-Star, DIALOG, ORBIT, STN |
| CURRENT BIOTECHNOLOGY ABSTRACTS | CAN/OLE, Data-Star, DIALOG, ESA-IRS |
| CURRENT CONTENTS SEARCH | BRS, DIALOG |
| ENGINEERED MATERIALS ABSTRACTS | DIALOG, ESA-IRS, ORBIT, STN |
| INPADOC | DIALOG, ORBIT, STN |
| INSPEC | BRS, CAN/OLE, Data-Star, DIALOG, ESA-IRS, ORBIT, STN |
| JAPAN TECHNOLOGY | DIALOG, ORBIT |
| KKF (Kunstoffe Kautschuk Fasern) | STN |
| MEDLINE | BRS, Data-Star, DIALOG, NLM, Questel, STN |
| METADEX | CAN/OLE, Data-Star, DIALOG, ESA-IRS, ORBIT, STN |
| NMRLIT (Nuclear Magnetic Resonance Literature Search System) | CIS |
| NORIANE | Questel |
| NTIS | BRS, CAN/OLE, Data-Star, DIALOG, ESA-IRS, ORBIT, STN |
| PASCAL | DIALOG, ESA-IRS, Questel |
| PATDPA | BRS |
| PHARSEARCH | Questel |
| PLASTICS RUBBER FIBRES DATABASE | STN |
| POLYMER ONLINE (Encyclopedia of Polymer Science and Engineering) | BRS, DIALOG |
| RINGDOC | DIALOG, ORBIT |
| SCISEARCH | Data-Star, DIALOG, ORBIT |

**Table 4.1:** (cont.)

| Database | Vendor |
|---|---|
| SOLID STATE AND SUPER-<br>CONDUCTIVITY ABSTRACTS | BRS, ESA-IRS |
| TOXLINE | BRS, DIALOG, ORBIT |
| WORLD PATENTS INDEX | DIALOG, ORBIT, Questel |

Data-Star and DIALOG both provide the EUROPEAN DIRECTORY OF AGROCHEMICAL PRODUCTS which corresponds to the print version by the same name. The Royal Society of Chemistry is the producer of the directory and its online service; it has also made the directory available on CD-ROM. CHEMLIST is available only on STN. Unlike those databases previously mentioned, CHEMLIST corresponds to several print sources, its primary function being to bring together sources dealing with United States toxic substance control legislation.

**Table 4.2: Selected referral databases**

| Database | Vendor |
|---|---|
| AGROCHEMICALS HANDBOOK | Data-Star, DIALOG |
| BIOQUIP (Biotechnology<br>Equipment Suppliers Data Bank) | STN |
| CASSI (Chemical Abstracts<br>Service Source Index) | ORBIT |
| CHEMICAL PLANT DATABASE | Data-Star, DIALOG |
| CHEMLIST | STN |
| CHEMQUEST | ORBIT |
| CUADRA DIRECTORY OF DATABASES | Data-Star, ORBIT, Questel |
| DEQUIP (DECHEMA Equipment<br>Suppliers Database) | STN |
| DERES (DECHEMA Databank on<br>Research Institutes) | STN |
| DETEQ (DECHEMA Environmental<br>Technology Equipment Databank) | STN |
| EUROPEAN DIRECTORY OF<br>AGROCHEMICAL PRODUCTS | Data-Star, DIALOG |
| FINE CHEMICALS DATABASE | DIALOG |
| HEILBRON | DIALOG |
| INTERNATIONAL PATENT<br>CLASSIFICATION | Questel |
| JANSSEN | Questel |
| THE MERCK INDEX | BRS, CIS, DIALOG, Questel |
| NUMERIGUIDE | STN |
| SUSPECT CHEMICALS SOURCEBOOK | CIS |
| TSCA CHEMICAL SUBSTANCES<br>INVENTORY | DIALOG, ORBIT |

*Numeric databases*

The numeric database is becoming increasingly important; consequently the number of these databases is increasing. Perhaps the easiest way of distinguishing this kind of file from the factual is by understanding who will use the database. The numeric database is for end-user access only. The function of these databases is the calculation and manipulation of compiled data, to be done by the practising chemist. The databases are developed by the scientific community; data are culled from articles and other documents, then entered into the ever growing pool of data; data contributions are then compiled and made available to the community at large.

Numeric databases are sometimes used in conjunction with other software packages for the purpose of calculation. For example, STN's TPROPS is a calculation package designed to perform with its DIPPR DATA COMPILATION database, created by the American Institute of Chemical Engineers. TPROPS calculates property information over a temperature range by implementing regression equations. STN also has developed DIST software to calculate interatomic distances and angles of molecular structures based on the data in its INORGANIC CRYSTAL STRUCTURE DATABASE (ICSD). These packages calculate by using set numbers retrieved from the online interactive search and are invoked from within the numeric databases by the special command RUN.

CIS, CAN/SND (like CAN/OLE, available from CISTI) and STN International are the vendors most actively involved in the development of numeric databases. The databases are most often produced by laboratories in large government or academic institutions which have traditionally been involved in the accumulation of data sets for in-house use. The commercial viability of these databases has now encouraged their marketing to external customers world-wide. These databases are often expensive and require a first-hand knowledge of the research in question in order to make proper and effective use of them. STN offers NUMERIGUIDE, the NUMERIC PROPERTY THESAURUS AND DATA DIRECTORY, as a key to all its numeric files. Table 4.3 provides a selective list of numeric databases and their vendors.

**Table 4.3: Selected numeric databases**

| Database | Vendor |
| --- | --- |
| BROOKHAVEN PROTEIN DATA BANK (formerly CRYSTPRO) | CAN/SND |
| CAMBRIDGE STRUCTURAL DATABASE | CAN/SND |
| CNMR (Carbon-12 Nuclear Magnetic Resonance Search System) | CIS |
| CRYSTMET (NRC Metals Crystallographic Data File) | CAN/SND |
| DIPPR DATA COMPILATION (Design Institute for Physical Property Data) | STN |
| F*A*C*T (Facility for the Analysis of Chemical Thermodynamics) | CAN/SND |
| INORGANIC CRYSTAL STRUCTURE DATABASE | CAN/SND (CRYSTIN), STN (ICSD) |
| IRSS (Infrared Search System) | CIS |
| JANAF THERMODYNAMICAL TABLES | STN |
| MSSS (Mass Spectral Search System) | CIS |

**Table 4.3:** (cont.)

| Database | Vendor |
|---|---|
| NBS CRYSTAL DATA IDENTIFICATION FILE | CAN/SND (CRYSTDAT) |
| NBSFLUIDS | STN |
| PLASPEC | STN |
| SPIR (Search Program for Infrared Spectra) | CAN/SND |
| THERMO | CIS, STN |
| TRC THERMO | STN |

*Factual databases*

Factual databases contain data or information that has been scrutinized and evaluated. For example, *Beilsteins Handbuch der Organischen Chemie/Beilstein Handbook of Organic Chemistry* and *Gmelin Handbuch der Anorganischen Chemie* are comprehensive reference works that contain data that have been evaluated by panels of experts and then organized by subject. The corresponding online files are BEILSTEIN ONLINE and GFI (GMELIN FORMULA INDEX). Viewing them as factual does not preclude their bibliographic nor numeric functions, nor does it exclude sections of these works being available in full-text version; factual refers to their primary function only. See Table 4.4 for the availability of the online files.

**Table 4.4:  Selected factual databases**

| Database | Vendor |
|---|---|
| BEILSTEIN ONLINE | DIALOG, ORBIT, STN |
| GMELIN FORMULA INDEX | STN |

*Full-text databases*

Full-text databases provide the text of a document in its complete, or near complete form (tables, graphs and graphics are still the exception rather than the rule). Full-text chemistry databases include those that cover journal articles and other primary literature (the source material for bibliographic files). Full-text databases also include many from the other categories described above - referral, numeric and factual. HEILBRON, the chemical properties database, is an example that is full-text in form but factual in function. Both the KIRK-OTHMER ENCYCLOPEDIA OF CHEMICAL TECHNOLOGY and THE MERCK INDEX are encyclopedic in nature and provide full-text retrieval. Many directories are full-text, for example the CUADRA DIRECTORY OF DATABASES is a full-text referral database. Table 4.5 lists some of the more important chemistry full-text databases.

**Table 4.5: Selected full-text databases**

| Database | Vendor |
|---|---|
| AGROCHEMICALS HANDBOOK | Data-Star, DIALOG |
| CEH ON-LINE (Chemical Economics Handbook) | DIALOG, ORBIT |
| CHEMICAL HAZARDS RESPONSE INFORMATION SYSTEM (CHRIS) | CIS |
| CJACS (Chemical Journals of the American Chemical Society) | STN |
| CJAOAC (Chemical Journals of the Association of Official Analytical Chemists) | STN |
| CJELSEVIER (Chemical Journals of Elsevier Science Publishers b.v.) | STN |
| CJRSC (Chemical Journals of the Royal Society of Chemistry) | STN |
| CJVCH (Chemical Journals of VCH) | STN |
| CJWILEY (Chemical Journals of John Wiley & Sons, Inc.) | STN |
| CUADRA DIRECTORY OF DATABASES | Data-Star, ORBIT, Questel |
| EUROPEAN CHEMICAL NEWS | Data-Star |
| HEILBRON | DIALOG |
| KIRK-OTHMER ENCYCLOPEDIA OF CHEMICAL TECHNOLOGY | BRS, Data-Star, DIALOG |
| THE MERCK INDEX | BRS, CIS, DIALOG, Questel |
| POLYMER ONLINE (Encyclopedia of Polymer Science and Engineering) | BRS, DIALOG |

STN International has taken the lead in the area of full-text chemistry journals with CJACS, CJAOAC, CJELSEVIER, CJRSC, CJVCH, CJWILEY, which as the mnemonic file names indicate are the chemistry titles published by American Chemical Society, Association of Official Analytical Chemists, Elsevier, Royal Society of Chemistry, VCH and Wiley respectively. These files contain an impressive number of titles from the publishers' lists in full-text version. Again photographs, graphs, graphics and tables are not yet available for search, display or retrieval. Some of the titles are available online with full-text going back to the early 1980s. Search 4.1 gives an abbreviated full-text example of an article retrieved from CJACS, showing a portion of the text (TX) and the first three references (RE).

**Search 4.1: Sample full-text display from STN's CJACS file**

```
=> file cjacs

FILE 'CJACS' ENTERED AT 17:09:00 ON 30 OCT 91
COPYRIGHT (C) 1991 AMERICAN CHEMICAL SOCIETY

FILE COVERS 1982 - 19 OCT 91 (911019/ED)
OTHER FULL TEXT FILES AVAILABLE: CJAOAC, CJELSEVIER, CJRSC, CJVCH,
AND CJWILEY
```

**Search 4.1:** (cont.)

```
=>  s  dinitrochlorobenzenes/bi
L1      1 DINITROCHLOROBENZENES/BI

=>  d l1 ti

L1 ANSWER 1 of 1
TI  Mechanism of Reaction of Hydroxide Ion with
      ***Dinitrochlorobenzenes***

=>  d l1 tx 1

L1 ANSWER 1 of 1

TX  TX(1) of 50. The mechanism of aromatic nucleophilic substitution of
***dinitrochlorobenzenes***  (1),  for example,  in polar, hydroxylic,
solvents has been assumed to involve rate-limiting formation of a.sigma.
or Meisenheimer complex (2), as in Scheme I .Scheme. for reaction of OH -
with 2,4- or 2,6-dinitrochlorobenzene (2,4- and 2,6-DNCB). 2 .Footnote.
Loss  of  Cl  -  from  2  should  be  fast  in  polar  solvents. Unproductive
Meisenheimer  complexes  form  in  the  course  of  some  reactions.

...

TX(50) of 50. Acknowledgment. We are grateful to a reviewer for thoughtful
comments. Support  by  the  National  Science  Foundation  (Organic  Chemical
Dynamics and International Program) and the donors of the Petroleum Research
Fund,  administered  by  the  American  Chemical  Society,  is  gratefully
acknowledged. Awards of a NATO grant to F.O. and a CNPq grant to C.Z. are
gratefully  acknowledged.


=>  d l1 re 1

L1 ANSWER 1 of 1

RE  RE(1) of 27. 1. Present address: (a) Department of Chemistry, Rutgers
SUNJ, Piscataway, NJ 08855. (b) Department of Physical Chemistry, Facultad
de  Ciencias  Quimicas,  Universidad  Complutense, 28040  Madrid,  Spain.  (c)
Departamento  de  Quimica,  Federal  University  of  Santa  Catarina,  88049
Florianopolis,  SC,  Brasil.

RE(2) of 27. 2. (a) Bunnett, J. F. Q. Rev., Chem. Soc. 1958, 12, 1. (b) Sauer,
J.; Huisgen, R. Angew. Chem. 1960, 72, 294. (c) Buncel, E.; Norris, A. R.;
Russell, K. E. Q. Rev., Chem. Soc. 1968, 22, 123. (d) Miller, J. Aromatic
Nucleophilic Substitution; Elsevier: New York, 1968. (e) Bernasconi, C. F.
Chimia 1980, 34, 1.

RE(3) of 27. 3. (a) Russell, G. A.; Janzen, G. E. J. Am. Chem. Soc. 1962,
84, 4153. (b) Shein, S. M.; Brykohovetskaya, L. V.; Pishchugin, F. V.;
Starichenko, V. F.; Panfilov, V. N.;Voevodski, V. V. Zh. Strukt. Khim. 1970,
11, 243. (c) Blumenfeld, L. A.; Brykohovetskaya, L. V.; Formin, G. V.; Shein,
S. M. Zh. Fiz. Khim.1970, 44, 931. (d) Ivanova, T. M.; Shein, S. M. Zh. Org.
Khim. 1986,16, 1221. (e) Abe, T.; Ikegami, Y. Bull Chem. Soc. Jpn. 1976,
49,3227; 1978, 51, 5, 196. (f) Mariani, C.; Modena, G.; Pizzo, G. P.;
Scorrano, G.; Kistenbrugger, L. J. Chem. Soc., Perkin Trans. 2 1979, 1187.

...
```

## Portable databases

Portable databases are proliferating in chemistry as in other subject areas. CD-ROM is the format showing the greatest activity, but diskette databases still have a role to play, particularly for the individual researcher. CD-ROM offers the opportunity for training and for trying alternative strategies without the time and financial pressures of dialup online searching.

Table 4.6 presents a selective listing of portable databases. (For additional titles, consult the Directory of Portable Databases [1] or the online file, CUADRA DIRECTORY OF DATABASES.) The majority listed are bibliographic in nature, capturing a limited period or subset of the corresponding online file. For example, Ei CHEMDISC covers the chemical engineering content of the COMPENDEX database from 1980 onwards. However, other types of databases are available. Several encyclopedias and handbooks are available full-text on CD-ROM, including the classic KIRK-OTHMER ENCYCLOPEDIA. The Institute for Scientific Information publishes two relevant citation indexes on CD-ROM - BIOTECHNOLOGY CITATION INDEX and CHEMISTRY CITATION INDEX. Spectral data is well represented in both CD-ROM and diskette formats. The portfolio of spectral data from Sadtler Research Laboratories is comprehensive, with advanced graphics and data analysis capabilities. As with other highly specialized, non-bibliographic databases, these spectral files are intended for and best utilized by the chemist.

BEILSTEIN ONLINE, one of the most challenging databases in chemistry, is now available in part in a CD-ROM product. BEILSTEIN CURRENT FACTS IN CHEMISTRY provides factual and structure searches for the data of approximately 300,000 compounds covered in the journal literature starting in 1990. The CD-ROM product provides links to the print *Beilstein Handbook* and to the BEILSTEIN ONLINE database through designated fields.

Despite the growing list of titles available in CD-ROM, the experienced chemistry searcher will not consider the field to be satisfactorily covered until CHEMICAL ABSTRACTS is available. Chemical Abstracts Service has only recently (Autumn of 1991) demonstrated an interest in creating a CD-ROM version of the CHEMICAL ABSTRACTS database, through a survey of its customers' potential interest in such a product. Given the size of the CHEMICAL ABSTRACTS database (ten million records for the last twenty-five years), it will be a challenge to the Chemical Abstracts Service to package the database in meaningful subsets.

**Table 4.6: Selected portable databases**

| Database | Type | Format |
|---|---|---|
| ADONIS | Bibliographic | CD-ROM |
| ANALYTICAL ABSTRACTS | Bibliographic | CD-ROM |
| BEILSTEIN CURRENT FACTS IN CHEMISTRY | Referral | CD-ROM |
| BIOTECHNOLOGY ABSTRACTS | Bibliographic | CD-ROM |
| BIOTECHNOLOGY CITATION INDEX | Bibliographic | CD-ROM |
| CD-CHROM | Bibliographic | CD-ROM |
| CHEMBANK | Referral | CD-ROM |
| CHEMISTRY CITATION INDEX | Bibliographic | CD-ROM |
| COMPENDEX | Bibliographic | CD-ROM |
| CURRENT CONTENTS ON DISKETTE | Bibliographic | Diskette |
| DIPPR DATA COMPILATION | Numeric | CD-ROM |
| Ei CHEMDISC | Bibliographic | CD-ROM |
| HEILBRON | Full-text | CD-ROM |

**Table 4.6:** (cont.)

| Database | Type | Format |
| --- | --- | --- |
| KIRK-OTHMER ENCYCLOPEDIA OF CHEMICAL TECHNOLOGY (3rd edition) | Full-text | CD-ROM |
| MASS SPECTROMETRY BULLETIN | Bibliographic | Diskette |
| METADEX COLLECTION | Bibliographic | CD-ROM |
| THE PESTICIDES DISC | Referral | CD-ROM |
| POLYMER ENCYCLOPEDIA | Full-text | CD-ROM |
| REGISTRY OF MASS SPECTRAL DATA | Numeric | CD-ROM |
| SADTLER INFRARED SPECTRAL LIBRARY | Numeric | Diskette |
| SADTLER $^{13}$C NMR LIBRARY | Numeric | Diskette |
| SADTLER UV/VISIBLE PEAK TABLE SEARCH LIBRARY | Numeric | Diskette |
| SADTLER SUB STRUCTURE SEARCH LIBRARY | Numeric | Diskette |
| SCIENCE CITATION INDEX | Bibliographic | CD-ROM |

## PRE-SEARCH PREPARATION

### Database selection

New databases are being developed constantly; some are the result of the parent index splitting into different parts, some are born as a result of new spurts in that area of research. Online databases reflect the trends in chemistry research. For example, during the mid-eighties there was a tremendous volume of polymer research being done resulting in many articles, conference papers and patents. Specific sections and chapters of the main databases in chemistry were dedicated to polymer research; databases were created covering polymer- related material.

As the number of online files grows it becomes increasingly difficult for the librarian/information scientist to know all appropriate databases. The *Directory of Online Databases* [2] or the online file, CUADRA DIRECTORY OF DATABASES, is an excellent tool to start any basic search; most online vendors including Data-Star, Questel and ORBIT now provide this online directory. The subject index of the July 1991 edition has two pages of chemical/chemistry-related database entries. An online search on the CUADRA DIREC-TORY using Data-Star retrieved ninety-four different database descriptions which have some level of toxicology relevance (see Search 4.2).

### Search 4.2: Selecting chemical toxicology databases using Data-Star's CUAD file

```
D-S - SEARCH MODE - ENTER QUERY
 1_: CHEMICAL$ AND TOXIC$

 RESULT    94

 2_: ..P TI/1-24
```

**Search 4.2:** (cont.)

```
    ...

    15
TI    TOXLINE; Aneuploidy; CIS Abstracts; Environmental Mutagen
      Information Center File;Environmental Teratology Information
      Center File; Epidemiology Information System; Hazardous Materials
      Technical Center; National Institute for Occupational Safety and
      Health;Pesticides Abstracts; Poisonous Plants Bibliography; Toxic
      Substances Control Act Test Submissions; Toxicity Bibliography;
      Toxicology Document and Data Depository; Toxicology/Epidemiology
      Research Projects; ANEUPL; CIS; CRISP; EMIC; EPIDEM; ETIC; HMTC;
      NIOSH; NIOSHTIC; NTIS; PESTAB.

    ...

    19
TI    CHEM-BANK; CHEMICAL HAZARDS RESPONSE INFORMATION SYSTEM; OIL AND
      HAZARDOUS MATERIALS-TECHNICAL ASSISTANCE DATA SYSTEM; REGISTRY OF
      TOXIC EFFECTS OF CHEMICAL SUBSTANCES; TSCA CHEMICAL SUBSTANCES
      INVENTORY; CHRIS; OHM-TADS; RTECS; TSCA INITIAL INVENTORY.

    20
TI    CCINFOdisc: SERIES A2; CESARS; CHEMINFO; INFOCHIM; PUBLICATIONS;
      REGISTRY OF TOXIC EFFECTS OF CHEMICAL SUBSTANCES; TRANSPORTATION
      OF DANGEROUS GOODS; VIDEOTEX INFORMATION PACKAGES; CCINFO Series
      A2; CHEM Data; RTECS.

    21
TI    PolTox: Pollution and Toxicology Abstracts on CD-ROM; Aneuploidy;
      Ecology Abstracts; Environmental Mutagen Information Center File;
      Environmental Teratology Information Center File; Epidemiology
      Information System; Food Science and Technology Abstracts;
      Hazardous Materials Technical Center; Health and Safety Science
      Abstracts; International Labour Office (CIS); National Institute
      for Occupational Safety and Health; Pesticides Abstracts;
      Poisonous Plants Bibliography; Pollution Abstracts; Toxic
      Substances Control Act Test submissions; Toxicity Bibliography;
      Toxicology Abstracts; Toxicology Document and Data Depository;
      Toxicology/Epidemiology Research Projects; TOXLINE; ANEUPL; CIS;
      Compact Cambridge: POLLUTION /TOXICOLOGY; CRISP; EMIC.

    ...
```

## Front end software

Pre-search preparation has come to mean more than selecting databases and preparing the search strategy. Nor is pre-search any longer synonymous with offline preparation. The advent of software for the purpose of uploading query input has made offline seem as much like online as possible but without the 'ticking metre' syndrome. All the major vendors which carry dictionary files for substance searching now have software available for purchase which will allow pre-search query input in the form of structure drawing, and in some cases, textual input.

*STN Express* (also used for Questel) and DIALOG's *Molkick* (available for Questel users as well), *ChemConnection* and *ChemTalk Plus* are all examples of software designed to execute more efficient structure searches. Each version has advantages and disadvantages that the other does not. The choice of software will depend on the system most often searched, whether or not structure searching is the only requirement of the software, and whether it can be used on more than one database.

## Vendor-specific documentation

Vendor-specific material includes the file data sheets provided by the vendors. These sheets are indispensable both before and during the search process. System manuals contain all the search term operators, truncation symbols and commands specific to the system. The expert searcher will not need to consult these manuals with every search but will rely on them for fine tuning in searches that require unique limiting functions. Generally, the online versions of the database indexes are more compact, comprehensive and up to date than the print versions.

## File-specific documentation

Besides vendor-specific information there is file-specific information, of particular importance when preparing for a search in the field of chemistry. Chemical Abstracts Service publishes a series of manuals, *Using CAS Online,* [3] on searching CHEMICAL ABSTRACTS and its associated nomenclature and structure files. Different volumes cover textual, nomenclature and structure searching. New search manuals are planned but not yet published as of late 1991. In addition to these manuals dealing specifically with the type of search being executed, manuals are also available for the specific files, each vendor system preparing its own manuals.

## Stand-alone documentation

Stand-alone material is reference material that is needed in preparing a strategy. Non-vendor thesauri and assorted handbooks may be required by the searcher to gain familiarity with vocabulary, analytical methods and control numbers such as a registry number. In chemistry, *The Merck Index,* the different CRC handbooks and chemical company catalogues are all possible reference sources. Many of these sources, including chemical catalogues, directories and thesauri, are themselves available online. Chemical industry directories are available online for both North America and Europe, with European coverage particularly strong in this area.

## RETRIEVAL METHODS

Retrieval methods will vary according to the category of database being searched, as well as the choice of host system being used. Retrieval methods will be discussed in the context of the database categories previously presented with examples from various host systems.

## Nomenclature searching

The rules governing the naming of organic or inorganic substances are complex and vary according to the agency presiding over their establishment. Librarians, students of chemistry and chemists themselves most often rely on reference books to acquaint themselves with the preferred term or registry number (a registry number being a unique numeric identifier assigned to a chemical substance). The sources most often consulted include: *The Merck Index*, Chemical Abstracts' *Chemical Substance Index* or the *Registry Index*, Aldrich's *Catalog Handbook of Fine Chemicals*, *CRC Handbook of Chemistry and Physics*, and *Pharmacological and Chemical Synonyms*. Many of these commonly used reference books are now available online at a very reasonable cost to the user.

Even more helpful than these texts are the chemical dictionary files. Most vendors provide what are called nomenclature and structure databases, also referred to as dictionary or registry files; for the purpose of this chapter these terms are used interchangeably. These files can stand alone and be used for the information as retrieved, or the information found can be used in conjunction with bibliographic or factual files on the same vendor. Because of the high level of interdependence between a bibliographic file and a dictionary file, the discussion of retrieval will seemingly 'jump' between the section on bibliographic and that on nomenclature and structure files. While their primary application is to be used in conjunction with the chemical literature bibliographic databases, such as CHEMICAL ABSTRACTS, dictionary files can serve to verify any substance name even if the searcher does not plan an online search. Reference librarians may be faced with queries regarding a certain substance that cannot be found as presented by the user in the traditional reference material.

These dictionary or registry files are the vendors' answer to nomenclature cross-indexing. The dictionary file is the analogue of a library catalogue authority file, providing nomenclature standardization, preferred terms and all synonyms including trade names. A dictionary file breaks each substance down into numerous fields of information. After registering all component parts of a substance including its structural depiction where available, the substance is assigned an arbitrary (arbitrary in meaning) number. This number is referred to as the registry number. Because it is a unique identifier, it is one of the most reliable ways of retrieving information on the substance in question. A record for a chemical compound can also contain the molecular formula, a registry number and the compound structure; information available varies by vendor.

The easiest method of retrieval in the dictionary file is by registry number (RN). Depending on the vendor, the nomenclature file may or may not require the use of the code RN. Database file sheets should be consulted for proper suffix/prefix placement and spacing. Database upgrades may make use of these codes unnecessary in the search statement; for example, the RN suffix is no longer required in STN's REGISTRY file.

Search 4.3 shows the dictionary file display from STN's REGISTRY file for dinitrochlorobenzene (registry number 97-00-7, this number having been found in one of the reference sources mentioned earlier in this section). Note the alternative chemical names (CN) given, as well as molecular formula (MF), the structure showing elements and bonds, and the number of references in CHEMICAL ABSTRACTS files (CA 1967 to date and CAOLD prior to 1967). The LC field is a useful cross-reference tool, alerting the searcher to other STN files in which this substance is indexed.

## Search 4.3: Dictionary file search and display for dinitrochlorobenzene using STN's REGISTRY file

```
=> S 97-00-7

L1       1   97-00-7
             (97-00-7/RN)

=> D L1 IDE

L1 ANSWER 1 OF 1
COPYRIGHT (C) 1991 AMERICAN CHEMICAL SOCIETY

RN    97-00-7
CN    Benzene, 1-chloro-2,4-dinitro-  (8CI, 9CI)   (CA INDEX NAME)
CN    1,3-Dinitro-4-chlorobenzene
```

**Search 4.3:** (cont.)

```
CN   2,4-Dinitrochlorobenzene
CN   2,4-Dinitro-1-chlorobenzene
CN   DNCB
CN   4-Chloro-1,3-dinitrobenzene
CN   1-Chloro-2,4-dinitrobenzene
CN   Dinitrochlorobenzene
CN   2,4-Dinitrophenyl  chloride
FS   3D  CONCORD
MF   C6 H3 Cl N2 O4
CI   COM
LC   ANABSTR,  BEILSTEIN,  BIOSIS,  CA,  CAOLD,  CASREACT,  CHEMLIST,  CIN,
     CJACS,  CSCHEM,  CSNB,  DIPPR,  DSL,  EINECS,  HODOC,  IFICDB,  IFIPAT,
     IFIUDB,  MEDLINE,  TSCA


O2N.    :C.     NO2
  .   :  .    .
     .C:     .C.
    .       :
    .       :
     C:      C
   .   :  .
   .    :C.
   .
  Cl


REFERENCES  IN  FILE  CAOLD  (PRIOR  TO  1967)
1709  REFERENCES  IN  FILE  CA  (1967  TO  DATE)
```

Although the registry number is extremely reliable, not all publications use registry numbers, and different abstract producers introduced these control numbers at different times. This is particularly the case for chemistry-related files such as MEDLINE, BIOSIS and NTIS. The searcher must refer to the file data sheets for information relating to retrieval by registry number. Some of these databases have only recently started using the registry number as a search term. However, the primary chemistry databases (CHEMICAL ABSTRACTS, BEILSTEIN ONLINE and ANALYTICAL ABSTRACTS) use these numbers consistently and effectively. They can be relied on to match registry number with relevant bibliographic references.

Currently Data-Star, DIALOG, ORBIT, Questel and STN provide a nomenclature file for CHEMICAL ABSTRACTS. The data sheets of the different vendors should be consulted in advance to verify that all the information required will indeed be provided by the database file in question and to verify the appropriate field designators. Information will vary, but its purpose is the same - to provide an authoritative record of all the substances encountered in the literature, specifically the literature covered by CHEMICAL ABSTRACTS. Similarly, CHEMLINE provides the dictionary/structure information for the National Library of Medicine's databases. A selective list of dictionary files can be found in Table 4.7.

Nomenclature problems can still arise even with the existence of these online dictionary files. The problems will most commonly be the result of input errors or trade names. A company may assign a root name to all its products of a certain line, the only distinction being some alphanumeric prefix or suffix. Should the searcher only be aware of the root name the search could retrieve a large number of substances. It saves a lot of time to go to the file with as full a name as possible. As with every aspect in online retrieval, the dictionary databases continue to evolve and improve. They can offer sophisticated facilities for the experienced searcher who wants to be precise, or straightforward searching for the novice user with minimal training.

Chemical nomenclature input is difficult; for productive searching, consult the database documentation and follow the examples. Greek letters cannot be keyed in; they must be spelled and offset by periods. A search on a compound name should start with an EXPAND command to check the index for similar names.

**Table 4.7: Selected nomenclature databases**

| Database | Vendor |
|---|---|
| CHEMLINE | NLM |
| REGISTRY NOMENCLATURE SERVICE (CAS) | Data-Star: CHEMICAL NOMENCLATURE; DIALOG: CHEMNAME and CHEMSEARCH; ORBIT: CHEMICAL DICTIONARY; STN: REGISTRY FILE |
| SANSS (Substructure and Nomenclature Searching System) | CIS |

All chemistry search and retrieval that includes a compound should start in the dictionary or registry file where available. These files are fine-tuned to a very high level allowing for retrieval based on many variations on a single compound. If a registry number is not known then the searcher must begin to search by compound name (CN). Compound name can include trade or trivial names, names based on alternative nomenclature rules, or Chemical Abstracts names. Some may prefer to search by name fragments. Name fragments are a good way of narrowing a search but cause difficulty in isolating the precise compound. The difficulties of fragment searching can best be understood if we consider the analogy of keyword searching using syllables rather than complete words. For example, 'ly' could be entered to retrieve the adverbial form; however, other words may have 'ly' as a syllable without being an adverb, resulting in irrelevant hits. In chemical nomenclature, fragments such as 'oxy', 'ethyl' or 'ol' will help refine retrieval. All the fragments ('syllables') taken together will retrieve the desired compound(s). However, unrelated compounds containing the same fragments will also be retrieved.

When entering compound names it is important to use the field designator CN (suffix or prefix depending on the system) as well as entering the name exactly as established by Chemical Abstracts. In STN's REGISTRY file, the input 'S dinitrochlorobenzene/CN' will result in no hits, whereas 'S 2,4-dinitrochlorobenzene/CN', which gives the full alphanumeric prefix, will provide the posting of one. This is precisely what the searcher wants. One posting does not mean one reference; rather it refers to the number of substances that match the chemical name.

CHEMICAL ABSTRACTS allows the registry number to be qualified in order to retrieve substances which are derived or produced from the compound in question. The qualifiers are 'D' for derivative and 'P' for product. However, this type of search, while still considered a nomenclature search, can only be done on a bibliographic file. This illustrates the 'jumping' phenomenon mentioned earlier. Search 4.4 shows that there are twenty-five references to products of dinitrochlorobenzene (RN 97-00-7) in STN's CA file.

**Search 4.4: Sample product search from STN's CA file**

```
S  97-00-7P

L1        25 97-00-7P

=> D L1 BIB ABS 1

L1 ANSWER 1 OF 25
COPYRIGHT  (C) 1991 AMERICAN CHEMICAL  SOCIETY

AN    CA113(21):190887s
```

**Search 4.4:** (cont.)

```
TI    Method  of  obtaining  2-bromo-4,6-dinitrochlorobenzene
AU    Andrievskii, A. M.; Gorelik, M. V.; Avidon, S. V.; Gordievskaya,
      E.V.; Al'tman, E. Sh.; Vorozhtsov, G. N.; Dyumaev, K. M. LO USSR
SO    PCT Int. Appl., 17 pp.
PI    WO 9007488  A1  12 Jul 1990
DS    W:  JP, US
      RW: AT, BE, CH, DE, ES, FR, GB, IT, LU, NL, SE
AI    WO 89-SU331  22 Dec 1989
PRAI  SU 88-4622749  30 Dec 1988
IC    ICM   C07C205-12
      ICS   C07C201-08; C07C201-06; C07C201-14; C07B039-00; C07B043-02 SC
      25-6 (Benzene, Its Derivatives, and Condensed Benzenoid Compounds)
      DT PCO PIXXD2
PY    1990
LA    Russ
AN    CA113(21):190887s
AB    The title compd. (I), useful as an intermediate for disperse and
      metallized dyes, pigments, herbicides, fungicides, and
      antioxidants,was prepd. by a simultaneous nitration and
      bromination of chloro(nitro)enzene(s) (reaction component A) with
      Br or alkali metal bromide (B or B1), HNO3 or alkali metal nitrate
      (C or C1), and H2SO4 or oleum (D) at 20-80.degree., at a mol.
      ratio A: (B or B1):(C or C1): D = 1.0: (0.5-1.5 or 1.0-3.0): (2.0-
      4.0 or 2.5-5.0): (6.0-70.9). Thus, a mixt of 4-(O2N)C6H4Cl, H2SO4,
      and HNO3 was stirred 4 h at 70.degree. to give 99.5% I.
```

## Structure searching

Retrieval by use of the chemical structure is often referred to as structure searching or sub-structure searching. The molecular structure is probably the most universal of languages used by chemists; it is the most definitive description of a compound or family thereof. It is also one of the most conventional and standardized chemical languages (although there can be some dispute where the drawing is concerned, it is generally more standard than the nomenclature of compounds). Structure searching is the process whereby the user searches the chemical information database using a molecular structure as the query term. The term 'sub-structure searching' is the same process but refers to a search for all possible compounds that fit the specifications of the query term, variables included.

Until recently structure searching was restricted to users of Questel or STN. This has changed in large part due to the introduction of BEILSTEIN ONLINE by the major vendors. In the early years of structure searching different systems were developed. Perhaps the most notable is the line notation method, WLN or Wiswesser Line Notation, which is still in use to a large extent. In overly simplified terms, the WLN compound description replaces the structure by a code which provides information on the compound's functional group, chain length and ring sizes. The WLN code is a combination of letters, numbers and symbols logically connected to depict a compound. Related compounds will be coded similarly, thus being indexed in close proximity.

Most commercial chemical database systems use the connection table method, of which ROSDAL is an example. ROSDAL (Representation of Organic Structure Description Arranged Linearly) provides a linear description of a compound. A compound's ring size, chain length, bond and atom descriptions are all encoded in a line giving the system enough information with which to draw the structure. Both STN and DARC have made their dictionary files retrieve using the connection table architecture. There are conversion programmes available for converting line notation data into connection table information. The commercial databases have very few compound dictionary files available through WLN retrieval. INDEX CHEMICUS' REGISTRY SYSTEM, which is no longer available online commercially, had line notation encoded structure retrieval ability. For an excellent review of chemical structure software file organization, refer to Warr's *Chemical Structure Information Systems* [4].

The 'drawing' of the structure is now widely used in structure searching. The drawing method will depend on the searcher's software and hardware capabilities. Certain terminal types will not handle graphic input or output. Where graphics are not possible, the searcher can opt for menu-driven, command-driven or free-hand drawn structure-building. Where the latter method is used the searcher is strongly urged to use a mouse. Many searchers have free-hand capabilities but prefer to use the command terms to achieve the structure.

Structure drawing is similar in concept to searching by words or chemical terms. Problems can arise due to ambiguity and too generous truncation. The chemical structure has its ambiguity problems with ring-isolation or ring-embedded, chain or bond connections. The searcher must be extremely vigilant with the structure to reduce ambiguity to a desired level. One would assume that zero ambiguity is desired. This is true except that a searcher will often want variability built into the structure. This would mean there will be desired 'free sites'. Free sites are positions where the searcher will allow connections to take place. When the system allows, a searcher will want to indicate whether a ring is embedded or isolated. Searchers should remember to be precise when they want an exact match and to indicate the appropriate range of options where they want some variability.

A high level of standardization makes the structure an ideal choice as a search term. Another reason for structure searching is to find out what kinds of compounds exist given a certain structural starting point. The searcher can retrieve all structurally-related compounds. This is also possible using term fragments and formula searching but with poorer results. It is also much easier to build variability into a structure than into a word or formula. It is probably worth mentioning again the different software available for structure searching offline: *Molkick* (DIALOG and Questel), *STN Express* (STN and Questel), *Darc Chemlink* (Questel), *MDL ChemTalk*, and *ChemConnection*.

## Bibliographic searching

Bibliographic databases are machine-readable versions of indexing/abstracting publications. Long before the advent of online searching, indexes and abstracts were developed to assist in the retrieval of information pertinent to the scientists' needs. Chemistry has a very long and healthy tradition in the area of secondary literature. For example, *Chemical Abstracts* dates from 1907. It is not surprising that the automated versions of chemistry secondary sources would be introduced at the earliest possible stages of text-retrieval technology.

Online bibliographic databases were one of the first categories of databases to be exploited fully. Their early arrival did not incite any revolution in the actual format and file system online. These databases are still a strong reflection of their printed relation. This partially explains some of the trickier online features. For example, STN's 'HEADING PARENT' or /HP is a feature used to retrieve all derivations of a single compound parent based on functional group organization. When searching the printed index this facilitates the users browsing through the terms. But the online usage of /HP requires a sound and undistracted view of the compound in question.

Chemistry bibliographic databases are unique in that their retrievable material is alphabetic, numeric and graphic. A searcher can use one or combinations of all three to obtain results. The most efficient retrieval is generally found in the bibliographic files where important fields have been controlled by means of companion or dictionary files, CHEMICAL ABSTRACTS and its REGISTRY file being an excellent example of this marriage between database files. The REGISTRY file can be seen as the central organization of all retrievable data. At present, Chemical Abstracts Service has over ten million substances in its REGISTRY file.

There are three general approaches to retrieval in the bibliographic databases: subject, compound name or number, or compound structure. Sometimes a searcher may also have only a chemical formula - MF - for search purposes; this can be extremely helpful where compound names have provided too many postings.

Subject retrieval is a matter of finding the term or terms that best describe the subject in question. Where no special stipulation has been placed by the searcher, the search will be conducted by default on what is referred to as the basic index (BI). A basic index may vary from vendor to vendor, but generally includes titles, identifiers and descriptors. STN International's CA file has the unique advantage of not only providing abstracts to the user but also making them searchable as well. Unlike ANALYTICAL ABSTRACTS, these abstracts do not form part of the basic index. The searcher must indicate by suffix (AB) in order for the abstract to be searched. The basic index combines controlled and natural vocabulary fields. Controlled fields in chemistry include: registry numbers, descriptors, identifiers and classification codes. A searcher can use offline thesauri to verify search terminology.

The scope of the database impacts the terminology selected by a searcher. CHEMICAL ABSTRACTS, with its comprehensive broad subject base, should be approached differently to a database with a narrower focus, such as ANALYTICAL ABSTRACTS, CHEMICAL ENGINEERING AND BIOTECHNOLOGY AB-STRACTS, patent databases, government report databases and SOLID STATE AND SUPERCONDUCTIV-ITY ABSTRACTS. The general rule of thumb is: the more specific the subject content of the database, the more specific the controlled vocabulary. For example, it is possible in ANALYTICAL ABSTRACTS to specify analyte, matrix or reagent. In the same way that D or P could be affixed to a chemical name or registry number in CHEMICAL ABSTRACTS, so too can suffixes be used in ANALYTICAL ABSTRACTS; for example, an A or M (for analyte or matrix) can be suffixed to a name or number. It is not necessary to indicate specific fields to be searched since ANALYTICAL ABSTRACTS has a very inclusive basic index (abstract, title, descriptor, identifier). The registry number field must be specified as it does not form part of the default index.

Bibliographic databases are collections of surrogate documents. They summarize an extensive amount of information in a very economic package. One method commonly used in the references to save space and money is the use of abbreviations. Abbreviations of commonly used chemical terms will be used in the abstract, as well as the descriptor fields. When searching it is important to include both the abbreviated term as well as the term in full, using the OR operator for maximum retrieval. It is easy to double your search postings by remembering to 'OR' your search term with its standard abbreviation. Examples include: 'dissociation OR dissocn.'; 'degradation OR degrdn.'; and 'evaporation OR evapn.'. When using CHEMICAL ABSTRACTS, all common chemistry terms should be checked before searching. Chemical Abstracts Service provides a handbook for this purpose, *CAS Standard Abbreviations* [5].

Searching the abstracts of CHEMICAL ABSTRACTS, ANALYTICAL ABSTRACTS (abstract included in basic index), CHEMICAL ENGINEERING AND BIOTECHNOLOGY ABSTRACTS (abstract included in basic index) and CHEMICAL SAFETY NEWSBASE (abstract included in basic index) should increase hits. Increased retrieval is often inversely proportional to relevancy. The quantitative advantages can quickly be offset by the qualitative disadvantage if the search strategy is not tailored to abstract searching; this reservation applies also to free-text rather than controlled term searching.

One method to control irrelevant retrieval is to anticipate as many contextual occurrences of the term as possible and allow for potential noise by using the 'NOT' and proximity operators creatively. There is more danger in using the 'NOT' than with proximity. In chemistry, there are numerous terms where proximity can and should be used: for named reactions, Diels(w)Adler, or analytical techniques, nuclear(w)magnetic (w)resonance. Liquid(w)liquid and gas(w)liquid should always be searched in proximity.

## Referral searching

Chemistry referral databases that are online directories and handbooks do not require any retrieval techniques that differ from directory searching in other subject areas. Refer to Table 4.2 for a selection of referral databases.

For the purposes of this chapter, the online thesaurus will be considered a reference or referral database. Alternatively, the thesaurus is sometimes considered to be a companion file to the bibliographic database and as such is included in the broader definition of bibliographic database.

Retrieval on thesauri files is an excellent starting point of any search. A good search will require some thesaurus referral before searching, and sometimes even during a search. It is important to input and to retrieve accurately on a thesaurus to ensure full results when searching on the companion bibliographic file. Expanding a term allows the searcher to browse as s/he would do in the print version. Thesauri expansions present possibilities that will improve the bibliographic file search. Not only will spelling variations be spotted (fiber/ fibre, sulfur/sulphur, etc) but term adjacency, preferred terminology, related, broader and narrower terms will all be displayed in an online thesaurus.

Another positive result of thesaurus usage online is the benefit of search term savings where the search term is a charged unit (that is where the searcher is charged for each term used). In chemistry one parent compound term can cover numerous variations. The searcher, by choosing the parent or umbrella term, will be charged for only the one compound name while searching for numerous others. This is a cost effective and comprehensive search strategy. Thesauri are sometimes only available off-line, but increasingly vendors are providing online versions. STN International provides thesaurus capability for the chemistry and related databases given in Table 4.8.

**Table 4.8: STN databases with thesaurus option**

BIOSIS
CIN (Chemical Industry Notes)
ENERGY
INSPEC
JICST-E (Japan Information Centre of Science and Technology - English)
MEDLINE
NUMERIGUIDE
PLASPEC
SDIM

**Reaction searching**

Reaction information, like spectral data or solubility data, need not be searched on a dedicated file. Reaction information is available on most of the relevant bibliographic, referral and full-text databases. A reaction database however treats reaction information as its only concern. Search and display fields are related to reaction specific information such as starting materials and end products. Mapping the path of chemical reactions is displayed graphically, with the different parts of the reaction separated by '- - -', as seen in Search 4.5 below.

There are two main reaction databases commercially available: STN's CASREACT and ORBIT's CHEMICAL REACTIONS DOCUMENTATION SERVICE (CRDS). CASREACT is searchable by keyword and/or registry number. Like many of the CHEMICAL ABSTRACTS related files on STN, the registry numbers obtained in the REGISTRY file either by dictionary or structure searching can be carried over to CASREACT to see the reaction information.

Obviously these two databases will provide specific reaction information, but it should be noted that a factual database like BEILSTEIN ONLINE will provide exactly the same information. The difference is that

BEILSTEIN ONLINE will provide many other types of information, so there are no defaults specific to reaction material.

Search 4.5 shows a reaction display based on a search in the CASREACT file using the registry numbers for two different dinitrochlorobenzene compounds retrieved from the REGISTRY file and carried over to the CASREACT file.

## Search 4.5: Reaction display from STN's CASREACT file

```
=> file reg

FILE 'REGISTRY' ENTERED AT 18:04:47 ON 11 NOV 91
USE IS SUBJECT TO THE TERMS OF YOUR CUSTOMER AGREEMENT
COPYRIGHT (C) 1991 AMERICAN CHEMICAL SOCIETY

STRUCTURE FILE UPDATES: HIGHEST RN 137252-02-9
DICTIONARY FILE UPDATES: 9 NOV 91 (911109/ED) HIGHEST RN 137202-39-2

=> s 606-21-3
L1      1 606-21-3
         (606-21-3/RN)

=> s 97-00-7
L2      1 97-00-7
         (97-00-7/RN)

=> file casreact

FILE 'CASREACT' ENTERED AT 18:05:45 ON 11 NOV 91
USE IS SUBJECT TO THE TERMS OF YOUR CUSTOMER AGREEMENT
COPYRIGHT (C) 1991 AMERICAN CHEMICAL SOCIETY

FILE CONTENT: 1985-1991 (VOL 102 ISS 1 - VOL 115 ISS 17)
All OFFLINE Prints or ONLINE Displays, use the ABS or ALL formats to
obtain abstract graphic structures. The AB format DOES NOT display
structure diagrams.

=> s 11 and 12
         9 L1
       108 L2
L3       5 L1 AND L2

=> D L3 1-5

L3 ANSWER 1 OF 5
COPYRIGHT (C) 1991 AMERICAN CHEMICAL SOCIETY
RX(5) OF 16   J + ***K*** ===> B...

-------------------------

                  F
                  .
H ......NH             .
     .     .C:     .CF
      . .    :    .
       C        C  .
       :      .  F
       :      .
      .C.    :C
     .   .   :
H...*...S.    C
```

**Search 4.5:** (cont.)

```
@  1/2  Zn


J

---------------------------

                   C        NO2
        O2N .   :  .      .
             .  C:   .  C.
                .        :
                .        :
                .        :
             .  C:      .C
          .     :  C.
             *
           .
        .
     Cl


K


---------------------------

        :C.                      .C:
        C:  .C * S          C.  `  :C
          .    :....... ..................:  .
          .    :                  :     .  F
          .    :                  :    .  .
        .C:  .C.              .C.   :C. .
     O2N.     :C.  .NO2         .   . C :  .CF
        .          .   H.......NH.      .
          .                             .

                                        F



B

YIELD  80%


RX(5)       RCT     J 368-75-2, K    ***97-00-7***
      PRO     B  1581-03-9
      SOL     64-17-5  EtOH
      RGT     1310-73-2  NaOH
```

CA111(1):7317c Synthesis of some substituted 8-trifluoromethylnitrophenothiazines. Malik, Seema; Anand, Madhu; Verma, S. S.; Prakash, L.; Mital, R. L. (Dep. Chem., Univ. Rajasthan,jaipur 302004, India). J. Fluorine Chem., 42(2), 201-14 (Eng) 1989. CODEN: JFLCAR.   ISSN: 0022-1139.

## Toxicology searching

In an earlier example (Search 4.2) a search for chemical toxicology databases retrieved ninety-four citations. Toxicology is a well-represented and highly important area of chemistry. Chemists need to know about any possible problem with compounds being used. Each laboratory is also responsible for providing safety data sheets on any substance that they produce. Suppliers must provide these sheets for any substance sold to the laboratories.

Many of these data sheets are available online. STN provides MSDS-CCOHS (Material Safety Data Sheets from the Canadian Centre for Occupational Health and Safety); Health and Welfare Canada provides the International Register of Potentially Toxic Chemicals (IRPTC database); the National Library of Medicine has HSDB (Hazardous Substances Data Bank) as part of TOXNET (see Table 4.9).

**Table 4.9: Selected toxicology databases**

| Database | Vendor |
| --- | --- |
| HAZARDLINE | BRS |
| MSDS-CCOHS (Material Safety Data Sheets) | STN |
| IRIS (Integrated Risk Information System) | CIS, NLM |
| IRPTC/RISCPT (International Register of Potentially Toxic Chemicals/Registre International des Substances Chimiques Potentiellement Toxiques) | Health and Welfare Canada |
| MALLIN (MSDS example) | CIS |
| RTEC (Registry of Toxic Effects of Chemical Substances) | CIS, DIALOG, NLM |
| TOXIC CHEMICAL RELEASE INVENTORY | CIS, NLM |

## PRIMARY CHEMISTRY DATABASES

## CHEMICAL ABSTRACTS

CHEMICAL ABSTRACTS is the most frequently used and most comprehensive database in the field of chemistry and related sciences and is available from the following vendors, with system-specific database name indicated:

| | |
| --- | --- |
| BRS: | CHEB, CHEM 1977-present |
| CAN/OLE: | CA 1977-present |
| Data-Star: | CH08, CH09, CH10, CH11, CHEM, CH22 1967-present |
| DIALOG: | CA SEARCH (files 308-312,399) 1967-present |
| ESA-IRS: | CHEMABS 1967-present |
| ORBIT: | CAS 1967-present |
| Questel: | CAS 1967-present |
| STN: | CA 1967-present |

CHEMICAL ABSTRACTS covers the literature from more than 150 countries in fifty languages. Source documents include ten thousand scientific and technical journals, patents, conference proceedings, technical reports, dissertations and monographs. Together with its associated nomenclature, structure and reaction files, CHEMICAL ABSTRACTS provides access to 14.5 million substance names, almost ten million CAS Registry numbers, nine million bibliographic references, eight million abstracts, 1.4 million patents, over 75,000 ring systems and over 680,000 reactions. STN's collective name for this family of inter-related files is CAS ONLINE. CAS ONLINE databases include the following:

- REGISTRY: The Registry File is an index to more than ten million chemical substances. It can be searched by partial or complete structure diagram, molecular formula, name or synonym. A Registry reference record will contain: CAS Registry number, CAS Index name, up to fifty synonyms per substance, molecular formula, structure image when available, the number of references in File CA and an indication of whether or not there are references in File CAOLD. Also included are all the STN files that contain records on the compound.

- CA: Includes all *Chemical Abstracts* references since 1967. Each record will contain all bibliographic information including an abstract when available.

- CAOLD: Includes references to substances in documents prior to 1967. The file can be searched by using a CAS registry number. No bibliographic information is available. The search result is the CAS abstract number which must be matched against the hard copy of *Chemical Abstracts* to identify the citation.

Content of a CHEMICAL ABSTRACTS record varies with the vendor, with STN's being the most complete. Search 4.6 gives a complete sample reference from STN's CA file. The format command ALL displays all fields in the record.

## Search 4.6: Sample citation in full format from STN's CA file

```
=> d l1 all

L1 ANSWER  1  OF  1  COPYRIGHT  (C)  1991  AMERICAN  CHEMICAL  SOCIETY

AN    CA111(1):7317c
TI    Synthesis  of  some  substituted  8-trifluoromethylnitrophenothiazines
AU    Malik,  Seema;  Anand,  Madhu;  Verma,  S. S.;  Prakash,  L.;  Mital,  R.  L.
CS    Dep.  Chem.,  Univ.  Rajasthan
LO    Jaipur  302004,  India
SO    J.  Fluorine  Chem.,  42(2),  201-14
SC    28-14  (Heterocyclic  Compounds  (More  Than  One  Hetero  Atom))
DT    J
CO    JFLCAR
IS    0022-1139
PY    1989
LA    Eng
OS    CASREACT  111:7317
GI

AB    The  syntheses  of  variedly  ring  substituted  phenothiazines,  e.g.  I,
      with  two  strong  electron-withdrawing  groups  (trifluoromethyl  and
      nitro)  have  been  accomplished  by  the  reactions  of  some  reactive
      halonitrobenzenes  with  the  zinc  mercaptide  of  2-amino-4-
      trifluoromethylbenzenethiol.   The  products  have  been  characterized
      by  elemental  anal.,  IR,  1H,  19F  NMR  and  mass  spectral  studies.
```

**Search 4.6:** (cont.)

```
KW    phenothiazine  trifluoromethylnitro;  aminobenzothiazol  zinc
      cyclization  halonitrobenzene
IT    Cyclocondensation   reaction
      (of  halonitrobenzenes  with  amino(trifluoromethyl)benzenethiol
      zinc  mercaptide,  phenylthiazines  from)
IT    88-88-0    606-21-3    2213-82-3    51686-79-4
      (cyclization  of,  with  amino(trifluoromethyl)benzenethiol  zinc
      mercaptide,  phenylthiazine  deriv.  from)
IT    1536-26-1P    121134-74-5P
      (prepn.  and  Smiles  rearrangement  of,  phenylthiazine  derivs.  from)
IT    1581-03-9P  121134-73-4P
      (prepn.  and  formylation  of)
IT    2069-32-1P  111280-98-9P  111280-99-0P  121134-75-6P
      121134-76-7P    121134-77-8P
      (prepn.  of)
IT    97-00-7  3698-83-7
      (reaction  of,  with  amino(trifluoromethyl)benzenethiols  zinc
      mercaptide)
IT    368-75-2
      (reaction  of,  with  halonitrobenzenes,  phenylthiazines  from)
```

## ANALYTICAL ABSTRACTS

ANALYTICAL ABSTRACTS, a Royal Society of Chemistry database, is available on the following systems, with system-specific database name indicated:

| | |
|---|---|
| Data-Star: | ANAB 1978-present |
| DIALOG: | ANALYTICAL ABSTRACTS (file 305) 1980-present |
| ORBIT: | ANALYTICA 1980-present |
| STN: | ANABSTR 1980-present |

ANALYTICAL ABSTRACTS is the only abstracting service devoted solely to analytical chemistry. All aspects of analytical chemistry appearing world-wide are covered, including applications of analytical techniques in inorganic, organic, agricultural, biochemical, environmental, food and pharmaceutical chemistry. In addition to the usual journal and conference proceedings coverage, there is also excellent coverage of monographs, technical reports and standards.

Retrieval from ANALYTICAL ABSTRACTS is similar to that from other chemistry databases. Chemical name and registry number are both acceptable query terms. ANALYTICAL ABSTRACTS is essential for the information needs of the analytical chemist. Obviously there will be some overlap between this file and CHEMICAL ABSTRACTS but there are enough unique titles to warrant a separate search on ANALYTICAL ABSTRACTS.

Abstracts are included with each reference (see Search 4.7). ANALYTICAL ABSTRACTS modified its index categorization in 1991. These changes are the result of editorial changes in its print equivalent. The modifications are in Section and Subsection headings. Cross-reference headings have also changed in format and content. This is an important change for searchers who narrow by section. Many searchers prefer to run their strategy on the entire database. The recent modifications will affect those who run periodic update searches (SDIs) from stored logic.

Another important feature of this database is the ability to search the basic index by stipulating analyte, matrix and concept. Depending on the choice of query term, be it registry number or chemical name, the searcher need only append the necessary abbreviation at the end of the query term. The appendages are easily remembered by the simple 'A' for analyte, or 'M' for matrix.

## Search 4.7: Sample citation in full format from ANALYTICAL ABSTRACTS (file 305) on DIALOG

```
s  au=rastegar, f?
      S1        11      AU=RASTEGAR,  F?
?  s  fluorescence?
      S2      6207      FLUORESCENCE?
?  s  s1 and s2
               11      S1
             6207      S2
      S3        10      S1 AND S2
?  s  py=1990
      S4      9838      PY=1990
?  s  s4 and s3
             9838      S4
               10      S3
      S5         1      S4 AND S3
?  t  5/5/1

  5/5/1
168833 AA Accession No.: 53-10-D-00042 DOC. TYPE: Journal
Application of energy-dispersive X-ray fluorescence for the
  determination of rare earths.
AUTHOR: Rastegar, F.; Hadj-Boussaad, D. E.; Heimburger, R.; Ruch, C.;
  Leroy, M. J. F.
CORPORATE SOURCE: Lab. Chim. Miner., Ecole Eur. Hautes Etud. Ind.
  Chim., 67008 Strasbourg, France
JOURNAL: Analysis, Volume: 18, Issue: 8, Page(s): 497-501
CODEN: ANLSCY ISSN: 0365-4877
PUBLICATION DATE: Oct 1990 (901000) LANGUAGE: French
ABSTRACT: Dil. HNO3 soln. (20 .mu.1) of such elements (10 to 50 .mu.g
  ml.minus.1) and Se (5 .mu.g ml.minus.1) as internal standard were
  analysed on a 4-.mu.m thick polypropylene foil in the instrument of
  Ruch et al. (Anal. Chem., 1985, 57, 1691) at 40 kV, 30 mA and
  irradiation time 1000 s. A Mo filter was used and calibration graphs
  were constructed from the rare-earth element L.alpha.1 and L.beta.1
  lines and the K.alpha. line of Se at 11.2077 keV. Precision and
  reproducibility were .ltoreq.2.2 and .ltoreq.4.9%, respectively, (n =
  5). Simultaneous multi-element determination was studied, but
  overlapping spectral L-peaks made precise determinations difficult.
  Mixtures containing all rare-earth elements should be separated
  before XRF.
ANALYTE: rare-earth metals —detmn. of, by energy-dispersive XRF
SECTION: D-23000 (Inorganic and Organic Analysis)
```

## BEILSTEIN ONLINE

The entire *Beilstein Handbook* should be available online by 1992 through various vendors. This database is likely to be as well used as is its hard copy counterpart, known more formally as *Beilsteins Handbuch der Organischen Chemie/Beilstein Handbook of Organic Chemistry*. The database, like the series, will be of most benefit to organic chemists, information scientists and librarians. Beilstein is considered to be the authoritative source for systematically organized evaluated data on organic compounds. Critically reviewed information is available for about 3.5 million compounds derived from over two thousand journals, patents, monographs and dissertations published world-wide since 1779.

Different types of databases were discussed earlier. BEILSTEIN ONLINE can be considered factual, full-text and bibliographic. This might appear contradictory except that many people use BEILSTEIN ONLINE not only for the evaluated data within but for references to the literature. A tremendous amount of flexibility is built into this file; users should take the time to read the documentation and discover what is available.

There are three helpful print sources when searching BEILSTEIN ONLINE depending on the vendor being used. A good detailed overview is *The Beilstein Online Database: Implementation, Content and Retrieval* [6], with a discussion of everything from file architecture to offline software availability. There is some good compare and contrast material available for searchers who have not yet committed themselves to a specific vendor. Springer has recently published *Online Searching on DIALOG: Beilstein Reference Manual* [7]. STN provides the usual volume that accompanies each of its files.

BEILSTEIN ONLINE is similar to Chemical Abstracts' REGISTRY File in that each record contains a verified structure in addition to evaluated and verified compound data (not all BEILSTEIN ONLINE information is evaluated, although the non-evaluated data is mainly from 1980 onward). It should be noted that structure searching is only available to those searchers with receptive hardware. For some searchers, the BEILSTEIN ONLINE database may present the first chance to perform structure searches online.

BEILSTEIN ONLINE, like several other related databases, allows searchers to cross over their answer sets from a search on the dictionary or registry file. It is a simple process, but users must remember when displaying the results to display the answer set carried over into BEILSTEIN ONLINE and not the original set number from the dictionary file.

Another advantage of a factual/numeric file like BEILSTEIN ONLINE is the ability to search for not just a value, but for ranges of values; this is particularly relevant where physical properties are being searched.

BEILSTEIN ONLINE can present surprises if the data sheets are not checked in advance. A check in the print version will present a general idea of how much information may be available on a given compound; some compounds could easily have twenty to thirty pages of information, some as high as two hundred pages of related information. It is an expensive database, so it is recommended to read as much preparatory information as possible. The searcher will be charged for fields even if they are not available for the compound requested. There is an excellent feature, the field availability feature (FA), which will list all fields present for a given request including the number of occurrences of the search term in each field (see Search 4.8).

## Search 4.8:  Field availability search on BEILSTEIN ONLINE

```
D L24 FA 1-2


L24   ANSWER 1 OF 2

   Code       Field Name                            Occur.
   -----+-----------------------------------+----
   MF         Molecular  Formula                    1
   FW         Formula  Weight                        1
   SO         Beilstein  Citation                    1
   LN         Lawson  Number                         1
   CTUNCH     Unchecked  Data                        1


   L24   ANSWER 2 OF 2
```

**Search 4.8:** (cont.)

```
       Code      Field  Name                          Occur.
       -----+--------------------------------+----
       MF        Molecular  Formula                 1
       CN        Chemical  Name                      1
       FW        Formula  Weight                      1
       SO        Beilstein  Citation                  1
       LN        Lawson  Number                        1
       RN        CAS  Registry  Number                 1
       RSTR      Related  Structure                    2
       PRE       Preparation                           17
       DM        Dipole  Moment                        4
       CTCPL     Coupling  Phenomena                   2
       CTMEN     Molecular  Energy                     1
       MP        Melting  Point                        49
       CTCRY     Crystal  Phase                        3
       CSYS      Crystal  System                       3
       CSG       Crystal  Space  Group                 3
       CLP       Crystal  Lattice  Parameter           1
       DEN       Density  (crystal)                    1
       BP        Boiling  Point                        4
       DEN       Density  (liquid)                     6
       ST        Surface  Tension                      1
       CTCAL     Calorific  Data                       1
       SREF      Entropy                               1
       RI        Refractive  Index                     3
       CTOPT     Optics                                1
       NMRS  NMR Spectrum                              1
       NMRA  NMR Absorption                            2
       CTNQR     Nuclear  Quadrupole  Resonance        1
       CTROT     Rotational  Spectrum                  1
       IRS       Infrared  Spectrum                    3
       RAS       Raman  Spectrum                       2
       EAM       Electronic  Absorption  Maximum       4
       CTEMS     Emission  Spectrum                    1
       DIC       Dielectric  Constant                  1
       CTELE     Electrical  Data                      2
       CTECB     Electrochemical  Behaviour            1
       DE        Dissociation  Exponent                1
       PHWP      Polarographic  Half-Wave  Potential   2
       SLB       Solubility                            6
       CTSOLM    Solution  Behaviour                   1
       CTLLSM    Liquid/Liquid  Systems                2
       CTLSSM    Liquid/Solid  Systems                 19
       CTLVSM    Liquid/Vapour  Systems                1
       CTENEM    Energy  of  MCS                       1
       CTASSM    Association                           3
       REA       Chemical  Reaction                    600
       CTUNCH    Unchecked  Data                       10
```

## GFI (GMELIN FORMULA INDEX)

STN's GFI database includes the Gmelin Formula Index supplemented by the abstracts and bibliographic information from the Complete Catalog. These two sources together provide the user with references to the entire set of Gmelin handbooks, formally known as *Gmelin Handbuch der Anorganischen Chemie*. The *Gmelin Handbuch,* published by the Gmelin Institute of the Max Planck Institute is the most comprehensive reference source for inorganic, organometallic and physical chemistry. Close to six hundred volumes have appeared since the early nineteenth century.

GFI provides refereed and verified information in the area of inorganic chemistry. It also serves the areas of physics, metallurgy, technology, geochemistry, mineralogy and crystallography, all in relation to inorganic compounds.

## ACKNOWLEDGEMENTS

We would like to thank the companies and individuals who granted us free search time and advice regarding their system's treatment of chemistry databases: Diane Chiasson at CAN/OLE, Irene Jarrett at Chemical Abstracts Service and DIALOG and ORBIT for granting free search time at our convenience. Also our colleagues in the Department of Chemistry at McGill University who were willing experimental subjects.

## REFERENCES

1.     *Directory of Portable Databases*. Santa Monica, CA: Cuadra Associates, 1990-
2.     *Directory of Online Databases*. Santa Monica, CA: Cuadra Associates, 1979-
3.     American Chemical Society. Chemical Abstracts Service. *CAS Online: the Chemical Search System*. Columbus, OH: American Chemical Society, 1983
4.     Warr, Wendy A. *Chemical Structure Information Systems: Interfaces, Communication, and Standards*. (ACS Symposium Series no. 400) Washington, DC: American Chemical Society, 1989
5.     American Chemical Society. Chemical Abstracts Service. *Standard Abbreviations, Acronyms, Special Characters and Symbols in CAS Computer Readable Files and Publications*. Columbus, OH: American Chemical Society, 1982
6.     Stephen R. Heller. *The Beilstein Online Database: Implementation, Content and Retrieval*. (ACS Symposium Series, no. 436) Washington, DC: American Chemical Society, 1990
7.     Stephen R. Heller and George W.A. Milne. *Online Searching on DIALOG: Beilstein Reference Manual*. New York: Springer, 1991

## FURTHER READING

Anthony, Arthur. *Guide to Basic Information Sources in Chemistry*. New York: J. Norton, 1979
Arnett, Edward McC. and Kent, Allen. *Computer-based Chemical Information*. New York: Dekker, 1973
Arny, Linda Ray. *The Search for Data in the Physical and Chemical Sciences*. New York: Special Libraries Association, 1984
Ash, Janet E. *Communication, Storage and Retrieval of Chemical Information*. Chichester, England: E. Horwood, 1985
Bottle, R.T. *Use of Chemical Literature*. 3d ed. London: Butterworths, 1979
Cain, B. Edward. *The Basics of Technical Communication*. Washington, DC: American Chemical Society, 1988
Chemical Information Transfer Review Committee. *Information Transfer and Use in Chemistry: Final Report*. London: British Library, 1978

Davis, Charles H. and Rush, James E. *Information Retrieval and Documentation in Chemistry.* Westport, CT: Greenwood Press, 1974

Grayson, Martin. *Information Retrieval in Chemistry and Chemical Patent Law.* New York: Wiley, 1983

*IUPAC International Symposium on Techniques for the retrieval of Chemical Information, London, England, 1976.* Oxford: Pergamon Press, 1978

Maizell, Robert E. *How to Find Chemical Information: A Guide for Practicing Chemists, Educators, and Students.* 2nd ed. New York: Wiley, 1987

Mellon, M.G. *Chemical Publications, Their Nature and Use.* 5th ed. New York: McGraw-Hill, 1982

Skolnik, Herman. *The Literature Matrix of Chemistry.* New York: Wiley, 1982

Warr, Wendy A. *Chemical Structures: the International Language of Chemistry.* Berlin: Springer, 1988

Warr, Wendy A. Online Access to Chemical Information: A Review. *In Training and Education for Online,* edited by Angela Haygarth Jackson. London: Taylor Graham, 1989. pp. 187-192

Wolman, Yecheskel. *Chemical Information: A Practical Guide to Utilization.* 2d ed. New York: Wiley, 1988

# 5 The biosciences

*Bonnie Snow*

## INTRODUCTION

The biosciences may be defined as those sciences concerned with the study of living organisms, including plants, animals, bacteria, viruses, and insects. Agronomy, anatomy, biochemistry, botany, cytology, ecology, entomology, forestry, genetics, horticulture, pharmacology, psychiatry, toxicology and veterinary medicine are but a few of the disciplines that can be classified as biosciences. With separate chapters in this volume already devoted to energy and the environment, agriculture, and chemistry, discussion here will focus on biomedical sources and those that provide access to related research with potential impact on human health, such as biotechnology databases.

The majority of bioscience online resources are bibliographic indexes, but two other general categories of databases are also available: (1) non-bibliographic (e.g., directories of companies, chemicals or people) and (2) full-text databases. Overviews of these two categories appear later in this chapter, but primary emphasis will be placed on factors to consider in formulating online strategies for bibliographic resources. Table 5.1 is a selective listing of English-language sources accessible through major online services likely to be available to readers of this book. No attempt has been made to provide an all-inclusive list. With just one directory of databases published in 1990 identifying more than 4,400 databases, 1,950 producers, and 645 vendors worldwide [1, p. v], it would be impossible to tabulate all files potentially relevant to the bioscience searcher.

**Table 5.1: Bibliographic databases in the biosciences: a selective listing**

| Title | Notes on scope, updating ** | Vendor(s)*** |
|---|---|---|
| AGELINE | Citations, with abstracts, to the literature of social gerontology. Focuses on social, psychological and economic aspects of ageing. 1978 + with bimonthly updates. | BRS DIALOG |
| AIDD* | AIDS Abstracts from the UK Bureau of Hygiene and Tropical Diseases. 1983 + with monthly updates. | BRS Data-Star |
| AIDSLINE* | Citations, with some abstracts, drawn from MEDLINE, CANCERLIT, HEALTH PLANNING & ADMINIS-TRATION databases. 1980 + , updated 2 x month | BRS DIALOG NLM |
| ALCOHOL AND ALCOHOL PROBLEMS | Citations, with abstracts, to litera-ture on alcoholism research. 1972 + , with monthly updates. | BRS |
| ALCOHOL INFORMATION FOR CLINICIANS & EDUCATORS | Citations to literature with emphasis on educational materials. 1978 + , updated quarterly. | BRS |
| AV-LINE | References to audiovisual and other nonprint teaching materials. 1975 + , updated weekly. | NLM |
| BIOBUSINESS | Citations, with abstracts, to litera-ture on business applications of bio-logical and biomedical research. 1984 + with weekly updates. | BRS Data-Star DIALOG |
| BIOCOMMERCE ABSTRACTS & DIRECTORY | Citations, with abstracts, to litera-ture on commercial aspects of biotech-nology, with focus on industry news. Profiles of over 1,500 organizations involved in biotechnolgy in U.K. and U.S. 1981 + , updated biweekly. | Data-Star DIALOG |

**Table 5.1:** (cont.)

| Title | Notes on scope, updating ** | Vendor(s)*** |
|---|---|---|
| BIOETHICS-LINE | Citations to literature 1973 +, updated bimonthly. | NLM |
| BIOSIS PREVIEWS* | Citations, with some abstracts, to the literature of the biological sciences. 1969 + , updated weekly. | BRS<br>Data-Star<br>DIALOG<br>STN |
| BIO-TECHNOLOGY ABSTRACTS | Citations, with abstracts. 1982 + . with monthly updates. | DIALOG<br>ORBIT |
| CA SEARCH | Citations drawn from *Chemical Abstracts*, 1967 +, with biweekly updates. | BRS<br>Data-Star<br>DIALOG<br>ORBIT<br>STN |
| CANCERLIT* | Citations, with abstracts. 1963 + . Updated monthly. | BRS<br>Data-Star<br>DIALOG<br>NLM |
| CATLINE | Citations to library collection of U.S. National Library of Medicine. 1300 + , updated weekly. | NLM |
| CCRIS | Chemical Carcinogenesis Research Information System. Bibliographic references and data extracted from literature on test conditions and results of tests on 1,400 chemicals. 1938 + , updated quarterly. | NLM |
| CHEMICAL ENGINEERING & BIOTECHNOLOGY ABSTRACTS | 1971 + , updated monthly. | Data-Star<br>DIALOG<br>ORBIT |
| CHEMICAL EXPOSURE | Citations to literature on over 1,800 chemicals identified in human and animal biological media and reported effects on the body. 1974 +, annual. | DIALOG |

**Table 5.1:** (cont.)

| Title | Notes on scope, updating ** | Vendor(s)*** |
|---|---|---|
| CHEMICAL INDUSTRY NOTES (CIN) | Citations, with abstracts. 1974 + , updated weekly. | Data-Star DIALOG ORBIT STN |
| CHEMICAL SAFETY NEWSBASE | Citations, with abstracts, to litera-ture on occupational hazards in industry. 1981 + , updated monthly. | Data-Star DIALOG ORBIT STN |
| CLINICAL ABSTRACTS | 1981 + , updated monthly. | DIALOG |
| CURRENT AWARENESS IN BIOLOGICAL SCIENCES | 1983 + , updated monthly. | BRS ORBIT |
| CURRENT BIOTECHNOLOGY ABSTRACTS | 1983 + , updated monthly. | Data-Star DIALOG |
| CURRENT CONTENTS SEARCH | Citations to articles in over 6,500 journals in the sciences, including clinical medicine and biology. Current year, updated weekly. | BRS DIALOG |
| DE HAEN DRUG DATA | Each record is a specially-prepared textual-numeric summary of a cited journal article. 1980 + , bimonthly. | DIALOG |
| DRUG INFO & ALCOHOL USE & ABUSE | Citations, with abstracts. 1968 + , updated quarterly. | BRS |
| EMBASE* | *Excerpta Medica* online. Citations, most with abstracts. 1974 + , updated weekly. | BRS Data-Star DIALOG |
| FOODS ADLIBRA | Citations, with abstracts, to litera-ture on food packaging and technology, with emphasis on business and regula-tory news. 1974 + , updated monthly. | DIALOG |

**Table 5.1:** (cont.)

| Title | Notes on scope, updating ** | Vendor(s)*** |
| --- | --- | --- |
| FORENSIC SCIENCE DATABASE | Citations, with abstracts. 1976 + , updated monthly. | Data-Star |
| FSTA* | FOOD SCIENCE AND TECHNOLOGY ABSTRACTS. 1969 + , updated monthly. | Data-Star DIALOG ORBIT STN |
| HEALTH AND SAFETY SCIENCE ABSTRACTS* | 1981 + , updated monthly. | BRS ORBIT |
| HEALTH DEVICES ALERTS | Citations, with abstracts or full text on reported medical device problems, hazards, recalls, and evaluations. 1977 + , updated weekly. | DIALOG |
| HEALTH INDUSTRY RESEARCH REPORTS | Citations, with abstracts, to research reports issued by security and investment firms.  1982 + , quarterly. | BRS |
| HEALTH PERIODICALS DATABASE* | Citations, with abstracts or full text, to literature on health, with a focus on summaries written for the layperson. 1976 + , updated weekly. | DIALOG |
| HEALTH PLANNING & ADMINIS-TRATION* | Citations, with some abstracts. 1975 + , updated monthly. | BRS DIALOG NLM |
| HISTLINE | Citations to literature on history of medicine.  1964 + , monthly. | NLM |
| HSELINE* | Citations, with abstracts, to literature of occupational safety and health.  1977 + , updated monthly. | Data-Star ORBIT |
| IDIS DRUG FILE | Citations to literature on human drug therapy taken from the Iowa Drug Information Service.  1966 + , updated monthly. | BRS |

**Table 5.1:** (cont.)

| Title | Notes on scope, updating ** | Vendor(s)*** |
|---|---|---|
| IPA* | INTERNATIONAL PHARMACEUTICAL ABSTRACTS. 1970 + , updated monthly. (Subfile of TOXLINE on NLM.) | BRS DIALOG NLM |
| LIFE SCIENCES COLLECTION* | Citations, with abstracts. 1978 + , updated monthly. | BRS DIALOG |
| MEDICAL AND PSYCHO- LOGICAL PREVIEWS | Citations, with some abstracts, from approximately 300 journals. Current six months, updated weekly. | BRS Data-Star |
| MEDLINE* | Citations, with some abstracts. 1966 + , updated weekly. | BRS Data-Star DIALOG NLM STN |
| MENTAL HEALTH ABSTRACTS | 1969 + , updated monthly. | DIALOG |
| NIOSHTIC* | Citations, with abstracts, to literature of occupational safety and health. 1973 + , quarterly. | BRS Data-Star DIALOG NLM ORBIT |
| NTIS* | Citations, with abstracts, to technical reports on government-sponsored research. 1964 + , with biweekly updates. | BRS Data-Star DIALOG ORBIT STN |
| NURSING & ALLIED HEALTH INDEX* | Citations 1983 + , updated monthly. | BRS Data-Star DIALOG |
| PASCAL | Citations, with abstracts, to litera-ture of science, technology, and medicine. 1973 + , updated monthly. | DIALOG |

**Table 5.1:** (cont.)

| Title | Notes on scope, updating ** | Vendor(s)*** |
|---|---|---|
| PHARMLINE | Citations, with abstracts, to journal literature on drugs and professional pharmacy practice. 1978 + , weekly. | Data-Star |
| PNI | PHARMACEUTICAL NEWS INDEX cites items in 20 newsletters focusing on business, legislative, and product developments. 1974 + , updated weekly. | BRS DIALOG ORBIT |
| PSYCINFO* | Citations, with abstracts, from *Psychological Abstracts.* 1967 + , updated monthly. | BRS Data-Star DIALOG |
| REHABDATA | Citations to print and audiovisual materials on rehabilitation of physically or mentally disabled. 1956 + , updated monthly. | BRS |
| RINGDOC | Citations, with abstracts, to pharmaceutical journal literature. 1964 + , updated monthly. | DIALOG ORBIT |
| SCISEARCH* | Citations to literature of science and technology. 1974 + , updated weekly. | Data-Star DIALOG ORBIT |
| SMOKING AND HEALTH | Citations, with some abstracts, to literature on tobacco and smoking. 1960 + , updated quarterly. | DIALOG |
| SPORT* | Citations, with some abstracts, to scientific and practical literature on sports, sports medicine, and physical fitness. 1949 + , monthly. | BRS DIALOG |
| TOXLINE* | Citations, with abstracts, to literature of toxicology. Selected subfiles derived from MEDLINE, NTIS, BIOSIS PREVIEWS, and IPA. 1981 + , monthly. | BRS DIALOG NLM |
| VETDOC | Citations, with abstracts, to literature on veterinary drugs. 1968 + , updated monthly. | ORBIT |

**Table 5.1:** (cont.)

| Title | Notes on scope, updating ** | Vendor(s)*** |
|-------|------------------------------|--------------|
| ZOOLOGICAL RECORD ONLINE | Citations to literature of zoology, with an emphasis on systematic taxonomic indexing. 1978 +, monthly. | BRS DIALOG |

\*     Also available on CD-ROM.

\*\*    Update frequency may vary from vendor to vendor.

\*\*\*   No attempt has been made to provide a comprehensive list of search services. For the sake of brevity, BRS is used to cover any service offered by that vendor, be it After Dark, Brkthru, Colleague, etc. In the same way, NLM covers MEDLARS and TOXNET, and DIALOG includes Knowledge Index.

## PROFILES OF OMNIBUS FILES

Even a quick glance at Table 5.1's admittedly selective list will show the proliferation of speciality files. Only a few databases contain information on virtually every category of the biosciences. Familiarity with these 'omnibus' files is essential.

### BIOSIS PREVIEWS

BIOSIS PREVIEWS heads the list of omnibus files for the bioscience searcher. Its subject scope encompasses all of the life sciences, including field, laboratory, clinical, experimental and theoretical work published on biological and biomedical topics, as well as botany, zoology, microbiology, pharmacology, biochemistry, biophysics and bioengineering. More than 8,500 journals published in over one hundred countries and in more than fifty languages are indexed in BIOSIS PREVIEWS. Approximately eighty-six per cent of BIOSIS records are citations to English-language sources. Since July 1986, abstracts have been provided for fifty-four per cent of references added to the online database. Hardcopy counterparts include *Biological Abstracts* (1969- ), *BioResearch Index* (1969-1979), and *Biological Abstracts/Reports, Reviews and Meetings (BA/RRM,* 1980 on). Updated biweekly on Data-Star, DIALOG, and STN and monthly on BRS, BIOSIS PREVIEWS offers access to books, theses, technical reports, bibliographies, and conference or symposia abstracts or papers, in addition to journal article indexing. Selective coverage of United States' patents began in 1986.

### SCISEARCH

A multidisciplinary index to the literature of science and technology, SCISEARCH also qualifies as an omnibus file in the life sciences. Its breadth of subject scope is particularly advantageous in answering questions on topics only selectively indexed in the more specifically subject-oriented databases. For example, searches involving biometrics, computer applications in medical care, drug delivery systems, epidemiology or bioengineering benefit from SCISEARCH's interdisciplinary journal list, which includes 4,500 titles originating in more than fifty countries. Thirty languages are represented in the database, but eighty-eight per cent of SCISEARCH records cite English-language source material. Hardcopy counterparts include *Science Citation Index* (1974- ) and selected subsets of the *Current Contents* series of publications from the Institute for Scientific Information (ISI). Updated weekly, SCISEARCH is notable for its currency and nearly cover-to-cover indexing.

## MEDLINE

For biomedical information, MEDLINE can be added to the list of omnibus resources. Although its focus is on clinical medicine, MEDLINE's subject coverage extends to preclinical research in key areas such as biotechnology, pharmacology and toxicology. Approximately 3,300 journals published in more than seventy countries and forty languages are cited in MEDLINE each year, with abstracts accompanying about sixty per cent of records added since January 1975. English-language sources account for seventy-five per cent of MEDLINE references, where online access is provided from 1966 to the present to material published in three hardcopy counterparts: *Index Medicus*, *International Nursing Index*, and the *Index to Dental Literature*. Update frequency on most databanks is now weekly.

## EMBASE

EMBASE (*Excerpta Medica* online) subject coverage reaches well beyond that traditionally defined as 'clinical medicine', making it a good starting point for searches on many bioscience topics, including environmental/occupational health, industrial medicine, pollution control, biophysics and bioengineering, developmental biology and teratology, clinical biochemistry and toxicology. This database offers unusually thorough indexing of the world's drug-related literature.

Like MEDLINE, EMBASE concentrates on journal articles, although approximately one thousand books per year were indexed 1975-1980. Approximately seventy-five percent of references are to English-language source material, but access to 4,500 journal titles published in thirty-six languages from more than 110 countries is provided in EMBASE (1974- ), updated weekly. The online file corresponds to forty-six speciality abstracting journals and two literature indexes published in hardcopy format to comprise *Excerpta Medica*. An additional 100,000 records per year are included in the online database that do not appear in its printed counterparts. Abstracts accompany approximately sixty percent of EMBASE citations.

## OTHER MULTIDISCIPLINARY BIOSCIENCE FILES

The LIFE SCIENCES COLLECTION contains information published in seventeen hardcopy abstracting journals in the fields of animal behaviour, biochemistry, ecology, endocrinology, entomology, genetics, immunology, microbiology, oncology, neuroscience, toxicology and virology. Most recently added subfiles include *Marine Biotechnology Abstracts* and *Growth Factor Abstracts*. Although limited in scope and size compared to BIOSIS PREVIEWS, THE LIFE SCIENCES COLLECTION offers selective indexing coverage

(1978-present, updated monthly) of approximately five thousand journals in most major bioscience disciplines.

PASCAL is a multidisciplinary database more familiar to European searchers than American information providers until its recent debut on DIALOG. Sources include journals, dissertations, technical reports, conference proceedings, books and selected patents in the area of biotechnology. Equivalent to seventy-nine hardcopy PASCAL journals, the online file contains major subject subfiles devoted to biology and medicine, chemistry and pollution, energy, food and agricultural sciences, and engineering. Records are bilingual (French and English) and about fifty percent provide abstracts. Spanish keyword indexing has been added to online citations dating from 1977 to the present. Updated monthly, PASCAL covers literature published from 1973 forward.

The United States Department of Commerce's National Technical Information Service (NTIS) is responsible for two online files frequently overlooked by life science searchers as sources of unique information not always found elsewhere. The NTIS database indexes reports of United States government-sponsored research, analyses and statistical compilations prepared by federal agencies, their contractors, or grantees (1964 to the present, updated biweekly). Truly ecumenical in scope, NTIS reflects the wide-ranging interests of national, state and local governments, including health planning, medicine and biology, environmental issues, agriculture and food science.

FEDERAL RESEARCH IN PROGRESS (FEDRIP), another NTIS-produced file online, offers access to information about ongoing federally-funded research projects in a variety of subject areas, including the life sciences. Records in the FEDRIP database include project title, principal investigator, performing organization and sponsoring organization, as well as a description of research. FEDRIP is updated monthly.

As the online record of all books and serials catalogued at the United States National Library of Medicine (NLM), CATLINE can be added to the list of multidisciplinary life science files, since the collection it documents supports research requiring hardcopy materials from many basic science disciplines.

## RESOURCE SELECTION

Multidisciplinary databases are a good place to begin research. Unless a comprehensive bibliography on a given topic is needed, results obtained from just one of the omnibus files discussed above may be sufficient to answer a query. Citations found in a broad-based file will help the researcher identify significant vocabulary and author names for future reference in building better search strategies for accessing more specialized databases when a thorough survey of the literature is required.

Resource selection will involve careful consideration of many factors beyond subject scope. A checklist could include:

1) types of publications cited and total number scanned
2) geographic origin and language of sources covered
3) frequency of file updates and lag time between source publication and online access
4) publication years of sources indexed
5) availability of abstracts online
6) indexing/access points provided.

Information on the first five database characteristics has been included, when available, in the previous discussion of omnibus files. How should each of these factors be weighted in making resource selection decisions? When, for example, will types of publications indexed be particularly important?

## Document coverage

Scientific communication appears in many forms: patents; meetings, symposia, and conference papers; notes, letters, case reports, and brief research communications; institutional and government technical reports; published theses and dissertations; bibliographies; and monographs. The most common form of scientific publication is journal articles.

### Depth as well as breadth

The number of periodical titles scanned each year for potential references to be included in a given database can serve as an indicator of that file's **breadth** of coverage. On the other hand, length of a database's journal list can be a misleading gauge of how comprehensive it is if many titles listed are only very selectively indexed. Comparing number of journals with number of citations (records) available would offer a more complete picture of **depth** as well as breadth in indexing the literature. For example, a rough calculation of depth for four omnibus files could be derived by determining the 'average' number of records added each year 1980-1989, then dividing this 'average' by the number of journal titles each scans annually.

| | Total records PY=1980-1989 | Annual 'average' | divided by number of journals | = | 'depth' ratio |
|---|---|---|---|---|---|
| BIOSIS PREVIEWS | 4,034,427 | 403,443 | 8,500 | = | 47.46 |
| SCISEARCH | 6,603,960 | 660,396 | 4,500 | = | 146.75 |
| MEDLINE | 3,054,935 | 305,494 | 3,300 | = | 92.57 |
| EMBASE | 2,518,391 | 251,839 | 4,500 | = | 55.96 |

True indexing depth calculations could only be made with accurate data on the number of journal articles and other indexable items actually published during the ten-year period in each source scanned by each database. Lacking these data, 'depth ratios' given here are useful only for comparison among files. Calculations also fail to take into account changes in the size of journal lists over the years and the number of records that may cite non-journal sources (although references to patents have been excluded from BIOSIS PREVIEWS totals). Despite these drawbacks, results nonetheless provide rough indicators of indexing depth from the perspective of selectivity.

Comparable data for a sample of subject speciality databases yield more food for thought.

| | Total records PY=1985-1989 | Annual 'average' | divided by number of journals | = | 'depth' ratio |
|---|---|---|---|---|---|
| BIOBUSINESS | 193,768 | 38,754 | 500 | = | 77.51 |
| CIN | 249,955 | 49,991 | 80 | = | 624.89 |
| IPA | 62,288 | 12,458 | 650 | = | 19.17 |
| RINGDOC | 255,070 | 51,014 | 800 | = | 63.77 |

A database with a relatively short journal list, such as CIN (CHEMICAL INDUSTRY NOTES), can nonetheless offer comparatively comprehensive coverage if titles scanned represent key resources within its stated scope. The nature of the primary literature itself must also be taken into account when comparing indexing depth. For example, the producers of IPA (INTERNATIONAL PHARMACEUTICAL AB-STRACTS) are forced to scan a large number of medical journals from which only a small selection of articles will fall within the boundaries of its subject speciality.

*Variety*

Bioscience searchers will also need access to forms of publication other than journal articles. Conference papers and patents are particularly important when information on new topics is sought. Monographs, annual reviews and symposia are helpful in gaining an overview of the state-of-the-art in past research. Case reports, often conveyed in the form of letters to editors of scientific journals, are a pivotal means of communication in medicine, pointing to new areas for investigation or new approaches to therapy. Technical reports assist researchers developing experiments by providing information on specific techniques and procedures.

Among the omnibus databases discussed above, BIOSIS PREVIEWS offers the most extensive coverage of non-journal literature (approximately forty-five percent of database records). It should be noted that EMBASE and MEDLINE both ceased coverage of non-journal literature in 1980 and 1981 respectively. Letters tend to be indexed fairly selectively by most life science files. Hence SCISEARCH's cover-to-cover indexing (reflected in its 'depth' or selectivity score above) is advantageous, picking up not only well-referenced letters and those reporting original research, but also equally important replies, corrections, etc.

*Updating*

Updating refers to the frequency with which a database supplier adds new or revised records to a file, passed along to the searcher with occasional variations in schedule from vendor to vendor. Lag time is less easily discernible. Although a supplier may be adding new references every week, these citations may actually refer to material published several months previously. The larger the journal list and the more special features routinely added to each record, the longer the lag time is likely to be. Some suppliers have designated a portion of their journal list as high priority for rapid input processing within one to three weeks of publication, but the average lag time in bioscience files overall is three to four months. Update frequency is nonetheless an indication of the emphasis placed on currency in a given source.

*Abstracts*

More abstracts online make the task of assessing relevance much easier and enhance the searcher's ability to retrieve concepts not identified in indexer-added keywords. Information provided in abstracts clarifies and augments titles and subject indexing terms and is particularly helpful in preliminary screening of non-English material. Table 5.2 compiles data on three factors that may serve as predictors of the potential utility of bibliographic database output: (1) the percentage of English-language source material cited, with or without an abstract; (2) the percentage of citations accompanied by abstracts online; and (3) the percentage of references to non-English sources which include English-language summaries online.

## SUBJECT INDEXING

The type of indexing provided in a database can determine its order of precedence on the searcher's list of candidate sources to be consulted. Three general types of subject indexing are available online: controlled

**Table 5.2: Language and abstracts data for key bioscience files**

| Database | % Citations to English-language | % Records with abstracts | % Non-English sources with English-language abstracts online |
|---|---|---|---|
| BIOSIS PREVIEWS | 86 % Language not directly search-able in full file until Jan. 1980. | 54 % July 1976+ | 67 % July 1976+ |
| EMBASE | 75 % | 60 % | 37 % |
| MEDLINE | 74 % | 65 % Jan. 1975+ | 26 % Jan. 1980+ |
| SCISEARCH | 88 % | No abstracts available online. | |

vocabulary, natural language, and classification codes. Careful analysis of the topic to be searched with a view to matching it with resource capabilities is important.

**When controlled vocabulary takes precedence...**

Vocabulary for a given topic grows as more and more people write about it. Predicting which words an author might use for concepts long established in the literature can be difficult; the list of synonyms or possible alternative search terms is likely to be extensive.

| | | |
|---|---|---|
| Crohn Disease | office surgery | prolonged-action |
| or | or | or |
| regional enteritis | ambulatory surgery | sustained-action |
| or | or | or |
| regional ileitis | outpatient surgery? | slow-release |
| or | | or |
| ileocolitis | | timed-release |
| or | | or |
| granulomatous colitis? | | delayed-action preparations? |

Trying to guess what terms may have been used to index the topic we have in mind is time consuming. Thus 'controlled' vocabularies have been developed: indexer-added keywords in many online records are chosen from a finite list of terms, rather than the entire English language, to ensure that all references that discuss a particular topic are indexed consistently with just one word or phrase, instead of a choice of synonyms. Many database suppliers publish their controlled vocabulary or 'authority list' in hardcopy format to assist frequent searchers in formulating efficient retrieval strategies before going online. The published list is often referred to as a database 'thesaurus' because it contains not only authorized terminology, but also includes numerous cross references from other common terms to the preferred keywords used in the online database.

MEDLINE's authority list, *Medical Subject Headings (MeSH)* [2], in many ways has set the standard for other database thesauri subsequently developed for bioscience databases. In addition to numerous cross references (for example, ILEOCOLITIS see CROHN DISEASE, OUTPATIENT SURGERY see AMBU-LATORY SURGERY), *MeSH* pre-coordinates frequently searched concepts such as PREGNANCY IN DIABETES; INFANT, LOW BIRTH WEIGHT; or CADMIUM POISONING. It defines editorial policy regarding use of terms which may be ambiguous. For example:

PUPIL     -      'of eye: do not use for STUDENTS.'
TANNING    -      'the leather industry, not suntanning.'
WOMEN     -      'for women only as a cultural, social, sociol, polit, force; do
                     not confuse with FEMALE for disease, organs, physiol, genetics, etc.'

*MeSH* also contains history notes indicating starting dates for consistent usage of indexer-added terms online and hints for retrospective searching on topics where preferred terminology has changed over time: for example, 'ROBOTICS...(87) search AUTOMATION 1966-86.'

Older, much-written-about concepts are easier to search in databases with highly controlled vocabularies. For example, a search on RECURRENCE OF CROHN'S DISEASE AFTER SURGERY is facilitated by MEDLINE's pre-coordinated indexing for CROHN DISEASE—SURGERY and the controlled *MeSH* descriptor RECURRENCE (see Search 5.1). In the majority of references retrieved (109 out of 132), author titles do not use the word RECURRENCE, but indexer-added *MeSH* terms indicate that this concept is discussed in the full text of the primary source cited. Samples of titles and indexing reproduced in Search 5.1 illustrate the utility of controlled vocabulary indexing in retrieving a concept such as RECURRENCE.

### Search 5.1: Example of controlled vocabulary search on MEDLINE

```
? b 154                                    The search begins in the
.                                          current segment of MEDLINE
.                                          on DIALOG.
File 154:MEDLINE _ 83-90/NOV (9011W2)

     Set   Items   Description             MeSH main heading/subhead-
     ---   -----   -----------             ing combination precoordi-
? select crohn disease --surgery?          nates two concepts.
     S1    618    CROHN DISEASE --SURGERY?
? s s1 and recurrence/de
           618    S1                       RECURRENCE is also a
           31002  RECURRENCE/DE            controlled MeSH descriptor.
     S2    132    S1 AND RECURRENCE/DE
? type s2/ti,de/2,4,8,13
2/TI,DE/2
  The results of surgery for large bowel Crohn's disease.
  Descriptors: *Crohn Disease—Surgery—SU; *Intestine,
Large—Surgery—SU; Anastomosis, Surgical; Colectomy; Intestine, Small
 —Surgery—SU; Postoperative Complications—Etiology-ET; Prognosis;
Recurrence; Time Factors

2/TI,DE/4
  Clinical course of Crohn's disease in older patients. A
retrospective study.
  Descriptors: *Crohn Disease; Age Factors; Aged;
Colitis—Surgery—SU;  Crohn  Disease—Diagnosis—DI;  Crohn
```

**Search 5.1:** (cont.)

```
Disease—Physiopathology—PP;  Crohn  Disease—Surgery—SU;
Ileitis—Surgery—SU; Middle Age; Recurrence; Retrospective Studies

2/TI,DE/8
 Resection margins and recurrent Crohn's disease.
 Descriptors: *Crohn Disease—Surgery—SU; Methods; Recurrence;
Reoperation; Review Literature; Short Bowel Syndrome—Prevention and
Control—PC

2/TI,DE/13
 Prognosis after surgery for colonic Crohn's disease.
 Descriptors: *Colitis—Surgery—SU; *Crohn Disease—Surgery—SU;
Adolescence; Adult; Aged; Child; Child, Preschool; Colitis—Mortality
—MO; Colitis—Pathology—PA; Crohn Disease—Mortality—MO; Crohn
Disease—Pathology—PA; Follow-Up Studies; Middle Age; Proctitis—
Surgery—SU; Prognosis; Recurrence; Reoperation; Time Factors
```

> Although author titles do not
> always indicate the concept
> of RECURRENCE, indexer-added
> MeSH terms ensure that
> potentially relevant items
> are not missed.

Life science databases other than MEDLINE do, of course, include controlled vocabulary indexing, but vary in the consistency of its usage and documentation. The complete *MALIMET* thesaurus for EMBASE is available in microform or machine-readable formats only (not hardcopy). Its size (more than 250,000 preferred terms compared to 15,000 in *MeSH*) indicates its tendency to provide a greater variety of possible terms and, in consequence, less consistent application in indexing. This proves to be the case in searching for RECURRENT DISEASE, as shown in Search 5.2. Although twenty-four citations are retrieved through controlled vocabulary indexing (Set 2), searching for the word root RECURREN? in titles and abstracts of EMBASE records reveals that additional, potentially relevant citations are available to which the indexer has not assigned the controlled phrase RECURRENT DISEASE. A sample of titles from Set 4 indicates relevance despite omission of the *MALIMET* descriptor.

Nowhere is the value of controlled vocabulary more apparent than in searching for topics where a subject population has been specified. Relatively few bioscience databases provide consistent indexing for subject populations (that is, humans or specific test animals) and related characteristics commonly requested, such as age groups, gender, occupation and racial or ethnic groups. Information compiled in Table 5.3 can affect database selection decisions.

> SELECT HISPANIC AMERICANS AND DIABETES/DE
> S1    62  hispanic americans and diabetes/de

For example, a bibliography is needed on 'Diabetes in Hispanic Americans'. As Table 5.3 indicates, MEDLINE provides controlled descriptors for ethnic groups, including Hispanic Americans.

Conducting a search on this topic in files without consistent indexing for the subject population desired is more difficult. Multiple keywords and more search time (and cost) are required.

> SELECT (HISPANIC? OR LATINO? OR CHICANO? OR (MEXICAN OR
> CUBAN OR SPANISH)(W)AMERICAN?) AND DIABET?

When executed in August 1990 on DIALOG, this textword search retrieved sixty-five references in MEDLINE, forty-nine in EMBASE, sixty-two citations in BIOSIS PREVIEWS, and forty-one references in SCISEARCH. Retrieval in all files was limited to material published 1987-1990. After duplicates were removed, MEDLINE contributed more than half of the 126 unique references remaining. The majority of these could have been retrieved with less effort by taking advantage of *MeSH* pre-coordinated indexing for HIS-PANIC AMERICANS which, when ANDed with the descriptor DIABETES, as illustrated above, led to sixty-two references.

**Search 5.2:  Controlled vocabulary augmented by natural language textword searching in EMBASE**

```
File    72:EMBASE  (EXCERPTA  MEDICA)_82-90/ISS37
(COPR. ESP BV/EM 1990)

        Set   Items    Description
        ---   -----    -----------
? select crohn disease and surgery/de              The initial strategy
          3484    CROHN DISEASE                     uses MALIMET terms
         83780    SURGERY/DE                        for each concept.
    S1     290    CROHN DISEASE  AND  SURGERY/DE
? s s1 and recurrent disease
           290    S1                                Set 2 = recall
from
          2492    RECURRENT  DISEASE               controlled  vocabu-
    S2      24    S1 AND RECURRENT DISEASE         lary.
? s s1 and recurren?
           290    S1                                Searching for the
         35312    RECURREN?                         word root RECURREN?
    S3      70    S1 AND RECURREN?                  as a textword.
? s s3 not s2
            70    S3
            24    S2                                Typing a sample of
    S4      46    S3 NOT S2                         items retrieved by
? type s4/ti,de/6,13,14                             textword searching
                                                    indicates relevance.

 4/TI,DE/6
  Multiple blood transfusions reduce the recurrence rate of Crohn's
disease
MEDICAL DESCRIPTORS:
*blood transfusion—surgery—su; *crohn disease; *immune deficiency;
adult

 4/TI,DE/13
  Recurrence after strictureplasty or resection for Crohn's disease
MEDICAL DESCRIPTORS:
*crohn disease—epidemiology—ep; *small intestine obstruction—
surgery—su ; *small intestine obstruction—epidemiology—ep
small intestine resection; reoperation; strictureplasty; aged; adult

 4/TI,DE/14
  Perforating and nonperforating Crohn's disease: An unpredictable
guide to recurrence after surgery
MEDICAL DESCRIPTORS:
*crohn disease—diagnosis—di; *crohn disease—surgery—su; *intestine
perforation; colon resection
```

**Table 5.3: Indexing of subject population characteristics**

| Identification of: | BIOSIS PREVIEWS | EMBASE | MEDLINE | SCISEARCH |
|---|---|---|---|---|
| Humans | * | [ ] | * | $ |
| Test animals | * | * | * | $ |
| Occupational groups | [ ] | [ ] | [ ] | $ |
| Racial/Ethnic groups | [ ] | [ ] | * | $ |
| Gender | $ | [ ] | * | $ |
| Age groups | [ ] | * | * | $ |

*  =  extensive, consistent controlled indexing.
[ ]  =  less consistency, fewer controlled terms available; augment with natural language keywords in strategies.
$  =  natural language approach required, multiple synonyms needed.

**Advantages of natural language indexing**

Online systems offer searchers the capability of accessing computer-produced indexes of all significant keywords that appear in titles or abstracts of records. This machine-generated natural language indexing is an important complement to controlled vocabulary descriptors. It allows searchers to plunge in without consultation of search aids and still retrieve some relevant items, provided that strategy keywords match those of authors writing about the topic under investigation. When no descriptors are available for a required concept, access to title and abstract keywords ensures that a bibliography can still be obtained, as was illustrated in recall from EMBASE, BIOSIS PREVIEWS and SCISEARCH on diabetes in Hispanic Americans noted above.

Not all natural language indexing is machine-generated and thus dependent on author vocabulary. Recognizing that a finite list of descriptors cannot accommodate all ideas likely to be discussed in the life science literature, some files offer non-thesaurus keyword indexing to augment author text in online records. Most BIOSIS PREVIEWS descriptors are natural language terms added by editors to enrich or clarify information provided in titles, identifying such factors as:

- specific scientific or common names of organisms discussed in a source, if not included in the citation title
- virus names
- organ systems or tissues used or affected
- diseases discussed
- geographic location, if pertinent
- instrumentation, apparatus, methodology, etc.

Accustomed to controlled vocabulary access, many bioscience searchers turn to the *BIOSIS PREVIEWS Search Guide* [3] for help in subject term selection. The 'Master Index' in the *Guide* lists keywords likely to be used as descriptors, 'based on how frequently they occur in the database and on their relevancy for searching' [3, p. B-1]. However, this index should not be regarded as an authority list or thesaurus, since it does not include all words or concepts that are searchable as indexer-added keywords in the online database.

EMBASE editors also add 'uncontrolled' drug terms to augment *MALIMET* descriptors in selected records. A search on a new development in biotechnology, 'Interleukin I receptor antagonist', will illustrate the advantage of such natural language access points. Two of the six references located in EMBASE are not retrieved elsewhere in the strategy reproduced in Search 5.3. Subsequent display reveals that although relevant keywords are not identified in either the author's title or indexer-added controlled medical descriptors, 'uncontrolled' (that is, natural language) drug terms assigned by EMBASE personnel identified interleukin I receptor antagonist.

MEDLINE also permits indexers to identify concepts lacking adequate descriptors in *MeSH*. Since June 1980, its identifier field has been used to index chemicals discussed in the full text of source documents, ensuring access to names or numbers of compounds whether or not they are included among *MeSH* descriptors. The MEDLINE record reproduced in Search 5.3 contains examples of 'uncontrolled' chemical identifiers.

Controlled vocabulary, by definition, is less dynamic and responsive to change than author terminology. Keywords for new concepts are not immediately added to thesauri. Until the volume of literature on a topic has grown and terminology coined to refer to it has become standardized by frequency of usage, consistency in indexing is unlikely. As a general rule, searches involving newer concepts must rely heavily on natural language access points and are best begun in databases with a high percentage of abstracted records or with indexer-added keywords drawn from terminology found in the full text of original sources. BIOSIS PREVIEWS, MEDLINE, and EMBASE fulfil these prerequisites.

**Search 5.3:  Strategy illustrating the advantages of uncontrolled terms added by indexers**

```
? b 5,34,72,76,149,155,159              The user plans to search
.                                        several files simultaneously
.                                        through DIALOG's OneSearch
.                                        capability.
System:OS  - DIALOG OneSearch

     File    5:BIOSIS PREVIEWS_69-90/SEP BA9007;RRM3907
               (C.BIOSIS 1990)
** The reloaded BIOSIS file will be available mid-September. **

     File  34:SCISEARCH _ 1990 WK 1-35
               (COPR. ISI INC. 1990)
* See also files 434 (1987-89), 433 (1980-86) & 432 (1974-79)
* Use 'BEGIN SCISEARC' to search all of SciSearch

     File  72:EMBASE (EXCERPTA MEDICA)_82-90/ISS37
               (COPR. ESP BV/EM 1990)
     File  76:LIFE  SCIENCES  COLLECTION _  78-90/JUN
               (Copr. Cambridge Scientific Abs.)

     File 149:HEALTH  PERIODICALS  DATABASE_1976-90/WEEK  37
               (COPR. IAC 1990)

     File 155:MEDLINE _  66-90/NOV  (9011W2)

     File 159:CANCERLIT 1963-90/SEPT
```

**Search 5.3:** (cont.)

```
        Set   Items   Description
        ---   -----   -----------
? select (interleukin or IL)(w)(1 or I)(w)receptor?(w)antagonist?
        81309   INTERLEUKIN
        66694   IL
      3045324   1
      1129078   I
       666155   RECEPTOR?
       409340   ANTAGONIST?
    S1      39   (INTERLEUKIN OR IL)(W)(1 OR I)(W)RECEPTOR?(W)ANTAGO
                 NIST?
```

? **t s1/5/19,21**

```
 1/5/19    (Item 2 from file: 72)
07723519 EMBASE No: 90153063
 Promising new arthritis drug awaits testing in humans
 N. Y. STATE J. MED. (USA) , 1990, 90/5 (281) CODEN: NYSJA
 ISSN: 0028-7628
 LANGUAGES: English
 SUBFILES: 031; 030
EMTAGS:
Joint 0965; Therapy 0160; Prevention 0165; Human 0888; Note 0063;
Priority journal 0007
MEDICAL DESCRIPTORS:
*arthritis—drug therapy—dt; *rheumatoid arthritis—drug therapy—dt;
* inflammation—prevention—pc
```

**DRUG TERMS (UNCONTROLLED): interleukin 1 receptor antagonist** protein
EMCLAS DRUG CODES:
03707030100; 03709010200; 03743000000

**Note that 'uncontrolled'
drug terms added by EMBASE
indexers identified
concept keywords.**

```
 1/5/21    (Item 4 from file: 72)
07679617 EMBASE No: 90108705
 Control of receptor appetite
 Whicher J.
 Department of Chemical Pathology and Immunology, University of
Leeds, Old Medical School, Leeds LS2 9JT  United Kingdom
 NATURE (United Kingdom), 1990, 344/6267 (584) CODEN: NATUA ISSN:
0028-0836
 LANGUAGES: English
 SUBFILES: 026

EMTAGS: Human 0888; Nonhuman 0777; Short survey 0002; Priority journal 0007
MEDICAL DESCRIPTORS:
*interleukin 1; *interleukin 2 receptor
```

**DRUG TERMS (UNCONTROLLED): interleukin 1 receptor antagonist** protein
—pharmacology—pd; interleukin 1 receptor antagonist protein—drug
  development—dv
EMCLAS DRUG CODES:
03707030100; 03746000000; 03743000000

? **t s1/5/34**                          **Sample MEDLINE record.**

**Search 5.3:** (cont.)

```
1/5/34  (Item 2 from file: 155)
07313867  90220867
   Purification, cloning, expression and biological characterization
of an interleukin-1 receptor antagonist protein [see comments]
   Carter DB; Deibel MR Jr; Dunn CJ; Tomich CS; Laborde AL;
Slightom JL; Berger AE; Bienkowski MJ; Sun FF; McEwan RN; et al
   Department of Molecular Biology Research, Upjohn Company,
Kalamazoo, Michigan 49007.
   Nature (ENGLAND) Apr 12 1990, 344 (6267) p633-8, ISSN 0028-0836
Journal Code: NSC
   Comment in Nature 1990 Apr 12;344(6267):584
   Languages: ENGLISH
   Journal Announcement: 9007
   Subfile: INDEX MEDICUS
   A human myelomonocytic cell line, U937, produced an interleukin-1
(IL-1) receptor antagonist protein (IRAP) which was purified and
partially sequenced. A complementary DNA coding for IRAP was cloned
and sequenced. The mature translation product of the cDNA has been
expressed in Escherichia coli and was an active competitive inhibitor
of the binding of IL-1 to the T-cell/fibroblast form of the IL-1
receptor. Recombinant IRAP specifically inhibited IL-1 bioactivity on
T cells and endothelial cells in vitro and was a potent inhibitor of
IL-1 induced corticosterone production in vivo.
   Tags: Animal; Human
   Descriptors: *Proteins—Isolation and Purification—IP; * Receptors,
Immunologic—Antagonists and Inhibitors—AI; Amino Acid Sequence; Base
Sequence; Binding, Competitive; Cell Adhesion; Cell Line; Cloning,
Molecular; Colony-Stimulating Factors—Pharmacology—PD;
Corticosterone—Blood—BL; DNA—Genetics—GE; Gene Expression;
Granulocytes—Metabolism—ME; Growth Substances—Pharmacology—PD;
Interleukin-1—Metabolism—ME; Interleukin-1—Pharmacology—PD; Mice;
Molecular Sequence Data; Monocytes—Metabolism—ME; Neutrophils—
Cytology—CY; Neutrophils—Physiology—PH; Proteins—Genetics—GE;
Proteins—Pharmacology—PD; Receptors, Immunologic—Metabolism—ME;
Recombinant Proteins; Tetradecanoylphorbol Acetate—Pharmacology—PD
   CAS Registry No.: 0 (interleukin 1 receptor antagonist
protein); 0 (interleukin 1 receptor); 16561-29-8 (Tetra
decanoylphorbol Acetate); 50-22-6 (Corticosterone); 83869-56-1
(granulocyte-macrophage colony-stimulating factor); 9007-49-2 (DNA)
```

**Since June, 1980 MEDLINE has
identified chemical sub-
stances by name and Chemical
Abstracts Service (CAS)
Registry Number (when
available), whether or not
these names are part of MeSH
vocabulary.**

```
?  t s1/3,de/7
 1/3,DE/7 (Item 7 from file: 5)
0021080534 BIOSIS Number: 39031633
   PRODUCTION AND CHARACTERIZATION OF MONOCLONAL ANTIBODIES TO A HUMAN
IL-1 INHIBITOR IRAP
   CHAPMAN D; LABORDE A; BERGER A
   UPJOHN CO., KALAMAZOO, MICH. 49001.
   JOINT MEETING OF THE AMERICAN SOCIETY FOR BIOCHEMISTRY AND MOLECULAR
BIOLOGY AND THE AMERICAN ASSOCIATION OF IMMUNOLOGISTS, NEW ORLEANS,
LOUISIANA, USA, JUNE 4-7, 1990. FASEB (FED AM SOC EXP BIOL) J 4 (7).
1990. A1751. CODEN: FAJOE
   Language: ENGLISH
```

**Sample BIOSIS PREVIEWS
record.**

**Search 5.3:** (cont.)

```
Descriptors/Keywords:   ABSTRACT   YT   CELLS   INTERLEUKIN-1   RECEPTOR
ANTAGONIST   PROTEIN   ELISA


                                        BIOSIS indexer-added un-
                                        controlled keywords augment
                                        and clarify author termin-
                                        ology. This record is also an
                                        example of conference paper
                                        indexing not found in
                                        MEDLINE, EMBASE, or SCISEARCH
                                        recall on this topic.
```

Results of the 'Interleukin I receptor antagonist' search also emphasize the importance of non-journal literature coverage when information on new concepts is needed. Eight of thirteen BIOSIS PREVIEWS records retrieved are citations to conference papers not found in MEDLINE, EMBASE, SCISEARCH or the LIFE SCIENCES COLLECTION. Although abstracts are omitted in BIOSIS references to non-journal literature, title keywords augmented by natural language descriptors provide access to scientific communications not found in many other life science databases. Note that indexer-added 'uncontrolled' terms led to the BIOSIS record reproduced in Search 5.3.

## Classification codes for broad concept searching

A third type of subject indexing offered in many bioscience databases is numeric classification of references to indicate their placement in broad conceptual categories of subject bibliography. In addition to assigning specific subject keywords to describe the content of a source document, indexers add codes to each reference which represent its general topical emphasis. Similar in rationale to codes used for shelving books in order to group volumes together by subject to facilitate browsing, classification schemes for online databases are perhaps more easily understood if related to hardcopy counterparts.

For example, each biweekly issue of *Biological Abstracts* arranges references under broad topical headings such as Behavioral Biology, Cardiovascular System, or Tissue Culture-Apparatus, Methods and Media. Thus readers can consult the Table of Contents to locate a subject area of interest, then turn to that section and find grouped together references which address the broad topic. A Concept Index is also provided in each issue to facilitate access to references printed under only one section heading but relevant to other sections as well. Online, each concept heading can be searched with a corresponding code, enabling BIOSIS PREVIEWS searchers to retrieve bibliography related to more than five hundred broad subject areas. Examples include:

    02504 Cytology and Cytochemistry - Plant
    02506 Cytology and Cytochemistry - Animal
    02508 Cytology and Cytochemistry - Human
            •
            •
    03504 Genetics and Cytogenetics - Plant
    03506 Genetics and Cytogenetics - Animal
    03508 Genetics and Cytogenetics - Human
    03509 Genetics and Cytogenetics - Population Genetics
    03510 Genetics and Cytogenetics - Sex Differences

A second scheme developed by BIOSIS focuses on subject populations. More than seven hundred Biosystematic Codes facilitate retrieval of a Phylum, Class, Order, Family, or other taxonomic grouping above the genus level for micro-organisms, plants, animals, and fossils. Human beings, for example, are classified as 86215-Hominidae. Thus BIOSIS PREVIEWS searchers need not construct lengthy lists of possible keywords used in the literature to refer to humans, such as Man, Woman, Child, Patient, Teenager, Adolescent, Infant, Males, Females, etc. (Several of these terms could also refer to animals.) BIOSIS transcends such terminology differences and ambiguities by consistently classifying subject populations discussed in source documents with appropriate Biosystematic Codes. Classification schemes serve to bring together references otherwise more difficult to retrieve with specific keyword strategies.

EMBASE provides a hierarchical classification system (EMTREES) [4] reflecting fifteen broad 'facets' of biomedicine, including, for example, Facet A - Anatomy, Facet B - Organisms, Facet C - Diseases, etc. A portion of Facet C will illustrate the structure of the scheme.

| | |
|---|---|
| C6.440.810 | Skin Infection |
| C6.440.810.10 | Bacterial skin disease |
| C6.440.810.10.270 | Erysipelas |
| C6.440.810.10.320 | Furunculosis |
| C6.440.810.10.440 | Impetigo |
| C6.440.810.10.480 | Leprosy |
| C6.440.810.10.720 | Pyoderma |
| C6.440.810.10.810 | Skin tuberculosis |

Prior to 1988, Section Headings based on medical speciality areas were used instead of EMTREES to index EMBASE citations. A portion of Section 13 - Dermatology and Venereology, shows a rough similarity in rationale to EMTREES.

| | |
|---|---|
| 013 32 | Infectious Skin Diseases |
| 013 32 01 | Bacterial infections |
| 013 32 02 | Protozoal infections, trepanomatosis |
| 013 32 03 | Tuberculosis and related conditions |
| 013 32 04 | Leprosy |

In both classification schemes, codes are constructed to facilitate broad concept retrieval through truncation. For example, SELECT DC=C6.440.810.10? on DIALOG would retrieve all references indexed with headings indented under 'Bacterial Skin Disease' in the EMTREEs. SELECT SH=01332? searches for headings indented under 'Infectious Skin Diseases' prior to 1988.

MEDLINE's *Tree Structures* [5] is the most detailed classification scheme developed for online searching. Each preferred *MeSH* descriptor has an equivalent code or codes which place it in the hierarchical 'Trees' intended to reflect, conceptually, the 'branches' of medicine. Trees can be 'exploded' or 'cascaded' to obtain references indexed under related terms for a given subject, as was seen with EMTREEs or Section Headings above. For example, SELECT DC=C17.838? on DIALOG retrieves records assigned to any of the 'Infectious Skin Disease' descriptors shown in Table 5.4.

**Table 5.4: Extract from MEDLINE's Tree Structures: an example of a hierarchical classification scheme**

| | |
|---|---|
| C17.838. | Skin diseases, infectious |
| C17.838.138 | Cellulitis |
| C17.838.208. | Dermatomycoses |
| C17.838.208.83. | Actinomycosis, cervicofacial |
| C17.838.208.165. | Candidiasis, chronic mucocutaneous |
| C17.838.208.170. | Candidiasis, cutaneous |
| C17.838.208.241. | Chromoblastomycosis |
| C17.838.208.557. | Maduromycosis |
| C17.838.208.883. | Tinea |
| C17.838.208.883.558. | Tinea capitis |
| C17.838.208.883.558.708. | tinea favosa |
| C17.838.208.883.658. | Tinea pedis |
| C17.838.208.883.758. | Tinea unguium |
| C17.838.208.883.858. | Tinea versicolor |
| C17.838.252. | Ecthyma |
| C17.838.292. | Erysipelas |
| C17.838.384. | Granuloma inguinale |
| C17.838.424. | Herpes simplex |
| C17.838.424.382. | Herpes labialis |
| C17.838.424.584. | Kaposi's varicelliform eruption |
| C17.838.556. | Molluscum contagiosum |
| C17.838.625. | Paronychia |
| C17.838.670. | Pinta |
| C17.838.722. | Pyoderma |
| C17.838.764. | Rhinoscleroma |
| C17.838.820. | Staphylococcal skin infections |
| C17.838.820.160. | Carbuncle |
| C17.838.820.387. | Furunculosis |
| C17.838.820.504. | Impetigo |
| C17.838.820.880. | Staphylococcal scalded skin syndrome |
| C17.838.835. | Syphilis, cutaneous |
| C17.838.887. | Tuberculosis, cutaneous |
| C17.838.887.329. | Erythema induratum |
| C17.838.887.603. | Lupus |
| C17.838.930. | Warts |
| C17.838.930.217. | Condylomata acuminata |
| C17.838.930.345. | Epidermodysplasia verruciformis |
| C17.838.960. | Yaws |

## OTHER ADDED-VALUE FEATURES

### Weighted Indexing

Several bioscience databases provide weighted indexing. Editorial personnel are asked to choose two or three out of all descriptive terms added to an individual record which they feel identify topics receiving primary emphasis in the original source. Searches on high recall topics can thus be qualified to major emphasis only. Search 5.4 shows a sample MEDLINE strategy to retrieve bibliographical items on 'Alternatives to in vivo animal skin toxicity testing'. Set 1, representing the toxicology concept, is coordinated with 'in vitro' OR Set 2, *MeSH* terms or *Tree Structures* for Cell, Tissue, OR Organ Culture. In an effort to fine tune output, the skin concept, Set 5, is subsequently qualified to MAJOR.

Alternatively, the toxicology Set 1 could be limited to MAJOR emphasis only. However, to limit both Set 1 and Set 5 to MAJOR is too restrictive. Several excellent references are lost, as illustrated in the sample records displayed.

### Search 5.4: Taking advantage of MEDLINE's weighted indexing: limiting *MeSH* descriptors to major emphasis

```
File 154:MEDLINE _ 83-90/NOV (9011W2)          Topic: Skin toxicity testing
                                               —alternatives to in vivo
       Set   Items    Description             animal tests.
       ---   -----    -----------
? select (toxicology or toxicity or models)/de
             1245     TOXICOLOGY/DE
            45304     TOXICITY/DE
            68546     MODELS/DE
       S1  113449     (TOXICOLOGY OR TOXICITY OR MODELS)/DE
? s cells, cultured or cell line or cell survival or dc=e5.909.813?
            56222     CELLS, CULTURED
            50307     CELL LINE
            14281     CELL SURVIVAL
             7997     DC=E5.909.813?
       S2  117089     CELLS, CULTURED OR CELL LINE OR CELL SURVIVAL OR
                      DC=E5.909.813?
? s in vitro
       S3   73463     IN VITRO
? s s1 and (s2 or s3)
           113449     S1
           117089     S2
            73463     S3
       S4   11822     S1 AND (S2 OR S3)
? s skin(L)drug effects
            54551     SKIN/DE
           344615     DRUG EFFECTS/DE
       S5    2923     SKIN(L)DRUG EFFECTS
? s s5 and (s4 or animal testing alternatives)
             2923     S5
            11822     S4
              205     ANIMAL  TESTING  ALTERNATIVES
       S6     110     S5 AND (S4 OR ANIMAL  TESTING  ALTERNATIVES)
? t s6/ti/1-2
```

**Search 5.4:** (cont.)

```
6/TI/1
Use of the chick embryo for pharmacological screening of retinoids.

6/TI/2
Transdermal dual-controlled delivery of contraceptive drugs:
formulation development, in vitro and in vivo evaluations, and
clinical performance.
```

the

**In an effort to 'fine tune' output, the set representing SKIN linked with**

**subheading DRUG EFFECTS is limited to MAJOR emphasis.**

**? s s5/maj and (s4 or animal testing alternatives)**
```
           1057    S5/MAJ
          11822    S4
            205    ANIMAL TESTING ALTERNATIVES
    S7       47    S5/MAJ AND (S4 OR ANIMAL TESTING ALTERNATIVES)
```
**? ds**

**DS = DISPLAY SETS to review strategy.**

```
Set    Items    Description
S1    113449    (TOXICOLOGY OR TOXICITY OR MODELS)/DE
S2    117089    CELLS, CULTURED OR CELL LINE OR CELL SURVIVAL OR
                DC=E5.909.813?
S3     73463    IN VITRO
S4     11822    S1 AND (S2 OR S3)
S5      2923    SKIN(L)DRUG EFFECTS
S6       110    S5 AND (S4 OR ANIMAL TESTING ALTERNATIVES)
S7        47    S5/MAJ AND (S4 OR ANIMAL TESTING ALTERNATIVES)
```

**Alternatively, the TOXICOLOGY SET 1 could be limited to MAJOR emphasis.**

**? s (s1/maj and (s2 or s3) or animal testing alternatives) and s5**
```
          50592    S1/MAJ
         117089    S2
          73463    S3
            205    ANIMAL TESTING ALTERNATIVES
           2923    S5
    S8       75    (S1/MAJ AND (S2 OR S3) OR ANIMAL TESTING
                   ALTERNATIVES) AND S5
```

**However, to limit both the TOXICOLOGY and SKIN concept sets to MAJOR is too restrictive.**

**? s s1/maj and (s2 or s3) and s5/maj**
```
          50592    S1/MAJ
         117089    S2
          73463    S3
           1057    S5/MAJ
    S9       37    S1/MAJ AND (S2 OR S3) AND S5/MAJ
```

**? s s7 or s8**
```
             47    S7
             75    S8
    S10      82    S7 OR S8
```

**Search 5.4:** (cont.)

```
?  s s10 not s9
              82   S10
              37   S9
       S11    45   S10 NOT S9
```

Several excellent references will be missed if too many concepts are limited to MAJOR emphasis.

```
?  t s11/ti,de/1-2,8-9
```

In the 1st sample record, SKIN—DRUG EFFECTS is WEIGHTED as MAJOR, but TOXICOLOGY is not. (* = MAJOR)

11/TI,DE/1
  Evaluation of a non-invasive human and an in vitro cytotoxicity method as alternatives to the skin irritation test on rabbits.
    Descriptors: *Animal Testing Alternatives; *Irritants; *KB Cells—Drug Effects—DE; **Skin—Drug Effects**—DE; Erythema—Chemically Induced—CI; Evaluation Studies; KB Cells—Metabolism—ME; Rabbits; Regional Blood Flow—Drug Effects—DE; Skin—Blood Supply—BS; **Toxicology**—Methods—MT; Uridine—Metabolism—ME

Here, TOXICOLOGY is identified as a MAJOR (*) concept, but SKIN is not.

11/TI,DE/2
  Do we find relevant parameters for in vitro cytotoxicity testing?
    Descriptors: *Cell Survival—Drug Effects—DE; **Toxicology**—Methods--MT; Cell Division—Drug Effects—DE; Cell Membrane—Drug Effects—DE; Eye—Drug Effects—DE; Nervous System—Drug Effects—DE; **Skin—Drug Effects**—DE

The subheading TOXICITY, when linked to an asterisked main *MeSH* heading, shares that heading's designation as MAJOR.

11/TI,DE/8
  Evaluation of in vitro predictive tests for irritation and allergic sensitization.
    Descriptors: *Allergens—**Toxicity**—TO; *Irritants—**Toxicity**—TO; Cells, Cultured; Dermatitis, Contact—Etiology—ET; Hypersensitivity Delayed—Etiology—ET; **Skin—Drug Effects**—DE

Still another example of a record that would have been missed if <u>both</u> key concepts had been limited to MAJOR.

11/TI,DE/9
  The isolated perfused porcine skin flap (IPPSF). I. A novel in vitro model for percutaneous absorption and cutaneous toxicology studies.
    Descriptors: *Skin Absorption; ***Skin—Drug Effects**—DE; Blood Pressure; Glucose—Metabolism—ME; **Models,** Biological; Perfusion; Skin—Metabolism—ME; Skin—Pathology—PA; Swine

Indeed, it must be acknowledged that any strategy that employs weighted indexing runs the risk of missing some relevant items. Judgments regarding major emphasis points in source documents are, after all, somewhat subjective. For example, a study on indexing consistency in MEDLINE has shown a mean consistency percentage for central concept main heading (equivalent to *MeSH* term/MAJOR, that is, *Toxicology in records) identification of 61.1 per cent, for central concept subheadings (for example, *MeSH* term - Toxicity) of 54.9 per cent, and for central concept main heading/subheading combinations (for example, *Skin - Drug Effects) of 43.1 per cent. [6, pp. 179-180]

Nonetheless, as a method for (albeit arbitrarily) reducing output while maintaining high precision, weighted indexing can be employed to good effect. A BIOSIS PREVIEWS strategy (reproduced in Search 5.5) for retrieving references to 'Alternatives to in vivo animal testing for eye irritancy' illustrates how weighted indexing can fine tune output. A quick scan of the first five titles resulting from the initial strategy reveals lack of precision. Display of indexing assigned to the first relevant record in Set 4 shows the searcher opportunities for weighting terms. Subsequent alterations in strategy confine output to more pertinent references where Toxicology and either Tissue Culture or Mathematical Biology are major concepts. The Concept Code 32600 for In Vitro Studies is less likely to be identified as a major concept by indexers. Hence /MAJ is deliberately omitted as a qualifier in the search example shown in Search 5.5. Sample titles displayed indicate higher precision achieved by taking advantage of weighted indexing in BIOSIS PREVIEWS.

**Search 5.5:  Taking advantage of weighted indexing in BIOSIS PREVIEWS: limiting concept codes to major**

```
                                        Topic: Alternatives to in
                                        vivo animal testing
                                        for eye irritancy.

File  55:BIOSIS PREVIEWS_81-90/SEP BA9007;RRM3907
        (C.BIOSIS 1990)
** The reloaded BIOSIS file will be available mid-September. **

      Set  Items   Description          LIMITing recall to records
      ---  -----   -----------          added from January 1990
? limitall/20767083-99999999,eng        forward, citing English-
>>>LIMITALL started                     language sources.
? select cc=22501
     S1   17503   CC=22501  (Toxicology-General; Methods and
                            Experimental)
? s cc=32600 or vitro
           8478   CC=32600  (In Vitro Studies, Cellular and
                            Subcellular)
          16133   VITRO
     S2   19727   CC=32600 OR VITRO
? s s1 and (s2 or cc=32500 or cc=04500)
          17503   S1
          19727   S2
          14515   CC=32500  (Tissue Culture, Apparatus, Methods and
                            Media)
          20188   CC=04500  (Mathematical Biology and Statistical
                            Methods)
     S3    2841   S1 AND (S2 OR CC=32500 OR CC=04500)
? s s3 and (eye or ocular or retina? or cornea? or iris or lens)
           2841   S3
           2073   EYE
            988   OCULAR
           2089   RETINA?
            758   CORNEA?
```

**Search 5.5:** (cont.)

```
            208   IRIS
            861   LENS
    S4       45   S3 AND (EYE OR OCULAR OR RETINA? OR CORNEA? OR IRIS
                  OR LENS)
? t s4/ti/1-5
  4/TI/1
  NEURONAL AND MICROVASCULAR ALTERATIONS INDUCED BY THE CHOLINERGIC
TOXIN AF64A IN THE RAT RETINA

  4/TI/2
  STRONG PASTEUR EFFECT IN RABBIT CORNEAL ENDOTHELIUM PRESERVES FLUID
TRANSPORT UNDER ANAEROBIC CONDITIONS
  4/TI/3
  CLASS II ALLOANTIGEN INDUCED ON CORNEAL ENDOTHELIUM ROLE IN CORNEAL
ALLOGRAFT REJECTION
  4/TI/4
  THE USE OF BALB-C 3T3 FIBROBLASTS AS AN AID IN DETECTING POTENTIAL
EYE IRRITANTS
  4/TI/5
  CHARACTERIZATION AND TOXICITY STUDIES UTILIZING PRIMARY CULTURES OF
RABBIT CORNEAL EPITHELIAL CELLS
```

**The first few titles indicate that the strategy may be less precise than desired. The searcher displays indexing for a relevant record to determine how to increase precision.**

```
? t s4/5/4

  4/5/4
  0021171751        BIOSIS Number: 39075630
  THE USE OF BALB-C 3T3 FIBROBLASTS AS AN AID IN DETECTING POTENTIAL
EYE IRRITANTS
  REECE B; BRYAN B; LONG D
  MARY KAY COSMETICS INC., DALLAS, TEX. 75247.
  FORTY-FIRST ANNUAL MEETING OF THE TISSUE CULTURE ASSOCIATION,
HOUSTON, TEXAS, USA, JUNE 10-13, 1990. IN VITRO CELL DEV BIOL 26
(3 PART 2). 1990.  65A.   CODEN: ICDBE
  Language: ENGLISH
  Document Type: CONFERENCE PAPER
  Subfile: BARRM (Biological Abstracts/RRM)

Descriptors/Keywords: ABSTRACT MOUSE PROTEIN RELEASE NEUTRAL RED
UPTAKE LACTATE DEHYDROGENASE CELL CULTURE IN-VITRO TOXICITY TESTING
Concept Codes:
  *02506 Cytology and Cytochemistry-Animal
  *10808 Enzymes-Physiological Studies
  *13012 Metabolism-Proteins, Peptides and Amino Acids
  *20006 Sense Organs, Associated Structures and Functions-Pathology
  *22501 Toxicology-General; Methods and Experimental
  *32500 Tissue Culture, Apparatus, Methods and Media
  *32600 In Vitro Studies, Cellular and Subcellular
  00520 General Biology-Symposia, Transactions and Proceedings of
        Conferences, Congresses, Review Annuals
  01054 Microscopy Techniques-Cytology and Cytochemistry
  10060 Biochemical Studies-General
  10064 Biochemical Studies-Proteins, Peptides and Amino Acids
  13002 Metabolism-General Metabolism; Metabolic Pathways
Biosystematic Codes:
  86375 Muridae
Super Taxa:
  Animals; Vertebrates; Nonhuman Vertebrates; Mammals; Nonhuman
Mammals; Rodents
```

**Search 5.5:** (cont.)

```
                                        'Weighting' Concept Codes for
                                        TOXICOLOGY and TISSUE CULTURE
                                        may help. (* = MAJOR CONCEPT)
      ? ds                              DS = DISPLAY SETS to review
                                        strategy.
      Set    Items     Description
      S1     17503     CC=22501 (Toxicology-General; Methods and
                                Experimental)
      S2     19727     CC=32600 OR VITRO
      S3      2841     S1 AND (S2 OR CC=32500 OR CC=04500)
      S4        45     S3 AND (EYE OR OCULAR OR RETINA? OR CORNEA? OR IRIS OR
                       LENS)
                                        Limiting selected Concept
                                        Codes to MAJOR emphasis.

      ? s s1/maj and (cc=32600 or cc=32500/maj or cc=04500/maj)
                 15961    S1/MAJ
                  8478    CC=32600      (In Vitro Studies, Cellular and
                                         Subcellular)
                  3871    CC=32500/MAJ (Tissue Culture, Apparatus, Methods
                                         and Media)
                  6931    CC=04500/MAJ (Mathematical Biology and Statistical
                                         Methods)
           S5      857    S1/MAJ AND (CC=32600 OR CC=32500/MAJ OR
                          CC=04500/MAJ)
      ? s s5 and (eye or ocular or retina? or cornea? or iris or lens)
                   857    S5
                  2073    EYE
                   988    OCULAR
                  2089    RETINA?
                   758    CORNEA?
                   208    IRIS
                   861    LENS
           S6       19    S5 AND (EYE OR OCULAR OR RETINA? OR CORNEA? OR IRIS
                          OR LENS)
      ? t s6/ti/1-5

       6/TI/1
        THE USE OF BALB-C 3T3 FIBROBLASTS AS AN AID IN DETECTING POTENTIAL
      EYE IRRITANTS

       6/TI/2
        CHARACTERIZATION AND TOXICITY STUDIES UTILIZING PRIMARY CULTURES OF
      RABBIT CORNEAL EPITHELIAL CELLS

       6/TI/3
        PRIMARY CULTURES OF RABBIT CONJUNCTIVA AND IRIS EPITHELIAL CELLS AS
      IN-VITRO TOXICITY TEST SYSTEMS

       6/TI/4
        THE MICROPHYSIOMETER AND ITS APPLICATION IN IRRITANCY TESTING

       6/TI/5
        MICROTOX A COMPARISON WITH TISSUE CULTURE AND ANIMAL EYE IRRITANCY
      DATA
                                        As this sample of titles
                                        indicates, higher precision
                                        has been achieved by taking
                                        advantage of 'weighted'
                                        Concept Codes.Cited Reference
                                        Indexing
```

SCISEARCH offers searchers a unique capability: the means to locate publications which have **cited** a given reference in their footnotes or bibliography. 'Citation indexing is based on the premise that a close subject relationship exists between an earlier published document and the current documents in the database which cite the earliest document.' [7, p.3]

To conduct a successful cited reference search, the user must first locate at least one bibliographic reference for a work already known to be relevant to the subject under investigation. Given a choice of starting references, the best candidates for citation searching are those published in well-known journals at least six months prior to the date of the search, and/or those written by authors who have published more than one article on the topic. The first author's surname, initial(s), and the year of publication are needed as minimum starting points. The following search will illustrate this technique.

References retrieved in the BIOSIS PREVIEWS search reproduced in Search 5.5 include a record that lists six types of in vitro tests currently undergoing investigation as alternatives to eye irritancy assessments using whole animals. Among them is 'Corneal Epithelial Plasminogen Activator Assay'. A subsequent search for this phrase in BIOSIS (SELECT CORNEA?(W)EPITHELI?(W)PLASMINOGEN?) yields only one additional reference. Further tracking of work by the same author in BIOSIS locates four more records discussing plasminogen activator in cultured corneal epithelial cells (see Search 5.6). These four core references will next be traced through citation indexing in SCISEARCH, where a subject phrase search results in no recall (see Search 5.7).

## Search 5.6: Core references to Chan's work on an in vitro ocular irritation test, located in BIOSIS PREVIEWS

```
Core reference #1:

0018194589 BIOSIS Number: 85095943
  DESIGN AND CORRELATION OF THE CEPA TEST AN IN-VITRO OCULAR
IRRITATION TEST
  CHAN K Y
  DEP.OPTHALMOL.RJ-10, UNIV. WASHINGTON, SEATTLE, WASH. 98195, USA.
  J TOXICOL CUTANEOUS OCUL TOXICOL 6 (3). 1987. 207-214.CODEN: JTOTD
  Language: ENGLISH
  Subfile:  BA (Biological Abstracts)
  An in vitro ocular irritation test, the corneal epithelial
plasminogen activator (CEPA) test, is proposed as an alternative
to the in vivo Draize eye ittitancy test. The scientific rationale
and basis, the test protocol, and the score system of this test are
described. The results of two correlation studies in which 15
chemicals and products were evaluated are summarized.  The
advantages, disadvantages, and areas for refinement of the CEPA test
are discussed.

Core reference #2:

0016685312 BIOSIS Number: 31096774
  AN IN-VITRO ALTERNATIVE TO THE DRAIZE TEST
  CHAN K Y
  DEP.OPTHALMOLOGY, UNIV. WASHINGTON, SEATTLE, WA 98195.
  GOLDBERG, A. M. (ED.). ALTERNATIVE METHODS IN TOXICOLOGY, VOL. 3.
  IN VITRO TOXICOLOGY: A PROGRESS REPORT FROM THE JOHNS HOPKINS
CENTER FOR ALTERNATIVES TO ANIMAL TESTING; THIRD SYMPOSIUM.
XVIII+722P. MARY ANN LIEBERT, INC.: NEW YORK, N.Y., USA ILLUS. ISBN
0-913113-05-0.  0 (0). 1985 (RECD. 1986).  405-422.  CODEN: AMTOE
  Language: ENGLISH
  Subfile:  BARRM (Biological Abstracts/RRM)
```

**Search 5.6:** (cont.)

**Core Reference #3:**

0016619238 BIOSIS Number: 82059208
CHEMICAL INJURY TO AN IN-VITRO OCULAR SYSTEM DIFFERENTIAL RELEASE
OF PLASMINOGEN ACTIVATOR
  **CHAN K Y**
  DEP.OPTHALMOLOGY,RJ-10,  UNIV.  WASHINGTON,  SEATTLE,  WA  98195,  USA.
  **CURR EYE RES   5 (5). 1986.  357-362.**   CODEN: CEYRD
  Language: ENGLISH
  Subfile: BA (Biological Abstracts)
  Primary cultures of corneal epithelial cells from adult albino
rabbits were exposed briefly to various concentrations of NaOH
and formaldehyde. The release of plasminogen activator from the
cells was stimulated or inhibited during a 6-day recovery period.
This differential effect was dependent on the chemical concentration
and duration of cell recovery. The modulation of plasminogen
activator release in the in vitro system would be useful for
predicting ocular toxicity of substances.

**Core Reference #4:**

0016618828 BIOSIS Number: 82058798
RELEASE OF PLASMINOGEN ACTIVATOR BY CULTURED CORNEAL EPITHELIAL
CELLS DURING DIFFERENTIATION AND WOUND CLOSURE
  **CHAN K Y**
  DEP.OF OPTHALMOL,RJ-10,UNIV.OF WASHINGTON,SEATTLE,WASH.98195,USA.
  **EXP EYE RES   42 (5). 1986.  417-432.**   CODEN: EXERA
  Language: ENGLISH
  Subfile: BA (Biological Abstracts)
  The release of plasminogen activator (PA) by corneal epithelium
was studied utilizing pure culture of rabbit corneal epithelial
cells and a sensitive photometric assay for the enzyme. The activity
of PA measured in conditioned medium collected from the cultured
cells was plasminogen-dependent, acid-stable, and free of
interference by endogenous PA inhibitors. When serum was included
in the culture medium, it was necessary to acid-treat the
conditioned medium before PA assay in order to inactivate plasma
derived inhibitors. During a month of culture in a serum-free medium,
the cells released a low basal level of PA in the first week of
growth and confluency. During the second week the cells
progressively increased PA secretion at the onset of cell
differentiation, reaching a peak (18-fold increase) in the third
week when focal multilayering of cells occurred. Thereafter, the
cells declined release, concomitant with globular aggregation of
cells. A delay in the elevated release of PA was observed when the
confluent phase was extended to 3 weeks, after which a substantial
rise in PA level occurred simultaneously with the onset of
multilayering. An in vitro model of corneal wound closure was
established....

## Search 5.7: Following up cited references in SCISEARCH

```
? begin scisearch                           Request for simultaneous
                                            multi-file access to SCISEARCH
                                            file segments on DIALOG via
                                            OneSearch

System:OS-DIALOG  OneSearch
     File   34:SCISEARCH _ 1990 WK 1-35
             (COPR. ISI INC. 1990)
* See also files 434 (1987-89), 433 (1980-86) & 432 (1974-79)
* Use 'BEGIN SCISEARC' to search all of SciSearch

    File 434:SCISEARCH _ 1987-1989
             (COPR ISI INC. 1990)
    File 433:SCISEARCH - 1980-1986
             (COPR ISI INC. 1988)
    File 432:SCISEARCH - 1974-1979
             (COPR ISI INC. 1988)
     Set   Items   Description            Subject keyword phrase
     ---   -----   -----------            yields zero recall
? s cornea?(w)epitheli?(w)plasminogen?
          9885   CORNEA?
         41783   EPITHELI?
          9154   PLASMINOGEN?
     S1      0   CORNEA?(W)EPITHELI?(W)PLASMINOGEN?
? expand cr=chan ky, 1985                   EXPANDing in the Cited
                                            Reference Index to trace core
                                            references shown in Search 5.6

Ref   Items   Index-term
E1      16    CR=CHAN KY, 1984, V306, P249, J CROMATOGR
E2       1    CR=CHAN KY, 1984, V39, P121, MICROBIOS
E3       0    CR=CHAN KY, 1985
E4       1    CR=CHAN KY, 1985, P405, ALTERNATIVE METHODS
E5       3    CR=CHAN KY, 1985, V14, P325, ARCH ENVIRON CON TOX
E6       8    CR=CHAN KY, 1985, V234, P192, J COMP NEUROL
E7      11    CR=CHAN KY, 1985, V234, P201, J COMP NEUROL
E8       1    CR=CHAN KY, 1985, V26, P92, INVEST OPTHALMOL VI
E9       1    CR=CHAN KY, 1985, V3, P405, ALTERN METHODS TOXIC
E10      5    CR=CHAN KY, 1985, V3, P405, ALTERNATIVE METHODS
E11      1    CR=CHAN KY, 1985, V3, P407, ALTERNATIVE METHODS
E12      9    CR=CHAN KY, 1985, V41, P687, EXP EYE RES
         Enter P or E for more
? s e4,e9:e11
     s2      8   E4,E9:E11
? p                                         Paging further down in the
                                            Cited Reference Index.
Ref   Items   Index-term
E13      1    CR=CHAN KY, 1986, EXP EYE RES
E14      1    CR=CHAN KY, 1986, UNPUB PRELIMINARY RE
E15      1    CR=CHAN KY, 1986, V17, P309, T AM SOC NEUROCHEM
E16      3    CR=CHAN KY, 1986, V27, P52, INVEST OPTHALMOL S
E17      1    CR=CHAN KY, 1986, V35, P137, EXP CELL RES
E18      1    CR=CHAN KY, 1986, V36, P52, B ENVIRON CONTAM TOX
E19     21    CR=CHAN KY, 1986, V42, P417, EXP EYE RES
E20      2    CR=CHAN KY, 1986, V45, P444, FED PROC
E21      7    CR=CHAN KY, 1986, V5, P357, CURR EYE RES
E22      1    CR=CHAN KY, 1986, V5, P387, CURR EYE RES
E23      1    CR=CHAN KY, 1986, V52, P1407, APPL ENV MICROBIOL
E24      6    CR=CHAN KY, 1986, V52, P1407, APPL ENVIRON MICROB
         Enter P or E for more
? s e13,e19,e21:e22
          1   CR=CHAN KY, 1986, EXP EYE RES
         21   CR=CHAN KY, 1986, V42, P417, EXP EYE RES
```

**Search 5.7:** (cont.)

```
                * 8    CR=CHAN KY, 1986, V5, P357, CURR EYE RES:CR=CH
         S3       24    E13,E19,E21:E22
? p
Ref     Items          Index-term
E25      1             CR=CHAN KY, 1986, V55, P1407, APPL ENVIRON MICROB
E26      1             CR=CHAN KY, 1987, IN PRESS VISION STRU
E27      2             CR=CHAN KY, 1987, V32, P1227, ELECTROCHIM ACTA
E28      1             CR=CHAN KY, 1987, V35, P57, MICROBIOS LETT
E29      6             CR=CHAN KY, 1987, V38, P791, AUST J AGR RES
E30      3             CR=CHAN KY, 1987, V45, P633, EXP EYE RES
E31      1             CR=CHAN KY, 1987, V52, P97, CYTOLOGIA
E32      2             CR=CHAN KY, 1987, V53, P125, A VAN LEEUW J MICROB
E33      1             CR=CHAN KY, 1987, V6, P207, J TOXICOL-CUTAN OCUL
E34      1             CR=CHAN KY, 1988, IN PRESS AUST J SOIL
E35      1             CR=CHAN KY, 1988, P47, VISION STRUCTURE FUN
E36      1             CR=CHAN KY, 1988, THESIS NATIONAL U SI
          Enter P or E for more
? s e33
     S4       1    CR=CHAN KY, 1987, V6, P207, J TOXICOL-CUTAN OCUL
? s s1:s4
     S5      27    S1:S4                        ORing together results.
? t s5/ti,au,so/all

5/TI,AU,SO/1       (Item 1 from file: 34)
  UROKINASE-TYPE PLASMINOGEN-ACTIVATOR IN RABBIT TEARS - COMPARISON
WITH HUMAN TEARS
  TOZSER J; BERTA A
  EXPERIMENTAL EYE RESEARCH, 1990, V51, N1, P33-37
     :
     :
5/TI,AU,SO/4       (Item 4 from file: 34)
  THE USE OF CULTURED EPITHELIAL AND ENDOTHELIAL-CELLS FOR DRUG
TRANSPORT AND METABOLISM STUDIES
  AUDUS KL; BARTEL RL; HIDALGO IJ; BORCHARDT RT
  PHARMACEUTICAL RESEARCH, 1990, V7, N5, P435-451
     :
     :
5/TI,AU,SO/8       (Item 8 from file: 34)
  USE OF PRIMARY RABBIT CORNEA CELLS TO REPLACE THE DRAIZE RABBIT
EYE IRRITANCY TEST
  WATANABE M; WATANABE K; SUZUKI K; NIKAIDO O; ISHII I; KONISHI H;
TANAKA N; SUGAHARA T
  TOXICOLOGY IN VITRO, 1989, V3, N4, P329-334

5/TI,AU,SO.9       (Item 9 from file: 34)
  TIME-LAPSE VIDEOMICROSCOPIC STUDY OF INVITRO WOUND CLOSURE IN
RABBIT CORNEAL CELLS
  CHAN KY; PATTON DL; COSGROVE YT
  INVESTIGATIVE OPTHALMOLOGY & VISUAL SCIENCE, 1989, V30, N 12,
P2488-2498
     :
     :
5/TI,AU,SO/13      (Item 4 from file: 434)
  ASSESSMENT OF CORNEAL WOUND REPAIR INVITRO
  TUFT S; EGGLI P; BOULTON M; MARSHALL J
  CURRENT EYE RESEARCH, 1989, V8, N7, P713-719

5/TI,AU,SO/14      (item 5 from file: 434)
  THE SDA ALTERNATIVES PROGRAM - COMPARISON OF INVITRO DATA WITH
DRAIZE TEST DATA
  BOOMAN KA; DEPROSPO J; DEMETRULIAS J; DRIEDGER A; GRIFFITH JF;
```

**Search 5.7:** (cont.)

```
GROCHOSKI G; KONG B; MCCORMICK WC; NORTHROOT H; ROZEN MG; SEDLAK RI
    JOURNAL OF TOXICOLOGY-CUTANEOUS AND OCULAR TOXICOLOGY, 1989, V8,
N1, P 35-49

5/TI,AU,SO/15        (Item 6 from file: 434)
   PLASMINOGEN-ACTIVATOR AND ITS INHIBITOR IN THE EXPERIMENTAL
CORNEAL WOUND
    TERVO T; TERVO K; VANSETTEN GB; VIRTANEN I; TARKKANEN A
    EXPERIMENTAL EYE RESEARCH, 1989, V48, N3, P445-449

5/TI,AU,SO/16        (Item 7 from file: 434)
   A CRITICAL-EVALUATION OF PREDICTING OCULAR IRRITANCY POTENTIAL
FROM AN INVITRO CYTO-TOXICITY ASSAY
    KENNAH HE; ALBULESCU D; HIGNET S; BARROW CS
    FUNDAMENTAL AND APPLIED TOXICOLOGY, 1989, V12, N2, P281-290
        :
        :
5/TI,AU,SO/18        (Item 9 from file: 434)
   INVITRO METHODS FOR ESTIMATING EYE IRRITANCY OF CLEANING PRODUCTS
PHASE-I- PRELIMINARY ASSESSMENT
    BOOMAN KA; CASCIERI TM; DEMETRULIAS J; DRIEDGER A; GRIFFITH JF;
GROCHOSKI GT; KONG B; MCCORMICK WC; NORTHROOT H; ROZEN MG; SEDLAK RI
    JOURNAL OF TOXICOLOGY-CUTANEOUS AND OCULAR TOXICOLOGY, 1988, V7,
N3, P 173-185
        :
5/TI,AU,SO/25        (Item 16 from file: 434)
   CORNEAL EPITHELIAL WOUND CLOSURE IN TISSUE-CULTURE - AN INVITRO
MODEL OF OCULAR IRRITANCY
    SIMMONS SJ; JUMBLATT MM; NEUFELD AH
     TOXICOLOGY AND APPLIED PHARMACOLOGY, 1987, V88, N1, P13-23
        :
        :
```

**Selected references can, in turn, be traced through citation indexing.**

First the searcher EXPANDs the author's name and starting date of references to be traced in the CR= (Cited Reference) index. E4 and E9 to E11 appear to represent citations to Chan's work published in the book *Alternative Methods in Toxicology* (BIOSIS PREVIEWS record #2 in Search 5.6). Note that variations in reference style used in primary sources can cause potentially relevant entries to become separated in the CR index: for example, E4 omits a volume number, E10 employs a different title format than E9, and E11 differs in page numbering. Thus EXPAND is always recommended as a first step in Cited Reference searching.

Paging down the EXPAND display, the searcher finds two likely entries (E13, E19) for citations to Chan's work published in *Experimental Eye Research* in 1986 (BIOSIS core reference #4 in Search 5.6). Line numbers E21 to E22 are probable references to BIOSIS core reference #3 and E33 appears to be a citation to Chan's 1987 article in the *Journal of Toxicology* that began the hunt (BIOSIS core reference #1).

A selection of records whose authors have cited Chan's core references, reproduced in Search 5.7, shows the advantage of citation indexing for tapping into the 'invisible college' in the scientific community: authors building on the work of others as they extend research in a given subject area - either supporting, enhancing, or refuting previously published findings. Although all authors may not use the same terminology when writing about a topic, many will cite the same precedents in the published literature. Hence cited reference searching often locates pertinent material otherwise missed in subject searching.

Work located in this initial search on Chan's core references can, in turn, lead to further relevant articles. Cited reference searching on new topics is especially useful, because recall from subject keyword strategies tends to be low when terminology is not yet clearly defined or standardized and is thus not consistently used by authors writing in the subject area. Each citation retrieved may yield new vocabulary for building better subject word searches.

## CHEMICAL NOMENCLATURE FILES AND CROSS-FILE SEARCH STRATEGIES

Bioscience information requests often involve chemical compounds, either exogenous or endogenous, including drugs, enzymes, hormones, food additives or ingredients in cosmetics, pesticides, detergents and other household, industrial or agricultural products. Unfortunately, by the time most chemicals are cited in life science literature they have acquired several names. Database thesauri typically devote many pages to establishing controlled vocabulary for chemical substances. In most bioscience files, simplified or 'generic' names take precedence. Before a generic name is established for a substance, however, several different types of names may appear as index terms for the compound: chemical names, investigational codes, Chemical Abstracts Service Registry Numbers (CAS RNs), or broader pharmacologic or therapeutic category names (for example, beta-adrenoceptor blocking agent, antihypertensive). Table 5.5 cross references types of pharmaceutical nomenclature with indexing practices and searching recommendations for selected bioscience databases.

**Table 5.5: Pharmaceutical nomenclature in selected bioscience files**

| Search term | BIOSIS PREVIEWS | CA SEARCH | EMBASE | MEDLINE | TOXLINE |
|---|---|---|---|---|---|
| Generic name | * | [ ] | * | * | [ ] |
| CAS Registry Number | * + | * | * + | * + | * + |
| Enzyme Commission Number | $ | $ | T | + | $ |
| Investigational code | $ | $ | T | $ | $ |
| Chemical name | $ | $ | T | $ | $ |
| Trade name | $ | $ | T | $ | $ |
| Classification by action/use | * | [ ] | * | * | $ |

* = preferred terminology, easy access
[ ] = less consistently indexed, augment in strategies with alternative names
$ = terminology inconsistent; use alternative names in strategies
T = cross-referenced to preferred terminology in thesaurus
+ = date, subfile, or vendor restrictions apply; consult vendor documentation for guidelines

What is evident from this tabulation is that alternate terminology may be needed to locate references to the same compound in different databases. Even within a single file, retrospective searching may require entry of other names used for the same substance at earlier stages in its developmental life cycle.

A sample search for references in the scientific literature to CARDIOLITE, a new radiopharmaceutical developed for myocardial imaging, will illustrate the importance of alternative terminology in cross-file search strategies. The initial request for more information arises from a monthly current awareness search conducted for competitive intelligence purposes in PHARMAPROJECTS. Users typically monitor this file for new formulations and compounds either associated with given companies or therapeutic activities. The strategy shown in Search 5.8 will retrieve, for example, records for products originating from Du Pont and updated in the May 1990 PHARMAPROJECTS.

For assistance with database selection to locate further background information on CARDIOLITE, the searcher next consults a cross-file index. Such index files as CROS on BRS or DIALINDEX on DIALOG enable searchers to check database indexes without entering the files themselves and paying the full royalty for each resource consulted. In Search 5.9, CARDIOLITE is searched across 165 files in the DIALINDEX Supercategory ALLSCIENCE and located in twenty-two databases. After ranking files by recall (RF), the user decides to access a selection of research-oriented bioscience databases (B N3, N7:N8, etc.) via OneSearch, where a composite bibliography merging output from all sources requested will be created automatically (Set 1). After duplicates are removed (RD), twenty-seven references to CARDIOLITE are available for display in Set 2. A quick scan of selected titles reveals that CARDIOLITE has several alternative names. If the literature search is intended to be comprehensive, each alternative name should be included in a revised strategy. Fortunately, there is no necessity to re-key all of these terms. Among items already retrieved is a reference in CHEMSEARCH.

## Search 5.8: Example of monthly current awareness search in PHARMAPROJECTS

```
File 928:PHARMAPROJECTS - OCT. 1990
        (COPR. PJB PUBLICATIONS, LTD)
DIALOG MAP feature can be used with NA, RN, SY.

      Set  Items   Description
      ---  -----   -----------
? s (dupont or du(w)pont)/co and may(w)1990/up
     S1     17   (DUPONT OR DU(W)PONT)/CO AND MAY(W)1990/UP
? t s1/5/all
        .
        .
        .


1/5/12
00015133 Pharmaprojects. PJB Publications Ltd, Richmond, Surrey, UK

Drug Name:   Cardiolite
Originator: DuPont  (US)

Cardiolite is a radiopharmaceutical, developed by DuPont for
myocardial imaging. An NDA has been granted for the diagnosis and
localization of myocardial infarction (Company communication, Feb
1990).

COUNTRY             STATUS
USA                 Registered
World               Registered
```

**Search 5.8:** (cont.)

```
    Activity:  V4A   Imaging agent
    Updated:   DEC   1989  New Product
               MAY   1990  First registration The US
    Revised:   900320
```

## Search 5.9: Sample cross-file search for a new drug

```
    ? b 411                                      BEGIN in DIALINDEX
    .
    .
    File 411:DIALINDEX(tm)
           (Copr. DIALOG Inf.Ser.Inc.)

    ? sf allscience                              SELECT FILES in
       You have 165 files in your file list.     'Supercategory'
       (To see banners, use SHOW FILES command.) ALLSCIENCE.
    ? s cardiolite
    Your SELECT statement is:                    SELECTing drug name.
       s cardiolite
          Items      File
          -----      ----
            10         5: BIOSIS PREVIEWS 69-90/SEP BA9007;RRM3907
             6        16: PTS PROMT - 72-90/September 28
             1        19: CHEM. INDUSTRY NOTES 1974-90ISS39
            16        42: PHARMACEUTICAL NEWS INDEX 74-90/SEP, WEEK 3
             5        72: EMBASE (EXCERPTA MEDICA) 82-90/ISS39
            10       103: DOE ENERGY _ 83-90/AUG(ISS17)
       Examined   50 files
             2       155: MEDLINE _ 66-90/NOV (9011W4)
             4       158: DIOGENES_ 1976 - SEP  17, 1990
             2       172: EMBASE (ExcerpTa Medica) 1980-81
             1       173: EMBASE (ExcerpTa Medica) 1974-79
             8       187: F-D-C REPORTS 1987-SEP 24, 1990
             1       226: TRADEMARKSCAN OG:09/11/90 AP:07/20/90
       Examined  100 files
             2       285: BIOBUSINESS _ 1985-1990/OCT WEEK 3
             3       319: CHEM BUS NEWSBASE 1984-90 ISS37 /UD=9037
             1       398: CHEMSEARCH(TM) 1965-Aug90 9,850,413 Subs
             2       434: SCISEARCH _ 1987-1989
            12       545: INVESTEXT = 82-90/SEP 19
             2       563: ICC IBR_04/SEP/90
       Examined 150 files
             1       621: PTS NPA _ 85-90/SEP WEEK 4
             5       648: TRADE AND INDUSTRY ASAP 83-90/OCT
             5       669: FEDERAL REGISTER 04 JAN 88 - 27 Sep 1990
             6       912: RINGDOC - UDB_(1983-90) UD=9008

       22 files have one or more items; file list includes 165 files.

    ? rf                                         RANK FILES by recall:
    Your last SELECT statement was:              highest to lowest.
       S CARDIOLITE
```

**Search 5.9:** (cont.)

```
Ref      Items        File
---      -----        ----
N1         16           42: PHARMACEUTICAL NEWS INDEX 74-90/SEP, WEEK 3
N2         12          545: INVESTEXT - 82-90/SEP 19
N3         10            5:  BIOSIS PREVIEWS 69-90/SEP BA9007;RRM3907
N4         10          103: DOE ENERGY _ 83-90/AUG(ISS17)
N5          8          187: F-D-C REPORTS 1987-SEP 24, 1990
N6          6           16: PTS PROMT - 72-90/September 28
N7          6          912: RINGDOC - UDB (1983-90) UD=9008
N8          5           72: EMBASE (EXCERPTA MEDICA) 82-90/ISS39
N9          5          648: TRADE AND INDUSTRY ASAP 83-90/OCT
N10         5          669: FEDERAL REGISTER_04 JAN 88 - 27 Sep 1990
```

     22 files have one or more items; file list includes 165 files.

          - Enter P or PAGE for more -

? **P**
Your last SELECT statement was:
    S CARDIOLITE

```
Ref      Items        File
---      -----        ----
N11         4          158: DIOGENES _ 1976 - SEP  17, 1990
N12         3          319: CHEM BUS NEWSBASE 1984-90 ISS37 /UD=9037
N13         2          155: MEDLINE _ 66-90/NOV (9011W4)
N14         2          172: EMBASE (ExcerpTa Medica) 1980-81
N15         2          285: BIOBUSINESS _ 1985-1990/OCT WEEK 3
N16         2          434: SCISEARCH _ 1987-1989
N17         2          563: ICC IBR 04/SEP/90
N18         1           19: CHEM. INDUSTRY NOTES 1974-90ISS39
N19         1          173: EMBASE (ExcerpTa Medica) 1974-79
N20         1          226: TRADEMARKSCAN OG:09/11/90 AP:07/20/90
```

     22 files have one or more items; file list includes 165 files.

          - Enter P or PAGE for more -

? **P**
Your last SELECT statement was:
    S CARDIOLITE

```
Ref      Items        File
---      -----        ----
N21         1          398: CHEMSEARCH(TM) 1965-Aug90 9,850,413 Subs
N22         1          621: PTS NPA _ 85-90/SEP WEEK 4
N23         0            6: NTIS - 64-90/ISSUE20
N24         0            8: COMPENDEX PLUS _ 70-90/SEP
N25         0           10: AGRICOLA _ 1979-90/SEP
N26         0           12: INSPEC _ 1969 Thru 1976
N27         0           13: INSPEC - 77-90/ISS20
N28         0           14: ISMEC: MECHANICAL ENGINEERING - 73-90/AUG
N29         0           18: F & S INDEX _ 1980-90/SEP, WEEK 4
N30         0           28: OCEANIC ABSTRACTS _ 64-90/OCT
```

     22 files have one or more items; file list includes 165 files.

          - Enter P or PAGE for more -

? **b n3,n7:n8,n13:n14,n16,n19,n21**                    **The searcher decides to**
     ...                                                **BEGIN in a selection of**
                                                        **research-oriented files.**

**Search 5.9:** (cont.)

```
System:OS  - DIALOG OneSearch

File   5:BIOSIS PREVIEWS_69-90/SEP BA9007;RRM3907
         (C.BIOSIS 1990)

File 912:RINGDOC - UDB_(1983-90) UD=9008

File  72:EMBASE (EXCERPTA MEDICA)_82-90/ISS39
         (COPR. ESP BV/EM 1990)

File 155:MEDLINE _ 66-90/NOV (9011W4)

File 172:EMBASE (ExcerpTa Medica) 1980-81
         (Copr. ESP BV/EM 1984)

File 434:SCISEARCH _ 1987-1989
         (COPR. ISI INC. 1990)
* See also file 34 (1990- ), 433 (1980-86) & 432 (1974-79)

File 173:EMBASE (ExcerpTa Medica) 1974-79
         (Copr. ESP BV/EM 1984)

File 398:CHEMSEARCH(TM) 1965-Aug90 9,850,413 Subs
         (Copr.1990 by Amer.Chem.Soc.)
*** Use is subject to the terms of user/customer agreement. ***
```

```
     Set   Items   Description          S1 is a composite
     ---   -----   -----------          bibliography merging out-
? s cardiolite                          put from all sources
     S1     29    CARDIOLITE            requested.  RD = Remove
? rd s1                                 duplicates.
>>>Duplicate detection is not supported for File 398.

>>>Records from unsupported files will be retained in the RD set.
...completed examining records
     S2     27    RD S1 (unique items)  S2 contains unique
? t s2/6/all                            citations after
                                        duplicates have been
2/6/1      (Item 1 from file: 5)        removed.
0020970900     BIOSIS Number: 89101108
  TECHNETIUM-99M CARDIOLITE METHOXYISOBUTYLISONITRILE SPECT
EXAMINATION BEFORE CORONARY BYPASS OPERATION

2/6/2      (Item 2 from file: 5)
0020828869 BIOSIS Number: 89029613
  DIAGNOSIS OF ACUTE MYOCARDIAL INFARCTION WITH TWO NEW TRACERS
INDIUM-111-RADIOLABELED ANTIMYOSIN AND TECHNETIUM-99M-LABELED
ISONITRILE

         .                              Display of sample titles
         .                              shows alternative names for
         .                              CARDIOLITE.


2/6/11     (Item 1 from file: 912)
0375880
ACCESSION NUMBER: 90-17442
THEMATIC GROUPS: T P S
TITLE: Single Photon Emission Computed Tomography with Technetium-99m
Hexakis 2-Methoxyisobutyl Isonitrile in Acute Myocardial Infarction
Before and After Thrombolytic Treatment.....
```

**Search 5.9:** (cont.)

```
      .
      .
      .
2/6/24     (Item 1 from file: 434)
08866183   Number of References: 0
  CLINICAL-EXPERIENCE WITH CARDIOLITE (RP-30A)
(TC(I)-99M-HEXAKIS-2-METHOXY-2-METHYLPROPYL ISONITRILE)
```

CHEMSEARCH is an example of a nomenclature authority file intended to help the searcher by providing known synonyms for chemical compounds. Data-Star, ORBIT, and STN offer similar files with data based on the CAS Registry Nomenclature and Structure Service. The coverage and size of these chemical 'dictionary' databases on each online service are somewhat different, but entries have in common data items such as alternative names and numbers for compounds registered by Chemical Abstracts Service. ORBIT's CHEMDEX, for example, covers all substances cited in *Chemical Abstracts (CA)* from 1972 to date. CHEMICAL NO-MENCLATURE on Data-Star offers retrospective coverage for substances cited in *CA* from 1967 to date. DIALOG, Questel, and STN nomenclature files provide the most comprehensive coverage, including all substances registered by CAS (whether cited in *CA* or not) since 1965. In addition to differences in scope and size, dictionary databases vary in their currency with update schedules ranging from quarterly to weekly.

**Search 5.10:  Importance of using alternative names in cross-file chemical searching**

```
  ? t s2/5/27                          Display of CHEMSEARCH
                                       record for CARDIOLITE.
  2/5/27     (Item 1 from file: 398)
CAS REGISTRY NUMBER: 109581-73-9
  FORMULA: C36H66N6O6Tc
  CA NAME(S):
    HP=Technetium(1+)-99Tc (9CI), SB=
        hexakis(1-isocyano-2-methoxy-2-methylpropane)-, ST=(OC-6-11)-
  OTHER CA NAMES:
    HP=Propane (9CI), SB=1-isocyano-2-methoxy-2-methyl-, NM=technetium
      -99 complex
  SYNONYMS: Cardiolite; RP 30A; Tc99m RP 30A; Technetium Tc 99m
      sestamibi; Technetium-99Tc sestamibi
  SUBFILE: CHEMNAME 12 LITERATURE REFERENCE(S) IN FILE 399.

Copyright 1990 by the American Chemical Society

? map sy temp s2 from 398              MAP SY automatically
                                       creates a search strategy
1 select statement(s)                  incorporating synonyms
serial#TA218                           found in the CHEMSEARCH
                                       (File 398) record.
? exs ta218
            29    CARDIOLITE           The stored strategy is
          8678    RP                   executed across the same
           264    30A                  group of databases
            39    RP(W)30A             originally queried with
           614    TC99M                the single term
          8678    RP                   CARDIOLITE.
           264    30A                  (see Search 5.8)
             2    TC99M(W)RP(W)30A
```

**Search 5.10:** (cont.)

```
                     .
                     .
                     .
              1      TECHNETIUM(W)99TC(W)SESTAMIBI
    S3       62      CARDIOLITE + RP()30A + TC99M()RP()30A +
                     TECHNETIUM()TC()99M()SESTAMIBI +
                     TECHNETIUM()99TC()SESTAMIBI          RD = Remove
? rd s3                                                      Duplicates.
>>>Duplicate detection is not supported for File 398.

>>>Records from unsupported files will be retained in the RD set.
...examined 50 records (50)
...completed examining records                   Synonyms have nearly
    S4       50      RD S3 (unique items)         doubled recall.
? s s4 not s2                                     S5 contains unique items
             50      S4                           missing from recall in
             27      S2                           Search 5.8
    S5       24      S4 NOT S2
? set detail on
DETAIL set on
? ds                                              Display Sets to review
                                                     search history.

Set          File    Items    Description
             5         10
    912      6                                    Recall in each file
     72      5                                    from the term CARDIOLITE.
    155      2
    172      2
    434      2
    173      1
    398      1
S1           29      CARDIOLITE
     5       10                                   RD eliminates one
    912      5                                    duplicate citation found
     72      4                                    in RINGDOC (File 912) and
    155      2                                    one in EMBASE (File 72).
    172      2
    434      2
    173      1
    398      1
S2           27      RD S1 (unique items)
     5       27
    912      13                                   Recall from each file
     72      6                                    when CHEMSEARCH MAPped
    155      4                                    synonyms are added to
    172      2                                    the strategy.
    434      8
    173      1
    398      1
S3           62      CARDIOLITE + RP()30A + TC99M()RP()30A +
                     TECHNETIUM()-TC()99M()SESTAMIBI +
                     TECHNETIUM()99TC()SESTAMIBI
     5       26
    912      9                                    RD eliminates one
     72      4                                    duplicate citation found
    155      2                                    in BIOSIS (File 5), four
    172      2                                    in RINGDOC (File 912),
    434      5                                    two in EMBASE (File 72),
    173      1                                    two in MEDLINE (File 155)
    398      1                                    and three in SCISEARCH
                                                  (File 434).
```

**Search 5.10:** (cont.)

```
S4              50    RD S3 (unique items)
       5        16
     912         5
      72         0                          Final set shows that,
     155         0                          after duplicates are
     172         0                          removed, synonyms added
     434         3                          to recall in BIOSIS,
     173         0                          RINGDOC, and SCISEARCH.
     398         0
S5              24    S4 NOT S2
```

Search 5.10 continues the CARDIOLITE search example. After displaying the CHEMSEARCH record for the compound, the user MAPs its synonyms. The MAP feature is a cost-effective way of transferring the contents of designated data fields from selected records into search statements for use in other files. MAP eliminates the need to scan records for needed data (for example, alternative names) and then re-key the strategy to incorporate new information.

In this example, the searcher is still connected to several bioscience bibliographic files in OneSearch. MAPped synonyms, saved under the code TA218, are now executed across the same group of databases originally queried with the single term CARDIOLITE. Results in Set 3 illustrate how use of alternative terminology can dramatically increase recall. After duplicate citations are removed, fifty unique items remain - nearly double the number of references originally found. The final Display Sets shows that additional citations have been retrieved in BIOSIS PREVIEWS, RINGDOC, and SCISEARCH.

Compiling a list of possible names for a chemical compound *before* beginning a bioscience literature search would eliminate the need to backtrack later to locate fugitive references indexed under alternative terminology. Chemical 'dictionary' databases are the best place to start this compilation. Although not all online vendors offer such files, access to a good nomenclature source is as important to the bioscience searcher as it is to the chemical research specialist.

**Registry Numbers in bioscience files**

Some readers may have noticed that one kind of name, the CAS RN, was absent from the CARDIOLITE strategy. To omit Registry Numbers in a search of *Chemical Abstracts* online (CA SEARCH) would be unthinkable. SELECT CARDIOLITE in CA SEARCH on DIALOG yields zero results. Additional MAPped synonyms also lead to no CA SEARCH citations. Yet the Registry Number 109581-73-9 retrieves eleven references.

Unfortunately, most bioscience files do not consistently index with CAS RNs. As Table 5.5 indicates, even major files such as EMBASE and MEDLINE have adopted RNs for a limited time period. The National Library of Medicine has been assigning Registry Numbers in MEDLINE records since June 1980, but use of synonyms is nonetheless advisable when searching compounds yet to be added as controlled MeSH descriptors. For example, a search for another investigational drug found in PHARMAPROJECTS, BITISTATIN, leads to three references in MEDLINE, as shown in Search 5.11. All three are located by using the generic name (Set 1), but only one can be found by using the compound's Registry Number (Set 2). A display of index terms assigned to the two BITISTATIN records missed in the RN strategy reveals that identifiers were confined to derivative components in one case (item #1, Search 5.11). In the other, the RN for BITISTATIN is listed as zero. Why?

## Search 5.11: CAS Registry Numbers should be augmented with synonyms when searching chemical compounds in MEDLINE

```
File 155:MEDLINE _ 66-90/NOV (9011W4)

      Set  Items   Description
      ---  -----   -----------
? s bitistatin                              Generic name (S1) versus
      S1      3    BITISTATIN               Registry Number (S2)
? s rn=124123-27-9                          recall in MEDLINE.
      S2      1    RN=124123-27-9 (BITISTATIN)
? s s1 not s2
              3    S1
              1    S2
      S3      2    S1 NOT S2
? t s3/5/all
```

3/5/1
07398100    90305100
   Inhibition of platelet adhesion to surfaces of extracorporeal
circuits by disintegrins. RGD-containing peptides from viper venoms.
   Musial J; Niewiarowski S; Rucinski B; Stewart GJ; Cook JJ; Williams
JA; Edmunds LH Jr
   Department of Surgery, Hospital of the University of Pennsylvania,
Philadelphia.
   Circulation (UNITED STATES) Jul 1990, 82 (1) p261-73, ISSN 0009-7322
Journal Code: DAW
   Contract/Grant No.: HL-19055; HL-15226; HL-36579
   Languages: ENGLISH
   Journal Announcement: 9010
   Subfile: AIM; INDEX MEDICUS
   Previous studies indicate that exposure of fibrinogen receptors
associated with glycoprotein IIb/IIIa complex contributes to platelet
loss during cardiopulmonary bypass. Recently, we isolated a number of
RGD (Arg-Gly-Asp)-containing, low molecular weight, cysteine rich
peptides from viper venoms. These peptides, which we propose to call
"disintegrins," block platelet-fibrinogen interaction and platelet
aggregation. We compared the effect of RGDS (Arg-Gly-Asp-Ser) and four
disintegrins (echistatin, flavoridin, albolabrin, and **bitistatin**) on
platelet behavior in a membrane oxygenator....
   Tags: Human; Support, U.S. Gov't, P.H.S.
   Descriptors: *Extracorporeal Circulation—Instrumentation—IS;
*Oligopeptides—Pharmacology—PD; *Peptides—Pharmacology—PD;
*Platelet Adhesiveness—Drug Effects—DE; *Viper Venoms—Analysis—
AN; Amino Acid Sequence; Oligopeptides—Analysis—AN; Peptides—
Analysis—AN; Peptides—Genetics—GE; Platelet Activation—Drug
Effects—DE; Platelet Count—Drug Effects—DE; Thrombin—Pharmacology-
PD
   CAS Registry No.: 0 (arginyl-glycyl-aspartic acid); 0
(arginyl-glycyl-aspartyl-serine) Enzyme No.: EC 3.4.21.5 (Thrombin)

                                        **BITISTATIN is not
                                        identified by name
                                        or CAS RN in
                                        indexing.**

3/5/2
07187324    90094324
   Characterization and platelet inhibitory activity of **bitistatin**, a
potent arginine-glycine-aspartic acid-containing peptide from the
venom of the viper Bitis arietans.
   Shebuski RJ; Ramjit DR; Bencen GH; Polokoff MA
   Department of Pharmacology, Merck Sharp and Dohme Research

**Search 5.11:** (cont.)

```
Laboratories, West Point, Pennsylvania 19486.
J Biol Chem (UNITED STATES) Dec 25 1989, 264 (36) p21550-6,
ISSN 0021 9258 Journal Code: HIV
   Languages: ENGLISH
   Journal Announcement: 9004
   Subfile: INDEX MEDICUS
   A platelet aggregation inhibitory protein, bitistatin, was isolated
from the venom of the puff adder Bitis arietans. This protein is a
single-chain peptide containing 83 amino acids and 7 disulfide bonds.
Bitistatin contains the sequence arginine-glycine-aspartic acid and
shows considerable homology to two previously described snake venom
platelet aggregation inhibitors, trigramin and echistatin. Bitistatin
inhibited human and canine platelet aggregation....
   Tags: Animal; In Vitro
   Descriptors: *Coronary Circulation—Drug Effects—DE; *Coronary
Vessels—Physiology—PH; *Peptides—Isolation and Purification—IP;
*Platelet Aggregation Inhibitors—Isolation and Purification—IP;
Adenosine Diphosphate—Pharmacology—PD; Amino Acid Sequence; Bleeding
Time; Blood Platelets—Drug Effects—DE; Blood Platelets—Physiology
-PH; Collagen—Pharmacology—PD; Coronary Vessels—Drug Effects—DE;
Dogs; Molecular Sequence Data; Platelet Aggregation; Sequence
Homology, Nucleic Acid
   CAS Registry No.: 0 (bitistatin); 58-64-0 (Adenosine
Diphosphate); 9007-34-5 (Collagen)

                                        CAS RN not found for
                                        BITISTATIN.
```

CHEMLINE is the chemical nomenclature file used in the NLM search system's MEDLARS and TOXNET. If an RN cannot be located in CHEMLINE at the time a record is added to MEDLINE, a zero appears in this data field. This does not mean that the compound in question has yet to be assigned a Registry Number by CAS. The zero designation simply indicates that no RN was found in CHEMLINE. There are two possible reasons for this omission: (1) the comparatively limited scope of CHEMLINE and (2) its update schedule (every two months). Of the more than nine million substances registered by CAS since 1965, CHEMLINE cites a total of approximately 900,000. Its coverage is confined to substances found in other NLM databases (MEDLINE, TOXLINE, CANCERLIT, RTECS, HSDB) or in the Toxic Substances Control Act (TSCA) Inventory. Compared to other 'dictionary' files based on the CAS Registry Nomenclature and Structure Service discussed above (for example, CHEMDEX, CHEMSEARCH, the REGISTRY FILE on STN), CHEMLINE's scope is somewhat restricted, thus leading to RN omission in many MEDLINE records.

A final MEDLINE search for an investigational drug, DUP 785, underlines the importance of augmenting RN strategies with synonyms. When the MAPped Registry Number Search-Save TA221 is executed in Search 5.12, no records are found. But when synonyms MAPped from CHEMSEARCH are used (TA222), twenty-four MEDLINE citations are retrieved. As indexing assigned to the sample record displayed illustrates, **a different Registry Number** (rather than the zero designation) is the problem this time. Backtracking to CHEMSEARCH, the user would find that 96187-53-0 is actually the RN for the parent compound BREQUINAR, rather than the salt BREQUINAR SODIUM. MEDLINE, in fact, consistently assigns the parent compound Registry Number to salts and stereoisomers. For this reason, as well as the possible omission of RNs due to the limited scope of CHEMLINE, experienced bioscience searchers soon learn to augment Registry Number retrieval in MEDLINE when no *MeSH* descriptor is available for a compound under investigation.

## Search 5.12: Registry Number indexing in MEDLINE: parent compound RNs for salts and stereoisomers

```
File 155:MEDLINE _ 66-90/NOV (9011W4)

       Set   Items    Description                      CAS RN for DUP 785 MAPped
       ---   -----    -----------                      from CHEMSEARCH is executed
    ? exs ta221                                         in MEDLINE.
       S1      0      RN=96201-88-6
    ? exs ta222                                         MAPped synonyms are now
              18      BREQUINAR                          executed.
          157048      SODIUM
              17      BREQUINAR(W)SODIUM
             246      DUP
             290      785
              24      DUP(W)785
            2130      NSC
              17      368390
              17      NSC(W)368390
       S2     24      BREQUINAR()SODIUM + DUP()785 + NSC()368390
    ? t s2/8/1-5
                                                        Display of title and indexing
    2/8/1                                               for selected records.
    07444490   90351490
      Structure-activity relationship of quinoline carboxylic acids. A
    new class of inhibitors of dihydroorotate dehydrogenase.
      Tags: Animal
      Descriptors: *Antineoplastic Agents—Pharmacology—PD; *Biphenyl
    Compounds—Pharmacology—PD; *Oxidoreductases—Antagonists and
    Inhibitors—AI; Leukemia L1210—Enzymology—EN; Leukemia L1210—
    Pathology—PA; Mice; Structure-Activity Relationship
      CAS Registry No.: 96187-53-0 (DuP 785) Enzyme No.: EC 1.
    (Oxidoreductases); EC 1.3.99.11 (dihydroorotate dehydrogenase)


    2/8/2
    07408630 90315630
      In vivo inhibition of the pyrimidine de novo enzyme dihydroorotic
    acid dehydrogenase by brequinar sodium (DUP-785; NSC 368390) in mice
    and patients.
      Tags: Animal; Human; Support, Non-U.S. Gov't
      Descriptors: *Antineoplastic Agents—Therapeutic Use—TU; *Biphenyl
    Compounds—Therapeutic Use—TU; *Dihydro-Orotate Oxidase-Antagonists
    and Inhibitors—AI; *Neoplasms—Drug Therapy—DT; *Oxidoreductases—
    Antagonists and Inhibitors—AI; Biphenyl Compounds—Pharmacology—PD;
    Biphenyl Compounds—Pharmacokinetics—PK; Dose-Response Relationship,
    Drug; Lymphocytes—Enzymology—EN; Mice; Mice, Inbred BALB C;
    Reference Values; Uridine—Blood—BL
      CAS Registry No.: 58-96-8 (Uridine); 96187-53-0 (DuP 785)
    Enzyme No.: EC 1. (Oxidoreductases); EC 1.3.3.1 (Dihydro-Orotate
    Oxidase)
     .                                                  96187-53-0 is the CAS RN for
     .                                                  BREQUINAR, the parent
                                                        compound.
```

## OVERVIEW OF NON-BIBLIOGRAPHIC DATABASES

Discussion of chemical 'dictionary' files above previewed the importance of a growing family of non-bibliographic bioscience resources online. Other examples include directories of people, products and companies, or compilations of research project descriptions and of treatment protocol summaries. The selective listing of non-bibliographic sources in Table 5.6 shows the tremendous variety of databases available.

**Table 5.6: Non-bibliographic bioscience sources online: a selective list**

| Title | Notes on scope, updating ** | Vendor(s)*** |
|---|---|---|
| ABLEDATA | Product descriptions and evaluations for more than 13,000 rehabilitation aids and equipment for disabled persons. Includes manufacturers, cost and user comments. Updated monthly. | BRS |
| AIDSDRUGS | References to more than 80 drugs being tested. Includes nomenclature, properties, manufacturers, adverse reactions, contraindications, pharmacology data. Monthly updates. | NLM |
| AIDSTRIALS | Companion file to AIDSDRUGS, with descriptions of approximately 230 clinical trials, both ongoing and completed. Updated biweekly. | NLM |
| AMERICAN MEN AND WOMEN OF SCIENCE* | Biographical directory of 127,000 biological and physical scientists in United States and Canada. 1979 +, updated every 3 years. | DIALOG ORBIT |
| CHEMDEX | Nomenclature file for chemical substances cited in *Chemical Abstracts* 1972 to date. | ORBIT |
| CHEMICAL NOMENCLATURE | Substances cited in *Chemical Abstracts* 1967 to date. | Data-Star |
| CHEMLINE | Nomenclature and structure information for more than 900,000 substances found in other NLM files. Updated bimonthly. | NLM |
| CHEMSEARCH | Nomenclature and structural data for substances registered with Chemical Abstracts Service 1965 to date, updated monthly. | DIALOG |
| CLINPROT | Summary descriptions of clinical | NLM |

**Table 5.6:** (cont.)

| Title | Notes on scope, updating ** | Vendor(s)*** |
|---|---|---|
| | investigations of new cancer agents and treatment modalities. 1960 +, updated monthly. | |
| CRIS/USDA | Current Research Information System, U.S. Dept. of Agriculture, provides descriptions of ongoing and recently completed research projects in agriculture, forestry, biology, and related life sciences, including food and nutrition, consumer health and safety, biotechnology applications in animal and plant production. Current two years, updated monthly. | DIALOG |
| DENTALPROJ | Citations, with abstracts, to ongoing dental research projects, including grants, contracts, and career awards. Current fiscal year, updated semi-annually. | NLM |
| DERES | DeChema Databank on Research Institutes provides descriptions of research activities in chemical engineering and biotechnology at European universities and institutes. Current, updated every 3 years. | STN |
| DIRLINE | References to about 15,000 U.S. organizations that provide information in their areas of specialization, e.g., poison control centres, medical libraries. Updated quarterly. | NLM |
| EVENTLINE | References to forthcoming conferences, symposia, trade fairs worldwide. October 1989 +, updated monthly. | Data-Star DIALOG |
| EXPERTNET | References to 1,300 U.S. physicians and others willing to serve as expert witnesses or consultants to attorneys. Updated twice a year. | DIALOG |

**Table 5.6:** (cont.)

| Title | Notes on scope, updating ** | Vendor(s)*** |
|---|---|---|
| FAIRBASE | References to exhibitions, confer-ences and meetings in more than 100 countries.  Past and future events in all industries, including medicine and food technology.  Selected abstracts and statistics included. 1986 +, updated monthly. | BRS Data-Star |
| FEDERAL APPLIED TECHNOLOGY DATABASE | Directory of products, processes, and services, including federal laboratories. 1981 +, updated monthly. | BRS |
| FEDERAL RESEARCH IN PROGRESS | FEDRIP includes descriptions of ongoing and recently completed U.S. government-sponsored research. Updated monthly. | DIALOG |
| HAZARDLINE | Textual-numeric data on over 78,000 hazardous chemicals.  Includes regulatory, health, and precautionary information.  Updated monthly. | BRS |
| HEALTH DEVICES SOURCEBOOK | Directory of U.S. manufacturers, distributors, and importers of medical devices.  Annual updates. | DIALOG |
| HEALTH INSTRUMENT FILE | Descriptions of assessment instru-ments: i.e., questionnaires, observation checklists, tests, etc. 1985 +, updated quarterly. | BRS |
| HSDB* | Hazardous Substances Data Bank offers textual-numeric data on more than 4,200 chemical substances. | Data-Star NLM |
| LINSCOTT'S DIRECTORY OF IMMUNOLOGICAL & BIOLOGICAL REAGENTS | Lists vendors of reagents used in biomedical research. Updated quarterly. | ORBIT |
| PDQ* | Physician Data Query compiles infor-mation on cancer treatment methods | BRS NLM |

**Table 5.6:** (cont.)

| Title | Notes on scope, updating ** | Vendor(s)*** |
|---|---|---|
| | and active treatment programmes. Both full-text summary and directory entries. Current, updated monthly. | |
| PHARMA-CONTACTS | Directory of more than 17,000 companies, agencies, and institutions. Updated monthly. | BRS Data-Star |
| PHARMA-PROJECTS | Descriptions of forthcoming and new pharmaceutical products. 1980 +, updated monthly. | BRS Data-Star DIALOG STN |
| RTECS | Registry of Toxic Effects of Chemical Substances compiles textual-numeric data on toxic effects of approximately 101,000 chemicals. Updated quarterly. | DIALOG NLM |
| SEDBASE | Full-text summaries, with references, of known data regarding drug adverse reactions and interactions. Corresponds to *Meyler's Side Effects of Drugs and Side Effects of Drugs Annual.* 1977 +, updated quarterly. | Data-Star DIALOG |
| TSCA | Directory of 116,900 chemical substances covered in the *Toxic Substances Control Act Inventory.* Offers alternative nomenclatures and, on ORBIT, a Reporting Companies directory. 1976 + . | DIALOG ORBIT |
| WHO'S WHO IN TECHNOLOGY | Biographies of contemporary scientists. Updated semiannually. | ORBIT |

*      Also available on CD-ROM.
**     Update frequency may vary from vendor to vendor.
***    No attempt has been made to provide a comprehensive list of search services.

Information found in a non-bibliographic source such as PHARMAPROJECTS can spur a query for further background from bibliographic files, as was seen in the CARDIOLITE example begun in Search 5.7. Factual data compiled in a non-bibliographic file are often essential ingredients in successful bioscience search strategies, as was illustrated in the continuation of the CARDIOLITE example in Search 5.9, when synonyms found in CHEMSEARCH nearly doubled recall. As sources of biographical, statistical and nomenclature information, of funding sources and research-in-progress summaries, non-bibliographic databases complement results obtained in the more traditional literature reference files.

## FULL-TEXT DATABASES

A third major category of bioscience databases yet to be discussed is full-text resources. Table 5.7 offers brief notes on examples available through several vendors. Searchers sometimes question the advantage of online access to reference books such as *Martindale: The Extra Pharmacopoeia, Merck Index, the American Hospital Formulary Service* (DIF), or *Meyler's Side Effects of Drugs* (SEDBASE) when such sources are readily available in most bioscience libraries, are easy to use in hardcopy format, and are relatively inexpensive compared to the cost of frequent online use.

**Table 5.7: Examples of full-text bioscience files online**

| Title | Notes on scope, updating ** | Vendor(s) *** |
|---|---|---|
| AIDS KNOWLEDGE BASE* | Full text of approximately 300 articles on AIDS written by physicians and other health professionals. Includes bibliographic citations to relevant literature. 1986 +, monthly. | BRS |
| CCML | Comprehensive Core Medical Library includes 20 major medical textbooks and 80 medical journals. Retrospective coverage and updating varies by source. | BRS |
| COMBINED HEALTH INFORMATION DATABASE | Contains 12 subfiles of information on health education and promotion topics for health professionals and the general public, including AIDS, Alzheimer's disease, arthritis, skin diseases, blood resources, cholesterol, high blood pressure and smoking education, diabetes, kidney diseases. Citations with selected full text. Updated quarterly. | BRS |
| CONSUMER DRUG INFORMATION FULLTEXT | CDIF covers more than 270 generic drugs. Updated quarterly. | BRS DIALOG |

**Table 5.7:** (cont.)

| Title | Notes on scope, updating ** | Vendor(s) *** |
|---|---|---|
| DIOGENES | Citations to FDA regulatory documents regarding drugs and medical devices as well as to industry newsletters. Selected full text. Updated weekly. | BRS<br>Data-Star<br>DIALOG |
| DIF* | DRUG INFORMATION FULLTEXT corresponds to the *American Hospital Formulary Service* and the *Handbook on Injectable Drugs*. Full text of 1,400 drug monographs summarizing actions and uses, adverse reactions, interactions, and stability, with manufacturer/trade names listed. Updated quarterly. | BRS<br>DIALOG |
| DRUG NEWS | Three ADIS Press publications: *BioPharma, Inpharma*, and *Reactions*. 1983 +, updated daily. | Data-Star |
| F-D-C REPORTS | Three pharmaceutical industry news-letters, popularly known as *The Pink Sheet, The Rose Sheet*, and *The Gray Sheet*, covering drug, cosmetics/toiletries, and medical device business and regulatory developments. 1987 +, updated weekly. | Data-Star<br>DIALOG |
| GENERAL PRACTITIONER | Three publications online: *GP, Medeconomics*, and *MIMs Magazine*. 1987 +, updated weekly. | Data-Star |
| HEALTH NEWS DAILY | Full-text newsletter on healthcare delivery. 1989 +, updated daily. | Data-Star |
| MARTINDALE ONLINE* | Corresponds to the highly-regarded *Martindale: The Extra Pharmacopoeia*. Annual updates. | Data-Star<br>DIALOG |
| MERCK INDEX ONLINE | More than 10,000 monographs describing 30,000 chemicals, including drugs and biologicals. Updated semiannually. | BRS<br>DIALOG |
| PHIND | Pharmaceutical and Healthcare Industry News Database contains the full text | BRS<br>Data-Star |

**Table 5.7:** (cont.)

| Title | Notes on scope, updating ** | Vendor(s) *** |
|---|---|---|
| | of four newsletters: *Scrip, Clinica, Animal Pharm,* and *Agrow,* covering business, regulatory, and scientific developments. 1980 +, updated daily. | DIALOG |
| PTS NEWSLETTER DATABASE | Full text of more than 100 speciality newsletters, including *Antiviral Agents Bulletin, Applied Genetics News, Biomedical Materials, CDC AIDS Weekly, FDA Drug Bulletin* | Data-Star DIALOG |
| SCIENTIFIC AMERICAN MEDICINE* | Textual summaries of developments in 15 subspecialities of internal medicine. Updated monthly. | BRS |

\*     Also available on CDROM.
\*\*    Update frequency may vary from vendor to vendor.
\*\*\*   No attempt has been made to provide a comprehensive list of all search services.

It is true that for 'one compound-one monograph' queries, manual access to hardcopy equivalents is less expensive and just as fast. But when information requests require retrieval of an entire class of compounds with a given characteristic (for example, antipyretics, or drugs that induce photosensitivity), or when a request calls for coordination of several different factors, online access is clearly advantageous. For example, which emetics can be administered orally, are soluble in water, are odourless with a taste that can be disguised in anisette, and have a fatal dose in small enough quantities to be administered in an egg-spoonful of liquid? When a fictional detective needed an answer to this question fifteen years ago, he had to resort to overnight study of the 2,025-page printed *Martindale* to correlate all of these properties.[8] Only the therapeutic concept in this question (emetics) would be easily accessible in the hardcopy index. Adding physical and chemical properties identified in drug monograph texts but not their indexing makes finding an answer other than via computer (whereby each textword becomes an access point) a time-consuming task.

Another advantage of machine-readable equivalents is greater currency. Between printed editions of *Martindale* or *Merck*, revisions and additions are regularly added online. Full-text sources such as newsletters also offer readers greater currency. Items destined for publication in *Scrip* or *Clinica* are, for example, available online through PHIND days before the printed newsletters will reach users.

Finally, special indexing and search features that are not offered in hardcopy editions are often provided in their online counterparts. MARTINDALE ONLINE developed a hierarchical thesaurus of more than 9,600 descriptors to facilitate searching on classes of drugs, but printed editions omit this feature. Sorting results by user-defined factors such as company or product names and the ability to create special tabular reports of selected data elements are examples of other value-added features in many online full-text files.

## COMPACT DISC (CD-ROM) DATABASES

By the end of 1986, eleven life science databases were available on compact disc for public preview, if not purchase.[9] Only two years later, MEDLINE alone had been licensed for availability through eighteen different suppliers.[10] The advent of CD-ROM technology in the past decade has obviously introduced an exciting new alternative in the information world. Resources offered on compact disc as well as online have been identified in Tables 5.1, 5.6, and 5.7. Other products unique to the CD-ROM format are listed in Table 5.8. With so many choices, what factors need to be considered in evaluating 'on disc' *versus* online products? A checklist could include:

- software capabilities
- cost
- currency
- scope/file size

**Table 5.8: Selected bioscience databases available in CD-ROM format\***

**BIOLOGICAL & AGRICULTURAL INDEX** - Corresponds to hardcopy bibliographic source of same title from H.W. Wilson.

**CANCER-CD** - Subsets from EMBASE, MEDLINE, and Yearbook Medical Publishers.

**CHEM-BANK** - Three databases on potentially hazardous chemicals: RTECS, OHMTADS (Oil and Hazardous Materials-Technical Assistance Data System from the Environmental Protection Agency), and CHRIS (Chemical Hazard Response Information from the U.S. Coast Guard).

**COMPACT LIBRARY: AIDS** - includes the electronic textbook AIDS KNOWLEDGE BASE, plus a subject subset of MEDLINE, and the full text of articles about AIDS from major medical journals such as *Annals of Internal Medicine, British Medical Journal, JAMA, Lancet,* and *New England Journal of Medicine.*

**COMPUTERIZED CLINICAL INFORMATION SYSTEM (CCIS)** - A full-text reference source from Micromedex.

**DRUGDEX** - Full-text Micromedex source consisting of two subfiles, one with 775 drug monographs covering actions and uses, and a second offering 5,300 patient-based consultations summarizing answers to drug-related problems documented by drug information centres and clinical pharmacology services nationwide.

**DRUGS DATABASE** - produced by the American Society of Hospital Pharmacists, combines DIP and IPA on one compact disc.

**Table 5.8:** (cont.)

---

**EMERGINDEX** - Contains more than 285 reviews of emergency and acute care treatment protocols as well as 17,000 citations with abstracts, to 50 journals. Produced by Micromedex.

**MAXX (MAXIMUM ACCESS TO DIAGNOSIS AND THERAPY)** - Covers 12 speciality areas and includes complete drug monographs from the U.S. Pharmacopeia.

**NATASHA** - National Archive on Sexuality, Health and Adolescence, a statistical file with access to 109 data sets and more than 39,000 variables from 82 major studies relevant to adolescent sexuality.

**NURSE LIBRARY** - A compilation of complete textbooks and manuals.

**ONCODISC** - The PDQ database, plus Lippincott books on oncology, including *Cancer, Principles and Practices of Oncology, Advances in Oncology,* and the *Manual for Staging Cancer.*

**OSH-ROM** - Contains NIOSHTIC database, HSELINE (Health & Safety Executive, UK), and CISDIC (United Nations International Occupational Safety and Health Centre of the International Labour Organization).

**PDR (PHYSICIANS' DESK REFERENCE)** - Full text of well-known drug reference sources from Medical Economics, including the PDR for ophthalmology and for OTC drugs.

**THE PHYSICIAN LIBRARY** - compilation of complete textbooks and manuals for major medical specialities.

**POISINDEX** - Substance identification information and management/treatment protocols, produced by Micromedex.

**POLTOX** - Pollution and toxicology database from Cambridge Scientific Abstracts.

---

\* See also CD-ROM sources identified in Tables 5.1, 5.6, and 5.7.

Access software deserves thorough evaluation. Finding a CD-ROM interface that fully exploits special features in the target database to the degree achieved in online databases, and at the same speed, can be difficult. Although CD-ROM products differ dramatically in response time, search processing on compact disc tends to be slow compared to counterparts online. Furthermore, if a database on compact disc has a highly controlled vocabulary, a classification scheme, and other less-than-transparent indexing features (like many bioscience files), the CD-ROM access program will need to do a great deal behind the scenes if it is to remain user-friendly, yet avoid superficiality.

Any CD-ROM interface which helps searchers bridge the gap between their limited keyword requests and the unpredictable vocabulary actually used by bioscience authors is a bonus. Flexible output options are an example of indirect search assistance taken for granted by online searchers, but often absent in user-friendly programs. Enabling users to browse retrieved records in short format (for example, title and indexing) can lead to additional candidate keywords otherwise missed.

If a CD-ROM database is intended for access by an end-user audience, prospective purchasers sometimes undervalue indexing and software features in favour of attractive design and a fixed-fee environment. In fact, it is all the more important in such situations that a compact disc resource perform the function of an expert searcher on behalf of the user. To equate user-friendliness with over-simplification, or to assume user satisfaction indicates a satisfactory product, are temptations best avoided if CD-ROM users are to rely on their search results, as many bioscience searchers do, as aids in patient care or in making important corporate research decisions.

Cost and frequency of use will also affect purchasing decisions. Subscription fees for life science CD-ROM sources identified here range from $500 to more than $20,000 per year. Anticipated frequency of use at a fixed fee must be weighed against estimated online charges on a pay-as-you-go basis. Creating a CD-ROM searching environment where time is less obviously linked with money is extremely attractive when projected usage is high and will include a novice end-user group. Convenience and increased accessibility to database searching may, of course, outweigh cost recovery in online versus on-disc selection decisions.

Frequency of file updates and file segmentation on compact disc *versus* online must also be considered. Few bioscience CD-ROM products are updated as frequently as their online counterparts. Another drawback is that only relatively small segments of the larger bibliographic databases fit on one compact disc, necessitating separate lookups on a succession of discs when a retrospective search is needed - in contrast to rapid access to several years' data in one search online. Because of disc storage space limitations, several CD-ROM databases are actually subsets of their larger online counterparts. Collections based on subject speciality areas or on selected journal titles are not uncommon. CD-ROM files sometimes omit older publication years, specific types of source documents covered in their online namesakes (for example, dissertations or technical reports), or selected data fields for searching and/or display. Author addresses or broad subject concept codes may, for example, be stripped from CD-ROM records.

Multifile searching facilitated by large online systems, not to mention simultaneous access to multiple databases with automatically merged output and duplicate detection, is, of course, not yet possible in the CD-ROM environment. Compact disc systems usually also lack increasingly important collateral services available online, such as electronic mail delivery of output to remote users, cross-file selection aids, automatic data extraction and transfer from one file to another (for example, MAPping), and source document delivery services.

## IMPLICATIONS

What will be evident from this introductory overview of online and CD-ROM resources in the biosciences is that with such a variety of options available, resource selection can be challenging. Most new sources in the life sciences focus on a specific subject area, reflecting increasing specialization within the professions they serve. This trend toward specialization will, no doubt, continue. The implication for searchers is that multifile access is now the norm, rather than an exception.

Regular consultation of cross-file indexes online will help define the group of complementary resources needed to answer a given query. Effective search sequencing within a database family thus defined involves consideration of many factors beyond subject scope or recall obtained from a necessarily 'generic' cross-file strategy. Knowledge of document coverage, types of subject indexing provided, availability of abstracts or full text, and other value-added features will assist searchers in determining an effective order of precedence among files to be consulted. Careful analysis of the topic to be searched with a view to matching it with resource capabilities highlighted in this chapter is important.

For example, are concepts to be searched old or new, much written about, or rarely discussed? Older concepts are easier to search in databases with highly controlled vocabularies. Newer or infrequently cited topics call for databases with more natural language or 'uncontrolled' access points and with document coverage beyond journal articles, such as conference papers, patents, letters and other brief research communications. Does the query involve searching broad concepts such as groups of chemicals, body or organ systems, or taxonomic classes? Files with classification schemes will not only facilitate retrieval of broad concepts, but also provide lists of relevant terms that can be used in building better strategies for searching files without classification schemes.

Are other special features needed? Is a subject population specified in the search request? Are characteristics such as age, gender, occupation or racial/ethnic group key factors? If a chemical is mentioned, what type of name is used to refer to the substance? Will trade or company name indexing be important?

Answers to questions such as these will influence search-sequencing decisions. What is learned in one resource can affect the strategy used in another. Above all, flexibility and iterative search techniques are essential ingredients in bioscience searching.

In conclusion, it should also be acknowledged that despite increasing specialization in database production, boundaries between disciplines are somewhat artificial in the context of information retrieval. Many databases discussed in other chapters in this book contain material relevant to bioscience topics. For example, the engineering files INSPEC and COMPENDEX are excellent sources in the medical device and instrumentation subject area. Searches involving administrative, economic, or societal aspects of life science topics (for example, personnel relations, law and medicine, rehabilitation and special education, ethics, family planning, gerontology) may benefit from bibliographical records provided in ABI/INFORM, MANAGEMENT CONTENTS, FAMILY RESOURCES or SOCIAL SCISEARCH. Crossfile index results shown in Search 5.9 underline the need for expanding search horizons to take into account potentially relevant news, business and regulatory information sources such as BUSINESS DATELINE, COURIER PLUS, PTS PROMT, INVESTEXT, TRADE & INDUSTRY INDEX or FEDERAL REGISTER. The Further Reading at the end of this chapter will, hopefully, provide background on additional databases and problem-solving applications beyond the basic principles discussed here.

## REFERENCES

1. *Directory of Online Databases.* New York: Cuadra/Elsevier, July 1990. [quarterly publication]
2. *Medical Subject Headings - Annotated Alphabetic List.* Bethesda, MD: National Library of Medicine, 1990. [annual publication]
3. *BIOSIS PREVIEWS Search Guide.* Philadelphia: Biological Abstracts, 1989. [annual updates]
4. *EMBASE Guide to EMTREES and Indexing Systems.* 2 vols. Amsterdam: Elsevier, 1989.
5. *Medical Subject Headings - Tree Structures.* Bethesda, MD: National Library of Medicine, 1990. [annual]
6. M.E. Funk and C.A. Reid.  Indexing consistency in MEDLINE. *Bulletin of the Medical Library Association* 71(2) 1983 176-183.
7. SCISEARCH. Chapter 34 in: *Guide to DIALOG Databases.* Palo Alto, CA: DIALOG Information Services, 1980.
8. B. Snow. MARTINDALE ONLINE: Drug info in a detective's toolkit. *Database* 11(3) 1988 90-98.
9. B. Snow. Life science sources on laser disk. *Online* 11(2) 1987 113-116.
10. A.J. Van Camp. The many faces of MEDLINE. *Database* 11(5) 1988 101-107.

# FURTHER READING

Barber, J. et al.  Case studies of the indexing and retrieval of pharmacology papers. *Information Processing and Management* 24(2) 1988 141-150.

Bowler, R.P. and Becker, C.E.  Computer searching for occupational medicine. *Journal of Occupational Medicine* 28(5) 1986 370-372.

Brahmi, F.A.  SCI CD edition: ISI's new CD-ROM product. *Medical Reference Services Quarterly* 8(2) 1989 1-13.

Branch, K.  Computerized sources of AIDS information. *Medical Reference Services Quarterly* 7(4) 1988 1-18.

Bronson, R.J.  Alcohol information for clinicians and educators database. *Medical Reference Services Quarterly* 8(2) 1989 65-76.

Bruce, N.G. and Farren, A.L.  Searching BIOSIS PREVIEWS in the health care setting. *Medical Reference Services Quarterly* 6(2) 1987 17-37.

Cassidy, S.L. and Kostrewski, B.J.  An evaluation of information sources in household product poisoning. *Journal of Information Science* 12(4) 1986 143-151.

Charen, T.  The Tree Trimmer. *NLM Technical Bulletin* 214 1987 10-11.

Dalrymple, P.W.  CD-ROM MEDLINE use and users: information transfer in a clinical setting. *Bulletin of the Medical Library Association* 78(3) 1990 224-232.

Eyers, J.E. and Taylor, A.E.R.  Online searching of parasitology literature. *Parasitology Today* 4(11) 324-328.

Fishel, C.C.  The Nursing and Allied Health (CINAHL) database: a guide to effective searching. *Medical Reference Services Quarterly* 4(3) 1985 1-26.

Fryer, R.K., Baratz, N. and Helenius, M.  Beyond MEDLINE: a review of ten non-MEDLINE CD-ROM databases for the health sciences. *Laserdisk Professional* 2(3) 1989 27-30.

Glaser, J.  Index to Dental Literature and MEDLINE: a guide to searching the dental literature. *Medical Reference Services Quarterly* 3(2) 1984 1-16.

Hewison, N.S.  COMBINED HEALTH INFORMATION database. *Medical Reference Services Quarterly* 6(2) 1987 71-81.

Hewison, N.S.  CURRENT CONTENTS SEARCH. *Medical Reference Services Quarterly* 7(4) 1988 57-66.

Hewison, N.S.  The SMOKING AND HEALTH database. *Medical Reference Services Quarterly* 6(4) 1987 53-63.

Janke, R.V. and Losinger, I.D.  Sports information online: searching the SPORT database. *Database* 11(1) 1988 15-25.

Judkins, D.Z.  Searching hints: A chronic disease hedge for use on MEDLINE. *Medical Reference Services Quarterly* 3(2) 1984 72-73.

Kahn, T.J. and Orr, C.  BIOETHICSLINE: overview for searchers. *Medical Reference Services Quarterly* 3(3) 1984 1-21.

Kelly, S.A.  Retrieving information on the neurophysiology of speech. *Medical Reference Services Quarterly* 7(4) 1988 31-45.

Kjellander, E., Olsson, P.O., and Zajicek, E.  Usefulness of the online database CANCERLIT: an evaluative study based on consecutive searches in CANCERLIT and MEDLINE for oncologists. *Journal of the National Cancer Institute* 74(6) 1985 1351-1353.

Klinkroth, M.M.  Full-text databases in the health sciences. *Medical Reference Services Quarterly* 5(3) 1986 1-15.

McCain, K.W.  Descriptor and citation retrieval in the medical behavioral sciences literature: retrieval overlaps and novelty distribution. *Journal of the American Society for Information Science* 40(2) 1989 110-114.

McGowan, A.T.  DIOGENES: a database for medical regulatory information. *Medical Reference Services Quarterly* 6(3) 1987 17-24.

McGowan, A.T. and Mater, D.A.  Identifying drugs in the chemical literature: a proposed strategy. *Medical Reference Services Quarterly* 4(4) 1985 1-16.

Nye, J.B. and Brassil, E.C.  Online searching on selected business databases for management aspects of health care. *Medical Reference Services Quarterly* 3(1) 1984 33-48.

Ojala, M.  The business of medicine. *Online* 12(6) 1988 88-93.

Perry, C.A.  Knowledge bases in medicine: a review. *Bulletin of the Medical Library Association* 78(2) 1990 271-282.

Perry, C.A.  Online information retrieval in pharmacy and related fields. *American Journal of Hospital Pharmacy* 43(6) 1986 1509-1524.

Price, C. and Burley, R.A.  An evaluation of information sources for retrospective literature searching on occupational diseases. *Journal of Information Science* 12(5) 1986 257-265.

Roeder, C.S.  Locating information on medical syndromes. *Medical Reference Services Quarterly* 7(2) 1988 23-30.

Schiftmann, G.N.  'Hedges'...the sometimes ignored search technique for example, that can save a lot of time. *Online* 9(6) 1985 40-41.

Self, D.A.  Searching the literature of veterinary medicine. *Medical Reference Services Quarterly* 4(4) 1985 17-28.

Snow, B.  Author address or corporate affiliations. *Database* 8(4) 1985 58-61.

Snow, B.  Competitive intelligence in the health device industry. *Online* 13(4) 1989 107-114.

Snow, B.  Consumer health information online. *Online* 11(4) 1987 110-116.

Snow, B.  *Database Search Aids: Health Sciences.*  Los Altos, CA: Database Services, 1982.

Snow, B.  Differences in CANCERLIT on MEDLARS and DIALOG. *Online* 10(6) 1986 118-123.

Snow, B.  DIOGENES sheds new light on FDA regulatory actions. *Database* 11(2) 1988 72-80.

Snow, B.  *Drug Information: A Guide to Current Resources.*  Chicago: Medical Library Association, 1989.

Snow, B.  Finding medical and health care statistics online. *Online* 12(4) 1988 86-95.

Snow, B.  General business statistics and r & d specifics: PHARMAPROJECTS has the answers. *Database* 13(5) 1990 111-115.

Snow, B.  Health care statistics online: business, news, and government resources. *Online* 12(5) 1988 102-109.

Snow, B.  In search of medical expert witnesses. *Database* 12(2) 1989 103-107.

Snow, B.  Keeping up-to-date with full-text F-D-C REPORTS. *Online* 14(3) 1990 94-97.

Snow, B.  Laboratory test modifications. *Database* 9(3) 1986 81-85.

Snow, B.  MAPping in medicine: creating and editing special search-saves. *Database* 10(3) 1987 100-107.

Snow, B.  Monitoring bioscience legal and regulatory news. *Online* 12(6) 1988 107-117.

Snow, B.  A new medical device directory online: ECRI's HEALTH DEVICES SOURCEBOOK. *Online* 13(3) 1989 103-107.

Snow, B.  Online database coverage of pharmaceutical journals. *Database* 7(1) 1984 12-26.

Snow, B.  Online puzzles: conference papers and proceedings. *Database* 11(4) 1988 94-103.

Snow, B.  Online searching for alternatives to animal testing. *Online* 14(4) 1990 94-97.

Snow, B.  Parenteral incompatibilities. *Database* 9(2) 1986 75-83.

Snow, B.  Patents in non-patent databases: bioscience specialty files. *Database* 12(5) 1989 41-48.

Snow, B.  Patents on non-patent databases: food, agriculture, and environment files. *Database* 12(6) 1989 115-119.

Snow, B.  People in medicine: searching names online. *Online* 10(5) 1986 122-127.

Snow, B.  Protecting patients and staff from medical equipment hazards: HEALTH DEVICES ALERTS online. *Database* 13(1) 1990 87-90.

Snow, B.  Review articles in MEDLINE: past and present. *Online* 13(2) 1989 101-105.

Snow, B.  Searching for drug interactions data. *Database* 9(1) 1986 69-74.

Snow, B.  SEDBASE online for drug side effects and interactions. *Database* 12(1) 1989 85-94.

Snow, B.  Special features in DE HAEN DRUG DATA. *Database* 10(5) 1987 116-126.

Snow, B.  Tapping into the 'invisible college'...online cited reference searching. *Online* 10(2) 1986 83-88.

Snow, B.  Trimming the thorns from MEDLINE's Trees. *Online* 12(3) 1988 70-76.

Snow, B.  When corporate human resource departments look for health care information. *Online* 13(5) 1989 112-118.

Snow, B.  When hospitals mean business: online sources for health care marketing information. *Online* 13(6) 1989 112-116.

Snow, B.  Why use a database thesaurus? *Online* 9(6) 1985 92-96.

Spala, J.L.  Sport science literature. *Medical Reference Services Quarterly* 4(2) 1985 15-37.

Tousignaut, D.R. and Spigai, F.  Searching pharmacy databases: nomenclature problems and inconsistencies. *Database* 5 1982 23-29.

Ulincy, L.D.  In search of information on aging: AGELINE. *Medical Reference Services Quarterly* 7(3) 1988 69-83.

Van Buskirk, N.E.  The review article in MEDLINE: ambiguity of definition and implications for online searchers. *Bulletin of the Medical Library Association* 72(4) 1984 349-352.

Van Camp, A.J.  HEALTH INSTRUMENT FILE. *Database* 12(3) 1989 104-108.

Van Camp, A.J.  Material safety data sheets: online and CD-ROM sources. *Online* 14(2) 1990 97-100.

Van Camp, A.J.  Searching the published conference literature. *Database* 13(4) 1990 100-102.

Van Camp, A.J.  Strategies and codes for finding cancer information online. *Online* 14(5) 1990 114-117.

Van Camp, A.J.  Subject code searching in biomedical databases. *Online* 14(1) 1990 90-94.

Van Camp, A.J.  Tips for finding sports medicine information online. *Database* 11(1) 1988 17-19.

Van Horn, L.J.  A hedge for searching nutrition and disease in MEDLINE. *Medical Reference Services Quarterly* 3(2) 1984 31-42.

Wexler, P.  HSDB and material safety data sheets. *NLM Technical Bulletin* 219 1987 10-13.

Wexler, P. and Goshorn, J.  Searching RTECS on TOXNET. *NLM Technical Bulletin* 224 1987 1, 5-8.

Williams, P.A.  Overview of on-line information data bases in orthopedics. *Orthopedic Clinics of North America* 17(4) 1986 519- 526.

Wycoff, L.W., Cable, L.G., and Buhman, L.  HEALTHLAWYER: an informal comparison with medical and legal databases. *Medical Reference Services Quarterly* 6(2) 1987 51-63.

Yonker, V.A., et al.  Coverage and overlaps in bibliographic databases relevant to forensic medicine - A comparative analysis of MEDLINE. *Bulletin of the Medical Library Association* 78(1) 1990 49-56.

# 6 Agriculture

*John Parkinson and Ian Snowley*

## INTRODUCTION

Agriculture belongs to that seemingly endless list of occupations that claim to be the second oldest profession in the world. It may well be that the assertion is justified in this case. It is now many centuries since the majority of the human race supported itself by a hunter/gatherer way of life. *The Shorter Oxford English Dictionary* [1] defines the subject as 'The science and art of cultivating the soil; including the gathering in of crops and the rearing of livestock'. E.A.R. Bush in his two volume bibliography of agriculture, observes more expansively that:

> 'Agriculture, as those who have anything to do with it well know, is not a single subject but a whole conglomeration which includes aspects of the social, the physical, the biological, the mechanical and the applied sciences...'[2]

Even since this definition was made back in 1974 the public perception of agriculture has changed. Increasing intensification of land use and increasing use of agrochemicals, mechanization, rationalization of farm labour, and the creation of vast 'prairies' where once was a patchwork of smaller fields, have all contributed to the feeling that agriculture is now an industry like any other, rather than the picturesque rural pursuit we had imagined. To some extent this is true, and the fact is reflected in the emergence of the term 'agribusiness' to denote agriculture's full-blooded participation in the commercial market place.

But agriculture still occupies a unique position in our society, and as the pressure for greater and greater production subsides, there is also increasing attention being given to the environmental impact of agriculture, both in the negative sense of examining its destructive effects, and in the positive sense which sees farmers as natural wardens of the countryside.

All these changes and more are reflected in the coverage of online databases. In this chapter we will deal with relatively few, but should you try the terms 'agriculture' or 'farm(ing)' in virtually any database, you will stand a good chance of coming up with something.

THE QUOTATIONS DATABASE on DIALOG is no exception and the two quotes below, though old and ancient respectively, seem to reflect (rightly or wrongly!) another popular perception of farming.

> 'Our farmers round, well pleased with constant gain,
> Like other farmers, flourish and complain'
> > George Crabbe from *The Parish Register*


> 'O farmers excessively fortunate if only they
> recognized their blessings!'
> > Virgil from *Georgics*


## USERS OF AGRICULTURAL INFORMATION

Those fortunate farmers are, ironically, probably the last people in the sphere of agriculture who would actually initiate an online search in the conventional sense. They may use some form of Videotex for up-to-date weather or market information, or general farming alerts, and we shall deal with access to these type of services elsewhere. But by and large this kind of searching consists of menu-driven access to the online equivalent of a daily news bulletin, and not the kind of complex, query answering search with which the present chapter will deal.

The main users of agricultural databases are usually outside the farm gate. They are mainly those doing agriculture-related research, either in a government laboratory or a large private company; agricultural advisors and consultants; or those engaged in agricultural education.


## CORE AGRICULTURAL DATABASES

There are three massive databases which are produced by the three organizations which dominate the world of agricultural information; these are AGRICOLA, AGRIS and CAB ABSTRACTS.


## AGRICOLA

AGRICOLA is produced by the National Agricultural Library (NAL) of the United States Department of Agriculture (USDA) and has been available since 1970, making it one of the earliest publicly available databases. Since 1984 it has also incorporated the records of other cooperating North American institutions such as the American Agricultural Economics Documentation Center and the Food Nutrition Information Center. More than two thousand serial titles are currently reviewed, and over the twenty years of the database's existence a total of around two and a half million records have been loaded.

It is updated monthly with approximately nine thousand records added at each update. It is used by the NAL to produce the printed *Bibliography of Agriculture* [3], and there is now also a CD-ROM version of the database available. It is worth noting that, since 1985, the NAL has adopted the *CAB Thesaurus* [4] for its indexing terms, thus creating a certain amount of compatibility between these two databases for the searcher. AGRICOLA is available on DIALOG in two files, 1970-1978, and 1979 to the present, and on DIMDI in one file from 1983 to present.

## AGRIS

AGRIS appears on DIALOG, ESA-IRS (IRS-Dialtech) and DIMDI. The file starts in 1975 on each, which corresponds to the commencement of publication of the hard copy equivalent, *Agrindex* [5]. However, only sixty-six per cent of the database is loaded on DIALOG; all the American entries are omitted in order to avoid duplication with AGRICOLA. DIMDI splits the file at 1983/84. The situation on ESA-IRS is also idiosyncratic in that ESA-IRS in this case is actually a gateway to another computer host, that of the International Atomic Energy Agency in Vienna where the database is actually held. Going through this gateway (and getting back out through it!) is now relatively simple, although having to change search language to the IAEA's 'STAIRS' language is a nuisance.

AGRIS is produced by the Food and Agriculture Organization (FAO) of the United Nations from the collected input of over one hundred national and multinational centres worldwide. None of these centres, however, is in the United States, so that there is a definite bias against United States' material. This is quite useful to the searcher as it militates against duplication with AGRICOLA which covers United States' material very well. On the other hand it uses its own thesaurus *Agrovoc* [6] to produce indexing terms, making it the odd-man-out in this respect. AGRIS is also updated monthly and contains over 1.1 million records.

## CAB ABSTRACTS

The Commonwealth Agricultural Bureaux (now CAB International) is a United Kingdom-based organization, administered and financed by its twenty-nine member governments. It has for many years produced printed abstracts covering different agricultural subject areas, and still currently produces over fifty of these. They form the basis of its database, most of the records in which (in contrast to the other major databases) contain abstracts. CABI scans over 8,500 journals in thirty-seven different languages. The database is updated monthly, and there are over 2.4 million records.

CAB ABSTRACTS is available on seven hosts, mostly commencing in 1972. On DIALOG it is held in two files split at 1983/84. On ESA-IRS it starts at 1973 and is split at 1985/86, but it is also held in one file going back to 1973. On DIMDI it is held in one file all the way back to 1972, but is also in two files split along subject lines - Animal and Plant. On STN it is held on one file from 1978. BRS have it back to 1980, Data-Star back to 1984, and CAN/OLE (available in Canada only) back to 1972.

As has been mentioned, CAB publishes its own thesaurus which has been adopted by AGRICOLA. Despite attempts to achieve agreement between the 'big three' on a universal agricultural thesaurus [7] little progress has yet been made. However a useful collaborative venture that has been achieved is the publication of an *International Union List of Agricultural Serials* [8], a compilation of the serials indexed in AGRICOLA, AGRIS and CAB, which greatly simplifies the searcher's task in finding which database indexes a given title.

## SAMPLE SEARCH AND ANALYSIS

Dealing with such huge databases as AGRICOLA, AGRIS and CAB, it is very difficult to design a search which both does justice to all of them, and is concise enough for analysis within the limits of a chapter in a book.

The search  shown as Search 6.1 has therefore been chosen from searches which the author has performed because it is reasonably typical, has a manageable number of retrieved records, and has one record which is present in each retrieved list, thus affording a direct comparison of database style.

For further brevity the search has been performed on DIALOG using the OneSearch facility, whereby the two files of AGRICOLA, the one of AGRIS, and the two of CAB are searched at once. Title and database information only have been displayed - file numbers are as given below. Aside from the aspect of comparison, however, it is worth focusing on some aspects of the search which demonstrate points worth bearing in mind when online searching in agriculture.

The search is for a pesticide called Larvadex in the context of controlling houseflies in poultry houses. The search is expressed in the form POULTRY AND (LARVADEX OR CYROMAZINE) AND (HOUSEFL? OR HOUSE(W)FLY OR HOUSE(W)FLIES OR MUSCA(W)DOMESTICA). The term POULTRY is left open as the ways that poultry housing can be referred to is somewhat unpredictable. In any event, if there is a reference to poultry in the context of fly control, the likelihood is that it will be about poultry houses!

The term LARVADEX is the common name of a pesticide whose chemical name is CYROMAZINE. There is no guarantee that a database will cross reference from common to chemical name (or vice versa) so it pays to look up the synonym [9] and include both terms. The point is borne out by this search where both terms occur in the title fields. CAB gives the chemical name in the Descriptor field when the common name occurs in the title, but not vice versa. The same rule applies to all animal and plant life (including insects) where common names will have a binomial scientific equivalent [10]; in this case MUSCA DOMESTICA for the common housefly. There is an added complication here in that 'housefly' can be given either as one word or two. As one word it is easy to truncate for the plural form, but not so when the 'FL?' is split off. On DIALOG, at least, the computer baulks at the suggestion of searching everything beginning 'FL...'! So there is nothing for it but to put in both singular and plural forms with suitable adjacency markers. To be strictly loyal to the dictum about binomials, of course, one should also enter all the scientific names (as well as all the common names) for birds falling into the class POULTRY. In reality that which belongs to the farmer tends to be cited by its common name, and, especially when searching the purely agricultural (as opposed to scientific) databases, there is probably little or nothing to be gained by entering farm animals by their Latin names as well as their common names.

## Search 6.1: Comparative search on AGRICOLA (c US Dept of Agriculture), AGRIS (c FAO) and CAB (c. CABI)

```
System:OS  - DIALOG OneSearch

File  10:AGRICOLA _ 1979-90/AUG

File 110:AGRICOLA - 70-78/Dec
See File 10(CurrenT)

File 203:AGRIS INTERNATIONAL_74-90/MAY

File  50:CAB ABSTRACTS _ 1984-90/JUL
SEE ALSO FILE 53 (1972-1983) COPR. CABI 1990.

File  53:CAB ABSTRACTS 1972-1983
SEE FILE 50 (1984+) COPR. CABI 1989

     Set      Items    Description
     ---      -----    -----------

             73953     POULTRY
                34     LARVADEX
               145     CYROMAZINE
```

**Search 6.1:** (cont.)

```
              1633    HOUSEFL
             18804    HOUSE
             19513    FLY
              1397    HOUSE(W)FLY
             18804    HOUSE
             15548    FLIES
               941    HOUSE(W)FLIES
              7417    MUSCA
              9903    DOMESTICA
              6034    MUSCA(W)DOMESTICA
     S1         23    POULTRY AND (LARVADEX OR CYROMAZINE) AND (HOUSEFL
                      OR HOUSE(W)FLY OR HOUSE(W)FLIES OR MUSCA(W)DOMESTICA)
```

?**t1/6/ALL**

```
 1/6/1        (Item 1 from file: 10)
86122124 86041245 Holding Library: AGL
Control of house flies in commercial poultry houses in Connecticut

 1/6/2        (Item 2 from file: 10)
84115911    84006023  Holding Library: AGL
Efficacy and  nontarget  effects  of  Larvadex  as  a  feed
additive for controlling house flies in caged-layer poultry manure (Musca
domestica, mites, Carcinops)

 1/6/3        (Item 3 from file: 10)
84074334 83113331 Holding Library: AGL
Control of manure breeding flies in poultry houses with Larvadex, 1981 (Musca
domestica)

 1/6/4        (Item 1 from file: 203)
0771658 Efficacy and nontarget effects of Larvadex as a feed additive for
controlling house flies in caged-layer poultry manure [Musca domestica,
mites, Carcinops]

 1/6/5        (Item 1 from file: 50)
0999005 0J078-03057; 7A016-01942
Flies are fast breeders.

 1/6/6        (Item 2 from file: 50)
0824607 0V059-02848; 7A015-01195; 0I057-00005; 7D010-01355; 0J078-02380
Control of house flies with larvicidal compounds and use of poisoned baits
against the adults in closed poultry and pig houses.

A hazi legy elleni vedekezes larvairto szerek es imagok elleni mergezett
csaletkek alkalmazasaval zart baromfi- es sertesistallokban.

 1/6/7        (Item 3 from file: 50)
0719697 7A014-01932; 0J076-01424; 0I056-00008
Stunting the spread of houseflies.

 1/6/8        (Item 4 from file: 50)
0677409 0J076-00747; 7A014-01100; 7E009-00512
An integrated pest management (IPM) approach [using Ophyra aenescens,
cyromazine, baits and insecticides] for controlling flies [Musca domestica]
in deep pit cage houses.

 1/6/9        (Item 5 from file: 50)
0671343 0J076-00501; 7A014-00811
Evaluation of the insect growth regulators cyromazine and diflubenzuron as
```

**Search 6.1:** (cont.)

surface sprays and feed additives for controlling houseflies Musca domestica
(L.) in chicken manure.

1/6/10        (Item 6 from file: 50)
0651654 0J076-00152; 7A014-00253; 0I056-00003
Trial of CGA-72662 (Larvadex) as a feed additive for controlling flies
breeding in caged chicken manure.


1/6/11        (Item 7 from file: 50)
0581041 0J075-01162; 7A013-01226; 0V057-04326; 0I055-00007
Control of house flies in commercial poultry houses in Connecticut.


1/6/12        (Item 8 from file: 50)
0568748 0J075-00941
Toxicity of cyromazine to strains of the housefly (Diptera: Muscidae)
variously resistant to insecticides.

1/6/13        (Item 9 from file: 50)
0563191 0J075-00917; 7A013-01003; 7E008-00948
Factors affecting the use of an IPM scheme at poultry installations in a
semi-tropical climate.

1/6/14        (Item 10 from file: 50)
0485144 0J074-01390; 7A012-02285
The efficacy of the insecticide Neporex 2 WSG against dipterous larvae.
Efikasi insektisida Neporex 2 WSG terhadap larva lalat (Diptera) pada lantai
kandang dan efeknya bagi kesehatan dan produksi telur ayam di sekitarnya.

1/6/15        (Item 11 from file: 50)
0396412 0J074-00067; 7A012-00258
House fly (Diptera: Muscidae) resistance to permethrin in a Georgia caged
layer poultry operation.

1/6/16        (Item 12 from file: 50)
0396411 0J074-00066; 7A012-00257; 7E007-00177
Ophyra aenescens: a potential bio-control alternative for house fly control
in poultry houses.

1/6/17        (Item 13 from file: 50)
0353257 0J073-02474; 7A011-01804; 0V055-06309; 0I053-00011
Fly control in feedlot, dairy, and poultry operations.

1/6/18        (Item 14 from file: 50)
0303703 0V055-02887; 0I053-00006; 0J073-01659; 7A011-01214
Cost-benefit evaluation of house fly (Diptera: Muscidae) control in caged
layer poultry houses.

1/6/19        (Item 15 from file: 50)
0177038 0V054-03397; 7A010-01996; 0J072-02392; 0I052-00004; 8A009-05041
Efficacy and nontarget effects of Larvadex as a feed additive for controlling
house flies in caged-layer poultry manure.

1/6/20        (Item 16 from file: 50)
0126224 7A010-00166; 0J072-00322
Evaluation of Larvadex, a new IGR for the control of pestiferous flies on
poultry ranches.


1/6/21        (Item 17 from file: 50)

**Search 6.1:** (cont.)

```
0126223 7A010-00165; 0J072-00321
Evaluation of the IGR Larvadex as a feed-through treatment for the control of
pestiferous flies on poultry ranches.

 1/6/22       (Item 1 from file: 53)
1609424 0V053-06477; 0I051-
[I] Evaluation of the IGR Larvadex as a feed-through treatment for the
control of pestiferous flies on poultry ranches.
[II] Evaluation of Larvadex, a new IGR for the control of pestiferous flies
on poultry ranches.

 1/6/23       (Item 2 from file: 53)
1342346 0J070-03401
A new triazine insect growth regulator for fly control on poultry ranches.
Proceedings and papers of the Forty-ninth Annual Conference of the California
Mosquito and Vector Control Association, Inc. April 26-29, 1981. Red Lion
Motor Inn, Redding, California.
```

CAB seems a clear 'winner' here, although it must be stressed that no single search could represent a valid total comparison of the three databases, and that the query is to some degree biased, especially for AGRIS which has only sixty-six per cent of its data on DIALOG, and whose worldwide coverage gives it a relatively greater strength in, for instance, tropical or third world agricultural questions.

The strength of CAB, even accepting these riders, however, is in its depth. In several titles in the CAB retrieved list, the pertinent terms are in little evidence, or not there at all. But the full record (too long for printing here) vindicates those references, as terms are contained either in the Abstract or the Descriptor fields. Again this may be slightly unfair to AGRIS and AGRICOLA which both have Descriptor fields in a proportion of their references (AGRICOLA in one out of the three in this retrieved list). AGRICOLA also carries Abstract fields in about ten per cent of its records. But the presence of those fields in CAB consistently, and as exampled by this search, more often than not means a larger retrieved list from this database than the other two.

In particular CAB's strength is in its Descriptor field, where in fifteen out of the nineteen hits, all three elements of the search query were represented in that field. This fact compensated for the oversight of the term Neporex as a synonym for Cyromazine in one article, where the term Cyromazine was provided as a cross reference in the Descriptor field. The Abstract field, though a blunter instrument, can also provide an additional safety net for the searcher, and from the end-user's point of view often provides enough information about the contents of the article to obviate the need of seeing it at first hand.

The record shown in Figure 6.1 was retrieved on all three databases and is shown below as an example of the different record styles in each database.

**Figure 6.1: Comparative record style on AGRICOLA, AGRIS and CAB**

**AGRICOLA**

```
84115911 84006023 Holding Library: AGL
Efficacy and nontarget effects of Larvadex as a feed
additive for controlling house flies in caged-layer poultry
manure (Musca domestica, mites, Carcinops)
Axtell, R.C. POSCA; Edwards, T.D.
Poultry science. v. 62 (12), Dec 1983. p. 2371-2377.
Champaign : , Poultry Science Association. ISSN: 0032-5791
NAL: 47.8 AM33P
Language: English
Includes  references.
```

**Figure 6.1:** (cont.)

```
Subfile: OTHER US (NOT EXP STN, EXT, USDA; SINCE 12/76);
Document Type: ARTICLE
Section Headings: PESTS OF ANIMALS-INSECTS(L821);
PESTICIDES-GENERAL(H000 ); FEED COMPOSITION(R300)
```

**AGRIS**

```
0771658 AGRIS No: 84-112951
Efficacy and nontarget effects of Larvadex as a feed additive for
controlling house flies in caged-layer poultry manure [Musca
domestica, mites, Carcinops]
Axtell, R.C.; Edwards, T.D.
Poultry Science, Dec 1983, v. 62(12) p. 2371-2377
Notes: Includes references ISSN: 0032-5791
Language: English
Place of Publication: USA
Availability: United States Center,(NAL 47.8 AM33P)
Document Type: Journal Article,
Journal Announcement: 1012 Record input by United States
Commodity Codes: 6000 (Domesticated birds - general); 3740
(Stimulants, growth substances, additives); 4020 (Injurious
insects); 4030 (Injurious mites)
Section Headings: L72 (ANIMAL PRODUCTION — Pests of animals) ;
H00 (PROTECTION OF PLANTS AND STORED PRODUCTS) ; L36 (ANIMAL
PRODUCTION — Feed composition)
```

**CAB**

```
0177038 0V054-03397; 7A010-01996; 0J072-02392; 0I052-00004;
8A009-05041
Efficacy and nontarget effects of Larvadex as a feed additive for
controlling house flies in caged-layer poultry manure.
Axtell, R. C.; Edwards, T. D.
Dep. Entomol., State Univ., Raleigh, North Carolina 27650, USA.
Poultry Science 1983. 62 (12): 2371-2377 (12 ref.)
Language: English
Document Type: NP (Numbered Part)
Status: REVISED
Subfile: 0V (Veterinary Bulletin); 7A (Poultry Abstracts); 0J
(Review Applied Entomology, Ser. B); 0I (Index Veterinarius); 8A
(Agricultural Engineering Abs.)
The insect growth regulator N-cyclopropyl-1,3,5-triazine-2,4,6
triamine (Larvadex, CGA 72662, cyromazine) was provided as a feed
additive (0.3% of feed) to caged laying hens under field
conditions in high rise, wide span and narrow poultry houses. The
chemical effectively controlled house flies (Musca domestica) and
soldier flies (Hermetia illucens). The feed additive had no
adverse effect on the populations of manure-inhabiting mites
(Macrochelidae and Uropodidae) and histerid beetles (Carcinops
pumulio), which prey on fly eggs and larvae. Satisfactory
fly control was demonstrated by use of the additive 50% of
the time when the interval without the additive in the feed was
4 days but not when the interval was 7 days. Use of a fly
monitoring programme to time the use of the feed additive is
advocated.
Descriptors: diptera; poultry; feed additives; fowl;
insecticides; cyromazine; manure; fly control; musca; musca
domestica; distribution; usa; hermetia illucens; carcinops
pumulio; control; growth regulators; against; poultry manure;
habitats;  effects  of  insect  growth  regulators macrochelidae;
```

**Figure 6.1:** (cont.)

```
uropodidae;  predatory  arthropods;  nontarget  effects;  effects
on predatory arthropods; in usa; poultry housing; manures;
flies
Geographic Names: USA
Section Heading Codes: 0VF47; 0I; 0J08071056; 7A1210; 8A56 ;
0J11002; 8A53
Section Headings: ARTHROPOD PARASITES (FROM 1976. SEE ALSO 0V12
TRUNCATED) - DIPTERA - FLIES (SC=0VF40); BOOKS (FROM 1983.
SEE ALSO 0H2100) (SC=0H2500); ARTHROPODS OF MEDICAL AND
VETERINARY IMPORTANCE - DIPTERA- OTHER DIPTERA (SC=0J08071056/);
GENERAL - PARASITIC DISORDERS (SC=7A1210); FARM BUILDINGS AND
EQUIPMENT - CLEANING AND WASTE DISPOSAL (SC=8A56) ;
PROTECTION AGAINST ARTHROPODS AND USE OF ARTHROPODS FOR
BIOLOGICAL CONTROL - CONTROL MEASURES- CONTR (SC=0J11002);
FARM BUILDINGS AND EQUIPMENT - POULTRY (SC=8A53)
```

## OTHER AGRICULTURAL DATABASES

Outside of the 'Big Three' there are few databases which can be considered uniquely agricultural. However, there are some which should be mentioned, and we shall deal with those here. Perhaps the first to consider are the agricultural research databases, AGREP - the Permanent Inventory of Agricultural Research Projects in the European Communities, and CRIS/USDA - Current Research Information System of the United States Department of Agriculture. Search 6.2 shows a sample entry from AGREP which is hosted on DIMDI.

### Search 6.2: Sample entry from AGREP on DIMDI

```
BASE COMMAND ACCEPTED FOR AP75;AGREP;ED=01.01.75 TO 31.12.89
?
F ALL RODENT PEST$

1.00   NUMBER OF HITS IS   8
?
S

1.00/000001 ZADI: -AGREP /COPYRIGHT ZADI
RN: 016326; AC: GB050365/78/0844; STA: cont'd; LA: ENGL
AU: Greaves, J.H.
TI: Investigating the genetics of rodent pest resistance to
rodenticides.
CS: Ministry of Agriculture, Fisheries and Food. [Great Westminster House,
Horseferry Road, London, SW1P 2AE.]; Agricultural Scientific Service, Slough
Laboratory. [London Road, Slough Berks, SL3 7HJ.]; Rodent Pests.; CE: RES.
ORG. GB050365
FC:   A2100    Protection against animals
      B5800    Mammals
      B6610    Pesticides
      B6800    Food and table luxuries in general
      C3510    Genetics
      D4420    Storage and conservation
NT:   PUBLICATIONS
```

CRIS/USDA is similar in principle to AGREP, but, while AGREP is an inventory file, CRIS/USDA is a current file which is updated monthly but purged annually so that only currently active and recently completed projects appear. Searching tends to be somewhat different in these databases as they are non-bibliographic and therefore employ different search terms and indexes. For instance, one does not search for an author on CRIS/USDA but for an Investigator (for example, IN=SMITH). A close examination of file documentation on potentially searchable indexes is recommended.

AGRIBUSINESS is perhaps one of the few databases in which farmers may be interested. Its claim is that it 'is utilized for strategic planning', and although a bibliographic database rather than a business database, in the sense of ICC or MOODY'S it does provide abstracts which one could imagine as being read with interest by the agricultural entrepreneur. A sample entry is given in Figure 6.2.

## Figure 6.2: Sample entry from AGRIBUSINESS on DIALOG

```
00183988
Ag suppliers increase role as lenders
Anon
Dairy Herd Management v27 n6 p6 np(1)  June 1990

ABSTRACT:   According to an article in the New York Times newspaper,
agricultural suppliers are becoming involved in farm lending. Three companies
who have started lending are Farmland Industries, Pioneer Hi-Bred
International, Inc., and Deere and Company, which generates $8 billion
annually for loans for farm equipment alone. Deere Credit Company is among
the 20 largest U.S. credit companies, with more than $3.2 billion in
farm-related loans. Some companies are loaning money strictly for
equipment sold by their dealers, while others are providing general-
purpose loans. The North American Equipment Dealers Association began a
lending program in March 1990, and has an initial loan fund of $100
million. Individual equipment dealers will loan $5,000-$50,000 at
competitive interest rates. Banks and insurance companies continue to
be wary of agricultural lending, and the government has placed stricter
lending limits and higher requirements on the reserves that must be
kept to cover bad loans. Financial analysts expect farm lending to shift from
local banks to companies that are delving into farm financing. The
increasingly competitive lending environment may lead to better lending rates
for producers.
```

AGRIBUSINESS is growing rapidly and had 171,288 records as at January 1990. The period covered is 1985 to present, although one would expect the most current information to be the most useful on a database such as this; one reason why it is updated as frequently as once a fortnight.

There are two other databases we shall mention here: the food databases FOOD SCIENCE AND TECHNOLOGY ABSTRACTS (FSTA) and FOODS ADLIBRA. Agriculture and food are so closely related that these can legitimately be regarded as being at the other end of the spectrum that begins in the field and the farmyard. FSTA in particular, with over 375,000 records going back to 1969, should be considered for any agricultural question erring on the 'foody' side. It should also be remembered that this database contains the subfile VITIS (also available separately on ORBIT and DIMDI) containing over 25,000 references to viticulture (see Figure 6.3).

**Figure 6.3: Sample record from FSTA on DIALOG**

```
00402044 90-12-p0049 SUBFILE: FSTA
Microbiological safety of cheese made from heat-treated milk. III.
Technology, discussion, recommendations, bibliography.
Johnson, E. A.; Nelson, J. H.; Johnson, M.
Correspondence (Reprint) address, J. H. Nelson, Food Res. Inst., Univ. of
Wisconsin, Madison, WI 53706, USA
Journal of Food Protection 1990 , 53 (7) 610-623 NOTE: 378 ref.
DOCUMENT TYPE: Review ISSN: 0362-028X
LANGUAGE: English

Heat treatment or pasteurization does not adversely affect the cheesemaking
process or the resulting physical properties of the cheese. Both types of
heat-treatments can correct chemical changes that occur in cold stored raw
milk. Thermization on the farm may help control psychrotrophic bacteria in
cold stored milk. Some denaturation of whey protein does occur during
pasteurization. Heat treatments slightly above current min. pasteurization
requirements can cause body/texture and moisture control problems in cheese.
Loss of functionality can adversely affect the marketing of whey protein
products. Cheeses made from pasteurized milk ripen more slowly and usually do
not exhibit the flavour intensity of cheeses made from raw or heat-treated
milk. Swiss and hard Italian type cheese, whose traditional flavour results
in part from native milk enzymes and microflora, would also be adversely
affected if milk pasteurization for cheesemaking were mandatory. The quality
of cheese made from pasteurized milk is consistently better than cheese made
from raw milk as evidenced by fewer body and flavour defects resulting from
the growth of undesirable bacteria. Either pasteurization or heat-treatment
enables improved uniform process control and quality during cheesemaking.
(Continued in following abstr.) (AS)
```

FOODS ADLIBRA is concerned with the business rather than the science of food, but is worth a mention in this context. Both databases are available on DIALOG, and FSTA is additionally available on ESA-IRS, DIMDI and STN.

## BIOLOGICAL DATABASES

Only experience and individual circumstances can tell you when a search of the purely agricultural databases may be sufficient. If it is definitely 'applied' agriculture, if comprehensiveness is not required, if the client is not 'science' based, then a search of the purely agricultural databases may well prove all that is needed. You should be aware, however, of the vast amount of agricultural information outside of this immediate sphere, and in particular in the biological and life science databases.

In a research environment questions often spread beyond the farm gate to include, for instance, animal, insect and microbial pests of agriculture, and the impact of agriculture on the environment. BIOSIS in particular is an invaluable resource. The online equivalent of *Biological Abstracts* and its various spinoffs, BIOSIS is available on DIALOG and STN for the period since 1969, and now carries over seven million records (DIMDI has it from 1970, and ESA-IRS from 1973 to date). Not only is it very large, but it also adheres to a very disciplined regime of keywording, enabling more sophisticated search strategies than most other databases.

In order to use the database to its full capabilities, however, one needs to acquire the BIOSIS manual, *BIOSIS PREVIEWS Search Guide* [11]. Basically, BIOSIS uses a system of Concept Codes and Biosystematic Codes to denote concept terms and groups of organisms, not only saving the searcher the bother of naming individually all the items and their synonyms within that group but automatically producing a context for further, more specific queries within that category. So, for instance, there is a Concept Code for Grain Crops under which are included, wheat, rye, oats, barley, corn, rice, millet, sorghum and buckwheat. The *Search Guide* entry under this code also tells you how many times the concept occurs as a major part of the record, and how many times as a minor, and searching with the suffix /MAJ allows you to restrict yourself to the major occurrences only, if you wish. 'Strategy Recommendations' (or to you and me 'See References'!) are also given as part of the Scope Notes on Concept Codes, providing pointers towards other areas of possibly fruitful examination.

The Biosystematic Codes group organisms by accepted taxonomic rules. With these codes it is possible to search references to large taxonomic groupings like Mammalia, or to families like Bovidae to include bull, calf, cattle, cow, heifer, etc. From the agricultural point of view one must be careful, however, as families often include wild as well as domesticated species - in this case bison, buffalo and gazelle! Concept Codes and Biosystematic Codes are, of course, an additional facility on top of the conventional free-text keyword search, and the *Search Guide's* Master Index provides a thesaurus of keywords, as well as an index to the codes. This is also well cross-referenced, although the non-American searcher needs to be aware here, as well as when searching, that American spellings are used as standard. A further point for the agricultural searcher to bear in mind is that domestic and laboratory animals are keyworded with the common name only, the scientific name only being added if it occurs in the source document.

LIFE SCIENCES COLLECTION, like BIOSIS, contains abstracts as well as bibliographic citations, and is the online equivalent of the twenty abstracting journals published by Cambridge Scientific Abstracts (Maryland, USA). These includes many that impinge either directly or indirectly on the agricultural sphere, including *Animal Behaviour, Ecology and Entomology Abstracts*. Although a fraction of the size of BIOSIS at 1,205,500 (September 1990) and covering only the period from 1978 to the present, LIFE SCIENCES often yields unique references in a search covering the two databases, and is therefore recommended if comprehensiveness is a requirement.

ZOOLOGICAL RECORD ONLINE is produced by BIOSIS and though minuscule by proportion, bears some similarity owing to the depth of its indexing, carrying master, subject, geographical, palaeotological and systematic indexes. Again acquisition of the manual, *The Zoological Record Search Guide* [12] is recommended if serious searching of this database is envisaged. In an agricultural research context ZOO RECORD would probably only come into its own in the case of the taxonomic type of query.

In 1990, CURRENT AWARENESS IN BIOLOGICAL SCIENCES is 'An ORBIT Search Service Exclusive!' Being the solitary biological database on a host with limited agricultural/biological coverage seems a dubious privilege, however. It means CABS tends to get overlooked because it is too much trouble to change hosts just to search one database! A regrettable human weakness in the world of automated information. CABS, nevertheless, boasts 1.2 million records, making it similar in size to LIFE SCIENCE COLLECTION, and covers the period from 1983 to present, making it well worth the effort if comprehensiveness, or that elusive particular reference, are being sought. Another worthwhile biological database is the surprising PHYTOMED on DIMDI and STN. Surprising because the database title doesn't immediately suggest the contents, which include a host of subjects around the central plant protection theme, including applied entomology, mycology, nematology, pesticides, storage protection, and ecology. PHYTOMED is also a relatively long established database, going back to 1965 with 374,000 references as of November 1990. DIMDI also carries the major agricultural databases, and PHYTOMED may well prove worth searching in an agricultural context as well as a biological.

Coming, perhaps, to the perimeter of agriculturally-useful databases in this direction, it may be worth mentioning a few that have sprung up in the burgeoning field of biotechnology. BIOTECHNOLOGY ABSTRACTS is available on DIALOG and ORBIT, and CURRENT BIOTECHNOLOGY ABSTRACTS is available on ESA-IRS and Data-Star. The longer established TELEGEN is available on ESA-IRS and DIMDI, and a new one on the economic aspects of agriculture and biosciences is BIOBUSINESS, also featured on ESA-IRS.

## CHEMICAL DATABASES

Chemistry might not seem a very promising area for the agricultural online searcher, but practice, especially in a research context, often proves otherwise. The chemical databases come into their own especially in the context of research into agrochemicals and biochemistry. The latter coverage also forms a bridge with the biological databases making it very worthwhile consulting the larger chemical files, especially CHEMICAL ABSTRACTS, in this context.

The virtue of CHEMICAL ABSTRACTS (variously known as CA, CA SEARCH, CHEMABS and CHEMICAL ABSTRACTS on different hosts) is that when searching for a particular compound there is a system to catch synonyms and ensure you get everything relating to your search term. This is achieved through a Registry system, which is searchable by substance name and Registry Number among others. On DIALOG for instance, this information is found in CHEMNAME. The search is then continued in the main database with the RN= prefix (or equivalent). Applying this principle to the chemical component of our agricultural search, cyromazine, we get thirty-seven hits for the period 1987-1990.

Chemical patent information is covered by AGPAT, an STN database of worldwide chemical and biochemical patents relating to agriculture and pest control, produced by Chemical Abstracts Service and covering the period from 1987 to present, which has now been merged with the CHEMICAL ABSTRACTS database (CA). For those with graphics terminals structure diagrams can be displayed online - otherwise it is necessary to wait for the offline prints.

As non-chemists, the authors will not dwell on the labyrinthine complexities of this database, which are in any case covered elsewhere in this volume. Suffice it to say, if intermediaries are not chemists, this is one area where the authors would recommend having the client present during the search.

There are very many databases in the chemical field, some or all of which may be useful depending on the individual interests of the search requester. We shall, however, only mention a few others which are of specific relevance to the agricultural searcher, and they are those that relate to agrochemicals. Three in particular deserve mention, although they are not the conventional database type in that they are non-bibliographic databases providing current information only. The type of information varies between the three so examples of their various entry types are included.

The first is from the AGROCHEMICALS HANDBOOK on DIALOG, which has already been mentioned in its printed form [7]. This database produces a single, comprehensive reference for each pesticide name - in this case Diflubenzuron - in Figure 6.4 printed in the full format.

## Figure 6.4: Sample entry from AGROCHEMICALS HANDBOOK

```
Common TAH Name: DIFLUBENZURON (BSI, ISO, ANSI, ESA)
ACTIVITY: Insecticide CAS REGISTRY NUMBER: 35367-38-5
MOLECULAR FORMULA: C14H9ClF2N2O2 MOLECULAR WEIGHT: 310.69
CHEMICAL NAMES: 1-(4-chlorophenyl)-3-(2,6-difluorobenzoyl)urea (IUPAC) N-
(((4-chlorophenyl)amino)carbonyl)-2,6-difluorobenzamide (CA)
OTHER NAMES:
DIFLURON
OMS 1804
ENT  29054
```

**Figure 6.4:** (cont.)

TRADE NAME(S): Dimilin; Astonex; Larvakil; DU 112307; PH 60-40; PDD 60-40-I ; TH 6040
MANUFACTURER: Duphar; Uniroyal
PHYSICAL STATE: Colourless crystals (technical: off-white to yellow crystals).
MELTING POINT: 230-232 Deg C (pure); 210-230 Deg C (technical).
BOILING POINT: Decomposes on distillation.
VAPOR PRESSURE: Less than 0.033 mPa at 50 Deg C.
SOLUBILITY: In water at 20 Deg C, ca. 0.14 mg/l. In acetone 6.5 g/l at 20 Deg C. In dimethylformamide 104, dioxane 20 (both in g/l at 25 Deg C). Moderately soluble in polar organic solvents very slightly soluble in non-polar organic solvents.
CORROSIVENESS: Non-corrosive.
STABILITY: Stable in acidic and neutral media (pH 2-7). Hydrolyzed in alkaline media above pH 9. Light-sensitive when in solution, but stable to sunlight as a solid.
ANALYSIS OF PRODUCTS: By HPLC with spectrometric detection (A. van Rossum et al. Anal. Methods Pestic. Plant Growth Regul. 1984, 13, 165).
ANALYSIS OF RESIDUES: By HPLC with spectrometric detection, or by GLC with ECD (H. N. Nigg et al. Bull. Environ. Contam. Toxicol. 1986, 36(6), 833-838; S. Smith et al. J. Agric. Food Chem. 1983, 31(3), 610-612; B. Rabenort et al. Anal. Methods Pestic. Plant Growth Regul. 1978, 10, 57-71). Also by enzyme-linked immunosorbent assay (S. I. Wie and B. D. Hammock J. Agric. Food Chem. 1982, 30(5), 949-957).
MODE OF ACTION: Non-systemic insect growth regulator with contact and stomach action. Interferes with chitin formation and moulting, leading to the death of larvae, pupae, and non-viable adults. Also prevents hatching of eggs.
USES: Control of leaf-eating larvae and leaf miners in forestry, tree fruit (including citrus), horticultural crops, cotton, soya beans, other field crops, and open areas. Particularly used for control of caterpillars of gypsy moths and pine processionary moths in forestry; codling moths and psyllids in pome fruit; boll weevils on cotton; velvetbean caterpillars on soya beans; large cabbage-white caterpillars on brassicas; etc. Also used for control of sciarid flies and phorid flies in mushroom cultivation; for control of fly larvae in animal houses, dung heaps, and other places where larvae may hatch; and control of mosquito larvae. Ineffective on mature adult insects and on sucking insect larvae and adults.
CROP TOLERANCE: Non-phytotoxic when used as directed.
FORMULATIONS: Wettable powder; 5LV liquid; Granules
TOXICITY: MAMMALS - Acute oral LD50 for rats and mice >4640 mg/kg. Acute percutaneous LD50 for rabbits >2000 mg/kg. Acute i.p. LD50 for mice >2150 mg/kg. In 2-year feeding trials, no-effect level for rats was 40 mg/kg diet. Non-teratogenic, non-mutagenic, and non-oncogenic. BIRDS - Eight-day dietary LC50 for bobwhite quail and mallard ducks >4640 mg/kg diet. FISH - LC50 (96 hours) for rainbow trout 140, bluegill sunfish 135 mg/l. BEES - Not dangerous to bees and predatory insects.

DEGRADATION AND METABOLISM: Rapidly degraded in soil, with a half-life of <7 days. The principal degradation products are 4-chlorophenylurea and 2,6-difluorobenzoic acid. In rats, following oral administration, elimination is partly as the unchanged parent compound in the faeces and partly as hydroxylated metabolites (for about 80%) and as 4-chlorophenylurea plus 2,6-difluorobenzoic acid (for about 20%). The intestinal

**Figure 6.4:** (cont.)

```
absorption is strongly related to the dosage administered -
the higher the dosage, the more is (relatively) excreted unchanged
in the faeces.
ANTIDOTES AND MEDICAL TREATMENT: No specific antidote known.
Symptomatic treatment.
PESTICIDE RESIDUE LEVELS IN FOODS (ppm): France: Pome fruit 1.
Germany (FRG): Wild berries 2; pome fruit, cabbage 1; mushrooms
0.2. Italy: Apples, pears 0.5. Netherlands: Cabbage, pome fruit 1;
mushrooms 0.1; egg, meat, milk, poultry meat, other 0.05.
Switzerland: Pome fruit, mushrooms 1; cabbage 0.5; milk 0.05.
CHEMICAL GROUP(S) OF PESTICIDE: urea
RECORD DATE: 900125
```

Like the AGROCHEMICALS HANDBOOK the EUROPEAN DIRECTORY OF AGROCHEMICAL PRODUCTS (EDAP) is a product of the Royal Society of Chemistry, and also has a printed equivalent [13]. Unlike AGROCHEMICALS HANDBOOK, however, EDAP is concerned with information about manufacturing companies and formulation type of a given agrochemical. Thus a search on EDAP for Diflubenzuron (trade name Dimilin) will yield many entries according to these two variables. One example is given in Figure 6.5.

**Figure 6.5: Sample entry from EUROPEAN DIRECTORY OF AGROCHEMICAL PRODUCTS**

```
009380
COUNTRY: Italy
PRODUCT NAME: Dimilin ACTIVITY: Insecticide
COMPANY: Du Pont
FORMULATION: Wettable powder
ACTIVE INGREDIENT(S): diflubenzuron
ACTIVE INGREDIENT PROPORTIONS: 5%
USES: INSECTICIDAL USES - Control of larvae and eggs of mining
microlepidoptera (Cemiostoma and Lithocolletis spp.), codling
moths, leaf rollers (Capua, Archips, and Orgyia spp.), and pear
suckers in pome fruit; and pine processionary caterpillars, oak
processionary caterpillars, gypsy moth caterpillars, spruce sawfly
larvae, and pine shoot moth caterpillars in forestry (fir, pine,
oak).
TOXICITY: MAN - Non-toxic.
LAST USE: Apples, pears - 45 days.
RECORD DATE: 880428
```

Also worthy of mention in this context are databases specifically dealing with toxicology, agrochemical toxicity included. CHEMLIST on STN, and EMTOX PLUS, TOXALL and RTECS on DIMDI deserve mention here. RTECS, the Registry of Toxic Effects of Chemical Substances, unlike the others is a non-bibliographical database produced by the National Institute for Occupational Safety and Health (NIOSH) in the United States. Its references tend to be lengthy, giving not only chemical information, but the details of various tests, usually on animals, to ascertain the toxicity of the chemical in question. The database header, however, makes the following disclaimer: 'The RTECS file contains toxicity data that have not been critically evaluated. Users whose requirements demand accurate toxicity data are reminded to consult the cited sources for verification of data.'

## PRESTEL

Since the last edition of this book there have been a number of changes to the information available on the British videotex service, Prestel. ADAS, the Ministry of Agriculture, Fisheries and Food (MAFF) Agricultural Development and Advisory Service, has ceased to be an information provider, and as a result much of the information previously described is no longer available. The main Agriculture section now includes the following:

- News for Farmers - general news, much of it supplied by the Meat and Livestock Commission (MLC), including some prices and market details. (some of which are private pages)
- Agricultural news - repeating much of the above.
- Farm Management & Finance - including details of some of the banks' services to agriculture.
- Agricultural commodities - giving detailed market prices for a range of commodities.

Prestel is now of limited value in the agricultural world, except for those market and commodity prices made available by the premium services.

## CD-ROM

### Introduction

The last five years have seen a revolution in online information retrieval, with the introduction and growth of databases on CD-ROM. This new technology has proved particularly amenable to the world of agriculture. The September 1990 catalogue of a major supplier (Microinfo) lists fifteen titles under the heading of earth sciences, all relevant to the work of the Ministry of Agriculture, Fisheries and Food and a further seven under other categories, all equally relevant.

The reasons for this are manyfold, but the portability of the databases and their ability to be used where telecommunications do not readily reach cannot be underestimated.

A recent issue of *CD-ROM EndUser* (July 1990) particularly concentrated on agricultural CD-ROMs under the heading, 'Harvesting information on CD-ROM'. Articles described a number of exciting and innovative projects ranging from that proposed by the secretariat of CIGAR (Consultative Group on International Agricultural Research) to place its research reports on disc (450,000 pages) as described by Pamela Andre [14], to the planned prototype multimedia disc on ornamental horticulture to be produced by the United States National Agricultural Library, described by Pamela Mason [15].

Whatever the reasons for this vast explosion, it is certain to continue - offering agricultural information centres all over the world an increasing choice and hopefully access to data not previously accessible.

### The databases

For the purposes of this chapter, the following discs were obtained on loan: from SilverPlatter - AGRIS, AGRICOLA and CABI; and from OCLC - AGRICULTURE LIBRARY, AGRICOLA and CRIS.

AGRIS is available on two discs 1986-1988 and 1989-1990 (mid) and covers material input to the AGRIS database by the national AGRIS centres around the world, maintained by the UN Food and Agriculture Organization (FAO).

AGRICOLA is available on four discs; three archival discs covering 1970-1984, and the current disc updated quarterly. AGRICOLA is compiled by the United States National Agricultural Library.

CABI currently has two discs available, 1984-86 and 1987-89 with the third planned for 1990-92. The discs contain 800,000 abstracts compiled by CAB International during the production of their invaluable Abstracts bulletins.

AGRICULTURE LIBRARY is a database taken from the OCLC Online union catalogue and consists of one disc holding 300,000 bibliographic records.

CRIS is a database of some thirty thousand abstracts and reports on current research, updated quarterly on one disc.

## Search software and installation

What follows is a brief and somewhat subjective comparison of the databases and their search software. Unfortunately the section has to be limited because of the short period the discs were available for trial. A true comparison can only come from sustained use of the discs in the field.

### SilverPlatter

The SilverPlatter discs use the SPIRS software which gives a common interface across all SilverPlatter discs. Installation is straightforward and gives the opportunity to specify all the discs which will be searched in the future. This obviates the need to reinstall the software, subject to a newer version being released.

As would be expected, the initial screen offers a standard layout showing the database title and date range, taken automatically from the disc, and a workspace. The standard function keys take the user into the search process from here, and allow search terms to be entered in the usual manner.

### OCLC

These discs are centred around the Search CD450 software, supplied on each CD-ROM disc. Here, the System Administration Module (SAM) allows the user to install each disc as it arrives. Installation was simple and trouble free.

The common interface is clear and easy to use, making good use of colour and the full size of the screen. From this point terms may be entered and searches combined using the search history screen.

## Summary - CD-ROM

These two groups of discs are very similar in use and functionality, a decision between them is most likely to be determined by the discs already in use. Obviously it will be necessary for any prospective CD-ROM user to carefully evaluate the possible combinations before choosing a particular set of discs - especially where funds are limited.

It is clear that online searching will continue; the CD-ROMs are most useful where searches requiring access to the backfiles are a particular feature or where end-user searching is particularly common. What is beyond doubt, is that a good agricultural library will need access to CABI, AGRIS and AGRICOLA as a minimum whether online or on CD-ROM, to ensure a comprehensive search of the literature.

## CONCLUSIONS

We have tried to cover here the central (and not so central!) subject areas that database searching in the agricultural field is likely to span. As mentioned at the outset, agricultural research is likely to take searchers into several areas that are not initially seen as being pertinent.

Even beyond the biological and chemical database areas mentioned, it is frequently productive to look at databases in other subject areas. Those concerned with the environment - ENVIROLINE, ENVIRONMENTAL BIBLIOGRAPHY, POLLUTION ABSTRACTS - could clearly be useful where a search is directed towards the ecological aspects of farming. Medical databases, MEDLINE in particular, often contain information on veterinary medicine as well as human. And finally the more generalized type of database, such as those covering theses, conferences or science in general, should also be remembered when the context seems appropriate.

## ADDENDUM

Since this chapter was written it has been announced that SilverPlatter is to take over most of OCLC's optical publishing interests; OCLC's CD450 discs will be entirely replaced by the SilverPlatter equivalent database.

## NOTES

1.    W. Little, H.W. Fowler, J. Coulson. *The Shorter Oxford English Dictionary.* Oxford: Clarendon, 1973.
2.    E.A.R. Bush. *Agriculture: A bibliographic guide.* London: Macdonald, 1974.
3.    *Bibliography of Agriculture.* Published monthly since 1942 by the US National Agricultural Library.
4.    CAB International. *CAB Thesaurus* (new ed) Wallingford: CABI, 1990.
5.    *Agrindex.* Published monthly since 1975 by the Food & Agriculture Organization of the United Nations.
6.    D. Leatherdale, G.E. Tidbury, R. Mack. *Agrovoc: a multilingual thesaurus of agricultural terminology.* Rome: Apimondia, 1982.
7.    A meeting to discuss the possibility of a universal agricultural thesaurus was held in Washington on 23 October, 1989. Copies of the minutes of this meeting are available from Nigel May, Science Librarian at the Polytechnic South West, Drake Circus, Plymouth, Devon PL4 8AA. England.
8.    National Agricultural Library of the US Department of Agriculture; Commission of the European Communities; Food and Agriculture Organization of the United Nations; CAB International. *International Union List of Agricultural Serials.* Wallingford: CAB International, 1990.
9.    Several publications will provide chemical/common name/trade name synonyms. One that can be recommended is: Royal Society of Chemistry. *The Agrochemicals Handbook* (2nd ed) Nottingham: RSC Information Services, 1987.
10.   An introduction to the concepts of taxonomy can be found in: C. Jeffrey. *Biological Nomenclature* (3rd ed) London: Arnold, 1989. However specific reference sources will need to be sought for whichever area of systematics the searcher finds themselves.

11.    Biosciences Information Services. *BIOSIS PREVIEWS Search Guide*. Philadelphia: BIOSIS, 1987.

12.    Biosciences Information Services. *The Zoological Record Search Guide*. Philadelphia: BIOSIS, 1985.

13.    H. Kidd, D. Hartley, J.M. Kennedy. *European Directory of Agrochemical Products, Parts 1-4*. Nottingham: Royal Society of Chemistry, 1985.

14.    Pamela Q.J. Andre. In the field of agriculture, CD-ROM delivers. *CD-ROM EndUser*. 2(3) 1990 26-27

15.    Pamela R. Mason. Ornamental horticulture on a multi-media CD-ROM. *CD-ROM EndUser*. 2(3) 1990 46-48

## FURTHER READING

Butler, R.W. AGRICOlearn: interactive laser videodisk technology for AGRICOLA instruction. *Agricultural Libraries Information Notes* 13 (10) 1987 1-4

Johnson, B.K. A comparison of online databases in relation to agricultural research and development. *Online Review* 5 (6) 1981 469-479

Kelly, S.A. Agricultural information: a comparison of information delivery alternatives. *Microcomputers for Information Management* 5 (2) 1988 113-128

Pritchard, E. & Scott, P.R. *Literature searching in science, technology and agriculture*. Westport: Greenwood Press, 1984

Reneau, F., Patterson, R. Comparison of online agricultural information services. *Online Review* 8 (4) 1984 313-322

Russell, H.M. Agricultural user populations and their information needs in the industrialized world. *Quarterly Bulletin of the International Association of Agricultural Librarians and Documentalists (NL)* 28 (2) 1983 40-52

Sepp, F.C. How good an online searcher are you? Twenty questions about AGRICOLA. *Online* 12 (4) 1988 56-57

## ACKNOWLEDGEMENTS

We should like to acknowledge the assistance of our colleagues in MAFF for their support, and the staff of Microinfo, CAB International and OCLC (Europe) in providing loan copies of the databases they either produce or market.

# 7 Energy and the environment

*John R. Luedtke*

## INTRODUCTION

Looking back over past editions of the introduction to this chapter, it is interesting to note how consistent energy-related environmental issues have been [1]. While the means of searching for information on this topic have undergone significant change, the subject matter has shown little variation. In some cases the emphasis has shifted, but the essential issues and relationships have not. Online literature searching on energy-related environmental issues remains as diverse and complex as the subject itself. Broad, multidisciplinary subject areas must be covered. Searchers must be aware of the intricate relationships among various energy technologies, their environmental impact, and their use of natural resources. In addition, they must be aware that policy and legislative decisions at the local, state, national and international levels have a very direct impact on energy-related environmental questions. All of this is further complicated by the uneven regional impacts of the various issues. The following outline of the energy and environment labyrinth will illustrate the potential subject difficulties faced by literature searchers. It will be followed by a discussion of how searchers can approach this information.

## ENERGY-RELATED ENVIRONMENTAL ISSUES

Energy production and use are still among the most important determinants of environmental quality. Current methods of fuel processing and combustion produce significant quantities of the major air pollutants. Most of the total suspended particulate and sulphur oxide emissions are produced by fossil fuel combustion (primarily coal) from stationary and transportation sources. Hydrocarbons and carbon monoxide emissions come primarily from fuels used in transportation. Radioactive emissions from nuclear power plants, though quite low under normal conditions, can have serious environmental consequences in the event of a reactor accident such as that at Chernobyl.

Water pollution is directly affected by effluent discharges of total dissolved solids, primarily from electric utilities; by oils and greases, primarily from petroleum refining; by heated effluents from power plants; and by chemical contamination of groundwater from leaking underground fuel storage tanks. In addition, atmospheric sulphur and nitrogen oxide emissions result in acid rain, lowering the pH of lakes as well as contributing to a worldwide decline in forest productivity. Atmospheric emissions of trace elements, particularly heavy metals, increase their concentrations in water bodies.

Coastal and marine environments receive a variety of energy-related contaminants from many sources, including land runoff *via* streams and rivers, atmospheric fallout, point source discharges, ocean dumping of dredged materials and other wastes, operational discharges from ships and offshore oil platforms, and accidental spills. The Exxon Valdez disaster is a well-known example of the latter. Most energy-related marine pollution results from petroleum-related activities. This is almost evenly divided between offshore production, marine terminals and tanker operations, and use and disposal activities. Some of these contaminants persist in the ocean environment for long periods and are relocated through the action of currents, sediment deposition and resuspension.

Non-combustible solid wastes are an important source of energy-related pollutants. They are generated by the removal of particulates, bottom ash, fly ash and dust from combustion and production processes. Industrial sludges and spent nuclear fuel and reactor parts comprise the remainder of the environmentally significant portion of the solid waste problem. These solid wastes help contaminate landfill sites as well as generate need for more landfill space.

## New resources and technologies

Development of additional energy resources or alternative energy technologies also has important environmental implications. Outer continental shelf oil and gas well drilling, pipeline and supertanker projects, and new coal mining increase the chances for oil spills, pipeline ruptures, mine runoff, groundwater contamination and land degradation. Major oil shale development entails the disposal of huge volumes of spent shale which contain toxic substances that could contaminate surface and groundwater. Wastes produced by coal liquefaction contain tars which are partially carcinogenic, requiring consideration of worker safety, handling and transportation safeguards, and combustion guidelines, in addition to waste disposal. Biomass energy production through use of wood-burning stoves generally has lower sulphur oxide, nitrogen oxide, solid waste and sludge levels than coal, but produces more total suspended particulates and is becoming a very important source in some localities, for example, in Denver's winter air quality. Solar technologies have much less direct environmental effects than either current energy practices or synthetic fuel development; however, toxic chemical discharges associated with the manufacture and construction of solar equipment and plants may offset some of these advantages. Ecosystem imbalances in fragile desert environments are one result.

Even energy conservation efforts, the most obvious way to reduce energy-related pollutant levels, can have significant environmental consequences. Programmes to save energy used by building ventilation systems have resulted in a slower rate of air exchange and a higher degree of indoor pollution. Health hazards have been created by the use of urea-formaldehyde foam insulation in homes and by construction of more energy-efficient buildings. These measures have increased the impact of indoor air pollutants detrimental to human health such as tobacco smoke, radon decay products, carbon monoxide, carbon dioxide, nitrogen dioxide, formaldehyde, asbestos fibres, viruses, bacteria, spores, and moulds.

## Water consumption

Energy-related environmental effects are not limited to pollution problems. Use of natural resources for energy production, particularly consumption of water, is another critical environmental issue. Electric utilities account for fifty per cent of the water consumed by energy and manufacturing industries. A shift toward more nuclear power plants would increase this, as nuclear plants consume almost two and a half times as much water per kilowatt hour as conventional fossil fuel plants. Synthetic fuel plants could have a major impact on water consumption in the future since they are likely to be located in water-scarce areas where they must compete with other uses of water, such as agricultural irrigation.

## Policy and legislation

Government policy, legislative and regulatory determinations will continue to play an important role in energy-related environmental issues. For example, in the United States seven major federal environmental laws which influence the way energy is produced and consumed have been established since 1976: The Clean Air Act as amended in 1977 and overhauled in 1990, The Clean Water Act of 1977 and 1987, The Resource Conservation and Recovery Act of 1976, The Toxic Substances Control Act of 1976, The Hazardous Waste Act of 1984, The Surface Mining Control and Reclamation Act of 1977, and The Comprehensive Environmental Response Compensation and Liability Act of 1980 and 1986 (Superfund). Three current energy-related laws also have environmental ramifications: The Energy Supply and Environmental Coordination Act of 1974, The Power Plant and Industrial Fuel Use Act of 1978, and The Acid Precipitation Act of 1980 (Title VII of the Energy Security Act of 1980). Consistent with federal energy policy to promote the domestic production of energy and reduce the importation of oil, the first two acts stipulate that coal replace oil and natural gas as fuel for new electric utilities and large industrial boilers. This will lead to sharp pollution increases, particularly in areas where oil and gas have been the primary sources of energy.

Choosing alternative energy strategies will have different impacts on energy and environmental relationships. For example, a moratorium on the use of nuclear energy would require increased use of coal and more energy conservation efforts. This would exacerbate coal-related environmental problems by increasing plant emissions and the discharge of total dissolved solids and solid wastes. It also would reduce water consumption, problems of radioactive waste disposal and the possibility of nuclear accidents. In dealing with energy and environmental concerns, policy and political trade-offs are as important as the scientific and technical aspects.

## Regional impact

Geographic considerations also play a part in defining the energy and environmental picture. The goals of energy self-sufficiency and environmental quality clash most acutely in the United States in the Rocky Mountain region where much of the new coal mining, oil shale production, and development of liquefaction and gasification industries are expected to be concentrated. Demographic shifts reflecting economic conditions in the Northeast of the United States are causing the closure of some traditional smokestack industries contributing to improvement of the area's water quality, while the growing population in the Southwest is causing water supply problems there. A shift from oil- and gas-fueled utilities in the south central USA will adversely affect that region's environmental quality. In areas already heavily reliant on coal, such as the Great Lakes region, the replacement of older, coal-fired plants with newer, more stringently controlled coal-fired boilers will cause some improvement.

**Long-range issues**

Lastly, certain broad, long-term effects not presently regarded as immediate threats may emerge as vital issues in the future. For example, atmospheric buildup of carbon dioxide caused primarily by fossil fuel combustion may significantly alter the earth's climate and adversely affect agricultural and coastal areas. The exact amount of warming produced by a given concentration of carbon dioxide in this so-called 'greenhouse' effect is currently unknown, but the alteration in the global air circulation pattern associated with atmospheric warming has some scientists concerned. Similar concern has been expressed with regard to the destruction of ozone in the stratosphere, acid rain, and impaired visibility or atmospheric discoloration such as found in the Grand Canyon.

From this overview, it can be seen that the boundaries to be covered in order to find information on energy-related environmental issues are far-reaching, cutting across many subject disciplines, encompassing legislative and policy matters, involving both short- and long-range scientific and technical aspects, and carrying geographic connotations. Within this broad framework, myriad information forms may also be required. Journal articles, conference proceedings, books, technical reports, patents, statistics, ongoing research, theses and dissertations, press releases, congressional hearings and newspaper articles are among the kinds of information needed. All of this places a huge challenge before the information seeker to identify and locate the appropriate information resources for each energy-related environmental request.

## THE DATABASES

The initial problem faced by searchers is to identify the most likely database(s). There are special difficulties for the searcher in this area because of the large number of databases which cover at least one aspect of energy or the environment. More than one hundred different databases could be used, depending on the specific question to be searched and the type of information needed. For the most part, these databases span four online services: BRS Information Technologies (BRS) and ORBIT Search Service (ORBIT), both now divisions of Maxwell Online, Inc., DIALOG Information Services, Inc. (DIALOG), and STN International: The Scientific and Technical Network (STN). Other services such as the Chemical Information System (CIS), the US Department of Energy-ITIS (DOE), Mead Data Central (LEXIS/NEXIS) and the National Library of Medicine (NLM) provide important topical files. In addition, some of these databases are available as CD-ROM searchable products through vendors such as SilverPlatter and DIALOG OnDisc as well as directly from the producers.

In order to deal with this multitude, it is useful to separate them into several groupings: (1) the primary comprehensive databases, which contain extensive information and cover most energy-related environmental issues; (2) the specialized subject databases, some of which contain extensive information, but are limited in subject coverage; and (3) the specialized document type databases, which may cover a wide range of subjects, but are limited to a specific form of literature, such as patents. Both bibliographic and complete or full-text databases can be classified in this way. While these groupings are somewhat arbitrary and may not work for every search topic, they do provide a practical approach to database selection in what would otherwise be an overwhelming maze, especially for new and relatively inexperienced searchers.

The primary comprehensive databases are suitable for most energy-related environmental topics. Included in this group are CA SEARCH, COMPENDEX (Computerized Engineering Index), ENVIROLINE, ENERGYLINE, ENVIRONMENTAL BIBLIOGRAPHY, INSPEC (Information Services for the Physics and Engineering Communities), NTIS (National Technical Information Service Bibliographic Database), PASCAL, POLLUTION ABSTRACTS, SCISEARCH, and the former DOE ENERGY DATABASE (EDB), now called ENERGY SCIENCE & TECHNOLOGY (EST). Each of these databases contains at least three hundred references per year on the overall subject, and many include considerably more. They each also cover most aspects of the subject. These databases are listed in Table 7.1.

**Table: 7.1: Primary comprehensive databases covering energy and the environment**

| NAME | PRODUCER | SEARCH SERVICE(S) |
|---|---|---|
| ENERGY SCIENCE & TECHNOLOGY | US DOE/Energy Technology Data Exchange | DIALOG, STN, DOE |
| CA SEARCH | Chemical Abstracts Service/ACS | BRS, DIALOG, ORBIT, STN |
| * COMPENDEX PLUS | Engineering Information, Inc. | BRS, DIALOG, ORBIT, STN |
| * INSPEC | Institute of Electrical Engineers | BRS, DIALOG, ORBIT, STN |
| * NTIS | National Technical Information Service | BRS, DIALOG, ORBIT, STN |
| * PASCAL | CNRS, Centre de Documentation Scientifique et Technique | DIALOG |
| +CURRENT CONTENTS SEARCH | Institute for Scientific Information | BRS, DIALOG |
| * SCISEARCH | Institute for Scientific Information | DIALOG, ORBIT |
| * SOCIAL SCISEARCH | Institute for Scientific Information | BRS, DIALOG |
| * ENVIROLINE | R.R. Bowker | DIALOG, ORBIT |
| * ENVIRONMENTAL BIBLIOGRAPHY | Environmental Studies Institute | DIALOG |
| * ENERGYLINE | R.R. Bowker | DIALOG, ORBIT |
| * POLLUTION ABSTRACTS | Cambridge Scientific Abstracts | DIALOG |

\*   Also available in CD-ROM format. *See* Table 7.7.
\+   Also available in microcomputer format.

## ENERGY SCIENCE & TECHNOLOGY

While any of the databases named above can provide useful results, for most searches the best file to start with in this group is the DOE ENERGY DATABASE (EDB), which recently has been renamed ENERGY SCIENCE & TECHNOLOGY (EST) to reflect better its diverse coverage and international origins. It has extensive subject coverage, includes most types of literature, covers more years, is well indexed and contains the most references on the subject. EST is available through DIALOG, DOE, and STN. However, the DOE-ITIS system only maintains the latest year of the database, while STN loads the FIZ Karlsruhe version of EST which is subject to information export restrictions.

*EST Coverage*

EST is produced by the Energy Technology Data Exchange (ETDE), an international consortium comprising members from Europe, Japan, Canada and the United States. The United States Department of Energy Office of Scientific and Technical Information is the operating agent for the ETDE. The database contains information published in *Energy Abstracts for Policy Analysis, Energy Research Abstracts, Solar Energy Update, Fossil Energy Update, Controlled Fusion Update, Energy Conservation Update, Geothermal Energy Update* and *Atomindex*. The broad subject coverage of EST is shown in Table 7.2.

Started in 1974, EST contains material dating back to the 1800s. Older literature has been added in many subject areas to increase the comprehensiveness of the database. All types of literature are covered by the more than 2,278,000 citations in EST. Approximately 7,500 new citations are added bi-weekly. The unit record for each item has an accession number, title, author, complete bibliographic information, subject descriptors, subject categories and abstracts for all entries added after June 1976.

**Table 7.2: Subject areas covered by EST**

| | |
|---|---|
| advanced automotive propulsion systems | economic and social aspects of energy technologies |
| biomedical sciences | explosives and explosions |
| safety and health | fusion energy |
| coal | geothermal energy |
| natural gas | hydro energy |
| petroleum | instrumentation |
| hydrogen | isotopes and radiation source technology |
| oil shales and tar sands | |
| natural and synthetic fuels | nuclear energy |
| electric power engineering | particle accelerators |
| energy conservation, consumption and utilization | physical sciences |
| | chemistry |
| energy conversion and storage | geosciences |
| energy policy and planning | materials |
| engineering | solar energy |
| environmental sciences: aquatic, atmospheric and terrestrial | tidal energy |
| | wind power |

*Indexing in EST*

The major subject approaches to EST are by controlled subject descriptors, subject categories or free-text searching. Descriptors are controlled by the *Energy Information Database: Subject Thesaurus*. Rules for assigning descriptors are given in the *Energy Information Database: Guide to Abstracting and Indexing*. Descriptors are picked on the basis of the most specific descriptor available to identify uniquely the subject content of each document. Broader terms are added only if information of a general nature is also included in the document. A journal article on air pollution control for coal liquefaction processes would be indexed using the descriptors AIR POLLUTION CONTROL and COAL LIQUEFACTION, but not the descriptor POLLUTION CONTROL unless the article also contained general information on pollution control (for example, on the economics of pollution control).

Approximately three major descriptors are assigned which best represent the main content of each document. These major descriptors are linked or paired with other descriptors or qualifiers which indicate the properties, characteristics, processes or actions determined. Descriptor pairs are the most specific form of subject access to EST because they indicate the major emphasis of the document as well as the precise relationship between each of the descriptors in the pair. The major descriptor 'COAL MINING' qualified by 'WATER POLLUTION' means that the document covers water pollution from coal mining, not merely that coal mining and water pollution are both discussed. For an example of this, see Figure 7.1.

## Figure 7.1: Sample EST record

```
14/5/6
1851269        GB-90:000189, EDB-90:054035
  Title: The challenge of environmentalism
  Author: Skea, J. (Sussex Univ., Brighton (UK). Science
Policy Research Unit)
  Title: European electricity: meeting the challenges of
the 1990s: a two-day conference held in the Churchill Hotel,
London, W1, Tuesday 7th and Wednesday 8th February 1989, in
association with BEAMA
  Corporate Source: European Study Conferences Ltd., Corby (UK)
  Conference Title: European electricity: meeting the
challenges of the 1990s conference
  Conference Location: London (UK) Conference Date: 7-8 Feb
1989
  Publisher: European Study Conferences Limited,Corby, GB
  Date: 1989 18 vp. p.
  Report No.: CONF-8902169-
  Document Type: Analytic of a Book; Conference literature
2 Language: English
  Journal Announcement: EDB9000
  Subfile: EPA (Energy Abstracts for Policy Analysis);
ETDE (Energy Technology Data Exchange). GB (United Kingdom
(sent to DOE from))
  Country of Publication: United Kingdom
  Work Location: United Kingdom
  Abstract: It is argued that the recent awakening of high
level political concern over environmental issues has
important implications for the electricity supply industry in
the UK. Four sets of issues which promise to be high on the
agenda during the 1990s are power plant siting, acid
emissions, the nuclear related problems of safety and
radioactive waste disposal and emissions of greenhouse
gases. In all of these, national, European and international
regulations will be important. (UK).
  Major Descriptors: *ELECTRIC POWER INDUSTRY — ENVIRONMENTAL
POLICY; *ELECTRIC POWER INDUSTRY — UNITED KINGDOM
  Descriptors: ACID RAIN; ENVIRONMENTAL EFFECTS; ENVIRONMENTAL
IMPACTS; GREENHOUSE EFFECT; NUCLEAR POWER; RADIOACTIVE WASTE
DISPOSAL; SAFETY; SITE SELECTION
  Special Terms: ATMOSPHERIC PRECIPITATIONS; EUROPE; GOVERNMENT
POLICIES; INDUSTRY; MANAGEMENT; POWER; RAIN; WASTE DISPOSAL;
WASTE MANAGEMENT; WESTERN EUROPE
  Class Codes: 290300*;296000;290600
```

Another very useful subject approach to EST is through subject categories represented by numeric class codes. These are used to arrange citations in the printed indexes and are assigned according to the content and purpose of the document. Multiple categories are assigned only where neither the content nor the purpose fits a single category. Unlike the approach to descriptors, no effort is made to categorize to the most specific level, and the purpose of the document is emphasized. Three pairs of two-digit numbers (category codes) are used to denote categories. The first two digits designate the main category. The second pair designates subsets of the first pair, and the third pair designates subsets of the second pair. For instance, radioactive effluents, as an environmental aspect of nuclear reactor technology, would be assigned the number 220502; the first two digits, 22, denote nuclear reactor technology, 05 denotes environmental aspects and 02 denotes radioactive effluents. Each level is searchable and may be combined with descriptors. A complete list of categories is given in *Energy Information Database: Energy Categories*. For additional details on the use of category codes, see the *Guide to Abstracting and Indexing*. Table 7.3 shows examples of representative environmental subject categories.

**Table 7.3: Representative EST subject categories**

| Category Code | Category Description |
|---|---|
| 500000 | ENVIRONMENTAL SCIENCES, ATMOSPHERIC |
| 500100 | BASIC STUDIES |
| | (Any basic atmospheric studies that establish information from which environmental effects of energy-related activities can be predicted, calculated, or measured.) |
| 500101 | RADIOMETRIC TECHNIQUES |
| | (Use of radioisotopes or ionizing radiations in basic atmospheric investigations.) |
| 500200 | CHEMICALS MONITORING AND TRANSPORT |
| | (Transport, monitoring, characterization, removal, or reactions of pollutants from the energy cycle during transit through or presence in the atmosphere, e.g., carbon, lead, nitrogen, or sulfur compounds, or respirable particulates. Also includes measures for control and abatement of these pollutants. Biological effects of these pollutants or chemicals are included under BIOMEDICAL SCIENCES, APPLIED STUDIES.) |
| 500300 | RADIOACTIVE MATERIALS MONITORING AND TRANSPORT |
| | (Atmospheric studies on, e.g., plutonium, krypton, xenon, iodine, and strontium radioisotopes; tritium; and other radioactive materials, especially from fission or fusion power plants and any phase of the fuel cycle.) |
| 500400 | THERMAL EFFLUENTS MONITORING AND TRANSPORT |
| | (Studies of atmospheric consequences of moisture and heat releases from power plant cooling towers or from any energy-related technology. Includes studies on cooling tower plume behavior, aerodynamic and thermal exchange over cooling ponds, meteorological and climate studies, Also includes effects from energy conservation measures such as thermal pollution from increased use of heat pumps. Also includes control and abatement. BIOLOGICAL SCIENCES, APPLIED STUDIES.) |

**Table 7.3:** (cont.)

| Category Code | Category Description |
|---|---|
| 500500 | SITE RESOURCE AND USE STUDIES<br>(Meteorological and atmospheric aspects of existing or potential sites for any phase of energy development and use.) |
| 500600 | REGULATIONS<br>(Legislation, ordinances, rules, litigation, hearings, decisions, etc. Recommended or adopted guides, criteria, and standards for allowable atmospheric emission limits or pollutant concentrations; air quality standards.) |
| 510000 | ENVIRONMENTAL SCIENCES, TERRESTRIAL |
| 510100 | BASIC STUDIES<br>(Any basic geological or soil studies that establish information from which environmental effects of energy-related activities can be predicated, calculated, or measured.) |
| 510101 | RADIOMETRIC TECHNIQUES<br>(Use of radioisotopes or ionizing radiation in basic terrestrial studies.) |
| 510200 | CHEMICAL MONITORING AND TRANSPORT<br>(Transport, monitoring, characterization, removal, or reactions of pollutants from the energy cycle during transit through or presence in the terrestrial environment or ecosystem, e.g., carbon, lead, nitrogen, or sulfur compounds. Also includes measures for control and abatement of these pollutants. Biological effects of these pollutants or chemicals are included under BIOMEDICAL SCIENCES, APPLIED STUDIES.) |

The third approach, free-text searching, uses title and abstract terms together with the descriptor words to provide broad, complete coverage of subject information. In addition, EST may be searched by type of document, language, country of publication, country of author affiliation and many other standard indexes. Figure 7.1 illustrates a sample EST record. The several printed tools available to assist searchers in becoming more familiar with EST are listed in Table 7.4.

## OTHER PRIMARY DATABASES

EST has been described in some detail because it is such a central database for energy-related environmental issues, and because it is comparatively unknown. However, the other ten primary databases should not be ignored. Six of these are large files covering broad, traditional scientific and technical fields, and for this reason

**Table 7.4: ENERGY SCIENCE & TECHNOLOGY (EST) searching aids**

| Document Number | Title |
|---|---|
| DOE/TIC-7000-R6 | Energy Information Database: Subject Thesaurus, DOE TIC, 1984 |
| DOE/TIC-4583-R3 | Energy Information Database: Guide to Abstracting and Indexing, DOE TIC, 1981. |
| DOE/TIC-4584-R5 | Energy Information Database: Subject Categories, DOE TIC, 1983. |
| DOE/TIC-4579-R13 | Energy Information Database: Serial Titles with ISSN Listing, DOE TIC, 1984. |
| DOE/TIC-85-R13 | Energy Information Database: Report Number Codes, DOE TIC, 1979. |
| DOE/TIC-4585-R4 | Energy Information Database: Corporate Author Entries, DOE TIC, 1984. |
| DOE/TIC-4045-S2 | Index to Conference Titles: Selected Conferences Cited in the Energy Database 1977-1982, DOE TIC, 1982. |

may not always be thought of as important energy/environmental databases. Four are smaller and more limited, specializing in energy or environmental topics. A brief description of each of these databases follows.

## CA SEARCH

Chemical Abstracts Service (CAS) covers worldwide literature of chemistry and its application from 1967 and contains approximately nine and a half million citations. About seventeen thousand new citations covering all types of literature, including patents, are added biweekly. The unit record available through all online services except STN does not include the abstract. Therefore online searching typically is based on a combination of author, uncontrolled terminology, controlled vocabulary from the *Chemical Abstracts Index Guide*, CAS Registry Numbers and Section Codes. Document type and language are also searchable. Full-text searching is available for a small group of core CAS journals through the CJACS database on STN. Particularly useful source journals for this topic are *Energy & Fuels* and *Environmental Science & Technology*. CAS is covered in detail in Chapter 4.

## COMPENDEX PLUS

COMPENDEX and its companion database, EI ENGINEERING MEETINGS (the online versions of *Engineering Index*), were merged into COMPENDEX PLUS in 1988. COMPENDEX PLUS covers all types of engineering and technology. Worldwide coverage of the literature is provided from 1970. The databases contain more than 2.6 million citations and abstracts, with 17,500 new records added each month. Online retrieval is facilitated in COMPENDEX PLUS by the ability to search terms in the title and abstract as well as the rather general main or sub-headings and the subject category codes. Treatment codes serve as a guide to the general orientation of the paper; theoretical versus practical, for example. Twenty-five per cent of the material is from a non-English-language source. Abstracts are available. COMPENDEX PLUS is covered in detail in Chapter 8.

## INSPEC

INSPEC corresponds to four *Science Abstracts* publications: *Physics Abstracts, Electrical and Electronics Abstracts, Computer and Control Abstracts* and *IT Focus* produced by the Institution of Electrical Engineers. Electrical power generation systems, of particular relevance to this chapter, form a major subject area. Material from 1969 to the present is covered online. While all types of literature are included in its 3,700,000 citations and abstracts, journal articles are emphasized. Approximately twenty thousand new entries are added per month. Descriptor terms assigned from the *Inspec Thesaurus* are a useful search tool in addition to title and abstract words. This thesaurus is available online. Chemical and numerical indexing fields have been added since February 1987. Category code schemes are available for each of the major publication areas, and are now uniform throughout as a result of INSPEC's recently completed database upgrade project. Treatment codes of the type described for COMPENDEX are provided. Fifteen per cent of the database is non-English material. This database is also covered in detail in Chapters 8 and 9.

## NTIS

The NTIS database consists of government-sponsored research and development reports plus analyses, reprints and translations from over 250 federal agencies. It contains all references published in *Weekly Government Abstracts* and *Government Reports Announcements*. Environmental pollution and control, and energy production and conservation are among the many topics covered by the more than 1,410,000 citations (dating form 1964 on DIALOG and STN, and from 1970 on ORBIT and BRS). Approximately 2,500 new reports are added biweekly.

Since the material is entered from a variety of agencies using different thesauri, controlled vocabulary is not consistent. Four major thesauri and five minor thesauri are currently used, while a number of others are used periodically. However, NTIS has compiled two composite thesauri, one on energy and another on the environment, which bring together similar terms from each of the major thesauri [2]. These tools assist the searcher by indicating which terms are used in each thesaurus to represent a particular concept. Subject category searching, when combined with keywords, can be helpful to eliminate false selections. Abstracts are available for most citations.

## PASCAL

PASCAL is produced by the Institut de l'Information Scientifique et Technique of the Centre National de la Recherche Scientifique (French National Research Council). It is a multidisciplinary database covering the world's scientific and technical literature, equivalent to the seventy-nine print publications now titled *Bibliographie Internationale*. The database consists of more than 2,572,000 records from 1973 to the present. Sources include all types of literature. Major subjects include: life sciences, biology, and medicine; chemistry, applied chemistry, and pollution; energy; metallurgy, mechanical and civil engineering; transportation; food and agricultural sciences; earth sciences; physics and space sciences; and computer sciences and engineering. It is bilingual. Titles and controlled descriptors are provided in French and English, and in some cases, Spanish. About fifty per cent of the records have abstracts.

## SCISEARCH and SOCIAL SCISEARCH

SCISEARCH and SOCIAL SCISEARCH are prepared by the Institute for Scientific Information (ISI) and correspond to the printed *Science Citation Index* and *Social Science Citation Index,* with additional items from selected *Current Contents.* They are multidisciplinary indexes to the journal literature of science and technology, and the social sciences, respectively. Several criteria, including citation analysis, are used to select the most significant journals for inclusion. Together these databases cover over 10.5 million citations. SCISEARCH, online since 1974, is updated weekly with about fifteen thousand new citations. SOCIAL SCISEARCH covers from 1972 and adds 2,500 new citations each week. Both files must be searched for scientific questions with social implications, a common situation for searches on energy-related environmental questions. Keyword searching is limited to title words - no additional vocabulary or abstracts are included. The strength of these files is in citation linking, which permits access to the literature by cited references. Searching by document type is also an important criterion since all significant articles, reports of meetings, letters, editorials and correction notices are entered into the databases.

Closely related to these databases is another online ISI product, CURRENT CONTENTS SEARCH. This weekly current awareness service reproduces the tables of contents of the latest issues of leading journals in the sciences, social sciences, and arts and humanities. Four of its seven subsets offer coverage of energy and environmental issues: *Life Sciences; Engineering, Technology and Applied Sciences; Agriculture, Biology, and Environmental Sciences;* and *Physical, Chemical, and Earth Sciences.* These individual subsets are also available as microcomputer diskette products. In addition, ISI has released a multidisciplinary, biweekly guide to current literature dealing with environmental change, FOCUS ON: GLOBAL CHANGE, in microcomputer diskette format.

## Smaller databases

The four smaller databases devoted to energy or environmental matters are ENVIROLINE, ENVIRONMEN-TAL BIBLIOGRAPHY, ENERGYLINE and POLLUTION ABSTRACTS.

ENVIROLINE contains citations from *Environment Abstracts,* a publication of the R.R. Bowker Company. It emphasizes coverage of the air environment, environmental health, the land environment, resource management, solid wastes management and the water environment. A new acid rain segment based on the Bowker publications *Acid Rain Abstracts* and *Acid Rain Index* has recently been added, significantly enhancing coverage on this important energy-environment issue. More than 150,000 citations are currently available, with about one thousand new references added each month. Roughly five thousand sources of information including technical, trade, professional and general periodicals, papers from conferences, research reports, Congressional hearing transcripts, environmental project reports and newspaper articles are scanned for enclosure. Rulings from the Federal Register and patents from the *United States Official Gazette* are also included. Journal papers comprise more than sixty per cent of the database. A significant amount of popular literature is also included. Title words, abstract terms and thesaurus-controlled descriptors along with review classifications and document type, form the basis for searching. Coverage starts in 1971. Abstracts are not available before 1975. A sample record is shown in Figure 7.2.

**Figure 7.2: Sample ENVIROLINE record**

```
    12/5/2
    0199750 Enviroline Number: 89-003844
      AIR QUALITY IMPACT ASSESSMENT (AIR POLLUTION CONTROL),
      SHEN THOMAS T. COLUMBIA UNIV,
      ENCYCLOPEDIA OF ENV CONTROL TECHNOLOGY, 1989, V2, P1(36)
      BOOK CHAPTER AIR QUALITY IMPACT ASSESSMENT (AQIA) IS A
    MECHANISM WHICH AIDS THE EFFICIENT USE OF AIR RESOURCES. AQIA
    INVOLVES THE IDENTIFICATION, PREDICTION, AND EVALUATION OF
    CRITICAL VARIABLES SUCH AS SOURCE EMISSIONS AND METEOROLOGICAL
    CONDITIONS, AS WELL AS POTENTIAL AIR QUALITY CHANGES AS A
    RESULT OF EMISSIONS FROM NEW PROPOSED PROJECTS. THE
    RESULTS OF THE PROCESS CAN PINPOINT THOSE IMPACTS WHICH
    ARE LIKELY TO HAVE THE MOST ADVERSE OR BENEFICIAL EFFECTS,
    AND CAN BE USED AS A SCREENING DEVICE FOR SETTLING POLLUTION
    CONTROL PRIORITIES. FACETS OF SUCH ASSESSMENT ARE
    DISCUSSED, INCLUDING REGULATORY REQUIREMENTS, BACKGROUND
    AIR QUALITY DETERMINATION, SOURCE EMISSIONS, AIR QUALITY
    MODELING, AND MITIGATION MEASURES. (2 DIAGRAMS, 18 REFERENCES,
    12 TABLES)
      Descriptors: *ENV IMPACT ASSESSMENT ; *AIR POLLUTION
    INDICATORS ; *MATHEMATIC MODELS-AIR ; *MONITORING, ENV-AIR
    ; *AIR QUALITY STANDS ; *STACK EMISSIONS ; *ATMOSPHERIC
    DIFFUSION ; INDUSTRIAL PLANT SITING ; POLYCHLORINATED
    BIPHENYLS ; POWER PLANT EMISSIONS
      Review Classification: 01
```

**ENVIRONMENTAL BIBLIOGRAPHY** is the online version of *Environmental Periodicals Bibliography* and is produced by the Environmental Studies Institute, in Santa Barbara, California. This database provides broad coverage of the environmental sciences, including human ecology, atmospheric studies, energy, land resources, water resources, and nutrition and health. Three hundred of the world's journals dealing with the environment are scanned to create the database. More than 372,000 citations are in the file from 1973 to the present, with 4,200 added bimonthly. Controlled indexing and title words provide subject access but there are no abstracts (see Figure 7.3 for a sample record).

**Figure 7.3: Sample ENVIRONMENTAL BIBLIOGRAPHY record**

```
    14/5/1
    1620031 An application of game theory in the design of optimal air pollution
    control measures
      Hati, S. K.; Lamb, R. G.
      Atmospheric Environment, 1987 VOL 21, NO. 8, p. 1833
        DESCRIPTORS: Power plant; Siting, optimal; Game theory;
    Air pollution
```

**ENERGYLINE**, like ENVIROLINE, is produced by the R.R. Bowker Company. It contains energy material from *Environment Abstracts* from 1971 to 1975, and all materials from *Energy Information Abstracts* starting with 1976. ENERGYLINE deals with a wide range of energy-related issues including economics, policy and planning, resources and reserves, solar energy, fuel processing and transport, electric power generation, nuclear resources and power, consumption and conservation, and environmental impact. Literature coverage and type is similar to that of ENVIROLINE. It is the smallest of the primary databases with more than 69,000 citations; 500 new citations are added monthly. Subject access is furnished through title and abstract terms, controlled vocabulary descriptors and review classification. Document type is also distinguished. Abstracts are not available before 1975. The record format is the same as that of ENVIROLINE.

POLLUTION ABSTRACTS corresponds to the printed *Pollution Abstracts* produced by Cambridge Scientific Abstracts. Subjects covered include air pollution, environmental quality, noise pollution, pesticides, radiation, solid wastes and water pollution. Technical literature from books, conference proceedings, government reports, periodicals and research papers is emphasized. The database contains more than 150,000 citations dating from 1970 and is updated bimonthly with 1,500 new citations. Controlled index terms, free language terms, title words and abstract terms beginning in 1978 are available for searching. Document type and language may also be used. See Figure 7.4 for an example of the record format.

## Figure 7.4: Sample POLLUTION ABSTRACTS record

```
87-04344
A social radiation risk criterion in nuclear power plant siting
Kollas, J.; Catsaros, N.
Nucl. Technol. Dep., Nucl. Res. Cent. "Domokritos", Aghia
Paraskevi 153 10, Attiki, Greece
INT. J. ENERGY SYST VOL. 6, NO. 3, pp. 81-85, Publ.Yr:
1986
SUMMARY LANGUAGE - ENGLISH
Languages: ENGLISH
A siting criterion accounting for the social radiation
risk in the presence of a large population centre is
formulated. The study performed led to the conclusion that for
distances of the order of a few tenths of kilometers and for
sites with favorable air flow patterns the social risk expressed
by the whole body population (collective) dose and resulting from
a severe postulate reference accident release which is of the
same order of magnitude as the collective dose due to
he natural background radiation- can be limited to levels
encountered historically in energy production as a whole.
Descriptors: nuclear power plants; radioactive emissions; risk
assessment ; public health; air quality
```

## SPECIALIZED SUBJECT DATABASES

The above are the eleven primary databases which cover energy-related environmental issues. For a number of questions, however, another group of databases, the specialized subject databases, should be considered as well.

The specialized subject databases (see Table 7.5) cover a variety of topical areas bearing on energy-related environmental matters. They are: atmospheric and climatological sciences, business and industry, electric power, energy/environmental issues specific to Japan or German-speaking countries, land resources, legislation and government policy, nuclear power, oil and gas, toxicology and health, transportation and water resources. Most specialized subject databases fall primarily into one of these areas, although a few have a somewhat broader orientation. Several of these databases are covered in some detail in other chapters. All are discussed briefly below.

**Table 7.5: Specialised subject databases covering areas related to energy and the environment**

| NAME | PRODUCER | SEARCH SERVICE(S) |
|---|---|---|
| **Atmospheric and climatological science** | | |
| * AEROSPACE DATABASE | American Inst. of Aeronautics & Astronautics | DIALOG |
| APTIC | Air Pollution Technical Information Center | DIALOG |
| METEOROLOGICAL & GEO-ASTROPHYSICAL ABSTRACTS | American Meteorological Society | DIALOG |
| **Business and industry** | | |
| * ABI/INFORM | University Microfilms (UMI)/Data Courier | BRS, DIALOG, ORBIT |
| BIOBUSINESS | BioSciences Information Service/Information Access Company(IAC) | DIALOG |
| * BUSINESS DATELINE | UMI/Data Courier | BRS, DIALOG |
| BUSINESSWIRE | BusinessWire | DIALOG |
| CHEMICAL INDUSTRY NOTES | CAS/American Chemical Society | DIALOG, ORBIT, STN |
| DETEQ | Deutsche Gesellschaft für Chemisches Apparatewesen Chemische Technik und Biotechnologie e.V | STN |
| FINANCIAL TIMES FULLTEXT | Financial Times Business Information, Ltd. | DIALOG |
| FOREIGN TRADE & ECONOMIC ABSTRACTS | Netherlands Foreign Trade Agency | DIALOG |
| * ICONDA | ICONDA Agency/Fraunhofer Society | ORBIT, STN |
| MANAGEMENT CONTENTS | Information Access Company | BRS, DIALOG, ORBIT |
| MCGRAW-HILL PUBLICATIONS ONLINE | McGraw-Hill, Inc. | DIALOG |
| MOODY'S CORPORATE NEWS | Moody's Investor Service, Inc. | DIALOG |
| NEWSWIRE ASAP | Information Access Company | DIALOG |
| PAPERCHEM | Institute of Paper Science & Technology | DIALOG |
| * PTS INDEXES | Predicasts, Inc. | BRS, DIALOG |
| PTS NEWSLETTER DATABASE | Predicasts, Inc. | DIALOG |
| RAPRA ABSTRACTS | Rapra Technology, Ltd. | ORBIT |
| TRADE AND INDUSTRY INDEX | Information Access Company | BRS, DIALOG |
| WORLD SURFACE COATINGS ABSTRACTS | Paint Research Association | ORBIT |

**Table 7.5:** (cont.)

| NAME | PRODUCER | SEARCH SERVICE(S) |
|------|----------|-------------------|
| **Electric power** | | |
| EPIA | Edison Electric Inst./Utility Data Institute | ORBIT |
| * EPRI | Electric Power Research Institute | DIALOG, DOE |
| **Energy/environment issues in Japan or German-speaking countries** | | |
| ENERGIE | FIZ Karlsruhe | STN |
| JICST-E | Japan Information Center of Science and Technology | STN |
| ULIDAT | FIZ Karlsruhe | STN |
| **Land-related resources** | | |
| * AGRICOLA | National Agricultural Library | BRS, DIALOG, ORBIT |
| * AGRIS INTERNATIONAL | National Agricultural Library | DIALOG |
| * BIOSIS PREVIEWS | BioSciences Information Service | BRS, DIALOG, ORBIT, STN |
| * CAB ABSTRACTS | CAB International | BRS, DIALOG, ORBIT, STN |
| CURRENT AWARENESS IN BIOLOGICAL SCIENCES | Current Awareness in Biological Sciences | BRS, ORBIT |
| GEOARCHIVE | Geosystems | DIALOG |
| * GEOBASE | Geo Abstracts Ltd. | DIALOG, ORBIT |
| * GEOREF | American Geological Institute | DIALOG, ORBIT |
| * LIFE SCIENCES COLLECTION | Cambridge Scientific Abstracts | BRS, DIALOG |
| **Legislation and government policy** | | |
| * CIS/INDEX | Congressional Information Service | DIALOG |
| CONGRESSIONAL RECORD ABSTRACTS | National Standards Association | DIALOG |
| FEDERAL REGISTER | US Government Printing Office | DIALOG |
| FEDERAL REGISTER ABSTRACTS | National Standards Association | DIALOG, ORBIT |
| LEXIS | Mead Data Central | MEAD |
| * PAIS INTERNATIONAL | Policy Review Information Service | BRS, DIALOG |
| **Nuclear power** | | |
| * INTERNATIONAL NUCLEAR INFORMATION SYSTEM | International Atomic Energy Agency (INIS) | CAN/OLE, ESA-IRS, JICST |

**Table 7.5:** (cont.)

| NAME | PRODUCER | SEARCH SERVICE(S) |
|---|---|---|
| NUCLEAR SAFETY INFORMATION CENTER | Nuclear Regulatory Commission | NRC |
| NUCLEAR SCIENCE ABSTRACTS | US Department of Energy | DIALOG, DOE |

**Oil and gas**

| | | |
|---|---|---|
| APILIT | American Petroleum Institute | DIALOG, ORBIT, STN |
| APIPAT | American Petroleum Institute | DIALOG, ORBIT, STN |
| ARAB INFORMATION BANK | Al Bayan Press | DIALOG |
| IPABASE | International Petroleum Abstracts | ORBIT |
| P/E NEWS | American Petroleum Institute | DIALOG, ORBIT |
| TULSA (PETROLEUM EXPLORATION & PRODUCTION) | Petroleum Abstracts/ University of Tulsa | DIALOG, DOE, ORBIT |

**Toxicology and health**

| | | |
|---|---|---|
| AQUIRE | Duluth Environmental Research Lab/EPA | CIS |
| * BIOSIS PREVIEWS | BioSciences Information Service | BRS, DIALOG, ORBIT, STN |
| * CANCERLIT | National Library of Medicine | BRS, DIALOG, NLM |
| CERCLIS | US EPA | CIS |
| CESARS | Michigan Dept. of Natural Resources/US EPA | CIS |
| * EMBASE | Elsevier Publishing Co. | BRS, DIALOG |
| ENVIROFATE | US EPA/Syracuse Research Corporation | CIS |
| * HEALTH AND SAFETY SCIENCE ABSTRACTS | Cambridge Scientific Abstracts | ORBIT |
| * HSELINE | Health and Safety Executive | ORBIT |
| * LIFE SCIENCES COLLECTION | Cambridge Scientific Abstracts | BRS, DIALOG |
| * MEDLINE | National Library of Medicine | BRS, DIALOG, NLM |
| * OCCUPATIONAL SAFETY AND HEALTH | National Inst. for Occupational Safety & Health | DIALOG |
| * OHM/TADS | US EPA | CIS |
| TOXNET | National Library of Medicine | NLM |
| * TOXLINE | National Library of Medicine | BRS, DIALOG, NLM |
| WASTEINFO | Waste Management Info Bureau/Harwell Lab | ORBIT |

**Transportation**

| | | |
|---|---|---|
| TRIS | US Department of Transportation | DIALOG |
| SIGLE | European Association for Grey Literature Exploitation | STN, BLAISE-LINE |

**Table 7.5:** (cont.)

| NAME | PRODUCER | SEARCH SERVICE(S) |
|---|---|---|
| ALTERNATIVE FUELS DATA BANK | US Department of Energy | DOE |
| **Water resources** | | |
| AQUALINE | Water Research Centre (UK) | ORBIT |
| * AQUATIC SCIENCES & FISHERIES ABSTRACTS | NOAA/Cambridge Scientific Abstracts | BRS, DIALOG |
| OCEANIC ABSTRACTS | Cambridge Scientific Abstracts | BRS, DIALOG |
| * WATER RESOURCES ABSTRACTS | US Department of the Interior | DIALOG |
| WATERNET | American Water Works Association | DIALOG |

\* Also available in CD-ROM format. *See* Table 7.7.

## Atmospheric and climatological sciences

Three databases are of interest; the AEROSPACE DATABASE which combines two publications, *Scientific and Technical Aerospace Reports* and *International Aerospace Abstracts*, the APTIC (Air Pollution Technical Information Center) file published as *Air Pollution Abstracts* and METEOROLOGICAL AND GEOASTROPHYSICAL ABSTRACTS (MGA) which corresponds to the printed publication of the same name. The AEROSPACE DATABASE provides extensive coverage of air pollution issues from key scientific and technical documents. APTIC was produced by the United States Environmental Protection Agency, but has not been updated since September 1978. It should be used when a comprehensive, retrospective search on any aspect of air pollution is required. MGA is produced by the American Meteorological Society in cooperation with the Environmental Science Information Center of the National Oceanic and Atmospheric Administration (NOAA), and is a good source of research information.

## Business and industry

A large number of databases cover business and industrial aspects of energy-environmental issues. Among the most useful are: ABI/INFORM which has no print counterpart, BIOBUSINESS, BUSINESS DATELINE, CHEMICAL INDUSTRY NOTES, FOREIGN TRADE & ECONOMY ABSTRACTS, MANAGEMENT CONTENTS, MOODY'S CORPORATE NEWS, NEWSWIRE ASAP (PR Newswire, Kyodo, Reuters, and Newsbyte), the PREDICAST series of databases such as PTS F&S INDEXES (*Funk & Scott*), PTS NEWSLETTER DATABASE, and PTS PROMT (*Predicasts Overviews of Markets and Technology*), TRADE AND INDUSTRY INDEX, BUSINESSWIRE and MCGRAW-HILL PUBLICATIONS ONLINE. Business and economics databases are covered in detail in Chapters 13 and 14. DETEQ, the DECHEMA Environmental Technology Equipment Data Bank, contains information on the manufacturers of apparatus and technical equipment in the field of environmental engineering. A few databases are devoted to individual industries such as PAPERCHEM and PIRA which cover the pulp and paper industry. Others are ICONDA, RAPRA ABSTRACTS and WORLD SURFACE COATING ABSTRACTS, covering construction, rubber, and paints respectively.

## Electric power

Information on the environmental effects of all types of electric power plants and associated transmission lines, power plant siting studies and methodologies, fuel transportation, storage and use, licensing and permit data, monitoring programmes, safety and risk assessment, coastal zone management plans and waste disposal facilities is contained in EPIA (Electric Power Industry Abstracts). It includes reports prepared by electric utilities and their consultants, United States federal and state agencies, siting commissions and control boards. The ELECTRIC POWER DATABASE (EPRI) covers United States and Canadian research and development projects of interest to the electric power industry, including environmental assessments.

## Energy/environment issues in Japan or German-speaking countries

ENERGIE contains citations, in German and English, on energy-related literature published in German-speaking countries. ULIDAT deals with the environmental problems of these same countries. It focuses on water, air, waste management and noise and is a German-language database with some titles and abstracts in English. JICST-E is a comprehensive bibliographic database with English-language citations and abstracts which covers literature published in Japan on all fields of science, technology and medicine.

## Land-related resources

AGRICOLA, produced by the United States Department of Agriculture, AGRIS INTERNATIONAL, which corresponds in part to the Food and Agriculture Organization's *AgrIndex* and CAB ABSTRACTS (CAB), a compilation of twenty-five abstract journals published by the Commonwealth Agricultural Bureaux cover agricultural and forestry aspects. BIOSIS PREVIEWS (BIOSIS) contains citations from *Biological Abstracts* and *BioResearch Index* and covers botanical as well as agricultural facets. CURRENT AWARENESS IN BIOLOGICAL SCIENCES is a broad biological database with coverage of ecology and environmental sciences. GEOARCHIVE, GEOBASE and GEOREF (Geological Reference File) deal with fossil energy sources and geothermal energy, mining geology and environmental geology. GEOREF offers better coverage of energy-related environmental questions. *Ecology Abstracts* is contained in the LIFE SCIENCES COL-LECTION database.

## Legislation and government policy

Extensive coverage is provided by CIS/INDEX which indexes the publications and working papers of the nearly three hundred committees and subcommittees of the United States Congress; CONGRESSIONAL RECORD ABSTRACTS (CRECORD) which covers the printed *Congressional Record*; FEDERAL REG-ISTER which provides the full text of the *Federal Register* and is updated daily; and FEDERAL REGISTER

ABSTRACTS (FEDREG) which includes federal regulatory actions as published in the Federal Register. FEDREG also covers existing and proposed rules and regulations, notices and hearings of the executive departments and agencies, presidential views, proclamations and final action on legislation, and court decisions and other judicial activities. Legal aspects, particularly United States federal code and case law, are found in LEXIS, a full-text database service of Mead Data Central. Contemporary public issues and the making and evaluation of public policy are covered by PAIS INTERNATIONAL (PAIS).

## Nuclear power

A great deal of information on environmental aspects of nuclear energy developments published before June 1976 is contained in NUCLEAR SCIENCE ABSTRACTS (NSA), which corresponds to the printed index of the same name. Literature on this topic published after June 1976 is found in the EST database. The INTERNATIONAL NUCLEAR INFORMATION SYSTEM (INIS) is a basic source on nuclear energy. Another useful file is the NUCLEAR SAFETY INFORMATION CENTER (NSIC) database. Siting of nuclear facilities, transportation and handling of radioactive materials, reactor accidents and all kinds of safety information is covered. NSIC also includes special studies or evaluations and operating experience data such as licensee event reports, which deal with environmental considerations.

## Oil and gas

Air, land and water pollution, along with solid wastes and health hazards resulting from petro-refining are encompassed in the APILIT (API Literature) database of the American Petroleum Institute (API). Another API database, P/E NEWS, covers petroleum and energy business news. All aspects of life in the Arab world are included in the ARAB INFORMATION BANK (AIB). AIB is based on Arabic-language newspapers and radio broadcasts along with periodicals specializing in Middle Eastern affairs. IPABASE contains petroleum and allied literature concerning oil field exploration and development, petroleum refining and products, and economics. Its printed equivalent is *International Petroleum Abstracts*. TULSA, which corresponds in part to *Petroleum Abstracts* published by the University of Tulsa, GEOARCHIVE and GEOREF are also appropriate in this field.

## Toxicology and health

The TOXLINE database provides coverage of toxicology information taken from eleven sources including CAS, MEDLINE and BIOSIS. *Toxicology Abstracts* is contained in the LIFE SCIENCES COLLECTION database. All aspects of environmental health are covered by EMBASE (EXCERPTA MEDICA), BIOSIS, MEDLINE, and CANCERLIT. HSELINE, OCCUPATIONAL SAFETY AND HEALTH (NIOSH), and HEALTH AND SAFETY SCIENCE ABSTRACTS have an industrial focus. WASTEINFO deals with all aspects of non-radioactive waste management. Several full-text databases on CIS contain toxicity data extracted from published literature and other sources. Among them are: CESARS (Chemical Evaluation Search and Retrieval System) which provides detailed information on a group of chemicals of particular importance to the Great Lakes Basin; OHM/TADS (Oil and Hazardous Materials/Technical Assistance Data System) which was established to aid spill response teams in the retrieval of chemical-specific response information; AQUIRE (Aquatic Information Retrieval) which contains information on acute, chronic, bioaccumulative and sublethal effects data from tests performed on freshwater and salt water species; ENVIROFATE (Environmental Fate) which covers data extracted from papers dealing with the ecological fate or behaviour of chemicals released into the environment; and CERCLIS, a database of hazardous waste sites being considered for cleanup under the EPA superfund programme. NLM's TOXNET system is a similar type of database with a broader subject orientation. Of particular interest is the TRI component which contains data on toxic chemicals released into the environment or transferred to waste sites.

## Transportation

TRIS (Transportation Research Information Service) produced by the Transportation Research Board and the United States Department of Transportation, is a major database for energy-related environmental aspects of air, highway, rail and maritime transport, mass transit and other modes of transportation. SIGLE contains European non-conventional literature in applied science and technology including propulsion and fuels. Pollutant emissions from alternative fuels for transportation uses, particularly alcohol fuels, are covered in the ALTERNATIVE FUELS DATA BANK (AFDB) of the DOE.

## Water resources

Energy issues which impact on the water environment are dealt with most extensively by AQUATIC SCIENCES AND FISHERIES ABSTRACTS (ASFA), WATER RESOURCES ABSTRACTS (WRA), AQUALINE, OCEANIC ABSTRACTS, and WATERNET.

## SPECIALIZED DOCUMENT-TYPE DATABASES

A third group of databases, the specialized document-type databases (see Table 7.6) also meets specific needs. These databases, covering government documents, popular or consumer-oriented information, ongoing research, patents, contracts and statistical information, are outlined below. As with the specialized subject databases, many are discussed more fully in other chapters.

**Table 7.6: Specialized document-type databases covering energy and the environment**

| NAME | PRODUCER | SEARCH SERVICE(S) |
|------|----------|-------------------|
| **Government documents** | | |
| EBIB | Texas A&M University/Gulf Publishing | ORBIT |
| FEDERAL APPLIED TECHNOLOGY DATABASE | National Technical Information Service | BRS |
| * GPO MONTHLY CATALOG | US Government Printing Office | BRS, DIALOG |
| * INDEX TO US GOVERNMENT PERIODICALS | Infordata International, Inc. | BRS |

**Table 7.6:** (cont.)

| NAME | PRODUCER | SEARCH SERVICE(S) |
|------|----------|-------------------|
| POWER | US Department of Energy | ORBIT |

**Popular or consumer-oriented sources**

| NAME | PRODUCER | SEARCH SERVICE(S) |
|------|----------|-------------------|
| AP NEWS | Press Association, Associated Press | DIALOG |
| CCML:SCIENCE | American Associationn for the Advancement of Science | BRS |
| COURIER PLUS | UMI/Data Courier | DIALOG |
| EARTHNET | Queens College | Queens College |
| ENERGY INFORMATION RESOURCES | US Department of Energy | DOE |
| * KIRK-OTHMER ONLINE | John Wiley and Sons, Inc. | BRS, DIALOG |
| * MAGAZINE INDEX | Information Access Company | BRS, DIALOG |
| MONUDOC | Information Center for Regional Planning & Building Construction/ Fraunhofer-Society | STN |
| * NATIONAL NEWSPAPER INDEX | Information Access Company | BRS, DIALOG |
| NATIONAL REFERRAL CENTER | US Library of Congress | NLM, SCOPIO |
| NEWSEARCH | Information Access Company | DIALOG |
| NEW YORK TIMES | New York Times Information Service | MEAD |
| * PAPERS | Individual newspaper publishers | DIALOG |
| PRESSNET ENVIRONMENTAL REPORTS | PressNet Systems, Inc. | CIS |
| UPI NEWS | United Press International | DIALOG |
| USA TODAY DECISIONLINE | Gannett News Media | DIALOG |
| * WASHINGTON PRESSTEXT | PressText News Service | DIALOG |

**Ongoing research**

| NAME | PRODUCER | SEARCH SERVICE(S) |
|------|----------|-------------------|
| * CRIS | US Department of Agriculture | DIALOG |
| FEDERAL RESEARCH IN PROGRESS | National Technical Information Service | DIALOG |
| JAPANESE GOVERNMENT & PUBLIC RESEARCH IN PROGRESS (JGRIP) | Japan Information Center of Science and Technology | STN |
| SSIE CURRENT RESEARCH | Smithsonian Science Information | DIALOG |
| UFORDAT | Umweltbundesamt | STN |

**Patents**

| NAME | PRODUCER | SEARCH SERVICE(S) |
|------|----------|-------------------|
| APIPAT | American Petroleum Institute | ORBIT, STN |
| INPADOC | International Patent Documentation Center | DIALOG, ORBIT, STN |

**Table 7.6:** (cont.)

| NAME | PRODUCER | SEARCH SERVICE(S) |
|---|---|---|
| WPI | Derwent Publications, Ltd. | DIALOG, ORBIT |
| **Procurement and contracts** | | |
| COMMERCE BUSINESS DAILY | US Department of Commerce | DIALOG |
| **Statistics** | | |
| * ASI | Congressional Information Service, Inc. | DIALOG |
| FEDERAL ENERGY DATA BASE INDEX | US Department of Energy | DOE |
| NATIONAL ENVIRONMENTAL DATA REFERRAL SERVICE | National Environmental Data Referral Service, US Department of Commerce | BRS |

\*    Also available in CD-ROM format. *See* Table 7.7.

## Government documents

Beside the government report coverage of NTIS, there are other significant energy collections and government databases which should be considered. Books, maps, government documents and technical reports in the Texas A&M University Library are indexed in EBIB (Energy Bibliography and Index). POWER contains catalogue records from the book collection of the DOE Energy Library. The GPO MONTHLY CATALOG (GPO) corresponds to the *Monthly Catalog of United States Government Publications*. Its sources are federal government agencies. Government-produced journals are covered in the INDEX TO THE US GOVERNMENT PERIODICALS and over half are not indexed elsewhere. The FEDERAL APPLIED TECHNOLOGY DATABASE provides access to United States government laboratory engineering and R&D activities.

## Popular or consumer-oriented information

News articles contain much energy-related environmental information and are indexed in such broad scope databases as COURIER PLUS, the NATIONAL NEWSPAPER INDEX (NNI), PAPERS (*Arizona Republic/ Phoenix Gazette, Boston Globe, Charlotte Observer, Chicago Tribune, Columbus Dispatch, Detroit Free Press, Fort Lauderdale News/Sun-Sentinel, Houston Post, Los Angeles Times, Newsday, Orlando Sentinel, Philadelphia Inquirer, Rocky Mountain News, Sacramento Bee, St. Louis Post-Dispatch, St. Paul Pioneer Press, San Francisco Chronicle, San Jose Mercury News, Washington Post Online*). Full-text coverage is provided by AP NEWS (Associated Press), UPI NEWS (United Press International), USA TODAY DECISIONLINE, WASHINGTON PRESSTEXT and NEW YORK TIMES. PRESSNET ENVIRONMEN-

TAL REPORTS contains summaries of articles on environmental issues published in American newspapers as well as original reporting on environmental questions relating to state governments. The MAGAZINE INDEX (MI) provides indexing to articles, news reports, editorials on major issues, product evaluations and reviews from several hundred popular American magazines. MI also comes in a full-text version. NEWSEARCH covers the most recent month of MI and NNI. A full-text version of the weekly journal, *Science,* is available as CCML:SCIENCE. Encyclopedia information on energy and environmental subjects can be found in KIRK-OTHMER ONLINE. MONUDOC, a German-language database, covers the preservation of historic monuments, with an emphasis on environmental damage to historic buildings. The EARTHNET database at Queens College, New York, takes a non-technical approach to energy and environmental concerns. Information sources such as organizations, laboratories and programme offices can be located in the ENERGY INFORMATION RESOURCES and NATIONAL REFERRAL CENTER databases.

## Ongoing research

Most current energy and environmental research information can be obtained from the FEDERAL RESEARCH IN PROGRESS databases. Research projects begun before February 1982 are found in the SSIE CURRENT RESEARCH (Smithsonian Science Information Exchange) file. JGRIP is an English-language file of current and recently completed research by public research organizations in Japan. The UFORDAT database covers current environmental research in the Federal Republic of Germany. Topical research is found in the CRIS (Current Research Information System).

## Patents

Patents are important in energy and environmental technology. The WPI (World Patents Index), INPADOC and APIPAT (API Patents) databases cover patents worldwide. The major patents databases are discussed in Chapter 3.

## Procurement and contracts

The United States federal government procurement and contracting system vets requests for proposals (RFPs) or bids on energy and environmental projects. These announcements along with lists of awarded contracts appear in the COMMERCE BUSINESS DAILY database produced by the Department of Commerce. Technical reports resulting from government contracts are found in NTIS.

## Statistics

The FEDERAL ENERGY DATABASE INDEX (FEDEX) yields bibliographic references to statistical publications of the DOE Energy Information Administration and in addition indexes tables and graphs contained within these publications. Other air quality, water supply, environmental measurements and energy data are furnished by the ASI (American Statistics Index) database.

## CD-ROM DATABASES

The emergence of CD-ROM products has provided another important means to search databases. The number of databases available on CD-ROM has increased rapidly and continues to grow. The CD-ROM databases listed in Table 7.7 should be viewed as indicative of what is developing rather than as a definitive inventory. In cases where the CD-ROM name is different from its online label, the online name is used in Table 7.7 to provide continuity. Also, though a number of the online databases grouped under the PAPERS label are available in CD-ROM format, they are not listed individually.

**Table 7.7: CD-ROM databases covering energy and the environment**

| NAME | PRODUCER | SOFTWARE |
|------|----------|----------|
| * ABI/INFORM | University Microfilms (UMI)/ Data Courier | UMI |
| ACID RAIN | University of Vermont | KAWARE |
| * AGRICOLA | National Agricultural Library | OCLC, SILVER-PLATTER, ROMWARE |
| * AGRIS INTERNATIONAL | National Agricultural Library | SILVERPLATTER |
| * AEROSPACE DATABASE | American Institute of Aeronautics & Astronautics | DIALOG |
| ALASKAN MARINE CONTAMINANTS DATABASE | US NOAA | RAIMA |
| * AQUATIC SCIENCES & FISHERIES ABSTRACTS | NOAA/Cambridge Scientific Abstracts | CAMBRIDGE |
| * ASI | Congressional Information Service, Inc. | QACCESS |
| * BIOSIS PREVIEWS | BioSciences Information Service | SILVERPLATTER |
| * BUSINESS DATELINE | UMI/Data Courier | UMI |
| * CAB ABSTRACTS | CAB International | SILVERPLATTER |
| * CANCERLIT | National Cancer Institute | CD PLUS, CAMBRIDGE, KNOWLEDGE FINDER, LIPPINCOTT, SILVER-PLATTER |
| * CIS/INDEX | Congressional Information Service, Inc. | QACCESS |
| * COMPENDEX PLUS | Engineering Information, Inc. | DIALOG |
| * CRIS | National Agricultural Library | OCLC, SILVERPLATTER |
| EARTH SCIENCES DATABASE | US Geological Survey | OCLC |
| ECODATA | Cedis Edizioni | CD SYSTEMS |
| * EI PAGE ONE | Engineering Information (EI) | EI |
| * EMBASE | Elsevier Science Publishers | SILVERPLATTER |
| ENFLEX INFO | Environmental Resources Management (ERMCS) | ROMWARE |
| ENVIRONMENT LIBRARY | OCLC, Inc. | OCLC |
| * ENVIRONMENTAL BIBLIOGRAPHY | Environmental Studies Institute | CD ANSWER |
| * ENVIRO/ENERGYLINE ABSTRACTS PLUS | R.R.Bowker | BOWKER |

**Table 7.7:** (cont.)

| NAME | PRODUCER | SOFTWARE |
|---|---|---|
| * EPRI (ElectriGuide) | Electric Power Research Institute | KAWARE |
| * GEOBASE | Geo Abstracts Ltd. | CD PUBCO |
| * GEOREF | American Geological Institute | SILVERPLATTER |
| GLOBAL CHANGE ENCYCLOPEDIA | Space Agency Forum | to be announced |
| * GPO MONTHLY CATALOG | US Government Printing Office | IAC, OCLC, SILVERPLATTER, WILSON |
| HAZARDOUS MATERIAL INFO SYSTEM (DOD) | US Department of Defense | GPO |
| * HSELINE (OSH-ROM) | Health and Safety Executive | SILVERPLATTER |
| * HEALTH & SAFETY SCIENCE ABSTRACTS (POLTOX) | Cambridge Scientific Abstracts | CAMBRIDGE |
| HYDRODATA | EarthInfo Inc. | EARTHINFO |
| * ICONDA | ICONDA Agency/Fraunhofer Society | SILVERPLATTER |
| * INDEX TO US GOVERNMENT PERIODICALS | Infordata International, Inc. | WILSON |
| * INSPEC | Institute of Electrical Engineers | UMI |
| * INTERNATIONAL NUCLEAR INFORMATION SYSTEM | International Atomic Energy Agency (IAEA) | BRS/SEARCH |
| * KIRK-OTHMER | John Wiley and Sons, Inc. | DIALOG |
| * LIFE SCIENCES COLLECTION (POLTOX) | Cambridge Scientific Abstracts | CAMBRIDGE |
| * MAGAZINE INDEX | Information Access Company | IAC |
| * MEDLINE | National Library of Medicine | CAMBRIDGE, CD PLUS, DIALOG, EBSCO, KNOWLEDGE FINDER, SILVERPLATTER |
| NATURAL RESOURCES METABASE | NISC/US Fish and Wildlife Service | CD ANSWER |
| * NATIONAL NEWSPAPER INDEX | Information Access Company | IAC |
| * NTIS | National Technical Information Service | DIALOG, OCLC, SILVERPLATTER |
| * OCCUPATIONAL SAFETY & HEALTH (OSH-ROM) | NIOSHDOC/HSELINE/ CISDOC | SILVERPLATTER |
| * OHM/TADS (CHEM-BANK, TOMES PLUS) | NIOSH/US DOT/US EPA | MICROMEDEX, SILVERPLATTER |
| * PAIS INTERNATIONAL | Public Affairs Information Service, Inc. | PAIS, SILVERPLATTER |
| * PASCAL | CNRS | CNRS/INIST |
| * POLLUTION ABSTRACTS (POLTOX) | Cambridge Scientific Abstracts | CAMBRIDGE |
| * PTS INDEXES | Predicasts, Inc. | SILVERPLATTER |
| RESORS | Remote Sensing On-Line Retrieval System | FINDIT |

**Table 7.7:** (cont.)

| NAME | PRODUCER | SOFTWARE |
|------|----------|----------|
| * SCISEARCH | Institute for Scientific Information | ISI |
| * SOCIAL SCISEARCH | Institute for Scientific Information | ISI |
| * TOXIC CHEMICAL RELEASE INVENTORY(TRI) | US EPA | GPO |
| * TOXLINE | National Library of Medicine | SILVERPLATTER |
| * WATER RESOURCES ABSTRACTS | US Geological Survey | CD ANSWER, OCLC |

* Also available online. *See* Tables 7.4 - 7.6.

CD-ROM databases are of two kinds: those that are based on online products and those that are not. Many CD-ROM databases have been derived from online databases. Currently ten of the primary energy-related environmental online databases and several of the specialized ones have CD-ROM counterparts. Despite some variation in names and generally fewer years of coverage, many of these correspond closely to their respective online databases and can be used accordingly. Others, however, have been repackaged.

ENVIROLINE and ENERGYLINE have been merged into a single CD-ROM database. EI PAGE ONE, from Engineering Information, Inc., lacks the abstracts of COMPENDEX PLUS but is scheduled to cover the table of contents of thirty per cent more journals. Some vendors have reproduced the online version of CANCERLIT, while another has added references from other sources. POLLUTION AND TOXICOLOGY ABSTRACTS ON CD-ROM (POLTOX) contains POLLUTION ABSTRACTS, HEALTH AND SAFETY SCIENCE ABSTRACTS, two sections from the LIFE SCIENCES COLLECTION and the toxicity segment of MEDLINE as well as other components. OSH-ROM comprises the OCCUPATIONAL SAFETY & HEALTH and HSELINE online databases plus the databases of the International Occupational Safety and Health Information Centre of the International Labour Organization and the British Major Hazard Incident Data Service. The OHM/TADS online database is a component of CHEM-BANK, a CD-ROM database which also contains the Registry of Toxic Effects of Chemical Substances (RTECS) and the Chemical Hazard Response Information System (CHRIS).

The CD-ROM databases beginning to appear in the secondary category generally have not had as much exposure as those derived from online databases. For the most part, they tend to be smaller, more specialized and text-based. The ACID RAIN database is a selection of more than one hundred Canadian federal and provincial documents, distributed by the University of Vermont. Data collected from thirty-five studies of the marine waters of Alaska make up the ALASKAN MARINE CONTAMINANTS DATABASE. This database was used to support damage assessments as a result of the Exxon Valdez oil spill. ECODATA contains more than 6,500 complete texts of Italian legislation and jurisprudence and EEC directives, as well as bibliographic selections on ecology. The full text of specific federal and state environmental regulations (Titles 29, 40 and 49), for fifteen states and six counties are provided by ENFLEX INFO. The GLOBAL CHANGE ENCYCLO-PEDIA, due to appear during the International Space Year of 1992, will be the first atlas of the world to show animated land and sea changes over an extended period of time. The United States Department of Defense's HAZARDOUS MATERIAL INFORMATION SYSTEM is intended to assist government installations to comply with regulations for the handling, storage and disposal of toxic substances. Streamer and water resource data from the USGS's WATSTORE database are available through HYDRODATA.

There are also CD-ROM databases which, though remaining specialized, are bibliographic in orientation. The EARTH SCIENCES DATABASE covers USGS library materials on earth sciences and natural resources. Environmental issues and policies from the OCLC Online Union Catalog are in the ENVIRONMENT LIBRARY. The NATURAL RESOURCES METABASE contains citations on wildlife and land management, wetlands and aquatic plants, and remote sensing literature is handled by the RESORS database

These are the databases which must be considered when energy-related environmental questions are being searched. The four groupings described are an attempt to provide a framework for them. Database selection methodologies are covered next, as part of search strategy development.


## THE SEARCH STRATEGY

The key to developing a successful search strategy on any topic is to determine the actual information need as accurately as possible in terms of the concepts expressed by the information request. A specific description of the question is required, including qualifying or limiting statements which help to define the context. Synonyms, closely related phrases and alternative spellings should be obtained for both scientific and technical terms and common vocabulary. The purpose or intended use of the search results, along with the amount of information needed, help the searcher to determine the required scope. Pertinent journals, known papers or authors help portray the subject. Language or geographic constraints, the time period to be covered and the type of information needed are also useful parameters. This information is typically collected through a pre-search interview, a search request form or a combination of both. Once the question has been set forth in as much detail as possible, it is necessary to select the appropriate database(s) and search terms.


### Database selection

As has been pointed out earlier, database selection in the energy-related environmental area can be difficult because of the enormous number of databases which may be applicable. Several factors influence the selection of databases: (1) the type of information desired, which can be bibliographic or non-bibliographic and can range from books, patents or current research to popular articles or statistics; (2) suitable subject coverage and degree of comprehensiveness required; (3) the timeliness or time lapsed between publication and appearance in a computerized database; (4) the number of years covered; (5) availability of appropriate indexes to search adequately the requested topic; (6) accessibility of the complete document; and (7) costs of the respective databases. Not all of these parameters are equally important for every search request. Most searches emphasize three or four of them. Tradeoffs may also be necessary depending upon the individual request.

To select the best database(s) for a specific energy-environment topic, it is essential to apply the database selection criteria to the database groups discussed in the preceding sections and listed in Tables 7.1, 7.5, 7.6 and 7.7. One method of doing this is described below and is illustrated in Figure 7.5.

First, determine from the interview or search request what type of literature is required. If a specialized document or literature type is needed, make the appropriate selection from the databases listed in Table 7.6. Sometimes a single database from this list will suffice.

Next, if specialized literature is ruled out, or if additional databases from the specialized subject database category are required, examine the databases in Table 7.5. Here again, one or two of these files may be sufficient for the request. If the request does not relate to the databases in either of these categories, or if additional databases are needed to complete the search, select the appropriate primary databases from Table 7.1.

**Figure 7.5: A database selection methodology**

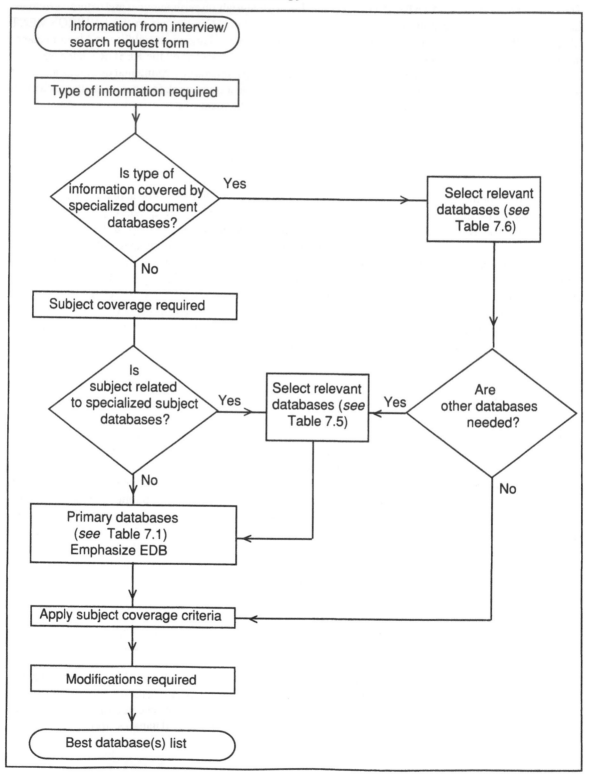

The final list of selected databases should be examined for best subject coverage of the request topic according to the following criteria: (1) searching experience and familiarity with the databases, (2) printed aids from database producers and online service vendors, (3) journal or document coverage of selected databases, and (4) crossfile search index files of online vendors.

Journal coverage of individual databases has long been available in printed form, either directly from individual database producers or through directories such as *Ulrich's International Periodicals Directory*. A new online database, DIALOG JOURNAL NAME FINDER, enhances the ability to select databases because of their journal coverage by showing which database(s) have the broadest coverage of specific journals.

The crossfile search index files are extremely useful tools for ranking subject coverage of databases, and for setting up crossfile searches. For multidisciplinary fields, where most energy and environmental questions fall, they are particularly valuable tools. They allow the searcher to scan a selected number of databases most likely to be useful. Databases other than those routinely searched are also suggested. Enhancements in the DIALOG crossfile, DIALINDEX, make running the technique more straightforward for this topic because one of its pre-established database groups includes an energy/environment section. Another section comprises all databases containing the full-text of journal articles, encyclopedias, newspapers and newswires. Also remember that EST deserves serious consideration for almost any energy-related environmental topic. When in doubt, EST is a good place to begin.

This refined list of databases, now ranked by type of information and subject coverage, should be modified further through use of the other selection factors. These will vary in importance for each request. Among them are the degree of comprehensiveness or amount of information required, timeliness, retrospective coverage, appropriate indexes, content of printout, availability of complete documents and database costs. This last step allows the searcher to fine tune the database list. For example, a request for citations on particulate emissions from coal-fired power plants would yield a sizeable list of potentially acceptable databases after the type of literature and subject coverage criteria are used. However, adding the criterion of only a few good, current citations, would help the searcher to single out a database such as SCISEARCH from this list, because of its coverage of journal literature, its quick processing time during preparation of the database updates and its use of title word searching which gives higher precision results. On the other hand, if thorough coverage of the subject is desired but the search budget is limited, the EST database would be a good choice because of its extensive coverage of journal and report literature and its relatively inexpensive print charges.

## Concept development

Search concept development, including the establishment of the logical relationships between concepts, is the last major step in search strategy formulation before going online. Returning to the information furnished in the interview or by the search request form, list each distinct concept and its relationship to the others. Next add all singular and plural keywords, synonyms, abbreviations, acronyms, jargon or other subject elements which describe the topic. Watch out for terms with different American and British spellings such as aluminum/aluminium, sulfur/sulphur and color/colour. Compound words such as power plant, wastewater and online are sometimes found with varying segmentation; that is, as powerplant, waste water and on-line.

Suggestions for relevant terms can be provided by the thesauri which cover the database(s) to be searched. In addition, there is an *Integrated Energy Vocabulary* which compiles energy terms from ten different database vocabularies [3]. A sample page from this compilation and the list of its vocabulary sources are displayed in Tables 7.8 and 7.9.

## Table 7.8: Sample entries from the *Integrated Energy Vocabulary*

| Source Code* | Term | Source Code* | Term |
|---|---|---|---|
| P | AIR PERMEABILITY<br>  USE   PERMEABILITY | D | AIR POLLUTION ABATEMENT<br>  USE   ABATEMENT<br>  and   AIR POLLUTION |
| T | AIR PERMEABILITY<br>  USE   PERMEABILITY | D | AIR POLLUTION CONTROL<br>  USE   AIR POLLUTION<br>  and   CONTROL |
| B | AIR POLLUTANT<br>  (LINK TO SPECIFIC POLLUTANTS)<br>  BT    WASTE MATERIAL<br>  NT    OXIDANT | G | AIR POLLUTION CONTROL ASSOCIATION<br>  USE   POLLUTION ASSOCIATIONS AND GOVERNMENT AGENCIES |
| D | AIR POLLUTANTS<br>  USE   AIR POLLUTION | | |
| B | AIR POLLUTION<br>  UF +   AIR POLLUTION CONTROL EQUIPMENT<br>          AIR POLLUTION SOURCE<br>  UF    ATMOSPHERIC POLLUTION | B | AIR POLLUTION CONTROL EQUIPMENT<br>  USE   AIR POLLUTION<br>  and    POLLUTION CONTROL EQUIPMENT |
| C | AIR POLLUTION<br>  UF    SMOG | T | AIR POLLUTION CONTROL EQUIPMENT |
| D | AIR POLLUTION<br>  UF    AIR CONTAMINANTS<br>          AIR POLLUTANTS<br>  UF +   AIR POLLUTION ABATEMENT<br>          AIR POLLUTION CONTROL<br>  UF    AIR POLLUTION EFFECTS<br>          AIR POLLUTION PROBLEMS<br>  UF +   AIR WATER POLLUTION<br>          ATMOSPHERIC POLLUTANT<br>  UF    ATMOSPHERIC POLLUTION<br>  UF +   CONTAMINATED AIR<br>          PARTICULATE AIR POLLUTANTS<br>          TOXIC AIR POLLUTANTS<br>  BT    CONTAMINATION<br>          POLLUTION<br>  NT    SMOG | D | AIR POLLUTION EFFECTS<br>  USE   AIR POLLUTION |
| | | D | AIR POLLUTION PROBLEMS<br>  USE   AIR POLLUTION |
| | | B | AIR POLLUTION SOURCE<br>  USE   AIR POLLUTION<br>  and   POLLUTION SOURCE |
| | | E | AIR POLLUTION-ANALYSIS |
| | | E | AIR POLLUTION-CONTROL |
| | | E | AIR POLLUTION-LEGISLATION |
| | | E | AIR POLLUTION-STANDARDS |
| | | E | AIR PREHEATERS |
| | | T | AIR PREHEATERS<br>  USE   AIR HEATERS |
| E | AIR POLLUTION<br>  UF    ATMOSPHERIC COMPOSITION-POLLUTION<br>          EARTH ATMOSPHERE-POLLUTION<br>          ENVIRONMENTAL ENGINEERING-AIR POLLUTION | D | AIR PURIFICATION<br>  USE   AIR<br>  and   PURIFICATION |
| G | AIR POLLUTION | I | AIR PURIFICATION<br>  USE   AIR CLEANING |
| I | AIR POLLUTION<br>  UF +   THERMAL POLLUTION (AIR)<br>  BT    POLLUTION | N | AIR PURIFICATION<br>  BT    PURIFICATION |
| N | AIR POLLUTION<br>  UF    ATMOSPHERIC IMPURITIES<br>  BT    ENVIRONMENTAL POLLUTION<br>          POLLUTION | T | AIR PURIFICATION<br>  USE   AIR CONDITIONING |
| P | AIR POLLUTION<br>  UF    ATMOSPHERIC POLLUTION<br>  BT    CONTAMINATION | D | AIR QUALITY<br>  UF +   AIR QUALITY MONITORING NETWORK |
| | | B | AIR QUALITY MEASUREMENTS |
| T | AIR POLLUTION<br>  UF    ATMOSPHERIC POLLUTION<br>  BT    POLLUTION | D | AIR QUALITY MONITORING NETWORK<br>  USE   AIR QUALITY<br>  and   MONITORING |
| | | N | AIR SAMPLING<br>  BT    SAMPLING |

* See Table 7.9

Source: *Integrated Energy Vocabulary,* PB-259000 (Washington, DC: National Technical Information Service, 1976).

**Table 7.9: Source thesauri comprising the *Integrated Energy Vocabulary* (*see* Table 7.8)**

| Source Code | Source Vocabulary or Thesaurus | Database(s) |
|---|---|---|
| B | American Petroleum Institute Thesaurus, 11th ed. (January 1974). | APILIT, APIPAT |
| C | Current concept file used by Chemical Abstracts. | CA SEARCH |
| D | Defense Documentation Center Thesaurus, AD-773 330 (January 1974). | DOD/RECON (now DROLS) |
| E | Subject Headings for Engineering (1972) used by Engineering Index. | COMPENDEX |
| G | Termatrex Thesaurus used by Institute of Gas Technology, publishers of Gas Abstracts (April 1971). | |
| I | INIS: Thesaurus, IAEA-INIS-13(Rev. 4), used by the International Nuclear Information System (includes USAEC vocabulary). | INIS |
| N | NASA Thesaurus (1976). Update (1971) and supplements. | NASA/RECON |
| P | Exploration and Production Thesaurus, 4th ed., used by University of Tulsa, publishers of Petroleum Abstracts (January 1970). | TULSA |
| R | GeoRef Index used by the American Geological Institute. | GEOREF |
| T | Thesaurus of Engineering and Scientific Terms, used by the National Technical Information Service (1967). | NTIS |

Source: *Integrated Energy Vocabulary,* PB-259000 (Washington, DC: National Technical Information Service, 1976).

Category codes for individual databases are another subject-related field which should be considered as part of concept development. While they usually cover broad areas, some contain hierarchical levels and can be truncated. Table 7.3 gives an example of EST subject categories and codes. All EST documents assigned to category 500000 ENVIRONMENTAL SCIENCES, ATMOSPHERIC shown in the example, would be retrieved by truncating to the first two digits, 50. This would include 500100 BASIC STUDIES, 500200 CHEMICAL MONITORING AND TRANSPORT, etc. Only general atmospheric environment studies would be retrieved with the code 500000.

Occasionally, corporate or organizational sources are also useful for subject access. Terms such as 'pollution' or 'environment' can appear as part of the organization title, providing in essence additional indexing. This is especially valuable for databases such as SCISEARCH, where the only other available subject field is the title. Other non-subject parameters or qualifiers such as date of publication, language restrictions or document type can also be included on the work sheet A sample work sheet illustrating concept development for the topic, 'air pollution aspects of siting electric power production facilities', is given in Table 7.10.

**Table 7.10: Sample concept development**

**Topic:** Air pollution aspects of siting electric power production facilities.

| Concept 1 | | Concept 2 | | Concept 3 |
|---|---|---|---|---|
| Siting | | Power plant(s) | | Air pollution |
| OR | | OR | | OR |
| Site selection | | Powerplant(s) | | Air pollutant(s) |
| OR | | OR | | OR |
| Site survey(s) | | Electric utility(ies) | | Air quality |
| OR | **AND** | OR | **AND** | OR |
| Site planning | | Electric plant(s) | | Emission(s) |
| OR | | OR | | OR |
| Site plan(s) | | Electric power | | Particulate(s) |
| OR | | OR | | OR |
| Site preparation | | Energy facility(ies) | | Nitrogen oxide(s) |
| | | | | OR |
| | | | | Nitrogen dioxide |
| | | | | OR |
| | | | | Sulfur oxide(s) |
| | | | | OR |
| | | | | Sulfur dioxide |
| | | | | OR |
| | | | | Sulphur oxide(s) |
| | | | | OR |
| | | | | Sulphur dioxide |
| | | | | OR |

( 500500 (EST subject code for SITE RESOURCE AND **AND** Concept 2 terms USE STUDIES *see* Table 7.3) (Concept 3 is not needed here as it is part of the subject code definition.) )

50 (EST subject code for ENVIRONMENTAL SCIENCES, ATMOSPHERIC *see* Table 7.3)

In the example listed in Table 7.10, the relationships between the concepts or subject elements are indicated by the general AND and OR Boolean logic. This approach will have a high recall; that is, it will retrieve a high percentage of the relevant citations to be had from the database. However, the precision of the search - the percentage of retrieved citations actually relevant to the topic - will be comparatively low.

**Multiple database searching**

Searching one database is often not adequate to satisfy energy-environmental requests. In these cases, a multiple database search strategy ought to be planned. The search strategy must be expanded to account for database variations. For example, databases use different thesauri resulting in diverse controlled vocabulary terms, some databases have a policy of segmenting words while others do not, numeric characters are sometimes converted to alphabet characters or vice versa, and searchable fields vary. Online vendor-supplied manuals and database producer search aids provide the searcher with much useful information on these differences.

Multiple database strategy planning follows the same work sheet approach outlined above, but relies more heavily on free-text searching, truncation and a less restrictive logic. Usually, the most efficient and effective technique is to use all possible forms and variations of keywords, including both controlled and uncontrolled vocabulary, together with a high recall logic. If the strategy produces an overly broad result in some databases, it is a relatively straightforward process to refine this outcome. The reverse is usually not true. Limiting by special fields such as language or document type, or by keyword fields such as titles and descriptors, should be left until last to avoid getting zero hits for databases without these fields. When searching multiple databases on the same computer system, the search-save, OneSearch and duplicate detection capabilities should be used to save time, energy and money. Use judgement in OneSearch, however; there will be times when a single database will provide what is needed, and there will be no need to search and pay for others.

**Full-text database searching**

The online availability of the complete text of documents such as directories, encyclopedias, journal and newspaper articles and textbooks has added a new dimension to searching. Because essentially every word in the text is both searchable and printable, requestors have immediate access to all the information. They no longer have to take a second step to locate the documents found in a computer search. Beside providing the complete text of documents, full-text databases can be searched for specific information such as names of products or people which are mentioned in the text of an article but do not appear in the title, abstract or indexing. Also, footnotes and bibliographies of important articles can be a good online source of additional secondary references.

Searching full-text databases differs from searching bibliographic files primarily because of the much larger size of the full-text record. Their basic indexes not only contain words from the title, descriptors, identifiers, abstract and section headings, but also words from the text field. The basic indexes of full-text databases may contain thousands of words per record. Consequently when searching for a broad concept the text field should be avoided. Broad concepts should be limited to title, descriptor, identifier and section heading fields. Conversely, text fields should be included when searching for a very specific concept. In order to increase the precision of full-text database searches, the most effective strategies make frequent use of narrower operators such as ADJACENT and WITH. An AND logic is seldom useful when dealing with large numbers of searchable terms. This is illustrated in Searches 7.1 and 7.2 run in the BRS search system.

**Search 7.1: AND logic in the full-text TRADE AND INDUSTRY INDEX database**

```
        1 :   (powerplant$1 or power adj plant$1) and siting

        RESULT            40 DOCUMENTS

            1
  TI  The public administrator: God?  Or entrepreneur?  Or are they the
      same in the public service?.

            2
  TI  CEC concerned about declining level of generation from geysers.
      (California  Energy  Commission).
```

**Search 7.1:** (cont.)

```
                3
TI  Utilities, coal group spell out what they want in transportation
    plan. (National Energy Strategy planning).

                4
TI  International developments in fuel cells.

                5
TI  Retiring a reactor. (decommissioning).

                3
TI  Utilities, coal group spell out what they want in transportation
    plan. (National Energy Strategy planning).
CP  COPYRIGHT Pasha Publications Inc. 1989.
TX  (6 OF 17) EEI also told DOT that utilities need flexibility to
    benefit from competing fuel types and among various methods of
    transporting these fuels; the marketplace should be allowed to
    determine rates where rail transportation rates are truly determined
    by competition; and ash from coal-fired power plants should be
    promoted for use in road construction projects.
TX  (7 OF 17) The right of federal eminent domain for construction of
    coal slurry pipelines is recommended by NCA and EEI, as are continued
    improvements to waterway and ocean ports. The use of eminent domain
    should be also used for the siting and construction of natural gas
    and oil pipelines, EEI said, and added that owners of existing oil,
    natural gas and product pipelines should be able to convert those
    systems to different products if market demands dictate they do.
```

## Search 7.2: WITH logic in the full-text TRADE AND INDUSTRY INDEX database

```
 2 :    (powerplant$1 or power adj plant$1) with siting

      RESULT            10 DOCUMENTS
 3 : ..p 2 ti/doc=6-8

                6
TI  Ferdinand's follies. (Ferdinand Marcos).

                7
TI  New England faces power shortages as it hesitates over coal power.

                8
TI  New England, facing power shortages, still hesitates over fossil energy.

                7
TI  New England faces power shortages as it hesitates over coal power.
CP  COPYRIGHT Pasha Publications Inc. 1990.
TX  (11 OF 38) However, there is hope for that project because siting
    decisions for power plants are made at the state level by the
    Facility Siting Council. "If the decision were subjected to a local
    referendum, you wouldn't build power plants anywhere," David
    Gilmartin of Eastern Energy said.
```

A search of the full-text TRADE AND INDUSTRY INDEX database for power plant siting information using an AND logic yielded forty documents. The first five titles are displayed along with the paragraphs which caused the retrieval of the third title. These titles are not very closely related to the search question. The reason for this can be seen by examining the paragraphs which caused the retrieval. The power plant term is in paragraph number 6 while the siting term is in paragraph number 7. There is no relationship between the two terms. Using a WITH logic to search the same database retrieved ten documents. In this case, both search terms are in the same sentence, causing the results to be much more specific.

## CD-ROM database searching

The recent trend to distribute databases in CD-ROM format has made searching more attractive to a wider audience. Despite some technical shortcomings, the improved interfaces and predictable charges of CD-ROM products have increased end user searching. A variety of menu- and command-driven systems with graphic displays are available to guide users. Fixed pricing removes the pressure to be fast and efficient, allowing more browsing and trial and error searching. Users accessing CD-ROM databases through libraries or other organizations may not have to deal directly with costs at all.

Searchers looking for energy-related environment information can choose from the CD-ROM databases listed in Table 7.7. Since publishing in the CD-ROM area is flourishing, many more databases should be available soon. However, because the accessibility of these products is site-specific, in practice many searchers may have a more limited choice.

Along with the benefits of accessing a wide range of CD-ROM-based subject matter, searchers must contend with a multitude of different search systems. Several of these are unique to a particular database. Others, such as the Cambridge, DIALOG, OCLC, and SilverPlatter systems, are used with a number of database products. Online searchers are likely to be most comfortable with CD-ROM search systems which closely replicate their familiar online counterpart. However, the scope of energy-related environment issues and the breadth of databases which cover them frequently will necessitate use of multiple systems with their attendant idiosyncrasies. Adoption of the CD-ROM Data Exchange Protocol proposed to the National Information Standards Organization (NISO) would be a major aid to searchers in this area.

One advantage of individual CD-ROM search systems is that they can be tailored to take advantage of specific database features. The CD-ROM version of SCISEARCH for example, provides a related record capability not available online. This feature is illustrated in Search 7.3. After finding a relevant reference, 'Site Selection of a Dual Purpose Nuclear-Power Plant in Saudi-Arabia', additional references sharing at least one bibliographic citation with the selected item can be displayed using the RELATED option. In this case twenty records are related.

The first related record has four references in common, Ahmed-S-1979..., Keeney-RL-1974..., Lugasi-Y-1985..., and Mehrez-A-1983..., as shown in Figure 7.6. The unique characteristics of CD-ROM databases and their search systems should be incorporated, where appropriate, as part of the searcher's overall approach.

All of these factors should be taken into account when developing the search strategy. Once the overall strategy is formulated, the search is ready to be undertaken.

**Search 7.3: RELATED search feature of the SCISEARCH CD-ROM database**

```
                        SCI (Jan 87 - Dec 87)
      Show results in title-only format.
           F1-Help    F2-Database    F3-Search    F4-Results    F5-Quit

                        Records:  2 of 4   (Set 3)

      Engineering Geophysical Studies of the Loviisa Nuclear-Power
      Plant Site, Finland

      Site Selection of a Dual Purpose Nuclear-Power Plant in
      Saudi-Arabia

      A Comparison of Retran-O2 and Trac-Pf1 simulations of a Loss of
      Off-Site Power Cooldown to Residual Heat Removal Entry
      Conditions at Calvert-Cliffs-Nuclear-Power-Plant

      Climatological Study of the Adrano Site of the Eurelios Solar
      Mirror Power-Plant


      Related    ReFerences Addresses Collect Print      Save
```

```
                        SCI (Jan 87 - Dec 87)
      Show results in title-only format.
           F1-Help    F2-Database    F3-Search    F4-Results    F5-Quit

      Record: 2 of 4
      Hussein-FM Site Selection of a Dual Purpose Nuclear-Power...

                        Related Records:  1 of 20       (Level 1)

      Discrete Multiattribute Utility Approach to Project Selection

      An Extension of the Analytic Hierarchy Process for Industrial
      R-and-D Project Selection and Resource-Allocation

      Approaches to Consistency Adjustment

      Use of Low-Grade in Driving Small Freezing Units for
      Desalination


      Related   ReFerences Addresses Collect  Print  Save    Makeset
```

**Figure 7.6:    Comparison of RELATED reference bibliographies in the SCISEARCH CD-ROM database**

```
      Retrieved Record:  Hussein-FM  Elmalahy-KS  Obeid-MA.  "Site
         Selection of a Dual Purpose Nuclear-Power Plant in
         Saudi-Arabia," NUCLEAR TECHNOLOGY, Vol 79 Iss 3 pp 311-321
         1987
```

**Figure 7.6:** (cont..)

```
        ABDULFATTAH-AF-1982-ATOMKERNENERGIE-KERN-V40-P282
        ABDULFATTAH-ARF-1982-NUCL-TECHNOL-V58-P404
       *AHMED-S-1979-NUCL-ENG-DESIGN-V51-P361
        BAAS-SM-1977-AUTOMATICA-V13-P47
        ELLIS-HM-1972-ANAL-PUBLIC-SYSTEMS-P376
        ELMALAHY-K-0000-IN-PRESS-COMPUTER-CO
        GRAINES-BR-1976-INT-J-MAN-MACHINE-ST-V8-P623
        HANNAN-EL-1983-DECISION-SCI-V14-P240
       *KEENEY-RL-1974-OPER-RES-V22-P22
        KEENEY-RL-1975-SLOAN-MANAGE-REV-V17-P63
        KEENEY-RL-1977-WILEY-IIASA-INT-SERI
        KEENEY-RL-1979-BELL-J-EC-MANAGE-SCI-V14-P49
        KEENEY-RL-1979-OPER-RES-V27-P49
        KENRANGUI-R-1979-T-AM-NUCL-SOC-V33-P617
        KIRKWOOD-CW-1982-J-OPL-RES-SOC-V33-P353
       *LUGASI-Y-1985-NUCL-TECHNOL-V69-P7
       *MEHREZ-A-1983-J-OPER-RES-SOC-V34-P621
        OBEID-MA-1975-ISLAMIC-SOLIDARITY-C
        SAATY-TL-1977-J-MATH-PSYCHOL-V15-P234
        SAATY-TL-1978-INTERFACES-2-V8-P37
        SAATY-TL-1980-ANAL-HIERARCHY-PROCE
        SAATY-TL-1982-LOGIC-PRIORITIES-APP
        WATSON-SR-1979-IEEE-T-SYSTEMS-MAN-C-V9-P1
        WIND-Y-1980-MANAGE-SCI-V26-P641
        ZADEH-LA-1972-J-CYBERN-V2-P4
        ZADEH-LA-1976-INT-J-MAN-MACHINE-ST-V8-P249

First RELATED Record: Sinuanystern-Z  Mehrez-A.  "Discrete
    Multiattribute Utility Approach to Project Selection,"
    JOURNAL OF THE OPERATIONAL RESEARCH SOCIETY, Vol 38 Iss 12
    pp 1133-1139 1987

References:
   *AHMED-S-1979-NUCL-ENG-DESIGN-V51-P361
    HOBBS-BF-1979-ANAL-MULTIOBJECTIVE
   *KEENEY-RL-1974-OPER-RES-V22-P22
    KEENEY-RL-1982-OPER-RES-V30-P803
   *LUGASI-Y-1985-NUCL-TECHNOL-V69-P7
    MEHREZ-A-1982-R-D-MANAGE-V12-P169
   *MEHREZ-A-1983-J-OPER-RES-SOC-V34-P621
    MEHREZ-A-1983-MANAGE-SCI-V29-P430
    MEHREZ-A-1983-WATER-RESOUR-RES-V19-P875
    RONEN-B-1981-OPER-RES-V29-P229
```

## SAMPLE SEARCH

The search to be illustrated is based on the question discussed in the search strategy section: a request for current technical information on the air pollution aspects of siting electric power production facilities. Formulation of the search strategy followed the approach outlined in the last section. After reviewing the question, the appropriate databases were chosen using the selection methodology depicted in Figure 7.5. Initially thirteen databases were picked for consideration: the eleven primary databases plus FEDERAL RESEARCH IN PROGRESS from the specialized document-type group and the EPIA and NSIC databases from the specialized subject group. The APTIC database was excluded because of the age of its information.

Cross database index searching was used with an abbreviated, indicative search strategy to check the subject coverage of these files. Since the databases are not all on the same search service, three different crossfile searches were used. NSIC was checked separately. Comparison of the results indicates that four databases seem best suited to the topic: EST, ENVIROLINE, EPIA and NTIS. The cross database search is shown in Searches 7.4 to 7.6. Note that the use of logical operators in the ORBIT system will not produce a ranked database list. However, a ranking of the single term 'siting' yielded enough information to confirm that the EPIA file was a good choice for this topic. No other factors were felt to be important enough to further modify the database list. Each of them was searched.

The search terms and term relationships used were those developed in Table 7.10, with the addition of a publication date parameter where applicable. A multiple database approach was employed, relying on a free-text strategy with numerous terms and synonyms, truncation and a high recall logic. The siting concept was represented by the term 'siting' together with 'site' truncated to one character and in close proximity to either 'select(ing,ion,ed)', 'survey(s,ing)' or 'plan(s,ning)'. The 'power plant' concept was searched with 'power plant(s)' as a single word and as a two-word phrase and the term 'electric' adjacent to 'power', 'plant(s)' or 'utility(ies)'. The 'air pollution' idea was represented by the broad 'air pollution', 'air pollutant(s)', 'air quality', 'emission(s)' or 'particulate(s)' terms along with the specific pollutants 'nitrogen oxide(s)', 'nitrogen dioxide', 'sulfur oxide(s)' or 'sulfur dioxide'. Both spellings of sulphur were used. In order to make sure that the siting concept was emphasized, siting terms were required to be in the title or keyword fields. Subject categories were added to the EST search strategy. The basic strategy was amended by using a specific subset of subject category 50, 500500 SITE RESOURCE AND USE STUDIES, in conjunction with the title or keyword requirement. Note that POWER PLANTS - SITE SELECTION appears as a paired descriptor in the sample EST record retrieved by the search. This phrase would be good to use if more precise results were required. In the EPIA database, the electric utility/power plant concept is implied and did not have to be included as a search term. The actual search strategy and a sampling of results are illustrated in Searches 7.4 to 7.6.

This multiple database strategy gave us several important citations on the topic of air pollution aspects of electric power plant siting. A similar strategy would help you find solutions to many requests on energy-related environmental issues.

## Search 7.4: Siting search in BRS: CROS and NTIS

```
CROS
1     LIFE SCIENCES        (LFSC)  2    MEDICINE/PHARMACOLOGY  (MDPH)
3     PHYSICAL/APPLIED SCI. (PHAS) 4    BUSINESS               (BUSN)
5     SOCIAL SCI/HUMANITIES (SOSC) 6    EDUCATION              (EDCA)
7     REFERENCE            (REFC)  8    ALL DATABASES          (FALL)
9     USER OPTION

ENTER CROS CATEGORY NUMBER DESIRED. _:  9

ENTER DATABASE NAMES SEPARATED BY COMMAS _:  insp,ntis

BRS SEARCH MODE - ENTER QUERY
1 _: siting and power adj plant$1 and (air adj pollut$5 or air
adj quality)

INSP                  7
  SEARCHING SEARCHING
NTIS                196

1 _:  ..c/ntis
```

**Search 7.4:** (cont.)

```
NTIS 1970 - AUG 1990
BRS SEARCH MODE - ENTER QUERY
1 _: siting.ti,de,id. or site$1.ti,de,id. with (select$5 or
survey$3 or plan or plans or planning)

RESULT        9941 DOCUMENTS
2 _: powerplant$ or power adj plant$1 or electric adj (power or
plant$1 or utilit$3)

RESULT        46043 DOCUMENTS
3 _: air adj (pollut$5 or quality) or emission$1 or
particulate$1 or nitrogen adj oxide$1

RESULT        69872 DOCUMENTS
4 _: nitrogen adj dioxide or sulfur adj oxide$1 or sulfur adj
dioxide or sulphur adj oxide$1 or sulphur adj dioxide$1

RESULT        8424 DOCUMENTS
5 _: 1 and 2 and (3 or 4)

RESULT        204 DOCUMENTS
6 _: ..l/5 yr gt 1986

RESULT        11 DOCUMENTS
BRS SEARCH MODE - ENTER QUERY
8 _:  ..p 6 ti/doc=1-5


          1
TI    DEVELOPMENT OF DREDGED ASH DISPOSAL AREA, PARADISE FOSSIL PLANT.
      FINAL ENVIRONMENTAL ASSESSMENT.


          2
TI    ENVIRONMENTAL REVIEW OF SOUTHERN MARYLAND ELECTRIC COOPERATIVE'S
      PROPOSED COMBUSTION TURBINE GENERATING FACILITY AT CHALK POINT.


          3
TI    AERIAL RADIOLOGICAL SURVEY OF THE BRAIDWOOD GENERATING STATION AND
      SURROUNDING AREA, BRAIDWOOD, ILLINOIS, AUGUST 1988.


          4
TI    CONCEPTUAL DESIGN OF A COAL-FIRED MHD (MAGNETOHYDRODYNAMIC) RETROFIT
      PLANT (SCHOLZ PLANT - SNEADS, FL): VOLUME 1. FINAL REPORT.


          5
TI    SOLID WASTE ISSUES ASSOCIATED WITH SULFUR DIOXIDE EMISSIONS CONTROL.

END OF REQUEST
ENTER DOCUMENT SELECTION. _: ..p 7 all/doc=1


          1
AN    DE90006572-XAB. 9012.
IN    TENNESSEE VALLEY AUTHORITY, KNOXVILLE.
      021113000 6172000.
TI    DEVELOPMENT OF DREDGED ASH DISPOSAL AREA, PARADISE FOSSIL PLANT.
      FINAL ENVIRONMENTAL ASSESSMENT.
NT    PROGRESS REPT. 38 PAGES.
YR    FEB 1989.
JN    N9023.
RN    TVA-RDG-EQS-89-1.
PR    NTIS PRICES: PC A03/MF A01.
AV    PORTIONS OF THIS DOCUMENT ARE ILLEGIBLE IN MICROFICHE PRODUCTS.
```

**Search 7.4:** (cont.)

```
CC    97I. 97R. 68.
MJ    FLY-ASH. PARADISE-STEAM-PLANT.
MN    AEROSOL-WASTES. CONSTRUCTION. COST-ESTIMATION. DREDGING.
      EVALUATION. FLOW-RATE. FOSSIL-FUEL-POWER-PLANTS. KENTUCKY. MAPS.
      PROGRESS-REPORT. SETTLING-PONDS. SITE-SELECTION. WASTE-DISPOSAL.
ID    EDB/200200.  EDB/200500.  *ENVIRONMENTAL IMPACT ASSESSMENTS.  *DREDGE
      SPOIL. *PONDS LAGOONS. WATER POLLUTION. AIR POLLUTION. NTISDEP.
AB    PARADISE STEAM-ELECTRIC PLANT COAL-FIRED FACILITY IN MUHLENBERG
      COUNTY, KENTUCKY. THIS PROJECT IS TO CONSTRUCT A DREDGE POND NEAR
      THE JACOBS CREEK ASH POND CAPABLE OF STORING FLY ASH DREDGED FROM THE
      ASH POND. THIS WILL PROVIDE APPROXIMATELY 10 YEARS OF ADDITIONAL FLY
      ASH STORAGE IN THE FLY ASH POND. EFFLUENT FROM THE DREDGE POND WILL
      BE RETURNED TO THE JACOBS CREEK ASH POND FOR DISCHARGE TO JACOBS
      CREEK. 4 FIGS., 5 TABS.
END OF   REQUEST
```

## Search 7.5: Siting search in DIALOG: DIALINDEX, EST and ENVIROLINE

```
File 411:DIALINDEX(tm)
?sf 8,34,40,41,68,69,103,144,266,312


       ----   -------------
   8: COMPENDEX PLUS _ 70-90/AUG
  34: SCISEARCH _ 1990 WK 1-31
  40: ENVIROLINE - 70-90/JUL
  41: POLLUTION ABSTRACTS _ 70-90/APR
  68: ENVIRONMENTAL BIBLIOGRAPHY - 74-90/FEB
  69: ENERGYLINE - 70-90/JUL
 103: DOE ENERGY _ 83-90/AUG(ISS14)
 144: PASCAL _1983 - 1990 APR
 266: FEDERAL RESEARCH IN PROGRESS - JUL 1990
 312: CA SEARCH _1987-1990 (UD=11306)

?s siting and power(w)plant? ? and (air(w)pollut? or air(w)quality)
File Items    Description
---- -----    -----------
8: COMPENDEX PLUS _ 70-90/AUG
       1855    SITING
     212835    POWER
     151814    PLANT? ?
      47140    POWER(W)PLANT? ?
     119017    AIR
      58568    POLLUT?
      27585    AIR(W)POLLUT?
     119017    AIR
      97532    QUALITY
       3278    AIR(W)QUALITY
         33    SITING AND POWER(W)PLANT? ? AND (AIR(W)POLLUT? OR
                 AIR(W)QUALITY)
34: SCISEARCH _ 1990 WK 1-31
         17    SITING
       2522    POWER
       5551    PLANT? ?
        136    POWER(W)PLANT? ?
       2032    AIR
        910    POLLUT?
```

**Search 7.5:** (cont.)

```
           112    AIR(W)POLLUT?
          2032    AIR
          2545    QUALITY
            53    AIR(W)QUALITY
             0    SITING AND POWER(W)PLANT? ? AND (AIR(W)POLLUT? OR
                  AIR(W)QUALITY)
40: ENVIROLINE - 70-90/JUL
          1620    SITING
         11294    POWER
         21147    PLANT? ?
          6952    POWER(W)PLANT? ?
         22993    AIR
         31807    POLLUT?
          9900    AIR(W)POLLUT?
         22993    AIR
         17031    QUALITY
          4637    AIR(W)QUALITY
            91    SITING AND POWER(W)PLANT? ? AND (AIR(W)POLLUT? OR
                  AIR(W)QUALITY)
41: POLLUTION ABSTRACTS _ 70-90/APR
           762    SITING
          7383    POWER
         21271    PLANT? ?
          4627    POWER(W)PLANT? ?
         24505    AIR
         44438    POLLUT?
         14200    AIR(W)POLLUT?
         24505    AIR
         15662    QUALITY
          4000    AIR(W)QUALITY
            29    SITING AND POWER(W)PLANT? ? AND (AIR(W)POLLUT? OR
                  AIR(W)QUALITY)
68: ENVIRONMENTAL BIBLIOGRAPHY - 74-90/FEB
           304    SITING
          7581    POWER
         22734    PLANT? ?
          3432    OWER(W)PLANT? ?
         11533    AIR
         20626    POLLUT?
          7828    AIR(W)POLLUT?
         11533    AIR
          8627    QUALITY
          1019    AIR(W)QUALITY
             4    SITING AND POWER(W)PLANT? ? AND (AIR(W)POLLUT? OR
                  AIR(W)QUALITY)
69: ENERGYLINE - 70-90/JUL
          1660    SITING
         24710    POWER
         20585    PLANT? ?
         15021    POWER(W)PLANT? ?
          6380    AIR
          3210    POLLUT?
          1145    AIR(W)POLLUT?
          6380    AIR
          2604    QUALITY
           651    AIR(W)QUALITY
            60    SITING AND POWER(W)PLANT? ? AND (AIR(W)POLLUT? OR
                  AIR(W)QUALITY)
103: DOE ENERGY _ 83-90/AUG(ISS14)
          2595    SITING
        196491    POWER (1974 DEC)
```

**Search 7.5:** (cont.)

```
   176510   PLANT? ?
    72956   POWER(W)PLANT? ?
   109120   AIR (1974 DEC)
    79794   POLLUT?
    43940   AIR(W)POLLUT?
   109120   AIR  (1974 DEC)
    55880   QUALITY
     7142   AIR(W)QUALITY
       76   SITING AND POWER(W)PLANT? ? AND (AIR(W)POLLUT? OR
            AIR(W)QUALITY)
144: PASCAL _1983 - 1990 APR
      287   SITING
    30686   POWER
   156194   PLANT? ?
    11609   POWER(W)PLANT? ?
    39023   AIR
    41709   POLLUT?
    11234   AIR(W)POLLUT?
    39023   AIR
    34936   QUALITY
      878   AIR(W)QUALITY
        1    SITING AND POWER(W)PLANT? ? AND (AIR(W)POLLUT? OR
            AIR(W)QUALITY)
312: CA SEARCH _1987-1990 (UD=11306)
      105   SITING
    10667   POWER (SEE ?IGNOTE)
    91999   PLANT? ?
     4224   POWER(W)PLANT? ?
    40905   AIR (SEE ?IGNOTE)
    44063   POLLUT?
    32001   AIR(W)POLLUT?
    40905   AIR (SEE ?IGNOTE)
    10102   QUALITY
      297   AIR(W)QUALITY
        1   SITING AND POWER(W)PLANT? ? AND (AIR(W)POLLUT? OR
            AIR(W)QUALITY)
266: FEDERAL RESEARCH IN PROGRESS - JUL 1990
       33   SITING
     2537   POWER
     9394   PLANT? ?
      256   POWER(W)PLANT? ?
     2402   AIR
     1472   POLLUT?
      428   AIR(W)POLLUT?
     2402   AIR
     6626   QUALITY
      121   AIR(W)QUALITY
        0   SITING AND POWER(W)PLANT? ? AND (AIR(W)POLLUT? OR
            AIR(W)QUALITY)

File 103:DOE ENERGY _ 83-90/AUG(ISS14)
* Use of File 103 is restricted. Please see ?RESTRICT *

     Set    Items    Description
     ---    -----    -----------
?s siting or site? ?(3n)(select? or survey? or plan or plans or planning)
            2595   SITING
           67747   SITE? ?
           86359   SELECT?
           47450   SURVEY?
           14252   PLAN
```

**Search 7.5:** (cont.)

```
            14254      PLANS
            46565      PLANNING  (1974 DEC)
            10120      SITE? ?(3N)((((SELECT? OR SURVEY?) OR PLAN) OR PLANS) OR
                       PLANNING)
     S1     11336      SITING OR SITE? ?(3N)(SELECT? OR SURVEY? OR PLAN OR PLANS
                       OR PLANNING)
```

**?s powerplant? or power(w)plant? ? or electric(w)(power or plant? ? or
utilit??? ?)**

```
              728      POWERPLANT?
           196491      POWER  (1974 DEC)
           176510      PLANT? ?
            72956      POWER(W)PLANT? ?
           141422      ELECTRIC
           196491      POWER  (1974 DEC)
           176510      PLANT? ?
            29710      UTILIT??? ?
            33222      ELECTRIC(W)((POWER OR PLANT? ?) OR UTILIT??? ?)
     S2     94886      POWERPLANT? OR POWER(W)PLANT? ? OR ELECTRIC(W)(POWER OR
                       PLANT? ? OR UTILIT??? ?)
```

**?s air(w)(pollut? or quality) or emission? ? or particulate? ? or
nitrogen(w)(oxide? ? or dioxide) or sulfur(w)(oxide? ? or dioxide) or
sulphur(w)(oxide? ? or dioxide)**

```
           109120      AIR  (1974 DEC)
            79794      POLLUT?
            55880      QUALITY
            46165      AIR(W)(POLLUT? OR QUALITY)
            73735      EMISSION? ?
            15041      PARTICULATE? ?
            79976      NITROGEN  (1974 DEC)
           108489      OXIDE? ?
            40671      DIOXIDE
            15313      NITROGEN(W)(OXIDE? ? OR DIOXIDE)
            64372      SULFUR  (1974 DEC)
           108489      OXIDE? ?
            40671      DIOXIDE
            15271      SULFUR(W)(OXIDE? ? OR DIOXIDE)
             5170      SULPHUR
           108489      OXIDE? ?
            40671      DIOXIDE
             1124      SULPHUR(W)(OXIDE? ? OR DIOXIDE)
     S3    121324      AIR(W)(POLLUT? OR QUALITY) OR EMISSION? ? OR PARTICULATE?
                       ? OR NITROGEN(W)(OXIDE? ? OR DIOXIDE) OR SULFUR(W)(OXIDE?
                       ? OR DIOXIDE) OR SULPHUR(W)(OXIDE? ? OR DIOXIDE)
```

**?c 1 and 2 and 3**
```
            11336      1
            94886      2
           121324      3
     S4       215      1 AND 2 AND 3
```
**`?s sc=50**
```
     S5     45827      SC=50
```
**?c 1 and 2 and (3 or 5)**
```
            11336      1
            94886      2
           121324      3
            45827      5
     S6       250      1 AND 2 AND (3 OR 5)
```
**?s sc=500500**
```
     S7       321      SC=500500
```
**?c 7 and 2**
```
              321      7
```

**Search 7.5:** (cont.)

```
              94886    2
       S8        50    7 AND 2
?s s1/ti,de
       S9      8206    S1/TI,DE
?c 9 and 6
              8206     9
               250     6
       S10     162     9 AND 6
?c 8 or 10
                50     8
               162     10
       S11     199     8 OR 10
?s py=1987:1990
       S12  477499     PY=1987:1990
?c 11 and 12
               199     11
            477499     12
       S13      44     11 AND 12
?t13/6/1-5
```

13/6/1
1881268 EDB-90:084038 TIC Accession No.: DE89008769
   Title: The Northern States Power Company reference FBC (fluidized bed combustion) plant
   Title: Proceedings: 1988 seminar on fluidized-bed combustion technology for utility applications
   Conference title: Fluidized-bed combustion technology for utility applications seminar

13/6/2
1873838 GRA-90:33333, EDB-90:076607
   Title: Environmental review of Southern Maryland Electric Cooperative's proposed combustion-turbine generating facility at Chalk Point

13/6/3
1873837 NOV-90:004166, EDB-90:076606
   Title: Solid waste disposal test program for a coal-fired power plant
   Series Title: Volume 2
   Conference title: 81. annual meeting of Air Pollution Control Association

13/6/4
1862740 NOV-90:004174, EDB-90:065508
   Title: Role of climate change predictions in siting a high-level radioactive waste repository
   Series Title: Volume 2
   Conference title: 81. annual meeting of Air Pollution Control Association

13/6/5
1856827 CANM-90:005030, EDB-90:059594
   Title: Environmental impact assessment on the proposal by NB Power to construct a thermal generating station in Belledune, New Brunswick Summary report
   Original Title: Etude d'impact environmental de la propostion faite par Energie N.-B. de construire et exploiter une centrale thermique a Belledune, Nouveau-Brunswick
   Series Title: Environmental impact assessment in New Brunswick

?t13/5/2
13/5/2
1873838 GRA-90:33333, EDB-90:076607
   Title: Environmental review of Southern Maryland Electric Cooperative's

**Search 7.5:** (cont.)

proposed combustion-turbine generating facility at Chalk Point
   Author: Peters, N.; Tomko, J.; Keating, R.; Corio, L.; Stern, M.
   Corporate Source: Environmental Resources Management, Inc., Annapolis, MD (USA)
  Date: Dec 1989 144 p.
  Report No.: PB-90-171992/XAB
  Document Type: Report
  Language: English
  Journal Announcement: EDB9000
  Availability: NTIS, PC A07/MF A01
  Subfile: ERA (Energy Research Abstracts); ETD (Energy Technology Data Exchange). GRA (NTIS NTS)
  Distribution Code: (Report): 6 (Microfiche): 9
  Country of Publication: United States
  Work Location: United States
  Abstract: The report provides an environmental assessment of a 70-100 MW gas turbine generating facility which the Southern Maryland Electric Cooperative, Inc. (SMECO) has proposed to construct on the site of Potomac Electric Power Company's (PEPCO) Chalk Point Generating Station. The facility, to be used as a peaking plant, will be SMECO's first generating station. Construction of the facility is expected to begin in March 1990, with completion scheduled for December 1990. Commercial operation is expected to begin prior to January 1, 1991. On the basis of the information available, no deficiencies have been identified which warrant finding the Chalk Point site unsuitable for construction of the proposed SMECO facility. Potential impacts from air emissions, ground water withdrawal, release of contaminants to ground water, noise emissions, discharge of effluent, and disturbance of the site were specifically examined. Recommendations for evaluations following construction are also provided.
  Major Descriptors: *GAS TURBINE POWER PLANTS -- ENVIRONMENTAL IMPACTS
  Descriptors: AIR POLLUTION; ELECTRIC UTILITIES; MARYLAND; NOISE POLLUTION ; PEAKING POWER PLANTS; SITE SURVEYS; SURVEYS; WATER POLLUTION
  Special Terms: FEDERAL REGION III; NORTH AMERICA; POLLUTION; POWER PLANTS ; PUBLIC UTILITIES; USA
  Class Codes: 200500*;296000

```
File  40:ENVIROLINE - 70-90/JUL
     Set   Items    Description
     ---   -----    -----------

           1620     SITING
           9470     SITE? ?
           5358     SELECT?
          10391     SURVEY?
           2895     PLAN
           2550     PLANS
          19325     PLANNING
            721     SITE? ?(3N)((((SELECT? OR SURVEY?) OR PLAN) OR PLANS) OR
                    PLANNING)
     S1    2231     SITING OR SITE? ?(3N)(SELECT? OR SURVEY? OR PLAN OR PLANS
                    OR PLANNING)
            126     POWERPLANT?
          11294     POWER
          21147     PLANT? ?
           6952     POWER(W)PLANT? ?
           3980     ELECTRIC
          11294     POWER
          21147     PLANT? ?
           3169     UTILIT??? ?
```

**Search 7.5:** (cont.)

```
            2110    ELECTRIC(W)((POWER OR PLANT? ?) OR UTILIT??? ?)
    S2      8204    POWERPLANT? OR POWER(W)PLANT? ? OR ELECTRIC(W)(POWER OR
                    PLANT? ? OR UTILIT??? ?)
           22993    AIR
           31807    POLLUT?
           17031    QUALITY
           12333    AIR(W)(POLLUT? OR QUALITY)
           11897    EMISSION? ?
            5098    PARTICULATE? ?
            6929    NITROGEN
            3965    OXIDE? ?
            6535    DIOXIDE
            3264    NITROGEN(W)(OXIDE? ? OR DIOXIDE)
            5936    SULFUR
            3965    OXIDE? ?
            6535    DIOXIDE
            4454    SULFUR(W)(OXIDE? ? OR DIOXIDE)
             205    SULPHUR
            3965    OXIDE? ?
            6535    DIOXIDE
              81    SULPHUR(W)(OXIDE? ? OR DIOXIDE)
    S3     22161    AIR(W)(POLLUT? OR QUALITY) OR EMISSION? ? OR PARTICULATE?
                    ? OR NITROGEN(W)(OXIDE? ? OR DIOXIDE) OR SULFUR(W)(OXIDE?
                    ? OR DIOXIDE) OR SULPHUR(W)(OXIDE? ? OR DIOXIDE)
            2231    S1
            8204    S2
           22161    S3
    S4       194    S1 AND S2 AND S3
>>>Prefix "SC" is undefined
    S5         0    SC=50
            2231    S1
            8204    S2
           22161    S3
               0    S5
    S6       194    S1 AND S2 AND (S3 OR S5)
>>>Prefix "SC" is undefined
    S7         0    SC=500500
               0    S7
            8204    S2
    S8         0    S7 AND S2
    S9      1321    S1/TI,DE
            1321    S9
             194    S6
    S10      159    S9 AND S6
               0    S8
             159    S10
    S11      159    S8 OR S10
>>>Prefix "PY" is undefined
    S12        0    PY=1987:1990
             159    S11
               0    S12
    S13        0    S11 AND S12
```

?**t11/8/1-5**

```
 11/8/1
0202516 Enviroline Number: *90-000040
  CARRYING  CAPACITY OF POLLUTANTS IN THE ATMOSPHERE IN RELATION TO THE NEW
ELECTRIC POWER PLANT PLANNED IN NORTHERN ISRAEL,
  Descriptors: *POWER  PLANT  EMISSIONS  ; *ISRAEL ; *POWER PLANT SITING ;
*POWER  PLANTS-COAL  FIRED  ;  *SULFUR  DIOXIDE  ; *ATMOSPHERIC DIFFUSION ;
```

**Search 7.5:** (cont.)

DIURNAL CHANGES ; STACK HEIGHT ; MATHEMATIC MODELS-AIR
  Review Classification: 01


  11/8/2
0199750 Enviroline Number: 89-003844
  AIR QUALITY IMPACT ASSESSMENT (AIR POLLUTION CONTROL),
  Descriptors:  *ENV  IMPACT  ASSESSMENT  ;  *AIR  POLLUTION   INDICATORS ;
*MATHEMATIC MODELS-AIR ; *MONITORING, ENV-AIR ; *AIR QUALITY STANDS ;
*STACK EMISSIONS  ;  *ATMOSPHERIC DIFFUSION ;  INDUSTRIAL  PLANT SITING ;
POLYCHLORINATED BIPHENYLS ; POWER PLANT EMISSIONS
  Review Classification: 01


  11/8/3
0198375 Enviroline Number: *89-002448
  A PROPOSED METRIC FOR ASSESSING THE POTENTIAL OF COMMUNITY ANNOYANCE FROM
WIND TURBINE LOW-FREQUENCY NOISE EMISSIONS,
  Descriptors:  *NOISE  EFFECTS  ;  *WIND  ENERGY  ;  *INDUSTRIAL  NOISE ;
*ATTITUDE  SURVEYS ; *TURBINE ENGINES-POWER PLANT ; *ACOUSTIC MEASUREMENT ;
NOISE LEVELS ; POWER PLANT OPERATION ; POWER PLANT SITING
  Review Classification: 10


  11/8/4
0194176 Enviroline Number: *88-061217
  ELECTRICITY: A PUBLIC HAZARD IN PRIVATE HANDS,
  Descriptors:  *U   K  CENTRAL  ELECTRIC  GEN  BRD  ;  *COMPETITION ; *ENV
MANAGEMENT,   NON   U S  ;  *POWER  PLANT  SITING  ;  *PUBLIC  HEARINGS ;
*TRANSMISSION LINES ; *NUCLEAR POWER PLANT OPERATION ; POWER PLANT EMISSION
CONTROL ; REACTOR SAFETY
  Review Classification: 03


  11/8/5
0191692 Enviroline Number: *88-011197
  INTEGRATED ENVIRONMENTAL CONTROL SYSTEMS: PAST, PRESENT, AND FUTURE,
  Descriptors:  *POWER  PLANT  DESIGN  ;  *ENV  MANAGEMENT ; *ENERGY IMPACT
ASSESSMENT ; *POWER PLANT OPERATION ; *POWER PLANT EMISSION CONTROL ; *LAW,
ENV-FED  ;  *WASTEWATER  REUSE,  INDUSTRIAL  ;  EFFLUENT  STANDARDS ;  AIR
POLLUTION CONTROL ; POWER PLANT SITING ; AVAILABILITY
  Review Classification: 03

  **?t11/5/1**


  11/5/1
0202516 Enviroline Number: *90-000040
  CARRYING  CAPACITY OF POLLUTANTS IN THE ATMOSPHERE IN RELATION TO THE NEW
ELECTRIC POWER PLANT PLANNED IN NORTHERN ISRAEL,
  GRABER  M. ISRAEL  MINISTRY  OF  ENV,  JERUSALEM,  ; DAYAN U. ; DORON E. ;
LURIA M. ; MAHRER Y. ; SHEHNAV R.
  ISRAEL ENV B, SUMMER 89, V12, N3, P17(8)
THE ORIGINAL DOCUMENT IS AVAILABLE FROM BOWKER
  RESEARCH  ARTICLE   THE PREFERRED SITE FOR A NEW 1100 MWE POWER STATION TO
BE  BUILT  IN  NORTHERN ISRAEL WAS INVESTIGATED ON THE BASIS OF AIR QUALITY
IMPACTS.   NUMERICAL   MODELS   WERE   USED  TO  DETERMINE  SULFUR  DIOXIDE
CONCENTRATIONS  AND  DISPERSION PATTERNS IN THE HAIFA AND HADERA AREAS, TWO
CANDIDATE  SITES.  THE  ANALYSIS  CONCLUDES  THAT  UNITS  3 AND 4 SHOULD BE
CONSTRUCTED  IN  HADERA  BECAUSE  OF  THE  UNFAVORABLE  POLLUTANT DISPERSION
CONDITIONS  IN  THE HAIFA AREA. DEGRADED AIR QUALITY IN HAIFA IS ATTRIBUTED
TO  THE  PROXIMITY  OF POLLUTION SOURCES IN THE HAIFA BAY REGION AND TO THE
HIGH  FREQUENCY  OF  LOW  ELEVATED  STABLE AIR LAYERS OVER MOUNT CARMEL. TO
ENHANCE  POLLUTANT  DISPERSION  EFFECTS  AT  HADERA,  THE POWER PLANT STACK
SHOULD BE AT LEAST 250 M HIGH. (1 GRAPH, 34 REFERENCES, 2 TABLES)

**Search 7.5:** (cont.)

```
   Descriptors:  *POWER  PLANT  EMISSIONS  ; *ISRAEL ; *POWER PLANT SITING ;
*POWER  PLANTS-COAL  FIRED  ;  *SULFUR  DIOXIDE  ; *ATMOSPHERIC DIFFUSION ;
DIURNAL CHANGES ; STACK HEIGHT ; MATHEMATIC MODELS-AIR
   Review Classification: 01
```

## Search 7.6: Siting search on ORBIT: DATABASE INDEX and EPIA

```
YOU ARE NOW CONNECTED TO THE DATA BASE INDEX DATABASE. THIS IS THE MASTER
INDEX TO ALL SEARCH SERVICE DATABASES.

SS 1 /C?
USER:
siting

PROG:
SS 1: (58) DATABASES

SS 2 /C?
USER:
prt rank 5

PROG:

-1-
DN - EPIA
PSTG- AT LEAST 1701.

-2-
DN - COMPENDEX PLUS
PSTG- AT LEAST 1601.

-3-
DN - ENVIROLINE
PSTG- AT LEAST 1501.

-4-
DN - ENERGYLINE
PSTG- AT LEAST 1501.

-5-
DN - NTIS
PSTG- AT LEAST 1401.

SS 2 /C?
USER:
air quality

PROG:
SS 2: (18) DATABASES

SS 3 /C?
USER:
prt rank 5

PROG:
```

**Search 7.6:** (cont.)

```
-1-
DN - NTIS
PSTG- AT LEAST 3101.

-2-
DN - EPIA
PSTG- AT LEAST 2201.

-3-
DN - COMPENDEX PLUS
PSTG- AT LEAST 1001.

-4-
DN - P/E NEWS
PSTG- AT LEAST 961.

-5-
DN - NIOSHTIC
PSTG- AT LEAST 481.

PROG:
YOU ARE NOW CONNECTED TO THE EPIA DATABASE.
COVERS 1975 TO (8403)

SS 1 /C?
USER:
/ti,iw siting or site(w)all select: or site(w)all survey: or site(w)all plan:

PROG:
SS 1 PSTG (1752)

SS 2 /C?
USER:
/ti,iw air(w)pollut: or air(w)quality or all emission# or all particulate# or
nitrogen(w)all oxide# or nitrogen(w)dioxide or sulfur(w)all oxide# or sulfur(
w)dioxide or sulphur(w)all oxide# or sulphur(w)dioxide

PROG:
MM (POLLUT:) (4)
      1      9      POLLUTANT/IW
      2     61      POLLUTANTS/TI
      3     27      POLLUTION/IW
      4      2      POLLUTIONAL/TI
SPECIFY NUMBERS, ALL, OR NONE

USER:
all

PROG:
SS 2 PSTG (2906)

SS 3 /C?
USER:
1 and 2

PROG:
SS 3 PSTG (145)

SS 4 /C?
USER:
prt ti 1-5
```

**Search 7.6:** (cont.)

```
PROG:

-1-
TI - Characterization of Transformer Noise Emissions - Volume 2: Transformer
     Environmental Noise Siting Guide.

-2-
TI - The Maryland Power Plant Siting Program (PPSP) Air Quality Model
     User's Guide.

-3-
TI - CONSIDERATIONS IN ELECTRIC POWER PLANT SITING: AIR QUALITY.

-4-
TI - STACK DESIGN AND EMISSIONS DATA FOR THE IPP PLANT.

-5-
 TI -AIR QUALITY CONSTRAINTS ON THE SITING OF COAL POWER PLANTS AND COAL
     CONVERSION FACILITIES IN EASTERN WY AND MT.

SS 4 /C?
USER:
prt full 5

PROG:

-5-
AN - 83-027199
TI - AIR QUALITY CONSTRAINTS ON THE SITING OF COAL POWER PLANTS AND COAL
     CONVERSION FACILITIES IN EASTERN WY AND MT.
AU - NORDSIECK, R.A.; TECOLOTE RESEARCH, INC.
SO - APPENDIX B, DES 82-77, U. S. BUREAU OF RECLAMATION, 34P., 07/81
DT - ENVIRONMENTAL IMPACT STATEMENT APPENDIX
IT - AIR QUALITY; STACK EMISSION; FEDERAL STANDARD; COAL PLANT; SYNTHETIC
     FUELS; ENERGY DEVELOPMENT; CONSTRAINT MAPPING
AB - REPORT PRESENTS THE RESULTS OF A GENERAL STUDY TO ESTABLISH THE AREAS
     OF POTENTIAL DEVELOPMENT AND THE MAXIMUM NUMBERS OF ENERGY FACILITIES
     THAT COULD OPERATE WITHIN THE SPECIFIED WATER SERVICE REGION OF
     MONTANA AND WYOMING GIVEN AIR QUALITY CONSTRAINTS. THREE TYPES OF
     FACILITIES WERE CONSIDERED: 1) A 500 MW COAL-FIRED POWER PLANT; 2) A
     250 MILLION CU. FT/DAY COAL GASIFICATION PLANT; AND 3) A 50,000
     BBL/DAY COAL LIQUEFACTION PLANT. THE ESTIMATED MAXIMUM LEVEL OF
     DEVELOPMENT OF THE MANDATORY AND PROPOSED AREA FOR A MIXTURE OF
     SINGLE-UNIT GASIFICATION AND LIQUEFACTION PLANTS RANGES FROM 19-42,
     ASSUMING AVERAGE SULFUR COAL AND CONSTRAINTS BY CLASS I AREAS ONLY.
     FROM 15-16 SINGLE-UNIT COAL-FIRED POWER PLANTS COULD BE BUILT UNDER
     THE SAME CONDITIONS.
```

## NOTES

1.    This chapter is an update of one on the same subject originally published in Ryan E. Hoover, ed. *Online Search Strategies*. White Plains, NY: Knowledge Industry Publications, 1982, pp 97-135 and C. J. Armstrong and J. A. Large, (eds). *Manual of Online Search Strategies*. Aldershot: Gower, 1988, pp. 355-393. Material in the Energy-Related Environmental Issues section has been taken from several reports, including: *Environmental Quality 1986: The Seventeenth Annual Report of the Council on*

*Environmental Quality together with The President's Message to Congress*. Washington, DC: Executive Office of the President, 1984 and *Environmental Outlook 1980*. Washington, DC: US Environmental Protection Agency, 1980.

2.  These are the *Energy Microthesaurus: A Hierarchical List of Indexing Terms used by NTIS*, PB-254800. Washington, DC: National Technical Information Service, 1976 and the *Environmental Microthesaurus: A Hierarchical List of Indexing Terms used by NTIS*, PB-265261. Washington, DC: National Technical Information Service, 1977.

3.  *Integrated Energy Vocabulary*, PB-259000. Washington, DC: National Technical Information Service, 1976.

## FURTHER READINGS

Alexander, W.A. *Use of DOE/RECON in Environmental Protection*. CONF-820418-21. Tennessee: Oak Ridge National Laboratory, 1982.

Bridges, K., Environmental Health and Toxicology: An Introduction for the Online Searcher. *Online* 5(1) January 1981 27-34.

Coyne, J.G., Carroll, B.C. and Redford, J.S. Energy Information Systems and Services. *Annual Review of Information Science and Technology* 18, 1983 231-274.

Crow, N.B. *On-line Information Retrieval Systems for Energy Studies*. UCID-16669, California: Lawrence Livermore Laboratory, 1975.

Holdren, J.P. *Integrated Assessment for Energy-Related Environmental Standards: A Summary of Issues and Findings*. LBL-12779, California: Lawrence Berkeley Laboratory, 1980.

Miller, B. Energy Information Online. *Online* 2(1) January 1978 27-30.

Miller, B. Overlap Among Environmental Databases. *Online Review* 5(5) October 1981 403-404.

Miller, Carmen. Detecting Duplicates: A Searcher's Dream Come True. *Online* 14(4) July 1990 27-34.

Milne, G.W.A., Fisk, C.L., Heller, S.R. and Potenzone, R. Jr. Environmental Uses of the NIH-EPA Chemical Information System. *Science* 215 22 January 1982 371-375.

Morris, A., Tseng, G., and Newham, G. The Selection of Online Databases and Hosts - An Expert System Approach. *Proceedings of the 12th International Online Meeting*. Oxford: Learned Information Ltd. 1988 139-148.

Mount, Ellis, ed. *Relation of Sci-Tech Information to Environmental Studies*. New York: The Haworth Press, 1990.

Niehoff, R.T. Development of an Integrated Energy Vocabulary and the Possibilities for On-line Subject Switching. *Journal of the American Society for Information Science* 27(1) January-February 1976 3-17.

Olson, R.J. *Data Resources for Assessing Regional Impacts of Energy Facilities on Health and the Environment*. CONF-810652-10, Tennessee: Oak Ridge National Laboratory 1981.

Robinson, J. and Hu, M. DOE's Energy Database (EDB) Versus Other Energy Related Databases: A Comparative Analysis. *Database* 4(4) December 1981 10-27. (Also LBL-12547)

Shriner, C.R. and Peck, L.J., (eds). *Inventory of Data Bases, Graphics Packages, and Models in Department of Energy Laboratories*. ORNL/EIS-144, Tennessee: Oak Ridge National Laboratory, 1978.

Walker, R.D. and Luedtke, J.R. DOE/RECON and the Energy Files. *Database* 2(4) December 1979 54-67.

Yska, G. and Martyn, J. Databases Suitable for Users of Environmental Information. London: Aslib, 1978.

# 8 Engineering

*M. Moon*

## INTRODUCTION

Engineering is 'the art of directing the great sources of power in nature for the use and the convenience of humans' according to the *McGraw-Hill Encyclopedia of Science & Technology* [1]. *Webster's Third New International Dictionary* defines engineering as 'the science by which the properties of matter and the sources of energy in nature are made useful to man in structures, machines and products' [2].

Both definitions are very broad and are used to illustrate the point that you need to be creative in your approach to online searching in this discipline. Relevant engineering information can be found in myriad databases including many which may not immediately come to mind, such as Predicasts' PTS NEWSLETTER DATABASE which includes the full text of newsletters like *Advanced Ceramics Report* or *Advanced Composites Bulletin* and NEWSNET which is host to *Sensor Technology* and *Advanced Manufacturing Technology*. Information can also be located in general science databases such as Wilsonline's APPLIED SCIENCE & TECHNOLOGY INDEX or in multidisciplinary files such as DISSERTATION ABSTRACTS. However, there is a core list of databases designed specifically to deal with all areas of engineering and a complementary list that deals with its specialities [3,4]. These databases reflect the diversity of engineering specialities that have been created and also the variety of forms their literature can take. Table 8.1 is a selective rather than exhaustive listing of engineering databases and their specialities extracted from the *Directory of Online Databases* [5] (this list does not cover chemistry, biology, agriculture, energy, environmental studies or computer science as they are contained in other chapters in this book).

This chapter is designed to aid the reader in learning more about the variety of engineering databases available and in using some of their features to develop effective search strategies. Most of the databases are mounted on multiple hosts (see Table 8.2) and usually the choice of which host to use is based on the availability of the host and your familiarity with it.

**Table 8.1: Engineering databases and their specialities**

| Database | Speciality |
| --- | --- |
| AEROSPACE DATABASE | Aerospace, general |
| AUSTRALIAN ENGINEERING DATABASE | Engineering |
| BEFO | Management, engineering |
| BIIPAM-CTIF | Engineering |
| BODIL | Construction |
| CERAMIC ABSTRACTS | Ceramics |
| CETIM | Mechanical engineering |
| CIVIL ENGINEERING DATABASE | Civil engineering |
| COMPENDEX*PLUS | Engineering, general |
| CONFERENCE PAPERS INDEX | General |
| CURRENT TECHNOLOGY INDEX | General |
| DKF | Automotive |
| DOMA | Mechanical engineering |
| EDF-DOC | Power |
| ENGINEERED MATERIALS | Materials |
| FhGPBULICA | Construction |
| FIESTA | General |
| FLUIDEX | Fluid engineering |
| GIDEP | Engineering |
| HAYSTACK | Engineering Products |
| HEATFLO | Heat |
| IBSEDEX | Construction |
| ICONDA | Construction |
| INSPEC | General |
| INTIME | Manufacturing engineering |
| ISMEC | Mechanical engineering |
| MATERIALS BUSINESS FILE | Materials |
| METADEX | Metallurgy |
| NONFERROUS METALS ABSTRACTS | Metallurgy |
| NTIS | General |
| PASCAL:BATIMENT,TRAVAUX PUBLICS | Construction |
| PASCAL:METAUX,METALLURGIE | Metallurgy |
| PLASPEC | Plastics engineering |
| RAPRA ABSTRACTS | Materials |
| RHEOLOGY | Rheology |
| ROBOMATIX ONLINE | Robotics |
| RSWB | Construction |
| SAE GLOBAL MOBILITY | Automotive, aerospace |
| SATELDATA | Aeronautics |
| SCISEARCH | General |
| SDIM | Metallurgy |
| SILICA | Ceramics |
| SOVIET SCIENCE & TECHNOLOGY | General |
| TRIBOLOGY INDEX | Engineering |

**Table 8.1:** (cont.)

| Database | Speciality |
|---|---|
| TRIS | Transportation |
| VDI-NACHRICHTEN | Engineering |
| VOLKSWAGEN | Automotive, transportation |
| WELDASEARCH | Welding |
| WORLD ALUMINUM ABSTRACTS | Metallurgy |
| WORLD CERAMICS ABSTRACTS | Ceramics |
| WORLD SURFACE COATINGS ABSTRACTS | Materials |
| ZDE | General |

**Table 8.2: Engineering databases and their host systems**

| Database | BRS | CEDOCAR | CISTI | Data-Star | DIALOG |
|---|---|---|---|---|---|
| AEROSPACE DATABASE | | | | | X |
| AUSTRALIAN ENGINEERING DB | | | | | |
| BEFO | | | | | |
| BIIPAM-CTIF | | | | | |
| BODIL | | | | | |
| CERAMIC ABSTRACTS | | | | | X |
| CETIM | | | | | |
| CIVIL ENGINEERING DATABASE | | | | | |
| COMPENDEX*PLUS | X | X | X | X | X |
| CONFERENCE PAPERS INDEX | | | | | X |
| CURRENT TECHNOLOGY INDEX | | | | | X |
| DKF | | | | X | |
| DOMA | | | | | |
| EDF-DOC | | | | | |
| ENGINEERED MATERIALS | | | | X | X |
| FhGPBULICA | | | | | |
| FIESTA | | X | | | |
| FLUIDEX | | | | | X |
| GIDEP | | | | | |
| HAYSTACK | | | | | |
| HEATFLO | | | | | |
| IBSEDEX | | | | | |
| ICONDA | X | X | X | | |
| INSPEC | X | X | X | X | X |
| INTIME | | | | | |
| ISMEC | X | | | | X |
| MATERIALS BUSINESS FILE | | X | X | X | X |
| METADEX | X | X | X | X | X |
| NONFERROUS METALS ABSTRACTS | | | | X | |

**Table 8.2:** (cont.)

| Database | BRS | CEDOCAR | CISTI | Data-Star | DIALOG |
|---|---|---|---|---|---|
| NTIS | x | x | x | x | x |
| PASCAL:BATIMENT,TRAVAUX PUB | | | | | x |
| PASCAL:METAUX,METALLURGIE | | | | | x |
| PLASPEC | | | | | |
| RAPRA ABSTRACTS | | | | | |
| RHEOLOGY | | | | | |
| ROBOMATIX ONLINE | | | | | x |
| RSWB | | | | | |
| SAE GLOBAL MOBILITY | | | | | |
| SATELDATA | | | | | |
| SCISEARCH | | | | x | x |
| SDIM | | | | | |
| SILICA | | | | | |
| SOVIET SCIENCE & TECHNOLOGY | | | | | x |
| TRIBOLOGY INDEX | | | | | |
| TRIS | | | | | x |
| VDI-NACHRICHTEN | | | | | |
| VOLKSWAGEN | | | | | |
| WELDASEARCH | | | | | |
| WORLD ALUMINUM ABSTRACTS | | | | | x |
| WORLD CERAMICS ABSTRACTS | | | | | |
| WORLD SURFACE COATINGS ABS | | | | | |
| ZDE | | | | x | |

| Database | ESA-IRS | Fiz Technik | Orbit | STN | Other |
|---|---|---|---|---|---|
| AEROSPACE DATABASE | | | | | |
| AUSTRALIAN ENGINEERING DB | | | | | CSIRO |
| BEFO | | x | | | |
| BIIPAM-CTIF | x | | | | |
| BODIL BYGGDOK | | | | | |
| CERAMIC ABSTRACTS | | | x | x | |
| CETIM | x | | | | |
| CIVIL ENGINEERING DATABASE | | | | | ATLIS |
| COMPENDEX*PLUS | x | | x | x | |
| CONFERENCE PAPERS INDEX | x | | | | |
| CURRENT TECHNOLOGY INDEX | | | | | |
| DKF | | | | | |
| DOMA | | x | | | |
| EDF-DOC | x | | | | QUESTEL |
| ENGINEERED MATERIALS | x | | x | x | |
| FhGPBULICA | | | | x | |

**Table 8.2:** (cont.)

| Database | ESA-IRS | Fiz Technik | Orbit | STN | Other |
|---|---|---|---|---|---|
| FIESTA | | | | | |
| FLUIDEX | x | | | | |
| GIDEP | | | | | GIDEP |
| HAYSTACK | | | | | ZIFF-DAVIS |
| HEATFLO | x | | | | |
| IBSEDIX | x | | | | BSRHA |
| ICONDA | | | x | x | |
| INSPEC | x | x | x | x | |
| INTIME | x | | | | |
| ISMEC | x | | | | |
| MATERIALS BUSINESS FILE | x | | x | x | |
| METADEX | x | | x | x | |
| NONFERROUS METALS ABS | x | | | | |
| NTIS | x | | x | x | |
| PASCAL:BATIMENT,TRAVAUX PUB | x | | | | |
| PASCAL:METAUX,METALLURGIE | x | | | | |
| PLASPEC | | | | x | PLASPEC |
| RAPRA ABSTRACTS | | | x | | |
| RHEOLOGY | | x | | | |
| ROBOMATIX ONLINE | x | | x | | |
| RSWB | | x | | x | |
| SAE GLOBAL MOBILITY | | | x | | |
| SATELDATA | x | | | | |
| SCISEARCH | | | x | | |
| SDIM | | x | | x | |
| SILICA | | x | | x | |
| SOVIET SCIENCE & TECHNOLOGY | | | | | |
| TRIBOLOGY INDEX | | x | | | |
| TRIS | | | | | |
| VDI-NACHRICHTEN | | x | | x | |
| VOLKSWAGEN | | x | x | | |
| WELDASEARCH | | | x | | |
| WORLD ALUMINUM ABSTRACTS | x | | | | |
| WORLD CERAMICS ABSTRACTS | | | x | | |
| WORLD SURFACE COATINGS ABS | | | x | | |
| ZDE | | x | | | |

## COMPENDEX*PLUS

COMPENDEX, COMPENDEX*PLUS and EI ENGINEERING MEETINGS are all bibliographic databases produced by Engineering Information, Inc. Together they comprise the best source of significant engineering information available throughout the world. COMPENDEX corresponds to the printed publication *Engineering Index* which has been published since 1884. It contains selective coverage of journal articles in addition to technical reports, engineering society publications, books and conference proceedings. Abstracts describing the documents' contents are included. EI ENGINEERING MEETINGS contains individual papers from engineering conferences, symposia or colloquia. Approximately two thousand conferences per year are referenced in the database with all papers from its sessions included.

COMPENDEX*PLUS was established in January 1988 as the sum of COMPENDEX and EI ENGINEERING MEETINGS. All duplicate records were eliminated and in DIALOG the accession numbers from both fields were changed. This merger was in response to searchers' requests for one-step access to the various types of engineering literature available. COMPENDEX*PLUS now contains more than 2.8 million citations (as of December 1990) and is updated monthly with about seventeen thousand additional citations. Table 8.3 shows which Engineering Information, Inc. databases are available on particular online services.

**Table 8.3: Availability of Engineering Information databases**

| Online Service | Database(s) | Starting Date(s) |
|---|---|---|
| BRS | COMPENDEX | 1970 |
| BRS/COLLEAGUE | COMPENDEX | 1970 |
| CEDOCAR | COMPENDEX, Ei MEETINGS | 1973,1982 |
| CISTI | COMPENDEX, Ei MEETINGS | 1970*,1982 |
| DATA-STAR | COMPENDEX*PLUS | 1983 |
| DIALOG | COMPENDEX*PLUS | 1970 |
| ESA-IRS | COMPENDEX PLUS | 1970 |
| KNOWLEDGE INDEX | COMPENDEX PLUS | 1975 |
| ORBIT | COMPENDEX*PLUS | 1970 |
| STN | COMPENDEX*PLUS | 1970 |

\*    abstracts from 1982

CEDOCAR & CISTI are in process of switching to COMPENDEX*PLUS

Engineering Information, Inc. (EI) publishes several aids that are of great value to searchers. *Ei Database Search Manual* is a looseleaf binder containing detailed user manuals for every online service that carries COMPENDEX or COMPENDEX*PLUS. There are nine different appendices that provide the Subheading index and Classification codes, complete special character list, in-depth abbreviations list and almost anything else you will need to formulate effective search strategies. If you have money for only one search aid, this is the one to buy.

*Ei Vocabulary.* The 1990 edition contains about twelve thousand controlled vocabulary terms of which three hundred are new to this edition. *Ei Vocabulary* combines and supersedes *SHE: Subject Headings for Engineering; SHG: Subject Heading Guide to Engineering Categories;* and *(CAL) Classification Codes.* It is organized into two major sections: (1) Subject Headings for Engineering and (2) Subject Headings by Classification Code. The first section includes subheadings as actual entries with references to the heading(s) under which the subheading can be used. The second section incorporates EI's classification codes and the controlled vocabulary terms (both headings and subheadings) used in that classification. *Notes and Comment* is a quarterly newsletter that reports news and information to users of EI products. It is distributed free to anyone requesting it. *PIE: Publications Indexed for Engineering* is published annually at the beginning of the year.

As of 1990, *PIE* will identify the journals and conferences that are to be covered in the current calendar year. This is a recent change of scope and coverage for the publication as it had been retrospective, that is, it covered journals indexed the previous year. 1990 also marked the time when EI expanded its core list of publications to approximately 1,900 from which all technical articles are indexed and abstracted. In addition, EI has identified two hundred cross-disciplinary publications from which all engineering-related technical articles are indexed.

The search aids are available through Engineering Information, Inc. (Dept. E, 345 East 47th Street, New York, NY 10017; 212/705-7600 or 800/221-1044). In addition to these search aids, EI will provide free online search assistance, and introductory plus advanced training workshops.

COMPENDEX*PLUS contains the standard fields found in most bibliographic databases - title, author, abstract, source, controlled vocabulary terms and so on. Major subjects in a record are shown in the Descriptor field; these can be retrieved by searching using the MAJ field on DIALOG (most online searching systems and databases provide a similar capability). This technique is one method of improving search precision and is illustrated in Search 8.1 along with another technique limiting a term to two specified fields: by limiting retrieval to only those documents that contain the term in the title or descriptor fields we are insuring that it is a significant part of the document but not necessarily the major thrust. Search 8.1 shows the difference in retrieval using these two techniques.

### Search 8.1: Limiting a search to particular fields or to MAJ: COMPENDEX*PLUS on DIALOG

```
File 8:COMPENDEX PLUS _ 70-90/DEC
      Copr. Engineering Info Inc. 1990)

      Set      Items      Description
      ---      -----      -----------
? S PROJECT()MANAGEMENT
               41140      PROJECT
               71091      MANAGEMENT
      S1        4346      PROJECT()MANAGEMENT
? S S1/TI,DE
      S2        3484      S1/TI,DE
? S S1/MAJ
      S3         998      S1/MAJ
? T3/8

 3/8/1
02997158
  Title: Managing data through naming standards.
  Descriptors: *ENGINEERING—*Project Management; COMPUTER
METATHEORY— Programming Theory; DATA PROCESSING—File Organization
  Identifiers: DATA MANAGEMENT; FILE SYSTEMS
  Classification Codes: 912 (Industrial Engineering & Management);
901 (Engineering Profession); 723 (Computer Software)
  91 (ENGINEERING MANAGEMENT); 90 (GENERAL ENGINEERING); 72 (COMPUTERS
& DATA PROCESSING)
```

Limiting to the title and descriptor fields eliminated about twenty per cent of the documents; limiting by MAJ eliminated over seventy-five per cent of the initial retrieval.

COMPENDEX*PLUS has many added search techniques to make retrieval as precise as needed. Some of the best to keep in mind when constructing searches are illustrated in Searches 8.2 and 8.3.

CAL Classification codes represent a broad subject classification scheme of over 175 technical disciplines. Each document may be assigned one to six classification codes. The present set of codes, defined in *Ei*

*Vocabulary*, has been used in COMPENDEX*PLUS since May 1970. Valid CAL codes are three-digit numbers but have also been cascaded to the two-digit level. This permits searching on a group of related subject areas with a single entry. On DIALOG CAL codes and their corresponding headings may be obtained by Expanding in the CC= index (see Search 8.2).

## Search 8.2: Use of CAL codes in COMPENDEX*PLUS on DIALOG

```
? e cc=65

Ref    Items   Index-term
E1     23772   CC=643 (SPACE HEATING & AIR CONDITIONING)
E2     15387   CC=644 (REFRIGERATION & CRYOGENICS)
E3    123405  *CC=65  (AEROSPACE ENGINEERING)
E4        23   CC=650 (AEROSPACE ENGINEERING)
E5     24529   CC=651 (AERODYNAMICS)
E6     29874   CC=652 (AIRCRAFT)
E7      7979   CC=653 (AIRCRAFT ENGINES)
E8      9053   CC=654 (ROCKETS & ROCKET PROPULSION)
E9     35428   CC=655 (SPACECRAFT)
E10     5631   CC=656 (SPACE FLIGHT)
E11    29792   CC=657 (SPACE PHYSICS)
E12      831   CC=658 (AEROSPACE ENGINEERING, GENERAL)

           Enter P or E for more


? s e7 and composite?
              7979   CC=653
             47354   COMPOSITE?
    S1         258   CC="653" AND COMPOSITE?
? s composite? and aircraft()engine?/de,id
             47354   COMPOSITE?
             33207   AIRCRAFT/DE,ID
            171798   ENGINE?/DE,ID
              7845   AIRCRAFT/DE,ID(W)ENGINE?/DE,ID
    S2         249   COMPOSITE? AND AIRCRAFT()ENGINE?/DE,ID
? s s1 or s2
               258   S1
               249   S2
    S3         285   S1 OR S2
? t3/6,cc/1-3

 02962641
   Title:   Strukturmechanische   Berechnung   und   Optimierung   eines
Propfanblattes unter Verwendung der finite-element-methode.
   Title:  Structural analysis and optimization of a propfan-blade by use of
the finite-element-method.
   Descriptors:  *AIRCRAFT   ENGINES,   JET AND TURBINE—*Blades;   MATHEMATICAL
TECHNIQUES—Finite Element Method;   STRUCTURAL   ANALYSIS—Computer   Aided
Analysis;   STRUCTURAL   DESIGN—Optimization;   AIRCRAFT—Propellers;   COMPUTER
PROGRAMMING—Algorithms
   Identifiers:  PROPFANS;   COMPOSITE   MATERIALS;   FIBER COMPOSITES; LAYERED
COMPOSITES; LAYERED FINITE SHELL ELEMENTS
   Classification Codes:  653  (Aircraft Engines); 921 (Applied Mathematics)
;  723 (Computer Software); 415 (Metals, Wood & Other Structural Materials)
   65 (AEROSPACE ENGINEERING); 92 (ENGINEERING MATHEMATICS); 72 (COMPUTERS &
DATA PROCESSING); 41 (CONSTRUCTION MATERIALS)

 02920709
   Title: Interfacial reactions in titanium-matrix composites.
   Descriptors:  *TITANIUM  AND  ALLOYS—*Metallic Matrix Composites; AIRCRAFT
```

**Search 8.2:** (cont.)

```
ENGINES,  JET  AND  TURBINE—Materials;  AIRCRAFT—Wings;  AIRCRAFT MATERIALS—
Composite  Materials;  SILICON  CARBIDE—Fibers;  TITANIUM  METALLOGRAPHY—
Microstructures
    Identifiers:  TITANIUM-MATRIX  COMPOSITES;  INTERFACIAL  REACTION  ZONE
    Classification Codes:  542  (Light  Metals & Alloys); 415 (Metals, Wood &
Other Structural Materials); 652 (Aircraft); 812 (Ceramics & Refractories);
531 (Metallurgy & Metallography)
    54  (METAL  GROUPS);  41  (CONSTRUCTION  MATERIALS); 65  (AEROSPACE
ENGINEERING);  81  (CHEMICAL  PROCESS  INDUSTRIES); 53  (METALLURGICAL
ENGINEERING)

  02828649
    Title: Applied technology in gas turbine aircraft engine development.
    Descriptors:  *AIRCRAFT  ENGINES,  JET AND TURBINE—*General Electric; GAS
TURBINES—Design;  STRUCTURAL  FRAMES;  CASTINGS;  HEAT  TRANSFER; COMPOSITE
MATERIALS—Applications
    Identifiers:  GAS  TURBINE  AIRCRAFT  ENGINE; POLYMERIC COMPOSITES; LIGHT
COMBAT  AIRCRAFT;  CAT-SCAN; STRUCTURAL INVESTMENT CASTINGS; COMPUTER AIDED
TOMOGRAPHY
    Classification Codes:  653  (Aircraft Engines); 612 (Combustion Engines);
408  (Structural  Design);  931  (Applied Physics); 534 (Foundry Practice);
641 (Heat & Thermodynamics)
    65  (AEROSPACE  ENGINEERING);  61  (PLANT & POWER ENGINEERING); 40 (CIVIL
ENGINEERING);  93  (ENGINEERING  PHYSICS);  53  (METALLURGICAL ENGINEERING);
64 (HEAT & THERMODYNAMICS)
```

In Search 8.2, EXPAND was used with cc=65 to see the codes related to Aerospace Engineering. As an example, we are searching for documents on the use of composites in jet engines. Therefore, we choose cc=653 (Aircraft Engines) and combine it with the term composites. We want to be certain of the highest relevant retrieval possible so we also search on aircraft engines as a descriptor or identifier. The difference in retrieval by using the two techniques can be seen. Finally, we combine the two sets and print the title and CAL codes to see a sampling of the items retrieved.

It is also possible to search CAL codes using the classification prose headings that correspond to the two- and three-digit codes. One thing to keep in mind when using lengthy headings is to enter the first forty-six characters exactly as they appear in the code; selecting the additional characters is optional on DIALOG. Truncation may be used with unique word stems, for example, S CC=ORE TREATMENT & METAL?.

There are several codes to help find conference proceedings. In COMPENDEX*PLUS two new document types have been added retrospectively to records since 1982: CP= for conference proceedings and PA= for proceedings article may be used to retrieve either the records for a conference as a whole or for individual conference articles. If you are searching for the proceedings of a particular conference you can use CL= if the conference location is known, or CD= for the conference date. Since 1982, EI has assigned a unique five-digit conference number to identify records for a particular conference. It is assigned to the main record and all individual articles from that conference. Once the conference number from one of the records is known, you can search on it to retrieve the other conference records using CN=. On DIALOG, the last record in a set retrieved using CN+ is always the main conference record. Conference title, CT=, is searchable in conference records only. Each significant word from the conference title is indexed and can be searched as a single word or using proximity operators. Finally, up to six sponsors of a conference are indexed in the conference sponsor, CS= field. The sponsor entries are indexed by individual word.

Journal names are indexed as complete phrases and are searchable with the JN= prefix. It is also possible to EXPAND on the journal name and select it directly from the list. This is desirable if you have not consulted

*PIE* for the correct form of entry. Journal names as displayed in the record may either be abbreviated or listed in full.

## Search 8.3:  Limiting to conference records on COMPENDEX*PLUS on DIALOG

```
File 8:COMPENDEX PLUS _ 70-91/JAN
       Copr. Engineering Info Inc. 1991)

       Set      Items   Description
       ---      -----   -----------
? s composite? and aircraft()engine?/de,id
                47712   COMPOSITE?
                33292   AIRCRAFT/DE,ID
               172457   ENGINE?/DE,ID
                 7859   AIRCRAFT/DE,ID(W)ENGINE?/DE,ID
       S1         249   COMPOSITE? AND AIRCRAFT()ENGINE?/DE,ID
? s s1 and eirev/id
                  249   S1
                12753   EIREV/ID
       S2           8   S1 AND EIREV/ID
? t s2/ct,cl,cd,sp/1-2 **

  2/CT,CL,CD,SP/1
    Conference Title: Papers Presented at NTSC87, The National Thermal
Spray Conference and Exposition.
    Conference Location: Orlando, FL, USA
    Conference Date: 1987 Sep 14-17
    Sponsor: ASM, Thermal Spray Div, Metals Park, OH, USA

  2/CT,CL,CD,SP/2
    Conference Title:  ICAS  Proceedings  1986:  15th  Congress of the
International Council of the Aeronautical Sciences.
    Conference Location: London, Engl
    Conference Date: 1986 Sep 7-12
    Sponsor: Int Council of the Aeronautical Sciences
```

NOTE: DIALOG allows the user to define the output to be printed if use
      of predefined formats is not desired. In this example, output
      includes conference title, location, date and sponsor.

As mentioned above, since 1982 EI has identified each conference record by type of document. Another way to identify conferences is to limit your subject retrieval to EIREV/ID as shown in Search 8.3. This limits the retrieval to *Ei Review* records that provide an overview of the entire conference and not just the individual papers. All other records added after 1985 are searchable by additional document types as listed in Table 8.4. These records may also have treatment codes (TC=) assigned to them to specify the orientation or approach taken in the document. As with document types, treatment codes can be specified as either a code or as the complete term. Valid treatment codes are also listed in Table 8.4.

Beginning in 1983, EI began to place the language of the document in a separate searchable field. Language(s) other than English also appear at the end of the abstract. All the major online searching vendors have made the language field searchable.

**Table 8.4: Document types and treatment codes in COMPENDEX*PLUS**

**DOCUMENT TYPES**

| | |
|---|---|
| PA | CONFERENCE PAPER |
| CP | CONFERENCE PROCEEDINGS |
| DS | DISSERTATION |
| JA | JOURNAL ARTICLE |
| MC | MONOGRAPH CHAPTER |
| MR | MONOGRAPH REVIEW |
| RC | REPORT CHAPTER |
| RR | REPORT REVIEW |
| ST | STANDARD |
| TX | TEXTBOOK |
| UP | UNPUBLISHED PAPER OR PREPRINT |

**TREATMENT CODES**

| | |
|---|---|
| A | APPLICATIONS |
| B | BIOGRAPHICAL |
| E | ECONOMIC/COST DATA/MARKET SURVEY |
| X | EXPERIMENTAL |
| G | GENERAL REVIEW |
| H | HISTORICAL |
| L | LITERATURE REVIEW/BIBLIOGRAPHY |
| M | MANAGEMENT ASPECTS |
| N | NUMERIC/STATISTICAL |
| T | THEORETICAL |

A number of saved searches have been developed by EI and stored on DIALOG to provide comprehensive strategies for broad topics involving numerous natural-language terms. While using the searches alone as a retrospective review would result in thousands of items retrieved, the searches can be effectively used when combined with additional concepts. A list of EI's saved searches (see Table 8.5) can be viewed by entering ?EISAVES. Use the DIALOG command to execute the saved search (for example, EXS SB2YTP/User 8303) and proceed with your search.

**Table 8.5: EI saved searches COMPENDEX*PLUS on DIALOG**

| | |
|---|---|
| Buildings/Structures | SB41DD/User 8303 |
| Consumer Attitudes | SB2YC5/User 8303 |
| Cost/Economics | SB2COX/User 8303 |
| Politics/Law | SB2PL3/User 8303 |
| Safety | SB2YTP/User 8303 |

EI now has a CD-ROM version of COMPENDEX*PLUS available from DIALOG as one of its OnDisc products. It is updated quarterly and may be purchased either as a Current File or the Complete File. The Current File contains the current year plus one year backfile in a two-disc set. The Complete File is the current year plus four years' backfile in a five-disc set. Yearly subscriptions are available for a stand-alone version or for a LAN licence fee for between two and ten workstations.

The COMPENDEX*PLUS CD-ROM can be searched in one of two ways. If you are familiar with DIALOG's search commands there is a command mode that will provide the same flexibility as the online version. If you are unfamiliar with searching DIALOG, there is a menu version that will easily move you through the steps to retrieving the information you seek. As the discs are updated less frequently than the online database, DIALOG has also provided its Communications Manager software with the CD-ROM. Use of this package will provide the searcher with the capability of signing on to the online system to pick up the latest information available.

Ei Engineering is also about to introduce a new product: the CITE Database, available either on magnetic tape or in CD-ROM format. CITE, as its name implies, will provide citations only and will be thirty per cent bigger than the equivalent span of COMPENDEX*PLUS, the additional material coming from journals that are only indexed selectively in COMPENDEX*PLUS. CITE will provide cover-to-cover indexing from these publications and is expected to be released sooner than COMPENDEX*PLUS which is slowed down by the addition of abstracts.

Most users will probably want the CD-ROM format, but larger organizations might want to investigate using magnetic tape as it includes citations since 1986. For example, Research Library Group (RLG) will be mounting CITE on its RLIN network. The CD-ROM version of CITE will cover a rolling twenty-four month time period. Approximately 300,000 records will be accessible on each disc, to be issued once a month. Ei Engineering purchased existing retrieval software which it has modified for its product and which was unavailable for review at the time of writing.

## The AEROSPACE DATABASE

The AEROSPACE DATABASE corresponds to *International Aerospace Abstracts (IAA)* and *Scientific and Technical Aerospace Reports (STAR)*. It describes itself as 'the most comprehensive collection publicly available on aerospace research and applied technology' and is especially valuable because of its comprehensive coverage of government reports and other unpublished literature not available elsewhere online and which may be difficult to locate [6]. Its coverage of literature from both western and eastern European countries is notable and its coverage of Japanese documents has been expanding. One caveat: the AEROSPACE DATABASE is available only in the United States, Canada and Australia. Access by other than United States Government organizations, or persons acting on their behalf, is not allowed without written approval from the American Institute of Aeronautics and Astronautics, Technical Information Service.

Although the database concentrates on aerospace, it includes a substantial amount of information on more generally related subjects that cut across engineering specialities. Subjects such as physics, quality assurance, mechanical engineering, structural mechanics and heat transfer are well represented. AEROSPACE DATABASE indexes over 1600 periodicals from world-wide sources and approximately fifty per cent of its overall coverage is of documents from outside the United States. The database is divided into ten major subject areas as shown in Table 8.6. Each main heading is divided into several sub-headings, all of which are searchable. COSATI codes are also present in the STAR portion of the database and can be used as search terms.

**Table 8.6: Major subject areas of the AEROSPACE DATABASE**

```
AERONAUTICS
ASTRONAUTICS
CHEMISTRY & MATERIALS
ENGINEERING
GEOSCIENCES
LIFE SCIENCES
MATHEMATICAL & COMPUTER SCIENCES
PHYSICS
SOCIAL SCIENCES
SPACE SCIENCES
```

AEROSPACE DATABASE has an online thesaurus that can be accessed to aid in obtaining keywords for your search (see Search 8.4). In this example, we have expanded the phrase 'aircraft engines' to enter the thesaurus. We then expanded the Reference number E3 to list the forty related terms available. To go even deeper into the thesaurus we expanded on Related Term 23 to find a record on the CF-700 engine which was then printed. This technique will prove of value when searching on any term that has multiple synonyms.

**Search 8.4: Use of online thesaurus AEROSPACE DATABASE on DIALOG**

```
? e aircraft engines

Ref  Items   RT   Index-term
E1      0     1    AIRCRAFT ENERGY EFFICIENCY PROGRAM
E2    374          AIRCRAFT ENGINE
E3   7706    40   *AIRCRAFT ENGINES
E4   2416    23    AIRCRAFT EQUIPMENT
E5     10          AIRCRAFT EXHAUST
E6     54          AIRCRAFT FUEL
E7     49          AIRCRAFT FUEL SYSTEM
E8    450     6    AIRCRAFT FUEL SYSTEMS
E9   1205    13    AIRCRAFT FUELS
E10  1308    11    AIRCRAFT GUIDANCE
E11    51          AIRCRAFT HAZARD
E12  1514    19    AIRCRAFT HAZARDS

            Enter P or E for more

 ? e e3

Ref  Items   Type  RT   Index-term
R1   7706          40   *AIRCRAFT ENGINES
R2      0     F     1    AIRCRAFT POWER SOURCES
R3    754     N    13    HELICOPTER ENGINES
R4      0     N     3    J-44 ENGINE
R5      6     N     7    J-52 ENGINE
R6     11     N     5    J-58 ENGINE
R7      0     N     2    J-84 ENGINE
R8     12     N     9    J-97 ENGINE
R9      2     N     9    T-34 ENGINE
R10     2     N     8    T-38 ENGINE
R11     6     N     6    T-55 ENGINE
R12    16     N     7    T-63 ENGINE
```

**Search 8.4:** (cont.)

```
        Enter P or E for more

Ref   Items   Type   RT   Index-term
R13      0    N       7   T-76 ENGINE
R14      0    N       8   T-78 ENGINE
R15     39    N       8   TF-30 ENGINE
R16     41    N       3   TF-34 ENGINE
R17     19    N       9   TF-41 ENGINE
R18    150    N       6   VARIABLE CYCLE ENGINES
R19     12    N       6   VARIABLE STREAM CONTROL ENGINES
R20    101    R       6   ACEE PROGRAM
R21     16    R       5   AIR START
R22    290    R       5   ENGINE AIRFRAME INTEGRATION
R23   7096    R      64   GAS TURBINE ENGINES
R24    163    R       5   HYDROGEN ENGINES

        Enter P or E for more

? e r23

Ref   Items   Type   RT   Index-term
R1    7096           64   *GAS TURBINE ENGINES
R2     762    B      43   AIR BREATHING ENGINES
R3   41306    B     203   ENGINES
R4    1192    B      98   INTERNAL COMBUSTION ENGINES
R5    1592    B      56   TURBINE ENGINES
R6      35    N      10   BRISTOL-SIDDELEY BS 53 ENGINE
R7      25    N       7   BRISTOL-SIDDELEY OLYMPUS 593 ENGINE
R8       1    N       7   BRISTOL-SIDDELEY VIPER ENGINE
R9       1    N       9   CF-700 ENGINE
R10     83    N       8   DUCTED FAN ENGINES
R11    163    N       5   HYDROGEN ENGINES
R12     17    N       8   INTEGRAL ROCKET RAMJETS

        Enter P or E for more

?s r9

    S1             1    CF-700 ENGINE ? t1/5

  1/5/1
0617913 N73-14984
  Pressures and temperatures on the lower surfaces of an externally
blown flap system during full-scale ground tests
    HUGHES, D. L.
    National Aeronautics and Space Administration. Flight Research Center,
Edwards, Calif.
    Place of Publication: Washington
    Publication Date: Jan. 1973 34P.
    Report No.: NASA-TN-D-7138; H-729
    Language: English
    Country of Origin: United States Country of Publication: United States
    Document Type: REPORT
    Documents available from AIAA Technical Library
    Other Availability: NTIS
    Journal Announcement: STAR7306
    Full-scale ground tests of an externally blown flap system were
made using the wing of an F-111B airplane and a CF700 engine.
Pressure and temperature distributions were determined on the under-
surface of the wing, vane, and flap for two engine exhaust
nozzles (conical and daisy) at several engine power levels and
```

**Search 8.4:** (cont.)

```
engine/wing positions. The test were made with no airflow over the
wing. The wing sweep angle was fixed at e6 deg; and the angle of
incidence between the engine and the wing was fixed at 3 deg; and the
flap was in the retracted, deflected 35 deg, and deflected 60 deg
positions. The pressure load obtained by integrating the local
pressures on the undersurface of the flap, F sub p was approximately
three times greater at the 60 deg flap position than at the 35 deg
flap position. At the 60 deg flap position, F sub p was between 40
percent and 55 percent of the engine thrust over the measured
range of thrust. More than 90 percent of F sub p was contained
within plus or minus 20 percent of the flap span centered around
the engine exhaust centerline with both nozzle configurations. Maxi-
mum temperatures recorded on the flaps were 218 C (424 F) and 180 C
(356 F) for the conical and daisy nozzles, repectively, (Author)
   Descriptors: *CF-700 ENGINE; *EXTERNALLY BLOWN FLAPS; *F-111
AIRCRAFT;*PRESSURE DISTRIBUTION; *TEMPERATURE DISTRIBUTION;AERODYNAMIC
CONFIGURATIONS; PERFORMANCE TESTS; VARIABLE SWEEP WINGS
   Subject Classification: 6501 Aerodynamics (1965-74)
   COSATI Code: 1B Aeronautics
```

There are several techniques available to limit retrieval to specific parts of the database. If you are interested only in items that are in *IAA* or *STAR*, enter JA=IAA or JA=STAR, respectively. If you have already used the NTIS database to retrieve records on your topic, you can use 'NOT AV=NTIS' to eliminate any records duplicated in both files.

AEROSPACE DATABASE has several free user tools that can be obtained by contacting the AIAA Technical Information Service, 555 W 57th St., New York, NY 10019, or (212)247/6500 ext. 243: a *List of Periodicals and Volumes Scanned for International Aerospace Abstracts* which is published annually; the *User's Guide to Scope and Coverage* is a subject indexed publication detailing the multidisciplinary coverage of published and report literature selected for inclusion in the database; the *Guide to Authority Lists* includes lists such as abbreviations used in the corporate source field, common acronyms, a country list, COSATI subject categories, subject category codes and names, and a language list.

The use of these publications along with the *NASA Thesaurus* will help in the development of more effective search strategies. In response to demands from its users, AIAA is also developing a product to be called AIAA Connection. This will provide AIAA members with several services including menu-driven access to the AEROSPACE DATABASE. The system is being produced in conjunction with DIALOG and is expected to be available by the end of 1991.

A CD-ROM version of AEROSPACE DATABASE was released at the end of 1990. It is available from DIALOG as another of its OnDisc products and is updated quarterly. AEROSPACE DATABASE can be purchased in either of two forms depending on the time periods you require - the current year plus one year backfile which represents over 102,000 records, or, the current year plus four years backfile representing over 296,000 records. The advantages of searching the CD-ROM product rather than the online version are the potential cost savings of searching without regard to hourly charges, and the availability of both an easy menu-driven system and a command mode for those acquainted with DIALOG's search software. Like other DIALOG OnDisc products, AEROSPACE DATABASE includes the Communications Manager that provides for quick access to DIALOG and the ability to search the online system for the latest information.

## INSPEC

While INSPEC primarily indexes the disciplines of electronic engineering and computer science which are outside the realm of this chapter, it does cover several interdisciplinary subjects and should not be overlooked. It should be considered when seeking information on materials, physics, instrumentation and education and training for engineers. Search 8.5 shows the file's coverage of titanium. Check the *INSPEC Thesaurus* for the broad range of subjects included in this file. INSPEC (International Information Services for the Physics and Engineering Communities) corresponds to the print copies originally known as *Science Abstracts* and now published as four complementary volumes: *Physics Abstracts, Electrical and Electronics Abstracts, Computer and Control Abstracts* and *IT Focus*. Since 1969 INSPEC has made this information available in its online database which is available on a number of hosts including BRS, CISTI, Data-Star, DIALOG, ESA-IRS, ORBIT and STN.

### Search 8.5: INSPEC on DIALOG

```
File    2:INSPEC 2 _ 69-91/9103B1
        (COPR. IEE 1991)
*****     Files 3 (1969-1982) and 4 (1983- )      *****
are also available

        Set     Items     Description
        ---     -----     -----------
? S TITANIUM/DE
        S1      23344     TITANIUM/DE (January 1969)
? S MECHANICAL PROPERTIES
        S2       9279     MECHANICAL PROPERTIES
? S MATERIAL PROPERTIES
        S3        591     MATERIAL PROPERTIES
? S S1 AND (S2 OR S3)
               23344      S1
                9279      S2
                 591      S3
        S4        631     S1 AND (S2 OR S3)
? T4/8/1-2

  4/8/1
03815659 INSPEC Abstract Number: A91030436
  Title: Structure and mechanical properties of Ti/sub 3/Al compact produced
by hot pressing of mechanically alloyed powder
  Language: Japanese
  Document Type: Journal Paper (JP)
  Treatment: Experimental (X)
  Descriptors: aluminium alloys; compressive strength; ductility; grain
refinement; grain size; mechanical alloying; plastic flow; powder
metallurgy; recrystallisation; superplasticity; titanium alloys;
transmission electron microscope examination of materials; X-ray
chemical analysis; X-ray diffraction examination of materials
  Identifiers: dynamic recrystallisation; grain refinement; grain structure
; superplastic flow; mechanical properties; hot pressing; mechanically
alloyed powder; X-ray diffraction; TEM observation; energy dispersive X-ray
analysis; ultra-fine grain; grain diameter; intermetallic compound; high
compressive strength; ductility; compressive fracture strain; 1173 K; 3.6
ks; 100 MPa; 1.5 micron; Ti/sub 3/Al compact
  Class Codes: A8120G (Specific metals and alloys (compacts, pseudoalloys))
; A8140L (Deformation, plasticity and creep); A8140E (Cold working, work
hardening; post-deformation annealing, recovery and recrystallisation;
textures); A8120E (Powder techniques, compaction and sintering);
```

**Search 8.5:** (cont.)

```
A6220F ( Deformation and plasticity)
  Chemical Indexing:
  Ti3Al bin - Ti3 bin - Al bin - Ti bin (Elements - 2)
  Numerical Indexing: temperature 1.173E+03 K; time 3.6E+03 s; pressure
1.0E+08 Pa; size 1.5E-06 m

  4/8/2
03815332 INSPEC Abstract Number: A91030611
  Title: Environmental effects on the mechanical properties of Co/sub 3/Ti
containing boron, carbon and beryllium
  Language: English
  Document Type: Journal Paper (JP)
  Treatment: Experimental (X)
  Descriptors: beryllium alloys; boron alloys; brittle fracture; cobalt
alloys; ductility; elongation; embrittlement; tensile strength; titanium
alloys; yield stress
  Identifiers: intergranular fracture; transgranular fracture; mechanical
properties; environmental effects; tensile testing; yield stresses;
elongation; ultimate tensile strength; embrittlement; ductility; 293 to
1173 K; Co/sub 3/Ti; Co/sub 3/Ti-C; Co/sub 3/Ti-B; Co/sub 3/Ti-Be
  Class Codes: A8140L (Deformation, plasticity and creep); A8140N (Fatigue,
embrittlement,  and  fracture);  A6220F  (Deformation  and  plasticity);  A6220M
(Fatigue,  brittleness,  fracture,  and  cracks)
  Chemical Indexing:
  Co3TiC ss - Co3 ss - Co ss - Ti ss - C ss (Elements - 3)
  Co3TiB ss - Co3 ss - Co ss - Ti ss - B ss (Elements - 3)
  Co3TiBe ss - Co3 ss - Be ss - Co ss - Ti ss (Elements - 3)
  Co3Ti bin - Co3 bin - Co bin - Ti bin (Elements - 2)
  Numerical  Indexing:  temperature 2.93E+02 to 1.173E+03  K
```

INSPEC was reloaded on both DIALOG and STN and the new version should be made available by other hosts during 1991. DIALOG now has INSPEC available in three files: the full INSPEC database from 1969, the older section of the Database, 1969-82 and the more recent information, 1983 to date. STN continues to offer only one INSPEC file covering 1969 to date.

Search aids in addition to the *INSPEC Thesaurus*  include the *INSPEC List of Journals and other Serial Sources* and the *User Update* newsletter. INSPEC also offers several free training workshops and customized, on-demand training. INSPEC has concluded an agreement with University Microfilms International to offer its database in CD-ROM format. It comprises a three-disc set, each disc containing approximately 250,000 records and covering a separate year (1989, 1990, 1991) with the most recent disc being updated quarterly. Additionally, three-year subsets of the INSPEC database will be available on CD-ROM: INSPEC PHYSICS and INSPEC ELECTRONICS/COMPUTER SCIENCE. University Microfilms International is introducing a new version of its search software which will include a dedicated thesaurus for precise subject definitions, a library holdings capability, inverted indexes for both words and phrases and a search option which will enable both American and British spellings to be retrieved.

There are additional general engineering and sub-speciality databases that may prove very useful. For the most part they are smaller databases; some may be difficult to access because availability is limited to the country of origin or they must be searched in non-English languages.

## AUSTRALIAN ENGINEERING DATABASE

This database, produced by the Institute of Engineers in Australia, has about twelve thousand citations with abstracts. Its focus is the Australian literature on engineering since 1980 including journal articles, monographs, conference papers and annual reports. It is updated with approximately 125 records per month. Australian Engineering Database is available on the CSIRO AUSTRALIS online service.

## BEFO

BEFO contains approximately 114,000 citations with abstracts primarily in German and titles also in English. It is produced by FIZ Technik and is an index to the world's literature on the management of engineering projects. It covers a variety of subfields including mechanical, electrical, electronic and biomedical engineering. The database is especially strong on quality control, project planning techniques and organizational aspects of production. DOMA and ZDE are two sources used to produce BEFO which is updated weekly with about 150 records. BEFO is mounted on the FIZ Technik online service.

## DOMA

DOMA, also produced by FIZ Technik and mounted on its online service, indexes primarily periodicals, monographs and conference proceedings dealing with mechanical engineering. DOMA contains approximately 530,000 records from 1970 and is updated weekly.

## ZDE

Dokumentation Elektrotechnik, ZDE, contains citations and abstracts of articles, books, patents, reports, dissertations and conference papers in the fields of control engineering, energy engineering, precision engineering, technical optics, measurement, communications and electrical engineering. It is available both from its producer, FIZ Technik and from Data-Star, and contains almost one million records with titles and index terms in English and German. Of the abstracts, approximately sixty per cent are in German and the remainder in English. ZDE is updated weekly with about 1,200 records.

## BIIPAM-CTIF

This database is mounted on ESA-IRS and is therefore widely available in both Europe and North America. It is produced by the Centre de Recherches de Pont-a-Mousson and the Centre Technique des Industries de la Fonderie. BIIPAM-CTIF contains about 85,000 citations with abstracts to industrial information in the field of engineering since 1979. Literature is covered in French, English and German, but searches must be conducted in French. Updating includes about 450 records every two months.

## CETIM

CETIM, produced by the Centre Technique des Industries Mecaniques covers primarily French mechanical engineering literature. It contains approximately 87,000 citations with abstracts and must be searched in French. It corresponds to *Bulletin de la Construction Mecanique*. It is updated monthly and spans the literature since 1975.

## CIVIL ENGINEERING DATABASE

CIVIL ENGINEERING DATABASE is available by subscription from the American Society of Civil Engineers. It contains about 35,000 citations with abstracts to the worldwide literature on civil engineering. It covers the subfields of aerospace, construction, structural engineering, and hydraulics among others. Sources include journals, books and conference proceedings. It is updated every two months and covers the literature since 1975.

## FLUIDEX

FLUIDEX is produced by BHRA, The Fluid Engineering Centre in Bedford, England. It provides indexing and abstracting of fluid engineering, including fluid mechanics, flow meters and measurements, flow dynamics, mixing and separation, fluid power, jet cutting and cleaning. Seventy per cent of the database is derived from twelve secondary abstract publications produced by BHRA. Nearly one thousand technical journals are indexed as well as books, conference proceedings, standards, patents and selected research reports from around the world. It is updated monthly with approximately 1,500 records added to the existing file of more than 230,000 items. FLUIDEX is useful for all types of fluid issues, aerospace as well as river and flood control.

## METADEX

METADEX, produced by Materials Information, a joint service of ASM International and The Institute of Metals, is available on most of the larger host systems. METADEX contains over 756,000 citations with abstracts (since 1979) to the world's technical literature on the science of metallurgy. The database covers from 1966 onwards on most hosts, but check the beginning date on your service as it can vary. METADEX corresponds to *Review of Metal Literature* (1966-67), *Metals Abstracts* (1968-date), *Alloys Index* (1974-date), *Steels Supplement* (1983-84) and *Steels Alert* (January-June 1985). It covers topics such as alloy production, properties, casting, melting, powder metallurgy, mining and ore preparation. Codes for specific alloys have been assigned to records since 1974 and allow access by alloy nomenclature, metallurgical systems and by the intermetallic compounds found in these systems.

DIALOG OnDisc offers a METADEX COLLECTION CD-ROM that includes three databases in one: METADEX (1985 to the present), MATERIALS BUSINESS FILE (1985 to the present) and ENGINEERED MATERIALS ABSTRACTS (1986 to the present).

## RAPRA ABSTRACTS

RAPRA ABSTRACTS is available on ORBIT and covers the time period from 1972 to the present. It is produced by RAPRA Technology Limited and corresponds to *RAPRA Abstracts, Adhesives Abstracts*, and *Advanced Materials Abstracts*. It is updated twice a month with about a thousand records and contains over 375,000 citations with abstracts to technical, commercial and research literature on the adhesives, plastics and rubber industries. Types of literature covered include periodicals, conference proceedings, books, patents, technical research reports, standards, trade literature, specifications and government publications. A CD-ROM version, THE PLASTICS AND RUBBER MATERIALS DISC, has just been announced and should be available in early 1991, containing records dating back to 1980. Updates are expected twice a year.

## TRIBOLOGY INDEX

TRIBOLOGY INDEX is offered online through FIZ Technik. It is produced by Bundesanstalt für Materialforschung und -pruefung - the German Federal Authority for Materials Testing. It contains over 64,000 citations to the worldwide literature on tribology, the science dealing with the design, friction, wear and lubrication of moving parts. It covers references to journals, standards, conference proceedings, books, reports and dissertations. Although produced in Germany, the database is in English with titles in the original language (if other than English). Updating is relatively infrequent - three times a year.

## WELDASEARCH

WELDASEARCH is produced by the Welding Institute and is currently available exclusively on ORBIT. It covers metallurgy literature since 1967 with emphasis on joining of metals and plastics, welding metallurgy, fatigue and fracture mechanics, thermal equipment, corrosion and quality control. It contains both citations and abstracts to research reports, patents, journal articles, books, standards, theses and special publications. There are about 100,000 citations in the database which is updated monthly.

## CONCLUSION

Engineering is well-represented in databases, especially some of the specialized databases that have been developed. Do not be afraid to try out a speciality database even if its name or primary focus does not appear to be relevant. Take advantage of the searching enhancements made available by the different vendors. For example, ORBIT's engineering database cluster or DIALOG's DIALINDEX or ONESEARCH. These are fast, inexpensive ways of checking files with which you might not be familiar. As you expand your knowledge of the various files you will be better aware of which subjects are on which databases and which will best fulfil your needs.

## REFERENCES

1.   Engineering. *McGraw-Hill Encyclopedia of Science & Technology*, vol 6. New York: McGraw-Hill, 1987, p.350

2.      Engineering. *Webster's Third New International Dictionary.* Springfield, MA: Merriam, 1976, p.752
3.      V.N. Anderson. Searching the engineering databases. *Database* 10(2) 1987 23-27
4.      D. T. Hawkins. Engineering. In C.J. Armstrong & J.A. Large (eds) *Manual of Online Search Strategies.* Aldershot: Gower, 1988, p.394
5.      *Directory of Online Databases* New York: Cuadra/Elsevier, 1990 (Updated quarterly)
6.      *COMPENDEX PLUS CHAPTER.* Palo Alto, CA: DIALOG Information Services, 1988, p.20

## FURTHER READING

Anderson, V. N. Searching the engineering databases. *Database* (10)2 1987 23-27

Ashling, J. K. INSPEC - The answer to the engineer's search for information. In *Conference Record - Electro volume 9.* Los Angeles: Electronic Conventions Management, 1984, pap19.4

Caputo, R. P. Survey of online bibliographic information databases useful to engineers. *Conference Record - Electro volume 8.* El Segundo, CA: Electronic Conventions Management, 1983, pap15.4

Schwarzwalder, R. COMPENDEX*PLUS improvements in engineering's premiere database. *Database* (12)4 1989 79-84

# 9 Computer and information science and technology

*David Raitt*

## INTRODUCTION

The purpose of this chapter is to give readers an overview of online and CD-ROM databases which could be searched for information in the fields of computer and information science and technology. These fields are rather broad - the computer field covering all aspects of mainframe and microcomputers, computer-aided design (CAD), software, data processing, computer applications, computer networks and communications; and information technology (IT) covering all aspects of information science and technology, not only in the more restricted sense of library and information scientists, but also including the aspects of chip manufacture, semiconductors, telecommunications, artificial intelligence (AI), microelectronics and so on, as IT is used in the context of the British and European information technology R&D programmes, Alvey and ESPRIT. Clearly this chapter is not able to describe all databases and show you how to do searches in all these areas!

Whilst there are well over one hundred databases dealing specifically with computers and software, most machine-readable databases - no matter what their primary subject coverage - will contain information on computers. Many will also contain material in the broad information science and technology domain. ERIC, the prime education database, for example, contains literature on computer-aided instruction and the use of microcomputers and IT in education as well as material on library automation. CHEMICAL ABSTRACTS contains information on the use of computers in chemistry; MEDLINE on computers in medicine; NASA/AEROSPACE on applications of computers in aerospace, and so on. Multidisciplinary databases like INSPEC, COMPENDEX, NTIS, SCISEARCH, PASCAL and WORLD PATENTS INDEX will also contain substantial numbers of references to computers and their applications, development or design. Even smaller or more specific databases will often contain much information on computers, software and IT: databases like MERLIN-TECH, ROBOMATIX, EDF-DOC and MATHSCI/MATHEMATICS. The latter database, for example, with strong coverage in the related disciplines of mathematics and statistics, recently announced coverage of *ACM Computing Reviews* and *ACM Guide to Computing Literature*. And then there are the databases which are more or less completely devoted to the subjects being looked at here.

Such databases are made available on a wide range of hosts - DIALOG, ESA-IRS, Telesystemes Questel, BRS, Pergamon ORBIT Infoline, Data-Star, CompuServe, NEWSNET, etc. Some, such as DIALOG and NEWSNET, have many of the specialist computer databases online; others have only one or two, often unique databases, such as the SERVICE DE BIBLIOGRAPHIQUE SUR L'INFORMATIQUE (SB-I) on G.CAM, which is produced by Paris Gestion Informatique and contains citations plus abstracts to French literature on such subjects as computer science, automation, robotics, microprocessors and videotex. This French-language database dates from 1978, contains around thirteen thousand references, mainly to journal articles, and is updated weekly with some three thousand items being added per year. COMPUTERS & MATHEMATICS SEARCH, from ISI, is a multidisciplinary index to the international literature of computer science, statistics, operations research and mathematics as well as computer applications in science, business, humanities etc. Besides articles, the database covers hardware, software and database reviews and includes citation indexing to enable searches by cited references. A special feature notes research fronts or areas covered by the articles and these equate to subject descriptors. The file dates from 1980 and contains some 420,000 records, being updated by one thousand items per week.

This chapter will describe some of the online databases which deal specifically with the computer and information science and technology fields on three hosts - ESA-IRS, DIALOG and NEWSNET. It will also cover their CD-ROM equivalents as well as some additional CD-ROMs in the field which could be profitably searched. A detailed comparison is all but impossible due to significant differences in subject orientation, scope and coverage, currency of information and database structure - all of which can affect the outcome of a search. However, while one cannot go into great depth on the philosophy and design behind the database, an attempt is made to note the indexing policy and consistency, update regularity, comparison with other databases where appropriate and so on. Such information can also be found in the documentation on the databases provided by each of the various hosts as well as in the specific user manuals from the database producers themselves. There are also several articles describing certain of the databases and these are noted in the appropriate places below when describing the databases. Several articles are, however, more general; Hawkins [1] mentions several databases covering computer sciences, such as THE COMPUTER DATABASE, INSPEC and SB-I, while Konings [2] compares and evaluates nine bibliographies/bibliographic databases in the field of computer science as regards their subject area, list of periodicals scanned, article coverage and overlap. A three-part series by O'Leary [3-5] surveys computer databases covering general information and news, applications and product databases.

## Finding out about the databases

Some databases, whether general or specific, will obviously be more useful than others for answering given questions. Clearly in trying to find out who has cited a certain paper on the use of public access microcomputers in municipal libraries, then SCISEARCH or SOCIAL SCISEARCH would be a logical place to start. For articles on the design of back-up power supplies for the onboard computers on the Space Shuttle, the NASA/AEROSPACE file would doubtless be best. Similarly to find out whether a particular paper in Russian had been translated into, say, Spanish, the WORLD TRANSLATION INDEX file would probably prove helpful. If you wanted to search with French keywords and retrieve French articles then PASCAL or SB-I would be first choice. For computer-related patents you might think of COMPUTERPAT or WPI while details on forthcoming computer or information industry conferences and meetings could be found in EI MEETINGS or MEETING AGENDA (on Questel) or FAIRBASE (on BRS, Data-Star and Fiz Technik). Computer company information could be sought on the KOMPASS files or the HOPPENSTEDT company databases on

Data-Star. If details were required, say, on an update of Fujitsu industrial statistics then you might try JAPAN COMPUTER INDUSTRY SCAN on NEWSNET, while if you were interested in the state of computer and information technology in the USSR, then you'd consider turning to SOVIET SCIENCE AND TECHNOL-OGY on DIALOG.

Obvious selections for obvious databases? Suppose you had a more general question which could probably be answered by searching several databases. For example, a search for information on the use and applications of onboard computers in cars (automobiles) might usefully be carried out on several databases like THE COMPUTER DATABASE, COMPENDEX, NTIS, MICROCOMPUTER INDEX or INSPEC. How do you know which is best? Indeed, how do you know about or find out about these databases in the first place? It's all very well to advise searching on SOVIET SCIENCE AND TECHNOLOGY or JAPAN COMPUTER INDUSTRY SCAN or SB-I - but how do you know such databases exist? Well, one way is to consult some of the many database and CD-ROM directories that are available (including online) such as the two-volume *Computer-Readable Databases* originally edited by Martha Williams. The subject index lists databases under computer hardware, computer industry, computer science, computer software, computers, data processing, information science, library science and so on. The main body of the text gives full details, including coverage, of the database and where they can be searched online. This Directory, with six thousand records, is online via DIALOG as COMPUTER-READABLE DATABASES (230) and is updated semi-annually. Another such directory is produced by Cuadra Associates and is also available online - on Data-Star as the CUADRA DIRECTORY OF DATABASES - while a third is Knowledge Industry Publication's DATABASE DIREC-TORY which is online via BRS. In the CD-ROM field one of the biggest and best publications is *The CD-ROM Directory* from TFPL Publishing. The 1991 fifth edition contains information on over 1,500 CD-ROM products as well as full details of the companies providing them. Meckler publishes *CD-ROMs in Print* and Cuadra Associates has produced the *Directory of Portable Databases* - which also includes databases on floppy diskette and magnetic tape.

Another way is to examine the listings of the databases made available by the different hosts - most publish a database catalogue as well as including the details online. A useful inventory of publicly-available online databases which are produced in the Nordic countries is published by SCANNET. Some hosts, for example ESA-IRS, DIALOG, and Data-Star, have a useful online facility which groups databases together (either pre-selected by the host or chosen or supplemented by the searcher) so that a search can be made automatically across all the databases in the group to see which (if any) contain references to the subject requested. Called QUESTINDEX on ESA-IRS and DIALINDEX on DIALOG, they give you, rapidly and economically, an idea of which databases may be best for your topic. The search is in reality only temporarily executed and it is still necessary to carry out the actual search in a particular database. (ESA-IRS also has a facility called QuestCluster where certain databases are grouped and the search is actually carried out in each of them. DIALOG's OneSearch command is similar, and NEWSNET also has a like capability.)

Among the many subject categories to choose from, ESA-IRS has a category for Computer Sciences and another for Information Science, Documentation and Information Management, while DIALOG has COMPSCI, SOFTWARE, PCINFO and INFOSCI. In addition, there is also EECOMP - a category for electrical engineering and computer science. It is possible to see which databases have been pre-selected in these categories by entering the commands ?EECOMP, ?SOFTWARE, ?PCINFO, ?COMPSCI and ?INFOSCI on DIALOG and the command ?QUESTINDEX on ESA-IRS (it will then be necessary to select various menu options to gain information on the category of interest). On both DIALOG and ESA-IRS it is also possible to create your own Dialindex or Questindex categories by selecting only the databases you want to be included. On NEWSNET there are three categories of interest: newsletters and services in the main category Electronics and Computers can be obtained by entering the command LIST EC; a list of services in two other relevant secondary categories can be viewed by entering HELP SOFTWARE and HELP INFOTECH. Unlike Dialindex and Questindex which give only temporary execution of a search, on NEWSNET a search is actually carried out on all the newsletters or services in a category with the results being displayable immediately (as in Questcluster and OneSearch available on ESA-IRS and DIALOG). In addition, NEWSNET has a somewhat similar feature to Questindex or Dialindex called Analyze though this is done after a search in a category rather than before and lists the actual newsletters in which hits appeared.

Tables 9.1 to 9.10 show the databases currently (late 1990) included in the various computer and information science and technology categories by ESA-IRS, DIALOG and NEWSNET. The choices for some might seem peculiar; for example, the Computer Engineering category on ESA-IRS omits such files as the BUSINESS SOFTWARE database (ABI/SOFT). A Questindex search on the Computer Engineering category (selected by entering simply Q T Computer) will actually be carried out on all the files in the list with the exception of EI MEETINGS and with the addition of HARD SCIENCES and TELECOM ABSTRACTS!

**Table 9.1: ESA-IRS Questindex databases relating to computer engineering**

| Name | File No. | Name | File No. |
|------|----------|------|----------|
| NASA | 1 | COMPENDEX | 4 |
| NTIS | 6 | INSPEC | 8 |
| PASCAL | 14, 205, 204 | SPACESOFT | 69 |
| ROBOMATIX | 84 | BUSINESS SOFTWARE | 89 |
| MATHEMATICS | 101, 80, 119, 191 | ARTIFICIAL INTELLIGENCE | 106 |
| CAD/CAM | 107 | EISD | 211 |

**Table 9.2: DIALOG Dialindex databases relating to computer science (COMPSCI)**

| Name | File No. | Name | File No. |
|------|----------|------|----------|
| NTIS | 6 | COMPENDEX PLUS | 8 |
| INSPEC 69-76 | 12 | INSPEC 77- | 13 |
| MICROCOMPUTER INDEX | 233 | MATHFILE | 239 |
| THE COMPUTER DATABASE | 275 | COMPUTER NEWS FULLTEXT | 674 |

**Table 9.3: DIALOG Dialindex files relating to personal computer information (PCINFO)**

| Name | File No. | Name | File No. |
|------|----------|------|----------|
| PTS PROMT | 16 | NEWSEARCH | 211 |
| MICROCOMPUTER INDEX | 233 | MICRO SOFTWARE DIR | 237 |
| SUPERTECH | 238 | BUSINESS SOFTWARE DB | 256 |
| THE SOFTWARE DIRECTORY | 263 | COMPUTER DATABASE | 275 |
| MICROCOMPUTER S/W GUIDE | 278 | MCGRAW-HILL PUBS ONLINE | 624 |
| BUSINESS DATELINE | 635 | PTS NEWSLETTER DB | 636 |
| TRADE & INDUSTRY ASAP | 648 | COMPUTER NEWS FULLTEXT | 674 |
| COMPUTER ASAP | 675 | | |

**Table 9.4: DIALOG Dialindex files relating to software (SOFTWARE)**

| Name | File No. | Name | File No. |
|------|----------|------|----------|
| MICRO SOFTWARE DIR | 237 | BUSINESS SOFTWARE DB | 256 |
| THE SOFTWARE DIRECTORY | 263 | MICROCOMPUTER S/W GUIDE | 278 |

**Table 9.5: DIALOG Dialindex files relating to electrical engineering and computer science (EECOMP)**

| Name | File No. | Name | File No. |
|------|----------|------|----------|
| NTIS | 6 | COMPENDEX PLUS | 8 |
| INSPEC 69-76 | 12 | INSPEC 77- | 13 |
| IHS INT. STANDARDS & SPECS | 92 | DOE ENERGY 83- | 103 |
| DOE ENERGY 74-82 | 104 | AEROSPACE DATABASE | 108 |
| PASCAL | 144 | COMPUTER DATABASE | 275 |
| COMPUTER ASAP | 675 | | |

**Table 9.6: NEWSNET newsletters in computers (main category EC - ELECTRONICS & COMPUTERS)**

| Newsletter Name | Service Code |
|-----------------|--------------|
| CONSUMER ELECTRONICS | EC01 |
| IMAGING UPDATE | EC05 |
| SEYBOLD OUTLOOK: PROFESSIONAL COMPUTING | EC20 |
| THE BUSINESS COMPUTER | EC22 |
| COMPUTER BOOK REVIEW | EC27 |
| JAPAN HIGH TECH REVIEW | EC28 |
| SEMICONDUCTOR INDUSTRY & BUSINESS SURVEY | EC35 |
| JAPAN COMPUTER INDUSTRY SCAN | EC39 |
| JAPAN SEMICONDUCTOR SCAN | EC43 |
| THE REPORT ON IBM | EC45 |
| OUTLOOK ON IBM | EC48 |
| JAPAN AUTOMATION REVIEW | EC49 |
| OPTICAL INFORMATION SYSTEMS UPDATE | EC51 |
| IDB ONLINE - THE COMPUTING INDUSTRY DAILY | EC55 |
| NASA SOFTWARE DIRECTORY | EC58E |
| MICROCOMPUTERS IN EDUCATION | EC59 |
| CAREER*EXCHANGE - THE COMPUTER FIELD | EC60 |
| HR/PC ONLINE | EC61 |
| MICROCOMPUTER RESOURCES | EC64 |
| CD COMPUTING NEWS | EC67 |
| THE VIDEODISC MONITOR | EC70 |

**Table 9.6:** (cont.)

| Newsletter Name | Service Code |
| --- | --- |
| CD-ROM DATABASES | EC71 |
| COMPUTERGRAM INTERNATIONAL | EC72 |
| TECHNICAL COMPUTING | EC73 |
| COMPUTER PROTOCOLS | EC74 |
| SUPERCONDUCTOR WEEK | EC75 |
| OPEN: OSI PRODUCT AND EQUIPMENT NEWS | EC76 |
| SNA COMMUNICATIONS REPORT | EC77 |
| SAA AGE - AN INSIDE LOOK AT IBM | EC78 |
| COMPUTER WORKSTATIONS | EC79 |
| PRODUCTIVITY SOFTWARE | EC80 |
| COMPUTERIZED PROCESSES | EC82 |
| NETLINE | EC86 |
| MAINFRAME COMPUTING | EC87 |
| NEWSBYTES NEWS NETWORK | EC89 |
| JAPAN CONSUMER ELECTRONICS SCAN | EC92 |
| AUDIO WEEK | EC93 |
| PC BUSINESS PRODUCTS | EC94 |
| NETWORKS UPDATE | EC95 |
| NETWORK MANAGEMENT SYSTEMS & STRATEGIES | EC96 |
| MODEM USERS NEWS | EC97 |
| LAN PRODUCT NEWS | EC99 |

**Table: 9.7: NEWSNET services covering computer software (secondary category - SOFTWARE)**

| Newsletter Name | Service Code |
| --- | --- |
| COMPUTER PROTOCOLS | EC74 |
| HR/PC ONLINE | EC61 |
| MAINFRAME COMPUTING | EC87 |
| MICROCOMPUTER RESOURCES | EC64 |
| NASA SOFTWARE DIRECTORY | EC58E |
| PRODUCTIVITY SOFTWARE | EC80 |
| SAA AGE - AN INSIDE LOOK AT IBM | EC78 |
| THE SOFTWARE LAW BULLETIN | LA13 |

**Table 9.8: NEWSNET services covering information technology (secondary category - INFOTECH)**

| Newsletter Name | Service Code |
|---|---|
| AUDIOTEX UPDATE | TE16 |
| CD COMPUTING NEWS | EC67 |
| COMMON CARRIER WEEK | TE26 |
| COMPUTERGRAM INTERNATIONAL | EC72 |
| DATA BROADCASTING REPORT | PB36 |
| EDI NEWS | TE80 |
| ELECTRONIC MESSAGING NEWS | TE05 |
| ELECTRONIC SERVICES UPDATE | PB33 |
| ENHANCED SERVICES OUTLOOK | TE81 |
| INSIDE MARKET DATA | PB37 |
| INTERACTIVITY REPORT | TE41 |
| MOBILE DATA REPORT | TE99 |
| NEWSBYTES NEWS NETWORK | EC89 |
| OPTICAL INFORMATION SYSTEMS UPDATE | EC51 |
| TELECOMMUNICATIONS REPORTS | TE11 |
| WORLDWIDE VIDEOTEX UPDATE | PB08 |
| THE VIDEODISC MONITOR | EC70 |
| VOICE TECHNOLOGY NEWS | TE02 |
| VIEWTEXT | TE18 |

**Table 9.9: ESA-IRS Questindex databases relating to information science, documentation and information management**

| Name | File No. | Name | File No. |
|---|---|---|---|
| NASA | 1 | NTIS | 6 |
| INSPEC | 8 | PASCAL | 14 |
| ABI/INFORM | 30 | INSPEC INFO SCI | 31 |
| ABI/SOFT | 89 | ELCOM | 93 |
| ULRICH'S | 103 | ARTIFICIAL INTELLIGENCE | 106 |

**Table 9.10: DIALOG Dialindex databases relating to library and information science**

| Name | File No. | Name | File No. |
|---|---|---|---|
| ERIC | 1 | NTIS | 6 |
| INSPEC 69-76 | 12 | INSPEC 77- | 13 |
| LISA | 61 | BRITISH EDUCATION INDEX | 121 |
| ONLINE CHRONICLE | 170 | INFORMATION SCIENCE ABS | 202 |

Taking the example above of onboard computers in cars, the quick and simple search (AUTOMOBILE? OR CAR? ?) AND ONBOARD(W)COMPUTER? showed that out of all the Questindex files in computer science INSPEC had twelve references, PASCAL and COMPENDEX had six each and NASA had one. All the other files in the category gave a zero response.

## DATABASES ON ESA-IRS AND DIALOG

It is apparent from the above figures that ESA-IRS and DIALOG cover a wide range of databases in their various computer and information science categories. They include multidisciplinary ones such as PASCAL and INSPEC; large subject-oriented ones like CHEMICAL ABSTRACTS, COMPENDEX, NASA/AERO-SPACE and MATHSCI; and smaller specialist ones like BUSINESS SOFTWARE and COSMIC. It is obvious that any multidisciplinary file and probably any large subject-oriented file will contain a reasonable proportion of references to computers, software, IT and information retrieval - thus, such files will not be considered here. Instead, some of the more specialist databases on ESA-IRS (E) and DIALOG (D) will be described briefly. CD-ROM versions of some of these databases are covered later in the chapter. Information is current as of December 1990 and has been taken in part from producer and host statements and descriptions.

Most of the databases on ESA-IRS and DIALOG have similar record structures and layouts, search fields, prefix/suffix codes (standardized) and limit and output possibilities. Because of space limitations the full record content with the complete range of access points or search fields for each database is not always given, and in most cases neither is a sample record (unless the database has unusual or different features) - these can be readily found in the general ESA-IRS and DIALOG user documentation for the system and databases as well as in the user aids from the database producers themselves. Such documentation will normally also include lists of classification/industry/category codes and lists of journals and other sources covered.

## COSMIC (E)

The COSMIC file (on ESA-IRS file 69 and formerly known as SPACESOFT) is produced by the Computer Software Management and Information Center (COSMIC), Georgia University, USA, and describes over 1,100 publicly available computer programs of interest to the aerospace industry and other high technology sectors. In addition to computer program packages developed under the auspices of NASA, a limited number of programs developed by other United States' government agencies, private concerns and universities is found in the COSMIC inventory. Subject fields include programs related to computer science and technology, aeronautics/astronautics, chemistry and materials, geosciences, physics and space sciences, life sciences, engineering, business and social sciences. The database dates from 1985 and is updated irregularly - the average annual increase being in the order of one hundred records. Each record contains a detailed description of the computer program and its capabilities, including abstract, program language, machine on which the program was developed, the program size, the standard distribution/media format, the price of the program source code and the supporting program documentation. Subject categories and controlled terms are also added for each record. Searchable fields include author, corporate source, program language and size, title, abstract, system (machine) requirements, distribution media, controlled terms and subject category. Each program source code and the supporting documentation is checked by COSMIC staff before being offered publicly to ensure that it is complete and can be implemented on designated machines. This database is the same as the one on NEWSNET called NASA SOFTWARE DIRECTORY and additional information will be found in the section on NEWSNET files below.

## NATIONAL COMPUTER INDEX (E)

The NATIONAL COMPUTER INDEX (NCI) database supplied by the National Computer Centre in England and on ESA-IRS as file 181, contains information on computer installations for organizations throughout the United Kingdom. For each organization the following searchable details are given: address, telephone and telex, name of DP manager, company turnover, budget, number of employees, hardware manufacturer, machine type, system value, software and peripherals, applications and comments. Several of the fields (such as the turnover and data processing budget) are grouped and searchable in ranges. The database is compiled from questionnaires returned to the National Computing Centre and is kept current by bi-monthly updates. There are around twenty thousand records online. As a gateway database, NCI is searchable with the BASIS retrieval language rather than ESA-QUEST. An NCI Database Manual is available from Pergamon Financial Data Services (PFDS).

## HARD SCIENCES (E)

This database consists of five subfiles: International Information Service in Mechanical Engineering (ISMEC 81-89); Solid State Abstracts; Health and Safety Sciences Abstracts; Electronics and Communications Abstracts; and Computer and Information Sciences Abstracts. The latter two subfiles constitute the ELCOM database which has been offloaded as a separate database from ESA-IRS. The HARD SCIENCES database (file 25 on ESA-IRS) is supplied by the Cambridge Information Group, Bethesda, USA and dates from 1981 to the present. It contains forty thousand records and adds some three thousand per month.

Subjects covered include: communications and telecommunications; computer engineering; data processing; hardware and software; electronics; information sciences; mechanical engineering; medicine (including pharmacology and toxicology); as well as related business and marketing aspects. The database covers worldwide journals, government reports, conference proceedings, dissertations and patents. Searchable fields include author and affiliation; bibliographic levels; classification codes and classification names; corporate source; environment; ISBN and ISSN; journal name; language; meeting details; report and patent numbers; patent details; as well as abstract, bio-taxonomic terms and controlled terms.

Marsden and Laub [6] describe the major characteristics and compare the strengths and weaknesses of three databases covering the computer science and electronics field - ELCOM (included in HARD SCIENCES), INSPEC and COMPENDEX. The selection policies of the databases are given, together with subject access possibilities and search aids. The comparison is made on coverage of disciplines (INSPEC and COMPENDEX being much broader than ELCOM), indexing (ELCOM does not use a controlled vocabulary unlike the other two - but this is not necessarily a disadvantage because of its narrower focus); journal coverage (ELCOM covers more newspapers and trade literature; INSPEC covers the most journals and more foreign-language ones); and currency of database content (INSPEC was most up-to-date, ELCOM the least). Sample searches were carried out on the three databases. The overall conclusion is that for comprehensive searches in computer science, all three databases would need to be searched.

## EISD (E)

The ENGINEERING AND INDUSTRIAL SOFTWARE DIRECTORY (EISD) file (number 211) is an objective, comprehensive and current reference guide to publicly available software for engineering, manufacturing and industrial applications. Produced by Engineering Information, Inc. (New York), its purpose is to enable the engineer, computer professional, manager or information specialist to identify available software packages and to obtain information about acquiring them.

The file covers programs that fall into key engineering disciplines, including: aerospace; architectural and civil; CAD/CAM; chemical, petroleum and mining; electrical, electronics, optical and control; environment; mechanical and materials; nuclear and energy; software engineering and transportation. It also includes programs that support engineering or industrial applications in, for example, physics, industrial engineering and mathematical methods, as well as general functions that are geared to the industrial and engineering communities such as accounting, information management and office systems.

The file is from 1980 to present (but also includes programs published from 1960 onwards), contains approximately 5,500 records and is updated semi-annually. Searchable fields include author/developer; classification name; subject headings; corporate source; country of vendor; distribution media; hardware; program language; operating system; source information; vendor; abstract; program name; and uncontrolled terms.

## ARTIFICIAL INTELLIGENCE (E, D)

This file, supplied by R. R. Bowker Company, New York, is concerned with all aspects of artificial intelligence and its related disciplines. The database covers such topics as expert systems; programming; image processing; computer architectures; algorithms; parallel processing; robotics applications; pattern recognition; CAD; and computer graphics. The time span covered by the file is from 1984 to the present and there are some ten thousand records with approximately two hundred being added per month. Search fields include author, corporate source, source data and classification codes as well as titles, abstracts and controlled terms. The database is available on ESA-IRS as file 106, while on DIALOG it forms a sub-file of SUPERTECH (file 238).

## CAD/CAM ABSTRACTS (E, D)

Again supplied by R. R. Bowker, New York, CAD/CAM covers articles, conferences, newspapers, market studies and government reports - on a worldwide basis - relating to computer aided design, testing and manufacture. The file includes aspects on: business and economics, human factors, graphics and imaging, computer-aided engineering, inspection and work monitoring, product design, product assembly, integrated factory systems, control systems and software, automation design and speciality applications as well as general and international news. The file dates from 1983 and updates by about two hundred references monthly. The current file size is nearly 11,500 items. Records include author and affiliation, title, abstract, source details, controlled terms, and classification codes. On ESA-IRS CAD/CAM is file 107; on DIALOG, however, it forms a subfile of SUPERTECH (file 238). ESA-IRS searchable fields include author, corporate source, classification codes, document type, source data, title, abstract and controlled terms. Additional searchable fields on DIALOG include document availability and patent numbers.

## BUSINESS SOFTWARE DATABASE (E, D)

The BUSINESS SOFTWARE database, from Information Sources Inc., Berkeley, California, consists of descriptions of software packages mainly for business use and covering applications such as: accounting; data processing; information management; economic analysis; financial analysis; financial management; marketing; advertising; sales; human resources and operations. The database places special emphasis on software for microcomputers and minicomputers and packages that are installed and supported including applications software, system software and utilities. Packages included are: database management programs, word processing, graphics, and commercial applications. IBM software is particularly well covered. The database was created in 1983 and adds some 250 new packages per quarter. The ESA-IRS version (file 69) contains nearly thirteen thousand items, while the DIALOG file (256) contains eighteen thousand.

There are two basic types of record - directory records and review records. Each directory record provides full company information, controlled index terms and a description of about 150 words plus operating systems, hardware, programming languages, price and terms, number of installations, training and documentation, and targetted users. All these fields are searchable on both ESA-IRS and DIALOG. In addition, there are review records which provide commentary about software products. These records come from reviews of individual packages as well as from evaluative, comparative and analytical articles. Each abstract may be up to 250 words. These review records are on DIALOG but not ESA-IRS. A cross-index links the software reviews with the directory records containing the basic information about the software products and vendors.

The BUSINESS SOFTWARE DATABASE can be used to find machine-compatible software, locate products or competitors, conduct competitive analyses, identify software for specific applications and so on. The producers, Information Sources Inc., also make available a guide to using the database. Called *Search Software* it covers the editorial policy, controlled terms, sample applications, rotated index, publication lists; search guides for DIALOG, Data-Star, BRS and the Human Resources Information Network, as well as search examples.

Critical user evaluations of BUSINESS SOFTWARE DATABASE have been carried out by Jacsó [7] who also compares it with two other online software directories - the ONLINE MICROCOMPUTER SOFTWARE DIRECTORY and .MENU - INTERNATIONAL SOFTWARE DATABASE [8]. Jacsó considers that the database provides good coverage of business software but its accuracy, currency and indexing policy leave much to be desired and result in lower search recall and precision than that of competitors. One of the major reasons for this is missing, incomplete or incorrect information on such matters as hardware or operating systems. Jacsó suggests that what is needed to improve the database is a precise, specific controlled vocabulary for hardware and operating system names and versions, as well as more complete and accurate information.

The BUSINESS SOFTWARE DATABASE is used as the base for SOFTWARE-CD - a CD-ROM produced by SilverPlatter.

## INSPEC (E, D)

INSPEC is produced by the Institution of Electrical Engineers in London, England. It indexes and abstracts journal articles, conference proceedings, books, reports, theses and patents in five main subject areas: physics; electrical engineering and electronics; control theory and technology; computers and computing; and information technology. Important relevant subject categories include: computer hardware; software and applications; business and industry applications; communications and computing systems; office automation; computer and information management; information science and technology; library automation; and computer and information science education. The database contains more than 3.6 million references and is growing at about 200,000 records per year. Journal articles comprise about eighty per cent of the file and some four thousand periodicals are regularly scanned.

About eighty per cent of the database is in English, though there is a significant proportion of Japanese and Russian material. Full bibliographical details plus an abstract are given and each record has controlled as well as free index terms. In addition, each document is assigned at least one classification code for the main subject with which it deals. Searchable fields include author, abstract, corporate source, patent and report numbers, source details, language, patent country and assignee, classification codes, document type, ISBN/ISSN, title, and controlled and uncontrolled terms. As INSPEC is a British file, both English and American spellings are used - much more so than in other (United States) databases. On ESA-IRS the database is file 8 and is updated two-weekly with some eleven thousand records, while on DIALOG file 12 contains the years 1969-1976 (nearly 950,000 items) and file 13 from 1977 to the present (over 2.5 million records, updated monthly).

Computing is a major subject area of the INSPEC database which currently contains some half a million abstracts with a further four thousand being added each month. The scope of computing ranges from circuits within computers to networks of computers, from microprocessor chips to superconductors, logic design, theory, computer vision, scientific and educational software packages, artificial intelligence, facsimile and electronic mail, teleconferencing, word processing, business applications and other related aspects.

INSPEC has been lengthily compared with COMPENDEX and ELCOM (see under HARD SCIENCES above) [6], and also with COMPENDEX and PASCAL (for a subject outside the scope of either computer or information science and technology); whilst INSPEC had a good coverage of the subject, inaccuracies in titles, abstracts and indexing made articles difficult to retrieve compared to the other two databases [9]. INSPEC is also compared with COMPENDEX and NTIS and other databases and with MICROCOMPUTER INDEX and THE COMPUTER DATABASE [10-12]. INSPEC has itself produced a thirty-five-page updated *Search Guide to Computing in the INSPEC Database* which is intended to serve as a guide to the many aspects of computers and their applications covered by INSPEC and to assist users when searching. The publication gives guidance in online (and manual) searching in the INSPEC database (and abstract journals) and provides an alphabetical index of thesaurus terms to the various areas of computing covered by INSPEC together with the classification codes used to specify them. The main INSPEC user manual also gives the classification codes not only for computing, but also for library and information science as well as all other subjects covered by the database.

It is worth noting that ESA-IRS has a special file called INSPEC TRAINING (file 39), which consists of some 45,000 records from 1977 and which allows users to gain search experience with the file at a cheap rate. DIALOG has a similar online file of some twenty thousand records from March 1987 called ONTAP INSPEC (file 213). These training files are mere frozen (in time) subsets of INSPEC and are thus not treated separately here. ESA-IRS also has another file called INSPEC INFORMATION SCIENCE (file 31) which dates from 1969, but does not appear to have been updated since 1986. Containing over twenty thousand records it is a subset of the main INSPEC database and covers references to the literature of information science and documentation, information services and centres, information generation, dissemination and use of information, publishing and reprography, translations, information analysis and indexing, and information storage and retrieval.

## THE COMPUTER DATABASE and COMPUTER ASAP (D)

THE COMPUTER DATABASE, produced by Information Access Company, Foster City, California, provides wide-ranging information on computers, telecommunications and electronics for the business and computer professional. The file contains abstracts from a wide range of predominantly North American literature sources - more than 650 journals, newsletters, tabloids and proceedings - indexed and abstracted cover-to-cover, and is designed to answer questions from business and computer professionals relating to hardware, software, peripherals and services. It also provides information on high-technology fields and gives product evaluations, comparisons, best buys, etc. By agreement with major publishers, significant coverage of the newest computer-related books and self-study courses are also available. The file began coverage in 1983 and now has over 453,000 references with weekly updates of approximately 1,500 citations. Records include author, title and source details, abstract, controlled descriptors, industry identifiers, etc. Additional useful information includes an indication of the role of the companies discussed in the articles, names of operating systems and products or people that are given significant mention. All these fields are searchable. Special features include bibliographies, illustrations and tables of contents for given journal issues. Records for hardware and software reviews are annotated as such and are indexed with the article type 'Evaluation'.

The database, on DIALOG as file 275, contains the full-text of records for more than fifty magazines, although the text is not searchable. For that you must turn to the companion COMPUTER ASAP database (file 675), also from Information Access and dating from 1988 (selected coverage from 1983) with currently over 121,000 records. Updated weekly, COMPUTER ASAP provides complete text and indexing for seventy per cent of the articles currently indexed in THE COMPUTER DATABASE (File 275). Contents include information on industry, products, companies, and people as well as technical information on programming, systems management and computer design. The full text of each article is searchable and complete articles may be retrieved and displayed online. As noted above, records in file 675 are also available in THE COMPUTER DATABASE where the text portion of these records is displayable but not searchable. COMPUTER ASAP provides coverage of the following computer-related areas: business and industry applications; company names and information; computer games; computer graphics; computer systems and equipment; consumer information; database management; electronics; computer-related financial information; hardware design; development; reviews; home computers; interfaces; letters to the editor; microprocessors; new products; performance evaluation; programming languages; operating systems; prototyping; robotics; software design and development; software reviews; telecommunications; and word processing. COMPUTER ASAP includes forty-six of the most widely circulated English-language journals and magazines on computers, electronics, and telecommunications including such titles as *UA+, Communications of the ACM, Datamation, Digital Review, Government Computer News, Infosystems, MacUser, MIS Week, PC Magazine, PC Tech Journal, PC Week* and *UNIX Review*. A training file, ONTAP COMPUTER DATABASE (file 805), containing some 20,500 records from 1986-1987 is available for online training and practice. While the training file does contain the full text of articles it is not searchable.

Bruckner summarizes the experience accumulated by computer professionals at Hungary's largest computer engineering and education company during use of THE COMPUTER DATABASE with regard to the subject coverage of the computing field, sources abstracted and indexed, record content and indexing practice [11]. Comparative quick-and-dirty searches were carried out on a number of databases including ERIC, COMPENDEX, NTIS, .MENU, and MICROCOMPUTER INDEX as well as THE COMPUTER DATABASE. Recall and precision of the retrieved references were measured and they showed favourable results for THE COMPUTER DATABASE. In addition the record content for the same document in different databases was compared and it was demonstrated that the records of THE COMPUTER DATABASE were very informative. Despite the fact that the majority of references in the database are from North American periodicals and there are only a few books and courses, THE COMPUTER DATABASE is considered to be a very useful source for computer professionals. A very brief comparison with INSPEC and MICROCOMPUTER INDEX is made by Jacsó [12], while Childress compares it with three other databases in the library and information science domain [13]. Broun examines THE COMPUTER DATABASE and COMPUTER ASAP in depth giving details of file organization, sample records and searches, documentation and support, and brief comparisons to closely-related sources [14].

Information Access Company also makes THE COMPUTER DATABASE available on CD-ROM.

## MICROCOMPUTER INDEX (D)

MICROCOMPUTER INDEX, from Learned Information Inc, Medford, New Jersey, corresponds to the print publication of the same name and is on DIALOG as file 233. It contains citations to the literature on the use of microcomputers in business, education and the home. Included are general articles, book reviews, software and hardware reviews, new product announcements, discussions of applications in various areas and so on, from over eighty mainly United States popular microcomputer journals, such as *Byte, Commodore, The Microcomputer Magazine, Home Computer Magazine, PC Magazine, PC Week, PC World*, etc. In addition, it covers some thirty-five other publications in the microcomputer field (for example, *Popular Electronics, Online, Educational Technology*). The INDEX is limited mostly to United States' and Japanese applications and products. Approximately ninety per cent of the records in the database contain informative abstracts and a controlled vocabulary is used for subject indexing. Searchable fields include abstract, title, controlled descriptors, identifiers, program listings, author, journal name, publication year, language, ISSN and geographic location. The abstracts give an indication of the rating a product received and also an indication of whether an article includes source codes. The file dates from 1981 and contains some 97,000 records with about one thousand records being added each month. Software review coverage has been expanded to include library, chemical engineering, medical and legal applications with information about specifications, list price and publisher/manufacturer being provided. The database also includes *Softwhere? Bargains Report* - a monthly buyers guide to the fifty topselling software packages. Details (easily identified using DT=DISCOUNT PRICE) include product name, price, lowest selling distributor, specifications and so on. Full *Softwhere? Bargains Report* records are displayed using Format 9. An additional special feature of the database is short, full-text computer book reviews provided by the publication, *Computer Book Review* (DT=BOOK REVIEW FULLTEXT or JN=COMPUTER BOOK REVIEW). These records are displayed in full using Format 5.

A user evaluation has been carried out by Jacsó [12], who critically reviews the scope, subject and source coverage, currency, indexing policy and searchability of the database. Results of example comparative searches for MICROCOMPUTER INDEX, THE COMPUTER DATABASE and INSPEC are given. The database was found to be adequate for any microcomputing-related searches. It provides informative though somewhat redundant bibliographic citations to publications of the popular and technical press, with fairly consistent indexing in terms of terminology, but rather unpredictable assigning of product names to the descriptor or identifier fields. Many of the additional indexes (prefix search fields) are considered to be unnecessary and do not enhance the searchability of the file, The database is recommended by Jacsó for computer practitioners who are satisfied with finding references to costly American computing magazines and newspapers and who want to learn the sources of product reviews, announcements, industry news and solutions to practical problems.

## LIBRARY AND INFORMATION SCIENCE ABSTRACTS (D)

LIBRARY AND INFORMATION SCIENCE ABSTRACTS (LISA) corresponds to the British Library Association's printed index of the same name and is on DIALOG as file 61. It covers the field of library and information science as well as such related areas as publishing, bookselling and reprography. Videotex, word processing, computer conferencing, archiving, education, mass media and non-book materials are included as well as information storage and retrieval, library automation, library history, library technical processes and library users and user behaviour. Material is drawn from more than 550 journals and periodicals from sixty countries as well as bulletins, conference proceedings, books, theses, technical reports and research project documentation. The file dates from 1969 and contains over 113,000 records and is updated monthly by about five hundred records. Searchable fields include authors and investigators, corporate sources, language, journal name, abstract, descriptors, section headings and section heading codes, which are the same as those in the printed version. As this is a British file, both English and American spellings will need to be employed in searches.

There are several articles discussing library and information databases, particularly LISA. LaBorie [15] attempts to answer the question 'what databases can information specialists use to find information about their field?' by examining several databases such as LISA, ERIC, INSPEC, NTIS and SCISEARCH. Format and language of material indexed, duplication of journal coverage and subject coverage are considered. LISA has the most divergent coverage of non-English language materials and, of course, specializes more than others in the library and information science literature. ERIC and NTIS cover a much greater proportion of technical report literature. Sample searches showed little difference in the average subject retrieval capability of LISA, ERIC, INSPEC and NTIS.

In an article by LaBorie and Halperin a study is described to assess the ability of the ERIC and LISA databases to support the research needs of library science students [16]. Subject searches on the two databases were performed to retrieve citations listed in students' bibliographies. The findings showed that a high percentage of the citations in the students' lists were not in either database (ERIC had thirty-six per cent, LISA twenty-eight per cent); that there was considerable duplication (thirty-one per cent) of citations retrieved from the two databases; and that ERIC was the preferred database when an exhaustive search was not required primarily because of the cheaper connect-time cost. A comparison of the indexing in LISA and ERIC of three journals devoted to online searching is made by Sievert and Verbeck [17]. On average LISA assigned more terms per document, though ERIC indexed more concepts per document. Childress [13] offers a critique of four databases covering the library and information science field (LISA, ERIC, INFORMATION SCIENCE ABSTRACTS (ISA) and THE COMPUTER DATABASE).

Although not referring to online databases, another paper gives some information on the coverage in this field by the printed abstract journal equivalents. The characteristics of library and information science literature were examined by Bottle and Efthimiadis who sampled issues of LISA, INFORMATION SCIENCE ABSTRACTS (ISA) and other relevant abstract journals [18]. Aspects looked at included language coverage (ISA worst, LISA next worst), currency of the abstract services (ISA and LISA both poor), coverage of journal titles (ISA had highest coverage of unique publications), and country of journal origin (LISA was good, especially for less-developed countries); LISA also had the most balanced coverage.

LISA is also available on CD-ROM from SilverPlatter - see below.


## INFORMATION SCIENCE ABSTRACTS (D)

This database, on DIALOG as file 202, is produced by IFI/Plenum Data Company, Alexandria, Virginia, and provides references and abstracts in the broad fields of information and library science. The international coverage includes over 450 journals as well as bibliographies, books and monographs, conferences, symposia, meetings, directories, patents, reports, theses and dissertations. INFORMATION SCIENCE ABSTRACTS (ISA) covers literature in the following broad subject categories: information science-documentation; libraries, information services; information generation, reproduction and distribution; information recognition and description; storing and retrieving of information; utilization of information; supporting studies and techniques (including psychology, mathematics, logic, etc.) as well as related fields such as computer science, translating, telecommunications, copyright, publishing, technical writing and education.

Core journals, report series and conference series are abstracted completely. Titles are generally given in the language of the original with an English translation; all abstracts are in English. Journal locations are also given within references to journal articles. Searchable fields include author and affiliation, source details, title, abstract, and controlled and uncontrolled index terms. Online since 1966 the file is updated nine times a year with approximately 1,500 records per update and currently contains over 131,000 records. (A comparison of ISA with other databases is given in references [13] and [18].)

## BUYER'S GUIDE TO MICRO SOFTWARE (SOFT) (D)

The BUYER'S GUIDE TO MICRO SOFTWARE (SOFT), produced by Online, Inc., is a directory of business and professional microcomputer software available in the United States. Online on DIALOG as file 237, it provides directory, product, technical, and bibliographic information on leading software packages, integrating this information into one succinct, composite record. The SOFT database can help professionals locate suitable packages compatible with specified hardware without sifting through large numbers of records. The file is highly selective, listing packages rated at least 'good' by the technical press, all packages from major software producers (even if negatively reviewed), and packages unique to specific business segments. In addition to leading microcomputer software packages and producers, emphasis is placed on library and medical software. Each record includes directory information, technical specifications including required hardware and operating systems, an abstracted product description, and, when available, a full citation to representative reviews. Different points of view are reflected by multiple reviews and reviews carry brief abstracts and evaluative comments.

Data are derived from information received directly from software producers, advertisements, press releases, and microcomputer magazines and books. Records are written, classified, and indexed by information professionals; listings are provided free to publishers selected for inclusion. Records are regularly updated and current reviews added when available. Controlled vocabulary is used to index the Application field. The database is current and contains over six thousand software descriptions.

## THE SOFTWARE DIRECTORY (D)

THE SOFTWARE DIRECTORY is a comprehensive database of information on current commercially available microcomputer software. The database corresponds to the print product of the same name. THE SOFTWARE DIRECTORY can help professionals in a variety of fields to find information on software packages relevant to their individual needs. Each entry includes vendor information; technical specifications such as required hardware and memory; a brief product description; special features; and, in many cases, a longer, more detailed product description. Controlled vocabulary is used to index the descriptor field. When available, records also contain information on warranties, demonstration disks, updates, backups, integrated packages, and shareware. Some records also contain brief citations to published software reviews. Most of these fields are searchable. Source data are derived from information received directly from over five thousand software publishers as well as industry sources, such as press releases, periodicals, and trade shows. Listings are regularly reviewed and updated. The database is on DIALOG as file 263 and contains over 36,000 currently available microcomputer software packages.

## ONLINE CHRONICLE (D)

File 170 is the ONLINE CHRONICLE - the electronic news journal of Online, Inc., serving as the much expanded online version of the news pages from these journals: *Online, Database* and *CD-ROM Professional*. Their news sections contain a wide variety of short items on all aspects of professional online and CD-ROM database activities and products, as well as public service announcements and notices, and information utilities. The file also contains a JOBLINE section - free classified advertisements for positions available and sought in the online industry, with a table of contents record for the previous six months. Each record may be a single news item or a cluster of related items, for example, peopleware, meetings and conferences, search aids and publications. Each news item is a textual record that is supplemented by keyword indexing from a controlled vocabulary. A table of contents record is included for each update.

Information for the ONLINE CHRONICLE comes from correspondents in the United States and Europe who are active in the online, CD-ROM, and other optical media fields. In addition, numerous press releases, professional and trade newsletters, and journals are scanned to keep ONLINE CHRONICLE users abreast of new research, development and late-breaking news. The file covers October 1981 to the present and contains nearly seven thousand records.

## MICROCOMPUTER SOFTWARE GUIDE (D)

The MICROCOMPUTER SOFTWARE GUIDE database (file 278 on DIALOG) contains information on virtually every microcomputer software program and hardware system available or produced in the United States. The database, produced by R. R. Bowker Company, New York, contains bibliographic records for all types of microcomputer software, including business, professional, consumer, educational, utility, and application. Each record includes ordering information, technical specifications, subject classifications and a brief description. Searchable fields include title, abstract, descriptors, programmer, hardware, operating system and programming language amongst others. Source data is derived from four thousand software publishers, as well as industry sources such as press releases, periodicals, and books. Reloaded monthly, the file, which is current, contains nearly 31,000 records.

## COMPUTER NEWS FULLTEXT (D)

The COMPUTER NEWS FULLTEXT database (file 674) contains cover-to-cover, full-text articles from *Computerworld* (since August 1989) and *Network World* (since October 1989), publications of IDG Communications, Inc., a leading publisher of nearly 120 computer-related magazines. As of July 1990 the file contains seven thousand records covering computers and networks as well as electronics and telecommunications. Emphasis is on news about industry developments and trends, systems management, hardware and software, management and marketing strategies, as well as product reviews. While the full text of the file can be searched it is also possible to search words in the titles, headlines and captions as well as authors, dateline phrase, journal name, section heading, publication year, etc.

## SEARCHING ON ESA-IRS AND DIALOG

### Basic features

The ESA-IRS QUEST and DIALOG search languages, since they both stem from the same root, are sufficiently similar in their basic commands for a user to be able to switch easily between the two. (Some history and several differences between the two search languages were given in the first edition of this chapter [19].) The basic commands for each are BEGIN (to choose a database in which to search); SELECT (to retrieve terms); EXPAND (to display database indexes); COMBINE (to manipulate sets logically); TYPE/DISPLAY (to show output of searches online); PRINT (for offline output); DISPLAY SETS (to get an overview of sets created); SAVE/EXECUTE (for storing, recalling and executing search strategies); LIMIT (for restricting a search to certain criteria); KEEP (to place selected references in a special set); ORDER (to permit online ordering of documents); and EXPLAIN (for online explanatory text of commands, searchable fields, database contents etc). In addition to the basic commands, each system has several unique commands and features such as REPORT, MAP, and SORT, ID/RD (duplicate elimination) in DIALOG and ZOOM, Cluster and the Common Command Language option in ESA-IRS.

Since the QUEST command language of ESA-IRS as well as the database record structures are so similar to those of DIALOG, it is proposed to treat the search aspects together. Databases on ESA-IRS and DIALOG can be searched pretty much the same way. In addition, most of the databases have similar record structures and layouts, search fields, prefix/suffix codes (standardized) and limit and output possibilities. The basic (subject) index is usually made up of words taken from the title, abstract and descriptors (controlled and uncontrolled terms) where these are provided. Additional indexes normally allow access via prefix codes to most of the other fields constituting the record. It is probably self-evident to any searcher, whether familiar with the computer literature or not, that it is always necessary to include synonymous terms (for example, microcomputer, microprocessor, personal computer, portable computer, desk top computer, laptop computer); abbreviations (micro, pc, etc); alternative spellings (CDROM, CD-ROM, CD ROM, CD/ROM); and to watch the different meanings of the same term (for example, APOLLO can refer to a computer, a satellite document delivery system and a space vehicle amongst other things). These quirks occur in all databases whether controlled or not and thus search strategies are not necessarily dependent on the subject field.

While, as a general rule, the databases can be searched in a standard and similar manner to most other databases, there are times when some of the special features that hosts offer may be usefully employed.

## Using term frequency lists

The ZOOM feature on ESA-IRS can be used to improve recall. ZOOM statistically analyses the contents of the current search results and provides a frequency list of terms appearing in selected fields of the records in a given set. There are many ZOOM options: most recent references, authors, corporate sources, words, controlled terms, classification codes, molecular formulae, titles, etc and more than twenty thousand records can be ZOOMed at a time. If no set is specified then the command samples the last set created (a maximum of fifty records unless more are specified) and if no fields are specified then only words from the controlled and uncontrolled terms fields (if present) will be extracted. The command format is Z followed by the set number, number of references required, and field - for example, Z6(100)AU.

A search on INSPEC on the full colour systems used in flat panel electronic displays devices provides an example. Knowledgeable searchers might add in the various types of active and passive flat panel display technologies such as electrochemical, vacuum fluorescent, light-emitting diode, cathodoluminescence, plasma, liquid crystal, electroluminescence and so on. But searchers new to the field of computer science and technology probably would not know these terms. So what approach could be used? You might start with a quick and dirty search using just the terms 'full colour' and 'flat panel displays'. On the resulting combination, the ZOOM command would produce a list of frequently occurring terms or keywords in the references some of which could then be incorporated into the search (Search 9.1). If, for example, you just augmented the search by selecting gas discharge displays, electroluminescent displays, plasma displays and liquid crystal displays, you would more than quadruple your search output from 36 to 162 references!

ZOOM can be used not only to find additional terms which are virtually synonyms of the original terms, but also to point to specific terms which are not synonymous. Say, for instance, you want to find out about microcomputer applications in libraries. Knowing no applications or possibilities, you do not know where to look. Simply by selecting and combining microcomputers and libraries followed by a ZOOM on the titles and

## Search 9.1: Use of ZOOM on ESA-IRS

```
ENTER-sflat(w)panel(w)display?
       1        741     FLAT(W)PANEL(W)DISPLAY?
ENTER-sfull(w)colour;sfull(w)color
       2        213     FULL(W)COLOUR
       3        411     FULL(W)COLOR
ENTER-c1*(2+3)
       4         36     1*(2+3)
ENTER-zoom

                       Text Analysis Results
Frq  Words/Phrases       Frq  Words/Phrases       Frq  Words/Phrases
---  -------------       ---  -------------       ---  -------------
41   FLAT PANEL               DISPLAYS            2    AIRCRAFT
     DISPLAYS            5    PLASMA DISPLAYS           INSTRUMENTATION
24   LIQUID CRYSTAL      5    VACUUM              2    AUTOMOBILES
     DISPLAYS                 FLUORESCENT         2    COMPUTERISED
9    ELECTROLUMINESCENT       DISPLAYS                 INSTRUMENTATION
     DISPLAYS           3    COLOUR TELEVISION   2    CONTRAST
9    LCD                      RECEIVERS           2    COST
9    THIN FILM          3    CRT                 2    DISPLAY AREA
     TRANSISTORS        3    DISPLAY DEVICES     2    DISPLAY
6    CATHODE RAY TUBE   3    FLAT DISPLAYS            INSTRUMENTATION
     DISPLAYS           3    HIGH RESOLUTION     2    ELECTROLUMINESCENT
6    FLAT PANEL DISPLAY       FULL COLOR         2    ELECTROLUMINESCENT
6    SILICON                  DISPLAY                 PANEL
5    AMORPHOUS          3    LIQUID CRYSTAL      2    ELECTRON
     SEMICONDUCTORS          DISPLAY                  MULTIPLIERS
5    ELEMENTAL          3    RESOLUTION          2    GRAPHICS
     SEMICONDUCTORS     3    SCREENS DISPLAY     2    HIGH RESOLUTION
5    GAS DISCHARGE      3    480 PIXEL           2    INSULATED GATE
...Pages.Lines: More=  7.47

5      2788     LIQUID(W)CRYSTAL(W)DISPLAY?
6       730     ELECTROLUMINESCENT(W)DISPLAY?
7       701     GAS(W)DISCHARGE(W)DISPLAY?
8      2014     LCD? ?
9       755     PLASMA(W)DISPLAY?
10      162     (2+3)*(1+5+6+7+8+9)
```

controlled and uncontrolled terms of the resulting set, applications of microcomputers for such tasks as cataloguing, word processing, collection development, circulation, etc would be readily apparent.

A different use of ZOOM is illustrated in Search 9.2 to find out which journals had recently published articles about the use of CD-ROMs in developing countries. On INSPEC, for instance, you could enter the terms and then ZOOM on journal names (cd?rom? will pick up both singular and plural versions of both cd rom and cd-rom).

## Search 9.2: Using ZOOM with journal names

```
ENTER-find (cd?rom? or cdrom?) and developing countr?
       1       1441     CD?ROM?
       2         55     CDROM?
       3       2228     DEVELOPING(W)COUNTR?
       4         17     (1+2)*3
```

**Search 9.2:** (cont.)

```
ENTER-zoom  jn

                       Text Analysis Results
Frq  Words/Phrases                    Frq  Words/Phrases
---  -------------------------        ---  -------------------------------------
4    Q BULL INT ASSOC AGRIC LIBR           MANAGEMENT
     DOC NETHERLANDS                  1    ELECTRON OPT PUBL REV UK
3    QUARTERLY BULLETIN OF THE        1    HER LIBR SCI INDIA
     INTERNATIONAL ASSOCIATION OF     1    HERALD OF LIBRARY SCIENCE
     AGRICULTURAL LIBRARIAN           1    INFORMATION DEVELOPMENT
2    INF DEV UK                       1    INT FORUM INF DOC USSR
2    MICROCOMPUT INF MANAGE USA       1    INTERNATIONAL FORUM ON
2    MICROCOMPUTERS FOR INFORMATION        INFORMATION & DOCUMENTATION
```

You could take this a stage further by then checking which authors had written anything on the subject as in Search 9.3.

**Search 9.3: ZOOMing on authors**

```
ENTER-zoom  au
                     Text Analysis Results
Frq  Words/     Frq  Words/       Frq  Words/       Frq  Words/
     Phrases         Phrases           Phrases           Phrases
---  ----------  --- ------------  ---  -----------  ---  -----------
2    BRITO C J   1   BALSON D      1    HUSAIN N     1    RAVI A
2    NAZIM ALI S 1   BEAUMONT J    1    JONES F G    1    RITZLER C
2    VAN         1   DEXTRE        1    METCALFE J R 1    SEVER S
     HARTEVELT       CLARKE S      1    MOORE N L    1    WEISS J W
     J H W       1   FENICHEL C H  1    MOORTHY A L
1    ABID A      1   HELAL A H     1    MURTHY S S
```

A new feature introduced by ESA-IRS in December 1990 is HYPERLINE which provides document and concept browsing as opposed to searching. The menu-driven interface allows a non-sequential associative way of reading documents - as in hypertext. Entering the command HL (or HYPERLINE) without specifying a topic will provide a list of the ten or so databases in which the feature can be run (those with a thesaurus). Once in a file, entering HL followed by a topic will set the system working (slowly!) to find related topics. Once the list of concepts is ready then the system will show the document references, or allow you to browse more terms. The main functions of HYPERLINE include navigating through the thesaurus network of broader, narrower, top and related terms; viewing documents (that is, references) containing terms in the thesaurus hierarchy; creating document sets; preparing a list of terms linked to the references conceptually related to the one currently being viewed; the preparation of a list of terms linked to documents on a given concept; and the ability to display a history of functions executed during the navigation process. In so far as computer and information technology searches are concerned HYPERLINE can be used in the INSPEC database and, less relevantly, on the COMPENDEX, NASA and NTIS databases.

DIALOG also has a facility to extract terms, though not in the same way as ESA-IRS. This is the MAP feature which automatically extracts and saves search terms from specified fields from records in a set. The strategy thus created can be executed later on in the same file or on different files exactly as the normal SAVE SEARCH command. Initially intended for use with the CHEMICAL ABSTRACTS Registry Numbers the MAP command can be used on many other databases with other search fields (for example, on patent and report numbers, patent assignees, D-U-N-S numbers, and other patent classification codes). This is presently not a command that can easily and usefully be used in the computing and library/information fields.

## Using classification codes

Recall can also be improved by the use of classification codes where these are available. Classification or category codes often provide an effective means for locating information on a given subject - though this can depend on indexing philosophy and consistency and the availability of full-text searching. INSPEC is a database where classification codes are extensively used, with every bibliographic reference being assigned at least one code to denote primary subject matter. COMPENDEX, as well as HARD SCIENCES, also uses codes to classify information into broad categories such that a search can be restricted to the more relevant portions of the database. As on INSPEC codes can be logically combined, truncated or used with free text words to focus a search.

As an example of their use on INSPEC, consider a search for information on the testing and performance of microcomputers. This could involve lengthy entry of terms such as performance, evaluation, benchmark tests, simulation, operating conditions, analysis and the like on one side and terms like microcomputers, microprocessors, portable computers, personal computers, laptops etc on the other. Such a search can quickly be done on INSPEC using classification codes because there is one which precisely covers the topic performance evaluation and testing of analogue and digital computers and systems (C5470) and another which covers microcomputers and its synonymous terms (C5430). Selecting and combining merely these two codes gives a total of 136 references (June 1990) which is probably ample.

## Using cross-file search capabilities

The power of Questindex and Dialindex should not be underestimated. They are extremely valuable to give you an idea of what a database is likely to contain on a given topic and so justify the expense of searching in it. Taking as an example a search on computer networks in the Soviet Union, Questindex and Dialindex show which of their computer category files might be suitable for a search proper (Searches 9.4 and 9.5). Note that while the number of references is ranked *here* for convenience, in the actual output databases are neither listed in file number order nor are they ranked by references retrieved.

## Search 9.4: Computer networks in the USSR - Questindex results

```
    ENTER-qf computer network? and (ussr or soviet union or russia)

        47      NTIS
        33      INSPEC
        19      NASA
        10      COMPENDEX
         6      MATHSCI
         6      PASCAL
         3      HARD SCIENCES
         1      TELECOM ABSTRACTS
         0      ISMEC
         0      SPACESOFT
         0      ROBOMATIX
         0      BUSINESS SOFTWARE
         0      ARTIFICIAL INTELLIGENCE
         0      CAD/CAM
```

**Search 9.5: Computer networks in the USSR - Dialindex results**

```
33        INSPEC
19        NTIS
12        COMPENDEX
 8        COMPUTER DATABASE
 6        MATHSCI
 2        COMPUTER NEWS FULLTEXT
 0        MICROCOMPUTER INDEX
```

The reason that the NTIS file on ESA-IRS has so many more references than the file on DIALOG is that the corporate source field in ESA-IRS is searched, as part of the basic index, along with subject terms, abstracts and titles, and the term USSR appears frequently in the corporate source field. It is worth noting also that for this particular search, you might very well consider searching on DIALOG file 270, SOVIET SCIENCE AND TECHNOLOGY (although it has not been updated for a few months). The search, if the same as the above formulation, would retrieve a disappointing twenty-one references. However, it should be borne in mind that the database covers Soviet rather than non-Soviet literature and thus there is no need for the indexers to add the various geographic terms for the country. If the search is simply done as computer(w)network? then the result is 360 references!

As noted earlier it is possible to specify whether to add extra databases to a Questindex/Dialindex category or take any out. Thus another way these cross-file search capabilities can be used is to point up databases which perhaps should not be included in the category at all and which could be omitted on a subsequent occasion to save even more time. PTS PROMT and PTS NEWSLETTER DATABASE might be suitable candidates for exclusion in the Dialindex PCINFO category, for example.

After using Questindex/Dialindex to identify a suitable database, the actual search must then be carried out in that database, that is to say, the cross-file search is only temporary and the results are not stored and useable. However, both ESA-IRS and DIALOG have another command which will actually execute a given search throughout any specified databases. On ESA-IRS, Questcluster permits the user to create temporary megafiles of up to eight individual databases. Three types of Questcluster are available: fixed (pre-defined) vertical file clusters where the databases are too big for normal use and thus have to be split into different time spans; fixed horizontal file clusters where predefined similar files have been grouped together for convenience; and user-defined clusters where files can be merged with other files, other clusters or even clusters with clusters. Simply entering the command, BEGIN followed by the desired file numbers will define the cluster which can then be searched by all Quest and CCL commands with the number of hits being given as the total of all the files in the cluster. Only at the reference output stage (DISPLAY, PRINT, etc) are the individual files distinguished. Duplicate citations are readily spotted and can be eliminated or merged in a post-processing stage after downloading.

On DIALOG, the similar OneSearch feature can be used to search up to twenty databases by entering them after the BEGIN command. Ranges of files may be given as well as Dialindex categories or combinations. Whereas ESA-IRS treats the individual files as one big file for retrieval purposes, DIALOG executes the search on each selected file so the user can see which files are producing hits or not. DIALOG, however, has the very useful facility of being able to identify and remove duplicates after a search of multiple databases. The ID (Identify Duplicates) command, followed by a set number, creates a sorted set of records in which duplicate records are grouped together by title for easy identification. The user then has the option of retaining the record with the most or best information or keeping all the records for post-processing into one composite, bumper reference. A different command, IDO (Identify Duplicates Only), creates a set containing only the records that are identified as duplicates. Using the RD (Remove Duplicates) command on the original set of all records creates a unique set in which only one copy from each set of duplicate citations is retained. The copy kept is dependent on the order in which the files were selected with the BEGIN command - though the priority can be changed at any time.

## NEWSNET AND ITS SERVICES

NEWSNET is a good source of specialized business information providing over 420 newsletters and services in fifty or so industry categories. Together these newsletters form one vast database with over seven thousand articles being added every day. Most of the newsletters are available electronically only on NEWSNET and many are available before the equivalent print version appears. Indeed, some are only available in electronic form. These newsletters and services are provided by independent publishers, who update them on a daily, weekly or monthly basis. Most of the newsletters currently on NEWSNET retain back-issues online. Several services are time-dependent and are kept for a certain period only (none so far in the computer field). Bulletin services (again none in the computer field) are typically updated as news breaks and items are retained for four weeks before being discarded. Encyclopedic services are updated at least annually and only the latest edition is kept online. To use NEWSNET efficiently it is helpful to know that the database is structured into industries, secondary selection categories, individual services and date ranges.

### NEWSNET structure

*Industry categories*

Some fifty industry categories are available on NEWSNET and each is identified by a two character code - thus EC for Electronics and Computers. Individual newsletters and services are assigned to the industry category which reflects their primary content. They are also cross-referenced to other categories selected by the publishers. So when using the SEARCH command for any given industry not only will the core newsletters be included but also all the related or cross-referenced ones (unless they are specifically excluded - see below) and some of these may or may not be relevant. For example, in the EC (Electronics and Computers) category, relevant cross-reference newsletters might be ONLINE LIBRARIES AND MICROCOMPUTERS (from the Publishing and Broadcasting category); SOFTWARE LAW BULLETIN and LAWYERS' MICRO USERS GROUP NEWSLETTER (both from the Law category); ADVANCED MILITARY COMPUTING (from the Defense category); and INVESTEXT/COMPUTERS AND OFFICE EQUIPMENT and INVESTEXT/ DATA PROCESSING (both from the Investext category). Table 9.11 shows the newsletters currently cross-referenced to the EC category as of July 1990 (core newsletters in the EC category are shown in Table 9.6). Typing HELP EC gives a description of the computer industry category, while LIST EC lists all the newsletters in or cross-referenced to it. HELP followed by a precise newsletter service code (for example, HELP PB42) will provide details on that newsletter in a similar way to the ?FILEn feature on ESA-IRS and DIALOG.

**Table 9.11: EC cross-referenced newsletters on NEWSNET**

| Newsletter Name | Service Code |
|---|---|
| SATELLITE WEEK | AE01 |
| SPACE STATION NEWS | AE13 |
| AVIONICS REPORT | AE14 |

**Table 9.11:** (cont.)

| Newsletter Name | Service Code |
| --- | --- |
| THE CHEMICAL MONITOR | CH15 |
| ADVANCED MILITARY COMPUTING | DE03 |
| MILITARY FIBER OPTICS NEWS | DE06 |
| DEFENSE R&D UPDATE | DE07 |
| DEFENSE INDUSTRY REPORT | DE08 |
| C3I REPORT | DE11 |
| MILITARY ROBOTICS | DE14 |
| VIDEO WEEK | EL01 |
| CARD NEWS | FI24 |
| TRADING SYSTEMS TECHNOLOGY | FI39 |
| BRANCH AUTOMATION NEWS | FI48 |
| THE INSIDER NETWORK MARKET REPORT | IV71 |
| INVESTEXT/COMPUTERS AND OFFICE EQUIPMENT | IX07 |
| INVESTEXT/DATA PROCESSING | IX09 |
| INVESTEXT/ELECTRICAL AND ELECTRONICS | IX11 |
| INVESTEXT/SEMICONDUCTORS | IX23 |
| LAWYERS' MICRO USERS GROUP NEWSLETTER | LA05 |
| THE SOFTWARE LAW BULLETIN | LA13 |
| LAW OFFICE TECHNOLOGY REVIEW | LA15 |
| ADVANCED MANUFACTURING TECHNOLOGY | MG12 |
| CIMWEEK | MG14 |
| CAD/CAM UPDATE | MG15 |
| SENSORS AND INSTRUMENTATION NEWS | MG16 |
| FACTORY AUTOMATION NEWS | MG17 |
| SMT TRENDS | MG18 |
| TELEVISION DIGEST | PB01 |
| WORLDWIDE VIDEOTEX UPDATE | PB08 |
| FRIDAY MEMO | PB15 |
| MORGAN REPORT ON DIRECTORY PUBLISHING | PB30 |
| ELECTRONIC SERVICES UPDATE | PB33 |
| ONLINE NEWSLETTER | PB41 |
| ONLINE LIBRARIES AND MICROCOMPUTERS | PB42 |
| WORLDWIDE DATABASES | PB44 |
| NEWSNET ACTION LETTER | PB99 |
| ELECTRONIC MATERIALS TECHNOLOGY NEWS | RD31 |
| COMMUNICATIONS DAILY | TE01 |
| VOICE TECHNOLOGY NEWS | TE02 |
| ELECTRONIC MESSAGING NEWS | TE05 |
| APPLIED NETWORKS REPORT | TE14 |
| AUDIOTEX UPDATE | TE16 |
| VIEWTEXT | TE18 |
| DATA CHANNELS | TE22 |
| COMMON CARRIER WEEK | TE26 |
| ONLINE PRODUCT NEWS | TE27 |

**Table 9.11:** (cont.)

| Newsletter Name | Service Code |
|---|---|
| JAPAN TELECOMMUNICATIONS SCAN | TE31 |
| INTERACTIVITY REPORT | TE41 |
| BOC WEEK | TE49 |
| REPORT ON AT&T | TE50 |
| OUTLOOK ON AT&T | TE56 |
| TDS TARIFF SEARCH | TE62 |
| TDS MARKET REPORT SEARCH | TE63 |
| TDS TELECOM CALENDAR | TE65 |
| NEW ERA: JAPAN | TE70 |
| ATC PRODUCTS AND SERVICES | TE74E |
| TELECOMMUNICATIONS ALERT | TE75 |
| WASHINGTON TELECOMMUNICATIONS DIRECTORY | TE77E |
| EDI NEWS | TE80 |
| ENHANCED SERVICES OUTLOOK | TE81 |
| THE SATELLITE DIRECTORY | TE82E |
| INTELLIGENT NETWORK NEWS | TE94 |
| TELECOM OUTLOOK | TE98 |
| MOBILE DATA REPORT | TE99 |

*Secondary selection categories*

Certain services are also grouped in secondary selection categories which work similarly to the industry categories. Normally these services are related in ways which could be more useful than the industry codes; for example, numerous newsletters cover the same geographical region such as Japan, thus the secondary category JAPAN has been created to pull together all the scattered newsletters on Japan, for example, KYODA NEWS SERVICE and JAPAN WEEKLY MONITOR (both from the International category); JAPAN SEMICONDUCTOR SCAN (from the Electronics and Computers category); NEW ERA: JAPAN (from the Telecommunications category) and so on. Such groups can be found by entering HELP SECONDARY at the command prompt. Other secondary categories of more use in the computer science context are SOFTWARE and INFOTECH. By entering, HELP SOFTWARE or HELP INFOTECH, you can get an overview of the newsletters in these secondary selection categories (Tables 9.7 and 9.8).

*Individual services*

Every NEWSNET newsletter has a unique service code. The first two characters show its industry category (for example, EC). The next two characters are numeric identifiers within that industry. Thus EC39 is the service code for JAPAN COMPUTER INDUSTRY SCAN in the Electronics and Computers industry category. A code may be followed by: a '#' to signify that it is a bulletin and thus updated irregularly as news breaks or develops (for example, PB99# - NEWSNET Action Letter); a 'T' to signify that the service is time-oriented and so updated more than once per day (for example, IV97T - Bechtel SEC Filings Index); an 'E' to show that it is an encyclopedic service and updated infrequently (for example, EC58E - NASA SOFTWARE DIRECTORY); or by a 'W' to signify that the service is a wirefeed where the news is available the instant it comes off the wire (for example, BW01W - BUSINESS WIRE). A description of each newsletter or service can be obtained by entering the command HELP followed by the four or five character service code (such as HELP EC39) at the command prompt.

*Date ranges*

Every issue of every newsletter (except the encyclopedic services) is dated thus enabling searching by date range (for example, 1/1/90-6/1/90), or by specific issue of a publication (04/13/90), or by the earliest or latest issue. Note that the date is entered in American format, that is month/day rather than *vice-versa*, thus 4/1/90-represents the period from 1st April 1990 to date and not from the 4th January!

### Newsletters and service on NEWSNET

Computer-related information will be found in the Electronics and Computers (EC) industry category whose coverage includes electronics, robotics, AI, computers, software, peripherals and new products. There are currently (December 1990) over forty newsletters in this category with another fifty or so related or cross-referenced to it - some being more relevant than others (see Table 9.6 and 9.11). Descriptions, partly based on publishers' statements, are given below for selected NEWSNET computer- and information technology-oriented services. Certain newsletters such as IDB ONLINE - THE COMPUTER INDUSTRY DAILY (EC55), while still online are no longer being updated by the publisher and are thus not included here. Many of the newsletters, of course, have a similar format, that is they have sections on products, reviews, industry news, events, analysis, people and so on.

*THE BUSINESS COMPUTER (EC22)*

Published by P/K Associates, Madison, Wisconsin, updated twice weekly and online since early 1983, THE BUSINESS COMPUTER has expanded from a weekly syndicated newspaper column and is claimed to be the world's widest-read computer publication. Indeed, it is known as the 'Bible of Silicon Valley'. THE BUSINESS COMPUTER provides twenty million computer users with reviews and advice, and aims to be the voice, eyes and hands for serious computer users through its tough user-oriented tests of equipment and software. No information about computers or computer programs reaches THE BUSINESS COMPUTER until they have been personally tested by the editorial staff. The service also gives innovative answers to problems facing computer users.

*CAREER\*EXCHANGE - THE COMPUTER FIELD (EC6O)*

CAREER\*EXCHANGE - THE COMPUTER FIELD is a nationwide clearinghouse for information on professional job opportunities in the hardware and software computer industry. The newsletter is in three parts - Part I (Software Design and Operations) and Part II (Hardware Production and Sales) both survey current industry conditions and news events affecting employment opportunities; Part III lists specific job vacancies nationwide, on a company-by-company basis with contact persons included. The electronic edition is online since February 1986 and is updated monthly. Although the newsletter groups items into one of the three parts, these parts do not have to be searched separately. Every item is given a running number and the user just selects one of these at the Headline prompt. The newsletter is published by Washington Research Associates, Arlington, Virginia.

## CD COMPUTING NEWS (EC67)

CD COMPUTING NEWS reports on the developments, applications, and business ventures concerned with compact optical discs and associated products used in computing. It covers not only CD-ROM and CD-I technologies, but every other type of optical medium now being developed for computing. It also reports on the application of this technology to new business areas such as document retrieval and storage, interactive computer training, database storage and access, and publishing. Online on NEWSNET since June 1987, the newsletter is published by Worldwide Videotex, Boston, Massachusetts and is updated monthly.

## CD-ROM DATABASES (EC71)

CD-ROM DATABASES is an electronic-only service from Worldwide Videotex with the earliest issue on NEWSNET dating back to September 1987. Updated monthly, the newsletter provides titles, purchase and subscription prices, and subject categories of all CD-ROM databases currently marketed. It also lists the names, addresses, and telephone numbers of all vendors who supply these CD-ROM databases. The information is listed first by title order and then by vendor name to facilitate finding desired titles, as well as for monitoring product lines of companies.

## COMPUTER BOOK REVIEW (EC27)

COMPUTER BOOK REVIEW critically reviews and rates over 1,200 computer books a year on all subjects and from most publishers. Supposedly the most comprehensive, widely acclaimed review journal in its field, COMPUTER BOOK REVIEW is published by Comber Press, Honolulu, Hawaii. Updated monthly on NEWSNET with each issue containing at least thirty concise reviews and the latest publishing news, the service is retained for the current year plus two previous years.

## COMPUTER PROTOCOLS (EC74)

COMPUTER PROTOCOLS covers developing news related to computer communication protocols and products such as bridges, gateways, and LANs. Other monitored products include software interfaces between personal computers and mainframes. Special coverage is provided on the development of international protocols. This includes ISO protocol development and testing activities of United States companies and the Corporation For Open Systems. The electronic version of the newsletter is on NEWSNET since June 1988 and is updated monthly by Worldwide Videotex, Boston, Massachusetts.

## COMPUTER WORKSTATIONS (EC79)

COMPUTER WORKSTATIONS provides news and information on computer workstations used in network applications, computer-aided design (CAD), computer-aided manufacturing (CAM), computer-aided engineering (CAE), and other business and industrial applications to improve productivity. It also covers the products, people, and companies using and making workstations. Emphasis is on product marketing strategies. The newsletter is published by Worldwide Videotex and updated monthly with the earliest issue in NEWSNET dating from August 1988.

## COMPUTERGRAM INTERNATIONAL (EC72)

COMPUTERGRAM INTERNATIONAL is the world's largest circulation daily newspaper for data processing, communications and microelectronics professionals, senior managers and investors in the high-technology field. It is compiled each day in London, England, from research submitted by journalists in New York, California, London, Tokyo, France and Germany. It focuses on the business side of the industry, presenting between forty and sixty articles each day. Financial results of over three thousand companies are reported each year. COMPUTERGRAM INTERNATIONAL is published by Apt Data Services, London, England and dates from November 1987 on NEWSNET.

## HR/PC ONLINE (EC61)

HR/PC ONLINE, updated monthly by DGM Associates, Marina Del Rey, California, and on NEWSNET since April 1986 provides up-to-date information about using personal computers in human resources. It helps the reader keep up with new products, software programs, product applications and professional services that are of particular interest to executives and professionals in human resources. Users get practical suggestions and guidance, news of general interest, reviews of products and services, and information about successful personal computer applications in different companies. Useful for the novice as well as for the computer expert, HR/PC ONLINE helps improve productivity and successfully manage the new and fast-changing methods of working a myriad human resource problems with the latest personal computer technology.

## THE INFORMATION REPORT (GT22)

THE INFORMATION REPORT, published by Washington Researchers Publishing, Washington DC, steers readers to sources of free and low-cost business information and assistance. On NEWSNET since May 1985 and updated monthly, each issue contains forty or more articles, most of which give details of free newsletters, magazines, directories, bibliographies, databases and other information sources from the federal government, regional organizations, state governments, associations, trade unions, commercial organizations and other bodies. Tips on how to gather intelligence on competitors and other corporate targets are also included. As an added benefit, readers can request added-value, in-depth directories and reports from the publisher.

## THE INTERNATIONAL INFORMATION REPORT (IT75)

Also from Washington Researchers Publishing and similar to the INFORMATION REPORT, each monthly issue of THE INTERNATIONAL INFORMATION REPORT features about forty news items that give descriptions of, and full contact information on, valuable information sources around the world. On NEWSNET since September 1988, the newsletter will be of use to company intelligence gatherers and analysts, as well as journalists, to aid them in getting information on foreign firms, multinationals, and United States' firms with facilities overseas.

## JAPAN COMPUTER INDUSTRY SCAN (EC39)

JAPAN COMPUTER INDUSTRY SCAN reports any major breakthroughs, research and development and Japanese computer marketing techniques as well as providing feature articles. Charts and statistics help to clarify production quotas and market shares. The newsletter is useful for learning how international computer manufacturers are collaborating and reaching licensing agreements with Japanese manufacturers. Published by Kyodo News International Inc., New York, the electronic-form only newsletter is online since January 1984 and is updated weekly.

## LAN PRODUCT NEWS (EC99)

Only on NEWSNET since January 1990, LAN PRODUCT NEWS from Worldwide Videotex aims to keep readers up-to-date on the fast-growing computer Local Area Network (LAN) industry. Each monthly issue covers new hardware and software products, research and development, user applications, and industry standards developments. The marketing strategies of LAN manufacturers and vendors are given special emphasis.

## MAINFRAME COMPUTING (EC87)

Also published by Worldwide Videotex, the monthly MAINFRAME COMPUTING provides news and information on computer mainframes, including supercomputers. Each issue provides articles covering new hardware peripherals, applications software, operating systems, and network systems. Special emphasis is placed on the marketing strategies of mainframe and peripheral vendors. The newsletter is on NEWSNET since December 1988.

## MICROCOMPUTER RESOURCES (EC64)

MICROCOMPUTER RESOURCES, a monthly electronic-form only service, published by VGL & Associates, Ashland, Oregon and online via NEWSNET since September 1986, assists readers in developing a clearer in-depth understanding of the rapid advances being made in the fields of data processing, telecommunications, and fibre optics. The newsletter features information and analyses on products that represent the leading edge of the new information technology revolution.

## MICROCOMPUTERS IN EDUCATION (EC59)

MICROCOMPUTERS IN EDUCATION, published by Custom Printing Service, Westerly, Rhode Island, is a monthly newsletter aimed at administrators, teachers, librarians, publishers and other professionals. The newsletter, on NEWSNET since October 1985 (although there is a gap from July 1987 to July 1988), gleans its information from a variety of sources in the microcomputer field. Each issue presents information on new software products, software education news, and book reviews.

## NASA SOFTWARE DIRECTORY (EC58E)

The NASA SOFTWARE DIRECTORY is published annually (online on NEWSNET since 1986) with monthly updates by High Tech Publishing, Greenfield, Massachusetts, and contains a comprehensive listing of abstracts in seventy-five subject categories describing more than 1,300 NASA sponsored and developed computer programs. These programs are available to the public via COSMIC which forms part of the University of Georgia. COSMIC is NASA's Computer Software Management and Information Center - a central office established to supply software developed with NASA funding. COSMIC's role as part of NASA's Technology Transfer Network is to ensure that business and industry, other government agencies, and academic institutions have access to NASA's advanced computer software technology. Utilizing its extensive computer resources, COSMIC staff verify the completeness of each computer program before it is made available to the public. Each program also receives a technical evaluation to ensure that the supporting documentation provides an adequate description of its capabilities, and detailed user instructions. Source code is always provided so that capabilities can be studied and modified or enhanced as needed.

Each listing in the NASA SOFTWARE DIRECTORY explains the program's capabilities, provides information to assist in the determination of the potential applications areas, and identifies the programming language, machine environment, size and prices for the source code and supporting documentation. The monthly updates contain full descriptions of newly available programs as well as summaries of any relevant applications notes and other information which may facilitate the transfer and utilization of NASA's software technology. Each program contains an average of six keywords selected from the *NASA Thesaurus* which can be used to assist subject searching.

The NASA SOFTWARE DIRECTORY is an encyclopedic NEWSNET service organized by chapters. Chapter 1 contains a general introduction to the Directory and offers suggestions for efficient use of the database. Chapters 2 to 7 contain the initial entries of the DIRECTORY arranged in NASA accession number order, which is roughly chronological. Other chapters contain new listings, also in chronological order. This file is the same as the COSMIC (formerly SPACESOFT) database on ESA-IRS (see above for additional details).

## ONLINE LIBRARIES AND MICROCOMPUTERS (PB42)

ONLINE LIBRARIES AND MICROCOMPUTERS covers new developments and their applications in libraries and information centres throughout North America. Feature articles report on trends in the use of CD-ROM and online databases, people in the news, and library networks. Also included are editorials and reviews of library-oriented software and hardware. The newsletter is published by Information Intelligence, Phoenix, Arizona, is updated monthly (it is not published in July or August) and is on NEWSNET since January 1989. This newsletter is also contained on the ONLINE HOTLINE NEWS SERVICE CD-ROM.

## ONLINE NEWSLETTER (PB41)

Also from Information Intelligence and international in scope, the monthly ONLINE NEWSLETTER covers all aspects of online and CD-ROM developments. Regular feature sections include reports of mergers and acquisitions, telecommunications and networks, forthcoming databases, and the people making news in the industry. Also included are editorials which analyse the events and product developments that impact online users. The newsletter is not published in July or August and is online since January 1988. It is also on the ONLINE HOTLINE NEWS SERVICE CD-ROM.

## OPTICAL INFORMATION SYSTEMS UPDATE (EC51)

OPTICAL INFORMATION SYSTEMS UPDATE, which began in 1982, is a monthly newsletter, published by Meckler Publishing, Westport, Connecticut, designed to provide its readers with current news on developing optical-based information systems, including videodiscs, optical discs and CD-ROMs. For each technology, the UPDATE covers recent technical developments, software announcements, courseware, executive movements, calendar items, and conferences. Other major features include new product releases, summaries of market research studies, contract announcements and developments outside the United States. The service is on NEWSNET since October 1985.

## PC BUSINESS PRODUCTS (EC94)

Yet another publication from Worldwide Videotex, the monthly-updated PC BUSINESS PRODUCTS provides the latest news and data on software, hardware, supplies and services. Intended for individuals and companies who use personal computers in business applications, this practical guide, on NEWSNET since July 1989, contains detailed product information, evaluations, and prices to help PC users select products that will meet their needs. Also included are the telephone numbers of dealers and manufacturers for readers who would like additional information regarding a product.

## PRODUCTIVITY SOFTWARE (EC80)

PRODUCTIVITY SOFTWARE, also produced by Worldwide Videotex, is a monthly updated newsletter online on NEWSNET since September 1988 which provides information and news on the latest business software products for PCs, minicomputers, and mainframes to increase productivity and cost-effectiveness. It covers the vendors who develop and market the programs as well as the end users and evaluates products, applications, and marketing strategies.

## THE REPORT ON IBM (EC45)

THE REPORT ON IBM is a weekly news, analysis, and forecasting letter on IBM, available to information industry executives worldwide. Each issue of THE REPORT provides full details of IBM products, systems and pricing announcements - together with background and expert analysis - within twenty-four hours of IBM releases each Tuesday. The NEWSNET edition is online by each Wednesday morning. Major coverage areas include personal computers, the computer marketplace, systems, international reports, software, communications, and services and support. THE REPORT ON IBM is an independent publication, researched, written and edited by a staff of industry journalists in New York and Washington, and supported by contributors and correspondents in London, California and around the world. Targeted for top IBM-watching executives among IBM users, customers, vendors, suppliers, competitors and market research groups, THE REPORT ON IBM is published six days before the industry trade papers. NEWSNET readers also benefit from special supplements - in-depth reporting on hot topics that are covered in periodic supplemental editions of the newsletter. Published by Capitol Publications, Arlington, Virginia, the NEWSNET file dates from November 1985.

## SAA AGE - AN INSIDE LOOK AT IBM (EC78)

SAA AGE - AN INSIDE LOOK AT IBM, on NEWSNET since March 1988, is published by Systems Educational Associates Inc., Irving, Texas, and brings timely monthly reports and commentaries on IBM's major new software technology - Systems Application Architecture. The report's coverage spans all software and associated systems (VSE, VM, MVS, OS/400 and OS/2). Specific topics featured each month include intelligent workstations, languages, business aspects, management topics, communications, and news updates.

## SEYBOLD OUTLOOK: PROFESSIONAL COMPUTING (EC20)

THE SEYBOLD OUTLOOK: PROFESSIONAL COMPUTING was launched in 1983 and presents a monthly focus on the next generation of computers and computing. The REPORT evaluates new office-oriented microcomputer software and hardware and analyses the transformation of office tasks in response to the desktop computer invasion. Coverage includes systems, industry news and forecasts, trade shows and reader feedback. It should be noted that issues from March 1987 to May 1989 are not available on NEWSNET.

### TECHNICAL COMPUTING (EC73)

Published by STICS, Inc., Houston, Texas, updated monthly and on NEWSNET since 1988, TECHNICAL COMPUTING combines information on technical, engineering, and scientific hardware and software into one newsletter. It is useful for those who use computers for chemical processing, laboratory work, scientific data processing or manufacturing. By abstracting publications, attending conferences, and contacting the manufacturers directly, TECHNICAL COMPUTING provides a concise synopsis of the market, the products, and the technology.

### THE VIDEODISC MONITOR (EC70)

Future Systems Inc., Falls Church, Virginia, is the publisher of THE VIDEODISC MONITOR which brings news and analysis on interactive video, compact disc, and related technologies. The MONITOR covers new applications of computers, video, and optical storage in areas such as training, retail, education, the military, and home entertainment - and how the convergence of these media will affect you and your business. Updated monthly the newsletter is online since September 1987 and includes short articles, conference coverage, charts, an events calendar, editorials, project and disc reviews, reference materials, and market statistics. The publication is international in scope, with correspondents in the United States, Britain, Europe, and Japan.

### WORLDWIDE DATABASES (PB44)

WORLDWIDE DATABASES is a new service (on NEWSNET since February 1990) from Worldwide Videotex and is updated monthly. It is a valuable source of information on online computer databases around the world. Each monthly issue contains features on new database products and enhancements, user applications and accessing requirements, as well as news on products in development. As with other Worldwide Videotex newsletters, special emphasis is placed on the marketing strategies of database services.

### WORLDWIDE VIDEOTEX UPDATE (PB08)

Videotex is a re-emerging business that is growing within the television broadcasting networks and cable industries. It is also used in electronic publishing, banking and teleshopping applications, as well as becoming a major information service for personal computer users. WORLDWIDE VIDEOTEX UPDATE reports news and information on videotex/teletext projects, services, and products around the world. Emphasis is on news that can be of value for formulating marketing strategies such as the activities of potential customers and emerging markets. Online on NEWSNET since December 1982, the service is published by Worldwide Videotex and is updated monthly.

### Using NEWSNET

A full overview of NEWSNET commands and their use was provided in the previous edition of this chapter [19]. Other overviews of the basic structure, search functions and coverage of NEWSNET are given by Fried [20] and Meyer [21]. Entire current or back issues of newsletters on NEWSNET can be selectively read, printed and downloaded. Keywords can be used to search a group of newsletters for articles on specific topics. An SDI facility (NewsFlash) is available which monitors new articles added each day, retrieves those matching your interest profile and presents them next time you log on. Unlike DIALOG or ESA-IRS, the NEWSNET command language consists basically of prompts and options. The main commands are READ, SCAN and SEARCH; each works in more or less the same way and the basic procedure to use them follows.

*The READ command*

READ is an efficient and straightforward way to display or print a complete specific issue of a newsletter - although this can be a lengthy, time-consuming process. Following entry of the command READ at a main command prompt, you are then prompted for a newsletter service code (you can enter up to three), and following this for an issue date. The full text of the entire newsletter for that issue is then displayed. When the output is finished you have the option of reviewing the text using the command AGAIN; seeing other issues if you requested other issues from the same publication by entering MORE; returning to the previous prompt by using BACK; entering STOP to return to the first prompt of the command currently being used; or typing HELP for assistance. In addition, QUIT takes you back to the main command prompt.

*The SCAN command*

The SCAN command is used to scan the headlines of the latest (or any other) issue of a particular newsletter (in fact up to three), look at the first paragraph of articles that are of interest and/or read the complete text of them. It can be likened to the titles only format (with up to five titles on a screen) of ESA-IRS. Scanning is efficient because most headlines are written to summarize the essence of the article. If no headline is given by the publisher, then the system automatically takes the first sixty characters of the first line of the article. SCAN works the same way as READ, that is, you enter the command, then up to three service codes, and specify the issue dates. Instead of displaying the complete text of every article in the issue (as in READ) the system gives numbered headlines; by entering specific headline numbers the complete text of interesting articles can then be called up.

In Search 9.6 the latest issue of PB42 (ONLINE LIBRARIES AND MICROCOMPUTERS) was scanned. The service code could have been entered directly after the command (that is, SCAN PB42). The full text of headline 13 was selected for viewing. Other possibilities would have been to enter ALL to see the text of them all, or several numbers (for example, 1 3 6), a range (2-5), or a mixture (1-3 6-9 14). You can also enter PREVIEW to get just the first paragraphs and MORE to see further issues. BACK, STOP, HELP and QUIT (see READ command above) are also applicable here.

## Search 9.6: Use of SCAN command on NEWSNET

```
Enter command or <RETURN>
-->scan

Enter service or industry code(s)
-->pb42

Enter Latest for latest issue, or other date options in MM/DD/YY
format
-->latest

Copyright
ONLINE  LIBRARIES  AND  MICROCOMPUTERS  via  NewsNet
JUNE  1990
```

**Search 9.6:** (cont.)

```
Head #    Headline                                           Words/Lines
------------------------------------------------------------------------
***************
*NEWS & TRENDS*
***************

1)  DIALOG FILES SUIT AGAINST THE AMERICAN CHEMICAL         1613/186
    SOCIETY
2) PROTOTYPE ROBOTIC BOOK RETRIEVAL AT CSU/NORTHRIDGE        243/23

********
*PEOPLE*
********

3)  JAMES R. BENN (AUTO-GRAPHICS)                              42/4

4)  RICHARD NOBLE (UMI DATA COURIER)                          61/6
•
•

10)  OCLC PERSONNEL PROMOTIONS IN MAY 1990                   102/20

******************
*LIBRARY NETWORKS*
******************

11)  CARL LOADS THE ONLINE HOTLINE NEWS SERVICE             410/43

12)  OCLC & RLG RENEW AGREEMENT ON LINKAGES USING THE       142/16
     OSI REFERENCE MODEL

***********
*DATABASES*
***********

13) ONLINE HOTLINE NEWS SERVICE ON CD-ROM UPDATE FOR          67/6
    1990
14) COMPTON'S MULTIMEDIA ENCYCLOPEDIA (CD-ROM REVIEW)      1896/204

15)  HEALTH INDEX PLUS & COMPUTER DATABASE/PLUS            1100/133
     CD-ROM REVIEW)

16)  QUOTEBASE: LITERARY QUOTATION DATABASES                262/34

************
*MISCELLANY*
************

17)  NEW FAXON TOLL-FREE NUMBERS                             86/8

18)  ABOUT ONLINE LIBRARIES AND MICROCOMPUTERS

 Enter headline number(s) or ALL to read; PREview; AGain; or More for
 more issues
 -->13


 Headline #13
 Copyright ONLINE LIBRARIES AND MICROCOMPUTERS via NewsNet
 JUNE 1990

 ONLINE HOTLINE NEWS SERVICE ON CD-ROM UPDATE FOR 1990
```

**Search 9.6:** (cont.)

```
ONLINE HOTLINE NEWS SERVICE ON CD-ROM UPDATE FOR 1990 - Annual
cumulative updating of this CD-ROM will change from June to December
to include the full volume years of the ONLINE NEWSLETTER and ONLINE
LIBRARIES AND MICROCOMPUTERS. The CD-ROM will be released annually
after the end of each calendar year. The 1990 (3rd edition) CD-ROM
will include full volume issues for both newsletters. (RSH)

 Enter headline number(s) or ALL to read; PREview; AGain; or More for
more issues
 -->stop
```

*The SEARCH command*

The other main command is SEARCH, used to search some or all of NEWSNET's services for articles on specific topics. Again, SEARCH works similarly to SCAN and READ. At the Enter Service Code prompt you can enter up to three service codes, industry codes or a combination of both, or ALL to search the entire database. This latter option is not recommended since it takes too long and will produce too much extraneous material. Following the date prompt, you are asked to enter keywords representing your topic. If a category code or more than one service code is entered the system gives an indication (a full stop) of when it has completed searching a newsletter and when it finds hits as the search progresses (an exclamation mark) - the total number of hits found is also given. On completion of the search you have the options to look at the headlines (command HEAD) or the complete text (command TEXT) in addition to entering BACK for new keywords or the command ANALYZE to see how many occurrences of the keywords there were in each newsletter. In Search 9.7 following a search for recent book reviews on expert systems, the option to look at article Headlines was chosen and the full text of one was displayed.

**Search 9.7: Use of SEARCH command on NEWSNET**

```
 Enter command or <RETURN>
 -->search

 Enter service or industry code(s)
 -->ec27
 Enter Latest for latest issue, or other date options in MM/DD/YY
format
 -->latest

 Enter keyword phrase
 -->expert systems
 !
     4 Occurrences

 Enter HEAd for headlines; TExt for full text; Analyze for
occurrences in each service; or Back for new keyword(s)
 -->head

Head # Date          Service Code and Title              Words /Lines
------------   ------------------------------------   --------------
 1) 07/02/90   EC27 - COMPUTER BOOK REVIEW                81/10
    HYPERSOURCE ON MULTIMEDIA/HYPERMEDIA
    TECHNOLOGIES. CHING-CHIH
```

**Search 9.7:** (cont.)

```
   2) 06/04/90   EC27 - COMPUTER BOOK REVIEW              71/10
      HANDBOOK OF ARTIFICIAL INTELLIGENCE, VOL. 4.
      AVRON BARR.

   3) 06/04/90   EC27 - COMPUTER BOOK REVIEW              76/11
      RESEARCH AND DEVELOPMENT IN EXPERT SYSTEMS VI.
      NIGEL SHADBOLT.

   4) 06/04/90   EC27 - COMPUTER BOOK REVIEW              77/10
      HANDBOOK OF ARTIFICIAL INTELLIGENCE AND EXPERT
      SYSTEMS IN LAW

   Enter headline number(s) or ALL to read; PREview; AGain to redisplay
   headlines
   -->3

   Headline #3
   Copyright COMPUTER BOOK REVIEW via NewsNet
   Monday June 4, 1990

   RESEARCH AND DEVELOPMENT IN EXPERT SYSTEMS VI. Nigel Shadbolt.
   Cambridge Univ. Press, 1989. 301 pp, $60 (p). R. ISBN 0-5213-
   8477-X
        Proceedings of Expert Systems 89, held in September 1989. The
   theme of the conference was Applications and Methods in
   Knowledge-Based Systems. Many papers describe applications in
   finance, engineering, manufacturing, and power utilities. Other
   papers report on theoretical work in knowledge representation,
   inference, knowledge base maintenance, human-computer interaction,
   distributed problem solving, and knowledge acquisition.

    Enter headline number(s) or ALL to read; PREview; AGain to redisplay
   headlines
   -->quit
```

A useful device when looking for material within categories with the SEARCH command, is the option -NOX which is used to exclude all the services and newsletters which have been cross-referenced to a category and which would otherwise be searchable along with the core ones. For most computer and IT topic searches many of these cross-referenced newsletters in the EC category may not be so useful (for example, SPACE STATION NEWS, DEFENSE R&D UPDATE, THE CHEMICAL MONITOR, TRADING SYSTEMS TECHNOLOGY) and using -NOX would exclude these and all the others. A further refinement is the -EX option to exclude certain publications from a category (either core or cross-referenced) or even whole categories. Several core newsletters in the EC category may also not be of interest for computer searches (for example, JAPAN SEMICONDUCTOR SCAN, SEMICONDUCTOR INDUSTRY & BUSINESS SURVEY or AUDIO WEEK). These could thus be excluded from the search. The -NOX and -EX features can be combined to create a tighter search and save execution time (Search 9.8).

The ANALYZE command is an interesting option which gives a tabulation of the results of a SEARCH, that is a listing of the number of hits per newsletter in the categories and date range specified. This is a bit like Questindex/Dialindex except that it is done after a search rather than before. In search 9.9 ANALYZE shows from which newsletter services the twenty hits obtained during the search on graphical user interfaces (Search 9.8) came.

## Search 9.8: Excluding services when SEARCHing NEWSNET

```
Enter command or <RETURN>
-->search ec -nox -ex

Enter service or industry code(s) to exclude
-->ec28 ec35 ec43

Enter Latest for latest issue, or other date options in MM/DD/YY format
-->latest

Enter keyword phrase
-->"graphical user interface*" or gui or guis
.......!!..................!........!!....!.!.......

    20 Occurrences

Enter HEAd for headlines; TExt for full text; Analyze for
occurrences in each service; or Back for new keyword(s)
-->head

Head # Date        Service Code and Title               Words /Lines
------------   ------------------------------------   ----------------
 1) 08/01/90   EC67 - CD COMPUTING NEWS                 396/49
             SUN OFFERS SUNOS 4.1 ON CD AND CUTS PRICES MORE
             THAN 30 PERCENT ON CD-ROM DRIVES

 2) 08/01/90   EC79 - COMPUTER WORKSTATIONS             859/121
             NEW HARDWARE PRODUCTS ENHANCE SUN'S SPARCSERVERS

 3) 08/01/90   EC79 - COMPUTER WORKSTATIONS             474/66
             SQL FROM SUN MAKES DATABASES EASY TO USE

 4) 07/24/90   EC89 - NEWSBYTES NEWS NETWORK            170/23
             MITAC JAPAN OFFERS IBM-COMPATIBLE PC WITH
             WINDOWS 3.0

   •

   •

   •

19) 05/01/90   EC20 - SEYBOLD OUTLOOK: PROFESSIONAL     2010/200
             HARDWARE FOR THE WINDOWS 3.0 WORLD

20) 05/01/90   EC20 - SEYBOLD OUTLOOK: PROFESSIONAL     460/43
             SUN MICROCOMPUTERSYSTEMS, INC.


Enter headline number(s) or ALL to read; PREview; AGain to redisplay
headlines
-->
```

## Search 9.9: Use of ANALYZE command on NEWSNET

```
   Enter HEAd for headlines; TExt for full text; Analyze for
   occurrences in each service; or Back for new keyword(s)
    -->analyze

   *** NEWSNET SEARCH ANALYSIS      WED 25 JUL 1990      12:19:08 ***
   =====================================================================

   Phrase: "GRAPHICAL USER INTERFACE*" OR GUI OR GUIS
   Database Range: EC -NOX -EX
   Date Range: LATEST

   CODE        TITLE                                      OCCURRENCES
   -----       ---------------------------------------    -----------

   EC20        SEYBOLD OUTLOOK: PROFESSIONAL COMPUTING          7

   EC21        EDGE: WORK-GROUP COMPUTING REPORT                1

   EC67        CD COMPUTING NEWS                                1

   EC78        SAA AGE - AN INSIDE LOOK AT IBM                  7

   EC79        COMPUTER WORKSTATIONS                            2

   EC86        NETLINE                                          1

   EC89        NEWSBYTES NEWS NETWORK                           1

   TOTAL OCCURRENCES. . . . . . . . . . . . . . . . . . . . 20

    Enter HEAd for headlines; TExt for full text; Analyze for
   occurrences in each service; or Back for new keyword(s)
    -->stop
```

*Other NEWSNET features*

NEWSNET has several other commands: HELP gives assistance on commands, service codes, date ranges, searching, etc; LIBRARY allows you to examine online a sample copy of a newsletter at a cheap rate to see whether or not that newsletter might be worth searching or subscribing to; ORDER enables you to order online anything offered by either NEWSNET or the newsletter publishers; MAIL can be used to send messages online to either NEWSNET or the publisher of a newsletter. There is also the NewsFlash electronic clippings service which allows users to monitor services of interest. The FLASH command lets you create, modify and delete SDI profiles - either totally personalized or using default settings. The NewsFlash service will notify you each time you log on to NEWSNET of any matches between your profile and the new material added daily to the system and you can either READ them there and then or SAVE them for later perusal.

The advantages of NEWSNET compared with many other systems are:

- most of the newsletters on NEWSNET are not covered by these other systems
- the newsletters are covered in their entirety
- you can scan or browse a whole issue rather than just search for an individual item or reference

Just about the entire text of every newsletter is searchable except for a few common stopwords and single letters and digits. The SEARCH function is not quite so powerful as the search possibilities on ESA-IRS or DIALOG - for example, no set numbers are given and intermediary results are not stored so there can be no combining or merging of previous sets or search statements. However, the SEARCH command on NEWSNET does permit Boolean operators, proximity searching, string searching, truncation and the use of parentheses.

As with other online systems, including ESA-IRS and DIALOG, NEWSNET offers a number of shortcuts to speed up searching. For instance you can abbreviate most commands, skip prompts, enter several codes at once, limit by date, and so on. The previous edition of this chapter [19] gave more details on keyword entry and short cuts. Meyer [21] also provides some useful search tips, although the best source available is the *NEWSNET User Documentation Reference Guide (1989)*.

NEWSNET is significantly different from DIALOG, although DIALOG has many full-text databases; as NEWSNET does not create reusable sets care must be taken to be accurate in specifying terms when searching the full-text newsletters. Otherwise it will either be necessary to scan through an awful lot of irrelevant references or else the search will have to be redefined - either way it will cost time and money. For example, do not just type 'DEC' for details on DEC computers because, as NEWSNET does not differentiate between upper and lower case, a lot of references to Dec(ember) will be produced!

Many of the newsletters and services on NEWSNET are valuable because they enable you to formulate vendor and information systems strategies, perform competitive analyses; spot and track industry trends; develop market strategies and make decisions, and plan and select the most cost-effective systems. Other services are useful in different ways. Suppose it was necessary to build up a collection of books on computers and programming. Of course, you could check BOOKS IN PRINT on DIALOG but this will not give much information about the book nor how useful it is. So you could start by looking at COMPUTER BOOK REVIEW (EC27). SCANning the latest issue would give a number of reviews of computer books under various subject headings, which could then be PREVIEWed or READ. As there can be quite a lot of reviews which might take some time to skim through, another approach might be to SEARCH on the same service code for a given topic, for example, X Windows. This would give a smaller list of books on the subject which can be quickly read.

## OVERVIEW OF DATABASES IN COMPUTER/INFORMATION SCIENCE/TECHNOLOGY

One problem encountered in searching is how many (relevant) references you want to find. For everything on or as much as possible about any given topic, it would be necessary to search a lot of files. On the other hand, for just a few relevant references almost any one file will do - whether its primary coverage is computer/information science/technology or not. For example, the BUSINESS SOFTWARE DATABASE, may be used to determine which mini- or micro-computer software packages are relevant for a given business application and what hardware is required to run the packages under consideration. The above notwithstanding, this section will attempt to provide an overview (not exhaustive) of which databases might be profitably searched for topics in certain areas (C = available on CD-ROM, D available on DIALOG, E on ESA-IRS and N on NEWSNET).

Clearly, some databases have a much greater coverage than others in certain areas. While, for instance, LISA and INFORMATION SCIENCE ABSTRACTS might contain a lot of articles on mainframes and library automation, and the problems of installing and using CD-ROMs in libraries, they do not carry much on popular microcomputers and software in general, extending back for a great length of time. NEWSNET carries very few library/information newsletters *per se* (and those that it does are very recent) - though some of the computer and telecommunication ones contain the occasional item on library automation or library software. Yerkey and Glogowski show that material relevant to library and information science is scattered throughout many databases and there are many documents of interest to library and information specialists in non-library databases [22]. Various tips and techniques to find software information are provided by Hewison [23] and Jacsó [24], while Stern covers databases in artificial intelligence [25] and Dueltger looks at supercomputers and supercomputing [26]. Many of the other references cited in this chapter also include search aspects.

The following summary may also prove useful if you are looking for information in any of the following areas:

### Hardware identification

For factual details and descriptions of hardware and computer products try BUSINESS SOFTWARE (C/D/E); or SEYBOLD OUTLOOK: PROFESSIONAL COMPUTING; TECHNICAL COMPUTING; MODEM USERS NEWS; OUTLOOK ON IBM; THE BUSINESS COMPUTER and PC BUSINESS PRODUCTS (all on NEWSNET); COMPUTER PRODUCTS INDEX (C); or MAC BUYER'S GUIDE (C)

### Software packages

For factual details and descriptions of software packages and applications:

* in the business field: BUSINESS SOFTWARE (C/D/E); PC BUSINESS PRODUCTS; CD COMPUTING NEWS; THE INFORMATION REPORT (all on NEWSNET)

* for science and engineering: COSMIC (E); COMPUTER DATABASE (C/D); CAD/CAM and INSPEC (both E/D); NASA SOFTWARE DIRECTORY; TECHNICAL COMPUTING; COMPUTER WORKSTATIONS (all on NEWSNET)

* in the public domain: COSMIC (E); ERIC (C/D); NTIS (C/D/E); MICROCOMPUTERS IN EDUCATION (N); NASA SOFTWARE DIRECTORY (N); PUBLIC DOMAIN SOFTWARE ON FILE CD-ROM (C); PUBLIC DOMAIN SHAREWARE HYPERCARD STACK (C)

* in the microcomputer field (in particular): BUSINESS SOFTWARE (C/D/E); BUYERS GUIDE TO MICRO SOFTWARE (D); MICROCOMPUTER INDEX (D); THE SOFTWARE DIRECTORY (D); MICROCOMPUTER SOFTWARE GUIDE (D); MICROCOMPUTERS IN EDUCATION (N)

* for mainframes: MAINFRAME COMPUTING; PRODUCTIVITY SOFTWARE; REPORT ON IBM; SAA AGE (all on NEWSNET)

* for program listings: CD-ROMs - PC-SIG LIBRARY; SHAREWARE GOLD; SHAREWARE GRAB BAG; PC BLUE LIBRARY; SHAREWARE EXPRESS; SIGCAT; SOFTWARE DU JOUR; BMUG; BUDGETBYTES; MACGUIDE USA; MEGAROM; ADA ROM and so on - there must be about fifty titles.

## Computer communications

For computer networks and file transfer try databases such as INSPEC (D/E); LISA (C/D); HARD SCIENCES (E); COMPUTER PROTOCOLS; COMPUTERGRAM INTERNATIONAL; MODEM USERS NEWS (all on NEWSNET); MICROSOFT PROGRAMMER'S LIBRARY (C).

## Optical computing

If you are interested in the growing optical information and communication field and in product reports of CD-ROMs, optical disk drives, multimedia systems and the like: CD COMPUTING NEWS; CD-ROM DATABASES; OPTICAL INFORMATION SYSTEMS UPDATE; VIDEODISK MONITOR (all on NEWSNET) in particular.

## Library/information applications

For general material in the library and information field consider BUSINESS SOFTWARE (C/D/E); INSPEC (D/E); ONLINE CHRONICLE (D); LISA (C/D); INFORMATION SCIENCE ABSTRACTS (D); ONLINE LIBRARIES AND MICROCOMPUTERS; ONLINE NEWSLETTER; WORLD WIDE DATABASES; THE INFORMATION REPORT; THE INTERNATIONAL INFORMATION REPORT (all on NEWSNET); ONLINE HOTLINE NEWS SERVICE (C).

## Company and persons identification

For information on company addresses, profiles, personnel, job vacancies, appointments, etc try BUSINESS SOFTWARE (C/D/E); ONLINE CHRONICLE; CAREER*EXCHANGE - THE COMPUTER FIELD; OUTLOOK ON IBM; COMPUTER WORKSTATIONS; JAPAN COMPUTER INDUSTRY SCAN (all on NEWSNET); ONLINE HOTLINE NEWS SERVICE (C); DIRECTORY OF LIBRARY AND INFORMATION PROFESSIONALS (C).

## Competitive intelligence

For tracking industry, finding out who's producing what at what price, reported sales and numbers of installations, potential users, marketing intelligence, advertisement campaigns and expenditure, select from BUSINESS SOFTWARE (C/D/E); COMPUTER WORKSTATIONS; JAPAN COMPUTER INDUSTRY SCAN; REPORT ON IBM; SAA AGE (all on NEWSNET).

## Reviews and tests

For critical reviews of software packages and hardware, together with reports of hands-on trials and experience plus problem solving consider looking at MICROCOMPUTER INDEX (D); COMPUTER DATABASE (C/

D), BUSINESS COMPUTER; SEYBOLD OUTLOOK ON PROFESSIONAL COMPUTING; COMPUTER BOOK REVIEW; PC BUSINESS PRODUCTS; MICROCOMPUTERS IN EDUCATION (all on NEWSNET).

## General and trade/industry news

While most of the databases will include general news, the following may be particularly helpful: JAPAN COMPUTER INDUSTRY SCAN; OPTICAL INFORMATION SYSTEMS UPDATE; ONLINE LIBRARIES AND MICROCOMPUTERS; OUTLOOK ON IBM; COMPUTER BOOK REVIEW (all on NEWSNET). In addition, more general news databases like WORLD REPORTER, AP and UPI NEWS, MAGAZINE INDEX, and MAGAZINE ASAP will also contain news and developments in the computer and information fields.

## Foreign rather than United States coverage

Most of the databases and newsletters are highly slanted to North American publications. For databases offering a high degree of European and/or other foreign news, product descriptions and references search PASCAL (E); NATIONAL COMPUTER INDEX (E); INSPEC (D/E); LISA (C/D); SOVIET SCIENCE AND TECHNOLOGY (D); JAPAN COMPUTER INDUSTRY SCAN; THE INTERNATIONAL INFORMATION REPORT; WORLDWIDE DATABASES; WORLDWIDE VIDEOTEX UPDATE; COMPUTERGRAM INTERNATIONAL (all on NEWSNET).

## Literature/references

If you are really interested in finding out about the literature rather than the products and want articles and papers discussing trends, developments, applications, designs, use, etc then you would be better off searching in databases such as INSPEC (D/E); NTIS (C/D/E); COMPENDEX (C/D/E); PASCAL (E); MICROCOMPUTER INDEX (D); LISA (C/D); INFORMATION SCIENCE ABSTRACTS (D); COMPUTER DATABASE (C/D) and ERIC (C/D); MICROSOFT PROGRAMMER'S LIBRARY (C); COMPUTER LIBRARY (C); ONLINE HOTLINE NEWS SERVICE (C) to mention just a few.

## CD-ROM COVERAGE

In the computer science and information technology domain there are a number of CD-ROM databases available. One or two of these are optical equivalents of the magnetic (and printed) versions are described earlier, for example: LISA; MATHSCI; COMPUTER DATABASE; BUSINESS SOFTWARE DATABASE. There are also quite a large number of CD-ROMs covering bibliographic and library catalogue information, such as BOOKBANK; BOOKS IN PRINT PLUS; BOOK REVIEW DIGEST; BRITISH NATIONAL BIBLIOGRAPHY; GERMAN BOOKS IN PRINT; LASERGUIDE; LASERQUEST; CD-MARC; ACCESS PENNSYLVANIA PACS; MAINECAT and so on. These are considered to be outside the scope of this particular chapter. An overview of CD-ROMs in cataloguing, acquisitions, public access catalogues; reference works and indices is provided by Desmarais [27]. There are a growing number of catalogues and directories listing CD-ROM products being provided by organizations making CD-ROMs available, such as Faxon,

EBSCO, Microinfo Ltd, Compact Data, Future Office Systems Ltd and the Bureau of Electronic Publishing, in addition to publications such as the annual *CD-ROM Directory* (5th 1991 edition published by TFPL, 1990) which provide more details about the discs. This Directory is also available on CD-ROM.

Journals such as *LaserDisk Professional, CD-ROM Librarian* and *The Electronic Library* amongst others carry reviews of CD-ROMs and provide sufficient information for the would-be buyer to decide whether to procure it or not. Particularly useful are the CD-ROM product directories in *CD-ROM Librarian* (for example those in the November and December 1990 issues) since they include bibliographic citations for reviews of the CD-ROMs listed. There are also a number of reference works such as the recent evaluative series by Armstrong and Large [28] which describe and review CD-ROM products.

Because such a vast amount of information can be easily, conveniently and succinctly stored on a CD-ROM, there are plenty of CD-ROMs providing computer program listings (such listings are also provided online via many bulletin boards on hosts other than the three considered in this chapter, for example CompuServe, BIX and PC MagNet). While it is relatively easy and cheap to log on to ESA-IRS, DIALOG or NEWSNET to check out and search online databases, it is not so easy to get hold of copies of CD-ROMs to evaluate, although the Bureau of Electronic Publishing (PO Box 43131, Upper Montclair, New Jersey 07043, USA; telephone: +1-201-746 3031) has established an online CD-ROM library where potential customers can dial-in and try out popular CD-ROMs for a limited period of time before deciding whether to buy the disc or not.

In addition there are a couple of CD-ROM catalogues available on the medium itself which give sample records and information of many different CD-ROMs. The DISC OF DISCS, produced by EURO-CD in both PC and Macintosh versions, begins with a general presentation of CD-ROM discs and technology and then gives details of all the CD-ROMs in the EURO-CD catalogue. Presentations on the hypermedia CD-ROM are interspersed with multilingual explanations and commentary as well as text, pictures and sound. The disc is updated at least every two months and is available in French, English or German. Helgerson Associates publishes the CD-ROM SOURCEDISC which provides descriptions and demonstrations of over eight hundred commercially-available CD-ROM products. Access is via title, publisher or subject headings and both PC and Macintosh versions are available.

Consequently this section will describe only a representative sample of the products available in the computer science and information technology fields.

## LIBRARY AND INFORMATION SCIENCE ABSTRACTS

LIBRARY AND INFORMATION SCIENCE ABSTRACTS (LISA) was described earlier in the section on databases on ESA-IRS and DIALOG. The CD-ROM version, published by SilverPlatter, contains over 81,000 references and is updated semi-annually. The SilverPlatter software, besides providing similar features to other retrieval software (for example, DIALOG), provides context-sensitive online help screens. LISA on CD-ROM has been reviewed by Hartley [29] and more recently by Terbille [30] among others.

## COMPUTER SELECT

COMPUTER SELECT, from Ziff Communications Co, New York, USA, provides access to over 45,000 article abstracts and over nineteen hundred full-text articles from more than 125 of the most popular and well-known computer-related journals and newsletters such as *Communications of the ACM, Computergram International, MacUser, PC Magazine, PC Week, Computer Design, IEEE Spectrum* and *Dr Dobb's Journal*. The annual subscription includes twelve, monthly, fully-updated CD-ROM discs, with each disc covering the previous twelve-month period. The search software is Lotus' BlueFish Searchware and it is included on the

CD-ROM itself. COMPUTER SELECT is the new name for the current version (with upgraded software) of the COMPUTER LIBRARY CD-ROM which has been reviewed by Hayne [31] and Anacker [32].

## SOFTWARE-CD

Also from SilverPlatter is SOFTWARE-CD - a CD-ROM software directory derived from the BUSINESS SOFTWARE DATABASE on ESA-IRS and DIALOG among others (and described earlier). The CD-ROM version contains over ten thousand entries which the user can access through many different entry points. Since the database is updated only semiannually, it is not as current as the online or print versions. The software is loaded from diskette rather than from the CD-ROM itself. Salomon reviews SOFTWARE-CD and compares searches done on it with searches done on another CD-ROM - the ICP Software Directory [33].

## ICP CD-ROM

The ICP CD-ROM is the equivalent of the printed *ICP Software Directory* published by International Computer Programs Inc. The directory contains industry-specific software, applications software, systems software, etc. The CD-ROM version, published by OCLC, contains over thirteen thousand records and is updated three times a year. OCLC's retrieval software permits searching by any of the numerous fields (product name, vendor, product category, hardware, software and so on) given in each record. The ICP CD-ROM has been reviewed by Salomon [33, 34].

## MICROSOFT PROGRAMMER'S LIBRARY

This CD-ROM provides an assortment of Microsoft programming references, for example, to Microsoft OS/2, Microsoft Windows, Microsoft Systems Journal, BASIC, DOS, Microsoft CD-ROM Extensions and so on. Version 1.1 contains the equivalent to over twenty thousand pages of text from seventy-two manuals, books and programmers' reference manuals to Intel chips.

The CD-ROM retrieval software permits access to the references in many different ways and there are powerful navigation features according to a review of the product [35]. A quick reference facility provides dictionary-type definitions of terms and concepts. The CD-ROM, produced by Microsoft itself, also provides over twenty-six Megabytes of sample codes.

## ONLINE HOTLINE NEWS SERVICE

This CD-ROM is a collection of five online databases providing access to more than six thousand full-text news articles covering the online and library automation industries from 1980 to 1989. These sources are ONLINE HOTLINE (1982-1987); ONLINE NEWSLETTER (1980-81, 1988-June 1989); ONLINE LIBRARIES AND MICROCOMPUTERS (1983-June 1989); JOBLINES (June 1989); and MAJOR ONLINE VENDORS (June 1989). The search software is TextWare and the disk is published by Information Intelligence Inc, Phoenix, Arizona. The first issue of the product was reviewed by Plaza [36].

## DIRECTORY OF LIBRARY AND INFORMATION PROFESSIONALS

The American Library Association has produced a CD-ROM directory of some 43,000 individuals (mainly in North America) in the library and information community. Details include address, employer, professional and subject interests, foreign language skills, job experience and other relevant biographical information.

## PC-SIG LIBRARY

The latest version of the PC-SIG LIBRARY CD-ROM contains the equivalent of 1,240 diskettes of personal computer sofware covering word processors, spreadsheets, teaching and educational software, business and financial software, communications software, language and program utilities, graphics and games, entertainment and home software, expert systems and the like. Many of the programs contain instructions and documentation on the CD-ROM. The annual subscription brings two discs.

## IEEE/IEE PUBLICATIONS ON DISC (IPO) and INSPEC

UMI have produced a CD-ROM containing the publications of the Institute of Electrical and Electronics Engineers (IEEE) and the Institution of Electrical Engineers (IEE) - the latter being the producers of the INSPEC database. The CD-ROM is not an equivalent of INSPEC - providing, as it does, the full text of IEEE and IEE published journals, standards and conference proceedings. For 1989/90 alone, forty discs are required. The beta test IPO disc is reviewed by Holland who looks at coverage, accessing and using the system, search features, indexing, printing, etc [37]. INSPEC OnDisc is now also available from UMI on three discs - each disc covering a full year from 1989 onwards.

## CONCLUSION

This chapter has attempted to give a feel for the coverage of computer and information science and technology on three vendors (addresses are given after the list of references below). As has been stressed throughout there are plenty of databases which cover, to a greater or lesser extent, these fields. The user has a bewildering job to determine which databases might be useful for any given search. This task is made more difficult because of the differences in subject; language and source coverage; indexing policy; editorial approach; consistency in spelling and grammar as well as record structure; file layout and search fields; and update regularity - thus making a comparison of one database with another a near impossibility. It is hoped that this chapter will have at least given some idea of what faces you. The rest is really up to individual searchers - to gain experience by searching the subjects here described. The references which follow describe some of the databases in more depth and thus might be of assistance. A perusal of the databases themselves will yield other references, primarily to the printed versions of the abstract journals, which may also be of interest.

# REFERENCES

1.  Hawkins, D.T. A review of online physical sciences and mathematical databases. *Database* 89(1) 1985 14-18
2.  Konings, C.A.G. Comparison and evaluation of nine bibliographies and bibliographic databases in the field of computer science. *Online Review* 9(2) 1985 121-133
3.  O'Leary, M. Computer databases: a survey. Part 1: General and new databases. *Database* 9(6) 1986 15-22
4.  O'Leary, M. Computer databases: a survey. Part 2: Applications databases. *Database* 10(1) 1987 27-34
5.  O'Leary, M. Computer databases: a survey. Part 3: Product databases. *Database* 10(2) 1987 56-64
6.  Marsden T. and Laub, B. Databases for computer science and electronics: COMPENDEX, ELCOM and INSPEC. *Database* 4(2) 1981 13-29
7.  Jacsó, P. The Business Software Database - a user evaluation. In: *Proceedings of the 9th International Online Information Meeting, 1985 Dec 3-5, London, England.* Oxford: Learned Information, 1985 pp423-436
8.  Jacsó, P. Comparison of online software directories. In: *Proceedings of the 10th International Online Information Meeting, 1986 Dec 2-4, London, England.* Oxford: Learned information, 1986 pp329-334
9.  Jong-Hofman, M.W. De. Comparison of selecting, abstracting and indexing by COMPENDEX, INSPEC and PASCAL and the impact of this on manual and automated retrieval of information. *Online Review* 5(l) 1981 25-36
10. Langlois, M.C. On-line information systems: comparison of COMPENDEX, INSPEC and NTIS search files via LMS/Dialog, SDC/Orbit and SDS/Recon. *Online Review* 11(39) 1977 231-237
11. Bruckner, H. The Computer Database - the first year. In: *Proceedings of the 8th International Online Information Meeting, 1984 Dec 4-6, London, England.* Oxford: Learned Information, 1984 pp289-299
12. Jacsó, P. Microcomputer Index - a micro evaluation. In: *Proceedings of the 7th National Online Meeting, 1986 May 6-8, New York, NY.* Medord: Learned Information, 1986 pp211-222
13. Childress, B. Database comparisons: library and information science. In: *Proceedings of the Online Conference, 1984 Oct 29-31, San Francisco, CA.* Online, Inc., 1984 pp37-42
14. Broun, K. Computer Database and Computer ASAP: centerpieces of computing literature online. *Database* 13(5) 1990 29-34
15. LaBorie, T. Databases for the information professional. In: *Proceedings of the 2nd National Online Meeting, 1981 March 24-26, New York, NY.* Medford: Learned Information, 1981 pp321-329
16. LaBorie, T. and Halperin, M. The ERIC and LISA databases: how the sources of library science literature compare. *Database* 4(3) 1981 32-37
17. Sievert, M.E. & Verbeck, A. The indexing of the literature of online searching: a comparison of ERIC and LISA. *Online Review* 11(2) 1987 95-104
18. Bottle, R.T. and Efthimiadis, E.N. Library and information science literature: authorship and growth patterns. *Journal of Information Science* 9(3) 1984 107-116
19. Raitt, D. Computer science and information technology. In: Armstrong, C.J. and Large, J.A. (eds.) *Manual of Online Search Strategies.* Aldershot: Gower, 1986 pp417-468
20. Fried, M. NEWSNET: an offering of current and specialized information. *Online* 9(4) 1985 99-105
21. Meyer, P. NEWSNET on a corporate library. *Database* 10(2) 1987 73-80
22. Yerkey, N. & Glogowski, M. Scattering of library and information science topics among bibliographic databases. *Journal of the American Society for Information Science* 41(4) 1990 245-253
23. Hewison, N.S. Tips and techniques for searching for software information online. *Database* 10(3) 1987 47-52

24.  Jacsó, P.  Special criteria in online searching of software for the correct environment. In: *Proceedings of the 8th National Online Meeting, 1987 May 5-7, New York, NY*. Medford: Learned Information, 1987 pp191-195

25.  Stern, D.  Artificial intelligence databases: a survey and comparison. *Database*  13(4) 1990 19-24

26.  Dueltger, R.R.  Supercomputers and supercomputing. *Database*  13(4) 1990 106-108

27.  Desmarais, N.  CD-ROMs proliferate. Part 1: Library/reference discs. *Optical Information Systems*  9(1) 1990 23-29

28.  Armstrong, C.J. and Large, J.A.  *CD-ROM information products: an evaluative guide and directory. Vol 1-*. Aldershot: Gower, 1990

29.  Hartley, R.J.  LISA on CD-ROM: an evaluation.  *Online Review*  13(1) 1989 53-56

30.  Terbille, C.  LISA on CD-ROM.  *CD-ROM Librarian*  5(8) 1990 26-28

31.  Hayne, P.J.  Computer Library. *Laserdisk Professional*  2(4) 1989 105-106

32.  Anacker, P.  Computer Library. *CD-ROM EndUser*  1(11) 1990 90-91

33.  Salomon, K.  Software CD: a CD-ROM guide to software.  *CD-ROM Librarian*  5(5) 1990 42-44

34.  Salomon, K.  ICP: a CD-ROM software directory.  *CD-ROM Librarian*  5(1) 1990 30-32

35.  Santos-Devries, A.E.  Microsoft Programmer's Library Version 1.1.  *CD-ROM Librarian*  5(2) 1990 42,44,45

36.  Plaza, J.  Online Hotline News Service, *Laserdisk Professional*  2(4) 1989 108-109

37.  Holland, M.  IEEE/IEE on CD-ROM: a review from a beta test. *CD-ROM Librarian*  5(2) 1990 34-42

Also, the various host and producer newsletters are invaluable for news and tips on the databases. Relevant ones include: *Chronolog* (DIALOG); *News and Views* (ESA-IRS); *NEWSNET Action Letter*; and *INSPEC Matters*.

## ADDRESSES OF THE HOSTS

### DIALOG

DIALOG Information Services, Inc.
3460 Hillview Avenue
Palo Alto
CA 94304
USA
Tel. +1 (415) 858 3810 or toll-free in the United States: 800-3-DIALOG
TeleM 334499 (DIALOG)
        DIALOG also has offices in Europe, Japan, Australia, Canada and elsewhere.

**ESA-IRS**

ESA - Information Retrieval Service
ESRIN
Via Galileo Galilei
CP 64
00044 Frascati (Roma)
Italy
Tel. +39 (6) 94011
Telex 610637 ESRIN I
    ESA-IRS also has representatives in various European and other countries including the United States.

**NEWSNET**

NEWSNET
945 Haverford Road
Bryn Mawr
PA 19010
USA
Tel. +1  (215) 527 8030  or  toll-free in the United States:  800-345-1301

# 10 Social and behavioural sciences

*Claire Drinkwater and Judith Barton*

## INTRODUCTION

What are the social and behavioural sciences? The list of subjects to be included under this heading seems to vary with every writer in the field, but sociology, psychology, anthropology, economics and political science are the most common candidates. White adds education, geography and history [1]. Sills also includes law and statistics [2], while the Behavioral and Social Sciences Survey Committee was prepared to consider material also drawn from linguistics, business administration, journalism, medicine, public health and social work [3]. For the purposes of this chapter law may be omitted as it is covered in separate chapters, and history and linguistics are usually included with the humanities and will not be considered here. Business, including marketing and management, is the subject of two other chapters, but economics as an academic subject and area of general interest is included with the social sciences. Of the remaining subjects, anthropology is an example of an area where the online searcher's contribution is necessarily limited as its major sources are still only available in print [4]. Geography falls into somewhat the same category: although useful information may be gleaned from other sources on some aspects of the subject (from sociology, geology or agriculture databases, for instance), there are few major sources concerned principally with geography. This chapter therefore will deal mainly with psychology and education, sociology and social welfare, with some reference to politics, current affairs and economics, although as boundaries are notoriously difficult to draw in the social sciences it may stray from time to time into neighbouring fields.

## CHARACTERISTICS AND PROBLEMS OF THE SUBJECT AREA

Before undertaking online searches in the social sciences, it is important to understand something of the nature of the subject area and the problems it presents to the searcher. The social and behavioural sciences can be described as those which study the activities of human beings, individually or in groups, rather than natural phenomena or artefacts. Human activities do not take place in a vacuum, nor is one activity clearly separated from another; all may be regarded from a variety of viewpoints. The act of learning to read, for instance, may at first sight appear to be the chief concern of the schoolteacher, and hence an aspect of education; but it may also be of interest to the psychologist, studying the mental processes involved, or to the sociologist studying levels of literacy in different social groups. Each of these three will place learning to read in a different context: the educationalist may relate it to other skills and areas of knowledge to be covered in the curriculum as a whole; the psychologist may consider it in relation to stages of intellectual development; the sociologist may link literacy to other social and cultural factors. In fact it is frequently difficult to draw any kind of dividing line between subjects in the social sciences; an overlap of interests is probably more common than a clear distinction. Areas such as social psychology and educational psychology reveal in their names that they draw on a combination of interests. Examples may also be found which extend beyond the social sciences: the neuropsychologist, for instance, will share much common ground with colleagues in the medical profession.

For the online searcher, this overlap of interests has a number of consequences. It necessitates a constant awareness of the variety of approaches, and hence the number of databases, which might be relevant to a particular topic. If a viewpoint is not stated at the outset, it will frequently be necessary to establish during the search interview whether, say, psychological or sociological studies will be relevant for this user. Some of the most difficult searches are those which take an unexpected viewpoint: 'I'm interested in rhythm in music education - particularly any philosophical discussions of the topic', or 'I'm studying people's idea of time - but as a sociologist, not a psychologist'.

Besides this variety of approach within the subject area, it is also important to take into account the wide variety of people who have an interest in the social sciences, and the effect this will have on the type of information required from a search. One type of enquiry will come from the academic: the researcher or higher degree student, for instance, who is embarking on a project and requires a comprehensive literature search to make sure that existing work is not being duplicated, and to provide background reading for the research. Besides other research findings in their own field, such people may be particularly interested in methodology, and wish to find theoretical discussions of a specific method or instrument. The requirements of practitioners - teachers, psychologists or social workers, for instance - are rather different. Instead of a comprehensive retrospective search, they are more likely to be satisfied with fewer references, providing they are recent and highly relevant. Case studies might be of particular value. Finally, many aspects of social science are also the concern of ordinary people in their everyday lives, as individuals, citizens or parents. Education is an obvious example where many topics will be of interest to parents as well as teachers or researchers. Again, the search will need to be adjusted so as to find items at an appropriate level, in this case popular rather than academic.

Associated with problems of definition and viewpoint in the social sciences are problems of terminology. Ways of dealing with terminology will be discussed in more detail later in this chapter, but the nature of the problem should be realized from the start. Unlike some of the pure sciences, the social sciences have no generally accepted rule of nomenclature. In established areas of study, an accepted scheme of terminology will eventually emerge; in new areas, new terms will be invented and will take time to become known and accepted. This may lead to conflicting usage between different groups working in the same area, or (quite commonly) between British and American sources. Moreover the new terms are frequently words which have some other more general meaning in common use, and are now given a specialized one, or one taken over from some other subject area. 'Stress', for instance, may mean one thing to an engineer, and something quite different to a psychologist, while in common usage it has a third sense (to emphasize). Perhaps one of the most confusing terms, 'development' has a neutral general sense in common usage, a specialized meaning for a child psychologist, and another quite different one for a student of economic and social progress in developing countries. In order to deal with this problem, as with the problems of viewpoint and overlap, detailed consultation with the user is essential.

Two more general points need to be considered before looking in more detail at searching in the social sciences: space and time. National and geographical factors can greatly affect the relevance of information in the social sciences. Where a question relates mainly to the behaviour of the individual, these factors are of less significance: psychologists will often be interested in work carried out in other countries (providing it can be obtained without difficulty). For any query relating to social factors, however, the origin and location of the research needs to be taken into account. In some cases, parallel studies may still be of interest (for instance, studies of inner city problems in Britain and the United States) but again the user needs to be consulted to see if this is so. If the question relates to specific institutions, systems or legislation on a national basis, information relating to one country may have no relevance to another. A question on the English school examinations system, for instance, would need to be answered from British sources: BRITISH EDUCATION INDEX would be the best database to use. Information on the American system, which might be obtained from ERIC, could only be used as a contrast. Thus in judging the suitability of a particular database for a search, the searcher should take into account not only subject coverage, but the geographical source of the database itself, as well as the information included in it: even databases which claim to be international in scope will frequently display a national bias towards their country of origin.

The currency of information is not usually so vital in the social sciences as it is in the pure sciences, as earlier material is not rendered obsolete so rapidly or to the same extent. However, online searches are often requested in order to see recent work in a particular field, or on subjects of topical interest, so that frequency of updating, and delays in indexing of sources are still factors which need to be noted. News databases will often provide more up-to-date comment than the conventional bibliographic ones. This is recognized in the complementary pair of databases ACOMPLINE and URBALINE, prepared by the London Research Centre. Both cover the same subject, urban issues, but whereas ACOMPLINE provides a full abstracting service for journal articles and reports, URBALINE is a news service, providing up-to-date coverage of items from the daily and weekly press, together with press releases and other sources of topical material. In many fields, however, there is no such source of recent information, and the searcher needs to note not only the latest update of the file in use but also the average delay between the date of publication of an article and its addition to the database. In cases where a full abstract and detailed indexing are provided, this can easily be several months. Length of retrospective coverage can also be an important question when considering databases. For anyone attempting a historical study or wishing to provide a historical perspective on, say, a social problem, a distinction needs to be made between historical studies recently published, and hence included in a database, and sources contemporaneous with the problem, which may not be included in any online file.

The extent to which any of these factors will affect a search will vary considerably, but in looking in more detail at choice of database and development of search strategy in the social sciences, their influence will frequently be apparent.

## CHOICE OF HOST

The first stage in planning a search will be choice of host and database. Major databases are often available on more then one host, and on CD-ROM as well; decisions as to which to use will depend largely on availability and cost. Most searchers will be limited in the first place to the range of hosts their organization usually accesses, and for which it has passwords, and to those CD-ROMs to which it already subscribes. Where the CD-ROM version of a database has been purchased, there will be no immediate cost in using it, less constraint on time spent searching, and less risk of technical failure, as no telecommunications link is required. However, it may well be less current than the online version of the same file (a quarterly update service is common for CD-ROM, rather than monthly or even weekly, as on the online files) and it may be necessary to repeat the search on several discs to cover the whole of a large database, such as ERIC. An online search will often be chosen, either to provide more up-to-date information, or to give access to a wider range of databases, some of which may not be available on CD-ROM, or may not be used frequently enough to justify the cost of a CD-ROM subscription. In this case, the databases required will often determine the choice of host. Some of the large databases, such as PSYCINFO, are available on a number of hosts, and here cost may again be the deciding factor in selecting one of them. At the other extreme, many databases are unique to one host, or only available through the producer's own system, and it may be necessary to register with that host or organization simply to take advantage of one important file. Thus, only Questel offers the FRANCIS family of databases, which covers a range of social science and humanities subjects, and is particularly strong on French and other European sources; BRITISH EDUCATION INDEX is only available on DIALOG; and POLIS, the database produced by the House of Commons Library to cover parliamentary proceedings and official publications, is hosted only by ICC. European sources in particular tend to be less widely available than American ones, and it may be necessary to have access to a range of European hosts in order to ensure thorough coverage.

It is a characteristic of social science searches that they often require access to more than one database if they are intended to be comprehensive. If a number of databases are found on one host, the task of multifile searching will clearly be made simpler and more economic; in some cases it may be possible to search files simultaneously. Where no other constraints apply, therefore, it is advisable to use one of the major online hosts which gives access to a wide range of databases in the social sciences and related fields.

## CHOICE OF DATABASE

There is now a very large number of databases available which may be of use to the social science searcher. Quite apart from those files which are clearly centred on a social science subject, useful information may often be obtained from sources primarily concerned with other fields: CAB ABSTRACTS, for instance, although chiefly concerned with agriculture, contains useful material on rural development in third world countries; the two main history files, HISTORICAL ABSTRACTS and AMERICA: HISTORY AND LIFE, are essential for any search in which social questions are considered from a historical perspective; LINGUISTICS AND LANGUAGE BEHAVIOR ABSTRACTS contains much information of interest to the psychologist and educationalist, as well as the linguist. General sources, such as the READERS' GUIDE TO PERIODICAL LITERATURE, often contain material relevant to the social sciences; at the other end of the scale, small specialized services exist, such as the EUDISED database, which contains details of recently completed and ongoing research projects in education in Europe. Table 10.1 contains a list of major social science databases, against the main hosts; it shows clearly which hosts provide the widest coverage of the social sciences. The following discussion looks firstly at single discipline databases, and attempts to identify the major sources available in each subject. It then examines multi-disciplinary databases of various kinds and their relevance to the social sciences.

### Single discipline databases

*Psychology*

A number of major databases in the social sciences are based on well-established indexing tools of the academic disciplines. Thus, in psychology, the PSYCINFO database corresponds to *Psychological Abstracts* (first published 1927). The PSYCINFO file dates from 1967, and covers all aspects of psychology, including developmental psychology, personality, physical and psychological disorders, psychometrics, social

**Table 10.1: Major social science databases and their hosts**

| | BLAISE-LINE | BRS | CAMPUS 2000 | CAN/OLE | CISTI | CompuServe | Data-Star | DIALOG | DIMDI | ESA-IRS | Ferntree | G.CAM Serveur | MARISNET | Mead Data Central | NewsNet | ORBIT | STN International | TECH DATA | Questel | Univ. of Tsukuba | WEFA Group | WilsonLine |
|---|---|---|---|---|---|---|---|---|---|---|---|---|---|---|---|---|---|---|---|---|---|---|
| Academic Index | | ✓ | | | | | | ✓ | | | | | | | | | | | | | | |
| Acompline | | | | | | | | | | ✓ | | | | | | | | | | | | |
| Africa News | | ✓ | | | | | | | | | | | | | | | | | | | | |
| Ageline | | ✓ | | | | | | ✓ | | | | | | | | | | | | | | |
| America: History and Life | | | | | | | | ✓ | | | | | | | | | | | | | | |
| AP Political File | | | | | | | | | | | | | | | ✓ | | | | | | | |
| ASSI | | | | | | | ✓ | | | | | | | | | | | | | | | |
| Australian Education Index | | | | | | | | | | | ✓ | | | | | | | | | | | |
| Australian Public Affairs Information Service | | | | | | | | | | | ✓ | | | | | | | | | | | |
| AV-MARC | ✓ | | | | | | | | | | | | | | | | | | | | | |
| British Education Index | | | | | | | | ✓ | | | | | | | | | | | | | | |
| British Official Publications | ✓ | | | | | | | ✓ | | | | | | | | | | | | | | |
| CAB Abstracts | | ✓ | | ✓ | ✓ | | | ✓ | ✓ | ✓ | | | | | | | | | | | | |
| CBT and Interactive Video Database | | | | | | | | | | | ✓ | | | | | | | | | | | |
| Cendata | | | | | | ✓ | | ✓ | | | | | | | | | | | | | | |
| Child Abuse and Neglect | | | | | | | | ✓ | | | | | | | | | | | | | | |
| Congressional Record Abstracts | | ✓ | | | | | | ✓ | | | | | | | | | | | | | | |
| Congressional Record Full Text | | | | | | | | | | | | | | ✓ | | | | | | | | |
| CRONOS | | | | | | | | | | | | | | | | | | | | | ✓ | |
| CSO | | | | | | | | | | | | | | | | | | | | | ✓ | |
| DHSS-Data | | | | | | | ✓ | | | | | | | | | | | | | | | |
| Dissertation Abstracts Online | | ✓ | | | | | | ✓ | | | | | | | | | | ✓ | ✓ | | | |
| ECCTIS | | | ✓ | | | | | | | | | | | | | | | | | | | |
| Economic Literature Index | | | | | | | | ✓ | | | | | | | | | | | | | | |
| Education Index | | | | | | | | | | | | | | | | | | | | | | ✓ |
| The Educational Directory | | | | | | | | ✓ | | | | | | | | | | | | | | |

**Table 10.1:** (cont.)

| | BLAISE-LINE | BRS | CAMPUS 2000 | CAN/OLE | CISTI | CompuServe | Data-Star | DIALOG | DIMDI | ESA-IRS | Ferntree | G.CAM Serveur | MARISNET | Mead Data Central | NewsNet | ORBIT | STN International | TECH DATA | Questel | Univ. of Tsukuba | WEFA Group | WilsonLine |
|---|---|---|---|---|---|---|---|---|---|---|---|---|---|---|---|---|---|---|---|---|---|---|
| Educational Testing Service Test Collection Database | | ✓ | | | | | | | | | | | | | | | | ✓ | | | | |
| ERIC | | ✓ | | | | | | ✓ | | | | | | | | | ✓ | | ✓ | | | |
| EUDISED | | | | | | | ✓ | | | | | | | | | | | | | | | |
| Exceptional Child Education Resources | | ✓ | | | | | | ✓ | | | | | | | | | | | | | | |
| Family Resources | | ✓ | | | | | | ✓ | | | | | | | | | | | | | | |
| Films and Video Database | | | | | | | | | | | | ✓ | | | | | | | | | | |
| FORIS | | | | | | | | ✓ | | | | | | | | | ✓ | | | | | |
| FRANCIS: Amerique Latine | | | | | | | | | | | | | | | | | | | ✓ | | | |
| FRANCIS: Bibliographie Geographique Internationale | | | | | | | | | | | | | | | | | | | ✓ | | | |
| FRANCIS: Bibliographie Internationale de Science Administrative | | | | | | | | | | | | | | | | | | | ✓ | | | |
| FRANCIS: ECODOC | | | | | | | | | | | | ✓ | | | | | | | ✓ | | | |
| FRANCIS: Emploi et Formation | | | | | | | | | | | | | | | | | | | ✓ | | | |
| FRANCIS Ethnologie | | | | | | | | | | | | | | | | | | | ✓ | | | |
| FRANCIS: Sciences de l'education | | | | | | | | | | | | ✓ | | | | | | | ✓ | | | |
| FRANCIS: Sociologie | | | | | | | | | | | | | | | | | | | ✓ | | | |
| GPO Monthly Catalogue | | ✓ | | | | | | ✓ | | | | | | | | | ✓ | | | ✓ | | |
| GPO Publications Reference File | | | | ✓ | ✓ | | | | | | | | | | | | | | | | | |
| HELPIS | ✓ | | | | | | | | | | | | | | | | | | | | | |
| Historical Abstracts | | | | | | | | ✓ | | | | | | | | | | | | | | |
| Humanities and Social Sciences | ✓ | | | | | | | | | | | | | | | | | | | | | |
| Linguistics and Language Behavior Abstracts | | ✓ | | | | | | ✓ | | | | | | | | | | | | | | |
| Magazine ASAP | | ✓ | | | | | | ✓ | | | | | | ✓ | | | | | | | | |

**Table 10.1:** (cont.)

| | BLAISE-LINE | BRS | CAMPUS 2000 | CAN/OLE | CISTI | CompuServe | Data-Star | DIALOG | DIMDI | ESA-IRS | Ferntree | G.CAM Serveur | MARISNET | Mead Data Central | NewsNet | ORBIT | STN International | TECH DATA | Questel | Univ. of Tsukuba | WEFA Group | WilsonLine |
|---|---|---|---|---|---|---|---|---|---|---|---|---|---|---|---|---|---|---|---|---|---|---|
| Magazine Index | ✓ | | | | | | | ✓ | | | | | | | | | | | | | | |
| Mental Health Abstracts | | | | | | | | ✓ | | | | | | | | | | | | | | |
| Mental Measurements Yearbook | ✓ | | | | | | | | | | | | | | | | | | | | | |
| Middle East: Abstracts and Index | | | | | | | | ✓ | | | | | | | | | | | | | | |
| National Newspaper Index | ✓ | | | | | | | ✓ | | | | | | | | | | | | | | |
| New Signposts | | ✓ | | | | | | | | | | | | | | | | | | | | |
| Newsearch | ✓ | | | | | | | ✓ | | | | | | | | | | | | | | |
| NTIS | ✓ | | | ✓ | ✓ | | ✓ | ✓ | | ✓ | | | | | | | ✓ | ✓ | ✓ | | | |
| Open Learning Bibliography | | | | | | | | | | | | ✓ | | | | | | | | | | |
| Organizations and Services Database | | | | | | | | | | | | ✓ | | | | | | | | | | |
| PAIS International | ✓ | | | | | | ✓ | ✓ | | | | | | | | | ✓ | | | | | |
| Papers | | | | | | | ✓ | | | | | | | | | | | | | | | |
| Peterson's College Database | ✓ | | | | | ✓ | | ✓ | | | | | | | | | | | | | | |
| Pickup Training Directory | ✓ | | | | | | | | | | | | | | | | | | | | | |
| Polytel | ✓ | | | | | | | | | | | | | | | | | | | | | |
| Population Bibliography | | | | | | | | ✓ | | | | | | | | | | | | | | |
| Psycinfo | ✓ | | | | | | ✓ | ✓ | ✓ | | | | | | | | | | | ✓ | | |
| Psyndex | | | | | | | | | ✓ | | | | | | | | | | | | | |
| Readers' Guide to Periodical Literature | | | | | | | | | | | | | | | | | | | | | | ✓ |
| Reuter News Reports | | | | | | | | ✓ | | | | | ✓ | ✓ | | | | | | | | |
| RSWB | | | | | | | | | | | | | | | | | ✓ | | | | | |
| Rural Learning Opportunities Database | | | | | | | | | | | | ✓ | | | | | | | | | | |
| SAGA | | | | | | | | | | | | ✓ | | | | | | | | | | |
| Self Study Materials Database | | | | | | | | | | | | ✓ | | | | | | | | | | |
| Short Courses Database | | | | | | | | | | | | ✓ | | | | | | | | | | |

**Table 10.1:** (cont.)

| | BLAISE-LINE | BRS | CAMPUS 2000 | CAN/OLE | CISTI | CompuServe | Data-Star | DIALOG | DIMDI | ESA-IRS | Ferntree | G.CAM Serveur | MARISNET | Mead Data Central | NewsNet | ORBIT | STN International | TECH DATA | Questel | Univ. of Tsukuba | WEFA Group | WilsonLine |
|---|---|---|---|---|---|---|---|---|---|---|---|---|---|---|---|---|---|---|---|---|---|---|
| Social Planning, Policy and Development Abstracts | | ✓ | | | | | | ✓ | | | | | | | | | | | | | | |
| Social Sciences Index | | | | | | | | | | | | | | | | | | | | | | ✓ |
| Social Scisearch | | ✓ | | | | | ✓ | ✓ | | | | | | | | | | | ✓ | | | |
| Social Work Abstracts | | ✓ | | | | | | | | | | | | | | | | | | | | |
| Sociological Abstracts | | ✓ | | | | | ✓ | ✓ | ✓ | | | | | | | | | | | | | |
| SOLIS | | | | | | | | | ✓ | | | | | | | | ✓ | | | | | |
| Supersite | | | | | | ✓ | | | | | | | | | | | | | | | ✓ | |
| The Times Network National Database | | | ✓ | | | | | | | | | | | | | | | | | | | |
| UCCA Course Vacancy Database | | | ✓ | | | | | | | | | | | | | | | | | | | |
| Urbaline | | | | | | | | | | ✓ | | | | | | | | | | | | |
| Urbamet | | | | | | | | | | | | | | | | | | | ✓ | | | |
| US Political Science Documents | | | | | | | | ✓ | | | | | | | | | | | | | | |
| World Affairs Report | | | | | | | | ✓ | | | | | | | | | | | | | | |

processes and issues, and treatment and prevention. It is prepared by the American Psychological Association, but attempts international coverage of the literature, with forty-four per cent of materials drawn from non-American sources. Since 1980, the PSYCINFO file has contained some information not included in its printed counterpart, notably references drawn from *Dissertation Abstracts International*. It is prepared using a controlled indexing vocabulary, published as the *Thesaurus of Psychological Index Terms*, 5th edition, 1988. PSYCINFO is also available in CD-ROM form, under the title PSYCLIT, from SilverPlatter. An archival disc covers the years 1974-82, and the current disc covers 1981 to the present, with quarterly updates. (See Searches 10.1, 10.8 and 10.9)

PSYCINFO is probably the most comprehensive source of bibliographic information in the field of psychology, but it is not the only one. Also available to the online searcher is another major database in a closely related field, MENTAL HEALTH ABSTRACTS, produced originally by the National Clearinghouse for Mental Health Information (NIMHI), and from 1983 onwards by IFI/Plenum Data Company. This, which has no printed counterpart, covers such fields as child development, psychiatry, psychology and social issues. In practice, although there is considerable overlap, these two databases have different strengths: MENTAL HEALTH ABSTRACTS lays more emphasis on clinical psychology and psychiatry, while PSYCINFO provides more academic and research material. An equivalent database of European origin is PSYNDEX, produced by the Zentralstelle für Psychologische Information und Dokumentation (ZPID), Trier University, and covering the literature of psychology and related fields from the German-speaking countries. It is available from the German host, DIMDI.

A more specialist source within the field is MENTAL MEASUREMENTS YEARBOOK, corresponding to the printed volumes of the same title, and providing descriptive information and reviews of English-language psychological and educational tests. Psychological information may of course also be found on databases covering related subjects: LINGUISTICS AND LANGUAGE BEHAVIOR ABSTRACTS, for instance, or most education files.

## Education

Owing to the differences between national education systems, databases in the field of education tend to be compiled on a national rather than an international basis, and the searcher frequently has to choose between them according to the geographical source and application of the material required. The largest and most important database is ERIC, produced by the Educational Resources Information Center (ERIC), United States Department of Education, Washington, D.C., and prepared in machine-readable form since its inception in 1966. The online file corresponds to two printed indexes: *Current Index to Journals in Education*, dating from 1969 and covering published journal articles, and *Resources in Education*, which includes unpublished papers, research reports and project reports from 1966 onwards. ERIC does cover some material from overseas, but is predominantly American. However, its wide coverage of education and related fields in published and unpublished materials makes it an essential source for many education searches. It too has a controlled indexing vocabulary, published as the *Thesaurus of ERIC Descriptors,* 12th edition, Oryx Press, 1990 (see Searches 10.1 and 10.10).

ERIC is available from several major online hosts, and also in three different versions on CD-ROM. Those used to searching ERIC on DIALOG may prefer to subscribe to the DIALOG version. This, which includes the whole file on two discs, offers the choice of a menu-driven approach for the less experienced, or a command driven mode which simulates the DIALOG online system, but it is the most expensive of the three. On SilverPlatter, three discs are required to cover the whole of the ERIC file. All the usual online searching methods are applicable, and the system is reasonably simple to learn. SilverPlatter also produces a range of other CD-ROM products, including PSYCLIT and SOCIOFILE, which makes this version attractive for the social scientist. ERIC has also been available from OCLC; it too offers a range of CDs, including some drawn from the main OCLC catalogue. Thus, the EDUCATION LIBRARY is a subset of the OCLC online union catalogue, covering educational material held in OCLC member libraries.

Another American education database is EDUCATION INDEX from the H.W.Wilson Company. In printed form this is the earliest indexing service in education, first published in 1929, but its online history is much shorter. It is available online from 1983, through H.W.Wilson's own host system, Wilsonline. It is much less comprehensive, and more exclusively American, than ERIC.

Other nationally based education databases include BRITISH EDUCATION INDEX and AUSTRALIAN EDUCATION INDEX. BRITISH EDUCATION INDEX covers journals on education and educational psychology published in Great Britain (many of them not indexed in ERIC), and is an essential source for any queries relating to education in this country. After a somewhat chequered career, from its first appearance in print in 1954, through a period in the hands of the British Library, it is now produced by the University of Leeds and available online on DIALOG. Earlier material in the online file (1976-1985) was indexed using the British Library's Precis system, not always a helpful one for online use. From 1986 onwards the file is indexed with terms drawn from the *British Education Thesaurus*, Leeds University Press, 1988, which was developed from the *ERIC Thesaurus*, and has many terms in common with it. AUSTRALIAN EDUCATION INDEX is available online from Ferntree Computer Corporation Ltd. It, too, has developed an indexing language based on ERIC, and plans exist for it, and also *Canadian Education Index* (not currently online) to join BRITISH

EDUCATION INDEX and ERIC on DIALOG as a cluster of files covering the literature of education in English-speaking countries.

Online sources for information on education in Europe are not numerous. The French indexing service *Bulletin Signaletique: Sciences de l'Education* is available online as FRANCIS: SCIENCES DE L'EDUCATION on Questel, and covers French and other European sources, with indexing in French and English. The German education indexing service is not available online. One service covering the whole of Europe, but limited in its scope, is the EUDISED database, produced by the Council of Europe Documentation Centre for Education in Europe, which indexes ongoing and completed projects of educational research and development. This corresponds to the printed *EUDISED R&D Bulletin*, and contains entries from 1975 onwards, contributed by Eudised agencies in twenty-one countries, indexed to a common standard using the *EUDISED Multilingual Thesaurus*. However, the database is limited in size, and contains, for instance, only a selection of the material received by the National Foundation for Educational Research (the British agency for EUDISED) for inclusion in its own printed *Register of Educational Research*.

Apart from the conventional bibliographic and research databases mentioned above, education is a field which has seen the development of a range of other online services, often aimed at particular groups or covering a specific type of information. Information about courses and course vacancies, and databases of educational materials and resources (that is, resources in all subjects, structured for use in teaching), are the most common. Among major hosts, BLAISE-LINE, for instance, offers two databases of audio-visual materials for teaching: AVMARC (Audio Visual Machine Readable Cataloguing Database) and HELPIS (Higher Education Learning Programmes Information Service). In addition, some hosts are specifically concerned with information of this kind, and intended principally for use in schools or further education institutions.

CAMPUS 2000 offers a number of databases of British courses, course vacancies and careers information: ECCTIS (Educational Counselling and Credit Transfer Information Service) provides information on courses in universities, polytechnics and colleges; POLYTEL gives details of current vacancies at polytechnics; UCCA (UCCA Course Vacancies Database) does the same for universities; the PICKUP TRAINING DIRECTORY provides information on work-related courses of up to three months' duration (full-time) or one year (part-time); NEW SIGNPOSTS is a database of careers information. Alongside these, CAMPUS 2000 also provides access to THE TIMES NETWORK NATIONAL DATABASE (DATAB) a much more general group of databases of education-related information, including curriculum information, resources for teaching, addresses of organizations, details of events and competitions, a software catalogue, a news file, and databases sponsored by commercial and industrial information providers.

MARIS-NET also has a range of databases in this field, dealing with Great Britain and particularly covering resources and open learning materials: CBT & INTERACTIVE VIDEO DATABASE and FILMS AND VIDEO DATABASE cover training packages and films respectively; SELF STUDY MATERIALS DATA-BASE concentrates on work-related training packages for individual use; the ORGANIZATIONS AND SERVICES DATABASE covers organizations and individuals offering products and services in education and training; RURAL LEARNING OPPORTUNITIES DATABASE and SHORT COURSES DATABASE provide information on training courses; the OPEN LEARNING BIBLIOGRAPHY is a bibliographic file covering the establishment and running of open learning schemes. Obviously, such specialized files are often small and of limited general use.

Finally NERIS (National Educational Resources Information Service) offers its own major database of materials and information for education. It includes full text of curriculum materials suitable for use in schools and colleges, references to further resources available elsewhere, and details of curriculum development projects. NERIS is also available on CD-ROM.

*Sociology*

In sociology, the major online source is SOCIOLOGICAL ABSTRACTS, produced by Sociological Abstracts Inc. It covers the broad field of sociology, with the focus on theoretical and academic materials. In July 1985, its coverage was enhanced by the introduction of SOCIAL PLANNING, POLICY AND DEVELOPMENT ABSTRACTS, dealing with practical applications and solutions to social problems rather than theoretical studies. Both are now indexed by the *Thesaurus of Sociological Terms*, 2nd edition, Sociological Abstracts Inc, 1989. International coverage is again attempted with forty-one per cent of references from outside the United States (see Search 10.1).

## Search 10.1: ERIC, PSYCINFO and SOCIOLOGICAL ABSTRACTS on DIALOG

```
File 1: ERIC 66-90/NOV

    Set     Items    Description
    ---     -----    -----------

?ss pregnancy/df or pregnant students

    S1      1168     PREGNANCY/DF
    S2       371     PREGNANT STUDENTS
    S3      1444     PREGNANCY/DF OR PREGNANT STUDENTS
?ss adolescents/df or secondary school students or high school students or
junior high school students

    S4     12271     ADOLESCENTS/DF (APPROXIMATELY 13-17 YEARS OF AGE)
    S5      3232     SECONDARY SCHOOL STUDENTS ((NOTE: COORDINATE WITH
                     THE APPROPRIATE MANDA...
    S6      6907     HIGH SCHOOL STUDENTS (STUDENTS IN GRADE 9 OR 10
                     THROUGH GRADE 12 (...)
    S7      2568     JUNIOR HIGH SCHOOL STUDENTS ((NOTE: COORDINATE WITH
                     THE APPROPRIATE MANDA..
    S8     23825     ADOLESCENTS/DF OR SECONDARY SCHOOL STUDENTS OR HIGH
                     SCHOOL STUDENTS OR JUNIOR HIGH SCHOOL STUDENTS

?ss early parenthood

    S9       535     EARLY PARENTHOOD (PARENTHOOD ASSUMED BEFORE AGE 20)
?ss s9 or (S3 and S8)

             535     S9
            1444     S3
           23825     S8
    S10      928     S9 OR (S3 AND S8)

?ts10/6/1-5

 10/6/1
EJ411312  UD515169
 The Timing of a First Birth and High School Completion.

 10/6/2
EJ411299  UD515156
 Pregnancies, Childrearing and Mental Health Problems in Adolescents.

 10/6/3
EJ410804  PS517718
 Unmarried Fathers: Perplexing Questions.
```

**Search 10.1:** (cont.)

```
   10/6/4
 EJ410792  PS517706
 Residential Program Serves Pregnant Teens and Young Mothers in Iowa.

   10/6/5
 EJ410791  PS517705
 Supporting Teens in Chicago's Humboldt Park
```

**?b11**

```
 File 11:PSYCINFO - 67-90/DEC
       (COPR. AM. PSYCH. ASSOC.)

     Set    Items   Description
     ---    -----   -----------
```

**?ss pregnancy/df**

```
     S1     2723    PREGNANCY/DF
```
**?ss adolescents/df or adolescence/df or high school students or junior high school students**

```
     S2     24915   ADOLESCENTS/DF
     S3     31911   ADOLESCENCE/DF
     S4     10975   HIGH SCHOOL STUDENTS
     S5      6424   JUNIOR HIGH SCHOOL STUDENTS
     S6     61022   ADOLESCENTS/DF OR ADOLESCENCE/DF OR HIGH SCHOOL
                    STUDENTS OR JUNIOR HIGH SCHOOL STUDENTS
```
**?ss adolescent pregnancy**

```
     s7      169    ADOLESCENT PREGNANCY
```
**?ss s7 or (s1 and s6)**

```
            169    S7
           2723    S1
          61022    S6
     S8     596    S7 OR (S1 AND S6)
```
**?ts8/6/1-5**

```
  8/6/1
 00761189     77-30714
 Teens at risk for pregnancy: The role of ego development and family
 processes.

  8/6/2
 00761180     77-30705
 Meaningful involvement in instrumental activity and well-being: Studies of
 older adolescents and at risk urban teen-agers.

  8/6/3
 00758788     27-59046
 An analysis of curriculum for pregnant and parenting adolescents.

  8/6/4
 00757491     77-28494
 A comparison and analysis of the presence of family problems during
 pregnancy of mothers of 'autistic' children and mothers of normal children.

  8/6/5
 00756915     77-27917
 Formal operational thinking: The role of cognitive developmental processes
 in adolescent decision-making about pregnancy and contraception.
```

**Search 10.1:** (cont.)

```
?b37

File 37:SOCIOLOGICAL ABSTRACTS - 63-90/OCT
     (COPR. SOC. ABSTRACTS)

     Set      Items    Description
     ---      -----    -----------

?ss pregnancy/df and (adolescents/df or high school students)

     S1       476      PREGNANCY/DF
     S2       3121     ADOLESCENTS/DF (Persons aged 13 to 17.)
     S3       350      HIGH SCHOOL STUDENTS
     S4       108      PREGNANCY/DF AND (ADOLESCENTS/DF OR HIGH SCHOOL
                       STUDENTS)
?ts4/6/1-5

 4/6/1
2092077   89W10802
Teen Pregnancy and Sexual Abuse: Exploring the Connection

 4/6/2
2089211   89U8561
Lifestyle and First Pregnancy among Finnish Adolescents

 4/6/3
2087395   89W9903
Sexuality, Pregnancy and Motherhood among Mexican-American Adolescents.

 4/6/4
2084493   89S21124
Size, Composition and Utility of Support Networks for Pregnant and Parenting
Adolescents.

 4/6/5
2084019   89U6583
Too Young, Too Soon, Too Fast: Rapid Repeat Pregnancy among Inner-City
Adolescents.
?logoff
```

From the European perspective, FRANCIS: SOCIOLOGIE, one of the family of FRANCIS databases produced by the French Centre National de la Recherche Scientifique Institute de l'Information Scientifique et Technique (CNRS/INIST), also covers the broad field of sociology, including social psychology, demography, economic and political sociology and social work. Its coverage corresponds to the *Bulletin Signaletique Sciences Humaines: Section Sociologie*, going back to 1972, and, although French-language based, its coverage is international.

For a general social science database, the Informationszentrum Sozialwissenschaften produces SOCIAL SCIENCES LITERATURE INFORMATION SYSTEM (SOLIS), a German-based database covering abstracts to social science literature, including sociology, social research methods, social psychology and social problems. The database covers material from 1945 to date, with abstracts from 1976, and provides titles and subjects in English. Sources include reports, conference proceedings and journals.

*Economics*

Economics, as an academic subject, is also covered by more than one database. ECONOMIC LITERATURE INDEX, from the American Economic Association, covers articles and book reviews from journals and books. It is the online equivalent of the *Journal of Economic Literature* and the annual *Index of Economic Articles*. Again, the French CNRS/INIST produces FRANCIS: ECODOC, covering selected French literature on economics and economic theory, from 1981.

*Politics*

Political science as a theoretical study is the subject of the US POLITICAL SCIENCE DOCUMENTS file, which corresponds to the printed source of the same name. It is indexed using the *Political Science Thesaurus* but coverage is limited to American sources. Also, PAIS, the broad-based international database on economics, political science, social sciences and the humanities, is a good source of political science information. The database corresponds to *PAIS Bulletin*, covering eight hundred English-language journals and six thousand non-serial publications, and *PAIS Foreign Language Index,* covering four hundred journals and two hundred non-serial publications in five languages. It also includes data on public administration, demography and sociology.

For many searches, especially those requested in an academic environment, databases rooted in a single discipline are the most obvious source of information. Their subject coverage is defined in terms of the subject disciplines with which the academic is familiar, and the level of material they contain is also appropriate to the researcher. Their subject approach is, however, also their limitation, as searches in the social sciences often draw on more than one discipline. Whether one single database will answer a given question will depend not only on the nature of the topic, but also on the amount of information and degree of comprehensiveness required. Inevitably, the files also overlap. In the area of educational psychology, for instance, there is some duplication between PSYCINFO and ERIC, but a search on the same topic carried out on both files will produce far from identical results. The PSYCINFO references are likely to include a high proportion of clinical and experimental material; the ERIC list will show far more material based on practical experience in school and classroom. The choice of one or other (or frequently both) will depend on the exact requirements of the user. Apart from actual overlap between databases, we have already seen that particular activities and problems in the social sciences may often be approached from the angle of different disciplines with equal validity. Thus, a search on 'pregnancy in adolescence' might be carried out on ERIC, PSYCINFO and SOCIOLOGICAL ABSTRACTS and produce useful references in each case. Search 10.1 uses this search and shows a small sample of results from each database. There is no overlap of results in this small sample, and some differences in emphasis can be detected. As might be expected, the PSYCINFO titles are concerned with psychological factors, while those from SOCIOLOGICAL ABSTRACTS look at social context. ERIC covers a range of materials, not only those dealing directly with education.

**Multi-disciplinary databases**

The traditional subject disciplines are by no means the only option for defining the content of a database. On the one hand, the growth of cross-disciplinary studies has led to the development of databases which focus on one topic or problem, but draw their material from a range of disciplines; on the other more practical considerations of form or source have produced databases which contain one type of information on many subjects: news databases are an obvious example. In addition, the searcher needs to be aware of databases with coverage broader than their name at first suggests. Thus NTIS (National Technical Information Service) is actually a multi-disciplinary database of United States government-sponsored research, development and engineering, and reports from government agencies covering administration and management, behaviour and society, business and economics, and health planning, among other subjects. A number of types of multi-disciplinary database useful to the social scientist are discussed in more detail below.

*Problem-centred databases*

An alternative approach, encouraged by the growth of cross-disciplinary studies, is to set up a database focused on one problem or area of interest, and draw relevant material from a range of sources and disciplines. CHILD ABUSE AND NEGLECT is a good example of this approach. Not only does it ignore traditional subject boundaries, but it includes a variety of materials; these include descriptions of ongoing research projects and of service programmes (in the United States only), bibliographic references, legal references, and descriptions of audio-visual materials. Abstracts of court case decisions are also included. The FAMILY RESOURCES database adopts a similar approach in the field of family studies, drawing on the disciplines of medicine, psychology, sociology and education as they relate to the family. It includes articles, audio-visual and instructional materials, books, government publications, dissertations and human resources. AGELINE, produced by the American Association of Retired Persons, is another example, focusing on aspects of middle age and ageing, and drawing together materials relating to such issues as economics, family relationships, demographic trends, political action and health care.

The socio-economic aspects of demography have been covered from 1966 to 1984 by the University of North Carolina, Carolina Population Center's POPULATION BIBLIOGRAPHY database, which contains references to studies in the areas of abortion, demography, migration, family planning, fertility and population policy and law. It focuses on demographic issues in the USA and developing countries, with most records in English. Its records have since been amalgamated with POPLINE (POPulation information onLINE), produced by John Hopkins University, Population Information Program in collaboration with other universities and research organizations in the United States. Its international coverage focuses on family planning and population, including contraception, child health care, AIDS in developing countries and demography.

DHSS-Data, the British database produced by the Library of the Department of Health and Social Security, covers the area in which the Department is actively involved - health service administration, social services and social security. It includes all types of material added to the library: official publications, research and conference reports, books and journal articles. Search 10.2 shows the range of material accessed in two brief searches on DHSS-Data. Similarly, SOCIAL WORK ABSTRACTS, an American database, covers areas of interest to social workers, including drug abuse, crime, child welfare and mental health. A new database for practitioners in community development and the voluntary sector is VOLNET, which spans material relating to economic development, social policy and social practice and which includes a good quantity of grey literature.

## Search 10.2: DHSS-Data on Data-Star search

```
    *SIGN-ON  15.52.45          07.09.90

    D-S/DHSS/1983 - 22. JULY 1990    SESSION 1487
    COPYRIGHT BY BRITISH CROWN COPYRIGHT, 1984

    D-S - SEARCH MODE - ENTER QUERY
      1_:  (residential adj care) and management and elderly

    RESULT    50
      3_:  ..p 2/au,ti,so,ab/1-5
```

**Search 10.2:** (cont.)

1
TI DELIVERY of health care in residential homes for elderly people : a
   seminar heldon 19 September 1989 : report of the proceedings<.
SO Heywood (DHSS Health Publications Unit, No. 2 Site, Manchester Road,
   Heywood, Lancs. OL10 2PZ) : Department of Health, 1990, 39 i.e. 94 p,
   ISBN (1851975322), Bliss (QLV : QEL 8P3 LR ), $4.50, DHSS=YES,
   UKGOV=YES.
AB The seminar, which this reports, was designed to help authorities in
   reviewing their current practices in respect of the health care
   arrangements for elderly people in residential settings. It addressed
   itself to practice and management issues arising from the Social
   Services Inspectorate (SSI) report 'Health in homes'. Five
   presentations looked specifically at : promotion of continence and
   the management of incontinence; administration of medicines; the
   needs of mentally ill elderly residents; and 'health inputs into
   residential homes'. Brief summaries of these papers are presented,
   with detailed related papers attached as annexes, together with the
   summary of the recommendations of the SSI report. The main issues
   arising from the small group sessions considering specific aspects of
   health care are also included.

2
TI Caring for quality : guidance on standards for residential homes for
   elderlypeople<.
SO London : HMSO, 1990, v,55p, ISBN (0113212720), Bliss (QLV ELG ),
   $6.00, DHSS=YES, UKGOV=YES.
AB This guide draws together information about standards used by the SSI
   (Social Services Inspectorate) in its recent work on the inspection
   of residential homes for elderly people and other relevant work. The
   compilation is being published in the expectation that it will be of
   value to a wide range of professionals who are concerned to provide,
   manage and evaluate homes. It is based on a review of existing SSI
   and related work on standards in residential homes and sets out to
   identify and systematise key principles and standards. It aims to
   provide: a way of thinking about standards for homes and their
   management; some clarification of the differences between standards
   for management, standards for care and good quality of life; and a
   compilation of the standards developed by SSI in recent years to
   apply to particular contexts and issues.

3
TI DIRECTORY of practice examples in residential care for elderly people
   <.
AU DOMONEY-L, HALVES-R, eds.
SO London (5 Tavistock Place, WC1H 9SS) : National Institute for Social
   Work, 1989, 287p, ISBN (0902789627), Bliss (QLV : QEL ), $5.00.
AB This directory is published as part of the 'Research into Practice :
   residential care of elderly people' programme of the Practice and
   Development Exchange at the National Institute for Social Work. It is
   concerned with examples of practice intended to embody the good
   practices described in phase one of the programme. Questionnaires
   were sent to all 123 statutory providers of social services in the
   United Kingdom, 45 voluntary providers of residential care and 21
   private providers (response rates were 48, 10 and 4 respectively).
   The 62 reports received are set out under the questionnaire headings
   of: alternative forms of care; assessment; information to applicants;
   choice, privacy and security; staff development training; and
   management of services. Contact addresses are included.

**Search 10.2:** (cont.)

4
TI DIRECTORY of practice examples in residential care for elderly people
   <.
AU DOMONEY-L, HALVES-R, eds.
SO London (5 Tavistock Place, WC1H 9SS) : National Institute for Social
   Work, 1989, 287p, ISBN (0902789627), Bliss (QLV : QEL ), $5.00.
AB This directory is published as part of the 'Research into Practice :
   residential care of elderly people' programme of the Practice and
   Development Exchange at the National Institute for Social Work. It is
   concerned with examples of practice intended to embody the good
   practices described in phase one of the programme. Questionnaires
   were sent to all 123 statutory providers of social services in the
   United Kingdom, 45 voluntary providers of residential care and 21
   private providers (response rates were 48, 10 and 4 respectively).
   The 62 reports received are set out under the questionnaire headings
   of: alternative forms of care; assessment; information to applicants;
   choice,  privacy and security; staff development training; and
   management of services. Contact addresses are included.


5
TI Taking good care : a handbook for care assistants<.
AU WORSLEY-J.
SO Mitcham (Bernard Sunley House, 60 Pitcairn Road, Mitcham, Surrey CR4
   3LL) : Age Concern England, 1989, 144p, ISBN (0862420725), Bliss (QLV
   : QEL ), $6.95.
AB This book offers practical advice for workers in residential homes.
   Topics discussed are the needs and views of older people, the
   management of common medical and social problems of old age and
   improving care and communication skills. It is arranged in nine
   chapters: (i) an overview of the book and brief guide to the workings
   of local authority, voluntary and private residential homes; (ii) the
   residents - a practical insight into the psychology of residents with
   comments from elderly residents; (iii) starting work - a manager
   describes the induction of a new care assistant in an inner-city
   home; (iv) the care assistant's role - the principles of care and
   practical procedures in the daily running of a home; (v) giving
   special care - promoting continence and helping with bowel problems,
   basic home nursing, pressure sores, care of the dying and procedures
   after death;  (vi) communicating with people - face to face
   communication and the reporting and recording of information; (vii)
   what is ageing? - changes in medical practice, body changes in old
   age, disease and illness, the care assistant's role in managing the
   problems of ageing; (vii) keeping active in mind and body; and (ix)
   training opportunities and further information.


        END OF DOCUMENTS

 _:..s

  D-S - SEARCH MODE - ENTER QUERY
   3_: **(under adj fives) and (child adj care)**

   RESULT    23
   4_: **..p 3/au,ti,so,ab/1-5**


    1
TI The Politics of child welfare : inequality, power and change<.
AU FROST-N, STEIN-M.
SO New  York  ; London : Harvester Wheatsheaf, 1989, 179p, ISBN
   (0745006132), Bliss (QLE : QAK ), $8.95.

**Search 10.2:** (cont.)

AB The authors declare the aim of this book as to present a political
analysis of the nature of child welfare in contemporary Britain - an
analysis in which inequality acts as the key organising concept.
There are chapters on: childhood in history; a history of child
welfare; abusing children - the politics of regulation; child sexual
abuse - a question of care; politicising juvenile justice; the care
and control of separated children; and caring for the under-fives. In
a final chapter the authors use their analysis as a basis for a new
framework for practice.

2
TI Caring for children : services and policies for children and equal
opportunities in the United Kingdom. Report for the European
Commissions Childcare Network<.
AU COHEN-B.
SO London    (8    Storeys    Gate, SW1) : Commission of the European
Communities, 1988, 147p, Bliss (QLE : TWX B ), Free.
AB The Childcare Network was formed as part of the European Community's
Second Action Programme on the Promotion of Equal Opportunities for
Women. The aims are to describe and analyse the current situation,
make recommendations, and initiate a programme of positive projects.
This report and recommendations are devoted to the situation in the
United Kingdom. A full list of conclusions and recommendations is
included, covering: equal opportunities in the UK; child care
policies; services for under-fives; services for school-age children;
employment provision; other policies affecting child care, e.g.
taxation; recommendations national action; priorities; and
recommendations for a European Community programme.

3
TI Voluntary organizations and childcare : issues and challenges<.
AU HOGG-C.
SO London (26 Bedford Square, WC1B 3HU) : National Council for Voluntary
Organizations, 1986, 79p, ISBN (0719911869), Bliss (QLP 5JV ), $1.50.
AB Survey of 26 national organizations working with the under-fives
which looks briefly at their roles, range of activities, funding,
working methods, training and performance review. In spite of wide
variations in approach, all organizations show a commitment to
working with children as part of a family, working with parents,
supporting    self-help    community    initiatives,    developing equal
opportunity and multi-cultural approaches to childcare, reviewing
activities more systematically, and developing a multi-disciplinary
approach to childcare. The bulk of the report consists of directory
information about the organizations studied.

4
TI Provision for the under-fives : one council's response 1980-87.
AU HAMILTON-D.
SO Children-and-Society, London, 1989, vol 3, no 2, p152-167, ISSN
(09510605), Bliss (QLP : QLE MPE J ).
AB Coordination of services for under-fives is a major concern in
efforts to achieve a reasonable level of services with low levels of
resources. This article relates the history of one attempt to develop
such a coordinated approach in one local authority - Leeds. A
specially appointed Council Committee led the way to breaking down
many barriers between services, to improving training, and to using
scarce professional skills to best advantage. Journal abstract  .

5
TI Protection through prevention.
AU PERRY-C.

**Search 10.2:** (cont.)

```
SO Community-Care, Haywards Heath, 1989, Jul 27, no 773, pvii, ISSN
   (03075508), Bliss (QLE T MRT ).
AB In 1983 South Glamorgan County Council adopted a strategy for
   services  to under-fives which placed major emphasis on abuse
   prevention and envisaged a network of locally-based family centres.
   The centres have facilities for counselling, group work and family
   therapy as well as being able to accommodate access visits and
   meetings of foster parents, childminders and playgroup leaders.
   Agreements have also been made with child care organizations such as
   Barnardo's. This article describes the organization of these services
   for under-fives, and also briefly explains how services to other
   groups, such as juvenile offenders and mentally handicapped children,
   have included within them some investment in the under-fives.

      END OF DOCUMENTS
```

Material on the social sciences can also be found in databases relating to urban planning. For instance, ACOMPLINE, from the Research Library of the London Research Centre, is a database on urban affairs originating in the information service provided to local government officers and members. It, too, covers a wide range of materials, including grey literature and published articles. Search 10.3 gives a sample of output from ACOMPLINE. PLANEX, produced by the Planning Exchange, again covers matters of interest to local government workers, including rural development and social and economic planning, whilst the French URBAMET database looks at worldwide literature on urban and regional planning. LOCAL GOVERNMENT INFORMATION NETWORK (LOGIN), an American database aimed at local government practitioners, also provides descriptions of innovative practice based on information from users, researchers and local government literature, whilst the German Fraunhofer Society, Information Centre for Regional Planning and Building Construction's German-language RSWB (RAUMORDNUNG, STADTEBAU, WOHNUNGSWESEN, BAUWESEN) covers urban and regional planning, architecture and construction.

**Search 10.3: ESA-IRS search on the ACOMPLINE database**

```
File 35:ACOMPLINE:74-90,06
? s right(w2)buy

     1        471     RIGHT(W2)BUY

? t 1/4/1-5

      TYPE 1/4/1
Quest Accession NUmber : 90034400
 90-NZ-06014 Acompline
 LONDON NEEDS HOMES: THE REAL COST OF HOUSING IN LONDON
 LHU, Feb 1990 5pp (LHU, Berkshire House, 168/173 High Holborn,
London WC1V 7AA) RP66047A
 Looks at the availablity and costs of housing in London, including
the influence of increased house prices, the decline of the private
rented sector, and changes to housing association and council
housing rents. Also highlights the need for low cost housing for
rent.
 Uncontrolled Terms: owner occupation / house purchase / right
to buy / council house sales / rented housing / private sector
 / first time buyer
```

**Search 10.3:** (cont.)

```
        TYPE 1/4/2
Quest Accession NUmber : 90030756
 90-NZ-05103 Acompline
 THE VALUATION ON TRANSFER OF LOCAL AUTHORITY HOUSING STOCK
 RICS, Sep 1989 29pp (RICS, 12 Great George Street, London SW1)
 RP66005A
 Provides guidance on the valuation of council housing for transfer
 under Section IV of the Housing Act 1988 and for voluntary
 transfers, in England. Gives background information on the legal
 framework, property portfolio, competence and liability, and
 discusses methodology, projected income from the stock, tenants,
 expenditure and future developments.
 Uncontrolled Terms: housing transfer / tenants choice /
 housing stock / local government expenditure / housing
 management / rent arrears / void / empty property / housing
 tenure / housing repairs / housing maintenance / right to buy
 / council house sales / discount / local government finance /
 landlord / sale


        TYPE 1/4/3
Quest Accession NUmber : 90030744
 90-NZ-05100 Acompline
 WHAT'S IT WORTH: THE VALUATION OF LOCAL AUTHORITY STOCK FOR
 TRANSFER TO NEW LANDLORDS
 LHU/LRC 1989? 28pp (LHU, Bedford House, 133 Camden High St, London
 NW1) (LRC, Parliament House, 81 Black Prince Road, London SE1 7SZ)
 RP65979A
 Describes the valuation process for the transfer of council
 housing under Part IV of the Housing Act 1988, voluntary transfers
 and the method used to determine the disposal price. Discusses the
 effect of negative valuations on local authority capital expenditure
 and procedures on referral to the district valuer, and includes a
 spreadsheet valuation model.
 Uncontrolled Terms: housing transfer / tenants choice /
 housing stock / local government expenditure / housing
 management / rent arrears / void / empty property / housing
 tenure / housing repairs / housing maintenance / right to buy
 / council house sales / discount


        TYPE 1/4/4
Quest Accession NUmber : 90030700
 90-NZ-05089 Acompline
 TAKING STOCK: COUNCIL TRANSFERS ONE YEAR ON
 Inside Housing, 2 Mar 1990 7(9) pp8-9
 Looks at the experiences of two local authorities who have already
 carried out voluntary transfers of their housing stock: Chiltern
 District Council and Sevenoaks District Council. Comments that there
 is still doubt about whether or not the spending of receipts is
 allowed, and the frustration this is causing to the councils.
 Uncontrolled Terms: housing associations / right to buy / West
 Kent Housing Association / rented housing / council housing /
 housing finance / Chiltern Hundreds


        TYPE 1/4/5
Quest Accession NUmber : 90030472
 90-NZ-05032 Acompline
 PRIVATISING BRITAIN'S HOUSING: AN ENGLISHMAN'S COUNCIL HOME
 Economist, 24 Feb 1990 314(7643) pp21-24
 Examines the reasons why the selling off of council housing has
```

**Search 10.3:** (cont.)

now come to a virtual standstill after the notable success of the
first eight years of the programme. Many more tenants are proving
harder to persuade of the merits of the right to buy and tenants'
choice schemes than the government anticipated. Also the
introduction of competition has had a striking impact on the
quality, efficiency and attitudes within local authorities.
 Uncontrolled Terms: housing policy / rented housing / housing
associations  /  Housing Act 1988 / tenants choice / council
house sales

? **limit/aco**

     LIMIT /ACO
? **s homelessness; s young(w)people**

     6        927      HOMELESSNESS
     7        2874     YOUNG(W)PEOPLE
? **c 6*7**

     8        134      6*7
? **t 8/4/1-5**

     TYPE 8/4/1
Quest Accession NUmber : 90034320
 90-NZ-05994 Acompline
HOMELESS AND HUNGRY: A SIGN OF THE TIMES
CS, 1989 34pp, tables (CS, 140A Glocester Mansions, Cambridge
Circus, London WC2H 8HD) RP65686A
Gives the results of the initial stage of research based on pilot
interviews with 49 people who stayed at the Centrepoint Nightshelter
in Soho, and on follow-up interviews with 23 of them two months
later. Updates a previous survey published in June 1988, repeating
and adding to the recommendations made then, arguing that despite
extensive media attention, the underlying causes of homelessness are
still not being addressed. Suggests a concerted programme bringing
together public, private, and voluntary groups is urgently required.
 Uncontrolled Terms: young people / night shelter

     TYPE 8/4/2
Quest Accession NUmber : 90033944
 90-NZ-05900 Acompline
THE TANHOUSE ESTATE AS AN ALTERNATIVE APPROACH TO HIGH RISE
HOUSING: A STUDY OF ESTATE IMPROVEMENT AND THE PROVISION OF HOUSING
FOR SINGLE PEOPLE IN DUDLEY
 BP, Nov 1989 34pp (Research Paper No.4) (BP, Perry Barr,
Birmingham B42 2SUE) RP66023A
 Examines the impact of the 1988 reform of the social security
system on public sector housing provision for single people in
Dudley, West Midlands. Shows how Dudley MBC has adapted its housing
management and lettings policy to improve its high rise housing to
provide accommodation for young single people or young childless
couples through Department of the Environment Estate Action funding,
questioning whether this innovative approach is being subverted by
Department of Social Security policies. 25 references.
 Uncontrolled Terms: house improvement / refurbishment /
housing estate / tower block / young people / homelessness /
 single homeless / Social Security Act 1986 / housing allocation

     TYPE 8/4/3
Quest Accession NUmber : 90033892
 90-NZ-05887 Acompline

**Search 10.3:** (cont.)

```
    REPORT ON HOMELESSNESS IN CENTRAL LONDON
    WECPCCG, Jan 1990 17pp (WECPCCG, PO Box 240, Victoria Street,
    London SW1E 6QP) RP65941A
    Examines the extent of homelessness in central London within the
    main categories of habitual vagrants, mentally ill, young people and
    transient people. Puts forward recommendations for alleviating the
    situation and possible police action, including the creation of more
    day  centres,  assessment  centres,  increasing  council  housing
    provision, and providing more information about services.
     Uncontrolled Terms: day care  / detoxification / alcohol /
    mental health / single homeless / social security


         TYPE 8/4/4
    Quest Accession NUmber : 90033612
     90-NZ-05817 Acompline
    CLOSING DOWN THE SPIKE
     Housing, Apr 1990 26(3) pp10-12
    Looks at some of the case histories of the residents of the
    squalid  350-bed  Shaftesbury Hostel, which Leeds Metropolitan
    District Council is in the process of closing down in order to
    provide decent accommodation for the single homeless. Despite a
    thoughtful closure programme, admissions to the Hostel of the young
    and abused are now increasing, and the it is filling up faster than
    it can be emptied.
     Uncontrolled  Terms:  domestic violence  /  sexual abuse  /
    homelessness / women / young people


         TYPE 8/4/5
    Quest Accession NUmber : 90032888
     90-NZ-05636 Acompline
    NOT AT HOME IN TORY BRITAIN
     Labour Res, Mar 1990 79(3) pp21-22
    Looks at the continuing problem of homelessness in Britain,
    arguing that the recent government review of the legislation has
    little new to offer. Claims that the deregulation of the private
    rented sector and the new proposals will only make things worse and
    that housing associations have not been given the resources to
    provide much help. Argues that only more public sector investment in
    housebuilding can provide the solution.
     Uncontrolled Terms: housing needs / young people
```

*Form-specific databases*

A totally different approach is provided by those databases which are not limited by subject matter, but only by the type of material they include. A number of these contain useful information for the social sciences. DISSERTATION ABSTRACTS ONLINE is one such. This is a multi-disciplinary database of dissertations presented at American universities or other accredited institutions. It includes almost all doctoral dissertations since 1861, and some Masters theses from 1962 onwards. Some Canadian dissertations are also listed. The question to be considered before using it, therefore, is not whether the subject approach is right, but whether studies of this type and length are appropriate for the user, especially bearing in mind that, for non-North American users, the dissertations may take some time to obtain. The file, which is equivalent to the printed source *Dissertation Abstracts International,* contains lengthy abstracts, but only rudimentary indexing, so that care is also needed in constructing an appropriate search strategy. Dissertation titles are usually explicit, so a search on titles alone may often prove the most satisfactory approach. Search 10.4 shows the difference this can make. The search for the development of the concept of time in children, carried out as a simple free text search without any restrictions produced 605 hits, but none of the sample titles displayed was really relevant. By limiting the search to title and descriptor fields only, the number of hits was reduced to five, of which three were highly relevant.

## Search 10.4: DISSERTATION ABSTRACTS on DIALOG

```
FILE 35: DISSERTATION ABSTRACTS ONLINE - 1861-NOV 90
     (Copr. University Microfilms)

     Set     Items    Description
     ---     -----    -----------

?ss time and concept and child?

     S1     87617    TIME
     S2     27367    CONCEPT
     S3     46295    CHILD?
     S4       605    TIME AND CONCEPT AND CHILD?

?ts4/6/1-5

 4/6/1
01124650 ORDER NO: AAD90-28566
CAREER MARGINALITY: CHARACTERISTICS AND EMPLOYMENT SITUATION OF REGISTERED
NURSES WHO WORK IN LONG-TERM CARE FACILITIES AND HOSPITALS

 4/6/2
01123749 ORDER NO: AAD90-25140
THE STABLE DISPOSITION CONCEPT AND SPONTANEOUS TRAIT INFERENCE:
DEVELOPMENTAL AND INDIVIDUAL DIFFERENCES

 4/6/3
01123638 ORDER NO: AAD90-20747
AN ASSESSMENT OF OBJECT-RELATIONS AND SELF-CONCEPT IN BLACK FATHER-ABSENT
MALE CHILDREN AS A CONSEQUENCE OF THE FATHER'S CONTROL OF HIS ABSENCE

 4/6/4
01122049 ORDER NO: AAD90-26662
HOME SCHOOL LITERACY: AN ETHNOGRAPHIC STUDY OF PARENTS TEACHING READING AND
WRITING

 4/6/5
01121666 ORDER NO: NOT AVAILABLE FROM UNIVERSITY MICROFILMS INT'L
EDUCATIVE TEACHING AS OWN AFFAIR: FUNDAMENTAL PEDAGOGICAL REFLECTION
(AFRIKAANS TEXT)

?limitall/ti,de


>>>LIMITALL started
?ss time and concept and child?

     S5     10658    TIME
     S6      8960    CONCEPT
     S7     29388    CHILD?
     S8         5    TIME AND CONCEPT AND CHILD?

?ts8/6/1-5
```

**Search 10.4:** (cont.)

```
    8/6/1
    0956970 ORDER NO: AAD87-13843
    FIRST-TIME FATHERHOOD: INTEGRATING CHILDBEARING EXPERIENCE INTO THE SELF-
    CONCEPT

    8/6/2
    834759 ORDER NO: AAD84-04061
    THE LEARNING DISABLED CHILD: AREA OF DYSFUNCTION, TIME IN SPECIAL EDUCATION
    AND DIMENSIONS OF SELF CONCEPT

    8/6/3
    681353 ORDER NO: AAD80-08428
    THE DEVELOPMENT OF THE CONCEPT OF PHYSICAL TIME: HOW CHILDREN COME TO
    RECOGNIZE SYNCHRONOUS DURATIONS AS EQUAL

    8/6/4
    396324 ORDER NO: AAD71-10212
    TIME CONCEPTION, SELF CONCEPT AND RESPONSIBILITY IN SEVEN AND TEN YEAR OLD
    CHILDREN OF A WHITE MIDDLE CLASS COMMUNITY

    8/6/5
    283772 ORDER NO: AAD66-02476
    AN INQUIRY INTO CHILDREN'S UNDERSTANDING OF THE TIME CONCEPT WITH
    IMPLICATIONS FOR WRITTEN COMPOSITION

?logoff
```

FORIS (Forschungsinformationssystem Sozialwissenschaften) contains descriptions of current, planned and completed research in the social sciences, in German-speaking countries. It covers communication, economics, education, political science, psychology and sociology from sources including research institutions, documentation centres and universities and colleges.

Other useful form-specific databases are those which deal with newspapers and magazines. Much news coverage is full text, but some databases provide an index and abstract approach to news. Thus URBALINE, produced as a subfile of the London Research Centre's ACOMPLINE database, contains abstracts of press comment and press reports on social policy and urban planning, with the aim of giving up-to-date coverage on the background to legislative changes. Similarly, Associated Press produces AP POLITICAL FILE, which has US local, state and federal political news and information. NATIONAL NEWSPAPER INDEX covers the entire content of three major American newspapers, the *Christian Science Monitor,* the *New York Times* and *The Wall Street Journal,* together with a selection of articles from the *Washington Post* and the *Los Angeles Times.* MAGAZINE INDEX provides cover-to-cover indexing for over four hundred American and Canadian popular magazines. Both serve as archive files to the daily updated NEWSEARCH file, which also covers legal journals. Material from these sources will be popular and topical rather than academic in approach, less appropriate to the research student or professional studying a topic in depth, but more useful in dealing with enquiries from those requiring up-to-the minute information. Search 10.5 shows a range of abstracts retrieved by an URBALINE search on the much debated subject of the British poll tax.

Databases of government publications also cover a wide range of subjects, but include much significant material for the social scientist. The BRITISH OFFICIAL PUBLICATIONS (HMSO) database is now available, covering British government publications. It includes parliamentary papers and non-parliamentary papers published on behalf of government departments and other national bodies, and also items published by

British and international organizations for which HMSO acts as an agent. Similar materials in the United States are included by the GPO MONTHLY CATALOG, which covers publications of US government agencies, and the GPO PUBLICATIONS REFERENCE FILE, which covers public documents published by the executive, judicial and legislative branches of the United States federal government. The activities of government are also covered by databases such as POLIS (Parliamentary Online Information System), from the House of Commons Library, which includes the proceedings and papers of the British Parliament, and selected official publications. A similar function is fulfilled in the United States by the CONGRESSIONAL RECORD ABSTRACTS and CONGRESSIONAL RECORD FULL TEXT databases.

## Search 10.5: ESA-IRS search on URBALINE

```
? limit/urb

    LIMIT /URB
? s community(w)charge; s poll(w)tax

    1       568     COMMUNITY(W)CHARGE
    2       627     POLL(W)TAX
? s poverty

    3       430     POVERTY
? c  (2+3)*4
    4       211     (2+3)*4
? t 4/4/1-5

        TYPE 4/4/1
Quest Accession NUmber : 88046893
 8807987 Urbaline
DIB
 Publication Date: 880908
  Extensive report and comment on the TUC annual conference
proceedings in Bournemouth yesterday; Congress voted to boycott the
Government Employment Training scheme, to support "every legal
effort" to oppose the introduction of the poll tax, and called for
the halt and phasing out of nuclear power; other issues discussed
include education, the post office strike, the Channel tunnel,
poverty and equal pay. Added Keywords: Neil Kinnock, Norman Fowler
 Controlled Terms: Trade unions
 Source: (Available for reference only ). (ES (WEF) 07/09 p2;
Financial Times 08/09 p10,28; Guardian p1,4,18; Ind p1,8,26; Times
p1,4,24; Daily Telegraph p1,7,48)

        TYPE 4/4/2
Quest Accession NUmber : 88033765
 8805677 Urbaline
DIB
 Publication Date: 880622
  According to 'Faith in the City of Birmingham', published
yesterday by the Church of England, a third of Birmingham's
population is living below the poverty line and despite an upturn in
prosperity 700,000 people are deprived. Added Keywords: inner city,
deprivation, ethnic minorities, racial discrimination,poll tax, job
creation, economic decline,
 Controlled Terms: Poverty / Birmingham
 Source: (Guardian 22/06 p5; Daily Telegraph p6)

        TYPE 4/4/3
Quest Accession NUmber : 88019881
 8803099 Urbaline
DIB
```

**Search 10.5:** (cont.)

Publication Date: 880405
 The Government is planning to issue students with poll tax
identity cards" to make sure that they do not escape paying the new
community charge; on the first day of registration for poll tax in
Scotland, Scottish Secretary Malcolm Rifkind said that people who
tried to avoid the poll tax could be fined by the courts; the Church
of Scotland is to publish soon a book 'Just Sharing - A Christian
Approach to the Distribution of Wealth, Income and Benefits', which
attacks  long  term poverty as "totally unacceptable" and is
understood to condemn the poll tax as "socially unjust"; report on
the launch by the People's Petition Against The Poll Tax, and
statistics released by the ALA, of a London Research Centre survey
which showed that the tax will cost people living in inner London at
least $700 a year on top of their current rates bill; letter from
Library Association Chief Executive George Cunningham criticising
the expected introduction into the Local Government Finance Bill of
measures affecting public libraries. Added Keywords: charging,
guillotine, enabling legislation
 Controlled Terms: Local government finance
 Source: (Guardian 01/04 p24; Ind p7; Times p4,17; Daily Telegraph
p4; Guardian 02/04 p3; Times p2; Daily Telegraph p4; Guardian 04/04
p11; Daily Telegraph p2; Guardian 05/04 p20; Time Out 07/04 p4)


        TYPE 4/4/4
Quest Accession NUmber : 88019457
 8802999 Urbaline
DIB
 Publication Date: 880330
 In a letter, Stanley Manchester, the Rev Tony Burnham, Prof Paul
Wilding and others of the Campaign Against Poverty announce the
setting up of a network to provide information and suggestions about
action over the "immorality or injustice" of the Budget, which "so
blatantly gives to the rich and leaves the poor yet again worse
off". Added Keywords: poll tax, community charge, cost of living,
Housing Bill, rent, gas prices, electricity prices
 Controlled Terms: Poverty
 Source: (Guardian 30/03 p18)


        TYPE 4/4/5
Quest Accession NUmber : 88018169
 8802788 Urbaline
DIB
 Publication Date: 880324
 Margaret Hodge, ALA Leader, announced yesterday results of a
major survey carried out by the London Research Centre for the ALA,
into the individual financial effects of the new poll tax system on
Londoners, which showed that most Londoners will be around $8 a week
worse off; Hounslow Council is supporting a national petition
against poll tax which is being launched on 28 March; the Scottish
National Party yesterday opened its local election drive, pledging
to lead a mass campaign of resistance to the poll tax. Added
Keywords: community charge, London, ethnic groups, black people,
evasion, SHAL,ion Unit, Shelter, Church Action on Poverty,
 Controlled Terms: Local government finance
 Source: (LB Hounslow Press Notice 138-88 16/03; ES (WEF) 23/03
p15; Guardian 24/03 p5)

*Citation indexes*

These are discussed in detail in another chapter, but mention should be made here of SOCIAL SCISEARCH, the online version of the *Social Science Citation Index*, as it is a significant file for the social science searcher. Citation searching, for works referring to an original book or article, is an important technique in the social sciences, where a key theory or approach is often taken as the basis for further work. The possibility of using this approach, instead of, or as well as, a conventional subject search should always be borne in mind, as it often produces highly relevant results. It does, of course, depend on the user being aware of a source document of sufficient significance and relevance. Occasionally, where the cited work is a very popular or influential one, it may be useful to combine a citation search with some subject elements. For instance, a request to discover if anyone has applied the ideas of Schumacher's *Small is Beautiful* (an economics text) to the field of education might be satisfied by carrying out a citation search, and then selecting only those documents which also include words such as 'education', 'school', 'college' etc. in their titles. As a source for subject searching, SOCIAL SCISEARCH has the advantage of being a very large file covering the whole range of social sciences, which makes it very suitable for dealing with those topics which include more than one traditional discipline. Its limitation lies in the fact that it contains no indexing, so that subject searching is carried out on titles alone. Where these are explicit and descriptive the results will be good, but the use of literary titles, chosen to catch the eye, is quite common in the social sciences, especially at a more popular level, and such items will be missed. A subject search carried out on SOCIAL SCISEARCH therefore is likely to produce results which score highly for relevance but not for total recall.

*Factual databases*

These are also discussed as ready-reference sources in a separate chapter, but their usefulness to the social scientist should not be overlooked. In addition to general sources such as encyclopedias, a number of which are now available both online and on CD-ROM, there are a number of files of factual and statistical information particularly relevant to the social sciences.

For those with permission from the United Kingdom's Department of Employment, access to NOMIS (the National Online Manpower Information System) can provide social scientists with about twelve billion historical, current and forecast British labour and population statistics from 1971, including Census of Employment data, 1981 Census of Population Small Area Statistics, unemployment data for the last eighteen years and population estimates for the year 2011. Search 10.6 illustrates data obtained from NOMIS. The Central Statistical Office's CSO database also contains about thirteen thousand monthly, quarterly and annual time series related to economics in Britain, corresponding to data covered by publications such as *Economic Trends, Financial Statistics* and the *Monthly Digest of Statistics*.

On a European basis, the European Commission produces the CRONOS database which contains economic data on EC member countries corresponding to the various EUROSTAT publications. The database covers material from the mid-1950s and includes data on population, employment and finance, as well as macroeconomic data for developing countries.

Both UK and US population and housing statistics are available on SUPERSITE and its GB SITE sub-file. The former holds data from the 1960, 1970 and 1980 US Census of Population and Housing, as well as updates and forecasts, which can be examined according to a particular geographical area. The latter holds data from the UK 1971 and 1981 Census of Population and Housing, by enumeration district, ward, civil parish, local authority and county. Again, areas of interest can be defined geographically.

Geographical and demographic data are particularly well-suited to CD-ROM, and a large number of products are available in this area. The information is unlikely to change to any great extent over ten years, or within a time series, and CD-ROM offers a significantly smaller storage space. For example, SUPERMAP 1980 provides US county and tract level census data with retrieval software to produce tables and maps, CD-

ATLAS DE FRANCE carries data from the national census of France, and the 1981 Census: Small Area Statistics for England, Wales and Scotland gives 1987 populations estimates and boundary mapping to ward level. Another factual database on CD-ROM is the United States National Institute of Justice's DRUGS AND CRIME, which carries statistics, full text, articles and graphics on all aspects of drugs and crime.

## Search 10.6: NOMIS search on census employment public access dataset giving industry breakdown in the City of London, 1981

```
     Ready for user input:
    *data=pe80
    *80big=1-8
    *percent=on
    *year=1981
    *1981lad=119
    *print

    Wait - Loading the Execution module.

    Wait - Command Execution begins.
     Census of Employment (1980 PSIC) SEP 1981 NOMIS (Crown Copyright Reserved)
    JUL 5, 1990

      1981LAD        City of London

        Persons    % Broad Industry Description (80 classification)

      1    ***       0.0  1 Agriculture, forestry and fishing
      2    2,800     0.9  2 Energy and water supply
      3   35,000    10.9  3 Manufacturing industries
      4    2,700     0.8  4 Construction
      5   27,000     8.4  5 Distribution, hotels/catering; repairs
      6  230,200    71.8  6 Transport/communication,banking,finance
      7    9,700     3.0  7 Public administration and defence
      8   13,300     4.2  8 Other service industries
         320,800   100.0    Column Totals

    Because of rounding, 'totals' may not agree.
    *** Negligible or Suppressed because of confidentiality.
```

*Full-text databases*

A growing number of databases now contain the full text of their source articles, rather than merely bibliographic references. MAGAZINE ASAP, for instance, contains a selection of the full text of 120 magazines drawn from the list covered by MAGAZINE INDEX. Similarly, PROFILE has a wide range of current affairs files containing the text of publications, including the *Financial Times, The Times, Daily Telegraph, The Independent, The Guardian, Keesings Record of World Events (formerly, Keesings Contemporary Archives), Washington Post,* and *Economist.* The TEXTLINE host also holds the full text of most British newspapers, as well as major European, African, Asian, Australian, Middle Eastern and Latin and North American sources. Both are valuable sources of articles on current affairs and searching is geared to the novice, with menu-driven searching on TEXTLINE and simple GET and PICK commands on PROFILE. Both provide facilities for displaying the context of search terms as well as the full text. Search 10.7 shows the same topic, ethnic minorities and unemployment, searched on both hosts, with very similar results. Full text of items from the REUTERS NEWS REPORTS is also available online, providing broad international coverage of news and current affairs, with updates throughout the day on DIALOG and within two days on MEAD.

## Search 10.7: PROFILE and TEXTLINE searches

```
                              PROFILE  search
   get  ethnic/minorit*

   GET ETHNIC/MINORIT*
      1557 ITEMS RETRIEVED
   >
   pick unemployment

   PICK UNEMPLOYMENT
       105 ITEMS RETRIEVED
   >
   ctx 1-5

   CTX 1-5
   SORTING

    1....
      DTL 19 Jul 90 North-West heads illegitimacy table: Population (332)
    ....
      'East Anglia and the South-West are regions with relatively high earnings,
      relatively low UNEMPLOYMENT and in recent years relatively good economic
      performance,' he said.
    ....
      Statistics show the South-East and the West Midlands have the highest
      proportion of ETHNIC MINORITY groups while Scotland, Wales and the
      South-West have the lowest.
    2....
      TMS 07 Jul 90 Catholics to discuss racism in church (364)
    ....
      RACISM in the Roman Catholic Church is to be discussed at a meeting of
      Catholics from ETHNIC MINORITY groups in London this month.
    ....
      The congress will be held at Digby Stuart College, London, and will discuss
      housing, UNEMPLOYMENT, education, the family, and other social and
      political
   ***PRESS RETURN TO CONTINUE, N FOR NEXT ARTICLE, OR X TO EXIT


      issues.
    3....
      FT 21 Jun 90 UK News (Employment): Employers find graduate demand easing
          (495)
    ....
      Thus, the researchers conclude, the next few years may be marked by growing
      graduate shortages co-existing with with rising levels of graduate
      UNEMPLOYMENT or underemployment.
    ....
      But the most disturbing trend, said Mr Pike, is the rising - and unmet -
      demand for technological graduates. The greatest difficulty is found among
      companies wishing to recruit graduates in scientific, engineering and
      research and development where one in three recruiters surveyed in 1989
      reported unfilled vacancies. No other subject caused problems for more than
      10 per cent of recruiters. Separately, the IMS study found that ETHNIC
      MINORITIES are far more likely to pursue higher education - at least at
      polytechnics and colleges - than are their white counterparts. Data on
      ETHNIC factors among students was collected the first time with the 1990
   ***PRESS RETURN TO CONTINUE, N FOR NEXT ARTICLE, OR X TO EXIT


      polytechnic round. While 13 per cent of applicants described themselves as
      non-whites, only 5 percent of the nation's 16- to 29-year-old population is
```

**Search 10.7:** (cont.)

```
   non-white.

All material subject to copyright
>
tx 6

TX 6

  6  IND 21 Jun 90 Weak graduates face lean time, jobs study says (386)

     By BARRIE CLEMENT, Labour Editor
  The first sign that the boom in the demand for graduates may be easing is
  reported today by the Institute of Manpower Studies.
  Employers will go on finding it difficult to recruit people with good
  degrees and those who are qualified in engineering and applied science, but
  weaker graduates may face problems getting suitable jobs.
  Geoffrey Pike, a co-author of IMS Graduate Review for 1990, launching the
  study, said the demographic downturn had not been such a constraint as
  expected.
  Most university students are drawn from social classes I and II where
  numbers have hardly fallen, and appetite for education has grown. The
  institute says the demand for graduates has eased in 1989/90 because of the
  economic slowdown, and because some employers are reassessing policies in
  anticipation of shortages.
  The proportion of graduates in engineering and the applied sciences is
  likely to fall in the 1990s while the proportion of women and mature
***PRESS RETURN TO CONTINUE, N FOR NEXT ARTICLE, OR X TO EXIT


  graduates, and those from ETHNIC MINORITIES and with non-traditional
  qualifications will rise. The proportion of 'traditional' young male
  graduates will decrease.
  Demand for graduates is expected to grow in the longer term, assuming there
  is no prolonged economic downturn. On present trends, demand could be 30per
  cent higher at the end of the century than it is now. This is above the
  projected growth in output of 15 percent. The introduction of student loans
  could mean that the projection of the numbers of students is optimistic.
  The shortfall is likely to push up starting salaries and bring more company
  sponsorships. At the moment salaries vary from pounds 8,000 to pounds
  14,000.
  The authors conclude that a growing shortage of graduates could co-exist
  with rising graduate UNEMPLOYMENT and underemployment in the next year or
  so, because of a mismatch of demand and supply in some specialities.
  The market is likely to become more complex in the 1990s with greater
  diversity among graduates. More are expected to delay choosing a career.
  Companies will probably recruit throughout the year and there will be more
  channels for advertising and finding jobs at home and in Europe.
***PRESS RETURN TO CONTINUE, N FOR NEXT ARTICLE, OR X TO EXIT


  The IMS Graduate Review; Institute of Manpower Studies, Mantell Building,
  University of Sussex, Falmer, Brighton BN1 9RF; pounds 24.
  Home News Page 005

  The Independent

All material subject to copyright
>
```

**Search 10.7:** (cont.)

*TEXTLINE  search*

**ethnic minorit \***

Databases sourced from these areas and industries are available for
searching:

| General: | Updated to | | | Updated to | |
|---|---|---|---|---|---|
| 1. Western Europe | 15- 8-90 | 6. | Central & S. America | 14- 8-90 |
| 2. USA | 14- 8-90 | 7. | USSR & E. Europe | 14- 8-90 |
| 3. Middle East | 14- 8-90 | 8. | Africa | 14- 8-90 |
| 4. Far East | 15- 8-90 | 9. | Canada | 15- 8-90 |
| 5. Australia & N.Z. | 15- 8-90 | 10. | India | 14- 8-90 |

| Specialist: | | | | |
|---|---|---|---|---|
| A. Banking & Finance | 10- 8-90 | G. Engineering | 19- 7-90 |
| B. Insurance & Investment | 2- 8-90 | H. Electronics & Computing | 14- 8-90 |
| C. Property | 2- 8-90 | I. Accountancy & Tax | 2- 8-90 |
| D. Marketing & Media | 13- 8-90 | J. Construction | 26- 7-90 |
| E. Retailing | 3- 8-90 | K. Travel | 6- 8-89 |
| F. Chemicals | 9- 8-90 | L. Aerospace & Defence | 23- 7-90 |

| Non-English Languages: | | | |
|---|---|---|---|
| S. German language | 13- 8-90 | T.   Italian language | 10- 8-90 |

'\*' indicates database not available for this account
Enter code(s) required or 'ALL' : **1**

Are the references to relate to material published:
    1. in the last month?
    2. in the last 3 months?
    3. in the last 6 months?
    4. in the last 12 months?
    5. since a specified date?
    6. before a specified date?
    7. between two specified dates?
Enter code number required: **3**

The database is now being searched.

There are 354 references meeting the specified criteria.
Frequency of each term is:

| | |
|---|---|
| ETHNIC | 2387 |
| MINORI\* | 5606 |

Options available in respect of this file are to
    1. inspect and print
    2. amend criteria
Enter code number required: **2**

Is the requirement to change
    1. Search terms?
    2. databases?
    3. time periods?
Enter code number required: **1**

**Search 10.7:** (cont.)

```
FULL SEARCH FACILITY


After display of criteria already specified
   * enter further requirements commencing with either an 'AND' (+)
     or 'NOT' (-) operator
   * separate additional terms by the 'AND' (+),'OR' (,) or 'NOT'(-)
     operators, used in conjunction with brackets [ ] if required
   * enter CANCEL to amend criteria already specified

ETHNIC
MINORI*
+  unemployment

The database is now being searched.



There are 23 references meeting the specified criteria.

Frequency of each term is:

ETHNIC            2387
MINORI*           5606
UNEMPLOYMENT      2972


Options available in respect of this file are to
   1. inspect and print
   2. amend criteria
Enter code number required: 1

Options available are to:
   1. display headlines singly for inspection
   2. display headlines and 'context' singly for inspection
   3. print all headlines
   4. print all headlines and contexts
   5. print all headlines and articles
   6. terminate enquiry
Enter code number required: 2

Is the order of presentation to be:
   1. chronological?
   2. reverse chronological?
Enter code number required: 2


After each context enter:
   1. for no further interest
   2. to retain for subsequent printing
   3. for immediate printing of article
   4. to end inspection


1 TEXTLINE * * * 19TH JUL 1990.
  _____

  UK: NORTH-WEST HEADS ILLEGITIMACY TABLE WITH 31% OF BABIES BORN TO
  UNMARRIED MOTHERS.
```

**Search 10.7:** (cont.)

..../ lifestyle.
"East Anglia and the South-West are regions with relatively high earnings,
relatively low UNEMPLOYMENT and in recent years relatively good economic
performance," he said.
Population movement also caused /....

..../ age – 21 per cent.
Statistics show the South-East and the West Midlands have the highest
proportion of ETHNIC MINORITY groups while Scotland, Wales and the South
West have the lowest. /....

SOURCES DT 19/7/90 P4
>2

2 TEXTLINE * * * 7TH JUL 1990.
_____

UK: CATHOLICS TO DISCUSS RACISM IN CHURCH.

..../ Daniel Treisman
Racism in the Roman Catholic Church is to be discussed at a meeting of
Catholics from ETHNIC MINORITY groups in London this month.
More than 200 Catholics from England and Wales will attend the Congress /..
.

..../ "joyous" not divisive.
The congress will be held at Digby Stuart College, London, and will discuss
housing, UNEMPLOYMENT, education, the family, and other social and
political issues.
Cardinal Hume will give the opening address, /....

SOURCES T 7/7/90
>2

3 TEXTLINE * * * 21ST JUN 1990.
_____

UK: WEAK GRADUATES FACE LEAN TIME, JOBS STUDY SAYS.

..../ sciences is likely to fall in the 1990s while the proportion of women
and mature graduates, and those from ETHNIC MINORITIES and with non
traditional qualifications will rise. The proportion of "traditional" young
male graduates /....

..../ #14,000.
The authors conclude that a growing shortage of graduates could co-exist
with rising graduate UNEMPLOYMENT and underemployment in the next year or
so, because of a mismatch of demand and supply in some specialities.
The /....

SOURCES IND 21/6/90 P5
>3

By Barrie Clement, Labour Editor
The first sign that the boom in the demand for graduates may be easing is
reported today by the Institute of Manpower Studies.
Employers will go on finding it difficult to recruit people with good
degrees and those who are qualified in engineering and applied science, but

**Search 10.7:** (cont.)

```
weaker graduates may face problems getting suitable jobs.
Geoffrey Pike, a co-author of IMS Graduate Review for 1990, launching the
study, said the demographic downturn had not been such a constraint as
expected.
Most university students are drawn from social classes I and II where
numbers have hardly fallen, and appetite for education has grown. The
institute says the demand for graduates has eased in 1989/90 because of the
economic slowdown, and because some employers are reassessing policies in
anticipation of shortages.
The proportion of graduates in engineering and the applied sciences is
likely to fall in the 1990s while the proportion of women and mature
graduates, and those from ETHNIC MINORITIES and with non-traditional
qualifications will rise. The proportion of "traditional" young male
graduates will decrease.
Demand for graduates is expected to grow in the longer term, assuming there
is no prolonged economic downturn. On present trends, demand could be 30
per cent higher at the end of the century than it is now. This is above the
projected growth in output of 15 per cent. The introduction of student
loans could mean that the projection of the numbers of students is
optimistic.
The shortfall is likely to push up starting salaries and bring more company
sponsorships. At the moment salaries vary from #8,000 to #14,000.
The authors conclude that a growing shortage of graduates could co-exist
with rising graduate UNEMPLOYMENT and underemployment in the next year or
so, because of a mismatch of demand and supply in some specialities.
The market is likely to become more complex in the 1990s with greater
diversity among graduates. More are expected to delay choosing a career.
Companies will probably recruit throughout the year and there will be more
channels for advertising and finding jobs at home and in Europe.
The IMS Graduate Review; Institute of Manpower Studies, Mantell Building,
University of Sussex, Falmer, Brighton BN1 9RF; #24.

Enter 1 for no interest, 2 to retain, 3 to waive selection: 1
```

Parliamentary proceedings are another type of material which is often made available in full text form. In Britain, *Hansard* references are limited to POLIS, but many other countries offer full text online versions of their parliamentary proceedings. These include the French government SAGA, the Spanish PARLAMADRID and sources in New Zealand, Canada and the United States.

With a wide range of potentially useful sources available, the searcher's problem is firstly to find which are at all relevant to a particular search, and secondly, which of those possibilities are the most appropriate. Database directories and hosts' catalogues and manuals will provide pointers to an initial selection, giving brief details of subject coverage, dates and sources. Assessment of individual files is more difficult to find. Even brief comments, such as those made by Gilreath, are useful when made by an independent assessor instead of a producer [5]. More detailed reviews and comparisons can be found in the periodical and conference literature. There is, however, no substitute for personal acquaintance with the database concerned. Where the searcher's own expertise in this area is limited, that of colleagues or users may usefully be exploited. Familiarity with an equivalent printed source is often a useful introduction to an online or CD-ROM file, giving a good indication of the type and level of material included, and the indexing practices employed. Apart from these external sources, most online hosts provide a cross-file searching facility, which may be of considerable help in identifying files containing relevant material.

# DEVELOPING A SEARCH STRATEGY

**Analysis**

The basic principles of search strategy are the same for the social sciences as for any other field, but the nature of the subject produces some characteristic problems. The first and most important step is to analyse the subject in terms of concepts and relationships, and to build a structure that will allow as far as possible for alternatives and for flexibility in developing the search, making full use of the interactive capabilities of the system. It is unusual for a single concept or term (unless it is a named individual, test, or case) to be sufficient to produce satisfactory search results: most topics can be approached from a surprising number of different angles. A combination of two or three concepts is more likely to be successful; more than this is likely to produce very few hits, or none at all. It is often helpful to start a search with the most important and specific concepts, and add more concepts only if the quantity and scope of the material found make further refinement necessary. More general concepts, such as age or educational level, are often usefully held in reserve in this way, as is the possibility of limiting the date range covered by the search. In Search 10.8, for example, the original request was for material on 'gender and moral development'. Using these two concepts only for a search on PSYCINFO produced a rather large, not very relevant set. Addition of a more precise term 'decision making' reduced this to only a few items, very relevant, but not sufficient for the user's purpose. Instead, a broader concept, defining the most significant age range involved was tried, and produced a larger, but still manageable set of references, noticeably more relevant than those found in the first set. The possibility of limiting the search by reducing the time span covered was also considered, but rejected in this case, on the grounds that influential work in this field had appeared over a considerable period of time.

## Search 10.8: PSYCINFO on DIALOG

```
FILE 11: PSYCINFO - 67-90/DEC
        (COPR. AM. PSYCH. ASSOC.)

      Set     Items    Description
      ---     ------   -----------

?ss moral development

      S1      2118     MORAL DEVELOPMENT

?ss gender or human sex differences or human females or human males or sex
roles or sex linked developmental differences

      S2      7425     GENDER
      S3     25045     HUMAN SEX DIFFERENCES
      S4     13523     HUMAN FEMALES
      S5      4639     HUMAN MALES
      S6      6219     SEX ROLES
      S7      1328     SEX LINKED DEVELOPMENTAL DIFFERENCES
      S8     48340     GENDER OR HUMAN SEX DIFFERENCES OR HUMAN FEMALES OR
                       HUMAN MALES OR SEX ROLES OR SEX LINKED DEVELOPMENTAL
                       DIFFERENCES
?ss s1 and s8

              2118     S1
             48340     S8
      S9       294     S1 AND S8

?ts9/6/1-5
```

**Search 10.8:** (cont.)

```
    9/6/1
00761168                77-30693
The development of moral orientation in elementary school children.

    9/6/2
00758884                27-59142
Gender differences in moral stage, moral orientation and sex-role
identity of academic administrators: A comparison of Kohlberg's and
Gilligan's theories.

    9/6/3
00758385                77-29396
Empathic response levels to Kohlbergian and nonKohlbergian counseling
analogs.

    9/6/4
00754220                27-57909
Moral development, courtship violence and sex roles in relationships of
adolescents.

    9/6/5
00753850                27-57539
Children's reasoning about sexual abuse reporting.
```

**?ss s9 and decision making**

```
                294    S9
     S10       5678    DECISION MAKING
     S11          6    S9 AND DECISION MAKING
```

**?ts11/8/1-2**

```
    11/8/1
00719093                27-51954
The role of context and gender in moral judgment.
Major Descriptors: *SEX ROLES; *CONTEXTUAL ASSOCIATIONS; *MORALITY;
 *MORAL DEVELOPMENT; *DECISION MAKING
Minor Descriptors: ADULTHOOD
Descriptor Codes: 46940; 11560; 32010; 32006; 13190; 01150
Identifiers: sex roles & context & moral dilemma, stage of moral
 reasoning & decision making & confidence, adults
Section Headings: 3100 -PERSONALITY

    11/8/2
00568063                24-56313
Beyond a unidimensional theory of moral development: An analysis of Jung's
personality typology and Kohlberg's theory of moral stages comparing career
military officers' wives and civilian women.
Major Descriptors: *PERSONALITY TRAITS; *JUNG (CARL); *PERSONALITY
 THEORY; *MORAL DEVELOPMENT; *MORALITY; *DECISION MAKING; *COGNITIVE
 PROCESSES; *EMOTIONAL RESPONSES; *MILITARY PERSONNEL: *HUMAN FEMALES
Minor Descriptors: THEORIES; WIVES; ADULTHOOD
Descriptor Codes: 37860; 27180; 37850; 32006; 32010; 13190; 10130;
 16860; 31470; 23450; 52590; 56900; 01150
Identifiers: Jung's psychological types & Kohlberg's moral development
 theory, affective & cognitive moral decision making, civilian vs
 military wives
Section Headings: 3100 -PERSONALITY; 3680 -MILITARY PSYCHOLOGY
```

**?ss s9 and adolescence/df**

**Search 10.8:** (cont.)

```
                  294   S9
        S12     31911   ADOLESCENCE/DF
        S13        45   S9 AND ADOLESCENCE/DF

?ts13/8/1-3

 13/8/1
 00754220                    37-57909
 Moral development, courtship violence and sex roles in relationships of
 adolescents.
  Major Descriptors: *SEX ROLES; *MORAL DEVELOPMENT; *CONFLICT
  Minor Descriptors: ADOLESCENTS; ADOLESCENCE
  Descriptor Codes: 46940; 32006; 11250; 00950; 00920
  Identifiers: sex roles & moral development, conflict tactics, 14-18 yr
   olds
  Section Headings: 2840 -PSYCHOSOCIAL AND PERSONALITY DEVELOPMENT

 13/8/2
 00753850                    27-57539
 Children's reasoning about sexual abuse reporting.
  Major Descriptors: *AGE DIFFERENCES; *MORAL DEVELOPMENT; *HUMAN SEX
   DIFFERENCES; *SEXUAL ABUSE
  Minor Descriptors: SCHOOL AGE CHILDREN; CHILDHOOD; ADOLESCENCE
  Descriptor Codes: 01360; 32006; 23510; 46965; 45540; 08750; 00920
  Identifiers: age & sex, moral reasoning about sexual abuse reporting, 10
   vs 13 vs 16 yr olds
  Section Headings: 3230 -BEHAVIOR DISORDERS & ANTISOCIAL BEHAVIOR; 2820
   -COGNITIVE & PERCEPTUAL DEVELOPMENT

 13/8/3
 00751408                    77-24972
 Early adolescents' acceptability of interventions: influence of problem
 severity, gender and moral development
  Major Descriptors: *HUMAN SEX DIFFERENCES; *PROBLEM SOLVING; *MORAL
   DEVELOPMENT; *CHILD DISCIPLINE; *BEHAVIOR PROBLEMS
  Minor Descriptors: SCHOOL AGE CHILDREN; CHILDHOOD; ADOLESCENCE
  Descriptor Codes: 23510; 40550; 32006; 08680; 05650; 45540; 08750; 00920
  Identifiers: problem severity & moral development, acceptability of
   disciplinary interventions, male vs female 12-14.7 yr olds
  Section Headings: 2840 -PSYCHOSOCIAL & PERSONALITY DEVELOPMENT

?logoff
```

Many social science subjects include a number of broad concepts which are very frequently used. Age ranges or levels of education are good examples, as are geographical groupings such as developing countries. In some cases, database producers make provision for this by a system of 'mandatory descriptors'. Thus, on ERIC, all documents should be given a descriptor for educational level, chosen from a list of fifteen alternatives, unless it is entirely inappropriate to their content. This system was introduced in 1975, but care is still needed in specifying educational level, as the mandatory descriptors include both narrower and broader terms, so that to achieve a comprehensive search for a broad area such as secondary education will still require several descriptors. On PSYCINFO, every entry since 1984 includes one of the three age identifiers 'childhood', 'adolescence' or 'adulthood', in addition to more specific terms where appropriate - a much simpler system. Searching for populations on this database on DIALOG was simplified still further in 1990 by the introduction of the age group prefix AG= which automatically collects together all materials, however indexed, in the groupings 'child', 'adolescent', 'adult' and 'elderly' ('elderly' is a subset of 'adult'). PSYCINFO on DIALOG also provides a number of saved searches, listing terms relevant to the concepts: Psychiatric Patients/Mental Disorders, Substance Abuse, Learning Disabilities, Communication/Language/Speech Disorders, Racial and Ethnic Groups, Tests and Measurement, Developing Countries, Mental Health Personnel, and 'Talking' Therapies. Search 10.9 illustrates two of these saved searches. Where such saved searches (or hedges) are not provided, it is well worth while to set them up, storing them either as saved searches on the host computer, or as named files on the searcher's own micro, ready to be called up and used whenever required.

## Search 10.9: Saved searches on PSYCINFO on DIALOG

```
FILE 11:PSYCINFO - 67-90/DEC
     (COPR. AM. PSYCH. ASSOC.)

     Set      Items    Description
     ---      -----    -----------

??psycsave

PSYCINFO (File 11) SearchSaves prepared by PsycINFO:

   Psychiatric Patients      SBMDIS/User 3471
   Mental Health Personnel   SBMHPRS/User 3471
   Racial/Ethnic Groups      SBRACE/User 3471
   Developing Countries      SBWORLD/User 3471
   Tests and Measurement     SBTEST/User 3471
   "Talking" Therapies       SBTHRPY/User 3471
   Substance Abuse           SBABUSE/User 3471
   Communication/Language/
    Speech Disorders         SBCDIS/User 3471
   Learning Disabilities     SBLDIS/User 3471

EXECUTE STEPS (EXS) at the beginning of a search before adding other
concepts
?exs sbtest/user 3471

     S1     26309    TEST/DE
     S2      3471    TESTS/DE
     S3      8499    TESTING/DE
     S4       763    SUBTESTS/DE
     S5       111    PRETESTING/DE
     S6        71    POSTTESTING/DE
     S7      5941    INVEN?/DE
     S8      1604    SURV?/DE
     S9      7072    SCALE?/DE
    S10      2453    QUESTIONNAIRE?/DE
    S11      4993    RATING/DE
    S12      3901    SCOR?/DE
    S13     45515    (TEST OR TESTS OR TESTING OR SUBTESTS OR PRETESTING
                     OR POSTTESTING OR INVEN? OR SURV? OR SCALE? OR
                     QUESTIONNAIRE? OR RATING OR SCOR?)/DE
    S14     15241    VALIDITY/DE
    S15      1108    PSYCHOMETRICS/DE
    S16        46    SOCIOGRAMS/DE
    S17      3487    ASSESSMENT/DE
    S18     32197    MEASURE?/DE
    S19      1741    SCREEN?/DE
    S20       475    EXAM?/DE
    S21       784    SEMANTIC DIFFERENTIAL
    S22       636    PIAGETIAN TASKS
    S23     46806    (VALIDITY OR PSYCHOMETRICS OR SOCIOGRAMS OR
                     ASSESSMENT OR MEASURE? OR SCREEN? OR EXAM?)/DE OR
                     SEMANTIC DIFFERENTIAL OR PIAGETIAN TASKS
```

**Search 10.9:** (cont.)

```
            45515    S13
            46806    S23
    S24     69537    S13 OR S23

?exs sbmdis/user 3471

    S25     10869    MENTAL DISORDERS/DE
    S26      6792    PSYCHOSIS/DE
    S27       247    PSYCHOTIC/DE
    S28      6222    NEUROSIS/DE
    S29       264    NEUROTIC/DE
    S30     20014    DEPRESSION/DE
    S31       822    DEPRESSIVE/DE
    S32     16538    SCHIZOPHREN?/DE
    S33       910    MANIA/DE
    S34      1926    DEMENTIA/DE
    S35      4546    PSYCHOPATH?/DE
    S36     60634    (MENTAL DISORDERS OR PSYCHOSIS OR PSYCHOTIC OR
                     NEUROSIS OR NEUROTIC OR DEPRESSION OR DEPRESSIVE OR
                     SCHIZOPHREN? OR MANIA OR DEMENTIA OR PSYCHOPATH?)/DE
    S37     12907    PSYCHIATRIC PATIENTS
    S38      2288    AFFECTIVE DISTURBANCES
    S39      1568    BORDERLINE STATES
    S40      1344    PERSONALITY DISORDERS
    S41       116    DYSTHYMIC DISORDER
    S42       770    PANIC DISORDER
    S43     18501    PSYCHIATRIC PATIENTS OR AFFECTIVE DISTURBANCES OR
                     BORDERLINE STATES OR PERSONALITY DISORDERS OR
                     DYSTHYMIC DISORDER OR PANIC DISORDER
            60634    S36
            18501    S43
    S44     74047    S36 OR S43

?logoff
```

Another common problem in the social sciences lies in the requirement for a normal or abnormal population as the subject of research in a particular field. If an abnormal population is specified, there is little difficulty - it can be included as one of the search concepts. The problem lies in dealing with normal populations, as this is not generally stated in title or indexing terms. Thus a search stating only 'children' will retrieve items relating to both normal and to mentally and physically handicapped children and other special groups. Where a comparison of normal and abnormal is required, this may be the best way to achieve it. If items only on normal children were wanted, the groups not required would have to be eliminated using the NOT operator. This cannot easily be done comprehensively, as there are many special groups; probably the best method is to review some references from the general search first to see which abnormal groups appear most frequently in connection with a particular topic. These can then be eliminated, bearing in mind that this may also remove some comparative material which includes both normal and abnormal cases.

A somewhat similar dilemma arises if a search requires a distinction to be made between a general, theoretical treatment of a subject, and case studies, experiments or individual examples in the same field. A subject search will normally include both types of material if both exist. It may be possible to use a term such as 'case studies' (ERIC or SOCIOLOGICAL ABSTRACTS) or 'case report' (PSYCINFO) to distinguish this type of material, although this may still include items on the theory of case study! In addition, in some areas, such as education, much material may be based on individual experience or particular projects without being strictly a case study. Perhaps more difficult is to retrieve only the general theoretical materials. Again, some help may be provided by thesaurus terms such as 'theories' or 'definitions' (ERIC) which can be used alongside the subject terms for the search.

Finally, particular care needs to be taken in formulating strategy for searches where a specific relationship between concepts is required. Concepts such as 'perception' and 'attitudes', for example, have a directional charge to them - they are held by one group of people about another. A search including the concepts teachers/ attitudes/children, would retrieve items on teachers' attitudes to children and on children's attitudes to teachers, as well as the attitudes of both groups to some third group or other issue. In some databases, this problem may be overcome by using pre-coordinated descriptors such as 'teacher attitudes' or 'student attitudes' which state explicitly who is holding the attitude. This kind of mismatch can occur in other combinations where only a Boolean operator is used to link concepts: thus a search for children/blind/parents will produce references on blind children with sighted parents and on sighted children with blind parents as in Search 10.10. This problem cannot always be avoided, although the use of pre-coordinated index terms or explicit free-text phrases may provide a solution in some cases.

## Search 10.10: Searching ERIC on SilverPlatter CD-ROM

```
SilverPlatter 1.6                                    ERIC (1/83 - 9/90)

No.                    Records      Request
1:                     >13072       PARENT*
2:                     >32070       CHILD*
3:                        574       BLINDNESS
4.                         16       (PARENT* in DE) and (CHILD* in DE)
                                    and (BLINDNESS in DE)
```

```
                                                            1 of 16
AN: EJ390660
AU: Preislar,-Gunilla; Palmer,-Christina
TI: Thoughts from Sweden: The Blind Child at Nursery School with Sighted
 Children.
py: 1989
JN: Child-Care,-Health-and-Development; v15 n1 p45-52 Jan-Feb 1989
AV: UMI
                                                            2 of 16
AN: EJ387201
AU: Abang,-Theresa-B.
TI: Blindisms: Possible Causes and Remedies.
PY: 1988
JN: British-Journal-of-Visual-Impairment;v6 n3 p91-93 Fall 1988
                                                            3 of 16
AN: EJ378808
AU: Joffee,-E.
TI: A Home-Based Orientation and Mobility Program for Infants and Toddlers.
PY: 1988
JN: Journal-of-Visual-Impairment-and-Blindness; v82 n7 p282-85 Sep 1988
AV: UMI
                                                            4 of 16
AN: EJ358080
AU: Deshen,-Shlomo
TI: Coming of Age among Blind People in Israel.
PY: 1987
JN: Disability,-Handicap-and-Society; v2 n2 p137-49 1987
                                                            5 of 16
AN: EJ341359
```

**Search 10.10:** (cont.)

```
AU: Rogers,-S.-J.;Puchelski,-C.-B.
TI: Social Smiles of Visually Impaired Infants.
PY: 1986
JN: Journal-of-Visual-Impairment-and-Blindness; v80 n7 p863-65 Sep 1986
AV: UMI
                                                                6 of 16
AN: EJ321062
AU: Arsnow,-George-F.; And-Others
TI: Blind Parents Rearing Sighted Children.
PY: 1985
JN: Journal-of-Visual-Impairment-and-Blindness; v79 n5 p193-98 May 1985
AV: UMI
```

## Terminology

The problems of terminology in the social sciences have already been touched upon: the lack of standard terminology in many fields; the use of natural language terms in a specific sense; the variety of specific senses for the same word which may emerge in different disciplines; the rapid development of new concepts and slow acceptance of new terms. Use of terminology may also change over time as concepts develop and fashions change: thus education of immigrants becomes multiracial, then multicultural and finally anti-racist education; the feeble-minded are reclassified as educationally subnormal, mentally retarded or learning disabled. To add to the confusion, usage may vary between European, British and American sources. Looking up the term 'pedagogy', for instance, in three different thesauri produces three quite different interpretations: the *EUDISED Multilingual Thesaurus for Information Processing in the Field of Education* (English Version) (1984) prefers the phrase 'sciences of education', the *British Education Thesaurus* opts for 'teaching process', and the *ERIC Thesaurus* directs one to use 'instruction'. Similarly, much space is devoted in British educational literature to the discussion of assessment and examinations; neither of these terms is an ERIC descriptor, 'evaluation' and 'tests' being the preferred terms. In addition, some articles may have literary or allusive titles which give no indication of their subject content.

Once a search has been analysed into basic concepts, the task of expressing these in appropriate terminology begins. Some concepts may be easily and accurately described by one term only: 'empathy', for example, has no real synonyms. It is much more common to find that a group of related terms, linked by the OR operator, is required to express one concept, and all aspects of it in which the user is interested. Undoubtedly the best help, if it is available, is provided by a properly constructed thesaurus, where this is also used in constructing the database. The *Thesaurus of Psychological Index Terms* (5th edition, 1988) used in compiling the PSYCINFO database is a good example, as is the *Thesaurus of ERIC Descriptors* (12th edition, 1990) used in the preparation of the ERIC and EXCEPTIONAL CHILD EDUCATIONAL RESOURCES databases, or its derivative, the *British Education Thesaurus* (1988) now used in preparing the BRITISH EDUCATION INDEX. The use of the thesaurus has a number of advantages. The controlled vocabulary will automatically eliminate a number of synonyms, while at the same time the relationship displays will direct attention to other useful terms, grouped in the categories of broader, narrower and related terms. A suitable list of terms for each concept can thus easily be built up. Searching on descriptors also has the advantage of ensuring that items with uninformative titles are not missed, while avoiding the high proportion of false drops which can arise from searching in the longer abstract field.

The disadvantage of using a thesaurus and controlled vocabulary is that it is always out of date; new concepts and terms must, necessarily, have been current in the literature for some time before they are accepted as part of the authoritative list of descriptors. Most major database producers include procedures for the regular updating of the thesaurus in the routine of compiling their database. The *Thesaurus of Psychological Index Terms,* for instance, is now in its fifth edition (1988) new versions having appeared at three to five year intervals since it was first published in 1974. This edition includes 250 new postable terms, intended to fill gaps and introduce new concepts: 'Acquired Immune Deficiency Syndrome', 'Child Neglect' and 'Disability Evaluation' are among the new additions. Similarly, the *Thesaurus of ERIC Descriptors* is produced in a new edition approximately every two to three years. Proposed new descriptors on ERIC appear first in the identifier field, and, once their utility has been proved, are then added to the next edition of the thesaurus. The *Thesaurus of Sociological Indexing Terms* is now in its second edition (1989) and arrangements are in hand for revision of the *British Education Thesaurus.* Between new editions, however, the searcher will frequently need to supplement descriptors with some free-text terms to express new or unusual concepts not covered in the thesaurus.

A printed thesaurus is usually the easiest to consult in preparation of a search, but some databases also have their thesauri available online. Where this is the case, the EXPAND command can be used to produce a display of related terms, which can then be selected directly by number, instead of being typed out in full. Social science files which offer this facility on DIALOG include ERIC, ECER, PSYCINFO, PAIS INTERNATIONAL and LLBA. Search 10.11 shows a search carried out on ECER, in which the online thesaurus was used to collect a large set of terms for the disabled or mentally retarded, including all types and degrees of disability.

## Search 10.11: EXCEPTIONAL CHILD EDUCATION RESOURCES (ECER) on DIALOG

```
      File 54: ECER/EXCEP CHILD - 66-90/JUL

            Set      Items    Description
            ---      -----    -----------

   ?e (disabilities)

   Ref      Items    Type          RT      Index-term
   R1       31529                   40      *DISABILITIES (PHYSICAL, MENTAL OR SENSORY
                                            IMPAIRMENTS THA...)
   R2        9669    U              1       DISABLED
   R3           0    U              1       HANDICAPPED (1966-1980)
   R4        5618    U              1       HANDICAPS
   R5          69    N              6       ADVENTITIOUS IMPAIRMENTS
   R6         469    N              10      COMMUNICATION DISORDERS
   R7         501    N              13      CONGENITAL IMPAIRMENTS
   R8        1279    N              11      DEVELOPMENTAL DISABILITIES
   R9         869    N              32      DISEASES
   R10       5549    N              27      HEARING IMPAIRMENTS
   R11        248    N              10      INJURIES
   R12       1766    N              20      LANGUAGE HANDICAPS

                       Enter P or E for more
   ?p

   Ref      Items    Type          RT      Index-term
   R13       9681    N              21      LEARNING DISABILITIES
   R14        360    N              19      MENTAL DISORDERS
   R15      10652    N              16      MENTAL RETARDATION
   R16        630    N              6       MILD DISABILITIES
   R17       1884    N              6       MULTIPLE DISABILITIES
   R18        468    N              22      PERCEPTUAL HANDICAPS
   R19       2637    N              25      PHYSICAL DISABILITIES
   R20       2102    N              10      SEVERE DISABILITIES
   R21       1414    N              21      SPECIAL HEALTH PROBLEMS
   R22       1835    N              20      SPEECH HANDICAPS
```

**Search 10.11:** (cont.)

```
R23       3300      N       22      VISUAL IMPAIRMENTS
R24       4877      R       21      ABILITY

              Enter P or E for more
?p

Ref       Items     Type    RT      Index-term
R25        500      R       12      ACCESSIBILITY (FOR DISABLED)
R26        257      R        5      ADAPTED PHYSICAL EDUCATION
R27        996      R       16      DAILY LIVING SKILLS
R28        342      R        7      DEINSTITUTIONALIZATION (OF DISABLED)
R29         15      R       29      EXCEPTIONAL PERSONS
R30        197      R       15      GROUP HOMES
R31       5025      R       38      HEALTH
R32       4596      R       14      MAINSTREAMING
R33        976      R       10      NORMALIZATION (HANDICAPPED)
R34       1209      R       14      PATIENTS
R35       3473      R       34      REHABILITATION
R36        267      R        9      RESIDENTIAL CARE

              Enter P or E for more
?p

Ref       Items     Type    RT      Index-term
R37        111      R        5      RESPITE CARE
R38        753      R        9      SELF CARE SKILLS
R39        372      R       10      SHELTERED WORKSHOPS
R40       2591      R       28      SPECIAL EDUCATION
R41       5412      R       23      THERAPY
```

**?ss r1 or r6 or r7 or r8 or r12 or r13 or r14 or r15 or r17 or r18 or r20 or r40**

```
      S1       31559     DISABILITIES
      S2         469     COMMUNICATION DISORDERS
      S3         501     CONGENITAL IMPAIRMENTS
      S4        1279     DEVELOPMENTAL DISABILITIES
      S5        1766     LANGUAGE HANDICAPS
      S6        9681     LEARNING DISABILITIES
      S7         360     MENTAL DISORDERS
      S8       10652     MENTAL RETARDATION
      S9        1884     MULTIPLE DISABILITIES
      S10        468     PERCEPTUAL HANDICAPS
      S11       2102     SEVERE DISABILITIES
      S12       2591     SPECIAL EDUCATION
      S13      42074     "DISABILITIES" OR "COMMUNICATION DISORDERS" OR
                         "CONGENITAL IMPAIRMENTS" OR "DEVELOPMENTAL
                         DISABILITIES" OR "LANGUAGE HANDICAPS" OR "LEARNING
                         DISABILITIES" OR "MENTAL DISORDERS" OR "MENTAL
                         RETARDATION" OR R17 OR R18 OR R20 OR R40
```

**?e r15**

```
Ref       Items     Type    RT      Index-term
R1        10652             16      *MENTAL RETARDATION (INTELLECTUAL
                                    FUNCTIONING THAT IS TWO OR MORE...
R2           0      U        1      MENTALLY HANDICAPPED (1966-1980)
R3           0      U        1      RETARDATION (1966-1980)
R4           0      U        1      RETARDED CHILDREN (1966-1980)
```

**Search 10.11:** (cont.)

```
R5          754      N      9      DOWNS SYNDROME
R6         3365      N      8      MILD MENTAL RETARDATION
R7         1815      N      7      MODERATE MENTAL RETARDATION
R8         1474      N      8      SEVERE MENTAL RETARDATION
R9        31529      B     40      DISABILITIES
R10        1680      R     33      ADJUSTMENT (TO ENVIRONMENT)
R11         705      R      6      CEREBRAL PALSY
R12        1279      R     11      DEVELOPMENTAL DISABILITIES

                 Enter P or E for more
?p

Ref        Items    Type         RT     Index-term
R13           15      R           29     EXCEPTIONAL PERSONS
R14         3750      R           21     INTELLIGENCE
R15          526      R           23     LEARNING PROBLEMS
R16         1153      R           28     NEUROLOGICAL IMPAIRMENTS
R17         1414      R           21     SPECIAL HEALTH PROBLEMS
```

**?ss r5 or r6 or r7 or r8 or r11 or r15**

```
S14      754      DOWNS SYNDROME
S15     3365      MILD MENTAL RETARDATION
S16     1815      MODERATE MENTAL RETARDATION
S17     1474      SEVERE MENTAL RETARDATION
S18      705      CEREBRAL PALSY
S19      526      LEARNING PROBLEMS
S20     7684      "DOWNS SYNDROME" OR "MILD MENTAL RETARDATION" OR
                  "MODERATE MENTAL RETARDATION" OR "SEVERE MENTAL
                  RETARDATION" OR "CEREBRAL PALSY" OR "LEARNING
                  PROBLEMS"
```

**?ss (s13 or s20) and word()process?**

```
        42074      S13
         7684      S20
S21      1851      WORD
S22      9510      PROCESS?
S23       130      WORD(W)PROCESS?
S24        87      (S13 OR S20) AND WORD()PROCESS?
```

**?ts24/2/1-3**

```
 24/2/1
EC221695
Word Processing for Learning Disabled Students.
Messerer, Jeffrey; Lerner, Janet W.
Learning Disabilities Focus v5 n1 p13-17 Fal 1989;   175P.
EDRS: NOT AVAILABLE
DOCUMENT TYPE: 052; 080

DESCRIPTORS: *Learning Disabilities; *Word Processing; *Writing
Instruction; *Computer Software; Elementary Secondary Education; Teaching
Methods; Computer Assisted Instruction
 IDENTIFIERS: FrEdWriter; Bank Street Writer; Talking Text Writer

 24/2/2
EC221327 ED312868
 Computers for Vocational Purposes: PAM Repeater No. 53.
Heiner, Donna; Ensign, Arselia S., Ed.
Physically Impaired Association of Michigan, Lansing, PAM Assistance
```

**Search 10.11:** (cont.)

```
Centre.
 1989-May  11P
 DOCUMENT TYPE: 055
 GEOGRAPHIC SOURCE: U.S.; Michigan

 DESCRIPTORS: *Physical Disabilities; Adults; *Microcomputers; *Computer
 System Design; Computer Peripherals; *Assistive Devices (for Disabled);
 *Selection; Decision Making; Input Output Devices

 24/2/3
 EC221086 ED311670
 Public Domain Software in Special Education. No Cheaper Software
Anywhere!
 Heiman, Brenda And Others
 1988-Dec  26+P
 NOTE: Paper presented at the National Conference on Special Education and
  Technology (Reno, Nevada, December 11-13,1988).
 DOCUMENT TYPE: 150; 055
 GEOGRAPHIC SOURCE: U.S.; New Mexico

 DESCRIPTORS: *Disabilities; *Computer Uses in Education; *Courseware;
 *Computer Assisted Instruction; *Computer Managed Instruction;
 *Instructional Materials
 IDENTIFIERS: *Public Domain Software

?logoff
```

## Interaction

However much preparation is done in advance, uncertainties over definitions and terminology make reviewing of results, followed by further online development of the search essential for the social science searcher. Only too often, scanning titles and descriptors (usually a cheap display format) after first entering a search, will reveal either some important term which has been omitted, or perhaps more frequently, some term used in a different sense from that which was expected, or simply of much broader application than anticipated. The search can then be continued, adding or subtracting terms as necessary. Even more disconcerting are those occasions when an apparently straightforward search strategy produces quite different results from those expected, as terms within it prove capable of combination in more than one sense. For instance, in a search on 'estimation of number and measurement by children', carried out on ERIC, the descriptor 'estimation' appeared from its thesaurus scope note to be an exact description of the process required. When combined only with terms for children, primary education, etc., it produced many articles where the estimation was on the part of the researcher, not the subject of the study. Only when the implied but unstated concept 'mathematics education' was added to the search strategy could the really relevant material be isolated.

An alternative approach to strategy which offers a quite different key to the maze of terminology is the technique sometimes known as pearl growing: one or two highly relevant articles are first found and displayed online, and suitable terms are then selected from these records and added to the search. This is a useful alternative approach, especially for searches which do not at first seem to conform to standard categories or terminology. It obviously depends less on advance preparation and far more on skill in interpreting results online; the final result may well be more relevant but less comprehensive than that obtained by the more conventional method.

**Output**

It has already become clear that desired output will influence search strategy at many points. Level, quantity and date of material required are all factors to be borne in mind when planning and executing a search. A final point to consider is availability. A long list of references which are not readily obtainable will be a source of more frustration than assistance to many users. Full text databases offer one solution to this problem, especially where downloading of data is possible. A few social science databases are also linked to document delivery services. Almost all ERIC documents, which comprise about half the ERIC file, are available on microfiche, either direct from the ERIC Document Reproduction Service (EDRS) or from libraries subscribing to the full collection. A list of these is available in the *Directory of ERIC Information Service Providers* [6]. Similarly, most dissertations listed in DISSERTATION ABSTRACTS ONLINE are available on microfilm from University Microfilms International, although, for British users, this can take some time. Where a database is prepared by a library, the latter will often supply source documents through an inter-library loan: both ACOMPLINE and DHSS-Data offer this service. In other instances, users will be dependent on the stock and inter-library loan services of their institution. It is particularly worth noting which files contain significant quantities of grey literature as this is likely to give most problems. In addition to those mentioned above, ECER, CHILD ABUSE AND NEGLECT, and FAMILY RESOURCES all scan a wide range of material relating to children and the family, including, for instance, legislation and project reports as well as journal articles; similarly in the field of current affairs, PAIS INTERNATIONAL and MIDDLE EAST: ABSTRACTS AND INDEX both cover a wide range of materials.

## CONCLUSION

Social science searches cover a great variety of subjects: although it is possible to select some common characteristics, variety is the most constant factor. Probably the only general conclusion that can be drawn, therefore, is that the best results can only be obtained by the closest collaboration between searcher and user. Ideally, users should be present at an online search to provide a full explanation of their requirements. They can then contribute to the planning of the search and follow this up by assisting in reviewing and assessing results while the search is in progress. This may provide valuable pointers to the way the search should be developed to arrive at a satisfactory final conclusion. Where users do their own searching, as is increasingly common with CD-ROM databases, advice and assistance from an experienced searcher will often be needed to make best use of the system. In both cases, it is the combination of the searcher's expertise and experience and the user's subject knowledge which allows the rich resources of online information to be exploited to the full.

## DATABASE DETAILS

**ACADEMIC INDEX**

| | |
|---|---|
| Subject: | Social sciences and humanities |
| File size: | 450,000 records |
| Coverage: | 1987 onwards with selected references for 1976-1986 |
| Updates: | Approx 15,000 records a month |
| Provider: | Information Access Company (IAC) |
| Hosts: | BRS, DIALOG |
| CD-ROM: | Available from IAC |

## ACOMPLINE
Subject:      Urban studies
File size:    146,000 records
Coverage:     1973 onwards
Updates:      Monthly. 12,000 references added per year
Provider:     Research Library, London Research Centre, 81 Black Prince Road, London SE1 7SZ
Host:         ESA-IRS

## AFRICA NEWS
Subject:      African affairs
File size:    Not available
Coverage:     July 1983 onwards
Updates:      Every 2 weeks
Provider:     Africa News Service Inc.
Host:         NewsNet
Note:         Full text file

## AGELINE
Subject:      Middle age and ageing
File size:    25,000 records
Coverage:     1978 onwards, with some earlier material
Updates:      About 500 records every 2 months
Provider:     American Association of Retired Persons
Hosts:        BRS,DIALOG

## AMERICA: HISTORY AND LIFE
Subject:      American history and culture
File size:    257,900 records
Coverage:     1964 onwards
Updates:      Quarterly, About 12,000 records per year
Provider:     ABC-CLIO, Santa Barbara, California
Host:         DIALOG

## AP POLITICAL FILE
Subject:      US politics and political science
File size:    Not known
Coverage:     1980 onwards
Updates:      Daily for news and commentaries, biographies periodically
Producer:     Associated Press
Hosts:        Mead Data Central, Inc: DataTimes Corporation, VU/TEXT Information Services, Inc

## ASSI
Subject:      Applied social sciences
File size:    68,000 records
Coverage:     1987 onwards
Updates:      Bi-monthly. Approx 3,000 records per update.
Provider:     Bowker-Saur Abstracts and Indexes, London
Host:         Data-Star

## AUSTRALIAN EDUCATION INDEX DATABASE

Subject:     Education and library and information science
File size:   40,000 records
Coverage:    1978 onwards
Updates:     Quarterly. About 4,700 records per year
Provider:    Australian Council for Educational Research
Host:        Ferntree Computer Corporation Ltd (formerly ACI Computer Services)
Note:        Some abstracts

## AUSTRALIAN FAMILY AND SOCIETY ABSTRACTS

Subject:     Families and family life
File size:   8,750 records
Coverage:    1980 onwards
Updates:     Monthly. About 2,000 records per year
Provider:    Australian Institute of Family Studies
Host:        CSIRO AUSTRALIS

## AUSTRALIAN GOVERNMENT PUBLICATIONS

Subject:     Government publications on all subjects
File size:   54,000 records
Coverage:    1983-1987
Updates:     Not updated
Provider:    National Library of Australia
Host:        OZLINE

## AUSTRALIAN PUBLIC AFFAIRS INFORMATION SERVICE

Subject:     Social sciences and humanities
File size:   120,000 records
Coverage:    1978 onwards
Updates:     Monthly. About 1,000 records per month
Provider:    National Library of Australia
Host:        Ferntree Computer Corporation Ltd (formerly ACI Computer Services

## AVMARC

Subject:     Audio-visual·materials, especially for teaching
File size:   9,000 records at 10/88
Coverage:    Not known
Updates:     Irregular
Provider:    British Library Bibliographic Services
Host:        BLAISE-LINE

## BRITISH EDUCATION INDEX

Subject:     Education and educational psychology
File size:   37,000 articles and 9,000 theses
Coverage:    1976 onwards (journals), 1950 onwards (theses)
Updates:     Quarterly. Journals 1,000 records per quarter, theses 1,000 records per year
Provider:    University of Leeds
Host:        DIALOG

## BRITISH OFFICIAL PUBLICATIONS (HMSO)
Subject:        British government publications
File size:      130,000 records
Coverage:       1976 onwards
Updates:        Approx 1,000 records per month
Provider:       HMSO Bibliographic Services, London
Hosts:          BLAISE-LINE; DIALOG

## CAB ABSTRACTS
Subject:        Agriculture and related fields
File size:      2.2 million records
Coverage:       1973 onwards
Updates:        Monthly. About 12,000 records per update.
Provider:       CAB (Commonwealth Agricultural Bureaux) International, Farnham Royal, Slough, England.
Hosts:          BRS, CISTI, Canadian Online Enquiry Service (CAN/OLE), DIALOG, DIMDI, ESA-IRS, The Japan Information Centre of Science and Technology (JICST), University of Tsukuba

## CBT AND INTERACTIVE VIDEO DATABASE
Subject:        Computer based and interactive video training packages
File size:      1,400 records at August 1988
Coverage:       Current
Updates:        Weekly
Provider:       MARIS-NET (Ely) Ltd
Host:           MARIS-NET (Ely) Ltd

## CENDATA
Subject:        Demography and population
File size:      53,569 records
Coverage:       Current
Updates:        Daily
Provider:       US Census Bureau, Washington DC
Hosts:          DIALOG, The Glimpse Corporation, CompuServe Information Service
Note:           Contains statistical data, press releases and product information

## CHILD ABUSE AND NEGLECT
Subject:        Child abuse and neglect
File size:      17,366 records
Coverage:       1965 onwards
Updates:        Semiannual
Provider:       National Center on Child Abuse and Neglect, US Department of Health and Human Services, Washington DC
Host:           DIALOG

## CONGRESSIONAL RECORD ABSTRACTS
Subject:        US government
File size:      340,000 records
Coverage:       1986 onwards
Update:         Weekly. Approx 1,000 records per week.

Provider:    National Standards Association, Inc.
Hosts:       BRS, DIALOG

## CONGRESSIONAL RECORD FULL TEXT
Subject:     US government
File size:   Not available.
Coverage:    1985 onwards
Update:      Daily
Provider:    National Standards Association, Inc.
Hosts:       Congressional Quarterly Inc.,Washington Alert Service (CQ); LEGI-SLATE Inc.; Mead Data
             Central. Inc.; West Publishing Company
Note:        Full text database

## CRONOS
Subject:     EEC economics
File size:   900,000 time series
Coverage:    1960s and 1970s to date
Updates:     Varies by series
Provider:    Commission of the European Communities
Hosts:       Datacentralen: GSi-ECO; The WEFA Group

## CSO
Subject:     UK economics
File size:   13,000 time series
Coverage:    Varies by series, some from 1947
Updates:     Monthly, revised annually
Provider:    CSO
Hosts:       DRI/McGraw-Hill; WEFA Group

## DHSS-Data
Subject:     Health care and social services
File size:   37,000 references
Coverage:    1983 onwards
Update:      Weekly. 250 records per week
Provider:    Department of Health and Social Security (*now* DSS) Library, Alexander Fleming House,
             Elephant and Castle, London.
Host:        Data-Star

## DISSERTATION ABSTRACTS ONLINE
Subject:     North American theses on all subjects
File size:   1,043,613 records
Coverage:    1861 onwards
Updates:     Monthly. Approx 3,500 records per month
Provider:    University Microfilms International, Ann Arbor, Michigan
Hosts:       BRS; DIALOG; TECH DATA; University of Tsukuba
Note:        Abstracts included for the majority of degrees granted after 1980
CD-ROM:      Available from UMI

## ECCTIS (Educational Counselling and Credit Transfer Information Service)
Subject:       Higher and Further Education courses
File size:     References to approx 60,000 courses
Coverage:      Current
Updates:       Continuous
Provider:      ECCTIS
Hosts:         CAMPUS 2000 (via gateway); TTNS
CD-ROM:        Available from ECCTIS

## ECONOMIC LITERATURE INDEX
Subject:       Economics
File size:     164,000 records
Coverage:      1969 onwards
Updates:       Quarterly. Approx 2,500 records per update
Provider:      American Economic Association, Pittsburgh, Pennsylvania
Host:          DIALOG
Note:          Abstracts added to approx 25 per cent of records since June 1984
CD-ROM:        EconLit from SilverPlatter

## EDUCATION INDEX
Subject:       Education
File size:     131,000 records
Coverage:      June 1983 onwards
Updates:       Twice weekly. 3,000 records per month
Provider:      H.W.Wilson Company, New York
Host:          WilsonLine
Note:          No abstracts
CD-ROM:        Available from H.W.Wilson

## THE EDUCATIONAL DIRECTORY
Subject:       Educational institutions
File size:     137,768 records
Coverage:      Current
Updates:       Semiannual reloads
Provider:      Market Data Retrieval Inc., Westport, Connecticut
Host:          DIALOG

## EDUCATIONAL TESTING SERVICE TEST COLLECTION DATABASE
Subject:       Educational tests
File size:     8,600 tests
Coverage:      Current information, some older materials
Updates:       Quarterly
Provider:      Educational Testing Service, Princeton, New Jersey
Hosts:         BRS; TECH DATA
Note:          Information provided about each item includes brief description, component subtests, and availability

## ENCYCLOPEDIA OF ASSOCIATIONS

Subject:     Associations and foundations directory
File size:   90,000 records
Coverage:    Current edition
Updates:     Twice yearly
Provider:    Gale Research Company, Detroit, Michigan
Host:        DIALOG

## ERIC

Subject:     Education and related information
File size:   691,750 records
Coverage:    1966 onwards
Updates:     Monthly, Approx 2,600 records per month
Provider:    Educational Resources Information Center (ERIC), US Department of Education, Office of
             Educational Research and Improvement (OERI), Washington DC
Hosts:       BRS; DIALOG; Orbit; University of Tsukuba
CD-ROM:      Available from DIALOG, OCLC and SilverPlatter

## EUDISED (European Documentation and Information System for Education)

Subject:     Educational research
File size:   8,500 references
Coverage:    1975 onwards
Updates:     Quarterly. Approx 200 records per update
Provider:    Council of Europe, Directorate of Education, Culture and Sport
Host:        ESA-IRS

## EXCEPTIONAL CHILD EDUCATION RESOURCES

Subject:     Special needs and gifted education
File size:   70,500 records
Coverage:    1966 onwards
Updates:     Monthly. Approx 250 records per month
Provider:    The Council for Exceptional Children, Reston, Virginia
Hosts:       BRS; DIALOG

## FAMILY RESOURCES

Subject:     Families and family life
File size:   102,000 records
Coverage:    1970 onwards (non-journal items), 1973 onwards (journals)
Updates:     Monthly BRS; Quarterly DIALOG
Provider:    National Council on Family Relations, St Paul, Minnesota
Hosts:       BRS; DIALOG; Executive Telecom Inc: The Human Resources Information Net

## FILMS AND VIDEO DATABASE

Subject:     Training films and video
File size:   1,500 records
Coverage:    Current
Updates:     Not available
Provider:    MARIS-NET (Ely) Ltd
Host:        MARIS-NET (Ely) Ltd

## FORIS (Forschungsinformationssystem Sozialwissenschaften)

| | |
|---|---|
| Subject: | Social sciences and humanities research in progress |
| File size: | 32,000+ records |
| Coverage: | German language |
| Updates: | 1,700 records three times a year |
| Provider: | Informationszentrum Sozialwissenschaften |
| Hosts: | DIMDI; STN International |

## FRANCIS: AMERIQUE LATINE

| | |
|---|---|
| Subject: | Social sciences and humanities in Latin America |
| File size: | 6,300 records |
| Coverage: | 1981 onwards |
| Updates: | Twice yearly. Approx 1,400 records per year |
| Provider: | Centre National de la Recherche Scientifique, Institut de l'Information Scientifique et Technique (CNRS/INIST) |
| Host: | Telesystemes-Questel |

## FRANCIS: BIBLIOGRAPHIE GEOGRAPHIQUE INTERNATIONALE

| | |
|---|---|
| Subject: | Geography |
| File size: | 80,000 references |
| Coverage: | 1976 onwards |
| Updates: | Quarterly. Approx 7,000 records per year |
| Provider: | Centre National de la Recherche Scientifique, Institut de l'Information Scientifique et Technique (CNRS/INIST, CNRS/INTERGEO |
| Host: | Telesystemes-Questel |

## FRANCIS: BIBLIOGRAPHIE INTERNATIONALE DE SCIENCE ADMINISTRATIVE

| | |
|---|---|
| Subject: | Administration and management |
| File size: | 60,000 records |
| Coverage: | 1972 onwards |
| Updates: | Quarterly. Approx 4,500 records per year |
| Provider: | Centre National de la Recherche Scientifique, Institut de l'Information Scientifique et Technique (CNRS/INIST) |
| Host: | Telesystemes-Questel |

## FRANCIS: CEGET (Tropical Geography)

| | |
|---|---|
| Subject: | Geography, urban and regional planning |
| File size: | 32,000 records |
| Coverage: | 1972 onwards |
| Updates: | 2,200 records per year |
| Provider: | Centre d'Etudes de Geographie Tropicale (CEGET); Centre National de la Recherche Scientifique, Institut de l'Information Scientifique et Technique (CNRS/INIST) |
| Host: | Centre National de la Recherche Scientifique, Institut de l'Information Scientifique et Technique (CNRS/INIST) |

## FRANCIS: ECODOC

| | |
|---|---|
| Subject: | Economics |
| File size: | 10,000 records |

Coverage:     1981 onwards
Updates:      Quarterly, about 1,300 records a year
Provider:     CNRS/INIST, Universite des sciences sociales de Grenoble
Hosts:        G.CAM Serveur; Telesystemes-Questel

## FRANCIS: EMPLOI ET FORMATION

Subject:      Employment and training
File size:    10,000 records
Coverage:     1974 - 1984
Updates:      Not updated
Provider:     Centre National de la Recherche Scientifique, Institut de l'Information Scientifique et Technique (CNRS/INIST)
Host:         Telesystemes-Questel

## FRANCIS: ETHNOLOGIE

Subject:      Ethnology and social anthropology
File size:    52,000 records
Coverage:     1972 onwards
Updates:      Quarterly. Approx 4,800 records per year
Provider:     Centre National de la Recherche Scientifique, Institut de l'Information Scientifique et Technique (CNRS/INIST)
Host:         Telesystemes-Questel

## FRANCIS: SCIENCES DE L'EDUCATION

Subject:      Education
File size:    96,600 records
Coverage:     1972 onwards (Telesystemes-Questel); 1979 onwards (G.CAM Serveur)
Updates:      Quarterly. Approx 4,500 records per year
Provider:     Centre National de la Recherche Scientifique, Institut de l'Information Scientifique et Technique (CNRS/INIST)
Hosts:        G.CAM Serveur; Questel

## FRANCIS: SOCIOLOGIE

Subject:      Sociology
File size:    72,700 records
Coverage:     1972 onwards
Updates:      Quarterly, about 4,000 records a year
Provider:     Centre National de la Recherche Scientifique, Institut de l'Information Scientifique et Technique (CNRS/INIST)
Host:         Questel
CD-ROM:       Available

## GPO MONTHLY CATALOGUE

Subject:      US government publications
File size:    282,000 records
Coverage:     July 1976 onwards
Updates:      Approx 2,500 records per month

Provider:     US Government Printing Office
Hosts:        BRS; DIALOG; TECH-DATA; WILSONLINE
CD-ROM:       Available from SilverPlatter, Information Access Company, and H.W.Wilson

## GPO PUBLICATIONS REFERENCE FILE
Subject:      US government publications
File size:    21,000 records
Coverage:     1971 onwards
Updates:      Every 2 weeks
Provider:     US Government Printing Office (GPO), Superintendent of Documents
Hosts:        CompuServe Information Service; DIALOG

## HELPIS (Higher Education Learning Programmes Information Service)
Subject:      Audio-visual materials for use in higher education
File size:    7,000 records at 10/88
Coverage:     Current
Updates:      Monthly
Provider:     British Universities Film and Video Council
Host:         BLAISE-LINE

## HISTORICAL ABSTRACTS
Subject:      World history, except US and Canada
File size:    308,788 records
Coverage:     1973 onwards
Updates:      Approx 4,000 records six times per year
Provider:     ABC-CLIO, Santa Barbara, California
Host:         DIALOG

## HUMANITIES AND SOCIAL SCIENCES
Subject:      Printed books on humanities and social sciences, acquired by the British Library
File size:    922,041 records at 8/88
Coverage:     1971 onwards
Updates:      Weekly
Provider:     British Library, Humanities and Social Sciences
Host:         BLAISE-LINE

## LINGUISTICS AND LANGUAGE BEHAVIOR ABSTRACTS
Subject:      Linguistics, psycholinguistics and language teaching
File size:    107,000 records
Coverage:     1973 onwards
Updates:      Quarterly. Approx 2,000 records per quarter
Provider:     Sociological Abstracts Inc., San Diego, California
Hosts:        BRS; DIALOG

## LOGIN (Local Government Information Network)
Subject:      US local government
File size:    35,000 records
Coverage:     1979 onwards

Updates:     Not known
Provider:    LOGIN Information Services
Host:        LOGIN Information Services

## MAGAZINE ASAP
Subject:     Full text of general interest magazines
File size:   213,229 records
Coverage:    1983 onwards
Updates:     Weekly
Provider:    Information Access Company, Belmont, California
Hosts:       BRS; DIALOG; Mead Data Central
CD-ROM:      Available from Information Access Company

## MAGAZINE INDEX
Subject:     North American general interest magazines
File size:   2,845,674 records
Coverage:    1959 onwards (BRS); 1959 to March 1970, 1973 onwards (DIALOG)
Updates:     Weekly
Provider:    Information Access Company, Belmont, California
Hosts:       BRS; DIALOG
CD-ROM:      Available from Information Access Company

## MENTAL HEALTH ABSTRACTS
Subject:     Psychology and mental health
File size:   475,830 records
Coverage:    1969 onwards
Updates:     Monthly. Approx 600 records per update
Provider:    National Clearinghouse for Mental Health Information (NIMHI), National Institute of Mental Health, Rockville, Maryland, to 1982; IFI/Plenum Data Company, Alexandria, Virginia from 1983 onwards
Host:        DIALOG

## MENTAL MEASUREMENTS YEARBOOK
Subject:     Psychological tests
File size:   1,850 tests
Coverage:    1972 onwards; selective coverage of older material
Updates:     Monthly
Provider:    Buros Institute of Mental Measurements
Host:        BRS
Note:        Contains descriptive information and reviews of English-language tests

## MIDDLE EAST: ABSTRACTS AND INDEX
Subject:     All aspects of the Middle East
File size:   36,174 records
Coverage:    1980 onwards
Updates:     Irregular. Approx 4,000 records per update
Provider:    Northumberland Press, Pittsburgh, Pennsylvania
Host:        DIALOG

## NATIONAL NEWSPAPER INDEX

Subject:      General coverage of North American newspapers
File size:    2,137,814 records
Coverage:     1979 onwards
Updates:      Monthly. approx 15,500 records per month
Provider:     Information Access Company, Belmont, California
Hosts:        BRS; DIALOG
CD-ROM:       Available from Information Access Company

## NERIS (National Educational Resources Information Service)

Subject:      Resources and information for education
File size:    29,000 records
Coverage:     Not known
Updates:      Weekly
Provider:     National Educational Resources Information Service
Hosts:        National Educational Resources Information Service; CAMPUS 2000
CD-ROM:       Available from NERIS

## NEW SIGNPOSTS

Subject:      Careers and occupational information
File size:    Approx 350 careers
Coverage:     Not known
Updates:      Not known
Provider:     Careers and Occupational Information Centre
Host:         CAMPUS 2000

## NEWSEARCH

Subject:      News and current affairs
File size:    1,200 - 54,000 records
Coverage:     Current month only
Updates:      Daily. Approx 2,000 records per day
Provider:     Information Access Company, Belmont, California
Hosts:        BRS; DIALOG

## NOMIS (National Online Manpower Information System)

Subject:      UK demography and population, labour market and employment
File size:    12bn time series
Coverage:     1971 to date
Updates:      Monthly
Provider:     University of Durham for Department of Employment Training Agency
Host:         University of Durham

## NTIS (National Technical Information Service)

Subject:      Research reports on all subjects
File size:    1.4 million records
Coverage:     1964 onwards
Updates:      2,600 records twice monthly
Provider:     NTIS

Hosts:      BRS; Centre de Documentation de l'Armament (CEDOCAR); CISTI; Canadian Online Enquiry Service; DATA-STAR; DIALOG; ESA-IRS; ORBIT; STN International; TECH DATA

CD-ROM:     Available from DIALOG, OCLC, and SilverPlatter

## OPEN LEARNING BIBLIOGRAPHY
Subject:    Open learning
File size:  1,200 records at 9/88
Coverage:   1983 onwards
Updates:    Monthly
Provider:   MARIS-NET (Ely) Ltd
Host:       MARIS-NET

## ORGANIZATIONS AND SERVICES DATABASE
Subject:    Training and education
File size:  3,000 records at 9/88
Coverage:   Current
Updates:    Weekly
Provider:   MARIS-NET (Ely) Ltd
Host:       MARIS-NET (Ely) Ltd

## PAIS INTERNATIONAL
Subject:    Economics, politics and social sciences
File size:  300,000 records
Coverage:   1972 onwards (Foreign Language Index); 1976 onwards (Bulletin)
Updates:    Monthly. Approx 1,500 records per month for Bulletin. Quarterly. approx 1,500 records per update for Foreign Language Index.
Provider:   Public Affairs Information Service, Inc., New York.
Hosts:      BRS; DIALOG; DATA-STAR; Knowledge Index; TECH DATA
CD-ROM:     Available from PAIS Inc.

## PAPERS
Subject:    Full text of a collection of American newspapers
File size:  2,200,000 records
Coverage:   Varies for each paper
Updates:    Daily
Provider:   Individual newspaper publishers
Host:       DIALOG

## PARLAMADRID
Subject:    Spanish government
File size:  35,000 parliamentary statements
Coverage:   1982 onwards
Updates:    Weekly
Provider:   Empresa Provincial de Information de Madrid
Host:       EPIMSA

## PETERSON'S COLLEGE DATABASE

| | |
|---|---|
| Subject: | Colleges and universities |
| File size: | 4,762 records |
| Coverage: | Current |
| Updates: | Annual |
| Provider: | Peterson's Guides  Inc., Princeton, NJ |
| Hosts: | BRS; CompuServe Information Service; DIALOG; Dow Jones and Company, Inc.; TECHDATA |
| CD-ROM: | Available from SilverPlatter |

## PICKUP TRAINING DIRECTORY

| | |
|---|---|
| Subject: | Short vocational courses |
| File size: | 14,000 courses at 9/88 |
| Coverage: | Current |
| Updates: | Fortnightly |
| Provider: | Guildford Educational Services (GES) Ltd for the Department of Education and Science |
| Host: | CAMPUS 2000 |

## PLANEX

| | |
|---|---|
| Subject: | Urban and regional planning |
| File size: | 17,000 records |
| Coverage: | 1981 to date |
| Updates: | 300 records a month |
| Provider: | Planning Exchange, Glasgow |
| Host: | PFDS |

## POLIS

| | |
|---|---|
| Subject: | British government |
| File size: | 741,000 references |
| Coverage: | 1979 onwards |
| Updates: | Daily. Approx 500 records |
| Provider: | House of Commons Library, Westminster, London |
| Host: | ICC |

## POLYTEL

| | |
|---|---|
| Subject: | Polytechnic course vacancies |
| File size: | Not known |
| Coverage: | Current |
| Updates: | Not known |
| Provider: | Committee of Directors of Polytechnics |
| Host: | CAMPUS 2000 (via Gateway) |

## POPLINE

| | |
|---|---|
| Subject: | International demography and population |
| File size: | Not known |
| Coverage: | 1970 onwards. Earliest materials from 1886. English language |
| Updates: | About 800 records a month |
| Provider: | Johns Hopkins University; Columbia University; Princeton University; University of North Carolina |

Host: National Library of Medicine
CD-ROM: SilverPlatter Information Inc. Updated semiannually

## POPULATION BIBLIOGRAPHY

Subject: Demography
File size: 67,827 records
Coverage: 1966 - 1984
Updates: Closed file
Provider: Carolina Population Centre, University of North Carolina, Chapel Hill, North Carolina
Host: DIALOG

## PROFILE

Subject: International news, current affairs and business
File size: Not known
Coverage: 1981 onwards
Updates: Daily
Provider: Profile Information
Host: Profile Information
Note: Full-text file

## PSYCINFO

Subject: Psychology
File size: 667,000 records
Coverage: 1967 onwards
Updates: Monthly. Approx 4,000 records per update
Provider: American Psychological Association, Washington, DC
Hosts: BRS; Data-Star; DIALOG; DIMDI; University of Tsukuba
CD-ROM: Available from SilverPlatter as PsycLIT

## PSYNDEX

Subject: Psychology
File size: Not available
Coverage: 1977 onwards
Updates: Monthly
Provider: Trier University, Zentralstelle fuer Psychologische Information und Dokumentation (ZPID)
Host: DIMDI
Note: Abstracts in English for about fifty per cent of records

## READERS' GUIDE TO PERIODICAL LITERATURE

Subject: General
File size: 324,000 records
Coverage: 1983 onwards
Updates: Twice weekly. Approx 5,300 records per month
Provider: H. W. Wilson Company, New York
Host: WilsonLine
Note: No abstracts
CD-ROM: Available from H.W.Wilson

## REUTER NEWS REPORTS

| | |
|---|---|
| Subject: | International news |
| File size: | Not known |
| Coverage: | 1979 to date (Mead); 1987 to date (DIALOG) |
| Updates: | Continuously (DIALOG, NewsNet), within two days (Mead) |
| Provider: | Reuters Information Services Inc |
| Hosts: | DIALOG; Mead Data Central, NewsNet Inc |

## RSWB (Raumordnung, Stadtebau, Wohnungswesen, Bauwesen)

| | |
|---|---|
| Subject: | Urban and regional planning, urban studies. German language |
| File size: | 360,000 records |
| Coverage: | 1976 onwards |
| Updates: | Monthly |
| Provider: | Fraunhofer Society |
| Hosts: | FIZ Technik; STN International |

## RURAL LEARNING OPPORTUNITIES DATABASE

| | |
|---|---|
| Subject: | Training in agriculture and related fields |
| File size: | 1,700 records at 9/88 |
| Coverage: | Current |
| Updates: | As necessary |
| Provider: | Owned by TAP/managed by Countryside Information Systems |
| Host: | MARIS-NET (Ely) Ltd |

## SAGA

| | |
|---|---|
| Subject: | French politics and political science |
| File size: | 3 files |
| Coverage: | 1974 onwards |
| Updates: | Monthly for Chronologie file, weekly for Communiques and Declarations |
| Provider: | Direction de la Documentation Francaise |
| Host: | G.CAM Serveur |
| Note: | French language |

## SELF STUDY MATERIALS DATABASE

| | |
|---|---|
| Subject: | Self study training packages |
| File size: | 9,000 at 9/88 |
| Coverage: | Current |
| Updates: | Weekly |
| Provider: | MARIS-MET (Ely) Ltd |
| Host: | MARIS-NET (Ely) Ltd |
| CD-ROM: | Available from MARIS-NET |

## SHORT COURSES DATABASE

| | |
|---|---|
| Subject: | Training courses |
| File size: | 6,000 at 9/88 |
| Coverage: | Current |
| Updates: | Weekly |
| Provider: | MARIS-NET (Ely) Ltd |
| Host: | MARIS-NET (Ely) Ltd |

## SOCIAL PLANNING, POLICY AND DEVELOPMENT ABSTRACTS (SOPODA)

| | |
|---|---|
| Subject: | Social welfare and policy |
| File size: | 18,500 records |
| Coverage: | 1975 onwards |
| Updates: | Twice a year. Approx 2,500 records per year |
| Provider: | Sociogical Abstracts, Inc., San Diego, California |
| Hosts: | BRS; DIALOG; Knowledge Index |
| Note: | On DIALOG, SOPODA is part of Sociological Abstracts |

## SOCIAL SCIENCES INDEX

| | |
|---|---|
| Subject: | Social sciences |
| File size: | 164,000 records |
| Coverage: | 1983 onwards |
| Updates: | Twice weekly |
| Provider: | H.W.Wilson Company |
| Host: | WilsonLine |
| CD-ROM: | Available from H.W. Wilson |

## SOCIAL SCISEARCH

| | |
|---|---|
| Subject: | Social sciences |
| File size: | 2.2 million records |
| Coverage: | 1972 onwards |
| Updates: | Weekly |
| Provider: | Institute for Scientific Information, Philadelphia, Pennsylvania |
| Hosts: | BRS; DIALOG; DIMDI; University of Tsukuba |
| Note: | Citation index |
| CD-ROM: | Available from ISI |

## SOCIAL WORK ABSTRACTS

| | |
|---|---|
| Subject: | Social work and related fields |
| File size: | 19,000 records |
| Coverage: | 1977 onwards |
| Updates: | Quarterly. Approx 575 records per update |
| Provider: | National Association of Social Workers, Inc., Silver Springs, Maryland |
| Host: | BRS |

## SOCIOLOGICAL ABSTRACTS

| | |
|---|---|
| Subject: | Sociology |
| File size: | 270,000 records |
| Coverage: | 1963 onwards |
| Updates: | Five times yearly |
| Provider: | Sociological Abstracts, Inc., San Diego, California |
| Hosts: | BRS; Data-Star; DIALOG; DIMDI; Knowledge Index |
| Note: | On DIALOG, SA includes SOPODA |
| CD-ROM: | Sociofile, available from SilverPlatter |

## SOLIS

| | |
|---|---|
| Subject: | Social sciences, humanities, sociology |

File size:      105,000+ records
Coverage:       1945 onwards, abstracts from 1976 onwards. German language
Updates:        1,000 records a month
Provider:       Informationszentrum Socialwissenschaften
Hosts:          DIMDI; STN International

## SUPERSITE
Subject:        UK and US demography and population
File size:      Not known
Coverage:       1960 onwards (US); 1971 onwards (UK)
Updates:        Annually
Provider:       CACI
Hosts:          CompuServe Business Information Service: COMSHARE Inc; DRI/McGraw Hill; Information Plus; WEFA Group

## TEXTLINE
Subject:        Business and industry news (international)
File size:      Not known
Coverage:       1980 onwards
Updates:        Daily. Approx 15,000 records per week
Provider:       Reuters Ltd.
Host:           Reuters Ltd.

## THE TIMES NETWORK NATIONAL DATABASE
Subject:        Resources and information for education
File size:      Not known
Coverage:       Not known
Updates:        Daily
Provider:       The Times Network System Ltd (TTNS)
Host:           CAMPUS 2000

## UCCA COURSE VACANCY DATABASE (UCCA)
Subject:        Vacancies at British Universities
File size:      Not known
Coverage:       Current
Updates:        Not known
Provider:       Universities Central Council on Admissions
Hosts:          CAMPUS 2000; ECCTIS

## URBALINE
Subject:        Urban and social policy, local government
File size:      90,000 records
Coverage:       1981 onwards
Updates:        Daily. Approx 9,000 records per year
Provider:       Research Library, London Research Centre, 81 Black Prince Road, London SE1 7SZ
Host:           ESA-IRS

## URBAMET

| | |
|---|---|
| Subject: | Transportation, urban and regional planning |
| File size: | 150,000 records |
| Coverage: | 1976 onwards, primarily English and French |
| Updates: | 1,000 records per month |
| Provider: | Reseau URBAMET (Represented by Institut d'Amenagement et d'Urbanisme de la Region d'Ile-de-France (IAURIF)) |
| Host: | Telesystemes-Questel |
| CD-ROM: | ACT Informatique; Euro-CD Diffusion. Annual updates |

## US POLITICAL SCIENCE DOCUMENTS

| | |
|---|---|
| Subject: | Politics and political science |
| File size: | 41,000 records |
| Coverage: | 1975 onwards |
| Updates: | Quarterly |
| Provider: | NASA Industrial Application Centre, University of Pittsburgh, Pennsylvania |
| Host: | DIALOG |

## VOLNET

| | |
|---|---|
| Subject: | Voluntary sector and community development |
| File size: | 18,000+ records |
| Coverage: | Not known |
| Updates: | 200 records per week |
| Provider: | Community Development Foundation; Volunteer Centre |
| Host: | Polytechnic of North London |

## WORLD AFFAIRS REPORT

| | |
|---|---|
| Subject: | World affairs as seen from Moscow |
| File size: | 34,810 records |
| Coverage: | 1970 onwards |
| Updates: | Monthly. Approx 400 records per update |
| Provider: | California Institute of International Studies, Stanford, California |
| Host: | DIALOG |

# CD-ROM DATABASES

## 1981 CENSUS: SMALL AREA STATISTICS FOR ENGLAND, WALES, AND SCOTLAND

| | |
|---|---|
| Subject: | Population maps and charts |
| Information provider: | OPCS |
| Publisher: | Chadwyck-Healey Ltd |

## A-V ONLINE

| | |
|---|---|
| Subject: | Audio-visual materials |
| File size: | 350,000 items |
| Coverage: | Not known |
| Updates: | Annual |

| | |
|---|---|
| Information provider: | National Information Center for Educational Media (NICEM) |
| Publisher: | SilverPlatter |

## CATALOGUE OF UNITED KINGDOM OFFICIAL PUBLICATIONS (UKOP)

| | |
|---|---|
| Subject: | British official publications, HMSO and non-HMSO |
| File size: | Not known |
| Coverage: | 1980 onwards |
| Updates: | Quarterly |
| Information provider: | HMSO Books, Chadwyck-Healey Ltd |
| Publisher: | HMSO Books, Chadwyck-Healey Ltd |

## CD-ATLAS DE FRANCE

| | |
|---|---|
| Subject: | Census data, maps, statistics |
| Information provider: | IGN Insee, GIP-Reclus |
| Distributor: | Chadwyck-Healey Ltd |

## DRUGS AND CRIME CD-ROM

| | |
|---|---|
| Subject: | Drugs and crime |
| File size: | 40,000 pages of text, 1,000 images from books and articles |
| Coverage: | 1970-1989 |
| Information provider: | National Institute of Justice |
| Distributor: | Abt Books, Inc (US), TBA (non US) |

## EDUCATION LIBRARY

| | |
|---|---|
| Subject: | Education books from OCLC union catalogue |
| File size: | 350,000 records |
| Coverage: | Not known |
| Updates: | Annual |
| Information provider: | OCLC |
| Publisher: | OCLC |

## EDUCATIONAL TESTING DATABASE

| | |
|---|---|
| Subject: | Educational tests |
| File size: | 90,000 test items |
| Coverage: | Not known |
| Updates: | Annual |
| Information provider: | Minnesota Department of Education |
| Publisher: | Minnesota Department of Education |

## NEWSPAPER ABSTRACTS ONLINE

| | |
|---|---|
| Subject: | American newspapers |
| File size: | Not known |
| Coverage: | Not known |
| Updates: | Quarterly |
| Information provider: | University Microfilms International (UMI) |
| Publisher: | UMI |

**SUPERMAP 1980 US CENSUS**
Subject:                          Census data, maps, statistics
Information provider:             US Bureau of Census
Distributor:                      Chadwyck-Healey Ltd

## REFERENCES

1.   C.M. White and others. *Sources of Information in the Social Sciences*. 2nd ed. Chicago:   American Library Association, 1973.
2.   D.L. Sills, ed. *International Encyclopedia of the Social Sciences*. New York: Macmillan and Free Press, 1968.
3.   Behavioral and Social Sciences Survey Committee. *The Behavioral and Social Sciences: Outlook and Needs. A Report, under the Auspices of the Committee on Science and Public Policy, National Academy of Sciences, and Committee on Problems and Policy, Social Sciences Research Council*. Englewood Cliffs, Prentice-Hall, 1969.
4.   S. Atkinson. Zero result searches.... how to minimize them. *Online* 10(3) 1986 59-66
5.   C.L. Gilreath. *Computerized Literature Searching: Research Strategies and Databases*. Boulder, London: Westview Press, 1984.
6.   S.Y. Fustukjian and B.J. Taheri, eds. *Directory of ERIC Information Service Providers*. Washington, DC: Educational Resources Information Center (ERIC), 1990.

## FURTHER READING

### General

Byler, Anne Meyer and Ravenhall, Mary. Using DIALINDEX for the identification of online databases relevant to urban and regional planning. *Online Review* 12(2) 1988 119-133
Hanstock, Terry. Information services for the elected member. *Public Library Journal* 2(3) 1987 47-50
Paige, Weston E. and Lauderdale, Diane S. How do we learn what a database includes? A case study using psychology dissertations. *RQ* 28(1) 1988 35-41

### Newspapers

Jaffurs, Alexa. Newspapers on CD-ROM: timely access to current events. *Laserdisk Professional* 2(3) 1989 19-26
Jewell, Timothy D. and Pearson, Glenda J. Newspaper Abstracts Ondisc and its competitors. *CD-ROM Librarian* 3(8) 1988 22-28
Long, Arlene. Full text newspaper retrieval is hard to manage: fact or fiction? In *Proceedings of the 9th National Online Meeting (New York 10-12 May 1988)* compiled by Martha E. Williams and Thomas H. Hogan; Medford, New Jersey: Learned Information Inc., 1988 213-216
Noras, Sibylle R. All the news that's fit to screen - the development of full text newspaper databases. *Australian Library Journal* 38(1) 1989 17-27

Ojala, Marydee. Newspaper data bases - the abstract and index approach. *Online* 13(1) 1989 90-97

Summit, Roger and Lee, Ann. Will full-text on-line files become electronic periodicals? *Serials Review* 14(3) 1988 7-10

Veccia, Susan H. Full-text dilemmas for searchers and systems: the Washington Post Online. *Database* 11(2) 1988 13-16, 19-32

## Online databases

Barrett, W. F. The EUDISED database: present situation and possible developments. *Liber News Sheet* (18) 1986 10-13

Capitani, Paola Costanzo. Grey literature in the field of education: the bibliographic databases. (La letteratura grigia nella scienze dell'educazione: le basi bibliografiche automatizzate.) *Bollettino d'Informazioni* 27(3-4) 1987 387-390

Conger, Lucinda D. Soviet information sources online. *Database* 10(2) 1987 119-121

Guyonneau, Christine H. Magazine Index Plus or Academic Index? *College and Research Libraries News* 49(7) 1988 430-433

Harris, Kevin and Whitcher, Angela. Online in the community and voluntary sector: old lessons for a new market. In *Proceedings of the 12th International Online Information Meeting (London, 6-8 December 1988)* Oxford: Learned Information (Europe) Ltd, 1988 665-670

Hirsch, Steven. ERIC and ECER. *Online Review* 11(5) 1987 315-321

Horn, Sharon K. and Clements, Stephen K. ERIC: the past, present and future federal role in education dissemination. *Government Information Quarterly* 6(2) 1989 183-197

O'Leary, Mick. AGELINE reflects oldsters' agenda. *Information Today* 6(6) 1989 11-12

Preschel, Barbara M. PAIS International: print, online, CD-ROM. In *Online 86. Proceedings of the Conference (Chicago, Illinois, 4-6 November 1986)* Weston, CT: Online Inc.,1986 200-203

Sanouillet, Anne. FRANCIS: a comparison with ERIC and Sociological Abstracts. In *Online Information 87. Proceedings of the 11th International Online Information Meeting (London 8-10 December 1987)* 259-265

Taylor, John. Educational counselling and credit transfer information service. *Learning Resources Journal* 2(3) 1986 125-136

Terris, Olwen. The British Universities Film and Video Council. *Audiovisual Librarian* 13(1) 1987 46-49

Ulincy, Loretta D. In search of information on aging: Ageline. *Medical Reference Services Quarterly* 7(3) 1988 69-83

## CD-ROMs

Anders, Vicki and Jackson, Kathy M. Online vs CD-ROM - the impact of CD-ROM databases upon a large online searching program. *Online* 12(6) 1988 24-32

Bacsanyi, Karen and Lynn, Patricia. CD-ROMs: instructional methods and user reactions. *Reference Services Review* 17(2) 1989 17-25

Bomta, Bruce D. CD-ROM in the social science reference room. *Inspel* 22(1) 1988 44-47

Ferl, Terry Ellen and Gordon, Margaret M. DIALOG's Ondisc ERIC in an academic library. *CD-ROM Librarian* 3(3) 1988 12-14

Holtmann, Susanne and Nicholls, Paul T. Research perspectives: Womens' issues searching with

DIALOG Ondisc ERIC: natural language and controlled vocabulary strategies. *Laserdisk Professional* 2(3) 1989 97-103

Lehmler, Wilfried. CD-ROM for self-service by users. Experiences with PsycLit in Konstanz university library. (CD-ROM zur Selbstbedienung von Benutzer. Erfahrungen mit PsycLit in der Bibliothek der Universitat Konstanz.) *Bibliotheksdienst* 22(1) 1988 27-33

Lewis, Mike. Experiences with CD-ROM in a university library. In *SCIL 89. Proceedings of the Third Annual Conference on Small Computers in Libraries (London, Feb 1989)* 133-136

Preschel, Barbara M. PAIS on CD-ROM. In *Online '87. Proceedings of the Conference (Anaheim, California, 20-22 October 1987) Part 1*. Weston, CT: Online Inc., 1987 178-181

Reese, Jean and Steffey, Ramona. ERIC on CD-ROM: a comparison of DIALOG Ondisc, OCLC's Search CD450 and SilverPlatter. *Online* 11(5) 1987 42-54

Reese, Jean. ERIC on compact disc: new software versions from DIALOG, OCLC and SilverPlatter. *Laserdisk Professional* 2(1) 1989 75-80

Siitonen, Leena. Advancing optical disc technology for social sciences in non-high tech societies. *Inspel* 22(1) 1988 70-83

# 11 Law: British and European legal systems

*John Williams*

## INTRODUCTION

The legal profession has a reputation for conservatism and a strong resistance to innovation. The manner of dress, the constant reference to earlier authority and the antiquated language all suggest a system with its feet firmly in the nineteenth century. Whereas such a view has much in common with truth, it does ignore the extent to which the legal profession has embraced modern technology. In legal education technology has been introduced as part of degree courses in universities and polytechnics. The establishing of the Law Technology Centre based at the University of Warwick, funded by the University Funding Council and the Computer Board, has greatly increased the profile of technology as an integral part of academic teaching and research. Similarly the British and Irish Legal Education Technology Association (BILETA) and the British and Irish Association of Law Librarians (BIALL) have done much to raise awareness of the implications of technology in legal education. Technology has also found its way into the lawyer's office. There is a wide range of computer software available for lawyers including standard form precedents, office management packages, databases and accounts systems. Many law firms have embraced such technology; this has not been confined to the larger City firms. Indeed it makes greater sense for the smaller and more remote law firm to avail itself of electronic database material to supplement its traditional law library which may, given the cost, be lacking in the more specialized material.

The use of electronic legal databases is a relatively new development for lawyers in the United Kingdom. It was not until the late 1970s that two commercial ventures - EUROLEX and LEXIS® - entered a somewhat wary market as competitors, each offering a differently biased database. EUROLEX contained the full text of materials covering the United Kingdom and European case law, legislation and secondary sources. LEXIS® originally contained the statute and case law of the United States of America, the United Kingdom and France. These two databases were eventually combined to produce a comprehensive online legal database for the United Kingdom market.

Developments in online legal databases have naturally reflected the greater unification of United Kingdom and European Community law. The JUSTIS Online Database is an excellent example of this containing European Community Law from 1952 onwards. The physical bulk of European Community law makes online an extremely attractive service for law firms and educational establishments.

It is essential that lawyers, when advising clients or representing them in court, are up to date. Law changes on a daily basis and a fast, efficient and comprehensive updating service is essential. The professional journals such as the *Law Society Gazette* and the *Solicitors Journal* provide specialist and general updating services covering case law, statutes and delegated legislation. A number of specialist encyclopedias are published in loose-leaf form which are regularly updated - for example the *Encyclopedia of Health Services and Medical Law* and the *Road Traffic Encyclopedia,* both published by Sweet and Maxwell. Other updating services are provided by publications such as *Current Law,* a monthly journal providing a comprehensive account of recent developments in case law, legislation and statutory instruments in addition to details of articles in journals and new books. Naturally the main draw-back is the delay in publication.

## LEGAL MATERIAL

A look around any law library attached to a law school or a large firm of lawyers will indicate the vast range of legal material available to the profession. This is reflected in the growth in the number of specialized law librarians being recruited by law schools and law firms. Searching for the appropriate legal authority is no longer the hit and miss affair it once was. It is now an essential skill which the complexity of law requires all lawyers to possess. The traditional *Law Reports* have been supplemented by reports covering specialist topics such as industrial tribunals, family law and planning law. The flow of legislation and delegated legislation from Parliament appears to be on the increase. Europe provides a bountiful supply of new law as does the more traditional international law. These developments have to be seen in the context of a society that is more aware of its legal rights and is more litigious. An example of this is found in the area of medical law. No longer are people prepared to leave important decisions to doctors, or to leave unchallenged acts of medical negligence. The courts are being used by individuals in such sensitive decisions as sterilization of people with mental handicap or suing for operations that have gone wrong. Thus the web of law which the lawyer has to untangle is growing more complex. In this environment the role of the electronic database becomes all the more crucial in the provision of high quality legal advice and assistance.

Traditionally lawyers rely on the following primary sources: statutes, case law, statutory instruments and European law.

### Statutes

The cardinal rule of the British constitution is that Parliament is supreme. It can, theoretically, do anything; its actions cannot be constrained by the courts. Whether this absolute supremacy of Parliament has been eroded by this country's membership of the European Community is a matter of some debate falling outside of the remit of this review. Acts of Parliament are the primary source of law which can overrule long established rules of common law. They may also amend, repeal or consolidate earlier legislation. In this context the original HMSO hard copy of an Act of Parliament does not necessarily provide an accurate picture of the law. A good example is provided by the Children and Young Persons Act 1969. The original 1969 Act was amended by a series of later Acts such as the Children Act 1975, the Health and Social Services and Social Security

Adjudication Act 1983 and the Criminal Justice Act 1988. This is not revealed in the original HMSO version. Nor does the original copy inform the reader that it has now been repealed by the Children Act 1989.

The implementation of a piece of legislation may be phased. Again this fact is not revealed by reading the original HMSO copy. It is essential for the practitioner to be aware of what is and what is not in force. Publications such as *Is it in Force?* contain details of which parts of legislation are in force.

The term the 'Statute Book' is somewhat misleading insofar as it creates the impression of one single reference work. A variety of different printed sources are available; very often these have different formats. These range from the official HMSO *Public General Acts* to the *Current Annotated Statutes* series which provides commentary on the legislation as well as the text. *Statutes in Force* endeavours to provide, through use of loose-leaf format, an official, up-to-date text of statutes currently in force. Unfortunately the series is, in places, considerably out of date.

## Case law

Case law is still an important source of British law. Common law principles still apply, and continue to be developed, in many important areas of law. Judges also have responsibility for interpreting Acts of Parliament. The system of binding precedent places great emphasis on the importance of accurately recording judicial decisions so that they may be cited before later courts.

A wide range of case law reports are available in the printed form. The *English Reports* contain most of the cases found in the nominate reports. From 1865 onward the Incorporated Council of Law Reporting started to produce semi-official reports of cases. These are now know as the *Law Reports*. It is practice for the courts to require citation of the *Law Reports* if a case presented in argument is reported in them. Currently the Council publishes the following reports:

- Appeal Cases
- Queen's Bench Division
- Chancery Division
- Probate and Family Division.

The Council is also responsible for publishing the generic series known as the *Weekly Law Reports*.

Commercial publishers produce a number of law reports. Of these the *All England Law Reports* are perhaps the best known. This is another generic series covering cases from different courts over a wide range of subject matter. In addition the *The Times, The Guardian* and *The Independent* produce daily law reports of the most important cases. However, these tend to be shortened versions of the decision and do not, as such, have any authority. As noted above, the *Law Society Gazette* and the *Solicitors Journal* provide updating services which include summaries of recently decided cases. Specialist reports include *Family Law Reports, Knight's Industrial Reports* and the *Planning Law Reports*.

Although having much in common with England and Wales, the jurisdictions of Scotland and Northern Ireland have their own specialist law reports. In Scotland these are the *Session Cases* and the *Scots Law Times*. In Northern Ireland cases are reported in the *Northern Ireland Law Reports*.

Some cases never make the law reports but are available only in transcript form. The procedure whereby a case does or does not reach the law reports is shrouded in mystery. This is a curious feature of the common law system as it operates in Britain. It presupposes that not all cases will be reported; if they were then the system would become unmanageable. The House of Lords in Roberts Petroleum Ltd v Bernard Kenny [1983] 2 AC 192 restricted the citation of transcripts. In its judgment the House of Lords held that leave to cite a transcript should only be allowed:

'upon counsel giving an assurance that the transcript contains a statement of some general principle of law, relevant to an issue in the appeal to this House, that is binding upon the Court of Appeal and of which the substance, as distinct from the mere choice of phraseology, is not to be found in any judgment of that court that has appeared in one of the generalised or specialised series of reports.'

The use of electronic databases requires some rethinking of the current situation. More cases will be available, many of them only in transcript form.

## Statutory instruments

Much of the detail surrounding legislation is to be found in statutory instruments. At times the Government is given wide powers to modify the law by means of statutory instruments. In order to obtain a complete picture of legislation it is essential to refer to the relevant statutory instruments. Statutory instruments are published by HMSO. They may be obtained individually or in the collected work known as *Statutory Instruments*. The same updating process that applies to Acts of Parliament also applies to statutory instruments. Of special assistance here is the publication, *A Table of Government Orders* which details the effects of statutory instruments on earlier ones.

## European material

A wide range of material is available dealing specifically with European law. *The Official Journal* is the primary source of European Community law containing legislation, directives, regulations and decisions, in addition to draft regulations and proceedings of the European Parliament. *The Official Journal* is published daily and is, therefore, an unmanageable amount of material. European case law is covered by the official series of the *European Court Report,* and the *Common Market Law Reports* published by the European Law Centre.

The above survey gives a brief account of the material sources of law. It illustrates the extensive nature of the source material to which lawyers must have regard when advising clients. Any legal database purporting to provide a comprehensive coverage of material must be up to date and reflect the law as it is today. In addition its searching facilities and the organization of its data must be such as to minimize irrelevant hits.

## LEXIS®

LEXIS® is now the market leader in British legal databases and achieves that position by virtue of the sheer bulk of material which it contains. Its main advantage over its rivals is the comprehensive nature of the material which it holds. This is of immense value to the lawyer. Upon getting into LEXIS® the user is presented with the library menu (Figure 11.1).

**Figure 11.1: The LEXIS® libraries**

```
LIBRARIES — PAGE 1 of 2
Please TRANSMIT the NAME (only one) of the library you want to search.
 - For more information about a library, TRANSMIT its page (PG) number.
 - To see a list of additional libraries, press the NEXT PAGE key.
 NAME  PG  NAME   PG  NAME    PG  NAME   PG  NAME   PG  NAME   PG  NAME   PG

  UK-LAW      EC-LAW      IR-LAW  - - - - U S - L A W - - - - -      FR-LAW
 ENGGEN 1   EURCOM  1   ITELIS 1   GENFED 3   FEDCOM 3   PUBCON 5   INTNAT 2
 UKTAX  1                          BANKNG 3   FEDSEC 4   PUBHW  5   LOIREG 2
 ADMRTY 1   CW-LAW                 BKRTCY 3   FEDTAX 4   STATES 5   PRIVE  2
 SCOT   1   COMCAS  1   INTL-LAWCORP      3   IMMIG  4   TRADE  5   PUBLIC 2
 UKJNL  1   AUST    1   INTLAW 3   ENERGY 3   ITRADE 4   TRANS  5   REVUES 2
 NILAW  1   NZ      1              ENVIRN 4   LABOR  4   ABA    5
                                   ESTATE 4   M&A    4   LAWREV 5
                                   FEDSEN 4   MILTRY 5   MARHUB 5
                                   INSRLW 4   COPYRT 9   LEXREF 5
                                   STENV  4   PATENT 9   INCORP 5
                                   ASSETS 4   TRDMRK 9   LEGIS  9   REALTY 9
   AC for AUTO-CITE       LXE (LEXSEE) to retrieve a case/document by cite

   SHEP for SHEPARD'S     LXT (LEXSTAT) to retrieve a statute by cite
```

**Basic searching techniques in the ENGGEN Library**

Each library is composed of a number of different files. The library 'ENGGEN' is the one which is of immediate value to municipal lawyers. Selecting ENGGEN (English General Law) reveals the files available in that library (see Figure 11.2).

**Figure 11.2: ENGGEN files on LEXIS®**

```
Please TRANSMIT the abbreviated NAME of the file you want to search. To see a
description of a file, type its page number and press the TRANSMIT key.
                         FILES — PAGE 1 of 1
 NAME    PG  DESCRIP

 CASES   1  Cases to  5/91
 INJURY  2  Summaries of Injury Cases to 2/91
 STAT    2  Public General Acts to 10/3/91*
 SI      2  Statutory Instruments to 10/3/91*
 STATIS  2  Combined STAT and SI files
 DTAX    2  Double Tax Instruments to 10/3/91*
 TAXMAT  2  Misc tax materials to  5/91
 LEARN   2  1981 Cases for practice research
 LRNSTA  2  Acts and SIs for practice research
               from 2/60 to 12/85

         * date of publication by HMSO

-Documents based on British Crown copyright materials are reproduced with the
permission of the Controller of Her Britannic Majesty's Stationery Office
```

The CASES file contains both reported and unreported cases. With one exception the reported cases cover those reported since 1st January, 1945 (with exception of the Tax Cases which go back only to 1975) in the main general and specialized law reports. Included in the list of general reports are the *All England Law Reports, Law Times Reports,* the *Weekly Law Reports* and *Weekly Notes.* The list of specialist law reports is extensive including obvious ones such as the *Criminal Appeal Reports* and the *Family Law Reports* in addition to the more esoteric *Ryde's Rating Cases* and the *Estates Gazette Digest.* The different volumes of the Law Reports are also in the CASES file.

Unreported cases go back to 1980. Transcripts of all unreported cases are available from the following courts or tribunals:

- House of Lords
- Privy Council
- Court of Appeal (Civil Division)
- Employment Appeal Tribunal
- Chancery Revenue Cases
- Queen's Bench Admiralty Court Cases
- Chancery Patent Court Cases
- Lands Tribunal Cases
- Crown Office List Cases

In addition, selected cases from the Queen's Bench Commercial Court and the VAT (Value Added Tax) Tribunal are available. Whether or not these unreported decisions are admissible depends upon the principle in the Roberts Petroleum Case referred to above.

Another category of unreported cases includes decisions of the High Court and above which are to be found in a wide range of academic and practitioner journals. There is an element of selectivity as to what is included or excluded. However, reports or summaries contained in such journals may be of value, especially if the case itself has not yet reached the more formal law reports. The list of journals is exhaustive and covers such disparate journals as the *Cambridge Law Journal, New Law Journal, Current Law* and *Pension Lawyer.* Reports in *The Times, The Independent* and *The Guardian Gazette* are covered under this group of reports.

Of the other files in ENGGEN particular mention should be made of STAT, SI and STATIS. STAT contains all the Public General Acts of England and Wales. SI covers the statutory Rules, Regulations and Orders of England and Wales which are published in the Statutory Instrument Series. STATIS is a combination of both these files allowing a search of statutes and statutory instruments at the same time. All three files are regularly updated (usually about one month following publication). They are presented in an amended form thus meeting the demand for a reliable up-to-date version of the legislation or instrument.

ENGGEN has two specialist tax files. DTAX is a complete and updated text of the statutory instruments containing the double taxation agreements to which the United Kingdom is a party. This saves searching the larger SI file. TAXMAT is a useful pot-pourri of tax material such as Inland Revenue Press Releases, VAT leaflets and extra statutory concessions. The United Kingdom Tax library (UKTAX, see below) provides a more comprehensive collection of tax material.

Searching the ENGGEN library is relatively easy provided sufficient thought is given to the structure of the search term. The recent changes to the National Health Service provide a good example of searching LEXIS®. Assume that the researcher is aware that under the legislation hospitals and other health service bodies can apply for self-governing status and that they are to be known as 'NHS Trusts'. What are the relevant statutory provisions? Have there been any statutory instruments? Has there been any case law? A starting point is to locate the precise statutory provision. By entering 'STAT' entry to the statutes files is effected. At this stage the search term 'NHS Trusts' must be entered.

This search reveals a number of hits. There are a number of ways in which this material may be viewed. By pressing CITE the hits will be listed in chronological order - the latest reference first as in Figure 11.3. Pressing CITE, the early references to the National Health Service and Community Care Act 1990 which is the principal piece of legislation can be seen. Scanning that list, s.5 National Health Service and Community Care Act 1990 is headed 'NHS Trusts'.

## Figure 11.3: Document citations on LEXIS

```
                    LEVEL 1 - 46 ITEMS


3. National Health Service and Community Care Act 1990 (c 19), 5 NHS trusts

4. National Health Service and Community Care Act 1990 (c 19), 6 Transfer of
staff to NHS trusts

5. National Health Service and Community Care Act 1990 (c 19), 7
Supplementary provisions as to transfer of staff

6. National Health Service and Community Care Act 1990 (c 19), 8 Transfer of
property, rights and liabilities to NHS trust

7. National Health Service and Community Care Act 1990 (c 19), 9 Originating
capital debt of, and other financial provisions relating to NHS trusts

8. National Health Service and Community Care Act 1990 (c 19), 10 Financial
obligations of NHS trusts

9. National Health Service and Community Care Act 1990 (c 19), 11 Trust funds
and trustees for NHS trusts

10. National Health Service and Community Care Act 1990 (c 19), 21 Schemes
for meeting losses and liabilities etc of certain health service bodies
```

Each individual hit can be viewed subsequently in one of two ways. Firstly, by pressing KWIC™ the search term will be highlighted together with approximately twenty-five words either side. This will enable the researcher to skim through the document to see if it is relevant to his or her needs.

The FULL key will provide the full text of the document in a very similar format to the printed copy (see Figure 11.4).

Reverting to the CITE list of hits there are a number of references to both later and earlier legislation. For example in Figure 11.5, it refers to the Voluntary Hospitals (Paying Patients) Act 1936. Using KWIC™ or CITE to view this hit will reveal that the 1936 Act has been amended to accommodate the setting up of NHS Trusts.

Having discovered the relevant statutory provision a search can be made of the statutory instruments file. Both statutes and statutory instruments could be searched together under STATIS, but in this case two separate searches are probably more convenient. At this stage there is a choice open to the researcher. A new search could be initiated using the reference to s.5 National Health Service and Community Care Act 1990. Alternatively the current search term could be used in the SI file. The latter is perhaps the easiest. Changing to SI is no problem - simply press the CHG FILE button to be presented with the choice of commencing a new search or continuing with the existing one in the SI file. By opting for continuing the existing search LEXIS® will identify references to 'NHS Trusts' in the SI file. These hits may be viewed using the CITE, KWIC™, and FULL buttons. The process can be repeated for searching the CASES file. It is interesting to note that the search of the CASES file actually identifies a case which was decided before the Act was in force. Traditional search methods might not have identified this case.

## Figure 11.4: Full text of document on LEXIS

```
                        LEVEL 1 - 3 OF 46 ITEMS


        National Health Service and Community Care Act 1990 (c 19)

                          29 June 1990

        CROSS-HEADING: Part I The National Health Service: England
                and Wales: National Health Service trusts

                    SECTION: 5  NHS trusts

                 DATE-IN-FORCE: 5 July 1990

     TEXT:
        (1) Subject to subsection (2) or, as the case may be, subsection (3)
     below the Secretary of State may by order establish bodies, to be known as
     National Health Service trusts (in this Act referred to as NHS trusts),--

        (a) to assume responsibility, in accordance with this Act, for the
     ownership and management of hospitals or other establishments or facilities
     which were previously managed or provided by Regional, District or Special
     Health Authorities; or
        (b) to provide and manage hospitals or other establishments or facilities
```

## Figure 11.5: KWIC™ view of LEXIS® document

```
                        LEVEL 1 - 46 OF 46 ITEMS


            Voluntary Hospitals (Paying Patients) Act 1936 (c 17)

                    SECTION: 1 Definitions

     TEXT:
        In this Act unless the context otherwise requires—

        "voluntary hospital" means an institution (not being an institution which
     is carried on for profit or which is maintained wholly or mainly at the
     expense of the rates [or which is vested in an NHS trust] [or which is vested
     in the Minister of Health]) which provides medical or surgical treatment for
     in-patients;

        "committee of management" includes any body or persons having the
     management or control of a voluntary hospital;

        ["NHS trust" means a National Health Service trust established under
     Part I of the National Health Service and Community Care Act 1990;]

        "Order" means an Order made by the Charity Commissioners for any of
     the ...
```

The above is an example of a relatively easy search designed to show the effect of a recent piece of legislation. At this stage it is worth mentioning another library that will be of use to those undertaking a general search of United Kingdom Law. United KingdomJNL is a library which contains in full text the *Law Society Gazette* (LSG) and the *New Law Journal* (NLJ) dating from 1st January, 1986. They may be searched separately (LSG or NLJ) or together (ALLJNL). The value of these two journals to practitioners and academics is enhanced by the ability to search them on LEXIS®.

A number of refining techniques are available on LEXIS®. The usual Boolean operators are available. Thus it is possible to search for the following:

> clean break AND child
> divorce OR judicial separation
> hospital NOT NHS Trust

Another useful tool, particularly when searching cases, is the proximity connector. When searching for cases dealing with intention and murder the command 'INTENTION W/10 MURDER' will reveal those cases where the two words appear within ten words of each other. Any combination of the above connectors may be used in a single search request.

Searches may be modified by date. A search for statutory instruments on NHS Trusts issued after October 1990 could be composed as follows:

> NHS Trusts AND DATE AFT OCT 1990

A LEVEL 1 search may be modified by pressing the MODIFY key and then refining the search using the techniques outlined above. It is then essential to commence the modification with a connector.

**Figure 11.6: Case segment searching on LEXIS**

```
                         LEVEL 1 - 1 OF 3 CASES


    {NAME}             Gillick  v West Norfolk and Wisbech Area Health Authority
                       and another

    {COURT}                            HOUSE OF LORDS

    {CITE}             [1986] 1 AC 112, [1985] 3 All ER 402, [1985] 3 WLR 830,
                       [1986] 1 FLR 224, [1986] Crim LR 113

    {HEARING          HEARING-DATES: 24, 25, 26, 27 JUNE, 1, 2, 3, 4 JULY, 17
    DATE}             OCTOBER 1985

    {CATCHWORDS}:
    National health service -- Family planning clinics -- Contraception --
    Circular containing guidance to area health authorities -- Legality of
    advice contained in circular-- Advice given regarding contraception for
    girls under 16 -- Whether doctor may give advice and treatment on
    contraception to girl under 16 without parental consent -- Whether
    doctor committing criminal offence or acting unlawfully by giving
    advice on contraception to girl under 16 -- Whether doctor interfering
    with parental rights -- Sexual Offences Act 1956, ss 6(1 ),
    contraception
```

Segments provide a more efficient way for searching cases, statutes and statutory instruments. Each document (that is each individual case, section of a statute or statutory instrument) is divided into a number of different segments (Figures 11.6 and 11.7). These may be searched rather than the entire document. This may speed up the search process.

### Figure 11.7: Headnote segment on LEXIS

```
HEADNOTE:
Minor — Medical treatment — Consent — Nature of consent which minor can give
to medical treatment without obtaining parental consent.

The Department of Health and Social Security issued a circular to area health
authorities containing, inter alia, advice to the effect that a doctor
consulted at a family planning clinic by a girl under 16 would not be acting
unlawfully if he prescribed contraceptives for the girl, so long as in doing
so he was acting in good faith to protect her against the harmful effects of
sexual intercourse. The circular further stated that, although a doctor
should proceed on the assumption that advice and treatment on contraception
should not be given to a girl under 16 without parental consent and that he
should try to persuade the girl to involve her parents in the matter,
nevertheless the principle of confidentiality between doctor and patient
applied to a girl under 16 seeking contraceptives and therefore in
exceptional cases the doctor could prescribe contraceptives without
consulting the girl's parents or obtaining their consent if in the doctor's
clinical judgment it was desirable to prescribe contraceptives. The
plaintiff, who had five daughters under the age of 16, sought an assurance
from her local area health authority that her daughters would not be given
advice and treatment on contraception without the plaintiff
```

A search using segments is relatively simple to conduct. LEXIS® will search for the relevant words within a specified sector. For example, when searching a case the following segments may be used:

> NAME(Gillick) - this will search for the case of Gillick v West Norfolk and Wisbech AHA (note that it will only find the actual case and not references to it in later cases);

> COURT(Family Division) - all cases in the Family Division - this may be refined by using the DATE AFT command to discover recent cases decided by that court;

> WRITTENBY(Latey) - all judgments delivered by Latey J;

> COUNSEL(Morgan) - all cases in which 'Morgan' appeared as counsel.

Similar use can be made of the other case segments and those for statutes and statutory instruments. One very useful feature of the use of segments is that statutory instruments made under a particular section of an Act may be identified. The DATE IN FORCE segments in statutes and statutory instruments also provide an up-to-date picture of the law.

## Moving through documents, files and libraries

There are a number of ways in which documents can be browsed in LEXIS®. The screen pages may be browsed by using the NEXT PAGE, PREV PAGE, ROLL UP, ROLL DOWN and FIRST PAGE keys. Moving from document to document is achieved by using the NEXT CASE, PREV CASE and FIRST CASE keys. Skipping pages or cases is achieved by entering the number of page/cases the user wishes to skip and then pressing the NEXT PAGE/CASE or PREV PAGE/CASE keys.

## Other libraries on LEXIS®

A number of special topic libraries are available on LEXIS®. UKTAX is a comprehensive collection of tax material which includes cases, press releases, statutes and statutory instruments. Similar libraries cover industrial cases (ENGIND), intellectual property (UKIP) and an extensive library on admiralty matters (ADMRTY). The latter, in addition to United Kingdom law, also includes American material. SCOTS contains a collection of Scottish cases as reported in the *Session Cases, Scots Law Times, Scottish Criminal Case Reports* and *Scottish Civil Law Reports*. All unreported cases of the House of Lords (if they relate to Scotland), Inner House and Outer House are also included. NILAW is the Northern Ireland database and covers the *Northern Ireland Law Reports* since 1945 and unreported cases from 1984.

Comparative material is also available. Irish case law is found in ITELIS. Reported cases from the *Irish Reports, Irish Law Reports Monthly, Irish Law Times* and the *Judgments of the Court of Criminal Appeal*. The Commonwealth law library (COMCA) is rather limited and covers case law from England, Australia (headnotes of cases in *Australian Law Reports, Australian Capital Territory Reports* and *Northern Territory Reports*), New Zealand and Northern Ireland. Files can be searched individually or collectively under ALL. An extensive collection of French Law is available on LEXIS®.

In the INTLAW library LEXIS® has recently expanded in the following areas:

AGREEMENTS AND TREATIES:

| | |
|---|---|
| BDIEL | Basic Documents of International Economic Law |
| ILMTY | Treaty Documents in ILM |
| DOSBUL | US Department of State Bulletin |
| TXINT | Tax Notes International |
| TREATY | United States Tax Treaties |

ASIAN LAW, AUSTRALIA/NEW ZEALAND LAW:

| | |
|---|---|
| CHINAL | CHINALAW Database |
| AUSCAS | Australian Case Headnotes |
| NZCAS | New Zealand Case Law |

US/CANADA FREE TRADE AGREEMENT:

| | |
|---|---|
| USCFTA | FTA Panel Review Decisions |

EUROPEAN COMMUNITY MATERIAL:

| | |
|---|---|
| ECLAW | European Community Law (CELEX database) |
| ECCASE | Cases in ECR, ECC, EHRR, CMLR |
| ECTY | European Community Treaties in BDIEL |
| COMDEC | European Community Decisions on Competition Policy |

In addition to the above files INTLAW also includes much of the material from other parts of the database. This includes, in particular, European Country Law from France, England, Ireland, Northern Ireland and Scotland. There is also a selection of International Law materials.

While the library contains material included elsewhere, it does have much that is new. Perhaps the most significant inclusion is that of the European Community material found on the CELEX database (European Community LAW). The CELEX database contains the online version of *The Official Journal* (Figure 11.8).

**Figure 11.8: *Official Journal* documents from the CELEX database on LEXIS**

```
              LEVEL 1 - 13 DOCUMENTS


1. Commission of the European Communities, PUBLICATION DATE: July 6, 1990,
1990 OJ L 173, DOCUMENT DATE: July 5, 1990, COMMISSION REGULATION (EEC) No
1911/90 of 5 July 1990 amending Regulation (EEC) No 1445/76 specifying the
different varieties of Lolium perenne L.

2. Commission of the European Communities, PUBLICATION DATE: July 13, 1989,
1989 OJ L 199, DOCUMENT DATE: July 12, 1989, COMMISSION REGULATION (EEC) NO
2088/89 OF 12 JULY 1989 AMENDING REGULATION (EEC) NO 1445/76 SPECIFYING THE
DIFFERENT VARIETIES OF LOLIUM PERENNE L.

3. Commission of the European Communities, PUBLICATION DATE: July 26, 1988,
1988 OJ L 200, DOCUMENT DATE: July 25, 1988, COMMISSION REGULATION (EEC) NO
2278/88 OF 25 JULY 1988 AMENDING REGULATION (EEC) NO 1445/76 SPECIFYING THE
DIFFERENT VARIETIES OF LOLIUM PERENNE L.

4. Commission of the European Communities, PUBLICATION DATE: June 23, 1987,
1987 OJ L 163, DOCUMENT DATE: June 22, 1987, COMMISSION REGULATION (EEC) NO
1731/87 OF 22 JUNE 1987, AMENDING REGULATION (EEC) NO 1445/76 SPECIFYING THE
DIFFERENT VARIETIES OF LOLIUM PERENNE L.

5. Commission of the European Communities, PUBLICATION DATE: June 24, 1986,
1986 OJ L 167, DOCUMENT DATE: June 23, 1986, COMMISSION REGULATION (EEC) NO
```

The ability to use this file in conjunction with the other United Kingdom and European Community material has provided LEXIS® with a distinct advantage over other databases and sets the standards for comprehensive coverage.

Finally, mention should be made of the considerable amount of American material available on LEXIS®, reflecting its American origins. In addition to Federal and State material, and the specialized libraries (Insurance, Environment and Labor), the LAWREV library contains many of the law journals published in the United States.

## Summary

There can be no doubt that LEXIS® is an all-embracing database which will provide most of the full text material or references for the practitioner or academic. In this respect it is difficult to beat. On the negative side the interface is slow, cumbersome and rather dated. Some thought needs to be given to how it can be improved to make its use less of a necessary chore and more of an enjoyable experience.

## JUSTIS ONLINE DATABASE

The JUSTIS Online database is produced by Context Ltd. It is based on the CELEX database of European Community law and is a development of the JUSTIS CD-ROM version. Although it is primarily a European database JUSTIS Online now contains some United Kingdom law material. Upon entering JUSTIS Online the menu shown in Search 11.1 appears.

### Search 11.1: JUSTIS opening menu

```
     1. JUSTIS database groups
     2. JUSTIN news and comment services
     3. database list
     4. new session identifier
     5. on-line guide
     6. terminal type
     7. notice board

PLEASE SELECT 1-7 , h (help) , x (exit)

        : 1
```

Entering the JUSTIS database groups reveals the three categories of data available.

Particular mention must be made of the JUSTIS CD-ROM Updates. One of the main strengths of JUSTIS Online is its interaction with the Context CD-ROM service. The update facility allows users to complete their search of the CD-ROM on the Online service to see what developments have occurred since the last issue. It is proposed to introduce a seamless interface between the two systems and its introduction should be keenly awaited. Constant users of the database will find this combination invaluable. The cost of online time will be minimized and yet up-to-date searches possible. With the introduction of CELEX on the LEXIS® database the off-line/online flexibility of JUSTIS will be an increasingly important factor in deciding which system is appropriate. On a more mundane matter the simple user interface on the JUSTIS Online service is preferred to the rather 'flash' CD-ROM screen.

The United Kingdom material on JUSTIS is more restricted than that on LEXIS®. The main component of the United Kingdom Law group is the *Weekly Law Reports* which go back to 1985. *The Times Law Reports* (1989 onwards) and the *Independent Newspaper Reports* (1987 onwards) provide a relatively fast update service for recent decisions. Searching on JUSTIS Online is simple. The types of searches available are shown in Searches 11.1 to 11.6.

## Search 11.2: JUSTIS data available

```
    1. European Community Law
       - CELEX treaties, legislation, proposals,
            cases, national provisions
       - Common Market Law Reports
       - SPEARHEAD
       - DRT Europe
       - The Treaty of Rome (EEC)

    2. UK Law  - Weekly Law Reports
       - Law Reports Index
       - Times Newspaper Law Reports
       -  Independent  Newspaper  Law  Reports
       - Criminal Appeal Office Index
       - Bulletin of Northern Ireland Law
       - After Dinner Stories

    3. JUSTIS CD-ROM Updates
       - CELEX treaties, legislation, proposals,cases (containing all the new
            documents since the latest JUSTIS CD-ROM was issued)

    PLEASE SELECT 1-3, r, x (exit)
                 : 2
```

## Search 11.3: JUSTIS search menu

```
  *

  1. simple query
  2. search within a zone
  3. search for a phrase
  4. proximity search
  5. stored queries
  6. sub-query
  7. another database

  r. return to 'database groups' menu

     PLEASE SELECT 1-7 , h (help) , x (exit)
     : 1
```

Once the search has been completed JUSTIS informs the user of the number of documents found and provides options as to how they may be viewed (Search 11.4).

## Search 11.4: JUSTIS search

```
Query : landlord & tenant


   Query being validated ...

   Searching ...

   130 DOCUMENTS FOUND

   display Documents, Titles only — or Escape (d/t/e) ?
>d
```

Searching is fast and the available search commands are easy to use. It is a much more agreeable interface than LEXIS®. Documents may be displayed in full as in Search 11.5.

## Search 11.5: WLR case on JUSTIS

```
TITLE
                              (1989) 1 WLR 408

                           *REGINA
                  v INNER LONDON CROWN COURT,
                       Ex parte BENTHAM

QUEEN'S BENCH DIVISION                                    Mann
LJ and Auld J.
1988 Nov. 22
881122

KEY CONCEPTS
   Public Health -- Nuisance - Abatement notice - proceedings brought by
TENANT against council LANDLORD - Council appealing against notice -TENANT
applying for legal aid to resist appeal - Whether council's appeal against
conviction or sentence - Whether TENANT eligible for

-- HIT No: 1 (of 130 documents) LINE No: 1 (of 300)
-- n/p next/previous followed by d(ocument), p(age),
s(earch term) or l(ine), c(ontinuous display), h(elp),
q(uit - new query)
     :nd
```

A frivolous, but enjoyable, part of the JUSTIS database is the after dinner stories found under the United Kingdom Law heading.

JUSTIS really comes into its own when used for searching the CELEX database. The material contained under European Community Law (see Search 11.2) is:

| | | |
|---|---|---|
| 1. | CELEX treaties | ( sectors 1 and 2 ) |
| 2. | CELEX legislation | ( sectors 3 and 4 ) |
| 3. | CELEX proposals | ( sector 5 ) |
| 4. | CELEX cases | ( sector 6 ) |
| 5. | CELEX national provisions | ( sector 7 ) |
| 6. | Common Market Law Reports | |
| 7. | SPEARHEAD | |
| 8. | DRT Europe | |
| 9. | The Treaty of Rome | (European Community) |

CELEX is the official legal database of the European Community. In its hard copy, the *Official Journal*, it is almost impenetrable. As with the CD-ROM version, the online database makes searching this mass of material much simpler. A title screen is shown in Search 11.6.

## Search 11.6: Title of Council Directive on JUSTIS

```
TITLE (Adopted)
     Council Directive 88/657/EEC of 14 December 1988 laying down the
requirements for the production of, and trade in, minced meat, meat in pieces
of less than 100 grams and meat preparations and amending Directives 64/433/
EEC, 71/118/EEC and 72/462/EEC.
     Official Journal Reference L382 of 31 December 1988 and (corrigendum)
L52 of 24 February 1989.
     Commission proposal: COM (87) 658 (Official Journal Reference C18 of 23
January 1988).


-- THIS IS TITLE No. 2 (of 2)
-- n(ext title), z(oom), c(ontinuous display), q(uit)
   : q
```

In addition to *The Official Journal* material and the *Common Market Law Reports*, JUSTIS Online also includes a Department of Trade and Industry database called SPEARHEAD. This is a database which monitors the progress of regulations and directives which relate to the introduction of the Single Market within the European Community in 1992. Included in this database are telephone numbers for the civil servant with responsibility for the regulation or directive.

## Summary

JUSTIS Online is an impressive product and reflects the considerable thought invested in it by Context. It suffers from not being as all-embracing as LEXIS® - particularly since LEXIS® now includes CELEX. However, its success must surely be guaranteed as an ancillary to the CD-ROM version. Once the seamless interface is available this database will have many advantages over its LEXIS® counterpart when searching for material common to both. Developing searches off-line and then updating online is an attractive proposition for regular users of electronic databases.

## LAWTEL

LAWTEL is quite different from LEXIS® and JUSTIS. It is a fast updating service available as a closed-user group through the British videotex service, PRESTEL. It is best described as an Online version of *Current Law*, although it is more up-to-date. LAWTEL is not a full text database. It provides summaries of the law and follows the format of an encyclopedia. The Main Index on LAWTEL details the services available (Figure 11.9).

**Figure 11.9: LAWTEL Main Menu**

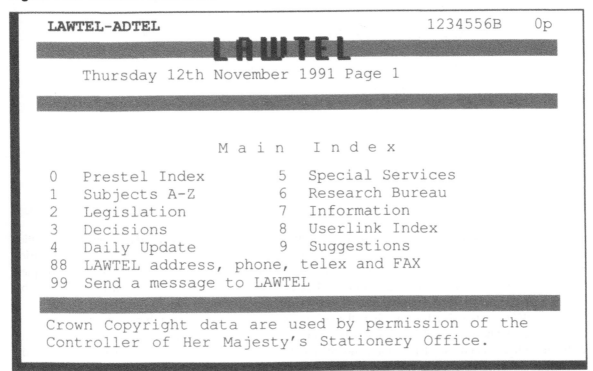

```
LAWTEL-ADTEL                          1234556B    0p
              L A W T E L
      Thursday 12th November 1991 Page 1


               M a i n    I n d e x

  0   Prestel Index       5   Special Services
  1   Subjects A-Z        6   Research Bureau
  2   Legislation         7   Information
  3   Decisions           8   Userlink Index
  4   Daily Update        9   Suggestions
  88  LAWTEL address, phone, telex and FAX
  99  Send a message to LAWTEL

  Crown Copyright data are used by permission of the
  Controller of Her Majesty's Stationery Office.
```

The material included on LAWTEL is as follows:

| | |
|---|---|
| Statutes | 01/01/80 onwards |
| SI (listed) | 11/07/83 onwards |
| Decisions and Practice Directions | 01/01/80 onwards |
| Injury | 01/11/78 |

A particular strength of LAWTEL is that it is invaluable in providing up-to-date references on legislation, case law, White and Green Papers, and the progress of Parliamentary Bills. The Daily Update (Figure 11.10) lists the main developments in the law with a brief summary.

**Figure 11.10: LAWTEL Daily Update**

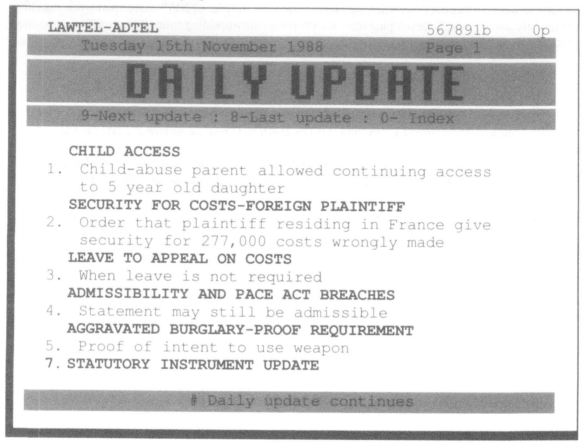

Statutes and statutory instruments on LAWTEL show the date of commencement and also the effect on other legislation. Case law is recorded in a manner that indicates the main thrust of the judgment. The summaries are very reliable and LAWTEL must be congratulated on its ability to encapsulate the gist of quite complex law in a few lines. The principal strength of LAWTEL is its ability to point the user in the right direction by referring him or her to the appropriate printed version of the document.

The LAWTEL screen is a little harsh on the eyes combining, as it does, a number of different colours to identify different headings and text. There is also a lot of information on the screen which may make reading difficult, particularly on a small monitor. However, these are features which the user will manage to live with.

**Summary**

It is rather unfair comparing LAWTEL with LEXIS® and JUSTIS as they do not seek to achieve the same objectives. As a means of obtaining information quickly and in an easily digestible form, LAWTEL is unbeatable. Its database is comprehensive and as up-to-date as could ever be desired. Searching is simple once the various commands are mastered. It is quick and the information may be downloaded onto a printer. LAWTEL is not an all-embracing research tool in the way that LEXIS® or JUSTIS are - but neither does it pretend to be. In terms of achieving what is sets out to do LAWTEL is a successful database.

## CONCLUSION

All three databases reviewed have their strength and their weakness. Much depends upon what end-users require of their online database as each offers a different service. This range of provision is most welcome and hopefully the trend towards conformity will be avoided. Each must concentrate on doing what it does best. LEXIS® will continue to be the all-embracing database covering a vast range of national and international material. JUSTIS, with its specialist European foundation, will continue to set new standards - particularly in the combination of CD-ROM and online flexibility. This combination seems to be the way forward for database technology in the fast changing area of law. LAWTEL has much to offer as a fast and efficient research facility.

It is interesting to speculate whether the future for online law databases lies with more specialist developments or the generic approach of LEXIS®. The breaking down of traditional barriers between national and international law, public and private law and criminal and civil law suggest that the LEXIS® approach is correct. However, the tendency for lawyers to know more and more about less and less points in favour of specialization. Whichever approach prevails one thing is certain: online law databases are here to stay. This has many implications for the teaching and practice of law. It is gratifying to see that in many respects those people responsible for education, training and practice are starting to consider the ramifications of these developments.

# 12 Law: North American legal systems

*Gary D Gott and Patricia M Young*

Mastering the realm of online legal research is not for the faint of heart or uninitiated and requires some understanding of traditional strategies for legal research using printed materials. The field of legal information is perhaps the most completely indexed and 'digested' of any field of human endeavour, yet pitfalls remain for the unprepared. This chapter will provide a brief summary of the development of legal publishing in the United States and Canada and the impact of automation on legal research.

## UNITED STATES: ONLINE

### Background

Publishers' editorial teams have been actively engaged in improving access to legal information for many years. These editors carefully read thousands of court opinions, extracting the key concepts and objectively categorizing the extracted paragraphs under 'key numbers' or other topical designators. Cases which refer back to earlier cases or statutes are thoroughly analysed in annotations written to guide the researcher in comprehending the legal concepts and relationships in dispute and finding relevant following cases. To use these tools successfully requires training and practice, and they continue to be fundamental to thorough legal research.

Legal publishing in the United States has been thoroughly integrated for the last hundred years. The leading exponent of such coverage is the West Publishing Company, whose comprehensive case reporting with detailed cross-references in a layered indexing scheme became the foundation of its considerable success. A major competitor, Lawyer's Cooperative Publishing, is more selective in case coverage but also intensively integrates the company's various series of publications and cross references them. SHEPARD'S CITATIONS, published by Shepard's/McGraw Hill, Inc., complements both systems with exhaustive tables of cited and citing cases.

Other companies provide extensive looseleaf-based research services. These looseleaf services are generally focused on particular areas of practice, such as tax law, family law or business associations. These systems emphasize the enormous editorial efforts that provide commentary, analysis and expert forecasting of developments regarding statutes, cases and administrative regulations. The case reporters from West Publishing, however, focus on the texts of the appellate court opinions themselves. LEXIS® and WESTLAW®, though extensively enhanced by secondary materials and replete with primary statutory authority, are above all perceived as case law databases.

Access to printed case law materials has been provided through a headnote/digest approach. Cases are read carefully and analysed into short topical abstracts. Each abstract is known as a headnote, and any given case may have many headnotes, each restricted to a particular legal topic or issue. Each headnote is assigned a number corresponding to the legal subject abstracted. These topics all come from a comprehensive numbering scheme, known in the West system as 'key numbers'. All headnotes are also reprinted in the 'digests', assembled under their respective topical numbers.

In the Lawyer's Cooperative Publishing system, selected cases are published along with extensive annotations. These annotations are actually articles synthesizing the particular area of law in detail and including references to all other leading cases on point.

Shepard's approach is to use only the citations to the cases, listed in such a manner that given the citation to the case in question, all subsequent cases which refer to it may be found. Special markings are included to correlate the citing cases with the headnotes of the cited case, and to indicate significant information regarding the history (affirmed, reversed, etc.) and treatment (criticized, distinguished, etc.) by the citing cases.

In the manual methods, the researcher searching for relevant cases must first know which headings in the West Key Number© or Lawyer's Cooperative Publishing system are appropriate. West's is the dominant scheme, and because this is a 'layered' system, with branching subheadings under subheadings under subheadings, the searcher's task is not necessarily straightforward. West's very success in descriptively pigeonholing every point of every case so thoroughly has made intimate familiarity with its indexing scheme a necessary prerequisite to comprehensive manual legal research. Furthermore the assignment of subject headings by West editors is subject to human error, though West's control procedures have been first class and have minimized this problem. The system itself, however, tends to rigidity while the common law it purports to delineate is constantly evolving in response to the changes in society. The key number system is so large that reflecting such changes with new or modified topical headings can be massively expensive and disruptive to existing headings. The system thus has a built-in tendency to try to fit new concepts into old ways of thinking. The non-legally trained researcher's problems in decoding the system and second-guessing the indexers are enormous. West argues, though, that these very features of its system work to the researcher's advantage in the online environment, by adding additional access points to the language of the cases themselves. LEXIS® users, on the other hand, dispute this and maintain that the headnotes generally reflect the identical language of the case in hand, thus adding no new access points, and that when the headnotes do introduce new terms they actually increase the imprecision of the search results.

*Online legal research*

Today's legal researcher has the option of using either the traditional print tools briefly sketched above or using their equivalents online. Legal databases were among the first full-text systems to come to market, eschewing the index/abstract approach common to many other online search systems. The advantages of speed, comprehensive coverage, and accuracy of computerized access seem obvious. The full-text method is thought to permit the researcher to become his or her own indexer and thus maximize flexibility in attacking the mass of information now available. Given the difficulty in using manual methods, the opportunity to escape the task of decoding the indexer's thinking is welcome, though formulating a successful search demands a clear understanding of the issues and the law in question.

When the search revolves around unique terms that have specific meanings, setting up a search is relatively straightforward. The searcher composes a string of terms, separated by proximity connectors to define the relationships of the terms, and sends the search request to a particular file. Files generally correspond to the jurisdiction of a court or set of courts, though both systems also collect materials into subject-specific categories. The researcher then reviews the cases retrieved and may select the best cases from the set presented or use new information gleaned from the screen to modify the search request and then re-transmit it. This interactivity between the searcher and the database is a great asset: the speed of the computer allows the searcher to act immediately on new information and bring relevant case law right to the desktop. Giving searchers the power to define exactly their search terms permits them to cut through the layers of controlled vocabulary index terms previously interposed between them and the relevant case law.

Some researchers, however, have questioned this online bonanza. Blair and Maron suggest that attorneys retrieving documents from large databases may not be obtaining anything close to the rate of recall that they believe they are getting [1]. Their research, the first to use Boolean search strategy in truly large-scale legal files, showed that attorneys were getting only about twenty per cent recall of relevant cases while under the impression that they were getting at least seventy-five per cent. Daniel Dabney's analysis [2] of Blair and Maron's experiment ascribes these results to the problems of linguistic imprecision: synonymous words, ambiguous words and complex expressions [3-6].

*Other databases*

Obviously, of the myriad databases on the market today, many have potential use in modern legal research. These 'non-legal' databases are thoroughly covered elsewhere in this book, and the legal searcher having need of them is referred to the appropriate chapters. Aside from the many non-legal databases, various legal publishers have put their products online, much as West has. Lawyer's Cooperative Publishing offers the AUTO-CITE electronic case citation service via LEXIS®. Using only the citation of a case, the legal researcher can access cases and annotations published in the *American Law Reports* since 1658 in these databases. No Boolean searching is supported in AUTO-CITE, but a separate file of these materials is searchable from within LEXIS®. The researcher must have an accurate citation to use as the search request. The boon to the searcher, however, is that once an annotation is retrieved a wealth of prior effort in thoroughly researching every point of law in the cases is instantly made available, with references to leading relevant cases and to other potential information sources.

SHEPARD'S CITATIONS are available on both LEXIS® and WESTLAW®, and are integrated with both systems. This integration permits instant 'shepardizing', or tracking of the subsequent history and treatment of a case, as well as the ability to call up the text of the case itself from the Shepard's citation listing. The online information is much more current than that found in the print versions.

Both Prentice-Hall and Commerce Clearing House, Inc., known for expert materials in tax and business, offer online services. Prentice-Hall's PHI-NET is targeted specifically at the tax researcher and emphasizes cost-effective access to that particular subject area. Commerce Clearing House offers its tax databases on both LEXIS® and WESTLAW® and independently offers the ELECTRONIC LEGISLATIVE SEARCH SERVICE (ELSS). This latter service tracks the status of bills on selected business-related topics in all state legislatures and at the federal level. This sort of research is particularly valuable to special interest groups and to businesses which must operate under the laws of multiple jurisdictions, as well as to students of the legislative process.

## WESTLAW®

WESTLAW® combines the full-text searching capabilities of LEXIS® with a form of controlled vocabulary searching based on the West Key Number and Digest Topic System. This approach allows both the experienced researcher and the novice great flexibility in structuring search requests.

### Equipment required

WESTLAW® can be accessed through almost any combination of microcomputer and modem. Special 'Westmate' software is available for most popular configurations which automates much of the dial-up process. WESTLAW® can also be reached via the company's dedicated terminals and personal computers with special keyboards. This approach provides the convenience of dedicated special function keys. Many other keyboards, however, can be equipped with function key templates that duplicate the special purpose keys.

### Query planning

Appropriate use of any database demands some forethought, and successful extraction of relevant data from WESTLAW® is no exception. Initially the legal issue must be clarified in the searcher's mind. Perhaps the best way to do this is simply to state it concisely on paper. Immediately, key search terms will appear as part of this statement which generate others that are suggested by those first considered. 'Are certain phrases or legal terms of art likely to occur in relevant documents?' 'Are particular statutory section numbers or sub-paragraph numbers likely to be mentioned?' 'Is this topic generally discussed in some form of legal shorthand?' The fundamental question is simply, 'What *must* be in a relevant document?'

WESTLAW® has programmed a user-friendly feature into the keyword selection process: the availability of normalized forms of compound words. This feature at once avoids problems due to inconsistencies in spelling and typographical errors. For example, one could find in the database occurrences of 'ill will', 'ill-will', or even 'illwill' (sic). But when the normalized form is selected ('ill-will', using the hyphen), the computer automatically finds all other occurrences of the other forms.

Along with alternative terms, the searcher also needs to choose expanders. Root expansion can be either a boon or a bane, and must be used with caution, especially in a full-text database. The possibilities for mischief are enormous when any variant of a root is inserted into a search strategy. The universal root expansion is accomplished by using the exclamation mark (!) and is particularly subject to abuse if the root is not carefully considered.

Using the asterisk (*) permits the selective replacement of one character at a time as a wild card. The asterisk may be used internally in a word (for example, dr*nk!) and if used internally, either the asterisk or exclamation mark may be used at the end of the same word. Multiple asterisks may be used to replace multiple characters either within or at the end of a word, but may not begin the search term. The process of generating terms should initially be as expansive as possible in order to consider all possible ways in which the necessary concepts may be expressed by the courts.

To use them all, though, would be impractical because of the extensive search time that would result without significantly improved results. The searcher needs, therefore, to omit terms which are not unique or which do not materially contribute to the query process, and implant root expanders judiciously.

### Connectors

Once these key terms have been identified, their relationship to one another needs to be decided. Must they occur in a particularly narrow proximity or can the net be woven more loosely? Connectors available to the

**Table 12.1: Connectors on WESTLAW®**

| | |
|---|---|
| **/s** | same sentence |
| **+s** | preceding in the same sentence |
| **/p** | same paragraph |
| **+p** | preceding in the same paragraph |

Numerical connectors include:

| | |
|---|---|
| **/n** | one term within a specified number of words of the next term |
| **w/n** | one term within a specified number of words of the next term |
| **+n** | one term preceding another by a specified number of words |
| **pre/n** | one term preceding another by a specified number of words |

General connectors include:

| | |
|---|---|
| **a space** | one term exclusive of another |
| **OR** | one term exclusive of another |
| **AND** | both terms inclusive of each other |
| **AND NOT** | all terms except the one specified |
| **%** | one term but not the next term |

searcher are based on the structure of the language as well as word proximity. This permits the searcher unparalleled flexibility. Connectors are shown in Table 12.1.

It is important to consider the effect the order of processing will have on your search results. The order in which the terms are processed, unless modified by the user, is: phrases (set off by quotation marks); OR; +n; /n; + s; /s; + p; /p; AND; AND NOT. If all of the proximity connectors are the same, WESTLAW® will process them sequentially from left to right. Terms in a phrase (enclosed in quotes), though separated by spaces, will not be treated as alternative search terms as they would have been had they not been in the quotation marks (for example, 'in forma pauperis'). The order of operation can be controlled more strictly by using parentheses to override the normal order of processing.

*Key number searching*

The controlled vocabulary equivalent in WESTLAW® is the system's use of the West Key Number Digest system. Topics and subtopics are assigned key numbers by West Publishing editors and placed in headnotes to cases. These key numbers are also separately published in multi-volume indexes known as digests, along with the appropriate excerpts from each case. The system thus attempts to organize the vast body of American legal case law into subject clusters. (Key numbers also have word equivalents, searchable in the topic field. Field searching is discussed below.)

The key number/topic advantage to the online researcher in a full-text environment arises when the search terms required are so common as to produce results so large as to be unusable. A key number, narrowly constructed to refer to only one subject, can be entered as the only search term or combined with others.

A great many lawyers in the United States have learned to do basic legal research based on the West Key Number system. As a result, and because this system has been automated, their learning curve on WESTLAW® can be shortened. They are, in effect, already trained on the system and have only the mechanics of manipulating the keyboard to master.

## Field searching

Another approach is to take advantage of WESTLAW®'s field searching option. Every full-text document in the database is invisibly segmented by the computer into separately searchable fields such as title, synopsis, digest, citation, court, and judge fields. By limiting the search to the topic field, the searcher can avoid false hits from occurrences in the full-text database. Also, the presence of unforeseen synonyms can sometimes mask the availability of relevant cases that did not use the particular terms selected for a full-text search. A topic search will often bring these cases to the researcher, as a trained indexer has already reviewed them and assigned them a standard key number heading.

## Options

One of WESTLAW®'s unique aspects is the options feature. By entering the term 'options' before beginning the query process, the searcher is taken to a screen which permits the alteration of a number of default settings. These include the 'Welcome to WESTLAW®' screen, 'EZ Access' and the display sequence for cases. The default for the latter is to present cases ranked from most recent to earliest, known as 'Age ranking'. Alternatively, the searcher can elect to have cases displayed in a ranking according to the frequency of search terms in the particular documents, known as 'Term ranking'.

Of perhaps more interest to the searcher unfamiliar with WESTLAW®, however, is the opportunity to ask the system to display suggestions for appropriate searching strategy as the search progresses. This option is known as 'Prompts' and must be requested from the 'Options menu', as the system defaults to a 'noprompts' mode designed for experienced searchers.

## Database organization

Selection of an appropriate database is an essential part of the search process. The WESTLAW® Database Directory is the first screen that the searcher sees after logging on, and can be reached at any time by entering the query 'db'. The Directory is an informational index designed to give more and more information as the searcher progresses into it (see Searches 12.1 and 12.2). The categories become more specific as choices are made. The Directory is divided into two major sections: Databases and Services. The tax databases serve here as an example of the topical databases available in WESTLAW®, and how they are organized in the Directory.

Some, but by no means all, of the databases parallel West publications. Others are jurisdictional. WESTLAW® contains both case law and statutory material. In the latter category the system is expanding to include the statutes of all fifty states in the United States, as well as the *United States Code*, which has been in the database for some time. The *Code of Federal Regulations* and *Federal Register* are online, as well as administrative law promulgated in the decisions of various government boards and agencies. Given the mushrooming of non-legislative, non-judicial law making that the Congress has found politically expedient to delegate to the administrative agencies, it is extremely valuable for citizens and businesses, as well as their lawyers, to have online access to this mass of legally binding material.

## Search 12.1: WESTLAW® directory - first and second screens

```
─────────────── WELCOME  TO  THE  WESTLAW  DIRECTORY ───────P1────
  GENERAL MATERIAL     TOPICAL MATERIAL    TEXT & PERIODICAL     SPECIALIZED MAT'L
Federal       P2     Gov't  Cont.  P159 Law Reviews,  P214 Gateways  (Dow P260
State         P5     Health Serv.  P162   Texts & CLE            Jones, D&B,
  TOPICAL  MATERIAL  Immigration   P165      CITATORS            Dialog,  etc.)
Admiralty    P123    Insurance     P167 Insta-Cite,   P244 Historical    P261
Antitrust    P125    Intell. Prop. P171 Shepard's PreView Newspapers     P277
Bankruptcy   P127    International P173   and Citations                  Other
Pubs         P278
Civil Rights P130    Labor         P175    SPECIALIZED  MAT'L Tax  Management P282
Communication P133   Legal  Service P182 ABA           P245 TaxSource       P283
Corporations P135    Military  Law P185 AJS            P247 WESTLAW         P284
Crim.  Justice P138  Products  Liab P187 BNA           P248   Highlights
Education    P141    Real  Property P190 Callaghan      P252 Other  Services P286
Energy       P144    Securities    P192 C.  Boardman    P253   & Databases
Environmental P148   Social  Secur. P199 CCH           P255   (NEW, FIND,
Family  Law  P153    Taxation      P202 Dictionary      P256   etc.)
Financial    P156    Transport     P209 Directories     P257 EZ  ACCESS       P287
First  Amend. P158   Worker  Comp. P211 Envtl L Inst    P259 CUSTOMER  INFO P288

If you wish to:
  View another Directory page, type P followed by its NUMBER and press ENTER
  Select a known database, type its IDENTIFIER and press ENTER
  Obtain further information, type HELP and press ENTER
```

```
──WESTLAW DIRECTORY WELCOME SCREEN──────────────────P1──
  ──GENERAL FEDERAL DATABASES                              P2──
FEDERAL DATABASES INDEX CASE LAW SPECIALIZED DATABASES
Case Law . . . This Page  CTA5   5th Circuit   BICENT       Bicentennial
Admin. Law . . Next Page  CTA6   6th Circuit   SCT-PREVIEW Preview of U.S.
Statutes . . . Next Page  CTA7   7th Circuit                Supreme Ct. Cases
Regulations. . Next Page  CTA8   8th Circuit   BNA-USLW     U.S. Law Week
Specialized. . This Page  CTA9   9th Circuit   BNA-USLWD    U.S.L.W. - Daily
                          CTA10 10th Circuit   WLD          West's Legal
      CASE LAW            CTA11 11th Circuit                Directory
ALLFEDS Federal Cases     CTADC D.C. Circuit   WLB-SCT      WESTLAW BULLETIN-
  SCT  Supreme Court      CTAF  Fed. Circuit                U.S. Supreme Ct.
  CTA  Courts of Appeals  DCT    District Courts GULFDEBATE Cong. Debate-Gulf
  CTA1 1st Circuit        DCTR  Reported Cases
  CTA2 2nd Circuit        DCTU  Unrepor. Cases  Note: For historical Case Law
  CTA3 3rd Circuit        CLCT  Claims Court    enter P273.
  CTA4 4th Circuit                              Note: For local, federal,
                                                district and bankruptcy court
                                                rules, enter P12.
If you wish to:
  Select a database, type its IDENTIFIER, e.g., ALLFEDS and press ENTER
  View information about a database, type SCOPE followed by its IDENTIFIER
    and press ENTER
```

**Search 12.2: Third level of WESTLAW® directory - two screens**

```
—WESTLAW  DIRECTORY  WELCOME  SCREEN——————————P1——
 —TAXATION  DATABASES                                        P202—
 —
 xxxxxxxxxxxxxxxxxxxxxxxxxxxxxxxxxxxxxxxxxxxxxxxxxxxxxxxxxxxxxxxxxx
     Taxation databases contain documents that relate to taxation by federal,
 state or local governments. Among the subjects included are excise, gift,
 income, inheritance, property, sales, and other taxes (but not customs
 duties), and collection and prosecution proceedings.
 xxxxxxxxxxxxxxxxxxxxxxxxxxxxxxxxxxxxxxxxxxxxxxxxxxxxxxxxxxxxxxxxxx
 INDEX TO TAXATION DATABASES                      TAXSOURCE
 Federal Databases —                    TAXSOURCE TaxSource Directory
  Case Law . . . . . . . Enter P203     This directory indexes the databases
  Statutes & Regulations. Enter P203    included in TaxSource, a comprehensive
  Administrative Law. . . Enter P204    collection of tax-related BNA, Tax
 State Databases —                      Management, federal and state databases.
  Case Law. . . . . . . . Enter P205          FEDERAL TAX
  Administrative Law. . . Enter P206    FTX-ALL  Combines federal case law,
 Specialized Databases  . Enter P207             statutes & regulations, and
 Texts & Periodicals  . . Enter P203             administrative law databases
 Historical Databases . . Enter P275
 If you wish to:
   Select a database, type its IDENTIFIER, e.g., TAXSOURCE and press ENTER
   View information about a database, type SCOPE followed by its IDENTIFIER
      and press ENTER
```

```
 —WESTLAW DIRECTORY WELCOME SCREEN——————————P1——
 —TAXATION DATABASES                                        P203——
 FEDERAL DATABASES                      FEDERAL DATABASES
 CASE LAW STATUTES & REGULATIONS
  FTX-CS      Federal Cases             FTX-TRA86 Materials on the Tax Reform
  FTX-SCT     Supreme Court                       Act of 1986
  FTX-CTA     Courts of Appeals         FTX-FR    Federal Register
  FTX-DCT     District Courts           FTX-CFR   Code of Federal Regulations
  FTX-CLCT    Claims Court              FTX-CODREG Combines FTX-USC, FTX-FR
  FTX-TCT     Tax Court                           and FTX-CFR
         STATUTES & REGULATIONS         FTX-REG   Combines FTX-FR and FTX-CFR
  FTX-USC     U.S. Code sections        FTX-TD    Treasury Decisions
  FTX-RULES   Federal Rules                    TEXTS & PERIODICALS
  FTX-PL      Public Laws               TX-TP     Law Reviews, Texts &
  FTX-USC-OLD U.S. Code before the                Journals
              Tax Reform Act of 1986 CASEY        Fed. Tax Practice (Casey)
                                    MERTENS       Law of Federal Income
                                                  Taxation (Mertens)
 If you wish to:
   Select a database, type its IDENTIFIER, e.g., FTX-CS and press ENTER
   View information about a database, type SCOPE followed by its IDENTIFIER
      and press ENTER
```

In the example which follows, the search will be restricted to a more common type of database, that of a particular state court's appellate decisions.

*Search example*

Privileged communications are those statements which the law protects that are made by certain persons within a protected relationship such as husband-wife, attorney-client, priest-penitent and the like. Defamation is an intentional false communication either published or publicly spoken, that injures another's reputation or good name.

Let us consider a hypothetical situation in which an employer has made inaccurate statements about an employee to other persons within the company. While the statements were not completely accurate, there was no evidence of malicious intent on the part of the employer. These statements were made in a situation, such as a performance evaluation report or hiring and promotion review, where candour was required and confidentiality was assumed, and thus the employer assumed he or she was protected by a form of privilege described above. Nonetheless, the employee is angry about these remarks and sues the employer for damage to reputation.

A lawyer-researcher would first distil from this situation a question or series of questions to sort out what legal issues are involved, or, stated another way, what is really at the heart of the controversy between the parties to the dispute. This must then be converted into a search query that would be most likely to retrieve relevant cases that decided similar controversies in the past. For example:

> ISSUE:   Are an employer's defamatory statements concerning an employee privileged, absent a showing of malice?
> QUERY:  defam! slander! libel /p employe* /p privilege* /p malice "ill-will"
> DATABASE TO BE SEARCHED:       NY-CS (New York state court decisions)

*Search strategy*

The key terms are obvious from the question which describes what is at issue. The addition of common alternatives such as 'slander' and 'ill will' broadens your search. When choosing alternatives, use only those words which you feel, based on your knowledge and experience, are likely to occur in relevant documents.

The ! (unlimited root expansion) should be used only after consideration of the superfluous words which might be generated. The * should be used when an expansion to a limited number of places is desired. Plurals will be generated from expanded words. (WESTLAW® refers to this function in its software as a 'pluralizer'.) Thus 'employe*' will generate 'employee' and 'employer' because of the *, and 'employees' and 'employers' because of the pluralizer. WESTLAW® will automatically generate plurals, possessives and irregular plurals without using any root-expansion. All connectors are /p in this query because a case that discusses all of these terms in the same paragraph has a high probability of being relevant. Grammatical connectors are generally to be preferred over numerical connectors. Since they are the basic units of the English language, searches based on grammatical relationships such as the sentence and the paragraph tend to yield more precise results. Since a space between words is read as 'OR', the phrase 'ill-will' must be enclosed in quotation marks to avoid retrieving occurrences of 'ill' OR 'will' in non-relevant contexts. By using the hyphen, the terms are treated as the normalized form for a compound word. WESTLAW® will therefore search for 'illwill', 'ill will', or 'ill-will'.

*Order of processing*

> Set 1   'ill-will'
> Set 2   (set 1 or malice)
> Set 3   (defam! or slander! or libel!)
> Set 4   (set 2 /p set 3 /p privilege* /p employe*)

Note that left to right processing is not used with grammatical connectors, but only with numerical connectors having the same value. To illustrate this, assume that this query was searched using '/30' instead of '/p'. The order of processing would be the same as above up to Set 4 and would then be processed as follows:

Set 4   (set 3 /30 employe*)
Set 5   (set 4 /30 privilege*)
Set 6   (set 5 /30 set 2).

The actual distance between 'defam!' and 'malice' could be as much as ninety words since the numerical proximities are additive. This also means that word order affects retrieval. In any query, leaving the numerical connectors the same and changing the order of the words could change the number of cases retrieved. The command is shown in Search 12.3.

The West Key Number for libel and slander, 237k44(3) (see Search 12.4) can also be used as a search term, as shown in Search 12.5. West's Key Number system has been in use in legal research in the United States since the last century, and many lawyers are familiar with the system and can use it to enhance the query formulation process. The same case, in a smaller set of cases, is retrieved.

## Search 12.3: WESTLAW® search and response

```
DEFAM!  SLANDER!  LIBEL!  /P  EMPLOYE*  /P  PRIVILEGE*  /P  MALIC! "ILL-WILL"


Please enter your query.

Your database is NY-CS




If you wish to:
    Enter your query, type it as desired and press ENTER
    View a list of available fields, type F and press ENTER
    View detailed information about this database, type SCOPE and press ENTER
COPR. (C) WEST 1991 NO CLAIM TO ORIG. U.S. GOVT. WORKS
```

```
                     COPR. (C) WEST 1991 NO CLAIM TO ORIG. U.S. GOVT. WORKS
Citation              Rank(R)          Page(P)        Database    Mode
557 N.Y.S.2d 209      R 1 OF 67        P 1 OF 8       NY-CS       T
(CITE AS: 557 N.Y.S.2D 209)
                         Lyn CLARK, Respondent,
                                   v.
                    David SOMERS, et al., Defendants,
                       Nina Somers, Appellant.
                  Supreme Court, Appellate Division,
                          Fourth Department.
                           June 22, 1990.
  In DEFAMATION action, the Supreme Court, Monroe County, Patlow, J., denied
defendant's motion for summary judgment, and she appealed. The Supreme Court,
Appellate Division, held that allegedly DEFAMATORY statements made by contract
computer consultant for company to other company EMPLOYEES, all of whom were
concerned with hiring of contract EMPLOYEES for company, were qualifiedly
PRIVILEGED and that PRIVILEGE was not defeated where there was no evidence
established that the comments were made with actual MALICE.
  Affirmed as modified.
```

## Search 12.4: Second page of case showing West Key Number

```
                          COPR. (C) WEST 1991 NO CLAIM TO ORIG. U.S. GOVT. WORKS
557 N.Y.S.2d 209          R 1 OF 67       P 2 OF 8       NY-CS       P
(CITE AS: 557 N.Y.S.2D 209)
[1]
237K44(1)
LIBEL AND SLANDER
K. In general.
N.Y.A.D. 4 Dept. 1990.
A communication made bona fide upon any subject matter in which party
communicating has an interest or in reference to which he has a duty is
privileged if made to a person having a corresponding interest or duty,
although it contained criminating matter which, without the privilege, was
slanderous or actionable.
Clark v. Somers
557 N.Y.S.2d 209
```

## Search 12.5: Key Number search on WESTLAW®

```
237K44(1)


Please enter your query.

Your database is NY-CS




If you wish to:
    Enter your query, type it as desired and press ENTER
    View a list of available fields, type F and press ENTER
    View detailed information about this database, type SCOPE and press ENTER
COPR. (C) WEST 1991 NO CLAIM TO ORIG. U.S. GOVT. WORKS
```

```
                          COPR. (C) WEST 1991 NO CLAIM TO ORIG. U.S. GOVT. WORKS
Citation              Rank(R)         Page(P)         Database    Mode
557 N.Y.S.2d 209      R 1 OF 37       P 1 OF 8        NY-CS       T
(CITE AS: 557 N.Y.S.2D 209)
                        Lyn CLARK, Respondent,
                                v.
                    David SOMERS, et al., Defendants,
                       Nina Somers, Appellant.
                  Supreme Court, Appellate Division,
                         Fourth Department.
                          June 22, 1990.
  In defamation action, the Supreme Court, Monroe County, Patlow, J., denied
defendant's motion for summary judgment, and she appealed. The Supreme Court,
Appellate Division, held that allegedly defamatory statements made by contract
computer consultant for company to other company employees, all of whom were
concerned with hiring of contract employees for company, were qualifiedly
privileged and that privilege was not defeated where there was no evidence
established that the comments were made with actual malice.
  Affirmed as modified.
```

**Search 12.5:** (cont.)

```
                        COPR. (C) WEST 1991 NO CLAIM TO ORIG. U.S. GOVT. WORKS
557 N.Y.S.2d 209           R 1 OF 37        P 2 OF 8       NY-CS        T
(CITE AS: 557 N.Y.S.2D 209)
 [1]
 237K44(1)
 LIBEL AND SLANDER
 K. In general. N.Y.A.D. 4 Dept. 1990.
 A communication made bona fide upon any subject matter in which party
 communicating has an interest or in reference to which he has a duty is
 privileged if made to a person having a corresponding interest or duty,
 although it contained criminating matter which, without the privilege, was
 slanderous or actionable.
 Clark v. Somers
 557 N.Y.S.2d 209
```

One of WESTLAW®'s features is the 'Locate' function. This permits a secondary level search for new terms to be run within the set of cases already retrieved without losing the original search result. For example, perhaps the researcher wishes to see how the issue of punitive damages was treated. A possible search strategy would be to depress the locate key and then enter the terms shown in Search 12.6 (remember that in WESTLAW® a space between words is the same as entering the connector 'OR').

**Search 12.6: WESTLAW® locate function**

```
PUNITIVE  EXEMPLARY  TREBLE  /3  DAMAGES


Please enter your LOCATE request.


   NOTE:   The same rules that apply to query formulation also apply to
           your LOCATE request;  you can use connectors, root expansion,
           field searches or phrases.









If you wish to:
   Submit a LOCATE request, type your LOCATE term(s) and press ENTER
   Use part of your query as your LOCATE request, type Q and press ENTER
   Cancel your LOCATE request, type XL and press ENTER
```

```
                        COPR. (C) WEST 1991 NO CLAIM TO ORIG. U.S. GOVT. WORKS
Citation                Rank(R)          Page(P)        Database    Mode
458 N.Y.S.2d 448        R 16 OF 37       P 1 OF 43      NY-CS       T LOCATE
 117 Misc.2d 162
(CITE AS: 458 N.Y.S.2D 448)
```

**Search 12.6:** (cont.)

Robert E. SCHULMAN, Plaintiff,
v.
ANDERSON RUSSELL KILL & OLICK, P.C., Peter J. Sprofera, Optical Concepts, Inc.,
Golden Aquarius, Inc., Rudolph Basso, Gerry Faulkner and Edward Faulkner,
Defendants.
Supreme Court, Special Term, New York County, Part I.
Dec. 13, 1982.
  Action was brought against law firm for libel, slander, prima facie tort,
abuse of process and tortious interference with plaintiff's accountancy
practice. On the law firm's motion for summary judgment as to all plaintiff's
causes of action save that for slander, the Supreme Court, New York County,
Special Term, Rena K. Uviller, J., held that: (1) law firm was not entitled to
privilege of absolute immunity from liability for defamation with respect to
letter sent by the firm seeking to elicit information and to identify potential
witnesses; (2) insofar as the letter included an explicit recounting of the law
firm's clients' grievances against plaintiff, such letter created a fact issue
as to whether the law firm acted with malice or recklessness, precluding
summary judgment for the law firm on libel claim; (3) fact issue existed as to
whether law firm invoked discovery process and obtained plaintiff's client list

---

COPR. (C) WEST 1991 NO CLAIM TO ORIG. U.S. GOVT. WORKS
458 N.Y.S.2d 448          R 16 OF 37      P 31 OF 43      NY-CS      T LOCATE
(CITE AS: 458 N.Y.S.2D 448, *451)
  In pursuit of the counterclaim against Schulman in the Laurel action, the
Firm sought compensatory and PUNITIVE DAMAGES for OCI and the individual
clients. To support the PUNITIVE DAMAGES claim, the Firm sought to show
that Schulman's conduct in negotiating a loan from Laurel without
disclosing to OCI his interest in Laurel was not an isolated incident,
but was part of a larger scheme to defraud the public. (Walker v.
Sheldon, 10 N.Y.2d 401, 223 N.Y.S.2d 488, 179 N.E.2d 497.)
  In an effort to prove that Schulman had planned to defraud the public at
large, the Firm sought and received by court order a list of all Schulman's
accountancy clients who had received loans from Laurel. At the Firm's
direction, Sprofera, the paralegal, telephoned Schulman's clients on the list
to learn of their dealings with Schulman. These telephone calls form the basis
of Schulman's slander action in that he asserts that in the course of these
calls Sprofera accused Schulman of dishonesty and of being a "crook".
Depositions of Schulman's clients to that effect are appended to Schulman's
answer to this motion.
  At least one of the persons whom Sprofera telephoned, Theodore Hillebrand, has
stated in deposition that Sprofera invited him to join the lawsuit against Schulman
*452 but that Hillebrand declined, stating that he had repaid his loan to Laurel
and had no interest in suing either Laurel or Schulman.
  Getting no better response by telephone from the others on the list, the Firm

---

*Additional features*

WESTLAW® has developed a number of enhancements to improve its utility to legal researchers. These include:

• *State Statutes:* WESTLAW® is in the process of mounting the complete statutes of all fifty states. This will affect the accessibility of state statutory material profoundly, much of which is poorly indexed and often difficult for out-of-state attorneys to research thoroughly.

- *WESTLAW® Gateway Services:* The Dow Jones News Service, DIALOG and VU-TEXT are easily accessed via the WESTLAW® connection. This significantly expands the scope of information available.
- *Commerce Clearing House Inc. (CCH):* THE CCH BLUE SKY LAW REPORTER, CCH TAX DAY: FEDERAL, CCH TAX DAY: STATE, and CCH TAX DAY: FEDERAL AND STATE are all available. The TAX DAY databases contain abstracts of publications from all possible government sources.

  Searching conventions are slightly different from West's proprietary databases. For example, to retrieve a chronological ranking of all documents in a CCH database, the researcher need only enter the word 'read'. This command can be combined with a date restriction, as in 'read & date (before 10-10-87 and after 10-15 -67)' to narrow the search to a particular date range.

  To search paragraph references, one could include paragraph numbers in a query such as 'fed + 1584.01'. This query would cause the computer to retrieve all abstracts containing references to CCH *Standard Federal Tax Reporter,* paragraph 1584.01.
- *Bureau of National Affairs:* Several of this publisher's titles are searchable in full text. These include DAILY TAX REPORT, INTERNATIONAL TRADE REPORTER, BNA'S PATENTS TRADEMARK & COPYRIGHT JOURNAL, BNA PENSION REPORTER, SECURITIES REGULATION & LAW REPORT and the BNA TAX UPDATES. Similar conventions apply as with other special databases.
- *American Bar Association (ABA):* The AMBAR database contains abstracts of a wide range of ABA programmes, activities, products and publications by ABA staff members, searched using the standard WESTLAW® protocols. In addition, the AMBAR-TP database includes selected documents from other ABA publications. The AMBAR-LE database covers legal education standards from the ABA Law Libraries Committee.
- *Center for Public Choice - George Mason University:* The BILLCAST database provides unique information on the chances for passage of major legislation as it passes through the current session of the United States Congress, with the exception of items introduced in the Appropriations and Budget Committees. Summary information on each bill is included.
- *H. W. Wilson Company:* The INDEX TO LEGAL PERIODICALS, with citations from over 460 legal periodicals, covers the period from 1981 to the present. Every topic of interest in American law is covered in the articles indexed.
- *Information Access Company:* The LEGAL RESOURCE INDEX includes references to more than 730 legal publications, from 1980 to the present. Sponsored by the American Association of Law Libraries, this index also includes Library of Congress subject headings and other descriptors as searchable terms.
- *National Forensic Center:* The FORENSIC SERVICES DIRECTORY includes names of scientific, medical and technical experts, translators, testing laboratories, investigators and other specialists available for trial support consultation or as trial witnesses.
- *Public Utilities Reports, Inc.:* Included in the PUBLIC UTILITY REPORTS are selected cases and regulatory decisions of state and federal courts and utility regulatory commissions. Coverage of headnotes begins in 1953 and of headnotes plus full text in 1974. Some portions of this database are augmented by West headnotes, annotations and key numbers, to enhance search access.
- *Private File Service:* This service enables a firm to create its own database and search its internal files and documents.
- *Shepard's:* SHEPARD's publishes citators which trace the subsequent history of all references to a case. This information is available in the online version months before it appears in print. The researcher can instantly 'shepardize' a case while viewing it by simply typing the letters 'sh' on the screen. When the SHEPARD's history is displayed, each case that is also in the WESTLAW® database is numbered. To see any case, the researcher merely types in the appropriate number. The researcher can immediately

return to SHEPARD's by typing 'gb' or 'goback'. Doing so again will take the researcher back to the original case from which the SHEPARD's excursion began.

- *INSTA-CITE:* INSTA-CITE provides immediate information about subsequent cases which affect the validity of the citing case. It also provides immediate verification of a case citation, including parallel official and non-official citations, state and/or district, docket number, filing date, indication of status as a table or memorandum decision, as well as the prior history of the case in a chronological listing. By first accessing INSTA-CITE, then locating further references through SHEPARD's online, a researcher can gain a complete picture of the history of a case. INSTA-CITE differs from SHEPARD's in that it traces only the direct line of a case's history. It also gives the exact relationship between cases in history, whereas SHEPARD's gives only the notation 'same case'.
- *Law Reviews:* Articles from more than two hundred university law reviews published in the United States are presently online in full text.
- *BLACK'S LAW DICTIONARY:* The Sixth Edition of *Black's Law Dictionary*, containing definitions of terms and phrases of American and English jurisprudence, is now available online. Once the dictionary has been selected, to see the definition of a term enter 'di' followed by the term, for example, 'di *inter vivos*'. Note that there is a slight variation of convention from the other WESTLAW® databases in that the rules for phrase searching do not apply. No quotation marks are necessary to set off the phrase.
- *EZ ACCESS:* WESTLAW® provides a menu-driven, 'fill-in-the-blanks' option to assist persons unfamiliar with its system to perform effective searches. The searcher is given lists of options from which to choose, and depending on what is chosen, fields in which to type relevant search terms or citations.

*Conclusion - WESTLAW®*

The WESTLAW® system once consisted of only the same headnotes found at the beginning of cases in the company's printed reports. It has grown to include both the full text and headnotes for a vastly expanded case law database. It also includes statutory and regulatory material in both jurisdictional and topical databases. The system includes titles in full text as well as abstracts from other publishers, and acts as a gateway to other online services in other scholarly disciplines and to business news sources.

The system's search options and connectors permit either or both numerical and grammatical word association in queries. A controlled vocabulary is available in the key number subject headings. 'Searches within searches' can be performed with the locate command, and case histories can be tracked with both the INSTA-CITE and SHEPARD's files. WESTLAW® thus provides a complete, sophisticated online resource for both large and small firms, solo practitioners or agency staff.

## LEXIS®

A product of Mead Data Central, Inc., LEXIS® is a full-text database consisting of primary and secondary legal materials as well as much non-legal information which can often be of value to the legal researcher. LEXIS® was the first major computer-assisted legal research (CALR) service and initially dominated the marketplace in CALR. The LEXIS® service continues to lead in the introduction of innovative products and services. The LEXIS® concept is straightforward: the system may be searched by any 'word' - that is, any string of characters or numerals separated from the rest of the text by spaces - found in any legal document in its database. These search terms may be joined using Boolean and proximity connectors. Thus the researcher becomes his or her own indexer, and is freed from the constraints of second-guessing what pre-assigned categories might have been imposed by a publisher's indexers.

## Search 12.7: First two menu screens of LEXIS® libraries

```
                         LIBRARIES -- PAGE 1 of 2
        Please TRANSMIT the NAME (only one) of the library you want to search.
         - For more information about a library, TRANSMIT its page (PG) number.
         - To see a list of additional libraries, press the NEXT PAGE key.
        NAME    PG NAME    PG NAME    PG NAME    PG NAME    PG NAME    PG NAME    PG

        - - - - - - L E X I S - U S - - - - - - - - - -PUBLIC    FINANCIAL --NEXIS--
        GENFED  1 CODES   1 LEGIS   1 STATES  1 ALR     6 RECORDS   COMPNY 15 NEXIS  13
                                                          ASSETS  6           BACKGR 13
        ADMRTY  2 FEDCOM  2 MILTRY  3 CORP    2 LAWREV  6 INCORP  6 -COUNTRY- SPORTS 13
        BANKNG  2 FEDSEC  3 PATENT  3 EMPLOY  2 MARHUB  6 LIENS   6 REPORT 16 INSURE 13
        BKRTCY  2 FEDTAX  3 PUBCON  3 HEALTH  3 LEXREF  6           INTNEW 16 LEXPAT 13
        COPYRT  2 IMMIG   3 PUBHW   4 INSRLW  3 ABA     6           ALERT  16 CMPCOM 13
        ENERGY  2 INTLAW  3 REALTY  4 STENV   4 BNA     6 —MEDIS—   EUROPE 16 LEGNEW 14
        ENVIRN  2 ITRADE  3 TRADE   4 STSEC   4 CCHSKY  6 MEDEX  12           MARKET 14
        ESTATE  2 LABOR   3 TRDMRK  4 STTAX   4                     POLITICAL BANKS  14
        FEDSEN  2 M&A     3 TRANS   5 UCC     5 -ASSISTS-           CMPGN  14 ENRGY  14
                            UTILTY  5           PRACT  12           EXEC   14 PEOPLE 14
                                                GUIDE  12                     TRAN   14

        LEXIS contains cases decided between the two dates given on the file menus.
        Some cases decided before the later date may yet arrive from some courts.
```

```
                         LIBRARIES — PAGE 2 of 2
        Please TRANSMIT the NAME (only one) of the library you want to search.
         - For more information about a library, TRANSMIT its page (PG) number.
         - To see a list of additional libraries, press the PREV PAGE key.
        NAME    PG NAME    PG NAME    PG NAME    PG NAME    PG NAME    PG NAME    PG

        - - - - - - - - L E X I S - U S - - - - - - - - LEXIS-UK  LEXIS-CW  LEXIS-FR
        ALA     7 GA      7 MD      7 NJ      8 SD      8 ENGGEN 10 COMCAS 10 INTNAT 11
        ALAS    7 HAW     7 MASS    7 NM      8 TENN    8 UKTAX  10 AUST   10 LOIREG 11
        ARIZ    7 IDA     7 MICH    7 NY      8 TEX     8 SCOT   10 NZ     10 PRIVE  11
        ARK     7 ILL     7 MINN    7 NC      8 UTAH    8 UKJNL  10           PUBLIC 11
        CAL     7 IND     7 MISS    8 ND      8 VT      9 NILAW  10           REVUES 11
        COLO    7 IOWA    7 MO      8 OHIO    8 VA      9
        CONN    7 KAN     7 MONT    8 OKLA    8 VI      9            EC-LAW
        DEL     7 KY      7 NEB     8 ORE     8 WASH    9           EURCOM 10
        DC      7 LA      7 NEV     8 PA      8 WVA     9
        FLA     7 MAINE   7 NH      8 PR      8 WISC    9           LEXIS-IR
                                      RI      8 WYO     9           IRELND 10
                                      SC      8
```

(These screens and those which follow from the LEXIS® Service are reprinted with the permission of Mead Data Central, Inc., provider of the LEXIS®/NEXIS® services.)

*Equipment required*

The LEXIS® service can be accessed through a variety of personal computers and can also be searched via dedicated terminals. The latter include the UBIQ® terminal, a compact desktop unit with an internal modem, dedicated to online research, and the LEXIS® 2000, an MS-DOS PC with a custom keyboard. LEXIS® was the first to offer 9600 baud access from forty-four cities in the United States at no additional charge, which powerfully enhanced the speed of searching.

LEXIS® dedicated terminals are extremely user-friendly, with clearly identified special function keys such as 'next page' and 'prev doc'. When accessing LEXIS® through a standard personal computer, the special functions are easily duplicated by using a template over the computer's function keys or by using 'dot commands'. For instance, the 'next page' function is achieved by entering the dot command '.np'; the 'prev doc' function becomes '.pd'. The use of dot commands allows the researcher to send several commands at once, telling the computer to do a new search in a new library, in a particular file, and to display the result in a particular format. This allows the experienced researcher to by-pass up to five menu screens, saving both time and money.

## Organization of data

Since finding case law is the most important component of research in the Anglo-American legal system, this discussion of LEXIS® will focus first on the system's access to court opinions. Unlike WESTLAW®, LEXIS® contains court opinions exactly as they are released for publication by the courts; headnotes are included only for cases originating from those courts which themselves assign headnotes to opinions. LEXIS® does not include a thesaurus or other editorial enhancement but it does include slip opinions and case law that is never published in printed format by the private reporters.

Free-text searching enables the LEXIS® user to escape the constraints of pre-defined indexing terms. Research has shown that this is a more efficient method of searching, as the inclusion of headnotes causes the search to retrieve large numbers of irrelevant cases which the researcher must nonetheless examine before discarding [7]. Even the user experienced in legal research and the language of the law, however, will benefit from a clear understanding of how materials in LEXIS® are organized in order to maximize search success.

LEXIS® is a menu-driven system. The first menu displayed after signing onto the system is a listing of 'libraries', the broadest subdivision of materials, categorized by subject matter or jurisdiction, within the database. Search 12.7 shows the first two menu screens of LEXIS® libraries.

By entering the page number which appears to the right of the abbreviation for a given library, the user may view a description of the materials included in the library. Once the user has chosen the desired library, a menu is displayed which lists the 'files' of further subdivisions within the library. For instance, upon entering the general federal ('genfed') library, the researcher views the menu of files shown in Search 12.8. This screen is typical of file menus within LEXIS®. The user may search in a file containing the opinions of only one court - such as the United States Supreme Court ('US') - or in a file containing opinions from several courts; for instance, all of the United States federal court opinions in the database may be searched in the 'courts' file.

At this point, an appropriate library and file having been selected, the system is ready to accept a search request. A successful search may retrieve one or more 'documents' which, in a file consisting of cases, are individual court opinions. Documents are further subdivided into fields (designated in LEXIS® as 'segments') a fact which has significant implications for searching. While searchable segments vary among the different files in LEXIS®, typical segments of an opinion include name, date, cite, court, disposition, counsel, opinion and judges.

## Search strategy

Much of what has been said about query planning in WESTLAW® is applicable to LEXIS®. The legal issue and factual pattern must be carefully examined and key words and phrases isolated. In choosing search words, the user must allow for synonyms, antonyms and alternative expressions. As with WESTLAW, the universal characters * and ! can be employed to locate alternative spellings and word endings.

LEXIS® does not automatically search for variant forms of compound words. A hyphen is treated as a blank space. Accordingly, to find all forms of 'antitrust' which are likely to occur in the LEXIS® database, the user would enter as alternatives 'antitrust' and 'anti trust' (the latter variant will also retrieve 'anti-trust'). LEXIS® does, however, search for simple plurals of singular words and the singular form of plural words.

## Search 12.8: Menu of files for the general federal library

```
Please TRANSMIT, separated by commas, the NAMES of the files you want to search
You may select as many files as you want, including files that do not
appear below, but you must transmit them all at one time. To see a
description of a file, TRANSMIT its page (PG) number.
            FILES - PAGE 1 of 6 (NEXT PAGE for additional files)


  NAME   PG DESCRIP        NAME  PG DESCRIP        NAME   PG DESCRIP

   ---COURT GROUP FILES--     ---U.S. COURT FILES----   -----LEGISLATIVE---------
  COURTS   1 Fed Cases & ALR USLIST 1 Sup.Ct Case List RECORD  9 CongRec aft 1984
  CURRNT   1 Cases aft 1989          Oct. 1990 Term  USCODE 20 USCS & PUBLAW
  NEWER    2 Cases aft 1944  US     1 US Supreme Court   --SUPREME COURT BRIEFS--
  SUPCIR   1 US,USAPP & CAFC          1790 - 1991     BRIEFS 16 Argued aft 9/79
   ----ADMINISTRATIVE----   USAPP  1 Court of Appeals  ----------RULES----------
  ALLREG  13 FEDREG & CFR             1789 - 1991     RULES  14 Federal Rules
  FEDREG  13 Fed. Register   DIST   1 District Courts CIRRUL 15 Circuit Ct Rules
             7/1/80- 5/02/91*         1789 - 1991     ----------NEWS-----------
  CFR     10 Code of Fed.Reg CLCT   1 Claims Court    USLW   17 US Law Week
  COMGEN  16 Comp.Gen.Decs.           1856 - 1991     USLWD  17 US Law Wk Daily
  * Part of 1/22/91 is temporarily unavailable.

To search by Circuits press NEXT PAGE.  NOTE:  Only court files can be combined.
```

```
Please TRANSMIT, separated by commas, the NAMES of the files you want to search.
You may select as many files as you want, including files that do not appear
below, but you must transmit them all at one time. To see a description of a
file, TRANSMIT its page (PG) number.
            FILES - PAGE 2 of 6 (NEXT PAGE or PREV PAGE for additional files)


  NAME   PG NAME   PG     NAME   PG NAME   PG       NAME   PG NAME  PG

  C I R & D I S T         C I R C U I T             D I S T R I C T


  1ST    3 8TH    4       1CIR   7 8CIR   7         1DIST   8 10DIST   8
  2ND    3 9TH    5       2CIR   7 9CIR   7         2DIST   8 11DIST   8
  3RD    3 10TH   5       3CIR   7 10CIR  7         3DIST   8 DCDIST   8
  4TH    3 11TH   6       4CIR   7 11CIR  7         4DIST   8 CIT      8
  5TH    4 CADC   6       5CIR   7 DCCIR  7         5DIST   8 CVA      8
  6TH    4 FED    6       6CIR   7 CAFC   7         6DIST   8 TC       8
  7TH    4                7CIR   7                  7DIST   8 BANKR    8
                                                    8DIST   8 CUSTCT   8
                                                    9DIST   8

-------------------CASES BY CIRCUIT AFTER 1911-----------------------

  Press NEXT PAGE for Cong. Record.  Note:  Only court files can be combined.
```

**Search 12.8:** (cont.)

```
Please TRANSMIT, separated by commas, the NAMES of the files you want to
search.
You may select as many files as you want, including files that do not
appear below, but you must transmit them all at one time. To see a
description of a file, TRANSMIT its page (PG) number.
        FILES - PAGE 3 of 6 (NEXT PAGE or PREV PAGE for additional files)

  NAME    PG DESCRIP        NAME  PG DESCRIP        NAME    PG DESCRIP

  -CONGRESSIONAL RECORD-    ------LEGISLATIVE MATERIAL-----------
  RECORD  9 1985 - 1991     BILLS 18 All Bills Files CNGRES 18 All CNGRES Files
  102ND   9 102nd Congress  BLTRCK18 Bill Tracking   CNGVOT 18 CNGRES Votes
  101ST   9 101st Congress  BLCAST18 Billcast        CNGFIN 18 CNGRES Financial
  100TH   9 100th Congress  BLTEXT18 Full Text Bills CNGMEM18 CNGRES Backgrnd
  99TH    9 99th Congress   CMTRPT18 Committee Rpts.  -LEGISLATIVE HISTORIES-
  102SEN  9 102nd Senate    ROLLCL17 Roll Call       BKRLH  21 Bkrtcy Leg. Hist
  102HSE  9 102nd House     BNAWI 17 Wash. Insider   ENVLH  22 *Envirn Leg.
  Hist                                                          Hist
  102RMK  9 102nd Remarks   ----U.S. CODE------      TAXLH  22 Tax Leg. Hist
  102DIG  9 102nd Digest    USCODE20 USCS & PUBLAW    -LEGISLATIVE ARCHIVES-
  SENATE  9 102 - 99 Senate USCS  20 US Code Service BLARCH18 Archived Bills
  HOUSE   9 102 - 99 House  PUBLAW20 US Public Laws  BTX101 18 BLTEXT Archive
  REMARK  9 102 - 99 Remark USCNST20 US Constitution BLT101 18 BLTRCK Archive
  DIGEST  9 102 - 99 Digest        *Compiled by Wilmer, Cutler & Pickering.
```

```
Please TRANSMIT, separated by commas, the NAMES of the files you want to
search. You may select as many files as you want, including files that do not
appear below, but you must transmit them all at one time. To see a description
of a file, TRANSMIT its page (PG) number.
        FILES - PAGE 4 of 6 (NEXT PAGE or PREV PAGE for additional files)

  NAME    PG DESCRIP        NAME  PG NAME   PG       NAME    PG DESCRIP

  -FEDERAL COURT RULES--     --CIRCUIT RULES--       ------RICO & CLSDRV-----
  RULES   14 Combined Rules CIRRUL15 7CRUL  15       RICO   13 RICO Related
  FRCP    14 Civil Proc.    1CRUL 15 8CRUL  15                  materials
  FRCRP   14 Crim. Proc.    2CRUL 15 9CRUL  15       CLSDRV 13 Class Action and
  FRE     14 Evidence       3CRUL 15 10CRUL 15                  Derivative Action
  FRAP    14 App. Proc.     4CRUL 15 11CRUL 15                  materials
  SUPRUL  14 Supreme Ct.    5CRUL 15 DCRUL  15        ----COURT GROUP FILES---
  CLRUL   14 Claims Ct.     6CRUL 15 FCRUL  15       COURTS  1 Fed Cases
  VACRUL  14 Vaccine Rules                           CURRNT  1 Cases aft 1989
  VETRUL  14 Ct. Vet. App.                           NEWER   2 Cases aft 1944
  TAXRUL  14 Tax Rules                               SUPCIR  1 US, USAPP & CAFC
  ADMRUL  14 Adm. & Mar.                             OLDER   2 Cases bef 1945
  BKRULE  14 Bankruptcy
  Press NEXT PAGE for Archived CFR Files. NOTE: Only court files can be combined.
```

**Search 12.8:** (cont.)

```
Please TRANSMIT, separated by commas, the NAMES of the files you want to
search. You may select as many files as you want, including files that do not
appear below, but you must transmit them all at one time. To see a description
of a file, TRANSMIT its page (PG) number.
        FILES - PAGE 5 of 6 (NEXT PAGE or PREV PAGE for additional files)

NAME    PG DESCRIP      NAME  PG DESCRIP        NAME   PG DESCRIP

  -----CFR-----        --------FARS---------    --------GROUP FILES--------
CFR     11 Current      ALLFAR17 Entire FAR &   COURTS  1 Fed Cases
CFR     12 Current         Supplements,         ALLREG 13 FEDREG & CFR
CFR88   13 1988 CFR          4/84 - date        RECORD  9 Cong. Record
CFR87   13 1987 CFR      -------FEDREG-------              1985 - 1991
CFR86   13 1986 CFR      FEDREG13 Fed. Register  USCODE 20 USCS & PUBLAW
CFR85   13 1985 CFR         7/1/80- 5/02/91     RULES  14 Combined Fed Rules
CFR84   13 1984 CFR      -----USAG OPINIONS---  PUBS   19 Legal Publications
CFR83   13 1983 CFR      USAG  16 1791 - Current  ------CONSENT DECREES------
CFR82   13 1982 CFR        --FEDERAL SENTENCING-- CONDEC 16 EPA Consent Decrees
CFR81   13 1981 CFR      GLINE 13 Fed Sent Guide
ALLCFR  13 81-89CFR      FSENR 13 Fed Sent Rptr
Press NEXT PAGE for additional GENFED Files including Presidential Documents.
NOTE: Only court files can be combined.
```

```
Please TRANSMIT, separated by commas, the NAMES of the files you want to
search. You may select as many files as you want, including files that do not
appear below, but you must transmit them all at one time. To see a description
of a file, TRANSMIT its page (PG) number.
        FILES - PAGE 6 of 6 (PREV PAGE for additional files)

NAME    PG DESCRIP        NAME  PG DESCRIP         NAME   PG DESCRIP

  -----------------LEGAL PUBLICATIONS-------------    ---COURT GROUP FILES---
PUBS    19 Legal Pubs     LGLTME 19 Legal Times     COURTS  1 Fed Cases
AMLAWR  19 American Lawyer MNLAWR 19 Manhattan Lawyer COURT2 16 Fed Cases
BUSLAW  19 ABA Bus. Lawyer NTLJNL 19 National Journal CURRNT  1 Cases aft 1989
EXPTLW  19 Expert and Law NTLAWJ 19 National Law Jnl NEWER   2 Cases aft 1945
INTLAW  19 ABA Int. Lawyer NYLAWJ 19 New York Law Jnl OLDER   2 Cases bef 1945
LGECON  19 Law Pract Mgmt  ----------------------  SUPCIR  1 US,USAPP & CAFC
                          GUIDE  17 Library Guides  ----------------------
                                                    PRESDC 17 Pres. Documents
                                                    DSPTCH 16 DOS Dispatch
Press PREV PAGE for additional files. NOTE: Only court files can be combined.
```

*Connectors*

In LEXIS®, the logical relationships among words and phrases are expressed by using one or more of eight connectors shown in Table 12.2. The LEXIS® Service does not use grammatical connectors based on sentence or paragraph structure *per se* (the /s and /p connectors used in WESTLAW). Some searchers believe grammatical connectors to be significantly slower, and thus more costly, than equivalent numerical connectors [7]. The first three of these connectors are the most commonly used as they are capable of expressing most relationships among search terms. The LEXIS® connectors have an established priority which will control their operation unless the user modifies it with parentheses. The standard priority is: OR; w/*n*; w/seg; not w/seg; AND; AND NOT. Pre/*n* and not w/*n* have the same priority as w/*n*. In a series of numerical connectors, the search will proceed from the smallest number to the largest.

## Table 12.2: LEXIS® connectors

| | |
|---|---|
| **OR** | alternative terms |
| **w/*n*** | terms within a specified number of words of each other |
| **AND** | terms both of which appear somewhere in the same document |
| **w/seg** | terms both of which appear in the same segment of the same document |
| **pre/*n*** | terms the first of which precedes the second by a specified number of words |
| **not w/*n*** | one term does not appear within a specified number of words of the other |
| **not w/seg** | one term appears in a least one segment in which the other term does not appear |
| **AND NOT** | the first term appears in a document in which the second term does not |

*Search example*

For purposes of comparison, the same search example will be used as with WESTLAW, elaborating only upon the differences apparent in LEXIS®.

ISSUE:    Are an employer's defamatory statements concerning an employee, absent a showing of malice, considered to be privileged communications?

SEARCH: defam! or slander! or libel! w/20 employe* w/20 privilege* w/20 malice or ill will

DATABASE TO BE SEARCHED: Library: NY

FILE: cases (New York state courts)

*Search strategy*

Since LEXIS® has no equivalent to the WESTLAW® /p connector for locating search terms within the same paragraph, it is necessary to use w/*n* as a proximity connector. Choosing the appropriate number of words of proximity is a matter of experience combined with trial and error. In the search example we chose twenty as the number of words; forty might have retrieved more cases, while ten might have retrieved fewer. The goal, of course, is to retrieve all relevant cases and to exclude, to the extent possible, irrelevant cases.

LEXIS® requires the OR connector between alternative terms; a blank space will not suffice. 'Ill will' will be read as a phrase and does not require enclosure in quotation marks; 'ill will' will also retrieve occurrences of 'ill-will'.

*Displaying search results*

When the search example was run on LEXIS® in January 1991, twenty-one cases were retrieved. These cases can be displayed in a variety of formats. The cite format displays only the citations of the retrieved cases; the full format displays the entire text of each case.

The most useful display format is KWIC™ (for key word in context). This format displays the portions of a case that contain one or more occurrences of the search query. These terms are highlighted and surrounded by twenty-five words of text on either side. Thus, the researcher can quickly scan a large number of retrieved cases for relevance. The screen reproduced in Search 12.9 shows the second case retrieved in the search example in KWIC format; the relevance of the case is immediately apparent.

## Search 12.9: Case displayed in KWIC format

```
                        LEVEL 1 - 2 OF 21 CASES

              TOFICK REZEY, Appellant, v GOLUB CORPORATION et al.,
                              Respondents.

              52 N.Y.2d 713; 417 N.E.2d 558; 436 N.Y.S.2d 264


                          Argued November 10, 1980
                            December 16, 1980

    HEADNOTES:   Libel and Slander   -- Qualified  Privilege -- Malice

    The Appellate Division properly reversed a judgment of the Supreme Court in
    favor of a former employee of a supermarket chain who was allegedly defamed
    by his employer and properly dismissed the complaint, where the jury was
    charged, without exception, that the defamatory statements were qualifiedly
    privileged, since the former employee failed to prove that the statements
    were false and that they were uttered with express malice or actual ill
    will.
```

*Additional features*

Due to the intense commercial competition between LEXIS® and WESTLAW®, there is pressure on each system to add the enhancements employed by the other. Thus, both systems now include the American Bar Association's AMBAR database; H. W. Wilson Company's INDEX TO LEGAL PERIODICALS; Information Access company's LEGAL RESOURCE INDEX; SHEPARD's citators; and many of the publications of Commerce Clearing House (CCH), the Bureau of National Affairs (BNA), and Tax Analysts, Inc.

LEXIS® has a feature similar to WESTLAW®'s 'Locate' feature, known as 'FOCUS™'. In LEXIS®, however, the results can be viewed in full, KWIC, or segment displays.

LEXIS® already includes statutes from all the fifty states in its database. The Michie Company, the largest publisher of state statutes in the United States (twenty-three states and the District of Columbia), is now owned by Mead Data Central, Inc., the publisher of LEXIS®.

An extremely powerful, versatile enhancement to LEXIS® is AUTO-CITE, a product of Lawyer's Cooperative Publishing. AUTO-CITE allows the user immediately to verify the correct name and official or parallel citations for a case, to check the current validity of a case, to see the prior and subsequent history of a case, and to find *American Law Reports (ALR)* annotations that discuss the case. In addition, the full text of the *American Law Reports* is available as a separately searchable library in LEXIS®. Experienced researchers know that to find an ALR annotation on point is to find a veritable cornucopia of finished research, thoroughly organized and analysed by experienced legal writers with supporting authorities provided for further review.

In its law review library, LEXIS® has taken an approach different from WESTLAW®. Though LEXIS® contains fewer law reviews (somewhat over seventy-five as of this writing) it includes the full text of *all* articles from those publications.

In addition to these enhancements it shares in common with WESTLAW, LEXIS® services include:

- NEXIS®: The NEXIS library provides full-text access to more than 750 publications devoted to general news, business, and finance including the *New York Times*, the *Washington Post, The Economist*, the *Legal Times*, and the *National Law Journal*. NEXIS is the exclusive online provider of some of the publications such as the *New York Times*.

- ALR: The American Law Reports (ALR) library contains the full text of thousands of annotations from *ALR2d, ALR3d, ALR4th, ALR Federal* and the *L. Ed.2d*. *ALR* is a product of Lawyer's Cooperative Publishing. Each annotation is a comprehensive collection and discussion of American case law on a particular legal question.

- UNITED KINGDOM AND FRENCH LAW: These libraries contain cases and statutory materials from the relevant jurisdictions.

- EUROPEAN COMMUNITIES: Cases from the Court of Justice of the European Communities and decisions of the Commission of the European Communities are included in this library.

- NAARS: The NATIONAL AUTOMATED ACCOUNTING RESEARCH SYSTEM (NAARS) database consists of annual reports for more than 25,000 publicly traded American Companies.

- LEXIS® FINANCIAL INFORMATION™ SERVICE: This service offers full-text corporate and industry reports, investment and research reports, SEC filings and company information on over 55,000 companies.

- MEDIS®: The Medis library contains the full text of more than sixty medical journals, newsletters and textbooks.

- H. W. Wilson Company: The *Index to Legal Periodicals*, with citations from over 460 legal periodicals, covers the period from 1981 to the present. Every topic of interest in American law is covered in the articles indexed.

- Information Access Company: The *Legal Resource Index* includes references to more than 730 legal publications from 1980 to the present. Sponsored by the American Association of Law Libraries, this index also includes Library of Congress subject headings and other descriptors as searchable terms.

- MARTINDALE-HUBBELL® LAW DIRECTORY: The leading directory of United States lawyers, Martindale-Hubbell includes biographical and geographical information on more than 700,000 attorneys and law firms. (Martindale-Hubbell is a registered trademark of Reed Publishing (USA) Inc.)

- ECLIPSE™ FEATURE: This feature automatically updates stored searches daily, weekly or monthly. This greatly facilitates staying current with developments in particular topics and jurisdictions.

- PAYBACK™ SERVICE: The *Payback* service allows attorneys to receive estimated bills for searches within one week of the online research which in turn helps firms produce much more timely invoices for services rendered.

- MEMBERSHIP GROUPS: This innovative program permits law schools and bar associations to act as sponsors to solo practitioners and small firms. By taking on certain responsibilities of billing and promotion, the membership group permits its members to use LEXIS® at rates similar to those enjoyed by the largest firms, to maintain privileges of access even during periods of little or no use without having to pay the overhead of large monthly access fees, and to leave the details of contracting with the vendor to the sponsor, much as an attorney in a large-firm partnership would rely on the firm's managing partner.

- LEXIS® PRIVATE DATABASE SERVICES: This service allows firms to store internal documents in full-text searchable files. One option permits these files to be stored on CD-ROM discs, thus combining the advantages of microform technology - storage of an actual image of the original documents, and not just the text thereof - with the powerful retrieval capacity of the computer.
- LEXDOC™ FEATURE: This feature provides the capability of ordering certified or uncertified public records from any jurisdiction in the United States and Canada while online.
- PRIVATE PUBLISHERS: The LEXIS®/NEXIS® services contain extensive databases of titles from other publishers, such as Commerce Clearing House, Inc. and The Bureau of National Affairs, similar to those described in the preceding section on WESTLAW®.

*Conclusion - LEXIS®*

The LEXIS® service has pioneered many areas of computer-assisted legal research. It includes not only published case law and statutes but also many unpublished opinions. Available directly on the system, almost all in full text, are many medical, business, financial and general interest journals, magazines, newspapers and news-wire services.

The LEXIS® service allows the legal researcher great flexibility in the selection of resources to be searched and in the viewing and electronic downloading of search results. Regardless of whether they have access to a well-stocked law library of printed materials, by using the LEXIS® service lawyers can obtain online virtually any legal publication needed to provide professional client services.


## CANADA: ONLINE

There are currently three major database vendors in Canada: QL Systems Limited, CAN/LAW and SOQUIJ. At the time of writing, a fourth is about to be launched: CANADIAN LAW ONLINE. There are, as well, a number of vendors offering useful legal databases as part of their more general systems.

This portion of the chapter will discuss briefly, the development of Canadian legal database vendors and follow this with short descriptions of other sources of online legal information. The three major online legal research systems will then be described in some detail.


**Background**

QL Systems Limited (QL), then known as QUIC/LAW, was developed in the late 60s and early 70s by Professor Hugh Lawford of Queen's University. Information provided was obtained both from the government and from commercial publishers. It was then reproduced in electronic format as it appeared in the original print version. Because data came from a number of sources, there was no standardization of such things as format, citations, style or vocabulary; nor was there any control over quality. There was also frequent duplication of decisions reported by different publishers. The database simply reproduced, in electronic format, what most libraries had on their shelves. What this first online legal database did provide, however, was speedier and improved access to these materials.

Canada Law Book was one of the early providers of information to QL Systems Limited. In mid-1987, after lengthy discussions, it withdrew from QL, setting up a new database system, CAN/LAW, based on its own printed publications. Because materials were published by one publisher and its affiliate (Western Legal Publishing), there was more standardization and less duplication within one system. A disadvantage was that researchers of Canadian law felt a need to learn a second search methodology and to use two systems in an attempt to 'get everything' on a given issue. The advantage is that the emergence of competitive systems nurtured responsiveness to user needs and requests.

The Société québeçoise d'information juridique is an agency created by the Government of Quebec to promote the publication and dissemination of Quebec legal information. From its inception in 1976, it has been heavily involved in both print and electronic publishing. The SOQUIJ system was first marketed in the early 1980s, offering access to primary (court records, statutes) and secondary (summaries of case law) materials. Since then it has expanded coverage in terms both of content and date range.

At the time of writing it appears that a fourth player is about to enter the Canadian legal database market. Thomson Professional Publishing Canada has indicated that it will introduce a new electronic legal research tool to be called CANADIAN LAW ONLINE incorporating and enhancing the content of the printed version of the *Canadian Abridgment*. It is expected that this product will offer online access to digests of more than 400,000 judgments dating back to 1811, as well as history and judicial information. The earliest case cited is an English case from 1254. Further comment is impossible until the product is made commercially available.

As with United States legal databases, the majority of Canadian legal databases are case law-based. Originally, only headnotes or summaries as provided by the original publisher were offered. With the growth of system capacity and of user demand came the introduction of full text.

QL has offered the full-text of statutes since the 1970s. This was followed by the full-text of decisions received directly from the Supreme Court of Canada. By 1988, all provincial governments, except Quebec which had its own agency marketing an online system, were providing the full-text of court of appeal and superior court decisions through QL Systems. Other databases are slowly being converted to full-text.

CAN/LAW also offers the full-text of Supreme Court of Canada judgments, as well as of selected other case law databases. In the late 1980s SOQUIJ made available the full-text of the decisions of the Cour d'Appel du Quebec. SOQUIJ also offers, in both English and French, the full-text of the statutes and regulations of Quebec.

The advantages of searching full-text, as opposed to searching keywords and headnotes only, have been discussed in the United States portion of this chapter. These comments hold true for Canadian research as well.

*Other databases*

In addition to those databases offered by the major Canadian legal online vendors, there are several others, important to legal research, available through more general or business systems. Several of these are covered elsewhere in this book. A few are worth mentioning here as they may prove useful to researchers of Canadian law.

There is as yet no Canadian equivalent of SHEPARD'S CITATIONS. Word is that such a service is currently being created.

CAN/LAW has offered FIRSTCITE since 1988. Similar to LEXIS®'s AUTO-CITE, FIRSTCITE provides both a history and a summary of judicial consideration of specific cases.

Online access to tertiary Canadian legal materials (journal articles) through a bibliographic database was introduced in 1989 with the availability of the INDEX TO CANADIAN LEGAL LITERATURE on INFOGLOBE. This is the online version of the legal periodical index portion of Carswell Publishing Company's (now Thomson Professional Publishing Canada's) *Canadian Abridgment*. Coverage dates from January 1987.

A selection of Canadian legal journals is also indexed by the two major United States legal periodical indexes, H. W. Wilson's INDEX TO LEGAL PERIODICALS and Information Access's CURRENT LAW INDEX. These online services are both available through WESTLAW® and LEXIS®.

CT ONLINE (CANADIAN TAX ONLINE) provides access to both legal and non-legal tax information. Owned by Thomson Professional Publishing Canada, it is available through the WISDOM network of STM Systems Corporation.

# QL Systems Limited

QL Systems Limited (QL) offers a wide variety of primary and secondary legal information including the full-text of federal and most provincial statutes and regulations*, of most major federal and provincial courts and of a variety of other materials. Summaries and/or headnotes are also provided for a number of case law reporters, both official (SUPREME COURT REPORTS) and commercial (CCH Canadian DOMINION REPORT SERVICE, Maritime Law Book's NATIONAL REPORTER SYSTEM). There are many quasi-legal (TAX RULINGS, HANSARD QUESTIONS) and non-legal (BUSINESS INFORMATION WIRE, MINING TECHNOLOGY PROJECTS) databases available as well. Coverage of these databases varies dramatically, with some going back to the late 19th century.

The full-text of any QL database is searchable, that is any word or string of characters can be searched using Boolean logic and a variety of connectors. Searchers who have used WESTLAW® will find the technique very similar to that used for QL. This is because the programs used by WESTLAW® were originally acquired from QL and were then modified and enhanced to meet the needs and demands of the United States market.

## *Equipment required*

QL can be accessed using nearly any personal computer equipped with communications software. It can also be accessed using a fixed function terminal or one of the company's dedicated terminals offering high speed communications capabilities. All configurations naturally require a modem and a link to DATAPAC, the Canadian telecommunications network. While most communications software packages are compatible, it is also possible to purchase the QUICKLINK package directly from the company. This package provides such things as programmed function keys, ease of downloading to disk or printer, help screens, access to WESTLAW® and other online vendors as required.

## *Search strategy*

It is very important to define clearly your search needs before going online. This involves three steps: clarification of the legal issue, selection of appropriate databases to be searched, and formation of the search query.

The basic approach to the first step is much the same as previously described for WESTLAW® and LEXIS®. Think about the issue, writing down key terms, phrases or statute references. What synonyms or variants of words are likely to be used? What date range should be covered? What jurisdiction? How should various search terms be connected? Is there another case on point? Is the topic searchable in a database offering key number searching capabilities (NATIONAL REPORTER SYSTEM)? If so, what is the appropriate key number?

## *Database selection*

Because there is such a wide variety of databases available on QL, many of which simply duplicate information found in others, it is wise to select appropriate databases before beginning the search. To review online the current list of databases available, simply enter DB. Taking into consideration jurisdiction, level of court, coverage, nature of contents (full-text, headnotes only), select accordingly.

---

\* Users should be aware that, while these statutes and regulations databases provide a useful means of access to the law on a given subject, they can be out-of-date by as much as several years.

QL's global searching feature allows the user to search different databases simultaneously. There are three options available: System Global, a permanent combination predefined by QL; User Global, a temporary combination predefined by the user, and Session Global, a temporary combination defined by the user. Not all databases can be searched globally. If the global feature is not used, other options exist to facilitate working with several databases. Searches can easily be transferred from one database to the next using the command: S DB [database]. Searches can also be modified, saved, combined and recalled.

*Query formulation*

When the issue has been clearly defined and the databases selected, it is best to formulate the search query on paper. All search terms should be listed with their variants. As with most online information retrieval systems, QL has a list of stop words which it will not search (the, and, their, etc.). QL automatically searches for all plural (but not singular) forms, all possessives and some irregular plurals, saving the searcher this effort. This function can be cancelled if so desired. As with WESTLAW® and LEXIS®, the character ! can be used to search variant word endings and * acts as a wild card replacement for one character anywhere in a string. Specific word endings can also be searched by enclosing the suffixes in parentheses immediately following the root, for example, tax(es, ing, ation). Hyphenated words can be searched by using a proximity connector (discussed below), causing the system to search a term as if it is one word, hyphenated or two words. QL is period-sensitive, that is it will search for periods. It is therefore wise to search a term which may have periods both with and without to be certain to retrieve what is required.

*Operators and connectors*

It is necessary to select which Boolean operators should be used. In QL these are: AND (&), implicit OR (*space*), explicit OR (OR), and BUT NOT (%). The searcher should be wary of using the 'BUT NOT' feature as it may inadvertently eliminate important materials.

**Table 12.3: Connectors on QL Systems Limited**

| | |
|---|---|
| **a space** | implicit 'or', searches alternative terms |
| **OR** | explicit 'or', searches alternative terms |
| **&** | both terms anywhere in the document |
| **%** | all terms except the one following the sign |
| **/n** | one term within a specified number of words of the next term |
| **/p** | terms appear in the same paragraph |

QL offers a limited number of proximity connectors (see Table 12.3) allowing the user to search for terms numerically (within a specified number of words, /n) or grammatically (within the same paragraph, /p). The order of terms cannot be specified.

The order in which the system processes these operators and connectors is as follows: implicit OR, proximity connectors (from those terms closest together to those furthest apart), explicit OR, AND, BUT NOT, working from left to right. Parentheses cannot be used, as in other systems, to create sets and affect the order of processing. Phrases can be searched by putting search terms in double quotation marks (""). Because of the way the system searches phrases, this is a very time-consuming feature. There are also certain limitations as to how this feature can be used. For these reasons, it is preferable to use proximity connectors if at all possible.

*Field searching*

As with WESTLAW®, QL is divided into separately searchable fields or segments, such as style-of-cause, date, court, citation, summary. These vary from database to database. The command F can be used to display a list of fields used in the database searched.

*Date range searching*

It is possible to limit searches to relevant dates on QL by specifying required dates in the DATE field, for example, @DATE 1991; @DATE BEFORE yy/mm/dd; @DATE AFTER yy/mm/dd; @DATE 45/11/12-50/07/24.

*Ranking method*

QL automatically displays search results in statistical order, that is with the documents containing the greatest number of usages of relevant terms appearing first. Should another ranking method (for example, chronological or reverse chronological) be desired, the appropriate command must be given before the search query is entered.

*Search example*

The same search example is used as in the United States section of the chapter in order to facilitate comparison.

> ISSUE:    Are an employer's defamatory statements concerning an employee privileged absent a showing of malice?
> QUERY: defam! slander! libel! /p employe* /p privilege* /p malice ill /l will illwill
> DATABASE TO BE SEARCHED: OR (ONTARIO REPORTS)

*Commentary*

The search statement in QL Systems Limited is almost identical to that for WESTLAW®. The only difference is found in the entry of the term ill-will. By using the proximity connector '/l' QL will search for the words 'ill' and 'will' within one space of each other (ill will or ill-will). The compound form will be searched as entered.

Because no method of ranking search results is specified, results will be displayed in statistically-weighted order, that is from the decision containing the most occurrences of search terms through to the decision containing the fewest occurrences.

The researcher searching Canadian case law should remember that there is not the same volume of court decisions as there is in the much larger United States. It is possible that, when a search query is too narrowly designed, there will be no results. This is the case with the above example. It then becomes necessary to restate the query in a less restrictive fashion.

> QUERY: defam! slander! libel! & employe* & privilege* & malice ill /l will illwill

The revised query replaces the first three proximity connectors with the straight Boolean operator '&'. The proximity connector '/1' remains to specify the connection between the words 'ill' and 'will'. The system, therefore, will search for all suffixes of any of the first three roots ('defam', 'slander' or 'libel') in the same document as the root 'employe' and the root 'privilege' each with only a one character suffix and either or any of the following 'malice', 'illwill', 'ill-will' or 'ill will'.

The danger of broadening a search query in this manner is that the possibility of retrieving cases which are not on point is greatly increased. This is particularly so in full-text databases, less so in databases providing only summaries or headnotes.

*Additional features*

The most distinctive feature of QL Systems Limited is the availability, either within hours or, at most, two weeks, of the full-text of recent unreported decisions of the Supreme Court of Canada and the provincial appeal courts. Other features include:

- *QL Mail,* the system's electronic mail service, provides, among other things, a means for the low cost transmission of recent judgments.
- *QUICKTAX* provides access to a variety of databases specific to the field of tax.
- *QUICKNEWS* provides access to the full-text of various wire services, both Canadian and international.

## CAN/LAW

CAN/LAW, which is owned and operated by Canada Law Book, provides databases which reproduce a selection of their published case reports and summaries, either entirely or in part. The whole of *ACWS (All Canada Weekly Summaries* - summaries of selected federal and provincial decisions since 1977) is available online, as are other such services (for example, *WCB - Weekly Criminal Bulletin*). Headnotes from the *Dominion Law Reports (DLR)* are available from 1955, with full-text included as of 1987 in the DLR database.

As with other systems discussed in this chapter, CAN/LAW is full-text searchable, that is any word or string of characters can be searched using basic Boolean operators and a variety of connectors. Because the content of the available databases is provided by one of two publishing houses (Canada Law Book and Western Legal Publishing), the searcher will find that there is some consistency in keywords used in summaries and headnotes. WLP (Western Legal Publishing) can be searched using a subject area number. CLAS (CANADIAN LABOUR ARBITRATION CASES) and LAC (LABOUR ARBITRATION CASES) can also be searched using paragraph reference numbers from Brown and Beatty's *Canadian Labour Arbitration*. While this may ease search preparation somewhat, the user should not rely entirely on such a method as it may limit results.

*Equipment required*

CAN/LAW can be accessed using virtually any personal computer with communications software, or with fixed function ('dumb') terminals. Any configuration requires a modem and a link to DATAPAC. Although the user can use nearly any generic communications software, it is also possible to purchase specially tailored software from CAN/LAW: Archway for Macintosh computers and CAN/LAW for IBM or compatible microcomputers. As with other such packages, these provide the user with programmed function keys and facilitate other manipulation of the database.

*Search strategy*

The planning of the search has been discussed above in the sections on WESTLAW®, LEXIS® and QL. The same holds true for CAN/LAW. It is important first to carefully define the issue to be searched, writing down keywords, variants and synonyms, and eliminating stop words. CAN/LAW provides users with a very nice query planner to assist in this process.

*Database selection*

Given the nature and number of databases available on CAN/LAW, selecting which should be searched is somewhat easier than on QL. The user must decide what is the nature of the issue: civil (DLR, ACWS, WLP), criminal (CCC - CANADIAN CRIMINAL CASES, WCB, WLP), labour (LAC, CLAS, WLP), or patent (CPR - CANADIAN PATENT REPORTER).

CAN/LAW does not offer the capability to search more than one database at a time. It is possible, however, to transfer a query from one database to another by first saving a search (SAVE) and then reissuing (REI*n) in another database. Note that searches must be SAVEd before results are displayed. Individual searches can be displayed by using the DIS command with the search number; all saved searches can be displayed by entering RECAP ALL.

*Query formulation*

The search query should be formulated on paper before going online. CAN/LAW is command driven. It is, therefore, necessary to indicate to the system what function it is to perform before entering any data. The command for search is SEA or S. The system automatically searches all regular plural forms of singular terms, all singular forms of all plural terms, some irregular plurals and all possessive forms. The character '!' can be used for truncation or root expansion. There is, however, no 'wild card' character to search variant spellings. A hyphen is treated as a space, so any search of a potentially hyphenated word should be entered as two separate words and as one word (for example, anti trust, antitrust). Periods are ignored unless they appear as a part of a number (such as section number 143.1)

*Operators and connectors*

Boolean operators in CAN/LAW are as follows: AND (AND); implicit OR (,); explicit OR (OR) and BUT NOT (NOT).

**Table 12.4: Connectors on CAN/LAW**

| | |
|---|---|
| **, [comma]** | implicit OR, searches alternative terms |
| **OR** | explicit OR, searches alternative terms |
| **AND** | searches both terms anywhere in the document |
| **NOT** | excludes following term(s) |
| **SAME** | searches terms in same paragraph |
| **WTHN*n*** | searches terms 0-7 lines apart in any order |
| **BSD*n*** | searches terms 0-7 lines apart in specified order |
| **NEAR*n*** | searches terms 0-7 words apart in any order |
| **ADJ*n*** | searches terms 0-7 words apart in specified order |

CAN/LAW offers a wider variety of proximity connectors than does QL (see Table 12.4). Terms can be searched grammatically (within the same paragraph, SAME) or numerically (within 0–7 lines). The order of terms can be specified. Parentheses are used to create sets of searches.

CAN/LAW processes operators and connectors in the following order: terms in parentheses, implicit OR, proximity connectors (from closest to furthest apart), NOT, explicit OR, AND, working from left to right. As in LEXIS®, phrases are searched automatically as entered, without quotation marks (for example, pay equity). For this reason it is important to remember to use a comma (,) when searching either of two terms.

*Field searching*

CAN/LAW is also divided into separately searchable fields such as citation, jurisdiction, style/of/cause, keyword. The command SHOW FIELD displays these segments.

*Date range searching*

The date range can be limited for all searches in a given database, (RANGE yymmdd; RANGE AFTER yymmdd *or* RANGE BEFORE 910119). Alternatively, the date range can be specified within a given query by searching the DATE field for the required date (for example, sea moreau and 1989 jdat).

*Ranking method*

CAN/LAW automatically displays search results in reverse chronological order (that is most recent first).

*Search example*

> ISSUE:   Are an employer's defamatory statements concerning an employee privileged absent a showing of malice?
> QUERY:   sea defam!,slander!,libel! SAME employe! SAME privilege! SAME malice,ill will,illwill
> DATABASE TO BE SEARCHED: DLR (DOMINION LAW REPORTS)

*Commentary*

The 'sea' instructs the CAN/LAW system to search the following terms. There are a few differences in this query from previous queries.

Unlike other systems CAN/LAW does not offer the option to limit suffixes to a specified number of characters. The '!' must therefore be used throughout the query and may bring more expansions of 'employe' and 'privilege' than found in examples where the suffix is limited to one character. The ',' is used between synonyms rather than a space or the word 'OR'. The results will, however, be the same.

Finally, when a space is left between a string of characters ('ill will') the system automatically searches for these words as a phrase. Because it does not 'read' hyphens, it will also retrieve ill-will. The compound form of the word is searched by including 'illwill' in the query.

*Additional features*

- *FIRSTCITE:*   The FIRSTCITE service on CAN/LAW offers users the ability to search the history of a court decision. The service to date is the only one of its kind for Canadian law. It is, unfortunately, somewhat limited in scope for decisions prior to 1988: only databases available on CAN/LAW are searched for judicial consideration of these. Most Canadian law reports, however, are searched for consideration of decisions since that time.

- *ELECTRONIC BULLETIN BOARDS:* A second feature of CAN/LAW is its electronic bulletin boards. Users have access to the Canada and Ontario Statute Citators through this service, as well as to recent decisions of the Supreme Court of Canada.

## SOQUIJ

SOQUIJ, the online legal database system of the Quebec Government agency, Société québeçoise d'information juridique, offers access to two major and very different kinds of legal information. The first of these is the records of the various Quebec Registry Offices (BUREAUX D'ENREGISTREMENT) and of various Court Registrars (SERVICES JUDICIAIRES); the second is legislation (BANQUE DE DOCUMENTATION LEGISLATIVE) and case law (BANQUE DE JURISPRUDENCE). The two parts of the system are very different in purpose and in structure, even to the point of using dramatically different software programs. The BUREAUX D'ENREGISTREMENT and the SERVICES JUDICIAIRES are databases providing factual information (for example, land titles) which is very specific to the needs of practising Quebec lawyers and notaries, and will not be dealt with here. The case law and legislation databases are, however, of interest to a wider market and will therefore be discussed in greater detail.

The full-text of the *Revised Statutes of Quebec 1977* in both English and French is available, as are all modifications since that time. This is a unique and occasionally useful feature. It does require, however, that the user be careful to note the version of any given article when conducting research of the LOIS or LAWS database.

The full-text of regulations (REGL, REGU) in force are also available in both English and French. Both statutes and regulations are found in the DOCUMENTATION LEGISLATIVE database.

The BANQUE DE JURISPRUDENCE database offers case law summaries in French from Quebec courts, the Federal Court of Appeal and the Supreme Court of Canada and the full-text in French of decisions of the Quebec Court of Appeal and the Supreme Court of Canada since 1987.

SOQUIJ, like the other systems described in this chapter, is free-text searchable. STAIRS software is the base program used and can be searched using simple Boolean operators and a variety of connectors. Like CAN/ LAW, much of the information provided to SOQUIJ has been produced by one publisher. There is, therefore, much consistency found in the terminology used in keywords and summaries. A list of keywords is available from the publisher and can prove helpful in query formulation.

### Equipment required

The SOQUIJ database runs on mainframe computers which are terminal sensitive. This means that a user must access the system through a terminal type which is recognized by the main computer. Dial-up access is possible with nearly any personal computer equipped with communications software and a modem; however, it is necessary first to pass through the intermediary of iNet, Telecom Canada's data network.

### Search strategy

Like CAN/LAW, SOQUIJ also offers a sample query preparation sheet for researchers. Once the issue to be searched has been clearly defined, the user can jot down keywords, variants and synonyms, connecting them with appropriate operators.

*Database selection*

The selection of databases is fairly straightforward on SOQUIJ. If the user is searching legislation, the options available in DOCUMENTATION LEGISLATIVE are as follows. English-language statutes (LAWS) or regulations (REGU); French-language statutes (LOIS) or regulations (REGL).

The BANQUE DE JURISPRUDENCE is offered only in French. Summaries are available for a wide range of Quebec cases and a limited number of Federal cases on the EXPRESS bank. This database also provides a roundabout way of accessing legislation, jurisprudence and doctrine cited. The TRAVAIL database contains summaries of Quebec labour cases. The APPEL database provides the full-text of judgments from the highest courts of Quebec and Canada respectively.

*Query formulation*

It is important to note that it is necessary to use accents when searching French terms on SOQUIJ. This is not a problem for users with a French keyboard. Users with an English keyboard will have to replace accents with special symbols (see Table 12.5).

**Table 12.5: Accents on SOQUIJ**

| Accents | Symbol | Example |
|---|---|---|
| Acute (é) | > | société = soci>et>e |
| Grave (è) | < | accès = acc<es |
| Circumflex (ô) | * | surcroît = surcro*it |
| Cedilla (ç) | ? | français = fran?cais |
| Diaeresis (ï) | % | aïeux = a%ieux |

SOQUIJ searches all other terms exactly as they are entered. There is no automatic pluralization or singularization. Root expansion is possible, however. The character $ will cause the system to search for variant endings of any root. The symbol $n will cause to be displayed only those endings of up to and including the number of characters (1 to 4) specified. Periods are ignored unless the string of characters in which they are included is isolated by the use of quotation marks (for example, 'c.c', '1042.3'). There are lists of stop words, English and French, which the system will not search.

Searches are automatically saved as they are run on the system. They can easily be recalled and combined as the session progresses.

*Operators and connectors*

SOQUIJ offers a wider range of operators and connectors than do either of its Canadian counterparts (see Table 12.6). Both Boolean and proximity (grammatical and numerical) capabilities are available to the users, as well as the ability to specify the order of search terms. Parentheses can be used to create sets of searches.

Operators and connectors are processed in the following order: ADJ, NEAR, AVEC/SANS, MEME/PASMEME, ET, NON, OU, XOR.

## Table 12.6: Connectors on SOQUIJ

| | | |
|---|---|---|
| **OU** | **OR** | OR - searches alternative term |
| **ET** | **AND** | searches both terms anywhere in the document |
| **NON** | **NOT** | excludes following term anywhere in the document |
| **MEME** | **SAME** | searches both terms in the same paragraph |
| **AVEC** | **WITH** | searches both terms in the same sentence |
| **PRES***n* | **NEAR***n* | searches terms 0-7 words apart in any order |
| **ADJ***n* | **ADJ***n* | searches terms 0-7 lines apart in specified order |
| **PASMEME** | **NOTSAME** | excludes following term in same paragraph |
| **SANS** | **NOTWITH** | excludes following term in same sentence |
| **XOR** | **XOR** | searches one or the other term but not both |

*Field searching*

SOQUIJ is divided into separately searchable fields or segments such as Parties, References and Resumé. Technical sheets are supplied outlining the structure of each of the three case law and legislative databases.

*Date range searching*

Specially formatted fields permit the user to search relevant dates with ease. These fields differ with each database, so it is necessary to check the technical sheets. Dates are written yymmdd (for example, 800416 for April 16, 1980) in the legislation database and yyyymmdd (for example, 19800416 for the same date) in the case law database and can be searched using the relational operators listed in Table 12.7.

## Table 12.7: Relational operators on SOQUIJ

| | |
|---|---|
| **EQ** | Equal to |
| **OL** | Outside the limits |
| **LE** | Less than or equal to |
| **LT** | Less than |
| **WL** | Within the limits |
| **NE** | Not equal to |
| **NL** | Not less than |
| **NG** | Not greater than |
| **GT** | Greater than |
| **GE** | Greater than or equal to |

*Sample search*

In order to provide a comparison with the systems discussed earlier in this chapter the example to illustrate SOQUIJ uses English terminology despite the fact that only French-language case law is available on SOQUIJ. Obviously the search could not, in fact, be conducted.

ISSUE:   Are an employer's defamatory statements concerning an employee privileged absent a showing of malice?

QUERY:   (defam$ ou slander$ ou libel$) MEME employe$l MEME privilege$l MEME (malice OU ill ADJl will OU illwill)

This query, if translated into French, should retrieve cases pertinent to the issue. The '$' will retrieve any expansion of the roots it follows. The '$1' will only retrieve suffixes of one character. The use of 'ADJ1' retrieves all instances where the word 'ill' appears before and adjacent to the word 'will' (ill will or ill-will), while 'illwill' will retrieve the compound version of the word. The use of the 'MEME' connectors instructs the system to retrieve only those documents containing search results from each set in the same paragraph.

## CD-ROMS FOR LEGAL RESEARCH: NORTH AMERICA

Legal publishers have been somewhat slower to produce information in CD-ROM format than many of their scientific counterparts. There are several reasons which could be postulated to explain this. One which is purely technological in nature is that the sheer volume of mainframe-based full-text systems such as those described earlier in this chapter could not be easily handled by early CD-ROM hardware. In a 1988 article published in *Trends on Law Library Management and Technology,* Stephen Burnett of West Publishing Company stated that despite the possibility of storing 250,000 pages of text per CD-ROM, it would take at least forty discs to store the first series of the *National Reporter* as a full-text searchable database [8]. The development of high capacity CD-ROM jukeboxes capable of holding two to three hundred CD-ROMs offers great potential for legal publishing.

In recent years legal publishers have produced single databases or portions of databases extracted from their larger systems. These tend to be bibliographic indexes to legal literature, directories or subject-oriented texts, documents and case law.

As with remote online systems, each vendor provides its own search software with its CD-ROM product. These are generally menu-driven and vary greatly in ease-of-use. Those systems which are very 'user-friendly' tend to prove frustrating to the experienced searcher who must work through menu after menu to obtain search results. Conversely, some systems require considerable user training before they can be effectively used.

Until supply and demand begins to work in the users' favour, subscriptions to legal CD-ROMs remain, in most cases, extremely high in cost compared to the benefit received. They are, for most law libraries, a luxury.

Unlike remote online legal vendors, of which there are perhaps five or six major North American systems, there is a wide variety of CD-ROM products for the legal market. As technology improves, more are being produced with greater regularity. A few of the major ones available at the time of writing are briefly described below. For the purposes of this chapter, only those intended primarily for legal research are discussed. Those touching on other disciplines are dealt with elsewhere in this book.

By far the majority of North American legal CD-ROMs are produced in the United States. Several of these also include selective Canadian and international information as well.

### Bibliographic CD-ROMs

*LEGALTRAC/INFOTRAC*

This is the CD-ROM version of Information Access Corporation's *Current Law Index* covering most major English language legal periodicals published in the United States, Canada, United Kingdom, Ireland, Australia and New Zealand, as well as selected French- and Spanish-language journals from these countries. All articles, case notes and book reviews found in the upwards of seven hundred law journals are indexed as well as articles of importance to the legal profession from more than two thousand other publications. Coverage begins in 1980 and the disc is updated monthly.

The search software for this product is extremely user-friendly. The researcher is led through a series of menus which assist in the retrieval of required information. Sophisticated search capabilities are not available.

Until January 1991 the database was searched in much the same way as the print index. The user was instructed to enter the required search term, either a subject (based on Library of Congress Subject Headings) or a name (personal, corporate, author, geographic, etc.). Titles of articles could not be searched. In 1991 the search software was upgraded to allow users to combine terms or concepts by using the Boolean 'AND' operator; to search keywords (not just Library of Congress Subject Headings) anywhere in the citation including title and annotation; to view the list of headings used to index any given article on point; and to download search results to disk.

## WILSONDISC®

WILSONDISC® is the CD-ROM version of the W.H. Wilson Company's print *Index to Legal Periodicals* and remote online retrieval system WILSONLINE. Over six hundred legal periodicals published in the United States, Canada, United Kingdom, Ireland, Australia and New Zealand are indexed. Unlike INFOTRAC, WILSONDISC® is somewhat more selective in its coverage indexing articles, case notes, bibliographies, biographies and notes of legislation only if they meet the criteria of minimum length. Coverage begins in August 1981 and the disc is updated quarterly. Users are expected to use the remote online version for recent citations.

WILSONDISC® provides more search flexibility for the user than INFOTRAC. Three search modes are possible: BROWSE, WILSEARCH and WILSONLINE. In BROWSE, the user is prompted to enter the subject to be searched. WILSONDISC® will respond with a list of related subject headings which can then be browsed or expanded through 'See Also' references. Citations can be retrieved by highlighting the desired subject. This mode is most like using the print index.

WILSEARCH is the search mode intended for novices. Users are guided through the system filling in search terms for any of a variety of fields covering subject, author, title, journal name, etc. Simple Boolean operation is possible. If several terms are entered on one line, they are automatically 'ANDed' together. To 'OR' terms, the line must be preceded by 'ANY'. The operator 'AND' is always understood between lines.

Experienced users will prefer WILSONLINE which offers greater flexibility and speed through its command-driven capabilities. Search elements and sets can be combined using simple Boolean operators (AND, OR, NOT). The colon (:) is the symbol used for truncation or root expansion; the hash mark (#) is used as a wild card replacing a single character. Virtually all the search capabilities of Wilson's remote online system are possible in the WILSONLINE mode.

## Directories

## MARTINDALE-HUBBELL LAW DIRECTORY

The CD-ROM version of this venerable sixteen-volume legal directory was first released in 1990. It contains information on over 800,000 lawyers, law firms, corporate legal departments, banks and legal services. All major United States firms, corporations and services are listed. There is also good Canadian and international coverage. Users of the *Law Digest* volumes of the print version should note that this information is not included.

The search software for the CD-ROM version of the MARTINDALE-HUBBELL LAW DIRECTORY is extremely simple to learn and use. The system is menu-driven and requires only that the user specify search terms beside any of twenty search criteria listed on the search workspace screen. Searchable categories include: City, Country, Law School, Languages, Firm Size, Fields of Law, Clients, etc. The only other search decision the user must make is which of the three record formats available (Brief, Lawyer/Firm or Full Firm) is required.

## Topical CD-ROMs

### Search Master

Matthew Bender & Company have began to produce a number of topical CD-ROMs of interest to the legal community, grouping several of their print texts and looseleaf services by subject and reproducing them on single CD-ROMs. Among those currently available are: INTELLECTUAL PROPERTY LIBRARY, TAX LIBRARY, FEDERAL PRACTICE LIBRARY, COLLIER BANKRUPTCY LIBRARY and BUSINESS LAW LIBRARY. As with their print versions, most of the information available takes the form of textbooks, treatises or legal commentaries, but access is also available to some case law. Subscriptions include updates which are generally monthly.

Matthew Bender CD-ROMs use a fairly sophisticated search strategy permitting full-text searches of all titles included on the disc with one search query. Searches can be saved and combined. The electronic bookmark function permits users to mark pertinent text, jump forward to another 'hit' and return to the marked text as required. A cross-referencing feature allows the user to move with one key-stroke from one text to a reference or citation which appears elsewhere on the disc.

### West CD-ROMs

West Publishing Company produces several topical CD-ROM databases, each focusing on specific subject areas (for example, BANKRUPTCY LIBRARY, BNA-TAX MANAGEMENT LIBRARY, FEDERAL TAXATION LIBRARY, FEDERAL CIVIL PRACTICE LIBRARY and GOVERNMENT CONTRACTS LIBRARY). Each CD-ROM includes a variety of topically-related information from original print sources including codes, regulations, procedure, case law, rulings and treatises. Subscriptions are monthly as are the updates.

The technique for searching West CD-ROMs is the same as that used for WESTLAW®. For a description of this see the description of WESTLAW® earlier in this chapter.

## Conclusion

There is an ever-increasing number of CD-ROMs available for the legal information researcher. Only a small sampling of existing products has been described. The New England Law Library Consortium (NELLCO), formed of sixteen law libraries including Harvard and Yale, is marketing the CD-ROM version of its union catalogue. The COMPACT DISC FEDERAL REGISTER is available from Counterpoint Publishing. Prentice-Hall is producing a number of topical CD-ROMs, including PHINet TAX COURT DECISIONS (U.S.) and the ELECTRONIC TAX ACT (Canada).

It is difficult to keep abreast of the market. Promises of new products are frequent: Mead Data (the producer of LEXIS®) is working on something which will, apparently, not be available in print form; Shepard-McGraw-Hill is promising to produce *Shepard's Legal Citations*; existing products are being enhanced. One thing in this era of change is certain: as technology and capacity improve, the number of legal CD-ROMs will continue to grow.

## REFERENCES

1.    David Blair and M. E. Maron. An evaluation of retrieval effectiveness for a full-text document retrieval system. *Com. ACM* 28 1985 289 (a publication of the Association of Computing Machinery)
2.    Daniel P. Dabney. The Curse of Thamus. *Law Library Journal* 78(5) 1986 9-17
3.    Jo McDermott. Another analysis of full-text legal document retrieval. *Law Library Journal* 78(10) 1986 337
4.    Craig E. Runde and William H. Lindberg. The Curse of Thamus: A response. *Law Library Journal* 78(10) 1986 345
5.    Daniel P. Dabney. A reply to West Publishing Company and Mead Data Central on The Curse of Thamus. *Law Library Journal* 78(10) 1986 349
6.    Robert C. Berring. Full-text databases and legal research: Backing into the future. *High Technology Law Journal* 1 1986 27
7.    John P. Doyle. Aiming at the Databases. *Trends in Law Library Management and Technology* 3(7) 1990 3-4
8.    Stephen Burnett. CD-ROM Technology. *Trends in Law Library Management and Technology* 1(6) 1988 1-3

## FURTHER READING

*Banques de données SOQUIJ: Manuel de l'utilisateur*. Montreal: SOQUIJ, 1990 - (looseleaf)

Baum, Marsha. The *Index to Legal Periodicals* on CD-ROM WILSONDISC®. *Trends in Law Library Management and Technology* 1(4) 1987 4-5

Best, Catherine. Summary of commands for computer assisted legal research. *Canadian Law Libraries/ Bibliothèques de droit canadiennes*. 16(1) 1991 13-16

Bintliff, Barbara B. Auto-Cite and Insta-Cite: The race to update case histories. *Colorado Lawyer* 15 1986 1675

*CAN/LAW News*. Aurora, Ont.: Canada Law Book, 19- (bimonthly)

*CAN/LAW User's Manual*. Aurora, Ont.: Canada Law Book, 19- (looseleaf)

Carrick, Kathleen M. *LEXIS® A Legal Research Manual*. Dayton, Ohio: Mead Data Central, Inc., 1989

Coco, Al J. Full-text vs. full-text plus editorial additions: Comparative retrieval effectiveness of the LEXIS® and WESTLAW® systems. *Legal Reference Services Quarterly* 4 1984 27

Griffith, Cary. Cost effective computer-assisted legal research, or when two are better than one. *Online* 10(6)1986 83-89

Harrison, Beverly and Russell, Gordon (eds). Focus on databases: Searching full-text databases: the good, the bad and the ugly. *Canadian Law Libraries/Bibliothèques de droit canadiennes*. 15(4) 1990 216 15

Harrison, Beverly and Russell, Gordon (eds). Focus on databases: Use the Abridgment or search online: Is the online search a viable alternative? *Canadian Law Libraries/Bibliothèques de droit canadiennes*. 15(1) 1990 32-3

Hood, Howard A. CD-ROM Products for Law Libraries: NELLCO's Union Catalog. *International Journal of Legal Information* 19(1) 1991 36-38

Kinsock, John E. *Legal Databases Online: LEXIS® and WESTLAW®.* Littleton, Colorado: Libraries Unlimited, 1985

*The Lawyer's Guide to the Online Galaxy: legal research and communication using computers.* Edited by Kate Welsh. Edmonton, Alberta: Legal Education Society of Alberta, 1991

*Learning LEXIS®: A Handbook for Modern Legal Research.* Dayton, Ohio: Mead Data Central, Inc., 1990

*LEXIS® Libraries Guide.* Dayton, Ohio: Mead Data Central, Inc., 2 vols., 1990

Marshall, Denis S. The history of computer-assisted legal research in Canada. *In Law Libraries in Canada* edited by Joan N. Fraser. Toronto: Carswell, 1988. pp 103-15

Marshall, Denis S. An introduction to Canadian legal research. *Law Library Journal.* 81(3) 1989 465-488

Morgan, Keith. The law library and the new technology. *Canadian Law Libraries/Bibliothèques de droit canadiennes.* 15(3) 1990 111-115

NELLCO (Harvard, Yale, etc.) Card Catalog on CD-ROM announced. *Trends in Law Library Management and Technology* 3(7) 1990 5

Pritchard, Teresa N. West's CD-ROMs. *Trends in Law Library Management and Technology* 2(9) 1989 1-3

*QUICKSEARCH: user's manual and database description manual.* Ottawa: QL Systems Limited, 1988 (looseleaf)

*Searching Canadian law online: a beginner's guide.* Edited by Johanne A.C. Blenkin, Robert T. Franson. Vancouver, B.C.: The Continuing Legal Education Society of British Columbia, 1991

Silverstein, Steven H. An Index Model for Query Formulation. *Legal Reference Services Quarterly* 3 1990 115

*SOQUIJ en ligne.* Montreal: SOQUIJ 1(1) 1990- (irregular)

User ratings of information retrieval services. *DATAPRO On-Line Services News* July 1984

*WESTLAW: A Guide to Legal Research with Workbook.* St. Paul, Minnesota: West Publishing Company, 1986

*WESTLAW Reference Manual.* St. Paul, Minnesota: West Publishing Company, 1986

# 13 Business and economics: United Kingdom

*Jacqueline Cropley*

## INTRODUCTION

Business databases offer a wide range of information on management and operational issues. There has been extensive growth in the number of business files over the last few years, covering numerous sources. In general the databases have evolved from a hard copy equivalent. The recent trend has been to load the full text of business publications online. In addition there are some key databases which do not exist in hard copy.

A prime characteristic of business research is the need to obtain information quickly. For this reason, users have been highly responsive to full-text and directory databases where all the available information can be retrieved immediately at the terminal. Several important data files provide abstracted information, but these also tend to be informative, digesting the main points of the end product. Truly bibliographic databases, which just index material or give indicative abstracts, are now rare and less used. The trend is towards one stop shopping, where the user can obtain the direct answer to an enquiry online.

In addition to supplying the basic information in full, many databases come equipped with software which permits its further utilization. This is especially the case with numeric information. The main economic sources have long supplied modelling and graphics facilities as standard, and this practice is now extending to the more structured company files. Ease of use and quick retrieval is becoming more important than sophisticated facilities.

## TYPES OF BUSINESS INFORMATION

The main types of information aimed at the business arena are:

- Company information. This includes principal directory information about a company, usually based on material lodged at Companies House or The International Stock Exchange. Details of ownership, directors, trading address, business history, product range, subsidiaries, and share structure are complemented by extensive financial information. This covers the company's capital structure, its accounting periods, dates of accounts filed, and balance sheet and profit and loss details.
- Credit status information. Financial and directory information for a company is again given, and is supplemented by a range of detail bearing on a company's credit-worthiness. This is compiled from official records and from reports based on the organization's trading history. Legal charges and judgements are recorded. The company's payment record is analysed. Credit databases contain recommendations on credit limits and whether guarantees should be sought. Similar information is available on individuals. Credit data are highly sensitive and can only be supplied to restricted categories of users.
- News information. With wide coverage of the United Kingdom and international business press, news services can be used to obtain snapshots of company activity and chronological events, as well as surveys and analyses. Broadly searchable on any topic, they contain a wide variety of material of potential business impact.
- Marketing information. These databases are mainly product-oriented. Many are aimed at the advertising and marketing professions, and give extensive detail on product launches, branding, market share and media activity.
- Industry information. This covers reviews, analyses and news on industrial sectors, outlining principal companies, sector activity and developments. Trade, production and import/export statistics are complemented by analytical breakdowns.
- Business opportunities. These contain details on invitations to tender for business and on sources of finance, together with contact details. Events such as exhibitions are also covered. Databases outlining and analysing regulatory changes can be used to establish the operating frameworks.
- Management databases. Issues of broad management concern are included in specialist and general databases, covering planning, finance, personnel, administration, legislation, and organizational activity.
- People. Information on individuals ranges from listings of directorships for executives through to profiles, appointments and reviews of business involvement.
- Economic information. This covers the main economic statistics, using both official and analytical sources, sometimes reaching back over forty years, as well as forecasting services. Textual services give commentary and analysis at both macroeconomic and microeconomic levels. There are databases covering economic theory as well as the analysis of politics and policy.
- Financial markets. The stock markets, international capital and money markets are covered extensively through statistical, real-time, and news services.

## THE ONLINE SEARCH

Because of the high perceived value of business information, databases in this area tend to be highly priced. The information is usually required quickly, and searching can be highly interactive, as the nature of a business enquiry may change in the light of information obtained.

Business databases are often packaged to meet defined user demands. Many are targeted at the originating enquirer rather than at an information intermediary. This means that attempts have been made to make the data easy to retrieve. The software used to interrogate the database is either formatted in menus which guide the user through the search, or uses a small range of fairly simple commands. This does sometimes limit the flexibility and sophistication which might be required if serious information research is needed, but it provides an easy entry point to the data for routine and speculative searching. Some databases offer alternative search methods according to the degree of experience or personal preference of the user. The existence of menus or simple searching techniques has meant that it is now possible to retrieve data from a broader range of services than used to be the case. Formerly the need to learn several complex command languages acted as a real barrier. Pricing structures permit browsing through general subject areas, instead of constantly demanding precise searching.

## Constructing an online search

It is important to work out the search strategy before going online. To get the best out of a database the searcher needs to be free to concentrate on the implications of the results, without having to ponder over the next command. Many business databases have a high time charge once the user is logged in, which means that thinking time or inefficient searching may prove expensive.

Some databases are much more structured than others. Data are posted in fields, or are indexed or coded. Using the predefined structure can greatly improve the search results. Business information is riddled with soft, imprecise terminology. The use of codes or restricting a search term to a particular part of the record can be of considerable assistance in homing in on relevant information. With so many business databases now on offer, the main problem is often the reduction of a surfeit of information to manageable proportions. This is particularly the case with full-text databases. Even a superficially specific search term, such as a company name, may generate a response full of passing references as well as material of direct relevance. Searches on subjects such as the shipping industry will probably be easier if a sector code can be used, to avoid loose usage of the word 'shipping' to mean general distribution. There are many words to describe motor vehicles, most of which are used in conjunction with components as well as the finished product. Words such as 'bond' or 'spring' have various meanings according to context.

The underlying purpose for the enquiry may be different from that originally expressed. Users have expectations for the possibility of retrieving data which influence the way they frame their requests. This may lead to results which are too broad, for example asking for a full set of financial figures for a company, when just a particular financial ratio was required. This may have been already calculated on the database, or software may be available to present the information in that format, to avoid the user having to work it out. Alternatively, the search may be too narrow. A request for a currency exchange rate may indicate the enquirer is planning to convert a series of figures to establish a comparison or ranking which could be obtained directly.

Determine how current the information must be. The latest financial return for a company may be too out-of-date for the purpose. Checking the last date the accounts were filed saves wasting time and money retrieving old information, so that another source can be tried instead. The most recent economic statistic from a news report may be more useful than a twelve-month time series which takes two months to update.

Ascertain the deadline for information. Lengthy searches or comprehensive reports may be useless if the user does not have time to digest the results. Credit data can be updated on request if a few days' delay can be tolerated.

Consider using the information iteratively. Think what the initial search may reveal, and how that may broaden the enquirer's interests. Confirmation that an individual is a director of a given company may be followed by a request for his other directorships. A reference to a company's growing interest in a particular sector may provoke a search for the major companies involved in that industry. Pursuing the enquiry or saving the search so that it can be retrieved and expanded later can reduce the overall cost.

Think about the reasons for the results obtained. Databases are neither perfect nor entirely predictable. Words are misspellt, indexing is not always clear, information appears in unexpected places. If the results are less than might have been expected expand the search or try another strategy. Remember also that a small number of relevant pieces of information is likely to be more useful than a large amount of unfocused material.

## BUSINESS DATABASES

### Company databases

A significant feature of the last few years has been the build-up of extensive data files on British companies. Basic directory data can be found on all the million or more companies registered at Companies House. This covers the name, registered address, registered number, and date of the latest accounts filed. ICC, Jordan and Sons Limited and Infocheck are major providers of this information.

In addition these suppliers provide detailed financial information on large companies, which is taken from their financial returns or annual reports. ICC is available directly from the company itself, and in varying levels also through Data-Star, DIALOG, Guardian Business Information (CCN), Global Report and Datastream, which was the first host for financial information on unquoted companies. Jordans, again available directly, is also accessible through Pergamon Financial Data Services (PFDS). Infocheck can be accessed directly, and through Data-Star, and as a gateway product, for example, through FT Profile.

Jordans' data is also found on CD-ROM, in the form of FAME from CD-ROM Publishing. Here it is accompanied by financial analysis software. CD-ROMs giving financial data also include LOTUS ONE SOURCE, from Lotus, using Extel data, and DISCLOSURE EUROPE from Disclosure, which is currently expanding its data content. Lotus's product has been constructed to interface directly with Lotus spreadsheet software. Extel provides company financial data through the diskette-based MICROEXSTAT, which again comes with analytical facilities.

At extra cost, Datastream information can be used with a simple graphics package for better presentation. DATALINE from Reuter:file provides financial data with basic modelling features.

Many of the well known hard copy company directories are now online. Most significant is KOMPASS ONLINE, from Reed Publications, covering the full range of Reed's directories. Included are the *Kompass Register*, which gives extensive details of companies' products and services, *Directory of Directors*, and *UK Exporters*. This information is also available on the KOMPASS CD-ROM. Pergamon Financial Data Services offers KEY BRITISH ENTERPRISES and WHO OWNS WHOM, listing companies' parentage and subsidiaries, both published by Dun and Bradstreet Limited.

### *Uses of company databases*

Information is readily retrievable by searching on company name, as it is in hard copy. The advantages of the online services are greater frequency of update in many cases and the ability to print out the data in a desired format.

In addition, company databases are regularly used for screening purposes - to compile a list of companies conforming to specific criteria.

### *Investigating individual companies*

For the purposes of example, the Jordans database, accessed through FT Profile, is used here to demonstrate a search for an individual company. The database is updated weekly, and grows by approximately fifty companies per week. A company record is updated whenever new documents or annual reports are filed at Companies House, or when changes are reported in the *London* or *Edinburgh Gazettes*. The file covers non-financial companies with a turnover above one million pounds, or pre-tax profits of fifty thousand pounds or minimum shareholder funds of one million pounds, plus those companies analysed as the result of a Jordans' business survey.

The quickest way to search for company information is to use the company registered number which, being unique, ensures that the correct organization is identified. If the number is not known the name can be used as the search term. The database offers a list of companies with that name or similar from which the desired company can be selected. This is a standard approach with most company financial databases. A full JORDANWATCH record is displayed as Search 13.1.

## Search 13.1: JORDANWATCH search and full company record on FT Profile

```
select jdn
Jordans Company Reports

    - for help with interpretation and advice on the information included
      and on the currency of update of the information please call Jordans on
      071-235-2030. The special terms and conditions relating to the data
      can be seen by typing 'DETAIL JDN' when online.

    "#" represents POUNDS STERLING on ASCII/teletype terminals
CHARGE GROUP(s): Q4 >
>

get pentos@headline

            6 ITEMS RETRIEVED >
>

h all              .
SORTING

  1   JDN  00032539 PENTOS PUBLIC LIMITED COMPANY
  2   JDN  01959624 PENTOS OFFICE FURNITURE PUBLIC LIMITED COMPANY
  3   JDN  00363306 PENTOS RETAILING GROUP LIMITED
  4   JDN  00939506 PENTOS OFFICE FURNITURE (RIPLEY) LIMITED
  5   JDN  00939506 PENTOS OFFICE FURNITURE LIMITED
  6   JDN  00300255 PENTOS GARDEN AND LEISURE PRODUCTS GROUP LIMITED

Copyright (C) 'Jordans' 1988, 1989, 1990 >
>

nobreak
YOUR TEXT WILL BE DISPLAYED WITHOUT PAGE BREAKS
>

text 1

  1   JDN 00032539 PENTOS PUBLIC LIMITED COMPANY

        SECTOR . . . . . HOLDING COMPANY RETAILING OFFICE FURNITURE
        SIC. . . . . . . 83962  65300
        Registered Number. . . . . 00032539    Incorporated . . . . .09/10/1890
        Latest Annual Return . . . 20/06/89     Accounting Ref. Date . . . 31/12
        Latest Accounts Filed. . . 31/12/89     Authorised Capital . #13,600,000
        Issued Capital . . . .   #10,400,000    Audit Fee. . . . . . . .#100,000
        Number of employees. . . . .  2,726     Total Remuneration . #26,100,000
        Soc. Security Cost . . . #2,600,000     Pension Cost . . . . . . . . .

This Company is officially listed on the Stock Exchange

        Registered Office     :   New Bond Street House, 1 New Bond Street, London
                                  W1Y 9PE
        R.O.Change Pending    :   13/11/85
        Trading Address(es)   :   New Bond St. Hse., 1-5 New Bond St., London,
                                   Gtr London W1Y.
                                  Tel: 071 499 3484
```

**Search 13.1:** (cont.)

```
Auditors              :    COOPERS & LYBRAND
Bankers               :    BARCLAYS BANK PLC
Secured Indebtedness  :    #0 as at 20/06/89
                           #0      23/06/87

Changes indicated by documents filed are as follows:
                      20/08/87      Change in Mem & Arts
                      29/06/90      Change in Share Capital
                      06/09/89      Change in Directors
                      10/05/85      Charge lodged
                      16/03/87      Mem.Satisfaction Lodged
A date is only displayed if there has been a new document filed since 1984
```

PROFIT AND LOSS ACCOUNT
-----------------------

|                               | 12/89 #'000 Consolid'd | 12/88 #'000 Consolid'd | 12/87 #'000 Consolid'd |
|-------------------------------|------------------------|------------------------|------------------------|
| Turnover                      | 143,200                | 120,800                | 90,012                 |
| Profit/Loss before interest   | 15,200                 | 12,400                 | 8,564                  |
| Interest Paid                 | 2,700-                 | 1,400-                 | 759-                   |
| Profit/Loss before Tax        | 12,500                 | 11,000                 | 7,805                  |
| Tax Charge/Credit             | 2,900-                 | 2,400-                 | 1,414                  |
| Profit/Loss after Tax         | 9,600                  | 8,600                  | 6,391                  |
| Minority Interests            |                        |                        |                        |
| Extraordinary Items           |                        | 1,000                  |                        |
| Profit/Loss  for  Period      | 9,600                  | 9,600                  | 6,391                  |
| Dividends                     | 2,300-                 | 1,400-                 | 1,009                  |
| Other  Appropriations         |                        |                        |                        |
| Retained Profit/Loss          | 7,300                  | 8,200                  | 5,382                  |

BALANCE SHEET
-------------

|                                      | 12/89   | 12/88   | 12/87   |
|--------------------------------------|---------|---------|---------|
| Fixed Assets                         | 54,900  | 41,700  | 27,595  |
| Tangible                             | 53,300  | 40,500  | 27,595  |
| Intangible                           |         |         |         |
| Investments & Others                 | 1,600   | 1,200   |         |
| Current Assets                       | 59,500  | 51,100  | 43,657  |
| Stock/W.I.P.                         | 38,100  | 32,700  | 25,590  |
| Debtors                              | 19,700  | 2,000   | 12,918  |
| Investments                          |         |         |         |
| Bank & Deposits                      | 400     | 4,100   | 4,332   |
| Others                               | 1,300   | 12,300  | 817     |
| Current Liabilities                  | 62,500- | 52,700- | 40,219- |
| Creditors                            | 35,900- | 35,300- | 27,594- |
| Loans/Overdraft                      | 12,300- | 7,700-  | 3,990-  |
| Others                               | 14,300- | 9,700-  | 8,635-  |
| Net Current Assets/Liabilities       | 3,000-  | 1,600-  | 3,438   |
| Assets  Less  Current  Liabilities   | 51,900  | 40,100  | 31,033  |
| Long  Term  Debt                     | 1,000-  | 1,600-  | 1,616-  |

**Search 13.1:** (cont.)

| | | | |
|---|---|---|---|
| Other Non-Current Liabilities | | 3,700- | 1,300- |
| 728- | | | |
| Minority Interests | | | 33- |
| | --------- | --------- | --------- |
| Total | 47,200 | 37,200 | 28,656 |
| | ========= | ========= | ========= |

RATIOS AND TRENDS
------------------

| Balance Sheet Ratios | 89/12 | 88/12 | 87/12 |
|---|---|---|---|
| Current Ratio | .95 | .97 | 1.09 |
| Acid Test Liquidity Ratio | .34 | .35 | .45 |
| Shareholder Liquidity Ratio | 10.04 | 12.83 | 12.06 |
| Solvency Ratio (%) | 41.26 | 40.09 | 40.22 |
| Gearing (%) | 36.02 | 28.49 | 22.22 |
| Share Funds/Employee (#'s) | 17,315 | 15,657 | 16,009 |
| Working Capital/Employee (#'s) | 8,034 | 253- | 6,097 |
| Total Assets/Employee (#'s) | 41,966 | 39,057 | 39,806 |

| Profitability Ratios | 89/12 | 88/12 | 87/12 |
|---|---|---|---|
| Profit Margin (%) | 8.73 | 9.11 | 8.67 |
| Return on Shareholders Funds (%) | 26.48 | 29.57 | 27.24 |
| Return on Capital Employed (%) | 24.08 | 27.43 | 25.15 |
| Return on Total Assets (%) | 10.93 | 11.85 | 10.95 |
| Stock Turnover | 3.76 | 3.69 | 3.52 |
| Debtors Turnover | 7.27 | 60.40 | 6.97 |
| Net Assets Turnover | 2.76 | 3.01 | 2.90 |
| Salaries/Turnover (%) | 18.23 | 17.63 | 15.56 |
| Turnover per Employee (#'s) | 52,531 | 50,842 | 50,286 |
| Average Remuneration (#'s) | 9,574 | 8,965 | 7,826 |
| Profit per Employee (#'s) | 4,585 | 4,630 | 4,360 |

| Balance Sheet Changes & Trends | 89/12 from 88/12 | | from 87/12 | |
|---|---|---|---|---|
| | (#,000's) | % | (#,000's) | % |
| Fixed Assets | 13,200 | 31.65 | 14,105 | 51.11 |
| Current Assets | 8,400 | 16.44 | 7,443 | 17.05 |
| Stock | 5,400 | 16.51 | 7,110 | 27.78 |
| Debtors | 17,700 | 885.00 | 10,918- | 84.52- |
| Total Assets | 21,600 | 23.28 | 21,548 | 30.24 |
| Current Liabilities | 9,800 | 18.60 | 12,481 | 31.03 |
| Creditors | 600 | 1.70 | 7,706 | 27.93 |
| Bank Overdraft | 4,600 | 59.74 | 3,710 | 92.98 |
| Long Term Liabilities | 1,800 | 62.07 | 523 | 22.00 |

| Profitability Changes & Trends | 89/12 from 88/12 | | from 87/12 | |
|---|---|---|---|---|
| | (#,000's) | % | (#,000's) | % |
| Turnover | 22,400 | 18.54 | 30,788 | 34.20 |
| Profit Before Tax | 1,500 | 13.64 | 3,195 | 40.94 |
| Interest Paid | 1,300 | 92.86 | 641 | 84.45 |
| Number of Employees | 350 | 14.73 | 586 | 32.74 |

**Search 13.1:** (cont.)

```
PRINCIPAL DIRECTORS
_____


Mr T.A. Maher        CHAIRMAN
And 004 other directors

ASSOCIATED COMPANIES
_____


Ultimate Holding Co.
NONE

UK Subsidiary Companies
AR MOWBRAY & CO. LIMITED                      00077496
RYMAN LIMITED                                 00081485
PENTOS PUBLISHING GROUP LIMITED               00094574
HK LEWIS & CO LIMITED                         00140815
GEORGE WEBB BOOKBINDERS LIMITED               00141225
VOUCHSOURCE LIMITED                           00188110
RYMAN DOWDESWELL LIMITED                       00244767
THORNBERS (UNITY WORKS) LIMITED               00262859
MESSENGERS (BIRMINGHAM) LIMITED               00273881
PENTOS GARDEN AND LEISURE PRODUCTS GROUP      00300255
PENTOS RETAILING GROUP LIMITED                00363306
W STRAKER LIMITED                             00423192
PENTOS CONSTRUCTION GROUP LIMITED             00444689
THORNBERS (GREET) LIMITED                     00491198
ATHENA INTERNATIONAL LIMITED                  00933506
PENTOS OFFICE FURNITURE (RIPLEY) LIMITED      00939506
PENTOS ASSETS LIMITED                         01080127
PARAMACE LIMITED                              01579373
PENTOS OFFICE FURNITURE PUBLIC LIMITED C      01959624

Jordan Information Services

Copyright (C) 'Jordans' 1988, 1989, 1990 >

>

end

TIME IN JDN 02 MINS 21 SECS - TOTAL SESSION TIME 6 MINS 11 SECS
```

Within Profile, data are displayed eighteen lines at a time. The user is then given the option to stop the display or to continue. Use of the "Nobreak" command gives an uninterrupted display. Alternatively the 'Break' command could be set at a lower or higher level, for instance, 'Break 12' or 'Break 28', for shorter or longer batches of text.

Whereas this sort of financial information can also be obtained fairly readily in hard copy, an advantage of the databases is that they can be used for screening purposes. By defining a set of criteria it is possible to identify companies which would be of interest. These can be used for sales and marketing purposes and competitor analysis, and are a basis for identifying potential mergers and acquisitions candidates.

If the enquirer interested in Pentos wanted to look for other retail booksellers as well, it would be easy to create a list from Jordans' data. A straightforward search would define the companies by size and location. In this example FAME CD-ROM is used (Searches 13.2 - 13.4). This is a CD-ROM database, updated monthly. The search is conducted through menus; each new screen is indicated by a lower frame.

Menu-driven searching is almost always a longer exercise than the command language approach shown in the previous example. The following is given in full to demonstrate how it is possible to sift through company financial data even when one is unsure what might be available. The detailed menus give all the options and define the enquiry precisely. The choices made are printed here in bold text. The disc itself displays the data in colour, with selections displayed in reverse video. The searcher requests companies in the retail bookseller industry with trading outlets in London and an annual turnover over ten million pounds.

## Search 13.2: FAME CD-ROM company search

```
                    FAME Financial Analysis Made Easy
      JORDANS DATABASE OF Accounts of Major Public & Private British Companies
                                 version 3.0
           FAME Retrieval Software: Copyright (c) Bureau van Dijk, 1990
                   Database: Copyright (c) JORDAN & SONS, 1990



                            Would you like to

      1.        Search by Company Name
      2.        Search by Registered Company Number
      3.        Search by Other Criteria
      4.        Select only Ultimate Holding Companies
      5.        Select all Subsidiaries
      6.        Go to FAME Financial Analysis Software
      7.        Record/Delete a Search Strategy
      8.        Load a Search Strategy
      9.        Printer Setup
      A.        Return to DOS

                Move            Select
```

```
                                Search by

      1.        SIC Code or Trade Description
      2.        Company Type
      3.        Date of Incorporation
      4.        Geographical Area
      5.        Financial Data
      6.        Accounts filed after 31 March 1990
      7.        Number of Employees
      8.        Ratios
      9.        Trends
      A.        Directors
      B.        Bankers
      C.        Auditors
      D.        Holding Company
      E.        Subsidiary

                Move            Select      Esc Go Back
```

```
                                Search by

      1.        SIC Code
      2.        SIC Description Index
      3.        Trade Description

                Move      Select           Esc Go Back
```

**Search 13.2:** (cont.)

```
Enter the Activity          BOOKKEEPING MACHINE MANUFACTURING      33010
You are searching for:      BOOKMAKER                              97912
                            BOOKSELLER, RETAIL                     65300
                            BOOT AND SHOE BOARD MANUFACTURING      47109
BOOK                        BOOT AND SHOE PATTERN MAKING AND DESIGN 45100
                            BOOT AND SHOE TIP AND PROTECTOR (MALLEA) 31110
                            BOOT CLOSING                           45100
                            BOOT LACE, BRAIDED, MANUFACTURING      43982
                            BOOT LAST, IRON, MANUFACTURING         31110
                            BOOT STIFFENER MANUFACTURING           45100
                            BOOT TREE, WOODEN, MANUFACTURING       46500
Selection in progress       BOOT UPPER MANUFACTURING               45100
                            BOOTBLACK                              98902
                            BOOTES, KNITTED, MANUFACTURING         43632
                            BOOTS AND SHOES, RETAIL DEALING IN     64600
                            BORER (MINING MACHINERY) MANUFACTURING 32510
Number of Activities        BORING (CIVIL ENGINEERING)             50200
Selected:         1         BORING MACHINE (METAL -CUTTING) MANUFAC 32221
Number of Companies         BORON CARBIDE ABRASIVE GRAIN MANUFACTUR 24600
Selected:       752         BOROUGH COUNCIL                        91120
                            BORSTAL                                91200
* All    Tab New entry
PgDn  PgUp  Home      Select      Correct    F2 Continue   Esc Go Back
```

```
1)   Activity : BOOKSELLER, RETAIL                                    752

                            Do you want to

     1.    Continue the Search
     2.    Display, Print or Transfer the Records Found
     3.    Show the Search Strategy
     4.    End the Current Search

                  Move          Select
```

```
                       Continue the search

     1.    Narrow down the Current Search
     2.    Broaden the Current Search
     3.    Exclude Companies from the Current Search

     Move              Select            Esc Go Back
```

```
                                         Narrowing down (stage 2)

                            Search by

     1.    SIC Code or Trade Description
     2.    Company Type
     3.    Date of Incorporation
     4.    Geographical Area
     5.    Financial Data
     6.    Accounts filed after 31 March 1990
     7.    Number of Employees
     8.    Ratios
     9.    Trends
```

**Search 13.2:** (cont.)

```
    A.      Directors
    B.      Bankers
    C.      Auditors
    D.      Holding Company
    E.      Subsidiary

    Move            Select          Esc Go Back
```

```
                                        Narrowing down (stage 2)

                        Search by

    1.      Registered Office Address
    2.      Trading Address
    3.      Telephone Area or Code of Registered Office or Trading Address

    Move            Select          Esc Go Back
```

```
                                        Narrowing down (stage 2)

                        Search by

    1.      Postcode Areas and Post Town
    2.      Postcode
    3.      Counties
    4.      Economic Planning Regions

    Move            Select          Esc Go Back
```

```
                                        Narrowing down (stage 2)


                                        County

                                        LONDON
    Select a county:                    MERSEYSIDE
        LONDON                          MID GLAMORGAN
                                        MIDDLESEX
                                        MIDLOTHIAN
                                        MORAYSHIRE
                                        NAIRNSHIRE
                                        NORFOLK
                                        NORTH HUMBERSIDE
                                        NORTH YORKSHIRE
    Would you like to                   NORTHAMPTONSHIRE
                                        NORTHERN IRELAND
1.  End the current stage of search     NORTHUMBERLAND
2.  Select another county               NOTTINGHAMSHIRE
                                        OXFORDSHIRE
                                        PEEBLESSHIRE

                                                140
    Move            Select          Esc Go Back
```

**Search 13.2:** (cont.)

```
                          Do you want to

        1.   Continue the Search
        2.   Display, Print or Transfer the Records Found
        3.   Show the Search Strategy
        4.   End the Current Search

        Move                Select
```

```
                       Continue the search

        1.   Narrow down the Current Search
        2.   Broaden the Current Search
        3.   Exclude Companies from the Current Search

        Move                Select           Esc Go Back
```

```
                                        Narrowing down (stage 3)


                          Search by

        1.   SIC Code or Trade Description
        2.   Company Type
        3.   Date of Incorporation
        4.   Geographical Area
        5.   Financial Data
        6.   Accounts filed after 31 March 1990
        7.   Number of Employees
        8.   Ratios
        9.   Trends
        A.   Directors
        B.   Bankers
        C.   Auditors
        D.   Holding Company
        E.   Subsidiary

        Move                Select           Esc Go Back
```

```
                                        Narrowing down (stage 3)


                          Search by

        1.   Sales - Turnover
        2.   Profit (Loss) before Taxation
        3.   Interest Paid
        4.   Net Tangible Assets
        5.   Fixed Assets
        6.   Current Assets
        7.   Current Liabilities
        8.   Long Term Debt
        9.   Stocks and W.I.P.
        A.   Debtors
        B.   Creditors
        C.   Total Remuneration
        D.   Audit Fee
        E.   Pension Contribution
```

**Search 13.2:** (cont.)

```
     F.   Shareholders Funds

     Move              Select          Esc Go Back
```

```
                                        Narrowing down (stage 3)


                              Search by

     1.   Average (all available years)
     2.   Latest year for which data is available
     3.   From 1st April 1989 to 31st March 1990 figures

     Move              Select          Esc Go Back
```

```
 Accounts: Sales - Turnover              Narrowing down (stage 3)

                                                            U T M
                                       Minimum value : 10
                                       Maximum value :


     U : Units
     T : Thousands
     M : Millions

                              Search by

     1.   Average (all available years)
     2.   Latest year for which data is available
     3.   From 1st April 1989 to 31st March 1990 figures

                     Move              Select
```

```
 3)   Accounts: Sales - Turnover (to 3/89):                    23
      Above 10,000,000
      (29.9 % of the companies give the data)
      (Narrowing down of the search)

 Do you want to

      1.   Continue the Search
      2.   Display, Print or Transfer the Records Found
      3.   Show the Search Strategy
      4.   End the Current Search

                     Move              Select
```

It is important to note in Search 13.2 that not all the company records give 1989 turnover details. This is a pitfall of screening. A blank field gives a negative result, even though the company actually does fit the criteria specified. Allowance must be made for this if the results are to be wholly accurate.

At this stage, with twenty-three company trading addresses identified, the user can request a set of printed labels to use for a mailshot (Search 13.3). These can be addressed to a specific job title in order to reach the right person in the target organization. Before printing, the companies can be sorted by various criteria, so that the most interesting - in this case the five most profitable - can be contacted first.

## Search 13.3: FAME search continued to produce mailing labels

```
            Would you like to display, print or transfer

        1.  Complete Company Records
        2.  Company Names
        3.  Company Profiles
        4.  Labels for Mailing (Registered Office Address)
        5.  Labels for Mailing (Trading Address)
        6.  SIC Codes and Trade Description
        7.  Profit and Loss Accounts and Number of Employees
        8.  Balance Sheet
        9.  Ratios and Trends
        A.  Directors
        B.  Holding Company
        C.  Subsidiaries
        D.  Miscellaneous Data
        E.  Data for FAME Financial Analysis Software
        F.  Data for Standard or Tailor-made Reports
        G.  Data for an ASCII file
        H.  Data into another format

        Move                Select            Esc Go Back
```

```
            Do you want a label addressed to

        1.  The company
        2.  Each director
        3.  A function to be specified

        ATT:  Managing Director

        Move                Select Esc      Go Back
```

```
            Do you want to

        1.  Display the Records
        2.  Print the Records
        3.  Transfer the Records
        4.  Sort the Records

        Move                Select            Esc Go Back
```

```
            Do you want to sort by

        1.  Name
        2.  Registered Company Number
        3.  Sales - Turnover
        4.  Profit (Loss) before Taxation
        5.  Net Tangible Assets
        6.  Shareholders Funds
        7.  Profit Margin
        8.  Return on Shareholders Fund
        9.  Return on Capital Employed
        A.  Liquidity
        B.  Gearing
```

**Search 13.3:** (cont.)

```
        C.   Number of Employees
        D.   Auditor
        E.   Registered Office Postcode

        Move              Select         Esc Go Back
```

```
                          Sort by

        1.   Average (all available years)
        2.   Latest year for which data is available
        3.   From 1st April 1989 to 31st March 1990 figures

        Move              Select      Esc Go Back
```

```
                   Do you want to sort in

        1.   Ascending  Sequence
        2.   Descending Sequence

        Move              Select      Esc Go Back
```

```
                      Do you want to

        1.   Display the Records
        2.   Print the Records
        3.   Transfer the Records
        4.   Sort the Records

        Move              Select      Esc Go Back
```

```
                      Select Records

        1.   All records
        2.   From Record ...
        3.   To Record ...
        4.   From Record ... to Record ...
        5.   One Record

        Move              Select      Esc Go Back
```

```
  To Record ... (min = 1, max = 23)

                              Maximum value :   5


                      Select Records

        1.   All records
        2.   From Record ...
        3.   To Record ...
        4.   From Record ... to Record ...
        5.   One Record

        Move              Select      Esc Go Back
```

**Search 13.3:** (cont.)

```
Do you want the software to test the status of your printer ?

   1.   Yes (to use for most recent printers)
   2.   No (in this case we will assume that the printer is always ready)

   Move              Select           Esc Go Back
```

```
REGISTERED OFFICE ADDRESS:

ATT: Managing Director
REED INTERNATIONAL P.L.C
6 CHESTERFIELD GARDENS
LONDON
W1A 1EJ

ATT: Managing Director
W H SMITH LIMITED
STRAND HOUSE
7 HOLBURN PLACE
LONDON
SW1W 8NR

ATT: Managing Director
W H SMITH GROUP PLC
STRAND HOUSE
7 HOLBEIN PLACE
LONDON
SW1W 8NR


ATT: Managing Director
PENTOS PUBLIC LIMITED COMPANY
NEW BOND STREET HOUSE
1 NEW BOND STREET
LONDON
W1Y 9PE


ATT: Managing Director
PROJECT OFFICE FURNITURE PLC
HAMLET GREEN
HAVERMILL
SUFFOLK
CB9 8QJ
```

Armed with the labels the searcher may want some further information to consider while awaiting a response to the mailshot. Ratio analysis gives a quick guide to the standing of a company. If the searching company is a potential supplier it could be concerned with the target company's ability to meet its debts. An acquisition predator might be aiming to pounce on an organization with cash flow problems. For these the current ratios field, showing working capital or the ease with which current assets can meet current liabilities, is a useful starting point.

$$\text{Current ratio} = \frac{\text{current assets}}{\text{current liabilities}}$$

Jordans supplies the most common ratios for direct searching. Others can be calculated using the FAME Financial Analysis Software supplied as part of the CD-ROM package. Calculated ratios can also be created in other databases, such as ICC's company database on Datastream. Ratios may be high or low through an imbalance on either side of the comparison. Rather than take the raw figures at face value, the underlying issues should be checked.

It is simple to produce a list of the desired companies on FAME, giving their name and registered number (Search 13.4). The registered number can be used at a later date to retrieve further material on the companies.

## Search 13.4: Company list on FAME

```
3)    Accounts: Sales - Turnover (to 3/89):              23
      Above 10,000,000
      (29.9 % of the companies give the data)
      (Narrowing down of the search)


                        Do you want to

   1.   Continue the Search
   2.   Display, Print or Transfer the Records Found
   3.   Show the Search Strategy
   4.   End the Current Search

        Move          Select
```

```
                    Continue the search

   1.   Narrow down the Current Search
   2.   Broaden the Current Search
   3.   Exclude Companies from the Current Search

   Move              Select          Esc Go Back
```

```
                                    Narrowing down (stage 4)


                        Search by

   1.   SIC Code or Trade Description
   2.   Company Type
   3.   Date of Incorporation
   4.   Geographical Area
   5.   Financial Data
   6.   Accounts filed after 31 March 1990
   7.   Number of Employees
   8.   Ratios
   9.   Trends
   A.   Directors
   B.   Bankers
   C.   Auditors
   D.   Holding Company
   E.   Subsidiary

   Move              Select          Esc Go Back
```

**Search 13.4:** (cont.)

```
                                              Narrowing down (stage 4)


                         Search by

   1.   Financial Ratios
   2.   Profitability Ratios

   Move              Select           Esc Go Back
```

```
                                              Narrowing down (stage 4)


                         Search by

   1.   Current ratio
   2.   Liquidity Ratio
   3.   Shareholder Liquidity Ratio
   4.   Solvency Ratio (%)
   5.   Gearing (%)
   6.   Share Funds per Employee
   7.   Working Capital per Employee
   8.   Total assets per Employee

   Move              Select           Esc Go Back
```

```
                                              Narrowing down (stage 4)


                         Search by

   1.   Average (all available years)
   2.   Latest year for which data is available
   3.   From 1st April 1989 to 31st March 1990 figures

   Move              Select           Esc Go Back
```

```
Financial Ratios: Current Ratio               Narrowing down (stage 4)

                                       Minimum value :
                                       Maximum value : 1.5

                         Search by

   1.   Average (all available years)
   2.   Latest year for which data is available
   3.   From 1st April 1989 to 31st March 1990 figures

   Move              Select           Esc Go Back
```

```
4) Financial Ratios; Current Ratio (to 03/89) :              16
Below 1.5
(100.00% of the companies give the data)
(Narrowing down of the search)

                       Do you want to
```

**Search 13.4:** (cont.)

```
    1.   Continue the Search
    2.   Display, Print or Transfer the Records Found
    3.   Show the Search Strategy
    4.   End the Current Search

         Move          Select
```

```
Would you like to display, print or transfer


    1.   Complete Company Records
    2.   Company Names
    3.   Company Profiles
    4.   Labels for Mailing (Registered Office Address)
    5.   Labels for Mailing (Trading Address)
    6.   SIC Codes and Trade Description
    7.   Profit and Loss Accounts and Number of Employees
    8.   Balance Sheet
    9.   Ratios and Trends
    A.   Directors
    B.   Holding Company
    C.   Subsidiaries
    D.   Miscellaneous Data

    E.   Data for FAME Financial Analysis Software
    F.   Data for Standard or Tailor-made Reports
    G.   Data for an ASCII file
    H.   Data into another format

    Move                Select           Esc Go Back
```

```
                       Do you want to

    1.   Display the Records
    2.   Print the Records
    3.   Transfer the Records
    4.   Sort the Records

    Move                Select           Esc Go Back
```

```
                       Select Records

    1.   All records
    2.   From Record ...
    3.   To Record ...
    4.   From Record ... to Record ...
    5.   One Record

    Move                Select           Esc Go Back
```

```
                    COMPANY NAMES :

Sorting criterion : None
        1   PENTOS PUBLIC LIMITED COMPANY
            00032539

        2   REED INTERNATIONAL P.L.C.
```

**Search 13.4:** (cont.)

```
              00077536

      3   W H SMITH LIMITED
          00237811

      4   PROJECT OFFICE FURNITURE PLC
          002353775

      5   W H SMITH GROUP PLC
          00471941

      6   SATEX LIMITED
          00473145

      7   OFFICE AND ELECTRONIC MACHINES P L C
          00477051

      8   AEG OLYMPIA (UK) LIMITED
          00529294

      9   BROTHER INTERNATIONAL EUROPE LIMITED
          00664172

     10   CONTINUOUS STATIONERY P L C
          00938016

     11   KARDEX SYSTEMS (UK) LIMITED
          00960163

     12   COPYGRAPHIC PLC
          00991049

     13   HUGIN SWEDA LIMITED
          01042296

     14   COTEVILLE LIMITED
          01111986

     15   CSS (SYSTEMS)LIMITED
          01555216

     16   SATEX GROUP PLC
          01992932

          PgDn   PgUp   Home   End     Move     Esc Go Back
```

```
 4) Financial Ratios; Current Ratio (to 03/89) :                    16
    Below 1.5
    (100.00% of the companies give the data)
    (Narrowing down of the search)

                          Do you want to

    1.        Continue the Search
    2.        Display, Print or Transfer the Records Found
    3.        Show the Search Strategy
    4.        End the Current Search

          Move      Select
```

**Search 13.4:** (cont.)

```
                        FAME Financial Analysis Made Easy
        JORDANS DATABASE OF Accounts of Major Public & Private British Companies
                                   version 3.0
            FAME Retrieval Software: Copyright (c) Bureau van Dijk, 1990
                    Database: Copyright (c) JORDAN & SONS, 1990



                             Would you like to

        1.         Search by Company Name
        2.         Search by Registered Company Number
        3.         Search by Other Criteria
        4.         Select only Ultimate Holding Companies
        5.         Select all Subsidiaries
        6.         Go to FAME Financial Analysis Software
        7.         Record/Delete a Search Strategy
        8.         Load a Search Strategy
        9.         Printer Setup
        A.         Return to DOS

             Move      Select
```

From the choices offered in the menus in this example, it can be seen that it is possible to search on a broad combination of data, for example to identify major subsidiary companies, newly formed or fast growing companies. The KOMPASS database, also available online or on CD-ROM, provides product information which permits business segments to be defined closely.

Once the desired companies have been identified, in addition to the normal convention of being able to repeat the search at regular intervals to obtain updated data, ICC and Jordans offer a company monitoring service whereby details are sent out whenever any changes are filed at Companies House. A microfiche of the company records can be ordered online. Both organizations provide extensive company information services in addition to their online data.

### Credit databases

Prior to its appearance online, credit information on companies was difficult to obtain. Most enquiries had to be conducted by recognized financial institutions. Now there are a variety of services, notably Dun and Bradstreet, UAPT Infolink, CCN and Advance Information.

The main difference between financial data from annual returns and that supplied on credit databases is its orientation. Credit data are tailored for the specific purpose of checking the financial standing of an organization in order to facilitate trade. They therefore contain a strong judgemental element, with credit ratings and opinions being a central feature. The accounts data furnished are principally a back-up to this.

Credit decisions are arrived at in varied ways. Some systems are based on credit-scoring techniques. Others rely strongly on trade references; the United Association for the Protection of Trade (UAPT) was established for the sharing of financial experience. The existence of court judgements and charges are also indicators of a company's trading record and ability to pay. Payment analysis records are compiled from reports from trading partners. The frequency of credit checks made on a company may be deemed significant. Credit reports exist where an enquiry has been made. This means that there are often data online for very small organizations which do not appear on the accounts-based databases. If there are no publicly available data, attempts may be made to build a picture by contacting the company itself, or by direct observation. It is possible to order a credit check online, or request that a report be updated. Some information suppliers remove out-of-date reports if they are not thought worthy of automatic renewal. Others leave them on, so that the date of compilation must be watched.

Because of the evaluative aspect, credit reports should be treated with caution. This is stressed by the information providers. Different sources may show totally divergent opinions on an organization's financial standing. There are many companies which appear on one database but not on another. Comparing records from two different credit agencies is not advisable because the criteria used are not the same.

Report formats for credit status tend to be standardized because it is important to see the whole picture. Looking at just one or two categories could be misleading and potentially damaging to a business relationship. It is dangerous, and usually impossible, to screen the data to build lists. The advantage of the structured reports is that most of the databases charge on a per report basis, so it is easy to estimate or allocate expenditure.

Credit reports contain much supplementary information or commentary not found in the accounts orientated databases. Now that they are widely available they can be used for many purposes other than credit checking. The information providers frequently offer reports at a lower unit cost the more that are used.

The example in Search 13.5 shows a search and standard report format from DUNSPRINT. Records are removed from this database when no longer current, so if there is material available it can be trusted to be up-to-date. Because of the sensitive nature of credit information this is not actual data on a genuine company, but an artificial reconstruction.

## Search 13.5: DUNSPRINT search and standard report

```
26/10/90 11:37
YOU ARE NOW ONLINE
TO DUN & BRADSTREET

ENTER ENQUIRY OR NEWS: MULSAND INDUSTRIES

 ENTER TOWN: POOLE

 ENTER COUNTRY CODE: UK

 ENTER REFERENCE OR CARRIAGE RETURN:

 MORE THAN ONE TOWN. POSSIBLE OPTIONS DISPLAYED BELOW.

    TOWN NAME                        POSTAL TOWN              COUNTY

    1  POOLE                         NANTWICH                 CHESHIRE
    2  POOLE                         POOLE                    DORSET
 ENTER SELECTION, NEW TOWN NAME OR CANCEL: 2

 NO MATCH ON THIS NAME.

 I=REQUEST BUSINESS INVESTIGATION
 V=ENQUIRY NAME VARIATION
 X=EXTENDED SEARCH ENTER
 SELECTION:X

 CHOOSE COUNTRY TO SEARCH
 EN=ENGLAND
 NI=NORTHERN IRELAND
 SC=SCOTLAND
 WA=WALES
 ENTER SELECTION: EN
```

**Search 13.5:** (cont.)

```
1     MULSAND INDUSTRIES (PURCHASING) 5 FORTUNE WAY  CHRISTCHU  293147896
2     MULSAND INDUSTRIES (U K) LTD    5 FORTUNE WAY  CHRISTCHU  230411537
3     MULSAND,MICHAEL,OVERSEAS LTD    53 HAMILTON PL LONDON     238678069
4     MULSITTER, F K                  3 MARK LA      LOUTH      226577054
5     MULSTHORPE,E,(BOURNE) LTD       31 MENTON ST   BOURNE     227537562
6     MULSTHORPE, E (BOURNE) LTD      31 MENTON ST   BOURNE     227537562  T
7     MULSTHORPE,E,(BOURNE) LTD       31 MENTON ST   BOURNE     227537562
8     MULSTHORPE, E (BOURNE) LTD      31 MENTON ST   BOURNE     227537562  T
```

```
I=REQUEST BUSINESS INVESTIGATION
V=ENQUIRY NAME VARIATION
ENTER 1 - 8, I OR V: 2
```

```
F=COMPREHENSIVE REPORT    A=ACCOUNTS ORDER        D=DUNS FINANCIAL PROFILE
S=STANDARD REPORT         B=DUNSMATCH             CAN=MOVE TO NEXT ENQUIRY
                                                  M=MAIL OPTIONS
```

```
ENTER SELECTION: S
```

```
PRINT NOW? ENTER Y OR N: Y
```

```
CONFIDENTIAL......THIS REPORT IS FURNISHED BY DUN & BRADSTREET LTD. IN STRICT
CONFIDENCE, AT YOUR REQUEST UNDER YOUR SUBSCRIPTION CONTRACT NO. 863-125267,
AND IS NOT TO BE DISCLOSED.
```

```
*IN DATE*
```

```
DUNS: 23-041-1537          STANDARD REPORT          DATE PRINTED 26 OCT 1990
```

```
MULSAND INDUSTRIES (U K) LTD                         RATING U
SUB OF: FAIRCROSS HOLLAND B V,
        AMSTERDAM,
        NETHERLANDS
5 FORTUNE WAY PRIORY IND PK
   CHRISTCHURCH
   DORSET BH23 4LD
   UK
```

```
TEL. 04252-72921                 BATHROOM & HSHLD ACCS MFRS
                                 SIC(S):    3079
```

```
       ANY AMOUNTS HEREAFTER ARE IN POUNDS STERLING UNLESS OTHERWISE STATED
```

```
SUMMARY
```

```
STARTED        1965          SALES         (EST) 4,000,000
DATE INC       1965          NET WORTH           406,453
LEGAL FORM     SEE BELOW     EMPLOYS             108
REG NO         836572        NOM CAP             50,000
CONDITION      GOOD          ISS CAP             ALL
TREND          UP
FINANCING      SECURED
```

```
PRINCIPALS
        Edward S Mullard, director.
        David F Lake, director.
        David J Bennett, director.
        Stephen Y Leith, company secretary.
```

**Search 13.5:** (cont.)

```
PAYMENT SUMMARY
DATE RANGE: 10.89 - 10.90    HI CREDIT: 2500        AVG HI CREDIT: 509

             ANTIC/DISC   PROMPT   SLOW TO 30  SLOW 31 TO 60   SLOW 61+   TOTAL
ALL SOURCES:      0          16         9            2             3       20
HIGHEST CR:       0         2500       2500         250           200
PLACED FOR COLLECTION:      0
In some instances, payments beyond terms can be the result of overlooked
invoices or disputed accounts.

PUBLIC RECORD
INFORMATION


MULSAND INDUSTRIES (U K) LTD              26 OCT 1990            PAGE 002


100123        MORTGAGES & CHARGES LODGED
              SATISFACTIONS
CO NAME: MULSAND INDUSTRIES (U.K.) LTD
DATE: 231285                            CRO: 0836572

2 satisfactions for 2 charges created 28.01.81 & 09.07.85.

CRO NOTICE    ADDRESS CHANGE
100823

CO NAME: MULSAND INDUSTRIES (U.K.) LIMITED
CO ADDR: 5 FORTUNE WAY
         CHRISTCHURCH
         DORSET
         BH23 4LD

CRO NBR: 0836623                     INSPECT FLAG:
CRO NOTICE    ADDRESS CHANGE
270387

CO NAME: MULSAND INDUSTRIES (U.K.) LIMITED
CO ADDR: 5 FORTUNE WAY
         CHRISTCHURCH
         DORSET
         BH23 4LD
CRO NBR: 0836623                     INSPECT FLAG:

CRO NOTICE    ACCOUNTS DATES
270373

CO NAME: MULSAND INDUSTRIES (U K) LTD
CRO NBR: 0836623                     INSPECT FLAG:
      ACCOUNTS MADE UP DATE: 000000
ANNUAL RETURNS MADE UP DATE: 161289

CRO NOTICE    ACCOUNTS DATES
300562

CO NAME: MULSAND INDUSTRIES (U K) LTD
CRO NBR: 0836623                     INSPECT FLAG:

      ACCOUNTS MADE UP DATE: 000000
ANNUAL RETURNS MADE UP DATE: 311288
```

**Search 13.5:** (cont.)

```
CRO NOTICE     ACCOUNTS DATES
210247


MULSAND INDUSTRIES (U K) LTD          26 OCT 1990          PAGE 003

CO NAME: MULSAND INDUSTRIES (U K) LTD
CRO NBR: 0836623                      INSPECT FLAG:
     ACCOUNTS MADE UP DATE: 000000
ANNUAL RETURNS MADE UP DATE: 311287


CRO NOTICE     ACCOUNTS DATES
010723

CO NAME: MULSAND INDUSTRIES (U K) LTD
CRO NBR: 0836623                      INSPECT FLAG:
     ACCOUNTS MADE UP DATE: 311286
ANNUAL RETURNS MADE UP DATE: 000000


CRO NOTICE     ACCOUNTS DATES
050444

CO NAME: MULSAND INDUSTRIES (U K) LTD
CRO NBR: 0836623                      INSPECT FLAG:
     ACCOUNTS MADE UP DATE: 311286
ANNUAL RETURNS MADE UP DATE: 000000
```

THIS PUBLIC RECORD INFORMATION HAS BEEN OBTAINED IN GOOD FAITH FROM THE
APPROPRIATE PUBLIC SOURCES. IN THE INTEREST OF SPEED SOME OF THIS INFORMATION
MAY BE PASSED TO YOU WITHOUT REVIEW OR COMMENT AND IS OFFERED TO YOU FOR YOUR
OWN ASSESSMENT.

BANKERS
     Yorkshire Bank PLC 12-14 Westgate Wakefield W Yorks WF1 1XC
     (40-99-23)

UPDATE
     In a communication received 5.3.90 and signed by The Secretary on
     2.3.90, it was indicated:
     Profits for the past six months were up.

FINANCES

* A FINANCIAL SPREAD SHEET OF COMPARATIVES, RATIOS AND INDUSTRY AVERAGES MAY
* BE AVAILABLE. ORDER A DUNS FINANCIAL PROFILE VIA YOUR DUNSPRINT TERMINAL
* OR LOCAL DUNSTEL CENTRE.

|                      | Fiscal Group 31.12.87 | Fiscal Group 31.12.88 | Fiscal 31.12.89 |
|----------------------|-----------------------|-----------------------|-----------------|
| Turnover             | 2,907,991             | 3,449,918             | 3,949,775       |
| Pre-tax profit(Loss) | 50,566                | (19,188)              | 113,491         |
| Net Worth            | 771,389               | 331,556               | 406,453         |
| Fixed Assets         | 320,508               | 312,111               | 315,347         |
| Total Assets         | 1,931,587             | 2,467,121             | 2,201,552       |

| MULSAND INDUSTRIES (U K) LTD | 26 OCT 1990 | | PAGE 004 |
|------------------------------|-------------|-----------|----------|
| Current Assets               | 1,611,079   | 2,155,010 | 1,886,205 |

**Search 13.5:** (cont.)

| | | | |
|---|---|---|---|
| Current Liabs. | 1,147,408 | 1,861,794 | 1,540,410 |
| Working Capital(Deficit) | 463,671 | 293,216 | 345,795 |
| Long Term Debt | 12,790 | 273,771 | 254,689 |
| Employees | 78 | 129 | 108 |
| goodwill | | 353,347 | 353,347 |

Abstract from consolidated fiscal balance sheet as at 31.12.89:

| | | | |
|---|---|---|---|
| Capital | 50,000 | Land & Bldgs | 26,127 |
| Retained Earnings | 709,800 | Fixtures & Equipment | 289,220 |
| Mortgages/Loans | 233,541 | Goodwill/Intangibles | 353,347 |
| hp | 21,148 | | |

| | | | |
|---|---|---|---|
| Current Liabilities: | | Current Assets: | |
| Trade Creditors | 798,018 | Stock & Work in Prog | 957,069 |
| Bank Overdraft/Loans | 140,170 | Debtors | 619,750 |
| Other Loans Payable | 38,178 | Prepaid Expenses | 52,059 |
| Taxation | 180,888 | Other | 75,269 |
| Due to Group Co's | 77,670 | Cash | 636 |
| accruals | 107,728 | Due from Group Co's | 161,134 |
| Other Current Liabs. | 197,758 | deferred expenditure | 20,288 |
| Total Current Liabs. | 1,540,410 | Total Current Assets | 1,886,205 |
| Total Liabilities | 2,554,899 | Total Assets | 2,554,899 |

Profit and Loss Account: Annual from 1.1.89 to 31.12.89.

| | |
|---|---|
| Sales | 3,949,775 |
| Cost of Goods Sold | 2,754,907 |
| Gross Profit | 1,194,868 |
| Selling/Admin. Exp. | 963,557 |
| Deprec./Amortisation | 93,280 |
| Payroll | 682,136 |
| Operating Income (Loss) | 207,795 |
| Other Income | 61 |
| Interest Expense | 94,365 |
| Income before Taxes | 113,491 |
| Income Tax | 10,503 |
| Profit After Tax | 123,994 |
| Extraordinary Items | 49,097 |
| Net Income | 74,897 |
| Retained earnings at start | 634,903 |
| Net Income | 74,897 |
| Dividends | 0 |
| Retained earnings at end | 709,800 |

The notes to the accounts give the number of employees as 108.

MULSAND INDUSTRIES (U K) LTD              26 OCT 1990              PAGE 005

Balance sheet obtained from Companies Registry 26.09.90
Tangible net worth is computed after deducting intangibles
consisting of: Goodwill 45,387
Registered in 1989 a debenture to Yorkshire Bank Plc.

**Search 13.5:** (cont.)

> Registered indebtedness at annual return date was shown as 571392
> On 26.3.90 Mr D F Lake submitted the following partial estimates.
> Turnover for 311289: 4,000,000.
> Profit for 311289: 250,000.
> On 28.3.90
> R L Spink confirmed certain general information in this report.
> Subject has plans for expansion which involve general expansion to
> keep up with the marketplace
> Informants consider subject trustworthy for normal engagements
> twenty five thousand pounds or so mentioned as a guide.

HISTORY

> Edward S. Mullard - appointed 10.06.85 - also associated with Mulsand
> Industries (Purchasing) Ltd, T P Bags Ltd, Mulpack Industries (U K)
> Ltd, Mulpack Ltd
>
> David F. Lake - appointed 04.06.88 - also associated with Mulpack
> Industries(U K) Ltd, Fibrex Ltd, Leyton Fabrics Ltd
>
> David J. Bennett - appointed 04.06.88 - also associated with Plastow
> Ltd, Leyton Fabrics Ltd, Fibrex Ltd
> Business started 1963.
> Registered as a private limited company 05.02.1963.
> Nominal Capital 50,000. All Issued.
> Search at the Companies Registry 26.09.89 showed annual return made
> up to 31.12.88

PARENT/ SUBSIDIARIES

> The company is a subsidiary of FAIRCROSS HOLLAND B V, AMSTERDAM,
> NETHERLANDS (Duns: 22-991-6536) , which holds 99% interest.
>
> Subsidiaries:
> Fibrex Ltd
> Trellware Curtain Rail Co Ltd, % of ownership: 100
> Leyton Fabrics Ltd, % of ownership: 100

OPERATIONS

> manufacturers of bathroom & houseware accessories
> EMPLOYEES: 108.
> Sells to: major retail chains and their own sales and marketing force.
> Terms are: 2.5 x 30 days. Territory: 100% National.
> Product Names: Aprex, Multil, Trellware
> Leases offices, factory, warehouse covering 30000 sq.ft.
> Registered office: Denman Ho 23/25 Denman Square London SW1
>
> A DUNSP.A.R. MAY BE AVAILABLE ON THIS BUSINESS. TO FIND OUT WHEN YOU
> ARE LIKELY TO GET PAID USE DUNSP.A.R.
> PRINT IT ONLINE USING DUNSPRINT OR PHONE YOUR DUNSTEL HOTLINE NUMBER.
>                    - STANDARD DISPLAY COMPLETE -

DO YOU REQUIRE FULL ALERT? ENTER Y OR N:N

| F=COMPREHENSIVE REPORT | P=PAR REPORT | D=DUNS FINANCIAL PROFILE |
|---|---|---|
| | A=ACCOUNTS ORDER | I=BUSINESS INVESTIGATION |
| | C=CREDIT APPRAISAL | CAN=MOVE TO NEXT ENQUIRY |
| | B=DUNSMATCH | M=MAIL OPTIONS |

ENTER SELECTION: **CAN**

**Search 13.5:** (cont.)

```
ENTER ENQUIRY: BYE

26/10/90  11:40

THANK YOU FOR DIALING.

PLEASE CALL AGAIN WITH YOUR FUTURE D&B ENQUIRIES.
```

## Company news information

The first major company databases to be offered online were news-based. The most commonly found are TEXTLINE, from Reuters, and FT PROFILE, which also incorporates the MCCARTHY service. Infomat, through Data-Star, and the American NEXIS, which is building its European coverage, are less comprehensive but worthy sources. All these services offer news information from the major newspapers either as abstracts or as full text.

Although not just containing company data, but any items of business interest, a predominant use of news services is for company searches. Most databases permit searching by company name or company field, which avoids the difficulties of irrelevant retrieval which might be encountered when looking for companies with common word names such as 'Preston' or 'Stone'.

The news databases carry long backfiles of data, in TEXTLINE's case from 1980, and are in the main very current. Profile Today's FT file means the database can be searched before the printed *Financial Times* is selling on the streets. Most services have newspapers up within a day or so of publication, and the availability of newswire information means the raw stories are searchable before they reach the printed press. As a separate development comprehensive news information is now available on CD-ROM, with *The Times* and *Sunday Times* full-text on THOR, as well as *The Financial Times, Independent* and *Guardian* CD-ROMs.

The most recent move in the company news area has been the introduction of searchable virtual real-time data. Reuters' COMPANY NEWSFILE and COMPANY NEWSYEAR show company information within five seconds to five minutes of an announcement. The example in Search 13.6 shows news of a British Aerospace order on the Equity News Page on the Reuters' MONITOR real-time service and the underlying summary. Searching on British Aerospace (BAE1) on Reuters COMPANY NEWSFILE not only brings up this story but also the previous five news stories and the most recent financial results.

## Search 13.6: Reuters' COMPANY NEWSFILE search

```
0000   REUTER EQUITIES NEWS - MAJOR EVENTS                    EQU1
1613--U.K. SHARES PLUNGE, FTSE INDEX DIPS BELOW 2,100         EQU2
1128   AMRO, ABN EXTEND SUBSCRIPTION PERIOD MERGER OFFER      EQU3
1154   GERMAN SHARES PLUNGE 5.2 PCT AS GULF TENSION GROWS     EQU4
1238   WANG GETS CONTRACT WORTH UP TO 841 MLN DLRS            EQU5
1303   BELGIAN FN NEGOTIATING 2 BLN BFR SAUDI ARMS DEAL       EQU6
1044   JAPAN BANKS REFUSE COMMENT ON UAL EMPLOYEE BUYOUT      EQU7
1523   FRENCH SHARES END SHARPLY DOWN ON FOREIGN SELLING      EQU8
1051   BAE ANNOUNCES JET ORDERS WORTH UP TO 900 MLN DLRS      EQU9
-------------------------------------------------------------------
TOKYO STOCKS - KABU * WALL STREET - WALL *  LONDON STOCKS - STOK
-------------- SPOT NEWS - AASS * FEATURES - ECRA --------------
MERGERS/ACQUISITIONS - MGR1 * NEW ISSUES - ISU1 * RESULTS - RES1
```

**Search 13.6:** (cont.)

```
AACC 1853 PERU'S CENTROMIN WORKING AT NEAR-NORMAL LEVELS DESPITE
STRIKE -SPOKESMAN

                                  MONITOR-SEE AAAA    1928


                                                    LINE #1
     ------------------------------------------------------------------


1051   BAE ANNOUNCES JET ORDERS WORTH UP TO 900 MLN DLRS       EQU9
       LONDON, AUG 21, REUTER - BRITISH AEROSPACE PLC <BAEL.L> SAID
IT HAD RECEIVED FIRM NEW ORDERS FOR 25 OF ITS BAE 146 JETS AND
OPTIONS ON A FURTHER EIGHT.
     BAE SAID IN A STATEMENT THE TOTAL VALUE OF THE ORDERS,
OPTIONS AND SPARES APPROACHES 900 MLN DLRS.
     THE COMPANY SAID THE ORDERS WERE PLACED BY NINE CARRIERS IN
SEVEN COUNTRIES.
     (FULL STORY BEGINS ON XXDF)


21-AUG-1204. EQU266 LA121804   HEADLINES     EQU1
                                             ENDS

AAUU 1449 DUN & BRADSTREET SAYS IS SEEKING BUYER FOR ITS IMS INT
L COMMUNICATIONS DIVISION


                                  MONITOR-SEE AAAA    1928


                                                    LINE #1
     ------------------------------------------------------------------


DATE       BRITISH AEROSPACE <BAEL.L> HEADLINES              BAE1
21AUG90--BAE ANNOUNCES JET ORDERS WORTH UP TO 900 MLN DLRS   VEGC
06AUG90    INDIAN AIR FORCE WANTS WESTERN-MADE FIGHTER JETS   VEGD
08AUG90    BRITISH AEROSPACE GETS 200 MLN DLR AMR0EAGLE ORDERVEGF
09AUG90    HONDA FORMS COMPANY TO IMPORT, SELL CARS IN ITALY VEGG
20AUG90    HUNTING PLC UNIT WINS BRITISH AEROSPACE CONTRACT  VEGH
-------    LATEST RESULTS - YEAR TO 31DEC89 --------- DIV DATES -
14MAR90    SHR ON NET DISTRIBUTION BASIS 82.8P VS 62P  REC 06APR90
           SHR ON NIL DISTRIBUTION BASIS 88.8P VS 62P  PAY 04JUN90
           TOTAL DIVIDEND 22.7 MLN VS 20.6P
           NET 238 MLN VS 171 MLN
           PRETAX PROFIT 333 MLN STG VS 259 MLN


AACC 1853 PERU'S CENTROMIN WORKING AT NEAR-NORMAL LEVELS DESPITE
STRIKE -SPOKESMAN

                                  MONITOR-SEE AAAA    1928


                                                    LINE #1
     ------------------------------------------------------------------
```

The main news databases, TEXTLINE, MCCARTHY and the other news files on Profile, quickly pick up the same story, either directly from a newswire or from a printed newspaper report. Unlike the real-time and virtual real-time products, the story will be kept on the database for retrospective searching. In the example in Search

13.7, TEXTLINE, as a Reuters product, has taken the story straight from the Reuters newswire. It has now been extensively indexed for retrieval in other ways, for example by the countries and people mentioned and the topic (T134 for company orders), as well as by company name.

TEXTLINE currently has two methods of searching: the original 'Standard Textline' and a new 'Enhanced Textline' service. The latter approach has been used here. TEXTLINE has always been menu-based. Enhanced Textline makes the search process a little faster. In the first display the responses to the questions about subject, database and time period have been stacked in one line for speed, using the '.' to separate each command. They could equally have been entered one by one in the appropriate place on the menu. TEXTLINE contains a variety of codes. In the search

$$\text{BAE}<1.1.5.20\text{-}8\text{-}90$$

the Textline company code for British Aerospace, 'BAE', has been used to select major references. The codes are not necessarily the same as the ones used for the real-time Reuters services. '<1' directs the search to company references only. The second '1' requests the main UK and Western European sources database. '5' asks for material since a certain date, that being specified as 20-8-90. Codes are given in the user manuals, or can be checked online, where the lists incorporate the latest revisions.

Five references are found and the headlines viewed. From this display screen, flagging the desired article, 'FL 1', selects it for further processing, in this case to be printed out in full. The '\' key is used to withdraw from the present menu.

## Search 13.7: Reuter TEXTLINE search

```
REUTER TEXTLINE              SEARCH ENTRY
version 1.14

1 . Enter search        :



2 . Select database(s) :
3 . Select time period :
---------------------------------------------------------------------

? for help                      !  Codes and examples
\ to return to list of services    Enter <space> to clear entry


BAE<1.1.5.20-8-90


\  to modify previous line

*** THE DATABASE IS NOW BEING SEARCHED ***

---------------------

REUTER TEXTLINE        PRINT/DISPLAY

TOTAL NUMBER OF ARTICLES FOUND : 5
     1.       Display headlines
     2.       Amend search
     3.       Display frequency of terms
     4.       Continuous display/print of all headlines
```

**Search 13.7:** (cont.)

```
       5.      Continuous display/print of all contexts
       6.      Continuous display/print of all full text
-------------------------------------------------------------------:
\ to return to search entry screen for new search
For display/print in chronological order, add C to entry, (eg 4C)
: 1


----------------------

REUTER TEXTLINE        HEADLINES DISPLAY
-------------------------------------------------------------------:
U/D to view more headlines           FL (to flag) or UF (to unflag) article
Article no. to view full article     (eg FL 1 2 or UF 3 4)
Article no. and C for context (eg 4C) \ to end selection & review options


1*21AUG90.UK: BAE ANNOUNCES JET ORDERS WORTH UP TO 900 MLN DLRS.
          (22 LINES) SOURCES REUTR      REUTUK LBA
2 21AUG90.JAPAN: BRITISH AEROSPACE SIGNS GYROSCOPE TECHNOLOGY TRANSFER DEAL
          WITH NIHON PRECISION.
          (7 LINES) SOURCES WMN 21/8/90 P8
3 20AUG90.UK: HUNTING PLC UNIT WINS BRITISH AEROSPACE CONTRACT.
          (10 LINES) SOURCES REUTR      REUTUK LBA
4 20AUG90.NETHERLANDS: TRUCKMAKER DAF SEEN TOO SMALL TO STAY INDEPENDENT.
          (77 LINES) SOURCES REUTR      REUTWE LBA
5 20AUG90.UK: TGWU FACES TUC SUSPENSION FOR 'POACHING' ROVER WORKERS.
          (18 LINES) SOURCES FT 20/8/90 P6

: FL 1

: \


----------------------------

REUTER TEXTLINE        PRINT/DISPLAY
TOTAL NUMBER OF ARTICLES FOUND : 5

   NUMBER OF FLAGGED ARTICLES : 1
1. Display headlines
2. Amend search
3. Display frequency of terms
4. Continuous display/print of all headlines
5. Continuous display/print of all contexts
6. Continuous display/print of all full text
7. Continuous display/print of flagged headlines
8. Continuous display/print of flagged contexts
9. Continuous display/print of flagged full text

-------------------------------------------------------------------:
\ to return to search entry screen for new search
For display/print in chronological order, add C to entry, (eg 4C)
: 9



-------------------------------------------------------------------:
<RETURN> when your printer has been switched on, and <RETURN> at end when your
printer has been switched off.
:
```

**Search 13.7:** (cont.)

```
    ------------------------------

    REUTER TEXTLINE
    ---------------

      1*21AUG90.UK: BAE ANNOUNCES JET ORDERS WORTH UP TO 900 MLN DLRS.
               (22 LINES) SOURCES REUTR    REUTUK  LBA

    LONDON, Aug 21, Reuter - British Aerospace Plc said it had received firm new
    orders for 25 of its BAe 146 jets and options on a further eight. BAe said in
    a statement the total value of the orders, options and spares approaches 900
    million dollars. The company said the orders were placed by nine carriers in
    seven countries. BAe said the new orders were from carriers in Europe, Asia-
    Pacific and Africa. Belgium's Sabena has ordered four 146-200s, with options
    on another four. Air U.K. has ordered two new 146-300s. Dan-Air and Princess
    Air have ordered a 146-300 and a 146-200QC (Quiet Convertible) respectively.
    Indonesian charter company PT National Air Charter has ordered two 146s (a
    series 100 and a series 200) and Air Botswana has ordered one 146-100. BAe
    said another three customers placed orders for 14 146s, with options on
    another four. Charles Masefield, managing director of the airlines division
    of BAe Commercial Aircraft, said the new orders raised the total number of
    BAe 146 orders and options to 293. BAe also announced the most comprehensive
    package of developments on the 70-122 seat airliner since it entered airline
    service in 1983. These include new engines from Textron Lycoming, part of
    Textron Inc, new avionics, increased design weights, an all-round increase in
    performance, capacity, payload and range, and the introduction of several new
    models of the aircraft, BAe said.


    REUTR    REUTUK  LBA


    REUTER TEXTLINE
    ---------------

    : ?END
```

With so many companies involved in mergers and acquisitions activity, the existence of specialist databases in this field has made the retrieval of merger information much easier than previously. The display from FT MERGERS AND ACQUISITIONS INTERNATIONAL on Profile shows news and bid information (Search 13.8). The database corresponds to the FT's monthly journal, *Mergers and Acquisitions*. Because everything is merger-related, there is no need to define the topic for a general search on merger activity. More specific detail can be requested, such as bid type or currency or sector. It should be noted that it is often possible to obtain more up-to-date information from the news databases.

JORDANS' SHAREHOLDER SERVICE and ICC SHAREWATCH are complementary resources for corporate finance work. They provide details of shareholdings, and in Jordan's case also give the underlying holders for nominee accounts.

Detailed financial and background information on companies is found in the highly specialized financial services databases such as IFR BONDBASE, EUROMONEY, BONDWARE and LOANWARE. They revolve around data on financial instruments, but also incorporate standing data and extensive notes fields which provide insight into a company's financing activity.

**Search 13.8: Profile's FT MERGERS AND ACQUISITIONS INTERNATIONAL**

```
>

GET RATNERS
        10 ITEMS RETRIEVED >

H ALL
SORTING

 1   MAA 30 Oct 89 RATNERS Group agreed bid for Weisfield's (133)
 2   MAA 30 Oct 89 RATNERS agreed bid for Weisfield's (149)
 3   MAA 11 Oct 88 RATNERS plans to acquire unit/division in Next
                   (Zales/Salisburys/Collingwood/Weir Shops) (230)
 4   MAA 13 Jul 88 RATNERS Group acquired Stephen's Jewellery Ltd (153)
 5   MAA 25 May 88 RATNERS agreed bid for Osterman's (221)
 6   MAA 19 May 88 RATNERS plans to acquire Time (Jersey) Ltd (193)
 7   MAA 22 Sep 87 RATNERS Group plans to acquire Westhall (116)
 8   MAA 07 Aug 87 RATNERS Group acquired Jones (Ernest) (207)
 9   MAA 06 Aug 87 RATNERS Group acquired Sterling Inc (130)
10   MAA 28 May 87 RATNERS Group bid lapsed for Combined English Stores (164)

Copyright (C) Financial Times Business Information 1988 - 1990
>

TEXT 3

 3   MAA 11 Oct 88 RATNERS plans to acquire unit/division in Next
                   (Zales/Salisburys/Collingwood/Weir Shops) (230)


Sector. . . . . . Bidder: Other Specialised Retailers.
                  Target: Other Specialised Retailers.

SIC . . . . . . . Bidder: 6540
                  Target: 6540

BIDDER . . . . . RATNERS
TYPE . . . . . . Public
COUNTRY. . . . . UK
CURRENCY . . . . Pounds sterling
ANNUAL SALES . . 95.13M(06)        PREV PRETAX PROFITS . . . . . 2.95M(06)
NET ASSETS/SHRE                    CURR PRETAX PROFITS . . . . . 2.65M(06)
EARNINGS/SHARE   31.61p

TARGET . . . . . Next (Zales/Salisburys/Collingwood/Weir Shops)

TYPE . . . . . . Public
COUNTRY. . . . . UK
BID DETAILS:
AREA . . . . . . New Uncompleted Bids for UK Companies
STATUS . . . . . plans to acquire unit/division in
ANNOUNCED. . . . 11/10/88

CURRENCY . . . . Pounds sterling
INIT BID(LOCAL)  150.80M
INIT BID(DLRS)   263.59M
```

TERMS: RATNERS is paying Pounds 150.8m for two businesses from rival group
Next. The businesses are Zales and Salisburys. As part of the deal RATNERS
is also taking over 73 other jewellery shops which traded under the
Collingwood and Weir names. RATNERS is raising part of the finance through
an Dollars 80m rights issue. Should the bid be stopped by the Monopolies &
Mergers Commission, the purchase of Salisburys would go ahead at a price of

**Search 13.8:** (cont.)

```
Pounds 80m and the rights issue would drop to Pounds 44m.

Reference No. 021    Issue 01:11:88
Mergers & Acquisitions

Copyright (C) Financial Times Business Information 1988 - 1990
>
```

## Sector information

Many textual business databases are useful for examining industries, sectors and markets.

Market research reports provide detailed analyses of a product or market segment. Several services are packaged to target advertising, media, and marketing companies, notably MAID and Harvest, which also supplies a back-up enquiry service for further detail. TEXTLINE and MCCARTHY contain many marketing news publications. MANAGEMENT AND MARKETING ABSTRACTS on PFDS, and PREDICASTS, through Data-Star or DIALOG, are excellent abstracting services. FT Profile has a number of marketing files which were originally presented as Datasolve's Magic service.

Marketing databases can be searched for broad concepts, the more so where the data are presented in full text. There are disadvantages to this, as the terminology may be very general, so that it is difficult to search precisely. It is important to think of the various terms which may be used to describe a subject. In the following example, ICC KEYNOTES on Profile is used to look for material showing the effects of prices on attitudes to 'green' products (Search 13.9).

The terms 'environment' and 'ecology' are chosen, using the truncation feature '*' to pick up references to derivatives such as 'environmentally' or 'ecological'. These are combined to appear in the same sentence as 'friendly' or 'sound'.

From the references found, those containing mention of terms such as 'pricing', 'expense', and 'cost', are selected:

```
>   GET (ENVIRONMENT*,ECOLOG*)/(FRIENDLY,SOUND)
45 ITEMS RETRIEVED

>   PICK PRICE*,PRICI*,COST,COSTS,EXPENS*
29 ITEMS RETRIEVED >
```

KEYNOTES is a database containing the full text of the *Keynotes* reports published by ICC. To make the information easy to find, it is segmented, meaning that there are separate references to different sections of the same report. Each is identified by its content, so the searcher can go directly to the relevant section. A quick way of seeing what is available is to view the headlines. The second page of headline display, items 16-24 in the example, suggests that item 20 may be of interest. This can be checked by using the context command, 'CTX'. This displays the lines either side of the place where the search terms appear. If the item looks relevant the full text can be printed, or the hard copy report consulted. The numbers at the end of the headlines refer to the word count of that section of the report.

High quality research and analyses of industrial sectors and companies can be found in the reports issued by stockbrokers and investment houses. Once restricted to a privileged circle, many are now released online through ICC STOCKBROKER RESEARCH and INVESTEXT from DIALOG and Data-Star. They are embargoed until about five weeks after their initial publication. This means they can be used for historical research but cannot be construed as investment advice, which was the original purpose. There is a strong financial orientation to these reports which differentiates them from the product/consumer bias of standard market research reports.

## Search 13.9: ICC KEYNOTES on Profile search for green products

```
H 16-24

16   ICK 05 Dec 89 TOILETRIES: Future Prospects (661)
17   ICK 22 Nov 89 SUPERMARKETS AND SUPERSTORES:
Supermarkets And Superstores (578)
18   ICK 22 Nov 89 SUPERMARKETS AND SUPERSTORES: Industry
Supply (3126)
19   ICK 24 Oct 89 Dry Batteries: 'Green' Cells (514)
20   ICK 09 Oct 89 Pollution Control: Consumer Awareness
(783)
21   ICK 09 Oct 89 Pollution Control: Industry Structure
(9188)
22   ICK 09 Oct 89 Pollution Control: Recent Developments
(1010)
23   ICK 09 Oct 89 Pollution Control: Future Prospects
(1503)
24   ICK 29 Sep 89 Cinemas and Theatres: Recent
Developments (572)

Copyright (C) ICC Key Note Ltd. 1987, 1988, 1989, 1990 >

CTX 20

20....
     ICK 09 Oct 89 Pollution Control: Consumer Awareness (783)
  ....
     Inevitably there is a trade-off between the long term
     planning of a business and a quick return on
     activities. The recent recession has promoted crisis
     management which tends to react primarily to external
     events. The concept of longer term strategic planning
     is re emerging within more responsible organizations.
     Recent trends indicate that there is already a strong
     movement away from the purchase of various products
     which are considered to be polluting the ENVIRONMENT.
     It appears that the green consumer demands products
     that 'won't COST the earth'.
     ....
     Green capitalists are promoting ENVIRONMENT FRIENDLY
     products. The Body Shop chain developed by Anita
     Roddick sells cosmetics which are not tested on
     animals. Richard Branson's enterprises are also 'green
     orientated'.

Copyright (C) ICC Key Note Ltd. 1987, 1988, 1989, 1990 >
```

Some of the earliest market-oriented databases were issued by Predicasts. The PTS PROMT database can be accessed through DIALOG and Data-Star. Its great advantage is its detailed coding system which means that enquiries can be defined precisely. The codes cover products and countries. Event codes represent aspects of an issue, for example a name change for a company, marketing procedures such as advertising, or research and development. This approach is no longer unique, as TEXTLINE offers similar facilities. Other benefits from PREDICASTS are its widespread coverage of magazines, reports and newspapers, and its informative abstracts. These permit the quick retrieval of large amounts of usable information, if researchers are not interested in looking elsewhere for the full text of the longer articles.

The following example of PROMT on DIALOG (Search 13.10), uses the product code '2013640' to search for articles on the bacon industry. If the results suggest that the term is too narrow, more general information on prepared meats, code '2013', may be relevant, perhaps used in conjunction with the word 'bacon' itself. Market information, event code 60, is specified. The search is limited to the UK. Many of the British articles on the database come from the *Financial Times*. This is information easily found elsewhere, so to reduce duplication all references from the newspaper are excluded from the search. This is done by requesting just material which is not in the *Financial Times,* defining this with the publication field JN=.

### Search 13.10: PROMT on DIALOG

```
     File 16:PTS PROMT -72-90/November 20
           (Copr. 1990 Predicasts)
   ** New FULL TEXT sources added to PROMT:
   ** Louisiana Industry Environmental Alert Money Laundering Alert
   ** New Jersey Industry Environmental Alert PRS Automotive Service

         Set      Items    Description
         ---      -----    -----------

 ?s pc=2013640
         S1         158    PC=2013640 (BACON)
 ?s py=1990
         S2      392370    PY=1990
 ?ss ec=60 and cc=4uk
         S3       87047    EC=60  (MARKET INFORMATION)
         S4      188259    CC=4UK  (UNITED KINGDOM)
         S5        6136    EC=60 AND CC=4UK
 ?s jn=financial times (london)
         S6       11159    JN=FINANCIAL TIMES (LONDON)
 ?s (s1 and s2 and s5) not s6
         S7         158    (S1 AND S2 AND S5) NOT S6

 ?t/7/5/1-2


  7/5/1
 02708660
 Dutch serve up more - but will Danes fight back?
 Grocer   August 18, 1990   p. 45 ISSN: 0017-4351

       UK: During first half 1990, supplies of bacon market fell by 4.1% to
 216,900 t vs 226,200 t in 1989. However, it was also seen from the figures
 that recovery was continuing in the market shares stakes by curers in the
 Netherlands, after forfeiting some of its ground during 1989 to the Danes. In
 first half 1990, Dutch exporters had a 26.8% share of the bacon trade, with
 58,100 t, vs 22.9% in 1989, with 51,800 t. Danish shippers had a 23.9% share,
 at 51,800 t, vs 26.2% in 1989, with 59,200 t. During first half 1990, the UK
 domestic market supplied 41.7%, with 90,600 t, a decline from 43.3% in 1989
 at 98k t.

 PRODUCT:  *Bacon (2013640)
 EVENT:    *Market Information (60)
 COUNTRY:  *United Kingdom (4UK)


  7/5/2
 02471799
 British Bacon drive pays off
```

**Search 13.10:** (cont.)

```
Meat Trades Journal February 22, 1990 p. 10

    UK: British bacon curers have a 44% share of the bacon market, with
sales of GBP1.3 bil/y. Some 95% of British bacon is produced by curers
belonging to the self-regulatory Charter Quality British Bacon Scheme. The
Meat & Livestock Commission launched its British Bacon's Brilliant campaign
in October 1989 which resulted in a slight increase in sales. The Netherlands
and Denmark are the UK's largest bacon suppliers.

PRODUCT:  *Bacon (2013640)
EVENT:    *Market Information (60)
COUNTRY:  *United Kingdom (4UK )
?
```

The most recent two articles are printed out in the predefined format 5 with all the indexing to show the classification codes used. A neater and cheaper method would be to use formats 4 or 7, which display the title, source and abstract only. An examination of the indexing may reveal other useful search terms. Amongst other format options, format 3 gives the bibliographic citation and word count, if the database is merely used as a reference point. Format 8 gives the title, indexing and word count, without the source, and is a quick and cost-effective method of checking the relevance of the articles without printing the records in full. If a large number of records is required, both DIALOG and Data-Star offer an off-line print service, whereby the records are printed out in their offices and mailed to arrive within three to five days.

In a specific search of this kind it is best to enter the elements one by one, in case the search becomes so narrow that nothing is retrieved. Each stage of the process can then be reviewed. It is possible, however, to enter all the elements of the search in one single command, thus:

```
? ss  (pc=2013640 and py=1990 and ec=60 and cc=4uk) not jn=financial times (london)
```

Where there is one search term the 'S' (SELECT) command is appropriate. Using the 'SS' command (SELECT STEPS) where terms are combined means that each consequent set is given a separate number. It can then be used in conjunction with any other. So, in the example on the bacon enquiry, if it was next decided to look at marketing information on bacon in the *Financial Times* this could be found using the search:

```
? s s1 and s3 and s6
```

or the alternative COMBINE command, (abbreviated as 'C'), which is slightly shorter:

```
? c 1 and 3 and 6
```

Either of these would now look for information on bacon anywhere in the world, as the geographical restriction 'cc=4uk' has been omitted. The 'S' and the 'C' commands do not create separate sets for each element of the search, so that intermediate steps cannot be picked up later. If the third step of the original search had been entered using 'S' instead of 'SS', the result would be:

```
?s ec=60 and cc=4uk
        87047   EC=60   (MARKET INFORMATION)
       188259   CC=4UK  (UNITED KINGDOM)
    S3    6136   EC=60 AND CC=4UK
?s jn=financial times (london)
    S4   11159   JN=FINANCIAL TIMES (LONDON)
?s (s1 and s2 and s3) not s4
    S5     158   (S1 AND S2 AND S5) NOT S6
```

It is now impossible to go back and pick up the concept of market information without restricting it to the United Kingdom, as the concepts of marketing and country are not given separate set numbers (S3 and S4 in the first search). The process is marginally quicker, but less flexible if more data are required later. Repeating a search for a term incurs a charge, and the advantage of set creation is to be able to retrieve any concept or to backtrack to any stage of the search. The SELECT STEPS command is therefore a useful habit to develop when using DIALOG.

In addition to general marketing databases, there are several specialist services. These are subject specific, such as MATERIALS BUSINESS FILE and PREDICASTS AEROSPACE AND DEFENCE MARKETS AND TECHNOLOGY on Data-Star and DIALOG. There are also newsletter files which cover their fields in great detail. Examples are FINANCIAL TIMES BUSINESS REPORTS on Profile and Data-Star, and COMPUTER INDUSTRY SOFTWARE SERVICES AND PRODUCTS on Data-Star. Again Predicasts features strongly with its NEWSLETTERS file on DIALOG and Data-Star.

## Management databases

Management issues can be found scattered throughout the business textual databases. Company and executive profiles appear on news databases and many articles of management interest appear in publications covered by the marketing databases. MANAGEMENT AND MARKETING ABSTRACTS is produced by PIRA, the Research Association for Paper & Board, Printing and Packaging Industries, in cooperation with the British Institute of Management (BIM). BIM has also established its own Helpline service, accessed directly. These are the main British-based data sources for management literature. SCIMP, available through Helecon, contains material selected and entered by the European business schools. The largest management databases are produced in the United States. Many management issues are universal, so an American bias may be acceptable; but it is also possible to obtain predominantly European information.

Management literature is beset by soft or ambiguous terminology. Often the article titles give little clue to their content. As concerns go into and out of fashion there may be large volumes of information to be found or virtually nothing. The introduction of jargon words such as 'perestroika' or 'greening' makes earlier articles on the same subject harder to trace.

The following two examples, looking for material on employee benefits, show the use of MANAGEMENT CONTENTS and ABI/INFORM on Data-Star (Search 13.11). Both are United States-based, but contain European material.

In the first example, simple search terms have been used to show that reasonable results can be achieved without too much effort. To use the term 'benefits' on its own would lead to many irrelevant articles, from the general meaning of advantages through to social security payments. One approach could be to combine the search term with another concept, such as 'remuneration', or 'compensation'. MANAGEMENT CONTENTS includes descriptive phrases as part of the indexing of the records, and in this case restricting the search to the descriptor field, DE, leads to precise retrieval. Using the additional search term 'UK' ensures that the articles found are of direct interest. This could be broadened by adding Great Britain or England as concepts, though in the latter case the American state of New England would have to be excluded. In practice on this database 'UK' produces good results.

As MANAGEMENT CONTENTS is a bibliographic database containing abstracts, the full article must be searched elsewhere. For this reason it is a cheap option on Data-Star just to display the title field, without the reference which is considered to be the true value of the record. This means that articles can be selected quickly without the need for further refinement of the search. As the term 'benefits' has to appear in the descriptor field for the record to be retrieved, the word may not be in the title, but it can be seen that the five items displayed could be of interest. The first record is printed out.

In the second example a different strategy is employed, avoiding the problems of soft terminology and the fact that American usage and spelling may differ from English. ABI/INFORM's records are all coded, and the codes for Employee benefits and compensation (6400) and Western Europe (9175) have been chosen. Code-based searches are fast and precise, avoiding the need to spend expensive time online. In the one record printed (Confusion over the Wages Act) the actual term 'benefits' does not appear in the descriptor field, so the article would not have appeared using the same search as in MANAGEMENT CONTENTS. Nonetheless, the abstract shows that the issue is relevant to the search.

## Search 13.11: MANAGEMENT CONTENTS and ABI/INFORM on Data-Star

```
ENTER DATA BASE NAME_:   mgmt

*SIGN-ON   20.03.35                    12.09.90

D-S/MGMT/1974 - VOL90/ISS08            SESSION   653

COPYRIGHT BY INFORMATION ACCESS COMPANY, FOSTER CITY, CAL. USA

D-S - SEARCH MODE - ENTER QUERY
    1_:  benefits.de.

    RESULT     6067

D-S - SEARCH MODE - ENTER QUERY
    2_:  1 and uk

    RESULT      10

    3_:  ..p/ti/1-5

    1
TI The cafeteria route to compensation. (cafeteria-style fringe
   benefits) (includes related article on Manufacturers National
   Corporation's benefit plan).

    2
TI The forgotten carers. (an analysis of care-friendly employment
   practices) (includes related article on elder care in the US and
   Canada).

    3
TI Company benefits: into a new age.

    4
TI Financial incentives pave the way ahead. (pension plans) (Pensions:
   Planning for the Future: a Special Report).

    5
TI ESOPs: fables no longer. (employee stock option plans).

R0601 * END OF DOCUMENTS IN LIST

D-S - SEARCH MODE - ENTER QUERY
    5_:  ..p/all/1

    1
AN 08510896 9007.
AU Woodley-C.
TI The cafeteria route to compensation. (cafeteria-style fringe
   benefits) (includes  related  article  on  Manufacturers  National
```

**Search 13.11:** (cont.)

```
          Corporation's benefit plan).
    SO Personnel-Management, v22, p42(4), issue: n5, May, 1990.
    YR 90.
    DE Cafeteria-benefit-plans; analysis; Employee-fringe-benefits;
       analysis; Personnel-management; Great-Britain.
    AB Cafeteria-style fringe benefits plans have grown in popularity in the
       US, but are not yet common in the UK because of tax complexity,
       ignorance, and administrative worries. However, it is predicted that
       the plans will soon be used by UK firms because they provide
       flexibility and a way to reduce costs while providing for the health
       care needs of workers. Firms considering implementing cafeteria-style
       benefits programs should consider a variety of issues, including:
       establishing effective pricing structures; making sure programs
       address cost control, simplicity, and legal issues; and communicating
       about programs to employees.
    PB Great Britain ENUK. IL illustration, photograph.

    -------------------
    D-S/INFO/1971-V90,I08/AUGUST/1990  SESSION  654  COPYRIGHT  BY  UMI/DATA
       COURIER.,  LOUISVILLE/KENTUCKY,  U.S.A.

    D-S - SEARCH MODE - ENTER QUERY
    1_:  6400.cc. and 9175.cc.

    RESULT 64
    2_:  ..p/all/1
            1
    AN 90-34942.
    AU Aikin-O.
    TI Confusion Over the Wages Act.
    SO Personnel Mgmt (UK), VOL: v22n7, P: 75,77, (2), Jul 1990.
    LG EN.
    PT JOURNAL PAPER.
    CD PTMAB.
    YR 90.
    DE UK; Federal-legislation; Employers; Wages-&-salaries; Payroll-
       deductions; Court-decisions.
    CC 4300: Law 6400: Employee benefits & compensation 9175: Western Europe.
    CO J-R-Masterton-&-Sons;   Foster-Wheeler-Ltd;  New-Centurion-Trust;  Star-
       Vehicle-Contracts-Ltd;  Chiltern-House-Ltd.
    DU -; 21-010-8486.
    JC PMA.
    IS 0031-5761.
    AV ABI/INFORM.
    AB Apart from any complaint about the drafting of the Wages Act 1986,
          there was a basic flaw in the concept in that the Act deals only with
          the mechanics by which the employer collects money from staff and
          ignores the question of entitlement. The Act itself also seems to
          give the term wage a wide definition. Section 7 refers to any sums
          payable to the worker by the employer in connection with employment.
          The Employment Appeal Tribunal (EAT) in Scotland has taken a wide
          interpretation of the definition of wages. In Kournavous versus J. R.
          Masterton and Sons, the EAT held . . . in Section 7 did not matter.
          The EAT in the UK and Wales has taken the opposite view. It clearly
          decided that wages  in lieu were not wages but damages for breach of
          contract. The narrow  UK line has also resulted in decisions to the
          effect that disputes do not come within the jurisdiction of the
          tribunals but should go to the County Clerk. Both treat a wage
          payment of less than a Wage Regulation Order as a deduction.

    R0601  *  END OF DOCUMENTS IN LIST
```

## Business opportunities

There are several databases to consult in the search for business opportunities. The lead-up to the Single Market in 1992 creates a European bias. An opportunity to tender for a project, to obtain funding, or to respond to a proposal or directive may not be open for long. Consequently opportunities databases have become useful because it is easy to check them quickly and regularly. They have been designed to be easy to search, as they are aimed at the people actually seeking the opportunities. At present they are probably considerably underused in relation to their potential value.

The three main databases covering 1992 prospects are SPEARHEAD and CELEX from the Department of Trade and Industry (DTI), and EUROSCOPE from Coopers and Lybrand Europe (formerly Deloitte Haskins and Sells). EUROSCOPE contains the company's reports on European Community developments, which are an excellent introduction to what is going on. SPEARHEAD is the DTI's summary of European Community measures, backed up by the full text of the legislation on CELEX. STARS, from EPRC Ltd in conjunction with the University of Strathclyde, deals with UK regulations and advisory bodies.

Opportunities for projects in the European Community are listed in TENDERS ELECTRONIC DAILY, which corresponds to Supplement S to the *Official Journal* of the European Communities. The file also covers Community-funded projects worldwide and Japanese tenders. Looking more widely afield, the British Overseas Trade Board's database, EXPORT INTELLIGENCE SERVICE, details export opportunities worldwide with direct contact details. All these opportunities databases are found on FT Profile. For trade fair details FAIRBASE on Data-Star can be used.

Financial assistance is announced through EPRC's AIMS, for the UK and EUROLOC, for Europe. On a broader scale Profile's INTERNATIONAL BUSINESS OPPORTUNITIES details current and forthcoming projects where World Bank funding is involved.

In the example from EXPORT INTELLIGENCE SERVICE a combination of cooperative ventures and specific opportunities can be seen (Search 13.12). The detail is sufficient for a preliminary judgement on relevance, and gives full contact details.

### Search 13.12: EXPORT INTELLIGENCE SERVICE

```
SELECT EIS
EIS ONLINE
 Crown Copyright (C) 1985,1986,1987,1988,1989,1990
CHARGE GROUP(S): Q1 >

>

GET AUTOMOTIVE/COMPONENT*
     274 ITEMS RETRIEVED
>

H 1-6
 SORTING

1     EIS 10 Aug 90 USA / MODERNIZATION OF GLASS PLANT / MARKET POINTER 33245
2     EIS 10 Aug 90 INDIA / AUTOMOTIVE PISTON RINGS / CO-OPERATION 33265
3     EIS 31 Jul 90 CHILE / LATHE/DRILLING MACHINES/MILLING MACHINE/AIR
                    COMPRESSOR/RIVETTING GUNS / SPECIFIC OPPORTUNITY 31415
4     EIS 19 Jul 90 USA / COMPONENT PARTS FOR AUTOMOTIVE ALTERNATORS AND
                    STARTERS / SPECIFIC OPPORTUNITY 29991
5     EIS 13 Jul 90 SOUTH AFRICA / AUTOMOTIVE HAND BRAKES / CO-OPERATION 29336
6     EIS 09 Jul 90 USA / AUTOMOTIVE COMPONENTS (OEM), OF METAL AND PLASTIC. /
                    AGENCY 28503

Crown Copyright (C) 1985, 1986, 1987, 1988, 1989, 1990
```

**Search 13.12:** (cont.)

```
> TEXT 4

4    EIS 19 Jul 90 USA / COMPONENT PARTS FOR AUTOMOTIVE ALTERNATORS AND
                    STARTERS / SPECIFIC OPPORTUNITY 29991

     REQUIREMENT - INFORMATION
     International Products And Manufacturing Inc (IPM), a subsidiary of
     Kearney-National, and a manufacturer of alternators and starters for the
     AUTOMOTIVE aftermarket, seeks British sources of supply for COMPONENT
     PARTS FOR AUTOMOTIVE ALTERNATORS AND STARTERS, specifically - alternator
     brush holds, roters, diodes, and starter solenoids, ameratures and
     bushings. Also interested in AUTOMOTIVE precision bearings.
     IPM employs 175, is one of the five largest US companies in the
     alternator/starter AUTOMOTIVE aftermarket. Company stocks over 7,000
     parts. Products are sold to distributors who in turn sell to AUTOMOTIVE
     rebuilders. Parts made for both domestic and foreign automobiles.
     Your response should mention the British Consulate-General in Chicago as
     the source of your information.

     RESPOND TO: Ms Diane R Mitzelfeld, Purchasing Manager, IPM Inc., 201 West
***PRESS RETURN TO CONTINUE, N FOR NEXT ARTICLE, OR X TO EXIT
     Oakton Street, Des Plaines, Illinois 60017. Tel: (708) 635 8080. Fax:
     (708) 635 0917.

     IF RESPONDING PLEASE INFORM: British Consulate General, 33 North Dearborn
     Street, Chicago, Il 60602. Attn: J Koestring.
     PRODUCT CODES: 851190    854110    87089906 87089985

     BOTB - Export Intelligence Service

Crown Copyright (C) 1985, 1986, 1987, 1988, 1989, 1990
>
```

## Economic databases

Economic information covers financial markets, trade statistics, econometric and socio-demographic data. This is often combined with forecasting or analytical services. The principal bibliographic databases are ECONOMIC LITERATURE INDEX on DIALOG, and FOREIGN TRADE AND ECONOMIC ABSTRACTS and PAIS INTERNATIONAL from DIALOG and Data-Star. KEESINGS RECORD OF WORLD EVENTS on FT Profile, formerly KEESINGS CONTEMPORARY ARCHIVES, digests economic stories.

Most economic research requires raw statistics. Many of the major sources are available online as numeric databases. These can be bought as magnetic tapes or downloaded services to be used directly with analytical software. For less frequent use there are comprehensive ranges of economic data hosted by Datastream, Wharton Economic Forecasting Associates (WEFA), Data Resources Inc. (DRI), and Reuter:file with its IP Sharp material. All provide a wide variety of time series covering everything from indices of production to interest rate movements, from gross national product to population figures.

These services are aimed mainly at economists and analysts, and at first sight appear difficult to use by the novice. Even more so than with text-based products, the searcher needs to know the full command language structure to use the data to best advantage. More pertinently, a good understanding of the underlying figures is essential. Many time series look similar but contain differences of statistical importance. The user needs to understand the source and the assumptions, not just to evaluate the data but to identify it in the first place. It is best to obtain a good comprehension of the information on paper before trying anything too complex online. It is significant that economic data may be published in hard copy before appearing online, so that the latest figures may not be searchable on the database. This is particularly the case with government data where the legal requirement to publish takes precedence. News databases such as TEXTLINE or PROFILE may supply more recent data.

Most econometric database services offer a second tier, more limited version which restricts the amount of data offered and the flexibility of manipulation, but instead makes the main material more accessible. A structured approach or menus make it easier to define the material required. DATASTREAM, which was menu-based from the start, has often been the entry level for searchers who do not have economics training. By asking all the necessary questions, the menu forces the user to define the series or instrument precisely, and displays the answer through report format options ranging from a single-figure answer to flexible graphics.

### Analytical/historical databanks

Originally the main economic services concentrated on offering powerful data manipulation software online. This means that raw statistics can be searched, reformatted and printed out exactly as the user requires. As well as providing ready insight into the trends so that supplementary material can be drawn from the database at the same time, this is an efficient use of research effort. The material can be retrieved from the information provider in a format which can be incorporated directly into the report for which it is required. This avoids the need for recalculation and rekeying.

With the growth of personal computers and the consequent widespread use of analytical software packages, the data suppliers have made it easy to download the data into local software, so that it can be processed off-line. This reduces the sometimes heavy and hard to predict charges which could be incurred by using the host's analytical capabilities. The example below shows population data from the International Monetary Fund (IMF) INTERNATIONAL FINANCIAL STATISTICS database, which has been downloaded into a Lotus 1-2-3 spreadsheet and presented as two graphs (Searchs 13.13 and 13.14). IMF and the Organisation for Economic Co-operation and Development (OECD) statistics are fundamental components of all the econometric hosts' offerings, and form an excellent reference point for comparisons with specialist data because of their standardized approach. Nonetheless it should be remembered that there may be an underlying political purpose behind the supply of statistics to these agencies, hence numbers should not always be taken at face value.

Many online searchers are reluctant to search numeric databanks because of the apparent complexity of the data and search language. In fact, simple data retrieval is not particularly difficult even without the menus. The commands follow a straightforward pattern which, once learnt, can be applied throughout. This is often easier than spreadsheet macros. For example DRI's EUROPE DATABANK contains, amongst other things, statistical data from the United Kingdom Central Statistical Office. To find United Kingdom crude oil exports using the command language EPS, the command is as follows:

```
SET   Q,86:1   TO   DATE(@NOW),SOURCE=@EUROPE/EXCRUDE@UK
```

Crude oil export statistics are reported quarterly, so the frequency is 'Q'. '86:1 to date(@now)' requests information from the first quarter of 1986 to the most recent data reported. The source is the EUROPE DATABANK, '@EUROPE'. The series is identified by a fairly recognizable mnemonic, 'EX' for exports, 'CRUDE' for crude oil, '@UK' for the country. The mnemonics can be found in the database guides. It is also possible to identify series online. The econometric databanks are supported by consultants who can assist the enquirer in understanding the data, as well as the conventional help-desk approach of formulating the search.

**Search 13.13: Output from International Monetary Fund INTERNATIONAL FINANCIAL STATISTICS database as Lotus 1-2-3 graph**

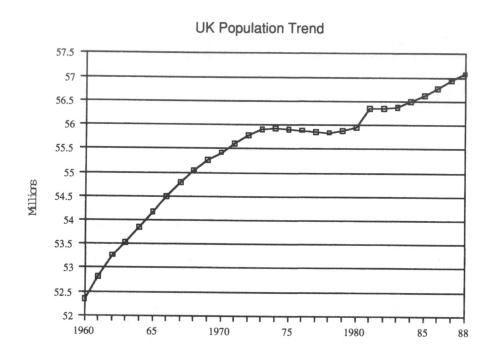

**Search 13.14: Output from International Monetary Fund INTERNATIONAL FINANCIAL STATISTICS database as Lotus 1-2-3 graph**

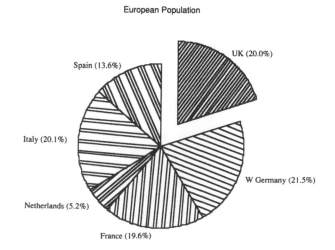

## REAL-TIME INFORMATION AND SHORT-TERM INFORMATION

The highest use of online business information is through real-time services. These are aimed at the end user, who may be a financial specialist, a research analyst or a corporate finance executive. There are many services which provide a wide range of live information fed directly to the screen from financial market, news and trade sources, either in digital or video format. Common names are Reuters, Telerate, Quotron, Telekurs, Pont Data, Bridge Data, and the International Stock Exchange's SEAQ and TOPIC services.

These services offer structured pages and the facility of user customization, so that traders or executives can monitor their own choice of perpetually changing data. Alerting services draw significant movements to the user's attention. Once real-time was prohibitively expensive for all purposes except constant use. Now several of the vendors offer cheaper packages which make the data more accessible. A low cost option is to use CITISERVICE on Prestel, the British videotext service which supplies a useful range of data at acceptable cost.

Search 13.15 shows the popular FXFX foreign exchange spot rates page from Reuters. Looking unimpressive when captured statically in black and white, the actual on-screen page is easy to read as the blue figures are overlaid with the dynamically updated data appearing in yellow.

### Search 13.15: Foreign exchange rates from Reuters real-time service

```
2008  CCY PAGE NAME   * REUTER SPOT RATES  * CCY        HI*AMER*LO FXFX
2006  DEM CIBB CAN IMPL TOR    1.4720/30    * DEM        1.4760    1.4650
2006  GBP CIBB CAN IMPL TOR    1.9725/35    * GBP        1.9775    1.9690
2007  CHF DBNY DEUTSCHE N.Y.   1.2455/65    * JPY        129.00    128.15
1959  FRF CINY CITIBANK N.Y    4.9670/00    * FRF        4.9790    4.9500
2001  ITL BCTO BCI      TOR 1108.50/9.25    * ITL        1111.50  1105.00
1642  ECU WMCS NATWEST  LDN    1.3980/90    * ECU        1.4032    1.3993
-----------------------------------------------------------------------
XAU RNBG 381.50/382.00 * ED3 7.87/ 8.00  * FED          PREB * MMKU 30Y
XAG CSSG    4.14/  4.15 * US30Y YTM 8.51 *7.50-          7.56 *102.18-20



AASS  2004  CORRECTED  -  PATHE  COMMUNICATIONS  3RD  QTR SHR LOSS 38 C
TS (CORRECTED FROM 36 CTS)


                         DEALING - SEE AADA 1954


                                                         LINE #1
-----------------------------------------------------------------------
```

In addition to the broadcast services, users may subscribe to customized digital feeds, dumping changes directly into their programs and portfolios. The recently launched FT FIRSTBASE furnishes information on *Financial Times* indices, Extel Examiner and other news services, the International Stock Exchange and the London options and financial futures markets, plus foreign exchange and capital markets data.

A wealth of data are available on the real-time services. In general the information is not searched in the conventional manner. Instead preformatted pages are consulted and constantly refreshed. Using windowing software, several pieces of information may be viewed simultaneously. Some initial work must be carried out to extract the data in the correct format, but then retrieval is virtually instant, usually by summoning a page or invoking a program. Significant players in the financial markets note a development, carry out a transaction, then see the results of their action on screen. Others may be content with more passive feeds of data into their management models.

## TEXTUAL ECONOMIC INFORMATION

Econometric databanks can also be used to obtain textual information about economic conditions. This ranges from simple summaries on DATASTREAM through to extensive forecasts on DRI. The abstracting services such as FOREIGN TRADE AND ECONOMIC ABSTRACTS review general economic literature. Latterly the range of country reports online has expanded greatly. REUTERS COUNTRY REPORTS is compiled from data obtained for the Reuters journalists. ABECOR (Associated Banks of Europe Country Reports) on Nexis's Country Report Service and FROST AND SULLIVAN POLITICAL RISK COUNTRY REPORTS on Data-Star look at information with a keen eye to financial stability. All these services give considerable detail about the political and business structure of the countries as well as the economic situation.

## DATABASE SUMMARY

There are so many business and economic databases that it is difficult in a review of this size to give more than a brief overview. Table 13.1 is a representative listing of major services, but is far from comprehensive. In some cases the databases compile data from several sources and combine them in different ways. Where a database is presented on more than one host it may not be exactly the same each time. Updating frequencies vary, not just by host, but also for individual elements of a data file. The scene alters constantly, so that hosts, databases and update schedules may change.

**Table 13.1: Database summary**

| Database | Content | Host/ Supplier | Update Frequency |
|---|---|---|---|
| Abecor | Country reports | Nexis | Monthly |
| ABI/Inform | Management & business literature | Data-Star, DIALOG, Nexis | Weekly |
| ABI/Inform CD-ROM | Management & business literature | Data Courier | 6 p.a. |
| Accountline | Company financial data | Reuter:file | Daily |
| Advance Information | Company credit data | Advance Information | Daily |
| AIMS | Financial assistance | EPRC | Daily |
| Analysis | Company financial data | Analysis Corporation, Infocheck | Daily |
| Automotive Information & News Service | Automotive industry news | Data-Star | Daily |
| Bank of England Financial & Economic Databank | Financial statistics | WEFA | Quarterly |
| Bondbase (diskette) | Financial instruments | IFR | Monthly |
| Bondware (diskette) | Financial instruments | Euromoney | Monthly |
| Bridge Data | Financial instrument data | Bridge Data | Constant |
| Business | Trade opportunities | Data-Star | Monthly |
| Business Base CD-ROM | Company financial data | Extel | Monthly |

**Table 13.1:** (cont.)

| Database | Content | Host/ Supplier | Update Frequency |
|---|---|---|---|
| CCN Business Info. | Company credit information | CCN | Daily |
| CCN Directors D'base | Company directors | CCN | Daily |
| Celex | European Community legislation | Profile | Monthly |
| Chemical Business News Base | Chemical industry news | Data-Star | Weekly |
| CitiService | Financial instrument data | Prestel | Constant |
| Computer Database | Computer marketing information | Data-Star, DIALOG | Weekly |
| Computer Industry Software Services & Products | Computer newsletters | Data-Star | Weekly |
| Corporate Actionline | Financial monitoring | Reuters | Daily |
| Country Report Service | Country reports | Nexis | Irreg. |
| CSO UK Macro-economic & Financial Databank | Economic statistics | Reuter:file | Monthly |
| Current Economic Indicators | Economic statistics | DRI | Daily |
| Dataline | Company financial modelling | Reuter:file | Daily |
| Datastream | Economic & company data | Datastream | Daily |
| Disclosure CD-ROM:Europe | Company financial data | Disclosure | Quarterly |
| Dow Jones News | News | Data-Star, Profile | Daily |
| Duns European Marketing Online | Company directory information | Data-Star, PFDS | 6 p.a. |
| Dunsprint | Company credit information | Dun & Bradstreet | Daily |
| Economic Forecasts | Economic analysis | Reuter:file | Monthly |
| Economic Literature Index | Economic analysis | DIALOG | Quarterly |
| EUROLOC | Financial assistance | EPRC | Daily |
| Euromoney | Financial data | Profile | Monthly |
| Euromonitor Market Reports | Market research | Profile | Monthly |
| Europe Databank | Economic statistics | DRI | Monthly |
| Europe's Largest Companies | Company directory information | PFDS | Monthly |
| Euroscope | European regulations | Profile | Weekly |
| Export Intelligence Service | Overseas trade | Profile | Daily |
| Exstat | Company financial data | DRI, Reuter:file, WEFA | Daily |

**Table 13.1:** (cont.)

| Database | Content | Host/ Supplier | Update Frequency |
|---|---|---|---|
| Extel Examiner | Company & financial news | Pont, Bridge | Constant |
| Extel Financial Cards | Company financial data | Data-Star, DIALOG, Profile | Weekly |
| Extel Price Plus | Financial instrument prices | Telecom Gold | Daily |
| Facts | News digest | Nexis | Monthly |
| Fairbase | Trade fairs | Data-Star | Monthly |
| FAME | Company information | Jordans | Monthly |
| Financial News Database | U.K. based financial institutions | PFDS | Fortnightly |
| Financial Times | News | Profile | Daily |
| Financial Times Actuaries Share Indices | London share data | Reuter:file | Daily |
| Financial Times Business Reports | Industry newsletters | Data-Star, Profile | Weekly |
| Financial Times Share & Rate Databank | Financial instrument data | WEFA | Daily |
| Financial Times Share Information | London share prices | Reuter:file | Daily |
| Finis | Financial marketing information | DIALOG, PFDS | Biweekly |
| Foreign Trade & Economic Abstracts | Economic analysis | Data-Star, DIALOG | Fortnightly |
| Frost & Sullivan Market Research | Market research | Data-Star | Quarterly |
| Frost & Sullivan Political Risk Country Reports | Country economic analysis | Data-Star | Irregular |
| FT Firstbase | Financial instrument prices | Financial Times | Daily |
| FT Mergers & Acquisitions International | Merger & bid information | Profile | Monthly |
| Harvard Business Review | Management concerns | Data-Star, DIALOG | 6 p.a. |
| Harvest Information | Market research information | Harvest | Daily |
| Helpline | Management literature | British Institute of Management | |
| ICC Companies | Company financial data | CCN, Data-Star, Datastream, DIALOG, Global Report, ICC, PFDS | Weekly |
| ICC Keynote Reports | Market research on companies | Data-Star, ICC Profile | Monthly |
| ICC Sharewatch | Company shareholder data | ICC, PFDS | |

**Table 13.1:** (cont.)

| Database | Content | Host/ Supplier | Update Frequency |
|---|---|---|---|
| ICC Stockbroker Research | Financial research on companies | Data-Star, ICC, DIALOG, PFDS, Profile | Weekly |
| IMSWorld | Pharmaceutical news | IMS International | Daily |
| Industrial Market Locations | Operational descriptions of companies | PFDS | 6 p.a. |
| Industry Data Sources | Market research | Data-Star, DIALOG | Monthly |
| Industry Monitor | UK economic statistics | WEFA | Daily |
| Infocheck | Company credit information | Infocheck, Kompass, PFDS, Prestel, Profile, Westcot | Weekly |
| Infolink ACE | Company credit information | UAPT Infolink | Daily |
| Infomat | Business news | DIALOG, Data-Star, Nexis, PFDS, Telecom Gold | Weekly |
| International Business Opportunities | Business project opportunities | Profile | Monthly |
| International Financial Statistics | Economic statistics | DRI, Reuter:file, WEFA | Monthly |
| International News | Business news | Nexis | Daily |
| Investext | Financial research on companies | DIALOG, BRS (PFDS), Data-Star | Weekly |
| Jordans Shareholder Service | Company shareholder data | Jordans, PFDS | Monthly |
| Jordanwatch | Company financial data | Jordans, PFDS | Weekly |
| Keesings Record of World Events | Economic news digest | Profile | Monthly |
| Key British Enterprises | Company directory information | PFDS | Monthly |
| Knight Ridder Financial News | News | DIALOG | Constant |
| Kompass CD-ROM | Company product data | Reed Information Services | 2 p.a. |
| Kompass Europe | Company directory information | DIALOG | Annually |
| Kompass Online | Company product data | Reed Information Services | Daily |
| Loanware (diskette) | Financial instruments | Euromoney | Monthly |
| Lotus CD/Corporate:UK | Company financial data | Lotus | Monthly |
| Lotus CD/M&A: Europe | Merger bid information | Lotus | Monthly |
| Lotus CD/Private+:UK | Company financial data | Lotus | Monthly |

**Table 13.1:** (cont.)

| Database | Content | Host/ Supplier | Update Frequency |
|---|---|---|---|
| Macmillan Directory of Corporate Affiliations | Company ownership | PFDS | Quarterly |
| MAID | Market research information | MAID | Daily |
| Management & Marketing Abstracts | Management literature | PFDS | Fortnightly |
| Management Contents | Business and management literature | Data-Star, DIALOG | Monthly |
| Materials Business File | Materials industry news | Data-Star | Monthly |
| Marketing Surveys Index | Market research | Profile | Monthly |
| McCarthy Online: Company Fact Sheets | Company directory information | Profile | Daily |
| McCarthy Online: Press Cuttings Service | Company & industry news | Profile | Daily |
| MEAL Quarterly Digest | Media expenditure | Profile | Quarterly |
| MicroExstat | Company financial data | Extel | Monthly |
| Mintel Daily Digest | Market research news | Profile | Daily |
| Mintel Reports | Market research | Profile | Monthly |
| MSI Market Reports | Market research | Profile | Irregular |
| Nexis | News & market research | Nexis | Daily |
| OECD Financial Statistics | Economic statistics | DRI, WEFA | Monthly |
| OECD Main Economic Indicators | Economic statistics | DRI, Reuter:file, WEFA | Monthly |
| PAIS International | Economic analysis | Data-Star, DIALOG | Monthly |
| Petroleum Industry/ Energy Business News | Energy news | Data-Star | Weekly |
| Pharma Marketing Service | Pharmaceutical marketing | Data-Star | Weekly |
| Pharmaceutical & Healthcare Industry News | Pharmaceutical news | Data-Star, DIALOG | Daily |
| Pont Data | Financial instrument data | Pont Data | Constant |
| Predicasts Aerospace Defense Markets & Technology | Aerospace marketing | Data-Star, DIALOG | Monthly |
| Predicasts Annual Reports | Company financial data | Data-Star, DIALOG | Monthly |
| Predicasts Forecasts | Industry & economic forecasts | Data-Star, DIALOG | Monthly |

**Table 13.1:** (cont.)

| Database | Content | Host/ Supplier | Update Frequency |
|---|---|---|---|
| Predicasts Marketing & Advertising Reference Service | Marketing information | Data-Star, DIALOG | Weekly |
| Predicasts New Products Announcements | Product news | Data-Star, DIALOG | Weekly |
| Predicasts Newsletters | Business newsletters | Data-Star, DIALOG | Daily |
| Predicasts PTS PROMT | Market research information | DIALOG, BRS (PFDS), Data-Star | Daily |
| Predicasts Time Series | Industry & economic statistics | Data-Star, DIALOG | Monthly |
| Pricelink | Financial instrument prices | Reuters | Daily |
| Profile | Company & industry news | Profile | Daily |
| Qui Credit | Company credit information | Qui Credit Assessment | Daily |
| Quotron | Financial instruments, news | Quotron | Constant |
| Quotron QST | Historical financial instruments | Quotron | Daily |
| Reuter Monitor | Financial instruments, news | Reuters | Constant |
| Reuters Company Newsfile | Company news | Reuters | Constant |
| Reuters Company Newsyear | Company news | Reuter:file | Constant |
| Reuters Country Reports | Country economic surveys | Reuter:file | Daily |
| SCIMP | Management literature | Helecon | Monthly |
| SCIMP (on CD-ROM) | Management literature | Helecon | 2 p.a. |
| SEAQ | Share price data | International Stock Exchange | Constant |
| Snapshot | Financial instrument prices | Reuters | Constant |
| Spearhead | European Community measures | Profile | Weekly |
| STARS | UK regulations | EPRC | Daily |
| Telekurs | Financial instruments, news | Telekurs | Constant |
| Telerate | Financial instruments, news | Telerate | Constant |
| Tenders Electronic Daily | Business opportunities | Profile | Daily |
| Textline | Company & industry news | Reuter:file | Daily |
| THOR | News stories | Times Newspapers | Quarterly |
| TOPIC | Share price data | International Stock Exchange | Constant |
| UK Importers | Importers directory | Data-Star | Monthly |

**Table 13.1:** (cont.)

| Database | Content | Host/ Supplier | Update Frequency |
|---|---|---|---|
| UK Mergers & Acquisitions Database | Merger deal information | DIALOG, Extel, Infocheck | Daily |
| Who Owns Whom | Company ownership | PFDS | Monthly |

## CONCLUSION

To be a fully knowledgeable business information researcher these days is virtually impossible. An enormous array of information is presented on a variety of systems. With increased effort on the part of the suppliers to make the systems easy to use, it is not too difficult to come to grips with the services that are necessary. Menus and cross-file searching facilities ease the path to the data. Unless a full commitment is essential it is best to select a few of the main suppliers and to become familiar with their particular wares. A combination of three or four hosts is enough for most purposes. The major hosts have comprehensive data ranges loaded, and there is usually a small specialist supplier to fill the gaps. The best policy is to choose the highest quality sources for the main business need.

The databases should be used with care, especially if major decisions are based on the material found. In most cases the information is presented in a fairly raw state, and it is up to the user to make of it what he or she can. A list of news stories may not give a comprehensive picture of a company's activities. Credit data can be misleading. Critical figures for acquisition screening may be absent. Where there are consultants on tap, as with the econometric services, it is a good idea to check on the detail.

This having been said, there is a wealth of material which can be easily retrieved. In many cases it can be reformulated and repackaged for direct use, as a mailing list or a report. By combining information from various sources it is possible to develop substantial insight into a business situation. A quick check may show that there is little or much to worry about, or may establish a common starting point. The data can be used as background reading or to confirm or preclude a course of action. New information sources are constantly added, and the suppliers are ready to listen to suggestions for more. Business information is not hard to find; there are plenty of good sources. Used wisely, they can provide a quick, cost-effective method of managing and developing a productive operating environment.

# 14 Business and economics: United States

*Mary Muenkel, Yve Griffith and Mike Koenig*

## BACKGROUND

Although we tend to think of the world of online database searching as evolving from Sci-Tech information systems, that is not quite accurate. The first commercial online database reviews were in fact in the business area. These services were of two types: stock market information retrieval systems such as Quotron and Telerate, and economics modelling packages such as those offered by DRI and IP Sharp. The former were conceptually very simple systems that could be searched by little other than ticker symbol (identifying initials used on ticker-tape machines). The latter were online software application packages of considerable complexity to which some data were appended.

What was introduced by the Sci-Tech community was the idea of an online vendor or host providing numerous databases, or more accurately datafiles, searchable by a common and rather sophisticated command language. Most of the first such databases were, in fact, Sci-Tech in nature, and most of the first users were from the Sci-Tech community, particularly in the pharmaceutical industry. Business databases, however, emerged rapidly, and an emphasis on business applications continues to characterize online database development today.

## CLIMATE

One of the most obvious trends in the business community today is the recognition of the importance of information as a corporate resource. A content analysis of bellwether, trend-setting journals such as the *Harvard Business Review* or *Sloan Management Review* over the last decade would show a marked increase in the number of articles devoted to information management or information technology. There are a number of converging reasons for that phenomenon.

## Recognition of external information

Until relatively recently information management in the context of the business organization meant the processing of data generated by the organization itself - typically reports based on the aggregation, summation and analysis of transaction data. The term Management Information Systems (MIS) was coined to describe such operations. MIS are now perceived as having been misrepresented and oversold in several regards. What has come to be recognized as chief among these reasons for misrepresentation was the failure to recognize that aggregated internal data are of only minor importance in the decisions made by senior management. In the higher organizational reaches, decisions become strategic rather than tactical. The importance of external information - that is, environmental or textual information - becomes greater; and the importance of data generated by or captured with the organization's own routine operations lessens. Interestingly, this most basic failing of the MIS concept was the last to be recognized. It is, for example, conspicuous by its absence in Ackoff's classic 1971 litany of MIS misperceptions and shortcomings, 'Management Misinformation Systems' [1]. Although elucidating the failings of MIS systems and the MIS concept has been fair sport for two decades [2], it is only in the last few years that the failure of MISs to incorporate external data meaningfully has been perceived as a major failing, indeed as *the* major failing.

However, the perception of the importance of external information to business decision-making is fast gaining strength. Perhaps the best indicator of that emergence, and also a very clear and useful articulation of the importance of information, is IBM's espousal of 'Enterprise Information Analysis', which at the highest level consists of three steps:

1. Decide what your enterprise is all about.
2. Decide what decisions have to be made correctly to be successful in that enterprise.
3. Decide what information is needed to make those decisions correctly.

## Competitive advantage

Another major theme that has appeared in business literature and in busines thinking is that information technology and information services can be much more than just better and more efficient ways of conducting backroom operations. Information technology can be a mechanism by which to obtain a significant competitive advantage. The competitive advantage of information technology has been the theme of many articles in those same bellwether journals, the *Harvard Business Review* and the *Sloan Management Review* [3-5].

Information technology, the thesis goes, changes how companies compete. Information technology allows differentiation by product configuration, by customer service, and by the elimination of transaction and friction costs. Any or all of those effects change the nature of competition and tend to bind purchasers to the supplier offering them. Needless to say, when a technology changes the nature of competition, that technology is rapidly perceived to warrant strategic top-level attention.

## Stage III of information systems development

Another theme that is emerging is that information technology itself is undergoing a major change, moving into a third stage in which operational information systems technology will be characterized by a Moore's Law rate of growth (doubling periods of one or two years) in all three components - computation, storage, and communication. Stage III technology, it is argued, will change the structure of both intracompany operations and extracompany operations - changing, among other things, where operations are conducted, changing indeed the very structural configuration of companies. These changes will require top management's attention to information systems in a fashion quite unlike that required before [6].

## Convergence of the archipelago

The convergence phenomenon of information technology has captured the attention of the business community. What have been organizationally distinct functions - data processing, telecommunications, information centres, records management and office automation, increasingly are perceived as needing integrated management. The islands in the archipelago report to distinct parts of the organization - for example, data processing to finance, telecommunications to administrative services, the library or information centre to research and development. The integration of these islands therefore will require either major organizational changes or complex cross-organization managerial structures. In either case, the solutions - as McFarlan and company have pointed out - will be difficult to implement well and will therefore demand top-management attention [7-9].

A final and little-enunciated point is that information services are becoming too large a component of an organization's operations to be regarded as minor overhead operations. As information functions become a larger slice of the organizational pie, they demand more management attention, particularly more attention to costing and to their relationship with the company's outputs.

What these themes have in common is that information or information systems management will increasingly become a strategic-level concern of top management.

## DOMAINS

Business databases can be characterized as those that specialize in:
1. General news and the business and management literature;
2. Company-specific data;
3. Marketing information;
4. Technology, particularly patents; and
5. Demographic information.

These categories are, as will be demonstrated, hopelessly overlapping, but they will provide some structure to what might otherwise simply be an almost random discussion of interesting and useful databases.

In presenting information about databases, this chapter cannot hope to be a substitute for the directories of databases mentioned below, and it cannot be complete, for the information world is now much too vast. This chapter will mention key and representative databases, but inevitably some will go unnoted. The authors take full credit and blame for the selection.

## News and management literature

The area of general business news is richly supplied with a number of good bibliographic and textual databases. MANAGEMENT CONTENTS, ABI/INFORM, FINIS, NEWSPAPER & PERIODICAL ABSTRACTS, and TRADE & INDUSTRY INDEX are a few of the most obvious.

Recent years have seen the trend from bibliographic to full-text databases continue. While some databases, most notably NEXIS, originated as full-text files, others are rapidly adding full-text options. At the same time, the distinction between traditionally bibliographic database vendors such as DIALOG and full-text vendors such as Mead is eroding, as each now supports both types. The convenience of early full-text documents was initially offset by a lack of indexing leading to less than precise search results, but recent products such as ABI/INFORM and PROMT have successfully applied index terms and codes to their full-text offerings.

As databases expand their coverage, they continue to incorporate specialized resources that were previously of limited availability. Brokerage houses, for example, typically provided investment analyst reports only to their customers; similarly, contract research firms frequently compiled market research reports exclusively for their industrial clients. The advent of databases like INVESTEXT and FINDEX gave access to powerful new classes of information. INVESTEXT alone provides the full text of over 90,000 research reports on companies and industries from investment houses such as Morgan Stanley, First Boston, and Salomon Brothers (see Search 14.1). FINDEX contains citations and abstracts to over 12,000 market research reports and studies. MARKET ANALYSIS AND INFORMATION DATABASE (MAID) offers the full text of reports from Frost and Sullivan, Business International, USA Monitor - Market Research USA, and other domestic and international research houses.

## Search 14.1: INVESTEXT search on DIALOG for reports on Federal Express Corp.

```
File  545:INVESTEXT - 82-91/NOV  07
              (Copr. 1991 Thomson Financial Networks, Inc)

?e  cr=federal exp


Ref     Items    Index-term
E1       147   CR=FEDDERS  CORP.
E2        31   CR=FEDERAL  CO.
E3         0  *CR=FEDERAL  EXP
E4      1057    CR=FEDERAL  EXPRESS  CORP.
E5       714    CR=FEDERAL  HOME  LOAN  MORTGAGE  CORP.
E6        53    CR=FEDERAL  INDUSTRIES  LTD.
E7      1667    CR=FEDERAL  NATIONAL  MORTGAGE  ASSOC.
E8       415    CR=FEDERAL  PAPER  BOARD  CO.,  INC.
E9         2    CR=FEDERAL  PIONEER  LTD.
E10      112    CR=FEDERAL  REALTY  INVESTMENT  TRUST
E11        8    CR=FEDERAL  RESOURCES  CORP.
E12        7    CR=FEDERAL  SAVINGS  BANK


              Enter P or E for more

?s  e4/1991
              1057     CR=FEDERAL   EXPRESS   CORP.
            401151     PY=1991
       S1     209     CR="FEDERAL   EXPRESS   CORP."/1991

?report  1/titles

                      DIALOG File 545: INVESTEXT
                      35 Analysts Reports Available

      Title / Date
      Report# / Source / Analyst / Pages
    --------------------------------------------
    1 Federal Express - Company Report / September 26, 91
         RN=1141862 / SHEARSON LEHMAN BRO / Becker, H. /  4 pages

    2 Federal Express Corp. - Company Report / September 25, 91
         RN=162758 / MARKET GUIDE INC. / Goodman, K. D. /  4 pages
```

**Search 14.1: (cont.)**

```
    3 Federal Express Corp. - Company Report / September 25, 91
      RN=161538 / MARKET GUIDE INC. / Vij, M. O. /   2 pages

    4 Federal Express Corporation - Company Report / September 5, 91
      RN=1137762 / MERRILL LYNCH CAPIT / Rockel, D.W. /   8 pages

Enter item number(s), P for next page, or EXIT to leave TITLES:
?exit
```

Another class of information that has mushroomed in electronic format is the trade or industry newsletter. These periodicals tend to be highly focused, with very specific areas of concentration in government and industry. The vendor that first claimed this niche and is often associated with it is NEWSNET. Predicasts' PTS NEWSLETTER DATABASE also gives excellent coverage of the full text of titles like *Affluent Markets Alert, Political Risk Letter, New Technology Week, Inside R&D, FCC Daily Digest*, and *Report on AT&T*. Predicasts nods to end-user searchers with a menu-driven version of its product.

Files dedicated to specific industries have become popular in recent years. The associations and special interest groups that tend to produce them have benefited from technological advances that simplify database production. The EBIS (EMPLOYEE BENEFITS INFOSOURCE) file on DIALOG, for example, covers the employee benefits and human resources industries and is an automated version of the print files maintained by the International Foundation of Employee Benefit Plans (see Search 14.2). Similarly, the INSURANCE PERIODICALS INDEX on DIALOG, which abstracts significant articles from the insurance literature, is produced by the Insurance and Employee Benefits Division of the Special Libraries Association in association with the NILS Publishing Company. The CONSUMER PACKAGED GOODS library in NEXIS is defined by product type rather than by industry. It focuses on consumer goods in the apparel, food, furniture, pharmaceutical, and tobacco industries. In like manner, the NEXIS ENTERTAINMENT library covers the film and television industries, drawing on sources like BASELINE, which provides box-office grosses for United States films, celebrity biographies and agents, and titles and credits to more than 30,000 American feature films and television shows.

**Search 14.2: DIALOG search on EBIS for salary survey data in the health care industry**

```
File    22:EMPLOYEE  BENEFITS  INFOSOURCE_86-91/NOV
          (COPR. 1991 IFEBP)

     Set     Items   Description
     ---     -----   -----------

?s salary survey?/de or (compensation?/de and survey results/de)
          536     SALARY  SURVEY?/DE
          5782    COMPENSATION?/DE
          6665    SURVEY  RESULTS/DE
     S1   1520    SALARY  SURVEY?/DE  OR  (COMPENSATION?/DE  AND  SURVEY
                  RESULTS/DE)

?s health care industry/de
     S2   2201    HEALTH  CARE  INDUSTRY/DE

?s s1 and s2
          1520    S1
          2201    S2
     S3     80    S1 AND S2
```

**Search 14.2:** (cont.)

```
?t  3/3/1-3

   3/3/1
   00085610
   Are  Managers  Compensated  for  Hospital  Financial  Performance?
   Pink,  George  H.;    Leatt,  Peggy
   Health  Care  Management  Review,  v16  no3    pp  37-45    Summer  1991
   ISSN/ISBN:  0361-6274

   3/3/2
   00085521
   Demand  From  HMOs  Raising  Primary-Care  Salaries.
   Wagner,  Mary
   Modern  Healthcare,  v21  no31    p  14    Aug  5,  1991
   ISSN/ISBN:  0160-7480

   3/3/3
   00084666
   Hospital  CEOs  Get  Top  Dollar.
   Agovino,  Theresa
   Crain's  New  York  Business,  v7  no24    pp  3,  34    Jun  17,  1991
   ISSN/ISBN:  8756-789X
```

**Company data**

Many of the previously-mentioned general business files provide access to company information as well. One of the most accurate sources for specific company research is the PREDICASTS OVERVIEW OF MARKETS AND TECHNOLOGY (PROMT), a multi-industry database drawing from the business and trade press, local, national, and international newspapers, newsletters, research reports, press releases, and corporate annual reports. Predicasts' superior indexing and its elaborate thesaurus of subject and event codes offer an admirable level of search precision. Information Access Company's TRADE & INDUSTRY ASAP is another solid source for company research. Additional databases for general company information are the NEXIS CURRENT and OMNI files, which are truly comprehensive in scope and benefit greatly from the recent streamlining opportunities offered by the 'Focus' command.

The search for financial data on American companies benefits from the very strict (by European standards) reporting requirements of the Securities and Exchange Commission (SEC) for all companies whose stock is publicly traded. Finding data on companies that are not publicly traded, however, is a much more problematic issue. Probably the best-known database for company financial data is DISCLOSURE, which provides detailed balance sheet and earnings information for over 12,000 publicly-traded companies. DISCLOSURE's source materials are the documents each company files with the United States Securities and Exchange Commission. MEDIA GENERAL PLUS is an authoritative source for company financial and stock price information. It covers all companies on the New York and American Stock Exchanges, as well as companies on the NASDAQ National Market System and selected Over-the-Counter companies. For each organization, MEDIA GENERAL PLUS provides daily, monthly, and yearly stock prices and volume; balance sheet data going back five years; financial ratios; and industry comparisons (see Search 14.3).

Standard & Poor's COMPUSTAT database is a useful tool for merger/acquisition/divestiture analysis, competitor and peer group analysis, and equity and fixed income securities research. The database includes annual and quarterly financial data for North American public companies, as well as price, dividends, earnings, and line-of-business information. It also tracks financial ratios and industry aggregates.

## Search 14.3: DIALOG search on MEDIA GENERAL PLUS for Apple Computer's annual ratios

```
File 546:MEDIA GENERAL PLUS - NOV 1   1991
          (Copr. 1991 Media General)

    Set     Items   Description
    ---     -----   -----------

?s ts=aapl;t 1/32

    S1        1    TS=AAPL

  1/32/1
  00011843
  APPLE COMPUTER INC

  Exchange:    NMS        Ticker:     AAPL
  Membership:  S&P

  SIC Code:    3571 (ELECTRONIC COMPUTERS)
               Number of Companies in Industry:    66
  This is a(n) COMPANY Record

  ANNUAL RATIOS

  PROFITABILITY
  Date                 09/90    09/89    09/88    09/87    09/86
  Profit  Marg-PreTax%  14.0     14.1     16.1     15.4     16.3
  Profit  Marg-PosTax%   8.5      8.6      9.8      8.2      8.1
  Return on Stk Eq  %   32.8     30.6     39.9     26.0     22.2
  Return on Inv Cap %   32.8     30.6     39.9     26.0     22.2
  Return on Assets  %   16.0     16.5     19.2     14.7     13.3

  VALUATION RATIOS
  Date                 09/90    09/89    09/88    09/87    09/86
  Price/Sales Ratio       .9       .8      1.2      2.0      1.3
  Price/Earning Ratio   11.4     10.0     13.1     25.5     16.9
  Price/Book  Ratio      3.4      3.0      4.9      6.3      3.7

  OPERATING RATIOS
  Date                 09/90    09/89    09/88    09/87    09/86
  Effective Tax Rate%   39.0     39.0     39.0     47.0     50.3
  Asset Turnover         1.9      1.9      2.0      1.8      1.6
  Inventory Turnover     5.8      5.5      5.6      7.3      6.1
  Receiv/Day  Sales     49.3     54.0     56.5     54.9     49.8

  FINANCIAL RATIOS
  Date                 09/90    09/89    09/88    09/87    09/86
  Current Ratio          2.3      2.6      2.2      2.7      3.2
  Quick Ratio            1.7      1.8      1.4      2.0      2.6
  Leverage Ratio         2.1      1.8      2.1      1.8      1.7
  Debt/Equity             .0       .0       .0       .0       .0
  Interest Coverage       NC       NC       NC       NC       NC
```

Newswires are an essential source for company information, for they report what a company is saying about itself as well as what the national news services are providing. A number of database providers carry the major newswires, including DIALOG, NEXIS, and Dow Jones. Regional newspapers are an additional source of company information, as local papers frequently cover local employers much more thoroughly than does the national business press. DIALOG's PAPERS file and the BUSINESS DATELINE file on DIALOG, NEXIS and Dow Jones provide good coverage of the local business press. DataTimes, traditionally known as a supplier of full-text regional newspapers, is expanding its base to include national and international newspapers and wires as well.

For stock information, there are a number of sources in addition to Quotron and Telerate, which are priced so as to be suitable only for high-volume operations needing immediate data.

Access to stock and similar trading information is an area of numerous options with very marked price/currency trade-offs. It is an area that bears close examination as both pricing and players change rapidly. At present, DOW JONES QUOTES gives stock market data with a fifteen-minute delay. MEDIA GENERAL offers end-of-week data, and the NEXIS QUOTE library provides real-time quotes from the North American stock exchanges and NASDAQ, as well as bond quotes traded on the North American exchanges.

For credit information, the dominant supplier is DUN & BRADSTREET. D&B distributes its credit rating reports through its own electronic access system. The standard Business Information Report records invoice payment histories as well as public filings, financial statements, histories of the organization and its executives, and a D&B rating. In addition, Dun's Marketing Services offers several files through DIALOG, including the comprehensive MARKET IDENTIFIERS file, which covers public and private companies with either five or more employees or at least one million dollars in annual sales.

### Marketing information

The marketing literature, in addition to defining a company's markets and its competitors, offers valuable insights into the organization's strategies and operations. The Predicasts family of files is particularly suited to searches for marketing information. The MARS (MARKETING AND ADVERTISING REFERENCE SERVICE) file, like the PROMT file, is thoroughly indexed to provide multiple access points. Although it focuses on the advertising and marketing of goods and services, it also provides insights on demographic markets and consumer preferences. It excels in its coverage of advertising agency business and its indexing of accounts won and lost, personnel changes, and new campaigns launched. Source materials include the advertising press - *Advertising Age, Adweek,* and *Campaign,* to name a few - as well as trade journals, news wires, product announcements, research reports, and company press releases (see Search 14.4).

### Search 14.4: PTS MARS search on DIALOG for new advertising campaigns for soft drinks in the United States

```
        File  570:PTS  MARS - 84-91/Nov.11
                   (Copr. 1991 Predicasts Inc.)

        ?s  ac=74
            S1      45107     AC=74    (AD=CAMPAIGN  LAUNCHED)

        ?s  pc=2086
            S2       7052     PC=2086

        ?s  cc=1usa
            S3      296495    CC=1USA   (UNITED  STATES)

        ?s  s1  and  s2  and  s3

                    45107     S1
                     7052     S2
                   296495     S3
            S4       1229     S1  AND  S2  AND  S3
```

**Search 14.4:** (cont.)

```
?t  4/7/7

 4/7/7

00498299      DIALOG FILE 570      PTS MARS
New 7-Up spots

        Seven-Up (Dallas) has a new TV ad campaign for 7-Up and Diet 7-Up
that will  bring  back  the 'UNCOLA' theme from past ads, reports Nancy
Millman.  The  ads  for  the soft drinks will include the Spot
character from current advertising.  Leo  Burnett  is handling the
campaign. A new design for 7-Up packages is debuting.

SLOGAN:  UNCOLA
TRADE NAME:  7-Up; Diet 7-Up
SPOKESPERSON:  Spot

Chicago Sun Times (IL)    September 30, 1991  v. 45  no. 205  p. 43
Article type:  EDITORIAL
```

Mead Data's MARKET library on NEXIS is another comprehensive source for marketing and advertising information. In addition to the full text of over thirty marketing-related sources, the MARKET library contains selected documents from the general business press. Within the MARKET library are the ADVERTISING & MARKETING INTELLIGENCE (AMI) file, which is limited to abstracts, and the MEDIA file, which contains contact information for major print and broadcast outlets in the United States.

For regional information, the advertising and marketing columns in local papers can be gold mines. The *Chicago Tribune's* daily 'On Marketing' column covers products, markets, and accounts in the Midwest and is accessible via NEXIS, DIALOG, and DataTimes. The daily columns in the *Wall Street Journal* (on Dow Jones) and in the *New York Times* (on NEXIS) focus on large national advertisers and their agencies, but not exclusively; as newspapers of record, they also report activity among small and mid-sized marketers.

Additional databases yield specialized information for marketers. Thomson & Thomson's TRADEMARKSCAN files (on DIALOG) identify active registered trademarks and servicemarks, as well as pending applications, filed with the United States Patent and Trademark Office. The PRODUCTSCAN database produced by Marketing Intelligence describes consumer products in over 170 categories in markets worldwide. Records provide manufacturer information; packaging, merchandising, and positioning analyses; and target market identifications. The PUBLIC OPINION ONLINE (POLL) database, recently accessible via DIALOG, offers marketers the full text of public opinion surveys, including those conducted by Roper, Gallup, and Harris, as well as those sponsored by national news services.

**Technology tracking**

A major concern for many companies is an awareness of what is happening, or will be likely to happen, in the relevant business, legal, political and technological environments. BIOBUSINESS (on DIALOG), for example, focuses specifically on the business applications of biomedical research. ENERGY SCIENCE & TECHNOLOGY, also on DIALOG, indexes references to basic and applied scientific and technical research literature. Relevant chapters in this volume describe sources for specific subject areas.

Another good source for technology analyses are the predictions and forecasts in the Predicasts PTS FORECASTS and PTS US TIME SERIES databases. The former provides abstracts of published worldwide forecasts with records that present historical base data, short-term forecasts, and long-term forecasts. The latter gives an average of twenty years of statistical data and a calculated growth rate for measurements of economics, finance, demographics, and products. This type of data is not normally associated with bibliographic databases, but it does furnish an excellent lead-in to discussions of technological developments, and it provides the trend data necessary to encourage educated predictions.

Patent literature and patent databases are well worth noting in any discussion of sources for the business sector. Patents are reviewed separately in another chapter, which precludes their inclusion here. Suffice it to say that technology tracking and patent literature have a utility far broader than in the obvious technology-based industries such as electronics and pharmaceuticals. For example, the number of patents regarding toothpastes, dentrifices, and the like is truly surprising, and the identity of the patent holders is frequently a clue to a corporation's product development plans.

## Demographic data

Most of the demographic databases are value-added extensions of Census Bureau data. CENDATA, the United States Census Bureau's own online database, offers timely access to selected full-text and numeric data from the Census Bureau's various reports and releases. Time-series data are frequently available within an hour of release to the media, and statistical briefs are often available online long before they appear in print form. This is especially true for 1990 Census Data (see Search 14.5).

### Search 14.5: DIALOG menu search in CENDATA for 1990 population information

```
   -  CENDATA  MAIN  MENU

     1    Introduction  to  Census  Bureau  Products  and  Services
     2    What's New  in  CENDATA  (Including  Economic  Survey  Release  Dates)
     3    U.S.  Statistics  at  a  Glance  (Including  Economic  Time  Series  Data)
     4    Press  Releases
     5    Census  User  News
     6    Product  Information
     7    CENDATA  User  Feedback
     8    Profiles  and  Rankings
     9    Agriculture  Data
    10    Business  Data
    11    Construction  and  Housing  Data
    12    Foreign  Trade  Data
    13    Governments  Data
    14    International  Data
    15    Manufacturing  Data
    16    Population  Data
    17    Genealogical  and  Age  Information
    18    1990  Census  Information

  Enter   choice:
  ?18

  18  -  1990  CENSUS  DATA  AND .INFORMATION

     1    1990  Census  Information
     2    Press  Releases  With  1990  Census  Data
     3    1990  Census  Data  for  the  US,  Regions,  &  Divisions
     4    Race,  Hispanic,  &  Housing  Unit  Counts  (States,  Co.,  Place)
     5    Persons,  Families,  Households  &  Housing  Units  (STF  1)
     6    1990  Population  Counts  for  Governmental  Units—States  &  Counties
```

**Search 14.5:** (cont.)

```
   7    1990 Population Counts for Governmental Units—Places
   8    1990 Census Terms (Definitions and Explanations)
Enter choice, or <return> to see previous menu:
?3

18.3 - 1990 CENSUS DATA FOR THE UNITED STATES, REGIONS, AND DIVISIONS

   1   Age By Race By Sex For All Persons
   2   Number of Households By Race
   3   Tenure By Race of Householder
   4   1990 Population By Age For All Persons
Enter choice, or <return> to see previous menu:
?4

18.3.4 - 1990 POPULATION BY AGE FOR ALL PERSONS

   1    1990 Population By Age For All Persons
   2    1990 Population By Age For White Persons
   3    1990 Population By Age For Black Persons
   4    1990 Population By Age For Am. Indian, Eskimo, & Aleut Persons
   5    1990 Population By Age For Asian & Pacific Islander Persons
   6    1990 Population By Age For Other Race Persons

Enter choice, or <return> to see previous menu:
?1

18.3.4.1 - November   7, 1991
1990 POPULATION BY AGE FOR ALL PERSONS

United States
Regions and Divisions                         Under 5      5 to 13     14 to 17
States                          All ages         years        years        years
-------------------------------------------------------------------------------

United States          248,709,873  18,354,443  31,970,321  13,279,668

   Northeast Region     50,809,229   3,504,805   5,883,950   2,524,252
      New England Div.  13,206,943     919,346   1,505,954     633,886
      Middle Atlantic Div. 37,602,286 2,585,459   4,377,996   1,890,366

   Midwest Region       59,668,632   4,404,822   7,941,650   3,268,311
      East North Central 42,008,942  3,095,230   5,533,963   2,320,628
      West North Central 17,659,690  1,309,592   2,407,687     947,683

   South Region         85,445,930   6,233,070  11,075,100   4,700,208
                           -more-
```

For time series data and projections, the most accessible source is DONNELLY DEMOGRAPHICS, which contains census data plus five-year projections. The data are organized and retrievable not only by the Census Bureau Metropolitan Statistical Areas (MSAs), but also by Arbitron Areas of Dominant Influence (ADIs) and A. C. Nielsen's Designated Marketing Areas (DMAs). The latter are media, particularly television, based categories and are useful for marketing-based analyses. The MAX system produced by National Planning Data Corporation provides current-year estimates and five-year projections of key demographics, as well as consumer spending patterns for various geographic designations.

The manipulative capabilities provided by online access has turned a staid old standby, the telephone book yellow pages, into a demographic resource for establishment information. The DUN'S ELECTRONIC

BUSINESS DIRECTORY on DIALOG is divided into fourteen sections (Agriculture, Business Services, Communications, etc.) which offer the creative searcher a number of options. A search of a census database, for example, might identify target areas, and a second search of those areas in the ELECTRONIC BUSINESS or the similar TRINET files would identify establishments in those areas.

## GENERAL COMMENTS

### SIC Codes

The Standard Industrial Classification (SIC) Code is used by a very large proportion of business databases, and the searcher should be familiar with it. SIC Codes are four-digit identifiers applied to all products tracked by the federal government. The first two digits define major groups of industries (for example, 20 is food industries); the first three digits define smaller groups of industries (202 is dairy products); and the four digits taken as a whole define individual industries (2024 is ice cream).

SIC Codes are clumsy and awkward to use. The main disadvantage of the Code is that industries and their products can appear in only one place. A computerized axial tomography (CAT) scanner, for example, must be classified as a mechanical device, an electrical one, or a health care device - but not all three, or even two of the three. In addition, the Code is outdated. The 1987 revision was three years in the making and already shows its age. Fax machines, for example, appear as 'Telephone and Telegraph Apparatus' (3661), sharing the same code with answering machines, switchboards, and modems.

Despite its drawbacks, the SIC Code is a useful tool, and the business database searcher is well advised to become familiar with it and its idiosyncrasies. It is much less expensive to peruse the Code in print form before formulating a search strategy than it is to explore online. Variations on the Code include the Predicasts extensions from four to as many as seven levels. Other classification methods, including CUSIP numbers and Dun's numbers, should be familiar to database searchers. CUSIP is the acronym for the Committee on Uniform Securities Identification Procedures, and a CUSIP number is a unique identifier assigned to securities in the United States since 1970. Dun's numbers are Dun & Bradstreet's method of uniquely identifying domestic and worldwide parent companies, branch locations, and subsidiaries or divisions (see Search 14.6).

## Search 14.6: DISCLOSURE search on DIALOG to identify DUNS and CUSIP numbers for insurance companies in New York City

```
File  100:DISCLOSURE_ ,  NOV  11  1991
            (Copr.  1991 Disclosure  (TM)  Incorporated)

      Set     Items    Description
      ---     -----    -----------

?s  sc=63?  or  sc=64?
              337    SC=63?
               95    SC=64?
      S1      393    SC=63?  OR  SC=64?

?s  cy=new  york
      S2      534    CY=NEW  YORK
```

**Search 14.6:** (cont.)

```
?s s1 and s2
                393     S1
                534     S2
        S3       39     S1 AND S2

?sort  3/all/co,a
        S4       39     Sort  3/ALL/CO,A

?report  4/co,dn,cu/1-5

Align  paper;   press  ENTER
?


Company                             D-U-N-S      CUSIP
Name                                Number       Number
------------------------------      ----------   ----------

ALEXANDER  &  ALEXANDER   SERVICES  06-487-0207  0000144761
ALLCITY  INSURANCE   CO             04-469-5955  0000167521
ALLEGHANY   CORP                    00-697-9652  0000171751
AMBAC  INC                          NA           0000231391
AMERICAN  INTERNATIONAL   GROUP  I  00-727-0028  0000268741
```

Note that although we tend to speak of the SIC Code, there is actually a family of SIC Codes - the United States, the Canadian, and the British, as well as the United Nations offshoot, the SITC (Standard Industrial Trade Classification) Code. These codes are all similar but not identical.


## CD-ROM

Much of the information discussed within this chapter is available, partially or fully, on compact disk. CD-ROM (Compact Disk Read Only Memory) offerings continue to multiply, proliferating at an incredible pace. Among the leading vendors offering business disks are SilverPlatter, DIALOG, Disclosure, and Lotus. By offering the advantage of fixed price with unlimited searching, CD-ROMs do away with the ticking clock and become ideal instruments for end-user environments.

Nevertheless, the technology is not without its drawbacks. Software requirements are not standardized, which can result in difficulties when trying to run products created to varying specifications by different vendors. In an environment where online billings are charged back to the customer, allocating the fixed cost of the disk to the variable use and changeable number of client-users presents a barrier to use in many business libraries. Premiums charged by vendors for linking compact disks to local area networks may also keep costs prohibitively high in some cases.

Financial information on CD-ROM comprises one of its widest areas of use. Outstanding among the offerings in this arena are LOTUS ONE SOURCE, COMPUSTAT PC+, and DISCLOSURE. LOTUS and COMPUSTAT can both be easily used in market analyses and are extremely powerful tools in the hands of a skilled user.

## Downloading and statistical manipulation

Many of the database hosts in the business area began as service bureau, selling computation rather than data. Vendors in this category include ADP, DRI, and IP Sharp. Because of the added value of manipulations as well as data provision, these vendors have tended to be rather more expensive than the vendors whose origin derives from the straightforward provision of data rather than computation. The implication of this is that for searching *per se*, alternative vendors are often cheaper.

Furthermore, the emergence of the powerful microcomputer and easy, cheap, local data manipulation independent of a corporate MIS centre implies that the same manipulation capability may now be more economically achieved by searching data via the least expensive source and manipulating the retrieved data locally. It is not apparent that the price structure of some of the vendors has adjusted to these new realities, or perhaps the more pertinent reality is that the inertia of users and their reluctance to change a procedure they are comfortable with inhibits price reduction. In any case, the business database searcher is well advised to examine costs carefully and to investigate thoroughly whether vendor-hosted data manipulation cannot now be done more economically locally.

Downloading can be a tricky business for database searchers. The process is usually attempted for one of two reasons: first, to import numeric data into a spreadsheet for automatic manipulation; and second, to improve the visual presentation of a textual document. The first, as implied above, is a straightforward procedure if the numeric database provides delimited fields and if the spreadsheet has been properly formatted. The second is, surprisingly, more cumbersome, because conversions from ASCII files to word-processing documents are still imperfect. The resulting documents frequently require extensive editing, which moves the database searcher from retrieval mode to word-processing mode. Desktop software such as VANTAGE can be programmed for automatic editing, but again with imperfect results.

## Trends

The entry of new players into the information marketplace, the beginnings of market saturation, and the increasing availability of primary data will have a dramatic effect on business information in the future. Legal barriers which prevented the entry of major telephone market players into the information business have been removed. The presence of companies with deep pockets, like Ameritech and NYNEX, may encourage consolidation or competition-induced growth in the industry, with accompanying price fluctuations and increasingly varied offerings.

The probability of a national fibre optic network linking businesses and homes and carrying a variety of data types is approaching reality. The capability of government and business to execute and maximize the potential of this technology will be key to the breadth of its use. Business information professionals will want to play a leading role in these developments.

The end-user market will heat up as the industry saturates. Dow Jones' DOWQUEST product is a current-day illustration of a product engineered to serve the end-user by providing plain-English searching. Market saturation is undoubtedly an opportunity for database searchers to lobby for lower prices.

Primary information is becoming increasingly more available. Electronic Data Interchange, or EDI, is being used by a growing number of businesses to replace paper documentation for ordering and purchasing parts and supplies. This data may ultimately become more widely dispersed into a larger network of product information. Another source of primary information which is bound to have continuing repercussions is scanner data, now spinning out of our retail establishments at a breathtaking clip. The integration of scanner data and credit files creates marketability down to a 'market of one'. The use and abuse of this data, its sale and availability, will be a key issue in research in the future.

Copyright issues are also becoming increasingly complex in the Information Age. Information providers and vendors will be asked to become more flexible in view of the electronic use of their data; the focus will undoubtedly have to move from one of 'pay per use' to a more complete service and functionality orientation. Vendors in particular will have to focus more clearly on the needs of key clientele and the individualized services which the vendor can provide.

The evolution of online business databases is accelerating, its pace exceeding the rate of growth at the industry's inception. With a complex world of online business data ahead, database searchers stand to be major beneficiaries of the change.

## REFERENCES

1.      Russel L. Ackoff. Management misinformation systems. *Management Science* 14 1967 B-147, B-156
2.      John Dearden. MIS is a mirage. *Harvard Business Review* 50(1) 1972 90-99
3.      Gregory L. Parsons. Information technology: A new competitive weapon. *Sloan Management Review* 25(1) 1983 3-14
4.      F. Warren McFarlan. Information technology changes the way you compete. *Harvard Business Review* 62(3) 1984 98-103
5.      Robert I. Benjamin, *et al.* Information technology: A strategic opportunity. *Sloan Management Review* 25(3) 1984 3-10
6.      Michael E. D. Koenig. The convergence of computers and telecommunications: Information management implications. *Information Management Review* 1(3) 1986 23-33
7.      James L. McKenney and F. Warren McFarlan. The information archipelago - Maps and bridges. *Harvard Business Review* 60(5) 1982 109-114
8.      F. Warren McFarlan, *et al.* The information archipelago - Plotting a course. *Harvard Business Review* 61(1) 1983 145-156
9.      F. Warren McFarlan and James L. McKenney. The information archipelago - Governing the new world. *Harvard Business Review* 61(4) 1983 91-99

## PRINCIPAL VENDORS

Some, but by no means all, of the principal vendors of business databases in North America are listed below, with brief descriptions of their emphases.

**BRS** - Exceptionally strong in the fields of medicine, science, and education, BRS has at times suffered from involvement in a multitude of projects ranging from software sales to joint publishing ventures. Business users will find a number of valuable files, however, including the HARVARD BUSINESS REVIEW and ABI/INFORM.

**COMPUSERVE** - A wholly owned subsidiary of H&R Block, Compuserve was originally designed as a system for the home computer user. Compuserve's Business Services unit, however, focuses on the business market, and has mounted S&P's COMPUSTAT and DISCLOSURE among other files. Its VALUE database provides daily stock history. Much of Compuserve's financial data is more easily retrieved elsewhere, however, via tools like Compustat's own PC+ product.

**DATA RESOURCES, INC. (DRI) -** A vendor of econumeric and time series data, DRI also makes available some textual and bibliographic databases (such as TRINET and the COMMERCE BUSINESS DAILY) as well as cross-sectional information (such as Census data).

**DATA-STAR -** A European-based direct competitor to DIALOG, Data-Star is launching an attack on the US market. Data-Star searching is based on BRS protocol; of 230 files, 112 are business-oriented. Overall pricing is competitive, and there is an after-hours discount (after 1:00 EST, thanks to its European base).

**DATATIMES -** Originally a provider of the full text of regional newspapers, DataTimes now operates as a gateway system with access to several Canadian and European databases, as well as Dow Jones and an expanding array of local, regional, and national US news services.

**DIALOG -** The 'supermarket of online databases', DIALOG provides a wide variety of information, maximizing the investment made in learning the system. A broad range of business databases - statistical, full-text, and abstract formats - are available. DIALOG also has a menu mode for end-user searching, and a number of CD-ROM products.

**DOW JONES -** With an almost purely business focus, Dow Jones is an important player. It exclusively offers the full text of the *Wall Street Journal*, as well as stock quotes (historical and current), investment reports, and more. Dow Jones is aggressively going after the executive market with its DowQuest plain-English searching and DowVision, which provides customized delivery of newswire and interactive data retrieval services through corporate computer systems direct to executives' desktops.

**DUN & BRADSTREET -** D&B's reputation was made on its collection of company data for credit rating purposes. It releases its credit reports through its own DunsPrint service, but it provides company financial and directory information through additional vendors including its own Duns Marketing Services Group and DIALOG. D&B is currently attempting to streamline its reporting procedures for faster delivery and to identify corporate linkages through its Duns numbers.

**MARKET ANALYSIS AND INFORMATION DATABASE (MAID) -** MAID is a British database which created a niche market by becoming an online supplier of research reports with detailed information on product categories and brands. The annual subscription fee ($10,000 at this writing) is prohibitive, but MAID's reports from prestigious research houses provide valuable insights into consumer markets, including hard-to-obtain market share data.

**MARKETING INTELLIGENCE -** Through its PRODUCTSCAN database, Marketing Intelligence provides descriptions of consumer products in worldwide markets including North America. Descriptions include product content, packaging information, manufacturer name and location, and target markets.

**MAX -** The database reporting system for National Planning Data Corporation's demographic estimates and projections, MAX offers current and historical census information. It also produces data for thematic maps by census tract, zip code area, county, and state.

**MEAD DATA -** Full text remains a stronghold for Mead, whose business services include NEXIS (news files, magazine files, etc.), EXCHANGE (brokerage reports), and NAARS (annual reports). Mead, more than any other vendor with the possible exception of Dow Jones, has targeted the end-user market. Search software and protocol are extremely user-friendly.

**NEWSNET** - Newsnet created a niche by putting trade and industry newsletters online. One of Newsnet's historical selling points has been its access to TRW credit reports with payment histories for millions of United States businesses. Newsnet also offers numerous publications which are unavailable online elsewhere.

**ORBIT** - The first to offer commercial online bibliographic database searching, ORBIT has maintained a focus in scientific and technical areas. With the termination of its exclusive arrangement with Derwent (patent databases), it is no longer a major business database provider.

**THOMSON FINANCIAL NETWORKS** - Formerly known for its INVESTEXT database, Thomson is attempting to target the end-user market with its new CORIS product. CORIS provides access to INVESTEXT, Business Dateline, Predicasts PROMT, and ABI/INFORM, among others, and produces 'Express' reports which pull selected current information from each datafile for a given company or industry.

**WEFA GROUP** - A result of the merger between Chase Econometrics and Wharton Econometric, the WEFA Group provides economic analysis, forecasting, and consulting services. (WEFA is an acronym for Wharton Econometric Forecasting Associates.) Its forecasting services focus on nine major areas of world economic activity, including automotive, food and agriculture, and financial. The WEFA Group's databases and econometric models are accessible via time-sharing, on disk for access by PCs, and on magnetic tape. Services are available on a fee or subscription basis.

# 15 Humanities

*Candy Schwartz*

## SCOPE

For the purposes of this chapter, humanities has been defined as including the visual and performing arts, philosophy, religion, literature, language and history. While history and language may be more appropriately characterized in part as social sciences, the problems encountered in searching files in these fields are similar to those associated with the 'true' humanities. In fact, many database vendors group social sciences and the humanities together when categorizing database offerings for directories or for training sessions (although the reasons for this have more to do with paucity of offerings than with shared features). In addition to commercially-available online databases, the chapter will include CD-ROM products (whether available by subscription or one-time purchase), and a brief digression into the world of electronic bulletin boards.

## OVERVIEW/HISTORY

There is a dearth of online offerings in the humanities (as compared with pure and applied sciences, business, and social sciences), and humanities files typically contain fewer records, have less frequent update schedules, and do not extend as far back in time. Very few humanities files do not also have a manual counterpart, and many print humanities indexes are not yet available in machine-readable form. On a brighter note, the past few years have seen a growth in the number of CD-ROM offerings in the humanities, and the increasing availability of dial-access to remote library catalogues and full-text general media files has improved the situation for the humanities scholar and online searcher.

The most obvious reason for the paucity of offerings in the humanities is the lack of a large and well-funded market. Historically database search service suppliers first turned their attention to the needs of the scientific and engineering communities, in response to national calls for control over the information explosion of the 1950s and 1960s. The problems of making large amounts of data accessible to large numbers of remote users were solved in the 1970s, and this expertise was then used to supply the demands of information-hungry and technologically-literate professions in business, law and health services. While new indexing and abstracting services continue to appear, most new offerings for the past decade have been in other file types: company and product directories; full-text journals, handbooks, encyclopedias, newspapers and news wires; and demographic, scientific, and economic data banks. To the advantage of search service suppliers, the target professional communities for these files are spread across a broad spectrum of society. Humanities scholarship, by contrast, is largely limited to academia, and humanities departments do not usually compare favourably in size (or support) with faculties in other fields. Research funds in the humanities are limited, with the result that humanities scholars (and their libraries) have little to spend on online searching, and search service suppliers cannot expect much in the way of revenue from this user group.

Demand for better offerings in the humanities has not been forthcoming from users, as there has been little to recommend online searching to the humanities scholar. Efforts to make humanities print indexing services available online have suffered from financial constraints and poor understanding of the search potential afforded by this different delivery mode. Up until recently, user aids and training sessions for humanities online searching have been poorly designed (or non-existent), and have not encouraged searching activity. Database publishers have marketed primarily to libraries rather than promoting awareness among humanities scholars, and libraries may have been reluctant to create a high demand which would then result in increased expenditures for online access, inter-library loan and staff time.

This rather unfortunate state is changing. New humanities files are appearing, CD-ROM subscriptions have offered a fixed-price method of information access which is also suitable to the individual nature of humanities research, and files are getting larger as time passes (and as retrospective conversion projects are put into place). Online searchers are more aware of the availability of humanities information in other subject areas and in general and interdisciplinary files, and full-text databases have alleviated some of the problems of document delivery. Scholars entering a career in the humanities are more likely to have been exposed to computer-based information seeking, whether through online catalogue use, 'home' systems such as Prodigy or CompuServe, bibliographic instruction programs, or (still rarely) online searching in high schools.

## A word on networking

The past two years have witnessed a tremendous surge in the use of electronic mail networks for scholarly interaction. While this is not really related to online searching, it is an important phenomenon in academic life. Systems such as Bitnet and Internet have enabled researchers to link with each other, to search large library catalogues world-wide, and to participate in electronic conferences in their areas of specialization, and all of this largely at no cost to the individual. National and international efforts to make such communication even more widely available are evident. A 1990 issue of *Online* carried a series of articles which not only discuss the issues, but provide practical tips on how to access the services [1]. A small sampling of humanities bulletin boards available on Internet as of November 1990 shows more than thirty in areas such as music, ethnomusicology, architecture, art, computers and the humanities, cinema, dance, Dante, folklore, *Finnegan's Wake*, Gaelic language, literature, morris dancing, philosophy, Shakespeare, theatre, and terminology. Most of these generate from academic institutions, and most are 'peered', meaning that someone oversees the circulating mail for appropriate content.

## THE NATURE OF HUMANITIES RESEARCH

Successful implementation of online searching in the humanities requires an understanding of the information needs and research habits of humanities scholars. These needs and habits differ from those of other disciplines in several respects which bear closely on the usefulness of online services.

### The humanities scholar

It is no longer (and perhaps never was) fair to say that humanities researchers are more likely than other groups to distrust, dislike or resist computers. It may be the case that humanists are more concerned with the impact of technology on the individual and society, but on a personal level most members of the academic community, whatever their department, conduct much of their business *via* computers, either directly or indirectly. From secretarial and personal word processing, through library catalogues, to machine-based humanities projects, the use of high technology in support of faculty life is not new.

What does create difficulties in a machine environment is the necessity of delegating research to an intermediary. Humanities scholars have not traditionally relied on assistance in conducting manual research. In a sense, the library is the scholar's laboratory, where basic research is conducted through secondary and primary sources. Collaboration among researchers (in the observable phenomenon of multiple authorship) is not as common in the humanities as in other fields. Research methods are personal and individualistic, demanding browsing and examination (both of which are difficult and expensive activities online). Information needs may change as a result of looking at sources while searching, and the whole process is highly interactive. This makes delegation difficult, and yet the complex nature of humanities files and the absence of good front-end software dictate the use of intermediaries.

### Information needs

Scientific research is evolutionary in that it seeks to test theories and discover new facts, and the results of these endeavours replace prior knowledge. Business information needs concentrate on the most current data - financial facts, mergers, acquisitions, and so on. By way of contrast, research in the humanities is cumulative and is concerned with the whole time span of human achievement. New information does not replace old information nor make it invalid. There is a greater need for retrospective sources, and first-hand examination of original (largely monographic) materials plays a greater role. Citation studies reveal that humanities information is scattered across a wider range of sources than in the sciences, and that journals remain actively useful for a longer time span.

Online services in the humanities do not speak to these needs. Few online indexing services extend back beyond the 1970s, and access to primary artefacts (other than current creative output in magazines and newspapers) consists principally of location information in various national and institutional MARC catalogues. Analytic indexing (for the individual contents of a collection of essays or other creative works) is rare. Information about non-print primary artefacts is very limited. Small wonder that humanities scholars find online search services limited at best and frustrating at worst.

# INFORMATION SEEKING PROBLEMS

Apart from the lack of suitable information sources, certain approaches to information seeking which are common among humanities scholars can create special problems for online searching.

## Names

Personal, institutional and geographic names and other proper nouns play an important role in humanities research, and are often the principal point of access in a search. The treatment of names is not only inconsistent across databases, it is usually inconsistent within one file. Names may or may not be included in the descriptor or identifier field, or in some separate index, and the fullness with which a name is cited in any of these fields may vary. No authority control is exercised over name forms in titles and abstracts, and these problems are compounded for names which have been converted from one script to another (for instance, Tchaikovsky) or are subject to variation because of their historical nature. Pen names and pseudonyms cause problems, and common names (such as Joyce) or names which are also common nouns (Wood, More, etc.) must be adequately contextualized.

## Time

Restricting a search to a particular time period has been called 'probably the most intractable problem in the humanities databases for producers as well as users...' [2, p.3]. Time may be implied in a word or phrase ('the Renaissance', 'the Middle Ages', 'the Woodstock era'), or it may be stated in natural language using words or numbers ('the seventeenth century', 'the 60s', 'the 60's', 'the sixties'), or it may be directly stated as a particular year or years ('1964', 'from 1963 to 1965', '1792-1793'). Some database publishers have attempted, without a great deal of success, to create time period indexes, but even these display error and inconsistency.

## Language and subject access

In addition to the problems outlined above, general text word searching in humanities files is difficult. Subject access is usually limited to titles and subject index fields, and where abstracts are present they are usually quite brief. Titles in the humanities are notoriously ambiguous, metaphorical and allusive. Titles of foreign language materials, which form a significant component of many files, may not be translated, and transliteration schemes for non-Roman titles vary from one file to another. Vocabulary control (that is, thesauri and subject headings schemes) in the humanities has always been problematic, whether for manual or online access. Publishers of print indexes developed idiosyncratic indexing schemes which suited the print environment. These tended to take a classificatory approach, grouping like items together by geographic region or time period. When most of these publications were converted into machine-readable databases, the indexing schemes were carried over. However, what works well for the human eye scanning a printed page does not provide effective specific access in an environment in which browsing is difficult and expensive. Many database publishers have subsequently modified their indexing methods for the online setting, but more work remains to be done.

Systematic classification schemes are rare, with the result that generic searching (for example, all the individual geopolitical units which form 'North America' or 'the United Kingdom') is laborious. Similarly, very few humanities files are accompanied by online thesauri to assist in the formation of groups of related concepts.

In general, indexing in humanities databases is neither exhaustive (covering all the topics in an item) nor specific (indexing concepts as narrowly as discussed in an item), which means that a great deal of effort is required on the part of the searcher to achieve reasonable levels of recall (finding relevant material) and precision (avoiding irrelevant material).

# DATABASES

The remainder of this chapter is devoted to discussions of specific databases or database types. The first five sections (humanities information in other fields, machine-readable cataloguing, general files, specialized files, and regional files) do not provide details of searching capabilities, but are intended to remind the reader of the wide range of online sources in which humanities information may be found. The final section examines the 'true' humanities files in depth. Most of the data and search examples were collected at the end of 1990, and file sizes and update rates are approximate (and are given for the online file rather than the CD-ROM equivalent). No attempt has been made to characterize price, as this varies with the vendor and searching institution. A list of search service suppliers and database publishers can be found in the Appendix to this chapter.

## Humanities information in other fields

In the absence of a large number of humanities files, searchers must be creative in investigating alternative sources. From the scholar's point of view, one of the real advantages of online searching is that it provides an attractive method of searching unfamiliar indexing services outside the domain of expertise. Large retrospective files in fields as diverse as agriculture, engineering, education, management, medicine and economics have been found to contain information on cultural life, creative arts, folklore and similar topics. These and other databases also support interdisciplinary research in areas such as computers and the humanities, humanities education, business and industrial aspects of the arts, demographic studies, and the history of science. Two admittedly broad searches in MEDLINE and INSPEC give an indication of the variety of materials which can be found (Searches 15.1 and 15.2).

## Search 15.1: Humanities information in science files: INSPEC on DIALOG

```
  ? e (humanities)
                                          Note  abundance  of
  Ref  Items  Type  RT  Index-term        humanities  descriptors
  R1     931         10  *HUMANITIES  (January  1969)
  R2   34382    N     5  ART  (January  1971)
  R3   50828    N     9  HISTORY  (January  1969)
  R4    2088    N    10  LANGUAGE  TRANSLATION  (January  1977)
  R5    8512    N     8  LINGUISTICS  (January  1977)
  R6   66610    N     5  LITERATURE  (January  1973)
  R7    8532    N     5  MUSIC  (January  1971)
  R8    1404    R     4  ARCHAEOLOGY  (January  1973)
  R9     574    R     9  HUMANITIES  DATA  PROCESSING  (January  1977)
  R10   2318    R     4  PHILOSOPHICAL  ASPECTS  (January  1969)
  R11  12496    R    10  CC=C7820  Humanities     Classification  code

  ? ss cc=c7820 and (medieval or mediaeval or middle(w)ages)/id
```

**Search 15.1:** (cont.)

```
         S1      6297    CC=C7820  Humanities
         S2       105    MEDIEVAL/ID
         S3        18    MEDIAEVAL/ID
         S4       567    MIDDLE/ID
         S5      1804    AGES/ID
         S6        18    MIDDLE/ID(W)AGES/ID
         S7        56    CC=C7820 AND (MEDIEVAL OR MEDIAEVAL OR MIDDLE(W)AGES)/ID

  ? ss s7 and (lexico? or dictionar? or linguist?)/de,id

                 56    S7
         S8      776    LEXICO?/DE,ID
         S9     2296    DICTIONAR?/DE,ID
         S10    5364    LINGUIST?/DE,ID
         S11      18    S7 AND (LEXICO? OR DICTIONAR? OR LINGUIST?)/DE,ID


  ? t 11/ti/1-3

   11/TI/1
   Title: The historical dictionary of the Hebrew language

   11/TI/2
   Title: An information-theoretic approach to the written transmission of
  Old English

   11/TI/3
   Title: Informatics and the humanities. Bibliography for 1984-7 from
  several specialist journals
```

**Search 15.2: Humanities information in science files: MEDLINE on DIALOG**

```
  ? e (art)                                          Note humanities
                                                     descriptors
  Ref   Items    Type   RT   Index-term
  R1     3080          12    *ART
  R2      671    X           DC=K1.93.  (ART)
  R3       59    N      4    ANATOMY,  ARTISTIC
  R4       69    N      3    CARICATURES
  R5       70    N      2    CARTOONS
  R6       26    N      3    ENGRAVING  AND  ENGRAVINGS
  R7      372    N      7    MEDICAL   ILLUSTRATION
  R8      365    N      2    MEDICINE  IN  ART
  R9       50    N      2    NUMISMATICS
  R10     279    N      2    PAINTINGS
  R11     276    N      3    PHILATELY
  R12    6021    N      2    PORTRAITS
  R13     109    N      2    SCULPTURE

  ? ss r8 and (middle(w)ages or medieval or mediaeval)

         S1       365    MEDICINE  IN  ART
         S2    454335    MIDDLE
         S3     14252    AGES
         S4       115    MIDDLE(W)AGES
         S5      1731    MEDIEVAL
```

**Search 15.2:** (cont.)

```
        S6          11      MEDIAEVAL
        S7          64      "MEDICINE  IN  ART"  AND  (MIDDLE(W)AGES  OR  MEDIEVAL  OR
                            MEDIAEVAL)

 ?  ss  s7  and  painting?

                    64      S7
        S8          521     PAINTING?
        S9          12      S7  AND  PAINTING?

 ?  t  9/ti/1-3
    9/TI/1
    [History  of  dentistry  in  western  painting]
    L'histoire  de  l'art  dentaire  a  travers  la  peinture  occidentale.

    9/TI/2
    [Facial  abnormalities  in  figurative  art  and  in  historical  documents]
    Gesichtsfehlbildungen  in  der  bildenden  Kunst  und  in  historischen
    Dokumenten.

    9/TI/3
    [Sources  on  the  Kral  hospital  in  Constantinople]
    Die  Quellen  zum  Kral-Spital  in  Konstantinopel.
```

### Machine-readable cataloguing

In most Western countries a national library or similar agency provides machine-readable cataloguing files which support local library automation activities and international exchange of records. The largest of these are produced by the British Library and the United States Library of Congress, and these institutions are also responsible for several retrospective cataloguing efforts which cover early imprints. It should be noted that the British Library applies both Library of Congress and PRECIS subject headings to its current cataloguing, which should result in improved subject access.

### BNBMARC

Producer:   British Library
Vendor:     BLAISE-LINE, OCLC, RLIN, Utlas
CD-ROM:     Chadwyck-Healey, Faxon (BNB ON CD-ROM)
Coverage:   Materials with British imprints published since 1950, including books, government publica-
            tions, conference proceedings, serials and series.
Size:       Well over a million records.
Update:     700 records per week.

### BRITISH LIBRARY CATALOGUE PREVIEW and BRITISH LIBRARY GENERAL CATALOGUE OF PRINTED BOOKS TO 1975 ON CD-ROM

Producer:   British Library
Vendor:     BLAISE-LINE
CD-ROM:     Chadwyck-Healey, Faxon
Coverage:   Between the online file and the CD-ROM, citations to items held by the British Library, in all
            languages, ranging in age from BC through 1975.

Size: Almost 9 million records.
Update: Irregular

## EIGHTEENTH CENTURY SHORT TITLE CATALOGUE
Producer: British Library
Vendor: BLAISE-LINE, RLIN
Coverage: Books, pamphlets, ephemera and other printed material from 1701-1800, including English-language items regardless of origin, and items published in the British Isles and colonies regardless of language.
Size: 260,000
Update: Varies with vendor.

## HUMANITIES AND SOCIAL SCIENCES
Producer: British Library
Vendor: BLAISE-LINE
Coverage: Current catalogue of several departments in the British Library, mostly from 1976 forward, including foreign language materials.
Size: 1,000,000
Update: 1,000 records per week.

## INCUNABLE SHORT TITLE CATALOGUE
Producer: British Library
Vendor: BLAISE-LINE
Coverage: Items in any language, of any origin, printed before 1501.
Size: 22,000
Update: Monthly

## LC MARC, LC FOREIGN MARC and REMARC
Producer: Library of Congress (LC MARC); Utlas (REMARC)
Vendor: Almost all vendors have some subset of the MARC files, and records are also available from the Library of Congress and cataloguing utilities.
CD-ROM: Various CD-ROM cataloguing systems include a subset of LC MARC records, and OCLC distributes LC MARC records on CD-ROM divided into 'subject libraries' (including THE MUSIC LIBRARY).
Coverage: The LC MARC and FOREIGN MARC files represent Library of Congress cataloguing since 1968 (or later for some non-English materials), including monographic and serial literature in almost all languages. REMARC covers items catalogued by LC and contributing libraries which are not in the LC MARC files, with imprints going back to the 1500s.
Size: 3,000,000 (LC MARC); 5,200,000 (REMARC)
Update: Varies with vendor, almost 300,000 new MARC records annually; REMARC is essentially a closed file.

## MUSIC LIBRARY CATALOGUE
Producer: British Library
Vendor: BLAISE-LINE
Coverage: All music published in the UK since 1981, and non-British music acquired by the British Music Library.

Size:        17,000
Update:      250 records per month.


## General files

Many leading English-language (particularly American) national and regional newspapers are now available on CD-ROM and online in full-text, or are abstracted and indexed by a variety of vendors. Apart from their utility as general news sources, these files are all noteworthy for including fiction, poetry, short stories, art, photographic essays and other original works, for reviews of all types of media, and for notices regarding current exhibits and performances. Visual images, with one exception (GENERAL PERIODICALS ONDISC), are not viewable online. Indexes to popular magazines and journals are an even better source for creative works, although fewer of these are available in full text.

Vendors such as Mead Data Central, Vu/Text, and DIALOG provide online access to news media. The Information Access Corporation (IAC) distributes MAGAZINE INDEX and NATIONAL NEWSPAPER INDEX in various guises on CD-ROM as well as online through several vendors, and provides full text online coverage for some magazines. H.W. Wilson sells online and CD-ROM access to READER'S GUIDE TO PERIODICAL LITERATURE and READER'S GUIDE WITH ABSTRACTS. UMI/Data Courier is a principal producer of some of the online newspaper files as well as several general CD-ROM indexes (NEWSPAPER ABSTRACTS ONDISC and PERIODICAL ABSTRACTS ONDISC) and GENERAL PERIODICALS ONDISC, which contains full-text images of 150 general interest magazines stored on some eighty CD-ROMs.

## DISSERTATION ABSTRACTS ONLINE and ONDISC
Producer:    University Microfilms International
Vendor:      BRS, DIALOG
CD-ROM:      University Microfilms International
Coverage:    All American doctoral dissertations since 1861, Canadian and some foreign doctoral dissertations from the 1980s forward, and masters' theses since 1988.
Size:        Approximately 1,000,000 items
Update:      Monthly, 6,000 items per year
             Author abstracts are available for records entered since 1980. Each record contains only one descriptor, corresponding to the broad departmental categories used by *Dissertation Abstracts International*. Searching therefore relies almost entirely on title and abstract, and names present a particular problem for lack of authority control.

Other general files which may hold information of interest to humanities scholars include BOOK REVIEW DIGEST, CUMULATIVE BOOK INDEX, BIBLIOGRAPHIC INDEX, BIOGRAPHY INDEX and ESSAY AND GENERAL LITERATURE INDEX, all available from H.W. Wilson online and most also on CD-ROM; DIALOG's BOOK REVIEW INDEX and BIOGRAPHY MASTER INDEX; and CONFERENCE PROCEEDINGS INDEX from BLAISE-LINE.

## Specialized files

*Sales catalogues*

There are several auction and art sales files available to the art scholar who is seeking information on location, provenance, artist information, and the like. ARTQUEST (Pergamon Financial Data Services) includes information on close to one million paintings, sculptures and other works of art sold at public auction. RLIN provides access to SCIPIO, which contains citations to over thirteen thousand art sales catalogues and publications held by a handful of the most important American art and museum libraries.

*Entertainment industry*

There is a wealth of large and small online files covering various aspects of the entertainment industries. Some are electronic bulletin boards and newsletters containing reviews, top ten lists, available properties, industry gossip, and so on. Most of these are available through services such as CompuServe, Dialcom, Dow Jones News/Retrieval and GEnie (General Electric Information Services). Examples include BASELINE (films, television, and theatre) CINEMA MOVIE REVIEWS, LAS VEGAS HOTLINE, ESI STREET, HOLLY-WOOD HOTLINE, ROCKNET, COMICS/ANIMATION FORUM, BILLBOARD INFORMATION NET-WORK and MUSIC INFORMATION SERVICE. DIALOG offer MAGILL'S SURVEY OF CINEMA, which contains essay-length reviews of international films produced since 1902. Newsreel Access Systems, Inc. distributes the CINESCAN CD-ROM which contains descriptions of film and videotape footage from major international film archives.

*Architecture*

Although the engineering and technical focus of architecture does not fall within the scope of this chapter, there is certainly much material in this field of interest to humanities scholars, especially with respect to decorative art, design and cultural aspects. THE AVERY INDEX TO ARCHITECTURAL PERIODICALS (DIALOG, RLIN), based on the holdings of Columbia University's Avery Architectural Library, covers the journal literature on all aspects of architecture. The British Architectural Library's ARCHITECTURE DATABASE (DIALOG) includes conference proceedings, monographs, exhibition catalogues and pamphlets as well as journal articles.

*Religion*

A variety of newsletters and bulletin boards serve the needs of clergy and others with an interest in religious affairs. Most of these are available through CompuServe, Newsnet and similar services. Examples include CATHOLIC NEWS SERVICE, CATHOLIC TRENDS, CHURCHNEWS INTERNATIONAL, LUTHERAN NEWS SERVICE, NATIONAL CATHOLIC REGISTER, ORIGINS: CATHOLIC DOCUMENTARY SERVICE, RNS DAILY NEWS REPORTS and UNITED METHODIST INFORMATION. The Bible, of course, is available in a myriad forms. The King James version is provided online by DIALOG, and there are CD-ROM and diskette versions of Bibles in various languages. Ellis Enterprises, FABS International and TriStar Publishing all publish CD-ROM products which contain multiple versions in English and other languages, accompanied by concordances, study aids, glossaries, and reference materials.

## Regional files

In almost every country whose population engages in online searching activities one can find regional files: databases which specialize in providing access to national sources, or to information of national interest. While most of these focus on the needs of the business community, some are of special interest to humanities researchers. Most of the files in the following sampling would not be easily accessible to users of standard North American or British online services, but may be worth the extra linguistic and/or telecommunications effort involved.

The AUSTRALIAN ARCHITECTURE DATABASE (Ausinet) contains citations to Australian and New Zealand literature on all aspects of architecture. In Canada, HISCABEQ (SDM) provides access to periodical and monographic sources on all aspects of the history of Quebec and Canada. The MUZIEK CATALOGUS NEDERLAND, from the company of the same name, includes citations to printed scores, sheet music and manuscripts in five Dutch music libraries. ICONOS (Questel) is a directory to the contents of French photography collections, whether personal or found in museums, libraries, companies, etc. Harvard University has produced the PERSEUS CD-ROM, which contains both textual and image data on Ancient Greek archaeological sites and objects. The French agency, CNRS, produces an online and CD-ROM database called TRESOR GENERAL DES LANGUAGES ET PARLERS FRANCAIS, the full-text of the *Tresor de la langues français*, a collection of sources published from the seventeenth through twentieth centuries.

Italian and Spanish cultural life is well documented online through the services of CNUCE (in Italy) and the Ministerio de Cultura (in Spain). The latter body is responsible for some dozen online files which provide directory and bibliographic information on architectural monuments, musical and theatrical performance, archaeology, museums, museology, art and cultural competitions, and art objects in museums. CNUCE online databases tend to centre on a particular object or school, including the works of Agostino Carraci, seventeenth century correspondence on the Venetian art market, the Chiesa di Santa Maria Assunta, and Roman sarcophagi.

Some files are more international in scope. Available online and on floppy diskettes, THE MEDIEVAL AND EARLY MODERN DATA BANK - MEMDB (RLIN) is still growing, and will eventually contain principally numeric data of historic interest, such as medieval currency exchange rates, pre-twentieth century demographic and economic data, glossaries of weights and measures, gazeteers and so on. MONUDOC (STN International) can be used to retrieve information on the preservation of historic buildings and monuments worldwide. DIANA (GEM) indexes international literature on art and literary criticism, with an emphasis on eighteenth-century German and European art. CNRS produces IMAGES DE LA MOSAIQUE and MOSAIQUE GRECQUE, which are both supplemented by the videodisc *Images de l'archeologie*.

## Humanities files

The rest of this chapter is devoted to the (relatively) large, 'true' humanities databases. Multidisciplinary and interdisciplinary files are discussed first, followed by individual subject files, organized by subject area. In most cases, basic information for a file is followed by a discussion of indexing practices, special features and problem areas. Where appropriate or possible, examples are given. A recent sample journal article record is given for most files, and where practices have changed over time an old record is also shown. Fields which are expected to be present (author, source citation, publication year, article type, standard book and serial numbers, codens, author affiliations and so on) are not discussed unless they exhibit peculiarities. In the discussion of titles, 'foreign' is taken to mean non-English, since most of the humanities files are English-language in origin.

The reader is assumed to be familiar with basic search techniques and concepts. The emphasis is on departure from the norm, especially with respect to double-posting, also known as 'word and phrase' indexing, or 'bound phrase' indexing. This refers to the common practice among database providers of allowing descriptors to be searched by individual word as well as by entire descriptor phrase as a separately indexed unit.

The user aids listed in each case do not include database chapters supplied as part of vendor documentation (some of which are more than ten years old). Although it may seem unusual to indicate 'print counterpart' as a user aid, in some cases the only method of examining controlled vocabulary is to look at an annual cumulation of the print subject index.

*Multidisciplinary and interdisciplinary files*

## ARTS & HUMANITIES SEARCH (AHCI)

| | |
|---|---|
| Producer: | Institute for Scientific Information |
| Vendor: | BRS, DIALOG |
| Coverage: | Fine arts and performing arts, archaeology, architecture, literature, philosophy, religion, and history. |
| Since: | 1980 |
| Size: | 1,120,486 (January 1990) |
| Update: | Weekly, approximately 4,300 records every two weeks. Tables of contents for journals in AHCI also form part of ISI's CURRENT CONTENTS database, for current awareness searching. |
| Materials: | 1,400 journals are fully indexed, 5,700 journals in related fields are scanned for items to be included. Citations include journal articles, letters, editorials, notes, chronologies, bibliographies, filmographies, books and monographs, conference proceedings, creative works (including scores), and reviews of print media, performances and exhibits. |
| Languages: | More than 30 languages are represented. |
| Printed as: | *Arts & Humanities Citation Index* |
| User aids: | *ISI Online Services User Guide: Arts & Humanities Search* (1988). |

## Figure 15.1: Sample record from ARTS & HUMANITIES SEARCH on DIALOG.

```
01202088    Genuine Article#: EK917    Number of References: 14
    NIETZSCHE GENEALOGY - OF BEAUTY AND COMMUNITY
    KEMAL S
      PENN STATE UNIV/UNIVERSITY PK//PA/16802
    JOURNAL OF THE BRITISH SOCIETY FOR PHENOMENOLOGY, 1990, V21, N3, P234-249
    Language: ENGLISH   Document Type: ARTICLE
    Geographic Location: USA
    Subfile: AHSearch; CC ARTS — Current Contents, Arts & Humanities
    Journal Subject Category: PHILOSOPHY
    Cited References:
      BURKE, ESSAY BEAUTIFUL SUBL
      BURKE E, REFLECTIONS REVOLUTI
      DERRIDA J, 1979, SPURS NIETZSCHES STY
      FULLER P, 1979, ART PSYCHOANALYSIS
      HOY DC, 1986, P20, NIETZSCHE AFFIRMATIV
      KAUFMANN W, 1969, GENEALOGY MORALS
      KAUFMANN W, 1968, TWILIGHT IDOLS
      KEMAL S, 1986, KANT FINE ART KANT P
      NEHAMAS A, 1985, NIETZSCHE LIFE LIT
      NIETZSCHE F, GAY SCIENCE
      NIETZSCHE F, 1986, HUMAN ALL TOO HUMAN
      NIETZSCHE F, WILL TO POWER
      SCHILLER F, AESTHETIC EDUCATION
      TIMPANARO S, 1972, MATERIALISM
```

A sample record appears in Figure 15.1. AHCI suffers from the difficulties associated with all of the citation databases (over-abbreviation, lack of standardization of variant citation practices, and so on), but the producer has addressed the special problems of humanities information in several ways. As with other citation files, subject search is limited to title words, but uninformative titles are enriched at input, and conference papers include the conference title. Except for creative works, all foreign titles are translated into English, and original titles are not included. Symbols appearing in titles are spelled out. Highly authoritative (that is, heavily cited) source records are entered with the phrase 'citation classic' as part of the searchable title. The objective is to allow the searcher to find the citation classic source records in a subject area, and then use the citation information to find works referring to the classic.

Since citation habits in the humanities are markedly different from those used in the sciences or social sciences, implicit citations for creative works (including films, pictures, scores, etc.) which are discussed in the text but not included in references are added to the cited reference list, sometimes followed by the words 'cited indirectly'. The cited reference field (searchable as CR=) is further broken down into cited work (CW=) for titles, cited author (CA=) and cited year (CY=). Each cited reference occupies a separate subfield. Cited titles can be searched by entire phrase or by individual word (Search 15.3). In general, apostrophes are removed rather than treated as a space for searching purposes (so 'Dante's Inferno' becomes 'Dantes Inferno'). Certain forms (such as illustrations) are 'flagged' in citation lists, and are part of CW= entry (best used with the S operator).

**Search 15.3: Using the CW= word index to find 'Raiders of the Lost Ark' as a cited reference title in ARTS AND HUMANITIES SEARCH on DIALOG.**
(Reprinted from the Arts and Humanities Search® database with permission of the Institute for Scientific Information®    copyright © 1991.)

```
   ?  ss  cw=(raiders(s)ark)                       Note use of S
                                                    operator
      S1        88    CW=RAIDERS
      S2       670    CW=ARK
      S3        35    CW=(RAIDERS(S)ARK)

   ? t 3/5/1

    3/5/1
    01082256   Genuine Article#: AP436  Number of References: 4
     STICK IT IN YOUR EAR (FILM SOUND DESIGNERS)
     SPOTNITZ F
     AMERICAN FILM, 1989, V15, N1, P40&
     Language: ENGLISH  Document Type: ARTICLE
     Subfile: AHSearch; CC ARTS — Current Contents, Arts & Humanities
     Journal Subject Category: FILM, RADIO, TELEVISION
     Cited References:
       LYNCH D, BLUE VELVET
       LYNCH D, ELEPHANT MAN
       SHATNER W, STAR TREK 5
       SPIELBERG S, RAIDERS OF LOSK ARK              Note error in
                                                     entry
```

Every author is indexed (with no punctuation, and no spaces in surnames) for source records, while cited references are indexed under first author only (or titles for anonymous works). Transliteration is taken as provided by the journal, so alternative spellings should be checked. For some authors, an online authority file will indicate the 'preferred' (but not necessarily consistently used) form (Search 15.4). Corporate affiliations

(CS=) are entered in separate subfields for each source author, and are word indexed (the use of the S operator ensures that two words will be part of the same affiliation).

### Search 15.4: The online authority file for cited authors in ARTS AND HUMANITIES SEARCH on DIALOG.

(Reprinted from the Arts and Humanities Search® database with permission of the Institute for Scientific Information®      copyright © 1991.)

```
? e cr=twain m

Ref    Items   RT  Index-term
E1      1           CR=TWADOWSKI J, 1921, V37, P3, PAU WYDZ HIST FILO
E2      1           CR=TWAGIRAYESCU M, 1982, DON QUE NOUS AVOS RE
E3      0    2  *CR=TWAIN M
E4      1           CR=TWAIN M, ADVENTURES HUCKLEBER
E5      3           CR=TWAIN M, CITED INDIRECTLY
E6      1           CR=TWAIN M, CONFIDENCE MAN
E7      1           CR=TWAIN M, GERMAN CHICAGO
E8      1           CR=TWAIN M, OLIVER TWIST
E9      1           CR=TWAIN M, PRINCE AND PAUPER
E10     1           CR=TWAIN M, SELECTED LETT
E11     1           CR=TWAIN M, UNCLE TOMS CABIN
E12     1           CR=TWAIN M, V2, P1329, AM LIT

? e e3

Ref    Items   Type  RT   Index-term
R1      0            2   *CR=TWAIN M
R2      0       U    1    CR=CLEMENS SL

? ss ca=twain m

    S1          24    CA=TWAIN M

? ss ca=clemens sl

    S2          782   CA=CLEMENS  SL              Note that most
                                                  entries are
                                                  under  Clemens
```

### Search 15.5: Using the journal category code (SC=) in ARTS AND HUMANITIES SEARCH on DIALOG.

(Reprinted from the Arts and Humanities Search® database with permission of the Institute for Scientific Information®    copyright © 1991.)

```
? e sc=film

Ref    Items   Index-term
E1      150     SC=FAMILY
E2      150     SC=FAMILY   STUDIES                Note that the SC=
E3      35332  *SC=FILM                            field is word and
E4      35332   SC=FILM,  RADIO,   TELEVISION      phrase  indexed
E5      31      SC=FINANCE
E6      8974    SC=FOLKLORE
E7      8       SC=FOOD
```

**Search 15.5:** (cont.)

```
    E8        8    SC=FOOD SCIENCE & TECHNOLOGY
    E9        1    SC=FORESTRY
    E10       2    SC=FUELS
    E11       4    SC=GASTROENTEROLOGY
    E12  138535    SC=GENERAL

    Enter P or E for more

? ss e3 and ca=tolkien jrr

    S1     35332    SC=FILM
    S2       451    CA=TOLKIEN JRR
    S3         4    SC="FILM" AND CA=TOLKIEN JRR

? t 3/5/1

 3/5/1
 00128206    Genuine Article#: LQ909    Number of References: 17
  AN INTERVIEW WITH BOORMAN,JOHN ON 'EXCALIBUR'
  CIMENT M; BOORMAN J
  POSITIF, 1981, N242, P18-31
  Language: FRENCH    Document Type: EDITORIAL
  Subfile: AHSearch; CC ARTS — Current Contents, Arts & Humanities
  Journal Subject Category: FILM, RADIO, TELEVISION
  Cited References:
    BOORMAN J, CATCH US IF YOU CAN
    BOORMAN J, EXCALIBUR
    BOORMAN J, QUARRY
    BOORMAN J, ZARDOZ
    ELIOT TS, WASTE LAND
    GRIFFITH DW, NAISSANCE DUNE NATIO
    MALORY T, MORTE DARTHUR
    ORFF C, CARMINA BURANA
    POWYS JC, GLASTONBURY ROMANDE
    TENNYSON A, IDYLLS OF KING
    TOLKIEN JRR, SEIGNEUR DES ANNEAUX
    WAGNER R, CREPUSCULE DES DIEUX
    WAGNER R, PARSIFAL
    WAGNER R, TRISTAN ET ISOLDE
    WESTON JL, RITUAL ROMANCE
    WHITE TH, ONCE AND FUTURE KING
    WOLFRAM ESCHENB., PARSIFAL
```

Searches can be limited to specific languages (LA=, including English), or can be limited to 'eng' or 'noneng'. Other limit commands allow restriction to articles ('art' and 'nonart'), reviews ('rev' and 'nonrev') and records with citations ('cr' and 'nocr'). The number of references in bibliographies can be searched in the NR= index, using numeric and range operators. Each journal is assigned to up to four subject categories (SC=), enabling broad subject searches. Search 15.5 shows an example of using the category code to retrieve articles in the field of film which make reference to J. R. R. Tolkien.

## ART INDEX (AI) and HUMANITIES INDEX (HI)

Producer:    H. W. Wilson
Vendor:      Wilsonline
CD-ROM:      Wilsondisc, Faxon

Coverage:    AI covers art and architecture, including city planning, crafts, fine arts, folk arts, graphic arts, industrial and interior design, film, museology, photography and television. HI is equally broad, covering archaeology, classics, film, folklore, journalism, linguistics, music, performing arts, philosophy, religious studies, world history and world literature.

Since:    1984

Size:    190,041 (AI); 188,038 (HI)

Update:    Semi-weekly, 24,000 (AI) and 36,000 (HI) new records annually.

Materials:    AI indexes more than 230 periodicals, and draws information from yearbooks and museum bulletins. In addition to articles, AI includes competition and exhibition notices, conference reports, anthologies, reviews, significant letters, editorials and reproductions. HI indexes articles in 295 journals and includes interviews, obituaries, reviews, and original works of fiction, drama and poetry.

Languages:    Primarily English, but both files include German, Italian, French, Spanish and a few other Western languages.

Printed as:    *Art Index, Humanities Index*

User aids:    None apart from online service documentation.

**Figure 15.2: Sample records from ART INDEX and HUMANITIES INDEX on Wilsonline.**

```
Who is the king of glory? The Byzantine enamels of an icon frame
and revetment in Jerusalem
Hetherington, Paul
bibl f il tabs
Zeitschrift fur Kunstgeschichte 53 no1:25-38 '90
Language: English
Subject heading: Icons
Subject heading: Picture frames and framing
Subject heading: Enamels, Byzantine
Subject heading: Jesus Christ in art
Special refs: Byzantine icons
Special refs: Man of sorrows
BART90022137
900920
Article

ART INDEX


Into the middleground: formula syntax in Stockhausen's Light
Kohl, Jerome
bibl
Perspectives of New Music 28:262-91 Summ '90
Language: English
Subject heading: Operas/Analysis
Subject heading: Composition (Music)
Stockhausen, Karlheinz:1928-
Special refs: Stockhausen, Karlheinz
BHUM90027280
901227
Article

HUMANITIES INDEX
```

An unqualified subject search in these files draws from titles, title enhancements, descriptors and corporate name subject headings. Up to four (AI) or six (HI) descriptor strings are assigned from Wilson's controlled list, which strongly resembles Library of Congress Subject Headings (see sample records in Figure 15.2). Each descriptor string (DS) consists of one or more subject headings (SH), which in any other system would be called main heading and subdivisions. Full descriptor strings and individual subject headings are posted in the index, along with individual words. Terminal unlimited truncation (using ':', rather than the single character '#') is useful to retrieve all subject headings and descriptor strings beginning with a particular phrase (see Search 15.6). As in all Wilsonline databases, query terms and phrases which are in the online thesaurus as 'use' references are automatically linked to the preferred term (Search 15.7). This also holds for personal and corporate names and for uniform titles.

## Search 15.6: Truncating descriptors in HUMANITIES INDEX on Wilsonline.

```
USER:   nbr folk music

        pstg    (Category) Term         File: HUM
        ----    ---------------
1         1     (DU) FOLK MEDICINE/UNITED STATES/ADDRESSES,
                     ESSAYS, LECTURES
2         1     (DU) FOLK MEDICINE/UNITED STATES/FORMULAE,
                     RECEIPTS, PRESCRIPTIONS
3         1     (DU) FOLK MEDICINE/UNITED STATES/HISTORY
4        10     (SH) FOLK MUSEUMS
5        10     (DS) FOLK MUSEUMS
6        73     (SH) FOLK MUSIC
7         2     (DS) FOLK MUSIC
8         2     (DU) FOLK MUSIC/AFRICA/ADDRESSES, ESSAYS, LECTURES
9         1     (DU) FOLK MUSIC/AFRICA/HISTORY AND
                     CRITICISM/ADDRESSES, ESSAYS, LECTURES
10        1     (DU) FOLK MUSIC/AFRICA/20TH CENTURY/HISTORY AND
                     CRITICISM
11        1     (DU) FOLK MUSIC/ALBERTA/HISTORY AND CRITICISM

-> UP : DOWN : GET : EXPAND :   ?

USER:   nbr folk music, a

        pstg    (Category) Term         File: HUM
        ----    ---------------
1         1     (DU) FOLK MUSIC/UNITED STATES/BIBLIOGRAPHY
2         3     (DU) FOLK MUSIC/UNITED STATES/CONGRESSES
3         1     (DU) FOLK MUSIC/UNITED STATES/DISCOGRAPHY
4         2     (DU) FOLK MUSIC/UNITED STATES/HISTORY AND CRITICISM
5         2     (DU) FOLK MUSIC/YUGOSLAVIA/PLANINICA (BUGOJNO,
                     BOSNIA AND HERCEGOVINA)
6         2     (SH) FOLK MUSIC, AFRICAN
7         2     (DS) FOLK MUSIC, AFRICAN
8         7     (SH) FOLK MUSIC, AMERICAN
9         6     (DS) FOLK MUSIC, AMERICAN
10        1     (DS) FOLK MUSIC, AMERICAN/BIBLIOGRAPHY
11        1     (SH) FOLK MUSIC, CANADIAN

-> UP : DOWN : GET : EXPAND :   ?
```

**Note use of both geographic subdivisions and ethnic/ national qualifiers**

**Search 15.6:** (cont.)

```
USER:  find folk music: and (ireland or irish or celtic)

    Generated terms from "FOLK MUSIC:"
    Generated terms from "FOLK MUSIC:"
    Generated terms from "FOLK MUSIC:"
    Generated terms from "FOLK MUSIC:"
    Generated terms from "FOLK MUSIC:"
    Generated terms from "FOLK MUSIC:"
    70 terms with 97 postings

            97    FOLK MUSIC:
           760    IRELAND
           565    IRISH
          1051    (IRELAND or IRISH)
            82    CELTIC
          1112    ((IRELAND or IRISH) or CELTIC)
             3    (FOLK MUSIC: and ((IRELAND or IRISH) or CELTIC))

    SEARCH 1 (3 FOUND)

    SEARCH 2 ?

USER:  prt fu 1

    1/1      (HUM)
    Institutions for the promotion of indigenous music: the case for
    Ireland's Comhaltas Ceoltoiri Eireann (link with nationalism)
    Henry, Edward O
    bibl il
    Ethnomusicology 33:67-95 Wint '89
    Language: English
    Subject heading: Folk music, Irish
    Subject heading: Nationalism/Ireland
    Subject heading: Music and politics
    Subject heading: Music patronage
    Subject heading: Musical societies
    Special refs: Patriotism in music
    BHUM89006331
    890322
    Article
```

**Search 15.7: Automatic linking of 'use' references to descriptors in HUMANITIES INDEX on Wilsonline.**

```
USER:  expand folk music

    REF  PSTS  #RTS  RELATION    TERM   (HUM)
    ---  ----  ----  --------    ----
      0     2    10  *           FOLK MUSIC
      1     0   140  BT          MUSIC
      2     4     0  NT          FOLK DANCING
      3     1     3  NT          FOLK ROCK MUSIC
      4     2     2  NT          GYPSIES/MUSIC
      5     9     1  NT          SOUND RECORDINGS/FOLK MUSIC
      6     6     5  NT          VIOLIN/METHODS (FOLK)
      7     2    15  RT          FOLK SONGS
```

**Search 15.7:** (cont.)

```
            8    0    1   USED FOR    FOLK TUNES
            9    0    1   USED FOR    INSTRUMENTAL FOLK MUSIC
           10    0    1   USED FOR    TUNES, FOLK

        "EXPAND n", or "GET n"

        SEARCH 1 ?

 USER:  find instrumental folk music

        HUM uses "FOLK MUSIC" instead of "INSTRUMENTAL FOLK MUSIC".

               73   FOLK MUSIC

        SEARCH 1 (73 FOUND)

        SEARCH 2 ?

 USER:  prt fu 1

        1/1     (HUM)
        Economic and transmission factors as essential elements in the
        definition of folk, art, and pop music
        Booth, Gregory D.
        Kuhn, Terry Lee
        The Musical Quarterly 74 no3:411-38 '90
        Language: English
        Subject heading: Music and society
        Subject heading: Music/Economic aspects
        Subject heading: Music/Classification
        Subject heading: Folk music
        Subject heading: Music, Popular (Songs, etc.)
        BHUM90025835
        901213
        Article
```

If a record in HI represents a creative work, one of several contents codes is assigned to the CT field. These may include 'shsto' (short story), 'drama', 'fictn', 'poems' and so on (Search 15.8). Reproductions which accompany an article in AI are searchable by title. Individual languages, including English, are searchable. Foreign titles are not translated. Ambiguous titles are enhanced, and AI also enhances the titles of exhibitions, reviews, anthologies and interviews. Abstracts are not included.

**Search 15.8: Using the CT field to isolate creative works in HUMANITIES INDEX on Wilsonline.**

```
 USER:  singer, isaac: (au) and shsto (ct)

                 7        SINGER, ISAAC:(AU)
              2206        SHSTO(CT)
                 4        (SINGER, ISAAC:(AU) and SHSTO(CT))

        SEARCH 1 (4 FOUND)

        SEARCH 2 ?
```

**Search 15.8:** (cont.)

```
USER:  prt fu 1

       1/1      (HUM)
       The last gaze
       Singer, Isaac Bashevis:1904-
       tr. by J. Singer
       Partisan Review 55:210-18 Spr '88
       Language: English
       Subject heading: Short stories/English language/Translations from
                         Yiddish
       BHUM88015684
       880720
       Literature
```

The main drawbacks of the Wilson databases are their small size and the inherent problems associated with subject access being limited to titles and a few pre-coordinated and rather broad subject headings (with no printed list other than the print index). The target audience for both files is broad, and some users may find AI and HI lacking with respect to in-depth scholarly research.

### FRANCIS

The FRANCIS files available to Questel users also present very valuable sources of humanities information [3]. Unfortunately, lack of access prevents an in-depth look at FRANCIS. However, searchers should note that these databases, corresponding to various sections of the *Bulletin signaletique*, offer excellent international coverage of the literature in a number of specialized areas. Titles of individual files of interest include ART ET ARCHEOLOGIE, HISTOIRE ET SCIENCES DE LA LITTERATURE, HISTOIRE ET SCIENCES DES RELIGIONS, PHILOSOPHIE, PREHISTOIRE ET PROTOHISTOIRE, REPERTOIRE D'ART ET D'ARCHEOLOGIE, and SCIENCES DU LANGUAGE. Indexing for many of these files consists of English and French descriptors, and in some cases German or Spanish as well.

*History*

### AMERICA: HISTORY AND LIFE (AHL) and HISTORICAL ABSTRACTS (HA)

| | |
|---|---|
| Producer: | ABC-Clio |
| Vendor: | DIALOG |
| Coverage: | AHL covers American and Canadian history, HA indexes the history of the rest of the world. General coverage in both files includes bibliography, cultural history, economic history, historiography, history of science, international relations, libraries and archives, military history, political history and teaching of history. AHL also includes American studies, ethnic studies, family history, folklore, Indian-White relations, local history, oral history, urban affairs and women's studies. HA adds area studies, diplomatic history and philosophy of history to its scope. |
| Since: | 1964 (AHL); 1973 (HA) |
| Size: | 151,618 (AHL - March 1990); 245,096 (HA - March 1990) |
| Update: | Three times a year, approximately 13,000 (AHL) and 22,000 (HA) records annually. |
| Materials: | Articles are selected from 2,100 journals published in ninety countries. Reviews (of various media), dissertations, collections and conference proceedings are also included. |

Languages:    Some forty languages are represented.
Printed as:    *America: History and Life*; *Historical Abstracts, Parts A and B*
User aids:    *Searching America: History and Life (AHL) and Historical Abstracts (HA) on DIALOG* (revised 1987) and a recent annual cumulation of the printed index.

Figures 15.3 and 15.4 show sample records from AHL and HA; in each case the second, newer, record includes indexing for subject and historical period. Records entered prior to 1975 (HA) or 1974 (AHL) do not have descriptors, and the historical period indexing was standardized to its current form in 1979.

## Figure 15.3: Sample records from AMERICA: HISTORY AND LIFE on DIALOG.

```
    109597    001-00604
THE FARMER, THE ARMY AND THE DRAFT.
  Blum, Albert A
  Agric. Hist. 1964 38(1): 34-42.
ABSTRACT: In spite of America's unsatisfactory experience with group
  deferment from selective service in World War I, numerous attempts were
  made early in World War II to obtain industry-wide deferments. The army
  opposed successfully all such demands except the one for West Coast
  aircraft workers. The American farmer, as a result, came close to
  receiving group deferment. The special deferment for farmers was
  achieved through political pressure on federal officials by members of
  the farm bloc rather than by mandatory legislation. The pressure on
  federal officials was reflected in instructions to local boards. (W. D.
  Rasmussen )
```

**Old record**

```
    1015238    27-14952
INQUIRY TEACHING AND FEMINIST PEDAGOGY.
  Maher, Frances A
  Social Education 1987 51(3): 186-192.
DOCUMENT TYPE: ARTICLE
ABSTRACT: Describes the essential features of feminist pedagogy" (a
  combination of teaching practices and curriculum content that explicitly
  relates students' viewpoints and experiences to the subject matter),
  concluding that attention to women's, and therefore to multiple
  experiences, in the teaching of American history encourages active
  learning and the acknowledgment of a variety of perspectives.
DESCRIPTORS: History Teaching ; Feminism ; Women's history ; 20c
HISTORICAL  PERIOD:  1900H
HISTORICAL  PERIOD  (Starting):  20c
HISTORICAL  PERIOD  (Ending):  20c
```

**New record**

**Figure 15.4: Sample records from HISTORICAL ABSTRACTS on DIALOG.**

```
      274338      019-00129
Hungarian-Slovak relations and the Slovak nationality movement in Hungary
after the Vienna Award (1938-41)
MAGYAR-SZLOVAK VISZONY ES SZLOVAK NEMZETISEGI MOZGALOM MAGYARORSZAGON A
BECSI  DONTES  UTAN  (1938-1941)
    Tilkovszky,   Lorant
    Szazadok (Hungary) 1964 98(3): 383-418.
    ABSTRACT: Analyzes the policy of the Hungarian government relating to the
      Slovak minority and the attitude of the Slovak government toward the
      Hungarian minority living in Slovakia. Discusses primarily the
      activities of Pal Teleki, Prime Minister of Hungary, and Vojtech Tuka,
      Prime Minister of Slovakia. Difficulties in establishing a Slovak
      national party in Hungary are discussed in detail, especially the actions
      of Emanuel Bohm, and Ludovit Obtulovic, who were among leaders of the
      Slovak minority in Hungary. Based chiefly on archival documents. (F. S.
      Wagner )

Old record


      1323648     41B-08283
Improving workers' material well-being in the Ukraine between the 1960's
and 1980's
PIDNESENNIA MATERIAL'NOHO DOBROBUTU TRUDIASHCHYKH URSR U 60-KH-80-KH ROKAKH
    Vitruk, L D
    Ukrains'kyi Istorychnyi Zhurnal (USSR) 1985 (3): 124-134.
    NOTE: Primary sources; 65 notes.
    DOCUMENT TYPE: ARTICLE
    LANGUAGE(s): Ukrainian.
    ABSTRACT: Details various sources describing ways of improving workers'
      material well-being. Istoria Ukrains'koi R.S.R. (History of the
      Ukrainian SSR) tackles the problem the most extensively, while general
      histories of factory existence are more specifically oriented. (E.
      Vynnycky )
    DESCRIPTORS: Ukraine ; Working Class ; Standard of Living ; Research
      sources ; 1960-1985
    HISTORICAL PERIOD: 1960D 1970D 1980D 1900H
      HISTORICAL PERIOD (Starting): 1960
      HISTORICAL PERIOD (Ending): 1985

New record
```

Titles are entered in original or transliterated form, and also in English if foreign titles. Up to three authors are indexed for each record. Abstracts or annotations are included for almost all articles and essays, but not for books, reviews and dissertations. Individual languages can be searched as LA= for records entered since 1980 (and only other than English in AHL). In HA a search can be limited to 'eng' or 'noneng', while in AHL this would have to be done by combining the final search statement with 'not LA=?' to select out foreign articles. HA searches can also be limited to articles with or without abstracts ('abs' vs. 'noabs').

The descriptors represent a combination of natural-language terms, subject headings, and authority-controlled proper names. Each entry contains an average of four descriptors, and these may include foreign terms (for instance 'Anschluss'). Book reviews are subject indexed. A comma or a hyphen in a descriptor (and this includes all inverted personal names) indicates that it is word indexed only, which is a departure from the norm, and will make a difference in search effectiveness (Search 15.9). Subdivisions are entered as parenthetical qualifiers, and are separately phrase and word indexed (Search 15.10).

**Search 15.9: Searching for descriptors containing commas in AMERICA: HISTORY AND LIFE on DIALOG.**

```
? e friends, society of

Ref  Items   Index-term
E1     1     FRIENDS OF WOMEN
E2     1     FRIENDS SEMINARY
E3     0     *FRIENDS, SOCIETY OF                Note absence of
E4     1     FRIENDSAND                          postings under
E5    671    FRIENDSHIP                          this descriptor
E6     1     FRIENDSHIP  (ORGANIZATION)
E7     1     FRIENDSHIP  (THEME)
E8     1     FRIENDSHIP  AIRPORT
E9     1     FRIENDSHIP  COMMUNITY
E10    1     FRIENDSHIP  HOUSE MOVEMENT
E11    1     FRIENDSHIP  PATTERNS
E12    1     FRIENDSHIP  SLOOPS

? ss  friends(l)society                          Note use of L
                                                 operator
    S1      576     FRIENDS/DE
    S2     2624     SOCIETY/DE
    S3      530     FRIENDS(L)SOCIETY

? t 3/ti,de/1-2

   3/TI,DE/1
Martha Schofield and the Re-Education of the South, 1839-1916.
(Studies in Women and Religion, vol. 24.)
 DESCRIPTORS: Friends, Society of ; Freedmen ; Slavery ; Social Reform ;
  Schofield, Martha ; Education ; South ; 1839-1916

   3/TI,DE/2
Forging Freedom: The Formation of Philadelphia's Black Community,
1720-1840.
 DESCRIPTORS: Friends, Society of ; Economic Conditions ; Race Relations ;
  Religion ; Pennsylvania -(Philadelphia) ; Blacks ; 1720-1840
```

**Search 15.10: Phrase indexing of headings and subdivisions in HISTORICAL ABSTRACTS on DIALOG.**

```
? ss russian revolution (review article)

    S1       20     RUSSIAN REVOLUTION (REVIEW ARTICLE)

? t 1/ti,de/1

  1/TI,DE/1
The Great October Revolution in bibliographic publications
VELIKII OKTIABR' V BIBLIOGRAFICHESKIKH IZDANIIAKH
 DESCRIPTORS: Russian Revolution -(review article) ; 1917 ; 1977-1986 ;
  Bibliographies

? ss russian revolution (l) review article

    S2     2142     RUSSIAN  REVOLUTION/DE
    S3    10179     REVIEW   ARTICLE/DE
```

**Search 15.10:** (cont.)

```
        S4          22     RUSSIAN REVOLUTION (L) REVIEW ARTICLE

? ss s4 not s1

                    22     S4
                    20     S1
        S5           2     S4 NOT S1

? t 5/ti,de/1

  5/TI,DE/1
New books on the important anniversary
NOVYE KNIGI K ZNAMENATEL'NOI GODOVSHCHINE
  DESCRIPTORS: Russian Revolution -(October) -(review article) ;
  Anniversaries ; 1917-1987

? ss russian revolution and review article

        S6        2142     RUSSIAN REVOLUTION
        S7       10179     REVIEW ARTICLE
        S8          53     RUSSIAN REVOLUTION AND REVIEW ARTICLE

? ss s8 not s4

                    53     S8
                    22     S4
        S9          31     S8 NOT S4

? t 9/ti,de/1

  9/TI,DE/1
RETHINKING THE RUSSIAN REVOLUTION.
  DESCRIPTORS: Working Class -(review article) ; Russian Revolution ;
  Revolutionary Movements ; 1880-1917
```

Place names are entered in the descriptor field according to local convention with respect to spelling, and according to the political breakdown at the time of indexing (a problem with African countries particularly). Even in the case of relatively fixed entities, variations may occur. In the light of this, and in the absence of a classification approach, a search containing a geographic aspect should include not only the generic word and its alternatives, but smaller units as well (Search 15.11). In AHL American places are entered with the state as the main heading, and the smaller unit in parentheses (for example, 'Massachusetts (Boston)'), except for New York City, which is entered directly. HA place name descriptors use the country name as main heading, as in 'Scotland (Edinburgh)'.

Date indexing (which the user aids suggest should only be used when absolutely necessary) is broken into three fields: HS= (historical starting date), HE= (historical ending data), and HP= (historical period). The HP= index has been used for decades ('HP=1980D') and centuries ('HP=1900H') since 1979, and although the HP= index will also display ranges, it should not be searched this way. Additionally, dates will appear in titles, abstracts, and in the descriptor field (not to mention that they will also be referred to by words and phrases such as 'Renaissance', 'the reign of Henry IV', '19th century', '19th c.' and so on). If date is a necessary part of a search, free text is probably the most effective way to retrieve it.

## Search 15.11: Including geographic aspects in HISTORICAL ABSTRACTS on DIALOG.

```
? ss great(w)britain or united(w)kingdom

    S1     38579    GREAT
    S2     29157    BRITAIN
    S3     27782    GREAT(W)BRITAIN
    S4     14509    UNITED
    S5      2041    KINGDOM
    S6       459    UNITED(W)KINGDOM
    S7     27921    GREAT(W)BRITAIN  OR  UNITED(W)KINGDOM

? ss s7 and marx?/de

           27921    S7
    S8      4105    MARX?/DE
    S9       104    S7 AND MARX?/DE

? ss s7 or wales or scotland or england or northern(w)ireland

           27921    S7
    S10     1692    WALES
    S11     2114    SCOTLAND
    S12    13711    ENGLAND
    S13     3946    NORTHERN
    S14     3503    IRELAND
    S15      503    NORTHERN(W)IRELAND
    S16    41622    S7 OR WALES OR SCOTLAND OR ENGLAND OR
NORTHERN(W)IRELAND

? ss s16 and marx?/de                        Note  higher  recall
           41622    S16                       when  smaller  units
    S17     4105    MARX?/DE                   are  included
    S18      156    S16 AND MARX?/DE

? ss s18 not s9

            156    S18
            104    S9
    S19      52    S18 NOT S9

? t 19/ti,ab,de/1

19/TI,AB,DE/1
THE COLLECTED ESSAYS OF CHRISTOPHER HILL.
 ABSTRACT: Reviews The Collected Essays of Christopher Hill  (3 vol.,
   1985-87). Christopher Hill has been commonly regarded as Britain's
   leading Marxist historian. Most of the essays reprinted here and some
   cast anew are recent responses to revisionist arguments. Hill defends
   his basic Marxist interpretation of the English Revolution and other
   aspects of English history, yet continues to show that he can be eclectic
   and frequently less than consistently Marxist. (G. P. Blum )
 DESCRIPTORS: Marxism ; Revolution ; Hill, Christopher -(review article) ;
   England ; 17c
```

*Art*

## ART LITERATURE INTERNATIONAL (RILA)

| | |
|---|---|
| Producer: | RILA, a bibliographic service of the Getty Art History Information Program of the J. Paul Getty Trust |
| Vendor: | DIALOG |
| Coverage: | All aspects of Western art from the 4th century to the present. |
| Since: | 1973 |
| Size: | 120,824 (January 1990) |
| Update: | Semi-annually, approximately 9,000 records annually. |
| Materials: | Journal articles, directories, bibliographies, monographs, collections, Festschriften, conference proceedings, museum publications, exhibition catalogues, dissertations, book and exhibition reviews, obituaries, interviews and published lectures. |
| Languages: | Almost 40 languages are represented. |
| Printed as: | *RILA, Repertoire international de la litterature de l'art* |
| User aids: | *RILA Subject Headings* (revised 1987) |

Figure 15.5 shows a sample record from the RILA database. Abstracts are included for more than half of the records (but not for reviews). Abstracts for collections consist of tables of contents, with RILA numbers for those individual items with their own records. A notes field includes details as to accompanying and illustrative material. Titles are entered in the original language (or transliteration), with English translations for foreign titles. Title words containing apostrophes and hyphens must be searched with the punctuation, which is not the usual case in DIALOG databases. Searches can be restricted by language using LA= (including English), and search results can be limited to 'eng' or 'noneng'.

## Figure 15.5: Sample record from ART LITERATURE INTERNATIONAL (RILA) on DIALOG.

```
0194851      15 7650 (1989)
The tree and the stump: hieroglyphics of the sacred forest
  MCGRATH, Robert L.
  Journal of Forest History, XXXIII/2, (Apr 1989), 60-69 12 illustrations
  PUBLICATION YEAR(S): 1989
  LANGUAGE(S): In English
  DOCUMENT TYPE: analytic
  Surveys 125 years of American landscape painting, emphasizing the 19th c.
      Discusses the representation of individual trees as symbols of specific
      regions as well as the use of trees as vanitas and memento mori
      symbols.
  DESCRIPTORS: landscape/painting/American, 19th-20th cs.
  forests/symbolism/painting, American, 19th-20th cs.
  trees/symbolism/painting, American, 19th-20th cs.
  vanitas/symbolism/painting, American, 19th-20th cs.
  memento mori/symbolism/painting, American, 19th-20th cs.
  painting, American/landscape/19th-20th cs.
  symbolism/landscape/painting, American, 19th-20th cs.
  SECTION HEADING(S): 13—GENERAL WORKS—iconography; 77—NEO-CLASSICISM AND
      MODERN ART—pictorial arts
  SUBJECT NATIONALITY: American
  SUBJECT PERIOD: 1825-1899; 1900-1950
  SUBJECT STYLE, MEDIUM, FORM: landscape; painting; secular iconography
```

All primary and secondary authors (editors, translators, etc.) are indexed, and corporate author names appear in the AU= index in the form 'city, state, country, name'. Exhibition catalogues and reviews thereof are indexed in the EX= and EY= (exhibition year) fields, and include city and abbreviated country name (and postal state code for the United States) as well as institutional name. The complexity of entry can make searching difficult, and an exhaustive search for exhibits should also include the descriptor field (Search 15.12).

**Search 15.12: Searching for exhibitions in the exhibition and descriptor fields in ART LITERATURE INTERNATIONAL on DIALOG.**

```
?  ss   ex=(boston(s)museum(s)fine(s)arts)              Note use of S
                                                         operator
       S1        263    EX=BOSTON
       S2       9863    EX=MUSEUM
       S3       1158    EX=FINE
       S4       2774    EX=ARTS
       S5         52    EX=(BOSTON(S)MUSEUM(S)FINE(S)ARTS)

? t 5/ti,ex,ey,de/1

5/TI,EX,EY,DE/1
Andrew Wyeth: the Helga pictures
 EXHIBITION  SHOWN: Washington, DC, USA, National Gallery of Art, 24 May-27
     Sept 1987
 EXHIBITION ALSO SHOWN: Boston, MA, USA, Museum of Fine Arts, Boston, 28
     Oct 1987-3 Jan 1988; Houston, TX, USA, Museum of Fine Arts, Houston, 31
     Jan-10 Apr 1988; Los Angeles, CA, USA, Los Angeles County Museum of Art
     , 28 Apr-10 July 1988; San Francisco, CA, USA, Fine Arts Museums of San
     Francisco, 13 Aug-16 Oct 1988; Detroit, MI, USA, Detroit Institute of
     Arts, 13 Nov 1988-22 Jan 1989
 EXHIBITION YEAR(S): 1987, 1988, 1989
 DESCRIPTORS: Wyeth, Andrew Newell, American painter, b.1917/art/Helga
     series, Andrews, Leonard E.B., collection
 Andrews, Leonard E.B., collection/art/Wyeth, A.N., Helga series
 Testorf, Helga, American, b.1932/portraits of/art, Wyeth, A.N.
 collectors and collecting/USA/Andrews, L.E.B.
 nude/art/Wyeth, A.N.
 portraits/art/Wyeth, A.N.
 women/art/Wyeth, A.N.
 human figure/art/Wyeth, A.N.
 preparatory studies, American/Wyeth, A.N.
 artists and models/Wyeth, A.N.
 artists' writings/Wyeth, A.N.
 Washington, DC (USA), National Gallery of Art/exhibitions/Andrew Wyeth:
     the Helga pictures
 Boston (MA, USA), Museum of Fine Arts, Boston/exhibitions/Andrew Wyeth:
     the Helga pictures
 Houston (TX, USA), Museum of Fine Arts, Houston/exhibitions/Andrew Wyeth:
     the Helga pictures
 Los Angeles (CA, USA), Los Angeles County Museum of Art/exhibitions/
     Andrew Wyeth: the Helga pictures
 San Francisco (CA, USA), Fine Arts Museums of San Francisco/ exhibitions/
     Andrew Wyeth: the Helga pictures
 Detroit (MI, USA), Detroit Institute of Arts/exhibitions/Andrew Wyeth: the
     Helga pictures

? ss boston(l)museum(l)fine(l)arts(l)exhibitions

       S6        882    BOSTON/DE
       S7      19276    MUSEUM/DE
```

**Search 15.12:** (cont.)

```
      S8      2185    FINE/DE
      S9      8086    ARTS/DE
      S10    30644    EXHIBITIONS/DE
      S11      292    BOSTON(L)MUSEUM(L)FINE(L)ARTS(L)EXHIBITIONS
```

? **ss s11 not s5**                              **Note number of**
                                                 **items without Boston**
              292    S11                          **Museum of Fine Arts**
               52    S5                           **in the exhibition**
      S12      240    S11 NOT S5                  **index**

? **t 12/5/1**

```
 12/5/1
 0186610       15 4476 (1989)     REVIEWED IN RILA 15 4477 (1989)
 Arp, 1886-1966
  EXHIBITION   SHOWN: Stuttgart, DEU, Wurttembergischer Kunstverein, 13
     July-31 Aug 1986
  EXHIBITION YEAR(S): 1986
  HANCOCK, Jane; POLEY, Stefanie
  CONTRIBUTOR(S): Konzeption von Ausstellung und Katalog: Jane HANCOCK und
     Stefanie POLEY
  (Stuttgart: Hatje: 1986) 315 p. Many illustrations, some color;
     bibliography; biographical summary; exhibition list; 289 works shown
  PUBLICATION YEAR(S): 1986
  LANGUAGE(S): In German
  DOCUMENT TYPE: review of an exhibition catalogue
  DESCRIPTORS: Arp, Jean, French sculptor, painter, printmaker, poet,
     1887-1966
  Stuttgart (DEU), Wurttembergischer Kunstverein/exhibitions/Arp, 1886-1966
  Strasbourg (FRA), Musee d'Art moderne/exhibitions/Arp, 1886-1966
  Paris (FRA), Musee d'art moderne de la ville de Paris/exhibitions/ Arp,
     1886-1966
  Minneapolis (MN, USA), Minneapolis Institute of Arts/exhibitions/ Arp,
     1886-1966
  Boston (MA, USA), Museum of Fine Arts, Boston/exhibitions/Arp, 1886-1966
  San Francisco (CA, USA), San Francisco Museum of Modern Art/ exhibitions/
     Arp, 1886-1966
  SECTION HEADING(S): 79—NEO-CLASSICISM AND MODERN ART—artists,
     architects, photographers
 REVIEW BY: MUNDY, Jennifer, Apollo, CXXVI/308, (Oct 1987), 296-297
  REVIEW YEAR(S): 1987
```

Descriptors, from the RILA thesaurus (Figure 15.6), consist of headings and subheadings, and are word and phrase indexed, but the separating dashes must be omitted in entry. Descriptors may include names, with dates and descriptive terms. The three fields displayed at the end of the sample record are word and phrase indexed identifiers, assigned to most but not all records. Identifiers include specific details as to nationality, time period, style, medium and form. There is substantial duplication between the descriptor and identifier fields, but an exhaustive search should not rely on one alone (Search 15.13).

**Figure 15.6: Descriptors in *RILA Subject Headings*, revised 1987**

RILA Subject Headings

    RT    environmental art
          installation works
          junk sculpture
          object art

asses, USE donkeys

associations  [na]
    RT    organizations
    UF    artists' associations

Assumption of the Virgin, USE Mary, Virgin/Assumption

Assyro-Babylonian inscriptions USE cuneiform inscriptions

Astarte  [ic]
    UF    Ashtaroth
          Ashtoreth

astrolabes  [md: scientific instruments]
    BT    astronomical instruments

astrology  [na]
    RT    occult sciences
          superstition
          zodiac

astronauts  [na]
    UF    cosmonauts

astronomers  [na]
    BT    scientists

astronomical charts  [na]
    UF    charts, astronomical

astronomical instruments  [md: scientific instruments]
    BT    scientific instruments
    NT    astrolabes
          meridians (astronomical instruments)
    UF    instruments, astronomical

astronomy  [na]
    BT    physical science
    RT    zodiac

Astyanax  [ic]

asylums  [bt]
    RT    almshouses
          charities
          hospitals
          orphanages

**Search 15.13: Importance of including identifiers in searching ART LITERATURE INTERNATIONAL on DIALOG.**

```
? ss (enamel and (irish or ireland or irl))/de
                                              IRL is an
     S1      291    ENAMEL/DE                 abbreviation used in
     S2      781    IRISH/DE                  descriptors
     S3      827    IRELAND/DE
     S4      448    IRL/DE
     S5        6    (ENAMEL AND (IRISH OR IRELAND OR IRL))/DE

? ss (enamel and (irish or ireland or irl))/de,id

     S6      315    ENAMEL/DE,ID
     S7      899    IRISH/DE,ID
     S8      827    IRELAND/DE,ID
     S9      448    IRL/DE,ID
     S10       8    (ENAMEL AND (IRISH OR IRELAND OR IRL))/DE,ID

? ss s10 not s5                               Note difference in
                                              recall when ID field
              8    S10                        is included
              6    S5
     S11      2    S10 NOT S5

? t 11/ti,de,id/1

  11/TI,DE,ID/1
  Enamels & glass
   DESCRIPTORS: Boston (MA, USA), Museum of Fine Arts, Boston/enamel/Medieval
   Boston (MA, USA), Museum of Fine Arts, Boston/glass/Medieval
   Medieval enamel/collections/Boston (MA, USA), Museum of Fine Arts, Boston
   Medieval glass/collections/Boston (MA, USA), Museum of Fine Arts, Boston
   Medieval stained glass/collections/Boston (MA, USA), Museum of Fine Arts,
      Boston
   media and techniques, enamel/Medieval
   media and techniques, glass/Medieval        ID field contains
   forgeries, enamel/Medieval                  useful national/
   forgeries, glass/Medieval                   ethnic terms
   SUBJECT NATIONALITY: French; British; German; Italian; Irish;
      Netherlandish
   SUBJECT STYLE, MEDIUM, FORM: enamel; stained glass; decorative arts;
      Medieval; museums
```

Each record is also assigned one or more section headings (/SH), which consist of a broad heading and a subdivision (Figure 15.7). Section headings are phrase and word indexed, and the S operator is useful in linking elements of one section heading. Each section heading has an equivalent code also in the /SH and basic index fields (Search 15.14).

**Figure 15.7: RILA section headings and codes**

The following is a list of Subject Heading Codes that are searchable at the time of preparation of this documentation:

| Subject Codes | Subject Headings |
|---|---|
| 01 | REFERENCE WORKS-bibliographies |
| 05 | REFERENCE WORKS-dictionaries and encyclopedias |
| 07 | REFERENCE WORKS-collected works |
| 08 | REFERENCE WORKS-art historians and critics |
| 10 | GENERAL WORKS-miscellania |
| 13 | GENERAL WORKS-iconography |
| 15 | GENERAL WORKS-architecture |
| 16 | GENERAL WORKS-sculpture |
| 17 | GENERAL WORKS-pictorial arts |
| 18 | GENERAL WORKS-decorative arts |
| 50 | MEDIEVAL ART-miscellania |
| 55 | MEDIEVAL ART-architecture |
| 56 | MEDIEVAL ART-sculpture |
| 57 | MEDIEVAL ART-pictorial arts |
| 58 | MEDIEVAL ART-decorative arts |
| 59 | MEDIEVAL ART-artists and architects |
| 60 | RENAISSANCE, BAROQUE AND ROCOCO ART-miscellania |
| 65 | RENAISSANCE, BAROQUE AND ROCOCO ART-architecture |
| 66 | RENAISSANCE, BAROQUE AND ROCOCO ART-sculpture |
| 67 | RENAISSANCE, BAROQUE AND ROCOCO ART-pictorial arts |
| 68 | RENAISSANCE, BAROQUE AND ROCOCO ART-decorative arts |
| 69 | RENAISSANCE, BAROQUE AND ROCOCO ART-artists and architects |
| 70 | NEO-CLASSICISM AND MODERN ART-miscellania |
| 75 | NEO-CLASSICISM AND MODERN ART-architecture |
| 76 | NEO-CLASSICISM AND MODERN ART-sculpture |
| 77 | NEO-CLASSICISM AND MODERN ART-pictorial arts |
| 78 | NEO-CLASSICISM AND MODERN ART-decorative arts |
| 79 | NEO-CLASSICISM AND MODERN ART-artists, architects, photographers |
| 80 | MODERN ART-miscellania and new media |
| 85 | MODERN ART-architecture |
| 86 | MODERN ART-sculpture |
| 87 | MODERN ART-pictorial arts |
| 88 | MODERN ART-decorative arts |
| 89 | MODERN ART-artists, architects, photographers |
| 90 | COLLECTIONS AND EXHIBITIONS-miscellania |
| 95 | COLLECTIONS AND EXHIBITIONS-public collections |
| 96 | COLLECTIONS AND EXHIBITIONS-private collections |
| 97 | COLLECTIONS AND EXHIBITIONS-exhibition list |

**Search 15.14: Searching section headings and codes in ART LITERATURE INTERNATIONAL on DIALOG.**

```
?  ss  medieval(s)art(s)decorative/sh          Note use of S
                                               operator
      S1      14579    MEDIEVAL/SH
      S2     120582    ART/SH
      S3      14010    DECORATIVE/SH
      S4       2834    MEDIEVAL(S)ART(S)DECORATIVE/SH

?  ss  58/sh                                   Equivalent  section
                                               heading code is also
      S5       2834    58/SH                   in /SH and basic
                                               index

?  t 5/ti,sh,de,id/1

 5/TI,SH,DE,ID/1
 Il trono di Massimiano Erculio e la Cattedra di San Pietro(The throne of
 Maximian Herculius and the Cathedra of S. Peter)
 DESCRIPTORS: Rome (ITA), Vatican, S. Pietro/thrones/Cathedra Petri
 thrones, Italian/Rome/Vatican, S. Pietro, Cathedra Petri
 Maximian (Marcus Aurelius Valerius Maximianus), Roman emperor, d.310/
     throne
 Roman thrones/throne of Maximian/and Cathedra Petri
 survival of antiquity/Roman thrones/throne of Maximian
 ivories, Italian/Rome/Vatican, S. Pietro, panels from Cathedra Petri
 Late Antique ivories/Italy/Rome, Vatican, S. Pietro, panels from Cathedra
     Petri
 ivories, Egyptian/and Cathedra Petri
 Hercules (mythical figure)/ivories/Late Antique
 Carolingian ivories/and Cathedra Petri
 SECTION HEADING(S): 58—MEDIEVAL ART—decorative arts
 SUBJECT NATIONALITY: Italian; Egyptian
 SUBJECT PERIOD: 300-310; 800-899
 SUBJECT STYLE, MEDIUM, FORM: church furnishings; ivories; Carolingian

?  ss  medieval(w)art(w)decorative/sh          Note that the W
                                               operator does not
      S6      14579    MEDIEVAL/SH              carry across
      S7     120582    ART/SH                   subdivisions in
      S8      14010    DECORATIVE/SH            headings
      S9          0    MEDIEVAL(W)ART(W)DECORATIVE/SH
```

## ARTBIBLIOGRAPHIES MODERN (ABM)

| | |
|---|---|
| Producer: | ABC-Clio |
| Vendor: | DIALOG |
| Coverage: | All aspects of 19th- and 20th-century art and design, including the fine arts, architecture, ceramics, costumes, folk art, furniture, glass, graphic design, iconography, posters, prints, textiles. ABM also includes significant artists and movements of the 18th century. |
| Since: | 1974 |
| Size: | 107,438 (early 1990) |
| Update: | Semi-annually, approximately 7,000 records annually. |
| Materials: | Monographs, dissertations, exhibition catalogues and articles from approximately 350 journals. |
| Languages: | Data not available. |

Printed as:    *ArtBibliographies Modern.*
User aids:    None, apart from online service documentation.

Figure 15.8 shows a sample record from ABM. Abstracts have been included for most records except exhibition reviews. Graphic materials have a descriptive note in place of an abstract. Titles are given in the original language, with English translations for foreign titles. All authors are indexed as AU=. Language is not a searchable field, but searches can be limited to 'eng' or 'noneng'.

**Figure 15.8: Sample record from ARTBIBLIOGRAPHIES MODERN on DIALOG.**

```
188024
   ZORN: PAINTINGS, GRAPHICS, AND SCULPTURE
   BIRMINGHAM, ALABAMA: MUSEUM OF ART (27 MARCH-6 JUNE 1986);MEMPHIS,
TENNESSEE: DIXON GALLERY AND GARDENS (15 JUNE-10 AUG. 1986);ST. PETERSBURG,
FLORIDA: MUSEUM OF FINE ARTS (14 SEPT.-26 OCT. 1986). SPONSORED
BY BIRMINGHAM FESTIVAL OF ARTS, NATIONAL ENDOWMENT FOR THE ARTS,
WASHINGTON, D.C., AND ALABAMA HUMANITIES FOUNDATION. D. K. S. HYLAND,
H. H. BRUMMER, M. J. HARBERT. 100PP. 68 ILLUS. BIOG. BIBLIOG.
   Document Type: EXHIBITION CATALOG
   CATALOGUE TO AN EXHIBITION OF PAINTINGS, DRAWINGS, PRINTS AND SCULPTURE
BY THE SWEDISH ARTIST ANDERS ZORN (1860-1920), WITH TWO ESSAYS. IN 'ZORN
AND HIS AMERICAN PATRONS' HYLAND DESCRIBES ZORN'S SWEDISH BACKGROUND AND
HIS EUROPEAN AND AMERICAN TRAVELS, NOTING HIS ABILITY TO ADAPT TO ANY
CULTURAL ENVIRONMENT. HE DEFENDS ZORN FROM THE CRITICISM THAT HE
HAD
NARROW-MINDED VIEWS ABOUT THE RACIAL SUPERIORITY OF THE NORDIC RACE, AND
STATES THAT TO AMERICANS HE SEEMED THE ESSENCE OF THE VIKING CHIEFTAIN. HE
DISCUSSES ZORN'S FASCINATION WITH THE FEMALE NUDE, PARTICULARLY IN
LANDSCAPES AND IN GENRE SCENES, AND CONSIDERS IN DETAIL ZORN'S
RELATIONSHIPS WITH AND PORTRAITS OF HIS AMERICAN PATRONS. IN 'ANDERS ZORN'
BRUMMER DISCUSSES ZORN'S EARLY CAREER AND HIS SOCIAL SUCCESS.
   Descriptors: ZORN (ANDERS); PAINTING (SWEDEN); DRAWING (SWEDEN); PRINTS
(SWEDEN); SCULPTURE (SWEDEN); PORTRAITS
```

Descriptors (using British spelling conventions) are assigned from a controlled list of almost two hundred headings, some of which have topical subdivisions (Figure 15.9). Descriptors which are asterisked in the printed list can be divided by centuries, countries, and some other terms. Only one subdivision appears with each main heading. A special list is given for subdivisions of 'Iconography (Themes- )'. Descriptors are word and phrase indexed, and the use of L is suggested to link main headings and subdivisions. Personal name descriptors are entered in a 'Surname (Forename)' pattern.

Entries in the gallery index (GI=) generally take the form of 'City, State/Province/Country (Gallery Name)'. For major cities, the country name is omitted. For galleries in non-English speaking countries, the name is in the local language. Searching is carried through only on the first forty-two characters of the GI= index, which might cause occasional problems. The gallery index field is word and phrase indexed, and expanding the GI= index is suggested (Search 15.15 shows some inconsistencies in entry for Berlin). Each entry is entered in a separate subfield, and the S operator is useful for accurate searching. Though all gallery names are indexed, only four or five names are displayed in the full record, which might be a bit disconcerting.

**Figure 15.9: Extract from ARTBIBLIOGRAPHIES MODERN descriptor list**

## ARTBIBLIOGRAPHIES MODERN Classification Headings (Descriptors)
### (SELECT words or phrases in the Basic Index with /DE)

This list contains all the subject classification headings used in the current online file except for personal names and the names of artists' groups. Those headings which are subdivided are indicated with an asterisk (*) and the main subdivisions, other than centuries and countries, are indicated where they occur.

Abstract Art
Abstract Expressionism
Academic Art
Academies
Aesthetic Movement
Affichisme
Air Art
Anamorphic Art
Architecture*
  (Architectural Drawing)
  (Design)
  (Ecclesiastical)
  (Ornamental Details)
  (Theory)
Art*
  (Collected Essays)
  (Criticism and Connoisseurship)
  (Ethnic and Tribal)
  (Inter-Cultural Influences)
Art and Ecology
Art and Environment
Art and Feminism
Art and Geometry
Art and Health
Art and History
Art and Language
Art and Literature
Art and Magic
Art and Mathematics
Art and Music
Art and Mysticism
Art and Nature
Art and Occultism
Art and Philosophy
Art and Photography
Art and Politics
Art and Psychology
Art and Psychoanalysis
Art and Racialism
Art and Religion
Art and Science
Art and Society
Art and Sound
Art and Space
Art and Spiritualism
Art and Sport
Art and Technology
Art and Time
Art Brut
Art Deco

Art Games
Art-Language
Art Legislation
Art Market
Art Nouveau
Art Performances
Art Publications
Art Sales
Arts and Crafts Movement
Art Thefts
Art Theory
Ash Can School
Auto-Destructive Art
Automatisme

Barbizon School
Basketwork
Bauhaus, The
Behavioural Art
Bibliography
Biedermeier
Black Art
Blaue Reiter, Der
Bloomsbury Group
Body Art
Book (Art of the)
Bruecke (Die)

Calligraphy**
Camden Town Group
Cameos
Carpets and Rugs
Cartoons and Caricatures
Celtic Revival
Censorship
Ceramics*
  (Theory)
Children's Art
Chinoiserie
Clocks and Watches
COBRA
Coins and Metals
Collecting and Collectors*
  (Theory)
Colonial Revival
Colour
Comic Strips
Computer Art
Conceptual Art
Concrete Poetry

Congresses
Constructivism
Copies, Replicas and Versions
Costume*
  (Details and Accessories)
  (Ecclesiastical)
  (Jewish)
  (Maternity)
  (Military)
  (Sporting)
  (Theatrical)
  (Theory)
  (Tribal Body Decorations)
  (Wedding Dresses)
Cowboy Art
Cubism
Cubo-Futurism
Cybernetic Art

Dada
Dance (Art of the)
Dealers and Dealing
Design*
  (Theory)
De Stijl
Drawing*
  (Theory)
Earth Art
Ecclesiastical and Religious Art
Education*
  (Theory)
Egocentric Art
Eight (The)**
Enamels
Environmental Art
Equipo Cronica
Erotic Art
Euston Road School
Exhibition Architecture and Design
Exhibitions (International)*
Expressionism

Fakes and Forgeries
Fantasy in Art
Fashion
Fauvism
Figurative Art
Film Art
Folk Art*
  (Theory)

\* Subdivided classification headings
\*\* Classification headings no longer used after 1974.

## Search 15.15: The gallery index in ARTBIBLIOGRAPHIES MODERN on DIALOG.

```
? e gi=berlin (nationalgalerie)

Ref    Items    Index-term
E1       1     GI=BERLIN (BAUHAUS-ARCHIV)
E2       1     GI=BERLIN (HAUS AM KLEISTPARK)
E3       3    *GI=BERLIN (NATIONALGALERIE)
E4       1     GI=BERLIN (NATIONALGALERIE, STAATLICHE MUSEEN PRE
E5       1     GI=BERLIN (STAATLICHE MUSEEN, KUNSTBIBLIOTHEK)
E6       1     GI=BERLIN (STAATLLICHE MUSEEN, KUPFERSTICHKABINET
E7       1     GI=BERLIN MUSEUM
E8       1     GI=BERLIN, E. GERMANY (KUNSTGEWERBEMUSEUM)
E9       1     GI=BERLIN, E. GERMANY (NATIONALGALERIE)
E10      1     GI=BERLIN, E. GERMANY (STAATLICHE MUSEEN)
E11      7     GI=BERLIN, G.D.R. (ALTES MUSEUM)
E12      1     GI=BERLIN, G.D.R. (GALERIE AM WEIDENDAMM)

? e gi=berlin, g.d.r. (nationalgalerie)

Ref    Items    Index-term
E1       1     GI=BERLIN, G.D.R. (GALERIE AM WEIDENDAMM)
E2       2     GI=BERLIN, G.D.R. (KUNSTGEWERBEMUSEUM SCHLOSS KOP
E3       1    *GI=BERLIN, G.D.R. (NATIONALGALERIE)
E4       3     GI=BERLIN, G.D.R. (NEUE BERLINER GALERIE)
E5       2     GI=BERLIN, G.D.R. (OTTO-NAGEL-HAUS)
E6       5     GI=BERLIN, G.D.R. (STAATLICHE MUSEEN)
E7       1     GI=BERLIN, G.D.R. (STADTBIBLIOTHEK)
E8       1     GI=BERLIN, G.D.R. (ZENTRUM FUR KUNSTAUSSTELLUNGEN
E9       1     GI=BERLIN, G.F.R. (AKADEMIE DER KUNSTE
E10     16     GI=BERLIN, G.F.R. (AKADEMIE DER KUNSTE)
E11      1     GI=BERLIN, G.F.R. (ALTEN MUSEM)
E12      1     GI=BERLIN, G.F.R. (AMERIKA HAUS)

? ss gi=(berlin(s)nationalgalerie(s)(e or d)
```

| | | | |
|---|---|---|---|
| S16 | 235 | GI=BERLIN | **Note use of S** |
| S17 | 32 | GI=NATIONALGALERIE | **operator** |
| S18 | 53 | GI=E | **For "E. Germany"** |
| S19 | 781 | GI=D | **For "G.D.R."** |
| S20 | 2 | GI=(BERLIN(S)NATIONALGALERIE(S)(E OR D)) | |

```
? t 20/ti,de,gi/1-2

20/TI,DE,GI/1
  RABINDRANATH TAGORE: WATERCOLOURS - GOUACHES - DRAWINGS
  RABINDRANATH TAGORE: AQUARELLE - GOUACHEN - FEDERZEICHNUNGEN
```
**BERLIN, G.D.R.: NATIONALGALERIE** (24 SEPT.-21 OCT. 1981). ORGANIZED BY THE MINISTERIUM FUR KULTUR DER DDR, THE MINISTERIUM FUR ERZIEHUNG UND KULTUR INDIENS, THE NATIONAL GALLERY OF MODERN ART, NEW DELHI, AND THE ZENTRUM FUR KUNSTAUSSTELLUNGEN DER DDR. 24PP. 6 ILLUS. BIBLIOG.
```
  Descriptors:  TAGORE  (RABINDRANATH);  PAINTING (INDIA);  WATERCOLOUR
PAINTING (INDIA); DRAWING (INDIA)

20/TI,DE,GI/2
  KARL  BLECHEN,  1798-1840: SKETCHES  IN OIL, WATERCOLOURS, SEPIA SKETCHES,
DRAWINGS,  DESIGNS
  KARL BLECHEN, 1798-1840: OLSKIZZEN,  AQUARELLE,  SEPIABLATTER, ZEICHNUNGEN,
ENTWURFE
```
**BERLIN,  E. GERMANY:  NATIONALGALERIE** (1 APRIL-15 JUNE 1973). 114PP. 48 ILLUS. BIOG. BIBLIOG.
```
  Descriptors: BLECHEN (KARL); IMPRESSIONISM; PAINTING (GERMANY)
```

*Language and literature*

## MLA [INTERNATIONAL] BIBLIOGRAPHY (MLA)

| | |
|---|---|
| Producer: | Modern Language Association |
| Vendor: | DIALOG, Wilsonline |
| CD-ROM: | Wilsondisc, Faxon |
| Coverage: | English, American, medieval and neo-Latin, and Celtic literatures and folklore; European, Asian, African and Latin American literature; theoretical, descriptive, comparative and historical linguistics. |
| Since: | 1963 (DIALOG); 1981 (Wilson) |
| Size: | 930,000 (DIALOG-January 1990); 378,033 (Wilson-November 1990) |
| Update: | Monthly. |
| Materials: | Monographs, collections, dissertations, bibliographies, source documents when accompanied by critical apparatus, articles from approximately 3,000 journals. |
| Languages: | Almost 60 languages are represented. |
| Printed as: | *MLA International Bibliography* |
| User aids: | None |

Figure 15.10 shows old and new sample MLA records from DIALOG, and Figure 15.11 shows a sample on Wilsonline (which does not include the older records). The following discussion is based on the DIALOG version. Abstracts are not included in MLA, although there is a notes field which is used for brief information on content, format or availability. Titles appear in the original language only, and non-Roman titles are transliterated. Hyphens and apostrophes in title words are retained in searching (or truncation should be used). All authors are indexed. Languages are searchable as LA= (including English) for records apart from those entered for 1970-1980, and this will be rectified shortly. With the same time restrictions, search results can be limited to 'eng' and 'noneng'.

## Figure 15.10: Sample records from MLA BIBLIOGRAPHY on DIALOG.
(Reprinted by permission of the Modern Language Association of America)

```
6301224       63-998
The Literary Epiphany in Some Early Fiction of Flaubert, Conrad, Proust,
    and Joyce
Sherwin, Jane King
Dissertation Abstracts, Ann Arbor, MI. 1963; 23: 3902.
PY: 1963
DOCUMENT TYPE: journal article
LANGUAGES(S): English
DESCRIPTORS: literature—themes—genres; literature—English—Great
    Britain—1900-1999—Joyce; literature—French—1800-1899—Flaubert;
    literature—French—1900-1999—Proust
DESCRIPTOR CODE(S): 010204000000; 010310000000; 020307000000;
020308000000

Old record
```

**Figure 15.10:** (cont)

```
9006252      90-1-478;  90-3-1173
Dialect in Irish Literature: The Hermetic Core
Wall, Richard
 Irish University Review: A Journal of Irish Studies, Dublin 4, Ireland.
   1990 Spring; 20(1): 8-18.
 PY: 1990
 ISSN 0021-1427
 DOCUMENT TYPE: journal article
 LANGUAGES(S): English
 DESCRIPTORS: SLT—Irish literature; LOC—1900-1999; AWK—Joyce, James; SJC
   —fiction; LTC—Irish English dialect; poetry; drama; LOC—1700-1999;
   SLN—English language (Modern); SLN—Irish English dialect; SJC—
   stylistics

New  record
```

**Figure 15.11: Sample record from MLA BIBLIOGRAPHY on Wilsonline.**
(Reprinted by permission of the Modern Language Association of America)

```
Wall,  Richard
Dialect in Irish Literature: The Hermetic Core
Irish University Review: A Journal of Irish Studies (Dublin 4,
Ireland) 1990 Spring; 20(1):8-18
Language: English
90-1-1037
90-3-2256
Article
(slt) Irish literature (sjc) fiction (tim) 1900-1999 (tim)
1700-1999 (sau) Joyce, James (ltc) Irish English
dialect/poetry/drama
(sln) English language (Modern) (sln) Irish English dialect
(sjc) stylistics
BMLA90002262
```

Discussion of descriptors must begin by pointing out that subject indexing practices changed radically in 1981, as is evident by looking at the sample old and new records. Prior to 1981, descriptors were limited to English language representations of the classification scheme used to organize the printed volumes. For literature, these typically take the form of an increasingly specific subject string designating [form, for example 'literature'] - [language] - [national origin] - [dates] - [specific named person or facet]. Each subdivision in the string is word and phrase indexed. Equivalent hierarchical descriptor codes (DC=) are also searchable and allow for generic search.

In 1981 a new system of supercoded descriptors replaced previous conventions, and descriptors now consist of a three-letter code (see Figure 15.12), followed by a more specific natural language term or phrase. These are word and phrase indexed, and retain hyphens and apostrophes. Many of the elements in both old and new descriptors are heavily posted, and can slow response time.

**Figure 15.12: Supercoded descriptors in MLA**

| | | | |
|---|---|---|---|
| AWK | Subject Author/Work/Folkwork | LWK | Alternative Language of |
| GEN | Genre | | Literary Work |
| GRP | Group | MED | Performance Medium |
| LFE | Feature | SAP | Scholarly Approach |
| LIF | Influence On | SCH | Scholar |
| LOC | Place/Time Period | SCP | Scholarly Theory/Discipline/Type |
| LPR | Process | SDV | Scholarly Tool/Device |
| LSO | Source | SJC | Subject Classification Term |
| LTC | Technique | SLN | Specific Language |
| LTH | Theme/Motif/Character | SLT | Specific Literature |

Under the new system, the descriptor field contains full names and titles; under the old system titles of works were usually not indexed, and names were limited principally to surname. A comprehensive search for James Joyce, for instance, would require 'joyce/df' for pre-1981 records, and 'joyce(l)(j or james)' for new records (Search 15.16). Searching for common names in the basic index presents a problem, since older records would only have the surname, but use of an unrestricted surname such as 'Joyce' will retrieve many other 'Joyce's' in old and new records besides James. Searching for a specific literary title in older records must rely on such information as may appear in source titles and occasional notes, and on the creative use of other clues. Search 15.17 shows many cases of 'Molly Bloom' having been mentioned where 'Ulysses' was not.

**Search 15.16: Searching for personal name subjects in MLA BIBLIOGRAPHY on DIALOG.**
(Reprinted by permission of the Modern Language Association of America)

```
? ss joyce/df or joyce(l)(j or james)

    S1      2578    JOYCE/DF                        For  records  prior
    S2      4637    JOYCE/DE                        to 1981
    S3      6647    J/DE
    S4      7246    JAMES/DE
    S5      1942    JOYCE/DE(L)(J/DE OR JAMES/DE)[for records since 1981]
    S6      4518    JOYCE/DF OR JOYCE(L)(J OR JAMES)

? t 6/ti,de/1,4518

  6/TI,DE/1                                         Example of new
James  Joyce's  Exiles:  Women  between  Men        record
  DESCRIPTORS: SLT—Irish literature; LOC—1900-1999; AWK—Joyce, James; AWK
     —Exiles; AWK—The Dead; drama; short story; AWK—Shelley, Percy Bysshe
     ; LSO—Shelley, Percy Bysshe; AWK—Ibsen, Henrik; LSO—Ibsen, Henrik

  6/TI,DE/4518                                      Example of old
La  lotta  con  Proteo                              record
  DESCRIPTORS: literature; literature—English—Great Britain—1900-1999—
     Joyce—Yeats; literature—English—United States—1800-1870—Melville;
     literature—English—United States—1871-1899—Whitman; literature—
     English—United States—1900-1999—Faulkner; literature—Italian—
     1900-1999—Montale

? ss joyce/de not s6                                Unspecified  /DE
                                                    search
```

**Search 15.16:** (cont.)

```
        S7        637      JOYCE/DE
                 4518      S6
        S8        119      JOYCE/DE NOT S6

? t 8/ti,de/1

8/TI,DE/1
Joyce Carol Oates in Berlin: The Birth of a Myth
  DESCRIPTORS: SLT—American literature; LOC—1900-1999; AWK—Oates, Joyce
     Carol; AWK—Lamb of Abyssalia; short story; LTH—Berlin Wall
```

## Search 15.17: Searching for specific literary works in MLA BIBLIOGRAPHY on DIALOG.
(Reprinted by permission of the Modern Language Association of America)

```
? ss ulysses and joyce/de

        S1       1360      ULYSSES
        S2       4637      JOYCE/DE
        S3       1226      ULYSSES AND JOYCE/DE

? ss molly(w)bloom

        S4         73      MOLLY
        S5        344      BLOOM
        S6         23      MOLLY (W) BLOOM

? ss s6 not s3

                   23      S6
                 1226      S3
        S7         13      S6 NOT S3

? t 7/ti,de/1-3

 7/TI,DE/1
Molly Bloom and the Rhetorical Tradition
  DESCRIPTORS: literature—English—Great Britain—1900-1999—Joyce

 7/TI,DE/2
Toward an Historical Molly Bloom
  DESCRIPTORS: literature—English—Great Britain—1900-1977—Joyce

 7/TI,DE/3
Molly Bloom and Lady Hamilton
  DESCRIPTORS: literature—English—Great Britain—1900-1977—Joyce
```

MLA includes date indexing, effected through the HP= (historical period), HS= (starting date) and HE= (ending date) indexes. The HP= index usually (but not always) contains a century range. Searching these indexes is subject to the same caveat as accompanies their use in HA and AHL. The SF= (subfile) index can be used to restrict a search to the equivalent of a particular volume of the MLA printed index (see Figure 15.13 for a display of this index). As the content of volumes has changed over time, the documentation should be read carefully, as is true for all subject searching in this database.

**Figure 15.13: Subfiles in MLA BIBLIOGRAPHY on DIALOG.**

```
E1         16   SE=98
E2         15   SE=99
E3          0   *SF=
E4     262676   SF=1  (VOLUME 1:  ENGLISH LITERATURE)
E5     368911   SF=2  (VOLUME 2:  FOREIGN LITERATURE)
E6     209852   SF=3  (VOLUME 3:  LINGUISTICS)
E7      19667   SF=4  (VOLUME 4:  GENERAL LITERATURE)
E8      19479   SF=5  (VOLUME 5:  FOLKLORE)
E9         22   SN=NO. 1-3 0761-2591; THEREAFTER 0994-5490
E10        12   SN=NONE
E11        54   SN=PP-76-1402
E12         7   SN=X-7200-9400-1
```

MLA has begun a retrospective conversion project that will eventually convert records from 1921 to 1969, which should considerably enhance the value of this file for humanities scholars. It is to the credit of the producers of MLA that they have gone to a great deal of effort to make subject access more specific and effective, and to standardize back files as they are mounted.

## LINGUISTICS AND LANGUAGE BEHAVIOR ABSTRACTS (LLBA)

Producer:     Sociological Abstracts
Vendor:       BRS, DIALOG
Coverage:     Linguistics and language behaviour.
Since:        1973
Size:         118,452 (January 1990)
Update:       Quarterly, approximately 8,000 records annually.
Materials:    Bibliographies, book reviews, monographs, conference proceedings, and articles selected from 1,200 worldwide journals.
Languages:    Over 40 languages are represented.
Printed as:   *Linguistics and Language Behavior Abstracts*
User aids:    *LLBA User's Reference Manual* (revised 1987)

A sample LLBA record is shown in Figure 15.14. Abstracts are provided for all records except dissertations. Abstracts may contain abbreviations, a list of which is provided in the user aid. The notes field (which contributes individual words to the basic index) contains information about a source or reprints, or may be used to indicate that an article is a comment, rejoinder, or reply. Titles appear in the original (transliterated) language, with English translations. Languages (including English) are searchable as LA=, and results may be limited to 'eng' or 'noneng'. All authors are indexed, with authors of reviewed books in the BA= index.

**Figure 15.14: Sample record from LINGUISTICS AND LANGUAGE BEHAVIOR ABSTRACTS on DIALOG.**

```
130709       9009867
Validity of Stanford-Binet IV with Linguistically Precocious  Toddlers
   Robinson, Nancy M.; Dale, Philip S.; Landesman, Sharon
   Center Study Capable Youth U Washington NI-20, Seattle 98195
   Intelligence 1990, 14, 2, Apr-June, 173-186. CODEN:NTLLDT
   PUB. YEAR: 1990
   COUNTRY OF PUBLICATION: United States
   LANGUAGE: English
   DOCUMENT TYPE: Abstract of Journal Article (aja)
   Standarized measures of cognitive & language development were administered
      at ages 20, 24, & 30 months to a group of toddlers identified as having
      above-average  language  development (N = 30). At the first assessment,
      the  Bayley Scales & Stanford-Binet IV were administered. At the second
      session,  the Bayley Motor Scale only, & the Peabody Picture Vocabulary
      Test-Revised  (PPVT-R)  were  given. At the final session, the PPVT-R,
      Stanford-Binet IV, & Stanford-Binet L-M were administered. Findings are
      discussed  with  relation  to  the  clinical  validity  of  the  new
      Stanford-Binet  instrument  with  very  young  children. Some specific
      problems  associated  with use of the test close to its lower age limit
      are  discussed. 2  Tables,  1 Figure, 17 References. dZ(O/V>>Y9 Murray
      (Copyright 1990, Sociological Abstracts, Inc., all rights reserved.)
   DESCRIPTORS: Preschool  (pr3aa);  Testing  (te7);  Child  Language (ch1);
      Peabody Picture Vocabulary Test (pe1)
   IDENTIFIERS: Stanford-Binet IV test  validity,  precocious  toddlers;
```

Four or five descriptors from a list of about eight hundred terms (Figure 15.15) are assigned to each item. Descriptors are word and phrase indexed, and there is an online thesaurus (the only example of this in the humanities files) (Figure 15.16). Descriptors can also be searched by their equivalent descriptor code (an asterisk beside a term in the thesaurus indicates that use of the code may not be effective). Identifiers, which are word indexed, are natural language 'mini-abstracts', containing details on variables, population, type of study, location, and so on.

**Figure 15.15: Descriptors in *LLBA User's Reference Manual*, revised 1987.**

# Authority File

| | |
|---|---|
| | Accent (see Foreign Accent or Suprasegmental Analysis) |
| ac1a | Achievement Testing |
| ac2 | Acoustic Phonetics |
| ac3 | Acoustic Theory of Speech Production |
| | Active Sentence (see Voice) |
| ad1 | Adjective (see also Article) |
| ad2 | Adolescent Language (see also Age Differences in Language) |
| ad3 | Adult Language (see also Age Differences in Language) |
| ad4 | Adverb |
| | Affects (see Emotions) |
| * af1 | Affix |
| * af2 | Afro-Asiatic Languages |
| ag1 | Age Differences in Language |
| ag2 | Aggression, Verbal |
| ai1 | Aided Recall |
| ai2 | Air Conduction |
| ai3 | Air Flow |
| | Alcoholism (see Neurotic Disorders) |
| | Algebraic Linguistics (see Computational Linguistics) |
| | Alliteration (see Phonological Stylistics) |
| al1 | Alphabet |
| al2 | Altaic Languages |
| am1 | Ambiguity |
| am2 | American Indian |
| am3 | American Linguistic Theory |
| am4 | American Negro |
| | Amerindian Language (see North, Mexican & Central, Caribbean & South Amerindian Languages) |
| | Anagrams (see Nonsense Syllables, Nonsense Words) |
| an1 | Animal Communication and Vocalization |
| an2 | Animate and Inanimate |
| an3 | Anomalous Strings |
| | Anomia (see Language Pathology) |
| an4 | Anthropological Linguistics (see also Ethnolinguistics) |
| an5 | Antonym |
| an6 | Anxiety |
| ap1 | Aphasia (see also Language Pathology, Nervous System Pathology) |
| ap2 | Applied Linguistics |
| ap3 | Aptitude Testing |
| | Arabic (see Afro-Asiatic Languages) |
| | Areal Linguistics (see Comparative Linguistics, Typology of Language) |
| ar1 | Art as Language |
| ar2 | Article |
| ar3 | Articulation |
| ar4 | Articulation Disorders (see also Stuttering) |
| | Articulation Structures (see Oral Structures, Phonation Structures) |
| ar5 | Articulatory Phonetics |
| | Artificial Languages (see Synthetic Languages) |
| | Aspect (see Mode) |
| at1 | Attention |
| | Attitude Change (see Attitudes, Persuasion) |
| * at3 | Attitudes |
| au1 | Audiolingual Language Teaching |
| au2 | Audiology |
| au3 | Audiometry |
| au4 | Audiovisual Language Teaching |
| | Auditory Evoked Response (see Evoked Response) |
| | Auditory Feedback (see Delayed Auditory Feedback, Feedback) |
| | Auditory Imagery (see Imagery) |
| au5 | Auditory Localization |
| au6 | Auditory Masking |
| au7 | Auditory Stimulation (see also Binaural Stimulation, Monaural Stimulation, Noise) |
| au8 | Auditory Thresholds |
| au9 | Austin |
| au9a | Australian Macro-Phylim |

| | |
|---|---|
| au9b | Austro-Asiatic Languages |
| * au10 | Austronesian Languages |
| | Authorship Attribution (see Statistical Analysis of Style) |
| au11 | Autism |
| | Automatic Data Handling (see Data Processing and Retrieval) |
| | Automatic Translation (see Machine Translation) |
| au12 | Auxiliary Verb |
| | Azerbaijani (see Altaic Languages) |
| az1a | Baltic Languages |
| | Bantu (see Congo Kordofanian Languages) |
| ba1 | Bar Hillel |
| | Basic English (see International Languages) |
| ba2a | Basque |
| be1a | Behavioral Disturbances |
| | Behavioral Therapy (see Psychoanalysis and Psychotherapy) |
| be2 | Behavioristic Linguistic Theory |
| be3 | Belief |
| | Bender Gestalt Test (see Projective Techniques) |
| be4 | Benveniste |
| be5 | Berber Languages (for post-1982 entries, see Afro-Asiatic Languages) |
| bi1 | Bilingualism (see also Plurilinguilism) |
| bi2 | Binaural Stimulation |
| * bi3 | Biological, Physical, Physiological |
| * bl1 | Black English |
| | Blindness (see Vision Disorders) |
| * bl3 | Bloomfield |
| bo1 | Bone Conduction |
| bo2 | Borrowing |
| | Braille (see Reading Aids for the Blind) |
| br1 | Brain Anatomy |
| | Brain Damage (see Nervous System Pathology) |
| | Brain Disease (see Nervous System Pathology) |
| | Broca'a Area (see Brain Anatomy) |
| | Caribbean Amerindian Languages (see Central Amerindian Languages) |
| ca2 | Carnap |
| ca3 | Case |
| ca4 | Case Grammar |
| ca5 | Caucasian Languages |
| ce1 | Celtic Languages (see also Indo-European Languages) |
| * ce1a | Central Amerindian Languages |
| | Central Nervous System (see Brain Anatomy, Nervous System Pathology) |
| ce2 | Cerebral Dominance (see also Handedness) |
| | Cerebral Palsy (see Nervous System Pathology) |
| ce4 | Chad (for post-1982 entries, see Afro-Asiatic Languages) |
| ch1 | Child Language (see also Age Differences in Language, Piaget) |
| ch2 | Chinese |
| ch3 | Chomsky |
| | Cinema (see Mass Media) |
| | Classical Conditioning (see Conditioning) |
| cl1 | Clause |
| cl2 | Cleft Lip and Palate |
| cl2a | Click Languages |
| cl3 | Clozes |
| | Cochlea (see Inner Ear) |
| * cm1 | Code, Coding |
| * cm3 | Code-Switching |
| * cm2 | Coding Instruction Strategy |
| co1 | Cognate |
| | Cognitive Function of Language (see Cognitive Processes) |
| co1b | Cognitive Processes |
| | College (see Undergraduate School) |
| | Colloquial (see Register) |
| co2 | Color (see also Stroop Color Word Test) |
| | Commercial Dialect (see Trade Languages) |

**Figure 15.16:  The online thesaurus in LINGUISTICS AND LANGUAGE BEHAVIOR
ABSTRACTS on DIALOG.**

```
    ? e bilingualism

    Ref   Items   RT   Index-term
    E1      3          BILINGUALE
    E2      4          BILINGUALEN
    E3    16272    3  *BILINGUALISM
    E4      2          BILINGUALISME
    E5      4          BILINGUALISMS
    E6      2          BILINGUALISMUS
    E7      1          BILINGUALISTIC
    E8      2          BILINGUALITE
    E9     16          BILINGUALITY
    E10     3          BILINGUALIZATION
    E11     2          BILINGUALIZE
    E12     1          BILINGUALIZING

    ? e e3                                      Accessing  the
                                                online thesaurus
    Ref    Items   Type RT   Index-term         from the basic
    R1     16272        3 *BILINGUALISM          index
    R2     15635    R   4   PLURILINGUALISM
    R3       100    R   2   SECOND DIALECT LEARNING
    R4     14777    R   6   SECOND LANGUAGE LEARNING

    ? e (second language learning)              Accessing  the
                                                online thesaurus
    Ref    Items   Type RT   Index-term         directly
    R1     14777        6 *SECOND LANGUAGE LEARNING
    R2         2    U   3   FOREIGN LANGUAGE LEARNING
    R3         5    U   3   LANGUAGE LEARNING
    R4     16272    R   3   BILINGUALISM
    R5     13889    R   4   FLES
    R6     15635    R   4   PLURILINGUALISM
    R7     23904    R   5   TESOL

    ? e r6

    Ref    Items   Type RT   Index-term
    R1     15635        4 *PLURILINGUALISM
    R2       249    U   1   MULTILINGUALISM
    R3     16272    R   3   BILINGUALISM
    R4       100    R   2   SECOND DIALECT LEARNING
    R5     14777    R   6   SECOND LANGUAGE LEARNING
```

Each item is assigned one (typically) or more of seventy-five section headings, which can be searched by word (/SH) or code (SH=). The current scheme (Figure 15.17) has been in use since 1977, and older items have been reclassified. The section headings codes are cascaded, and allow for generic and range search (Search 15.18).

**Figure 15.17: Section Headings and Codes in *LLBA User's Reference Manual*, revised 1991 (in press).**

# APPENDIX I
## LLBA CLASSIFICATION SCHEME

|  |  |
|---|---|
| **4000** | **PSYCHOLINGUISTICS** |
| 4010 | Psycholinguistics |
| 4011 | Theories and Models |
| 4012 | Language and Cognition |
| 4013 | Syntactic Processing |
| 4014 | Semantic processing |
| 4015 | Child Language Acquisition |
| 4016 | Verbal Learning |
| | Paired Associate, Serial Learning |
| | Memory, Recognition |
| 4017 | Psychoacoustics |
| 4018 | Neurolinguistics |
| **4100** | **APPLIED LINGUISTICS** |
| 4110 | Applied Linguistics |
| 4111 | Native Language Pedagogy |
| 4112 | Non-Native Language Pedagogy |
| 4113 | Non-Native Language Acquisition |
| 4114 | Language Testing |
| 4115 | Adult Language Development |
| 4116 | Reading Readiness |
| 4117 | Reading Instruction and Remediation |
| 4118 | Reading Materials |
| 4119 | Reading Processes |
| 4120 | Reading Testing |
| 4121 | Writing |
| 4122 | Bilingualism, Bilingual Education |
| 4123 | Translation |
| **4200** | **PHONOLOGY** |
| 4210 | Phonology |
| **4300** | **SYNTAX** |
| 4310 | Syntax |
| **4400** | **SEMANTICS** |
| 4410 | Semantics |
| **4500** | **MORPHOLOGY** |
| 4510 | Morphology |
| **4600** | **DISCOURSE ANALYSIS/TEXT LINGUISTICS** |
| 4610 | Discourse Analysis/Text Linguistics |
| 4611 | Text Linguistics |
| 4612 | Stylistics |
| **4700** | **THEORY OF LINGUISTICS** |
| 4710 | Theory of Linguistics |
| **4800** | **HISTORY OF LINGUISTICS** |
| 4810 | History of Linguistics |
| **4900** | **ANTHROPOLOGICAL LINGUISTICS** |
| 4910 | Anthropological Linguistics |
| **5100** | **DESCRIPTIVE LINGUISTICS** |
| 5110 | Descriptive Linguistics |
| 5111 | Diachronic Linguistics |
| 5112 | Comparative Linguistics |
| 5113 | Computational and Mathematical Linguistics |
| 5114 | Language Universals |
| 5115 | Language in Contact |
| 5116 | Language Area Studies |
| 5117 | Dialectology |
| 5118 | International Languages |
| 5119 | Onomastics |
| 5120 | Creole Studies |
| 5121 | Paleolinguistics |

|  |  |
|---|---|
| **5200** | **LEXICOGRAPHY** |
| 5210 | Lexicography |
| 5211 | Lexicology |
| **5300** | **ORTHOGRAPHY, WRITING SYSTEMS** |
| 5310 | Orthography, Writing Systems |
| **5400** | **LANGUAGE CLASSIFICATION** |
| 5410 | Typological Classification |
| 5411 | Genetic Classification |
| 5412 | Areal Classification |
| **5500** | **INTERPERSONAL BEHAVIOR AND COMMUNICATION** |
| 5510 | Interpersonal Behavior and Communication |
| 5512 | Communication in Groups |
| 5513 | Mass Media |
| **5600** | **SOCIOLINGUISTICS** |
| 5610 | Sociolinguistics |
| 5611 | Language Planning |
| **5700** | **POETICS/LITERARY THEORY** |
| 5710 | Poetics |
| 5711 | Literary Criticism |
| 5712 | Literary Theory |
| **5800** | **NONVERBAL COMMUNICATION** |
| 5810 | Human Nonverbal Communication |
| 5811 | Animal Communication |
| 5812 | Art as Language |
| **5900** | **SEMIOTICS** |
| 5910 | Semiotics |
| **6000** | **PHILOSOPHY OF LANGUAGE** |
| 6010 | Philosophy of Language |
| **6100** | **PHONETICS** |
| 6110 | Phonetics |
| 6111 | Speech Synthesis |
| **6200** | **HEARING AND SPEECH PHYSIOLOGY** |
| 6210 | Hearing and Speech Physiology |
| **6300** | **HEARING-PATHOLOGICAL AND NORMAL** |
| 6310 | Hearing-Pathological and Normal |
| 6311 | Auditory Perception |
| **6400** | **LANGUAGE-PATHOLOGICAL AND NORMAL** |
| 6410 | Language-Pathological and Normal |
| **6500** | **LEARNING DISABILITIES** |
| 6510 | Learning Disabilities |
| **6600** | **MENTAL RETARDATION** |
| 6610 | Mental Retardation |
| **6700** | **PSYCHOPATHOLOGY** |
| 6710 | Linguistics and Psychiatry |
| **6800** | **SPECIAL EDUCATION** |
| 6810 | Special Education |
| 6811 | Hearing Therapy |
| 6812 | Language Therapy |
| **6900** | **PSYCHOMETRICS** |
| 6910 | Psychometrics |

## Search 15.18: Section headings in LINGUISTICS AND LANGUAGE BEHAVIOR ABSTRACTS on DIALOG.

```
? e sh=4111

Ref    Items    Index-term
E1     30011    SH=41
E2       537    SH=4110
E3      3276    *SH=4111
E4      9656    SH=4112
E5      4659    SH=4113
E6       793    SH=4114
E7       380    SH=4115
E8       230    SH=4116            Reading   readiness
E9      2528    SH=4117            Reading   instruction...
E10      581    SH=4118            Reading   materials
E11     1642    SH=4119            Reading   processes
E12      437    SH=4120            Reading   testing

? ss sh=4116:4120

     S1        5387     SH=4116:4120

? ss reading(w)(readiness or instruction or materials or processes or
testing)/sh
                                           Note  equivalence
     S2        5387     READING/SH          between codes and
     S3         230     READINESS/SH        headings
     S4        2528     INSTRUCTION/SH
     S5         581     MATERIALS/SH
     S6        1642     PROCESSES/SH
     S7        1226     TESTING/SH
     S8        5387     READING(W)(READINESS OR INSTRUCTION OR MATERIALS OR
                        PROCESSES OR TESTING)/SH

? ss s1 and kindergarten/de

               5387     S1
     S9         316     KINDERGARTEN/DE
     S10        113     S1 AND KINDERGARTEN/DE

? t 10/ti,de,sh/1

10/TI,DE,SH/1
The Impact of the Writing to Read Program on Reading, Spelling, and Writing
    of Kindergarteners
 DESCRIPTORS: Kindergarten (ki1); Written Language Instruction (wr3);
    Reading Instruction (re4); Orthography (or5)
 SECTION HEADINGS: applied linguistics- writing (4121) applied
    linguistics- reading instruction and remediation  (4117)
```

## OTHER FILES

Two indexing services in this category were not examined first-hand, but certainly deserve mention here. One is the online file BIBLIOGRAPHIE LINGUISTISCHER LITERATUR (GEM), which offers German and English keyword indexing for worldwide sources on linguistics. The second is RLIN's RESEARCH IN PROGRESS database, which indexes forthcoming journal articles, dissertations, conference papers and presentations, grant proposals, and various nonprint materials in the fields of linguistics, literature, and women's studies. The scope is expected to broaden in coming years, and one recent addition of interest is the *MLA Thesaurus of Linguistic and Literary Terms.*

In addition to the indexing services discussed above, a number of dictionaries have been issued on CD-ROM. The most notable of these is the OXFORD ENGLISH DICTIONARY (Oxford University Press), the full-text of the current edition (with periodic updates). Users can search by definition, part of speech, quoted author and text, etymology, and other features [4]. Other electronic offerings of note in literature include SHAKESPEARE ON DISC (CMC ReSearch), containing the complete works in full text, and the LIBRARY OF AMERICA COLLECTION (Electronic Text Corporation), consisting of the full text of selected works of a dozen noted American authors.

*Philosophy*

### PHILOSOPHER'S INDEX (PI)

| | |
|---|---|
| Producer: | Philosophy Documentation Center |
| Vendor: | DIALOG |
| Coverage: | Aesthetics, epistemology, ethics, logic, metaphysics, and the philosophy of various disciplines. |
| Since: | 1940 |
| Size: | 151,116 (January 1990) |
| Update: | Quarterly, approximately 4,800 records annually. |
| Materials: | Monographs and articles selected from over 270 journals. |
| Languages: | More than 20 languages are represented. |
| Printed as: | *Philosopher's Index* |
| User aids: | *Searching The Philosopher's Index Database on DIALOG* (1988 - for end users); *Philosopher's Index Thesaurus* (1975). |

Figure 15.18 shows a sample PI record. Abstracts are principally author abstracts, and may be in languages other than English. Greek letters are coded with capital letters between quote marks ('logos'), and other symbols are entered as a descriptive phrase between double dollar signs ($$less than$$). Titles are entered in the original language only, unless they are non-Roman, in which case a Roman title is taken from the table of contents of the journal, preferring English if available. Individual languages (excepting English) are searchable as LA=, and results can be limited to 'eng' or 'noneng'. Up to three authors are indexed in the AU= field; in the case of more than three authors only the first is indexed.

### Figure 15.18: Sample record from PHILOSOPHER'S INDEX on DIALOG.

```
170076
    "THE TRIALS AND TRIBULATIONS OF SELECTIONIST EXPLANATIONS" IN "ISSUES IN
EVOLUTIONARY EPISTEMOLOGY", HAHLWEG, KAI (ED), 413-432.
    AMUNDSON, RON
    "ALBANY, SUNY PR,
    Languages: ENGLISH
    Journal Announcement: 241
    EVOLUTIONARY EPISTEMOLOGISTS STRESS SIMILARITIES AMONG NATURAL SELECTION,
TRIAL AND ERROR LEARNING, AND OTHER SELECTIVE MECHANISMS OF CHANGE. IT IS
INFREQUENTLY RECOGNIZED THAT SELECTIONIST SCIENTIFIC THEORIES HAVE TYPICAL
KINDS OF COMPETITORS, WHICH COMPETITORS SHOW SIMILARITIES OF THEIR OWN. THE
```

**Figure 15.18:** (cont.)

```
CHALLENGES  ARE  OFTEN  WELL  FOUNDED  AND  HAVE  LED  TO  MODIFICATION  OR  REJECTION
OF   SELECTIONIST   THEORIES.  THIS   PAPER   CITES   HISTORICAL   CASES   SHOWING
PERSISTENT   PATTERNS   IN  SELECTIONIST/NONSELECTIONIST  DEBATES.  THE  PATTERNS
EXPOSE  A  SET  OF  "CENTRAL  CONDITIONS"  FOR  THE  FORCE  OF  SELECTIONIST
EXPLANATIONS,   WHATEVER  THEIR  DOMAIN.  IMPLICATIONS  ARE  DRAWN  FOR  THE  LIMITS
OF   SELECTIONIST   EXPLANATION,   AND   FOR   THE   PROJECT   OF   EVOLUTIONARY
EPISTEMOLOGY  ITSELF.
   Descriptors:  EPISTEMOLOGY;  NATURAL  SELECTION
```

Descriptors come from a thesaurus of about five thousand terms (Figure 15.19). Three to four are assigned for journal articles, and ten to fifteen for books. Descriptors may include names of nationalities, specific subject terms, and form descriptors 'bibliography' and 'biography' where appropriate, and each record must have one or more of the following major field or historical period terms:

| | | | |
|---|---|---|---|
| aesthetics | metaphysics | | |
| axiology | philosophical anthropology | | |
| education | philosophy | | |
| epistemology | political phil | | |
| ethics | religion | ancient | modern |
| history | science | medieval | nineteenth |
| language | social phil | renaissance | twentieth |
| logic | | | |

The abbreviation 'phil' is common, and must be used when searching (Search 15.19). Descriptors are word and phrase indexed. Some descriptors were hyphenated prior to 1975, and must be searched in that form in older records (Search 15.20).

**Search 15.19: Abbreviated descriptors in PHILOSOPHER'S INDEX on DIALOG.**

```
? ss social philosophy

     S1          1     SOCIAL PHILOSOPHY

? ss social phil

     S2      13128     SOCIAL PHIL

? ss euthanasia and (s1 or s2)

     S3        406     EUTHANASIA
                 1     S1
             13128     S2
     S4         21     EUTHANASIA AND  (S1 OR  S2)

? t 4/ti,de/1-2

 4/TI,DE/1
  SUICIDE AND EUTHANASIA: HISTORICAL AND CONTEMPORARY THEMES.
  Descriptors: SOCIAL PHIL; SUICIDE; EUTHANASIA
```

**Search 15.19:** (cont.)

```
4/TI,DE/2
THE SANCTITY-OF-LIFE DOCTRINE IN MEDICINE: A CRITIQUE.
Descriptors: SOCIAL PHIL; MEDICAL ETHICS; EUTHANASIA; DEATH; QUALITY OF
LIFE; LIFE; INTENTION; KILLING; SANCTITY OF LIFE; RESPONSIBILITY
```

**Figure 15.19: Descriptors in *Philosopher's Index Thesaurus*, 1975**

**Anatta - Armenian**

Anatta
Ancient
  see also
  Greek
  Roman
Angel
Anger
Anguish
Animal
Animal Experimentation
Animation
Animism
Anisotropy
Annihilation
Anomaly
Anomie
Anonymity
Answer
Antagonism
Anthropocentrism
Anthropogenesis
Anthropology
  see also
  Cultural Anthropology
Anthropomorphism
Anti-Art
Anti-Communism
Anti-Conceptual Mentality
Anti-Formalism
Anti-Intellectualism
Anti-Matter
Anti-Science
Anti-Semitism
Antichrist
Anticipation
Anticlericalism
Antologism
Antinomianism
Antinomy
Antipater
Antipositivism
Antipsychiatry
Antiquarianism
Antiquity
  see also
  Ancient
Antithesis
Anxiety
APA
  see American Philosophical Association
Apartness

Apathy
Ape
Aphasia
Aphorism
Apocalypse
Apollo
Apollonian
Apologetics
Apology
Apostle
Apostolate
Apparitions
Appearance
Appearing
Apperception
Appetite
Appetition
Applicability
Application
Appositive
Appraisal
Appreciation
Appreciatives
Apprehension
Apprenticeship
Appropriation
Approval
Approximation
Aptitude
Arabic
Arbitration
Archeology
Archetype
Architect
Architecture
Argentine
Arguer
Argument
  see also
  Ad Hominem
  Analogical Argument
  Priority Arguments
  Transcendental Arguments
Argumentation
Arianism
Aristocracy
Aristoteleans
Aristotelianism
Arithmetic
Arithmetization
Armenian

**Search 15.20: Hyphenated descriptors in PHILOSOPHER'S INDEX on DIALOG.**

```
?  e social-

Ref   Items    Index-term
E1      46     SOCIAL WELFARE
E2      39     SOCIAL WORK
E3       0     *SOCIAL-
E4      11     SOCIAL-CHANGE
E5       7     SOCIAL-CLASS
E6      10     SOCIAL-CONSCIOUSNESS
E7      14     SOCIAL-CONTRACT
E8    2059     SOCIAL-PHIL
E9       1     SOCIAL-PHILOSOPHY
E10      1     SOCIAL-PHYSICS
E11     10     SOCIAL-PSYCHOLOGY
E12      7     SOCIAL-ROLE

?  e social con

Ref   Items    Index-term
E1       2     SOCIAL CHOICE
E2     101     SOCIAL CLASS
E3       0     *SOCIAL CON
E4       3     SOCIAL CONDITION
E5     108     SOCIAL CONSCIOUSNESS
E6     242     SOCIAL CONTRACT
E7      35     SOCIAL CONTROL
E8       9     SOCIAL CONTROLS
E9      56     SOCIAL CRITICISM
E10     18     SOCIAL DARWINISM
E11     23     SOCIAL DETERMINISM
E12     30     SOCIAL ENGINEERING

?  ss social contract or social-contract

      S1      242     SOCIAL CONTRACT
      S2       14     SOCIAL-CONTRACT
      S3      256     SOCIAL CONTRACT OR SOCIAL-CONTRACT

?  ss  social(w)contract/de                        Note effectiveness
                                                    of W operator in
      S4    17791     SOCIAL/DE                     masking  hyphens
      S5      424     CONTRACT/DE
      S6      256     SOCIAL(W)CONTRACT/DE

? t 6/ti,de/1

 6/TI,DE/1
  "TOULMIN TO RAWLS" IN "ETHICS IN THE HISTORY OF WESTERN PHILOSOPHY",
CAVALIER, ROBERT J (ED), 399-420.
   Descriptors: SOCIAL CONTRACT

? t 2/ti,de/1

 2/TI,DE/1
  PHILOSOPHERS' CONTRACTS AND THE LAW
   Descriptors: SOCIAL-PHIL; SOCIAL-CONTRACT; LAWS; RATIONALITY
```

The named person (NA=) field contains names of persons whose philosophies are discussed. Well-known personages are entered by surname only, the less well-known receive initials as well. In early records the space between the surname and the initial is lacking, and this has not been corrected. Transliterated names may vary. The most interesting quirk in PI is that owing to severe field size restrictions some descriptors are found in the named person field (NA=), and some named persons appear in the descriptor field. While this is not the case very often, it is still important to remember for high recall (Search 15.21).

### Search 15.21: Overlap between descriptor and named people fields in PHILOSOPHER'S INDEX on DIALOG.

```
? ss structuralism/de and na=marx

    S1       477     STRUCTURALISM/DE
    S2      2885     NA=MARX
    S3        20     STRUCTURALISM/DE  AND  NA=MARX

? t 3/ti,de,na/1

  3/TI,DE,NA/1
   THE STATE AND POLITICAL THEORY.
    Descriptors: POLITICAL PHIL; STATE; STRUCTURALISM; DEMOCRACY;
SOCIALISM;
ECONOMICS; POLITICAL THEORY
    Named People: MARX; GRAMSCI, A

? ss s1 and marx/de

             477     S1
    S4         4     MARX/DE
    S5         1     S1 AND MARX/DE

? t 5/ti,de,na/1

  5/TI,DE,NA/1
   LE STRUCTURALISME ENTRE LA SCIENCE ET LA PHILOSOPHIE.
    Descriptors: EPISTEMOLOGY; STRUCTURALISM; MARX; HISTORY; FREEDOM;
PHILOSOPHY
    Named People: LEVI-STRAUSS,C; ALTHUSSER,L; KANT

              Named people in the descriptor field


? ss (catholicism and abortion)/de

    S1       560     CATHOLICISM/DE
    S2       468     ABORTION/DE
    S3        18     (CATHOLICISM AND ABORTION)/DE

? ss s1 and na=abortion

             560     S1
    S4         2     NA=ABORTION
    S5         2     S1 AND NA=ABORTION

? t 5/ti,de,na/1

  5/TI,DE,NA/1
   PHILOSOPHY AND SEX.
    Descriptors: ETHICS; SEX; WOMAN; SEXUAL INTERCOURSE; MALE CHAUVINISM;
```

**Search 15.21:** (cont.)

```
SEXISM; MORALITY; PERVERSION; SEXUALITY; LOVE; MARRIAGE; BIRTH CONTROL;
PARENTHOOD; PROCREATION; CATHOLICISM; HEDONISM; ADULTERY; PROMISCUITY;
SADISM
   Named People: MASOCHISM; HOMOSEXUALITY; INCEST; FEMINISM; ABORTION
```

*Descriptors in the named people field*

*Religion*

## RELIGION INDEX (RI) [also known as ATLA RELIGION DATABASE]

Producer:     American Theological Library Association
Vendor:       BRS, DIALOG, Wilsonline
CD-ROM:       Wilsondisc, Faxon
Coverage:     Church history, biblical literature, theology, history, sociology and psychology of religion, and related areas in the social sciences and in current events.
Since:        Periodicals are covered from 1949-1959 and 1975 on; multi-author books from 1960; dissertations from 1981; book reviews from 1975. The Wilson file covers 1975 onwards.
Size:         611,290 (DIALOG - January 1990); 423,868 (Wilson - November 1990)
Update:       Monthly
Materials:    Over four hundred journals are regularly indexed for articles and book reviews, many other journals are scanned; monographs include Festschriften, directories, dissertations, collections, proceedings and irregular series.
Languages:    Sixty per cent English, the remainder principally German, French, Scandinavian languages, Italian and Spanish.
Printed as:   *Religion Index One: Periodicals*; *Religion Index Two: Festschriften*; *Religion Index Two: Multi-Author Works*; *Research in Ministry*; *Index to Book Reviews in Religion*.
User aids:    *Religion Indexes: Thesaurus* (5th ed. 1989); *Online Searching in Religion Indexes*.

Figure 15.20 shows sample RI records on DIALOG and Wilsonline. The DIALOG version is used in the rest of this discussion. Summary abstracts are provided for most journal articles only between 1975 and 1985 (some in European languages other than English). Dissertations have abstracts from 1986 forward. Monographs are represented by tables of contents in the original language (and occasionally in English for foreign items). Abstracts may also contain illustrative matter, notes, title enrichments, biblical citations, etc.

## Figure 15.20: Sample records from RELIGION INDEX on DIALOG and Wilsonline.

```
1049255      J2217329
Peacemaker woman? Theological perspectives on women, war and peace
Herzog, Kristin
Ref W, 41 no 2, 41-56, 1990
Language: English

Descriptors: WOMEN  IN  WAR;  PEACE;  SEX  ROLE;  WAR—RELIGIOUS ASPECTS—
    CHRISTIANITY

DIALOG
```

**Figure 15.20:** (cont.)

```
Monograph
RIT
B8515766
Jegen, Carol F.:ed.
Mary according to women
Leaven Pr:Kansas City, Mo
163
1985
Contents: Introduction, C Jegen. Mary in the mystery of the
church: Vatican Council II, A Carr. Mary, seat of wisdom:
reflection on the femininity of God, M Healy. Comforter of the
afflicted: Christian pastoral care and new ministries for women,
R Lorentzen. Mary, mirror of justice: a challenge for the church
to reflect justice, M Donahey. Mary of Nazareth: paradigm of a
peacemaker, M Lifka. Our Lady of Guadalupe: symbol of
liberation?, M De Cock. Mary Immaculate: woman of freedom,
patroness of the United States, C Jegen.
conf papers, Mundelein College, chicago, 1983
0-934134-31-6
Language: English
Subject heading: CONFERENCE PROCEEDINGS/THEOLOGY
Subject heading: MARY, VIRGIN
Subject heading: SISTERS OF CHARITY OF THE BLESSED VIRGIN MARY
Subject heading: THEOLOGY, CATHOLIC
890928
BREL85019202
```

**Wilsonline**

Titles are entered in the original, except for Japanese and Chinese, which are translated into English. Non-Roman titles are usually transliterated, or may be translated into English. Titles may contain enrichment. Individual languages are indexed as LA= (including English), but the LIMIT command is not available for use with language. All authors are indexed, and reviewers are in the RE= index (in early records, joint reviewers appear as one entry). Compound surnames are treated variously, so comprehensive search under all possible entry points is recommended.

Descriptors are assigned from the thesaurus (Figure 15.21), but book reviews and some other records do not have descriptors. Descriptors consist of headings and subdivisions, and may include proper names (with titles and dates). The thesaurus provides a list of standard subdivisions, which includes geographic designation for some headings. Each part of the string is word and phrase indexed. Descriptors may contain standard abbreviations (listed in the user aid). Some spellings have changed over time, and must be searched both ways (for instance, 'phenicians' and 'phoenicians', or 'a-posteriori' and 'a posteriori'). In a departure from the norm, words in the abstract, title and descriptor fields which contain hyphens and apostrophes must be searched that way (Search 15.22).

**Figure 15.21: Descriptors in *Religion Indexes: Thesaurus*, 5th edition, 1989**

AA-AB

1

RELIGION INDEX THESAURUS

**AACHEN, SYNODS OF**
<XX>
  COUNCILS AND SYNODS
**AARHUS, DENMARK**
**AARON (BIBLICAL CHARACTER)**
**ABBASIDS**
<XX>
  CALIPHS
  IRAQ--HISTORY--0634-1534
  ISLAMIC EMPIRE
ABBEY OF SANKT GALLEN
see
  SANKT GALLEN (ABBEY)
**ABBEY OF THE PARACLETE (NOGENT-SUR-SEINE**
<>
  PARACLETE, ABBEY OF THE
**ABBEYS**
also
  ABINGDON (BENEDICTINE ABBEY)
  BURY ST EDMUNDS, ENGLAND (BENEDICTINE ABBEY)
  CITEAUX, FRANCE (CISTERCIAN ABBEY)
  DOWNSIDE ABBEY
  EINSTEDELN ABBEY
  SANKT GALLEN (ABBEY)
<XX>
  MONASTERIES
**ABBOTS**
<XX>
  SUPERIORS, RELIGIOUS
**ABDERA (ANCIENT CITY)**
<XX>
  CITIES AND TOWNS, ANCIENT
ABDIAS, VISION OF
see
  BIBLE (OT)--OBADIAH
ABECEDARIUM
see
  ALPHABET
ABEL AND CAIN
see
  CAIN AND ABEL
**ABELAM (NEW GUINEA PEOPLE)**
<XX>
  ETHNOLOGY--OCEANIA
**ABELARD, PETER, 1079-1142**
ABHIDHARMAKOSA
see
  VASUBHANDU--ABHIDHARMAKOSA
ABIHU AND NADAB
see
  NADAB AND ABIHU
**ABILITY**

**ABIMELECH (BIBLICAL CHARACTER)**
**ABINGDON (BENEDICTINE ABBEY)**
<XX>
  ABBEYS
**ABKHAZIANS**
ABLUTIONS (JUDAISM)
see
  BAPTISM--JUDAISM
ABODE OF ISLAM
see
  DAR AL-ISLAM
ABODE OF PEACE
see
  DAR AL-SULH
ABODE OF WAR
see
  DAR AL-HARB
**ABOLITIONISTS**
<X>
  ANTISLAVERY
ABORIGINES, AUSTRALIAN
see
  AUSTRALIAN ABORIGINES
**ABORTION**
<XX>
  MEDICAL ETHICS
  SEXUAL ETHICS
**ABORTION--LAW**
<X>
  LAW, ABORTION
ABOTH (TRACTATE)
see
  MISHNAM- NEZIKIN--AVOT
ABOTH D'RABBI NATHAN
see
  TALMUD- MINOR TRACTATES--AVOT D'RABBI NATHAN
ABOU GOSH
see
  PALESTINE--ANTIQUITIES--ABU GHOSH
**ABRABANEL, JUDAH, 1460?-1535?**
<X>
  HEBRAEUS, LEO
  JUDAH ABRABANEL
  LEO HEBRAEUS
  LEONE EBREO
**ABRAHAM**
also
  AKEDAH
<X>
  BIBLE (OT)- GENESIS 12-25
  PATRIARCHS (BIBLE)
ABRAHAM, BOOK OF (MORMONSM)
see
  PEARL OF GREAT PRICE (MORMON BOOK)

ABRAHAM, TESTAMENT OF
see
  TESTAMENT OF ABRAHAM
**ABRAHAM BEN DAVID OF POSQUIRES, 1125?-1198**
<X>
  IBN DA'UD, ABRAHAM
ABRAHAM IBN EZRA
see
  IBN EZRA, ABRAHAM BEN MEIR, 1089-1164?
**ABSALOM**
ABSENCE OF GOD
see
  GOD--HIDDENNESS
**ABSOLUTE, THE**
also
  ONE, THE
<XX>
  INFINITE
  METAPHYSICS
  ONE, THE
**ABSOLUTES**
**ABSOLUTION**
also
  CONFESSION
  PENANCE
  POWER OF THE KEYS
<XX>
  CHURCH DISCIPLINE
  FORGIVENESS
  PENANCE
ABSOLUTISM
see
  DESPOTISM
**ABSTRACTING AND INDEXING SERVICES**
<XX>
  DOCUMENTATION AND INFORMATION SERVICES
**ABSTRACTION (PSYCHOLOGY)**
also
  CATEGORIZATION (PSYCHOLOGY)
  CONCEPTS
<XX>
  ATTENTION
  EDUCATIONAL PSYCHOLOGY
  LOGIC
  PSYCHOLOGY
**ABSURD**
also
  IRRATIONALISM
<XX>
  DESPAIR
  EXISTENTIALISM

**Search 15.22: Searching for terms with apostrophes in RELIGION INDEX on DIALOG.**

```
? ss women's(w)(liberation or rights or movement)

>>>Warning: unmatched quote found
      S1      1425    WOMEN'S
      S2      3867    LIBERATION
      S3      2580    RIGHTS
      S4      8160    MOVEMENT
      S5       312    WOMEN'S(W)(LIBERATION OR RIGHTS OR MOVEMENT)

? ss s5 and south(w)africa

               312    S5
      S6      3883    SOUTH
      S7      5748    AFRICA
      S8      1931    SOUTH(W)AFRICA
      S9         4    S5 AND SOUTH(W)AFRICA

? t 9/5/1

 9/5/1
1026344    J2119425
The importance of feminism for the women's movement in SA
Bertelsmann-Kadalie, Rhoda
J Th So Africa no, 66, 48-52, Mr 1989
Language: English
Descriptors: WOMEN- SOUTH AFRICA; WOMEN'S LIBERATION MOVEMENT; LODGE, TOM

? ss women?(1w)(rights or liberation or movement)
                                            Note that use of W
      S10     8151    WOMEN?                does not retrieve
      S11     2580    RIGHTS                terms with
      S12     3867    LIBERATION            apostrophes
      S13     8160    MOVEMENT
      S14        8    WOMEN?(1W)(RIGHTS OR LIBERATION OR MOVEMENT)

? ss women(w)s(w)(rights or liberation or movement)

      S15     8149    WOMEN
      S16     9663    S
      S17     2580    RIGHTS
      S18     3867    LIBERATION
      S19     8160    MOVEMENT
      S20        0    WOMEN(W)S(W)(RIGHTS OR LIBERATION OR MOVEMENT)
```

## REX ON CD-ROM

FABS International publishes REX ON CD-ROM, the electronic equivalent to *Religious and Theological Abstracts*, containing upwards of 65,000 citations from scholarly journals. This product was not available for illustration.

*Music*

## MUSIC LITERATURE INTERNATIONAL (RILM)

| | |
|---|---|
| Producer: | City University of New York |
| Vendor: | DIALOG |
| CD-ROM: | Faxon, NISC |
| Coverage: | All aspects of music, including historical musicology, ethnomusicology, instruments and voice, pedagogy, liturgy, performance practice and notation and interdisciplinary studies (including acoustics). |
| Since: | 1972 |
| Size: | 95,197 (January 1990) |
| Update: | Three times a year, approximately 4,500 records annually (but RILM suffers from a severe updating problem - the most recent update as of the time of writing is December 1984). |
| Materials: | Monographs, dissertations, catalogues, iconographies, and articles and reviews from over 300 journals. |
| Languages: | Almost forty languages are represented. |
| Printed as: | *RILM Abstracts of Music Literature* |
| User aids: | *RILM English-Language Thesaurus, Vols I-X* (revised 1976); *RILM English-Language Thesaurus, Vols XI-* (1983). |

Figure 15.22 shows a sample RILM record. Abstracts are included for most items, except for book reviews and books in translation. For collections, the abstract consists of a list of authors and abstract numbers of individual items which are separately indexed (and authors and titles for items which are not). Although the abstracts are English, place names and titles contained in the text may be in the original language. Abbreviations used in the abstracts are listed in the print index volumes. Original titles (or transliterations) and English translations are included. All authors and reviewers appear in the AU= index. Individual languages are searchable as LA= (including English), but the LIMIT command cannot be used to restrict search results by language.

## Figure 15.22: Sample record from MUSIC LITERATURE INTERNATIONAL on DIALOG.

```
8316507    83/7772ap94
  Luther's hymns
  Les cantiques de Luther
  VEIT, Patrice
  CNRS, Paris, F
  Positions  lutheriennes  XXXII/1  (Jan-Mar  1984) 2-77. Illus., bibliog.,
discog.  In French.
  DOCUMENT TYPE: article in periodical or yearbook
  ABSTRACT:  French  translation  of  the  collection of 36 hymns by Martin
Luther  published between 1524 and 1543. Includes notes on the collection's
history; gives for each hymn the date and place of initial publication,
and
the possible source. (Author, abridged)
  DESCRIPTORS:  Luther, Martin-- works-- hymns-- French translation; hymn--
Luther,  M.--  French  translation; translation-- Luther, M.-- hymns-- into
French
  SECTION HEADINGS: MUSIC AND LITURGY - Protestant (94)
```

**Figure 15.23: Descriptors in *RILM English-Language Thesaurus,* Vols XI- , 1983.**

---

**impressionism**

Improperia <u>see</u> chant--Gregorian

**improvisation**
  sa  aleatory music; avant-garde
      music; jazz, ornamentation
  x   countering
  xx  keyboard playing

**incidental music**
  sa  dramaturgy; melodrama
      theater
  xx  dramaturgy; melodrama;
      orchestral music; theater

indexes <u>see</u> catalogues and indexes

**indexing**
  sa  cataloguing and classification;
      computer applications

Indians--North and South American
  sa  place headings
  x   Eskimos; Inuit

**Indonesia**
  x   Bali; Java

**industrial applications**
  x   Muzak

inégales <u>see</u> notes inégales

**information theory**
  sa  analysis; computer
      applications
  xx  analysis; computer
      applications

**instrumental music**
  sa  specific genres, instruments

**instrumentation and orchestration**
  sa  performance practice
  x   arranging; density; orchestration;
      scoring; transposition
  xx  orchestra

**instruments**
  sa  electronic sound generation
      families of instruments, e.g.
      string instruments; specific
      instruments by name
  x   organology
  xx  folk instruments

**instruments--collections**
  sa  catalogues and indexes
  x   collections
  xx  libraries, museums, collections

**intermezzo**
  sa  opera headings
  x   opera

**interpretation**
  sa  ensemble playing; ornamentation;
      performance practice; performers;
      specific instruments by name
  x   accent; articulation; dynamics;
      phrasing; rubato; tone color
  xx  ensemble playing; notes inégales;
      ornamentation; performance
      practice; tempo

**intervals and scales**
  sa  modality; tonality
  x   microtone; modes; quarter tones;
      proportions; scales; tonus;
      tritone
  xx  modality; tonality

---

The main heading portion of a descriptor comes from the thesaurus (Figure 15.23); the subheadings may or may not appear in the thesaurus. An entire descriptor phrase can be searched (using quote marks to mask hyphens, or using the L operator), and so can an entire main heading or subdivision phrase (Search 15.23). Names of musical or literary works in the descriptor field are entered in the original (or transliterated) form. When a personal name forms the main heading in a descriptor, the surname, first name and second name or initial are entered. When a personal name is the second part of a subject heading, the surname and initials appear. In any other position, only the surname is used, unless initials are required for disambiguation. There is a list of standard subheadings which must be used under names of people (for example, 'aesthetics', 'autographs', 'interviews' and 'relation to') and which may be followed by more specific information. Expanding in the index is recommended (Search 15.24), as is use of the L operator, keeping in mind the variation in fullness of name (see for example Search 15.25).

## Search 15.23: Searching descriptors in MUSIC LITERATURE INTERNATIONAL on DIALOG.

```
? e folk music - ireland

Ref   Items    Index-term
E1      1      FOLK MUSIC - IRAN - PERSIAN TASNIF
E2      1      FOLK MUSIC - IRAQ
E3      5     *FOLK MUSIC - IRELAND
E4      1      FOLK MUSIC - IRELAND - G. PETRIE AS COLLECTOR
E5      1      FOLK MUSIC - IRELAND - HISTORY AND DEVELOPMENT
E6      1      FOLK MUSIC - IRELAND - INFLUENCE ON 18TH-C. BA
E7      1      FOLK MUSIC - IRELAND - JOURNAL OF FOLK MUSIC S
E8      1      FOLK MUSIC - IRELAND - NORTHWEST - RURAL BILIN
E9      1      FOLK MUSIC - IRELAND - OLD BALLADS
E10     1      FOLK MUSIC - IRELAND - RECENT RESEARCH - DISCO
E11     1      FOLK MUSIC - IRELAND - STREET BALLADS
E12     1      FOLK MUSIC - IRELAND - SURVEY
```

```
? ss folk music "-" ireland?                    Using quotes to
                                                mask hyphen

    S1         14    FOLK MUSIC "-" IRELAND?
```

```
? ss folk music(l)ireland                       Using the L
                                                operator achieves
    S2       1802    FOLK  MUSIC/DE              higher recall
    S3        146    IRELAND/DE
    S4         27    FOLK  MUSIC(L)IRELAND
```

```
? t 1/ti,de/1

 1/TI,DE/1
  Songs of Irish rebellion: political street ballads and rebel songs
  DESCRIPTORS: folk music-- Ireland; politics--  Ireland- - street
ballads and rebel songs;
```

```
? ss s4 not s1

          27    S4
          14    S1
    S5    13    S4 NOT S1
```

```
? t 5/ti,de/1                                   Note difference in
                                                subject heading word
 5/TI,DE/1                                       order
  The  need  for  a  sociology of Irish folk music: A review of writings on
"traditional" music in Ireland, with some responses and proposals
  DESCRIPTORS: Ireland-- folk music-- state of  research ; ethnomusicology--
national  and   regional   studies-- Irish music-- state of research; culture
and music-- Ireland--  folk music
```

## Search 15.24: Variations in fullness of subject heading in MUSIC LITERATURE INTERNATIONAL on DIALOG.

```
? e bach, johann sebastian - influence

Ref    Items    Index-term
E1       1     BACH, JOHANN SEBASTIAN - ICONOGRAPHY - PORTRAI
E2       1     BACH, JOHANN SEBASTIAN - ICONOGRAPHY - TONHALL
E3       0    *BACH, JOHANN SEBASTIAN - INFLUENCE
E4       1     BACH, JOHANN SEBASTIAN - INFLUENCE - 1750-1800
E5       2     BACH, JOHANN SEBASTIAN - INFLUENCE ON BARTOK
E6       1     BACH, JOHANN SEBASTIAN - INFLUENCE ON BEETHOVE
E7       1     BACH, JOHANN SEBASTIAN - INFLUENCE ON BEN-HAIM
E8       7     BACH, JOHANN SEBASTIAN - INFLUENCE ON BRAHMS
E9       1     BACH, JOHANN SEBASTIAN - INFLUENCE ON BRUCKNER
E10      1     BACH, JOHANN SEBASTIAN - INFLUENCE ON BUSONI
E11      1     BACH, JOHANN SEBASTIAN - INFLUENCE ON C.P.E. B
E12      1     BACH, JOHANN SEBASTIAN - INFLUENCE ON CHOPIN

? ss e8

    S1        7    "BACH, JOHANN SEBASTIAN - INFLUENCE ON BRAHMS"

? t 1/ti,de/1

 1/TI,DE/1
  Musical influences on Brahms
   DESCRIPTORS: Brahms, Johannes-- style-- influences; Beethoven, Ludwig van
-- influence on Brahms ; Bach, Johann Sebastian-- influence on Brahms ;
folk music-- influence on Brahms ; Schumann, Robert-- influence on Brahms ;
Mozart, Wolfgang Amadeus— influence on Brahms ; Haydn, Joseph— influence
on Brahms ; Schubert, Franz— influence on Brahms

? ss bach, johann sebastian(1)influence on brahms

    S2     1526    BACH, JOHANN SEBASTIAN/DE
    S3       25    INFLUENCE ON BRAHMS/DE
    S4        8    BACH, JOHANN SEBASTIAN(L)INFLUENCE ON BRAHMS

? ss s4 not s1

           8     S4
           7     S1
    S5     1     S4 NOT S1
```

**? t 5/ti,de/1**            **Note presence of intervening subdivision**

```
 5/TI,DE/1
  Brahms's organ works
   DESCRIPTORS: Brahms, Johannes-- style-- chorale preludes, op. 122; Bach,
Johann Sebastian-- works-- organ music-- influence on Brahms ; chorale
prelude--    Brahms, J.; instruments--keyboard (organ family)-- organ music--
Brahms, J.

? ss bach(1)influence(1)brahms

    S6     1923    BACH/DE
    S7     3634    INFLUENCE/DE
    S8      616    BRAHMS/DE
    S9       12    BACH(L)INFLUENCE(L)BRAHMS

? ss s9 not s4
```

**Search 15.24:** (cont.)

```
                  12    S9
                   8    S4
      S10          4    S9 NOT S4
```

? **t  10/ti,de/1-4**                          **Note extension of**
                                               **"Brahms" subdivision**
   10/TI,DE/1                                  **to include work**
   Adagio  in B minor: remarks on the intermezzo op. 119, no. 1, by Johannes
Brahms
      DESCRIPTORS:  Brahms,  Johannes--  style--  intermezzos,  op. 119, no. 1;
   dance  music--  sarabande--  influence on Brahms intermezzo op. 119, no. 1;
   Billroth, Theodor Christian Albert--  views  about Brahms intermezzo op. 119,
   no. 1;  **Bach,  Johann Sebastian-- works-- sarabandes-- influence on Brahms**
   **intermezzo op. 119, no. 1;**  Schumann, Clara Wieck--  works--  romance, B minor
   --  influence  on  Brahms  intermezzo  op. 119, no. 1; Reger, Max--
   works--  Silhouetten—  relation  to Brahms intermezzo op. 119, no. 1

**Search 15.25: Variations in fullness of name in MUSIC LITERATURE INTERNATIONAL on DIALOG.**

? **ss  bach(n)j(n)s**

```
      S1      2524     BACH
      S2      6370     J
      S3     28300     S
      S4      1267     BACH(N)J(N)S
```

? **ss bach(n)johann(n)sebastian**

```
      S5      2524     BACH
      S6      3550     JOHANN
      S7      1858     SEBASTIAN
      S8      1757     BACH(N)JOHANN(N)SEBASTIAN
```

? **ss s4 not s8**

```
              1267     S4
              1757     S8
      S9       223     S4 NOT S8
```

? **t  9/ti,de/1**

   9/TI,DE/1
   Court  musician,  cantor, beer fiddler: The training and social status of
the musician in the time of **J.S. Bach**
   DESCRIPTORS: Germany-- musical life-- performers-- 18th c.; performers--
Germany-- 18th c.; sociology-- Germany-- influence on musicians-- 18th c.

? **ss s8 not s4**

```
              1757     S8
              1267     S4
      S10      713     S8 NOT S4
```

? **t  10/ti,de/1**

**Search 15.25:** (cont.)

```
10/TI,DE/1
  Aus  Liebe will mein Heyland sterben : The change in the understanding of
the Passion in the early 18th century
  DESCRIPTORS:    Passion--   Lutheran--   early   18th   c.;   religious
music--Christian (Protestant)-- Lutheran-- Passion-- early 18th c.; Bach,
Johann Sebastian--  works--  Passions; Enlightenment-- relation to Lutheran
Passion-- early 18th c.
```

Each record is assigned one section heading (/SH). Section headings consist of seven broad categories divided into more than eighty subheadings (Figure 15.24). Each heading is phrase and word indexed, and is also searchable by equivalent code in the SH= index. Since the words used in section headings have varied over time, the codes (which have been consistent) are more effective, although the contribution of section heading words to the basic index is useful for high recall. The codes lend themselves to generic and range searching (Search 15.26). Section headings are particularly useful when searching specific time periods.

**Search 15.26: Using section heading codes in MUSIC LITERATURE INTERNATIONAL on DIALOG.**

```
? e sh=23

Ref   Items   Index-term
E1      171   SH=22
E2      235   SH=22 ANTIQUITY
E3      791   *SH=23
E4      900   SH=23 MIDDLE AGES
E5       52   SH=23 MIDDLE AGES+
E6     1346   SH=24
E7     1713   SH=24 RENAISSANCE
E8     2532   SH=25
E9     2929   SH=25 BAROQUE
E10    2320   SH=26
E11    2732   SH=26 CLASSIC AND PRE-CLASSIC
E12    4251   SH=27

? ss e3,e4,e5

      S1      791    SH=23
      S2      900    SH=23
      S3       52    SH=23
      S4     1743    E3,E4,E5

? t 1/ti,sh/1                           Different   section
                                        heading phrases used
  1/TI,SH/1                             over time
  Organicum melos . The musical perspective of John Scotus Erigena
  SECTION HEADINGS: HISTORICAL MUSICOLOGY (Western music) - To ca. 1400
(Middle Ages) (23)

? t 2/ti,sh/1

  2/TI,SH/1
  Music in Provence in the 14th century
  SECTION HEADINGS: HISTORY, WESTERN ART MUSIC - Middle Ages (23)
```

**Search 15.26:** (cont.)

```
? t 3/ti,sh/1

3/TI,SH/1
The lady, the lyrics and the letters
SECTION HEADINGS: HISTORICAL MUSICOLOGY - Middle Ages+ (23)
```

## Figure 15.24: RILM section headings and codes

**REFERENCE AND RESEARCH MATERIALS**
01 Bibliography and librarianship
02 Libraries, museums, collections
03 Encyclopedias and dictionaries
04 Catalogues and indexes
05 Catalogues, thematic
06 Bibliographies, general
07 Bibliographies, music
08 Bibliographies, music literature
09 Discographies
10 Iconographies
11 Chronologies and almanacs
12 Directories

**Collected writings**
14 Periodicals and yearbooks
15 Festschriften
16 Congress reports and symposium proceedings
17 Essays, letters, documents, literary texts

**HISTORICAL MUSICOLOGY**
20 The discipline
21 History, general; collected biography
22 Antiquity
23 Middle Ages
24 Renaissance
25 Baroque
26 Classic and pre-Classic
27 Romantic and post-Romantic
28 Twentieth century, history
29 Twentieth century, musical life

**ETHNOMUSICOLOGY**
30 The discipline
31 General
32 Africa
33 Asia
34 Europe
35 North America (north of Mexico)
36 South and Central America
37 Australia and Oceania
39 Jazz, pop, and rock

**INSTRUMENTS AND VOICE**
40 General
41 Voice
42 Keyboard, organ
43 Keyboard, general
44 String
45 Wind
46 Percussion
47 Mechanical
48 Electronic

**PERFORMANCE PRACTICE AND NOTATION**
50 Performance practice, general
51 Performance practice, to ca. 1600
52 Performance practice, ca. 1600-1825
53 Performance practice, ca. 1800-1900
54 Performance practice, twentieth century
55 Notation and paleography
58 Editing

**THEORY AND ANALYSIS**
60 General
61 Rhythm, meter, tempo
62 Melody
63 Harmony and counterpoint
64 Form
65 Orchestration, instrumentation, timbre
66 Style and structural analysis
68 Techniques of composition

**PEDAGOGY**
70 General
71 Primary and secondary schools
72 Colleges and universities
73 Conservatories

**MUSIC AND OTHER ARTS**
75 General (cultural history)
76 Dance
77 Dramatic arts (including film)
78 Poetry and other literature
79 Plastic arts

**MUSIC AND RELATED DISCIPLINES**
80 General
81 Philosophy, aesthetics, and criticism
82 Psychology and hearing
83 Physiology, therapy, medicine
84 Archaeology
85 Engineering and sound recording
86 Physics, mathematics, acoustics, and architecture
87 Sociology
89 Printing, engraving, publishing

**MUSIC AND LITURGY**
90 General
91 Jewish
92 Byzantine (and other Eastern)
93 Catholic
94 Protestant
95 Buddhist
96 Hindu
97 Islamic
99 Other

## OTHER FILES

While MUSIC LITERATURE INTERNATIONAL covers the periodical literature, two large, significant music libraries were mentioned in the 'Machine-readable cataloguing' section above. THE MUSIC LIBRARY (OCLC) contains LC and other North American MARC records on CD-ROM, and MUSIC LIBRARY CATALOGUE (BLAISE-LINE) represents holdings of the British Music Library.

## PROSPECTS

In the light of the problems identified above, search strategies which obtain a satisfactory balance between precision and recall are not easily designed. Pre-search preparation using traditional reference tools (encyclopedias, biographical dictionaries, and so on) can be helpful in revealing variant name forms, finding alternative expressions for specialized or metaphorical word usage, and disambiguating common terms through contextualization. Subject indication is a problem in humanities databases, although the past few years have seen improvements in user aids, and most publishers are prepared to be quite frank about changes in practice and errors which have accrued in their files. It is the responsibility of searchers to read documentation thoroughly and to use all possible print and intellectual resources when framing strategies. Even so, searchers can expect to engage in 'trial and error', examining preliminary online results, consulting with users, and modifying queries in an iterative process.

Although there is little hope that large retrospective conversion projects will be implemented (MLA being an exception), the limited time coverage that is currently evident in humanities files is becoming less of an issue as time passes. With the advent of CD-ROM, and generally decreasing costs of electronic publication, it is likely that more publishers will find online or optical products an attractive addition to print services. Any growth in offerings, humanities and otherwise, underscores the point that online searchers in the humanities must be specialists as well as generalists. They must be familiar with the content, coverage, structure and indexing practices of humanities files, and they must also be able to retrieve humanities information in a wide range of databases targeted to other fields. Unlike most of their colleagues, who are able to specialize in a relatively small set of files which they search frequently, humanities searchers must acquire and retain a large skill set in a wide array of databases, most of which they will only search infrequently. This condition emphasizes the importance of taking advantage of training opportunities and online workshops, and keeping abreast of the online professional literature.

With all this in mind, the role of the humanities searcher is to act as an advocate for both user and service, understanding the needs of the former and making explicit the capabilities of the latter. Marketing activities, promotion, demonstration and online ready reference are the responsibility of any academic search service, and efforts to reduce or subsidize costs and to present attractively packaged results will help substantially in making the case for the value of online searching to humanities scholars. Improved document delivery and full-text availability may alleviate some dissatisfaction. Unpressured browsing through CD-ROM indexes (or tapes mounted in-house in some cases) can address some of the problems associated either with finances, or with the difficulty of delegating what is essentially a personal interactive process of discovery. Support for humanities research is best provided by a trained and up-to-date staff, thoroughly familiar with the available resources in whatever format, and fully prepared to cope with the constraints imposed by the nature of humanities research and by the nature of humanities information online.

## REFERENCES

1.    *Online* 14(5) 1990
2.    A. Lowry. A consumer's report on humanities databases. *Technicalities*  2(8) 1982 1-3, 11-12
3.    J. Le Maguer. FRANCIS database: the social sciences files. In *Databases in the Arts and Humanities*. Medford, N.J.: Learned Information, 1987 pp.391-409
4.    D.J. Grogan. Oxford English Dictionary. In C.J. Armstrong and J.A. Large, eds., *CD-ROM Information Products: an Evaluative Guide and Directory*. Aldershot: Gower, 1990, pp. 213-238

## FURTHER READING

Falk, J. D. Database characteristics and search problems in the humanities. In *Online '85 Conference Proceedings* Weston, Conn.: Online, 1985 pp.102-106

Garfield, E. Is information retrieval in the arts and humanities inherently different from that in science? The effect that ISI's Citation Index for the Arts and Humanities is expected to have on future scholarship. *Library Quarterly* 50(1) 1980 40-57

Goudy, A. W. Music coverage in online databases. *Database* 5(4) 1982 39-57

Hoffman, H. H. *et al*. Online access to the embedded literature of 'Literature'. *Database* 4(1) 1985 55-63

Kiresen, E.-M. *et al*. The use of online databases for historical research. *RQ* 21(4) 1982 342-351

Mackesy, E. M. A perspective on secondary access services in the humanities. *Journal of the American Society for Information Science* 33(3) 1982 146-151

Muratori, F. RLIN special databases: serving the humanist. *Database* 13(5) 1990 48-57

Raben, J. Information systems and services in the arts and humanities. *Annual Review of Information Science and Technology*  16 1981 247-266

Stebelman, S. D.  On-line searching and the humanities: relevance, resistance, and marketing strategies. In *National Online Meeting Proceedings - 1981*. Medford, N.J.: Learned Information 1981, pp.443-453

Walker, G. Searching the humanities: subject overlap and search vocabulary. *Database* 13(5) 1990 37-46

Wiberly, S. E. Subject access in the humanities and the precision of the humanist's vocabulary. *Library Quarterly* 53(4) 1983 420-423

## ONLINE SERVICES AND CD-ROM DISTRIBUTORS

**America: History and Life**
*Online*:    DIALOG

**Architecture Database**
*Online*:    DIALOG

**Art Index**
*Online*:    Wilsonline
*CD-ROM*:    Faxon Company; Wilsondisc

**Art Literature International**
*Online*:       DIALOG

**ARTbibliographies Modern**
*Online*:       DIALOG

**ArtQuest**
*Online*:       Pergamon Financial Data Services

**Arts and Humanities Search**
*Online*:       BRS; DIALOG

**ATLA Religion Indexes**
                *see* Religion Index

**Australian Architecture Database**
*Online*:       Ausinet

**Avery Index to Architectural Periodicals**
*Online*:       DIALOG; RLIN

**BaseLine**
*Online*:       Baseline Inc.

**Bible**
*Online*:       DIALOG
*CD-ROM*:       Abt Books; Bureau of Electronic Publishing; Ellis Enterprises Incorporated; FABS International, Inc.; Faxon  Company; Tri Star Publishing

**Bibliographic Index**
*Online*:       Wilsonline

**Bibliographie linguistischer literatur**
*Online*:       GEM (Gesellschaft für elektronische Medien)

**Billboard Information Network**
*Online*:       Billboard Information Network

**Biography Index**
*Online*:       Wilsonline
*CD-ROM*:       Faxon Company; Wilsondisc

**Biography Master Index**
*Online*:       DIALOG

**BNBMarc, BNB on CD-ROM**
*Online*:     BLAISE-LINE; OCLC; RLIN; Utlas
*CD-ROM*:     Chadwyck-Healey Limited; Faxon Company

**Book Review Digest**
*Online*:     CompuServe; Wilsonline
*CD-ROM*:     Faxon Company; Wilsondisc

**Book Review Index**
*Online*:     DIALOG

**British Library General Catalogue of Printed Books to 1975 on CD-ROM**
*Online*:     BLAISE-LINE
*CD-ROM*:     Chadwyck-Healey Limited; Faxon Company

**Catholic News Service**
*Online*:     NewsNet

**Catholic Trends**
*Online*:     NewsNet

**ChurchNews International**
*Online*:     NewsNet

**Cineman Movie Reviews**
*Online*:     Delphi; Dialcom, Inc.; Dow Jones News/Retrieval; FYI News; GEnie; MCI Insight; Prodigy; Q-Link; U.S. Videotel

**Cinescan**
*CD-ROM*:     Newsreel Access Systems, Inc.

**Comics/Animation Forum**
*Online*:     CompuServe

**Conference Proceedings Index**
*Online*:     BLAISE-LINE

**Cumulative Book Index**
*Online*:     Wilsonline
*CD-ROM*:     Faxon Company; Wilsondisc

**Diana**
*Online*:     GEM (Gesellschaft für elektronische Medien)

**Dissertation Abstracts Online** (and **Ondisc**)
*Online*:     BRS; DIALOG
*CD-ROM*:     University Microfilms International; Faxon Company

**Eighteenth Century Short Title Catalogue**
*Online*:        BLAISE-LINE; RLIN

**ESI Street**
*Online*:        Dialcom, Inc.

**Essay and General Literature Index**
*Online*:        Wilsonline
*CD-ROM*:     Faxon Company; Wilsondisc

**Francis**
*Online*:        Questel

**General Periodicals OnDisc**
*CD-ROM*:     UMI/Data Courier

**Hiscabeq**
*Online*:        SDM, Inc. (Services documentaires multimedia)

**Historical Abstracts**
*Online*:        DIALOG

**Hollywood Hotline**
*Online*:        CompuServe; FYI News; GEnie; MCI Insight; NewsNet; Q-Link

**Humanities and Social Sciences**
*Online*:        BLAISE-LINE

**Humanities Index**
*Online*:        Wilsonline
*CD-ROM*:     Faxon Company; Wilsondisc

**Iconos**
*Online*:        Questel

**Images de la mosaique**
*Online*:        CNRS (Centre national de la recherche scientifique)

**Incunable Short Title Catalogue**
*Online*:        BLAISE-LINE

**Inspec**
*Online*:        BRS; CISTI; CAN/OLE; Data-Star; DIALOG; ESA/IRS; Orbit; STN International

**Las Vegas Hotline**
*Online*:        CompuServe

**LC Marc, LC Foreign MARC, and REMARC**
*Online*:     BLAISE-LINE; DIALOG; OCLC; RLIN; Utlas; Wilsonline; WLN
*CD-ROM*:   Faxon Company; Gaylord Information Services; Library Corporation; Library of Congress; Utlas; WLN

**Library of America Collection**
*CD-ROM*:   Electronic Text Corporation

**Linguistics and Language Behavior Abstracts**
*Online*:     BRS; DIALOG

**Lutheran News Service**
*Online*:     NewsNet

**Magazine Index**
*Online*:     BRS; CompuServe; DIALOG; Mead Data Central
*CD-ROM*:   Information Access Company

**Magill's Survey of Cinema**
*Online*:     CompuServe; DIALOG

**The Medieval and Early Modern Data Bank (MEMDB)**
*Online*:     RLIN
*CD-ROM*:   RLG (Research Libraries Group)

**Medline**
*Online*:     BRS; Data-Star; DIALOG; Mead Data Central; National Library of Medicine; PaperChase; Questel; STN International
*CD-ROM*:   Aries System Corporation; Bureau of Electronic Publishing, Inc.; Cambridge Scientific Abstracts; CD Plus; DIALOG; Digital Diagnostics Incorporated; EBSCO; Faxon Company; Massachusetts Medical Society; SilverPlatter

**MLA International Bibliography**
*Online*:     DIALOG; Wilsonline
*CD-ROM*:   Faxon Company; Wilsondisc

**Monudoc**
*Online*:     STN International

**Mosiaque grecque**
*Online*:     CNRS (Centre national de la recherche scientifique)

**Music Information Service**
*Online*:     CompuServe

**Music Library**
*CD-ROM*:   OCLC

**Music Library Catalogue**
*Online*:　　BLAISE-LINE

**Music Literature International**
*Online*:　　DIALOG
*CD-ROM*:　　Faxon Company; NISC DISC

**Muziek Catalogus Nederland**
*Online*:　　Muziek Catalogus Nederland

**National Catholic Register**
*Online*:　　NewsNet

**National Newspaper Index**
*Online*:　　BRS; DIALOG
*CD-ROM*:　　Information Access Company

**Newspaper Abstracts Ondisc**
*CD-ROM*:　　Faxon Company; UMI/Data Courier

**Origins: Catholic Documentary Service**
*Online*:　　NewsNet

**Oxford English Dictionary**
*CD-ROM*:　　Abt Books; Bureau of Electronic Publishing, Inc.; Faxon Company; Oxford University Press;
　　　　　　　Tri Star Publishing

**Periodical Abstracts Ondisc**
*CD-ROM*:　　Faxon Company; UMI/Data Courier

**Perseus CD-ROM**
*CD-ROM*:　　Harvard University, Department of the Classics

**Philosopher's Index**
*Online*:　　DIALOG

**Reader's Guide to Periodical Literature** and **Reader's Guide with Abstracts**
*Online*:　　Wilsonline
*CD-ROM*:　　Faxon Company; Wilsondisc

**Religion Index**
*Online*:　　BRS; DIALOG; Wilsonline
*CD-ROM*:　　Faxon Company; Wilsondisc

**Research in Progress**
*Online*:　　RLIN

**Rex on CD-ROM**
*CD-ROM*:    FABS International, Inc.

**RILA**        *see* Art Literature International

**RILM**       *see* Music Literature International

**RNS Daily News Reports**
*Online*:    NewsNet

**Rocknet**
*Online*:    CompuServe; Q-Link

**Scipio**
*Online*:    RLIN

**Shakespeare on Disc**
*CD-ROM*:    Bureau of Electronic Publishing, Inc.; CMC ReSearch, Inc.; Faxon Company

**Tresor general des langues et parlers francais**
*Online*:    CNRS (Centre national de la recherche scientifique)
*CD-ROM*:    CNRS

**United Methodist Information**
*Online*:    NewsNet


**NOTE**:    H. W. Wilson databases will be available through BRS at the end of 1991, according to a
             February 1991 press release.

# 16 Databases for ready reference

*S. Koshman and J. Beheshti*

## INTRODUCTION

The diversity of ready reference queries - questions which require fact or data retrieval - and the proliferation of databases present searchers with a maze of information needs and sources. Information specialists are challenged by the prospect of online ready reference work since almost any database may be used to answer these kinds of queries.

In contrast to complex reference questions that require lengthy online searches, ready reference queries require specific pieces of data and information [1, p.101] such as 'Who is the president of Apple Canada?' or 'What is the nonresident tuition fee at the University of Pittsburgh?'. Usually such queries exhibit three characteristics:

      (1) they contain unambiguous concepts;
      (2) they require minimal online search time;
and    (3) they retrieve a small quantity of data.

The purpose of this chapter is to guide searchers in the development of search techniques for online and CD-ROM databases. Referral and source databases will be focused upon but bibliographic databases will be briefly considered in the context of ready reference work. The chapter describes the advantages and disadvantages of using online databases as opposed to print sources and the search techniques which optimize efficient information retrieval. Online databases are considered first and then the growing number of databases available for ready reference on CD-ROM. Search examples taken from databases available on DIALOG are used to illustrate specific databases' access points and system features which enhance this type of reference work.

## Online databases versus print sources

The outlay for using online resources includes calculating the cost for items such as computer equipment, telecommunications charges, documentation, online training, online connect time costs, etc. Print costs include: subscriptions, update costs, labour costs, etc. It is difficult to compare online and print costs for ready reference work although various researchers have suggested formulae which attempt to establish cost differences; however, none has proved particularly successful.

Assessing online ready reference costs is problematic because the variety of databases used results in diverse pricing of information. Also, the calculation of mean online connect time costs may be skewed by the diversity of expertise among specialists who conduct the searches.

The issue of estimating online and manual ready reference search costs may not be resolved, but it is interesting to note that cost has been widely used as a guideline for deciding if certain ready reference queries merit an online search. For example, the Haas study shows that one of the guidelines established for conducting ready reference searches online was to use a database that did not exceed US$108.00 per connect hour [2, p.149].

Related to the cost factor is that of the time required to conduct an online versus a manual ready reference search. The calculation of search time using online or print sources is related to the number of concepts in the ready reference query and the quantity of information being retrieved. Generally, a one-fact ready reference query is more quickly answered using a print source than an online source [3, p.67]. Havener studied search time differences between print and online sources, and his findings show that the average time for the online treatment of factual questions was 6.6 minutes whereas the average manual search time for the same questions was 3.2 minutes [4, p.26]. However, searching online sources becomes more time efficient if the queries require several pieces of information to answer the question or if two or more concepts are being searched [4, p.25].

Service is linked to resources and often online sources are used when print sources are unavailable or the library lacks sufficient shelf space for various hardcopy ready reference sources. The library may subscribe to online versions of standard ready reference works because they provide advantages in terms of currency, linkage to related information and flexibility in retrieval [5, p.172]. But using online sources to replace print copies is limited because online databases specifically categorized as standard ready reference works (such as almanacs, dictionaries, yearbooks, etc.) are scarce. Hence, the application of online databases to ready reference work is perhaps best considered an extension of available print sources during the reference process.

## DATABASES

The standard categories were used to organize the databases available for ready reference work on DIALOG. (BRS databases are also listed wherever possible.) The categories used are:

**Reference Databases**
    Bibliographic
    Referral
        biographical directories
        dictionaries, thesauri and other language aids
        directories
        handbooks

**Source Databases**
> Full-text
>> encyclopedias
>> news sources
>> graphics, images
> Textual-Numeric

## REFERENCE DATABASES

Reference databases are defined by Harter as those which contain representations of original sources of data, information or knowledge [1, p.97]. This class can be divided into bibliographic and referral databases.

### Bibliographic

Bibliographic databases contain citations leading to other literary sources such as books or journals. Subject-specific bibliographic databases are covered elsewhere in this manual, but it is important to recognize the utility of these databases for ready reference queries that require bibliographic verification or subject-specific factual information. For these types of queries, the bibliographic database is used as a source of information, not as a tool for further information retrieval.

Bibliographic verification is perhaps the best known ready reference technique and online sources which may assist the searcher in answering these queries online include: DIALOG's BOOKS IN PRINT (FILE 470) (BRS: BBIP); BRITISH BOOKS IN PRINT (FILE 430); LC MARC - BOOKS (FILE 426); REMARC (FILES 421-425); ULRICH'S INTERNATIONAL PERIODICAL DIRECTORY (FILE 480) (BRS: ULRI) and CURRENT CONTENTS SEARCH (FILE 440) (BRS: CCON).

*QUERY: Who is the author of a book whose title contains the words: sex and librarian?*

The query in Search 16.1 asks for a book title but does not contain the year of publication so the database choice is narrowed to LC MARC - BOOKS since it contains English-language books catalogued since 1968. To expedite the search the DIALOG commands are stacked. The stacking feature is limited to 240 characters and each command must be separated by a semicolon. The search statement limits the two words recalled by the user to the title (/TI) field. The Boolean operator AND is used to retrieve the words in the title, and parentheses are used to ensure that all terms are searched in the same field.

### Search 16.1: LC MARC - BOOKS (FILE 426)

```
?b 426; s (sex and librarian)/ti
.
.
File  426:LCMARC  -  BOOKS  1968-1991/9107W3
      Set     Items   Description
      ---     -----   -----------
              3242    SEX/TI
               327    LIBRARIAN/TI
      S1         2    (SEX  AND  LIBRARIAN)/TI

?t  s1/3/1-2
1/3/1
```

**Search 16.1:** (cont.)

```
2938077  LCCN:  88039488  //r90
The young adult librarian's knowledge of and attitudes about sex / by
Susan Steinfirst
Steinfirst, Susan
Metuchen, N.J. : Scarecrow Press, x, 49 p. ; 23 cm.
PUBLICATION  DATE(S):  1989
ISBN:  0810821850
LC CALL NO.: Z682.4.Y68 S73 1989 DEWEY CALL NO.: 306.7

1/3/2
0323994  LCCN:  73014707
Sex and the undecided librarian; a study of librarians' opinions on
sexually oriented literature
Pope, Michael, 1940-
Metuchen, N.J., Scarecrow Press, x, 209 p. 22 cm.
PUBLICATION  DATE(S):  1974
ISBN:  0810806789
LC CALL NO.: Z711.4 .P66 1973 DEWEY CALL NO.: 025.2/1
```

A second application of bibliographic databases to ready reference work is the subject-specific factual query. Search 16.2 illustrates how a ready reference search may be conducted when the subject databases are unfamiliar to the searcher. DIALOG's DIALINDEX/OneSearch categories were used to aid database selection. OneSearch was selected because it makes a multiple file search look like a single file search. The SET DETAIL ON command can be used in OneSearch to view the number of items retrieved in each database. The DETAIL command is useful if the search is to be limited to just one database - that with the highest number of hits.

*QUERY: What does the acronym PCTE represent in the field of computer science?*

DIALOG's DIALINDEX/OneSearch feature (option five) was selected from the opening HOMEBASE main menu. Computer technology (option six) was selected from the next menu, then the stacked search statement was entered in the COMPSCI (Computer Science) files. It included B (BEGIN) COMPSCI files, then S (SELECT) PCTE and then the RD (REMOVE DUPLICATES) command was used to remove duplicate citations. REMOVE DUPLICATES creates a second set of records excluding the duplicate records found in Set 1. (In lengthy bibliographic output the ID (IDENTIFY DUPLICATES) command should be used first to check the duplicate records that were removed. ID creates a separate set for the duplicate records.) Fifty records are scanned at a time and the remaining citations are kept in order of the database selection.

The first three citations of Set 2 were displayed in the KWIC (keyword in context) format, and PCTE (Portable Common Tools Environment) was found in the first two records.

**Search 16.2: DIALOG OneSearch**

```
?b compsci; s pcte; rd s1
•
•

      Set    Items   Description
      ---    -----   -----------
      S1      188    PCTE
>>>Duplicate detection is not supported for File 674.
>>>Records from unsupported files will be retained in the RD set.
...examined 50 records (50)
```

**Search 16.2:** (cont.)

```
...examined 50 records (100)
...examined 50 records (150)
...completed examining records
    S2         149   RD S1 (unique items)
?t  s2/k/1-2
>>>KWIC option is not available in file 6
>>>KWIC option is not available in file 233
>>>KWIC option is not available in file 239
  2/KWIC/1   (Item 1 from file: 2)
  Abstract: This paper primarily reports on semantic aspects of how a
formal specification of the PCTE interfaces (Portable Common Tool
Environment interfaces) has been achieved in a situation where only
a...
  .
```

Duplicate detection is not available for all DIALOG files and a list of databases which do not have this feature may be obtained by typing HELP DUP. Likewise KWIC is not available in all files, and HELP KWIC provides a list of databases which have the KWIC display format. KWIC may be used for example, in conjunction with another display format, t s2/3,K/1 will display the record in the bibliographic citation and the KWIC formats.

**Referral**

*Biographical directories*

Biographical directories are frequently consulted for ready reference queries when information is needed about particular persons, living or dead. Databases such as DIALOG's MARQUIS WHO'S WHO (FILE 234), AMERICAN MEN AND WOMEN OF SCIENCE (FILE 236) and STANDARD & POOR'S REGISTER-BIOGRAPHICAL (FILE 526) contain biographical summaries of persons. BIOGRAPHY MASTER INDEX (FILE 287) is an index to sources of biographical information on a person, and it is most useful if information is difficult to find.

Most biographical databases may be searched by the name of the individual (usually the NA= prefix or /NA suffix). If a person's name is used to retrieve the record, the EXPAND command should be used to check how the name was entered on the database (see Search 16.3 in File 236). File 287, DIALOG's BIOGRAPHY MASTER INDEX indexes over 600 biographical dictionaries and directories, and may be searched by name, the year of birth (YB=) and year of death (YD=). The MARQUIS WHO'S WHO database (FILE 234) contains detailed biographical information which is divided into categories such as vital statistics, career and educational information. The person's business address may be retrieved along with information such as research specialty (RS=), titles of creative works (/TI) and political/religious affiliations (AF=).

STANDARD AND POOR'S REGISTER - BIOGRAPHICAL (FILE 526) contains 'personal and professional data' on business executives. The database may be searched by access points such as company name (CO=), graduate college (GC=), graduate year (GY=), undergraduate college (UC=), undergraduate year (UY=), position (PO=), fraternal organization (FO=). The AMERICAN MEN AND WOMEN OF SCIENCE (FILE 236) has access points such as honours and awards (HA=), honorary degree (HD=), and memberships (ME=).

DIALINDEX/OneSearch (FILE 411) contains a BIOGRAPH category which includes Files 162, 234, 236, 287 and 526. A second DIALINDEX/OneSearch category to search for biographical information is PEOPLE.

In this category encyclopedia and newspaper indexes are included to find more detailed information on individuals who may not be listed in the biographical directories. DIALINDEX allows the searcher to compare the number of records among various databases. It creates no sets, but the search may be saved temporarily (SAVE TEMP) and then executed in the files which contain the largest number of hits.

Other notable files include EXPERTNET (FILE 183) which has information on American medical experts who offer opinions on legal matters. Fields include typical hourly fee and willingness to testify. This database is not searchable by name or address; however, access points include state of residence (ST=), state of licensure (SL=), geographic limitation (GL=) and past experience (PE=).

The CAREER PLACEMENT REGISTRY (FILE 162) contains qualification summaries of people seeking employment. Some interesting access points include language skills (LA=), occupational preference (OP=) and special skills (SK=). These files, in addition to the directories mentioned earlier, may be used to locate an expert in a particular field.

*QUERY: What is the current address of the chemist John Polanyi?*

If sufficient information is given in a ready reference inquiry, then only one file need be selected. Search 16.3 illustrates a search for an address in the AMERICAN MEN AND WOMEN OF SCIENCE database. This database was chosen because the query contained the person's name and occupation. As has been said, most biographical directories are searchable by the individual's name (usually the NA= prefix or /NA suffix). Here, the EXPAND command was used on the name prior to the actual search to verify the name format. (This step should not be neglected because search time will be prolonged by inaccurate name entry.)

## Search 16.3: AMERICAN MEN AND WOMEN OF SCIENCE (FILE 236)

```
?b 236; e na=polanyi, j

File 236:AMERICAN  MEN  &  WOMEN  OF  SCIENCE  17TH  ED.
(COPR.  R.R.  BOWKER  INC.  1989)
*  FILE CONTAINS THE  17th EDITION  OF  AMWS.  *
      Set      Items     Description
      ---      -----     -----------


Ref   Items    Index-term
E1      1      NA=POLANER,  JEROME  L(ESTER)
E2      1      NA=POLANSKY,  MARILYN  MACARTHUR
E3      0     *NA=POLANY,  J
E4      1      NA=POLANYI,  JOHN  CHARLES
E5      1      NA=POLATNICK,  JEROME
E6      1      NA=POLAVARAPU,  PRASAD  LEELA
E7      1      NA=POLCYN,  DANIEL  STEPHEN
E8      1      NA=POLEJES,  J(ACOB)  D
E9      1      NA=POLEN,  PERCY  B
E10     1      NA=POLESTAK,  WALTER  JOHN  S
E11     1      NA=POLET,  HERMAN
E12     1      NA=POLGAR,  GEORGE
      Enter  P  or  E  for  more

?s e4; t s1/4/1
      S1            1   NA="POLANYI,  JOHN  CHARLES"

  1/4/1
0071145
Polanyi,  John  Charles
ADDRESS: Dept  of  Chem,  Univ  of  Toronto
Toronto  ,  ON  M5S  1A1
Can
```

In Search 16.3 the entire concept need not be mapped out and it is important to confine the search to the specific name. Format 4 is used to display the biographee's name and address. (Noteworthy is the fact that the person is Canadian so coverage is extended to non-American persons in this database despite its restrictive name.)

Biographical information on historical persons may be best retrieved from encyclopedias (for example, EVERYMAN'S ENCYCLOPEDIA: FILE 182). Current information may be retrieved from news sources; DIALINDEX (FILE 411) contains the PEOPLE category comprising files such as MAGAZINE INDEX (FILE 47), ACADEMIC INDEX (FILE 88) and NATIONAL NEWSPAPER INDEX (FILE 111).

*QUERY: Locate an obituary on the musician Leonard Bernstein who died in 1990.*

Search 16.4 shows the retrieval of an obituary from the PAPERSNE (PAPERSNE) database. The death was recent; therefore, current news sources were suitable for the search. PAPERSNE contains three newspapers from the North-Eastern United States and it was chosen because Bernstein was from New York.

The BEGIN and SELECT STEPS commands were stacked and each concept was limited to a particular field in order to ensure precise retrieval. The 1W (WITH) proximity operator was used in the name to allow for a middle initial. The W (WITH) proximity operator specifies that two terms must occur next to each other in the order specified. The operator may be numerically qualified to indicate the number of words between the two terms. The name was limited to the headline field (/TI). The section heading suffix (/SH) was used to retrieve the obituary section and the publication year (PY=) was used as a limitation since the year of death was known.

Both records were obituaries from the *Boston Globe*. The records were displayed in reverse chronological order, so record one contained the third edition obituary and the second record, the first edition obituary. The records were displayed in Format 5 which shows the bibliographic citation, indexing, lead paragraph and word count; however, the entire obituary could be retrieved using Format 9 (full record).

## Search 16.4: PAPERSNE search

```
?b papersne; ss leonard(1w)bernstein/ti and obituary/sh and py=1990

SYSTEM:OS  -  DIALOG  OneSearch
File  631:BOSTON  GLOBE_  1980  -  28  Jun  1991
(c)  1991  Globe  Newspaper  Company
File  633:PHILADELPHIA  INQUIRER_  1983  -  24  Jun  1991
(c)1991  Phil.  Newspapers  Inc
File  638:NEWSDAY/NEW  YORK  NEWSDAY_  1988  -  29  Jun  1991
(c)  1991  Newsday  Inc.
     Set      Items    Description
     ---      -----    -----------
     S1        684     LEONARD/TI
     S2        197     BERNSTEIN/TI
     S3         35     LEONARD/TI(1W)BERNSTEIN/TI
     S4      37443     OBITUARY/SH
     S5     203218     PY=1990
     S6          2     LEONARD(1W)BERNSTEIN/TI  AND  OBITUARY/SH  AND  PY=1990
?t s6/5/1-2
6/5/1 (Item 1 from file: 631)
05789056
LEONARD  BERNSTEIN  DEAD  AT  72
BOSTON  GLOBE  (BG)  -  MONDAY  October  15,  1990
By:  Edgar  J.  Driscoll  Jr.,  Globe  Staff
Edition:  THIRD  Section:  OBITUARY  Page:  1
Word  Count:  1,066
LEAD  PARAGRAPH:
Leonard  Bernstein,  the  internationally  known  conductor,  composer,
pianist,  teacher  and  writer  who  thrilled  audiences  with  his  impassioned
works,  died  yesterday.  He  was  72 . . .
```

*Dictionaries, thesauri and other language aids*

There is a paucity of online databases in this category; DIALOG contains only one dictionary: THE QUOTATIONS DATABASE (FILE 175) which is the online version of *The Oxford Dictionary of Quotations*. The database contains quotations of over 650 notable writers, public figures, the Bible, Vulgate, Book of Common Prayer, Latin Mass, Greek and Latin classics, modern European language classics and famous historical notes, dicta, quips and utterances.

Strategic access points include searching by author (AU=), note (/NT) or source (SO=) or by quotation in the text (/TX) field. Other access points include the author's year of birth (YB=) and year of death (YD=). All DIALOG stopwords are searchable in the quotation field and Boolean operators (AND, OR, NOT) must be enclosed by quotation marks.

*QUERY: Who said 'a wit with dunces and a dunce with wits'?*

Search 16.5 shows the frequent use of the W proximity operator. It is used to replace a stopword in full-text databases, and in this instance it is used to specify word order and to replace 'with' within the quote in order to shorten the search statement. The entire quote was not entered in the statement; however, this technique may not apply to all quotes and partial quotes should be searched cautiously. If the entire quote was searched, then the statement would appear as follows:

s a(w)wit(w)with(w)dunces(w)"and"(w)a(w)dunce(w)with(w)wits/tx

The W operator is used extensively and the boolean operator is enclosed in double quotation marks. This statement may be shortened by using 1W to replace 'with' and 'and'. However, the search is still cumbersome to type and long search statements are prone to more typing errors.

## Search 16.5: QUOTATIONS DATABASE (FILE 175)

```
?b  175;  s  a(w)wit(1w)dunces?/tx
•
•
File  175:Quotations  Database
        (Copr.  Oxford  U.  Press  1979)
     Set      Items     Description
     ---      -----     -----------
              5308    A/TX
               102    WIT/TX
                 2    DUNCES?/TX
     S1          1    A(W)WIT(1W)DUNCES?/TX

?t  s1/5/1
 1/5/1
00008951  DIALOG  File  175:  QUOTATIONS  DATABASE
POPE,  ALEXANDER  1688-1744
A  wit  with  dunces,  and  a  dunce  with  wits.
SOURCE/NOTES:  The  Dunciad  (1728),  bk.iv  (1742),  1.90
Oxford  Dictionary  of  Quotations
```

If word order is unknown, then the N (NEAR) proximity operator may be used. NEAR is used when terms appear next to one another, but the order of the terms are unknown. (The N operator is used to search names in biographical sources if the order of the first and last names is unknown, for example, s george(1n)michael. If precision is more important, then the W operator would be used since it specifies word order. Like the W proximity operator, the N may be qualified by a numeral that indicates a certain number of words.

A sample of more standard language aids available on other systems include the following: Data-Star's EXCERPTA MEDICA VOCABULARY - EVOC and MEDLINE VOCABULARY - MVOC; ECHO Service's EURODICAUTOM which covers terms, phrases and abbreviations in the languages of the European Community and in all subject fields, and West Publishing Company's BLACK'S LAW DICTIONARY which covers legal terminology and phrases.

*Directories*

Online directories contain lists of organizations, products, people, etc. in a prescribed order. Directories are useful for solving ready reference queries because of their factual composition and numerous directories are found on systems such as DIALOG, BRS or Data-Star.

A large proportion of directories contain corporate information; hence, business directories are excluded from this discussion since they are covered in the chapter on business information.

It is impossible to discuss the details of each database within the confines of this chapter, so a sample list of files is listed below. The asterisks denote the databases which are used in the forthcoming search examples. The sample list of files is broadly categorized into organizations and products.

### Organizations

AMERICAN LIBRARY DIRECTORY (460)*
D&B - DUN'S ELECTRONIC BUSINESS DIRECTORY (FILE 515)
    (Formerly referred to as the ELECTRONIC YELLOW PAGES.)
EDUCATIONAL DIRECTORY, THE (511)
ENCYCLOPEDIA OF ASSOCIATIONS (114)*
FOUNDATION DIRECTORY (26)
FOUNDATION GRANTS INDEX (27)
GRADLINE (273)
GRANTS (85)
PUBLISHERS, DISTRIBUTERS, WHOLESALERS (450)*
PETERSON'S COLLEGE DATABASE (214)
RESEARCH CENTERS AND SERVICES DIRECTORY (115)

### Products - Industrial

EUROPEAN DIRECTORY OF AGROCHEMICAL PRODUCTS (316)
FINE CHEMICALS DATABASE (360)
HEILBRON (303)
REGISTRY OF TOXIC EFFECTS OF CHEMICAL SUBSTANCES (336)
TRADE NAMES DATABASE (116)*

### Products - Consumer - Computer

BUSINESS SOFTWARE DATABASE (256)
BUYER'S GUIDE TO MICRO SOFTWARE (237, SOFT)
COMPUTER-READABLE DATABASES (230)
MICROCOMPUTER SOFTWARE GUIDE (278)
SOFTWARE DIRECTORY, THE (263)

**Products** - Health

HEALTH DEVICES SOURCEBOOK (188)
HEALTH DEVICES ALERTS (198)

*QUERY: To which publishers is the ISBN 0-8143 assigned? [6,p.136]*

File 450 is most suitable to answer this query as it contains the ISBN prefix code (BN=). The answer is quickly retrieved online and is shown in Search 16.6.

### Search 16.6: PUBLISHERS, DISTRIBUTERS, WHOLESALERS (FILE 450)

```
?b  450;  s  bn=0-8143
.
.
File  450:PUBLISHERS,  DISTRIBUTORS  &  WHOLESALERS  JUN  91
        (COPR.  1991  R.R.  BOWKER)
     Set     Items    Description
     ---     -----    -----------
     S1         1     BN=0-8143
?t  s1/5/1
  1/5/1
0039480   051287400
    RECORD  TYPE:  BIP  PUBLISHER;  DISTRIBUTOR  STATUS:  ACTIVE  ENTRY
    COMPANY  NAME:  Wayne  State  University  Press
    VARIANT  COMPANY  NAME:  Wayne  State  Univ.  Pr.
    IMPRINTS:  Detroit  Institute  of  Arts;  Savoyard  Books;  Waynebooks;
Great    Lakes  Books
    SYMBOL:  Wayne  St  U  Pr  ISBN  PREFIX:  0-8143
    ADDRESS:  Leonard  N.  Simons  Bldg.,  5959  Woodward  Ave.
      Detroit,  MI  48202
      TEL.:   313-577-4600
      SAN:   202-5221
```

*QUERY: What is the address of the company which produces Timex watches? [6,p.135]*

The answer was sought in File 116 since the trade name was given (see Search 16.7). The search statement limits 'timex' to the trade name field (/TN) which includes alternative and former trade names, and enters the truncated term 'watch?' in the goods/services description field (/DE). Three items were retrieved because the company has three locations.

### Search 16.7: TRADE NAMES DATABASE (FILE 116)

```
?b  116;  s  timex/tn  and  watch?/de
.
.
File  116:Trade  Names  Database_1991S1/JAN
        (COPR.  GALE  RESEARCH  INC.  1991)
**FILE116:  FREE  TIME  for  July!  See  HOMEBASE,  or  BEGIN  410  and
TYPE  063494/5  for  details.
     Set     Items    Description
     ---     -----    -----------
                4     TIMEX/TN
```

**Search 16.7:** (cont.)

```
                   2218   WATCH?/DE
        S1            3   TIMEX/TN  AND  WATCH?/DE
?t  s1/5/1
1/5/1
09795000  DIALOG File 116:  TRADE NAMES DATABASE
SUBFILE: Brands and Their Companies
TRADE NAME: TIMEX
DESCRIPTION: Watches  and  clocks
COMPANY:
TIMEX  Corp.
Box 2126 Waterbury, CT 06722
  Telephone: (203)  573-5000
.
.
```

*QUERY: What type of works make up the holdings of the National Science Foundation Library in Washington?*
*[6, p.135]*

The name of the library was entered using the W (WITH) proximity operator and the name was limited to the 'name, former name, parent institution' field (/ON). Format 6 was used to display the record because it displayed address and holdings information (see Search 16.8).

**Search 16.8: AMERICAN LIBRARY DIRECTORY (FILE 460)**

```
?b  460;  s  national(w)science(w)foundation/on
.
.
File 460:AMERICAN LIBRARY DIRECTORY 43RD EDITION
       (COPR. 1990 R.R.BOWKER)
     Set    Items   Description
     ---    -----   -----------
            566    NATIONAL/ON
            505    SCIENCE/ON
            225    FOUNDATION/ON
     S1       1    NATIONAL(W)SCIENCE(W)FOUNDATION/ON
?t  s1/6/1

  1/6/1
00032320  0629145XX  LIBRARY  RECORD
   OFFICIAL NAME: NATIONAL  SCIENCE  FOUNDATION  LIBRARY
   LIBRARY TYPE: SPECIAL
   ADDRESS: 1800 G St NW, Room 245
     Washington,  DC
     20550
   SAN (Standard Address Number): 302-735X
   TELEPHONE NUMBER(S): 202-357-7811
   LIBRARY HOLDINGS:
 BK VOLS: 15,000 PER SUB: 800
   SPECIAL COLLECTIONS: Current College & University Catalogs, microfiche
```

*QUERY: When was Beta Phi Mu founded? What are some of its publications and committees?*

The ENCYCLOPEDIA OF ASSOCIATIONS (FILE 114) was selected for this search because it includes Greek and non-Greek Letter Societies, Associations and Federations. The organization name does not require the W operator because the field is phrase as well as word indexed. The /ON suffix is the organization name and abbreviation field (see Search 16.9).

## Search 16.9: ENCYCLOPEDIA OF ASSOCIATIONS (FILE 114)

```
?b 114; s beta phi mu/on
•
•
File 114:ENCYC. OF ASSOCIATIONS - MAY 1991
        (COPR. GALE RESEARCH INC.1990-1991)
**FILE114: May91: File updated with Nat'l Orgns-1992 ed. & Int'l Orgns
Supplement. Display codes AD,TE,CY,ST,ZP or CN are $1.50/type, $1.80/prt.
        Set     Items   Description
        ---     -----   -----------
        S1        1     BETA PHI MU/ON
?t s1/9/1
  1/9/1
09978327 EA ENTRY NO.: 021681 (National Organizations of the U.S.)
 Beta Phi Mu
 School of Library & Info. Science, Univ. of Pittsburgh, Pittsburgh, PA
   15260
 (412) 624-9435
 Dr. Blanche Woolls, Exec.Sec.
 FOUNDED: 1948.
  •
  •
 PUBLICATIONS: Newsletter, semiannual. Also publishes monographs
  •
  •
```

## Handbooks

Handbooks contain information which is limited to specific disciplines or fields of knowledge. Four online handbooks are available on DIALOG: THE AGROCHEMICALS HANDBOOK (FILE 306), BEILSTEIN ONLINE (FILE 390) which contains chemical information, CHEMICAL ECONOMICS HANDBOOK (CEH) (FILE 959) and CONSUMER DRUG INFORMATION FULLTEXT (FILE 271) which has 'handbook' data on frequently prescribed drugs.

*QUERY: What is the technical name for actifed and what other products are similar to it?*

The CONSUMER DRUG INFORMATION FULLTEXT file was searched on DIALOG in Search 16.10. The antihistamine 'actifed' was entered and one record was retrieved. The partial record is displayed in Format 3 which displays the AHFS Class Number and name, monograph title, generic name, record title, trade name(s) and CAS Registry Number. Additional information about the drug such as use, storage and side effects is given in the full record.

**Search 16.10: CONSUMER DRUG INFORMATION FULLTEXT (FILE 271)**

```
?b 271; s actifed
File  271:Consumer  Drug  Information  File  (DEC.1990)
       (COPR. ASHP 1991)
     Set    Items   Description
     ---    -----   -----------
     S1       1     ACTIFED/NA
?t  s1/3/1
  1/3/1
00000303
Monograph  Title:  PSEUDOEPHEDRINE  and  TRIPROLIDINE
Pronunciation:  soo  doe  e  fed'  rin  trye  proe'  li  deen
     Synonyms:  Actifed;  Allerfrin;  Triacin;  Trifed;  Triphed;  others  Copr.,
1991,  Am.  Soc.  of  Hospital  Pharmacists,  Inc.  All  Rights  Reserved.
```

## SOURCE DATABASES

Source databases contain complete representations of information sources and are here divided into two classes: full-text and textual-numeric.

### Full text

*Encyclopedias*

In general, online encyclopedias deviate from the standard definition of a hardcopy encyclopedia which is regarded as a collection of knowledge on a variety of subjects. Only DIALOG's EVERYMAN'S ENCYCLO-PEDIA (FILE 182) conforms to this definition; whereas, others contain information in a specific discipline. They include: THE KIRK-OTHMER (ENCYCLOPEDIA OF CHEMICAL TECHNOLOGY) ONLINE (FILE 302) (BRS: KIRK), POLYMER ONLINE (FILE 322) which is the online version of the second edition of the *Encyclopedia of Polymer Science and Engineering* and the MERCK INDEX ONLINE (FILE 304) - a one-volume encyclopedia of chemicals and drugs.

Encyclopedias such as EVERYMAN'S support a wide range of queries. For example, certain types of biographical information may be retrieved as well as quick facts or brief histories. The EVERYMAN'S ENCYCLOPEDIA's basic index includes country name (/CO), historical period (/CS), descriptor (/DE), bibliography (/SB), article title (/TI) and text (/TX). The remaining access point is article type (AT=). Searches must emphasize key concepts and employ proximity operators to ensure precision.

However, the utility of online encyclopedias for ready reference work is questionable because the search output is frequently cumbersome. The EVERYMAN database does not provide the KWIC (keyword in context) print format; therefore, enormous search results can easily be produced. For example, 'Fabian Socialism' was searched in order to find the term's origin. The term was located in a lengthy general article on Socialism. Hence, it is preferable to search CD-ROM encyclopedias rather than the online versions because CD-ROMs offer more flexibility in displaying and printing search results.

*QUERY: What is the basket called in the game of jai alai?*

Search 16.11 shows that 'basket' was searched with the term 'jai alai' which was qualified by empty parentheses that imply the W operator. One hit was retrieved.

*News sources*

Online news sources include newspapers, wire services and magazines which report current events. News sources are multidisciplinary and their application for ready reference work includes current factual information as well as archival information.

### Search 16.11: EVERYMAN'S ENCYCLOPEDIA (FILE 182)

```
?b 182; s jai()alai and basket
•
•
File  182:Everyman's  Encyclopaedia
         (Copr.  J.M.  DenT  &  Sons,LTd.)
         Set     Items     Description
         ---     -----     -----------
                     5     JAI
                     6     ALAI
                     4     JAI(W)ALAI
                    32     BASKET
         S1          1     JAI()ALAI  AND  BASKET

?t s1/5/1
 1/5/1
1974869
 Jai Alai
... leading  finally  to  the  use  of  a  curved  wicker  basket  (cesta)
attached  to  the  hand,  about  76  cm  in  length...
```

Online access to full-text news databases allows the searcher to filter through a vast quantity of information in a much speedier and more sophisticated fashion than is possible with print equivalents. The same searches conducted manually would be rendered cumbersome and time consuming, partly because of the sheer size of the print collection and partly because indexes to the print products are usually lacking in detail, if available at all.

The key to successful searching in online news sources is precise search statements and terminology. Free text searching is problematic because word usage is unpredictable, and searches may result in a large number of false drops.

If the searcher establishes a context for the query's concepts through the use of proximity operators and field limiters in the search statements, then the level of precision may increase. Further, synonyms may be used to establish context but this deviates from the simple search statements which characterize ready reference work. The use of proper names, places and events offer the searcher more precise access and if possible, these terms may be limited to a specific field such as 'lead paragraph' to improve precision.

DIALOG's PAPERS (PAPERS) database is updated daily and comprises twenty-six American newspapers as of June 1991, and includes the following fields in the basic index: captions (/CP), descriptor (/DE), lead paragraph (/LP), memo (/ME), section heading (/SH or SH=), headline (/TI) and text (/TX). Some of the additional indexes which are useful access points and limiters include: byline (AU=), dateline (DL=), United States region (RG=), publication date (PD=) and edition (ED=). The length of retrieved text may be controlled by the limit features /SHORT (word count less than 1,000) and /LONG (word count of 1,000 or more).

*QUERY: Which countries make up the Group of Seven?*

The PAPERS newspaper database was selected to answer this question in Search 16.12. The search statement included searching the name of the organization using 1W to replace 'of' and limiting the name to the lead paragraph (/LP). The S (SUBFIELD) proximity operator was used to specify that the terms must occur in the same subfield and in this example, the terms are in the same paragraph. (If there are no subfields, then the terms will be retrieved from the entire field.)

The latter phrase was enclosed in parentheses to ensure the order of processing (W then the S operator). The words, 'countries' and 'include' were incorporated into the search statement on the assumption that journalists might use this wording to list the Group of Seven's membership in a news story. This technique is based upon knowledge of journalistic style and may not always prove successful, so it should be used with caution. Finally, the search results were displayed using Format 3 (bibliographic citation) and the KWIC format.

## Search 16.12: PAPERS (PAPERS)

```
?b  papers;  s  group(1w)seven/lp(s)(countries(w)include)
.
.

    Set     Items    Description
    ---     -----    -----------
            254727   GROUP/LP
            172230   SEVEN/LP
            241392   COUNTRIES
            643645   INCLUDE
    S1           1   GROUP(1W)SEVEN/LP(S)(COUNTRIES(W)INCLUDE)

?t  s1/3,k/1
1/3,K/1 (Item 1 from file: 630)
01263603  08690
IN BRIEF
DOLLAR MIXED AS DEALERS AWAIT NEWS
LOS ANGELES TIMES (LT) - THURSDAY February 2, 1989
By: Times wire services
Edition: Orange County Pm Final Section: Business Page: 3 Pt. A Col.1
Story Type: Brief; Wire
Word Count: 74
LEAD PARAGRAPHS:
    ...were lower.
  Most dealers said they were moving to the sidelines before the so-
called Group of Seven meeting of industrialized nations late Thursday.
The G-7 countries include the United States, West Germany, Japan,
France, Britain, Italy and Canada.
```

DIALINDEX/OneSearch news source categories include: Archival News (NEWSFILE), Current News - daily updates (NEWSDAY), Newspapers (NEWSPAP) and Newswires (NEWSWIRES) and Full-Text United States Newspapers (PAPERS). Other categories to be considered are United States Public Affairs (PUBAFF) and Regional United States Business News (REGIONAL). Individual news databases are listed below:

> BNA DAILY NEWS (FILE 655) (Covers Government and private sector activities.)
> BUSINESSWIRE (FILE 610) (Contains news releases.)
> CHEMICAL BUSINESS NEWSBASE (FILE 319)
> COMPUTER NEWS FULLTEXT (FILE 674)
> FACTS ON FILE (FILE 264)
> MAGAZINE INDEX (FILE 47)
> NATIONAL NEWSPAPER INDEX (FILE 111)
> NEWSEARCH (FILE 211)
> NEWSPAPER ABSTRACTS (FILE 603)
> NEWSWIRE ASAP (649)

ONLINE CHRONICLE (170)
PAPERS (PAPERS)
PHARMACEUTICAL NEWS INDEX (FILE 42)
PTS NEWSLETTER DATABASE (636, PTSNL)
STANDARD & POOR'S NEWS (FILES 132, 134)
USA TODAY DECISIONLINE (FILE 644)

Other features which may be used in full-text databases include the proximity operators F (FIELD) and L (LINK). The FIELD operator specifies that both terms must occur in the same field. (For example, the title field or the abstract field.) However, if the fields are lengthy, then the terms may be far apart and therefore the search results may be inaccurate.

The LINK proximity operator specifies that both terms must occur in the same descriptor. LINK is more precise than FIELD because the two terms must occur in the same descriptor, not the entire field.

## Graphics/images

Ready reference queries often require visual data and full-text databases are deficient in this respect because they do not include their graphics component.

The print versions of encyclopedias, newspapers and magazines contain pictorial data which are used to solve queries such as 'Locate an illustration of the solar system' or 'Can you find a photograph of Margaret Thatcher for my essay?', etc. The PAPERS database contains a special feature field (SF=) that is used to retrieve information about a photo, graph, drawing, chart, table, diagram and/or map. Search 16.13 shows how newspaper photographs of former British Prime Minister Margaret Thatcher may be located online.

*QUERY: Locate a newspaper photograph of Margaret Thatcher.*

The name was searched using 1W proximity operator to specify the order of the terms and to allow for a middle initial. The name was limited to the headline (/TI) field to ensure that the subject was given emphasis in the article. The special features prefix (SF=) was used to limit the search results to photographs. It should be noted that the system reported that the SF prefix is not available in all files. Format 3, bibliographic citation and the SF field were used to display the search results.

The practical use of online databases for retrieving graphics location information needs to be weighed against the cost of conducting these searches online. Search 16.13 required a few seconds' system processing time and a more complicated search would have resulted in a greater time delay. To narrow search results, it is probably better to limit the search to a particular newspaper. For example, when Set 1 in Search 16.13 was combined with the newspaper code (JC=) LT (Los Angeles Times), the search results were reduced to four hits. However, to ensure speedy retrieval, it is more efficient to access a particular newspaper database directly (that is, search the LOS ANGELES TIMES (FILE 630).

Certain types of images lend themselves to easier retrieval and the TRADEMARKSCAN - FEDERAL (FILE 226) database comprises approximately 400,000 trademarks which may be retrieved by using certain software and hardware. Searchers use six-digit design codes to query the database and retrieve the most pertinent images. Similarly, seventy per cent of the records in the HEILBRON database provide images of chemical structures and they may be retrieved online.

Since online databases are still unsatisfactory in regard to their graphics component, CD-ROM databases may be a better choice because they provide more flexibility for image retrieval. Images on CD-ROM may be viewed online even if they cannot be printed out successfully.

**Search 16.13: PAPERS (PAPERS)**

```
?b  papers;  s  margaret(1w)thatcher/ti  and  sf=photo
.
.


     Set     Items    Description
     ---     -----    -----------
>>>One or more prefixes are unsupported
>>> or undefined in one or more files.
Processing
              1861     MARGARET/TI
              3670     THATCHER/TI
               113     MARGARET/TI(1W)THATCHER/TI
           1839568     SF=PHOTO
     S1       50      MARGARET(1W)THATCHER/TI  AND  SF=PHOTO
?t  s1/3,sf/1
>>>No matching display codes found in file 146
1/3,SF/1 (Item 1 from file: 492)
05829054
ONE WE'LL REMEMBER MARGARET THATCHER HAD A DRAMATIC IMPACT ON WORLD
EVENTS DURING HER TIME IN OFFICE. IT WILL BE A LONG TIME BEFORE WE SEE
ANOTHER LEADER LIKE HER
ARIZONA REPUBLIC (AR) - SUNDAY November 25, 1990
By: Geoffrey Smith Special for The Arizona Republic
Edition: FINAL CHASER Section: PERSPECTIVE Page: C1
Word Count: 1,146
SPECIAL FEATURE: PHOTO
```

**Textual-numeric databases**

The application of textual-numeric databases to ready reference work is apparent since typical queries often require a statistic, date, cost, etc. Charts and tables are a primary feature for databases which contain numeric information and contrary to image retrieval, they are easier to retrieve online. DIALOG's REPORT feature may be used to organize numeric data output.

DIALOG's CENDATA (FILE 580, CENDATA), DONNELLY'S DEMOGRAPHICS (FILE 275) and PUBLIC OPINION ONLINE (FILE 468, POLL) provide textual-numeric information on a myriad of topics ranging from the average production of alfalfa sprouts to the percentage of people who approve of extramarital sex.

*QUERY: What is the most recent total voting population of California?*

Search 16.14 shows that the LV= prefix was used to indicate the geographic level, the state name was entered and the term 'vot?' was truncated to retrieve voting, votes, voters, etc. Truncating the root of vote may prove inefficient in most databases, but variations on 'vot' is limited in this type of database so the risk of several false drops is minimal.

**Search 16.14: CENDATA (FILE 580, CENDATA)**

```
?b  580;  s  lv=state  and  california  and  vot?
.
.
File  580:CENDATA
```

**Search 16.14:** (cont.)

```
        ( 01 Jul 91 )
     Set     Items   Description
     ---     -----   -----------
             3152    LV=STATE
            14906    CALIFORNIA
              169    VOT?
     S1         3    LV=STATE  AND  CALIFORNIA  AND  VOT?
  .
  .
  .
  1/5/2
  00100540
  May 16, 1989
  TABLE 2.  REPORTED VOTING AND REGISTRATION, BY RACE, HISPANIC ORIGIN,
  AND SEX, FOR STATES: PART 2 (ALABAMA - GEORGIA)
  (November 1988. Numbers in thousands. Consistent with all-age
  resident population shown in Press Release CB88-205)
  CALIFORNIA            (1)persons  Percent     error    Percent
       Total......     20,194      59.1        0.9      51.7
       Per cent...      100.0       (X)         (X)       (X)
  .
  .
```

PUBLIC OPINION ONLINE (File 468) contains the survey questions and statistics from public opinion polls conducted by various organizations such as Decima, Gallup and Roper. This database may be used to answer ready reference queries such as 'I am giving a talk on sexual ethics in the 1990s and I would like to know what people think about extramarital sex.' A specific search query with 'extramarital(w)sex' limited to the descriptor field yielded two records. The first hit was precise whereas the second record dealt with political scandals and which type of moral offence would be considered most scandalous. Fields such as survey beginning and survey ending dates (SB= and SE= respectively), survey population (SP=), source (SO=) and interview method (IM=) may be used as specific access points.

## Miscellaneous databases

DIALOG contains several databases which may be useful for ready reference work that were not discussed in the prescribed categories. For example, JOURNAL NAME FINDER (FILE 414) is a useful searching tool to find out which databases index a particular journal. This is achieved by searching on the journal's name (JN=).

The A-V ONLINE (FILE 46) database covers non-print educational materials including 16mm films, 35mm filmstrips, overhead transparencies, audio tapes, video tapes, phonograph records, motion picture cartridges and slides.

The BIBLE (KING JAMES VERSION) (FILE 297, MENU) is available online and EVENTLINE (FILE 165), which is a diverse database covering information about past and forthcoming worldwide events such as conferences, exhibitions, symposia and trade fairs, may also be used to respond to queries such as 'Where is the Grey Cup final being held next year?' EVENTLINE - EVNT is also available on Data-Star.

Also noteworthy is the OAG ELECTRONIC EDITION (FILE OAG, MENU) on DIALOG. This database contains current information on international flight schedules, fares, seat availability and hotel/motel information. The 'worldwide travel facts' may be useful for factual retrieval.

Data-Star has FAIRBASE-FAIR which contains references to conferences, exhibits, trade shows, etc. and MARTINDALE ONLINE - MART which has information on various types of drugs.

A sample of BRS databases includes the AIDS KNOWLEDGE BASE (ASFG), which is an online textbook covering all aspects of the acquired immune deficiency syndrome and the VOCATIONAL EDUCATION CURRICULUM MATERIALS database (VECM) which contains abstracts to instructional materials in technical and vocational education. The MENTAL MEASUREMENTS YEARBOOK (MMYB) database contains labels such as testname (TN), purpose (PP), classification (CL), authors (AU), etc., as well as 'factual information, critical reviews, reliability and validity information on all English language tests' covered in three editions of the print version.

The skill in matching online databases with ready reference queries increase with the searcher's experience. There are several online aids on BRS, Data-Star and DIALOG, however which are worth mentioning. BRS/ FILE (FILE), DATA-STAR NEWS-NEWS and the DIALOG BLUESHEETS (FILE 415) contain information regarding the databases on their respective systems.

Databases on any search system may be found in directories of databases: BRS has the KNOWLEDGE INDUSTRY PUBLICATIONS DATABASES (KIPD); Data-Star contains the CUADRA DIRECTORY OF DATABASES (CUAD) and DIALOG has COMPUTER READABLE DATABASES (FILE 230).

After surveying the databases on BRS, Data-Star and DIALOG, it appears that the number of online databases which are considered standard ready reference tools is limited, several databases are redundant and with the exception of directory databases, the ready reference database growth rate is seemingly stagnant.

The lack of growth may be attributed to the high costs associated with online searching for this particular type of reference work and the amount of online training which is required to prepare information specialists for the diversity of ready reference queries. Also, the increasing number of CD-ROM databases available for ready reference work may further diminish the number of online databases since CD-ROM technology has proved a much more successful and effective means of storing reference information.

## CD-ROM DATABASES

Since their debut in 1985, the number of CD-ROM databases has grown exponentially to over two thousand. The 1987 edition of *CD-ROMS in Print* listed one hundred databases available on CD-ROMs, the 1988-1989 edition covered 240 titles, the 1990 publication listed six hundred databases, and the 1991 edition produced a list of over 1,400 titles. A more recent estimate has put the total number of CD titles at 2,250 [7, p.28]. With the current growth rate, the total number of CD-ROM databases may surpass the number of online databases by the mid 1990s.

The nature of quick, ready, or factual reference questions has already been discussed in the previous sections of this chapter. In an online environment in general, a limited amount of time is allocated to factual reference questions and the search strategy is aimed towards highest precision. Users have to pay for online time, telecommunications costs, and in some cases for each record retrieved. In the CD-ROM environment, the time factor is much less significant. The initial cost of a database may rationally be distributed over the total number of searches resulting in a substantive reduction in cost per search.

The storage capacity of a CD-ROM, though not comparable to online services, may be considered ideal for a reference department. It can hold the equivalent of 1,500 diskettes or approximately five hundred books including all the pertinent indexes. Many reference questions may be readily answered by using one of the hundreds of CD-ROM databases available today. Indexes to periodicals in business, medicine, education and psychology, to name a few, are now accessible on this medium. Many academic, special and public libraries have incorporated CD-ROM databases in their reference departments to augment and enhance reference tools used by patrons. The results of one study show that users expressed a high level of satisfaction with the online substitution for the printed sources of information. However, when online was replaced with CD-ROM, patrons' and librarians' satisfaction levels were significantly increased [8]. Similar results have been obtained in other institutions [9].

Another reason for relying on CD-ROM products for reference queries is the availability of many titles in the market. CD-ROM databases, like their online counterparts, may be categorized into two groups: reference and source. Reference databases can be further divided into bibliographic and referral, while source databases consist of full-text, numeric, graphical, sound and moving images. Together, the referral and source databases comprise over seventy-four per cent of all CD-ROM titles [10]. Such a high proportion of commercially-available databases makes the CD-ROM medium an ideal candidate for ready reference or factual queries.

## Physical standards

The proliferation of CD-ROM databases has been made possible through the rapid adoption of standards by the industry. From the outset, specialists and developers were aware of a need for standards. Hence several standards were devised to assure compatibility at different levels. The first set of standards which were readily adopted by many producers were proposed by Philips and Sony in 1980 for the physical structure of the CD-ROMs. These are contained in the Red Book for the digital audio CDs (CD-DA). *The Yellow Book*, published in 1983, is a variation of CD-DA standards. Both standards suggest use of the Constant Linear Velocity (CLV) format on a single-sided disc with a recording density of 16,000 tracks per inch [11, p.28].

The second set of standards deals with the logical format of files and directories and has been referred to as the High Sierra standards. These standards were first proposed in 1986 by representatives from industry and various organizations including the American Library Association. They were later approved by the International Standards Organization (ISO 9660). A year later Microsoft Corporation introduced the Disk Operating System Extensions to alleviate the problem of operating a disc on different drives. Philips, Sony and Microsoft, in August, 1988, proposed the CD-ROM Extended Architecture (CD-ROM XA) to address the problems associated with retrieval of data in several different media simultaneously. CD-ROM XA is conceived to reduce the incompatibilities of text, audio and graphics on a single disc. The Optical Publishing Association (OPA) has recently proposed a standard for the transfer of multimedia data to compact disc manufacturers. The standard, called the Disc Description Protocol (DDP) is intended to reduce the problems which may arise from sending different media to manufacturers to be incorporated into one disc.

While existing and draft standards address storage issues for CD-ROMs, they do not discuss the internal data and file structures. The ability to retrieve information effectively from the CD-ROM depends on a basic understanding of the internal data structures and the logical file arrangements. Essentially, information is stored in two types of logical files: data files which contain the actual data, such as bibliographical data, full text and graphics, and the index files. While the data files are normally arranged sequentially, the index files may have different structures, for example, hashed files, ISAM and B-Tree files [12, p.90]. Larson states that producers of CD-ROM products choose the most appropriate retrieval software based on storage requirements, speed of access and efficiency of retrieval engine. For the end users 'these design decisions determine the methods of searching available, such as whether truncation or wildcard searches can be performed, whether Boolean operations are supported and so forth. The searching software used in any CD-ROM system is intimately tied to the file structure chosen for the database' [12, p.101].

## Interfaces

The increase in storage capacity of a medium results in the accumulation of an increasingly vast amount of information. Software, along with the logical and physical organization of data, plays a vital role in retrieving the required information. However, the implications of lack of software standards and the potential problems in retrieval have not been contemplated to any extent. CD-ROM vendors and developers have produced many colourful interfaces which are designed to be 'user friendly' or 'user sensitive'. In fact, so many different interfaces have been produced that according to one industry expert, 'soon we'll have the user interface equivalent of cola wars' [13, p.28]. Although these interfaces are designed to help the retrieval needs of end users, the results of recent research suggest 'very few users are able to formulate totally efficient searches on the CD-ROM system' [14, p.43]. The proliferation of different types of databases exacerbates the situation and creates additional obstacles in developing standard retrieval interfaces.

Currently, three basic classes of interfaces are available for the CD-ROM databases: Command driven, menu driven and graphical/object driven. In addition several software vendors have produced hybrid systems which combine different features of the three basic classes.

The command line interface (CLI) in its basic form is used in a few CD-ROM products, and is designed to emulate online systems. DIALOG produces some databases which use CLIs as one of the available search options. In these systems, the CLIs use identical commands to their online counterparts. In general, the CLI's advantage lies in its speed of operation. Instead of moving through countless menus or endless pointing and clicking, the user types the exact commands which will produce the desired results. In addition, many systems which employ CLIs provide other attributes such as Boolean searching, truncation and proximity operators which enable users to control the search outcome. Lack of consistency across applications and systems, however, is the CLI's major disadvantage. To appreciate all the CLIs' features and to use them effectively, users are compelled to develop expertise in each one of many available command languages. CLIs can be effective interfaces for information retrieval only if they are standardized. Such standards have been proposed for the online industry which has been reluctant to adopt them. The Common Command Language (CCL), proposed by National Information Standards Organization (NISO), and ISO, has many features which could be incorporated into a CD-ROM interface [15].

Menu mode consists of provision of prompts and choices on the screen. The items presented on the screen are usually manipulated by highlighting the choice or filling the blank spaces of a pre-defined 'form'. Many systems use search aids implicitly to help the users. H. W. Wilson Company, a major publisher of print, online and CD-ROM products, offers a choice to the users. Among the three available search modes, Browse, Wilsearch and Wilsonline, the first relies almost exclusively on menus.

Purely menu or command driven systems, however, are uncommon among CD-ROM interfaces. Many producers, such as Online Computer Systems Inc., and SilverPlatter Information Services rely on hybrid interfaces for their products. These systems combine features from both menu and command interfaces to create unique front-ends to a retrieval engine.

SilverPlatter is one of the largest distributors of CD-ROM databases with over sixty titles in its 1991 catalogue, including CAB ABSTRACTS, CANCER-CD, DISCAMERICA, ERIC, MEDLINE and LISA. SilverPlatter's interface is designed to show primary search, display and auxiliary commands on the screen. These commands are located at the bottom of the screen and may be chosen by moving the curser and highlighting them. To initiate a search, the FIND command is highlighted, followed by several commands which may be typed in to refine the search. The proximity operator is NEAR for any order specific searching and the WITH operator is used for retrieving terms in the same field. Full Boolean operators, truncation, field qualification and nested logic are also available through commands. A combination of commands, function keys and options on the menus are used to display the results of a search. The main advantage of a hybrid system is its relative ease of use for novice patrons. With the basic commands already displayed on the screen, users do not need extensive knowledge of the interface to conduct an elementary search. As the need for complex searches increases, so does the requirement for expertise in applying more sophisticated strategies and hence a better knowledge of the interface.

Graphical or object oriented interfaces use a graphical user interface (GUI), icons and direct manipulation techniques to guide the user through the data. The number of databases which utilize this technique is relatively small, but with the introduction of hypertext and multimedia in the form of CD-I (Compact Disk-Interactive) and DVI (Digital Video Interactive), it is expected that the numbers will grow substantially in the near future.

CD-ROM Consistent Interface Committee (CD-CINC) and its UK counterpart, the CD-ROM Standards and Practices Action Group (CD-ROM SPAG) have, in 1990, begun discussion on standardization of CD-ROM interfaces. In addition, the Information Handling Committee of NISO is working on an ambitious standardization proposal referred to as CD-ROM Read-Only Data Exchange (CD-RDx). The main objective of this proposal is to help 'the United States government to foster an environment in which access to data on CD-ROM discs would be system independent (functionally interoperable across systems) and software independent (functionally interoperable with any search and retrieval program)' [16]. A system which utilizes CD-RDx will enable the user to choose the most familiar interface, submit a query and obtain the results without any knowledge of search engine or database structure.

Until these standards have been implemented, CD-ROM users need to rely on their own expertise and knowledge for retrieving information from this medium. Unlike the online environment, however, conventional search strategies may not be useful for obtaining information from CD-ROM databases. Retrieval techniques will depend on individual interfaces and file structures, and often the end user may have no choice but to follow the path provided by the vendors.

## READY REFERENCE CD-ROM DATABASES

The number of CD-ROM databases suitable for ready reference or factual queries is estimated to be just over 760 [10, p.24]. It is neither possible nor appropriate to review each title and to examine the retrieval interface of each product. Hence this section has been limited to a sample of those CD-ROM databases which *are not* available online, are considered useful for ready reference questions, and are either accessible to the authors for evaluation or a review has already been published.

The following sources in particular have been consulted for existing reviews of CD-ROM databases: *CD-ROM Librarian, CD-ROM EndUser, CD-ROM Professional* and volumes one and two of *CD-ROM Information Products: the evaluative guide,* edited by C. J. Armstrong and J. A. Large.

### Almanacs

Using the formal definition of an almanac, approximately twenty-five per cent or more of all CD-ROM products should be discussed under this heading. However, very few databases are available which would fit the conventional definition of an almanac.

TIME Magazine produces the ALMANAC, annually updated and containing five thousand articles. The coverage consists of the full text of the last available year as well as articles on major events from 1923 to 1988. As an almanac, it contains four hundred tables from the *United States Statistical Abstracts,* colour charts and maps of the world, *United States Congressional Directory* and recent recommended books and non-print materials. It uses three different types of searching mode: pull-down menus for browsing, key word searching by entering up to three key words or using an index and hypertext links in major articles to move around in the database. Articles may be marked and saved to be used later.

Quanta Press, Inc. over the last few years has produced several inexpensive CD-ROM databases, one of which is THE WORLD FACTBOOK. This database is updated annually and is based on The Directorate of the United States Central Intelligence Agency, the United States Bureau of the Census, the United States Defense Intelligence Agency, the United States Defense Nuclear Agency, the United States Department of State, the United States Department of the Interior and the United States Coast Guard. It covers 249 countries and territories providing extensive examinations, including socioeconomic, geopolitical, demographic and other country-specific data, as well as map images for each country. The retrieval engine and interface designed by TextWare is command-driven using wild cards, truncation and Boolean operators. The index consisting of some 24,000 terms may be browsed with the INDEX command followed by a letter or word. Searching precision in this database increases by using phrases or word proximity operators, as index terms do not include every field in each record [17].

The SOFTWARE TOOLWORKS WORLD ATLAS, published by The Software Toolworks, Inc., contains demographic, economic, political and travel information for more than two hundred countries and twenty-eight regions. It also includes 240 country and topographic maps as well as more than three thousand statistical maps. The database is based on a variety of sources including the CIA, the United States Bureau of Public Affairs, the World Meteorological Association, the United States Department of State, the United Nations Food and Agriculture Organization (FAO), the World Health Organization (WHO) and the World Bank. Six different elements are covered in each record in the WORLD ATLAS: people, government, geography, economy, communication and travel. Records contain information such as climate, land use, language, infant mortality rate, national holidays, GNP, airfields, highways and required travel documents.

LIBRARY REFERENCE PLUS is produced by Bowker and covers library professionals, libraries, book publishers and distributors. The coverage is based on five Bowker products: *American Book Trade Directory, American Library Directory, The Bowker Annual Library and Book Trade Almanac, Literary Market Place (LMP),* and *Publishers, Distributors, and Wholesalers of the United States.* LIBRARY REFERENCE PLUS, which first appeared in 1989, contains over 130,000 records and is updated annually.

YEAR BOOKS ON DISC is a medical yearbook published by Year Book Medical Publishers, Inc. It contains the complete text of the preceding year's Year Books describing advancements in different fields of medicine: pediatrics, cardiology, family medicine, dermatology, drug therapy, emergency medicine and psychiatry.

### Dictionaries, thesauri and other language aids

A dictionary may be defined as a 'reference book containing words usually alphabetically arranged along with information about their forms, pronunciations, functions, etymologies, meanings and syntactical and idiomatic uses' (Webster). The strict definition of a dictionary may not apply to CD-ROM products. The distinction between an encyclopedia and a dictionary has become obscure, with many products featuring characteristics of both types of media.

The OXFORD ENGLISH DICTIONARY (OED), produced by Oxford Electronic Publishing, contains the complete text of the original twelve-volume *Oxford English Dictionary*. The file contains some 252,000 main entries which list the entire known vocabulary of the English language from 1150 to 1933. The four volumes of the supplement to OED has not been included, although Oxford has promised an upgrade in the early 1990s. Records in the database contain such information as headword (Lemma), etymology, definitions, label (part of speech) and quotations. Eight indexes may be searched, four of which are about the word, the remainder relating to quotations where the word's usage is illustrated. Search statements are composed in a search panel using a combination of menu and function keys. Boolean operators, right-hand truncation and nested logic may be used to enhance the search. One of the advantages of the OED software is its ability to search while it displays a list of tagged items, reducing response time. A drawback, typical of many textual database management systems, is the inherent problem of displaying text on a small screen. This problem becomes acute when a long list of entries, such as different definitions, has to be browsed.

Harrap's CD-ROM is published by Harrap and distributed in the United States by NTC Publishing Group. This multilingual dictionary which is called the LANGUAGES OF THE WORLD in the United States and CD-ROM MULTILINGUAL DICTIONARY in Europe, contains the complete text of eighteen dictionaries of translations, definitions and synonyms for more than seven million words in Chinese, Danish, Dutch, English, Finnish, French, German, Italian, Japanese, Norwegian, Spanish and Swedish. The search software, a memory-resident program, is based on choosing a specific dictionary, a particular translation, or a list of synonyms, from a menu. Searches may be conducted by using headwords, subheadwords, list of compound entries and equivalency in eleven languages. The screen is divided into two sections; the upper half holds the information from the CD, while the lower half is reserved for the user supplied text. Although LANGUAGES OF THE WORLD has numerous capabilities, one potential limitation lies in its lack of direct links among all the language pairs.

MERRIAM WEBSTER NINTH NEW COLLEGIATE DICTIONARY is published by Highlighted Data, Inc. It contains definitions, etymologies and line illustrations for words and includes three hundred hours of recordings of the pronunciations of words which can be heard using a speaker or headphones. The file consists of 160,000 records, over 200,000 definitions, six hundred line drawings, the *Handbook of Style* and other features. The software allows for two types of searching: *Thumbguide* enables the user to select a letter then utilize the *Page Turner* to move forward and backward in the database, Search menu enables the user to utilize the *Find Word* command. The interface also uses hypertext to link different entries.

MICROSOFT BOOKSHELF is a well-known product, chosen as Best Educational Product by the Optical Publishing Association in the Fifth International Conference on CD-ROM in February 1990, and designed to be a 'Jack-of-all-trades'. Produced by Microsoft Corporation, it contains the complete text of ten reference sources and writing tools: *The American Heritage Dictionary, Roget's II: Electronic Thesaurus, The World Almanac and Book of Facts, Bartlett's Familiar Quotations, The Chicago Manual of Style, Forms and Letters, United States ZIP Code Directory, Houghton Mifflin Spelling Verifier and Corrector, Houghton Mifflin Usage Alert* and *Business Information Sources*. It is a reference work and writing tool for use in business and personal communications.

THE AMAZING MOBY is produced by ALDE Publishing and covers more than one million English-language words and phrases. It consists of four files: Moby Words contains over half a million words and phrases, and includes the *Yale Bright Star Catalog* of nine thousand stars with their individual coordinates and magnitudes; Moby Hyphenator which contains 150,000 fully hyphenated words; Moby Part of Speech - contains more than 200,000 words and phrases categorized according to their principal uses in the English language; Moby Pronunciator - contains 150,000 fully enunciated words and phrases and distinguishes the part of speech for nine hundred of those entries.

## Directories

The majority of directory databases deal with business, banking and financial information. In 1987, Datext, the original developer of a number of the corporate and financial databases, was acquired by the Lotus Development Corporation along with Computer Access Corporation, the developer of the CD-ROM search software BlueFish [18, p.15]. Today, Lotus is one of the major producers of directories on CD-ROMs with a number of such databases marketed under the title One Source prefixed with the letters 'CD'. The search software incorporated in the Lotus databases is menu-driven and has the ability to screen companies using different variables and attributes. In addition to the menus, the software allows experts to search the database through a Screensheet facility which allows more efficient data manipulation.

CD/BANKING contains financial performance information on banks and bank holding companies, and has four files: Commercial Banks (14,000 records), Savings & Loans (3,100 records), Bank Holding Companies (six thousand records), and Mutual Savings Banks (five hundred records). In addition, it provides data on 90,000 branch offices. The data are collected by Sheshunoff Information Services from United States government sources, such as the Federal Deposit Insurance Corporation, the Federal Reserve Board and the Federal Home Loan Bank.

CD/CORPORATE: United Kingdom is produced by the European branch of Lotus and provides information on five thousand public companies registered in the United Kingdom. It contains five years of financial data, interim reports and news items. The data are derived from company annual reports and accounts, corporate records, consolidated profit and loss accounts and interim reports and news items maintained by Extel Financial Limited's United Kingdom Services.

CD/INTERNATIONAL includes financial and stock performance data on five thousand large industrial corporations and other companies. The WORLDSCOPE database and Moody's Investors Service are used to provide financial information extracted from twenty-five countries and twenty-seven industries, including income statements, balance sheets and funds flow statements. It lists 250 financial variables per company.

CD/INVESTMENT: United States EQUITIES and CD/INVESTMENT: United States RESEARCH provide over 25,000 company listings, 35,000 stock listings, data on five hundred utilities and historical research files covering twenty years of data on twelve thousand active and inactive companies. In addition, CD/INVESTMENT includes income statments comparative analyses, technical analyses and price and volume. Most of the information has been supplied by COMPUSTAT, FORD DATA BASE, SECURITY DATA BASE and the BONDS DATABASE (Interactive Data Services, Inc.).

CD/M&A and CD/M&A: EUROPE supply data on more than 45,000 mergers, acquisitions, leveraged buyouts and other major American and European settlements for public and private companies. Data are derived from IDD United States Mergers, IDD United Kingdom Mergers & Acquisitions, IDD European Mergers & Acquisitions and the Disclosure II database. Each record in the database contains information on: Targets, acquirers, advisors and fees, considerations, proxy/tenders, shareholdings and stock prices.

CD/PRIVATE PLUS and CD/PRIVATE PLUS: UNITED KINGDOM include financial information on 210,000 private and public parent companies, subsidiaries and major divisions derived from Ward's *Business Directory,* ICC *British Companies,* Macmillan's *Directory of Leading Private Companies* and DISCLO-SURE. Each record contains company name, address, telephone number, CEO name, sales, number of employees, year formed, parent company, Standard Industrial Classification (SIC) codes, executive names, market segment, geography, income statement items, assets, liabilities, financial ratios and growth rates. In addition, the British database contains information on profitability ratios, revenue ratios, credit ratios, productivity ratios, value-added rates and ICC scores.

In an interesting development, one of the two marketing databases which were introduced by Lotus had to be withdrawn from the market. Public opposition to LOTUS MARKETPLACE: HOUSEHOLDS forced Lotus and the information supplier, Equifax Inc., to suspend production of the databases and cancel further developmental work in January, 1991. This database provided marketing information on 120 million people in eighty million American households. Consumer groups around the nation voiced their strong concerns about such a database which they viewed as an infringement on their privacy. In a similar move, Lotus has announced the cancellation of LOTUS MARKETPLACE: BUSINESS which contained information on more than 7.5 million American businesses.

Other business directories include CORFILE ON DISC, published by Bowker Business Research and providing portfolio information on fifteen thousand public and private companies and their divisions and subsidiaries, government agencies and not-for-profit institutions. The database, updated quarterly, contains financial data, shareholder information, the complete text of annual reports, investment analysts' reports and company newsletters.

Several telephone directories have appeared on CD-ROM. PHONEDISC USA contains residential and business names, addresses, zip codes and telephone numbers for the entire United States. The data for the three disc set have been derived from some five thousand directories. The search software is proprietary and designed to be as simple as possible, using menus, windows and function keys. The opening screen asks the user to Enter Name, after which a list of names appear on the screen. The list may be limited by pressing the F2 function key, invoking a pull-down menu which enables the user to limit the search by street, city, state and zip code. As a name is highlighted on the list, a window on the right-hand corner of the screen displays a mailing label for that name.

Searching a telephone directory, as in any large database, needs to be tailored towards maximum precision. Common names such as Smith and Jones must, for example, be accompanied by limiting factors such as full first name and middle initials, state, city, or zip code. By entering common names without limitations, not only does the response time significantly diminish, but the risk of overloading and possibly crashing the system increases. Another problem with telephone directories is the accuracy and integrity of data. Since the sources of data are existing directories, these databases do not, in general, achieve accuracy rates above eighty per cent.

Postal information has also been available on disc for some time. The British Post Office has produced the POSTCODE ADDRESS FILE, listing over twenty-three million addresses. The disc contains private and business names and addresses which are linked to the postal codes from Ordnance Survey Grid Reference Numbers. The retrieval software, provided by Dataware Technologies, allows searching by name, street, town, postal code and other fields such as User Category or Sortcode. The software has two basic modes, Search and Display. Searching is conducted through a number of function keys and pull-down menus. In addition, the interface allows implicit use of Boolean operators as well as right-hand truncation and masking. POSTCODE ADDRESS FILE is similar to the telephone directories in its rate of data accuracy.

J + W COMMDISC INTERNATIONAL by Telex-Verlag Jaeger + Waldmann GmbH is similar to the postal and telephone directories listing worldwide subscribers of telex, teletex and facsimile communications services and providing country codes, subscriber numbers and answerback codes. J + W is published semi-annually with each record containing information on company name, address, telex or teletex numbers, answerback code, telefax number, country code and line of business.

## Handbooks

Many handbooks are available in the CD-ROM format, some of which have been produced by the United States Department of Defense (DoD). DOD STANDARDIZATION SERVICE is distributed by Information Handling Services (IHS) and contains the complete text of more than 50,000 active Department of Defense (DoD) standardization documents. It also contains information on 180,000 historical documents, DoD adopted industry standards, naval instructions, DoD directives and NASA documents. A subfile called DODISS PLUS summarizes the active documents. A related database is the SPECMASTER, produced by the National Standards Association, Inc. (NSA), consisting of the complete text and graphics of 50,000 DoD standards and specifications documents which specify terminology, performance, testing, safety, or other requirements and characteristics of a particular technology of interest. In addition, the database contains four subfiles including American Society for Testing & Materials (ASTM) standards, National Aerospace Standards (NAS), Society of Automotive Engineers (SAE) standards and specifications and vendor catalogues. Each record in the SPECMASTER database contains Federal supply class; title; scope; date of last change; current revision level; and list of related documents. The database which has an annual suscription rate of $12,000 is updated monthly.

Hopkins Technology produces the FOOD ANALYST. This numeric database contains the entire United States Department of Agriculture's food database (Handbook 8) and provides nutritional breakdowns for more than eighty nutrients found in over five thousand foods. The nutritional analysis is reported for protein, carbohydrates, fat, sugar, vitamins, minerals and fibre in a variety of food groups. FOOD ANALYST PLUS covers one hundred nutrients and 20,000 foods. The search software is menu-driven, with the opening screen providing eight options to the user: Person, Meal, Date, Recipes, Graph, Analysis, Utilities and Quit. Each option provides the user with a different screen and additional information and options to choose from. In the Meal option, implicit Boolean operators have been implemented: by using the '+' the software searches for foods with words on both sides of the sign included in the food description.

Various religious databases have been available in the electronic format for some time. The optical version of these databases, however, has provided new opportunities for reseachers. THE BIBLE LIBRARY, published by Ellis Enterprises, containing several translations of the Bible, THE FABS REFERENCE BIBLE SYSTEM, produced by the Foundation for Advanced Biblical Studies and the MASTER SEARCH BIBLE: COMPARATIVE BIBLE RESEARCH produced by Tri Star Publishers, may be considered as handbooks on the subject. The latter contains the complete text of the following three versions of the Bible: the King James Version (KJV), the New American Standard Bible (NASB), and the New International Version (NIV). The user can simultaneously display particular phrases from selected versions with material from ten authoritative Bible reference books using hypertext links. The ten references include biblical geography, archeology, language, history and ancient culture. The interface uses a combination of windows and menus, as well as other features such as Boolean, proximity and phrase searching. In addition to standard searching aids, FABS also includes lexical and grammatical aids to different biblical languages.

Several handbook databases in science are now available on CD-ROM: DANGEROUS GOODS, THE PESTICIDES DISC and CCINFODISC. DANGEROUS GOODS is produced by Springer-Verlag and provides information on more than 100,000 environmentally hazardous substances. The database consists of several files, including: HOMMEL, the *Handbook of Dangerous Goods* which contains physical data, reactions, environmental data and instructions concerning medical treatment for 1,500 substances; CHEMDATA providing German- and English-language safety measures for eighteen thousand substances; Operation Files supplying instructions on procedures based on actual chemical incidents of the Swiss Fire Brigades Association; and other such information. Each record in the database contains: substance names, description, classification, appearance, danger symbols and colours, health risks, measures for controlling results of an accident, safety measures, water pollution, first aid, medical advice and manufacturers addresses. The retrieval and interface software is produced by Lasec GmbH and is called OptiSearch. The interface provides two modes of searching: menu driven and command language. In the menu mode, a form is presented on the screen to be filled by the user. The form consists of 'labels' about the substance: unique identification number or class code, name, CAS number, transport class code and the International Maritime Dangerous Goods transport class code. Two additional fields may also be filled on the form: Select hazard label which displays several symbols on the screen for the user to choose from, and the Personal database enabling the user to 'footnote' information. The OptiSearch command language includes features such as Boolean operators and truncation.

THE PESTICIDES DISC is produced by the Royal Society of Chemistry (RSC) Information Services. It contains data on pesticides consisting of four files: *The Agrochemical Handbook* covering 750 substances; *The European Directory of Agrochemical Products* encompassing some 23,000 agrochemical products; *Pesticides Index* consisting of 25,000 pesticide commodities produced worldwide; and *World Directory of Pesticide Control Organisations* containing information on 1,500 companies which are involved in the manufacturing and marketing of pesticide products worldwide. For each product, the database contains the chemical, common and trade names, active ingredients and activity and marketing company details. The database is updated semi-annually.

CCINFODISC, published by the Canadian Centre for Occupational Health & Safety, provides data on chemical substances which may affect health and safety. The database consists of two parts, one about the actual substances (Series A), and the second covering safety information (Series B). The Series A database contains information on trade names, regulatory information on pesticide products, Pest Management Research Information System (PRIS), residual limits in foods, parasitic information, Registry of Toxic Effects of Chemical Substances (RTECS), Transportation of Dangerous Goods (TDG), and New Jersey Hazardous Substance Fact Sheets. CCINFODISC uses the FindIt search engine, produced by Reteaco, which utilizes function keys and menus to carry out a search.

One of the most interesting databases in the handbook category is the GUINNESS DiSC OF RECORDS. Published by Pergamon Compact Solutions, it won the Optical Publishing Association's Most Innovative CD-ROM Title. GUINNESS DISC OF RECORDS contains information on current world record holders in fields such as sports, business, science, space and the living world. It includes photographs, animations and audio reproductions for relevant record categories. Each record in the database consists of: category name, record holder name, record data, description, visual reproduction of some events and audio reproduction. The disc includes five thousand 'cards' and three indexes. The interface is based on Knowledge Retrieval System (KRS) which in the opening screen provides five methods of searching: browsing the indexes of What, Where and Who; searching terms by using limited Boolean operators; random viewing of records in three areas of Natural, Physical, or Sporting; random viewing of pictures; and random display of records. The interface uses pull-down menus and windows in a typical Apple Macintosh environment.

MULTI-MEDIA BIRDS OF AMERICA contains the information in the seven-volume first edition of John James Audubon's *Birds of America* published in 1840. It holds five hundred full colour and black-and-white illustrations, as well as many bird calls and songs. The retrieval software can search the entire database including the colour illustrations and bird calls through a series of menus. Searching is conducted by using one of the three access methods: Search, Browse, or Contents. Search utilizes a form on the screen to be filled out, enabling the user to choose Boolean operators. Truncation and proximity capabilities are additional features of the Search option. Browse provides an alphabetical list of words and Contents displays the table of contents.

AUTOMATED PATENT SEARCHING (APS) by MicroPatent is a comprehensive database for all patents issued by the United States Patent and Trademark Office (PTO). It is updated weekly from the PTO files with each record containing: patent number, issue year, patent assignee, state or country, patent classification codes, title and abstract. The European equivalent of APS is ESPACE CD-ROM, produced by the European Patent Office (EPO) and containing the complete text of European patent applications. ESPACE is updated annually and encompasses three languages: English, French and German.

ALDRICHEM DATA SEARCH is produced by Aldrich Chemical Company and provides information on 50,000 chemicals as well as descriptions of six thousand laboratory equipment products. Each record in the database contains: chemical name, synonyms, Aldrich catalog number, chemical structure, physical data, chemical class and CAS Registry Number.

D.A.T.A. DIGESTS consists of a number of reference manuals on the characteristics of commercially available semiconductor or integrated circuits manufactured worldwide. This quarterly database covers 750,000 devices made by 1,600 international manufacturers. The information is derived from manufacturers, military specifications and association standards. Records in the database contain information on manufacturer name, address, glossary of terms and definitions, tables of technical specifications, electronic connection information, number index of devices and manufacturers covered. IC/DISCRETE PARAMETER DATA-BASE is produced jointly by Information Handling Services (IHS) and D.A.T.A. It identifies over one million active discontinued components from one thousand worldwide manufacturers. The bimonthly database contains information on specific technological and functional parameters of engineering devices, and includes 272,000 manufacturer datasheets and parts ordering information. Each record in IC includes replacement and alternative parts, standard parts specifications, package outlines, national stock numbers, Commercial and Government Entity (CAGE) numbers, SIC numbers, manufacturer addresses and their datasheet items.

Another handbook on semiconductor technology is Cahners Technical Information Service's CAPS (Computer Aided Product Selection) containing specifications and scanned images of manufacturers' data-sheets for integrated-circuit devices and related components from more than four hundred manufacturers. The scope of the database is augmented by its coverage of information on 150,000 obsolete components. CAPS is updated quarterly with each record containing information on: part name, alternative sources, upgrades and downgrades, manufacturers' addresses and telephone numbers, military part numbers and military reliability levels.

Sweet's Group, a McGraw-Hill Information Services Company, is the producer of ELECTRONIC SWEET'S consisting of SweetSearch, SweetSpec, CodeCONTROL and CodeANALYST. It provides descriptions of more than 20,000 building products, based on Sweet's *General Building & Renovation* and *Engineering & Retrofit Catalog* files. SweetSearch is the name of the retrieval software which enables the user to search for product characteristics based on their specific design requirements. The interface is menu-driven with each screen including an explanatory note. The Building Product Search System allows five access points to the database: Product Search, Manufacturer Search, Trade Name Search, Catalog Search and Association/Agency Search. Each selection from the menu leads to another menu with more choices, for example, the Product Search selection allows the user to browse a list of sixteen standard product categories. Manufacturer Search and Trade Name Search produce alphabetical lists of manufacturers and names respectively. Records in the database contain information about product characteristics, material, size, energy performance, product brand name and manufacturers' print catalogues.

## Encyclopedias

An important contribution of the CD-ROM to the information industry is in the area of encyclopedias. When the NEW GROLIER ELECTRONIC ENCYCLOPEDIA first appeared on the market in 1986, it was viewed as avant-garde. One CD-ROM contained the entire textual content of the twenty-one volumes of the *Academic American Encyclopedia*. It had over nine million words and thirty thousand entries covering a variety of topics. Many public and school libraries have embraced CD-ROM technology to take advantage of the ELECTRONIC ENCYCLOPEDIA. The online industry, for all practical purposes, has abandoned encyclopedia databases.

In 1990, Grolier introduced an enhanced edition of its 1986 publication winning the Best Consumer Product from the Optical Publishing Association. The main enhancements to the second edition are three thousand updated or new articles, images and links among the articles in a move toward a multimedia product. The documentation of the second edition also contains some procedural errors and lacks a comprehensive index. Aside from these differences, the search interface which is designed by Online Computer Systems Inc., has not changed significantly from the first edition. It uses a combination of commands and pull-down menus to search for individual words within articles or entire titles of articles, as well as browse lists of words and images. Selecting 'Word Search' enables the user to choose up to four words and use various combinations of Boolean operators to refine the search. Once articles about the search topic have been found, their entire texts may be browsed for desired information. Capitalization of certain words in the content of the articles designates links to other related articles. Images and illustration, although of relatively poor quality, may be browsed directly or viewed in the context of specific articles.

One drawback of the retrieval interface lies in its inability to search dates directly. Dates for births and deaths are rich sources of biographical information included in many articles. Unfortunately, Online Computer Systems' interface does not allow direct manipulation of the dates or the use of arithmetic operators, such as greater than or less than. To retrieve the names of all famous people who were born in the same year, several intermediary steps have to be followed.

Two searches on Grolier's produced interesting results. The first was to answer the reference question 'what is the largest bell in the world?' The combination of menus proved very useful in this search; the term BELL was entered ALONG WITH the term LARGE (truncated with an asterisk). These words were searched using a proximity operator available in the pull-down menu and limiting them to within two words of each other. One article was retrieved on BELL, the first paragraph of which stated that the 'largest bell ever cast is the Tsar Bell in Moscow: it is 5.75 m (19 ft) high, 6.75 m (22 ft) in diameter, and weighs 181 metric tons (200 United States tons)'. The search was fast and efficient retrieving the required information in less than one minute.

The second search on 'why do people throw rice at weddings?' was not as successful. Terms such as RICE, CONFETTI, WEDDING and MARRIAGE were entered in truncated forms using different searchable fields and various Boolean operators. The results were disappointing. Articles on FOLK DANCE, RICE and MARRIAGE were retrieved without any mention of ceremonial customs and traditions.

In spite of minor shortcomings, the NEW GROLIER ELECTRONIC ENCYCLOPEDIA represents a user friendly system designed to bring CD-ROM technology to the home market.

Another award winning CD-ROM is the new COMPTON'S MULTIMEDIA ENCYCLOPEDIA (CMME). CMME, which was named the 1990 Consumer Product of the Year by *CD-ROM Professional,* was jointly developed by Encyclopaedia Britannica, Inc., Jostens Learning Corp., and Del Mar Group. It contains all the information in the twenty-six volumes of *Compton's Encyclopedia,* and includes fifteen thousand illustrations of which five thousand are high resolution charts, four thousand are full colour, six thousand are black-and-white photographs and eight hundred are maps. There are also forty-five animated sequences and sixty minutes of music, speech and sound. In addition, it contains the complete 65,000 *Merriam Webster Intermediate Dictionary* entries with 1,500 glossary terms which have audio pronunciation. The retrieval engine and interface are different from other CD-ROM products. The Main Menu offers eight access points to the database: Idea Search, Title Finder, Topic Tree, Picture Explorer, United States History Timeline, World Atlas, Science Feature Articles and Researcher's Assistant.

The CMME interface has been designed for novice users but assumes familiarity with icons and mouse. Its main retrieval engine is based on a proprietary software called SmarTrieve which does not use explicit Boolean or proximity operators. In the Idea Search, a term may be typed in directly for free-text searching. SmarTrieve then uses the 'contextual relationships among words, to link one's personal vocabulary to the index terms of a data or a knowledge base' [19, p.15]. The algorithm is based on relevance ranking which, theoretically, presents the best match for a searched term. In practice, however, SmarTrieve does not always produce the desired results. Truncation, phrase searching and some type of limited Boolean operators are implied in CMME searches, but without any user control. Icons on the left margin of the screen indicate use of animation and sound for specific passages. One of CMME's interesting features is the World Atlas which enables the user to browse the entire globe through the arrow keys. It has seven levels of zoom to expand on the features of a particular region or country. 'Hot' points on the maps let the user move directly to a related article. CMME has additional features such as bookmarks, cut and paste and notebook which facilitates customization of the results of a search.

The two reference questions which were used in previous examples were again used to test CMME. From the Main Menu the Idea Search was chosen and the two terms BELL and LARGE were entered. The result was one major entry, indicated by an asterisk and several other articles. By clicking on the designated article, the first page of a thirteen-page article on BELL appeared. As CMME does not highlight the searched terms in the text of the article, many pages of text have to be read before the required information is found. The second search on 'why do people throw rice at weddings?' produced very peculiar results. It listed several articles ranging from RICE and CHINESE LITERATURE to JAPAN and ARKANSAS. It seems that the 'contextual relationships' applied by SmarTrieve are based on preconceived notions which may not reflect the objectives of a search.

CMME represents a new approach to information retrieval. It may not be the best vehicle for expert searchers and professional librarians, but it introduces the novice and occasional searchers, particularly the younger audience, to the joys of information retrieval.

In a move towards an appropriate multimedia application, the National Geographic Society in collaboration with IBM has produced MAMMALS: A MULTIMEDIA ENCYCLOPEDIA. The database covers over two hundred animals using seven hundred colour photographs, six hundred pages of text, 155 animal vocalizations, forty-five full-motion movie segments, glossaries and animal classifications. The interface is completely menu driven presenting the user with a main menu consisting of a glossary and six selections for mammals names. The retrieval engine is based on an authoring tool produced by IBM called Link Way software. Icons are presented in the lower right corner of the screen enabling the user to move forward and backward in the database. Vital statistics are also presented for each animal. The description of many animals is accompanied by a full-motion video and sound vocalization. These features set MAMMALS apart from other encyclopedias and enhance the learning environment particularly for young audiences.

WORLD BOOK INFORMATION FINDER is an encyclopedia based on the *World Book Dictionary* and selected material from the *World Book Encyclopedia,* containing 139,000 entries in seventeen thousand articles, 1,700 tables, 1,600 reading lists and sixty thousand links. The retrieval interface provides the user with different options for searching including Boolean operators and keyword searching, as well as notebook and cut and paste capabilities. Links or cross-references have been provided in many articles.

A specialized encyclopedia is the INTERNATIONAL ENCYCLOPEDIA OF EDUCATION (IEE) produced by Pergamon Press Ltd. It encompasses the complete text of about 1,500 articles in the ten-volume print version in the areas of human development, planning, research methodology and comparative education and national systems. Each record contains article title, bibliography, fact box and tables and article text. IEE uses hypertext links enabling the user to move around the database. Other features include separate windows for user's notes, scrolling for browsing, zooming into graphs and charts, truncation, adjacency and proximity and Boolean operators.

## News sources

One of the first newspaper databases on CD-ROM was PRAVDA '87 by ALDE Publishing. This database contains the text of English-language translations of selected articles published in *Pravda,* the official newspaper of the (then) Soviet Union's Communist Party. PRAVDA '87 includes 5,853 articles which generate an index of over 100,000 unique words. Entries or cards are accessed through a series of menu-driven screens. Each card can be retrieved directly by using its unique number. Boolean operators and truncation, both left and right-hand, have been implemented in PRAVDA's retrieval engine.

A number of British newspapers are now available on CD-ROM, among which is *The Guardian.* Produced and marketed by Chadwyck-Healey Ltd., THE GUARDIAN ON CD-ROM uses Clarinet Systems Ltd.'s Clearview software engine. The interface allows for expert and novice searching as well as the use of mouse for menu-driven screens or direct manipulation of keywords. Headlines, bylines, date and page numbers are separately searchable. The software also allows browsing the indexes for each field to aid the user in spell checking and rekeying the words. Since the physical layout and location of articles in a newspaper may be as important as the content, the front pages of *The Guardian* have been scanned and incorporated into the database. In addition, hypertext has been used to establish links between the front page and the ASCII text of the newspaper. This is a unique feature which provides more access points for the users.

PERIODISC La PRESSE is one of the first applications of CD-ROM to full-text newspapers in Canada. The database, produced by CEDROM Technologies Inc., contains the text of the French daily newspaper *La Presse,* with the first disc appearing on March 1, 1991. PERIODISC is one of the first full-text databases to use the Microsoft Windows graphical user interface. The retrieval software is designed to search every word in the database with a maximum combination of fifteen keywords. A mixture of pull-down menus, window presentations, keyboard and mouse is used to search the database through sixteen access points: Texte intégral, Auteur, Photographe, Agence, Date, Jour de la semaine, Longueur, Section, Centre d'Intérêt, Centre Géographique, Chronique, Dossier, Type Bas de vignette, Lead and Journalliste. Boolean and proximity operators have been implemented to accommodate expert searchers.

Other types of news databases are also available on CD-ROMs. CLUBMAC by Quantum Access, Inc. (QA) contains articles and technical notes on Apple Macintosh computers. It includes a variety of information, comprising six sections: Articles, BBS providing name, system operator and phone number for six hundred worldwide bulletin board systems sorted by area code, Mac User Group listing the name and telephone number of eight hundred user groups, classified advertisements, reviews and software. The data are collected from many sources including magazines, online databases and public access broadcasting.

THE SEYBOLD REPORT ON PUBLISHING SYSTEMS, produced by Seybold Publications, Inc., reports on the emerging technology of the publishing industry. The CD-ROM database consists of evaluation of new systems, industry news, trade-show coverage and reader feedback. The topics covered by SEYBOLD REPORT include computer composition and typesetting, editing, formatting and transmission of text. Its coverage dates back to 1982 and it is published bi-weekly.

## Image and sound sources

CD-ROM has created new opportunities for storage and retrieval of information regardless of the medium used. While the online systems have been unable to offer image and sound databases, many CD-ROM products currently on the market provide access to this type of information. A number of CD-ROM databases consist of clip art images which are photographs, diagrams, drawings and maps that can be 'clipped' from the database and incorporated into a document. CLIP ART 3-D, produced by NEC Home Electronics, contains 2,500 three-dimensional, full colour graphics in different file formats including PICT, TIFF (Tag Image File Format), and EPS (Encapsulated Postscript). Images cover a wide variety of topics such as people, toys, nature, vehicles and theatre. The interface allows seven graphic categories to be selected. Each category is sorted into sixty additional divisions. CLIP ART 3-D is accompanied by an image management software which enables the users to manipulate selected images.

THE RIGHT IMAGES produced by Tsunami Press contains 103 images in colour and grey-scale. The general theme of the database is space, with the majority of images provided by NASA. The retrieval interface displays very small images on the screen allowing their selection as well as browsing the basic index. Once an index number has been chosen, an image management software must be used to manipulate the image - change colours, crop, rotate, zoom, etc.

VOYAGE TO THE PLANETS is a collection of three CD-ROMs containing images of Mars, Jupiter, Neptune and other planets. The discs are produced by Astronomical Research Network and include more than 1,500 images. The retrieval interface is based on pull-down menus and allows three-dimensional displays, zooming and data analysis.

IMAGE LIBRARY for ModelView consists of six hundred high resolution 24-bit colour images of interior and exterior material finishes and background images of buildings. IMAGE LIBRARY, produced by ModelVision Inc., was created specifically for use with ModelView image management system and Intergraph Computer-Aided Drafting (CAD). Records in the database are indexed by type of materials such as brick, tile, fabric, wood and type of background such as ocean views, mountains, skies, etc. The background images can be integrated into the finished models.

CD-ROM DIGITAL SOUND SERIES, produced by Reflective Arts International, is a two-volume database encompassing the sounds of hundreds of instruments, synthesizers, sound effects, percussion and ambient backgrounds. Sounds include those made by animals, the weather, and aircraft as well as combat, industrial, household and science fiction noises and human vocals.

CHART-NAV 20/20 is published by Laser Plot Inc. and contains navigational charts produced by the United States National Oceanic and Atmospheric Administration. By overlaying a ship's position on the stored charts, route planning is accomplished. The database contains over one thousand charts and is updated annually.

## Statistical sources

Many CD-ROM databases consist of textual as well as numerical information. Some, however, are exclusively statistical. Slater Hall Information Products (SHIP) is one of the major publishers of numeric or statistical databases. Three of its products are COUNTY AND CITY STATISTICS, AGRICULTURAL STATISTICS and POPULATION STATISTICS. COUNTY AND CITY STATISTICS contains 1980 United States demographic and statistical data, including about one thousand data items for each county, state and metropolitan area from the United States Bureau of the Census. The database consists of three files: County, City and Local Area population statistics. The database contains data on United States population for counties and cities with a population of 25,000 or more, housing, business, health, agriculture, education, crime, manufactures and other statistics. Data have been derived from: United States Department of Commerce and the Bureau of the Census and the *County and City Databook* published by the Bureau of the Census. SEARCHER, the retrieval software developed by Slater Hall, is menu-driven which allows access through geographical locations and attributes of interest such as income, crime and education. Once a location has been selected and different attributes identified, the strategy must by EXECUTED. This approach is somewhat similar to mainframe operation using batch processing.

AGRICULTURAL STATISTICS includes data from the 1982 and 1987 Censuses of Agriculture and United States Bureau of the Census County File, as well as farm income covering 1969 to the present. It covers such topics as acreage, operating expenses, sales, production, crops and livestock.

POPULATION STATISTICS contains population and housing characteristics for the United States. It covers metropolitan areas, counties, places of ten thousand or more population and Congressional districts. The database consists of Census Bureau population estimates by age, race and sex for counties through 1984, estimates by population and per capita income for counties and places in 1986, and estimates by Commerce Department for states and metropolitan areas to the year 2010.

Hopkins Technology produces CONSU/STATS I containing the latest publicly released United States Survey of Consumer Expenditures. The database consists of interview and diary data covering many consumer and family characteristics in one hundred selected United States geographical areas. These characteristics include such information as major appliance purchases, trips and vacations and vehicle purchases.

Other databases produced by Hopkins Technology are AGRI/STATS I and ECON/STATS I. AGRI/STATS I includes United States Department of Agriculture's Statistical Service data covering crops and livestock. It contains approximately three-quarters of a million records dating back to 1939 and including data on corn production in forty-two African countries since 1966. ECON/STATS I contains a variety of United States economic data, including the Consumer Price Index, Producer Price Index, Industrial Production Index, Export-Import Price Indices, Industry Employment Hours & Earnings by State and Areas, Money Stock and Selected Interest Rates.

A different type of numeric database is a series produced by EarthInfo Inc., called HYDRODATA. The series covers a wide range of water resources data for Canada and the United States. The databases are based on the National WATer Data STOrage and REtrieval System (WATSTORE), produced by the United States Geological Survey (USGS).

HYDRODATA: CANADIAN SURFACE WATER DATA provides daily water flow, instantaneous peak flow and lake level historical values for Canada, including precalculated summary statistics. Data have been derived from observations from collecting stations compiled by Environment Canada for the HYDAT database. The search software is menu-driven and allows six access Views: Index, Summary, Daily, Peak, Hydex and Mean. The Index View displays the station name, flow or water level, time coverage and the first year of record. Summary View shows information about stations and daily/monthly minimum and maximum data. Hydex View displays gauge information such as type, location, operation schedule and history. HYDRODATA: USGS DAILY VALUES has a similar interface to CANADIAN SURFACE WATER DATA and includes about one hundred years of streamflow data observations from gauging stations in all fifty states.

HYDRODATA: USGS PEAK VALUES contains one hundred years of annual and partial flood peak data observations from 25,000 present and historical gauging stations in all fifty States. The retrieval interface is similar to EarthInfo's other products and offers four formats of access: Index View provides a separate listing for each gauging station and indicates the time span of the record; Summary View shows the maximum and minimum peak and data on the annual and partial series; Annual View lists the annual peaks chronologically; Partial View displays the partial peaks chronologically; Rank View ranks the annual and partial peaks in descending order of discharge and exceedance probability; and Remarks View provides a text summary of the station history, current year and period of record. Other products in the HYDRODATA series include HYDRODATA: USGS QUALITY OF WATER, containing more than three million surface and ground water quality analyses gathered from approximately 200,000 sites in the United States, and including information for 2,600 parameters. Each record in the database contains information on latitude/longtitude, station name or ID, drainage area, aquifer type, date/time, sample medium and type, geologic unit code, analysis source and status, hydrologic condition and event. The interface has a main menu of seven options, with each option using a pull-down menu. A Station menu allows searching by the station name, identification number and state or county. Searches can further be limited by the Analysis menu which enables the users to define the analytical attributes related to the observing stations. A parameters menu lists water quality parameters, but keying in the desired parameter as a search term through the use of function keys may be a more efficient retrieval method. Other menus are designed to aid users refine, store and display their search results.

EarthInfo also produces a series of CD-ROMs on climate and global weather patterns. CLIMATEDATA: CLIM-20 contains statistics for climate data observations from more than 1,800 present and historical weather stations in the United States provided by National Climatic Data Center (NCDC). It includes daily and monthly temperatures, precipitation and snowfall, as well as frost-free and agricultural planting statistics. CLIMATEDATA: NCDC HOURLY PRECIPITATION holds precipitation data observations from 5,500 active and abandoned weather stations in the United States that have recorded hourly precipitation measurements for the past forty-five years. The interface is similar to EathInfo's other products with different Views available for searching: Index, Summary, Hour, Daily, Event and Storm. Hour View shows a matrix with all precipitation which allows the user to trace a storm from start to finish. Daily View displays precipitation total per day in month columns for each year or for the whole period of record. Storm View provides data on the longest enduring storms for each station, including those with a duration between one hour and thirty days.

CLIMATEDATA: NCDC SUMMARY OF THE DAY consists of one hundred years of climate data observations from 25,000 weather stations in the United States. The interface includes EarthInfo's standard Views as well as Bin View, Extreme View and History View. Bin View displays statistics, such as counts of days based on the entire historical period for specific ranges. Extreme View shows maximum and minimum daily statistics, and History View tracks changes in location and name reporting status and identifies specific stations. For all of its databases, EarthInfo recommends the use of fast processors for searching due to very large file sizes.

Data Base Products, Inc., publishes several databases on international and domestic air traffic. INTERNATIONAL holds monthly and quarterly airline passenger traffic data. It is updated quarterly and covers international air carrier onboard traffic, traffic flow and origin and destination data. Data have been input from United States Department of Transportation and the United States Immigration and Naturalization Service. O & D PLUS provides airline passenger origin, destination and itinerary data from the United States Department of Transportation (DOT). O & D PLUS is updated quarterly and covers historical data dating back to 1979. ONBOARD contains monthly, quarterly and annual domestic onboard traffic and service segment data. It covers the period 1972 through to the available months/quarters of the current year and includes information on domestic onboard traffic and service segment data. Data have been derived from carrier filings with the United States Department of Transportation.

## CONCLUSIONS

Online and CD-ROM databases improve the selection of information sources for ready reference work. The introduction of these databases has expanded the reference skills needed for retrieving factual information. Accuracy and precision are particularly important skills for solving ready reference queries online. To become an efficient searcher, a basic knowledge of the appropriate database, the database structure and the retrieval software of the various systems must be achieved.

Selecting the appropriate CD-ROM database for answering ready reference queries may prove more challenging than for online systems. With the exception of directories, the number of online ready reference databases seems to be reaching a plateau or is on the decline. By contrast, the number of CD-ROM databases has grown exponentially in the past few years.

The most important facet of the database structure for information specialists is a fundamental knowledge of the database access points. Systems such as DIALOG and BRS maintain a consistent structure for many of their databases. DIALOG's Bluesheets and BRS's AidPages and their equivalents online provide ample information for the searchers on various fields and indexes. By comparison, the vast number of CD-ROM producers create their own unique engines which may prove to be an obstacle in maintaining a consistent structure for many databases. A CD-ROM database may have from two or three to hundreds of access points depending on the nature of stored data and the end-users' information needs.

However, the search software of CD-ROM databases, their ease of use and their flexibility in retrieving information render them a more viable option than online databases for solving ready reference queries. CD-ROM databases, like the traditional print sources, allow end-users to satisfy their information needs with minimal assistance from an intermediary. By comparison, the retrieval software of the online systems require the knowledge of many commands; therefore, the intermediary plays a crucial role in the search process.

The ready reference process will probably undergo further changes with the advent of new technologies including multimedia databases and the application of artificial intelligence to the information retrieval process. These advances will assist end-users and possibly relieve the intermediaries of many ready reference queries in the future.

## REFERENCES

1.     Stephen P. Harter. *Online Information Retrieval: Concepts, Principles and Techniques*. San Diego: Academic Press, Inc. 1986.

2.     Leslie M. Haas. Online Ready Reference Searching for Company and Market Share Information. In *Proceedings of the Eleventh National Online Meeting*. Medford, NJ: Learned Information, Inc. 1990 149-153.

3.     Carol Tenopir. Online Databases: Decision Making by Reference Librarians. *Library Journal* 113 (16) 1988 66-67.

4.     Michael W. Havener. Answering Ready Reference Questions: Print vs. Online. *Online* 14 (January) 1990 22-28.

5.     Charles M. Goldstein. Online Reference Works and Full Text Retrieval. In *Proceedings of the Eleventh National Online Meeting*. Medford, NJ: Learned Information, Inc. 1990 171-177.

6.     Thomas P. Slavens. *Reference Interviews, Questions and Materials*. Metuchen, NJ: The Scarecrow Press, Inc. 1985.

7.     *BYTE* 16(6) 1991 28.

8.     R. Loomis, et al. Electronic versus printed access to reference tools: Two approaches. *RSR* 15(3) 1987 49-53.

9.     CD-ROM for reference: A panel discussion. In: *CD-ROM in the library today and tomorrow*. Ed. Mary Kay Duggan. Boston, Mass.: G.K.Hall 1990 27-42.

10.    Paul Travis Nicholls. A survey of commercially available CD-ROM database titles. *CD-ROM Professional* 4(2) 1991 23-28.

11.    Ahmed M. Elshami. *CD-ROM technology for information managers*. Chicago: American Library Association 1990.

12. R. Larson. CD-ROM Search Software: From Menus to Hypertext. In: *CD-ROM in the Library Today and Tomorrow* 1990 85-119.
13. *BYTE* 15(7) 1990 28.
14. P.M. LePoer and C.A. Mularski. CD-ROM's Impact On Libraries And Users. *Laserdisk Professional* 2(4) 1989 39-45.
15. Jamshid Beheshti. Retrieval interfaces for CD-ROM bibliographic databases. *CD-ROM Professional* 4(1) 1991 50-53.
16. CD-ROM Read-Only Data Exchange (CD-RDx) Standard. *CD-ROM Librarian* 6(3) 1991 10-27.
17. C.J. Armstrong. CIA World Fact Book. In: *CD-ROM information products: the evaluative guide.* Vol. 2. Ed. C.J. Armstrong and J.A. Large. Brookfield, Vermont: Gower Publishing Company 1991 57-74.
18. Norman Desmarais. *The Librarian's CD-ROM handbook.* Westport, CT: Meckler Corporation 1989.
19. H. Urrows and E. Urrows. Children's encyclopedias on CD-ROM. *CD-ROM Librarian* 6(2) 1991 15.

## ONLINE DATABASES

| | |
|---|---|
| **ACADEMIC INDEX** | BRS, DIALOG |
| **AGROCHEMICALS HANDBOOK** | Data-Star, DIALOG |
| **AIDS KNOWLEDGEBASE** | BRS |
| **AMERICAN LIBRARY DIRECTORY** | DIALOG |
| **AMERICAN MEN AND WOMEN OF SCIENCE** | DIALOG, ORBIT |
| **A-V ONLINE** | DIALOG |
| **BEILSTEIN ONLINE** | DIALOG, ORBIT, STN |
| **BIBLE (KING JAMES VERSION)** | DIALOG |
| **BIOGRAPHY MASTER INDEX** | DIALOG |
| **BLACK'S LAW DICTIONARY** | Westlaw |
| **BNA DAILY NEWS** | DIALOG |
| **BOOKS IN PRINT** | BRS, DIALOG |
| **BRITISH BOOKS IN PRINT** | DIALOG |
| **BRS/FILE** | BRS |
| **BUSINESS SOFTWARE DATABASE** | BRS, Data-Star, DIALOG, ESA-IRS |
| **BUSINESSWIRE** | American Library Association, Bridge Information systems, BT Tymnet Dialcom Service, CompuServe, DIALOG, Dow Jones News/Retrieval, General videodex Corporation/DELPHI, Mead Data Central, NewsNet, VU/TEXT |
| **BUYER'S GUIDE TO MICRO SOFTWARE** | BRS, DIALOG |
| **CAREER PLACEMENT REGISTRY** | DIALOG |
| **CENDATA** | CompuServe, DIALOG |
| **CHEMICAL BUSINESS NEWSBASE** | Data-Star, DIALOG, Pergamon Financial Data Services, Reuters Limited |
| **CHEMICAL ECONOMICS HANDBOOK** | DIALOG |
| **COMPUTER NEWS FULLTEXT** | DIALOG |
| **COMPUTER-READABLE DATABASES** | DIALOG |
| **CONSUMER DRUG INFORMATION FULLTEXT** | BRS, DIALOG |
| **CUADRA DIRECTORY OF DATABASES** | Data-Star, ORBIT Search Service, Questel |
| **CURRENT CONTENTS SEARCH** | BRS, DIALOG, DIMDI |

| | |
|---|---|
| DATA STAR NEWS | Data-Star |
| D&B-DUN'S ELECTRONIC BUSINESS DIRECTORY | CERVED, DIALOG |
| DIALOG BLUESHEETS | DIALOG |
| DONELLY'S DEMOGRAPHICS | DIALOG |
| EDUCATIONAL DIRECTORY | DIALOG |
| ENCYCLOPEDIA OF ASSOCIATIONS | DIALOG |
| EURADICAUTOM | Echo |
| EUROPEAN DIRECTORY OF AGRO-CHEMICAL PRODUCTS | Data-Star, DIALOG |
| EVENTLINE | DIALOG, Data-Star, SiteSelex On-Line |
| EVERYMAN'S ENCYCLOPEDIA | DIALOG |
| EXCERPTA MEDICA VOCABULARY | Data-Star |
| EXPERTNET | DIALOG, West Publishing Company |
| FACTS ON FILE | DIALOG, Mead Data Central |
| FAIRBASE | BRS, Data-Star, FIZ Technik, National Center of Scientific and Technological Information |
| FINE CHEMICALS DATABASE | DIALOG |
| FOUNDATION GRANTS INDEX | DIALOG |
| FOUNDATION DIRECTORY | DIALOG |
| GRADLINE | DIALOG |
| GRANTS | DIALOG |
| HEALTH DEVICES ALERTS | DIALOG |
| HEALTH DEVICES SOURCEBOOK | DIALOG |
| HEILBRON | DIALOG |
| KIRK-OTHMER (ENCYCLOPEDIA OF CHEMICAL TECHNOLOGY) ONLINE | BRS, Data-Star, DIALOG |
| KNOWLEDGE INDUSTRY PUBLICATIONS DATABASES | BRS |
| LC MARC - BOOKS | BLAISE-LINE, DIALOG, Library of Congress Information System, Universitetsbiblioteket i Oslo, WILSONLINE |
| MAGAZINE INDEX | BRS, CARL Systems Inc., Data-Star, DIALOG |
| MARQUIS WHO'S WHO | DIALOG |
| MARTINDALE ONLINE | Data-Star, DIALOG |
| MEDLINE VOCABULARY | Data-Star |
| MENTAL MEASUREMENTS YEARBOOK | BRS |
| MERCK INDEX ONLINE | BRS, Chemical Information Systems, DIALOG, Questel |
| MICROCOMPUTER SOFTWARE GUIDE | DIALOG |
| NATIONAL NEWSPAPER INDEX | BRS, DIALOG |
| NEWSEARCH | BRS, DIALOG |
| NEWSPAPER ABSTRACTS | DIALOG |
| NEWSWIRE ASAP | DIALOG |
| NORMATERM | Minitel |
| OAG ELECTRONIC EDITION | DIALOG |
| ONLINE/CD-ROM DATABASE NEWS | DIALOG |
| PAPERS | DIALOG |

| | |
|---|---|
| **PAPERSNE (PAPERSNE)** | DIALOG |
| **PETERSON'S COLLEGE DATABASE** | BRS, CompuServe, DIALOG, Dow Jones News/ Retrieval |
| **PHARMACEUTICAL NEWS INDEX** | DIALOG |
| **POLYMER ONLINE** | BRS, DIALOG |
| **PTS NEWSLETTER DATABASE** | DIALOG |
| **PUBLIC OPINION ONLINE** | DIALOG |
| **PUBLISHERS, DISTRIBUTERS, WHOLESALERS** | DIALOG |
| **QUOTATIONS DATABASE** | DIALOG |
| **REGISTRY OF TOXIC EFFECTS OF CHEMICAL SUBSTANCES** | DIALOG |
| **REMARC** | DIALOG, UTLAS International |
| **RESEARCH CENTERS AND SERVICES DIRECTORY** | DIALOG |
| **SOFTWARE DIRECTORY** | Apple Computer, Inc., DIALOG |
| **STANDARD & POOR'S NEWS** | DIALOG, Mead Data Central |
| **STANDARD & POOR'S REGISTER - BIOGRAPHICAL** | DIALOG, Mead Data Central |
| **TDFK-DFK** | Data-Star |
| **TRADE NAMES DATABASE** | DIALOG |
| **TRADEMARKSCAN - FEDERAL** | DIALOG |
| **ULRICH'S INTERNATIONAL PERIODICAL DIRECTORY** | BRS, DIALOG, ESA-IRS |
| **USA TODAY DECISIONLINE** | DIALOG, Gannett News Media Services, Quantam Computer Services Inc., Western Union Telegraph Company |
| **VOCATIONAL EDUCATION CURRICULUM MATERIALS** | BRS |

# Appendix:
# A selective list of directories, bibliographies and reference works

Anthony, L.J. and Deunette, J. European Hosts and Databases. *Online* 9(3) 1985 88-89

Armstrong, C.J. (ed). *World Databases in [subject]*. 1992- (Series in preparation)

Armstrong, C.J. and Large, J.A. (eds). *CD-ROM Information Products: An Evaluative Guide*. Aldershot: Gower, 1990- (Irregular)

Ball, S. *Directory of International Sources of Business Information*. Southport: Pitman, 1988

*Les Banques de Donnees Utiles aux Collectivites Locales et Territoriales*. Paris: FLA Consultants, 1989 (in French)

Bater, P. and Parkinson, H. *Online Business and Company Databases 1989*. London: Aslib, 1988

*Britline: Directory of British Databases*. New York: McGraw-Hill, 1987- (Biennial)

Brownstone, D. and Carruth, G. *Where to find business information*. (2nd ed). New York: Wiley, 1982

*Business Information Yearbook*. Cleveland: Headland Press (Annually)

*Business Line Finance: the international directory of online financial information*. London: Euromonitor, 1987

Byerly, Greg. *Online Searching: A Dictionary and Bibliographic Guide*. Littleton, CO: Libraries Unlimited, 1983

*CD-ROM Directory*. London: TFPL Publishing, 1989- (Annually)

*CD-ROMs in Print*. London: Meckler, 1987- (Annually)

*CICI Directory of Information Products and Services*. London: Longman, 1989

Cox, John. *Online Building, Construction and Architectural Databases, 1990*. London: Aslib, 1990

Cox, John. *Online Environmental Databases, 1990*. London: Aslib, 1990

*Database Directory 1989*. White Plains: Knowledge Industry Publications, 1989

*Data on Display: A Guide to Numeric Databases*. Helsinki: Central Statistical Office of Finland, 1991 (in English)

*Datapro Complete Guide to Dial-Up Databases*. 3rd ed. Delrun, NJ: Datapro, 1985

*Datapro Directory of Online Services.* 2 vols. Delrun, NJ: Datapro, 1985

Davies, Owen and Edelhart, Mike. *Omni Online Database Directory 1985.* New York: Collier Macmillan, 1984

*Directory of French Videotex Databases for Companies.* Paris: FLA Consultants, 1991 (in English)

*Directory of Online Databases.* Andover: Cuadra/Gale, 1979- (Quarterly)

*Directory of Online Information Resources.* 11th ed. Kensington, MD: CSG Press, 1983

*Directory of Portable Databases.* Andover: Cuadra/Gale, 1990- (Semiannually)

*Directory of United Nations Databases and Information Systems.* 4th ed. New York: United Nations, 1990

*Encyclopedia of Information Systems and Services 1990.* 10th ed. 2 vols. Detroit: Gale Research, 1989

*European Business Information Sourcebook.* Cleveland: Headland Press, 1992- (Annually)

*European Business Intelligence Briefing.* Cleveland: Headland Press, 1989- (11/year)

*European Company Information: EEC Countries.* 3rd ed. London: London Business School Information Service, 1989

Feldman, Beverly. Database Directories: Review and Recent Developments. *Reference Services Review* 13(2) 1985 17-19

Fletcher, Paul. *CD-ROM in the UK - Market Report 1990/91.* Oxford: Learned Information, 1991

*Guide des Banques de Donnees Factuelles Français sur les Materiaux.* Paris: FLA Consultants, 1991 (in French)

*Guide International des Banques de Donnees sur les Brevets et les Marques.* Paris: FLA Consultants, 1989 (in French)

Gunn, A.A. and Moore, C. *CD-ROM: A Practical Guide for Information Professionals.* London: LITC/ UKOLUG, 1990

Haddon, Angela. *Online Management and Marketing Databases, 1989.* London: Aslib, 1989

Hall, James L. and Brown, Marjorie J. *Online Bibliographic Databases: An International Directory.* 4th ed. London: Aslib, 1986

*Handbuch der Datenbanken für Naturwissenschaft, Technik, Patente 1991.* Darmstadt: Hoppenstedt, 1991

Hargreaves, D. *Company Information in the UK: an examination and analysis of the problems.* Aberystwyth: University of Wales, 1989

Harter, Stephen P. *Online Information Retrieval: Concepts, Principles, and Techniques.* London: Academic Press, 1986

Hartley, R.J.; Keen, E.M.; Large, J.A. and Tedd, L.A. *Online Searching: Principles and Practice.* London: Bowker-Saur, 1990

Howitt, Doran and Weinberger, Marvin. *Inc Magazine's Databasics: Your Guide to Online Business Information.* New York: Garland, 1986

*Information Industry Directory 1992.* Andover: Gale Research, 1992

Ingebretsen, D.L.; Borgman, C.L. and Case, D. Database Guides: An Annotated Bibliography. *Database* 8(3) 1985 89-100

Jones, C. and Dowsland, W. *Online Sources of European Information: their Development and Use.*

Killen, D. *Directory of Australian Databases.* 3rd ed. Hawthorn, Victoria: Australian Database Development Association, 1991

Kingston, I. *Directory of European Business Information Sources, 1979*

Lambert, S. *Online: A Guide to America's Leading Information Services.* Bellevue WA: Microsoft Press, 1985

Lesko, Matthew. *Computer Data and Database Source Book.* New York: Avon, 1984

Lyon, Elizabeth. *Online Medical Databases, 1989.* London: Aslib, 1988

Marcaccio, K.Y. (ed). *Computer-Readable Data Bases* 8th ed. Andover: Gale Research, 1991

Marchant, Peter. *Online Patents and Trademarks Databases, 1989.* London: Aslib, 1988

Nicholas, D. and Erbach, G. *Online Information Sources for Business and Current Affairs: An evaluation of Textline, NEXIS, Profile and DIALOG.* London: Mansell, 1989

Nicholls, P. and DenElshout, R. Van. Survey of Databases Available on CD-ROM: Types, Availability and Content. *Database* 13(1) 1990 18-23

*Nordic Databases 1990*. 3rd ed. Esbo, Finland: SCANNET, 1991 (mostly in English)

*Online Business Information*. Cleveland: Headland Press (Biannual)

*Online Business Sourcebook*. Cleveland: Headland Press (Biannual)

*Online Database Selection: A User's Guide to the Directory of Online Databases*. Amsterdam: Elsevier, 1989

Parker, N. *Online Marketing and Management Databases 1991*. London: Aslib, 1991

Peterkin, K. and Black, D.V. *The Directory of Online Healthcare Databases*. 5th ed. Alpine Guild, 1990

*Portable Business Databases* (Business Research Guide Series). Cleveland: Headland Press, 1990

Radford, Fred. *Database Finding Aid*. Byron Center, MI: Alert Consultants, 1984

*Repertoire International des Banques de Donnees Biomedicales*. Paris: FLA Consultants, 1991 (in French)

*Repertoire International des Banques de Donnees Juridiques 1990-91*. Paris: FLA Consultants, 1991 (in French)

*Repertoire International des Banques de Donnees Teletel pour l'entreprise*. 3rd ed. Paris: FLA Consultants, 1991 (in French)

Shafritz, Jay M. and Alexander, Louise. *The Reston Directory of Online Databases*. New York: Prentice-Hall, 1984

Sims, M. (ed). *Directory of Periodicals Online: Indexed, Abstracted and Full Text. Volume 2: Medicine and Social Science*. Washington, DC: Federal Document Retrieval, [in press]

Sims, M. (ed). *Directory of Periodicals Online: Indexed, Abstracted and Full Text: News, Law and Business*. 4th ed. Washington, DC: Federal Document Retrieval, 1988

Sims, M. (ed). *Directory of Periodicals Online: Indexed, Abstracted and Full Text: Science and Technology*. Washington, DC: Federal Document Retrieval, 1988

Smith, G. *Business Information Sourcebook*. Revised ed. Cleveland: Headland Press, 1985

*The Source Book*. London: Key Note Publications, 1990

Spencer, N. *Instant Guide to Company Information Online - Europe*. London: The British Library SRIS, 1991

Tookey, D.A. (ed). *Accessible Databases: A Directory of Online and Machine-Readable Information Sources*. London: Spicer and Pegler, 1987

Tudor, J. *Macmillan Directory of Business Information Sources*. 2nd ed. London: Macmillan, 1989

UK Online User Group. *UKOLUG Quick Guide to Online Commands*. 3rd ed. London: UKOLUG, 1991

Vernon, K. (ed). *Information Sources in Management and Business*. London: Butterworths, 1984

Walsh, B. P.; Butcher, H. and Freund, A. *On-line Information: a cComprehensive Business Users Guide*. Oxford: Blackwells, 1987

Webb, J.A. (ed). *Optical Publishing Directory 1990/91*. 4th ed. Oxford: Learned Information, 1991

*Which European Database?* Cleveland: Headland Press, 1990- (Annually)

Woodsmall, R.M.; Lyon-Hartmann, B. and Siegel, E.R. (eds). *MEDLINE on CD-ROM: National Library of Medicine Evaluation Forum*. Oxford: Learned Information, 1989

# Database, Host and Information Provider index

# Source material and search aids index

# Subject index

Printed and bound by CPI Group (UK) Ltd, Croydon, CR0 4YY

21/10/2024

01777098-0005